The Renaissance & Early Modern Era

1454 - 1600

Great Lives from History

The Renaissance & Early Modern Era

1454 - 1600

Volume 2
Leonardo da Vinci-Huldrych Zwingli
Indexes

Editor
Christina J. Moose

Editor, First Edition
Frank N. Magill

SALEM PRESS
Pasadena, California   Hackensack, New Jersey

Editor in Chief: Dawn P. Dawson
Acquisitions Editor: Mark Rehn
Research Supervisor: Jeffry Jensen
Manuscript Editors: Desiree Dreeuws, Andy Perry
Assistant Editor: Andrea E. Miller

Production Editor: Joyce I. Buchea
Graphics and Design: James Hutson
Editorial Assistant: Dana Garey
Layout: Eddie Murillo
Photograph Editor: Philip Bader

Cover photos: Library of Congress
(Pictured left to right, top to bottom: Montezuma II, Henry VIII, Francis Bacon, Elizabeth I, African sculpture from Benin Empire, Süleyman the Magnificent, Wang Yangming, William Shakespeare, Catherine Parr)

∞ The paper used in these volumes conforms to the American National Standard for Permanence of Paper for Printed Library Materials, Z39.48-1992 (R1997).

Some of the essays in this work originally appeared in the following Salem Press sets: *Dictionary of World Biography* (© 1998-1999, edited by Frank N. Magill) and *Great Lives from History* (© 1987-1995, edited by Frank N. Magill).

Library of Congress Cataloging-in-Publication Data

Great lives from history. The Renaissance & early modern era, 1454-1600 / editors, Christina J. Moose, Frank N. Magill.— 1st ed.
    p. cm.
    Includes bibliographical references and indexes.
    ISBN 1-58765-211-0 (set : alk. paper) — ISBN 1-58765-212-9 (v. 1 : alk. paper) — ISBN 1-58765-213-7 (v. 2 : alk. paper)
    1. Biography—15th century. 2. Biography—16th century. 3. Renaissance. I. Title: Renaissance & early modern era, 1454-1600. II. Moose, Christina J., 1952-   . III. Magill, Frank Northen, 1907-1997.
CT115.G74 2005
909′.5′0922—dc22

2004028875

First Printing

CONTENTS

KEY TO PRONUNCIATION

Many of the names of personages covered in *Great Lives from History: The Renaissance, 1454-1600* may be unfamiliar to students and general readers. For these unfamiliar names, guides to pronunciation have been provided upon first mention of the names in the text. These guidelines do not purport to achieve the subtleties of the languages in question but will offer readers a rough equivalent of how English speakers may approximate the proper pronunciation.

Vowel Sounds

Symbol	Spelled (Pronounced)
a	answer (AN-suhr), laugh (laf), sample (SAM-puhl), that (that)
ah	father (FAH-thur), hospital (HAHS-pih-tuhl)
aw	awful (AW-fuhl), caught (kawt)
ay	blaze (blayz), fade (fayd), waiter (WAYT-ur), weigh (way)
eh	bed (behd), head (hehd), said (sehd)
ee	believe (bee-LEEV), cedar (SEE-dur), leader (LEED-ur), liter (LEE-tur)
ew	boot (bewt), lose (lewz)
i	buy (bi), height (hit), lie (li), surprise (sur-PRIZ)
ih	bitter (BIH-tur), pill (pihl)
o	cotton (KO-tuhn), hot (hot)
oh	below (bee-LOH), coat (koht), note (noht), wholesome (HOHL-suhm)
oo	good (good), look (look)
ow	couch (kowch), how (how)
oy	boy (boy), coin (koyn)
uh	about (uh-BOWT), butter (BUH-tuhr), enough (ee-NUHF), other (UH-thur)

Consonant Sounds

Symbol	Spelled (Pronounced)
ch	beach (beech), chimp (chihmp)
g	beg (behg), disguise (dihs-GIZ), get (geht)
j	digit (DIH-juht), edge (ehj), jet (jeht)
k	cat (kat), kitten (KIH-tuhn), hex (hehks)
s	cellar (SEHL-ur), save (sayv), scent (sehnt)
sh	champagne (sham-PAYN), issue (IH-shew), shop (shop)
ur	birth (burth), disturb (dihs-TURB), earth (urth), letter (LEH-tur)
y	useful (YEWS-fuhl), young (yuhng)
z	business (BIHZ-nehs), zest (zehst)
zh	vision (VIH-zhuhn)

COMPLETE LIST OF CONTENTS

VOLUME 1

VOLUME 2

LIST OF MAPS, TABLES, AND SIDEBARS

VOLUME 1

VOLUME 2

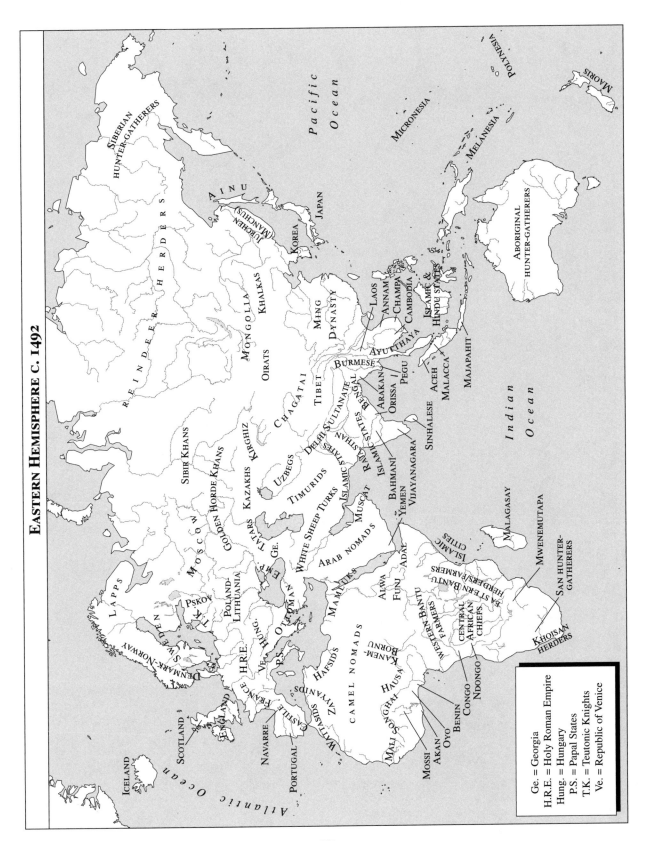

EASTERN HEMISPHERE C. 1492

Ge. = Georgia
H.R.E. = Holy Roman Empire
Hung. = Hungary
P.S. = Papal States
T.K. = Teutonic Knights
Ve. = Republic of Venice

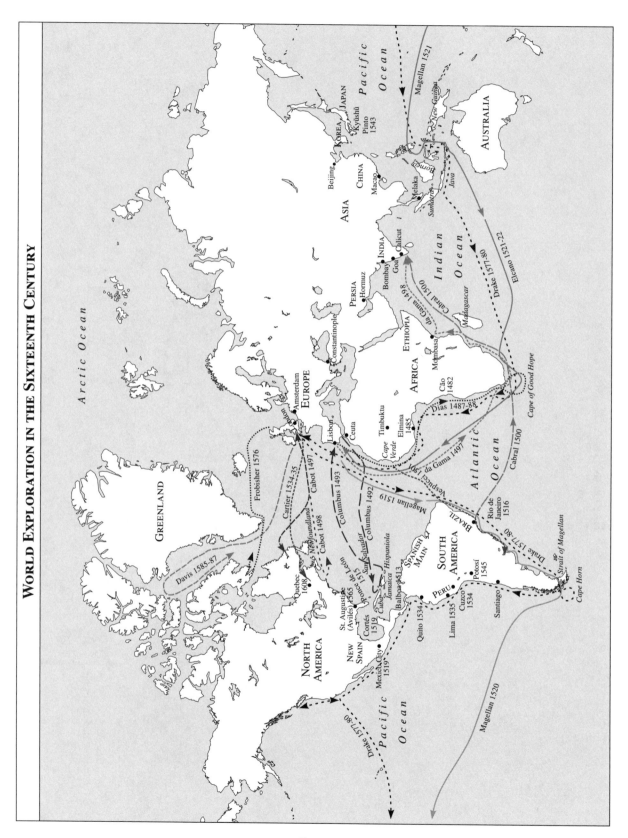

WORLD EXPLORATION IN THE SIXTEENTH CENTURY

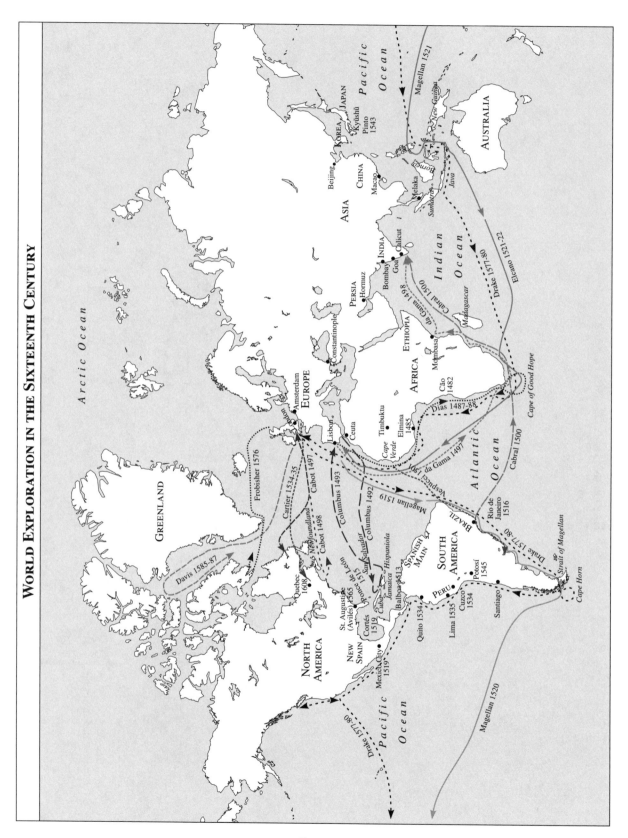

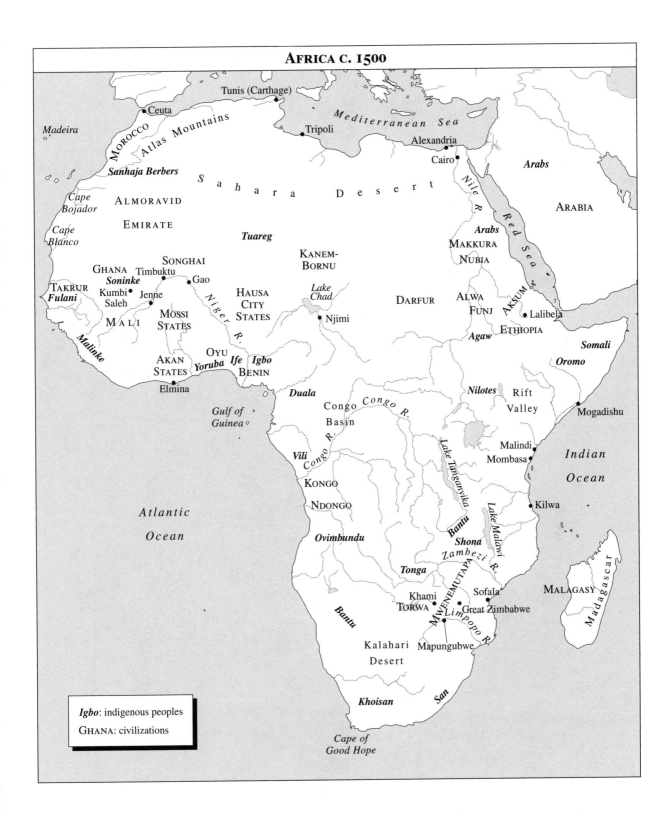

AFRICA C. 1500

Madeira

Tunis (Carthage)

Ceuta

Mediterranean Sea

Tripoli

Alexandria

MOROCCO Atlas Mountains

Cairo

Arabs

Sanhaja Berbers

S a h a r a   D e s e r t

Nile R.

Red Sea

ARABIA

Cape Bojador

ALMORAVID

EMIRATE

Tuareg

Arabs

MAKKURA

NUBIA

Cape Blanco

KANEM-
BORNU

SONGHAI

GHANA Timbuktu

Soninke

Gao

Lake Chad

DARFUR

ALWA

FUNJ

AKSUM

Lalibela

TAKRUR

Fulani

Kumbi
Saleh   Jenne

HAUSA
CITY
STATES

Njimi

ETHIOPIA

Somali

M A L I

MOSSI
STATES

Niger R.

Agaw

Oromo

Malinke

AKAN
STATES

OYU
Yoruba   *Ife*   *Igbo*
BENIN

Nilotes

Rift
Valley

Mogadishu

Elmina

Duala

Congo
Basin

Congo R.

Malindi

Mombasa

Indian

Ocean

Gulf of
Guinea

Vili

Congo R.

Lake Tanganyika

KONGO

Bantu

Kilwa

Atlantic

Ocean

NDONGO

Ovimbundu

Shona

Lake Malawi

Zambezi R.

Tonga

MWENEMUTAPA

Sofala

MALAGASY

Madagascar

Khami
TORWA

Great Zimbabwe

Linpopo R.

Bantu

Mapungubwe

Kalahari
Desert

Khoisan

San

Cape of
Good Hope

Igbo: indigenous peoples

GHANA: civilizations

THE AMERICAS: SIXTEENTH CENTURY EUROPEAN SETTLEMENTS

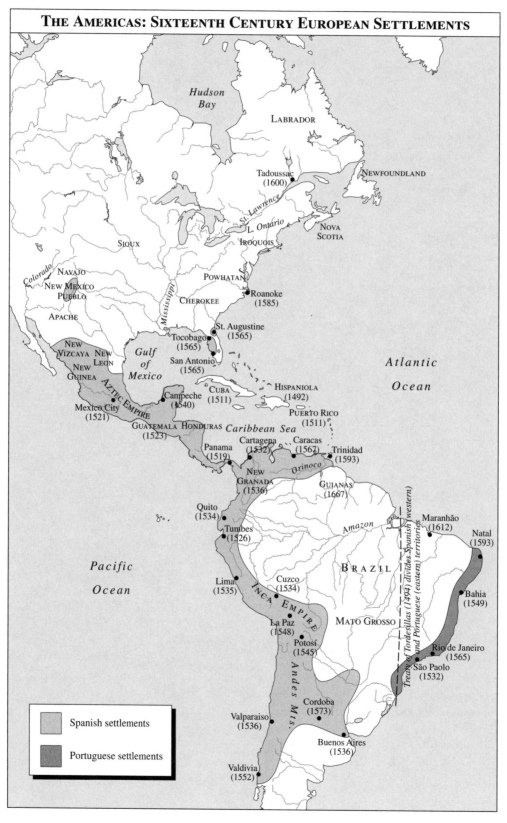

Hudson Bay

LABRADOR

NEWFOUNDLAND

Tadoussac (1600)

St. Lawrence

L. Ontario

NOVA SCOTIA

IROQUOIS

SIOUX

POWHATAN

Colorado

NAVAJO

NEW MEXICO PUEBLO

Mississippi

CHEROKEE

Roanoke (1585)

APACHE

St. Augustine (1565)

NEW VIZCAYA

NEW LEON

Tocobago (1565)

Gulf of Mexico

NEW GUINEA

San Antonio (1565)

Atlantic Ocean

AZTEC EMPIRE

Campeche (1540)

CUBA (1511)

HISPANIOLA (1492)

Mexico City (1521)

GUATEMALA (1523)

HONDURAS

Caribbean Sea

PUERTO RICO (1511)

Panama (1519)

Cartagena (1532)

Caracas (1567)

Trinidad (1593)

NEW GRANADA (1536)

Orinoco

GUIANAS (1667)

Quito (1534)

Amazon

Maranhão (1612)

Tumbes (1526)

Natal (1593)

Pacific Ocean

Lima (1535)

Cuzco (1534)

B R A Z I L

Bahia (1549)

Treaty of Tordesillas (1494) divides Spanish (western) and Portuguese (eastern) territories

La Paz (1548)

MATO GROSSO

Potosí (1545)

Rio de Janeiro (1565)

São Paolo (1532)

Cordoba (1573)

Valparaiso (1536)

Andes Mts.

Buenos Aires (1536)

Valdivia (1552)

☐ Spanish settlements

☐ Portuguese settlements

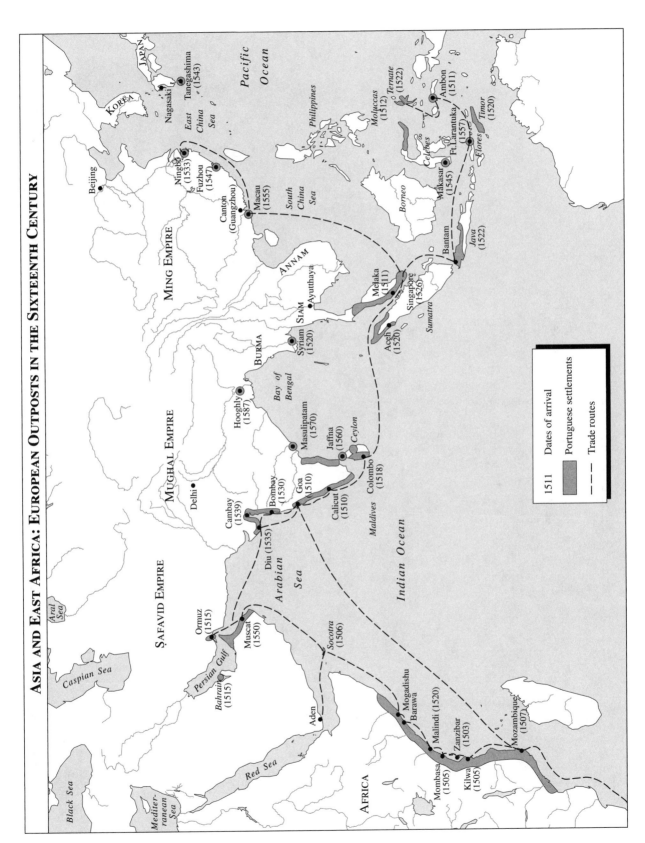

ASIA AND EAST AFRICA: EUROPEAN OUTPOSTS IN THE SIXTEENTH CENTURY

Dates of arrival: 1511

Portuguese settlements

Trade routes

JAPAN

KOREA

Nagasaki
Tanegashima (1543)

Pacific Ocean

East China Sea

Beijing

MING EMPIRE

Ningbo (1533)
Fuzhou (1547)

Canton (Guangzhou)

Macau (1555)

South China Sea

Philippines

Moluccas (1512)
Ternate (1522)
Ambon (1511)
Ft. Larantuka (1557)
Timor (1520)
Flores

Makasar (1545)

Celebes

Borneo

Bantam
Java (1522)

ANNAM

Ayutthaya

STAM

Syriam (1520)

BURMA

Bay of Bengal

Melaka (1511)
Singapore (1526)

Aceh (1520)

Sumatra

MUGHAL EMPIRE

Delhi

Hooghly (1587)

Masulipatam (1570)

Jaffna (1560)
Ceylon
Colombo (1518)

Cambay (1539)
Bombay (1530)
Goa (1510)
Calicut (1510)

Maldives

Indian Ocean

ŞAFAVID EMPIRE

Aral Sea

Caspian Sea

Diu (1535)

Arabian Sea

Ormuz (1515)

Muscat (1550)

Persian Gulf

Bahrain (1515)

Socotra (1506)

Aden

Red Sea

Mogadishu
Barawa (1520)

Malindi
Mombasa (1505)
Zanzibar (1503)
Kilwa (1505)

Mozambique (1507)

AFRICA

Black Sea

Mediterranean Sea

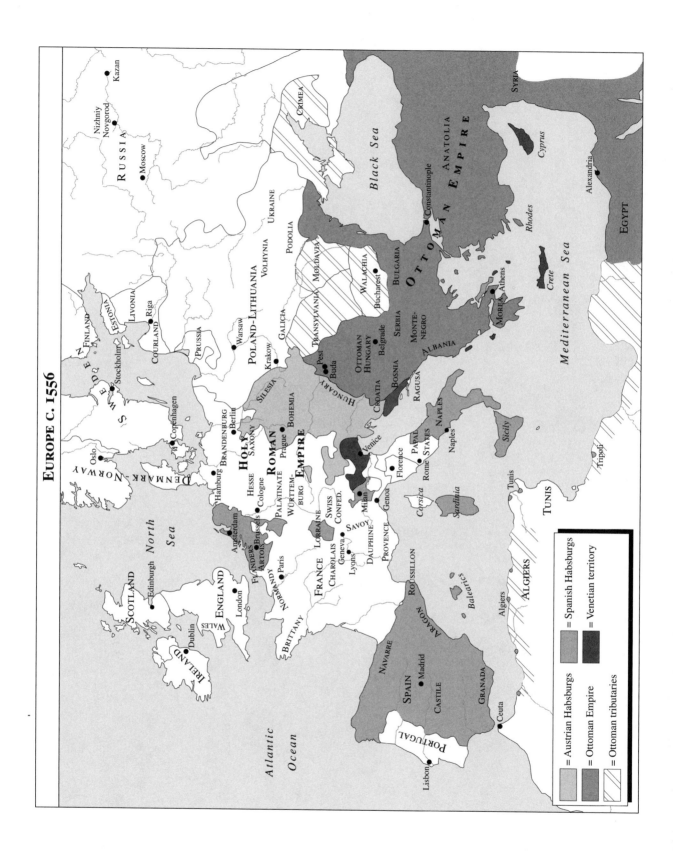

EUROPE C. 1556

= Austrian Habsburgs

= Spanish Habsburgs

= Ottoman Empire

= Venetian territory

= Ottoman tributaries

Great Lives from History

The Renaissance & Early Modern Era

1454 - 1600

Leonardo da Vinci
Italian painter and inventor

Leonardo da Vinci, who laid the foundation for the High Renaissance style in painting, drawing, sculpture, and architecture, is considered by many the best painter and draftsman of all time. In addition, he made a number of unprecedented discoveries in botany, anatomy, mechanical engineering, and medicine that were unparalleled until the twentieth century.

Born: April 15, 1452; Vinci, Republic of Venice (now in Italy)

Died: May 2, 1519; Cloux (now Clos-Lucé), near Amboise, France

Areas of achievement: Art, engineering, science and technology

Early Life

Leonardo da Vinci (lay-oh-NAHR-doh deh VIHN-chee) was born the illegitimate son of Piero da Vinci, descendant of a long line of Florentine minor officials, and a local woman known only as Caterina. Nevertheless, he was reared as a member of his father's household, first in Vinci and then in Florence; a notarized attestation of his birth by his grandfather signifies his family's recognition of him and of its responsibilities toward him. Still, there are few documented facts about his early life. Furthermore, since the first biography of him—by the historian Giorgio Vasari—appeared only some thirty years after his death, conjectural reconstructions have flourished.

Leonardo himself recorded only one event from his childhood, recalled years later, when he was compiling notes on the flight of birds in his notebooks. He simply comments that he was probably fated to write about the flight of kites "because in the earliest memory of my childhood it seemed to me that as I lay in my cradle a kite came down to me and opened my mouth with its tail and struck me with its tail many times between the lips." As open to Freudian reconstruction as this seems to be, it may only document Leonardo's memory of the closeness of the physical environment that was natural to an upbringing in a Tuscan hill village. This is more likely, since his fascination with horses also seems to date from this period. Both interests continued throughout his life.

There is no evidence earlier than Vasari's biography that Leonardo served an apprenticeship under Andrea del Verrocchio, but legend, as well as some internal evidence, seems to make this likely. Under Verrocchio, Leonardo would have worked with fellow apprentices Pietro Perugino, later the teacher of Raphael, and Lorenzo di Credi, both to become masters in their own right.

Of Leonardo's work at this early period little survives, other than some sketches in his notebooks. One page of these, consisting of a series of portraits of the same head—a head that also appears in some of his earlier paintings—seems to record various impressions of himself. If they are self-portraits, they correspond to early reminiscences on the part of his contemporaries of his remarkable beauty and grace; the delicacy of his profile coincides with memories of fluid, dancerlike movement, of a luminous presence and carriage, of an unusually sweet singing voice, of considerable ability as a lutanist, together with quite unexpected physical strength.

One early account credits him with contributing the head of an angel to Verrocchio's painting *Baptism of Christ* (c. 1474-1475), and one head is clearly by a hand subtler and more delicate than Verrocchio's; Vasari reports improbably that Verrocchio was so dismayed by the contrast that he refused to paint thereafter, confining himself to sculpture.

A final event from this period deserves mention. While staying at the house of Verrocchio—long after his apprenticeship had come to an end—Leonardo was twice accused of having visited the house of a notorious boy prostitute, which was tantamount to being accused of sodomy, a crime punishable at best by exile, at worst by being burned at the stake. In neither case was the evidence necessary for conviction brought forth, but the incident suggests something about Leonardo's sexual orientation and perhaps foreshadows his never having a deep relationship with a woman.

Life's Work

Leonardo remains best known for his painting, even though it is now nearly impossible to restore his works to their original splendor. Yet his qualities announce themselves almost immediately in his first Florentine period (1472-1482). In *Baptism of Christ* of Verrocchio, for example, his hand can be seen not only in the angel's head long attributed to him but also in the delicate treatment of the watercourse in the foreground and in the fantastic mountain landscape to the rear. Two similar paintings, both called *The Annunciation*—one in the Louvre, one in the Uffizi, both from around 1475—display advances in structure, delicacy of detail, and a personal iconography unlike that of any previous painter.

LEONARDO DA VINCI ON EXPERIENCE, MOTHER OF ALL CERTAINTY

Leonardo da Vinci's notebooks contain entries that examine painting and the arts, but they also address the sciences and mathematics. Leonardo disagreed with the common belief that painting is purely mechanical, that it requires no special knowledge and is simply putting brush to canvas. Instead, he believed that painting is possible—and scientific in its own right—because it comes from an experiential knowledge made certain by the senses.

They say that knowledge born of experience is mechanical, but that knowledge born and consummated in the mind is scientific, while knowledge born of science and culminating in manual work is semimechanical. But to me it seems that all sciences are vain and full of errors that are not born of experience, mother of all certainty, and that are not tested by experience, that is to say, that do not at their origin, middle, or end pass through any of the five senses. (For if we are doubtful about the certainty of things that pass through the senses, how much more should we question the many things against which these senses rebel, such as the nature of God and the soul and the like, about which there are endless disputes and controversies. And truly it so happens that where reason is not, its place is taken by clamour. This never occurs when things are certain. . . .) The scientific and true principles of painting first determine what is a shaded object, what is direct shadow, what is cast shadow, and what is light, that is to say, darkness, light, colour, body, figure, position, distance, nearness, motion, and rest. These are understood by the mind alone and entail no manual operation. . . .

Source: The Middle Ages and Renaissance. Vol. 1 in *A Documentary History of Art*, edited by Elizabeth Gilmore Holt (New York: Anchor Books, 1957), pp. 275-277.

Among other masterpieces from this period are a portrait of Ginevra de' Benci (c. 1474), *Head of a Woman* (c. 1475), and the *Madonna Benois* (c. 1478). Here the distinctive element is sensitivity of character, so that the figures rendered seem to take on a life of their own, almost as if establishing eye contact through the pictorial plane. Great as these are, the *Adoration of the Magi* (1481) completely transcends them. This unfinished painting occupied Leonardo's attention for the remainder of his stay in Florence, yet he completed only the preliminary underdrawing. Nevertheless, it displays an absolutely unprecedented sense of fantasy and imagination, all accomplished within the norms of accurate Albertian perspective. With this painting, Leonardo broke free from the confines of traditional Nativity iconography, relegating the ruined stable to the background and replacing it with the powerful symbol of the broken arch. He also regrouped the figures of the traditional scene so that they could appear both as individuals with distinct motives

and as participants in a communal activity. Leonardo gives a theological doctrine a real psychological dimension.

Following this stay in Florence, Leonardo resided in Milan for nearly twenty years. Although he apparently hoped to be taken into the service of Duke Ludovico Sforza as military engineer, his principal activities were artistic. His first major work was the *Madonna of the Rocks*, two versions of which survive, one in the Louvre and one in the National Gallery in London, both from around 1485. This work was commissioned by the Convent of the Conception in Milan, and, although the doctrine of the Immaculate Conception had not yet been officially adopted, Leonardo chose to depict it in his painting.

The Last Supper (1495-1497), a fresco, is a true masterwork and a ruin. To get the effects he wanted, Leonardo invented new methods of applying color to wet plaster. At first he seemed to have succeeded, but by 1517, the work had already begun to deteriorate, and by 1566, Vasari pronounced it a jumble of blots. Only in the late twentieth century did restoration recover the core of the original. What is there is astonishing in itself, but what is lost is irreplaceable. The work at first seems firmly rooted in tradition; the framing derives directly from previous treatments of the subject by Andrea del Castagno and Ghirlandajo. Where they focused on the moment when Christ confronted Judas, Leonardo chose to treat the instant when Christ revealed the presence of a traitor in the midst of the faithful. Leonardo thus transfixed the immediate response as with a candid lens; all the apostles save one act out their unique forms of the question, "Is it I, Lord?" In this way, he reveals their responses both as individuals and as members of a communion.

To get the expressions he wanted, he walked the streets for hours, sketching memorable faces on his portable pad, then fitting expression to individual character and working at the combinations until he got the exact effect he wanted. The unveiling of this fresco must have been explosive, for the moment catches the apostles' regrouping after the shock wave has passed. Few spectators would have noted that Leonardo had here also transcended the laws of Albertian perspective.

In 1500, Leonardo left Milan. Thereafter, except for a return lasting from 1508 to 1513, he was a transient. At first this did not keep him from painting. In Florence in 1501, he displayed a preliminary drawing for a *Virgin and Child with Saint Anne and the Infant Saint John,* though he did not complete the painting. The cartoon itself is marvelous in the integrity of the grouping, the revelation of movement in a fixed moment, and the combination of the casual with the intense. An equally celebrated and similar contemporary cartoon for the painting of *Virgin and Child with Saint Anne* (1508-1513) reveals how much has been lost, for this work again shows Leonardo's carrying his ideas one step further. In this painting, he places his subjects against a barren and forbidding backdrop and concentrates on the

physical and theological fecundity of the Virgin, who is shown rocking in the lap of her mother while trying to contain her Child, who is evading her to clasp the lamb—the emblem of his sacrifice. Their expressions are joyful, serene, and supernally oblivious to the implications: Leonardo presents a quiet portrait of a family doomed to be ripped asunder to bring life to the world.

This painting, along with a late *Saint John the Baptist,* was among the three works taken by Leonardo when he moved to France in 1515. The third was the *Mona Lisa* (1503), easily the most celebrated and most identifiable painting in the world as well as one of the most controversial. Historians cannot even agree on the subject of the work, so that its proper title is still questioned; critics argue about whether the painting was finished, about the meaning of the famous smile, and about the significance of the background. Yet several points are indisputable. One is that Leonardo created a pose that would dominate portrait painting for the next three centuries. Another is

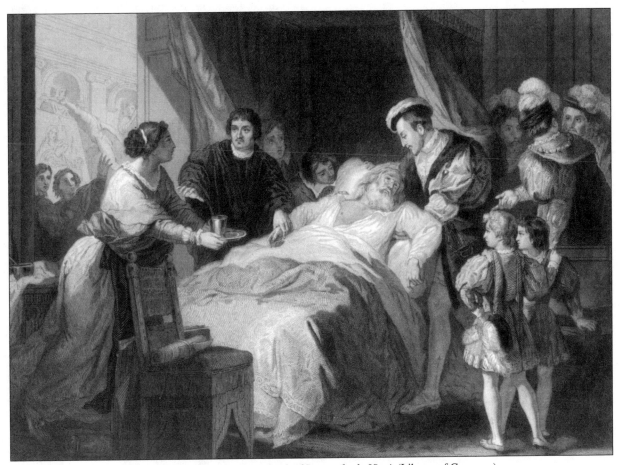

An engraved depiction of the death of Leonardo da Vinci. (Library of Congress)

that he made the depiction of arms and hands an indispensable element in the disclosure of character. A third is that the effect of the painting has much to do with the contrast between the savage, uninhabitable background of crag and moor and the ineffable tranquillity of the woman's face. This woman is ascendant over the barren land. That apparently meant everything to the artist as he aged.

For the last ten years of his life, Leonardo did little painting, though he was much sought after; instead, he occupied himself with problems in mathematics, botany, optics, anatomy, and mechanics. He left unfinished his last commission, a battle piece for the Palazzo Vecchio in Florence, in which he was in direct competition with Michelangelo. At sixty-three, out of touch with the monumental achievements of his successors Michelangelo and Raphael, he accepted an appointment with the king of France to settle at the château of Cloux, near Amboise, where his only duty was to converse with the king. There he died, still pursuing his research, on May 2, 1519.

SIGNIFICANCE

Leonardo da Vinci's achievement was nothing less than the foundation of the High Renaissance style in the arts, in theory or practice or both. His equally significant accomplishments in establishing the groundwork for the scientific study of botany, anatomy, physiology, and medicine fall short only because he did not publish his theories and observations and because his secretive manner of recording kept them from discovery until long after most of them had been superseded.

His career presents a unique paradox. He is unique in having accomplished so much during his lifetime—he seems to be a compendium of several men, all geniuses. Yet he is also unique in having left so little behind and in having disguised or obscured much of that; some of his legacy was still being rediscovered in the middle of the twentieth century, and much of it will never be restored.

Leonardo's discoveries ranged across the boundaries of art and science, because for him there were no boundaries to the inquiring intellect. The key to opening up these realms of inquiry was the eye, for Leonardo the principal instrument of observation, with which discovery began. In both art and science, Leonardo held that observation had to take precedence over both established authority and established method. What was true to the eye was the supreme truth; the eye alone opened the window to the intellect and to the soul.

—James Livingston

FURTHER READING

Atalay, Bülent. *Math and the Mona Lisa: The Art and Science of Leonardo da Vinci.* Washington, D.C.: Smithsonian Books, 2004. This study of the relationship between science, art, mathematics, and nature treats Leonardo as a mathematician working out his ideas in art instead of numbers, or as an artist whose medium is fundamentally scientific. Includes photographic plates, illustrations, bibliographic references, and index.

Clark, Kenneth. *Leonardo da Vinci: An Account of His Development as an Artist.* Rev. ed. Baltimore: Penguin Books, 1967. One of the best overall treatments of the technical and compositional qualities of Leonardo's work. Contains excellent plates and good illustrations. Makes fine connections between Leonardo's innovations in optics and anatomy and their effects on his painting techniques.

Goldscheider, Ludwig. *Leonardo da Vinci.* 6th ed. London: Phaidon Press, 1959. Presents a thorough survey of the life and accomplishments of Leonardo, with outstanding plates. Also presents a clear account of Leonardo's relations with other artists and with his patrons.

Hartt, Frederick. *History of Italian Renaissance Art: Painting, Sculpture, Architecture.* 5th ed. New York: Harry N. Abrams, 2003. Certainly the best-written overall account of its subject, with clear technical exposition, sumptuous illustrations, and finely tuned tracing of the cultural complex. Written by an expert in the iconography of the period.

Heydenreich, Ludwig H. *Leonardo da Vinci.* 2 vols. New York: Macmillan, 1954. This standard scholarly biography abounds in illuminating detail about Leonardo's life, accomplishments, and environment.

Kemp, Martin. *Leonardo da Vinci: The Marvelous Works of Nature and of Man.* Cambridge, Mass.: Harvard University Press, 1981. Kemp concentrates on the revelations in the published notebooks and in other writings of Leonardo, reproducing the illustrations brilliantly and bringing them to bear on Leonardo's paintings. Kemp also pieces together Leonardo's detached observations into a coherent philosophical system, focusing on the priority of the eye.

Leonardo da Vinci. *Selections from the Notebooks of Leonardo da Vinci.* Edited by Irma Richter. Reprint. New York: Oxford University Press, 1977. The best succinct introduction to the wealth of material contained in Leonardo's notebooks, deciphered and fully published only in the twentieth century. Richter selects the material intelligently and provides the right amount of explanation.

Marani, Pietro C. *Leonardo da Vinci: The Complete Paintings.* New York: Harry N. Abrams, 2000. A truly remarkable book, this text includes reproductions and scholarly analysis of all known paintings by da Vinci in loving detail, including double foldout reproductions of his frescoes, extreme close-ups of select details, and a host of sketches and works by Leonardo's contemporaries. Also includes checklists of all extant paintings and all known lost paintings, an appendix of all known primary documents that refer directly to the artist's life, extensive bibliography, and index.

Parr, Adrian. *Exploring the Work of Leonardo da Vinci Within the Context of Contemporary Philosophical Thought and Art.* Lewiston, N.Y.: Edwin Mellen Press, 2003. A reinterpretation of Leonardo's aesthetic project from the point of view of modern and postmodern criticism, especially the work of Gilles Deleuze. Looks at the dynamics of identification and the impossibility of pure verisimilitude. Includes illustrations, bibliographic references, and index.

Payne, Robert. *Leonardo.* Garden City, N.Y.: Doubleday, 1978. Payne provides an extremely readable and nicely detailed discussion of Leonardo's life and work, avoiding technical jargon and guiding clearly through obscure and confusing material.

Pedretti, Carlo. *Leonardo: A Study in Chronology and Style.* London: Thames and Hudson, 1973. An accessible book on Leonardo by the foremost modern authority. Pedretti is full of insights and useful knowledge, particularly on the relation between the artist's writings and his work.

Wasserman, Jack. *Leonardo da Vinci.* New York: Harry N. Abrams, 1975. A solid art historian's approach to the life, reflections, and art of Leonardo, this book is more readable than most and provides solid background material as well as illuminating discussion of the paintings. Particularly good on the relationship between written material and art.

SEE ALSO: Andrea del Sarto; Donato Bramante; Correggio; Francis I; Giorgione; Michelangelo; Raphael; Ludovico Sforza; Giorgio Vasari; Andrea del Verrocchio.

RELATED ARTICLES in *Great Events from History: The Renaissance & Early Modern Era, 1454-1600:* 1469-1492: Rule of Lorenzo de' Medici; c. 1478-1519: Leonardo da Vinci Compiles His Notebooks; 1481-1499: Ludovico Sforza Rules Milan; Beginning 1490: Development of the Camera Obscura; 1495-1497: Leonardo da Vinci Paints *The Last Supper;* c. 1500: Revival of Classical Themes in Art; c. 1510: Invention of the Watch; 1517: Fracastoro Develops His Theory of Fossils.

PIERRE LESCOT
French architect

Lescot was long regarded as the first of France's great architects, chiefly because of his redesign and reconstruction of the original Louvre castle. Although modern scholarship modifies this estimate, he remains ranked among the premier French architects and designers of the sixteenth century.

BORN: 1510?; Paris, France
DIED: September 10, 1578; Paris
AREAS OF ACHIEVEMENT: Architecture, art

EARLY LIFE

Biographical material on the early life of Pierre Lescot (pee-ehr lehs-koh) is limited and often unverifiable. He was born probably in Paris in 1510 into a well-positioned seigneurial family. His father, for whom he was named,

was King Francis I's crown attorney, an attorney for one of the courts of relief, or assistance, as well as the leader of the Parisian merchant guilds. The elder Lescot held estates at Lissy near Brie and, among others, at Clagny close to the royal residences at Versailles. Originally, the Lescots came to France from Italy, where their connections with the Alessi family affected the younger Lescot's later career.

While a young man, Lescot inherited the paternal estate at Clagny. Favored by Francis and Henry II, Lescot served as their principal chaplain, as their honorary church canon, as an associate abbey at Clermont near Laval, and as a canon at Nôtre Dame in Paris. Advantaged by such royal associations and family position, the younger Lescot began displaying talents as a painter, while at the same time studying mathematics and architecture. Very likely while young, Lescot journeyed to Italy, where, under the auspices of old family friends, he absorbed decorative and architectural concepts later manifested in his work. Unquestionably, he studied Italian architectural writings and examined many of France's Roman ruins many years prior to his official visit to Rome in 1556.

Under absolutist monarchs who were forging France into Europe's first nation-state, Paris during Lescot's lifetime was also changing. Whether engaged in the monarchs' hodgepodge administrative structures or in the small manufacturies producing luxuries for Crown and court, most of the 250,000 inhabitants of Paris clustered around the Île de la Cité, the Seine River island that from time immemorial simultaneously offered the people their best opportunities for defense and the first ford bridge linking both riverbanks. During Lescot's lifetime, royalty, its retainers, and courtiers began converting the Marais (swamp), the oldest district on the Seine's north bank, into an aristocratic enclave, where services of architects—builders and artists—were ineluctably drawn.

LIFE'S WORK

Lescot's architectural work commenced during a period of brilliance in French Renaissance architecture, translating into its own idiom characteristics of Italian styles, while subduing elements of its own Gothic traditions. Among his contemporaries and colleagues were the great French sculptor Jean Goujon and Philibert Delorme, an innovative engineer. Encouraged by relative domestic peace, the Crown, its court, and other aristocrats not only began new constructions but also planned to redesign buildings and residences that formerly functioned as fortified positions. New or remodeled, these structures were intended as the abodes of people enjoying the money and leisure to live more ostentatiously, surrounded by what they conceived to be the ultimate in style.

Francis's own building obsession, which included several châteaus, was epitomized in 1519 by his redesign of Chambord, initially a feudal strong point, which, on completion, reflected Italian symmetries imposed on a functionally banal fortress. Partly a consequence of French and Italian architects and artists crossing one another's borders more frequently, Chambord, as an exemplar, inspired more imaginative, eclectic, and sophisticated architectural design in France.

Francis then turned his attention to the three-hundred-year-old Louvre in Paris, whose pattern closely conformed to other thirteenth century castles, many then still built of wood. It was replete with a strong tower and a donjon, and was surrounded by sturdy masonry walls.

Because the Louvre's poor drainage and *odeurs* made its precincts unfashionable and its proximity to religious houses and the raucous students of the Left Bank undesirable, Francis decided in 1526 on the Louvre's modernization, though aside from removing the donjon, nothing was done until 1546. That year, Lescot was selected to construct a new structure on the site of the old château's west wing—the Old Louvre—then lying outside the old city walls. Considering the restricted Parisian work space available, Lescot planned for two floors of detached buildings, with a central pavilion and its staircase. Each side was to be flanked by large public reception rooms. Within five years, however, these plans had been revised, providing for a grander gallery (*salle*) and shifting the staircase to the north wing: in all, requiring construction of two new pavilions at each end with a new staircase for one of them. Moreover, the façade was raised one floor so construction of the King's Pavilion to the southwest would not overpower these two new pavilions.

Monarchs, the times, and styles altered events even as Lescot's revisions were under way. Sometime between 1551 and Henry's death in 1559, Lescot was called on by the Crown to develop more ambitious plans, which he did. His new plans called for building a court enclosed by blocks double the length of his original wing. The Louvre façade was visually unified with pilasters of the then-preferred Corinthian and Composite orders. Pediments over windows were alternated between triangular and rounded ones: a variety demanding attention. Each of his three pavilions divided into separate bays, differing from the wings uniting them. Ground-floor windows were set inside rounded arches; those windows of the second floor featured open pediments; and attic windows were capped by sculpted crossed torches. All three pavilions, devoid of horizontal lines, were designed to accentuate the vertical: Double columns, among other devices, carried eyes upward. Overall, Lescot (with Goujon) successfully blended classical and traditional French architecture into his own style of French classicism.

Lescot's interior work on the new wing was brilliantly enhanced by Goujon's caryatids—ornamentation unknown in France and rare even in Renaissance Italy—and by the four groups of sixteen richly decorated Doric columns separating—yet affording monumentality—to the southern end of the great gallery. Their genius combined, Lescot's and Goujon's interior collaborations were almost inseparable: Both added distinctions to an architectural masterwork.

Although his career was preempted for years by the Louvre, Lescot managed many other commissions. Again in collaboration with Goujon, he built the Hôtel Carnavalet in 1545, filling the space between the Hôtel de Ville and the Bastille, thereby luring more courtiers and aristocrats into the Marais district. His use at Carnavalet of a wide street flanked by stables and a kitchen in lieu of a plain wall shortly became the rage among wealthy Parisians. Lescot worked on these other projects with great craftspeople. When Henry tired of his bedroom ceiling, Lescot and the Italian wood-carver Scribec di Carpi produced a new ceiling that rivaled any other of the period, including the magnificent ceilings for which Venice was famous.

After Henry's death in 1559, Lescot's personal life disappears from the historical record. Francis, who previously extended him his first commissions, enthusiastically supported him, partially repaying him by designating him the canon of Paris's metropolitan church (with its many perquisites) and by making him the abbey of Clermont and a royal councillor as well. Francis's successors reconfirmed these prerogatives for him, and throughout his career he maintained his Clagny estate. There is no other substantial knowledge of him, except that his death occurred on September 10, 1578, in Paris.

SIGNIFICANCE

For some modern architectural historians, Lescot has been a source of debate: He was basically an amateur architect, and he was not a critical figure in the development of French architecture, particularly the distinctive Gallic version of Renaissance architecture—French classicism.

In addition, many of Lescot's plans and constructions were flawed, and some believe that as a mere overseer, he assumed credit for the genius of men such as Jean Goujon. Whatever modicum of credibility may be accorded these views, in the light of the overall evidence available, they fail to diminish significantly his contribution to his singularly imaginative plans and designs combining Italianate Renaissance elements with traditional French elements that produced a uniquely French architectural style. This was no more pronouncedly evident than in the original reconstruction of the Louvre and in the designs and plans that substantially determined the shape of that magnificent structure's future.

Moreover, the design and embellishment of the Louvre and other of his original work represents a rare conjunction of architectural, engineering, and sculpting genius—that is, the collaboration of Lescot, Goujon, and Scribec di Carpi. In addition to all their other accomplishments, they produced a nucleus around which, architecturally, one of the world's most visual and magnificent urban cultural centers would develop to the wonderment of many subsequent generations.

—Clifton K. Yearley

FURTHER READING

Blunt, Anthony. *Art and Architecture in France, 1500-1700.* 5th ed. Revised by Richard Beresford. New Haven, Conn.: Yale University Press, 1999. Excellently and authoritatively written for general readers by a distinguished art critic and historian. Descriptions of Lescot's work on the Louvre are clear and detailed. Contains notes for each chapter and many illustrations and plates.

Cloulas, Ivan, and Michèle Bimbenet-Privat. *Treasures of the French Renaissance.* Translated by John Goodman. New York: Harry N. Abrams, 1998. Survey of French Renaissance architecture, the chateaux and palaces of the period, and the treasures contained within. Includes illustrations, bibliographic references, and index.

Gardner, Helen, et al. *Gardner's Art Through the Ages.* 11th ed. Fort Worth, Tex.: Harcourt College, 2001. Chapter 14 is especially pertinent to the work of Lescot and his colleagues. The book is beautifully illustrated in both color and black and white and includes plates and schematics. The text is well written. Contains a glossary, a bibliography, and an index.

Hamlin, Talbot. *Architecture Through the Ages.* Rev. ed. New York: Putnam, 1953. Chapter 16 bears particularly on the Renaissance in France and Italy, and hence on Lescot's work on the Louvre. Older and less critical than Blunt's book, it is still accurate and substantial in its major features. Contains many fine photographs and schematics and an excellent, double-columned index.

Janson, H. W. *History of Art.* 3d ed. Revised and expanded by Anthony F. Janson. New York: Harry N. Abrams, 1986. Clearly written, this is a large, lavishly illustrated work with splendid black-and-white and color photographs. Part 3 of the book deals specifically with the Renaissance and Chapter 5, the subject of which is the Renaissance in the North, has excellent materials, including photographs of Lescot's old Louvre.

Lévêque, Jean-Jacques. *The Louvre: A Palace, a Museum.* Translated by Geoffrey Finch, Ellen Krabbe, and Kirk McElhearn. Courbevoie, France: ACR, 1999. Details the history of the Louvre and its transformation from palace to museum. Includes color illustrations.

Ranum, Orest. *Paris in the Age of Absolutism.* Rev. and exp. ed. University Park: Pennsylvania State University Press, 2003. This extended essay is very important to an understanding of the general social, political, and intellectual climate prevalent in Lescot's day. Lescot is mentioned in connection with the Louvre and other works. Contains prints of local scenes, a fine view of the Louvre front, and portraiture paintings. Includes an excellent select bibliography and an extensive, double-columned index.

SEE ALSO: Leon Battista Alberti; Donato Bramante; Francis I; Henry II; Michelangelo; Andrea Palladio; Piero della Francesca; Raphael; Jacopo Sansovino; Diego de Siloé.

RELATED ARTICLE in *Great Events from History: The Renaissance & Early Modern Era, 1454-1600:* c. 1500: Revival of Classical Themes in Art.

MICHEL DE L'HOSPITAL
French statesman

An eminent jurist and Humanist, L'Hospital was a conciliatory officeholder under Henry II and into the French Wars of Religion. Despite the failure of his policy of moderation during his lifetime, his plea for civil peace still inspires advocates of religious tolerance.

BORN: c. 1505; Aigueperse, Auvergne (now Puy-de-Dôme), France
DIED: March 13, 1573; Belesbat, France
ALSO KNOWN AS: Michel de L'Hôpital
AREAS OF ACHIEVEMENT: Government and politics, law

EARLY LIFE

A first-born nobleman, Michel de L'Hospital (loh-pee-tahl) studied law and classical literature in Toulouse and also was drawn to Latin verse writing. In 1523, he had to leave for Italy with his father, Jean, who was the physician and councilor of the constable of Bourbon—a traitor to King Francis I. They fled to join Charles V's retinue, and young L'Hospital was then suspected and long imprisoned in Toulouse, from 1523 to 1526, when the king released him.

After assisting his father in Milan, he completed his juridical training and taught civil law in Padua, from 1526 to 1531, surrounded by Christian Humanists. He was briefly named auditor of the Rota in Rome, then attended the University of Bologna (1531-1533). When he returned to France in late 1533, due to amnesty, he intended to become a magistrate.

In 1537, in order to gain a position as a councilor in the Paris Parlement (the judiciary and legislative court), he married Marie Morin, a moderate Protestant. Once in Parlement, he gained a solid reputation as an exacting lawyer. In his writings, he deplores the corruption of Paris and the severity of growing religious dissent and repression. Eager to influence events, he participated in national meetings (Moulins, 1540; Riom, 1542), and soon solicited appointments to positions in public affairs.

Henry II first sent him to the ecumenical Council of Trent, then in Bologna (1547-1548), as an ambassador. There, disheartened by the multiple postponements of the council, he associated with Italian Humanists. He frequented the court of Duchess Renée in nearby Ferrara, which was a refuge for French Protestants and liberal thinkers and a place that deepened L'Hospital's secular piety. He became the tutor of Renée's daughter, Anne d'Este, and he arranged her marriage to François of Lorraine, second duke de Guise, who became his new patron. When he returned to Paris and the Parlement in 1548, he also befriended the powerful cardinal Charles of Lorraine.

LIFE'S WORK

When Henry II's sister Marguerite married, she appointed L'Hospital chancellor of Berry in 1550 (a title he held until 1560). Faithful to his other patrons, the duke of Guise and the cardinal of Lorraine, he became "Master of the Requests" in 1553 and first president of the Court of Exchequer in 1555. His correspondence with the chancellor of France, François Olivier, displays their common moral and pragmatic concerns regarding rising religious tensions between the Roman Catholics and the Protestant Calvinists, called the Huguenots, in France. On the accession to the French throne of fifteen-year-old Francis II (1559), and while still serving Marguerite in Nice, L'Hospital entered the Privy Council and dedicated a Humanistic memoir on kingship to the young monarch. The young king, however, died a year later.

After the death of Chancellor Olivier, L'Hospital was unexpectedly named chancellor of France on April 1, 1560. Francis II's mother, Catherine de Médicis, now regent, worked to reconcile the two religious camps. L'Hospital labored for conciliation and toleration for sedition by the Protestants and two noble families: the Guises, who aligned themselves the Spanish crown and Catholicism, and the generally Protestant Bourbons, who were next in line to the French crown after Catherine's children. He promoted the Edicts of Romorantin for national unity (May, 1560), and he induced Catherine de Médicis to call the assembly of notables at Fontainebleau in August, 1560, which Bourbon leaders boycotted. Another failed conspiracy from the Guises against the Bourbons in September and the unexpected death of Francis II in December aggravated civil disorder.

At the Estates-General of Orléans in January, 1561, L'Hospital rejected seditious violence in the name of ethics and faith. The Edicts of February, April, and July, 1561, which suspended all prosecutions for private religious opinion and forbade seditious gathering, were soon abolished. At the Colloquy of Poissy (September 9-14, 1561), L'Hospital managed to get the Catholic and Huguenot leaders to sit together, but it turned into a riot. Despite the colloquy's failure, the chancellor kept striving for moderation and national unity.

At the Estates-General of Saint-Germain, he proposed the liberal and later acclaimed Edict of January (1562), granting Huguenots liberty of worship outside cities and the right to hold meetings in private homes. Yet such pacifying gestures only increased seditious rage, which soon led to the first War of Religion (1562-1563). When the Crown provided no justice for the assassinated Protestants at the Massacre of Wassy, the French civil war started. L'Hospital retreated to his estate in Vignay, though still in office. He was recalled after the precarious Pacification of Amboise, which favored the Protestants. Facing increasing turmoil, the chancellor and Catherine declared Charles IX of age and accompanied him on a tour of the kingdom from 1564 to 1566. Factions, however, kept quarreling over the means to reform the kingdom and questioning royal authority.

Also active in foreign policy, L'Hospital wrote the thirty-four articles representing France at the Council of Trent in 1564, but it appears that he faced the powerful pope and Philip II of Spain as the only statesman in Europe advocating moderation and peace. Still endeavoring toward pragmatic balance and civil concord, he insisted

that the Protestant ruler Jeanne d'Albret grant Catholics in Béarn (a region in southwestern France) the same rights Protestants demanded in the north. France finally declined the Council of Trent's decrees.

While growing hostilities deprived L'Hospital of actual power, he concentrated on administrative efficiency, reforming court justice and the royal treasury. He is said to have elaborated the Ordinance of Moulins (February, 1566), an edict that sealed an apparent reconciliation by balancing royal and local governments' authority. This reform was one of L'Hospital's last and most enduring juridical legacies.

When a new civil war threatened in September, 1567, L'Hospital once again advocated tolerant measures, but his policy of moderation was faulted for aggravating dissent. Still believing in appeasement, however, he personally addressed party leaders and notables, trying to curb national dissent, until pacification was reached in March, 1568. When L'Hospital, however, refused to seal the papal bull authorizing aggression that Catherine had requested, the regent allied herself with the ultra-Catholics to eliminate the Huguenots. The chancellor, therefore, had to surrender his official seals in 1568 as the third war of religion began.

L'Hospital retired in grief and seclusion. His 1570 *Discours politiques, 1560-1568* to Charles IX explicates his integrity and pacifism. The massacre of Protestants on St. Bartholomew's Day (August 24, 1572) not only marked his failure but also made him fear for his daughter, who was saved by the duchess of Guise, while Marguerite protected him. He resigned after the Peace of Saint-Germain was made official on February 1, 1573, and died only six weeks later, before civil war again broke out.

SIGNIFICANCE

L'Hospital embodies the committed Christian Humanist. A jurist and scholar, he reformed justice, protected French poets (La Pléide), and wrote letters and speeches (in Latin and French) advocating peace, ethics, and irenic faith. As a public servant, he strengthened the monarchy through treasury control, trade regulation, and criminal justice, thereby partly prefiguring Cardinal de Richelieu's absolutist policy.

A realist statesman in wartime, he supported civil toleration and regarded moral and lawful patriotism as a pillar of politics. To his mind, national unity stemmed from the interdependence of "one faith, one law, one king" (faith as a moral bond, law as a reminder of it, with the king incarnating religious and temporal unity). He pragmatically advocated religious pluralism in order to avoid civil conflict—a largely incomprehensible mind-set at the time.

L'Hospital's policy of moderation and toleration is now viewed as one of the first attempts at the separation of church and state, and at entrusting temporal authority against partisan sedition. Variously called Civil Evangelicism, Gallican irenicism, or the third-party Politiques, his followers succeeded when Henry IV's Edict of Nantes (1598) ended the civil war by reaffirming the right to private worship for Huguenots. Civil pluralism, a concept L'Hospital's work foreshadowed, soared with Enlightenment philosophers, who demanded genuine toleration and limited church power.

—*Corinne Noirot Maguire*

FURTHER READING

Beame, Edmond. "The Politiques and the Historians." *Journal of the History of Ideas* 54, no. 3 (July, 1993): 355-379. Surveys polemical designations of the Catholic moderate party during and after the religious wars.

Holt, Mack, et al. *The French Wars of Religion, 1562-1629*. New York: Cambridge University Press, 1995. Provides authoritative and extensive historical background with a description of L'Hospital's chancellorship in the first section.

Hunt, Richard. *Religion and Law: The Chancellorship of Michel de L'Hospital (1560-1562)*. Philadelphia: University of Pennsylvania Press, 1973. Covers L'Hospital's first two years in office and his attempt to avoid civil war by reinstating legal justice as a civil ward.

Kim, Seong-Hang. "The Chancellor's Crusade: Michel de L'Hôpital and the Parlement of Paris." *French History* 7, no. 1 (1993): 1-29. Portrays L'Hospital as a sponsor of royal authority opposed by the Parlement and misunderstood by royalty.

_____. "'Dieu nous garde de la messe du Chancelier': The Religious Belief and Political Opinion of Michel de L'Hôpital." *Sixteenth Century Journal* 24, no. 3 (1993): 595-620. Explains toleration of Protestantism as a means for the Catholic statesman to maintain national unity under a strong monarchy.

_____. *Michel de L'Hôpital: The Visions of a Reformist Chancellor During the French Religious Wars*. Sixteenth Century Essays and Studies 36. Kirksville, Mo.: Sixteenth Century Journal Publishers, 1997. Exhaustive, acute, and accurate biographical account of L'Hospital's ideas and practice.

Turchetti, Mario. "Religious Concord and Political Tolerance in Sixteenth and Seventeenth Century France." *Revue de Théologie et de Philosophie* 118 (1986): 255-267. Analyzes the 1560-1562 toleration edicts as a compromise to attain religious unity.

SEE ALSO: Catherine de Médicis; Charles V; Henry II; Henry IV.

RELATED ARTICLES in *Great Events from History: The Renaissance & Early Modern Era, 1454-1600*: 1545-1563: Council of Trent; March, 1562-May 2, 1598: French Wars of Religion.

SIR THOMAS LITTLETON
English legal scholar

Littleton's fame rests on a short treatise titled Tenures, *in which he gives a full and clear account of the several estates, tenures, and doctrines pertaining to landholding that were then known to English law. This work is the primary source of the land law of medieval England, and it is considered to be the first great book on English law not written in Latin and wholly uninfluenced by Roman law.*

BORN: 1422; Frankley, Worcestershire, England
DIED: August 23, 1481; Frankley
ALSO KNOWN AS: Thomas de Littleton (given name); Thomas Lyttelton; Thomas Luttelton
AREA OF ACHIEVEMENT: Law

EARLY LIFE

Thomas Littleton was one of four sons and four daughters born to Thomas Westcote of Westcote, near Barnstaple, England, a courtier to the king, and Elizabeth de Littleton, daughter and sole heir of Thomas de Littleton, lord of the manor of Frankley and esquire of the body to three kings: Richard II, Henry IV of Castile, and Henry V. It was agreed at the time of the marriage that, since the estate that would ultimately come to Elizabeth was large and that it was desirable to maintain the Littleton name, the firstborn son would have the name Littleton rather than Westcote. Therefore, although the other children of the marriage used the name Westcote, Thomas, the eldest son, was named

Thomas de Littleton (spelled Luttleton prior to the reign of Henry VI).

What is known of Littleton's early personal life is very spare. He received his training in law at the Inns of Court, where he was a member of the Inner Temple. Between the years 1440 and 1450, in addition to his marriage to Joan, the widow of Sir Philip Chetwynd, of Ingestrie, Staffordshire, and one of the daughters and coheirs of Sir William Burley of Bromscroft Castle, he started to gain considerable prominence in the county of Worcestershire: His professional services were requested against the famous family of the Pastons; he became in 1444 escheator of the county, undersheriff of that county from 1447 to 1448, and in 1450 recorder of the town of Coventry, who had the honor of receiving Henry VI when that king came to visit in 1450. On his appointment as reader of the Inner Temple in or about 1450, he began to study and explain the great Statute of Westminster II, otherwise known as *De donis conditionalibus*, which in 1285 had revolutionized the alienation of land, and in 1451 or 1452, he was granted for life, as a result of his great and good counsel, the manor of Sheriff Hales in Staffordshire by Sir William Trussel.

On July 2, 1453, about the time when the Wars of the Roses were beginning in England, Littleton was called to the degree of serjeant-at-law, and then on May 13, 1455, was appointed Henry VI's serjeant, where he rode the northern circuit as a justice of assize. Although this appointment did not bring him an increase in legal business, it did bring him an advance in dignity and responsibility. The king's serjeants were actually advisers to the Crown, standing at the head of the legal profession, and even outranking, according to the historian Eugene Wambaugh, the attorney general. He was under the protection of Richard of York (Richard III), one of the contenders for the throne in the Wars of the Roses, and must have been of high repute, for he was placed on a commission under the privy seal for raising funds for the defense of Calais, was one of the commissioners of array for Warwickshire, and was justice of the county palatine of Lancaster. High in favor with Edward IV, who came to the throne in 1461, Littleton was first reappointed as king's serjeant and then raised to the position of justice of the Court of Common Pleas in Westminster on April 27, 1466, retaining that position until his death. It was in that position that he was drawn particularly close to the matter of land questions, because the Court of Common Pleas largely dealt with real estate issues.

LIFE'S WORK

According to Sir John Fortescue, the noted judge of the Court of King's Bench, in his *De laudibus legum Angliæ* (wr. 1470, pb. 1537; *Learned Commendation of the Politique Lawes of Englande*, 1567), the judges of England sat in the king's courts only about three hours in the day, from eight in the morning until eleven, the courts being closed in the afternoon so that the judges would have time to study the laws, read the Holy Scriptures, and busy themselves with other "innocent amusements," so that the life of a judge appeared to be one of contemplation. Therefore, Littleton's appointment as a judge gave him the opportunity to devote himself to the writing of his work on tenures. Also, the position gave Littleton a certain freedom from care; even though the Crown changed hands two times, the judges of the Courts of Common Pleas and the Court of the King's Bench were not affected, being given new patents to retain their positions.

Honors came to Littleton fairly rapidly, for he was employed on a commission to arbitrate a dispute between the bishop of Winchester and several of the bishop's tenants with regard to their services and the quality of their tenure under him; he was chosen to be trier of petitions from Gascony in the parliaments of 1467 and 1472; he was made a Knight of the Bath on April 18, 1475; and he was allowed extensive expenditures for salary and personal expenses. He executed his will on August 22, 1481, died the following day, August 23, 1481, and was interred in the Cathedral Church of Worcester, "under a fair tomb of marble, with his statue or portraiture on it, together . . . with a memorial of his principal titles," in the words of the great English jurist Sir Edward Coke. Out of the mouth of the statue, which Littleton had finished while yet alive, was inscribed the prayer "Fili Dei miserere mei" (Jesus Christ have mercy on me).

According to Coke, Littleton had a "grave and reverend countenance," as he observed from the figure of Littleton shown kneeling in coif and scarlet robes that adorned the east window of the chancel of the Chapel of St. Leonard, Frankley, and a portrait of him in one of the windows of the church at Halesowen, both of which were destroyed at some point after Coke's observation. There is, however, an engraving of the Frankley portrait in Coke's second (1629) edition of his *The First Part of the Institutes of the Law of England: Or, A Commentary upon Littleton* (1628). One can also view the effigy on his tomb in the nave of Worcester Cathedral, which Littleton erected himself. The chances are that the effigy is more a stereotype of how distinguished men of that time wanted to appear than an actual portrait of Littleton. The portrait of Littleton on the brass plate set on top of his tomb disappeared during the Puritan Revolution in England (1642-1660).

Littleton's work on *Tenures* (c. 1480) is one of the five great books on the history of English law, the others being those of Ranulf de Glanville, Henry de Bracton, Coke, and William Blackstone. Written originally as a source of information for one of his sons, Richard, a lawyer, it was composed in the law French of Littleton's day and translated into English by John Rastell, an author, printer, and serjeant-at-law (1514-1533). It must have been accepted as a classic from the very first, because the poet John Skelton, who died in 1529, remarked on one occasion that Littleton was well known in his own time.

Although the book gives little hint of new developments that characterize the land law, such as uses and contingent remainders, it does present a fine summary of the medieval English land law and was so admired by Sir Edward Coke that he referred to Littleton's *Tenures* in the preface to his *Institutes* (1628-1644), in which he wrote a commentary on Littleton, as "a work of as absolute perfection in its kind, and as free from error, as any book that I have known to be written of any humane learning, shall to the diligent and observing reader of these Institutes be made manifest." Coke also touched on the real reason for Littleton's fame, claiming that "by this excellent work which [Littleton] had studiously learned of others, he faithfully taught all the professors of the law in succeeding ages." What Littleton did was to make sense and order out of the growing chaos of the land law of the preceding 150 years, thereby giving future generations of lawyers a point of departure from which to develop a land law in conformity with changing social and political conditions.

The work is divided into three books: book 1, dealing with the types of holdings or estates; book 2, with the rights by which these estates are held and their incidents of holding; and book 3, with holdings by more than one person, and miscellaneous items.

Much of what Littleton wrote about at the end of the fifteenth century is no longer valid today, because Littleton's land law was based on the feudal system, a system that no longer operates, but whatever of Littleton pertains to modern practice, such as his doctrines on joint tenancies and tenancies in common, remains generally valid at the core of the land law. As more than one historian has noted, Littleton summed up the medieval land law and passed it on to future generations of lawyers before that land law was altered by the needs of the Industrial Revolution and the rise of equity, just as Blackstone's *Com-*

mentaries on the Laws of England (1765-1769) summed up and passed on the common law as developed to his time by the work of lawyers before it was remodeled by the direct legislation inspired by the teachings of Jeremy Bentham. No mere collection of decisions, Littleton's *Tenures* is rather a creative work based on the practical knowledge and needs of the time. Trying to get beneath the surface of the decisions, Littleton studied and assessed the arguments of the lawyers and the reasoning of the judges to construct a coherent body of legal knowledge.

Before Littleton wrote his *Tenures*, the land law, despite its importance as the major portion of the English law during medieval times, had given rise to a small treatise generally known as *The Old Tenures*, probably composed during the preceding, fourteenth century, which gives brief descriptions, among other things, of the various tenures and their incidents, of villeinage, villein tenure, and creditors' rights. Its main claim to fame is that its brevity suggested to Littleton that he might write an expansion of this little treatise.

The exact date when Littleton's book was published is not known, but it is known that during Littleton's lifetime, two complete manuscripts were available. The first edition, or *editio princeps*, of the work is a folio published at London by Lettou and Machlinia without date or title, which was followed by an edition issued by Machlinia alone, also without date or title. Many other editions followed, although Coke's remains the most famous.

SIGNIFICANCE

Littleton provided, in a reasonably easy-to-understand work, a clear and full account of the various estates known to English law through the fifteenth century in England, together with the incidents of ownership and the legal doctrines pertinent to them. The first great book on English law not written in Latin and generally uninfluenced by Roman law, his *Tenures* served as the foundation on which, gradually, succeeding generations of lawyers and courts of law fashioned what are today the modern concepts of the land law. Although the book was founded on the Year Books, which are the law reports of the Middle Ages in England, Littleton's work is not merely a compilation of court decisions. Rather, it is a study of the judicial decisions with interpretations and commentary by its author. There can be no understanding of the development of the English feudal system without an understanding of the land law—as described by Littleton—on which that feudal system was based.

—*Robert M. Spector*

FURTHER READING

Coke, Sir Edward. *The First Part of the Institutes of the Laws of England: Or, A Commentary upon Littleton.* London: Societie of Stationers, 1628. 17th ed. 2 vols. London: W. Clarke and Sons, 1817. Although written in rather florid seventeenth century style, Coke's preface is an excellent introduction to the life of Littleton. Coke's commentary on Littleton's work is, however, difficult reading.

Foss, Edward. *The Judges of England, with Sketches of Their Lives and Miscellaneous Notices Connected with the Courts at Westminster from the Time of the Conquest.* 9 vols. London: Longman, Brown, Green and Longmans, 1848-1864. Reprint. New York: AMS Press, 1966. Like most of the early sketches of judges of England, Foss's sketch of Littleton is relatively brief, giving only the barest details of his life and no presentation of the material contained in Littleton's book. It does, however, give some information on Littleton's descendants.

Hicks, Michael. *Bastard Feudalism.* New York: Longman, 1995. Exploration of the feudal structure and land tenure in England from 1150 to 1650 is especially strong in its discussion of the fifteenth century. Includes bibliographic references and index.

Holdsworth, Sir William. *The Mediaeval Common Law.* 3 vols. Reprint. London: Methuen, 1977-1980. Constitutes the first three volumes of Holdsworth's great multivolume *History of English Law.* Both a very readable presentation of the life of Littleton and an excellent digest of the estates, incidents of tenure, and doctrines of law emanating from these estates and tenures, as given by Littleton. At times difficult for the general reader. Probably the best introduction to Littleton.

Kynell, Kurt von S. *Lyttleton: His Treatise of Tenures in French and English.* Edited by Thomas Ellyne

Tomlins. London: S. Sweet, 1841. Rev. ed. New York: Russell and Russell, 1970. This work is important to the general reader for the editing of Coke's preface. Tomlins annotates the preface with commentary on Coke's presentation of Littleton's life. Also provides Littleton's will and other pertinent documents, and an account of the various editions of *Tenures.*

_____. *Saxon and Medieval Antecedents of the English Common Law.* Lewiston, N.Y.: Edwin Mellen Press, 2000. Traces the development of common law in England from Saxon times to the nineteenth century. Includes bibliographic references and index.

Littleton, Sir Thomas. *Littleton's Tenures.* Edited by Eugene Wambaugh. Washington, D.C.: J. Byrne, 1903. Reprint. Littleton, Colo.: Fred B. Rothman, 1985. This book is most valuable because it gives the most complete presentation of Littleton's life and the editions of his *Tenures.* Also, although it gives no commentary or explanation of Littleton's work, it does give the student the opportunity to read what Littleton himself wrote in as correct a translation as possible, Wambaugh having spared no effort to introduce what he believed to be an accurate translation of French law of the fifteenth century.

Maitland, Frederic W., and Francis C. Montague. *A Sketch of English Legal History.* Edited by James F. Colby. Reprint. Union, N.J.: The Lawbook Exchange, 1998. Reprints a series of essays on the major epochs in English legal history by one of the major scholars of the turn of the twentieth century.

SEE ALSO: Edward IV; John Fortescue; Henry IV of Castile; Henry VI; Richard III.

RELATED ARTICLES in *Great Events from History: The Renaissance & Early Modern Era, 1454-1600:* 1536 and 1543: Acts of Union Between England and Wales; 1531-1540: Cromwell Reforms British Government.

LOUIS XI
King of France (r. 1461-1483)

Louis XI rebuilt France from the Hundred Years' War, prevented renewed English invasion, demolished Burgundy as a great power within France, ended the era of feudal dominance, restored the extent and influence of the royal domain, and reorganized medieval France as a modern nation-state, with himself as the prototype of Renaissance despotism.

BORN: July 3, 1423; Bourges, France
DIED: August 30, 1483; Plessis-les-Tours, France
ALSO KNOWN AS: Louis de Valois
AREA OF ACHIEVEMENT: Government and politics

EARLY LIFE

When Louis (loo-ee) was born to Charles VII and Mary of Anjou, the misfortunes of the Hundred Years' War saw most of France controlled by the English or their Burgundian allies following the 1415 Battle of Agincourt. Louis was reared with middle-class companions at Castle Loches in Touraine and was educated on broad lines, while his father, disinherited by the 1420 Treaty of Troyes, dawdled at Bourges, essentially waiting on events. Joan of Arc's victories in 1429 and 1430 revived confidence in the Valois cause, and following the Franco-Burgundian alliance of 1435 and the 1436 recapture of Paris, Charles VII felt secure enough to bring the dauphin, Louis, into public affairs.

In 1436, Louis entered an arranged political marriage to eleven-year-old Princess Margaret of Scotland, an unhappy union without children. His soldiering also began in 1436, and by 1439, he held independent commands. As a general, Louis was energetic, courageous, and moderately successful. As king, he would prefer diplomacy to war from his personal experience that "battles are unpredictable."

From 1436 to 1445, Louis and his father agreed on broad royal policy, but not on specific men and measures, and in 1440, the dauphin was persuaded by powerful magnates to head a rebellion dubbed the Praguerie. The revolt failed, and reconciliation followed. After his wife's death in 1445, the dauphin resumed his demand for new royal advisers, and in 1447, Charles sent his heir to semibanishment as governor of Dauphiné.

Louis reorganized the government in Dauphiné and took his own line in foreign policy, including his 1451 marriage to Charlotte of Savoy, which Charles refused to accept. The crucial father-and-son quarrel centered on the efforts of each to control or bribe the advisers of the other. In 1456, Charles sent his troops to Dauphiné to enforce his authority, and Louis fled to the court of Burgundy.

Louis spent five years in the Burgundian Netherlands as a guest of Duke Philip the Good and his son, the future Duke Charles the Bold. Louis could see that their wealth, army, and ambition were all organized toward making Burgundy an independent power in France and Europe. Charles VII died on July 22, 1461, and Louis at last came to the throne of France. He was thirty-eight years old.

LIFE'S WORK

As king, Louis initially replaced most of his father's advisers but continued basic royal policy. External defense and internal coordination were still the great national problems. Territorial feudalism still defied control by wreaking local havoc, but the feudal levy of lance-wielding knights could not defend France in wars of gunpowder and missiles. Yet the king's expensive, new standing army of middle-class professionals threatened the whole structure of feudal government, and the great magnates resisted in four separate rebellions against Louis.

In the first of these feudal revolts, audaciously advertised as The League of the Public Weal, Charles led a concerted advance on Paris in 1465. The indecisive Battle of Montlhéry on July 16 left Paris saved by Louis but besieged by Charles and the magnates. To keep Paris, the king was forced to give the rebels territories later expensively regained. The Burgundian settlement was challenged by Charles after his 1467 accession, and Louis was then forced to make humiliating concessions at the Peronne Conference of 1468.

The 1468 marriage alliance of Charles and Margaret of York, sister of Edward IV of England, posed an open threat to Louis of invasion. His bold support of the Lancastrian restoration of 1470 seemed ill-judged when Edward resumed power in 1471. By the time Edward invaded France in June of 1475, however, Charles was preoccupied with a Rhineland siege. Louis came to terms with Edward in the August 29 Peace of Picquigny, offering him money and a pension; the two monarchs exchanged sardonic compliments through an iron grill.

Charles, meanwhile, pursued his claims in other quarters. In 1476, the duke and his army advanced to Lake Neuchâtel and began a campaign in which he was three times soundly beaten in unexpected attacks by Swiss infantry—at Grandson, Murten, and Nancy, where Charles died fighting in 1477. His heir was his nineteen-year-old daughter, Mary of Burgundy.

Louis gave the Swiss money only until they began to win and then moved decisively, bringing Nevers, ducal Burgundy, Charolais, Picardy, Artois, Boulogne, and Rethel under the control of France. Mary, to protect Franche-Comté, Luxembourg, and the remaining Burgundian Netherlands, married Maximilian I of Habsburg. Louis broke the power of Burgundy in France by being ready and able to invade in the hour of Burgundian defeat.

By inheritance and pressure, Louis acquired Provence, Anjou, Maine, and Bar. The emerging geographic outline of modern France was accompanied by a strategic linkage of royal lands in the Loire and Seine river valleys. With the duke of Alençon under control, the estates of Armagnac partitioned, the heir of Bourbon married to Louis's daughter Anne, and the elderly duke of Brittany now harmlessly isolated, Louis was now the feudal master of France, which he had to be in order to change the feudal system.

Louis XI. (Library of Congress)

Externally, Louis managed to gain Roussillon from the aged and wily John II of Aragon, but John's revenge was masterful. His son Ferdinand II married Isabella I of Castile in 1469, commencing an age of increasing Spanish unity, nationalism, and anti-French sentiment. In Burgundy, Spain, Italy, and elsewhere, the fear of French strength prepared the way for the future Habsburg-Valois wars.

Domestically, Louis replaced military, police, administrative, tax, and judicial institutions of the territorial lords with agencies of the Crown. The nobles who had ruled fiefs became a privileged class of patriotic military and civilian servants sworn in loyalty to the king. The 1472 concordat with the pope gave Louis somewhat comparable powers in the appointment of new bishops. Significantly, the king's taxes, such as *taille, aides,* and *gabelle,* were now collected without representative consent, and the remaining parlements merely registered the king's laws.

Additionally, Louis invested in and promoted new industries such as silk production and modernized mining as well as many commercial enterprises. A royal messenger system became a sort of postal service, conveying not only government business and privileged letters but also the publications of the new printing industry Louis helped to develop.

This rebuilding and modernization of French life depended on the safety of commerce and the tranquillity of a country no longer beset by ravaging armies. In the revised order of the new French state, the greatest economic benefit went to the bourgeoisie and the wealthiest peasants, but political power in France was concentrated in the hands of the king. On the whole, Louis governed wisely and well, but he institutionalized despotism.

Great in his accomplishments for France, Louis was not impressive in appearance. His dress and manners were informally bourgeois rather than royal. Louis was witty, garrulous, and even charming in conversation or letters, but he lacked the touch of dignity, heroism, generosity, or even understandable vice that would cause men to overlook the cruelties of which, like his contemporaries, he was sometimes capable.

Apoplexy crippled Louis as early as February, 1481, and eventually killed him. He died at Plessis-les-Tours on August 30, 1483, hopeful that his religious observances, his generosity to the Church, and his sincere faith would gain for him a fair judgment from God. His only son succeeded as Charles VIII with his sister Anne as regent. A younger daughter, Jeanne, became duchess of Orléans.

SIGNIFICANCE

When Louis XI ascended the throne in 1461, the postwar lives of Frenchmen were still dominated by territorial feudal lords whom the king could not control. When Louis died in 1483, a centralized nation-state monarchy was the new great fact for the future of France. The scattered royal domain lands of 1461 were increased in extent, geographic cohesiveness, and economic leadership. Most conspicuously, Louis's policy helped to shatter the Burgundian power, that, in alliance with the external foes and internal rivals of the French crown, had long constituted a threat to the survival of France itself as a nation of consequence.

The nation-state that Louis created gave the country more security, peace, and order, as well as better laws and justice; new industry, production, commerce; and a better life, especially in the towns, than feudal Europe had ever sustained. High taxes were the naturally unpopular price for the benefits. Louis's political system endured basically unchanged for three centuries, until the old regime was swept away in 1789.

Despite the greatness and importance of Louis's achievements, legend, fiction, and even some historians have distorted and diminished his reputation. Most scholars agree that he deserves a better place in public estimation. Apart from the problem of misrepresentation, however, the evidence at hand suggests that, while Louis XI was in his own time respected and feared, he did not, for whatever reason, capture great sympathy and affection.

—*K. Fred Gillum*

FURTHER READING

Bakos, Adrianna E. *Images of Kingship in Early Modern France: Louis XI in Political Thought, 1560-1789.* New York: Routledge, 1997. Explores the legacy of Louis XI and the representation of his kingship during the two hundred years leading up to the French Revolution, as a means of understanding the ideological evolution of France during this period. Includes bibliographic references and index.

Champion, Pierre. *Louis XI.* Translated by Winifred Stephens Whale. New York: Dodd, Mead, 1929. Once the standard biography on Louis XI, this work is weakened by its reliance on Philippe de Commynes, a sparsity of detail, and lack of footnotes, but it is still a clear and enjoyable account.

Commynes, Philippe de. *The Memoirs of Philippe de Commynes.* Edited by Samuel Kinser. Translated by Isabelle Cazeaux. Columbia: University of South Car-olina Press, 1969. These memoirs are the contemporary source most used by later biographers. The author, an adviser and confidant to Louis for eleven years, combines an intimate and generally favorable account of the king with his own reflections on politics.

Kendall, Paul Murray. *Louis XI.* New York: W. W. Norton, 1971. The most useful single volume on Louis XI. Kendall's research is comprehensive. This book is scholarly, informative, and accurate, with an extensive bibliography and footnotes that give the reader the sources for everything consequential. Although it is well written, the complex story is not as easy to follow as in Champion.

Lewis, D. B. Wyndham. *King Spider.* New York: Coward, McCann, 1929. A popular work, now dated, but useful for the section translating a short selection of Louis's letters from the eleven-volume French edition. The book's title comes from Charles the Bold's description of Louis as "the universal spider," a label that has lasted.

Mosher, Orville W., Jr. *Louis XI, King of France.* Toulouse, France: Édouard Privat, 1925. Many biographers complain of the distortion and legend surrounding Louis without adequate explanation. Mosher supplies this, although the work should be read with later works.

Potter, David. *A History of France, 1460-1560: The Emergence of a Nation State.* New York: St. Martin's Press, 1995. Charts French history from the reign of Louis XI to the Wars of Religion, arguing that a fundamental continuity exists throughout this time, which should belie attempts to demarcate a clear division between late medieval and early modern France. Includes illustrations, genealogic tables, maps, appendices, bibliography, and index.

Spencer, Mark. *Thomas Basin (1412-1490): The History of Charles VII and Louis XI.* Nieuwkoop, the Netherlands: De Graaf, 1997. Study of the life of Louis XI written by Thomas Basin, a prelate who was forced to flee from Louis, then write his biography while wandering from town to town seeking refuge.

SEE ALSO: Charles the Bold; Charles VII; Charles VIII; Edward IV; Ferdinand II and Isabella I; Mary of Burgundy; Maximilian I; Pius II.

RELATED ARTICLES in *Great Events from History: The Renaissance & Early Modern Era, 1454-1600:* July 16, 1465-April, 1559: French-Burgundian and French-Austrian Wars; August 29, 1475: Peace of Picquigny.

LOUIS XII
King of France (r. 1498-1515)

Louis helped to make France the European state with the greatest potential political power and most centralized government in all Europe by the mid-sixteenth century. To many in France, Louis came to be regarded as the ideal monarch.

BORN: June 27, 1462; Blois, France
DIED: January 1, 1515; Paris, France
ALSO KNOWN AS: Father of the People
AREAS OF ACHIEVEMENT: Government and politics, warfare and conquest

EARLY LIFE

Louis (loo-ee) was born the son of Charles d'Orleans and Mary of Cleves. He was on an indirect path to the throne because his house was several bloodlines removed from the royal family. As duke of Orleans, Louis never expected to become king of France. He had hoped to become the regent for the underage Charles VIII when Charles became king in 1483, but was rebuffed and instead led a rebellion against the young Charles. After a period of imprisonment, he returned to the king's good graces and campaigned with him in his invasion of Italy of 1494-1495.

By the time Charles died childless in 1498, Louis had emerged as the presumptive heir. Louis mounted the throne with a life full of experiences already behind him: He had been imprisoned for treason, been captured in battle, commanded a fleet at sea, and led the defending force of a city under siege.

LIFE'S WORK

As king, Louis's style of rule was hardworking and economical, and he displayed a keen interest in administration. He had an open manner with those at his court, but his stubborn streak and lack of patience and subtlety often frustrated his advisers. His reputation for plain speaking was not necessarily an asset in the cutthroat world of Renaissance politics. Louis himself seemed to regard the primary purpose of kingship as the dispensation of justice rather than the accretion of power, but some features of his reign nonetheless predict the absolutist experiment characteristic of the early modern French monarchy.

The open sales of offices in parlement began under Louis XII, and his reign can be seen as a part of the ongoing process of territorial consolidation and centralization under the French monarchs that reduced eighty great fiefs of the French realm in 1480 to less than forty by 1530. These were achievements that would crumble in the religious and civil bloodletting of the second half of the century.

Early in his reign, Louis set out to secure the annulment of his marriage to Jeanne de France, the homely daughter of King Louis XI, who had pressured the younger Louis into the match. Louis desired to marry the widow of the recently deceased Charles VIII, Anne of Brittany, largely to prevent her from withdrawing her duchy of Brittany from the French crown's jurisdiction. After a lengthy and dubious inquest into the legal status of his marriage, Louis received an annulment and was free to marry Anne.

Louis's rule was characterized chiefly by domestic tranquility and prosperity. The *taille*, the most important of French taxes, remained at a low level until the exigencies of war required him to raise it in 1512. He held consultative assemblies regularly and acknowledged the right of provincial bodies to consent to the imposition of new taxes. An oft-repeated tale, most likely apocryphal, had it that Louis would weep when he had to impose a tax. For the king, such active consultation was a means of creating loyal subjects, without compulsion, which was probably beyond the capacity of the Crown to do anyway.

Louis provided France with perhaps the most efficient government of any of the French Renaissance monarchs. There was an air of professionalism about Louis's rule, as he appointed a great many middling nobles and members of the haute bourgeoisie to government offices close to him, especially in the fiscal and judicial spheres.

Louis also solidified the territorial integrity of France, assuring that newly acquired Brittany, Burgundy, and the lands of the House of Orléans would become integrated into the French state.

Louis's wisdom and pragmatism in domestic affairs was not replicated in his foreign policy, and he found himself repeatedly involved in the quicksand of Italian politics. Louis continued the obsession of his predecessor Charles VIII in an Italian venture. He inherited Charles's claims to the Kingdom of Naples and brought his own Orleanist claims to the duchy of Milan. J. X. Hexter remarked that Louis, like Charles before him and Francis I after, was intent on "pouring the human and material resources of his kingdom down the rat hole of Italy." His ventures in Italy led to nothing but failure and frustration.

Two unsuccessful invasions of Italy during his reign left France increasingly isolated politically. Louis ultimately saw his army routed by the Swiss at Novara in

Louis XII. (Hulton|Archive by Getty Images)

1513, and the French were subsequently driven out of northern Italy almost completely, while at the same time facing invasions by the Aragonese in Navarre and the English in Picardy.

The death of Louis's implacable foe, Pope Julius II, helped rescue the king from his predicament, as did a peace treaty with Henry VIII of England, by which he agreed to marry Henry's daughter Mary (Anne died in 1514). Louis was succeeded as king by his cousin Francis of Angoulême, who would reign as Francis I.

SIGNIFICANCE

Louis XII was labeled the father of the people during a meeting of the estates in 1506. His reign represents a bridge in the history of the French monarchy, situated somewhere between the feudal regimes of the Middle Ages and absolutist kings of the early modern period. Louis's rule was in fact a mixture of the two models of rule.

Louis mortgaged many of these achievements with his ill-fated interventions in the Wars of Italy. Here he continued the ongoing dynastic struggle with the king of Spain, a conflict that would dominate European politics for the next several decades. The gap between Louis's successes

at home and his failures abroad is a distinctive feature of his reign. To some extent, this foreign policy was forced on Louis, for, like many monarchs of his age, he had to give his nobility an outlet for their martial energies and the opportunity to win honor and glory. Thus, Louis's reign represents a prime example of how the task of creating a modern monarchy came up against, and was complicated by, the enduring social structures of the Middle Ages.

—Paul M. Dover

FURTHER READING

Baumgartner, Frederic. *Louis XII.* New York: St. Martin's Press, 1994. A biography of Louis and a reasonably sympathetic portrait that incorporates French and English-language historiography.

Cruikshank, C. G. *Army Royal: Henry VIII's Invasion of France.* Oxford, England: Clarendon Press, 1969. A military and diplomatic history of the English invasion of Picardy in 1513.

Holt, Mack, ed. *Renaissance and Reformation France.* New York: Oxford University Press, 2002. Part of the Oxford Shorter History of France series, a collection of thematic essays by top scholars of sixteenth century French history. Maps, lengthy bibliography.

Lewis, P. S. *Late Medieval France.* New York: St. Martin's Press, 1968. This survey examines the social, cultural, and economic milieu of France in the fourteenth and fifteenth centuries.

Major, J. Russell. *From Renaissance Monarchy to Absolute Monarchy: French Kings, Nobles, and Estates.* Baltimore: Johns Hopkins University Press, 1994. Traces the political and institutional challenges to the extension of state power in the early modern period. Written by one of the leading experts in the field.

Potter, David. *A History of France, 1460-1560: The Emergence of a Nation State.* Basingstoke, England: Macmillan, 1995. A survey of French history from the end of the Hundred Years' War to the Wars of Religion, focusing primarily on the relationship between the Crown and the people and the expansion of the state in this period. Maps, genealogical tables.

SEE ALSO: Anne of Brittany; Charles VIII; Francis I; Julius II; Louis XI.

RELATED ARTICLES in *Great Events from History: The Renaissance & Early Modern Era, 1454-1600:* 1481-1499: Ludovico Sforza Rules Milan; 1499: Louis XII of France Seizes Milan; 1504: Treaty of Blois; 1508: Formation of the League of Cambrai; April 11, 1512: Battle of Ravenna; August 18, 1516: Concordat of Bologna.

ISAAC BEN SOLOMON LURIA
Jewish mystic and religious leader

Luria was the culminating figure in the Jewish mystical tradition known as Kabbalah. His revision of key Kabbalist concepts and his theory of a dynamic creation—altered by sin but capable of regeneration and final redemption—had a profound influence on subsequent Jewish thought, including Hasidism, and on messianic movements in both the Jewish and the Christian worlds.

BORN: 1534; Jerusalem, Palestine, Ottoman Empire (now in Israel)
DIED: August 5, 1572; Safed, Syria (now Zefat, Israel)
ALSO KNOWN AS: ha-Ari
AREAS OF ACHIEVEMENT: Religion and theology, philosophy

EARLY LIFE

Isaac ben Solomon Luria (I-zihk behn SAHL-uh-muhn LUHR-yah), also known as ha-Ari (acronym for Ashkenazic Rabbi Isaac), was born in Jerusalem. His father was an Ashkenazi who had come from Germany or Poland, and his mother was of Sephardic stock. At his father's death, his mother took him to Egypt, where he grew up in the household of his wealthy uncle, a tax collector. Details of his life are sparse; the principal source is the *Toledot ha-Ari* (life of the Ari), an account written fifteen or twenty years after his death in which fact and legend are freely mingled.

Luria was highly precocious, and his uncle provided him with able tutors, including David ben Solomon ibn Abi Zimra and Bezalel Ashkenazi. He collaborated with the latter in producing legal commentaries and wrote a study of the Book of Concealment section of the *Zohar*, the central text of the Kabbalist tradition. In later life, he disdained to write, however, preferring personal teaching and communication with his disciples; his mature thought is known only through their accounts, particularly those of Ḥayyim Vital (1543-1620), who claimed to have recorded his master's thoughts verbatim.

Luria married at the age of fifteen and later went into commerce, in which he was engaged to the end of his life. At the age of seventeen, he began an intensive study of the Kabbalah, focusing on the *Zohar* and on the works of his elder contemporary, Moses ben Jacob Cordovero (1522-1570), the leading figure of the major Kabbalist school at Safed in Palestine. In early 1570, he took up residence in Safed with his family and studied briefly with Cordovero himself, who was said to have appointed him his spiritual successor.

LIFE'S WORK

At Cordovero's death, Luria became the head of a group known as the Cubs (his own nickname of Ari meant Holy Lion in Hebrew), who formed a core of devoted disciples about him. They lived as a community, with quarters for themselves and their families. Luria lectured to them on the Sabbath, after they had donned ritual white garments and marched processionally into the neighboring fields. He also worked with them on an individual basis, imparting the techniques of mystical meditation and elucidating the spiritual ancestry of each in accordance with the Kabbalist principle of transmigration.

The impact of Lurianic doctrine may be attributed not only to its intrinsic power as a revision of Kabbalist tradition but also to the condition of Jewry in the aftermath of the Spanish expulsion of 1492 and the revived anti-Semitism of Reformation Europe. For Jews seeking a divine meaning in these calamities and thrown back anew on the painful consciousness of their *Galut*, or exile, Luria's thought had both explicative and consolatory appeal.

Traditional Kabbalism described the creation of the universe as a wholly positive event, emanating from God's benevolence and unfolding in orderly stages. Luria, in contrast, described this process as involving an act of privation, a contraction or concentration (*tzimtzum*) of the Godhead into itself to create a space outside itself (the *tehiru*, or void) in which the universe could be formed.

The divine light of creation was released into the void, but some of the forms or vessels (*sefirot*) created to receive it were overwhelmed by its force. This "breaking of the vessels" (the *shevirah*) caused a catastrophic scattering of light. The intact vessels constituted a perfected but incomplete upper realm, while the broken ones (including the highest, Adam Kadmon, or Primal Man, which consisted not only of Adam but of the souls of all his progeny as well) produced a lower, fallen world, to which, however, many sparks of divine light still clung. The sin of Adam then produced further ruin, increasing the alienation of the fallen world from the Godhead.

Adam having failed, God turned to the people of Israel to accomplish the redemption (*tikkun*) of the fallen world and to liberate the divine sparks from their material prison. Each Jew could advance or retard this process by his or her ethical conduct; with each pious act, a spark was redeemed, but with each wicked or impious one, a spark of the sinner's own soul was lost to chaos. The individual thus not only sought personal salvation by his or her acts but also participated in the process of universal redemption.

The most esoteric part of Luria's doctrine concerned the divine motive for creating the world and its abortive realization. Luria suggested that there were elements of disunity within the Godhead itself, although the divine essence was seamless and could be conceptualized only as light. In the act of *tzimtzum*, God differentiated these elements (the *reshimu*), which cleaved to the "surface" of the *tehiru* in the manner of water clinging to a bucket. From this exteriorized residue, the vessels were to be composed, and this formed emptiness,

---

THE PLACE OF THE SEFIROT IN LURIA'S KABBALISTIC THOUGHT

Isaac ben Solomon Luria's model of the universe places great importance upon a group of finite vessels through which the infinity of reality assumes discrete forms. In the passage below, this aspect of Luria's thought is explained.

The characteristic feature of Luria's system in the speculative Cabala [Kabbalah] is his definition of the Sefirot and his theory of the intermediary agents, which he calls "parzufim" (from [the Greek word for] face). Before the creation of the world, he says, the En Sof [God] filled the infinite space. When the Creation was decided upon, in order that His attributes, which belong to other beings as well, should manifest themselves in their perfection, the En Sof retired into His own nature, or, to use the cabalistic term, concentrated Himself. From this concentration proceeded the infinite light. When in its turn the light concentrated, there appeared in the center an empty space encompassed by ten circles or dynamic vessels ("kelim") called "Sefirot," by means of which the infinite realities, though forming an absolute unity, may appear in their diversity; for the finite has no real existence of itself.

Source: The Jewish Encyclopedia: A Descriptive Record of the History, Religion, Literature, and Customs of the Jewish People from the Earliest Times to the Present Day, edited by Cyrus Adler et al., eds. (New York: Funk & Wagnalls, 1903-1906), p. 210.

---

penetrated by retained light from the Godhead. Thus, the creation of the universe was to accomplish the reintegration of the Godhead with itself. The world of evil resulted when the refractory vessels failed (or refused, since they were composed both of and by the *reshimu*) to contain the Godhead's light; yet even that world was penetrated by divine goodness in the form of the sparks.

Luria's explanation of the fallen world may be regarded as an abstract reconceptualization of the story of the rebel angels, filtered through Manichaean and Gnostic thought. His attempt, as with all theodicy, was to account for the presence of evil without imputing it directly to God. Despite its abstract nature, it presented a powerfully compelling picture of creation itself as the process of God's own self-exile and redemption, and the *tikkun* as Israel's opportunity to participate in the completion of his design for the universe. Israel's own exile, and the tribulations heaped on it by the forces of evil, could thus be seen as a mirror of the divine travail. The more closely the final victory of *tikkun* approached, the more violently evil resisted. Thus, the expulsion of the Spanish Jews and the general persecution of Israel were indications not of the weakness of the Jews in the face of their enemies but of their gathering strength against all opposition to the divine will.

Luria's brief ministry ended with his death in August,

1572, during an epidemic in Safed, but such was the force of his personality and doctrine that his teachings were rapidly propagated throughout the Jewish world, where they profoundly influenced both contemporary messianic movements and the theological, liturgical, and literary traditions of Judaism.

The Safed Kabbalists believed that the moment of redemption was imminent. Luria may have conceived of himself as the Messiah ben-Joseph, the first of the two messiahs prophesied in Jewish tradition, whose fate was to be slain in the war of Gog and Magog; he was apparently so regarded by his admirers, and his sudden death did nothing to dispel the notion. Messianic expectation, nourished by Lurianic doctrine, flourished widely in the Jewish world for the next hundred years, culminating in an attempted mass migration to Palestine in 1665-1666 under Sabbatai Zevi. Christian chiliasts, who believed that the Jews' return to Palestine was the prelude to the Second Coming of Jesus, were deeply stirred by this ferment, and the Lurianist Menasseh ben Israel paid a state visit to England at the behest of Oliver Cromwell.

SIGNIFICANCE

Isaac ben Solomon Luria was the culminating figure in the Kabbalist movement, the major tradition of Jewish mysticism and speculative theology in the late medieval and early modern world. Menasseh ben Israel declared that "the wisdom of Rabbi Isaac Luria rises above the highest mountains," and a modern scholar, Joseph Dan, has called the concept of *tikkun* "the most powerful idea ever presented in Jewish thought." After 1620, almost all works of ethics in Hebrew used Lurianic symbolism, and, as Dan further comments, "Lurianism became a national theology for Judaism for several generations."

Although Luria's influence reached its apogee in the seventeenth century, it remained important in the eighteenth and nineteenth centuries, and passed directly into Hasidism. Luria's emphasis on the world-altering significance of each believer's acts revitalized Jewish ethics and continued to animate it long after his arcane theology had become, for most, a historical curiosity. The critic Harold Bloom has tried to revive Lurianic Kabbalism as a device of literary scholarship, and a current periodical of Jewish American thought calls itself *Tikkun*. Luria thus remains one of the most seminal figures in the past five hundred years of Judaism.

—Robert Zaller

FURTHER READING

Bloom, Harold. *Kabbalah and Criticism*. New York: Seabury Press, 1975. A modern reinterpretation of Luria's Kabbalism as a "psychology of belatedness" that anticipates Freudian doctrine, a philosophy of suffering that anticipates Friedrich Nietzsche, and a system of signs with affinities to Charles Sanders Peirce. Bloom also proposes Luria's thought as a paradigm for literary interpretation.

Fine, Lawrence. *Physician of the Soul, Healer of the Cosmos: Isaac Luria and His Kabbalistic Fellowship*. Stanford, Calif.: Stanford University Press, 2003. Major study of Lurianic Kabbalah emphasizes the importance of seeing it as a material, social, lived tradition, rather than a set of detached ideas. Discusses the relationship of Luria to his disciples and the influence of that relationship on his thought. Includes illustrations, bibliographic references, index.

_____. *Safed Spirituality: Rules of Mystical Piety, the Beginning of Wisdom*. Ramsey, N.J.: Paulist Press, 1984. Focuses on the customs and rituals practiced by Luria and his disciples.

Klein, Eliahu, and Isaac ben Solomon Luria. *Kabbalah of Creation: Isaac Luria's Earlier Mysticism*. Northvale, N.J.: Jason Aronson, 2000. Radical new poetic translation of Luria's early Kabbalah, as well as commentary on its meaning and its historical and bibliographic importance. Includes illustrations, glossary, bibliographies, and appendices.

Lenowitz, Harris. *The Jewish Messiahs: From the Galilee to Crown Heights*. New York: Oxford University Press, 1998. Reads Luria as an apocalyptic messiah, "adhering to a mystic worldview that seeks the repair of the world in a cosmic sense." Includes illustrations, bibliographic references, and indexes.

Schechter, Solomon. "Safed in the Sixteenth Century: A City of Legists and Mystics." In *Studies in Judaism*. 1896. Reprint. Freeport, N.Y.: Books for Libraries Press, 1972. A classic essay, still valuable, on the Kabbalists of Safed and especially Luria.

Scholem, Gershom. *Major Trends in Jewish Mysticism*. 3d ed. Reprint. New York: Schocken Books, 1995. Scholem was the foremost twentieth century scholar of Jewish mysticism and the Kabbalah. His work has been so dominant that it has spawned a major literature of reinterpretation and revision, best summarized in Joseph Dan's *Gershom Scholem and the Mystical Dimension of Jewish History* (1987). Luria's system is treated in the eighth chapter of Scholem's book, which was first published in 1941. Includes an analysis of the textual issues in reconstructing the system from the writings of the disciples, with special emphasis on Joseph ben Tabul.

_____. *On the Kabbalah and Its Symbolism*. New York: Schocken, 1965. Another of Scholem's major works, indispensable for understanding the Kabbalist tradition and containing a chapter on Luria. See also his book-length essay, "Kabbalah," in the *Encyclopedia Judaica* (Jerusalem: Keter Publishing House, 1971).

SEE ALSO: Isaac ben Judah Abravanel; Joseph ben Ephraim Karo.

RELATED ARTICLE in *Great Events from History: The Renaissance & Early Modern Era, 1454-1600:* 1486-1487: Pico della Mirandola Writes *Oration on the Dignity of Man*.

MARTIN LUTHER
German religious leader and church reformer

Out of his own personal struggle and his conflict with the Church, Luther developed a theology and a religious movement that rejuvenated the Christian faith and had a profound impact on the social, political, and religious thought of Western society.

BORN: November 10, 1483; Eisleben, Saxony (now in Germany)

DIED: February 18, 1546; Eisleben

AREAS OF ACHIEVEMENT: Religion and theology, philosophy, church reform

EARLY LIFE

Martin Luther (LEW-thur) was born to Hans and Margarethe Luther. Soon after his birth, the family moved to Mansfield, where his father worked in the copper mines, prospering sufficiently to become one of the town's councillors in 1491. Possessing a strong, forceful character, Hans Luther had a great impact on his son. He could be exceptionally stern; years later, Luther stated that his father gave him a sense of inferiority that took years to overcome. Yet, recognizing that his son had a promising intellect, his father sent Luther to Latin school at Mansfield. At age twelve, Luther spent a year at a school in Magdeburg operated by the Brethren for the Common Life and in 1498 attended a school at Eisenach. In 1501, he entered the University of Erfurt, one of the best universities in Germany, obtaining his bachelor's degree in 1502 and his master's degree in 1505.

His father wanted Luther to pursue a legal career. Luther, however, was suffering from depression, a lifelong chronic condition. On July 2, 1505, as he was returning to Erfurt from Mansfield, a lightning bolt knocked him to the ground. Fearful, facing eternity, Luther at that moment vowed to become a monk. Without consulting his father, Luther immediately entered the Augustinian monastery in Erfurt. He was ordained in 1507 and was selected for advanced theological studies, receiving his doctorate in theology from the University of Wittenberg in 1512. Luther then succeeded his mentor, Johann von Staupitz, to the chair of biblical theology at Wittenberg.

Beneath his successful exterior, however, all was not well with Luther. Between 1505 and 1515, Luther underwent an acute personal crisis. Harboring terrible anxieties about sin and his own salvation, Luther believed that no matter how irreproachably he lived, he was unable to satisfy God. Luther was clearly headed for a breakdown. At this juncture, Staupitz interceded and told Luther to abandon the concept of God as judge, to focus on Christ, and simply to love God. This was a revelation for the young monk. While studying Paul's Epistle to the Romans, Luther realized that humankind is saved by faith and not by works. Thus, the essential theology of Protestantism arose to a large extent from Luther's inner, personal struggle.

LIFE'S WORK

The issue that ignited Luther's conflict with the Church was the sale of indulgences in Germany by the Dominican friar Johann Tetzel. Indulgences were the remission for money of part of the temporal (priest-assigned) penalties for sin. They were granted on papal authority and sold by licensed agents. While the Church never maintained that divine forgiveness could be obtained through an indulgence, unscrupulous agents such as Tetzel employed such claims with great success. Luther, disturbed that ordinary people were having their salvation endangered by these false claims, authored Ninety-five Theses attacking indulgences and fastened them to the door of All Saints Church in Wittenberg on October 31, 1517. Contrary to Luther's wishes, the theses were widely circulated, striking a responsive chord among the Germans. What Luther had intended as a local, scholarly debate was becoming a public controversy.

The archbishop of Mainz, who was profiting directly from the sale of indulgences, forwarded copies of the Ninety-five Theses to Rome, requesting that Luther be disciplined. Pope Leo X, viewing the dispute as an argument between the Augustinians and Dominicans, simply told the former to deal with Luther. At this point, the scope of the controversy suddenly widened. A colleague of Luther at Wittenberg, Bodenstein von Karlstadt, responding to criticisms of Luther's positions by Johann Eck, published 405 theses, some of which attacked Eck personally. Eck's order, the Dominicans, were outraged, and heresy proceedings against Luther began to move forward in Rome. Luther himself inflamed the situation by publishing a sermon on excommunication that clearly questioned papal authority.

Rome sent a summons for Luther to appear at Rome to Cardinal Thomas Cajetan, who was at Augsburg. For political reasons, however, the pope could not afford to antagonize Frederick III of Saxony, an elector of the Holy Roman Empire and Luther's protector. Luther was instead given a safe-conduct to have a personal interview with the conservative Cajetan.

History will always note the dramatic presentation of the Ninety-five Theses in 1517 and the even more significant confrontation at Worms in 1521, but the meeting at Augsburg in 1518 probably had more impact than either. In 1517, Luther was insulated by his anonymity; in 1521, he was famous, with possibly half of Germany supporting him. Yet in 1518, Luther was vulnerable, not yet famous and not certain how the Church would deal with him. The Church had an opportunity to silence Luther without suffering severe damage and failed to do so. Cajetan had no intention of hearing Luther's statements,

Martin Luther. (Library of Congress)

and, although he promised to forward Luther's "explanations" to Rome, he demanded that Luther recant. Luther refused and, in fear for his life, fled Augsburg.

While he had been in Augsburg, Luther had met with Eck and had agreed to a debate at Leipzig in July, 1519. This dispute did not go well for Luther. Eck was able to maneuver him into supporting some Hussite positions and into questioning papal authority as well as the authority of ecclesiastical councils. The Church responded on June 15, 1520, with a papal bull condemning many of Luther's teachings. The papal legate sent to circulate the bull among the German cities was shocked to discover German opinion solidly behind Luther. Luther's friends, aware of his dangerous position, tried to have him moderate his beliefs, but Luther had already moved beyond that point and in 1520 published three of his most famous treatises.

In January, 1521, the Church formally excommunicated Luther. At this juncture, Frederick obtained a promise from Emperor Charles V to provide Luther with an opportunity to defend himself before the Imperial Diet then meeting at Worms. At the meeting, it became clear that Luther had been summoned only to recant. Since his life could depend on his answer, Luther requested time to think. The next day, Luther made a skillful statement, and the chancellor of Trier made an equally skillful reply from the papal perspective. He concluded with a demand that Luther give a simple answer to the question, "Do you recant, yes or no?" Luther responded with a reply that changed the course of history. Unless he were proved wrong on the basis of the Scriptures and sound reason—for popes and councils had erred and might do so again—he was bound by his conscience to the Word of God. He concluded in German, "May God help me. Amen."

There was no doubt that Luther had won a great moral victory, but his enemies also gained something important: the Edict of Worms, which declared Luther an outlaw and proscribed his writings. This edict would dog him all his days, but while it could restrict his freedom of movement, it could not restrict Luther's ideas. It did mean that his protector, Frederick, could not openly support Luther, so for political reasons and for Luther's own safety, Luther was "kidnapped" to the castle at the Wartburg. He found this enforced inaction tiresome and depressing, but he did use the time to begin the translation of the New Testament from Greek into German. Published in September, 1522, it was a historic work that would have a tremendous influence on German language, life, and religion. Luther remained informed about developments beyond the Wartburg, and when he left in March, 1522, he faced a situation that gravely concerned him.

Religious doctrine can easily have social and political ramifications, and Luther was very alarmed by the political and social unrest his theological cornerstones—justification by faith and the priesthood of all believers—had engendered. Luther, always a conservative, feared that the new radical teaching by Karlstadt and others would lead to revolution. In response, Luther in 1523 postulated the Two Realms theory. There is the spiritual realm, where humans exist only in relation to God, and the temporal realm, where humans exist as flesh, subject to sin and the needs of the flesh. Since both realms are divinely inspired, humans have a duty to obey civil authority, and thus it is sinful to rebel against lawful authority. Freedom for Luther consisted of humanity's freedom to obey the Gospel. These views help explain Luther's strong condemnation of the Peasants' War of 1524-1526.

The year 1525 was pivotal for Luther and the Protestant Reformation. Luther was married to Katherina von Bora, a former nun, who proved to be a wonderful wife, bringing much-needed stability into his life. Also that year, relations were severed between Luther and Desiderius Erasmus. Early in the Reformation, Erasmus had supported its goals, but he had counseled caution, peace, and change through a reforming council. He feared a catastrophic split in the Church. As Luther's theology evolved and it became clear that the Reformation was no longer a reformation but a religious revolution, Erasmus parted company with Luther and chose the Church.

By the end of 1525, the lines were clearly drawn. From this point, Luther was the leader of a great religious movement. He would have to deal with doctrinal problems, the more radical Protestant leaders such as John Calvin and Huldrych Zwingli, and, as he grew older, others, especially Philipp Melanchthon, who would share the mantle of leadership with Luther. Early in 1546, Luther traveled to Eisleben to settle a quarrel between two young princes. The weather was awful and cold. On February 17, he suffered a heart attack and died the next day. When news of his death reached Wittenberg, Melanchthon announced to his class, "Alas, gone is the horseman and the chariots of Israel," citing the words spoken by Elisha when Elijah was taken to heaven.

SIGNIFICANCE

Luther rejuvenated and restored the Christian faith. Rather than canon law, it was now the Bible that was at the center, leading people to a life of faith, love, and good works. Jesus of Nazareth was once again considered to be a personal savior and not a distant, judgmental God approachable only through priestly mediation. The Church returned to being a community of believers and not a legalistic, bureaucratic institution. In accomplishing these reforms, Luther transformed the face of Europe as radically as Napoleon I or Otto von Bismarck and dramatically changed the course of Western civilization.

LUTHER ON CHRISTIAN FAITH

In his translation of the Bible into German, Martin Luther clearly outlines in the introduction to one section what he believes marks Christian faith: doing not just "good works" but doing "God's work," God's work being faith.

Faith is not what some people think it is. Their human dream is a delusion. Because they observe that faith is not followed by good works or a better life, they fall into error, even though they speak and hear much about faith. "Faith is not enough," they say, "You must do good works, you must be pious to be saved." They think that, when you hear the gospel, you start working, creating by your own strength a thankful heart which says, "I believe." That is what they think true faith is. But, because this is a human idea, a dream, the heart never learns anything from it, so it does nothing and reform doesn't come from this "faith," either.

Instead, faith is God's work in us, that changes us and gives new birth from God. (John 1:13). It kills the Old Adam and makes us completely different people. It changes our hearts, our spirits, our thoughts and all our powers. It brings the Holy Spirit with it. Yes, it is a living, creative, active and powerful thing, this faith. Faith cannot help doing good works constantly. It doesn't stop to ask if good works ought to be done, but before anyone asks, it already has done them and continues to do them without ceasing. Anyone who does not do good works in this manner is an unbeliever.

He stumbles around and looks for faith and good works, even though he does not know what faith or good works are.

Source: Excerpted from "An Introduction to St. Paul's Letter to the Romans," translated by Robert E. Smith. Luther's German Bible of 1522. Project Wittenberg, http://www.iclnet.org/pub/resources/text/wittenberg/wittenberg-luther.html#sw-work. Accessed September 20, 2004.

Luther himself is more difficult to summarize. He was clearly constrained by his love of God and the Scriptures. He was often depressed by the evil he found in the world but was ultimately confident of the salvation and glory that awaited after death. That this attitude gave Luther tremendous courage and confidence in the face of powerful opposition is seen in an incident that occurred early in the Reformation. While at the Wartburg, in hiding from his enemies under the ban of the empire, and with his own future far from certain, Luther wrote, "Our enemies threaten us with death. They would do better to threaten us with life."

—Ronald F. Smith

FURTHER READING

Atkinson, James. *Martin Luther and the Birth of Protestantism.* Reprint. Atlanta: John Knox Press, 1981. This book is essentially a theological account of Luther that is engagingly written and very understandable. Luther comes alive on these pages as a theologian and as a historical figure. Includes a subject index, an index of biblical references, a select bibliography, and a chronological table. Highly recommended.

Boehmer, Heinrich. *Road to Reformation: Martin Luther to the Year 1521.* Translated by John W. Doberstein and Theodore G. Tappert. Philadelphia: Muhlenberg Press, 1946. Based thoroughly on primary sources, the book's detail and insight into Luther's life and thinking to the conclusion of the Diet of Worms are exceptional. Lucid and well written, this work is considered by many Luther scholars to be a classic in the field. Includes an index.

Ebeling, Gerhard. *Luther: An Introduction to His Thought.* Translated by R. A. Wilson. Philadelphia: Fortress Press, 1964. Although this work is not a popular discussion of Luther's thought, it does not assume any special knowledge on the part of the reader. It concentrates on the dynamics of Luther's thought. The discussion of Luther's view of philosophy and theology is particularly insightful.

McKim, Donald K., ed. *The Cambridge Companion to Martin Luther.* New York: Cambridge University Press, 2003. Anthology of essays by noted scholars covering Luther's theology, moral thought, skill with words, direct effects, and lasting legacy, among other topics. Includes bibliographic references and index.

Marty, Martin. *Martin Luther.* New York: Viking Penguin, 2004. Subtle and balanced portrayal of Luther's theology and its cultural context, explaining the importance of the debates in which he intervened as well as tracing the ultimate results of that intervention. Luther's character gets an equally nuanced treatment. Includes maps and bibliographic references.

Oberman, Heiko A. *The Two Reformations: The Journey from the Last Days to the New World.* Edited by Donald Weinstein. New Haven, Conn.: Yale University Press, 2003. Posthumous collection of essays by one of the foremost Reformation scholars of the twentieth century. Revisits debates on Luther's anti-Semitism. Argues that medieval religious thought was essential to both Calvin's and Luther's understandings of Christianity. Includes bibliographic references and index.

Schwiebert, Ernest G. *Luther and His Times.* St. Louis, Mo.: Concordia, 1950. Schwiebert stresses the philosophical and sociogeographical factors that contributed to the molding of Luther. The first three chapters give an excellent historical background to the Reformation. This highly impressive, scholarly, yet accessible book should be a standard in any bibliography of Luther. Includes an index, chapter notes, bibliographical notes, numerous photographs, and illustrations.

Smith, Preserved. *The Life and Letters of Martin Luther.* Reprint. New York: Barnes & Noble Books, 1968. The author is considered one of the great Reformation scholars. An excellent introduction to Luther's letters with comments by the author placing them in historical context. Includes an index, chronological tables, and a detailed bibliography.

Thompson, W. D. J. Cargill. *The Political Thought of Martin Luther.* New York: Barnes & Noble Books, 1984. Thompson, a leading authority on Luther's political thought, places Luther's political views in the context of his complete theology. The discussion of the Two Realms theory is outstanding. Includes an index and a select bibliography of secondary sources.

Todd, John M. *Luther: A Life.* New York: Crossroad, 1982. Like all top biographers of Luther, Todd draws heavily from Luther's own writings. This historical and theological account of Luther is lucid, providing an excellent discussion of the historical currents and events that helped to shape the Reformation. Includes an index, an excellent appendix on indulgences, numerous illustrations, and a map of Germany.

Wengert, Timothy J., ed. *Harvesting Martin Luther's Reflections on Theology, Ethics, and the Church.* Grand Rapids, Mich.: W. B. Eerdmans, 2004. Anthology of essays focused on the practical value of Luther's teachings for daily life. Discusses a range of issues, both doctrinal and secular, to give a full portrayal of Luther's thought and its applications. Includes illustrations, bibliographic references, index.

SEE ALSO: Martin Bucer; John Calvin; William Caxton; Charles V; Miles Coverdale; Lucas Cranach, the Elder; Desiderius Erasmus; Saint John Fisher; Henry VIII; Balthasar Hubmaier; Saint Ignatius of Loyola; Leo X; Marguerite de Navarre; Maximilian II; Philipp Melanchthon; Menno Simons; Philip the Magnanimous; Pius V; Huldrych Zwingli.

RELATED ARTICLES in *Great Events from History: The Renaissance & Early Modern Era, 1454-1600:* 1499-1517: Erasmus Advances Humanism in England; October 31, 1517: Luther Posts His Ninety-five Theses; April-May, 1521: Luther Appears Before the Diet of Worms; November 3, 1522-November 17, 1530: Correggio Paints the *Assumption of the Virgin*; June, 1524-July, 1526: German Peasants' War; February 27, 1531: Formation of the Schmalkaldic League; March, 1536: Calvin Publishes *Institutes of the Christian Religion*; 1543: Copernicus Publishes *De Revolutionibus*; 1550's-c. 1600: Educational Reforms in Europe.

NICCOLÒ MACHIAVELLI
Italian politician and philosopher

Machiavelli's posthumous reputation rests primarily on his having initiated a pragmatic mode of political discourse that is entirely independent of ethical considerations derived from traditional sources of moral authority, such as classical philosophy and Christian theology.

BORN: May 3, 1469; Florence (now in Italy)
DIED: June 21, 1527; Florence
AREAS OF ACHIEVEMENT: Philosophy, government and politics, historiography, literature

EARLY LIFE

The year 1469 has a dual significance in the historical annals of Florence, since it marks both the date of Lorenzo de' Medici's ascension to power and that of the birth of Niccolò Machiavelli (NEE-koh-loh mahk-yah-VEHL-lee). The boy was reared in a household consisting of his parents, Bernardo and Bartolomea, along with two older sisters and a younger brother.

Bernardo, a tax lawyer and petty landowner of modest means, had pronounced scholarly proclivities and a genuine passion for Roman literature. Machiavelli's own schooling in the principles of Latin grammar and rhetoric began at the age of seven. The study of arithmetic, however, was deferred until several years later. Although the family was too poor to own many books, it did possess a copy of the first three decades of Livy's survey of ancient Roman history. This work must have been a favorite of both father and son because it was eventually sent to the bindery when Niccolò was seventeen years of age. Little is known for certain about the next decade in Machiavelli's life. There is some evidence that indicates that he may have spent most of the years between 1487 and 1495 in Rome working for a prominent Florence banker.

The political climate in Florence had altered drastically in the years immediately preceding Machiavelli's return from Rome. Lorenzo de' Medici died in 1492 and had been succeeded by his eldest son, Piero, an inept youth barely twenty years of age. Piero was soon confronted with a major crisis when King Charles VIII of France invaded Italy in 1494 to lay claim to Naples, and Piero's feckless conduct in relation to the French monarch met with such revulsion on the part of his fellow citizens that they resolved to banish the entire Medici clan from the city forever. Soon thereafter, control of the Florentine republic fell into the hands of an austere Dominican friar from Ferrara, Girolamo Savonarola.

While Savonarola made considerable headway in mitigating the dissolute moral conditions that pervaded Florence, he had considerably less success with his self-imposed mission to restore Christian virtue to the Roman Catholic Church. His adversary in this struggle was Rodrigo Borgia, whose reign as Pope Alexander VI is generally conceded to represent the moral nadir in the history of the Papacy during the Renaissance. Savonarola's persistent challenges to papal authority led to his being formally excommunicated by the Roman pontiff; this event emboldened the friar's political adversaries into taking direct action to destroy him. The climax of this struggle occurred on May 23, 1498, when Savonarola and his two closest confederates in the Dominican Order were escorted to the main square in Florence and hanged atop a pile of brush and logs that was thereupon promptly set ablaze by the hangman. Several hours later, the charred remains of the three men were tossed into the Arno River. Machiavelli witnessed Savonarola's rise and fall at first hand and viewed the episode as an object lesson as to the danger of being "an unarmed prophet."

LIFE'S WORK

Savonarola's demise turned out to be highly beneficial with respect to Machiavelli's own personal fortune, for a few months thereafter he was called on to serve in the newly reconstituted municipal government in several important posts. Its chief executive, Piero Soderini, appointed him both head of the Second Chancery and secretary to the Council of Ten for War. It remains unclear why an inexperienced twenty-nine-year-old from an impoverished family should have been elevated to these key offices. Most likely, it was his keen intelligence that recommended him to Soderini, for each of the artists for whom Machiavelli chose to pose has fully captured this character trait. In addition to the bemused cynicism manifested in his facial expression, Machiavelli is depicted as slender, with thin lips and penetrating eyes. He was, in short, one whose crafty countenance must have caused others to be on their guard while conducting official business with him.

Despite his initial lack of diplomatic experience, Machiavelli was routinely commissioned to undertake sensitive missions to other Italian states as well as to the courts of Louis XII in France and Maximilian I in Germany. Diplomatic activities such as these played a vital role in Machiavelli's development as an uncompromis-

Niccolò Machiavelli. (Library of Congress)

ing exponent of political pragmatism. Most instructive of all in this context were his extensive contacts with Cesare Borgia in Romagna during 1502-1503. It was this illegitimate son of Pope Alexander VI who best exemplified the quality of manliness (*virtù*) that Machiavelli most admired in a political and military leader. Cesare Borgia's meteoric career was, however, terminated abruptly as a result of the death of his father in 1503. The new pope, Julius II, was an inveterate enemy of the entire Borgia clan and soon sent Borgia into exile, where he later died.

Julius was also responsible for terminating Machiavelli's career as a civil servant. When Louis XII of France invaded Italy and succeeded in establishing control over the duchy of Milan, Julius proceeded to form in 1511 a political coalition known as the Holy League, whose aim was to drive the invader from Italian soil. Soderini, despite Machiavelli's advice, refused to permit Florence to join the coalition and insisted on its maintaining strict neutrality throughout the entire conflict. After the expulsion of the French, Julius decided to punish the Florentine republic and compelled its citizenry to accept the return of the Medicis. Both Soderini and Machiavelli were immediately dismissed from office. On February 23, 1513, moreover, Machiavelli was falsely accused of being part of a conspiracy to reestablish the republic and

was put to torture on the rack. Though lack of evidence compelled the authorities to release him, he feared rearrest and decided to retire to his ancestral villa at Sant' Andrea, near Florence, together with his wife, Marietta Corsini, and their six children.

His premature retirement from public life at age forty-three enabled Machiavelli to study Roman literature and to compose many original works. His major political treatises are *Il principe* (wr. 1513, pb. 1532; *The Prince*, 1640) and *Discorsi sopra la prima deca di Tito Livio* (wr. c. 1513, pb. 1531; *Discourses on the First Ten Books of Titus Livius*, 1636). Since Machiavelli focuses on issues pertaining to the governance of principalities in *The Prince* and of republics in the *Discourses on the First Ten Books of Titus Livius*, these works constitute, in effect, a unified exposition of the author's political theories and should therefore be studied in conjunction with each other. The title of the *Discourses* is, however, misleading to the extent that this work is not really a commentary on Livy's history of ancient Rome. Machiavelli subscribed to a cyclical view of history based on the theories propounded by the Greek historian Polybius, and he used the *Discourses on the First Ten Books of Titus Livius* to draw parallels between the events depicted by Livy and the political situation of his own time.

He next tried his hand at writing comedies for a brief period. The most celebrated of his works in this genre is *La Mandragola* (c. 1519; *The Mandrake*, 1911), the other two being adaptations of plays by Terence. Foremost among the other books that Machiavelli wrote at Sant' Andrea are *Dell'arte della guerra* (1521; *The Art of War*, 1560) and *Istorie fiorentine* (1525; *The Florentine History*, 1595). In *The Art of War*, Machiavelli argues strongly in favor of the greater efficacy of native militias as opposed to mercenary armies, and in *The Florentine History* he chronicles the city's fortune from the fall of the Roman Empire to the death of Lorenzo de' Medici.

Even though Machiavelli had been an ardent supporter of the republic headed by Soderini, he considered himself to be a professional civil servant above all else and burned with a desire to be of service to his native city. Machiavelli, in fact, wrote *The Prince* for the express purpose of getting the Medici family to recognize his political sagacity and offer him employment in the new regime. Within a few years, the responsibility of governing Florence passed into the lands of Lorenzo de' Medici, to whom Machiavelli decided to dedicate *The Prince*. Lorenzo, however, showed no interest in the treatise. Lorenzo died prematurely in 1519 at the age of twenty-seven and was succeeded by Cardinal Giulio de' Medici, under whose administration of the city's affairs Machiavelli's personal fortunes improved somewhat. He was entrusted with a few minor diplomatic missions on behalf of the Medicis. More important, it was Giulio who commissioned Machiavelli to write *The Florentine History*.

Giulio de' Medici became Pope Clement VII in 1523 when the immediate successor to Pope Leo died after a brief reign of twenty months. A series of diplomatic missteps on the part of Clement led to the horrendous sack of Rome in 1527 by mercenaries in the service of the German emperor Charles V. The citizens of Florence took advantage of the occasion and expelled the Medicis from their own city for the sake of reestablishing the republic. Machiavelli expected to be reinstated in the posts that he had held under Soderini. The Florentines, however, took a dim view of Machiavelli's previous association with the Medicis and declined to entrust him with any posts in the new regime. Bitterly disappointed, Machiavelli died in Florence a scant few months after the city had regained its liberty. The eclipse of the Medicis turned out to be a short one since Pope Clement and Emperor Charles were quick to reconcile their differences. The Medicis returned to Florence in 1530, but this time they did so as a hereditary nobility. The city's days as an independent republic were thus ended forever.

SIGNIFICANCE

Machiavelli's political writings have elicited an unusual number of disparate reactions over the course of time. The negative viewpoint was initiated by the Roman Catholic Church when it decided to ban open dissemination of Machiavelli's works by placing his entire oeuvre on its *Index librorum prohibitorum*, or Index of Prohibited Books, in 1559. Oddly enough, even though an English translation of *The Prince* did not appear until 1640, it was the frequent allusions to Machiavelli that occur in plays by Elizabethan dramatists such as Christopher Marlowe and William Shakespeare that did the most to popularize his image as an evil counselor. It is generally assumed that the Elizabethan public had already derived a measure of familiarity with the contents of *The Prince* from earlier French translations of the work. Sir Francis Bacon, on the other hand, took a more favorable view of Machiavelli and hailed him as a fellow empiricist who described "what men do, and not what they ought to do." Jean-Jacques Rousseau went even further in vindicating Machiavelli by contending that the real purpose of *The Prince* was to expose the modus operandi of tyrants

MACHIAVELLI'S MAJOR WORKS

1503	*Descrizione del modo tenuto dal Duca Valentino nello ammazzare Vitellozzo Vitelli, Oliverotto da Fermo, il Signor Pagolo e il Duca di Gravina Orsini*
1504	*Decennale primo (First Decennial, 1965)*
1507	*Discorso dell'ordinare lo stato di Firenze alle armi (Discourse on Florentine Military Preparation, 1965)*
1508	*Rapporto delle cose della Magna*
1509	*Decennale secondo (Second Decennial, 1965)*
1512-1513	*Ritratto di cose di Francia*
1513	*Il principe (pb. 1532; The Prince, 1640)*
1513	*Discorsi sopra la prima deca di Tito Livio (pb. 1531; Discourses on the First Ten Books of Titus Livius, 1636)*
1513-1514	*Serenata (Serenade, 1965)*
1517	*L'asino d'oro (rev. 1549; The Golden Ass, 1965)*
c. 1517	*Andria (based on Terence's play; English translation, 1969)*
c. 1519	*La Mandragola (The Mandrake, 1911)*
1520	*Discursus florentinarum rerum post mortem iunioris Laurentii Medices*
1520	*Discorso delle cose fiorentine dopo la morte di Lorenzo (Discourse on the State of Florence After the Death of Lorenzo, 1965)*
1520	*La vita di Castruccio Castracani (The Life of Castruccio Castracani, 1675)*
1521	*Dell' arte della guerra (The Art of War, 1560)*
1523-1524	*Canti carnascialeschi (Carnival Songs, 1965)*
1525	*Istorie fiorentine (The Florentine History, 1595)*
1525	*La Clizia (based on Plautus's play Casina; Clizia, 1961)*
1525	*Discorso: O, Dialogo intorno alla nostra lingua (Discourse: Or, Dialogue About Our Language, 1961)*

and thereby to advance the cause of democracy. In modern times, however, *The Prince* has frequently been called "a handbook for dictators."

Whatever may be said for and against Machiavelli's political doctrines, it is necessary to recognize that he himself was deeply committed to a republican form of government. Even after one concedes Machiavelli's genuine patriotism and his deeply held commitment to republican virtues, there are a number of disquieting elements in his political philosophy that cannot easily be dismissed. There is, for example, his excessive taste for violent and cruel solutions to political problems, as reflected in his unabashed admiration for the bloody deeds of Cesare Borgia. Similarly, he held the view that morally reprehensible actions in terms of Christian standards are fully justifiable if perpetrated for what have come to be known as "reasons of state." For these and other reasons, Machiavelli continues to be a disturbing figure in the cultural pantheon of Western culture.

—*Victor Anthony Rudowski*

FURTHER READING

Bondanella, Peter E. *Machiavelli and the Art of Renaissance History.* Detroit: Wayne State University Press, 1973. This astute study constitutes a chronological survey of Machiavelli's development as a literary stylist. Focuses on the compositional techniques that he employed in depicting the character and conduct of heroic personages. Lacks a formal bibliography, but there are copious endnotes for each chapter.

Hale, John Rigby. *Machiavelli and Renaissance Italy.* New York: Macmillan, 1960. Hale's primary objective is to demonstrate the extent to which Machiavelli's writings are a reflection of the political events that were unfolding in Italy during his own lifetime. Generally viewed as the best introduction to the study of Machiavelli and his age. Contains two maps and a brief annotated bibliography.

Kocis, Robert A. *Machiavelli Redeemed: Retrieving His Humanist Perspectives on Equality, Power, and Glory.* Bethlehem, Pa.: Lehigh University Press, 1998. An attempt to reposition Machiavelli as a Humanist in order to rescue him from his pervasive portrayal as an amoral advocate of anti-Humanist political practices. Includes illustrations, bibliographic references, index.

Machiavelli, Niccolò. *Machiavelli: The Chief Works and Others.* Edited and translated by Allan Gilbert. 3 vols. Durham, N.C.: Duke University Press, 1965. The most extensive collection of Machiavelli's writings currently available in English translation. Although textual annotations are dispensed with, there are succinct introductions to the individual selections as well as an outstanding index to the entire corpus.

Pitkin, Hanna Fenichel. *Fortune Is a Woman: Gender and Politics in the Thought of Niccolò Machiavelli.* Berkeley: University of California Press, 1984. This pioneering study of gender as a factor in political theory depicts Machiavelli as a misogynistic authoritarian. It is particularly useful in clarifying the manner in which Machiavelli employs the concepts of *fortuna* and *virtù.* The text is extensively annotated and supplemented by a highly detailed index and a useful bibliography of works cited.

Pocock, J. G. A. *The Machiavellian Moment: Florentine Political Thought and the Atlantic Republican Tradition.* 2d ed. Princeton, N.J.: Princeton University Press, 2003. Classic study of Machiavelli's conception of a republic and its need to preserve itself, followed by an extended discussion of Machiavelli's influence on English republicanism and the American Revolution. Includes bibliographic references and index.

Ridolfi, Roberto. *The Life of Niccolò Machiavelli.* Translated by Cecil Grayson. Chicago: University of Chicago Press, 1963. This biography is generally regarded as superior to the earlier efforts of Pasquale Villari and Oreste Tommassini by virtue of its focus on the course of Machiavelli's life rather than on his ideas or his cultural and historical milieu. Exhaustive documentation of sources.

Skinner, Quentin. *Machiavelli: A Very Short Introduction.* Rev. ed. New York: Oxford University Press, 2000. Summary of Machiavelli's life and of his thought as revealed in *The Prince,* the *Discourses,* and *The Florentine History.* Includes illustrations, bibliographic references, and index.

Strauss, Leo. *Thoughts on Machiavelli.* Glencoe, Ill.: Free Press, 1958. The author, one of the most renowned political scientists of the modern age, argues that Machiavelli was a teacher of wickedness. This work is especially helpful in evaluating the relationship between the ideological content of *The Prince* and the *Discourses.* Minimal index, but each chapter is accompanied by extensive endnotes.

Viroli, Maurizio. *Machiavelli.* New York: Oxford University Press, 1998. A wide-ranging survey and reexamination of Machiavelli's philosophy, covering his political and social theories and his thoughts on love, women, religion, humanity, and the good life. Includes bibliographic references and index.

SEE ALSO: Alexander VI; Francis Bacon; Cesare Borgia; Charles the Bold; Charles V; Charles VIII; Clement VII; Thomas Cromwell; Desiderius Erasmus; Alberico Gentili; Francesco Guicciardini; Ivan the Terrible; Julius II; Louis XII; Christopher Marlowe; Maxi- milian I; Lorenzo de' Medici; Girolamo Savonarola; William Shakespeare.

RELATED ARTICLE in *Great Events from History: The Renaissance & Early Modern Era, 1454-1600:* July-December, 1513: Machiavelli Writes *The Prince.*

FERDINAND MAGELLAN
Portuguese explorer

Although he died while trying, Magellan was the first person to command an expedition that would eventually circumnavigate the globe. During the expedition, he discovered the southernmost point of South America (later called the Strait of Magellan), was the first to sail across the Pacific Ocean (which he named), and discovered the Philippine Islands. His feat also proved that the earth is indeed round.

BORN: c. 1480; probably Sabrosa, Portugal
DIED: April 27, 1521; Mactan Island, the Philippines
ALSO KNOWN AS: Fernão de Magalhães; Fernando de Magallanes
AREA OF ACHIEVEMENT: Exploration

EARLY LIFE
Ferdinand Magellan (FEHRD-ehn-and muh-JEHL-luhn) was born the third child of Dom Roy and Donha Alda Magalhães. His father was high sheriff of the district and city of Aveiro, located south of the city of Pôrto on the Atlantic coast. Magellan grew up with his siblings—sister Isabel and brother Diogo—in the Torre de Magalhães, the family farmhouse, and had a pleasant childhood in this rustic setting. At the age of seven, he attended school in the nearby monastery of Vila Nova de Mura, where he learned basic arithmetic, Latin, and the importance of harboring a strong faith in the power of Christianity.

When he was twelve, Magellan, with his father's influence, was able to travel to Lisbon and attend Queen Leonora's School of Pages with his brother, Diogo. The king of Portugal, John II, was a great supporter of marine exploration, and the young pages were expected to master such subjects as celestial navigation, cartography, and astronomy as well as the regular court subjects such as court etiquette, hunting, jousting, and swordsmanship.

LIFE'S WORK
In March, 1505, Magellan, his brother Diogo, and his cousin Francisco Serrano sailed with the fleet of Fran- cisco de Almeida to the Orient, the three young squires having signed for a three-year service with the fleet. Magellan would serve eight years in the Orient, leaving as an extra sea hand and returning as an accomplished captain. During his service in the East, he helped establish major ports from the East African coast all the way to the Malay Peninsula. He was also involved in major confrontations with Muslim and Indian forces and was wounded several times.

Magellan, stocky in height with dark, swarthy features and piercing yet sympathetic eyes, developed strong leadership qualities and a keen appetite for adventure during his years in the East. He was also known as a fair and just man who many times risked his life for his fellow crewmen. He was a soldier, one who could remain calm and decisive during a crisis, but one who preferred the excitement of discovery to the life of a military officer.

In July, 1511, Magellan captained a Portuguese caravel to a destination that remains unclear but was probably the Moluccas, or Spice Islands, in Indonesia. Pepper, which was used as a food preservative by all the major countries and was therefore nearly as valuable as gold, was exported largely from the Spice Islands. During his travels, Magellan became convinced that there was an alternate route to the Spice Islands and the East Indies, one that could be attained by sailing west from Europe as Christopher Columbus had done. Unlike Columbus, Magellan had knowledge of a passage around the newly discovered South American continent, previously explored by a fellow navigator and friend, John of Lisbon. John had also informed Magellan that an unexplored ocean existed through the South American passage and that the Spice Islands could be reached in a few weeks time by sailing across this ocean.

When Magellan returned to Portugal in 1512, he was eager to find backing for an expedition to discover the new sea route. He found no support from John II's successor, King Manuel I, who was much less receptive to new exploratory ventures. Rebuffed by Portugal, Magellan sailed to Spain in October, 1517, hoping to present his proposal to King Charles I. Magellan's chief contact in Spain was Diogo Barbosa, a former Portuguese navigator who had made a fortune in the spice trade and who was now the wealthy governor of the Castle of Seville. Magellan married Barbosa's daughter, Beatriz, in December, 1517. The marriage gave Magellan much pleasure, as well as a son, Rodrigo. On March 22, 1518, Magellan secured an audience with Charles. Charles was so impressed with Magellan and his proposal that he approved the expedition that same day. Preparations were then made for what would turn out to be the most epic voyage in the history of exploration.

During the year it took to prepare for the voyage, Magellan dealt with all details, from the rigging and loading of the ships to preventing riots and pilferage caused by spies sent from Portugal and Venice to sabotage the voyage. In the end, Magellan triumphed and finally set sail on September 20, 1519, from San Luca, Spain, with 277 crewmen and five ships: the *Victoria*, the *Santiago*, the *Concepción*, the *San Antonio*, and the *Trinidad*.

Soon after leaving Spain, Magellan's Spanish captains, led by second-in-command Juan de Cartagena, began ridiculing Magellan's authority, attempting to provoke him so that they could justify a mutiny and take command of the voyage. Magellan, however, refused to be provoked.

After suffering major storms along the African coast and disturbing doldrums near the equator, the ships successfully crossed the Atlantic by early December, 1519. On December 8, the coast around Cape Roque in northern Brazil was sighted. Knowing that this area was under Portuguese domain, Magellan headed south into unclaimed territory and landed in what is now Rio de Janeiro on December 13. There the crewmen secured provisions and had friendly relations with the South American Indians. Two weeks later, they set sail down the coast, looking for *el paso*, the pathway first revealed to Magellan by his friend John of Lisbon.

Three months later, when no trace of *el paso* had materialized, the crew was at its breaking point. Winter storms, the worst of the expedition, began battering the ships. Magellan gave the command to seek a harbor where the ships and crew would wait out the winter for five months. The Spanish captains thought that he was mentally unstable and urged him to sail eastward for Africa's Cape of Good Hope and follow the old route to the Indies. The crew wanted him to return to the idyllic harbor at Rio de Janeiro and spend the winter there. Magellan, however, held firm.

The armada anchored at San Julián in southern Argentina on March 31, 1520. The following evening, the Spanish captains mutinied. Under the leadership of Juan de Cartagena, they quickly secured three of the five ships. During a confusing boat exchange of crewmen between mutinous ships, Magellan was able to capture one of the small boatloads of men, substitute his own men for the mutiny sympathizers, and send the boat back to one of the Spanish captains along with another boatload of Magellan's men. While the Spanish captain was dealing with the first boatload, one of Magellan's men suddenly pulled out a knife and stabbed the mutinous captain as the second boat reached the ship. The rest of the boat's passengers scrambled on deck, ready to do battle with the rebellious crew. The crew, shocked by the sudden turn of events, became sympathetic to Magellan once more. With three ships in his control, Magellan surrounded the other two ships and forced the remaining captains to surrender.

A trial was held for the mutineers. Two men were beheaded, and their ringleader, Juan de Cartagena, was set adrift in a small boat, never to be seen again. Through the ordeal of the mutiny, in fact through every ordeal the ex-

Ferdinand Magellan. (Library of Congress)

pedition faced, Magellan remained strong and decisive. The fact that he never doubted his ability to succeed with his mission ultimately inspired his crew to follow him, even when conditions were nearly unbearable.

The expedition spent a total of seven months waiting for the storms to subside, first at San Julián and then farther south at Puerto Santa Cruz, where the *Santiago* was smashed against the shoreline and lost. Finally, on October 18, they set sail once again in search of *el paso*. Three days later, they came to a narrow inlet protected on either side by jagged cliffs. The inlet seemed too dangerous to navigate, but Magellan, by now appearing nearly insane to his crew, ordered the *Concepción* and the *San Antonio* to explore the inlet.

The two ships had just entered the pathway when a storm suddenly arose and swept the ships through the inlet and out of sight, while simultaneously forcing Magellan's *Trinidad* and the *Victoria* out to sea. For two days, Magellan fought the storm until he was able to return to the inlet where the *Concepción* and the *San Antonio* had disappeared. Close to panic, fearing that the two ships had been destroyed, Magellan entered the treacherous pathway. The following morning, a cloud of smoke was sighted. Then, miraculously, the two lost ships sailed into view, flags and pennants waving and crewmen cheering excitedly. They had found *el paso*.

Navigation of the strait (which Magellan called the Strait of Desire, but which was later named for him) was not complete until mid-November. During that period, the *San Antonio* disappeared. Magellan searched for the missing ship until it became apparent that the *San Antonio* had deserted and returned to Spain. Because the *San Antonio* was the largest ship and carried the bulk of their provisions, the crew urged Magellan to turn back as well. Magellan, however, would not be deterred. After the three remaining ships had sailed out of the treacherous strait and into the surprisingly calm waters of a new ocean, Magellan spoke to his men: "We are about to stand into an ocean where no ship has ever sailed before. May the ocean be always as calm and benevolent as it is today. In this hope, I name it the Mar Pacifico [peaceful sea]."

No one encountering the Pacific Ocean for the first time could have anticipated its immensity. In the following three months, nearly half of the remaining men died of starvation and scurvy. Magellan was unfortunate in that his course across the Pacific Ocean led him away from all the major groups of islands that would have supplied him with necessary provisions. During the ghastly voyage across the Pacific Ocean, Magellan threw his maps overboard in anguish, knowing that they were uselessly inaccurate. Some of the men began to believe the old superstition that the ocean would lead them not to the other side of the world but to the end of the world. When the food rotted and the water turned to scum, the dying men began eating rats and sawdust. On March 4, 1531, all the food was gone. Two days later, after ninety-eight days and about eleven thousand miles across the mightiest ocean on the planet, they reached Guam and salvation.

Taking on provisions at Guam was made difficult by the weakened state of the men and the hostility of the people of Guam. As quickly as he could, Magellan set sail and, on March 16, found the island of Samar in the Philippines. Magellan had now achieved his personal goal, having discovered a new chain of islands for Spain. Here the expedition rested and the sick were tended, Magellan personally nursing his emaciated men.

On March 28, during the start of Easter weekend, the crew held a pageant to which the native Filipinos were invited. Magellan had made friends with the local raja and began encouraging him and his followers to convert to Christianity, which they did by the thousands. Inspired by this enthusiastic acceptance of his religion, Magellan decided not only to claim the island chain for Spain but also to convert as many of its inhabitants to Christianity as he could. His desire to reach the Spice Islands, always of secondary importance to him, faded as he became more determined to make the Philippines his ultimate destination.

One month later, after exploring more of the Philippines and being favorably accepted, Magellan attempted to force the powerful raja of the island of Mactan to honor his presence. When the raja refused, Magellan assembled a small army of volunteers and the next morning, on April 27, 1521, led an attack on the raja and his followers. Because of all the hardships he had encountered and conquered, and because his expedition had now taken on a divine mission, Magellan must have come to think of himself as invincible. Unfortunately, he realized too late that he was not.

Magellan quickly realized that he and his men were hopelessly outnumbered. When he ordered a retreat, a panic ensued in which his men scrambled to the shoreline and frantically rowed back to the ships, leaving Magellan and a handful of men stranded. For more than one hour, the men defended themselves as the rest of the crew watched from the ships, until finally Magellan was struck down and killed. Antonio Pigafetta, the chronicler of the voyage, was one of the men who fought beside Magellan when he was struck down. Pigafetta was able to escape during the frenzy that followed. Later he wrote: "And so they slew our mirror, our light, our comfort and our true and only guide."

SIGNIFICANCE

On September 8, 1522, sixteen months after Magellan's death, a floating wreck of a ship with an emaciated crew of eighteen men sailed into the harbor of Seville, Spain. The ship was the *Victoria*. The men, led by Juan Sebastián de Elcano, a former mutineer, staggered out of the ship and marched barefoot through the streets to the shrine of Santa Maria de la Victoria, Our Lady of Victory, the favorite shrine of their fallen leader. They lit candles and said prayers for their dead comrades, then proceeded through the streets of Seville, shocking the citizens with their wasted appearance. The *Victoria* had returned laden with riches from the Spice Islands, which had indeed been reached on November 8, 1521. As for the fate of the remaining two ships, the *Concepción* had been burned before reaching the Spice Islands and the *Trinidad* had been captured by the Portuguese, its fifty-two crewmen hanged.

Magellan's reputation was at first defiled and degraded by his contemporaries as they learned about his behavior from the crew of the *San Antonio*, the ship that had deserted in South America. Later, however, the magnitude of his accomplishments could not be denied. He had proved that the Indies could be reached by sailing west, had discovered a pathway around the southern tip of South America, had named and crossed the largest body of water on the planet, had discovered a new chain of islands, had accumulated a mountain of new information about navigation, geography, and exploration, and had commanded an expedition which, after three years and possibly forty-two thousand miles, had circumnavigated the world.

—James Kline

FURTHER READING

Bergreen, Laurence. *Over the Edge of the World: Magellan's Terrifying Circumnavigation of the Globe.* New York: William Morrow, 2003. Engaging and dramatic narrative of Magellan's famous voyage, which is portrayed day by day according to ship's logs and the journals of crew members. Includes photographic plates, illustrations, maps, bibliographic references, and index.

Cameron, Ian. *Magellan and the First Circumnavigation of the World.* New York: Saturday Review Press, 1973. Generously illustrated with maps, woodcuts, and drawings, this biography of Magellan details his life and his voyage and uses generous quotes from other biographers as well as passages from the journal of Antonio Pigafetta. Includes a selected bibliography.

Humble, Richard. *The Explorers.* Alexandria, Va.: Time-Life Books, 1978. Contains an overview of the accomplishments of the four most significant Renaissance explorers: Bartolomeu Dias, Christopher Columbus, Vasco da Gama, and Magellan. Nearly one third of the book is devoted to Magellan. Includes excellent maps and charts plus an illustrated section on the ships and navigational instruments used by the explorers, as well as a detailed description of the *Victoria*. Includes a selected bibliography.

Joyner, Tim. *Magellan.* Camden, Maine: International Marine, 1992. Detailed biography that balances impressionistic detail of the voyage with historical analysis of its consequences and importance. Includes illustrations, maps, bibliographic references, and index.

Oliveira, Fernando. *Another Report About Magellan's Circumnavigation of the World: The Story of Fernando Oliveira.* Translated by Pedro Sastre. Edited by Karl-Heinz Wionzek. Manila, Philippines: National Historical Institute, 2000. Firsthand account of Magellan's voyage, written by a member of his crew. Includes illustrations, maps, and bibliographic references.

Parr, Charles McKew. *So Noble a Captain: The Life and Times of Ferdinand Magellan.* New York: Thomas Y. Crowell, 1953. Reprint. Westport, Conn.: Greenwood Press, 1975. The definitive biography of Magellan that traces his ancestry, details the lives of all the principal men and women who affected or were affected by Magellan, vividly re-creates the time in which he lived, and chronicles his accomplishments in minute detail. Contains an extensive bibliography, including books on such related subjects as the history of Spain and Portugal, sailing-ship construction, navigation, and various locations visited by Magellan.

Pigafetta, Antonio. *Magellan's Voyage: A Narrative Account of the First Circumnavigation.* Translated by R. A. Skelton. New Haven, Conn.: Yale University Press, 1969. Reprint. Mineola, N.Y.: Dover, 1994. An English translation from a French text of Pigafetta's Italian journal. It is full of detailed descriptions of the events of the voyage, the lands discovered, the natives encountered and their habits and customs, and the tales told by the natives and examples of their vocabulary.

Sanderlin, George. *First Around the World: A Journal of Magellan's Voyage.* New York: Harper & Row, 1964. An interesting reconstruction of Magellan's life and voyage using letters and journals of Magellan's contemporaries. The early texts are linked by comments from the author. Most of the book is composed of excerpts from Pigafetta's journal. Illustrated, with a selected bibliography.

Zweig, Stefan. *Conqueror of the Seas: The Story of Magellan.* Translated by Eden Paul and Cedar Paul. New

York: Viking Press, 1938. A full account of Magellan's life from the time of his first voyage in 1505 to his death, and the results of his epic voyage. Contains maps and illustrations of the principal events taken from early texts.

SEE ALSO: Charles V; Juan Sebastián de Elcano; John II; Miguel López de Legazpi; Manuel I.

RELATED ARTICLES in *Great Events from History: The Renaissance & Early Modern Era, 1454-1600:* 1519-1522: Magellan Expedition Circumnavigates the Globe; 1565: Spain Seizes the Philippines.

MUḤAMMAD IBN ʿABD AL-KARĪM AL-MAGHĪLĪ
Muslim religious leader

Al-Maghīlī was a major figure in the movement of classical Sunni Islam from North Africa to other African states. He corrected what he believed were violations of Islamic law by non-Muslims, particularly Jews. The corpus of his writings represents how Islamic culture migrated from one major ethnic and cultural region to another.

BORN: c. 1440; Tlemcen (now in Algeria)
DIED: Between 1503 and 1506; Tamantit (now in Algeria)
AREA OF ACHIEVEMENT: Religion and theology

EARLY LIFE

Very little is known about the early life of Muḥammad ibn ʿAbd al-Karīm al-Maghīlī (moh-KAWM-mawd ib-ehn ehb-dawl-kaw-REEM ahl-mawg-EEL-ee). The place in which he was born had been for several centuries a recognized seat of Islamic learning. Tlemcen was tied, symbolically at least, to the Qādirīyah Sufi tradition in Islam, which harks back to its twelfth century founder ʿAbd al-Qādir al-Jīlānī (d. 1166).

During al-Maghīlī's early life in Tlemcen, reigning authority was held by the Zayyanids, Berber successors to the prominent Almohad Dynasty seated in Marrakech (now Morocco). Whereas the Almohads had represented a rigorous Islamic reformist policy, the Zayyanids seem to have been much less involved in religious affairs and were mainly concerned with maintaining regional political hegemony.

Al-Maghīlī's primary teacher was ʿAbd al-Raḥmān al-Thaʾālabī (d. 1470), who was at that time established in Tunis, capital of the Ḥafṣid Dynasty, another successor to earlier Almohad rule. Another teacher who left a strong impression on al-Maghīlī was Ibn Yadir (d. 1473). To study with him, it is possible that al-Maghīlī went as far as the Saharan oasis region of Tuwat, nearly 620 miles (1,000 kilometers) south of Tlemcen. The latter had moved to the oasis zone in the 1440's to pursue his own studies and also to serve as Islamic judge, or *qadi*, in Tuwat.

Al-Maghīlī was exposed early in his life to applied Islamic law, not only through his association with the *qadi* Ibn Yadir but also through a major work he may have studied while still in Tlemcen: *Tuhfat al nazir* (virtue of the minister), by Muḥammad al-ʿUqbani (d. 1409). This work was a law treatise in a field known to Islamists as *hisba* (legal control over public mores), which focuses on the daily lives of Muslims. The *Tuhfat* was particularly detailed on matters having to do with the status of non-Muslims, protected people called *dhimmis* (singular *dhimma*), living in Islamic society. The entire field of *hisba* was something that attracted the young al-Maghīlī, and this interest carried over into later years when he gained a major reputation as a reformer and preacher.

LIFE'S WORK

The exact date of al-Maghīlī's decision to move to Tamantit, a main town dominating the oasis of Tuwat, is not known. Events in Tamantit itself helped establish al-Maghīlī's reputation as a reformist. It was in Tamantit that he had his first exposure to the major trans-Saharan trade caravans that traveled through Tuwat to the black African kingdoms of the general region referred to as the

AL-MAGHĪLĪ ON THE RIGHT PRACTICE OF ISLAM IN NORTHERN AFRICA

Al-Maghīlī answered a series of questions from Songhai king Mohammed I Askia, the first Muslim ruler of Songhai, about establishing and administering Islamic government and correct Islamic practices in West Africa.

Mohammed: Among the people [of the Songhai Empire], there are some who claim knowledge of the supernatural through sand divining and the like, or through the disposition of the stars . . . [while] some assert that they can write (talismans) to bring good fortune . . . or to ward off bad fortune. . . . Some defraud in weights and measures.

Al-Maghīlī: The answer—and God it is who directs to the right course—is that everything you have mentioned concerning people's behavior in some parts of this country is gross error. It is the bounden duty of the commander of the Muslims and all other believers who have the power to change every one of these evil practices.

As for any who claims knowledge of the supernatural in the ways you have mentioned . . . he is a liar and an unbeliever. . . . Such people must be forced to renounce it by the sword. Then whoever renounces such deeds should be left in peace, but whoever persists should be killed with the sword as an unbeliever; his body should not be washed or shrouded, and he should not be buried in a Muslim graveyard.

Source: Quoted in *The Heritage of World Civilizations*, edited by Albert M. Craig et al., vol. 1, 5th ed. (Upper Saddle River, N.J.: Prentice Hall, 2000), p. 504.

Sudan (*bilad al-sudan*, land of the blacks), the area that includes the great Niger River bend (now Mali, Niger, and the northern regions of Nigeria).

After he had established himself in Tamantit, al-Maghīlī began a crusade to correct what he claimed was a lack of adherence by non-Muslims, particularly Jews, to provisions of Islamic law governing their status. Apparently, he was concerned with conditions not only in Tamantit but also in the entire oases frontier zone in the northern Sahara. The main points at issue were legal questions, such as required payment by non-Muslims of the so-called head tax for protected people, or *jizya*. Al-Maghīlī, apparently, went beyond mere debate. According to one of his main biographers, Ibn 'Askar, he claimed that if protected non-Muslims did not honor the legal provisions for their special status in Islam, physical action against them was justifiable, since they were effectively giving up their right to protection. He also maintained that maintenance of a synagogue in Tamantit was contrary to the assumption that protected peoples should remain in a subordinate position and that synagogues, if allowed to exist, might be considered

equal in importance to the Islamic mosque.

Whether he called for mob action to deal with assumed illegal actions by Jews, surviving contemporary reports and later historical accounts confirm that violent attacks were carried out in various places in the Tuwat zone during the time of al-Maghīlī's residence there. Indeed, the well-known early sixteenth century account by Leo Africanus states that an actual massacre of Jews took place in 1492 (the same year in which the Jews were expelled from Spain by King Ferdinand II and Queen Isabella I), implying al-Maghīlī's direct involvement in inciting the violence.

Al-Maghīlī is best known for his extended travels, beginning between 1490 and 1493, in the Middle Niger region. The decision to leave the Tuwat oasis region may or may not have been connected to the tumultuous events in Gurara (and other places) in and around 1492. His first trip across the Sahara could have been the result of an invitation from Muhammad Rumfa, sultan of the Hausa state of Kano (now in northern Nigeria). Unlike his contemporary King Sonni 'Alī of the Songhai Empire, who held sway at that time over the major trade termini once contained in the empire of Mali, Muhammad Rumfa appeared to be fully devoted to Islam, and he took pride in the fact that Muslim scholars came from afar to assist and apparently to advise his court.

During his extended stay in Kano, al-Maghīlī composed two manuscripts that might be compared to what in the Western world are called traditional "mirrors for princes." The strictly political sections of these works deal with statecraft, or the development of skills necessary to govern. Al-Maghīlī, however, was concerned especially with proper Islamic behavior in society. Thus, the subject of *hisba*, or formal control over mores, appeared in a section dealing with, among other subjects, gender relations and prohibition of alcoholic beverages. Another section is more specifically concerned with administration of justice under Shari'a law (canon law). Al-Maghīlī spent several years in Kano and may have contracted a local marriage, since to this day there is still a group of people there who claim to be his descendants.

After visiting Katsina, a second well-known Hausa state, sometime in the mid-1490's, al-Maghīlī traveled farther west, reaching Gao, the capital of the Songhai Empire, around 1498. The political situation in Songhai had changed considerably since the death in 1492 of King Sonni ʿAlī, a ruler who seems to have either neglected Islamic guidelines or perhaps even opposed them openly. After a succession struggle, the much more pious Muslim ruler, Mohammed I Askia, ascended the throne in 1493 and confirmed his dedication to Islam by making the pilgrimage to Mecca. Perhaps Mohammed I Askia passed through the Hausa states returning from Mecca and Cairo, which would explain how al-Maghīlī met him before journeying to Gao.

In any event, and even though al-Maghīlī's name does not appear in major Arabic language chronicles of Songhai history, it was there that he composed his best-known work, the *Ajwibatu* (*Shariʿa in Songhay*, 1985). This work purports to be al-Maghīlī's responses to a set number of questions posed by the new ruler of Songhai. The subjects range from straight governmental questions through choice of trained Islamic advisers, and from *tajdid*, or Islamic revival and revolution, to responsibilities for jihad, or effort in advancing the faith.

SIGNIFICANCE

Al-Maghīlī was an intermediary between the centuries-old North African tradition of Islam and the nascent Islam of sub-Saharan Africa. His role in *tajdid* remains significant for its time. Al-Maghīlī's role also marked the extension of literary Arabic as a shared mode of communication between the Niger zone and the rest of the Islamic world.

—Byron Cannon

FURTHER READING

Fisher, Humphrey. "Leo Africanus and the Songhay Conquest of Hausaland." *International Journal of African Historical Studies* 11 (1978): 86-112. This article studies an early firsthand account of the political relations between the two regions of the Niger basin affected by al-Maghīlī's teachings.

Hunwick, John. "Religion and State in the Songhay Empire, 1464-1591." In *Islam in Tropical Africa*, edited by I. M. Lewis. Bloomington: Indiana University Press, 1980. Discusses the complexities of Islam's role in the politics of an African society that was only partially converted during al-Maghīlī's time.

_____, trans. and ed. *Shariʿa in Songhay*. New York: Oxford University Press, 1985. A translation of al-Maghīlī's *Ajwibatu*.

SEE ALSO: Amina Sarauniya Zazzua; Askia Daud; Leo Africanus; Mohammed I Askia; Sonni ʿAlī.

RELATED ARTICLES in *Great Events from History: The Renaissance & Early Modern Era, 1454-1600:* 1454-1481: Rise of the Ottoman Empire; 1481-1512: Reign of Bayezid II and Ottoman Civil Wars; May, 1485-April 13, 1517: Mamlūk-Ottoman Wars; 1525-1600: Ottoman-Ruled Egypt Sends Expeditions South and East; 1529-1574: North Africa Recognizes Ottoman Suzerainty.

SIR THOMAS MALORY
English writer

Combining French prose, Arthurian romances, and some English materials with stories of his own invention, Malory set the Arthurian legend in its enduring form in Le Morte d'Arthur.

BORN: Early fifteenth century; Warwickshire, England
DIED: March 14, 1471; Newgate Prison, London
AREA OF ACHIEVEMENT: Literature

EARLY LIFE

The problem in writing the biography of Thomas Malory (MAL-ohr-ee), the most famous author of Arthurian stories, is that it is not known with any certainty who he was. At one time or another, scholars have championed no fewer than nine Thomas Malorys, but perhaps only three of those men deserve serious attention.

The primary conditions for establishing the author's identity come from the text of *Le Morte d'Arthur* itself. Modern scholars have available to them the first printed edition, produced in 1485 by William Caxton, and also the late fifteenth century manuscript version, found in the library of Winchester College in 1934 by Walter F. Oakeshott. "Syr Thomas Maleoré, Knyght" tells his readers that he has completed the work in the ninth year of the reign of Edward IV (that is, March 4, 1469, to March 3, 1470) and asks them to pray for his "good delyuerance" from prison. In the "explicit," the formal statement ending the first of the eight tales that make up the whole book in the Winchester manuscript, Malory again suggests that he is a knight prisoner. Thus, one knows that the author was a knight, was of an age to write the work in 1469-1470, and was a prisoner of some sort. That the printer Caxton knew so little about Malory suggests further that Malory had died by the time the book was printed, or before July, 1485.

Throughout most of the twentieth century, the one who was thought to have best met these qualifications was Thomas Malory of Newbold Revel in Warwickshire. George L. Kittredge had made this identification most forcefully in his influential article "Who Was Sir Thomas Malory?" written in 1896. As Kittredge and other scholars supported this choice of the Warwickshire Malory with further evidence in later publications, the link appeared to become increasingly sound. Some scholars began to treat it as established fact: Sir Thomas Malory was the author, and a man by that name and rank could be identified who seemed to meet the qualifications; therefore, Sir Thomas Malory of Newbold Revel had written

Le Morte d'Arthur. In many ways, he fit the part. This Malory was a member of an old Warwickshire family; he had served for a quarter of a century in the wars in France, following Richard Beauchamp, earl of Warwick, a mirror of chivalry to his contemporaries; and he had been a member of Parliament for Warwickshire in 1445-1446.

Yet there were troublesome aspects to this identification, for the Warwickshire Malory was at least accused of committing a remarkable series of crimes between 1450 and 1460. The list of charges included attempted murder, rape (twice, against the same person), cattle raiding, extortion, and raids on an abbey. He was imprisoned eight times and twice escaped dramatically. Could this man actually have written the great chivalric tale of Arthur and his knights of the Round Table? Could one who seemed so immoral have produced what many readers considered a moral book? Some scholars tried to excuse Malory, arguing that he had been simply indicted, not convicted. Others merely shrugged off the charges as evidence of the vigorous acts of living in a violent age. Eugène Vinaver, the editor of the standard edition of *Le Morte d'Arthur,* frankly stated that the morality of the author was not the same issue as the morality of his artistic work.

Until 1966, those scholars troubled by the "morality issue" or, more generally, by the identification of the Warwickshire knight with the author had no strong opposition candidate. In that year, however, William Matthews criticized the case for the leading candidate and advanced a previously unknown Thomas Malory who came from Hutton Conyers in Yorkshire. He supported this Malory from the north of England by pointing to northern elements in the Winchester text—in vocabulary and usage, in a preference for northern geographical locations, and in a frequent use of northern romances as sources. That this Thomas Malory could not be proved either a knight or a prisoner presented obstacles, but Matthews argued that "knight prisoner" might mean "prisoner of war." Some scholars found these arguments appealing; few found them convincing. Specialists, for example, have cast doubts on the validity of the linguistic evidence. Yet the question of identity, formerly more or less considered settled on the Warwickshire knight, once again seemed to be a matter for debate.

The likelihood of further debate increased in 1981, when Richard R. Griffith reopened a case for a candidate from Papworth St. Agnes, a tiny village in Cambridgeshire on the border with Huntingdonshire. This Thomas Malory had been considered as long ago as 1897 but had been dismissed ever since. Griffith thinks the dialect, age, and political affiliations of the Cambridgeshire Malory fit the author perfectly. He argues that his candidate was briefly imprisoned before his execution (for reasons of politics, not crime) in September of 1469 (Malory's prayer for good deliverance thus being in vain). Griffith suggests that this Malory had access to the one library in England likely to have contained all the French romances that went into *Le Morte d'Arthur*. Though there is no incontrovertible proof that this Malory was a knight, Griffith makes a plausible case that he possessed the status so crucial to his identification with the author.

Supporters of the traditional author, the Warwickshire knight, have continued to advance and modify their case. P. J. C. Field, for example, having eliminated a claim for a second Warwickshire knight, a Thomas Malory of Fenny Newbold (by proving that Newbold Revel and Fenny Newbold were simply two names for the same place), has clarified the birth date of Malory, altering the chronology for his entire career. Field suggests a birth date of about 1416, putting the Warwickshire Malory in his mid-thirties and early forties when imprisoned and about age fifty-five when he died in 1471. This chronology eliminates the idea of Malory's long wartime service with that great knight, the earl of Warwick, but it provides a chronology that fits the author quite well.

LIFE'S WORK

Whoever Sir Thomas Malory the author was, his enduring achievement was the writing of *Le Morte d'Arthur*. Yet this work has no more been free from controversy than its author. Two issues in particular have attracted attention and generated debate. In the nineteenth century, many scholars concentrated on identifying Malory's sources and began to debate the issue of his originality. By the twentieth century, scholarship on Malory had tended to focus instead on the structure of *Le Morte d'Arthur* and debated the issue of the unity of the work.

The emphasis on Malory's sources focused first on his numerous French sources (such as the Prose *Tristan* and the Vulgate *Queste del Saint Graal*, both written in about 1230) and only later considered his English sources (such as the *Alliterative Morte Arthure*, which also dates back to about 1230). The emphasis on sources coincided with the tendency during the nineteenth century to consider Malory a "mere" translator or compiler, rather than an author of much originality. Yet, increasingly, scholars

began to describe Malory as a conscious artist, selecting and adapting his sources, creating from their immense diversity and bulk a set of Arthurian stories that above all bear the stamp of his own originality and style. From the complex French tales, with their elaborately interwoven incidents (using a technique called intertwining, or *entrelacement*), Malory wrote a long story of eight sequential, cumulative, major sections (as in the Winchester manuscript, though there are twenty-one books as printed by Caxton), culminating in the dramatic collapse of the fellowship of the Round Table.

The question of originality led to the discussions of unity more common in twentieth century scholarship on Malory: What was the structure of *Le Morte d'Arthur*? Did Malory intend and achieve a unified work of art? Vinaver placed such questions at the forefront of discussion by giving his 1947 edition of the work (based on the Winchester manuscript) the controversial title *The Works of Sir Thomas Malory*. Although Vinaver softened his views in a second edition published in 1967, he considered Malory primarily a translator of French Arthurian tales and argued that he actually adapted eight separate romances, not a single book. This latter contention was hotly debated for at least the following two decades. Robert M. Lumiansky and Charles Moorman vigorously argued that in *Le Morte d'Arthur* Malory shows clear intent of linking the eight tales and that he succeeded in making them a unified book. The views of Vinaver's critics appear most clearly in a volume edited by Lumiansky and significantly titled *Malory's Originality: A Critical Study of "Le Morte d'Arthur"* (1964) and in Charles Moorman's *The Book of Kyng Arthur: The Unity of Malory's "Morte d'Arthur"* (1965).

SIGNIFICANCE

The uncertainties and the scholarly debates about Sir Thomas Malory and his work must be considered, but they should not obscure his achievement and importance. It is through Malory and his great book (or books) that English-language readers know the stories of King Arthur, Queen Guinevere, Sir Lancelot, Sir Gareth, and Sir Tristram, and of the Quest for the Holy Grail, the Round Table, and Camelot. In telling these stories, Malory has delighted his readers for hundreds of years. As Vinaver wrote:

> Perhaps none of this would have seemed real to us if so much of it were not conveyed in a form which in a very true sense creates its own substance, a prose both crisp and resonant, blending the majesty of epic eloquence

with the freshness of living speech. How strange and yet how instructive the contrast between the appeal of the work to English readers and the neglect into which the Arthurian legend fell in the country where it found its first poetic expression!... [Malory's] magic spell...had revived in English prose the quests of Arthurian knights, the epic grandeur of their grim battles, and the "piteous tale" of the fall of Arthur's kingdom.

—Richard W. Kaeuper

FURTHER READING

Batt, Catherine. *Malory's "Morte d'Arthur": Remaking Arthurian Tradition.* New York: Palgrave, 2002. Analysis of Malory's achievement in synthesizing the French and English traditions to create a distinctive version of the Arthur legend. Looks at the cultural function of Malory's work in relation to nationalism, history, identity, and gender. Includes bibliographic references and index.

Bennett, J. A. W., ed. *Essays on Malory.* New York: Oxford University Press, 1963. Seven essays by various scholars debating significant aspects of Malory's work.

Bloom, Harold, ed. *King Arthur.* Philadelphia: Chelsea House, 2004. Anthology of essays on Arthurian legend, focusing especially on Malory's *Le Morte d'Arthur* and Alfred, Lord Tennyson's *Idylls of the King* (1859-1885). Includes bibliographic references and index.

D'Arcy, Anne Marie. *Wisdom and the Grail: The Image of the Vessel in the "Queste del Saint Graal" and Malory's "Tale of Sankgreal."* Dublin, Ireland: Four Courts, 2000. Comparison of Malory's secular version of the quest for the Holy Grail with a thirteenth century religious version of the story. Looks at the history of Grail symbolism and Malory's incorporation of the story into his Arthurian mythos.

Field, P. J. C. *The Life and Times of Sir Thomas Malory.* Rochester, N.Y.: D. S. Brewer, 1999. A careful, rigorous analysis of all existing evidence as to the identity of the author of *Le Morte d'Arthur,* including documents that were unavailable to Matthews in 1966. Concludes that the Warwickshire Malory is the author, then provides a full biography. Includes bibliographic references and index.

Griffith, Richard R. "The Authorship Question Reconsidered: A Case for Thomas Malory of Papworth St. Agnes, Cambridgeshire." In *Aspects of Malory,* edited by Toshiyuki Takamiya and Derek Brewer. Woodbridge, Suffolk, England: D. S. Brewer, 1981. Elaborate argument for the Malory from Papworth St. Agnes.

Kim Hyonjin. *The Knight Without the Sword: A Social Landscape of Malorian Chivalry.* Rochester, N.Y.: D. S. Brewer, 2001. Study of the relationship between Malory's representation of chivalry within his work and actual conceptions of chivalry and aristocracy in his society. Argues that Malory's knights embody the aspirations and the anxieties of contemporary English nobles. Includes bibliographic references and index.

Kittredge, George Lyman. "Who Was Sir Thomas Malory?" *Harvard Studies and Notes in Philology and Literature* 5 (1896): 85-106. The essay that placed the Warwickshire Malory in the front rank among contenders for authorship of *Le Morte d'Arthur.*

Lumiansky, Robert M., ed. *Malory's Originality: A Critical Study of "Le Morte d'Arthur."* Baltimore: Johns Hopkins University Press, 1964. Eight essays by different authors, each examining the function of an individual tale in Malory's book as a whole.

Malory, Sir Thomas. *The Works of Sir Thomas Malory.* Edited by Eugène Vinaver. 3d ed. 3 vols. Revised by P. J. C. Field. New York: Clarendon Press, 1990. The standard edition. Oxford also published a one-volume paperback edition in 1971, minus the introduction, critical apparatus, index, and bibliography, but including a revised glossary, summaries of Vinaver's original commentary on each romance, and explanatory notes.

Matthews, William. *The Ill-Framed Knight: A Skeptical Inquiry into the Identity of Sir Thomas Malory.* Berkeley: University of California Press, 1966. Matthews's attack on the Warwickshire Malory as author and his case for the Yorkshire Malory.

Moorman, Charles. *The Book of Kyng Arthur: The Unity of Malory's "Morte d'Arthur."* Lexington: University Press of Kentucky, 1965. Incorporates a number of his articles published earlier, discussing important aspects of Malory and themes of his work.

SEE ALSO: William Caxton; George Chapman; Edward IV; Christopher Marlowe; Thomas Nashe; William Shakespeare; Sir Philip Sidney; Edmund Spenser.

RELATED ARTICLE in *Great Events from History: The Renaissance & Early Modern Era, 1454-1600:* c. 1589-1613: Shakespeare Writes His Dramas.

ANDREA MANTEGNA
Italian artist

Mantegna contributed to the growth of Renaissance art in northern Italy and created an individual style that shows his powers of invention, directness of presentation, illusionism, and detailed realism. He was a transmitter of the Florentine Renaissance to his northern Italian contemporaries and was an artistic interpreter of antiquity for his own and succeeding generations.

BORN: c. 1431; Isola di Cartura, Republic of Venice (now in Italy)
DIED: September 13, 1506; Mantua (now in Italy)
AREA OF ACHIEVEMENT: Art

EARLY LIFE

Andrea Mantegna (ahn-DRAY-ah mahn-TEHN-yah) was born near Padua in northern Italy. His probable birth date of around 1431 is based on an inscription, preserved in early documents, from a lost altarpiece of 1448 executed for the Church of Santa Sofia in Padua. It lists his age as seventeen when the project reached completion.

Little is known of Mantegna's life before he reached the age of ten. At that time, his father, Biagio, a carpenter, gave him up for adoption to the painter Francesco Squarcione, who appears to have acted as adoptive father to several talented boys. In addition to his activities as a painter, collector, and dealer, Squarcione trained his young charges while providing them with a home and the necessities of life. Once their schooling was complete, the master contracted with wealthy patrons for the services of his young protégés.

Mantegna served his apprenticeship in the workshop of his adoptive father from 1442 to 1448. During the 1440's in Padua, Squarcione's *bottega* functioned as an exchange for ideas and methods among important artists and craftsmen. In this ambience, Mantegna was introduced to the best talents and the latest artistic developments of the time. The superior genius of Donatello, the Florentine sculptor, provided a focus for Paduan art from 1443 to 1453. Donatello's works must have been a major topic of conversation among artists and patrons who frequented Squarcione's workshop.

Other Florentine artists influenced Mantegna's development through the agency of Squarcione's *bottega*. In 1447, the master and his apprentices moved to Venice and resided there for several months. Paolo Uccello, Fra Filippo Lippi, and Andrea del Castagno had preceded them by the period of a decade or more, and at different times. These artists had all left the mark of the Florentine Renaissance on the city of canals and lagoons. It should also be noted that Lippi had executed in Padua works that Mantegna would already have seen. Elements peculiar to the individual styles of these artists were transmitted to Mantegna at that formative period in his career.

The atmosphere of Squarcione's shop, with its constant activity and opportunity for dialogue, provided Mantegna with all the conditions necessary for his accelerated development as a painter. Squarcione's own approach to painting appears to have had minimal impact on Mantegna. The importance, however, of Donatello and the new Florentine art in the formation of Mantegna's style is universally recognized and may be clearly distinguished in the young artist's paintings of the 1450's. In addition to providing Mantegna with an entrée into the contemporary art circles, Squarcione instilled in his adopted son a love of antiquity. The influence of classical art and literature appears constantly in Mantegna's earliest and latest work.

Mantegna's early training came to a close in 1448. In January, the young man sued Squarcione over the terms of his adoption and what he considered to be insufficient compensation for his six years as an apprentice. The two men reached a compromise that enabled Mantegna to declare his independence and to take control of his own finances. It seems extraordinary that Mantegna was able to do this at the tender age of seventeen, unless he had made significant contributions as a member of Squarcione's *bottega*, thereby establishing his reputation as a painter of great potential.

LIFE'S WORK

Mantegna received his first major independent commission in May, 1448. The plan for decoration of the Ovetari Chapel in the Church of the Eremitani in Padua included provisions for an altar and frescoes with scenes from the lives of Saints James and Christopher, who were patron saints of the church. At the outset, Mantegna shared this work with several other artists. For several reasons, including the death of two participants and withdrawal from the project by the others, Mantegna was left with a large number of scenes to finish by himself. The three standing figures of Saint Peter, Saint Paul, and Saint Christopher in the vault of the chapel's apse were probably the earliest frescoes that Mantegna completed. If this is true, they were done while Niccolò Pizzolo, a Paduan painter who initially shared Mantegna's half of the commission, was still alive.

Modern scholarship supports the conclusion that Pizzolo may have had an even stronger influence on Mantegna's artistic formation than Squarcione. As Mantegna's older associate in the Ovetari venture, Pizzolo may have cemented the connection between the younger artist and the new Florentine art. Mantegna's three saints do not have the strong sculptural quality of Pizzolo's adjacent figures, but the draperies are carefully studied and the poses are harmonious and symmetrically balanced in the new manner.

Saint James Baptizing Hermogenes and *Saint James Before Herod Agrippa* are the first completely mature works by Mantegna in the Ovetari Chapel. The painter's thorough knowledge of Leon Battista Alberti's perspective system, published in *De pictura* (1435; *Of Painting*, 1726), is visible in the precisely measured perspective grid of each fresco as well as in the common vanishing point employed for these two adjacent scenes. The classical derivation of the architectural settings and the sculptural decorations in these works reveal Mantegna's growing love of the antique. Although there is no direct proof, the soldier standing in the right foreground of *Saint James Before Herod Agrippa* is often identified as a self-portrait. The sharp angular features and the distinct frown fit written descriptions of Mantegna's serious and often severe demeanor.

Two other scenes, *Saint James Led to Execution* and *Martyrdom of Saint James*, are impressive in their continued exploration of perspective and figural relationships. Their position on the wall places the lower edge of each composition approximately at eye level, making the figures and architecture appear to move down the picture plane as they recede in the picture space. Several of the figures in the foreground seem to violate the picture plane and project into the viewer's space. By this time, such effects were common in Florentine painting but still quite unusual in northern Italian art. The sculptural, stony quality of Mantegna's figures was very likely a result of his love of ancient sculpture and an appreciation for the work of Donatello. This sculpturesque quality combined with the northern Italian penchant for detailed realism are two of the major components of Mantegna's mature style. During the nine years the painter worked in the Ovetari Chapel, from 1448 to 1457, his formation as a major Renaissance artist occurred.

Between 1457 and 1459, Mantegna was occupied with the commission for a major altarpiece for the Church of San Zeno in Verona. The main part of this

Andrea Mantegna. (Library of Congress)

polyptych consists of three panels that depict a *Madonna Enthroned with Saints*. The carved and gilded wooden frame with its arched pediment and entablature form a temple format using the Corinthian order. Its design and the general placement of the figures in the painting are thought to reflect the original disposition, now much changed, of the principal elements in Donatello's altar for Sant' Antonio. Mantegna visually attached the columns of the frame to piers in the painting and continued the illusion by creating a square loggia that encompasses the Madonna, the Christ Child, and the saints, while defining the perspective space of the picture. A "classical" frieze of cherubs, clearly Mantegna's own invention, surrounds the level above the piers. The spatially conceived garland of fruit painted at the front of the picture, the crisp detail, and the bright colors show Mantegna at his best. The San Zeno altarpiece sets the tone for a whole group of works of this category in northern Italian art in the fifteenth and sixteenth centuries.

By 1459, Mantegna had accepted the invitation of the Marchese Ludovico Gonzaga, lord of Mantua, to become his court painter. As one of the first Renaissance artists officially attached to a princely court, Mantegna found himself painting altarpieces, frescoing churches, decorating palaces, and even designing costumes and entertainments for lavish court pageants. The frescoes of the Camera degli Sposi (chamber of the bride and groom) in the Gonzaga Palace were painted between 1465 and

1474, and are considered to be major works in Mantegna's mature style. He covered the walls and ceiling of the square chamber with scenes from the life of the Gonzaga family. The left wall contains a depiction of the meeting between Ludovico Gonzaga and his son, Cardinal Francesco. The Gonzaga court is shown on the right wall, and the ceiling fresco takes the form of a circular architectural opening, the eye, or oculus, of a dome. The intermediate zone, which ties the lower scenes to the oculus, consists of illusionistically painted transverse arches that crisscross a flattened domical ceiling and encompass wreathed medallions containing the busts of Roman emperors. Although there is a wealth of classical allusion juxtaposed with scenes from the life of the Gonzaga family, the exact meaning and relationship of the parts have not yet been satisfactorily explained. The overall design and meticulous detail of the chamber reveal Mantegna's genius as a decorator and his skill with *trompe l'oeil* effects. The oculus in particular is a tour de force of perspective and foreshortening and, when viewed from the proper vantage point beneath, surprises and amuses the viewer with the artist's expertise and gentle sense of humor.

Mantegna continued in the service of the Gonzagas after Ludovico's death in 1478, first for Federico and then for Francesco. Francesco presented Mantegna to Pope Innocent VIII in June, 1488, and this trip to Rome gave Mantegna the opportunity to study the classical antiquities of the Eternal City. In addition, he was commissioned by the pope to paint a small chapel in the Vatican. On his return from Rome in 1491, a change occurred in Mantegna's style. The paintings of his late period, such as the *Madonna of the Victory* (1495), are almost overrefined. Linear elements increase in complexity and tend to rob figures and objects of their three-dimensional form. The brilliance of the earlier works is exchanged for softer tones. While still the works of a great painter, the later productions lack the force and vitality of his youth, and instead evoke an idyllic mood of quiet and gentleness.

The *Triumph of Caesar* (begun c. 1486) was the last great series created by Mantegna. These enormous canvases painted in tempera are 108 by 108 inches (274 by 274 centimeters) and represent a theme based on Petrarch's description of a triumphal procession. Clearly inspired by Mantegna's trip to Rome, these works are the masterpieces of his late style. They are carefully planned and executed to provide a continuity of atmosphere from one canvas to the next as the procession unfolds. They are also so precisely detailed that they present an unparalleled feeling of truth to nature. Yet, in all their complexity of line, foreshortening, and changes in scale, designed to portray the noise and clamor of such an event, they exude the same curious quietness and serenity that mark many of Mantegna's late works.

A letter from Mantegna's son to Francesco Gonzaga tells of the artist's death at seven in the evening on Sunday, September 13, 1506. Although Mantegna suffered from recurring ill health and financial problems toward the end of his life, he remained an active and innovative figure in northern Italian art to the end.

SIGNIFICANCE

Andrea Mantegna stands forth as a major figure in the history of Renaissance art. For his northern contemporaries, he functioned as an important interpreter of the new Florentine art. He was among the very few artists working in Padua, Venice, or the other princely states of the north who was intellectually prepared to understand and absorb the full meaning and potential of the art of Paolo Uccello, Fra Filippo Lippi, Andrea del Castagno, and Donatello.

Mantegna's coherent and consistent vision of the physical world, fostered by his Florentine contacts, became the standard to which his contemporaries conformed. His passion for perspective devices and foreshortening was also born of this connection. Mantegna combined his knowledge of the new Florentine experiments with the native northern Italian tradition of detailed realism and created a style that guided his own generation and the next into a full-fledged Renaissance.

Mantegna was also the principal interpreter of antiquity for his generation. His constant use of classical references, real or invented, resulted in the synthesis of ancient and contemporary forms and ideas central to any definition of the Italian Renaissance. Mantegna had the courage to use his artistic genius to the fullest, to give free rein to his intellectual curiosity about the distant past, and to use his talent to explore the latest contemporary developments in art. He was truly and completely of his time and deserves to be remembered as a major contributor to the northern Italian Renaissance.

—*John W. Myers*

FURTHER READING

Ames-Lewis, Francis, and Anka Bednarek, eds. *Mantegna and Fifteenth-Century Court Culture: Lectures Delivered in Connection with the Andrea Mantegna Exhibition at the Royal Academy of Arts, London, 1992.* London: Department of History of Art, Birkbeck College, 1993. Anthology of essays detailing the influence of court culture on Mantegna's life and art.

Includes forty-four pages of photographic plates, bibliography, and index.

Camesasca, Ettore. *Mantegna.* New York: Harper & Row, 1981. A well-illustrated survey that contains a discussion of all the major works of the artist and includes reference to the most recent primary evidence that sheds light on the artist's career and production. Presents summaries of many of the scholarly arguments relative to questions about Mantegna's work in an attempt to arrive at a consensus concerning perennial problems in the artist's oeuvre. Includes excellent color reproductions and a good general bibliography.

Carr, Dawson W. *Andrea Mantegna: The "Adoration of the Magi."* Los Angeles: J. Paul Getty Museum, 1997. Thorough analysis of Mantegna's masterpiece, detailing the artist's life in Padua at the time he created it, the formal innovations of the painting, and the modern-day difficulties of preserving the work. Includes illustrations and bibliographic references.

Fiocco, Giuseppe. *The Frescoes of Mantegna in the Eremitani Church, Padua.* Introduction by Terisio Pignatti. New York: Phaidon Press, 1978. This definitive study of the Ovetari frescoes was first published in 1947, after the destruction of the chapel by stray bombs during World War II. Updated by Pignatti to include all the more recent research, which includes new documentation that confirms Fiocco's original assertions about Mantegna's part in the frescoes and the influences at work on him.

Hartt, Frederick. *History of Italian Renaissance Art: Painting, Sculpture, Architecture.* 5th ed. New York: H. N. Abrams, 2003. The most recent comprehensive survey of Italian Renaissance art, including painting, sculpture, and architecture. Written for the general reader and copiously illustrated with black-and-white and color illustrations.

Kristeller, Paul. *Andrea Mantegna.* London: Longmans, Green, 1901. The earliest definitive monograph on Mantegna, marked by a scholarly and thorough use of all available documentary evidence related to the life and work of the artist. This monograph is a valuable and comprehensive study that will reward the serious reader with many insights about Mantegna's contributions to Renaissance painting.

Lincoln, Evelyn. *The Invention of the Italian Renaissance Printmaker.* New Haven, Conn.: Yale University Press, 2000. Study of the careers of Mantegna and two other printmakers, Domenico Beccafumi and Diana Mantuana. Details the lifestyle and vocation of Renaissance printmakers, as well as the culture in which they flourished. Includes illustrations, bibliographic references, index.

Mantegna, Andrea. *All the Paintings of Mantegna.* Text by Renata Cipriani. Translated by Paul Colacicchi. 2 vols. New York: Hawthorn Books, 1964. Illustrates in black and white all the known and attributed works of the artist. Contains a general essay on Mantegna's life and work, biographical notes and dates, a brief catalog of works, selected criticism, and a selected bibliography. Good as a quick reference.

Pächt, Otto. *Venetian Painting in the Fifteenth Century: Jacopo, Gentile and Giovanni Bellini, and Andrea Mantegna.* Edited by Margareta Vyoral-Tschapka and Michael Pächt. Translated by Fiona Elliott. London: Harvey Miller, 2003. Extended study of the Bellini family, including in-law Mantegna. Focuses on Mantegna's distinctively fifteenth century use of perspective to construct depth and space. Includes illustrations, bibliographic references, index.

SEE ALSO: Leon Battista Alberti; Giovanni Bellini; Donato Bramante; Correggio; Albrecht Dürer; Isabella d'Este.

RELATED ARTICLE in *Great Events from History: The Renaissance & Early Modern Era, 1454-1600:* 1528: Castiglione's *Book of the Courtier* Is Published.

MANUEL I
King of Portugal (r. 1495-1521)

Manuel I was one of Portugal's most illustrious monarchs. His reign represents the zenith of Portuguese imperial strength. Continuing the centralizing trends and overseas expansion policies of his predecessors, Manuel brought both to a climax, while presiding over a court remarkable for its splendor.

BORN: May 31, 1469; Alcochete, Portugal
DIED: December 13, 1521; Lisbon, Portugal
ALSO KNOWN AS: Manuel the Fortunate
AREA OF ACHIEVEMENT: Government and politics

EARLY LIFE

Manuel I (mahn-WEHL) of Portugal was born in the town of Alcochete on the east bank of the Tagus River. He came from a prominent family, the youngest of nine children of Prince Fernão, the duke of Viseu. He was a grandson of King Afonso V, a cousin to King John II, and the younger brother of John's queen Leonor. Despite the prominence of his family, Manuel's upbringing was filled with turmoil. Four of his elder brothers died before he reached adulthood. In 1484, in reaction to the growing threat of royal absolutism, his brother, the duke of Viseu, became involved, along with other members of the nobility, in a plot against John. The plot was discovered, and the duke died by the king's own hand. Yet the intervention of his sister the queen protected Manuel's interests.

When John's only legitimate son, Afonso, died in 1491, Leonor was able to block his attempts to have his illegitimate son, Jorge, declared his heir. Instead John was forced to accept Manuel, Leonor's last surviving brother, as the future king. When John died on October 25, 1495, Manuel, duke of Beja and Master of the Order of Christ, ascended the throne as the fifth monarch from the House of Avis. Historian H. V. Livermore describes the twenty-six-year-old monarch as "fair, rather thin, diligent, sparing in his food and drink, musical, vain, and fond of display." These personal traits would also be characteristic of Manuel's administration.

LIFE'S WORK

As king, Manuel continued the centralization of royal power begun by his predecessors. Ironically, he benefited from the results of John's ruthless policy of breaking the independent power of the nobility, the very policy that had led to his elder brother's death. There was now much greater acceptance of royal authority. Manuel was able to strengthen royal authority further in a number of ways. The three military orders came under the control of the Crown, and memberships were dispensed as rewards for royal service. A system of royal allowances encouraged the nobility to reside at court, where their actions could be more easily monitored, while at the same time increasing their financial dependency on the Crown.

The system of justice was centralized and the laws codified by the compilation of the first modern legal code, called the Ordinances of King Manuel. Administrative power began to pass from the old privileged groups into the hands of an expanding royal bureaucracy, much of it consisting of university-trained legists dependent on the monarch for their livelihood. Manuel called the Cortes only four times in his twenty-six-year reign, reflecting the Crown's lessening dependence on it as a source of revenue. Weights and measures were standardized after 1499 to facilitate national trade. In the early sixteenth century, Manuel introduced Portugal's first postal system, which helped to link the countryside to Lisbon and the royal court.

The greatest achievements attributed to Manuel's tenure as king came in overseas expansion. After nearly a century of success in exploring and mapping the African coast, as Manuel took the throne, Portuguese navigators were poised to open an all-water trade route to India. Vasco da Gama's groundbreaking voyage (1497-1499) had been authorized and planned before John's death, and it was left to Manuel to implement his predecessor's plans. Following da Gama's triumphal return from India, the king obtained papal confirmation of the discoveries and assembled a huge fleet under Pedro Álvars Cabral to follow up on contacts. On this voyage, Cabral made contact with lands on the western side of the southern Atlantic, thus establishing Portugal's claim to Brazil. He then completed his voyage to India.

Portuguese trade contacts in India and other lands bordering the Indian Ocean continued to expand during Manuel's reign. This trade, transacted at enormous profit, made Portugal the richest kingdom in Europe. Manuel maintained the Portuguese presence in North Africa and, during this same time, Portuguese explorers visited Greenland, Labrador, and Nova Scotia, failing to find the fabled Northwest Passage, but in the process opening the bountiful waters off Newfoundland to Portuguese fishermen.

Manuel not only sought to enlarge the empire through further exploration but also hoped to increase his dominions by marriage alliances with other royal houses. Yet these dreams came to nothing in the end. Manuel hoped to join the crown of Portugal with those of Ferdinand II and Isabella of Aragon and Castile by producing a joint heir. As this coincided with Ferdinand's own dynastic designs, a marriage was arranged in 1497 between Manuel and their eldest daughter, Princess Isabella, the widow of John's son Afonso and second in the line of royal succession after her brother Juan. Following the death of Juan, Manuel and Isabella were proclaimed heirs of Castile (although not Aragon); Isabella died in childbirth, however, and their son died soon after. Manuel then married a younger daughter of Ferdinand and Isabella, Maria, who produced his heir in 1502.

One major aspect of Manuel's reign that brought him no glory was his vacillating policy toward the Jewish population of Portugal. Prior to Manuel's tenure, the small but significant Jewish community was generally tolerated and allowed to follow its religious and cultural traditions. In fact, many Spanish Jews were allowed to settle in Portugal following their 1492 expulsion from Spain. The Jewish community made important intellectual and economic contributions that served the Crown in a number of important ways in the fifteenth and sixteenth centuries. Manuel began his reign continuing this liberal policy of toleration, but he soon changed his mind.

Manuel I. (Hulton|Archive by Getty Images)

Manuel had wished to marry Isabella for reasons of dynastic union. Under Spanish pressure, as part of that marriage agreement, Manuel promised to expel all unconverted Jews. All were ordered out of the country by October, 1497, the month the marriage took place. This decree proved to have far-reaching economic consequences as large numbers of Jews prepared to liquidate their holdings and move their families out of the country. Faced with financial dislocations, the king settled on a controversial policy of forced conversion as a way to meet his obligations yet preserve for Portugal the Jewish community's financial assets. To soften the blow of forced conversion, Manuel embarked on a policy of gradual assimilation of the so-called New Christians. They were to be given a twenty-year grace period, during which their religious practices and social customs would not be scrutinized. Yet even converted Jews would not be allowed to leave, underscoring the essentially economic rather than religious motivation of this policy.

Manuel's policy of gradual assimilation, tied to the trend toward royal centralization, created an atmosphere of resentment against the New Christians, many of whom continued to practice Judaism under the protection of the royal decrees. Only after serious rioting in Lisbon in 1506 and the massacre of thousands of New Christians did Manuel give in to the converts' pleas and again grant permission to leave and reenter Portugal at will. Nevertheless, at the same time Manuel secretly requested from the pope the establishment of the Inquisition (a request granted only in the reign of Manuel's successor), apparently as a means of controlling Judaization among the population he had agreed to protect from such scrutiny.

The fabulous material wealth flooding in from Portugal's overseas trade, estimated at more than one million cruzados a year, created opulence at home. Manuel's court was known for its splendor and ostentation. In 1513, for example, Manuel sent to Rome richly bejeweled vestments, an Eastern manuscript, and a selection of exotic animals that included a trained elephant as gifts to the newly elected Pope Leo X. Yet the money went for more than luxury and waste. The wealth pouring in from the empire not only supported a sumptuous court but also financed patronage for artists and intellectuals.

The reign of Manuel saw the first blossoming of Humanism in Portugal, which would reach its rather modest peak in the reign of John III. Manuel provided patronage for Portuguese students abroad and undertook the reform of the University of Lisbon in the early sixteenth century. The wealth arriving from the Portuguese Indies also provided commissions for buildings, decorative sculptures, and numerous paintings. The buildings were often designed in the late Gothic style (marked by lavish decoration on a basic Gothic structure) called "Manueline" by art historians, although the style remained popular in Portugal long after Manuel's death.

Manuel died in Lisbon on December 13, 1521. His son John inherited a prosperous kingdom, but one beginning to show the strains of rapid growth, which would lead to a noticeable decline in Portuguese fortunes by the end of John III's reign.

SIGNIFICANCE

Manuel I, aptly called the Fortunate, ruled Portugal at the high point of its imperial fortunes. His reign represents the culmination of several trends begun earlier in the fifteenth century by the Avis monarchs, most notably the growth of royal power and the search for a water route to India, which Manuel completed. His tenure marks the clear emergence of the Renaissance state in Portugal. He was an able administrator who built on John II's accomplishments to establish firmly the dominance of royal authority and completed the centralization of bureaucratic power.

Manuel's approach to government was practical. Even his inconsistencies with regard to the Jews are best understood in terms of administrative rather than religious imperatives. It was Manuel's good luck to ascend the throne at the precise moment in which the all-water trade route to India, proved by the voyage of Bartolomeu Dias, was about to be activated. The enormous profits accruing to the Crown provided the funds to support Manuel's other policies. He is justly credited with generously patronizing intellectuals, artists, and architects, and in so doing helping to usher in a golden age in Portugal. Yet his royal absolutism, harsh treatment of the economically important Jewish community, and lavish spending of the Indies wealth on ostentation blocked modern economic development and thus hastened the decline in Portugal's economic fortunes that would follow his reign.

—*Victoria Hennessey Cummins*

FURTHER READING

Anderson, James M. *The History of Portugal.* Westport, Conn.: Greenwood Press, 2000. Brief but comprehensive political, social, economic, and cultural history of Portugal. Manuel is discussed in the chapter on the early House of Avis. Includes timeline, appendices, maps, bibliographic references, and index.

Bedini, Silvio A. *The Pope's Elephant.* Nashville, Tenn.: J. S. Sanders, 1998. Original, offbeat, and illuminating study; uses Hanno the elephant, a gift from Manuel to Pope Leo X, as a lens through which to explore Leo, Manuel, and Renaissance culture.

Diffie, Bailey W., and George D. Winius. *Foundations of the Portuguese Empire, 1415-1580.* Minneapolis: University of Minnesota Press, 1977. The best summary in English of Manuel's involvement in the Portuguese overseas expansion in the late fifteenth and early sixteenth centuries. Voyages of discovery and the evolution of Portuguese policy are both addressed. Includes an extensive bibliography.

Greenlee, William Brooks. *The Voyage of Pedro Álvares Cabral to Brazil and India from Contemporary Documents and Narration.* London: Hakluyt Society, 1938. Reprint. St. Clair Shores, Mich.: Scholarly Press, 1972. The extensive introduction to this volume of documents gives considerable information on Manuel's involvement in the voyages of discovery undertaken under his auspices. The work is also valuable for its translated documents, which include letters written to Manuel describing the discovery of Brazil and from Manuel to other monarchs concerning Cabral's voyage.

Katz, Israel J., and M. Mitchell Serels, eds. *Studies on the History of Portuguese Jews from Their Expulsion in 1497 Through Their Dispersion.* New York: Sepher-Hermon Press, 2000. Details Manuel's role in the expulsion of the Jews from Portugal. Includes illustrations, maps, bibliographic references, and index.

Livermore, H. V. *A New History of Portugal.* Cambridge, England: Cambridge University Press, 1966. Gives a chapter-long overview that covers the main aspects of Manuel's reign. While royal centralization, the Jewish question, and Manuel's dreams of dynastic union with Spain are all addressed, the greatest attention is given to Portugal's successes in overseas expansion.

Oliveira Marques, A. H. de. *History of Portugal.* 2 vols. New York: Columbia University Press, 1972. Presents a concise description of the development of the Renaissance state under kings John II, Manuel I, and John III. Useful in tracing institutional developments in Manuel's reign. This work covers intellectual and artistic achievements in addition to tracing political and religious change.

Payne, Stanley G. *A History of Spain and Portugal.* Vol. 1. Madison: University of Wisconsin Press, 1973. Contains an overview describing major political, economic, religious, and cultural aspects of Manuel's reign. Gives attention to fiscal and economic matters as well as social and demographic factors contributing to the rise and eventual decline of Portuguese power in the sixteenth century. Includes a bibliography, but most works cited are written in Portuguese or Spanish.

Resende, André de. *Biographies of Prince Edward and Friar Pedro.* Edited and translated by John R. C. Martyn. Lewiston, N.Y.: E. Mellen Press, 1997. Biographies of Manuel's son and of one of his contemporaries, written in the sixteenth century by Prince Edward's tutor, which provide much information about Manuel and his court, as well as the life and education of the young prince. Includes illustrations, bibliographic references, and a brief biography of the author.

Yerushalmi, Yosef Hayim. *The Lisbon Massacre of 1506 and the Royal Image in the "Shebet Yehudah."* Cincinnati, Ohio: Hebrew Union College-Jewish In-

stitute of Religion, 1976. A critical view of Manuel's relationship with the New Christian community in Portugal and his handling of the 1506 riot in Lisbon. It cites resentment of royal centralization as the real cause of the 1506 pogrom and the New Christians as the convenient targets for pent-up frustration. The notes provide a bibliography on the subject of the Jews in Portugal.

SEE ALSO: Bartolomeu Dias; Ferdinand II and Isabella I; Vasco da Gama; John II; John III; Julius II; Leo X; Tomás de Torquemada.

RELATED ARTICLES in *Great Events from History: The Renaissance & Early Modern Era, 1454-1600:* 1500-1530's: Portugal Begins to Colonize Brazil; 1505-1515: Portuguese Viceroys Establish Overseas Trade Empire.

ALDUS MANUTIUS
Italian scholar

Manutius's printing company helped to spread the central texts and ideas of Humanism to European readers. Manutius also was the first printer to use the italic font, and he pioneered the use of the pocket-sized book for literary classics, a precursor to the modern paperback.

BORN: c. 1450; Bassiano, Papal States (now in Italy)
DIED: February 6, 1515; Venice, Republic of Venice (now in Italy)
ALSO KNOWN AS: Aldo Manuzio; Aldo Mannucci
AREAS OF ACHIEVEMENT: Science and technology, art, scholarship, literature

EARLY LIFE

Aldus Manutius (AWL-duhs mah-NYEW-shee-uhs) was born near Rome. Although next to nothing is known about his family, he was certainly educated in some of the most eminent Humanist circles in fifteenth century Rome and Ferrara. Alongside the traditional Latin, he also learned Greek, which was to become the focal point of his printing program.

By the early 1480's, Aldus had moved into the circle surrounding the great scholar Giovanni Pico della Mirandola and was soon appointed tutor to Pico's nephews, Alberto and Leonello Pio, the princes of Carpi. In these circles he encountered other significant Humanists and established a range of distinguished contacts and

friends that was to serve him well in his later career. In the late 1480's, some of his poetic compositions were published, dedicated to his royal patrons. In 1493, the established Venetian printer Andrea Torresani, soon to become his business partner, printed an elementary Latin grammar that Aldus had written, which was reprinted by his own press several times.

Probably motivated by the desire to ally his pedagogical ideals to the new power of print, Aldus settled in Venice around 1490. At that time Venice was the biggest center of printing in Europe, less than half a century after the invention of the printing press. Aldus set in motion the printing enterprise that was to produce its first works in 1495. A most important step was the partnership he formed with Torresani (whose daughter Maria he wed around 1505), with the financial backing of the powerful Pierfrancesco Barbarigo, the nephew of the then doge of Venice. Although Aldus put in less capital than his partners, he was the "brains" behind the business. The new company became known as the Aldine Press.

LIFE'S WORK

Manutius's first dated work was Constantine Lascaris's Greek grammar *Erotemata.* Publishing this work, in 1495, was typical of the pedagogical motive that drove Aldus: to help his readers build a firm foundation in the Greek (and Latin) languages from which to pursue their studies in what he called "good letters." The next few years saw the publication of an ambitious collection of Greek works, most importantly the series of the works of Aristotle (1495-1498), dedicated to the publisher's old patron, Prince Alberto Pio of Carpi.

In the long, elegant prefaces and dedication letters he appended to a great many of his works from the very first days of his business, Aldus clearly set out his guiding ideals and reported on the progress of his business. Like other Humanists, he believed strongly that most social ills could be remedied by the resurrection and publication of the great works of classical antiquity, particularly Greek. Although classical works had been numerous from the earliest days of Italian printing, Aldus thought his press, armed with the most elegant types and meticulous and learned editors (including himself), could contribute to this process more than any previous printing firm.

Although his focus was on Greek, Aldus also printed a number of Latin and vernacular works in the years to 1500. These included Pietro Bembo's *De Aetna* (1496), featuring a newly cut and incredibly influential Roman typeface; Francesco Colonna's *Hypnerotomachia Poliphili* (1499), a fanciful, lavishly illustrated vernacular work; and the letters of Saint Catherine of Siena in Italian (1500).

Around 1500, probably because of financial demands, Aldus was forced to shift somewhat the emphasis of his printing enterprise from scholarly and Greek works toward more popular and salable texts. In 1501, the press began to issue a new type of book, and a new font type, for which it was to become even more renowned: the pocket-sized octavo editions of classic texts such as Vergil and Cicero, printed in the novel italic font. Significantly, Aldus also chose to present the texts stripped of the marginal commentaries with which they were traditionally burdened, allowing for a smaller, more manageable text. Perfectly suited to the itinerant lifestyle of many European scholars, these works were eagerly embraced. They were more affordable than the expensive and weighty earlier publications and featured works that were established classics, thus finding a ready market.

Although these octavo books cemented the success of the Aldine Press and its fame across Europe, the later years of Aldus's career were full of travails and disruptions. The times in which he had chosen to found his enterprise, as Aldus often reminded readers, were war-torn and tumultuous ones for Europe. This made the search for ancient manuscripts as sources, as well as the editing, printing, and distribution of these printed books, a difficult task. In 1505, Aldus interrupted his work and left Venice with his new wife, probably to search for manuscripts. He resumed work eighteen months later but

Aldus Manutius. (Hulton|Archive by Getty Images)

abandoned it again from 1509 to 1512, when Venice was engaged in war. From this time until his death in 1515, he worked continuously, although his prefatory letters often lamented the constant stress and toil of trying to run an enterprise such as his own.

The press's notable publications also include Bembo's *Gli Asolani* (1505); the collected *Adagia* (1500) of the Dutch Humanist Desiderius Erasmus, who stayed for a time in Aldus's household while his work was prepared for publication; and the works of Plato in Greek (1513), dedicated to Pope Leo X.

Aldus's prefaces and dedications promoted the ideal of a Republic of Letters linked across Europe by its commitment to learning and literature and linked by the new technology of print; Aldus's press itself became a focal point for the scholars of his time. A great variety of the most important Italian and European scholars and authors frequented the Aldine circle, helping to edit and track down manuscripts. This learned circle was known as the Aldine Academy, and it was the publisher's fervent hope for many years that he would be able to found a true educational institution from this nucleus, so that Greek and Latin language and literature could continue to flourish in Europe. Although several eminent potential patrons showed an interest in his project, the dream was never realized. Nevertheless, the printing company established by Aldus was carried on for a century by his heirs, who often harked back to the legacy of their great forebear and proudly adopted his famous emblem of the dolphin and anchor.

SIGNIFICANCE

The place of Aldus in printing and intellectual history is justified on a number of fronts. Stylistically, the introduction of the typefaces he oversaw, particularly the italic and the Roman, were much-copied across Europe and have remained standards into the twenty-first century. Likewise, his octavo format, a cheaper, more portable vehicle for popular texts, prefigured the paperback books popularized in the twentieth century.

Setting into print a great number of Greek and Latin (as well as a few vernacular Italian) works for the first time was also critical to the development and dissemination of European scholarship. Aldus's efforts contributed to the spread of Renaissance-era ideas far beyond the borders of Italy.

—Rosa M. Salzberg

FURTHER READING

Davies, Martin. *Aldus Manutius: Printer and Publisher of Renaissance Venice.* Tempe: Arizona Center for Medieval and Renaissance Studies, 1999. Useful, succinct account of Aldus's career, placed in the context of late fifteenth century Italy.

Fletcher, H. George. *In Praise of Aldus Manutius: A Quincentenary Exhibition.* New York: Pierpont Mor-

gan Library, 1995. A well-illustrated and annotated catalog of a major exhibition of Aldine books that includes a helpful overview of the company's progress to the late sixteenth century.

_____. *New Aldine Studies: Documentary Essays on the Life and Work of Aldus Manutius.* San Francisco, Calif.: Bernard M. Rosenthal, 1988. Draws together the available evidence to fill out the details of Aldus's life.

Lowry, Martin. *The World of Aldus Manutius: Business and Scholarship in Renaissance Venice.* Ithaca, N.Y.: Cornell University Press, 1979. Still the definitive biography of Manutius. Evaluates his work and legacy in the context of the Venetian intellectual and commercial world. Contains tables of his publications and an extensive bibliography.

Zeidberg, David S., ed. *Aldus Manutius and Renaissance Culture: Essays in Memory of Franklin D. Murphy.* Florence, Italy: Leo S. Olschki, 1994. A collection of scholarship on Aldus, looking at both the stylistic and intellectual aspects of his business.

SEE ALSO: William Caxton; Miles Coverdale; Desiderius Erasmus; Leonhard Fuchs; Charlotte Guillard; Hans Holbein, the Younger; Leo X; Giovanni Pico della Mirandola.

RELATED ARTICLES in *Great Events from History: The Renaissance & Early Modern Era, 1454-1600:* 1490's: Aldus Manutius Founds the Aldine Press; 1528: Castiglione's *Book of the Courtier* Is Published.

LUCA MARENZIO
Italian composer

Marenzio took over the idiom of the late Renaissance Italian madrigal as shaped by elder contemporaries and became its most admired and productive master. Despite his short life, he created the classic corpus of madrigal composition at its most expressive.

BORN: 1553; Coccaglio, near Brescia, Republic of Venice (now in Italy)
DIED: August 22, 1599; Rome, Papal States (now in Italy)
AREA OF ACHIEVEMENT: Music

EARLY LIFE

The father of Luca Marenzio (LEW-kah mah-REHNTS-yoh) was a notary in Brescia, the nearest city to the small

town of his birth. The region was far from major cultural centers of the day. Nevertheless, presumably through his father's efforts, the boy received good training. He seems to have had some good basic education, and tradition has it that he studied music with the choirmaster at Brescia's cathedral, Giovanni Contino. There is virtually no firm information on Marenzio's youth, so beyond several statements by contemporaries of uncertain accuracy, the claim that he sang as a boy chorister under Contino is now discredited.

It is speculated, however, that Marenzio might have accompanied Contino for at least part of the latter's stay at the Gonzaga court of Mantua during the years 1568 to 1574. About the time of Contino's death, and perhaps through his influence, Marenzio was taken into service by a former patron of Contino, Cardinal Cristoforo Madruzzo, who by then had taken up residence in Rome. Madruzzo was an enthusiastic patron and connoisseur of music, and Marenzio served him until the cardinal's death in 1578. Marenzio enjoyed a smooth transition into the service of a friend of Madruzzo, the worldly and pleasure-loving Cardinal Luigi d'Este. To that point, Marenzio had functioned primarily as a singer and expert lutenist for his patrons, only a single madrigal of his appearing in print in 1577, but this new period of the next eight years in the employ of Cardinal Luigi witnessed the blossoming of Marenzio's productivity and reputation as a composer.

LIFE'S WORK

Cardinal Luigi settled in Rome, with Marenzio in his retinue. The terms of service seem to have been flexible, and the composer apparently secured income from other patrons or sources. Cardinal Luigi himself seems to have been eager to advance the career of his protégé beyond his own household. In 1579, he attempted in vain to win him a post in the papal choir. Marenzio did, however, establish ties, as both singer and composer, to some of the important confraternities in Rome, although efforts to place him in positions at the royal court of France and the Gonzaga court of Mantua were unsuccessful.

Meanwhile, Marenzio won his first attention as a composer, producing his initial books of madrigals, published between 1580 and 1587: five books of madrigals for five voices, four books for six voices, his first book of four-voice madrigals, a collection of five-voice *madrigali spirituali*, four books of light, three-voice *villanelle*, and his first volume of four-voice Latin liturgical motets. In this first half of his output, and with an extraordinary range of emotional variety—from charm to passion—Marenzio perfected in his madrigals (especially those for five voices) a style of highly rhetorical structure, rich in word-paintings and increasingly filled with daring harmonic surprises. His choice of poetic texts stressed the lyrics of such authors as Petrarch, Torquato Tasso, and the younger Giovanni Battista Guarini.

Cardinal Luigi's death in late 1586 left Marenzio briefly without a patron, but about a year later, he was taken into the service of Ferdinand I de' Medici, grand duke of Tuscany. His primary activity in Florence was to contribute music for two of the six *intermedii* grafted into the play *La pellegrina*, performed at the lavish celebrations of his master's marriage in May, 1589. He was dismissed from Medici service later that year, however. New connections allowed him to move back to Rome, which served as his base for most of his remaining years.

By this time, he could arrange rather loose and multiple relationships with patrons. He enjoyed the favors of Duke Virginio Orsini and Cardinal Montalto, but he eventually established a particular closeness to the papal court, which allowed him to take up residence in the Vatican—though an alleged appointment to the papal choir seems not to have been the case. Indeed, Marenzio succeeded in avoiding the professional obligations of any appointment as a church musician, the normal livelihood for musicians of the time. During these years, Marenzio continued his outpouring of compositions, embodied in new publications: following a 1588 collection of madrigals for four, five, and six voices, there came the fifth and sixth books of six-voice madrigals, books six through nine of his five-voice madrigals, and book two of his four-voice madrigals (now lost), as well as his second collection of Latin motets (also lost). In his central madrigal writing, Marenzio moved in this later period to greater darkness and intensity, his leaner, more daring and dissonant textures suggesting some influence of the new monodic experiments of his contemporaries. His choice of texts shifted, too, away from simpler lyrics toward more dramatic or more sentimental writings of Guarini (in his *Il pastor fido*, pb. 1590, pr. 1596; *The Faithful Shepherd*, 1602) and Livio Celiano.

It was at papal insistence that Marenzio undertook a journey to Poland, from 1595 to 1598, to serve as *maestro di cappella* (choir master) to King Sigismund III. In that capacity, he contributed to some important court occasions, including a Mass setting (now lost) that was the most ambitious of his polychoral liturgical works.

Back in Rome, Marenzio saw his last publications through the press and made at least one visit to Milan. His health deteriorated, however, whether from the exertions of the Polish residence or under a cloud of papal displeasure, and in 1599, he died in Rome, at the Villa Medici, domain of his former Florentine patrons. The attractions of his music outlived him in the inclusion of his secular and sacred pieces in anthologies past his death, and in two posthumous publications (one lost) of his liturgical compositions.

SIGNIFICANCE

Despite his activity as a composer for the Church, Marenzio's sacred music has suffered by comparison with his madrigals. Their wide popularity and dissemination—not only from his earliest printed collections, but extending to their samplings in many printed anthologies of the day—was based on Marenzio's facile technique and daring scope of dramatic expression.

By his death, he was regarded as Italy's leading composer, and his music continued to be widely circulated beyond his homeland, all over Europe, and with special attraction for musical circles in England. Claudio Monteverdi was soon to match Marenzio in his own terms and then, as he drew the madrigal out of the vocal-consort idiom into the radically new forms of early Baroque concert writing, to overshadow the older master, though without ever effacing "the Schubert of the madrigal."

—*John W. Barker*

FURTHER READING

Arnold, Denis. *Marenzio.* London: Oxford University Press, 1965. A brief, trenchant, and perceptive study of Marenzio's music and its characteristics.

Chater, James. *Luca Marenzio and the Italian Madrigal, 1577-1593.* 2 vols. Ann Arbor, Mich.: UMI Research Press, 1981. Vol. 1 is a thorough and critical study of the composer's life, output, and stylistic features. Vol. 2 contains critical editions of six of Marenzio's madrigals, followed by examples of the music of a number of his contemporaries.

Einstein, Alfred. *The Italian Madrigal.* Translated by A. H. Krappe, R. H. Sessions, and O. Strunck. 3 vols. Princeton, N.J.: Princeton University Press, 1971. The classic study of this musical form, its first two volumes a comprehensive but detailed survey of the idiom and its composers (including an eighty-page section on Marenzio), and its third volume containing transcriptions of ninety-seven madrigals by various composers.

Kirkendale, W. *The Court Musicians in Florence During the Principate of the Medici.* Florence, Italy: Olschki, 1993. Includes treatment of Marenzio's service in Florence, especially his involvement in the extravaganza *La pellegrina.*

Macy, L. W. *The Late Madrigals of Luca Marenzio: Studies in the Interactions of Music, Literature, and Patronage at the End of the Sixteenth Century.* Ph.D. dissertation. University of North Carolina, Chapel Hill, 1991. An analysis of Marenzio's later period of composition in its cultural context.

Maniates, Maria Rika. *Mannerism in Italian Music and Culture, 1530-1650.* Chapel Hill: University of North Carolina Press, 1979. Reconsidering the broad concept of mannerism as a cultural label for this period, this intensive and probing study presents Marenzio as perhaps the central figure in its musical dimensions.

SEE ALSO: Andrea del Sarto; William Byrd; Andrea Gabrieli; Giovanni Gabrieli; Orlando di Lasso; Thomas Morley; Giovanni Pierluigi da Palestrina; Torquato Tasso.

RELATED ARTICLES in *Great Events from History: The Renaissance & Early Modern Era, 1454-1600:* 1588-1602: Rise of the English Madrigal; 1590's: Birth of Opera; October 31, 1597: John Dowland Publishes *Ayres.*

MARGARET OF AUSTRIA
Regent and governor of the Netherlands (1507-1530)

Margaret of Austria gained fame during her long and colorful life as the highly regarded regent and governor of the Netherlands, as a patron of the arts, and as a musician.

BORN: January 10, 1480; Brussels, duchy of Brabant (now in Belgium)
DIED: December 1, 1530; Mechelen, Spanish Netherlands (now in Belgium)
AREAS OF ACHIEVEMENT: Government and politics, music

EARLY LIFE

Habsburg princess Margaret of Austria was born in Coudenberg Palace, Brussels, which later became the capital of the Netherlands (now in Belgium). She was the daughter of archduke Maximilian of Austria—who later became Holy Roman Emperor Maximilian I—and Mary of Burgundy, who died after a fall from her horse when Margaret was still an infant.

The Habsburg family, which spread throughout much of Europe, had been the bloodline of royalty of the Austrian Holy Roman Empire for more than four hundred years. As a Habsburg, Margaret's title was Austrian; however, the Netherlands was Burgundian at the time of her birth. Margaret's maternal grandfather was the powerful duke of Burgundy, Charles the Bold.

In 1483, when she was only three years old, Margaret became engaged to the thirteen-year-old dauphin of France, who was soon to become King Charles VIII.

She was to be reared at the French court under the guardianship of Louis XI; however, he died in August of that year. Although Margaret's stay in France was ostensibly designed to form her into a proper French queen, the demand that Princess Margaret be reared in France was actually Louis XI's insurance that her father, Maximilian I, would not attack. Thus, the princess was essentially a hostage. Her primary caretakers were her future sister-in-law and Louis XI's daughter, Anne de Beaujeu, and her governess. She received from these women a distinguished education that was particularly rich in the arts.

When the dauphin became King Charles VIII in 1483, his sister, Anne, and her husband acted as provisional regents. With the perceived lack of strength on the French throne, various noble families tried to shift some of that power into their own hands. The last independent fief in France was inherited by Anne of Brittany. She became betrothed to Maximilian I in a political and military alliance. Charles VIII, however, renounced his engagement to Margaret in an effort to prevent Maximilian I from making Anne of Brittany his second wife. Charles also backed out of the Treaty of Arras and married the eleven-year-old Anne of Brittany himself.

Furthermore, Charles refused to let Margaret return home because it would have meant returning her dowry. War was declared, and Margaret remained yet longer as a hostage at the French court. On May 23, 1493, the Treaty of Senlis was signed and most of the dowry was returned to the Netherlands. Consequently, Margaret was returned to her father.

LIFE'S WORK

Margaret of Austria gained recognition in three separate areas: as a leader in government and politics, as a patron of the arts, and as a musician. Although it would seem Margaret was doomed to unhappiness after being rejected in marriage, that incident instead directed her to her destiny as an important European political figure.

After returning to her father's court, Margaret unfortunately suffered through two more difficult marriage situations. In 1497, intent on finding an advantageous political match for Margaret, and one that would keep his French enemy under control, Maximilian I arranged for the seventeen-year-old Margaret to marry the nineteen-year-old John of Spain. John was the son of King Ferdinand II and Queen Isabella I of Spain and heir to the throne of Castile and Aragon. They were wed at

Margaret of Austria. (Hulton|Archive by Getty Images)

Burgos, but John was to die less than a year later. The widowed Margaret married yet again, this time to Duke Philibert II of Savoy, whom she loved desperately. History, however, was quick to repeat itself, and within three years she was again widowed. When Maximilian I attempted to arrange yet another marriage for now twice-widowed daughter, this time with the old king of England, Henry VII, she adamantly refused. Margaret of Austria swore to remain a widow forever. This declaration allowed her to gain a great deal of autonomous power as a ruler.

In 1508, Margaret's talents as a powerful and sharp negotiator were brought to public light when she played an important role in the formation of the League of Cambrai. The league was an alliance between her father, Holy Roman Emperor Maximilian I, France (now under Louis XII), Pope Julius II, and other European states, against the Republic of Venice, which was aggressively intent on territorial expansion. In addition, again acting as an intermediary for her father, Margaret successfully negotiated a commercial treaty profiting Flemish cloth interests with England.

It was the sudden death of her brother, Philip I, the Handsome, in 1506, however, that determined Margaret's destiny. First, she became a brilliant ruler when Maximilian I, without Margaret's permission, appointed her regent and governor of the Netherlands in 1507. In this capacity, the widowed Margaret found her true calling. She ruled the Netherlands as a wise and highly respected regent.

Second, Philip I was married to Joan, daughter of Ferdinand and Isabella. He thus brought the Habsburg line into Spain. When Philip died, Joan became insane, and Margaret became guardian of their children: Eleonora, Isabella, Mary, and, in particular, her nephew, Charles. Margaret built a palace and a court of her own. Her influence in the political arena and as a patron of the arts reached far and wide, even to Rome. Her nephew Charles was to inherit a vast empire on the death of his grandfather Maximilian I, as Charles I, king of Spain (1516-1556), and as Charles V, Holy Roman Emperor (1519-1558).

Although Charles, for a time, revolted against her authority, he nevertheless continued to entrust Margaret of Austria with the regency of the Netherlands. He also came to depend on her insightful judgment and to view her as one of his most loyal allies until her death in 1530.

In 1529, representing the beleaguered Charles, she achieved great fame by shrewdly negotiating and signing the Treaty of Cambrai, or what became known as the Ladies' Peace. For ten years, Charles and France had remained continually at war over land disputes and were repeatedly unable to achieve peace. Margaret successfully negotiated the Ladies' Peace with Louise of Savoy (1476-1531), regent of France for her son Francis I. They ended the ten-year war. The Treaty of Cambrai renewed the Treaty of Madrid, except that it did not demand the surrender of Burgundy to Charles. At its signing, the future of Europe lay in Margaret of Austria's hands.

Margaret of Austria's prominent patronage of the arts included the support of literature, the visual arts, and the music associated with the early sixteenth century Northern Renaissance. Until recent scholarship showed differently, women at this time were not known to have taken on patronage roles. In this era of turmoil, when the arts could no longer depend on the Church for support, as they had during medieval times, Europe's courts developed into cultural centers, with musicians and artists becoming highly regarded members of the court. Musicians, writers, and artists found refuge at Margaret of Austria's court, among them the French composers Antoine Brumel, Perrequin de Thérache, the Franco-

Flemish Pierre La Rue, and the French poet and historiographer Jean Lemaire. Of particular interest are the manuscripts familiarly known as the "Chanson Albums of Marguerite of Austria." In addition, Margaret was an extremely skilled musician.

Margaret lived by the motto "Fortune makes every woman very unfortunate." She died at the age of fifty as the result of an infection and at the hands of an incompetent surgeon.

SIGNIFICANCE

As a Habsburg ruler and as governor of the Netherlands for her nephew, Holy Roman Emperor Charles V, Margaret of Austria helped consolidate Habsburg dominion in the Netherlands. In an era when few women had any power, Margaret achieved great fame as a wise and popular ruler. She was especially noted for her shrewd diplomatic skills and was responsible for bringing about the Ladies' Peace with Louise of Savoy, which ended ten years of war with France.

Furthermore, as a well-known patron of the arts, she cultivated cultural centers in the Netherlands that housed and supported artists. These centers contributed greatly to the intellectual life of the sixteenth century Northern Renaissance. She also was a highly regarded and talented musician, contributing both vocal and instrumental compositions to early sixteenth century Renaissance music.

—M. Casey Diana

FURTHER READING

Farquhar, Michael. *A Treasury of Royal Scandals: The Shocking True Stories of History's Wickedest, Weirdest, Most Wanton Kings, Queens, Tsars, Popes, and Emperors.* New York: Penguin, 2001. Discusses in great detail the Habsburg family, of which Margaret of Austria was a member. In particular, it provides an effective Habsburg family tree.

Iongh, Jane de. *Margaret of Austria, Regent of the Netherlands.* Translated by M. D. Herter. New York: Norton, 1953. The long-standing primary biography for Margaret of Austria in English.

Picker, Martin. *The Chanson Albums of Marguerite of Austria.* Berkeley: University of California Press, 1965. Offers information on Margaret as regent of the Netherlands, her role and contributions as a patron of the arts, and her personal career as a musician.

Sautman, Francesca Canadé, and Pamela Sheingorn, eds. *Same Sex Love and Desire Among Women in the Middle Ages.* New York: Palgrave, 2001. Chapter 11, "Laudomia Forteguerri Loves Margaret of Austria," discusses Renaissance poet Forteguerri's affection for Margaret of Austria through an examination of five surviving sonnets.

Wheatcroft, Andrew. *The Habsburgs: Embodying Empire.* New York: Viking, 1995. Provides a historical overview of the colorful Habsburg family, which acts as a historical and political framework in which to place Margaret of Austria.

SEE ALSO: Anne of Brittany; Charles V; Ferdinand II and Isabella I; Julius II; Louis XI; Louis XII; Maximilian I

RELATED ARTICLES in *Great Events from History: The Renaissance & Early Modern Era, 1454-1600:* July 16, 1465-April, 1559: French-Burgundian and French-Austrian Wars; 1508: Formation of the League of Cambrai; June 5-24, 1520: Field of Cloth of Gold.

MARGARET OF PARMA
Governor-general of the Netherlands (1559-1567)

Margaret of Parma, who faced almost insuperable difficulties during her time as governor-general of the Netherlands, held her office against the Protestant revolutionaries attempting to bring about the collapse of Spanish—and Catholic—rule of the Netherlands.

BORN: 1522; Oudenaarde, Spanish Netherlands (now in Belgium)
DIED: January 18, 1586; Ortona, Kingdom of Naples (now in Italy)
ALSO KNOWN AS: Margarita de Parma
AREA OF ACHIEVEMENT: Government and politics

EARLY LIFE

Margaret of Parma was descended from a complex line of royalty, her direct lineage stemming from her father, Charles V, the Holy Roman Emperor. Through inheritance, Charles became the ruler of Spain, Italy, the Netherlands, and the Austrian territories of the Habsburgs.

Margaret was Charles's illegitimate daughter, the product of his clandestine union with Johanna van der Gheenst. She was a direct lineal descendant of such luminaries as Queen Isabella of Castile, and Maximilian I, her grandfather, who presided over the largest and most powerful European empire since Charlemagne. Margaret was acknowledged and accepted as Charles's daughter despite her illegitimacy. Her half brother, Philip II, king of Spain, did not hesitate to appoint her governor-general of the Netherlands.

Because Charles's mother was insane and his father died when he was six years old, Margaret's great-aunt, Margaret of Austria, essentially raised Charles and also, along with Mary of Hungary, played a considerable role in the early education of Margaret of Parma. Margaret of Austria served as Charles's regent for the Netherlands from 1507 until 1515 and again from 1519 until 1530, a post Margaret of Parma would assume.

In 1536, at age fourteen, Margaret married Alessandro de' Medici, duke of Florence. Their marriage of less than a year ended with Alessandro's murder. At age sixteen, Margaret married Ottavio Farnese, who, in 1547, became duke of Parma. In 1545, Margaret bore Ottavio a son, Alessandro, named after her first husband.

LIFE'S WORK

In 1559, Philip II appointed Margaret governor-general of the Netherlands, a capacity in which she served until 1567. At that time Spanish control of the Netherlands was much disputed by the French and by many of a growing number of Protestants who inhabited the Low Countries, which included the Netherlands.

Margaret assumed her post as governor-general, having authority over the Spanish troops that occupied the Netherlands. The presence of troops evoked considerable resentment among longtime residents of the Low Countries.

Antoine Perrenot de Granvelle, a Roman Catholic priest, was Margaret's chief adviser. Following his advice, she enforced a papal order that created new bishoprics during the first year of her rule. This order alienated local residents because they were to lose the privilege of self-rule in both political and religious matters.

Granvelle used his position as a stepping-stone to higher office, being named archbishop of Mechelen in 1560 as a reward for helping to reorganize the Church according to the papal bull and placing in power many minions of the pope and of King Philip II. With Margaret's acquiescence, Granvelle was made a cardinal in 1561, as his power became consolidated.

As Granvelle's power increased, however, his imperiousness appalled the local nobility. They organized opposition, led by William the Silent and Lamoraal, count of Egmond. By 1564, agitation against Granvelle and, by

615

Margaret of Parma. (Hulton|Archive by Getty Images)

extension, against Margaret's rule became so great that her position was seriously threatened and a revolution seemed a distinct possibility. Her administration had moved from one of relative beneficence to one of pronounced authoritarianism.

The loss of local rule was anathema to most of the people who lived under Margaret's reign. Finally, she conceded that the only reasonable solution to her problem was to dismiss Granvelle, which she summarily did in 1564.

With Granvelle's dismissal, Margaret was forced to pay heed to and acknowledge the validity of some of the complaints of the lower nobility, whose chief spokesperson was William the Silent. William was actually an eloquent speaker but was tagged with the sobriquet the Silent because he was renowned for his moderation, for holding his tongue and evaluating situations before he spoke for or against them.

The Spanish occupation of the Netherlands had led to excessive taxation, which seemed especially onerous to people who were consistently losing their right to self-determination. Even more fundamental to their discon-

tent was that they felt they were being discriminated against and harassed because of their break from the Roman Catholic Church and because of the spread of Protestantism throughout the Low Countries.

The members of the dissident lower nobility called themselves Les Gueux (the Beggars). In 1566, they presented Margaret with a petition that called for even-handed treatment of Protestants. She acceded to some of the demands, but in August, 1566, the more radical elements of Les Gueux, convinced that Margaret was not acting in their best interests, sprang into action, attacking and badly damaging Roman Catholic churches.

Margaret, realizing that a revolution was imminent, imported a large force of German mercenaries to the Netherlands early in 1567. This act pushed Les Gueux into further action. The situation became so grave that Philip II sent the duke of Alva to the Netherlands with a substantial Spanish army for backup. The duke, who had assumed the role of governor-general, imposed strong sanctions on the Protestants, who then openly rebelled against the Spanish rule of their land.

In the wake of this upheaval, Margaret tendered her resignation and departed for Italy, where she remained until 1580. Her son, Alessandro Farnese, was appointed commander in chief and, shortly thereafter, governor-general of the Netherlands. Margaret, who had an insider's understanding of the sociopolitical situation in the Low Countries, returned to the Netherlands as head of her son's civil administration. She retired and returned to Naples, where she died in 1586.

SIGNIFICANCE

Considerable blame for Margaret of Parma's resignation can be attributed to her early exploitation by Antoine Perrenot de Granvelle, whose personal ambitions led her to abandon her role as a benevolent monarch and become a monarch who grew increasingly oppressive, largely through fear that she might lose control. It was this oppressiveness that led to Margaret's final downfall.

Her resignation did herald the success of the dissidents. Nevertheless, Spanish rule of the Netherlands continued for several more decades, during which Margaret returned, once again in an influential position. She was in charge of civil administration from 1580 to 1583 during her son Alessandro's governorship.

Both as the illegitimate daughter of Charles V and because of her own abilities, Margaret was accepted and placed in positions of considerable importance and influence, which was unusual for women in her day. Her great aunt, Margaret of Austria, had established a precedent when she earlier held the post Margaret of Parma later assumed.

—*R. Baird Shuman*

FURTHER READING

Darby, Graham, ed. *The Origins and Development of the Dutch Revolt*. New York: Routledge, 2001. Several of the essays in this collection touch on the rule of Margaret of Parma in the Netherlands as governor-general and later as head of civil administration.

DuPlessius, Robert S. *Lille and the Dutch Revolt: Urban Stability in an Era of Revolution, 1500-1582*. New York: Cambridge University Press, 1991. Looks at Lille in Walloon Flanders (now in Belgium), an island of tranquillity and stability during the time of greatest unrest in the Netherlands.

Israel, Jonathan. *The Dutch Republic: Its Rise, Greatness, and Fall, 1477-1806*. Oxford, England: Clarendon Press, 1995. Israel's treatment of the Dutch revolt and Margaret of Parma's involvement is brief but penetrating.

Limm, Peter. *The Dutch Revolt, 1559-1648*. New York: Longman, 1989. Viewing the Dutch revolt during Margaret's rule and afterward, Limm addresses particularly religious concerns and also the role of Granvelle.

Parker, Geoffrey. *The Dutch Revolt*. New York: Penguin Books, 1988. Parker considers the entire sequence of events from 1556 to 1648 that led to the freedom of the Netherlands from rule by Spain and other countries. He gives passing attention to both Margaret and her son, Alessandro Farnese.

Van Gelderen, Martin, ed. and trans. *The Dutch Revolt*. New York: Cambridge University Press, 1993. This contribution to a series of texts in the history of political thought presents a document that details the Dutch revolt. This is a highly specialized text, however, valuable for scholars but not easily accessible to general readers. Its presentation of the role played by Margaret of Parma in the revolt is significant. Margaret is seldom mentioned by name but rather by the identifier the Governess.

SEE ALSO: Duke of Alva; John Calvin; Charles V; Elizabeth I; Alessandro Farnese; Kenau Hasselaer; Martin Luther; Margaret of Austria; Mary of Hungary; Maximilian I; Bernardino de Mendoza; Philippe de Mornay; Johan van Oldenbarnevelt; Philip II; William the Silent.

RELATED ARTICLES in *Great Events from History: The Renaissance & Early Modern Era, 1454-1600*: 1568-1648: Dutch Wars of Independence; July 26, 1581: The United Provinces Declare Independence from Spain.

MARGUERITE DE NAVARRE
French poet and queen of Navarre (r. 1544-1549)

Patron of Church reformers and poets, Marguerite helped introduce the new Humanism into French culture. She invented the idea of the salon, or learned courts, which were centers for discussing religion, literature, and politics. She was also a poet and writer and was the first society woman of learning—what the eighteenth century would call a bluestocking.

BORN: April 11, 1492; Angoulême, France
DIED: December 21, 1549; Odos, Bigorre, France
ALSO KNOWN AS: Marguerite d'Angoulême; Margaret of Angoulême; Marguerite of Angoulême; Marguerite of Navarre; Margaret of Navarre; Marguerite d'Alençon
AREAS OF ACHIEVEMENT: Literature, social reform, church reform, patronage of the arts, philosophy, women's rights, government and politics, scholarship

EARLY LIFE

Marguerite de Navarre (mawr-gyew-reet deh naw-vawr), born Marguerite of Angoulême to distinguish her from her grand-niece, Marguerite of Valois, who also married a king of Navarre, was the first child of the ambitious and dominating Louise of Savoy. Marguerite was two years older than her brother Francis (later king of France). Their mother reared the children to become queen and king, insisting that they both master the so-called new learning (essentially classical literature, the Bible, and Latin).

Tall and fiercely intelligent, Marguerite charmed by her wit rather than her beauty. Until she became a queen in her own right by virtue of her second marriage in 1527, her early life revolved around that of her Valois brother, the glorious King Francis I. She would later recollect their childhood and adolescence under the guise of a *ro-*

man à clef, or a story whose characters are known only to readers who have the "key."

In 1509, with her fifteen-year-old brother already betrothed to the ten-year-old princess of France, Marguerite was married by the scheming Louise to the duke of Alençon, a simple nobleman with a pious and unworldly mother. Marguerite took her books with her to Normandy and proceeded to set up at Alençon one of the earliest salons, in imitation of the society in which her mother had reared her and Francis. Her husband the duke left Marguerite to her cultivated guests, preferring his horses and hounds to the new learning. Illiterate himself, he was embarrassed to visit the royal court with a wife who knew how to discuss the Italian poet Dante Alighieri (1265-1321) and the Italian writer Giovanni Boccaccio (1313-1375). There began Marguerite's patronage of Clément Marot (1466?-1544) and other poets, and there she met the great Humanist scholar Jacques Lefèvre d'Etaples.

Lefèvre was the French counterpart of Desiderius Erasmus, the famous Dutch Humanist, and the teachings of both scholars attracted the intelligent noblewoman, who was still in her twenties. In this context, one must recall that Martin Luther did not begin the Reformation. The movement to reform the church (which was still the Christian church, with no distinction of Protestant or Catholic) had been underway for a generation by the time Luther nailed his theses to the church door in 1517. Among the various reform movements that ensued, Catholic reformers outnumbered Protestant by at least three to one. Like Erasmus, Lefèvre wanted to strip the institutional trappings from religious experience so that the believer might communicate more directly with Christ. In particular, these men hoped to "make everyone his or her own theologian," as Erasmus wrote in his preface to the New Testament, which he edited in its original Greek. Educated Christians could pray to God and think for themselves, without the help of priests or doctors of theology. These Humanists expressed their hostility to theologians by insisting that the teachings of the great pa-

gan moralists—including Socrates, Plato, and Cicero—were closer to the spirit of biblical Christianity than were the doctrines debated at the Sorbonne in Paris.

To Marguerite, living with an ignorant husband and his puritanical mother, the Humanist teaching came like the dawn of a new epoch. After ten years of marriage, she still had no children, and, knowing herself the intellectual and social equal of any aristocrat in France, she embraced Lefèvre's cause as her life work. He put her in touch with the bishop of Meaux (near Paris), and with her letters in 1521 she began her thoughtful writing on religion and the Scriptures. Without ever condoning Luther's radicalism, Marguerite lent her protection to a number of Catholic reformers and even to Luther's follower John Calvin. This earned for Marguerite the hatred of the doctors at the Sorbonne, who were determined to root out "Lutheran heretics" and burn them at the stake. When the Sorbonne's activists overstepped their authority and condemned one of Marguerite's religious tracts, her brother the king was furious and banished their ringleader from the country.

Protecting and nourishing the new ideas and encouraging her brother to do likewise were perhaps Marguerite's greatest historical accomplishments. In 1534, following the Affair of the Placards (when, overnight, all Paris was plastered with signs denouncing the Church's main dogmas, such as the presence of Christ in the host), Francis was powerless to stop the mob reaction against Protestantism, and the Sorbonne hunted down Lefèvre. Marguerite sheltered the old man and was at his bedside when he died.

LIFE'S WORK

The year 1525 was a critical one for Marguerite. She wrote her first serious poem, a discussion of the afterlife conducted in a dialogue with the imaginary spirit of her eight-year-old niece, who had just died. Her brother the king had led an army into Italy, where he was defeated and captured at the Battle of Pavia. Sent to Spain as the prisoner of his archrival Emperor Charles V, Francis languished in a cell until his sister came to Madrid to negotiate with the astonished emperor. Francis was eventually released after promising to cede all of Burgundy to Charles (a promise Francis never kept).

In the meantime, Marguerite's husband, who had run away from the encounter at Pavia, died in disgrace. Charles immediately wrote to Lou-

MARGUERITE DE NAVARRE'S MAJOR WORKS	
1524	*Dialogue en forme de vision nocturne* (pb. 1533)
1531	*Le Miroir de l'âme pécheresse* (*The Mirror of the Sinful Soul,* 1548)
1547	*Les Marguerites de la Marguerite des princesses*
1547	*Suyte des marguerites*
1549	*Les Prisons*
1559	*L'Heptaméron* (*The Heptameron,* 1597)

Marguerite de Navarre. (Hulton\Archive by Getty Images)

ise (who was governing the country as regent for her imprisoned son) and asked for her daughter's hand in marriage. Marguerite had dealt with the emperor and loathed him; she preferred the handsome Henri d'Albret, king of Navarre and eleven years her junior. They were married in January, 1527. Late in 1528, in her thirty-seventh year, Marguerite gave birth to a daughter, Jeanne d'Albret; later, she would have a son who lived only a few months, as well as twins who died at birth. Her only surviving child, Jeanne, would marry a Bourbon and become the mother of Henry IV, France's most illustrious king between Louis IX and Louis XIV.

After the Affair of the Placards, Marguerite retired from Paris to her court at Nérac in Navarre (Gascony). There she hosted several evangelical Humanists; besides Lefèvre and Calvin, she patronized Maurice Scève, the poet, and her old friend Marot. From Paris, the church doctors complained that she was "accompanied by her Lutheran demons under the name of advisers." It was probably her court at Nérac that served as William Shakespeare's model for his brilliantly witty comedy *Love's Labour's Lost* (pr. c. 1594-1595).

During the final decade of her life, Marguerite wrote not only her most profound religious poems and dialogues but also five of her seven comedies, as well as the work for which she is best known, *L'Heptaméron* (1559; *The Heptameron*, 1597). At the same time, she realized that she was losing her power to protect the Humanist reformers from the Inquisition, which with her brother's encouragement was then raging in Paris. Marguerite had always felt herself to be part of the intellectual avant-garde. Like Erasmus when Luther challenged him to choose between a corrupt establishment and anarchical reform, Marguerite was now caught between the conservative reaction known as the Counter-Reformation, on one side, and Calvin's uncompromising Protestantism on the other. Still hopeful, Calvin had dedicated his explosive *Christianae religionis institutio* (1536; *Institutes of the Christian Religion*, 1561) to the king in 1540. Marguerite might have appreciated that gesture, but she must have been dismayed by Calvin's attack on a fellow Humanist, François Rabelais, who in 1546 dedicated to Marguerite his *Tiers Livre* (*Third Book*, 1693), which ridiculed Calvinism. These fallings-out among her gifted protégés must have greatly discouraged the queen, who had found her guiding vision in their eager collaboration to harmonize the new learning with true religion.

Marguerite had also grown estranged from her adored brother. Perhaps she experienced some disillusionment when Francis broke his oath to Charles; however, she could not have expected Francis to give away Burgundy if he was to remain king of France. Francis not only ignored the birth of her daughter in 1528, but he also schemed in 1540 to marry Jeanne for his own advantage to a man she detested. Jeanne was a headstrong young woman who was later to win fame as a military leader, a woman able to campaign with her army while taking a day off to give birth to her son Henry. Francis had removed her from her mother's care when she was two because he was afraid Marguerite would betroth her to Charles V's son, Philip. Marguerite might have been expected to intercede for Jeanne when the king had her married against her will; instead, Marguerite chose to fall in with the king's state policy, and she ordered her twelve-year-old daughter to be lashed until she submitted. Jeanne, who had to be forcibly carried to the altar, never forgave her mother. After Marguerite's death, Jeanne came to admire her abilities and oversaw the publishing of *The Heptameron*, but she could never love her. (Fortunately for Jeanne, when her detested husband allied himself with Charles three years later, the king decided to annul her marriage. That left Jeanne free to marry the man of her choice, Anthony of Bourbon.)

SIGNIFICANCE

From his fortieth year, King Francis, who had been perhaps the most notorious philanderer in Europe—he easily outdid England's Henry VIII—was afflicted with syphilis. Partly to distract him from his constant pain, his estranged sister began the series of tales modeled on Boccaccio's *Decameron: O, Prencipe Galeotto* (1349-1351; *The Decameron*, 1620; literally "ten days"). She imagined five men and five women stranded at a spa in the Pyrenees and entertaining one another by telling a tale each day. Marguerite left *The Heptameron* unfinished after starting the eighth day—hence the title, meaning seven days. Unlike Boccaccio, Marguerite—who appears as one of the storytellers, Parlamente—stipulates that all the tales are to be true narratives. Despite the stories' factual appearance, however, Marguerite contrives to discuss the political and religious quarrels of her time under the veil of fable, just as Rabelais does. Scholars have only begun to discover *The Heptameron*'s complex art and its hidden meanings.

Francis's death in 1547 devastated Marguerite. She lived two more years in a monastery in Poitou, completing her finest long poem, *Les Prisons* (1549). In this six-thousand-line Neoplatonic masterpiece, the queen of Navarre proceeds in her imagination from one prison to another as her soul looks for a way to escape from the dungeon of life. One of the "prisons" is the sun-flooded palace of love, where pleasures blind the soul and keep it from taking flight. The Renaissance Humanist in Marguerite had receded into the background, giving way to the medieval ascetic that had always lurked deep in her nature.

—*David B. Haley*

FURTHER READING

Erasmus, Desiderius. *The Paraclesis*. In *Christian Humanism and the Reformation*, edited by John C. Olin. New York: Harper & Row, 1965. Erasmus's brilliant preface to his 1516 version of the New Testament distills the essence of Christian Humanism on the threshold of the Lutheran Reformation.

Lyons, John D., and Mary B. McKinley, eds. *Critical Tales: New Studies of the "Heptameron" and Early Modern Culture*. Philadelphia: University of Pennsylvania Press, 1993. Anthology of essays interpreting *The Heptameron* as a series of commentaries on different aspects of Renaissance and Reformation culture. Includes bibliographic references and index.

Marguerite de Navarre. *The Heptameron*. Translated by P. A. Chilton. Harmondsworth, England: Penguin Books, 1984. Contains a useful introduction, a key to the characters, and summaries of the seventy-two stories.

More, Thomas. *Utopia*. Edited by Edward Surtz. New Haven, Conn.: Yale University Press, 1964. This classic dialogue, with a prefatory letter from Guillaume Budé, the star of Francis I's court, is an excellent example of the witty discussions sponsored by Marguerite in her salons.

Putnam, Samuel. *Marguerite of Navarre*. New York: Coward-McCann, 1935. The only modern biography in English, by a famous translator of Rabelais and Miguel de Cervantes.

Stephenson, Barbara. *The Power and Patronage of Marguerite de Navarre*. Burlington, Vt.: Ashgate, 2004. Based on a reading of her correspondence, this study of Marguerite's political career discusses the various direct and indirect ways in which she exercised power to benefit and protect her allies and relatives. Includes map, bibliographic references, and index.

Stone, Donald. *France in the Sixteenth Century: A Medieval Society Transformed*. Englewood Cliffs, N.J.: Prentice Hall, 1969. An accessible overview of French society in Marguerite's day.

Thysell, Carol. *The Pleasure of Discernment: Marguerite de Navarre as Theologian*. New York: Oxford University Press, 2000. Original reading of *The Heptameron*, arguing that while it appears to be a secular work, it was actually written to further a surreptitious theological project. Includes bibliographic references and index.

SEE ALSO: Ludovico Ariosto; John Calvin; Charles V; Vittoria Colonna; Desiderius Erasmus; Henry IV of Castile; Aemilia Lanyer; Jacques Lefèvre d'Étaples; Martin Luther; François Rabelais; Pierre de Ronsard; William Shakespeare; Torquato Tasso; François Villon.

RELATED ARTICLE in *Great Events from History: The Renaissance & Early Modern Era, 1454-1600:* March, 1536: Calvin Publishes *Institutes of the Christian Religion*.

DOÑA MARINA
Mexican-Indian interpreter, translator, and guide

Doña Marina aided conquistador Hernán Cortés during the Spanish conquest of the Aztec Empire in Mexico. She has been celebrated as a protector of the Spanish conquerors and for helping to bring Christianity to the Mexican Indians, but she also has been vilified as a traitor to her family's indigenous roots for having mixed-race children.

BORN: c. 1502; Tenochtitlán, Aztec Empire (now Mexico City, Mexico)
DIED: 1527 or 1528; place unknown
ALSO KNOWN AS: Malintzin (given name); Malinalli; La Malinche
AREA OF ACHIEVEMENT: Warfare and conquest

EARLY LIFE

While there are many sixteenth century visual and textual sources that refer to Doña Marina (DAWN-yah mah-REE-nah), the details of her life remain sketchy. Hernán Cortés referred to her twice, briefly, in his own writings.

Most known biographical information about Marina comes from the pen of Bernal Díaz del Castillo, a conquistador who accompanied Cortés during the conquest of Mexico. Díaz del Castillo left a vivid narrative account of those events, with some mention of Marina, in his *Historia verdadera de la conquista de Nueva España* (wr. 1560's-1570's, pb. 1632; *The True History of the Conquest of New Spain*, 1908-1916). There are also many surviving depictions of Marina, including those in a massive illustrated account of the Aztecs that was compiled from indigenous sources by the Spanish priest and missionary Bernardino de Sahagún. It is called *Historia general de las cosas de Nueva España* (pb. 1829, 1831; *General History of the Things of New Spain*, 1950-1982), is better known by scholars as the *Florentine Codex*, and was compiled by Sahagún between 1576 and 1577.

Marina's multiple names reflect her role as a transitional figure between Aztec and Spanish cultures and highlight the linguistic transformations and miscommunications that took place in the century of conquest. Her original name was likely Malinalli. The Spanish gave her the name Marina, and the conquistador Díaz del Castillo always referred to her as Doña Marina, "doña" being an honorific title given to Spanish woman of rank. Native peoples called her Malintzin (the Nahuatl -tzin was also a suffix of respect). The Nahuatl "Malintzin" turned into "Malinche" (Marina is also known as La Malinche) when pronounced by the Spanish, and it has since become a pejorative word used to designate traitors.

When she was still a child known as Malinalli, Marina's world changed when her father died; he was a cacique (a native Indian chief). Her widowed mother married another cacique and, after she had borne a son by this second marriage, she sold Marina into slavery, presumably to protect the inheritance of the son. Marina was first sold to Mayan traders, who in turn sold her to Tabascan Indians settled on the Bay of Campeche. When a group of Spanish conquistadores led by Hernán Cortés attacked the Tabascans in 1519, the Mexican Indians gave twenty women to the invaders as a gift, and Marina was among them. Thus, Marina came to be in the service of Cortés, who was on his way to conquer the Aztec Empire.

LIFE'S WORK

Cortés was a Spanish explorer charged with leading an expedition from Hispaniola to the North American mainland. He landed in the Yucatán in February of 1519, and after conquering Tabasco he headed north to Tenochtitlán, the capital of what was then the Aztec Empire and what is now Mexico City.

Doña Marina and nineteen other women were given to the Spaniards to serve as cooks and mistresses. (They first had to be baptized, which made them suitable partners for the Christian soldiers, whose religion forbade them from sleeping with heathen women.) It soon became apparent, however, that Marina had other skills that would serve the Spanish enterprise. Marina came from the border area between Nahuatl-speaking Central Mexico and the Maya-speaking Yucatán, giving her fluency in both languages.

Marina's bilingual skills were immeasurably valued by the Spanish. She became a key player in the linguistic relay that took place when Cortés needed to communicate with the Nahuatl. Cortés would speak Spanish to Jerónimo de Aguilar, a Spanish priest who had been shipwrecked in 1511 and spent eight years in captivity among the Maya, during which time he learned the Mayan language and culture. Aguilar in turn would speak Mayan to Marina, who would translate into the language of the Aztecs. After Marina learned sufficient Spanish, Aguilar was no longer needed. Marina became not only Cortés's translator and negotiator but also his eyes and ears and his point of entry into understanding indigenous culture. Indeed, the pair were so closely associated that they were

TRANSLATING SPANISH-AZTEC CONTACT

Doña Marina, also called La Malinche, was instrumental in mediating contact between the Spanish-speaking conquistador Hernán Cortés and the Nahuatl-speaking Montezuma through her translations of the words of the two leaders. Here she "speaks" for the two at their first meeting in Tenochtitlán.

When Motecuhzoma [Montezuma] had finished, La Malinche translated his address into Spanish so that the Captain [Cortés] could understand it. Cortés replied in his strange and savage tongue, speaking first to La Malinche. "Tell Motecuhzoma that we are his friends. There is nothing to fear. We have wanted to see him for a long time, and now we have seen his face and heard his words. Tell him that we love him well and that our hearts are contented."

Then he said to Motecuhzoma: "We have come to your house in Mexico as friends. There is nothing to fear."

La Malinche translated this speech and the Spaniards grasped Motecuhzoma's hands and patted his back to show their affection for him.

Source: The Broken Spears: The Aztec Account of the Conquest of Mexico, edited by Miguel Leon-Portilla (Boston: Beacon Press, 1970), pp. 64-65.

practically inseparable as individuals to the Mexican Indians, who called Cortés Captain Malinche.

Marina not only interpreted for the Spanish, she also saved them from almost certain destruction. In the city of Cholula, a noble indigenous woman confided to Marina a plot to trap and murder the Spanish in the city. When Marina revealed the plan to Cortés, he massacred the Cholulans instead.

When Cortés and his men arrived in the Aztec capital, Tenochtitlán, the Aztec Empire was at its height and the city bedazzled the Spanish soldiers. The empire was ruled by Montezuma II, and Marina served as a go-between for the Spanish commander and the Aztec emperor. Marina spoke the noble form of the language, in a way suitable for communicating with a person of such exalted status, and she did so with appropriate ceremony. Cortés eventually took Montezuma hostage, and the Spanish soldiers attacked the city. By August of 1521, Montezuma was dead and the great Aztec capital had fallen to the Spanish.

After the fall of Tenochtitlán, Marina bore a child by Cortés, a son named Martín. Marina was not Cortés's only mistress, nor was Martín his only illegitimate child. Martín was eventually legitimized by Pope Clement VII, along with two of Cortés's other illegitimate children, as a special favor to the conqueror of Mexico.

Young Martín was left behind when Cortés called on Marina to accompany him to Honduras in 1524. During this expedition, Marina was married to one of Cortés's lieutenants, Juan de Jaramillo, but Marina continued to serve Cortés as his interpreter. While traveling in Honduras, Marina had a daughter named María with Jaramillo, and she died shortly thereafter, in 1527 or 1528.

SIGNIFICANCE

Doña Marina's importance lies as much in her posthumous symbolic role as it does in her actual life. In colonial Mexico, Marina was celebrated for protecting the Spanish from harm and for helping to bring Christianity to the Mexican Indians. Following Mexican independence from Spain in 1821, her reputation sank, and Marina came to be seen as the betrayer of her race for her collusion with the conquerors. Her having been a mistress to the Spanish is the most-remembered part of her life story. As the mother of two mestizo children—children of both Indian and European parentage—Marina is a fitting symbol for the conflicted birth of modern-day Mexican society.

—*Amanda Wunder*

FURTHER READING

Cypess, Sandra Messinger. *La Malinche in Mexican Literature: From History to Myth*. Austin: University of Texas Press, 1991. Literary study of changing representations of Marina from colonial to modern times. Focuses on issues of gender, ethnicity, and identity.

Díaz del Castillo, Bernal. *The Discovery and Conquest of Mexico*. Translated by A. P. Maudslay and edited by Genaro García. New York: DaCapo Press, 2004. Account of Cortés's conquest of Mexico by a conquistador who accompanied him. Provides most of the known information about Marina's life and her role in the conquest.

Karttunen, Frances. "Rethinking Malinche." In *Indian Women of Early Mexico*, edited by Susan Schroeder et al. Norman: University of Oklahoma Press, 1997. Summarizes Marina's debated symbolism and redefines her as neither a hero for the Spanish nor a traitor to the indigenous of Mexico, but as a talented woman who did what was necessary to survive her turbulent times.

Leon-Portilla, Miguel, ed. *The Broken Spears: The Aztec Account of the Conquest of Mexico*. Boston: Beacon Press, 1992. Compilation of various Mexican Indian accounts of Cortés's conquest of Mexico, with many references to Doña Marina's role as translator.

Restall, Matthew. "The Lost Words of La Malinche: The Myth of (Mis)Communication." In *Seven Myths of the Spanish Conquest*. New York: Oxford University Press, 2003. Argues against the conventional wisdom that only the Spaniards benefited from miscommu-nication, with an emphasis on Marina's role in the process of communication.

SEE ALSO: Clement VII; Hernán Cortés; Cuauhtémoc; Guacanagarí; Montezuma II.

RELATED ARTICLE in *Great Events from History: The Renaissance & Early Modern Era, 1454-1600:* April, 1519-August, 1521: Cortés Conquers Aztecs in Mexico.

CHRISTOPHER MARLOWE
English dramatist

Marlowe was complex, lyrical, and frequently erotic in both his dramatic and his poetic writing and was concerned in his work largely with the question of power and how it affects human beings.

BORN: February 6, 1564; Canterbury, England
DIED: May 30, 1593; Deptford, England
AREAS OF ACHIEVEMENT: Literature, theater

EARLY LIFE

Dead at twenty-nine from stab wounds suffered in a tavern brawl, Christopher Marlowe (MAHR-loh) led a life of violence, intrigue, mystery, and remarkable productivity. His dramas and poetry have established him as an Elizabethan dramatist second only to William Shakespeare. It is tempting to speculate on what he might have produced had he lived a normal life span.

The son of John and Catherine Arthur Marlowe, Christopher was born on February 6, 1564, and was thus almost an exact contemporary of Shakespeare, who was born on or near April 23 of the same year. Marlowe was the second child in a family of nine children, six of whom, two boys and four girls, survived infancy. John Marlowe was a leatherworker and a member of an affluent guild in Canterbury, the Kentish cathedral town in southeastern England in which the shrine of Saint Thomas Becket is located.

Despite the prosperity of the guild to which he belonged, John Marlowe was not wealthy. His family had gained the reputation of being contentious and litigious. John, judging from court records of the time, followed in his ancestors' footsteps, as did his offspring. John was said to be loud, arrogant, demanding, and profligate.

Marlowe was enrolled in the King's School in Canterbury—a noble institution of which Roger Ascham had been headmaster in the generation before Marlowe—at fifteen, the top age for admitting new students. The school was renowned for its emphasis on theater and was considered one of the best schools in Elizabethan England. The young Marlowe, fair of countenance, with unruly dark hair and the bright eyes of one ever alert to and aware of his surroundings, read selectively in the extensive private library of the headmaster, concentrating on medieval romances, particularly Sir Thomas Malory's versions of the Arthurian legends. Marlowe favored blood-and-thunder romances, indicating that perhaps the legendary Marlowe combativeness had been passed on to this young member of the family. Much of his writing appears to have as its source works from the library available to him during his days at King's School.

In 1581, two years after he had entered King's School, Marlowe became a student at Corpus Christi College of Cambridge University, where he was considered an excellent student and an accomplished poet, writing at that time primarily in Latin. He was named a Canterbury Scholar for his six years at Cambridge, apparently because he had expressed his intention of entering the clergy.

Marlowe's college career was marked by long absences from the university, and it is now assumed that he was engaged in some sort of espionage activities in Europe for the Crown. This assumption is substantiated by the fact that when Cambridge moved to withhold Marlowe's master's degree from him in 1587, Queen Elizabeth's Privy Council intervened to see that Marlowe received his degree, saying in a letter to university officials that his absences from the university had benefited the Crown. It is known that Marlowe worked for Sir

An imaginative depiction of the English dramatist Christopher Marlowe. (Hulton\Archive by Getty Images)

Francis Walsingham, the secretary of state for Queen Elizabeth, who was much involved in espionage.

In the early summer of 1591, Marlowe shared a workroom with Thomas Kyd, renowned for writing *The Spanish Tragedy* (c. 1585-1589). Marlowe and Kyd were at that time both under the patronage of Thomas Walsingham, cousin of Sir Francis, who provided the workroom. Queen Elizabeth finally knighted Thomas Walsingham.

LIFE'S WORK

After he received the master's degree from Cambridge University in 1587, Marlowe rushed to London, England's cultural and theatrical center. By that time, he had already completed two plays, *Dido, Queen of Carthage* (pr. c. 1586-1587, pb. 1594; with Thomas Nashe) and *Tamburlaine the Great* (in two parts, pr. c. 1587, pb. 1590), as well as translations of Lucan's *Pharsalia* (first century) and, between 1595 and 1600, Ovid's *Amores* (c. 20 B.C.E.).

Certainly, these two plays established Marlowe's reputation as an important playwright, but they also left him open to charges of atheism by people of established repu-

tation. Charges of atheism and pederasty, both capital offenses in Elizabeth's England, were to follow Marlowe throughout his brief life. The latter charges stemmed initially from Marlowe's statements that all men who do not love tobacco and boys are fools and later from the fact that his *Edward II* (c. 1592, pb. 1594) is about a homosexual king. Because Marlowe reveled in shocking people, it is difficult to know whether he spoke out of conviction or out of a desire to get reactions from his listeners when he made his statements about boys. Certainly, writing a historical play whose protagonist is homosexual does not make the writer homosexual. Marlowe's own sexuality has not been convincingly established. It is interesting, but not surprising, that one of Marlowe's most vigorous attackers, Robert Greene, was also his most fervent imitator.

By 1589, Marlowe was living in Norton Folgate, close to London's theatrical district. In September of that year, Marlowe was involved in a street fight with William Bradley. Marlowe's friend, the poet Thomas Watson, came to Marlowe's assistance and killed Bradley by inflicting stab wounds. Marlowe ran from the scene, but soon Watson was arrested and taken to Newgate Prison. Shortly thereafter, Marlowe was arrested and imprisoned in Newgate for a fortnight. Watson was held until February, when he was exonerated on the grounds of self-defense.

In 1587, *Historia von Doctor Johann Fausten* was published in German in Frankfurt. Although Marlowe is not known to have read this seminal book in German and although it was not translated into English until 1592 as *The History of the Damnable Life and the Deserved Death of Doctor John Faustus*, Marlowe appears to have begun working on his renowned *The Tragicall History of D. Faustus* (known more commonly as *Doctor Faustus*) shortly after his two Tamburlaine plays were produced. The Stationers' Register shows that a play presumed to be *Doctor Faustus* was registered on February 28, 1589, and other dramatists writing before 1592 show evidence in their work of having borrowed heavily from Marlowe's play.

In 1589, the Lord Admiral's Company performed Marlowe's *The Jew of Malta*, a play to which Shakespeare's *The Merchant of Venice* (c. 1596-1597) bears a strong resemblance. Marlowe's play, deemed atheistic by many of his contemporaries, should probably be viewed as a biting satire rather than as the tragedy that some critics have considered it to be. Barabas's annihilation of a whole convent full of nuns is the sort of bloody, melodramatic theme that Marlowe liked and that Kyd also exploited in *The Spanish Tragedy*.

MARLOWE'S MAJOR WORKS

c. 1586-1587	*Dido, Queen of Carthage* (with Thomas Nashe)
c. 1587	*Tamburlaine the Great, Part I* (commonly known as *Tamburlaine*)
1587	*Tamburlaine the Great, Part II*
c. 1588	*Doctor Faustus*
c. 1589	*The Jew of Malta*
c. 1592	*Edward II*
1593	*The Massacre at Paris*
1595-1600	*Elegies* (translation of Ovid's *Amores*)
1598	*Hero and Leander* (completed by George Chapman)
1599	"The Passionate Shepherd to His Love" (in *The Passionate Pilgrim*)
1600	*Pharsalia* (translation of Lucan's *Bellum civile*)

The three parts of *Edward II*, which Pembroke's Men first performed in 1592, represent Marlowe's most mature and well-crafted writing. Also, the text for the play is the most reliable extant text of any Marlowe play save *Tamburlaine the Great*. In *Edward II*, Marlowe's chief concern is with the question of civil authority. Edward's homosexuality is incidental, although Marlowe deals head-on with the king's proclivity. The death scene in this play is among the most affecting death scenes in the whole of Western literature.

Four months after *The Massacre at Paris* was first staged on January 26, 1593, Marlowe was arrested as an atheist, a capital charge in his day. On May 12, Kyd was arrested on a charge of atheism, and on the rack, he attributed the documents that had led to his arrest to Marlowe. On May 18, a warrant was issued for Marlowe's arrest, and he was apprehended at the estate of Sir Thomas Walsingham, his patron. On May 20, having answered the charges against him to the Privy Council, he was directed to attend the council daily, a lenient sentence for one charged with a capital offense. Ten days later, on May 30, 1593, Ingram Frizer, Lady Walsingham's business agent, fatally stabbed Marlowe in a tavern in Deptford during a dispute over a bill. Marlowe was interred in the Walsingham tomb in Deptford on June 1, 1593, and Frizer was promptly acquitted of his murder on grounds of self-defense.

SIGNIFICANCE

In his short and colorful life, Christopher cut a swath in British drama that no other playwright of his time equaled except Shakespeare. Indeed, Calvin Hoffman, in *The Murder of the Man Who Was "Shakespeare"* (1955),

argues that Marlowe, living under a cloud in 1593, was not actually murdered but, rather, went to the Continent and continued to write, producing before his death many of the plays attributed to Shakespeare. Hoffman's claim has been thoroughly discredited but suggests something of Marlowe's dramatic stature.

After Marlowe's premature death, which many of his contemporaries took to be God's judgment of a man who was an atheist and homosexual, a steady stream of his writing continued to appear. His incomplete poem *Hero and Leander* and his translation of *Lucan's First Book* (the first part of *Pharsalia*) were entered in the Stationers' Register in September, 1593, the former published in 1598 and the latter in 1600.

In 1594, *Edward II* and *Dido, Queen of Carthage* were published, and Marlowe's translation of Ovid's *Amores*, publicly burned around 1600 as heretical, appears also to have been published in the late 1590's, although it is not dated. *The Massacre at Paris* was probably also published in 1594, followed ten years later by the publication of *Doctor Faustus*.

Marlowe was a literary giant, a genius who wrote some of the most compelling dramas of his day. He had a lyrical gift that showed both in his drama and in his poetry. His full power as a dramatist has yet to be fully recognized, although it is generally conceded that Marlowe's only real peer in Elizabethan drama is Shakespeare, whose dramatic gifts generally exceeded those of Marlowe.

—*R. Baird Shuman*

FURTHER READING

Hilton, Della. *Who Was Kit Marlowe? The Story of the Poet and Playwright*. New York: Taplinger, 1977. This great admirer of Marlowe seeks to explain his alleged atheism and homosexuality and also comments interestingly on some of his mysterious espionage work. The book is at times lacking in objectivity, and the conjecture that Marlowe committed suicide is not credibly presented.

Kendall, Roy. *Christopher Marlowe and Richard Baines: Journeys Through the Elizabethan Underground*. Madison, N.J.: Fairleigh Dickinson University Press, 2003. This study is a life of Marlowe disguised as a biography of his associate Richard Baines. It consists of a chronological examination of Baines's life, but one which is constantly interrupted by analyses of Marlowe's life and works whenever they were affected by Baines. Includes bibliographic references and index.

Knoll, Robert E. *Christopher Marlowe.* New York: Twayne, 1968. Knoll provides a useful overall coverage of Marlowe, dealing forthrightly with interpreting his work and with the controversies surrounding some of its interpretation. The standard Twayne format is useful for beginning readers of Marlowe. Knoll is quite successful in identifying Marlowe's basic themes and in discussing them.

Kuriyama, Constance Brown. *Christopher Marlowe: A Renaissance Life.* Ithaca, N.Y.: Cornell University Press, 2002. A self-consciously speculative approach to biography, asserting that so few facts about Marlowe are known that one must look to his culture and political milieu to invent likely if unverifiable details of his life. Includes illustrations, bibliographic references, index.

Levin, Harry. *The Overreacher: A Study of Christopher Marlowe.* Cambridge, Mass.: Harvard University Press, 1952. One of the best assessments of Marlowe, this book calls for a less romanticized portrayal of the author than most of the treatments of him have been. Levin shows a Marlowe who was deeply intelligent, highly complex, and given to a hyperbole that many critics have taken more seriously than Marlowe apparently intended it.

Lunney, Ruth. *Marlowe and the Popular Tradition: Innovation in the English Drama Before 1595.* New York: Manchester University Press, 2002. A study of the dramatic conventions that Marlowe inherited and his simultaneous debt to and intervention in those conventions. Looks especially at audience expectations and response to late sixteenth century drama in general and Marlowe's works in particular. Includes bibliographic references and index.

Marlowe, Christopher. *The Complete Works of Christopher Marlowe.* 2 vols. Edited by Fredson Bowers.

New York: Cambridge University Press, 1973. This standard edition of the works of Marlowe includes introductions to each work. It summarizes bibliographical problems associated with the canon and contains detailed notes of help to both the scholar and the general reader.

Norman, Charles. *Christopher Marlowe: The Muse's Darling.* Indianapolis, Ind.: Bobbs-Merrill, 1971. A well-written, often-reprinted biography of Marlowe that gives shrewd appraisals of his life and work. A thoroughly readable book that somewhat romanticizes its subject. The 1971 revision of Norman's 1960 edition includes additional information on Walsingham, Peele, and Watson.

Oz, Avraham, ed. *Marlowe.* New York: Palgrave Macmillan, 2003. Anthology about Marlowe and his work contains essays by several scholars of Renaissance studies, including Stephen Greenblatt, Catherine Belsey, and Jonathan Dollimore. Includes timeline, bibliography, and index.

Pinciss, Gerald M. *Christopher Marlowe.* New York: Frederick Ungar, 1975. A brief discussion of Elizabethan theater, of Marlowe's life and contributions, and of each of Marlowe's seven plays. This is a good starting point for someone unfamiliar with Marlowe's work.

Trow, M. J., and Taliesin Trow. *Who Killed Kit Marlowe? A Contract to Murder in Elizabethan England.* Stroud, Gloucestershire, England: Sutton, 2001. Suggests that Marlowe was assassinated by those in power, because he knew too much about their affairs and flouted their wishes in his plays. Includes photographic plates, illustrations, bibliographic references, and index.

SEE ALSO: William Caxton; George Chapman; Elizabeth I; Sir Thomas Malory; Thomas Nashe; William Shakespeare; Sir Philip Sidney; Edmund Spenser.

RELATED ARTICLES in *Great Events from History: The Renaissance & Early Modern Era, 1454-1600:* 1576: James Burbage Builds The Theatre; c. 1589-1613: Shakespeare Writes His Dramas.

MARY, QUEEN OF SCOTS
Queen of Scotland (r. 1542-1567)

Through the misfortunes of her personal life, Mary precipitated a political and religious struggle in Scotland that ultimately led to her death in England as a Catholic martyr.

BORN: December 8, 1542; Linlithgow Palace, West Lothian, Scotland

DIED: February 8, 1587; Fotheringhay Castle, Northamptonshire, England

ALSO KNOWN AS: Mary Stuart; Mary Stewart

AREAS OF ACHIEVEMENT: Government and politics, religion and theology

EARLY LIFE

Mary Stuart was born just six days before the death of her thirty-year-old father, King James V. His death, hastened by the physical and mental anguish of the English defeat of the Scots at Solway Moss in November, brought to the throne one of the most remarkable and tragic women of the sixteenth century: Mary, Queen of Scots.

Mary's infancy ensured a regency under her French-born mother, Mary of Guise. In the midst of the war, Henry VIII proposed a marriage between his young son Edward and the infant queen. Ancient Scottish fears of English domination, and the regent's family connections, led to marriage negotiations with France. Thus, at the age of five, Mary Stuart was sent abroad.

Her departure from Scotland was marked by storms and the danger of shipwreck on enemy shores, but despite the perils, Mary landed in France to receive a warm welcome. Her formidable grandmother Antoinette of Guise met the child and introduced her to the French court at Moulin. There, for the first time, Mary met Francis, the dauphin of France and her future husband. The two children became fast friends. Mary at five was a vivacious, charming, and happy child. Her four-year-old fiancé was frail and shy but affectionate. The French court was enchanted, and King Henry II proclaimed Mary the "most perfect child" he had ever seen.

The education of such a child could not be ignored, but Mary's training would be much more conventional and less rigorous than that of her Tudor cousins in England. Fortunately, Renaissance France offered much that could challenge and captivate a bright child. Mary learned the traditional Latin and a smattering of Greek as well as Italian and Spanish. More important socially, she learned how to draw, to sing, to play the lute, and to dance elegantly. Hunting and riding became passions shared with the nobility of Europe. Moreover, she absorbed the Catholic faith of the French court with youthful devoutness. Mary became the very model of a French princess. In April, 1558, she and Francis were married, but because of his ill health, the marriage may never have been consummated.

Queen Mary I's death in England in November, 1558, stirred the French court deeply. Mary, like her English cousin Elizabeth, was a Tudor descendant of Henry VII. Mary's blood claim to the English throne was, however, untainted by the questions that surrounded Henry VIII's marriages and children. Indeed, for Catholics, her claim to the throne of England was more pure constitutionally than that of Elizabeth. Henry II responded immediately to Elizabeth's accession by having Mary Stuart proclaimed queen of England, Ireland, and Scotland. It was a decision that would haunt Mary for three decades and would play a role in her death sentence.

Nevertheless, the year 1559 opened joyously. The royal family, despite family rivalries, the stirrings of religious dissent, and the unpopular treaty of Cateau-Cambresis, celebrated a number of royal weddings. The balls and pageants were magnificent enough to obscure the national tensions. Then suddenly, it all collapsed.

On June 30, 1559, at the conclusion of a tournament, Henry II, wearing the black-and-white colors of his mistress Diane de Poitiers, was injured in a bizarre accident. The lance of an opponent struck the king viciously, splintering into his eye and throat. Nine days later, he died in agony. With his death, Francis II became king and Mary, Queen of Scots, was now queen of France as well. For a timid boy of fifteen and a carefree girl of sixteen it must have been a shattering transition.

Not surprisingly, a tug of war ensued between the young king's mother, Catherine de Médicis, and the powerful Guise family of the young queen. Yet, in this period Catherine's example may have been a great influence on her daughter-in-law. Mary watched Catherine maneuver, intrigue, and balance quarreling factions, for the sake of the Bourbon Dynasty. The lessons were not lost. Mary would never match her mother-in-law's ability as intriguer, but it would not be for want of trying.

In November, 1560, Francis returned from a hunting expedition with a terrible earache. Three weeks later, the young king was dead of a massive infection. Mary had lost both her husband and her closest childhood friend.

She was eighteen, and it was time to return to Scotland, a home she had never really known.

LIFE'S WORK

Mary arrived at Leith, Scotland, early on a typically damp and dismal day. Her reception would have daunted any but the most obtusely cheerful. Barely a handful of local fisherman were on hand to greet the queen of Scotland, and only the generosity of a local inhabitant provided some shelter until a royal welcoming committee arrived.

Her entry into Edinburgh was, however, a triumph. As crowds poured out to greet her, bonfires were lit, bells rang, and bagpipes played. The queen made a vivid impression on all who saw her. Nearly six feet tall, Mary had a delicate-boned elegance that set off her golden blonde hair, white complexion, and hazel eyes. Her voice was light but commanding, her high forehead deemed a sign of intellect, and her long, thin hands a sign of aristocracy. Her most compelling physical feature was probably her sensual, heavy-lidded eyes. Not

classically beautiful, she had an indefinable charisma that drew others to her and earned for her the romantic title "the queen of Hearts." Certainly, she captured the hearts of those who saw her return to Holyrood Palace in 1561.

Mary was equally pleased with her subjects and was thrilled by the rugged, misty beauty of Scotland. Yet the problems she now faced were daunting. Thirteen years of absence gave her little knowledge of her country. Furthermore, she had little real political or administrative experience. Scotland was beautiful but impoverished. A warring nobility and a feudal governmental structure made it more a relic of the medieval era than a modern emerging nation. Moreover, while Mary was growing up in France, the force and fury of the Protestant Reformation had swept across the land. The fiery Calvinist leader John Knox and other adherents of the new faith viewed the queen's return with alarm.

Despite such problems, Mary's reign began auspiciously. Indeed, with the advice of her illegitimate half brother James, earl of Moray, her first months of govern-

An engraved depiction of Mary, Queen of Scots (seated, right) in prison. (F. R. Niglutsch)

ment went well. It was her rash decision to remarry that began a series of crises that would destroy her throne.

In July, 1565, Mary married her cousin Henry Stewart, earl of Darnley, the son of the fourth earl of Lennox. Although a love match, it was, nevertheless, a choice that was certain to antagonize Elizabeth, whose support Mary needed. Elizabeth, always hostile to the Scottish queen and fearful of her claims, was incensed. Darnley, a Tudor descendant, doubly underscored Mary's rights in England. The earl of Moray despised Darnley personally and hated the Lennox family. He would continually incite other Scottish nobles against the queen.

The real and continuing problem was Darnley himself. Under a tall, thin, elegant, exterior that won Mary's heart if not her mind, Darnley was at best an amiable dolt. At his worst, which was more often the case, he was weak, spoiled, vain, and silly. Unfortunately, he also possessed a cruel, even vicious streak. In March of 1566, he conspired in the brutal murder of David Riccio. Mary's hapless Italian secretary was hacked to death in front of the queen, despite her pleas for his life. Mary, who was expecting her first child in June, never forgave Darnley. After the birth of her son James VI, she turned increasingly for support to a group of powerful nobles under the leadership of James Hepburn, earl of Bothwell.

On February 9, 1567, the house at Kirk o'Field near Edinburgh, where Darnley was staying, was destroyed by an explosion. When the crowds came running, Darnley's nearly naked body was found in the garden, where he had apparently been caught and strangled. Whether Mary was privy to the conspiracy, which had been led by James Hepburn, the fourth earl of Bothwell, is unclear. The only evidence ever introduced against Mary as an accomplice was the highly suspect collection of "Casket Letters." The letters, however, are a puzzling mixture of genuine documents and outright forgeries.

Whatever Mary's knowledge of the events, her dependence on Bothwell and his faction was obvious. Bothwell was acquitted of any involvement in Darnley's death after a farcical hearing. Less than three months later, Mary married Bothwell, after an alleged abduction and rape.

The public was outraged. All over Scotland, placards with the arms of Bothwell went up, depicting the queen as a mermaid, an ancient symbol of prostitution. The implication that she had condoned the murder of Darnley for love of Bothwell was clear. On June 15, 1567, an army led by Mary was defeated at Carberry Hill. The queen was forced to abdicate in favor of her infant son. After nearly a year of incarceration, she escaped and rallied her supporters for a fight at Langside. With Langside

lost, Mary fled south. Her advisers agreed that her return to France was essential; there she could appeal to her powerful Guise relatives and to Catholic sentiment to finance a return. At Dundrennan Abbey, she startled her followers by deciding to enter England and seek aid from Elizabeth. Thus, Elizabeth suddenly found herself hostess to the one woman in Europe who might threaten her throne. Mary remained in England for nineteen years under increasingly tight captivity. She proved too valuable a diplomatic prize and too dangerous a rival to set free.

The Rebellion of the Northern Earls in 1569 was the beginning of a long series of plots to overthrow Elizabeth on Mary's behalf. Over the years, the Norfolk plot, Ridolfi plot, and the Babington plot, all financed by King Philip II of Spain, would exhaust the patience of Elizabeth's government. In late 1586, Mary was sentenced to death for conspiring to assassinate Elizabeth. On February 8, 1587, she was beheaded at Fotheringhay Castle.

SIGNIFICANCE

Mary, Queen of Scots, met her death as she had lived her life: with courage and a sense of adventure. A prisoner, she still captivated the hearts of those who knew her and stirred the dreams of those who did not. Her famous motto had been "in my end is my beginning." She knew that Elizabeth was aging, barren, and bitter and that Mary's son James would be the logical successor to the English crown. The Stuarts would triumph in the end. Despite the turbulence of her early years, she had finally found an inner serenity. In an age of martyrs, she would be surely the most royal. Her end, like her beginning, would capture romantic imaginations forever.

—*E. Deanne Malpass*

FURTHER READING

Dunn, Jane. *Elizabeth and Mary: Cousins, Rivals, Queens.* New York: Alfred A. Knopf, 2004. Study of the rivalry and political intrigue between Elizabeth I and Mary, Queen of Scots, attempting to portray the private emotions behind their public acts. Includes photographic plates, illustrations, bibliographic references, index.

Fraser, Antonia. *Mary Queen of Scots.* London: Weidenfeld and Nicolson, 1969. A colorful and sympathetic biography of Mary, written with tremendous zest and extensive research. Fraser is, perhaps, overly antagonistic to Elizabeth's political situation but is so readable that the reader forgives any imbalance.

Froude, J. A. *History of England from the Fall of Wolsey to the Defeat of the Spanish Armada.* London: J. W. Parker and Son, 1862. Reprint. New York: AMS

Press, 1969. A panoramic work by a distinguished historian that sets the stage for Anglo-Scottish policies on a national and international scale.

Girouard, Mark. *Robert Smythson and the Architecture of the Elizabethan Era.* London: Country Life, 1966. Provides illustrations of several of the places Mary was held during her nineteen-year stay in England. In particular, some of the properties of the earl of Shrewsbury and his formidable wife, Elizabeth, are depicted.

Gore-Browne, R. *Lord Bothwell.* London: Collins, 1937. Remains the only work to study Bothwell in some detail and is useful if somewhat romanticized on the family background.

Guy, John. *Queen of Scots: The True Life of Mary Stuart.* Boston: Houghton Mifflin, 2004. Exhaustive reexamination of Mary's life and rule, attempting to rejuvenate her reputation somewhat by blaming her fall on the plots and intrigues of those around her. Reinterprets correspondence usually used to condemn Mary to show how it may actually enhance history's judgment of her. Includes photographic plates, illustrations, maps, bibliographic references, and index.

Hosack, John. *Mary, Queen of Scots, and Her Accusers.* Edinburgh: W. Blackwood and Sons, 1869. An old but interesting examination of the enemies of the queen, and their motives and weapons in attacking her rule and reputation.

MacNalty, Sir Arthur Salusbury. *Mary Queen of Scots: The Daughter of Debate.* London: C. Johnson, 1960. A good, readable biography of Mary and the attitudes of those who knew her. While interesting, it does not have the depth of interpretation of character that makes Fraser's Mary so vivid.

Merriman, Marcus. *The Rough Wooings: Mary Queen of Scots, 1542-1551.* East Linton, Scotland: Tuckwell, 2000. Study of Mary's childhood and her early efforts to preserve Scottish autonomy from England by marrying France's Francis I.

Phillips, J. E. *Images of a Queen: Mary Stuart in Sixteenth Century Literature.* Berkeley: University of California Press, 1964. An interesting and scholarly work that reflects both the concept of royalty and the life of Mary in the literature of her own times.

Strickland, Agnes. *Lives of the Queens of Scotland.* London: Coburn, 1854. A pioneering work in the use of historical sources. Strickland was deeply stirred by the tragedy of Mary's life and devoted considerable energy to understanding the queen's personality and the conflicts within sixteenth century Scotland.

Weir, Alison. *Mary, Queen of Scots, and the Murder of Lord Darnley.* London: Jonathan Cape, 2003. Exonerates Mary of complicity in the murder of her husband, asserting instead that the evidence against her was the product of a cover-up by Bothwell and his coconspirators. Includes photographic plates, color illustrations, map, bibliographic references, and index.

SEE ALSO: Bess of Hardwick; George Buchanan; Catherine de Médicis; William Cecil; Diane de Poitiers; Edward VI; Elizabeth I; Henry II; Henry VII; Henry VIII; James V; John Knox; Mary of Guise; Mary I; Philip II; Pius V; First Earl of Salisbury; First Duke of Somerset; The Tudor Family.

RELATED ARTICLES in *Great Events from History: The Renaissance & Early Modern Era, 1454-1600:* August 22, 1513-July 6, 1560: Anglo-Scottish Wars; February 27, 1545: Battle of Ancrum Moor; May, 1559-August, 1561: Scottish Reformation; July 29, 1567: James VI Becomes King of Scotland; November 9, 1569: Rebellion of the Northern Earls; February 25, 1570: Pius V Excommunicates Elizabeth I.

MARY OF BURGUNDY
Duchess of Burgundy (r. 1477-1482)

Mary of Burgundy granted the Great Privilege, which restored local rule to the provinces and towns of Burgundy. Her marriage to Maximilian I meant Spanish and Habsburg control of the Netherlands and formed the basis of the worldwide Habsburg Empire.

BORN: February 13, 1457; Brussels, duchy of Brabant (now in Belgium)

DIED: March 27, 1482; Brugge, Flanders (now in Belgium)

ALSO KNOWN AS: Marie de Bourgogne

AREAS OF ACHIEVEMENT: Government and politics, diplomacy

EARLY LIFE

Born the only child of Charles the Bold and Isabel of Bourbon, Mary of Burgundy grew up in a wealthy but troubled environment. Mary's great-grandfather, John the Fearless, and her grandfather, Philip the Good, had enlarged Burgundy's power by conquest, heritage, and purchase. Burgundy reached its greatest extent under Charles the Bold, who aimed to concentrate power in his hands, which weakened the states general, the representation of the provincial estates. Mary's godfather, King Louis XI of France, proved to be an enemy who strived to seize Burgundian estates and insisted that the duchy had once been a fief of the French crown.

Mary had a solid education: Having French as her mother tongue, she studied Flemish, the duchy's second language, and Latin, the language of science and diplomacy. She was interested in history and had artistic abilities. Mary combined her sense of aesthetics with Christian education in the books of hours she used, one of which has been preserved in Austria (Codex Vindobonensis, 1857). The princess's favorite hobby was falconry.

Mary's mother died early, but Mary found a friend for life in Margaret of York, who married Charles in 1468 and became a caring duchess. Monarchs from all over Europe courted Mary, yet Charles was mostly interested in the Habsburg proposals, hoping to be crowned king by the Holy Roman Emperor Frederick III for giving Mary in marriage to Maximilian, the successor to the throne. Marriage negotiations at Trier (1473) came to an abrupt end, since Frederick was not willing to accept Charles's conditions. Nevertheless, the engagement was announced in 1476, when Charles was already troubled by

the Swiss. He died at Nancy in 1477, leaving Mary an unstable throne.

LIFE'S WORK

After the death of Charles the Bold, the French invaded the south of Burgundy. Louis XI reclaimed the duchy as a fief of France through the doctrine of strict male primogeniture, and he urged Mary to marry his son. Finding herself between threats of war and a marriage proposal to six-year-old Charles, and realizing that by such a marriage Burgundy would be swallowed up by France, Mary took up negotiations with the states general.

Burgundy was on the verge of revolt, since the large cities were demanding autonomy and some groups were even likely to ally with Louis. After making financial concessions, Mary realized that she could hold Burgundy together only by abolishing the unifying and centralizing reforms that had been undertaken mainly by her father. In February, 1477, she agreed to the Great Privilege, a treaty that made a federation out of the Burgundian estates and granted Mary the title of general princess. Shortly afterward, she was sworn in as countess of Flanders. The condition of Burgundy remained a critical concern.

Two of Mary's counselors were decapitated—a sign of continuing protest to centralized ruling powers—and Louis XI continued stirring up the provinces. Mary felt spied on and, firmly determined not to yield Burgundy to Louis, she appealed to her fiancé for help. Maximilian was willing to come to her aid immediately, but displaying the lack of money typical of the Habsburgs, he still had to raise money for undertaking an impressive journey. Nevertheless, a preliminary marriage was performed, assisted by imperial officials and dukes. This marriage, *per procurationem* (by power of attorney or by agent), which took place in Brugge without Maximilian in April, 1477, and later was repeated in Ghent, increased Mary's authority.

Yet the marriage was not accepted by Louis XI, who continued to cause disturbances, conquering Picardy as well. He tried to block Maximilian on his bridal journey, the adventures of which are described in two autobiographical epic poems by Maximilian: *Theuerdank* (1517; *The Theuerdank of 1517*, 2003) and *Weisskunig* (c. 1515; the white king). The obstacles to the wedding, which was solemnized in August, 1477, are worth mentioning, since it was Mary's determination to fulfill her father's wedding plans that kept Burgundy from falling apart or being

An engraved depiction of Mary of Burgundy confirming the charter of rights known as the "Great Privilege." (F. R. Niglutsch)

archduchess of Austria and duchess of Burgundy, died at the age of twenty-five from internal injuries sustained in a riding accident during falconry. Although Maximilian married again and had many affairs later on, he is said to have never loved again.

Mary and Maximilian's son, Philip, became famous as Philip I, king of Castile and regent of the Netherlands. Their daughter, Margaret of Austria, became a conscientious governor of the Netherlands after her brother's death. Initially, Margaret had been married to—among others—John, the heir to the Castilian throne, who died young. Mary's third child, Francis, died shortly after his birth in 1481. Maximilian grew to appreciate his wife's authority posthumously. He had become a member of the prestigious Burgundian Order of the Golden Fleece in 1478. He was a grand master and was followed by his son in 1482. Moreover, he was installed, through Mary's will, as the regent of the provinces during the minority of Philip. Nonetheless, it took him more than a decade to get his status as legitimate ruler accepted. The Treaty of Senlis (1493) finally restored Franche-Comté and the Netherlands to the House of Habsburg (Burgundy and Picardy remained French). That same year Maximilian became Holy Roman Emperor Maximilian I.

annexed by France. Saving her inheritance by marrying Maximilian meant giving up Burgundy's independence, however. Mary's descendants devolved the rights of the House of Burgundy to the House of Habsburg, and so the conflicts between Burgundy and France were transferred to the war between the House of Austria and the Kingdom of France.

Still, and importantly, this marriage founded the basis for a global Habsburg Empire, as Mary's and Maximilian's children ultimately were given in marriage to members of the House of Aragón. Because of this rise of a worldwide empire, the marriage of Mary of Burgundy and the later Maximilian I achieved mythical status, intensified by the couple's legendary deep love. Mary, the

SIGNIFICANCE

After the death of her father, the harsh ruler Charles the Bold, Mary of Burgundy's diplomatic negotiations with the states general of the Netherlands led to the formation of a surprisingly modern federal governmental system in the duchy of Burgundy, still under the unifying figure of the duchess. This system developed through Mary's granting of the Great Privilege.

By carrying out the marriage planned by her father, Mary transferred Burgundy to the House of Habsburg, so the duchy depended on a foreign ruler. Its largest province remained autonomous yet still a fundamental part of the Habsburg Empire. Parts of Mary's heritage were lost to France after the marriage of Mary and

Maximilian, yet their children not only would be regents of the Netherlands, but they also connected the Habsburgs to Spain.

Mary gained the image of a decisive and graceful duchess because of her diplomacy, beauty, and early death, and also through her contribution to the foundation of an empire in which the sun never set.

—*Veronika Oberparleiter*

FURTHER READING

Blockmans, Wim, and Walter Prevenier. *The Promised Lands: The Low Countries Under Burgundian Rule, 1369-1530*. Philadelphia: University of Pennsylvania Press, 1999. Part of the Middle Ages series, this work includes an analysis of how the fief of Burgundy turned into a ruling power over other estates.

Bruges à Beaune: Marie, l'héritage de Bourgogne. Edited by the Hospices Civils de Beaune. Paris: Somogy, 2000. Illustrations of the legendarily graceful duchess, and other informative items.

Grössling, Sigrid-Maria. *Maximilian I: Kaiser, Künstler, Kämpfer.* Vienna, Austria: Amalthea, 2002. Written from the Habsburgs' point of view, rich in descriptions of Mary's and Maximilian's administrative achievements.

Tanner, Marie. *The Last Descendant of Aeneas: The Hapsburgs and the Mythic Image of the Emperor.* New Haven, Conn.: Yale University Press, 1993. Explains why the wedding of Mary and Maximilian became mythical.

Vaughan, Richard. *Charles the Bold: The Last Valois Duke of Burgundy.* 4th rev. ed. Woodbridge, Suffolk, England: Boydell Press, 2004. Points out the critical condition of Burgundy in 1477, and useful for understanding Mary's political background.

Vossen, Carl. *Maria von Burgund: Des Hauses Habsburg Kronjuwel.* Stuttgart, Germany: Seewald, 1982. Though rich in romanticizing anecdotes, important as one of the very few biographies of Mary.

Wellens, Robert. *Les États Généraux des Pays-Bas, des origines à la fin du règne de Philippe le Beau (1464-1506).* In *Anciens Pays* 64 (1974). Illustrates why the states general could exert surprising power on Mary's father, herself, and Maximilian.

Wheatcroft, Andrew. *The Habsburgs: Embodying Empire.* 2d ed. New York: Penguin Books, 1997. Study of the Habsburgs' imperial ideology, useful for reflecting on Mary's inheritance within a broader context.

SEE ALSO: Charles the Bold; Frederick III; Louis XI; Margaret of Austria; Maximilian I.

RELATED ARTICLES in *Great Events from History: The Renaissance & Early Modern Era, 1454-1600:* July 16, 1465-April, 1559: French-Burgundian and French-Austrian Wars; August 17, 1477: Foundation of the Habsburg Dynasty.

MARY OF GUISE
Queen of Scotland (r. 1554-1560)

French-born Mary of Guise, attaining the regency of Scotland after the death of her husband, James V, exploited her connections to French elites, which frustrated English attempts to force an alliance with Scotland. Though Mary's resistance to the Reformation failed and she was deposed by English-backed Protestant insurgents, she succeeded in paving the path to power for her daughter, Mary, Queen of Scots, whose upbringing and marriage she carefully arranged.

BORN: November 22, 1515; Lorraine, Bar-le-Duc, France
DIED: June 11, 1560; Edinburgh, Scotland
ALSO KNOWN AS: Marie de Guise; Mary of Lorraine
AREAS OF ACHIEVEMENT: Government and politics, religion and theology, warfare and conquest

EARLY LIFE

Mary of Guise was born into the French nobility, the daughter of Claude de Lorraine, the duke of Guise, and Antoinette of Bourbon. Insofar as her father was the leading magnate of the powerful House of Guise, Mary would have been raised in an environment of material wealth and high culture, and she also would have received a grounding in the arts of court politics, which would later serve her as a political leader in her own right.

Mary had ties to numerous relatives in positions of power in French society, and clearly she cultivated these close relations with her French family for the remainder of her political life. Born into a leading Catholic family in a predominantly Catholic country, Mary would later consistently maintain her sense of national and religious identity, even though much of her later life would be spent outside her native France.

In 1534, Mary married Louis d'Orléans, the second duke of Longueville. Mary and Louis had two sons: Francis and a second son, who did not survive infancy. In 1537, Mary's husband, Louis, died, leaving the young Mary an eminently eligible candidate for a marriage to a powerful noble. Though negotiations for a marriage between Mary and the English king Henry VIII were begun soon after the death of Louis, Mary rejected the proposal. Mary probably sought to avoid a marriage alliance with the ruler of her nation's perennial enemy, England—the first sign of an anti-English ideology that would characterize her later political career.

LIFE'S WORK

In 1538, Mary married James V, king of Scotland, at St. Andrews. James and Mary had three children: two sons, James and Arthur, who both died in 1541, as well as James's sole surviving heir, Mary (the future Queen of Scots), who was born December 8, 1542.

For the remainder of James's reign, Mary enjoyed a position of prestige in a court teeming with material wealth and flourishing with the culture of the Renaissance. Weeks after a disastrous defeat by English forces at Solway Moss and just days after the birth of his heir, Mary, James V died at Falkland on December 14, 1542, creating a chaotic political environment in which numerous Scottish factions resisted Mary of Guise's assumption of the regency during her daughter's minority.

In 1542, James Hamilton, earl of Arran, who sought to ally Scotland with England, became regent of Scotland. Mary of Guise, who was committed to her late husband's policy of maintaining Scotland's alliance to France, immediately began to maneuver to replace Hamilton as regent.

In 1543, Hamilton succeeded in negotiating the marriage of Mary, Queen of Scots, to Henry VIII's heir, the English prince Edward (the future Edward VI). Mary of Guise successfully nullified the planned marriage, convincing the Scottish parliament, on July 7, 1548, to agree to the Treaty of Haddington, which not only repudiated the marriage of the vulnerable Scottish queen to the English heir but also ensured that the French king, Henry II, would guarantee French military support as Scotland's "protector." Henry VIII reacted to the rejected marriage by leading several destructive raids into southern Scotland, winning some support from Protestant Scots, such as James Stewart, earl of Moray, who resented the presence of French troops brought into Scotland by Mary.

As she maneuvered to replace Hamilton as regent, Mary sought aid and advice from two of her brothers,

Charles, the cardinal of Lorraine, and Francis, the duke of Guise, seeking to use her ties to France to ensure her position of power in Scotland, France's perennial ally. After arranging for Mary's future marriage to the French dauphin (the future French king, Francis II), Mary sent her young daughter, in 1547, to be raised in Francis's household in France. Mary sought to ensure that Scotland's heir would share the French cultural background that she felt made herself best suited to govern Scotland until her daughter came of age. By 1554, her careful arrangements for her daughter's ties to France had paid off, and Mary succeeded in replacing the earl of Arran as the regent of Scotland.

Mary of Guise's reign as queen regent was beset by the rising tide of Protestantism within her traditionally Catholic realm. At first, Mary sought a lenient policy toward Reformers, but, as their numbers grew and their backing by English supporters began to pose a grave threat to Scotland's stability, Mary soon began a campaign to violently suppress the Reformation movement. In 1557, Protestant insurgents, led by John Knox, formed an ideologically Calvinist group calling itself the Lords of the Congregation. In 1559, the Lords of the Congrega-

Mary of Guise. (Hulton|Archive by Getty Images)

tion sought to bring about the overthrow of Mary of Guise by forming an alliance with England; soon, they were in open rebellion against Mary's rule. Although Mary gained support in the civil war from French forces, the Reformers, empowered by English support, prevailed, successfully deposing Mary in 1559.

In 1560, Mary died, shortly after urging the competing sides to unite in loyalty to Mary, Queen of Scots, advice that led the many competing parties to agree to the Treaty of Edinburgh. Mary's body was removed to the Convent of Saint-Pierre in Reims, where her sister Renée held the position of abbess, ensuring that her final resting place would be in her native and beloved France.

SIGNIFICANCE

Throughout her political life, Mary of Guise proved committed to the cause of her native France, successfully avoiding any ties through marriage to her nation's perennial enemy, England, even as she worked to acquire the most powerful position in the government of France's traditional ally, Scotland.

Mary proved a patient and very effective political operator, securing the regency in the chaotic political landscape of Scotland created by the death of James V, even as she worked to attain for her daughter, Mary, Queen of Scots, an acceptably French and well-placed marriage.

Throughout her tenure in Scotland, Mary effectively exploited her connections to power-players in France, working to frustrate English military incursions by securing French military backing, while simultaneously countering England's attempts to ally itself to Scotland during the volatile period of her daughter's minority. Although Mary's resistance to the rise of the Reformation in Scotland ultimately failed, she managed, even after being driven from power, to convince her opponents to agree to the Treaty of Edinburgh, which strengthened the hand of her daughter, Mary, whose upbringing and marriage she had so carefully engineered.

—*Randy P. Schiff*

FURTHER READING

Cowan, Ian Borthwick. *The Scottish Reformation: Church and Society in Sixteenth Century Scotland.* London: Palgrave Macmillan, 1982. A broad survey of the impact of the Reformation as it swept into the formerly Catholic Scotland. Offers detailed discussion of Mary's unsuccessful struggle against Protestant reformers.

Fraser, Antonia. *Mary, Queen of Scots.* London: Weidenfield and Nicolson, 1977. Detailed biography of Mary's daughter, featuring in-depth analysis of Mary's efforts to raise her daughter in a French household to prepare her to assume the throne of Scotland. Plates, genealogical tables.

Marshall, Rosalind K. *Mary of Guise.* Edinburgh: National Museums of Scotland, 2003. A revised edition of Marshall's 1977 biography of Mary, offering a narrative of the entirety of Mary's life. Plates, genealogical tables.

_____. *Scottish Queens, 1034-1714.* East Linton, Scotland: Tuckwell Press, 2003. Incorporating gender studies into the study of Scottish queenship, this broad survey offers analysis of the status of queens and consorts in Scottish history. Includes brief biographies of key female rulers of Scotland, including Mary of Guise. Color plates, dynastic tables.

Ritchie, Pamela E. *Mary of Guise in Scotland, 1548-1560: A Political Career.* East Linton, Scotland: Tuckwell Press, 2002. Revises the view that Mary was concerned primarily with defending Catholicism, arguing that Mary had personal, "dynastic" motives that centered on the advancement of Mary, Queen of Scots, and the strengthening of the alliance between Scotland and France.

Schama, Simon. *A History of Britain: At the Edge of the World? 3000 B.C.-A.D. 1603.* New York: Hyperion, 2000. A broad survey of British history through the sixteenth century, featuring numerous color plates, maps, and genealogical tables. Offers in-depth discussion of Mary of Guise's role in resisting the English-backed Reformation movement in Mary's Scotland.

SEE ALSO: Edward VI; Henry II; Henry VIII; James V; John Knox; Mary, Queen of Scots.

RELATED ARTICLES in *Great Events from History: The Renaissance & Early Modern Era, 1454-1600:* August 22, 1513-July 6, 1560: Anglo-Scottish Wars; May, 1559-August, 1561: Scottish Reformation.

MARY OF HUNGARY
Queen of Hungary (r. 1521-1526), regent of the Netherlands (r. 1531-1555)

Both as queen consort of the Hungarian kingdom and as regent of the Netherlands, Mary of Hungary showed significant governmental and administrative skills that were highly regarded in her time. She continued the Spanish-Austrian empire's centralization of the Low Countries.

BORN: September 17, 1505; Brussels, Brabant (now in Belgium)

DIED: October 18, 1558; Cigales, Castile (now in Spain)

ALSO KNOWN AS: Mary of Habsburg; Maria von Ungarn; Maria van Hongarije; Marie de Hongrie; Marie d'Autriche

AREAS OF ACHIEVEMENT: Government and politics, patronage of the arts

EARLY LIFE

Like most daughters of royal families of the age, Mary of Hungary's fate was to be a pawn in family politics from the moment of her birth. Born the fifth child of Philip I and Joan of Castile, she was barely six months old when she was selected to play an important role in the eastern European politics of her grandfather, Holy Roman Emperor Maximilian I.

Mary spent the first nine years of her life at the court of her aunt, Margaret of Austria, in Malines (now Mechelen, Belgium), and was brought up with her oldest brother, Charles (later Holy Roman Emperor Charles V), and her elder sisters Eleonora and Isabella.

Maximilian's efforts to bring the Kingdoms of Hungary and Bohemia under Habsburg dominion had led him to arrange a double marriage treaty with King Vladislav II of Hungary and Bohemia in March of 1506. According to this treaty, the daughter of Vladislav, Anne (later Queen Anne of Austria), would be married to one of Mary's brothers, while Mary herself would be the spouse of Vladislav's younger child. Although not yet born when the treaty was signed, this younger child was, nevertheless, assumed to be the male heir to the throne.

The expectation expressed in the treaty materialized with the birth of prince Louis (later King Louis II). In 1514, Maximilian had his granddaughter brought to the Austrian territories to prepare her for her role as future queen of Hungary and Bohemia. The double marriage was contracted in Vienna on July 22, 1515. Because of the young age of the couples, the actual consummation of the marriage was postponed, and Mary and Anne held a joint princess-court in Innsbruck to 1521.

After Anne married Mary's brother, Archduke Ferdinand (later Ferdinand I, Holy Roman Emperor), in Linz, she traveled to Hungary to be crowned queen. She arrived in a country that was in the shadow of the ever-increasing threats and attacks of the Ottoman Turks on its southern borders, weakened further by chaotic political circumstances, an impoverished royal court, and a weak king, barely sixteen years old. In the summer of 1521, Sultan Süleyman the Magnificent led an attack against the southern border of the Hungarian kingdom. On August 28, 1521, the Turkish troops seized Belgrade, the key fortress on its southern defense line, hereby leaving the central areas of Hungary and the royal residence of Buda defenseless against further attacks. After the sack of Belgrade, the Ottoman troops withdrew, only to return five years later in 1526, when they would conquer a large part of the country and bring an end to the independent Hungarian kingdom.

LIFE'S WORK

Mary was crowned queen of Hungary on December 11 in the royal coronation town of Székesfehérvár. Shortly after the celebration of her wedding with Louis II in Buda (January, 1522), the royal couple traveled to Bohemia, where Anne also was crowned queen of Bohemia (June, 1522). On their marriage, Mary received a great amount of property and other rights as morning gifts from her husband, a practice in accordance with the rights of the queens of Hungary and Bohemia. The gifts made her one of the country's richest feudal lords, and they gave her the power to influence large numbers of people and to gain significant political power.

Mary's efforts to centralize royal power came to an abrupt end with the defeat of the Hungarian troops by the Turks at the Battle of Mohács (August 29, 1526), a battle that also caused the death of her husband. Mary fled from Buda to Pressburg (now Bratislava, Slovakia), where she tried to secure the Hungarian crown for her brother Ferdinand, against the claims of John Zápolya (King John). She also acted as a regent for her brother until Ferdinand's coronation on November 3, 1527.

Mary's next years were marked by serious financial difficulties and by uncertainty about her future position. Despite her family's renewed efforts to arrange a second marriage for her, she vowed to stay a widow. This decision, together with the skill she had demonstrated in state matters, persuaded her elder brother, Holy Roman Emperor Charles V, to appoint her as his regent in the Netherlands in 1531, after the death of the previous regent, Margaret of Austria.

As regent of the Netherlands, Mary devoted her intelligence and administrative skills to furthering the traditional Burgundian-Habsburg aims of territorial unification, resulting in the annexation of the provinces of Groningen in 1536 and Gelder and Zutphen in 1543. She promoted the centralization of the government, aided by collateral councils dealing with the state, finance, and everyday administration (1531). Throughout her regency, she stayed in contact with her brother and discussed with him policy, financial, and administrative matters, and asked his advice, but she did not hesitate to act according to her own judgment.

Mary of Hungary mediated between the imperial demands and the interests of the Netherlands. She was able to translate the frequently unrealistic expectations of her brother into more practical requirements, and she had enough authority to govern the Netherlands in a period of wars, famine, and religious dissent.

In addition to politics, Mary of Hungary was keenly interested in the intellectual currents of her age. At the Buda court earlier, she came into contact with the ideas of Humanism and the teachings of Martin Luther. After the death of her husband, both Desiderius Erasmus, whom she admired greatly, and Luther dedicated treatises to her. Though never formally conceding to Luther's teaching, she showed interest in and sympathy to Reformation ideas in the earlier years of her life, as well as in the years after assuming the regency. She tried to persuade the aging master scholar Erasmus to return to the Netherlands. Throughout her life Mary's passion for hunting and her love of music provided outlets from her strenuous political responsibilities.

With the abdication of Charles V in favor of his son, Philip II, in 1556, Mary of Hungary resigned her responsibilities as regent. Mary and Charles left the Netherlands, accompanied by their sister, Eleonora, to sail to

An engraved depiction of Mary of Hungary's rescue by the Venetians. (F. R. Niglutsch)

Spain, where they planned to spend their final years in retirement.

In the last two years of her life, Mary was repeatedly put under pressure by her nephew Philip to return to the Netherlands and to continue her regency or act as an adviser in state matters. After having declined the request several times, ultimately, she could not resist the pressure, which mounted after Charles ordered her belongings packed and made ready for travel. Before she could embark, however, she became seriously ill, and she died about a month after the death of her brother, Charles.

SIGNIFICANCE

Mary of Hungary's situation and choices made her an exceptional figure of her times. After the dramatic loss of her crown, lands, and husband—all by the young age of twenty-one—she was faced with the few possibilities traditionally open to women in such a position: remarrying, entering a convent, or taking care of her ill mother. Instead, as a highly talented and strong-willed individual, she chose to accept the extremely difficult task of governing the Netherlands. For the rest of her life, Mary devoted herself completely to the interests of the House of Habsburg.

—Orsolya Réthelyi

FURTHER READING

Daniel, David P. "Piety, Politics, and Perversion: Noblewomen in Reformation Hungary." In *Women in Reformation and Counter-Reformation Europe: Private and Public Worlds*, edited by Sherrin Marshall. Bloomington: Indiana University Press, 1989. This chapter summarizes the generally known facts about Mary's life against the background of the Reformation.

De Jongh, Jane. *Mary of Hungary, Second Regent of the Netherlands*. New York: Norton, 1958. This traditional biography is still the best source of general information on the subject in English, with thorough knowledge of sources and an enjoyable style.

Goss Thompson, Glenda. "Mary of Hungary and Music Patronage." *Sixteenth-Century Journal* 15 (1984): 401-418. Using the records of Mary's regency period, this study analyzes the evidence of significant music patronage.

Kubinyi, András. "The Road to Defeat: Hungarian Politics and Defense in the Jagiellonian Period." In *War and Society in East Central Europe*, edited by János M. Bak and B. K. Király. New York: Columbia University Press, 1982. This study provides a very thorough analysis of politics in pre-Mohács Hungary.

Spruyt, Bart Jan. "Mary of Hungary and Religious Reform." *English Historical Review* 431 (April, 1994). This article investigates Mary's attitude and actions regarding the Reformation from the years spent in Hungary and in the Netherlands.

Tracy, James D. *Holland Under Habsburg Rule, 1506-1566: The Formation of a Body Politic*. Berkeley: University of California Press, 1990. Analyzes the effect of the Habsburg Dynasty on the Netherlands, including the years of Mary's regency.

SEE ALSO: Duke of Alva; Charles V; Desiderius Erasmus; Alessandro Farnese; Kenau Hasselaer; İbrahim Paşa; Martin Luther; Margaret of Austria; Margaret of Parma; Maximilian I; Bernardino de Mendoza; Philippe de Mornay; Johan van Oldenbarnevelt; Philip II; Süleyman the Magnificent; Vladislav II; William the Silent.

RELATED ARTICLES in *Great Events from History: The Renaissance & Early Modern Era, 1454-1600:* January 23, 1516: Charles I Ascends the Throne of Spain; August 29, 1526: Battle of Mohács; 1528-1536: Narváez's and Cabeza de Vaca's Expeditions; September 27-October 16, 1529: Siege of Vienna; 1555-1556: Charles V Abdicates; 1568-1648: Dutch Wars of Independence; November, 1575: Stephen Báthory Becomes King of Poland.

MARY I
Queen of England (r. 1553-1558)

Mary I, the first woman to rule England in her own right and not simply as a consort to a king, also restored Catholicism to her country.

BORN: February 18, 1516; Greenwich, England
DIED: November 17, 1558; London, England
ALSO KNOWN AS: Mary Tudor; Bloody Mary
AREAS OF ACHIEVEMENT: Government and politics, religion and theology

EARLY LIFE

Mary I was the first surviving child of King Henry VIII and his first wife, Catherine of Aragon. Although Henry VIII wanted a male heir and although he could still hope a son would be born, Mary received more than the normal attention due a royal child. Catherine commissioned the Spanish Humanist Juan Vives to devise an educational program for Mary and employed Thomas Linacre as her daughter's first tutor. Henry often proudly displayed the young princess to foreign ambassadors. She played the expected role in diplomacy as Henry tried to arrange marriages for her with the heir to the French throne as well as with her older cousin, the Holy Roman Emperor, Charles V. In 1524, Henry made her the first princess of Wales, with her own household and administrative staff at Ludlow.

The king's "Great Matter," Henry's decision to end his marriage to Catherine in order to marry Anne Boleyn, reversed Mary's fortunes in her teenage years. Henry had every reason to expect a favorable response from Rome, but just as he needed an annulment, the Papacy came under the control of Charles V, Catherine's nephew.

Consequently the pope, Clement VII, was not free to dissolve the marriage. Henry was genuinely fond of Mary, so her position did not change immediately. Although she was seldom at court while the king and his council struggled to obtain the "divorce" from 1529 to 1533, Mary developed a hatred of Anne and a fierce loyalty to her mother. When the new archbishop of Canterbury, Thomas Cranmer, declared the marriage to Catherine void in the spring of 1533, Mary became illegitimate. After the birth of Elizabeth, on September 7, Mary's material circumstances changed radically. To punish Mary for her loyalty to Catherine, Henry separated her from her mother, revoked her title, and placed her in the hostile atmosphere of Princess Elizabeth's household. Despite intense pressure, she refused to accept the separation from Rome and the altered succession

to the Crown; as a result of this psychological conflict, she suffered recurring physical ailments. She did not submit until after her mother's death and Anne Boleyn's execution in 1536. After that, her situation improved, but she never regained her former favored position. Mary lived quietly for the rest of Henry's reign, but as a result of her previous experiences, she firmly identified herself with her mother's memory and Catholicism.

The reign of her half brother Edward VI (r. 1547-1553) tested Mary's religious conviction. Mary's position became precarious as Protestantism grew, under the leadership of Edward Seymour, duke of Somerset, and then John Dudley, duke of Northumberland. Because she had become a symbol of the old religion, the council challenged her right to hear Mass in her household after the rebellious summer of 1549. Mary consistently resisted. Ultimately, her closest advisers and household servants were sent to the Tower of London, but she was not harmed. In the spring of 1553, as it became obvious that Edward would not live, the young king and the duke of Northumberland altered the established succession by replacing Mary with Lady Jane Grey, a Protestant, the granddaughter of Henry VIII's younger sister Mary. When Edward died on July 6, Mary was warned in time to escape to Framlingham castle in Suffolk, from where she could either flee to the Continent or resist the new government. Lady Jane was proclaimed queen, but to the surprise of many, the East Anglian nobility and gentry responded to Mary's call for aid. Within nine days, she had a council and an army strong enough to convince the officials in London to proclaim her queen on July 19, 1553.

As she ascended the throne at the age of thirty-seven, Mary's attitudes were shaped by her past experiences. She remained devoted to her mother's religion and continued to rely on the advice of Charles V, whose ambassadors had often been her only consistent support and comfort. Given her history, Mary could have been an embittered, vengeful woman, but she was not. She enjoyed the elegant clothes and jewels that she used to enhance her auburn hair and small stature. Although she loved to gamble, she appeared serious and pious, more like a kindly maiden aunt than a queen regnant.

LIFE'S WORK

History has not treated Mary well. Her persecution of Protestants earned for her the epithet "Bloody Mary," and her marriage to Philip II of Spain, the son of Charles V, was a serious mistake. At the beginning of her reign, Mary faced many problems. Her right to rule had been challenged, she had to form a government using the same officials who had supported Lady Jane, and she had to overcome the factionalism and economic distress of the previous reign. Initially, without advisers whom she could trust implicitly, Mary relied on the Spanish ambassador, Simon Renard. She energetically devoted her first months as queen to selecting her councillors, establishing her government, beginning to restore Catholicism, and choosing a husband.

Although she had been accepted as the legitimate ruler, most believed a woman was naturally too weak to rule alone, and she had a duty to produce a Catholic heir to the throne. During those first months, she made only one disastrous decision, rejecting the single viable English candidate for her hand, Edward Courtenay, the earl of Devon, and accepting Philip II of Spain. The

choice was not popular from the beginning. It split her council and partially caused Wyatt's Rebellion (January-February, 1554), the most serious insurrection of the reign. During the rebellion, Mary showed herself a true Tudor. She resisted Renard's advice to flee. Her speech at the Guildhall, in London, rallied the city to her cause, and the rebellion failed.

The initial steps toward reunion with Rome were taken in 1553 by Mary's first Parliament. It repealed all the religious legislation of Edward VI's reign, but papal absolution was required to return England to the Catholic fold. Reginald Pole, Mary's cousin, was sent as papal legate to end the schism in the fall of 1554. While he had gained a reputation for wisdom and learning during his twenty-year exile, Pole revealed his ignorance of English conditions by insisting that former monastic lands be returned to the Church. Mary, her councillors, and Charles V persuaded Pole to relent, and in December, he presided over the formal reconciliation.

Religion was considered the cement of society in the sixteenth century, so religious diversity could not be tolerated: It would subvert a spiritually healthy commonwealth and an orderly government. In that spirit, Parliament revived the medieval heresy laws. The passage of laws could not ensure a Catholic revival, and Pole's plan for a progressive, reformed English Catholicism did not have time to work. As a result, Mary's reign is remembered for heresy trials and the fires of Smithfield. About 293 heretics were burned at the stake after February, 1555. To varying degrees, Bishop Edmund Bonner of London, Bishop Stephen Gardiner of Winchester, the lord chancellor, and Cardinal Pole supported the persecution, but the chief responsibility belongs to Mary. She acted, not out of cruelty, but out of a deep concern for the spiritual health of her realm. Still, her firm conviction, which would have been better tempered with a dose of political consideration as Philip advised, led to failure. Far from eliminating heresy, the persecution of the Protestants elevated them as martyrs associated with courage and national pride.

The marriage to Philip failed to produce an heir. Worse, Philip drew Mary into his

Mary I (Mary Tudor). (Library of Congress)

foreign entanglements. Ironically, in 1557, Mary agreed to aid Philip against the Papacy and France. The following January, England lost Calais, her last outpost on the Continent and a symbol of England's past military glory. The loss was more symbolic than real. Although Mary has been criticized for entering the war and thus straining her financial resources, it had positive results. The navy was overhauled. A new administrative structure and new men produced a naval policy that defeated Philip's armada in 1588. Mary's death in 1558 was welcomed and celebrated by many of her subjects.

SIGNIFICANCE

Accounts of Queen Mary I's reign are still clouded by the liberal Whig vision of history, because England took a more modern direction under Elizabeth I. Mary's accomplishments are often overlooked, and she is unfairly compared to Elizabeth, who ruled forty-five years, not five. In the important area of government finance, the revenue courts were consolidated, austerity measures were employed, and a new book of rates (customs duties) began to increase royal revenue. England's trade position improved when the government recognized that England had been too dependent on trade through Antwerp (now in Belgium). Mary and her advisers supported exploration by the Merchant Adventurers and encouraged northern trade though the Muscovy Company. These initiatives outweighed the loss of Calais.

Mary's council has traditionally been criticized for being inefficient and factional because of its size. An informal inner ring that functioned with energy and discretion directed policy, and genuine discussion of opposing views on important questions such as religion and her marriage should not be mistaken for factionalism. Parliament showed little organized opposition to the return to Catholicism. Members were more concerned with preserving their monastic lands than with religious issues, and a spirit of compromise and flexibility marked Mary's relationship with them.

Mary faced economic and social crises which were a true test of her skill as a ruler, and her solutions compare favorably with Elizabeth's handling of a similar crisis at the end of her reign. After harvest failures in 1555 and 1556, followed by a flu epidemic the next year, the government worked to stimulate the economy. The establishment of London's charitable and welfare institutions, which Mary encouraged, served as a model for the whole country. Many of Mary's initiatives bore fruit in Elizabeth's reign. Although personally the most attractive of the Tudors by modern standards, and perhaps the most

merciful toward her political enemies, Mary lacked the redeeming political skill of the other Tudors, who instinctively understood and shared the hopes, prejudices, and desires of their subjects. She proved that a woman could rule, if not entirely wisely in terms of policy, at least competently.

—Ann Weikel

FURTHER READING

Erickson, Carolly. *Bloody Mary*. Garden City, N.Y.: Doubleday, 1978. A colorfully written, popular biography that takes a traditional approach and relies on standard sources.

Harbison, E. Harris. *Rival Ambassadors at the Court of Queen Mary*. Princeton, N.J.: Princeton University Press, 1940. Reprint. Freeport, N.Y.: Books for Libraries Press, 1970. A classic study of the important role played by the French and Spanish ambassadors in Mary's reign.

Loach, Jennifer. *Parliament and the Crown in the Reign of Mary Tudor*. New York: Oxford University Press, 1986. The only study of Mary's reign from the standpoint of this very important institution of Tudor governance. This study rejects the traditional interpretation of conflict between Crown and Parliament, and Catholics and Protestants, in her reign.

Loades, David. *Chronicles of the Tudor Queens*. Stroud, Gloucestershire, England: Sutton, 2002. A study and comparison of the reigns of Mary and Elizabeth, including the period of transition from the former to the latter. Includes photographic plates, illustrations, maps, bibliographic references, and index.

_____. *The Oxford Martyrs*. New York: Stein and Day, 1970. A scholarly account of the Marian persecution of Protestants.

_____. *The Reign of Mary Tudor: Politics, Government, and Religion in England, 1553-58*. 2d ed. New York: Longman, 1991. The most original, scholarly, and complete account of Mary's reign. It does not include much biographical material, but it does thoroughly analyze the events of the reign.

_____. *Two Tudor Conspiracies*. Cambridge, England: Cambridge University Press, 1965. An account of Wyatt's Rebellion in 1554 and the Dudley Conspiracy in 1555. Some points in the discussion of Wyatt's Rebellion have been disputed, but the book gives invaluable information about some of the discontented.

Prescott, H. M. F. *Mary Tudor*. New York: Macmillan, 1962. While some aspects of the political and administrative treatment need revision in the light of subsequent scholarship, this is the standard biography.

Ridley, Jasper. *Bloody Mary's Martyrs: The Story of England's Terror.* New York: Carroll & Graf, 2001. Somewhat sensationalistic account of Mary's terror and the horrors perpetrated at her command or in her name. Includes photographic plates, illustrations, bibliography, and index.

Tittler, Robert. *The Reign of Mary Tudor.* New York: Longmans, Green, 1983. Designed for college students, Tittler's work presents both positive and negative aspects of Mary's reign through a short commentary and documents.

Weikel, Ann. "The Marian Council Revisited." In *The Mid-Tudor Polity: c. 1540-1563*, edited by Jennifer Loach and Robert Tittler. London: Macmillan, 1980. Contests the traditional view of Marian government through an examination of her council.

Weir, Alison. *The Children of Henry VIII.* New York: Ballantine Books, 1996. Study of Henry VIII's de-

scendants and of the intrigues for the throne in the years following his death. Includes photographic plates, illustrations, bibliographic references, and index.

SEE ALSO: Anne Boleyn; Catherine of Aragon; Charles V; Clement VII; Thomas Cranmer; Edward VI; Elizabeth I; Lady Jane Grey; Henry VIII; Philip II; First Duke of Somerset; The Tudor Family.

RELATED ARTICLES in *Great Events from History: The Renaissance & Early Modern Era, 1454-1600:* December 18, 1534: Act of Supremacy; May, 1539: Six Articles of Henry VIII; 1544-1628: Anglo-French Wars; July, 1553: Coronation of Mary Tudor; January 25-February 7, 1554: Wyatt's Rebellion; 1558-1603: Reign of Elizabeth I; January 1-8, 1558: France Regains Calais from England; April or May, 1560: Publication of the Geneva Bible; January, 1563: Thirty-nine Articles of the Church of England.

MATTHIAS I CORVINUS
King of Hungary (r. 1458-1490)

Matthias I moved Hungary from feudal particularism toward a more centralized state, and through his lavish patronage promoted remarkable Humanist literary and artistic achievements on the model of the Italian Renaissance.

BORN: February 24, 1443; Kolozsvár, Transylvania (now Cluj, Romania)
DIED: April 6, 1490; Vienna, Austria
ALSO KNOWN AS: Mátyás Corvin; Mátyás Hunyadi
AREAS OF ACHIEVEMENT: Government and politics, military, patronage of the arts, literature

EARLY LIFE

Matthias I Corvinus (mah-THI-uhs kawr-VI-nuhs) was the second son of János Hunyadi, a self-made individual of the Hungarian nobility. Hunyadi won great military renown fighting against the Ottoman Turks and in the process had become the largest single landowner in the kingdom, arousing the fear and resentment of the magnates, to Matthias's later detriment.

As a boy, Matthias received under his father a rigorous military training. He polished his soldierly skills in battle and was knighted at the age of fourteen during a victorious engagement with the Turks at Belgrade. Matthias's

father also provided him with a superior education through private tutors headed by János Vitéz, who had strong Humanist sympathies. Matthias became fascinated with Italian Renaissance culture.

On the sudden death of his father in 1456, Matthias and his elder brother were seized by feudal enemies of the Hunyadi family, with the approval of the impressionable boy-king Ladislas V. Matthias's brother was executed, but Matthias was spared, apparently because of his youth. When Ladislas died without an heir in late 1457, the diet of Hungarian nobles decided, with some qualms, to elect as king the fifteen-year-old Matthias, preferring him both for his native birth and for the heroic image left by his father. The candidates of assorted Polish, Saxon, and Austrian Habsburg dynasties were passed over. At his accession, Matthias was a vigorous, powerfully built youth. He had a charming manner that belied a sometimes-fiery temper.

LIFE'S WORK

The new king faced a desperate situation. The royal treasury was empty, while hostile forces pressed from virtually all sides. As Czech marauders and Hungarian rebels plagued much of northern Hungary, Turkish armies to

Matthias I Corvinus (standing in front of desk) becomes king of Hungary at age fifteen. (F. R. Niglutsch)

the south held Serbia in its entirety and raided Hungarian territory continually. Meanwhile, to the west, Holy Roman Emperor Frederick III, who coveted the Hungarian crown, plotted Matthias's overthrow with the help of an alienated faction of the Hungarian magnates. Finally, a crippling condition of Matthias's election was that he submit during the first five years of his reign to a regency government under his uncle and a council of state composed mainly of magnates. In meeting these challenges, Matthias soon demonstrated that Hungary had acquired no ordinary monarch.

Matthias I rejected from the outset the authority of the regency council. Within months, he had deposed his uncle, the regent, and replaced the magnates on the council with his personal choices. The young king then drew on his private resources to crush the northern rebellion and clear that region of its roving Czech military bands. By 1462, he had met temporarily the challenge of the Austrian emperor from the west through a skillfully negotiated treaty. That gave Matthias the breathing space to turn finally to the south, where Turkish forces had ad-

vanced from Serbian bases to overrun the neighboring Hungarian region of Wallachia. In a series of brilliant campaigns, Matthias recovered northern Serbia and most of Wallachia. He consolidated his gains with a chain of forts.

Matthias's impressive military and diplomatic successes were attributable largely to a complete restructuring of the Hungarian army accomplished during his first years in power. Believing the traditional feudal levy inadequate to his needs, the king recruited an army composed mostly of Czech and German mercenaries, professional soldiers who could be mobilized on short notice. These troops, supplemented by native feudal contingents, he personally trained and maintained with firm discipline and good pay. At its peak, the new standing army numbered some thirty thousand men, about two-thirds of them heavily armed cavalry. Known from their garb as the Black Army, these forces became the chief instrument in carrying out Matthias's foreign policy objectives.

To support his large military establishment, the king had to overhaul the tax system. A decree of 1467 became the cornerstone of a fiscal policy designed to produce the funds not only for the army but also for Matthias's extensive political and cultural projects. Previously inviolate tax exemptions for the magnates were drastically curtailed, while heavy new taxes were imposed on the free peasantry. Old taxes were given new names and expanded in scope. To handle the windfall of revenue, Matthias staffed his treasury office with specialists. Despite widespread protests and occasional tax rebellions, Matthias's fiscal reforms yielded a tenfold increase in royal income over that of his predecessor.

The king pursued other administrative and social reforms. Deeply suspicious of the feudal magnates, Matthias chose to run his government through a professionalized chancellery office staffed by men of humbler social background. He also won the gratitude of many towns through royal grants of autonomous status through the local feudal jurisdictions. To improve the administration of justice generally, Matthias revamped the court system. He installed a new appeals procedure that ran from local jurisdictions through an intermediate level to the royal court itself, at each stage conducted by judges knowledgeable in the law. Also, new laws were decreed that protected the rights of the free peasantry, softening the impact of his taxes by improving the peasantry's status in relation to the magnates, while other legislation prohibited the tightening of bonds on serfs. Matthias's legal reforms culminated in a royal decree of 1486, in which he sought to provide a synthesis or codification of the best principles of Hungarian jurisprudence, both in criminal and in civil law.

Following his early military and diplomatic victories, Matthias determined to use the Black Army to unite the Czech and Austrian realms with Hungary. Although his long-range policy goals were never clearly stated, it is possible that he contemplated the building of a coalition of central European Christian states to deal decisively with the Muslim Turkish menace in the Balkans, something he felt unable to achieve alone. In any case, from 1468 onward, Matthias began to compete more aggressively for the crown of Bohemia.

By 1478, after defeating a combined Czech, Polish, and Austrian force four times the size of the Black Army, Matthias had his prize. Under terms of the Peace of Olomouc, the Hungarian monarch took not only the title of king of Bohemia but also the associated lands of Moravia, Silesia, and Lusatia. Then, Matthias fought three wars against his old antagonist the Austrian emperor Frederick III. By 1485, the Black Army had occupied the Habsburg capital of Vienna, and it occupied

most of southern Austria soon afterward. Matthias triumphantly took up residence in Vienna, but the imperial crown itself would elude him, as Frederick III refused to designate Matthias his heir.

The most enduring achievement in Matthias's reign would lie not in his political and military exploits but in the prodigious cultural energies he brought to focus in Hungary. Convinced that cultural distinction was essential to a prince of his eminence in the Renaissance era, Matthias determined early to create a court life that was at once enlightened, elegant, and cosmopolitan. To this end, he gathered Humanist scholars around him, mostly from Italy, and drew many of his officials from their ranks. Further, he subsidized with great generosity the work of painters, sculptors, architects, and goldsmiths. Himself highly educated, the king often was a participant in the lively philosophical and scientific discussions he encouraged at court. His marriage in 1476 to Beatrix, daughter of the king of Naples, further intensified the impact of the Italian Renaissance on Hungarian elite society.

Resident Italian historians such as Antonio Bonfini now wrote histories of Hungary in which Matthias, to his delight, was hailed as a "second Attila." The same flattering Humanist Bonfini also stretched Matthias's genealogy to include as forebear a distinguished ancient Roman consul whose family crest, a crow (*corvinus*), Matthias promptly made his own. Finally, the king imported artwork from Italy and ordered the decoration of his various palaces with appropriate Renaissance paintings and statues.

Matthias's reputation as "friend of the muses" would rest above all on the splendid Corvina library he assembled in his Buda palace. The estimated twenty-five hundred manuscripts of the Corvina at its peak contained some six thousand distinct Greek and Latin works. These titles, by pagan and Christian alike, reflected the breadth of Matthias's interests. The books ranged in subject from military strategy and law through art and theology to Renaissance literature. Matthias also employed transcribers and book illuminators to copy and adorn selected works and emboss them with gems and precious metals. The Corvina would remain his greatest cultural legacy.

Matthias Corvinus died at age forty-seven in Vienna, the victim of a stroke that ended prematurely his grand scheme of a Hungarian empire embracing south-central Europe. He was interred near Budapest. He left only an illegitimate son who was quickly passed over by the Diet of magnates. They elected a Polish youth who seemed malleable enough and who, above all, was not of the house of Corvinus. In the grim generation that followed, the Black Army was disbanded, and Matthias's other major reforms were allowed to lapse. In 1526, an overwhelming Hungarian defeat at Mohács began two centuries of Turkish occupation.

Significance

Most of King Matthias's achievements proved fleeting because of the lack of capable successors. Yet the thirty-two years of his reign remain among the most remarkable in Hungarian history. Against heavy odds, Matthias I Corvinus managed to reverse several generations of feudal anarchy. He did so by remodeling the central government in ways similar to innovations then being ventured in the major Renaissance monarchies of the West. In particular, Matthias's administrative and legal reforms laid the foundations for a regime perceived as more stable and more just in its relations with its citizens generally. The renown of his judicial measures is reflected in the popular lament that followed his passing: "Matthias is dead; justice has fled."

In addition to his judicial and economic reforms, Matthias created in the Black Army one of the earliest standing armies in Europe. It made Hungary for a time the major power of central Europe. Yet there is some validity to the criticism that Matthias became so obsessed with the conquest of the Habsburg lands and the imperial crown that he badly neglected the critical problem of the Turks.

Matthias is remembered not only as a warrior, statesman, and lawgiver, but also as an extremely generous patron of arts and letters. The Corvina library ranked with the Vatican and the Medici collections in Italy as the foremost in Europe.

Matthias I, the Renaissance king of Hungary, was inspired by a larger vision than most princes of his time regarding the distinctive values of a civilized society and how to achieve them. A generation of prosperity and promise for his people expired with the man himself.

—*Donald D. Sullivan*

Further Reading

Bibliotheca Corviniana, 1490-1990: International Corvina Exhibition on the Five Hundredth Anniversary of the Death of King Matthias, National Széchényi Library, 6 April-6 October 1990. Budapest, Hungary: The Library, 1990. Catalog of an exhibition of materials from Matthias's library. Includes color illustrations and bibliographic references.

Birnbaum, Marianna D. *Thr [sic] Orb and the Pen: Janus Pannonius, Matthias Corvinus, and the Buda Court.* Budapest, Hungary: Balassi, 1996. Collection of eleven interdisciplinary essays on the Hungarian Renaissance, focusing especially on Pannonius's poetry and Matthias's library. Includes color illustrations, bibliographic references, and index.

Csapodi, Csaba. *The Corvinian Library: History and Stock.* Translated by Imre Gombos. Budapest: Akadémiai Kiadó, 1973. The definitive descriptive and historical account of Matthias's library. Provides valuable information on the scribes and illuminators of the books and where manuscripts are to be found. Provides an informed estimate that the Corvina originally contained at least twenty-five hundred manuscripts.

Feuer-Tóth, Rózsa. *Art and Humanism in Hungary in the Age of Matthais Corvinus.* Translated by Györgyi Jakobi. Edited by Péter Farbaky. Budapest, Hungary: Akadémiai Kiadó, 1990. A study of Matthias's court, his patronage of the arts, and the spread of Humanism in the Hungarian Renaissance. Include eight pages of photographic plates, illustrations, bibliographic references, and index.

Klaniczay, Tibor, and József Jankovics, eds. *Matthias Corvinus and the Humanism in Central Europe.* Budapest, Hungary: Balassi Kiadó, 1994. Anthology of essays originally presented at a conference on Matthias I and Humanism in Székesfehérvár, Hungary in May, 1990. Includes photographic plates, illustrations, bibliographic references, and index.

Kosáry, Dominic G. *A History of Hungary.* Foreword by Julius Szekfü. New York: Benjamin Franklin Bibliophile Society, 1941. Reprint. New York: Arno Press, 1971. An admiring but solid account of Matthias's chief policies and achievements. Kosáry argues that Matthias's efforts at erecting a central European empire of Austria and Bohemia, along with Hungary, was intended only as a prelude to ending decisively the Turkish threat in the south.

Kosztolynik, Zoltan J. "Some Hungarian Theologians in the Late Renaissance." *Church History* 57 (1988): 5-18. A good overview of an important segment of intellectual life in Matthias's Hungary, focused especially on the distinguished theologian Pelbart of Temesvar. Valuable for aspects of Matthias's relationship with the Hungarian church, particularly in substantiating the underlying resentment and hostility of leading Hungarian churchmen toward their Renaissance king.

Sinor, Denis. *History of Hungary.* New York: Praeger, 1959. Reprint. Westport, Conn.: Greenwood Press,

1976. The most balanced, scholarly, and informative account available in English. Provides a careful appraisal of the weaknesses as well as the strengths of Matthias's impressive reign. Sinor argues, contrary to Kosáry, that Matthias's pursuit of an elusive Hungarian empire that would include Austria and Bohemia was an end in itself, not directed toward building an anti-Turkish alliance.

Vámbéry, Arminius, with Louis Heilprin. *The Story of Hungary.* New York: G. P. Putnam's Sons, 1886. Reprinted as *Hungary in Ancient, Medieval, and Modern Times.* Freeport, N.Y.: Books for Libraries Press, 1972. Lacking a good modern biography in English, this rather uncritical treatment remains useful for the vivid, extensive detail relating to Matthias himself, especially the earlier years, on which little is available elsewhere.

Varga, Domokos G. *Hungary in Greatness and Decline: The Fourteenth and Fifteenth Centuries.* Translated by Martha S. Liptaks. Budapest, Hungary: Corvina Kiadó, 1982. The most extensive treatment available in English on the core period of Matthias's regime. The main value of this work lies in its extensive citations of original chronicle sources and its excellent illustrations.

SEE ALSO: Frederick III; İbrahim Paşa; Mehmed II; Mehmed III; Süleyman the Magnificent.

RELATED ARTICLES in *Great Events from History: The Renaissance & Early Modern Era, 1454-1600:* April 14, 1457-July 2, 1504: Reign of Stephen the Great; 1458-1490: Hungarian Renaissance; June 12, 1477-August 17, 1487: Hungarian War with the Holy Roman Empire.

MAXIMILIAN I
Holy Roman Emperor (r. 1493-1519)

Maximilian I revived and strengthened both the concept and the actual position of Holy Roman Emperor by a great reform movement. These accomplishments were short-lived, however, and his enduring contribution lies in the development of German and Austrian nationalism.

BORN: March 22, 1459; Wiener Neustadt, Austria
DIED: January 12, 1519; Wels, Austria
ALSO KNOWN AS: Maximilian von Habsburg
AREAS OF ACHIEVEMENT: Government and politics, social reform

EARLY LIFE

Maximilian (mak-suh-MIHL-yuhn) was the only son of the Holy Roman Emperor Frederick III and Eleanor of Portugal. The varied cultural background of Maximilian (he was also the great-great-grandson of John of Gaunt and had a Polish, Lithuanian, and Russian background from his paternal grandmother) combined to produce a highly interesting character. He was energetic, vivacious, and restless; he was an adventurer, an avid hunter, and a mountaineer; he was friendly, gregarious, and popular because he inspired confidence; and he loved writing, music, and the study of different languages. He was filled with curiosity, a love of learning, and a desire to meet people.

With his dynamic personality, it is not surprising that even before he became emperor, on the death of his father in 1493, Maximilian could boast of an impressive string of accomplishments. On February 16, 1486, he was crowned king at Aix-la-Chapelle, becoming coruler with his father. In 1486, he was also granted the title king of the Romans. Frederick worked patiently with Maximilian to teach him the concepts of governing an empire, a sense of responsibility, and political ethics. Maximilian also gained from his father personal strength and dignity. These lessons would prove valuable when Maximilian assumed full control of the imperial office.

In 1477, with his career just beginning, Maximilian married the heiress of the Burgundian lands, Mary, daughter of Charles the Bold. Charles had just been killed in battle against the Swiss, who, along with the French, moved quickly to appropriate portions of his inheritance, which Charles had carefully and laboriously assembled in the hope of Burgundy's becoming a kingdom. Maximilian, often called the last knight, arrived just in time to prevent the dismembering of Burgundy. By his marriage to Mary, he added her lands, consisting of the Netherlands, Luxembourg, Artois, and Picardy, to the Habsburg holdings. Maximilian also recovered Franche-Comté and lands in Austria and the Tyrol. By 1491, he had made claim to Hungary and Bohemia. Maximilian not only acquired lands but also emerged as a recognized leader in the field of European politics, giving rise to the power of the house of Habsburg. Thereafter, the Habsburgs retained control of the imperial office, and France was forced to pursue its expansionist policies in Italy.

Maximilian's relationship with Mary resembled a storybook romance. He loved her sincerely, spending much time with her at sporting activities, social events, and government functions. Together they had two children, Philip and Margaret. Mary was killed in 1482, however, as a result of a fall from a horse, causing Maximilian to have to face the resistance of Netherlanders who did not want to see Mary's children entrusted to his guardianship. In 1488, the citizens of Bruges even took him prisoner, although he was rescued by his father. All the events, however, successful and frustrating, of his involvement with Burgundian politics taught him valuable lessons in statecraft and gave him insights about the Flemish people that he could use later.

LIFE'S WORK

Maximilian became Holy Roman Emperor in 1493 after the death of his father. His great popularity, untiring energy, and capacity for work aroused the concern of the electors, who did not want to see the imperial office regain real power. The leader of the opposition was his life-long enemy, Prince Berthold, elector of Mainz. Berthold attempted to increase opposition to the emperor and create an administrative machine that would weaken Maximilian's hand and require approval for his acts. Berthold proposed a regency council (*Reichsregiment*), which the emperor bitterly fought. It was adopted in 1500 but failed two years later. Had it continued, it would have represented a great victory for the electors and the estates of Germany. Maximilian, trying to sabotage the council, acted independently of it, gaining support from the young princes of Germany, with whom he was highly popular. He also took advantage of the quarrels and dissension among council members.

His need for money to deal with the threat of invasion by the Turks forced him into a meeting with the electors and princes in 1495. This assembly, the Diet of Worms, marked the real beginning of his reign. Maximilian showed his capability as a ruler by dealing with the demands of the jealous nobility through compromises in which he gained more than the nobility. One of the results was the Common Penny, a tax collected from subjects throughout the realm to provide funds for Maximilian's campaign against the Turks. In return, he allowed the estates the opportunity to be included in his new bureaucratic offices. As a counterpoise to the pro-

Maximilian I. (Library of Congress)

posed *Reichsregiment*, Maximilian established the Imperial Chamber (*Reichskammergericht*), a supreme court of justice with a president appointed by the emperor and sixteen justices appointed by the estates. The chamber acted as a court of appeals in private cases and as a court to settle disputes among princes. It is important to note that the chamber implemented Roman law and served as a court of the empire rather than of the emperor. It also served as a rival to the regency council and gave the emperor considerable influence in judicial proceedings.

Perhaps the most significant accomplishment of the Diet of Worms was the peace (*Landfriede*), which effectively brought an end to personal warfare. With the decline of feudal power and the loss of feudal restraints, private vendettas were rife in Germany. This peace, to be eternal, meant that private disputes would now be settled in a court of law.

In another move to centralize power, Maximilian activated the six administrative circles originally planned by Emperor Albert II in 1438. In 1512, Maximilian added four circles. Each major district of the empire contained the organization for both war and peace, as each circle had a military commander and an administrative director. In 1501, Maximilian created the Aulic Council, which had eight members appointed by the emperor. This council allowed the emperor to hear appeals and to exercise supreme jurisdiction, extending the emperor's authority even into Italy.

Maximilian also had a separate financial administration dependent on him alone and a modern chancery with judges whom he appointed. Within a few years, Maximilian was able to replace the old feudal power of the electors and the estates of Germany with a new, modern, centralized bureaucracy. By 1505, Berthold was dead, leaving Maximilian with no enemies. He had gained the support of the young leaders, and he had reached the apex of his power and influence. In 1508, Pope Julius II approved for him the title Roman emperor elect. Maximilian took very seriously his religious responsibilities, believing that he was born destined to be a new Constantine who would strengthen and extend the borders of Christ's kingdom. He also took quite seriously the concept that he was destined to perpetuate the ancient Roman Empire as a new Augustus.

As important as Maximilian's modernized bureaucracy was to the enhancement of Habsburg power, perhaps more important were the dynastic marriages he arranged. He promoted a double marriage between his son Philip and Joan, the second daughter of Ferdinand II and Isabella I of Spain, and between his daughter Margaret and the Spanish prince John. The untimely deaths of the heirs to the Spanish throne placed Philip in a position to inherit the Spanish empire. He later arranged a marriage between his granddaughter and Louis II, son of Vladislav II, the king of Hungary and Bohemia, and between his grandson Ferdinand and Louis's sister. These dynastic marriages extended Habsburg control to include an extensive empire.

Maximilian's apparent genius as a leader and his successes attracted the attention of the scholarly community of Europe, who looked to Maximilian to establish an enlightened Christian empire. Humanists, whose vision centered on classical antiquity and the days of imperial Rome, were drawn to the patronage of Maximilian's court. They sincerely believed that Maximilian was destined to restore glory to Germany; Maximilian felt keenly this sense of his own destiny to be the founder of a new world order. At the same time, he found the Humanists useful in spreading the good news of his glorious reign. Maximilian worked hard to upgrade learning in the empire; he turned the University of Vienna into one of the most significant universities in Europe. He also composed works of his own: the *Weisskunig* (c. 1515), an account of his life; *Freydal* (1513); and *Theuerdank* (1517; *The Theuerdank of 1517*, 2003).

The least successful of Maximilian's policies was his involvement in Italian affairs. Maximilian made an alliance with Ludovico Sforza, tyrant of Milan, sealing it by marrying Ludovico's niece, Bianca Maria Sforza, in 1494. His purpose was to counteract the growing French influence in Italy, caused to a large degree by Maximilian's expulsion of the French from Burgundian lands. In 1495, he joined the Holy League with the pope, Milan, England, and Aragon to stop the French in Italy. In 1508, he joined the League of Cambrai against Venice, and, in 1513, he joined the Holy League (formed 1511) against the French. The league forced the French king Louis XII to withdraw, but the French returned later under Francis I. Maximilian's anti-French policy contributed to the protracted war between German and French forces in Italy, which escalated into a series of bloody conflicts over both politics and religion that did not end until 1648. Maximilian also struggled in vain against the Swiss. They fought his forces to a standstill in 1499 during the Swabian War, resulting in the de facto independence of the Swiss, recognized officially at the Peace of Westphalia in 1648. In his declining years, Maximilian spent his time preparing his young grandson Charles to assume the throne. (His son Philip had died in 1506, leaving Charles as heir to the entire Habsburg holdings.) Maximilian died on January 12, 1519, in Wels.

SIGNIFICANCE

Maximilian I was able to restore the effectual authority of the emperor and the prestige and prominence of the Holy Roman Empire to its greatest degree of strength since the downfall of the Hohenstaufens. The empire had now at least the appearance of a united state. His own position as a Habsburg ruler was the strongest of any of his family, largely because of his timely dynastic marriages. He was responsible for a more cohesive Germany and for the cultivation of a spirit of national pride within the German people. His *Landfriede* program brought about peace and order, ending the tyranny of robber barons. Maximilian faced political realities and could conceive of modern alternatives to feudal traditions and institutions.

He was not an original thinker, but he was able to take ideas from others and make them work, creating an effective political machine. He was an enlightened ruler who showed an interest in church reform and the advancement of learning. He showed a modern adroitness in political propaganda—a politician's skill in disarming his opponents—usually coming out on the winning side.

Maximilian's reform, however, was short-lived. Internally, his power was never more than an uneasy balance between imperial and feudal elements. Although the Aulic Council continued to the end of the empire, generally his efforts to create permanent centralized institutions failed. His efforts probably had more to do with the rise of Austrian and German national states than with the preservation of the empire. Some consider him to be the last ruler of the Holy Roman Empire. Certainly he is a transition figure from the old medieval empire to the modern national states. He had energy and a dedication to work, but he lacked clear objectives and persistence.

The death of his wife was not only an emotional catastrophe for him but also a political one. His involvement in Burgundy drove the French to Italy, and his involvement in Italy resulted in war and great distress for Germany. Switzerland was lost to the empire; Burgundy became an area fought over by France and Germany for centuries.

The most important and lasting achievement of Maximilian was the cultivation and the institutionalizing of German nationalism. In years to come, the efforts of this "last knight"—who himself was the bridge to the modern world—contributed to the rise of the nineteenth and twentieth century political realizations of the German Reich.

—J. David Lawrence

FURTHER READING

Bouckaert, Bruno, and Eugeen Schreurs, eds. *The Burgundian-Habsburg Court Complex of Music Manuscripts (1500-1535) and the Workshop of Petrus Alamire*. Leuven, Belgium: Alamire, 2003. Proceedings of a colloquium discussing the court musicians of Maximilian and his successors and their contribution to the culture of the Habsburg dynasty. Includes illustrations, sheet music, bibliographic references, and index.

Bryce, James. *The Holy Roman Empire*. Rev. ed. London: Macmillan, 1913. Reprint. New York: AMS Press, 1978. Important for the discussion of the transfer of the imperial consciousness from Roman to German and the carrying forth of the concept that the one empire is eternal. Somewhat dated but thorough, especially in the discussion of the relationship of Germany to the Church.

Cuneo, Pia, ed. *Artful Armies, Beautiful Battles: Art and Warfare in Early Modern Europe*. Boston: Brill, 2002. Includes two essays on Maximilian I, one on chivalry and his conduct of warfare, and one on artistic portrayals of war designed to legitimate Maximilian's foreign policies. Includes photographic plates, illustrations, bibliographic references, and index.

Fichtner, Paula Sutter. *The Habsburg Monarchy, 1490-1848: Attributes of Empire*. New York: Palgrave Macmillan, 2003. History of the Habsburg monarchy beginning with Maximilian's period of corule with his father and his assumption of the throne. Argues that the monarchy was a European empire comparable to those of Britain, France, and Spain, and that it should be studied in those terms. Includes illustrations, maps, genealogical table, bibliographic references, and index.

Gilmore, Myron P. *The World of Humanism, 1453-1517*. New York: Harper & Row, 1952. A valuable source for the study of Humanism, which provides the intellectual context for Maximilian's time. The chapter on dynastic consolidation is interesting, especially as it pertains to Germany. The discussion of Maximilian is highly informative.

Heer, Friedrich. *The Holy Roman Empire*. Translated by Janet Sondheimer. New York: Praeger, 1968. A most valuable source for students of medieval German history. Begins with the birth of the Roman Empire and traces the development of imperial consciousness. Excellent discussion of Maximilian and his relationship to the general picture. Good illustrations, an excellent index, and a bibliography.

Holborn, Hajo. *The Reformation*. Vol. 1 in *A History of Modern Germany*. New York: Alfred A. Knopf, 1959. Reprint. Princeton, N.J.: Princeton University Press, 1982. Begins with the German migrations and continues through the history of the empire to the sixteenth century. Very good for setting forth ideas and underlying causes; good analysis. Overview of Maximilian's life is good; main points delineated well.

Maehl, William H. *Germany in Western Civilization*. Tuscaloosa: University of Alabama Press, 1979. This critical and very comprehensive work begins with ancient times and follows the history of Germany to the post-World War II era. An excellent index, a bibliography, a glossary, and a chronological list of German rulers. Especially good discussion of Maximilian's dedication to scholarship, his marriage alliances, and his Italian policy.

Meconi, Honey. *Pierre de la Rue and Musical Life at the Habsburg-Burgundian Court: Beginnings.* New York: Oxford University Press, 2003. Study of the life and work of the major court composer of several Habsburg monarchs, beginning with Maximilian.

Stubbs, William. *Germany in the Later Middle Ages, 1200-1500.* Edited by Arthur Hassall. New York: Howard Fertig, 1969. First published 1908, this work consists of a series of lectures which the author delivered at the University of Oxford. Provides a detailed view of Germany in the thirteenth, fourteenth, and fifteenth centuries.

SEE ALSO: Charles the Bold; Albrecht Dürer; Ferdinand II and Isabella I; Francis I; Frederick III; Henry VII; James IV; Julius II; Louis XII; Niccolò Machiavelli; Mary of Burgundy; Philip the Magnanimous; Pius V; Ludovico Sforza; Vladislav II.

RELATED ARTICLES in *Great Events from History: The Renaissance & Early Modern Era, 1454-1600:* July 16, 1465-April, 1559: French-Burgundian and French-Austrian Wars; August 17, 1477: Foundation of the Habsburg Dynasty; 1481-1499: Ludovico Sforza Rules Milan; 1482-1492: Maximilian I Takes Control of the Low Countries; August 19, 1493-January 12, 1519: Reign of Maximilian I; 1499: Louis XII of France Seizes Milan; 1504: Treaty of Blois; 1508: Formation of the League of Cambrai; August 18, 1516: Concordat of Bologna; June 28, 1519: Charles V Is Elected Holy Roman Emperor; 1531-1585: Antwerp Becomes the Commercial Capital of Europe.

MAXIMILIAN II
Holy Roman Emperor (r. 1564-1576)

Maximilian II's defense of the Peace of Augsburg, a religious compromise between Lutheran and Catholic rulers, contributed to a period of relative internal peace in most of the Roman Empire and in the Habsburg lands during his reign.

BORN: July 31, 1527; Vienna, Austria
DIED: October 12, 1576; Regensburg, Bavaria (now in Germany)
AREAS OF ACHIEVEMENT: Government and politics, religion and theology

EARLY LIFE

Maximilian II was born to Ferdinand I and Anna of Bohemia and Hungary. Six years before Maximilian II's birth, Ferdinand I, the brother of Holy Roman Emperor Charles V, inherited the Habsburg lands, and in 1556, he succeeded his brother as emperor.

In 1529, Ferdinand I moved his family to Innsbruck, in part because the Ottoman Turks threatened Vienna and because it was free of the plague. Maximilian grew up in Innsbruck and learned the local Tirolian German dialect, which he used in adult life. He received a solid education from his tutors, young nobles from the Habsburg lands who were brought to the court to teach Maximilian. As Maximilian matured, he also became an enthusiastic hunter and horseman.

The Protestant Reformation's impact on Germany, and Europe in general, made religion a contentious issue. In 1536, Maximilian's tutor was Wolfgang Schiefer, who had been at Wittenberg with Martin Luther. Two years later, Ferdinand I issued an order that there would be no discussion of Luther's religious teachings. In 1539, Schiefer was replaced by an orthodox Catholic tutor and Maximilian was confirmed in the Catholic faith.

LIFE'S WORK

Beginning in 1538, Ferdinand I introduced Maximilian and his brothers to their future tasks. In Linz, Maximilian became acquainted with foreign diplomats, and in Vienna he met other officials. At age sixteen, Maximilian accompanied his father to the Reichstag. In 1544, his uncle, Charles V, summoned him to his court in Brussels. Maximilian supported his uncle in his war against the Protestant Schmalkaldic League and fought at the Battle of Mühlberg in 1547. Charles also arranged his daughter's 1548 marriage to Maximilian in Spain. Maria and Maximilian had sixteen children, ten surviving childhood. Devoutly Catholic, Maria outlived Maximilian and died in a cloister in Spain in 1603.

In Spain, Maximilian became Charles's regent for two years (1548-1550) and learned much about administration and government. In October, 1551, he returned to

Maximilian II. (Hulton|Archive by Getty Images)

Germany and was later joined by his wife. From 1552, Maximilian lived in Vienna and administered his father's Habsburg lands as regent of Austria, where he became the center of anti-Spanish opposition. He grew to dislike Charles V because Charles attempted to have his own son, Philip II, succeed Ferdinand as emperor of Germany. Naturally, Maximilian urged his father to reject Charles's dynastic plans. In 1554, Ferdinand I divided his Habsburg possessions among his three sons, granting Maximilian Upper and Lower Austria and Hungary and Bohemia.

Because of Maximilian's ambivalent attitude toward Catholicism, his dynastic future was first uncertain. Ferdinand had negotiated the Peace of Augsburg in 1555, which recognized Lutheranism along with Catholicism in the empire. As German king in 1557, however, Ferdinand was confronted with Pope Paul IV's threat to refuse to recognize him as emperor unless he gave assurances that no Protestant would succeed him to the throne in Germany. The Spanish Habsburg relatives were also concerned about Maximilian's friendly relations with Protestant princes in the empire. By 1560, solutions were found.

With the religious issue seemingly solved, Maximilian became king of Bohemia on September 20, 1562.

In November, 1562, he was crowned German king, and in September, 1563, he was named king of Hungary, even though much of that country was occupied by the Turks. Also, after having satisfied Pope Pius IV that he was committed to Catholicism, Maximilian succeeded his father as emperor on July 25, 1564.

As German emperor, Maximilian was confronted by a series of problems, ranging from religious issues in the empire and in his Austrian lands, to the Turkish threat on his eastern borders and the need for imperial reforms in the empire. The Turks had occupied large parts of Hungary after 1526, and because of Maximilian's conflict with the prince of Transylvania, John Zápolya (later King John of Hungary), a new Turkish war broke out. In November, 1565, Sultan Süleyman the Magnificent attacked and defeated Maximilian in 1566, forcing him to agree to the Peace of Adrianople in 1568. Both parties accepted the status quo, and Maximilian was forced to recognize Zápolya as prince of Transylvania. In 1574, Maximilian again agreed to renew the peace treaty with the Turks.

Maximilian's religious policy was contentious as far as the Papacy and his Spanish relatives were concerned. Maximilian wanted reconciliation between Lutheranism and Catholicism. Personally, he was willing to receive both bread and wine during Mass. Maximilian was horrified by the St. Bartholomew's Day massacre in Paris on August 24, 1572, which resulted in the mass murder of Protestant French Huguenots by Catholic leaders; he disagreed with the pope's excommunication of Queen Elizabeth I of England in 1570; and he initially thought Spanish repressive policy in the Netherlands in 1567 a mistake. All he could do, however, was to forbid the recruiting of troops in the Reich for the Dutch and the Huguenots. In the end, he was not successful in moderating Spanish policies in the Netherlands, nor could he contain Spanish expansion in Italy, an area of special interest because five of Maximilian's sisters were married to Italian princes. His inability to control his Spanish cousin undermined his position with the German Protestant princes.

The need for finances to meet the constant Turkish threats allowed the Austrian estates to win concessions from Maximilian. To the disgust of his Spanish relatives and the pope, in 1568, he allowed Austrian and Bohemian nobles to practice the Augsburg Confession on their estates. At the Reichstag in 1566, he had to accept Calvinism in addition to Lutheranism and Catholicism. Maximilian became increasingly skeptical about the Hussite tradition and Calvinism, and, by 1572, he seems to have moved closer to equating Calvinism with treason.

Maximilian also faced frustrations with his dynastic policies. In the election for king of Poland in 1575, Maximilian was defeated by Stephen Báthory, prince of Transylvania. In Hungary, he had to acknowledge the principality of Transylvania under Zápolya, which was a dependency of the Ottoman Empire. Maximilian also failed to achieve major reforms in the empire. In 1567, he allowed Augustus I of Saxony to execute Wilhelm von Grumbach, a knight who had hoped to work with the emperor against the princes. This strengthened territorial power in the empire even more. He also failed to convince the Reichstag in 1570 to agree to military reforms, which would have increased the powers of the emperor. All he was able to do in that year was to ban German service in foreign military forces.

Throughout his adult life, Maximilian suffered from a variety of ailments, ranging from gout and urinary difficulties to heart problems. In 1571, he had a seizure. On October 12, 1576, he died in Regensburg, having refused the Catholic holy sacraments before his death.

SIGNIFICANCE

Given the short period of Maximilian's reign, the increasingly divisive role of religion, and the empire's political realities, he found it impossible to accomplish major administrative reforms in the empire. Nevertheless, his acceptance of the Peace of Augsburg between Lutherans and Catholics helped keep peace in much of the empire and in the Habsburg domains. Compared to the bloody religious strife in France and in the Netherlands, this was no mean accomplishment. Maximilian could control neither the expansion of the Reformed Church (Calvinism) nor the growth of the Catholic Counter-Reformation in Germany. His successors, however, were no more successful, and they witnessed a bloody religious war in the empire in the early seventeenth century.

Maximilian's policy of religious compromise increased the power of the regional estates in the empire and in Austria. His attempts to heal the split between the

Catholics and Lutherans also brought him into conflict with his Spanish Habsburg relatives. Maximilian's pressures on his father to reject Charles V's plans to rotate the Crown between the Spanish and Austrian families, however, played a major role in ensuring that the Austrian Habsburgs would retain control of the imperial title. Furthermore, on October 9, 1576, he was able to get his son, Rudolf II, elected king of Germany, designating him as his successor and ensuring dynastic continuity.

—*Johnpeter Horst Grill*

FURTHER READING

Fichter, Paula Sutter. *Emperor Maximilian II*. New Haven, Conn.: Yale University Press, 2001. The only comprehensive, although very critical, biography of Maximilian II in English.

Kaufmann, Thomas da Costa. *Variations on the Imperial Theme: Studies in Ceremonial Art and Collecting in the Age of Maximilian II and Rudolf II*. New York: Garland, 1978. Discusses ceremonies and rituals as acts of state.

Lindell, Robert. "New Findings on Music at the Court of Maximilian II." In *Kaiser Maximilian II: Kultur und Politik im 16. Jahrhundert*, edited by Friedrich Edelmayer and Alfred Kohler. Vienna, Austria: Verlag für Geschichte und Politik, 1992. Evaluates Maximilian's patronage of music.

Louthan, Howard. *The Quest for Compromise: Peacemaking in Counter-Reformation Vienna*. New York: Cambridge University Press, 1997. Examines Maximilian's tolerant religious views and policies.

SEE ALSO: John Calvin; Charles V; Elizabeth I; Martin Luther; Maximilian I; Giovanni Pierluigi da Palestrina; Philip II; Rheticus.

RELATED ARTICLES in *Great Events from History: The Renaissance & Early Modern Era, 1454-1600:* September 25, 1555: Peace of Augsburg; 1576-1612: Reign of Rudolf II.

COSIMO I DE' MEDICI
Grand duke of Tuscany (1569-1574)

Cosimo I centralized the governmental and cultural institutions of the Tuscan state, giving permanence to its transition from a republic to a hereditary principality. He provided the city of Florence and the Medici halls of state with ornamentation fit for the seat of a duchy, employing an outstanding group of artists and architects.

BORN: June 12, 1519; Florence (now in Italy)
DIED: April 21, 1574; Villa di Castello, near Florence (now in Italy)
ALSO KNOWN AS: Cosimo de Medici; Cosimo I; Cosimo the Great
AREAS OF ACHIEVEMENT: Government and politics, patronage of the arts

EARLY LIFE
Cosimo I de' Medici (KAW-see-moh day MEHD-ee-chee) was born to a celebrated military leader, Giovanni delle Bande Nere de' Medici, descended from the younger son of Giovanni di Bicci de' Medici. The junior, or younger, branch of the family had always been active in Medici business enterprises but not in Florentine politics. Cosimo's mother, Maria Salviati, was a member of the senior Medici line descended from Giovanni di Bicci's first son, Cosimo the Elder. Cosimo I was born in the Salviati palace in Florence, and his great uncle on his mother's side, Giovanni de' Medici (later known as Pope Leo X), chose the boy's name in honor of his illustrious ancestor.

The unstable political climate in Florence forced the family to move frequently. When Cosimo was seven, his father died in battle near Mantua, and after having spent much of his early childhood in Venice, the boy was shuttled between Bologna, Genoa, Naples, and his family's villa, Il Trebbio, north of Florence, where he could indulge his passion for hunting. Surrounded by his father's former officers, Cosimo aspired to become a soldier. He often dressed as one until his great uncle, Pope Leo's successor Clement VII, ordered him to stop.

On January 7, 1537, Lorenzino de' Medici assassinated his unpopular cousin Duke Alessandro of Florence, who had ruled the city with a heavy hand. Lorenzo's subsequent flight and the illegitimacy of Alessandro's four-year-old son Giulio left the seventeen-year-old Cosimo the logical successor. At the time of his formal election on January 8, 1537, he and his mother were staying in a house next to the Palazzo Medici in Florence.

LIFE'S WORK
Many politically active members of Florence's patrician families welcomed the accession of Cosimo. Since the boy was neither deeply familiar with Florence nor schooled in the arts of statecraft, political veterans such as Francesco Guicciardini expected to manipulate or lead him, governing in his stead. Showing surprising acumen, however, Cosimo outmaneuvered his would-be handlers, managing to gather the reins of power into his own hands. In 1540, he moved into the Palazzo Vecchio, former seat of Florence's republican government, an event that heralded his dominance. He was assisted by his dashing father's popularity among the lower classes, his mother's intimate knowledge of the Florentine elite, and the astute advice of his secretary Francesco Campana. Eventually, he would succeed in transforming the old governing class into courtiers, appointing them to honorary posts in which they exercised little real power.

Decisive in strengthening Cosimo's rulership was the Battle of Montemurlo, fought near Prato on July 31, 1537, in which he defeated an army led by Piero Strozzi and other anti-Medici Florentine exiles. On October 4, 1539, he augmented his international stature by marrying Eleonora de Toledo, daughter of the imperial viceroy of Naples, Pedro de Toledo. Otherwise secretive and often cold, Cosimo was a loving husband, fathering eleven children with Eleonora. It was Eleonora who purchased Florence's spacious Pitti Palace, which, enlarged by sculptor and architect Bartolommeo Ammannati and others, became the permanent Medici seat.

Cosimo developed Florence's diplomatic and intelligence network to serve his dynastic plans, which included territorial expansion. In 1546, he sought to annex Lucca after discovering a plot by the Lucchese Franceso Burlamacchi, who wanted to free Pisa from Medici rule and rally other Tuscan cities to expel the Spanish and overthrow Cosimo. Loyal Lucchese officials, however, appealed to the emperor and forestalled the duke's plans. Cosimo enjoyed more success with Siena, when, after an expensive three-year war, he managed to win that city for Holy Roman Emperor Charles V in 1555.

Although failing once again in negotiations that would have allowed his victorious army to assault Lucca, and unsuccessfully petitioning Pope Pius IV in 1559 to be crowned king of Tuscany, he succeeded in other efforts. In 1562, he arranged for Pius IV to found the military order of Santo Stefano with Cosimo as its head, a privilege reserved normally for royalty. In 1565, he wedded his son and eventual successor, Francesco, to the Austrian archduchess Joanna, daughter of the Habsburg emperor Ferdinand I and sister of Holy Roman Emperor Maximilian II. Since Cosimo had supported certain Counter-Reformation measures of Pius V, that pope granted him the hereditary title of grand duke on August 27, 1569, in a lavish ceremony in Rome.

At home, Cosimo also sought through a wide variety of means to strengthen his state. The year 1550 saw the maiden voyages of *La Saetta* and *La Pisana*, the first warships of Florence's soon-considerable navy based at Elba Island. Like the military order of Santo Stefano, the navy was designed to protect shipping from Barbary Coast pirates, or corsairs. With foresight, he also promoted the development of Livorno, reducing dependence on Pisa as a mercantile port.

Yet he did not neglect Pisa, posting the engineer Luca Martini there to devise and oversee the construction of a canal system for that city. Cosimo's other engineering projects included a scheme to drain the malarial marshes of the Sienese coastal plain following the Treaty of Cateau-Cambrésis (April 3, 1559), which gave him formal possession of those territories. In Florence, after the

Cosimo I de' Medici. (Hulton|Archive by Getty Images)

Arno flood of 1557, Cosimo commissioned Ammannati to rebuild the Ponte alla Carraia and to construct another bridge, the Ponte Santa Trinità (begun 1566).

Overshadowing Cosimo's architectural improvements in the Palazzo Vecchio was his project, begun in 1559, to consolidate the government offices in a single complex next to the Palazzo Vecchio. Giorgio Vasari designed the grand buildings known simply as the Uffizi (offices), which today houses a famous art collection.

Between March and September of 1565, Vasari constructed an elevated corridor through the city for ducal use, befitting Cosimo's status and reflecting his continual security concerns. Known simply as the Corridoio (corridor), it connects the Palazzo Vecchio and Uffizi with the Pitti Palace across the Arno River. Cosimo also established a tapestry workshop at Florence's Foundling Hospital to compete with the lucrative near-monopoly of the Flemish on that highly prestigious product, complementing Florence's long-standing wool and silk industries (the latter of which he also sought to revive). Also, to stimulate commerce, he offered tax incentives to non-Florentine businesses willing to relocate to his territory.

Cosimo was also a shrewd sponsor of the arts. He founded the Accademia Fiorentina (Florentine Academy) in 1541 to promote and publicize the virtues of the Florentine language. Its illustrious membership included Italian scholar Benedetto Varchi, who wrote a history of Florence for the period 1527-1538 for Cosimo. Six years later, he ensured a publishing outlet for academy members by bringing Lorenzo Torrentino from Bologna as ducal printer, although the press foundered twenty years later. Since commissioning the spectacular decorations for his own wedding, Cosimo had attracted a circle of gifted artists, among them architect Vasari, sculptors Giovanni da Bologna (Giambologna) and Benvenuto Cellini, and painters Cecchino Salviati, Agnolo di Cosimo (Il Bronzino), and Jacopo da Pontormo.

After the mid-1560's, Cosimo started few major enterprises. Plagued by advanced uricemia and arteriosclerosis and saddened by the premature deaths of his wife and several children, Cosimo began in 1564 to delegate official duties to his son Francesco. After illicitly fathering a son, Giovanni, by Eleonora degli Albizzi, he began a liaison with another Florentine woman, Camilla Martelli, which, in May of 1568, produced a daughter, Virginia. He astonished the court by marrying Camilla on March 29, 1570, although she never assumed the title of grand duchess. In the following years, Cosimo suffered a series of strokes that disabled him and left him inarticulate. After two months of semiconsciousness, he died on April 21, 1574.

SIGNIFICANCE

Cosimo greatly strengthened the machinery of state, rationalizing its bureaucracy and making it more meritocratic. The measures he took for attracting new industry, revitalizing existing textile production, and reclaiming arable land brought Tuscany's economy to the high point of its sixteenth century fortunes. His development of Leghorn also proved farsighted. On the cultural front, he transformed loosely structured local academies into state-supervised institutions and promoted the use of the Florentine idiom in literary and scientific works, preparing the way for Tuscan to become a pan-Italian language.

—*James Carlton Hughes*

FURTHER READING

Booth, Cecily. *Cosimo I.* Cambridge, England: Cambridge University Press, 1921. The most thorough treatment in English of Cosimo's life.

Cox-Rearick, Janet. "Art at the Court of Duke Cosimo I de' Medici." *The Medici, Michelangelo, and the Art of Late Renaissance Florence.* New Haven, Conn.: Yale University Press, 2002. An overview that clearly re-

lates phases of Cosimo's patronage of painters and sculptors and discusses stages in his political career.

_____. *Dynasty and Destiny in Medici Art.* Princeton, N.J.: Princeton University Press, 1984. Analyzes the cosmological and dynastic aspects of imagery that Cosimo used to propagandize his absolute rule, comparing it to the less-overt symbolism of fifteenth century Medici art.

Eisenbichler, Konrad, ed. *The Cultural Politics of Duke Cosimo I de' Medici.* Burlington, Vt.: Ashgate, 2001. A many-faceted collection of essays examining, through case studies, Cosimo as a statesman and a patron of art, literature, and craft industries.

Hibbert, Christopher. "Duke Cosimo I." *The House of Medici: Its Rise and Fall.* New York: Perennial Press, 1999. Vividly depicts Cosimo as guarded and imperious but tenderly devoted to his family, and alludes in passing to his major enterprises.

SEE ALSO: Benvenuto Cellini; Andrea Cesalpino; Charles V; Clement VII; Leonhard Fuchs; Francesco Guicciardini; Leo X; Maximilian II; Pius V; Giorgio Vasari.

RELATED ARTICLE in *Great Events from History: The Renaissance & Early Modern Era, 1454-1600:* 1469-1492: Rule of Lorenzo de' Medici.

LORENZO DE' MEDICI
Italian statesman

Florence's Lorenzo de' Medici was the most important statesman in Italy during the latter part of the fifteenth century. Lorenzo was also a noted banker, poet, and patron of the arts, and he epitomized the concept of the Renaissance man.

BORN: January 1, 1449; Florence (now in Italy)
DIED: April 8, 1492; Careggi, near Florence
ALSO KNOWN AS: Lorenzo il Magnifico; Lorenzo the Magnificent
AREAS OF ACHIEVEMENT: Government and politics, diplomacy, literature, patronage of the arts

EARLY LIFE

Lorenzo de' Medici (loh-REHNT-soh day MEHD-ee-chee) was born in Florence. His father, Piero, died at age fifty-three in 1469. Lorenzo's grandfather, Cosimo, building on the accomplishments of his father, Giovanni,

had established himself as the most powerful individual in the Florentine republic. Medici influence resulted in the wealth accumulated through banking activities. Financial abilities were joined to political talents and ambitions, which made them the most formidable nonroyal family in fifteenth century Europe.

The Medicis were not unique. By the 1400's, there were other influential families in Florence whose wealth and power also came from banking and commerce. Although a republic, Florence was not a democracy; political rights came from membership in the various guilds that had evolved in the later Middle Ages. At the apex were a small number of Florentines, and it was this wealthy oligarchy that controlled the government. All offices were constitutionally open to all guild members, but through various techniques it was possible to manipulate the system. In Renaissance Florence, however, life was more than simply wealth and power for their own sakes.

Civic responsibilities went together with political ambition; one was expected to provide public buildings, sponsor schools, or be a patron of the arts. Participation in politics was also expected, as the Medicis well understood, and other Florentine families matched them in wealth and ambition.

In addition to his banking and political responsibilities, Piero, Lorenzo's father, was a patron of the sculptor Donatello and the painter Sandro Botticelli. Lorenzo's mother, Lucrezia Tornabuoni, was a poet of note. Privately tutored, Lorenzo received a Humanist education through the Latin and Greek classics. Education was not merely intellectual: The body and spirit were equally important. He played the lyre, sang his own songs, and wrote his own verse. He rode well and was an accomplished athlete, and he enjoyed talking to both peasants and popes. Piero arranged for Lorenzo's marriage to Clarice Orsini, from an aristocratic Roman family; political and economic considerations were more important than love. Lorenzo was not handsome, with his dark complexion, irregular features, jutting chin, and misshapen nose that denied him a sense of smell. Yet he had a brilliant mind and a charismatic personality.

Lorenzo de' Medici. (Library of Congress)

LIFE'S WORK

Lorenzo was only twenty when Piero died. Given his age, he was reluctant to assume the various political and economic responsibilities, but it was impossible for him not to do so. As he himself noted, it did not bode well for someone of wealth to evade his civic obligations. The same techniques that the Medicis had used to gain influence at the expense of others could equally be used against them; if they wished to maintain their position, they had to participate in the political arena. Not only had Lorenzo been trained by scholars, but also he had been sent on several diplomatic missions before Piero's death. At that time, modifications were made in the Florentine constitution that assured the continued primacy of the Medici party, both for Lorenzo and for those other oligarchs who had attached their ambitions to the Medici banner. Nevertheless, Florence remained officially a republic and Lorenzo ostensibly a private citizen.

During Lorenzo's lifetime, the Medici banks continued to be influential throughout Europe, but less so than earlier. Lorenzo was not particularly interested in banking. Over time, the Medicis became relatively less powerful in banking matters as other cities and nations of Europe rose to positions of power. During Lorenzo's era,

his resources were occasionally put under pressure and he was accused of manipulating the economy of Florence to the benefit of the Medicis. Lorenzo could argue that his position, unofficial as it was, benefited all Florentines and that he deserved to be recompensed. Given the nature of Florentine politics, it was perhaps impossible to separate Lorenzo's private needs from the republic's welfare.

Other Italian city-states and European nations were accustomed to dealing with the head of the Medici family directly instead of through the official Florentine government. Lorenzo's position of primacy was never officially avowed: He remained merely a citizen, although the most important citizen. While Lorenzo was the unquestioned leader of a banking and merchant oligarchy, he did not always enjoy absolute freedom to commit his city to a particular course of action, freedom such as the hereditary dukes of Milan or the popes in Rome exercised.

The Medicis had a close relationship with the kings of France: Louis XI had granted Piero the right to incorporate the three lilies of the French royal house of Valois onto the Medici arms. Lorenzo realized, however, that it was necessary to keep that large kingdom's military might out of Italy. The peninsula was divided by various mini-states and their rivalries. To the south lay the Papal States and the Kingdom of Naples, and to the east, the Republic of Venice. To balance those powers, the Medicis relied on an alliance with the dukes of Milan.

In 1471, Francesco della Rovere ascended the papal throne as Pope Sixtus IV. Initially, the relationship between Sixtus and Lorenzo was cordial, but within a few years it soured. The pope had a large family to support, and Lorenzo feared that those needs threatened the security of Florence and of the Medicis. For several decades, the Medicis had been the papal bankers, a connection that was beneficial to both parties, but when Sixtus requested a loan to purchase Imola for one of his nephews, a city Lorenzo considered to be within the Florentine sphere of influence, Lorenzo refused. Sixtus ended the papal connection with the Medici bank and turned to another Florentine banking family, the Pazzis.

The Pazzis, though connected to the Medicis through marriage, were political and economic rivals. In addition to the Imola loan, other issues combined that led to a plot, known as the Pazzi conspiracy, to remove the Medicis from power. Sixtus stated that while he wished the Medicis to be gone, he did not want it accomplished by murder. It is doubtful, however, that Sixtus truly believed that such an end could be attained without violence. The other conspirators turned to assassination.

The conspirators struck on a Sunday in April, 1478, during the High Mass in the cathedral of Florence. They were partially successful: Giuliano, Lorenzo's brother, was stabbed to death. Lorenzo, however, though injured, survived. Florence rallied to Lorenzo. Most of the conspirators, including leading members of the Pazzi family, were quickly seized and brutally executed. Sixtus responded by accusing Lorenzo and Florence of murder. Lorenzo was excommunicated from the Church, and Florence was placed under an interdict. Because of the animosity toward Sixtus, however, the churches of Florence remained open.

Sixtus also declared war on Florence. As a result of the assassination of its duke, Galeazzo Maria Sforza, Milan was of no assistance to Florence, and with King Ferrante of Naples allied to the Papacy, with an economic downturn in part caused by the military situation, and with the onset of plague, life in Florence soon became very difficult. Finally, in an act of calculated courage, Lorenzo journeyed to Naples and placed himself in the hands of Ferrante. Although he had some indication that

Naples might be willing to agree to a treaty with Florence, Lorenzo's action was still a gamble. A treaty was agreed to, and Lorenzo was returned to Florence as a hero.

Afterward, Lorenzo took an even greater interest in public affairs. His power in Florence increased, although constitutionally he was still only a private citizen. In 1484, Sixtus died, and his successor, Innocent VIII, developed a close relationship with Lorenzo, sealed with the marriage of one of Lorenzo's daughters to one of Innocent's sons. Lorenzo also concerned himself with the relations of the other Italian states, and until his death, major conflict was avoided. To what degree his policies were responsible for peace is impossible to ascertain, but Lorenzo received the credit. As Scipio Ammirato noted, Florence

> remained free of all troubles, to the great reputation of Lorenzo. The Italian princes also enjoyed peace, so that, with everything quiet beyond her frontier and with no disturbances at home, Florence . . . gave herself up to the arts and pleasures of peace.

The arts and pleasures of peace were an integral part of Lorenzo's life and character. He arranged festivals and took part in jousts. He was a patron as well as a colleague of various writers and artists, including Michelangelo. He himself was a poet of considerable ability and a supporter of the Universities of Florence and Pisa. Suitably, on his deathbed, one of his last statements was to express regret that he was not going to live to assist in completing a friend's library.

SIGNIFICANCE

Lorenzo de' Medici died in the spring of 1492 at Careggi, one of the family's villas outside Florence. Inheriting his father's medical maladies, Lorenzo in his last years suffered increasingly from gout and other illnesses. He was only forty-three. Shortly before his death, Lorenzo received Girolamo Savonarola, a Dominican monk who had earlier become a notable figure in Florentine life for his vehement condemnations of Renaissance society in general and Lorenzo in particular. Within two years, Savonarola became the ruler of Florence. Lorenzo's son, Piero, had neither his father's abilities nor his luck, and the Medicis were forced into exile.

Yet Medici wealth and influence were not extinguished. Just before Lorenzo's death, one of his sons, Giovanni, age sixteen, had become a cardinal in the Catholic Church. In 1512, the Medicis returned to Florence from exile, and in the following year, Giovanni was elected pope as Leo X. He died in 1521, and after a brief hiatus his cousin, Giulio, the illegitimate son of Lorenzo's brother, ascended the papal throne as Clement VII. In 1533, Clement performed the marriage of Catherine de Médicis to the son of King Francis I of France. She became one of the most powerful women of the sixteenth century. In Florence, the Medicis became hereditary dukes. The republic was over.

Lorenzo was a controversial figure in his own era and has remained so ever since. His status is suggested by the epithet that frequently accompanies his name: Il Magnifico (the Magnificent). During his era that appellation was used as an honorary title for various Florentine officials; in time, however, it was applied only to Lorenzo. Fifteenth century Florence epitomizes the civilization of the Renaissance, and Lorenzo the Magnificent remains inseparable from the history of that civilization and that city. His reputation has fluctuated; he has been praised for qualities he perhaps did not possess, and he has been condemned for activities that were not within his responsibility. One of his critics was his fellow Florentine, the historian Francesco Guicciardini, an avid republican in ideology. Still, even Guicciardini had to admit that if Florence was not free under Lorenzo, "it would have been impossible for it to have had a better or more pleasing tyrant."

—Eugene Larson

FURTHER READING

Ady, Cecilia M. *Lorenzo dei Medici and Renaissance Italy*. London: English Universities Press, 1970. There has been no major biography of Lorenzo in English in recent decades; Ady's work is the most satisfactory substitute.

Hale, J. R. *Florence and the Medici: The Pattern of Control*. London: Thames and Hudson, 1977. This study of the Medicis traces the family from its earliest days through its decline in the eighteenth century. Hale places Lorenzo within the overall context of Florentine politics.

Hibbert, Christopher. *The House of the Medici: Its Rise and Fall*. New York: William Morrow, 1975. The author is a prominent narrative historian who has written many works on English and Italian subjects. A well-written survey of the Medicis.

Mallett, Michael, and Nicholas Mann, eds. *Lorenzo the Magnificent: Culture and Politics*. London: Warburg Institute, University of London, 1996. Anthology of papers presented at a colloquium marking the five

hundredth anniversary of Lorenzo's death. Covers the arts, politics and social history, and public spectacle at the heart of Lorenzo's rule. Includes illustrations, maps, bibliographic references, and index.

Marchand, Eckart, and Alison Wright, eds. *With and Without the Medici: Studies in Tuscan Art and Patronage, 1434-1530*. Brookfield, Vt.: Ashgate, 1998. Anthology of essays on Renaissance art and the Medici family. Includes illustrations, bibliographic references, and index.

Martines, Lauro. *April Blood: The Plot Against the Medici*. New York: Oxford University Press, 2003. Somewhat revisionist view of the assassination of Lorenzo's brother and Lorenzo's subsequent crackdown. Argues that the plot was a reaction to the Medici's corruption and that Lorenzo's over-reaction harmed his family's reputation with the citizens of Florence and helped to bring about the Medicis' eventual downfall. Includes illustrations, maps, bibliographic references, index.

Medici, Lorenzo de'. *The Autobiography of Lorenzo de' Medici the Magnificent: A Commentary on My Sonnets Together with the Text of "Il comento" in the Critical Edition of Tiziano Zanato*. Translated by James Wyatt Cook. Binghamton, N.Y.: Medieval & Renaissance Texts & Studies, 1995. Modern edition of Lorenzo's autobiography. Includes bibliographic references and index.

Pulci, Luca. "Lorenzo the Magnificent's Utopian State." In *Images of Quattrocento Florence: Selected Writings in Literature, History, and Art*, edited by Stefano Ugo Baldassarri and Arielle Saiber. New Haven, Conn.: Yale University Press, 2000. A study of the goals and vicissitudes of Lorenzo's political machinations.

Rowdon, Maurice. *Lorenzo the Magnificent*. Chicago: Henry Regnery, 1974. This brief work traces the story of the Medicis through the fifteenth century to Lorenzo's death in 1492. The author tells the tale adequately and is especially helpful on the broad economic issues affecting the Medicis. Includes many illustrations.

Williamson, Hugh Ross. *Lorenzo the Magnificent*. New York: G. P. Putnam's Sons, 1974. This volume is similar to Rowdon's work although somewhat more extensive. Like Rowdon, Williamson recites the history of Lorenzo and his family. Includes illustrations.

SEE ALSO: Sandro Botticelli; Catherine de Médicis; Clement VII; Marsilio Ficino; Francis I; Francesco

Guicciardini; Leo X; Louis XI; Niccolò Machiavelli; Cosimo I de' Medici; Michelangelo; Girolamo Savonarola; Sixtus IV.

RELATED ARTICLES in *Great Events from History: The Renaissance & Early Modern Era, 1454-1600:* Early 1460's: Labor Shortages Alter Europe's Social Struc-

ture; 1462: Founding of the Platonic Academy; 1469-1492: Rule of Lorenzo de' Medici; April 26, 1478: Pazzi Conspiracy; 1486-1487: Pico della Mirandola Writes *Oration on the Dignity of Man*; c. 1500: Revival of Classical Themes in Art; May 6, 1527-February, 1528: Sack of Rome.

MEHMED II
Sultan of the Ottoman Empire (r. 1444-1446, 1451-1481)

Mehmed II expanded Ottoman territory and reunited a fragmented empire following lengthy civil strife. His greatest achievement was the seizure, sacking, and rebuilding of the Byzantine Empire's capital Constantinople, marking an end to Christian rule in Asia Minor and a virtual end to the Middle Ages.

BORN: March 30, 1432; Adrianople, Ottoman Empire (now Edirne, Turkey)
DIED: May 3, 1481; Hunkârçayırı, near Maltepe, Ottoman Empire (now in Turkey)
ALSO KNOWN AS: Mehmet II; Mehmed Fatih; Muḥammad II; Mehmed the Conqueror
AREAS OF ACHIEVEMENT: Warfare and conquest, military, government and politics, religion and theology

EARLY LIFE

Mehmed (meh-MEHT) II was the third son of Sultan Murad II and, possibly, Devlet Hatun, a slave girl of non-Muslim origin. Mehmed's father voluntarily retired from his throne in 1444, yielding the reins of government to his twelve-year-old son.

Mehmed's early years were spent in the harem, the women's quarters, of the Edirne palace. Under the tutelage of Murad's grand viziers (chief ministers), Mehmed was sultan from August of 1444 to May of 1446, after his father's abdication. Mehmed lost his first reign, however, when Murad was recalled to his throne to lead an army against an advancing coalition of Hungarian, Byzantine, Venetian, and papal forces at Varna, now in Bulgaria.

Mehmed's second accession as the seventh sultan of the Ottoman Empire was on February 18, 1451. After his initial training, Mehmed became a provincial governor and was in charge of Rumelia, the European (Balkan) portion of the empire. In December, 1447, or January, 1448, Mehmed had a son with a slave girl named Gülbahar. The child was to become Sultan Bayezid II. In 1449, Mehmed's father arranged Mehmed's marriage to

Sitt Hatun, a wealthy girl, without prior consultation. Another son, Mustafa, was born, possibly from this marriage, in 1450.

LIFE'S WORK

Mehmed's thirty-year rule was marked by a series of major conquests but also some setbacks. His crowning glory, for which he had been preparing both diplomatically and militarily since his accession, was the fifty-day siege of the Byzantine Empire's capital, Constantinople, in April and May of 1453, earning the sultan the sobriquet Fatih (the conqueror). The Ottomans managed this climactic event by breaching the walls of the city with very heavy artillery and through skillful strategy by land and water, including the building of forts to control the naval approaches to the city. Byzantine emperor Constantine XI Palaeologus was killed on the battlefield.

Mehmed moved his capital to the city from Adrianople and also repopulated it after a long decline. This had been only the beginning of his military conquests, however. In rapid succession, the sultan launched campaigns in Serbia, the Black Sea region, Moldavia, Trabzon, Morea (now Peloponnese, Greece), Amastrias, Wallachia, Lesbos, Bosnia, Hungary, Albania, Karaman, Euboea, Transylvania, Crimea, and points in between. Despite this sizable extension of Ottoman territory in the Balkans, Anatolia, the Black Sea region, and the Aegean, it was not always smooth sailing for Mehmed. He was repulsed at Belgrade in 1456 and in Hungary in 1474. Also, after repeated attacks, the well-fortified island of Rhodes stood firm. Even Albania could not be subjugated until 1479, after the death of its hero, Skanderbeg (George Kastrioti). Otranto, now in Italy, barely remained under Ottoman rule for a few months following Mehmed's death.

In the meantime, Mehmed founded a system of secondary-level palace schools to educate Christian boys, ages eight to eighteen, who were selected from among the brightest and sturdiest of their age through the *devshirme*, the levy of conscripts who were not Turkish,

Mehmed II. (Library of Congress)

charitable foundations for the benefit of the imperial treasury. His land reform enabled the administration to regain direct control of thousands of villages that had lapsed into private hands, and he codified the functions of public officials. He legalized the custom of fratricide, by which an heir-presumptive was entitled to eliminate his siblings—who were potential political rivals—in the interest of avoiding civil strife on account of the succession. For this reason, the sultan had ordered the drowning of his own infant brother.

Mehmed clearly had a complex personality. He was wary, ruthless, calculating, vengeful, and cruel at times, but also magnanimous, being very tolerant in religious matters, for example. He was a patron of the arts, a poet, and an accomplished linguist, demonstrating competence in Turkish, Arabic, Greek, Persian, and even some Italian and Serbian. He ordered the building of mosques and other public facilities, and he was an accomplished gardener. His Topkapi Saray (Topkapi Palace) at the entrance of the Bosporus remained the chief domicile of sultans for centuries.

His death occurred at the start of yet another military campaign. Mehmed left two sons, Bayezid II and Cem (or Jem), but his favorite son, Mustafa, died during illness in 1475. Some have accused Bayezid, who was on bad terms with his father, of killing his father, who died, ostensibly, from a sudden, acute ailment.

SIGNIFICANCE

The fall of Constantinople, signifying the end of millennial Christian rule in Asia Minor and the close of the Middle Ages, was significant in many ways. With the Byzantine Empire's fall, Mehmed managed to extend the Ottoman Empire substantially in the Balkans, the Black Sea region, Central Europe, the Caucasus, the Arabian peninsula, and North Africa. In fact, the overthrow of the Byzantines marked the real beginning of the Ottoman Empire, even though by that time, six other sultans had girded themselves with the sword of Osman, the founder of the dynasty.

These often-successful military feats, dependent on an expanded army and a large navy, were paralleled by civilian accomplishments. These involved the ruling institution and Ottoman policy toward the increasing number of non-Turkish and non-Muslim minorities in the far-flung empire. The booty from conquests and the collection of tribute funded much public spending. An Islamic military theocracy was thus launched toward a long period of dynamic expansion and development.

—*Peter B. Heller*

in the Balkans. Following their conversion to Islam, these students emerged from the palace schools as soldiers or officials. Some of them also learned skills such as shipbuilding and architecture.

Mehmed regularized the millets—semiautonomous nations or communities—on a religious basis. There were four millets initially: the Muslim, which had priority, the Greek Orthodox, the Armenian Gregorian, and the Jewish. The Catholic millet was not established until the reign of Süleyman the Magnificent. Each was under the jurisdiction of its own religious head and subject to its own legal system. They were expected to be loyal to the sultan, with their heads being responsible for the good behavior of their coreligionists. They also had to pay the appropriate taxes.

Mehmed also created an artillery corps, which was critical in many sieges. In cases of need, he managed to stay on the right side of the elite Janissary (infantry) corps, when there were rumblings in their ranks. He lavished them with gifts and even demobilized some of the war-weary men.

Mehmed was also skillful in public administration, establishing state monopolies and confiscating Muslim

FURTHER READING

Babinger, Franz. *Mehmed the Conqueror and His Time*. Translated by Ralph Manheim Edited by William C. Hickman. Princeton, N.J.: Princeton University Press, 1978. An authoritative annotated biography of the sultan that focuses on diplomacy and military and political history. Appendices, glossary, illustrations, and index.

Beg, Tursun. *The History of Mehmed the Conqueror*. Translated by Halil Inalcik and Rhoads Murphey. Minneapolis, Minn.: Bibliotheca Islamica, 1978. A summary English translation of the original Turkish version by a member of Mehmed's inner circle. Appendix, glossary, chronology, map, and Turkish-text index.

Imber, Colin. *The Ottoman Empire, 1300-1481*. Istanbul, Turkey: Isis Press, 1990. A detailed chronological narrative of the empire's political and military history, based on a thorough analysis of primary sources. Glossary, bibliography, maps, and index.

Inalcik, Halil. "Istanbul: An Islamic City." *Journal of Islamic Studies* 1 (1990): 1-23. A well-known Turkish scholar describes the early years of Constantinople as the Ottoman capital and Mehmed's urban policies.

McNeese, Tim. *Constantinople*. New York: Chelsea House, 2003. Concise and basic account of the circumstances that led to the imperial city's siege in 1453.

Nicolle, David. *Constantinople, 1453*. London: Osprey, 2000. Military history of the city's siege, fall, and aftermath. Chronology, bibliography, appendix, and index.

Runciman, Steven. *The Fall of Constantinople, 1453*. 1965. Reprint. New York: Cambridge University Press, 1990. A thoroughly researched and detailed account by a celebrated British historian. Appendix, bibliography, map, and illustrations.

SEE ALSO: Bayezid II; Charles V; İbrahim Paşa; Matthias I Corvinus; Mehmed III; Pius II; Qāytbāy; Süleyman the Magnificent.
RELATED ARTICLES in *Great Events from History: The Renaissance & Early Modern Era, 1454-1600:* 1454-1481: Rise of the Ottoman Empire; April 9, 1454: Peace of Lodi; April 14, 1457-July 2, 1504: Reign of Stephen the Great; 1463-1479: Ottoman-Venetian War; 1469-1508: Ak Koyunlu Dynasty Controls Iraq and Northern Iran; 1478-1482: Albanian-Turkish Wars End; 1481-1512: Reign of Bayezid II and Ottoman Civil Wars.

MEHMED III
Sultan of the Ottoman Empire (r. 1595-1603)

Mehmed III was a weak ruler whose reign was marked by political corruption, rebellion in Anatolia, and war with Austria, which continued the slow decline of the Ottoman Empire. He was successful, however, in developing initial defenses against Austrian encroachment into Ottoman territory in the Balkans.

BORN: May 26, 1566; Manisa, Ottoman Empire (now in Turkey)
DIED: December 22, 1603; Constantinople, Ottoman Empire (now Istanbul, Turkey)
AREAS OF ACHIEVEMENT: Government and politics, warfare and conquest

EARLY LIFE

Mehmed (meh-MEHT) III, who became ruler of the Ottoman Empire, was the son of the Ottoman sultan Murad III. As was the custom among Ottoman rulers, the caring and raising of the heir-apparent was controlled by the sultan's advisers, so Mehmed was separated from his father and his mother, Safiye Sultan, possibly an Albanian.

As the eldest of Murad's twenty sons and presumptive heir to the Ottoman throne, Mehmed lived in luxury and was educated by tutors. He spent much of his youth, however, in fear for his own life. Because the eldest son was considered a threat by each sultan, those sons would have been watchful of assassination attempts. Constantinople was a dangerous place for him. The political intrigue in the capital and his close proximity to the Murad clan heightened fears that political power would be lost if he were killed. Mehmed was saved because he spent much of his early adult life in exile. Mehmed had been sent to the provinces by his father because of his uncontrollable temper and proneness to violence, keeping him out of Constantinople for more than a dozen years; he returned to preside over his father's funeral.

LIFE'S WORK

Mehmed III's mother and chief adviser was the daughter of Venetian nobility. According to legend, Safiye Sultan was either forced by the Ottomans to become part of Sultan Murad's harem or was planted there as a high-level spy. Safiye dominated the thirteen-year-old Murad, was mother to his first son, Mehmed, and clashed with Murad's equally dominating mother, Nur Banu. When Murad's mother died, Safiye became highly influential, making many of the political and military decisions for the empire. When Murad died, Safiye sought to expand her influence over her son Mehmed.

After Murad's body was interred, Mehmed saw his mother for the first time in twelve years. Safiye was able to convince him to abide by Ottoman law, which allowed him to eliminate Murad's other children, the males of which might have a claim to the throne. The law, enacted under Sultan Mehmed II, allowed any sultan to kill family members who might challenge his rule. Mehmed exhibited the weakness that he would show throughout his rule by following his mother's suggestion to conduct mass murder.

The murder of Mehmed's nineteen brothers proceeded in the fashion typical of the Ottomans. Mehmed gathered his brothers in his throne room and ordered them to be ritually circumcised. After this procedure, all nineteen were murdered by strangulation by persons unable to speak or hear, which prevented the appointed assassins from spreading gossip about the brothers' deaths. The brothers were given a lavish funeral with full honors, then were interred with their father, possibly a sign that Mehmed was upset and embarrassed by the slaughter. Most of Mehmed's brothers were under the age of ten, making his actions even more horrifying. He was the last sultan to dispose of family members in such a manner. After Mehmed's reign, male members of a sultan's family who might have claim to the throne would be exiled and isolated from the world.

Mehmed's twenty-seven sisters fared better than his brothers. They were exiled to a convent. At the same time, Murad's concubines and personal servants were also exiled from Constantinople. Seven of Murad's wives were pregnant with his children, so they were murdered by being sewn into bags and drowned to ensure that no one would challenge the sultan.

An imaginative depiction of the death and violence that occurred upon Mehmed III's accession to the throne. (F. R. Niglutsch)

Mehmed III followed in the footsteps of his father, gathering a large harem that kept his focus away from ruling. Safiye, free of challenges from the sultan's relatives, became the main political force in the empire. She was responsible for many of the political appointments, including those of governors of provinces and of lower officials. Bribery was the main strategy for getting Safiye to approve an appointment to and for keeping a high government position. Once in office, the official would have to maintain payments to Safiye to prevent other "bidders" from taking the office away. This corruption weakened the Ottoman political system, as the most competent were prevented from rising to important positions.

Safiye also seized control over foreign policy from her son. While Mehmed was enjoying the good life of Constantinople, his mother negotiated with the Ottomans' allies and enemies. Her close relationship with Catherine de Médicis prevented a war with the Venetians. She was less successful when handling the Austrians, who had attacked the empire in 1593. It was the military crisis in the Balkans that raised Mehmed from his comfort to join his troops along the Danube River.

In 1596, Mehmed III took personal control of the Ottoman army in Europe. The Ottomans had suffered a series of setbacks against the Austrians and were facing revolts in some of their eastern European territories. Mehmed believed that his presence would bolster troop morale and drive them to push the Austrians from Ottoman territory.

Mehmed's troops were successful, though his own military abilities were limited. During a three-day battle on the Hungarian plain, the sultan watched his army from a distance. When the Austrians swarmed forward and appeared ready to rout the Ottomans, the sultan counseled retreat. Only a late cavalry charge on the third day of the battle drove the Austrians back and killed some thirty thousand men as they struggled to cross a nearby river.

Mehmed's personal leadership did instill, at least initially, a sense of victory in the Ottoman army. His departure in 1597 to return to Constantinople, however, saw the Turkish forces descend into chaos and once again lose battles to the Austrians. The Austrian war continued through the remainder of Mehmed's reign, but he never became directly involved. Instead, his attention was drawn to a gathering rebellion in the main region of the empire known as Anatolia.

The Ottoman Empire was made up of a mix of ethnicities and religions, and the army was drawn from this population, creating many armed, clashing groups. During Mehmed's reign, the *Jelalis*, a peasant army that received less pay and fewer perks than thse regular army, challenged Ottoman rule because of a series of economic and social crises. Led by Deli Hassan, the *Jelalis* rampaged across Anatolia. The regular army was able to quell the revolt, but not until thousands were killed or forced to flee their homes.

Mehmed lived long enough to see the end of the revolt. In October, 1603, it was prophesied that disaster would befall him soon, and before the end of the year, he was dead. His passing was followed by the murder of Safiye and the rise of the inept Ahmed I, Mehmed's son, as sultan.

SIGNIFICANCE

Mehmed III's reign suffered from political corruption and a series of wars and rebellions. Raised separate from his family and father, Mehmed III had little experience in directing government or the military. He delegated much of that power to his mother, who directed the domestic policies of the empire.

Mehmed followed in the footsteps of his father but was lost in the pleasures and privileges of being a sultan. When he died in 1603, he left an empire struggling with outside enemies and a political system that was so corrupt it was unable to solve many of the problems it faced.

—Douglas Clouatre

FURTHER READING

Barber, Noel. *The Sultans*. New York: Simon and Schuster, 1973. This work focuses on the Ottoman sultans and their role in the rise and decline of the empire. It examines the major trends and leaders in Ottoman politics and explains how the declining quality of the empire's leadership led to its collapse.

Goffman, David. *The Ottoman Empire and Early Modern Europe*. New York: Cambridge University Press, 2002. This works examines the relationship between the Muslim Ottomans and the Christians in eastern and western Europe. It discusses political and military conflicts and how they affected both regions.

Goodwin, Jason. *Lords of the Horizon: A History of the Ottoman Empire*. New York: Henry Holt, 1999. A broad-based work that examines the Ottomans from their capture of Constantinople in 1453 to their decline and fall at the end of World War I. The book discusses the political, social, and military aspects of the empire.

Hathaway, June. *Mutiny and Rebellion in the Ottoman Empire*. Madison: University of Wisconsin Press, 2003. Hathaway's work examines how the Ottomans dealt with the various ethnic and religious groups within their borders, the military rebellions by these groups, and military organizations such as the Janissaries.

SEE ALSO: Bayezid II; Catherine de Médicis; Charles V; İbrahim Paşa; Matthias I Corvinus; Mehmed II; Pius II.
RELATED ARTICLES in *Great Events from History: The Renaissance & Early Modern Era, 1454-1600:* 1574-1595: Reign of Murad III; 1589: Second Janissary Revolt in Constantinople; 1593-1606: Ottoman-Austrian War.

PHILIPP MELANCHTHON
German religious scholar

Melanchthon, a Humanist scholar who became a close associate of Martin Luther in the Protestant Reformation, was the author of the Augsburg Confession of 1530, basically a summary of Luther's teachings, which remains the fundamental confessional platform of worldwide Lutheranism. Melanchthon also is credited with having established the German school system.

BORN: February 16, 1497; Bretten, Palatinate (now in Germany)
DIED: April 19, 1560; Wittenberg, Saxony (now in Germany)
ALSO KNOWN AS: Philipp Schwartzerd
AREAS OF ACHIEVEMENT: Religion and theology, education, scholarship

EARLY LIFE

Philipp Melanchthon (meh-LANK-tehn) was born in the village of Bretten in the German Rhineland, some twenty miles south of Heidelberg. His given name was Philipp Schwartzerd; his father, Georg Schwartzerd, was an armorer under the Palatinate princes. His mother, Barbara Reuter, was a niece of the great Humanist and Hebrew scholar Johannes Reuchlin, whose influence over Philipp can be seen not only in his early studies but also in his Humanist leanings.

The eldest of five children, Philipp proved himself something of a child prodigy under the direction of his great-uncle Reuchlin, at that time regarded as the best Greek and Hebrew scholar in Germany. It was Reuchlin who first recommended Johann Unger of Pforzheim as Philipp's private tutor and who later caused him to enroll in the Pforzheim Latin school, one of the most celebrated in the Palatinate. At Pforzheim, Philipp came under the influence of Georg Simler and John Hiltebrant, both classicists and excellent scholars of Latin, Hebrew, and Greek. It was there that Reuchlin, in recognition of Philipp's accomplishments in the Greek classics, fol-

lowed a contemporary custom and declared that such a brilliant young man should no longer be known by the humble name Schwartzerd (meaning black earth) but should henceforth be called by its Greek equivalent—"Melanchthon."

In October, 1509, Melanchthon followed the advice of Reuchlin and Simler and enrolled in the University of Heidelberg. During his years at Heidelberg, he seems to have pursued his studies for the most part by himself, preferring the Greek classics, such as the orations of Cicero and Demosthenes, to the medieval Scholastic orientation of Heidelberg. There, he also studied the writings of Rodolphus Agricola and the warm devotional sermons of Johann Geiler von Kaysersberg.

In 1511, Melanchthon, not yet fifteen years of age, was awarded the bachelor of arts degree from Heidelberg. Yet after another year of devoted study of Scholastic philosophy, his application for the master of arts degree was denied, primarily because of his youth and boyish appearance. Small for his age, Melanchthon had a somewhat shy and awkward manner about him and suffered from attacks of fever from time to time. Later portraits of him reveal a more serious demeanor, a thoughtful face marked by a very high forehead, penetrating eyes, and an aquiline, craggy nose. When lecturing on a topic of particular interest, he is said to have visibly changed in appearance, with his voice becoming clear and forceful, his actions animated, and his large blue eyes sparkling with delight and excitement.

In the fall of 1512, again at the advice of Reuchlin, Melanchthon left Heidelberg and moved south to Tübingen, Reuchlin's own university, where he would reside as a student and later as professor for the next six years. A much newer university than Heidelberg, Tübingen had been founded in 1477 and was less under the influence of medieval Scholastic philosophy. At Tübingen, Melanchthon heard lectures on Aristotle that fascinated him for years. There, he came under the influence of the great Desiderius Erasmus, as well as certain "reformers before the Reformation," such as John Wessel. He also began serious study of Hebrew and Latin. In 1514, he was awarded the master of arts degree, the first among eleven in his class. He then became a tutor at the university and, two years later, professor of rhetoric and history. During his Tübingen years, he published translations of Plutarch, Pythagoras, Agricola, and Terence Lucidas, as well as a Greek grammar and a handbook of general history, and began major works on Aristotle and Aratus. Melanchthon and his work were highly praised by Erasmus, and at Tübingen he became widely recognized as the finest Humanistic scholar in Germany.

LIFE'S WORK

In the autumn of 1518, at the age of twenty-one, Melanchthon was called to become professor of Greek at the University of Wittenberg, once again largely as a result of the highest recommendation of his kinsman Reuchlin. At Wittenberg, he would spend the rest of his career; marry and rear a family; come under the powerful influence of Martin Luther, his closest friend for nearly thirty years; and become intimately involved in the Protestant Reformation and the education of Germany's youth. Only four

Philipp Melanchthon. (Library of Congress)

days after he arrived in Wittenberg, on August 29, 1518, Melanchthon delivered a lecture on the improvement of studies, in which he called for fresh study not only of the Latin and Greek classics but also of Hebrew and the Bible. This was an indication of his early interest in education, which would bear fruit in later years.

Melanchthon began his own lectures in Wittenberg with Homer and the Epistle to Titus. Luther was so inspired by Melanchthon's lectures, some of which attracted as many as two thousand persons, including professors, ministers, and various dignitaries as well as students, that he made much more rapid progress in his translation of Scripture into German than he had made before. Melanchthon assisted Luther in collating the various Greek versions and revising some of his translations.

In November, 1520, Melanchthon married Katharine Krapp, daughter of the Wittenberg burgomaster, apparently primarily because Luther had concluded that it was time for Melanchthon to marry. Four children were born of this apparently happy union, which lasted thirty-seven years.

Melanchthon was first drawn into the Reformation controversies when he accompanied Luther and others to Leipzig in June and July of 1519 for the Leipzig Disputation between Luther and Andreas Carlstadt on one side and Johann Eck of Ingolstadt on the other. Melanchthon attended as a spectator but was shortly afterward attacked by Eck for aiding Luther and Carlstadt. Melanchthon replied to Eck in a brief treatise, in which he supported Luther's argument on the supreme authority of Scripture and denied the authority of the church Fathers on whom Eck had relied so heavily in Leipzig. From that point onward, Melanchthon's die was cast with the Protestant Reformers. Shortly thereafter, at Luther's insistence, Melanchthon was made lecturer in theology in addition to his professorship in Greek. The degree bachelor of divinity was conferred on him; it was the only theological degree he ever accepted.

In 1521, during Luther's confinement in Wartburg, Melanchthon became the main leader of the Reformation in Wittenberg. At that time, he had chosen Paul's Epistle to the Romans as the subject for his lectures and had compiled from that letter a series of classified statements of scriptural truths that were to become one of the most influential manuals of Protestant theology. He wrote them primarily for his own personal use and called these statements "common places," or *Loci communes rerum theologicarum* (1521; *The Loci Communes*, 1944), following a phrase of Cicero. At the encouragement of others, he allowed them to be published, and this document almost immediately established him in the theological forefront of the Reformation. Luther once even praised *The Loci Communes* as worthy of a place in the canon of Scripture.

For most of the remainder of his career, Melanchthon was greatly occupied with theological controversy and debate, largely in defense of Luther against charges brought by the Roman Catholics. He insisted that Luther was accused of heresy not because of any departure from Scripture but because he opposed the universities, the Fathers, and the councils of the Church in their theological errors. During Luther's absence from Wittenberg in 1521 and 1522, a much more radical group of Reformers took control, primarily under the leadership of Carlstadt. Ecclesiastical vestments were abolished; persons were admitted to communion without confession or repentance; and pastoral oversight was neglected, as were hospitals and prisons. Melanchthon, the scholar, opposed such radical changes but was powerless to check them until Luther's return in March, 1522. After he had restored some semblance of order to the Reformation in Wittenberg, Luther, with Melanchthon's encouragement, completed his translation of the entire Bible into German, in many ways his own most important work and the one which introduced the Reformation to the masses.

After the First Diet of Speyer in 1526, Melanchthon was one of those commissioned to visit the various reformed states and issue regulations for the churches. This resulted in the publication, in 1528, of his *Unterricht der Visitatorn* (visitation articles), which contained not only a statement of evangelical Protestant theology but also an outline of education for the elementary grades. This was shortly thereafter enacted into law, and, as a result, Germany had the first real Protestant public school system, one which was soon copied far and wide. Hundreds of teachers were also trained in Melanchthon's methods and thousands of students instructed by his textbooks. He encouraged the establishment of universities and revised dozens of schools' curricula. All this earned for him the title "preceptor of Germany." His influence on German education can hardly be overstated.

Moderate and at peace, Melanchthon was also present at the Second Diet of Speyer, when the protest, from which the name "Protestant" originated, was lodged against the Roman Catholic majority in 1529. He was the leading representative of Protestant theology at the Diet of Augsburg in 1530 and the author of the Augsburg Confession of 1530. This document remains the basic confessional statement of worldwide Lutheranism, which has influenced nearly every subsequent major Protestant creed. Melanchthon tried very hard to be conciliatory in the Augsburg Confession without sacrificing important convictions. He met with papal representatives amid frequent charges of collaboration in an effort to reconcile Protestant-Roman Catholic differences. Eventually, he wrote a spirited defense of the Augsburg Confession entitled *Apologie der Confession aus dem Latin verdeudschet* (1531; *The Apologie*, 1536), also generally recognized as one of the best writings of the Reformation.

Melanchthon staunchly held the middle ground between more radical Reformers and the Roman Catholic theologians. He defended the Reformation doctrines of justification by faith and the authority of the Scriptures; yet for the sake of unity, he was willing to accept a modified form of the Papacy. After Luther's death in 1546, Melanchthon's later years were marked by poor physical health and major theological disputes, especially the so-called adiaphoristic controversy and arguments concerning the role of humans in salvation.

Adiaphora, religious beliefs and practices of indifference, were areas where flexibility or compromise may be necessary. Melanchthon, however, was unfairly accused of including among the adiaphora such essentials to the Protestant cause as justification by faith. He was, indeed, willing to recognize the necessity of good works for salvation, not as in any way meriting God's favor but as the inevitable fruits of faith. Melanchthon eventually also seems to have rejected the doctrine of predestination, which he earlier shared with Luther. In *The Apologie*, he represented the mercy of God as extended to all, yet he insisted that God draws to himself only those who are willing to turn to him. Humans thus have an important role in the process of salvation, although a secondary one of response to God's initiative in the written and preached Word. Melanchthon was unjustly accused of the heresy of Pelagianism as a result of his theological views, and his influence declined during his lifetime. It is only in modern times that his contributions have come to be fully appreciated.

SIGNIFICANCE

Melanchthon is a prominent example of an outstanding theologian and scholar whose works have been neglected. His was a melding of the twin influences of the Renaissance and the Reformation. His services to educational reform in Germany, as well as to classical scholarship and Humanism, were outstanding, but it was as a theologian that he excelled. Throughout his lifetime, he tried to be a reconciler, and his influence was consistently thrown on the side of moderation and peace. Yet he was misunderstood and unappreciated by many of those on both sides of the great theological controversies of his age.

—*C. Fitzhugh Spragins*

FURTHER READING

Hildebrandt, Franz. *Melanchthon: Alien or Ally?* Cambridge, England: Cambridge University Press, 1946. Reprint. New York: Kraus Reprint, 1968. An exploration of the complex relationship between Luther and Melanchthon, this volume is primarily an examination of the five main "concessions" said to have been made by Melanchthon to elements outside the inner circle of Protestant evangelicals. Particularly valuable in highlighting some of the most important doctrinal differences between Luther and Melanchthon.

Maag, Karin, ed. *Melanchthon in Europe: His Work and Influence Beyond Wittenberg.* Grand Rapids, Mich.: Baker Books, 1999. Anthology of essays on Melanchthon covers such topics as his correspondence with John Calvin, his strategic alliance with the Swiss reformers, and the theological function of his rhetoric. Includes illustrations, bibliographic references, and index.

Mann, Jeffrey K. *Shall We Sin? Responding to the Antinomian Question in Lutheran Theology.* New York: Peter Lang, 2003. Examination of the responses of five major Lutheran thinkers to the question of the consequences of sin for those justified by faith. Evaluates the responses given by Luther himself, by Melanchthon, and by Philip Jakob Spener, Søren Kierkegaard, and Dietrich Bonhoeffer. Includes bibliography.

Manschreck, Clyde L. *Melanchthon: The Quiet Reformer.* New York: Abingdon Press, 1958. One of the most important works on Melanchthon currently available in English. Basically a historical approach. Manschreck also gives a sympathetic and lively description of the doctrinal issues that preoccupied so much of Melanchthon's career. The volume is copiously documented and indexed, with a variety of interesting illustrations.

Melanchthon, Philipp. *Melanchthon on Christian Doctrine: Loci Communes, 1555.* Edited and translated by Clyde L. Manschreck. New York: Oxford University Press, 1965. The first translation into English of the 1555 (final) edition of *The Loci Communes*, this volume was translated and edited by the English-speaking world's foremost Melanchthon scholar. Contains a valuable preface by Manschreck and an introduction

by Hans Engelland, a German Melanchthon scholar. Good bibliography and index.

Richard, James W. *Philip Melanchthon: The Protestant Preceptor of Germany, 1497-1560.* New York: G. P. Putnam's Sons, 1898. Reprint. New York: B. Franklin Reprints, 1974. One of the best nineteenth century biographies of Melanchthon available in English. Richard includes many quotations from Melanchthon's letters and other writings in this volume. Carefully documented and includes a helpful index and many illustrations.

Vajta, Vilmos, ed. *Luther and Melanchthon in the History and Theology of the Reformation.* Philadelphia: Muhlenberg Press, 1961. A series of addresses on the relationship between Luther and Melanchthon delivered before the Luther Research Congress. Most are in German, but among the English contributions of particular interest are "Luther and Melanchthon" by Wilhelm Pauck, in which the inseparability of the two theologians' works is clearly demonstrated, and "Melanchthon in America" by Theodore G. Tappert, which explores the revival of interest in Melanchthon during the first half of the nineteenth century in the United States.

Wengert, Timothy J. *Human Freedom, Christian Righteousness: Philip Melanchthon's Exegetical Dispute with Erasmus of Rotterdam.* New York: Oxford University Press, 1998. Argues against the common view that Melanchthon was sympathetic to Erasmus in his dispute against Luther. Explores Melanchthon's Humanist theology in relation to issues such as free will, divine vs. human righteousness, and the proper biblical interpretation of political order. Includes bibliographic references and index.

Wilson, George. *Philip Melanchthon: 1497-1560.* London: Religious Tract Society, 1897. Published after the death of its author, this brief biographical work is a more personal memoir than the volumes by Manschreck and Richard. Wilson had planned a much more complete work on Melanchthon than this but did not live to finish it.

SEE ALSO: Martin Bucer; John Calvin; Miles Coverdale; Desiderius Erasmus; Hugh Latimer; Martin Luther; Rheticus; William Tyndale; Huldrych Zwingli.

RELATED ARTICLES in *Great Events from History: The Renaissance & Early Modern Era, 1454-1600:* c. 1510: Invention of the Watch; 1550's-c. 1600: Educational Reforms in Europe; September 25, 1555: Peace of Augsburg.

BERNARDINO DE MENDOZA
Spanish diplomat

Bernardino de Mendoza was head of Spanish diplomatic and intelligence services at the court of England's Queen Elizabeth I and later at the French court of King Henry III. He was involved in the Throckmorton and the Babington plots to overthrow Elizabeth, and he played a prominent role supporting the Catholic League during the French Wars of Religion. Bernardino also wrote one of the most important treatises on the theory and practice of war.

BORN: February 21, 1541; Guadalajara, Spain
DIED: August 3, 1604; Madrid, Spain
AREAS OF ACHIEVEMENT: Government and politics, diplomacy, military, religion and theology

EARLY LIFE

Bernardino de Mendoza (behr-nahr-DEE-noh day MAYN-doh-zah) was the tenth son of Alonso Suárez de Mendoza and Doña Juana Jiménez de Cisneros, counts of Coruña and vice-counts of Torija. He belonged to a small branch of the powerful Mendoza family, which had acquired enormous wealth and influence in Castile since the late 1300's.

Bernardino studied at the prestigious University of Alcalá and graduated in June, 1556, with a degree in arts and philosophy. In October of the same year, he received his master's degree and was elected fellow of the College of San Ildefonso, where he spent some time with the future government and military elites of Spain.

He began his military career in 1563-1564, participating in campaigns against the Berbers in North Africa. He also took part in the defense of Malta against the Turks in 1565, fighting under the command of Don Juan of Austria, brother of King Philip II of Spain. In 1567, he accompanied the duke of Alva to Flanders to fight the Protestant rebels, and he distinguished himself as a cavalry captain in the battles of Mook, Mons, and Nijmegen and in the Siege of Haarlem.

In 1574, he received his first serious diplomatic mission and traveled to England to obtain the promise of refuge and succor in English ports for the planned Spanish armada against the Dutch rebels. His mission was successful and, as a reward for his services, he was inducted into the prestigious military order of Santiago and was appointed resident ambassador to the English court in 1578.

LIFE'S WORK

Bernardino de Mendoza's talents as a military officer were matched only by his abilities as a spy and a diplomat. Much of what he accomplished militarily reflects the aggressiveness he had displayed in the battlefields of North Africa and Flanders. Since his arrival in England, Bernardino had fought and plotted indefatigably in defense of his master, King Philip II, and the Catholic cause. The essence of his mission was to prevent Queen Elizabeth I from helping the Dutch rebels and to protect and give support to the English Catholics in whatever manner he could.

Bernardino realized that the policy of coexistence that had informed Spanish-English relations in the first half of the sixteenth century was reaching an end and that a more aggressive approach was needed in order to stop the troublesome and defiant English Tudor monarchy. Spanish ships were suffering from constant harassment and attacks at the hands of English privateers in the high seas, and the religious persecution and repression of Catholic subjects of the queen convinced Bernardino that the policy of coexistence was ending.

In 1583, one of these Catholic subjects, Francis Throckmorton, convinced Bernardino to take part in a plot to murder Elizabeth and enthrone her cousin, Mary, Queen of Scots, with the help of a French invading army. The plot was discovered, and the confession obtained from Throckmorton left no doubt as to Bernardino's involvement. In January, 1584, Bernardino was declared persona non grata (unwelcome) by the English authorities and was ordered to leave the country immediately. He departed with the defiant retort, "Bernardino de Mendoza was not born to disturb countries, but to conquer them."

During his stay in England, Bernardino developed an extensive network of informants and contacts and created very sophisticated methods for encoding and transmitting messages to his king. This experience would serve him well in his next diplomatic mission, at the French court of Henry III. At the time of Mendoza's arrival, Henry was a dissolute and corrupt king who found himself in a difficult political situation. In 1584, his younger brother Francis, duke of Anjou, had suddenly died, which made Henry of Navarre, a Huguenot prince, the new heir apparent to the throne. Navarre looked for support with the Dutch Protestants and, at the same time, the French Catholic League rallied around the powerful aristocrat Henry I of Lorraine, duke of Guise, whom they saw as a stronger and more reliable leader than their own king. Henry I was able to obtain the favor of Philip II, who gave precise instructions to his ambassador to offer military and financial support to the league. Although Bernardino had been busy with the internal affairs of the French court, he kept in touch with his English contacts and managed to contribute to the Babington plot in 1586—another failed attempt to murder Queen Elizabeth and put her Catholic cousin on the English throne.

Bernardino also provided logistic assistance to the Spanish Armada and persuaded Henry I and the Catholic League to enter Paris and overthrow Henry III. Henry I was murdered by Henry III in 1588, and the Armada project became a monumental fiasco that weakened Spanish policy all over the Continent. In 1590, Henry of Navarre laid siege to Paris, and Bernardino helped the Parisians with food and with fortifying the walls of the city.

By this time, he had lost his eyesight completely from chronic glaucoma, a condition that he started to suffer during his years as ambassador at Elizabeth's court. Consumed by the pain of disease and the grief of political failure, he retired from his post and went back to Madrid in 1591. He bought a house next to a convent and died on August 3, 1604. His body was buried in the church of his native Torija, next to a Latin inscription that reads "Nec timeas nec potes" (neither fear nor wish).

Bernardino's role as a schemer and a diplomat has secured him a place in the history of early modern politics and espionage. The range of his talents, however, was much broader. He was a prolific writer and an accomplished military scholar. His *Theorica y practica de guerra* (1595; *Theorique and Practise of Warre*, 1597; theory and practice of war) was one of the most popular and respected books on warfare of the sixteenth and seventeenth centuries (it was translated into Italian in 1596 and then into French and English in 1597). He also wrote *Comentarios de Don Bernardino de Mendoça de lo sucedido en las guerras de los Payses Baxos* (1591; commentaries of Don Bernardino de Mendoza on the events of the wars in the low countries), which he dedicated to the French Catholics. Finally, in the year of his death, he sent to the press a translation of *Los seys libros de la politica o doctrina civil* (1604; *Six Bookes of Politickes or Civil Doctrine*, 1970), a 1594 text by the Dutch Humanist scholar Justus Lipsius, one of the most eminent political thinkers of the Renaissance.

SIGNIFICANCE

Bernardino de Mendoza's career as a soldier, diplomat, and writer exemplifies the diverse profile identified commonly with the figure of the Renaissance man. He also epitomizes, along with Niccolò Machiavelli, Francis Walsingham, and Cardinal Richelieu (Armand-Jean du Plessis), the image of the ruthless Renaissance politician who will stop at nothing in service to his country. His rise to military and political prominence was the result of talent, self-determination, and powerful family connections.

He was a shrewd diplomat and spy, but his views of political reality were clouded by intransigence and his staunch religious zeal. As a writer, his greatest contribution was the understanding of war as a global and state-sponsored enterprise, which he approached in a scientific and almost managerial fashion.

—*Javier Lorenzo*

FURTHER READING

Jensen, De Lamar. *Diplomacy and Dogmatism: Bernardino de Mendoza and the French Catholic League.* Cambridge, Mass.: Harvard University Press, 1964. Still the best scholarly study on Bernardino. The book focuses primarily on Bernardino's mission in France, but it also offers a good summary of his endeavors at Elizabeth I's court.

Morel-Fatio, Alfred. "Bernardino de Mendoza, sa vie, son œvre." *Bulletin Hispanique* (1906). The first modern biography of Bernardino, by an authoritative scholar, which gathers most of the data collected by nineteenth century scholars.

Oman, Charles. *History of the Art of War in the Sixteenth Century.* Mechanicsburg, Pa.: Stackpole Books, 1999. Discusses in detail the military and historical background of Bernardino's work and explains their practical and theoretical significance in the context of sixteenth century warfare.

SEE ALSO: Duke of Alva; Elizabeth I; Henry III; Niccolò Machiavelli; Mary, Queen of Scots; Philip II.

RELATED ARTICLES in *Great Events from History: The Renaissance & Early Modern Era, 1454-1600:* 1558-1603: Reign of Elizabeth I; March, 1562-May 2, 1598: French Wars of Religion; June 17, 1579: Drake Lands in Northern California.

ANA DE MENDOZA Y DE LA CERDA
Spanish noblewoman

Ana de Mendoza was an intimate friend of the queen of Spain and a patron of the Discalced Carmelite nuns. After her husband's death, she became involved in various courtly intrigues that led to her exile from court and eventual imprisonment at her estate at Pastrana.

BORN: June 29, 1540; Cifuentes, Guadalajara Province, Spain

DIED: February 2, 1592; Pastrana, Guadalajara Province, Spain

ALSO KNOWN AS: Ana de Silva (given name); Ana de Mendoza; princess of Eboli; countess of Mélito; duchess of Pastrana; Ana Hurtado de Mendoza

AREAS OF ACHIEVEMENT: Government and politics, religion and theology

EARLY LIFE

The only surviving legitimate offspring of Diego Hurtado de Mendoza, viceroy of Aragon and Catalonia, Ana de Mendoza y de la Cerda (AH-nah day men-DOH-zah ee day lah SEER-dah) was born into the wealthy and powerful Mendoza family. Although she was given the last name of Silva at baptism, according to historian James M. Boyden, she used the surnames de Mendoza and de la Cerda later in life, since their use was a condition of her assumption of the title of countess of Mélito. During her lifetime, she was commonly referred to as Ana de Mendoza, her paternal last name, or one of her noble titles.

In contrast to many Renaissance noblewomen who entered the historical record, Ana de Mendoza is not remembered solely because of her marriage contract. Historian Helen H. Reed suggests that the young Ana was educated by her mother, Catalina de Silva—owner of a large library and a woman celebrated for her intelligence—and her aunt María de Mendoza. In a marriage contract dated 1553, Ana was betrothed to Ruy Gómez de Silva, then an attendant to Prince Philip, heir to the Spanish throne.

LIFE'S WORK

Since Ruy Gómez de Silva spent much of the next few years outside Spain accompanying Philip II to England and the Netherlands, Ana remained at the court in Spain in the company of her parents. Beginning with Gómez de Silva's first trip and throughout her adulthood, Ana maintained an active epistolary life with her family members. When Philip II's third wife, Isabel de Valois, arrived at court in 1560, Ana became her close friend. It is likely that Sofonisba Anguissola painted the famous portrait of Ana dressed as a shepherdess during this period. The canvas, portraying a young, beautiful woman wearing an eye patch, created an enduring and mysterious image of Ana de Mendoza; it is not known how (or whether) her eye was injured.

Like all nobles who resided at court, Ana was surrounded by lively social activities. In all likelihood, she attended jousts and other courtly festivals and, along with other noblewomen, maintained a busy schedule of visits. In addition to this whirl of activities, in the course of Ana's marriage, she bore ten children; six survived their childhoods.

After the deaths of prince Carlos, heir to the throne, and his mother Isabel de Valois in 1568, Ana and her husband withdrew somewhat from life at court in favor of their estate in Pastrana. Philip II had rewarded Gómez de Silva with the title duke of Pastrana in 1572. During this period, the princess of Eboli founded a number of religious institutions, monasteries, and convents, as well as a Carmelite college, in and around Pastrana. At Ana's request, the celebrated mystic—and later saint—Teresa of Ávila established a religious community at Pastana. On her husband's death in 1573, like many Renaissance widows, Ana de Mendoza retreated to a convent. Not surprisingly, the princess of Eboli chose to enter the convent of the Discalced Carmelites, which she founded at Pastrana.

Conflict soon developed between Ana and other members of the religious community, apparently because of the patron's failure to follow the strict seclusion required of the Discalced Carmelites. Largely as a result of this disagreement, Teresa and her nuns abandoned the convent at Pastrana in the dead of night. At the same time, royal authorities insisted that the princess leave the convent in order to administer her estates for her children.

Because of this mandate, Ana returned to the court in Madrid in 1576. While at court, she actively negotiated marriage contracts for her children and attempted to protect their inheritance after the remarriage of her father. Her maneuvering might have affected several importance historical events, especially the Spanish position in the Netherlands and the question of succession to the Portuguese throne in 1578. Although her inheritance was seemingly ensured after her father's posthumous child was stillborn in 1578, Ana was forced to enter into a lengthy legal battle when her uncle contested a woman's right to inherit entailed property.

On her return to Madrid, Ana established a friendship with Antonio Pérez, a friend of her deceased husband and Philip II's secretary. Despite the courtly gossip that detailed an amorous affair between the two, historians remain divided as to whether this was actually the case. Whatever the nature of their relationship, Ana was implicated in Pérez's successful plot to murder Juan de Escobedo, secretary to Philip II's half brother Don Juan of Austria. Although Ana's precise role in the conspiracy to eliminate Escobedo has not come to light, in 1579, a year after the murder, both the princess of Eboli and Antonio Pérez were arrested.

From the date of the princess's arrest until her death in 1592, she lived under increasingly restrictive imprisonment. Nevertheless, as Reed amply demonstrates through the princess's correspondence, her confinement restricted neither her written contact with the world at large nor her active defense of her family's legal position. By 1592, the princess was walled into one room at her palace at Pastrana, where she died in February of that year.

SIGNIFICANCE

Since one of Ana's most vital social roles was motherhood, an important portion of her significance lies in the positions her offspring attained in Spanish society and government. One son, Diego de Silva y Mendoza, served as viceroy of Portugal, and his sibling Rodrigo assumed the title of duke of Pastrana. A third son, Pedro, entered the church and became bishop of Sigüenza. Furthermore, scholars are still discovering the details of Ana de Mendoza's role as a patron of both religious orders and the arts.

Yet the murky events surrounding the princess's exile from court have most determined her place in history. Although historians often represent the princess of Eboli as an unscrupulous courtesan, more recent historiography portrays Ana de Mendoza as a highly educated woman constrained and ultimately punished because of the gender expectations of her era. Ana's most enduring fame, however, results from creative endeavors inspired by her life circumstances. The nineteenth century Italian composer Giuseppe Verdi made her a character in his opera *Don Carlos* (1867). She is also a frequent character in novels, both in Spanish and in English. Largely as a result of this legacy, her palace at Pastrana remains a popular tourist attraction in Spain.

—*Patricia W. Manning*

FURTHER READING

Boyden, James M. *The Courtier and the King: Ruy Gómez de Silva, Philip II, and the Court of Spain.* Berkeley: University of California Press, 1995. Emphasizes Ana de Mendoza's role as wife to Gómez de Silva. Also delves into the princess of Eboli's lineage and its impact on her spouse. Mentions monastic foundations at Pastrana. Includes bibliographical references and an index.

Elliott, John Huxtable. *Imperial Spain, 1469-1716.* 1963. Reprint. New York: Penguin Books, 1990. Highly detailed overview of Spain's empire. Focuses on the Eboli faction at court in opposition to the duke of Alva.

Kamen, Henry. *Philip of Spain.* New Haven, Conn.: Yale University Press, 1997. References to Ana de Mendoza center on her role in the Pérez plot. Maintains that Ana's relationship with Pérez was political, not romantic.

Parker, Geoffrey. *Philip II.* 4th ed. Chicago: Open Court, 2002. Implicates Ana de Mendoza as an active participant in Pérez's plot. Includes bibliographical references and an index.

Reed, Helen H. "Mother Love in the Renaissance: The Princess of Eboli's Letters to Her Favorite Son." In *Power and Gender in Renaissance Spain: Eight Women of the Mendoza Family, 1450-1650,* edited by Helen Nader. Urbana: University of Illinois Press, 2004. Discusses Ana de Mendoza, with emphasis on her familial relationships, particularly with her son Diego. Includes citations from Eboli's correspondence. Other chapters in the greater work provide valuable context for the princess of Eboli's life through analysis of other prominent female members of her family.

Weber, Alison. "Saint Teresa's Problematic Patrons." *Journal of Medieval and Early Modern Studies* 29, no. 2 (Spring, 1999): 357-379. Describes disagreements between Teresa of Ávila and her patrons, including the particularly stormy relationship with Ana de Mendoza.

SEE ALSO: Barbe Acarie; Sofonisba Anguissola; Philip II; Saint Teresa of Ávila.

RELATED ARTICLES in *Great Events from History: The Renaissance & Early Modern Era, 1454-1600:* Beginning c. 1495: Reform of the Spanish Church; August 15, 1534: Founding of the Jesuit Order.

PEDRO MENÉNDEZ DE AVILÉS
Spanish explorer

Menéndez de Avilés developed the Florida peninsula of North America as a colony of the Spanish crown.

BORN: February 15, 1519; Avilés, Spain
DIED: September 17, 1574; Santander, Spain
AREA OF ACHIEVEMENT: Exploration

EARLY LIFE

One of twenty-one brothers and sisters, Pedro Menéndez de Avilés (PAY-droh may-NAYN-dayz day ah-bee-LAYS) was born in the seaport town of Avilés on Spain's northern coast. A member of a family with claims to Hidalgo (minor nobility) status, he was related also by marriage to the important Valdés clan. Like many of his relatives, friends, and contemporaries who lived in this port city, Menéndez turned to the sea in pursuit of a career.

The young seaman served initially with a leading local privateersman, Alvaro Bazán, in battles with French corsairs operating off the coast of Western Europe. Soon he bought his own small ship with the prize money that he had earned and began the pursuit of French raiders under royal commissions granted by the Spanish Crown. His successes led him to expand his operations across the Atlantic to the Indies. He became a captain-general and commander of the Spanish treasure fleets plying the routes between their colonies and the homeland.

His rising reputation as a naval leader caused Spain's King Charles I (Holy Roman Emperor Charles V) to assign Menéndez to accompany the emperor's heir, young Prince Philip, to England for the latter's wedding to Mary Tudor, the eldest daughter of King Henry VIII and the future queen Mary I. While the close relationship that he had developed with the heir to the throne during this period helped Menéndez throughout his subsequent career, he incurred also the enmity of the powerful merchant circle in Seville, which had to bear the expense of maintaining the armed fleet needed to protect the sea lanes to Spain's colonies. The merchants saw the young seaman as a potential rival for the profits emanating from transatlantic trade.

LIFE'S WORK

By the middle of the sixteenth century, open hostilities had broken out between Spain and France, exacerbated by the militant Protestant movements that had swept Europe. Philip II, now king of Spain, turned south to stem the Protestant tide both on the European continent and in Spain's colonial empire.

Rumors had reached the Spanish court of French incursions and the establishment of settlements on the coast of Florida, territory claimed by Spain by right of discovery. Loss of control of this strategic area would seriously jeopardize Spanish sovereignty over the whole Caribbean zone. Philip II decided that he had to take strong countermeasures as quickly as possible. Previous attempts by Spain to establish a permanent colony under its explorers Hernando de Soto and Juan Ponce de León had ended in failure.

Philip now turned to his successful, experienced captain-general Menéndez to evaluate and to make recommendations on how to deal with the Florida problem. The veteran sailor replied quickly that the French threat was a real one and that the so-called Protestant heretics, if they were successful in enlisting Florida's Native Indians in their cause, could threaten the Spanish political and economic status quo throughout the area. Menéndez recommended the dispatch of an expedition immediately to rout the French if they had indeed established bases there, to institute agricultural settlements with Spanish immigrants, and to employ missionaries to convert the indigenous peoples to Catholicism. He estimated the cost of such an expedition, together with a necessary year's supplies after landing, to be in the neighborhood of eighty thousand ducats to the royal treasury.

The king and his advisers countered the proposal by offering to license Menéndez as *adelantado*, or governor, promising him lands, revenues, and titles if he would undertake the expedition largely at his own expense, but with some financial and material support by the Crown. Such an arrangement had become a common practice employed by Spanish royalty at the time, since it reduced the burden on the Crown's own finances. Menéndez accepted this risky venture involving exploration, the probabilities of serious conflict, the transfer of a substantial group of immigrants, and the religious conversion of the indigenous population.

Although the new *adelantado* initially received moral support, military men, supplies, and missionaries to aid him, he encountered resistance from another quarter, the merchants of Seville and the Casa de Contratación—powerful groups that played a major role in the transatlantic trade between Spain and its colonies. They delayed the aid pledged by the Crown in furnishing the ships and supplies Menéndez required to start his enterprise.

Undaunted, Menéndez not only employed all his own

personal resources in the project but also secured the support of family and friends in and about Avilés. These loyal comrades became the key personnel on which he depended in building and administering the new colony. The group pledged not only their wealth but also their lives in support of their kinsman and close friend.

Meanwhile, powerful French Huguenot interests had begun assembling a fleet of their own. They did indeed have a colony started at Fort Caroline on the Florida coast, and they planned to reinforce this fledgling operation before Menéndez arrived.

By the time the Spanish expedition had reached Florida in mid-1565, the enterprising French had already reinforced their settlement at the Caroline location. On September 8, Menéndez landed north of the French fort at a beach that he named St. Augustine and dedicated to the Spanish Crown. It became the headquarters for the new *adelantamiento*, or seat of government.

Two weeks later, the Spanish leader marched south, carried out a surprise attack on Fort Caroline, captured it, and killed most of the inhabitants. Later, when some of the survivors of the initial battle who had escaped attempted to surrender, Menéndez executed the majority of them as well. Such massacres of the vanquished were all too common in the bloody encounters among European rivals. In this case, the Spaniards had quickly and forcefully ended the French threat to their control of Florida.

The *adelantado* then proceeded to launch his three-fold plan of action for the colony: the establishment of military bases, the preparation for the influx of permanent settlers, and the religious conversion of the indigenous peoples. The progress proved to be slow. Food remained in short supply during the settlement's initial stages, causing low morale within the garrisons, and the North American Indians proved to be difficult to convert to a new religion.

The relationships between the conquistadores and their North American Indian charges were tumultuous. The missionaries who accompanied the soldiers insisted that the Indians give up their traditional gods and adopt Catholicism exclusively. The friars demanded that the converts discontinue their practices of polygamy, sodomy, and child sacrifice, customs that were accepted traditionally within their culture. The Spanish soldiers also took by force what they wanted from the Indians and abused the women. Moreover, when the Spaniards adopted a particular tribe as allies, they immediately incurred the enmity of that group's traditional adversaries.

Vital supplies continued to be a problem for Menéndez's Floridian colonies. Officials both in Cádiz and in Havana either ignored the *adelantado*'s requests or demanded prepayment for goods to be delivered. The scarcity of provisions critical to the settlements' welfare kept the outposts at a bare survival level.

Despite the hazards facing the Spaniards throughout Florida, Menéndez managed to establish a string of forts along the shores of the peninsula. Unfortunately, sporadic raids by Indians, food shortages, and mutinies created problems for the Spanish leader whenever his duties called him away from the peninsula. On many occasions, he was forced to punish drastically, and in some cases to execute, malefactors.

The cost involved in establishing and supplying these outposts proved to be much higher than anticipated. The colony's backers lost many ships and much cargo in the process of navigating through uncharted waters. Menéndez and his associates also suffered severe financial reverses, because Florida's natural resources offered little in the way of immediate return on investment. Disorder broke out constantly among the unruly soldiery when they came to realize that there was little loot to be acquired from the Indian population. Menéndez decided to return to Spain and present his problems to the Crown.

Unfortunately for the Spanish colony's leader, Philip II had turned his attention to more pressing difficulties closer to home. Both France and England threatened

Pedro Menéndez de Avilés. (Hulton|Archive by Getty Images)

Spain's control over its spheres of interest on the European continent itself. Accordingly, faraway Florida ranked low on the king's list of priorities.

Nevertheless, a visit to court by Menéndez did produce some favorable results. King Philip added to Menéndez's Florida command the post of governor of Cuba as well. Menéndez acquired command of a newly formed armada to operate as Spain's main line of defense throughout the Caribbean. Recalcitrant Seville and Cádiz merchants received orders from the Crown to furnish Menéndez with overdue money and supplies.

The *adelantado* was not left to govern his Florida enterprises for much longer. Philip recalled him to Europe for a new, somewhat more mysterious, assignment in mid-1573. He gave Menéndez command of a great two-hundred-ship armada, the purpose of which was to launch an attack against English home ports and to cut off supplies to English raiders harassing Spanish shipping in the Americas.

On September 17, 1574, while in the midst of organizing this undertaking, Pedro Menéndez de Avilés suddenly died, perhaps poisoned by English spies. Certainly Spain's outstanding seaman represented a serious threat to the English Crown. When Philip attempted an invasion of England some fourteen years later under a less experienced and less successful admiral, the undertaking proved to be a disaster.

Although Philip II had heaped honors of all kinds on his captain-general, the huge expenses of the Florida expedition left Menéndez penniless at the time of his death.

SIGNIFICANCE

Pedro Menéndez de Avilés has been criticized by some historians for his brutal repression of the French colonists who attempted to secure Florida for their own king. He is credited with being the first European to colonize the peninsula on a permanent basis as well as founding the oldest city in the continental United States, St. Augustine. Although he sustained prohibitive financial losses personally in his attempt to develop the colony, Menéndez never wavered in his loyalty to the Spanish ruler or in his commitment to introduce Catholicism to the indigenous peoples of Florida. He must be recognized as one of Spain's outstanding colonial explorers and military leaders. He lies buried in his hometown of Avilés.

—*Carl Henry Marcoux*

FURTHER READING

Barrientos, Bartolomé. *Pedro Menéndez de Avilés: Founder of Florida.* Translated by Anthony Kerrigan. Gainesville: University of Florida Press, 1965. Barrientos, a historian, was a contemporary of Menéndez.

Folmer, Henry. *The Franco-Spanish Rivalry in North America, 1524-1723.* Glendale, Calif.: Arthur H. Clark, 1954. The author attributes the Fort Caroline massacre of the French by the Spaniards to direct orders by Philip II to Menéndez to kill all of those he might find in Florida. Folmer also describes the severe reprisals that the French took against the Spaniards during their raid on the Spanish settlement that had replaced Fort Caroline in 1568.

Gallay, Alan, ed. *Voices of the Old South: Eyewitness Accounts, 1528-1861.* Athens: University of Georgia Press, 1994. Menéndez's account of his travels in Florida is one of many first-person narratives reproduced in this anthology of antebellum primary sources. Includes bibliographic references.

Glete, Jan. *War and the State in Early Modern Europe: Spain, the Dutch Republic, and Sweden as Fiscal-Military States, 1500-1660.* New York: Routledge, 2002. An account of the development of Spain into an empire founded on military power and economic exploitation of foreign territories. Provides the larger context for Menéndez's life and career. Includes bibliographic references and index.

Kenny, Michael. *The Romance of the Floridas.* 1934. Reprint. New York: AMS Press, 1970. This work is divided into two parts: "The Finding: From Ponce de León to Pedro Menéndez de Avilés, 1512-1565" and "The Founding: The Menéndez-Jesuit Period, 1565-1575." The emphasis is on the Jesuit missionary activity that took place during the Menéndez expeditions.

Larsen, Clark Spencer, ed. *Bioarchaeology of Spanish Florida: The Impact of Colonialism.* Gainesville: University Press of Florida, 2001. Anthology of essays detailing the effects of the colony first founded by Menéndez on all aspects of indigenous life in Florida, from diet to disease to everyday behavior. Includes illustrations, bibliographic references, and index.

Lyon, Eugene. *The Enterprise of Florida: Pedro Menéndez de Avilés and the Spanish Conquest of 1565-1568.* Gainesville: University Presses of Florida, 1976. An account of the initial era of exploration and settlement of Florida by the Menéndez expeditions.

_____, ed. *Pedro Menéndez de Avilés.* New York: Garland, 1995. Volume 24 in the Spanish Borderlands Sourcebooks series, this work includes bibliographical references, illustrations, and maps.

Solís de Merás, Gonzalo. *Pedro Menéndez de Avilés.* Translated by Jeannette Thurber Connor. Gainesville: University of Florida Press, 1964. Solís de Merás was Menéndez's brother-in-law. The writer furnished an intimate knowledge of the explorer and his times.

SEE ALSO: Pedro de Alvarado; Vasco Núñez de Balboa; Álvar Núñez Cabeza de Vaca; Charles V; Christopher Columbus; Francisco Vásquez de Coronado; Hernán Cortés; Juan Sebastián de Elcano; Ferdinand II and Isabella I; Henry VIII; Miguel López de Legazpi; Mary I; Philip II; The Pinzón Brothers; Francisco Pizarro; Juan Ponce de León; Hernando de Soto.

RELATED ARTICLES in *Great Events from History: The Renaissance & Early Modern Era, 1454-1600:* 1493-1521: Ponce de León's Voyages; September, 1565: St. Augustine Is Founded.

MENNO SIMONS
Dutch religious reformer and scholar

Menno contributed a stabilizing influence to the Anabaptist movement of the sixteenth century and also to a defense of religious toleration. His most lasting contribution has been his emphasis on the Bible as the authority in religion and theology.

BORN: 1496; Witmarsum, Friesland (now in the Netherlands)

DIED: January 31, 1561; Wüstenfeld, Holstein (now in Germany)

ALSO KNOWN AS: Menno Simonsz; Menno Simonszoon

AREAS OF ACHIEVEMENT: Church reform, religion and theology

EARLY LIFE

Menno Simons (MEHN-oh SIHM-ohnz) was born in the Dutch village of Witmarsum, between the cities of Franeker and Bolsward, less than ten miles from the North Sea. His parents were devout Roman Catholics who consecrated their son to the service of their church. Menno's education for the priesthood was most likely at the Franciscan monastery in Bolsward. While there, he performed the duties of a monk but never took the vows. He studied Roman Catholic theology, learned to read and write Latin, acquired a basic knowledge of Greek, and became familiar with the writings of the early church fathers. Conspicuously absent from Menno's studies was the Bible.

Menno was ordained as a Roman Catholic priest in 1524 and remained faithful to that calling for twelve years. The last five years (1531-1536), he served as parish pastor in his home village of Witmarsum. Outwardly, he was the average country priest of the sixteenth century, performing his duties faithfully but with the least possible effort. With two fellow priests, his leisure time was spent "playing [cards], . . . drinking, and in such diversions as, alas, is the fashion . . . of such useless people."

Inwardly, Menno was troubled by doubts concerning the ceremony of the Mass. He could not escape the thought, which he first attributed to Satan, that the bread and wine were not really transformed into the body and blood of Christ as he had been taught. Menno's doubts may have been prompted by the Sacramentists, a group that denied the physical presence of Christ in the Lord's Supper. Two years after becoming a priest, Menno sought and found his answer in the Bible. He later wrote, "I had not gone very far when I discovered that we were deceived. . . ." Menno then faced the same decision that faced other reformers: Would he rely on his church for authority, or would he take the Bible as his sole authority for doctrine and practice? His decision to accept the latter came in 1528.

Privately rejecting Roman Catholic authority did not mean an immediate break between Menno and the Church. Although not in agreement, he was willing to continue performing the Mass in the traditional way; at the same time, he became more deeply involved in personal Bible study.

Menno's second question concerning the traditions of his church, and the one that eventually led to his departure from it, concerned infant baptism. In 1531, a man was beheaded in nearby Leeuwarden because of Anabaptism (rebaptism based on baptism for believers only). Menno's Bible study soon convinced him that believers' baptism (baptism of adolescents and adults who consent to the ritual) was the biblical position. By this time, small groups of Anabaptists were forming throughout the Netherlands, but Menno did not join any of them, partly because he enjoyed the comfortable life of a priest and partly because of the radical nature of some Anabaptists, such as those who violently captured Münster in 1534.

The greatest change in Menno's life came in April, 1535, when he accepted, as a "sorrowing sinner, the gift of His [God's] grace. . . ." He then rejected both the Roman Catholic Mass and infant baptism. On January 30, 1536, Menno renounced the Roman Catholic Church and joined the Anabaptists.

LIFE'S WORK

Following his break with Rome, Menno began a period of wandering that would last about eighteen years, in which he served as an underground evangelist to the scattered Anabaptist communities. In late 1536, he settled briefly in the northern Dutch province of Groningen, where at least a semblance of religious freedom existed. While there, he was baptized with believers' baptism and ordained as an elder in the Anabaptist movement. Soon thereafter, Menno was forced to resume his wandering. His exact points of residence can be traced only by noting those who were executed for sheltering him. On January 8, 1539, Tjard Reynders, a God-fearing Anabaptist in Leeuwarden, was executed solely because he had given a temporary home to Menno.

Until late 1543, Menno's work was concentrated in the Netherlands. The authorities in Leeuwarden, the capital of West Friesland, seemed determined to be rid of Menno, whose hometown of Witmarsum was in their province. In 1541, they offered a pardon to any imprisoned Anabaptist who would betray him, but the offer was not accepted. On December 2, 1542, with the support of Charles V, emperor of the Holy Roman Empire as well as ruler of the Netherlands, they offered a reward of one hundred gold guilders, plus a pardon for any past crime, to anyone who would deliver Menno. These efforts testify to the importance ascribed by that time to Menno's leadership of the movement.

The exact time and place when Menno married Geertruydt are not known; in 1544, however, he wrote "to this hour I could not find in all the country . . . a cabin or hut . . . in which my poor wife and our little children could be put up in safety." Menno continued throughout these years to express concern for his family, all of whom, except one daughter, preceded him in death. From 1541 to 1543, Menno concentrated his labor farther south around Amsterdam, but details of this work are scarce. He evidently baptized many, although the names of only two have been preserved.

The most enduring part of Menno's work is his writ-

Menno Simons. (Hulton|Archive by Getty Images)

ing. By 1543, at least seven books from the pen of Menno Simons were circulating throughout the Netherlands, including *Dat fundament des christelycken leers* (1539; *A Foundation of Plain Instruction*, 1835), *Van dat rechte christen ghelooue* (c. 1542; *The True Christian Faith*, 1871), and *Verclaringhe des Christelycken doopsels* (c. 1542; *Christian Baptism*, 1871). Rather than being academic treatises designed for theologians, they are commonsense presentations for the average layperson. Precisely because Menno's works were so accessible, church authorities were particularly determined to destroy them.

In the fall of 1543, Menno and his family left the Netherlands, and for the last eighteen years of his life, he labored primarily in northwest Germany. His first German refuge was Emden, in East Friesland, ruled by the tolerant Countess Anna of Oldenburg. Menno had visited the province, which had become a haven for all Anabaptists, many times previously. By this time, however, Anna was being pressured by Charles V to suppress all the outlawed sects.

The superintendent of the East Friesland churches, on whose advice Anna relied, was John a'Lasco, a Zwinglian reformer of Polish descent. Although on friendly terms with Menno, a'Lasco's goal was a state-controlled Reformed church. Countess Anna decided to suppress those whom a'Lasco declared to be heretical. To this end, a theological discussion was held on January 28-31, 1544, involving a'Lasco, who hoped to bring the Anabaptists into the state church, and Menno, who hoped to preserve the tolerant spirit in East Friesland. The discussion revealed three irreconcilable differences. First, Menno strongly opposed the concept of a state-controlled church, which he believed always led to compromise and spiritual lethargy. Second, a'Lasco could not reconcile believers' baptism to a state church. The final point concerned Menno's unique understanding of the Incarnation of Christ; he taught that the body of Christ, to be completely sinless, had to be given completely to the Virgin Mary by the Holy Spirit. A'Lasco interpreted this as a denial of the humanity of Christ, weakening his position as the savior of humankind; he therefore declared that Menno was guilty of heresy.

In 1545, Anna issued a decree that the more radical Anabaptists were subject to execution, while the "Mennisten" were to be examined and, if they did not conform to the state church, were to leave the province. This decree was the first official document to recognize Menno's leadership by applying his name to the peaceful branch of the Anabaptist movement.

Menno left East Friesland in May, 1544, for the lower Rhine area of Cologne and Bonn, where he spent two fruitful years; the last fifteen years of his life were spent in the province of Schleswig-Holstein. There, in 1554, Menno finally found a permanent home for his weary family in Wüstenfelde, between Lübeck and Hamburg.

Menno's final years were productive in that he had time for more writing, including revising some of his earlier books. They were also troublesome years in which Menno had to settle disputes and defend himself within the Anabaptist movement. The most serious dispute concerned the ban and shunning of excommunicated members; Menno took the strict position that all human ties, even those of marriage and family, had to be broken under the ban of the church.

By 1560, Menno's health was failing. The years of hardship and privation, as well as the burden of the church, had taken a heavy toll. He often used a crutch as a result of an injury suffered in Wismar around 1554. Menno died in his own home on January 31, 1561, exactly twenty-five years after his break with Rome, and was buried in his own garden. Unfortunately, Wüstenfelde was destroyed during the Thirty Years' War (1618-1648), and the site of Menno's grave could only be approximated in the early twentieth century, when a simple memorial was erected.

SIGNIFICANCE

The Anabaptist movement began in 1525; for the next eleven years, Menno Simons was a Roman Catholic priest. Therefore, he was only a leader, not the founder, of the church that bears his name: the Mennonite church. Menno's role in the Reformation is not as obvious as that of his contemporaries, Martin Luther, Huldrych Zwingli, and John Calvin; yet his true significance is revealed in three areas of influence: his character, his message, and his work.

The character of Menno was ingrained with a sensitivity for the truth, an unswerving devotion to his convictions, and a deep trust in God. These traits enabled him to have a steadying influence on the diverse Anabaptist communities of the Netherlands and northern Germany.

The foundation of Menno's message was the Bible. He declared that he "would rather die than to believe and teach my brethren a single word or letter . . . contrary to the plain testimony of the Word of God. . . ." He identified the heart of his message when he said, "I strive after nothing . . . but . . . that all men might be saved. . . ." As a reward for this message, however, "we can expect nothing from them (I mean the evil disposed) but the stake, water, fire, wheel, and sword. . . ."

The significance of Menno's work is that he united the northern wing of the Anabaptist movement, thus preventing its disintegration through persecution. Unlike other reformers, he did this without the aid of the state. The endurance of the Mennonite church throughout the centuries is the best testimony that his work was in the providence of God.

—Glenn L. Swygart

FURTHER READING

Doornkaat Koolman, Jacobus ten. *Dirk Philips: Friend and Colleague of Menno Simons, 1504-1568*. Translated by William E. Keeney. Edited by C. Arnold Snyder. Kitchener, Ont.: Pandora Press, 1998. Biography of one of Menno's closest colleagues and an important leader of the Dutch Anabaptists in his own right. Includes bibliographic references and index.

Estep, William R. *The Anabaptist Story: An Introduction to Sixteenth-Century Anabaptism*. 3d ed. Grand Rapids, Mich.: William B. Eerdmans, 1996. Emphasizes the calming influence of Menno on the diverse Anabaptist groups in the Netherlands. Estep argues that Menno's leadership enabled the movement to survive the persecution, as well as the violent and visionary elements within the movement. Includes bibliographic references and index.

Horsch, John. *Mennonites in Europe*. 2d ed. Scottdale, Pa.: Mennonite Publishing House, 1950. Includes an account of Menno's doubts about Roman Catholic doctrine. Covers his early contacts with the Anabaptist movement. Identifies sources of information about Menno's early labors as an Anabaptist evangelist.

Littell, Franklin H. *A Tribute to Menno Simons*. Scottdale, Pa.: Herald Press, 1961. Written to recognize the historical significance of Menno Simons on the quadricentennial of his death. Emphasis on his contributions to the Anabaptist movement, in particular, and to Protestantism, in general. Author's position is that Menno has great significance to modern Christianity.

Menno Simons. *The Complete Writings of Menno Simons*. Edited by J. C. Wenger, Scottdale, Pa.: Herald Press, 1956. Complete English translation of Menno's literary works. Includes an introduction and a good brief biography. Also includes the location of the writings in other editions. Contains books, tracts, letters, hymns, and all other available writings. Gives direct insight into the philosophy and theology of Menno. Good illustrations.

Miller, Keith Graber. "Complex Innocence, Obligatory Nurturance, and Parental Vigilance: 'The Child' in the Work of Menno Simons." In *The Child in Christian Thought*, edited by Marcia J. Bunge. Grand Rapids, Mich.: W. B. Eerdmans, 2001. Study of Menno's theology and teachings about the nature of childhood and the obligations of parents and other adults to children. Includes bibliographic references and indexes.

Smith, C. Henry. *Smith's Story of the Mennonites*. 5th ed. Newton, Kans.: Faith and Life Press, 1981. Includes a good summary of the inner conflicts experienced by Menno in his relationship to the Roman Catholic Church. Illustrations, bibliography, and index.

Voolstra, Sjouke. *Menno Simons: His Image and Message*. North Newton, Kans.: Bethel College, 1997. An attempt to recover the authentic voice of Menno, emphasizing his belief in sincere penitence and forgiveness, his understanding of the importance of baptism, and his break with the Catholic church. Includes illustrations, bibliographic references, and index.

SEE ALSO: John Calvin; Charles V; Balthasar Hubmaier; Martin Luther; Huldrych Zwingli.

RELATED ARTICLES in *Great Events from History: The Renaissance & Early Modern Era, 1454-1600:* October 31, 1517: Luther Posts His Ninety-five Theses; April-May, 1521: Luther Appears Before the Diet of Worms; June, 1524-July, 1526: German Peasants' War.

GERARDUS MERCATOR
Flemish cartographer and geographer

Mercator invented a map projection that is particularly useful for ocean navigation. He was the first person to use the word "atlas" for a volume of maps. His maps represented the best geographic knowledge available at his time.

BORN: March 5, 1512; Rupelmonde, Flanders (now in Belgium)
DIED: December 2, 1594; Duisburg, duchy of Cleves (now in Germany)
ALSO KNOWN AS: Gerhard Kremer (given name); Gerard de Cremer; Gerard de Kremer; Gerhard Mercator
AREAS OF ACHIEVEMENT: Cartography, geography

EARLY LIFE
Gerardus Mercator (jeh-RAHR-duhs muhr-KAYT-uhr) was christened Gerhard Kremer at birth but took the Latinized form of his given name and surname; Latinizing one's given name and surname was common practice for many scholars of his day. In a sense, Mercator upgraded his name. *Kremer* was the German word for trader, and *mercator* is the Latin word for world trader.

Mercator's parents both died while he was young. He was provided for by his uncle, Gisbert Kremer, who financed his way at the University of Louvain, where he studied philosophy, mathematics, astronomy, and cosmography (geography of the cosmos).

After graduation, he established a workshop in Louvain, where he made globes, sundials, mathematical instruments, armillary spheres, astrolabes, and other measuring instruments. He drew, engraved, and colored maps. His first known map was of the Holy Land. In 1538, he engraved and published his first world map. It was drawn on a double, more or less heart-shaped projection that was interrupted at the equator. The Northern

Hemisphere was drawn in the left-hand heart, and the Southern Hemisphere in the right. This map claims the distinction of being the first known map to give two names to the Americas: *Americae pars septemtrionalis* and *Americae pars meridionalis*, North and South America respectively. While in Louvain, he also published a map of Flanders that was based on his own survey rather than being an edited copy of another's map or a compilation of data reported by others. He also made celestial and terrestrial globes, several of which have a certain renown because of their large size and the fact that they belonged respectively to Emperor Charles V and his prime minister.

Mercator lived at the time of the Protestant Reformation and the reactionary Counter-Reformation of the Roman Catholic Church. This religious conflict was particularly strong in the Low Countries. For some reason, Mercator was arrested for heresy in 1544. After Mercator was in prison for several months, some influential friends obtained his release, which very possibly may have saved his life. This experience caused Mercator to move his business to Duisburg, Germany, where he spent the rest of his life.

Gerardus Mercator. (Library of Congress)

LIFE'S WORK

Mercator's 1554 map of Europe was one of the largest maps available at that time. It was enlarged on fifteen copper plates, and, when assembled, it was 132 by 159 centimeters (52 by 62.5 inches) in size. Mercator used italic lettering for the first time on a map drawn in northern Europe. These changes were important but superficial. The map is more important in three items of content that it corrected. A careful study of the accounts of navigators on the Mediterranean Sea and travelers in Eastern Europe led him to shorten the length of the Mediterranean Sea ten degrees of longitude. He increased the distance between the Black and the Baltic Seas by several degrees of latitude and made the Black Sea several degrees longer. These corrections made his map of Europe the most accurate of his day.

In 1564, Mercator produced a 129-by-89-centimeter (51-by-35-inch) map of the British Isles. This map seems unusual to a modern map reader in that it was oriented with West instead of North to the top of the map. Mercator is best known for his world map of 1569, which he drew on a projection that he invented and is known by his name. It was another large map in the Mercator tradition measuring 131 by 208 centimeters (51.5 by 82 inches). It contained the latest geographic information known by 1569. The map showed three land masses (Africa, Eu-

rope, and Asia), the New Indies (North and South America), and a large southern continent antipodal to Africa, Europe, and Asia. In the latter case, Mercator seems to have been perpetuating the belief of ancient philosophers rather than reporting the findings of explorers.

South America is more rectangular on this map than it is in reality, and North America is much wider. Baja California is shown as a peninsula in this map, correcting other maps of the time that showed it as an island. Little was known of the interior of North America, so Mercator used this space to explain the features of his projection. Mercator drew North America as separated from Asia, which encouraged explorers to mount efforts to find the Northwest Passage to China. Europe, the best-known part of the world to Mercator, was drawn with the most accuracy. The coastlines of Africa and Asia are easily recognized, except for eastern India, Southeast Asia, and China.

The interior of Asia was not well known. The Caspian Sea is not recognizable except for its general location. This map shows that Mercator was aware that the magnetic north pole was not located at the geographic North Pole. He placed it where the Bering Strait now appears. Mercator inserted items within cartouches placed in what would have been blank spaces in the area occupied by the great southern continent. These items included notes on measuring distances on this projection, a map of the North Polar Region, and the like. Today the map is an important historic document in that it reveals what was known about the world in the mid-sixteenth century.

The projection Mercator invented for this map was a very important cartographic invention that is still being used with modifications today. Yet the importance of this projection was not appreciated until almost one hundred years after his death. The Mercator projection draws the spherical earth within a rectangular frame. It is characterized by equally spaced parallel lines of longitude and parallel lines of latitude that become farther and farther apart as the distance from the equator increases. Since lines of longitude are not parallel and lines of latitude are equally spaced, the projection introduces two errors that magnify each other. The result is that the areas of places located away from the equator are significantly distorted.

The Mercator projection is soundly rejected by editors of modern-day textbooks, magazines, and atlases. It must be remembered, however, that Mercator drew this map for navigators, not geographers. The remarkable thing about his map was that every straight line drawn on this map plotted a course of constant compass direction. Thus, if the true locations of two places were known and correctly plotted on this projection, the navigator could connect the two places with a straight line and find the compass direction to follow in order to reach the place at the other end of the line. Mercator knew that this would not be the shortest possible course between two places, but he believed that the ease with which the course could be found fully compensated for the extra distance that would have to be traveled as the result of not following a great circle route.

While Mercator's projection is little used for world maps, several forms or derivations of his projection are still in common use, and his name can still be seen on many large-scale maps of small areas and on many aeronautical maps. When Mercator drew his world map in 1569, he drew it as if a cylinder were placed around the globe, tangent at the equator. It is common now to place this cylinder tangent to the earth at the North and South poles. When this is done, it is called a transverse Mercator projection. This form is used for most U.S. military maps. It is also used for medium-scale topographic maps published by the United States Geological Survey and by the Canadian Department of Mines and Technical Surveys. Aeronautical maps are drawn with the cylinder tangent to the earth along the great circle, connecting the starting place with its destination.

Mercator had what could be called a life's goal. He believed that the world needed a cosmography. His cosmography was made of three parts: The first part was about the beginnings of the world, the second part was the geography of the ancient world, and the third part was about the world geography of his day. The year 1569 marked the publication not only of his world map but also of the first part of his cosmography, *Chronologia*. Mercator tried to establish the beginning of the world and to reconcile the chronologies of the ancient Hebrews, Greeks, Egyptians, and Romans with that of the Christian world.

In 1578, he published his version of Ptolemy's *Geographike hyphegesis* (geography), which contained twenty-seven plates engraved especially for this edition that are generally agreed to be the finest ever prepared for this work. This edition became the second part of his cosmography.

Mercator envisioned that the third part of his cosmography, *Atlas sive cosmographicae meditationes de fabrica mundi et fabricati figura* (1595; *Historia mundi: Or, Mercator's Atlas*, 1635), would include some one hundred maps, and he spent the last sixteen years of his life working on it. Since this work contained many maps bound together in one volume, it has given its name—Mercator's atlas—to all other such map collections.

Mercator's atlas was long in coming. In fact, it was published in parts, the first of which covered France, Belgium, and Germany. The second part contained twenty-two maps covering Italy, Yugoslavia, and Greece. The last section, which contained thirty-four maps, twenty-nine drawn by Mercator and five by his son Rumold and two grandsons, was published in the year after his death.

SIGNIFICANCE

Gerardus Mercator is renowned for four things: his terrestrial and celestial globes of 1541; his large map of Europe in 1554 and of the British Isles in 1564; his world map of 1569, particularly the projection on which it was drawn; and his three-part cosmography, which included a chronology of the world from creation to his day, an edition of the works of Ptolemy, and his atlas of the then-known world.

Few books in English are dedicated to Mercator and his work. What little is known about Mercator's life came first from a very short biography written by a neighbor and fellow mapmaker, who described him as "a man of calm temperament and exceptional candor and sincerity." Much is known about Mercator's works, however, many of which have been preserved in rare-book libraries around the world. Mercator was the leading cartographer of the last half of the sixteenth century. He was more than a skilled engraver and publisher of maps; he was an innovator and geographer as well.

—*Theodore P. Aufdemberge*

FURTHER READING

Brown, Lloyd A. *Map Making: The Art That Became a Science.* Boston: Little, Brown, 1960. This book contains a portrait of Mercator and a reproduction of his world map that first used separate names for North and South America. It also tells the story about his book of maps.

_____. *The Story of Maps.* Boston: Little, Brown, 1949. Reprint. New York: Dover, 1979. A scholarly book on the history of cartography that contains information on the life and work of Mercator. It puts Mercator into the historical context of his time. Contains extensive notes, bibliographic data, and several illustrations of Mercator's maps.

Crane, Nicholas. *Mercator: The Man Who Mapped the Planet.* New York: H. Holt, 2003. Biography of Mercator that does an impressive job of assembling documents and evidence to cover the entire span of his life and accomplishments. Includes photographic plates, illustrations, maps, bibliographic references, and index.

Crane, Gerald R. *Maps and Their Makers: An Introduction to the History of Cartography.* London: Hutchinson University Library, 1966. This book contains some biographical material. It is more concerned, however, with Mercator's works, particularly the geographic contents of his world map of 1569 and his cosmography. Illustrated, with bibliographic references.

Greenhood, David. *Mapping.* Chicago: University of Chicago Press, 1964. Contains little information about Mercator himself. Instead, the chapter on projections clearly describes Mercator's projection and how it is constructed. Well illustrated.

LeGear, C. E. "Gerardus Mercator's Atlas of 1595." In *A La Carte: Selected Papers on Maps and Atlases,* compiled by Walter W. Ristow. Washington, D.C.: Library of Congress, 1972. This chapter is a reprint of an article that originally appeared in the *Library of Congress Quarterly Journal of Acquisitions* in May, 1950. It describes the contents of Mercator's atlas and provides a short biography of Mercator. Contains three reproductions of illustrations that appeared in his atlas, Mercator's portrait, and two of his maps, one of the New World and one of the British Isles.

Mercator, Gerardus. *The Mercator Atlas of Europe: Facsimile of the Maps by Gerardus Mercator Contained in the "Atlas of Europe," Circa 1570-1572.* Edited by Marcel Watelet. Translated by Simon Knight. Pleasant Hill, Oreg.: Walking Tree Press, 1998. Reproduction of Mercator's original maps of Europe with commentary by James R. Akerman. Includes bibliographic references.

Stevenson, Edward Luther. *Terrestrial and Celestial Globes: Their History and Construction Including a Consideration of Their Value as Aids in the Study of Geography and Astronomy.* New Haven, Conn.: Yale University Press, 1921. Reprint. New York: Johnson Reprint, 1971. In addition to the usual short biography and the study of Mercator's projection and atlas, this book contains a lengthy description of Mercator's globes.

Thrower, Norman J. W. *Maps and Man.* Englewood Cliffs, N.J.: Prentice-Hall, 1972. A short history of cartography. The unique contribution of the chapter on Renaissance cartography is Thrower's description of Mercator's map rather than the projection on which it is drawn. Contains bibliographic citations.

Wilford, John Noble. *The Mapmakers.* Rev. ed. New York: Alfred A. Knopf, 2000. History of mapmaking from antiquity to the present. Explains the importance of Mercator's projection method, both at the time and for later cartographers. Includes illustrations, maps, bibliographic references, and index.

SEE ALSO: John Cabot; Sebastian Cabot; Charles V; John Dee.

RELATED ARTICLE in *Great Events from History: The Renaissance & Early Modern Era, 1454-1600:* 1569: Mercator Publishes His World Map.

MICHELANGELO
Italian artist

Michelangelo excelled in sculpture, painting, architecture, and poetry. He was the supreme master in representing the human body, especially the male nude, and his idealized and expressive treatment of this theme was enormously influential, both in his own day and in subsequent centuries.

BORN: March 6, 1475; Caprese, Tuscany, Republic of Florence (now in Italy)

DIED: February 18, 1564; Rome, Papal States (now in Italy)

ALSO KNOWN AS: Michelangelo Buonarroti (full name)

AREAS OF ACHIEVEMENT: Art, architecture, literature

EARLY LIFE

Michelangelo (mee-kuh-LAHN-juh-loh) was the second of five sons of an aristocratic but impoverished Florentine family. He was born in the village of Caprese, near Arezzo, where his father was serving as magistrate, but before he was a month old the family returned to Florence.

From childhood Michelangelo was strongly drawn to the arts, but this inclination was bitterly opposed by his father, who considered artistic activity menial and hence demeaning to the family social status. The boy's determination prevailed, however, and at the age of thirteen, he was apprenticed to the popular painter Ghirlandajo. From Ghirlandajo he presumably learned the technique of fresco painting, but his style was formed on the study of the pioneers of Renaissance painting, Giotto and Masaccio. It was, in fact, while copying a Masaccio fresco that he was punched in the face by another apprentice. The resulting broken nose gave his face its distinctive bent profile for the rest of his life.

About a year after entering his apprenticeship, Michelangelo's precocious talent attracted the notice of Lorenzo de' Medici, the unofficial ruler and leading art patron of Florence, and the boy was invited to join the Medici household. There he had the opportunity to study both classical and modern masterpieces of sculpture and to absorb the Humanistic culture and Neoplatonic philosophy that pervaded the Medici court. From this period date Michelangelo's two earliest surviving works, both reliefs, *The Battle of the Centaurs* (c. 1492) and *The Madonna of the Steps* (c. 1492). When Lorenzo died in 1492, Michelangelo left the Medici palace and undertook the study of anatomy based on the dissection of corpses from the Hospital of Santo Spirito, for which he carved a wooden crucifix in gratitude.

In 1494, the populace of Florence, stirred by the puritanical monk Girolamo Savonarola, ousted the Medici family and reestablished a republic. Michelangelo, although he seems to have admired Savonarola and supported the republic, evidently felt threatened because of his close ties to the Medici family and fled the city, staying briefly in Venice and then in Bologna. There he supported himself with relatively minor sculpture commissions.

The year 1496 found him in Rome, where he undertook two important projects, the *Bacchus* (1497), which effectively replicated the Hellenistic style, and the Vatican *Pietà* (1499), an image of the Virgin Mary supporting the dead Christ. In this work Michelangelo minimizes the painful aspect of the subject by showing the Virgin as a lovely, surprisingly youthful woman gazing down serenely at the classically beautiful body of her son. To overcome the awkwardness of balancing an adult male body on the lap of a woman, he enlarges the Virgin but masks her size with billowing drapery and wraps the body of Christ around her to create a compact, pyramidal group. The contract called for the *Pietà* to be "the most beautiful work in marble which exists today in Rome." When Michelangelo completed the piece, there was no question that he had met this requirement.

LIFE'S WORK

In 1501, Michelangelo returned triumphantly to Florence and to a new challenge. An enormous marble block was assigned to him. It had been abandoned decades earlier because its tall, shallow proportions seemed unsuitable for a figure sculpture. From it he carved the *David* (1501-1504). David was a favorite Florentine subject, but Michelangelo's treatment broke with tradition in representing the shepherd boy as a Herculean nude, twice life-size, before, rather than after, the battle so as to incorporate greater physical and psychic tension. The statue was placed in the square outside the governmental palace, but it has since been moved inside to protect it from the weather.

Contemporary with the *David* or slightly later are several powerful representations of the Madonna and Child, including the artist's only unquestioned panel painting, the *Doni Madonna* (c. 1503-1505).

In 1504, the Florentine republic ordered two large battle scenes for its council chamber, one from Leonardo da Vinci and the other from Michelangelo. Neither fresco was actually painted, and even Michelangelo's preliminary drawing survives only in a copy. It shows a group of bathing soldiers struggling out of a stream at the battle alarm, and the treatment of the straining, foreshortened bodies was to provide instruction and inspiration to a whole generation of Italian artists.

This painting and a series of sculpted apostles for Florence Cathedral were interrupted when the newly elected pope, Julius II, called Michelangelo to Rome. The pope's first commission was for his tomb, a grandiose, multilevel structure that was to include more than forty figures. Michelangelo had hardly begun this project when the pope changed his mind and ordered the artist instead to paint the ceiling of the Sistine Chapel. Michelangelo vigorously objected that he was a sculptor, not a painter, but in the end he spent the years 1508-1512 covering the surface, approximately fifty-eight hundred square feet, seventy feet above the floor, with scenes from Genesis, enframed by nude youths and surrounded by enthroned prophets and Sibyls. In keeping with his preference for sculpture, emphasis is placed on the monumental figures with rather minimal background. Nevertheless, as cleaning of the fresco has revealed, the coloring is both subtle and brilliant.

On completion of the ceiling, Michelangelo resumed his work on the pope's tomb, producing *The Dying Slave* (1513-1516), *The Rebellious Slave* (1513-1516), and *Moses* (1505-1545). Julius, however, died in 1513, and his successors would include two members of the Medici family, both boyhood companions of Michelangelo, Leo X (1513-1521) and Clement VII (1523-1534). Both preferred to keep Michelangelo employed largely on family projects in Florence, so that progress on the Julius tomb was slow and sporadic. The first Medician commission, an elaborate facade for the family church of San Lorenzo, was never executed, but the next, a new sacristy in the same church containing tombs of the Medici dukes, although never finished, was to be the artist's most complete architectural and sculptural ensemble. Probably the most celebrated figures from this complex are the personifications of *Night* and *Day*, *Dawn*, and *Dusk* (1520-1534), which recline uneasily on the curved and sloping sarcophagus lids. Above them sit idealized effigies of the dead dukes, who turn toward a statue of the Madonna and Child, the so-called *Medici Madonna* (1525). There is a noticeable change in Michelangelo's style in the 1520's, the decade of this chapel. His figures become more restless, with spiraling rhythms and sometimes elongated or otherwise distorted proportions, the overall effect of which is disturbing.

The same quality is found in the architecture that Michelangelo executed in the same decade, especially the vestibule of the Laurentian Library, which includes a number of unconventional and even bizarre features. This change corresponds to a more general anticlassical and antinaturalistic trend in Italian art at this time that is often characterized as mannerism. When, in 1527, the Florentines again expelled their Medici rulers and restored the republic, Michelangelo sided against his pa-

Michelangelo. (Library of Congress)

trons and supported it. During the ensuing conflict, he played a major role in designing the fortifications of the city, and when Medici forces recaptured it in 1530, he went into hiding. Pope Clement amnestied the artist, but Michelangelo felt threatened and estranged under the new autocratic regime and spent increasing amounts of time in Rome. Finally, in 1534, he left Florence forever. Two days after he arrived to settle in Rome, Clement VII died.

Michelangelo expected now to be free to return to the long-delayed and repeatedly scaled down Julius tomb, but again he was frustrated. The new pope, Paul III, declaring that he had waited thirty years to have Michelangelo work for him, induced Julius's heirs to accept a modest wall tomb featuring *Moses*, from the original project, and two more female figures from Michelangelo's hand. The monument was completed in 1545, and Michelangelo was at last free of what he himself described as "the tragedy of the tomb."

Meanwhile, he was engaged on several major projects for Pope Paul III, beginning with the fresco of *The Last Judgment* on the altar wall of the Sistine Chapel, painted between 1536 and 1541. The expressionist tendency in Michelangelo's art, already noted, is dominant here. Clusters of swirling figures alternate with empty sky, and the scale of the figures changes unaccountably, with the more distant becoming larger. A poignant personal note is the inclusion of a grimacing self-portrait of the artist on the discarded skin of one of the saints.

The Last Judgment was followed by two more frescoes painted during the 1540's for Paul III's private chapel, *The Conversion of Saint Paul* (1542-1545) and *The Crucifixion of Saint Peter* (1542-1550). The pope also placed Michelangelo in charge of several architectural projects, including the rebuilding of the cupola at St. Peter's Basilica and the remodeling of the Piazza del Campidoglio. Neither, however, was to be completed in the artist's lifetime.

In his last years, Michelangelo returned to sculpture with two devotional and deeply personal works. The Florence *Pietà* (1550-1556) was intended for Michelangelo's own tomb and contained his self-portrait. In 1555, however, he attacked and damaged the piece in a fit of frustration. Thereafter he sculpted the Rondanini *Pietà* (1552-1564), on which he was still working six days before his death, in 1564, when he was eighty-eight.

SIGNIFICANCE

Michelangelo gave eloquent expression, in sculpture, painting, and poetry, to his own ideals and those of his

---

MICHELANGELO'S POEM ON PAINTING THE SISTINE CHAPEL

Michelangelo endured physical and mental strain in the years it took him to paint the ceiling of the Sistine Chapel. Here, in a witty verse written around 1511, he tells of the pain.

I've got myself a goitre from this strain,
As water gives the cats in Lombardy
Or maybe it is in some other country;
My belly's pushed by force beneath my chin.

My beard toward Heaven, I feel the back of my brain
Upon my nape, I grow the breast of a harpy;
My brush, above my face continually,
Makes it a splendid floor by dripping down.

My loins have penetrated to my paunch,
My rump's a crupper, as a counterweight,
And pointless the unseeing steps I go.

In front of me my skin is being stretched
While it folds up behind and forms a knot,
And I am bending like a Syrian bow.

And judgment hence must grow,
Borne in the mind, peculiar and untrue;
You cannot shoot well when the gun's askew.

John [Giovanni da Pistoia], come to the rescue
Of my dead painting now, and of my honor;
I'm not in a good place, and I'm no painter.

Source: The Middle Ages and Renaissance. Vol. 1 in A Documentary History of Art, edited by Elizabeth Gilmore Holt (New York: Anchor Books, 1957), pp. 23-24.

---

contemporaries as they moved from the confident Humanism of the High Renaissance to the anxious spirituality of the Counter-Reformation period. His early work seems to harmonize the pagan sensuality of antiquity with Christian themes and to celebrate human beauty as a reflection of divine creation. As his art and thought evolved, however, he increasingly conveyed a tension between spirit and body, form and matter, and he came to depreciate physical perfection in favor of psychological and spiritual expression. In his late Roman years, he became associated with the Catholic reform movement, and his growing religious fervor gives a highly personal and sometimes mystical flavor to the art of this period.

Michelangelo's genius was recognized and venerated by his contemporaries, and he exerted enormous influence on generations of younger artists. It was, however, the superficial aspects of his style—serpentine poses and muscular anatomies—that were easiest to assimilate. None of his followers was able to match his profundity of thought and feeling.

—Jane Kristof

FURTHER READING

Condivi, Ascanio. *The Life of Michelangelo*. Edited with an introduction by Hellmut Wohl. Translated by Alice Sedgwick Wohl. Baton Rouge: Louisiana State University Press, 1976. An essential primary source, this biography was written during Michelangelo's lifetime by one of his students and is based on the artist's own recollections. Illustrations and bibliography.

De Tolnay, Charles. *Michelangelo*. 5 vols. 2d ed., rev. Princeton, N.J.: Princeton University Press, 1969-1971. The definitive scholarly study of the artist in five volumes, each devoted to a particular aspect of his life or work. Catalog of works, extensive notes, illustrations, and bibliography.

Gill, Anton. *Il Gigante: Michelangelo, Florence, and the David, 1492-1504*. New York: T. Dunne Books, 2003. Study focuses on the twelve years between the death of Lorenzo de' Medici and the unveiling of Michelangelo's most famous statue. The author claims that these twelve years are the most dramatic, not just in Michelangelo's life, but in Florentine history as well. Includes photographic plates, illustrations, map, bibliographic references, and index.

Goffen, Rona. *Renaissance Rivals: Michelangelo, Leonardo, Raphael, Titian*. New Haven, Conn.: Yale University Press, 2002. A study of the importance of artistic rivalry to both the great artists of the Renaissance and their patrons. Looks at many primary documents of the period, including letters, contracts, and treatises. Includes illustrations, bibliographic references, and index.

Hartt, Frederick. *Michelangelo*. New York: Harry N. Abrams, 1965. Limited to Michelangelo's paintings, which are dealt with in an introductory essay, followed by color plates with interpretive comments. Biographical chronology and bibliography.

_____. *Michelangelo, the Complete Sculpture*. New York: Harry N. Abrams, 1969. Contains lavish illustrations, many in color, with fine interpretive text geared to plates. Includes biographical chronology and bibliography.

Hibbard, Howard. *Michelangelo*. 2d ed. Cambridge, Mass.: Harper & Row, 1985. A highly readable, unobtrusively scholarly survey of Michelangelo's life and career. Illustrations and bibliography.

King, Ross. *Michelangelo and the Pope's Ceiling*. London: Chatto & Windus, 2002. Extremely detailed narrative of the creation of the Sistine Chapel fresco, from the political intrigues behind Michelangelo's receipt of the commission through its completion. Details both the artist's daily life and rivalries of the period, and the technical details of the creation itself, as well as emphasizing the importance of Michelangelo's work to the history of art. Includes photographic plates, illustrations, maps, bibliographic references, and index.

Murray, Linda. *Michelangelo: His Life, Work, and Times*. New York: Thames and Hudson, 1984. Focus on the artist's historical setting, with extended quotes from contemporary sources. Numerous illustrations relate both to Michelangelo's works and to his background. Bibliography.

Vasari, Giorgio. "Michelangelo." In *Lives of the Artists*, translated by George Bull. New York: Penguin Books, 1965. A major primary source, this biography by a friend and fellow artist was written shortly after Michelangelo's death and includes firsthand impressions and recollections.

SEE ALSO: Alexander VI; Andrea del Sarto; Sofonisba Anguissola; Donato Bramante; Clement VII; Vittoria Colonna; El Greco; Julius II; Leo X; Leonardo da Vinci; Lorenzo de' Medici; Paul III; Raphael; Jacopo Sansovino; Girolamo Savonarola; Tintoretto; Titian; Giorgio Vasari.

RELATED ARTICLES in *Great Events from History: The Renaissance & Early Modern Era, 1454-1600:* 1469-1492: Rule of Lorenzo de' Medici; 1477-1482: Work Begins on the Sistine Chapel; c. 1500: Revival of Classical Themes in Art; 1500: Roman Jubilee; 1508-1512 and 1534-1541: Michelangelo Paints the Sistine Chapel.

MOHAMMED I ASKIA
King of the Songhai Empire (r. 1493-1528)

Mohammed I Askia greatly expanded and consolidated the Songhai Empire, which dominated much of West Africa in the fifteenth and sixteenth centuries. His policies resulted in a rapid expansion of trade and the imposition of the stamp of Islamic civilization on the empire.

BORN: c. 1442; probably near Gao, Songhai Empire (now in Mali)

DIED: 1538; near Gao

ALSO KNOWN AS: Moḥammad I Askia; Askia Muḥammad; Muḥammad Ture; Mohammed Ture ibn Abi Bakr (given name); Muḥammad ibn Abī Bakr Ture; Askia the Great

AREAS OF ACHIEVEMENT: Government and politics, religion and theology

EARLY LIFE

Mohammed I Askia (moh-HAH-mehd AS-kyah) was born Mohammed Ture ibn Abi Bakr, probably of parents of the Soninke people. Although the Soninke frequently are cited as the source of the royal lineage of ancient Ghana, a large West African kingdom that flourished before 1000, most Soninke, including Mohammed's clan, were subject in the fifteenth century to the Songhai Empire, centered at the Niger River entrepôt of Gao.

Mohammed's family was of a military caste, providing soldiers and officers for the Songhai cavalry regiments. His childhood and education no doubt reflected that experience. He probably received systematic religious instruction in some Islamic institution as a child. In early adulthood, Mohammed became a trusted lieutenant in the service of the Songhai emperor, Sonni ʿAlī. Mohammed's early years were a time of unprecedented expansion and turmoil for Songhai. Although oral dynastic history of Songhai goes back to the eighth or ninth century, prior to the fifteenth Songhai had been only a small principality.

Sonni ʿAlī's leadership transformed Songhai into a regional influence. Taking advantage of the progressive disintegration of its powerful western neighbor Mali, after 1450, his forces swept westward, capturing the fabled city of Timbuktu, pushing back the Saharan nomads who menaced the river towns, and punishing recalcitrant Mossi chieftains to the south. In the process of forming an empire, however, Sonni ʿAlī revealed a streak of barbaric cruelty. Furthermore, many of the newly conquered areas west of Songhai proper were heavily Islamic and thought to be culturally more sophisticated than Songhai itself, and often related more to North African than sub-Saharan ethnic types. Sonni ʿAlī's vicious temperament and cavalier attitude toward Islam set his subjects to plotting. His death in 1492, before consolidation of Songhai's considerable territorial gains could be completed, prepared the way for Mohammed to emerge as a national leader.

LIFE'S WORK

In April, 1493, Mohammed allied himself with the Muslim clerics and disaffected Muslim portions of the empire against Sonni ʿAlī's son and would-be successor, whose support lay primarily in the Songhai homeland. Ethnic and religious divisions ran deep in the ranks of the large Songhai army. Mohammed avoided what otherwise might have become a bloody and prolonged civil war by staging a coup, seizing the capital, and forcing Sonni ʿAlī's son into exile. He took the dynastic title of askia (*askiya*).

Mohammed's first task was to obtain recognition as the legitimate ruler of Songhai. That he achieved, at least initially, by purging or deporting as many members of earlier Songhai dynastic lines as possible. His long-term strategy, however, involved cultivation of tighter alliances with Muslim intellectuals and clerics. Mohammed viewed Islam as the logical counterpoint in Songhai to the power and influence of the traditional priesthood and political leadership. He lavished attention, gifts, and titles on Muslim notables, particularly those in the newly conquered, western part of the empire. He also strove to develop the city of Timbuktu—already known for its concentration of Muslim clerics and scholars—into a first-rate center of learning, a cultural focus that could rival the traditional religious center of Kukia in the eastern Songhai homeland.

Mohammed must have perceived the enormous advantages of Islam in transforming Songhai from a peripheral state into a partner in what was, in the sixteenth century, the world's most diverse and extensive civilization and commercial network. Songhai, and its predecessors Ghana and Mali, depended on the export of gold and ivory to North Africa for hard currency, and on crucial imports such as horses for cavalry. There is evidence too that, by Mohammed's time, the presence of European trading stations on the West African coast was beginning to affect traditional commercial networks in the region.

For these reasons, doubtless also as an expression of his own piety, Mohammed in late 1496 undertook the *hajj*, or pilgrimage, to Mecca. The expedition was a stupendous effort to eclipse the pomp and splendor of the pilgrimage by Mansa Mūsā some 175 years earlier. In Egypt, the titular ʿAbbāsid caliph bestowed on Mohammed the title caliph of the Blacks. In addition to donating enormous amounts of gold to the poor and needy, Mohammed endowed a hostel for future pilgrims from West Africa. Mohammed was away nearly two years, which suggests that he was firmly in control of affairs in Songhai.

Mohammed's *hajj* was a boon to the fortunes of Islam in West Africa. He established visibility for the kingdom and returned determined to purify the practices of West African Muslims and bring them into line with orthodoxy. The *hajj* attracted scholars and religious notables from all over the Middle East; many accompanied Mohammed back to Songhai and greatly strengthened the scholarly community there. Timbuktu, in particular, developed an international reputation as an academic and religious center. Farther to the west, amid the serpentine courses of the Niger floodplain, protected from invasion by the annual inundation, the city of Djenné developed a reputation throughout West Africa comparable to that of Timbuktu.

Mohammed continued to expand Songhai's frontiers, often in the cause of a jihad, or holy war. His soldiers battled the Mossi tribes of modern Burkina Faso to the south and captured most of the important salt mines and oases in the Sahara as far as the frontiers of modern Algeria and Libya. Even some of the powerful Hausa city-states of northern Nigeria fell under Mohammed's sway. The Songhai army featured a mobile cavalry and levies of conscripts, very likely the first such standing army in Africa, supported by a strong riverine navy on the Niger. (Firearms, however, though apparently known, were not used by the Songhai forces.) By the end of Mohammed's active reign, these forces had created what most likely was the largest political entity in African history to that time.

The administrative structure of Songhai shows little of the Islamic influence so pervasive in other facets of the state. It was a simple system of provincial governors responsible to Mohammed. There was a ministerial council of sorts but with little real power and usually dominated by members of the royal family in any case. The court protocol that was reported by foreign travelers—

among them the famous Leo Africanus—suggests that Mohammed continued to behave as a traditional West African king, wielding almost absolute power. Despite his commitment to Islam, there is no evidence of persecution of unbelievers. Gao, in fact, became a haven for Jewish refugees from the Saharan oases when persecution broke out there in the early sixteenth century. Many of Mohammed's gestures toward traditionalism may have resulted from the fact that the people of the Songhai capital of Gao continued to resist Islamic influence.

Signs of despotism reappeared in Mohammed's later years. Moreover, the large and unprecedented administrative apparatus of the court and provincial government had to be supported by a growing system of landed aristocrats, a network of royal estates producing food and military supplies through slavery and forced labor. Newly conquered peoples found themselves assigned to the production of weapons and armor or to service to the army. Others plied the Niger to produce fish for the court.

In his declining years, Mohammed lost his grip on the empire. In order to foster the continued growth of Islam, the king had designated a western governor as successor, but his ambitious sons were determined to seize power. In 1528, they deposed Mohammed, who was already blind and infirm, exiling him to an island in the Niger. Nearly a decade of turmoil elapsed before the Askia rivals settled on a system of succession and power sharing.

SIGNIFICANCE

Mohammed I Askia belongs to a tradition of warrior-kings who periodically unified and integrated the Niger basin and adjacent areas, a tradition beginning perhaps as early as 800. This periodic unification greatly affected the economic history of lands around the Mediterranean, especially with respect to the export of gold and other precious commodities. In the Niger region itself, it established a level of political order and stability necessary for commerce to thrive. In the period of Mohammed, as well as in earlier decades when Mali was prominent, Islam made important advances, which conferred a measure of cultural unity on the region and also stimulated interaction with the outside world.

Mohammed himself was among the foremost of the unifiers, administrators, and purveyors of Islam. Evidence from the era of his predecessor, Sonni ʿAlī, strongly suggests that Islam was in decline, actively challenged by pagan and traditional elements in West African society. Given the importance of Muslim merchants in the economic life of the region, it is also likely that the Niger basin was in a state of economic disarray owing to the disintegration of Mali and growing hostility to outsiders. These trends Mohammed dramatically reversed, restoring and greatly expanding commerce and drawing the Niger basin closer than ever before to the world economy. His contributions toward an Islamic cultural order laid the foundations for the eventual emergence of Islam as a mass religion in West Africa.

Mohammed's Askia Dynasty continued after his death. His sons ruled ably for fifty years in the mid-sixteenth century, during which time Songhai maintained relations with the newly established Ottoman Empire in North Africa, and Songhai was able to withstand some of the commercial turmoil resulting from increased European activity on the African coast.

On the other hand, the limits of Mohammed's Islamic campaign in Songhai are clear. Neither he nor his successors managed to close the gap between the predominantly Muslim west and the still-pagan Songhai heartland in the eastern part of the empire. Civil war eventually resulted in a disastrous reverse for Mohammed's Islamic edifice in 1588. Three years later, an invasion from Morocco brought the empire crashing down and the Askia Dynasty to a humiliating close.

—Ronald W. Davis

FURTHER READING

Boahen, A. Adu, Jacob F. Ade Ajayi, and Michael Tidy. *Topics in West African History.* 2d ed. Burnt Mill, England: Longman Group, 1986. An excellent description of Songhai within the wider context of medieval West African history.

Bovill, E. W., and Robin Hallet. *The Golden Trade of the Moors.* 2d ed., rev. 1958. Reprint. Princeton, N.J.: Markus Weiner, 1999. An excellent treatment of medieval West African history and its connections with European events. Gives a detailed account of the rise of Songhai and the contributions of its major rulers.

Hale, Thomas A. *Scribe, Griot, and Novelist: Narrative Interpreters of the Songhay Empire.* Gainesville: University of Florida Press, 1990. Comparative study of written Arabic narratives from the sixteenth and seventeenth centuries, a modern francophone Malian novel, and an oral epic telling of Mohammed's rule. The epic, newly recorded, transcribed, and translated, is reproduced in its entirety.

Includes one photographic plate, map, bibliography, and index.

Hunwick, J. O. "Religion and State in the Songhay Empire." In *Islam in Tropical Africa*, edited by I. M. Lewis. London: Oxford University Press, 1966. Discusses the tensions between Islamic and pagan religious and philosophical ideas in Songhai and how the major rulers borrowed and elaborated on ideas from both sources to organize and administer the empire.

_____, ed. and trans. *Timbuktu and the Songhay Empire: Al-Saʿdi's "Taʾrīkh al-Sūdān" Down to 1613, and Other Contemporary Documents.* Boston: Brill, 2003. Translation and analysis of a chronicle of the Songhay court and other primary documents recording the acts of Mohammed and his successors. Includes illustrations, genealogical tables, maps, bibliographic references, and index.

Kaba, Lansine. "The Pen, the Sword, and the Crown: Islam and Revolution in Songhay Reconsidered, 1464-1493." *Journal of African History* 25 (1984): 241-256. Traces the rise of Songhai to changing trade patterns and discusses Sonni ʿAlī's antagonism toward Muslim elites which, by contrast, Mohammed supported and used to build his administration.

Malio, Nouhou, et al. *The Epic of Askia Mohammed.* Translated, edited, and annotated by Thomas A. Hale. Bloomington: Indiana University Press, 1996. Newly annotated and revised translation of the epic first published in Hale's book, together with a new introductory essay. Includes illustrations, bibliographic references, and index.

Pardo, Anne W. "The Songhay Empire Under Sonni Ali and Askia Muhammad: A Study in Comparisons and Contrasts." In *Aspects of West African Islam*, edited by Daniel F. McCall. Boston: Boston University Press, 1971. An unusually critical treatment of chronicles and other sources in an effort to determine the precise ideological and religious attitudes of Sonni ʿAlī and Mohammed.

Saad, Elias. *A Social History of Timbuktu: The Role of Muslim Scholars and Notables, 1400-1900.* New York: Cambridge University Press, 1983. An important study of social and intellectual life in precolonial West Africa. Provides extensive coverage of the zenith of Songhai civilization in the early sixteenth century, using indigenous chronicles and a wide variety of other documentary sources.

Trimingham, J. Spencer. *A History of Islam in West*

Africa. New York: Oxford University Press, 1962. One of the most painstaking studies of the development of Islamic influence and practices in the region. Particularly harsh on Sonni ʿAlī and critical of other accounts suggesting a high level of Islamic intellectual activity in Songhai and the center of learning in Timbuktu.

SEE ALSO: Amina Sarauniya Zazzua; Askia Daud; Leo Africanus; Muḥammad ibn ʿAbd al-Karīm al-Maghīlī; Sonni ʿAlī.
RELATED ARTICLES in *Great Events from History: The Renaissance & Early Modern Era, 1454-1600:* c. 1464-1591: Songhai Empire Dominates the Western Sudan; 1493-1528: Reign of Mohammed I Askia.

Michel Eyquem de Montaigne
French writer and scholar

In an age of violent religious and political struggles, Montaigne mediated for tolerance. His gift to literature was the invention of the essay.

Born: February 28, 1533; Château de Montaigne, Périgord, near Bordeaux, France
Died: September 13, 1592; Château de Montaigne, Périgord, near Bordeaux, France
Also known as: Michel de Montaigne
Areas of achievement: Literature, philosophy, government and politics, scholarship

Early Life

Michel Eyquem de Montaigne (mee-shehl ehk-ehm deh mahn-tayn) was born in his father's château in Périgord, a French county east and north of Bordeaux that became a part of France in 1607. His father, Pierre Eyquem, held many important posts, including that of mayor of Bordeaux, and afforded an unusual model of religious tolerance by heading a Catholic family that included a Protestant wife of Spanish and Jewish blood and two Protestant children.

Montaigne dearly loved his father, who was responsible for his receiving a gentle and cultured life. At age six, he was sent to the finest school in Bordeaux, where he completed the twelve-year course in seven years. Sometime during the next eight years, he very likely studied law.

From 1557 to 1570, Montaigne was a councillor in the Bordeaux Parlement and took numerous trips to Paris. During this period, he made a close and erudite friend, Étienne de La Boétie, who in the remaining four years of his life came to be more important to Montaigne than anyone else and influenced Montaigne throughout his life. It was La Boétie's stoic acceptance of suffering and his courageous death, at which Montaigne was present despite the danger of contagion, that turned Montaigne toward Stoicism and probably inspired him to begin writing.

In 1565, Montaigne married Françoise de La Chassaigne. He seldom mentions her in his writing. Of his six children, only one, Léonor, survived childhood.

About 1567, Montaigne's father had him translate a work that was strongly opposed to Protestantism and atheism: *Theologia naturalis, sive Liber creaturarum* (1485; the book of creatures: or, natural theology), written in medieval Latin by a fifteenth century Spaniard, Raymond Sebond. His father, although terminally ill, arranged for the publication of the translation.

After his father's death, Michel became lord of Montaigne, owner of the château and the estate, and at thirty-eight years of age retired to what he hoped would be a life of quiet study and composition. Much of his time was spent in the tower, which he asked to be added to his castle and which even his wife was forbidden to enter. There he wrote his life's work, *Essais* (1580-1595; *The Essays*, 1603), which was placed on the *Index librorum prohibitorum*, or Index of Prohibited Books, in 1676 but was viewed favorably by the Vatican in Montaigne's day.

Life's Work

Over a period of thirty years, Montaigne dealt with every conceivable aspect of a person's life by describing in detail his own thoughts, beliefs, experiences, and habits of living. Nothing was too abstruse to be tackled or too insignificant to be mentioned. His essay titles range from "Sur des vers de Virgile" ("On Certain Verses of Virgil") to "Des coches" ("Of Coaches"). His early essays were compilations of views followed by a brief moral, often showing the influence of the first century Roman philosopher Seneca the Younger or of the first-second century Greek biographer Plutarch, both of whom he admired immensely. These were followed by what is called his skeptical period, during which he coined his motto: "What do I know?" The years from 1578 onward are

Michel Eyquem de Montaigne. (Library of Congress)

termed his Epicurean period, wherein he endeavored to find his own nature and to follow its dictates. His hero during this period was Socrates, and life was a great adventure to be lived as happily as possible, with due regard for the rights of others and guided by common sense. He counseled moderation in all things, freedom with self-control, and honesty and courage.

In the essay "De la proesumption" ("About Presumption"), Montaigne describes himself as below average in height but strong and well-set, with a face not fat but full. A portrait of him in the Condé Museum at Chantilly depicts him as handsome, with regular features, fine eyes, short-cropped hair, a small mustache, and a neat beard. Evidently he was not given to vanity. He enjoyed horseback riding, travel, and conversation with intelligent men. He also enjoyed the company of his "covenant daughter," Marie de Gournay, who became his literary executor.

After Montaigne's retirement, all his time was not spent in seclusion: Between 1572 and 1576, he attempted to mediate between his friend Henry of Navarre (later King Henry IV) and the extremist Catholics of the Holy League. At the accession of Henry III in 1576, Mon-

taigne was made a gentleman of the Bedchamber, an office that gave access to the king without requiring residence at court. His disgust at the excesses of the Wars of Religion gave him a strong distaste for government, and, while he loved the city of Paris, he avoided the royal court.

In 1580, Montaigne journeyed to take the waters at Lucca on the west coast of Italy. He hoped, but probably did not really believe, that the baths could cure his recurring misery caused by a kidney stone. Accompanied by his younger brother, two nobles, and a secretary, he left on horseback with no planned itinerary.

En route to the baths, he visited Paris, Switzerland, and Germany. In Rome, he was declared a citizen of that city, an honor he greatly coveted. During his second stay in Lucca, he learned to his dismay that he had been elected mayor of Bordeaux. He tried to refuse the responsibility but finally capitulated and arrived home after an absence of seventeen months.

Montaigne served two terms as mayor, from 1581 to 1585, and without showing undue zeal managed to initiate some reforms that included improving the lot of foundling children and imprisoned women and helping the poor by refusing to allow the rich to be exempt from taxation. He showed his concern for education by improving the Collège des Jésuites and also his own old school, the Collège de Guyenne. He left office somewhat ignominiously, tendering his resignation outside the city, which was at that time stricken by the plague.

Although no longer mayor, Montaigne was unable to avoid for long his involvement in the turbulent political situation. After a peaceful year at home working on *The Essays*, he found his unprotected estate overrun by soldiers and himself suspect to both the Catholics and the Protestants. In early 1588, he was sent to Paris on a secret mission to Henry III from Henry of Navarre. En route, he was detained by Protestants, and a few months later, he found himself briefly imprisoned in the Bastille by the Catholics. After nearly a year spent in following the king from Paris to Chartres to Rouen and attending the estates-general at Blois, Montaigne returned home and helped to keep Bordeaux loyal to the king. In his remaining years, he continued to add passages to *The Essays*. There is no eyewitness account of his death, but numerous contemporaries claim that he died peacefully while hearing Mass in his room.

Significance

Montaigne's writing style is vivacious and strong, with unexpected images, picturesque details, and often ironic humor. He reaches his highest level when he discusses the interdependence of mind and matter; modern psychologists and even psychiatrists might well claim him as their forefather. It is said that the nineteenth to twentieth century psychoanalyst Sigmund Freud was interested in *The Essays*.

Perhaps it is the surprising intimacy that Montaigne creates that is the most novel characteristic of his work: The reader believes that he knows the author better than he knows his closest friends or his family and maybe better than he knows himself. This kind of writing was new to literature.

In politics and in religion, Montaigne was opposed to change; his aim was peace, and he worked toward that end. Despite personal reservations, he remained a loyal subject of the Crown and a practicing Catholic, proclaiming that one ought to accept the government of one's country and its religion.

In education, Montaigne was centuries ahead of his time: In his essay "De l'institution des enfants" ("Of the Education of Children"), he advocated training a child to be an efficient human being by exposing him or her not to pedants but to individuals of all social stations. The child must be taught to observe and to judge for himself or herself.

In literature, Montaigne established the great principle of the seventeenth century: respect for and imitation of the classics. He insisted that the only subject suitable for a person's study is humankind itself. There is no doubt that his essays influenced Francis Bacon, François de La Rochefoucauld, Blaise Pascal, Jean de La Bruyère, and Joseph Addison.

While Montaigne was describing himself in his writings, he was also depicting humans in general; in fact, he was dealing with the human condition. In the twentieth century, Albert Camus, André Malraux, Jean-Paul Sartre, and a host of other eminent writers and philosophers in Europe and the United States devoted their talents to examining the human condition. Whether they

---

MONTAIGNE ON THE INCONSISTENCY OF HUMAN ACTIONS

Montaigne developed the genre of the personal essay, which reflected his belief in the importance of the little things in life, of the trivial actions of the individual heart and mind, and of the fits and starts—the inconsistencies and incoherencies—that define us as human. In effect, there is nothing Montaigne finds "more difficult to believe than man's consistency, and nothing more easy than his inconsistency."

It seems reasonable to judge a man by the most ordinary acts of his life, but in view of the natural instability of our habits and opinions, I have often thought that even good authors are wrong in obstinately attributing to us a steadfast and consistent character. . . .

We do not go, we are carried along, like things floating, now smoothly, now perturbedly, according as the water is angry or calm. . . .

Every day a new fancy; and our humours move with the changes of weather. . . .

These so supple changes and contradictions which we manifest have made some imagine that we have two souls, others, that we have two powers which, each in its own way, accompany and stir us, the one to good, the other to evil, since so abrupt a diversity is not to be reconciled with a single subject. . . .

All the contradictions are to be found in me, according as the wind turns and changes. Bashful, insolent; chaste, lascivious; talkative, taciturn; clumsy, gentle; witty, dull; peevish, sweet-tempered; mendacious, truthful; knowing, ignorant. . . .

We are all made up of bits, and so shapelessly and diversely put together, that every piece, at every moment, plays its own game. And there is as much difference between us and ourselves, as between us and others.

It is not enough for a sober understanding to judge us simply by our external actions: we must sound the innermost recesses, and observe the springs which give the swing.

Source: From Essais, *by Montaigne, excerpted in* The Norton Anthology of World Masterpieces, *vol. 1, edited by Maynard Mack (New York: W. W. Norton, 1980), pp. 1313-1318, passim.*

---

acknowledged it, directly or indirectly, they were all indebted to Montaigne.

—*Dorothy B. Aspinwall*

FURTHER READING

Burke, Peter. *Montaigne*. New York: Hill & Wang, 1981. Each of the ten chapters is devoted to a special aspect of Montaigne. Each chapter has its own bibliography, and there is an index. The style is straightforward, the information accurate. For students and general readers.

Frame, Donald M. *Montaigne's Discovery of Man: The Humanization of a Humanist*. New York: Columbia University Press, 1955. Reprint. Westport, Conn.:

Greenwood Press, 1983. An account of the life of Montaigne and the development of his thought as conveyed in *The Essays*.

_____. *Montaigne's "Essais": A Study*. Englewood Cliffs, N.J.: Prentice-Hall, 1969. A detailed study of Montaigne's life and an erudite examination of the evolution of his talent as revealed in *The Essays* as well as an estimate of his impact during the last four centuries. Contains a chronology, a bibliography, and an index.

Hartie, Ann. *Michel de Montaigne: Accidental Philosopher*. New York: Cambridge University Press, 2003. This study of Montaigne's work seeks to counter the perception that his achievements were primarily literary rather than philosophical. Argues for the philosophical originality and importance of his ideas. Includes bibliographic references and index.

Hoffman, George. *Montaigne's Career*. New York: Oxford University Press, 1998. This study of the relationship between politics and writing in the sixteenth century charts Montaigne's various occupations and sources of income in order to determine the influence of financial and practical considerations on his writings and his thought. Includes bibliographic references and index.

Levine, Alan. *Sensual Philosophy: Toleration, Skepticism, and Montaigne's Politics of the Self*. Lanham, Md.: Lexington Books, 2001. Based on the presumption that until now practitioners of various disciplines (literary criticism, political science, philosophy, history) have each studied and appropriated only fragments of Montaigne's work, this study aims to be the first to synthesize his model of the self, his attitudes toward Native Americans, his skepticism, and his arguments in favor of tolerance into a single comprehensive model of Montaigne's thought showing how each piece relates to the whole. Includes bibliographic references and index.

Montaigne, Michel de. *The Essays of Michel de Montaigne*. Translated and edited by M. A. Screech. New York: Penguin Classics, 1993. A contender for the definitive edition of Montaigne's *Essais* in English. Includes an extremely useful introduction and extensive notes by the translator. Bibliographic references and index.

O'Neill, John. *Essaying Montaigne: A Study of the Renaissance Institution of Writing and Reading*. 2d ed. Liverpool, England: Liverpool University Press, 2001. Examines Montaigne's practice of writing, its cultural context, and his personal understanding of what it meant to write, as well as the reception of Montaigne's work, both by his contemporaries and by successive generations up to the present. Includes bibliographic references and index.

Sichel, Edith. *Michel de Montaigne*. London: Constable, 1911. Reprint. Port Washington, N.Y.: Kennikat Press, 1970. Divided into "Montaigne the Man" and "Montaigne the Philosopher," this is a leisurely and rather personal view of his times, his life, and his work based largely on quotations from *The Essays*. Facsimiles of portraits as well as manuscript and bibliographical notes.

SEE ALSO: Henry III; Henry IV; François Hotman; François Rabelais.

RELATED ARTICLE in *Great Events from History: The Renaissance & Early Modern Era, 1454-1600:* 1580-1595: Montaigne Publishes His *Essays*.

MONTEZUMA II
Aztec emperor (r. 1502-1520)

Montezuma II expanded the Aztec Empire to its greatest size but died as his empire crumbled under the pressures of the Spanish conquistador Hernán Cortés.

BORN: 1467; Tenochtitlán, Aztec Empire (now Mexico City, Mexico)
DIED: June 30, 1520; Tenochtitlán
ALSO KNOWN AS: Moctezuma
AREA OF ACHIEVEMENT: Government and politics

EARLY LIFE

Axayácatl named his fourth son Montezuma (mawn-tay-SEW-mah), the Younger, after the child's great-grandfather. Montezuma I was the Mexica *Uei Tlatoani* (great speaker, or emperor) of the Aztec Empire, centered in Anahuac, an intermontane valley in central Mexico. At Montezuma the Younger's naming ceremony, held four days after his birth in 1467, the priests dedicated the infant to Quetzalcóatl, that year's patron deity, and prophesied that he would earn greatness as both ruler and priest.

The prophecy was not a guarantee. Young Montezuma was born into an oligarchy called the *Pipiltin* (sons of lords) that was composed of the putative descendants of Acamapichtli, founder of the Mexica state, and a princess of the fading Culhuacán dynasty. The office of emperor was not hereditary. A council of *Pipiltin* elders elected a successor on the basis of merit rather than on degrees of kinship to the deceased emperor. For Montezuma to become emperor when his generation came of age, his accomplishments would have to set him apart from his brothers and cousins.

After spending five years in the *Calmécac*, an elite preparatory school, twelve-year-old Montezuma moved into the barracks for a two-year apprenticeship before joining the warriors in combat. He soon excelled in battle and captured enough enemies to be inducted into the exclusive Order of the Eagle. In 1483, at age sixteen, he resumed religious studies and became a priest of the war god Huitzilopochtli (Blue Hummingbird). The next year, Montezuma had to decide whether to take an oath of celibacy and devote his entire life to the priesthood or to marry and continue his military career.

He chose the middle route and became a warrior-priest. He had, eventually, four legitimate wives and participated in most of the major military campaigns until his installation as emperor in 1503. Through his first wife, he inherited the title *tlatoani* (speaker, or ruler) of the city-state Ehecatepec. Prowess in war made him an army commander at age thirty, and later he became *Tlacochcalcatl* (prince of the house), one of the four closest advisers to the emperor. He also retained his priestly office and rose through clerical ranks to become high priest of Huitzilopochtli.

LIFE'S WORK

This warrior-priest bore the markings of both professions on his body. Among warriors, he was a *Tequihua* (master of cuts) and had the sides of his head shaved, leaving on top a stiff tuft bound with a red thong. A sizable plug through his lower lip and large studs through extended ear lobes identified him as an aristocrat. A band of black paint across his face signified his priestly status, as did the streaks of cuts and scars on his ears, arms, and thighs. Montezuma had made these cuts with cactus thorns as he propitiated the deities with his own blood. He was of average height, slight but of wiry build; he had little wisps of hair on his upper lip and chin and a yellowish-brown skin color. In demeanor, he was grave, reserved, almost aloof. To his reputation of bravery was added respect for his soft-spoken advice on political and religious affairs of state.

The Aztec Empire was relatively young. The Mexica themselves were the last branch of the Aztec tribe to leave the ancestral home of Aztlán. They had arrived in Anahuac in 1258. Called *Chichimeca* (sons of dogs) by the remnants of the disintegrating Toltec-Culhuacán civilization, the Mexica had been treated as outcasts for a century. In 1375, Acamapichtli had secured recognition as a fellow *tlatoani* from the rulers of the city-states around Lake Texcoco. Having risen from abasement to parity, Acamapichtli and his three successors had forged alliances and waged wars until the Mexica dominated Anahuac.

Montezuma I, the fifth *tlatoani*, had sent conquering armies down the slopes of the central valley in all directions and built an empire that reached the oceans to the east and west, the deserts to the north, and the tropical forests to the south. His next three successors, his grandsons—the father and uncles of Montezuma II—had inherited the title *uei tlatoani* and continued the policy of constant expansion.

The Aztec Empire was built by war and sustained by blood. Conquered nations paid annual tributes of young men and women who were sacrificed to gods that consumed human hearts. The victims' beating hearts were ripped out of their chests, heads severed then stacked in enormous pyramids, and bodies butchered for consumption by the victorious Mexica.

When Emperor Ahuitzotl died in 1502, Montezuma's piety and prowess convinced the council of elders that he was preferable to his elder brother Macuilmalinaltzin. Following his election, Montezuma II spent a brief time in prayer and meditation, then led an invasion of two neighboring provinces. He brought back fifty-one hundred prisoners to be sacrificed and eaten as part of the enthronement festivities the following year. As emperor, Montezuma had to let his hair grow to shoulder length,

An imaginative depiction of Montezuma II's reception of Hernán Cortés. (Library of Congress)

wear a thin gold tube through his nose, and exchange his copper lip and ear plugs for larger, golden plugs. He wore a half-miter crown and gold sandals. Once installed, he launched a series of startling actions.

He purged from all government positions *Pipiltin* supporters of his brother and dissolved the council of elders. He then directed the massacre of Macuilmalinaltzin, two younger brothers, and twenty-eight hundred Texcoco warriors. With his power consolidated, Montezuma turned his attention to the empire's subject states. He required all conquered nations to send their nobles to Tenochtitlán, where they replaced the commoners in Montezuma's palace as servants. Tribute payments were increased, and each nation had to erect its own temples to Huitzilopochtli. He then sent armies to the south to add new territories to the empire and to bring more oblations to Huitzilopochtli. By 1519, Montezuma's empire encompassed about 200,000 square miles and contained more than twenty million people. Montezuma had created a chasm between himself and commoners by surrounding himself with only nobles. He had elevated Huitzilopochtli in importance throughout the empire and had identified himself more closely with Huitzilopochtli. Soon, however, his patron god Quetzalcóatl overtook the war god in importance for Montezuma and his empire.

The principal deities of the primitive Mexica had been their tribal goddess Mexitli and Huitzilopochtli. When the Mexica arrived in Anahuac, the principal Toltec deity was Quetzalcóatl, the god of divine wisdom who had taught humans agriculture and all the other arts of civilization. The Toltecs had an elaborate cosmogony that included a cyclical theory of time and a conviction that quarrelsome gods had created and destroyed the world four times. At a reconciliation, some of the gods had created a fifth world by immolating themselves. Quetzalcóatl traveled to the netherworld and collected the bones of humans who had lived in the previous worlds. He then ground the bones into powder and re-created humanity by mixing his own divine blood into the powder.

In the ninth century, three hundred years before the Mexica began their trek, the Toltecs were ruled by a high priest who had taken Quetzalcóatl as his own name. This Quetzalcóatl introduced radical religious reforms. He ended human sacrifice, took a vow of celibacy, and sought spiritual unity with his divine namesake through prayer, meditation, and penance. When the priest was an old man, three sorcerers gave an intoxicant, which they called a medicine, to Quetzalcóatl. When the priest was inebriated, the sorcerers put him in bed with a princess, who successfully tempted him to break his vow of chastity. On awakening, Quetzalcóatl felt his disgrace so keenly that he fled the Toltec nation, which promptly restored human sacrifice. When Quetzalcóatl reached the Gulf of Mexico, he sailed eastward on a magic raft and vowed to return once he found the place of perfect wisdom.

In their cyclical reckoning of time, the Toltecs and their successors calculated the possible return of Quetzalcóatl and the possible destruction of the fifth world. In the third year of Montezuma's reign, 1506, a fifty-two-year cycle of time was completed. A campaign to Oaxaca garnered twenty-three hundred captives, who were sacrificed en masse in a petition for fifty-two more years of life. If Quetzalcóatl were to return in this new cycle, the light-skinned, bearded priest would return from the east on a magic raft in 1519.

While Hernán Cortés and his five hundred Spaniards sailed up the Yucatán coast in early 1519, Montezuma received regular reports of their activities. After consulting with his priests, Montezuma concluded that the Spaniards were either Quetzalcóatl himself and his entourage or emissaries of the fabled priest. The return of Quetzalcóatl not only was predicted by the calendar but also explained the series of fantastic events that had baffled the Mexica since 1489. There had been earthquakes, a solar eclipse, a flood, and comets that appeared both in the day and at night. Grotesque people and wondrous animals mysteriously appeared and magically disappeared. Huitzilopochtli's temple burst spontaneously into flames, and its replacement was struck by lightning. A woman rose from the dead and told Montezuma that he was the last emperor, and a disembodied woman's voice frightened residents of Anahuac by wailing in lament at night. To Montezuma, the arrival of Cortés gave meaning to these bizarre events; they foretold the return of Quetzalcóatl, who would reclaim the empire he had left years ago.

Reluctant to face the religious reformer who had ended human sacrifice, the high priest of Huitzilopochtli tried to hold onto the throne without defying Quetzalcóatl. Montezuma sent Cortés rich gifts, pledged his fealty, exaggerated the difficulties of the journey from the coast to Anahuac, and asked the Spaniards to return east. When Cortés led his Spaniards and six thousand Mexican Indian allies across the mountains, Montezuma desperately tried to have Cortés ambushed. When all efforts failed, Montezuma accepted his fate and on November 8, 1519, greeted Cortés with these words:

> Thou hast arrived on earth; thou hast come to thy noble city of Mexico. Thou hast come to occupy thy noble mat and seat, which for a little time I have guarded and watched for thee. . . . [N]ow it is fulfilled: thou hast returned.

Montezuma's advisers were appalled at their emperor's behavior. They regarded the Spaniards as dangerous aliens who should be repulsed rather than welcomed. The Spaniards' Indian allies were the rebellious Cempoalans and the intransigent Tlaxcalans who already had encouraged the subject states to renounce their loyalty to the empire. Sensing danger, Cortés arrested Montezuma and hoped that his royal hostage would guarantee the Spaniards' safety. When the Spaniards massacred the priests of Huitzilopochtli and placed crucifixes in the temples, Montezuma tried to secure his freedom through intrigue, but it was too late. The *Pipiltin* deposed Montezuma, replaced him with his brother Cuitláhuac, and assaulted the Spaniards. When Cortés had Montezuma taken to the rooftop to restore calm, the infuriated warriors threw stones at their former *Uei Tlatoani* and wounded him seriously in the head. Montezuma died three days later, on June 30, 1520. That night, the Spaniards fought their way out of the city and vowed to return. When the *Pipiltin* found Montezuma's body, they first threw it into a sewage canal and then burned it in a trash heap.

SIGNIFICANCE

Since the time of the Spanish Conquest and the destruction of the Aztec culture, Montezuma II has entered the world of symbolism. For centuries, he was seen as the embodiment of barbarism, cruelty, and evil. His image was rehabilitated by *indigenistas* (admirers of Mexican Indian culture) during the Mexican Revolution of 1910, and he has been portrayed as the epitome of an innocent America violated by a corrupt, greedy, ruthless Spain. With the waning of *indigenista* fervor by the mid-twentieth century, the name Montezuma has come to be associated with the concept of an "authentic" Mexico.

—Paul E. Kuhl

FURTHER READING

Brundage, Burr Cartwright. *A Rain of Darts: The Mexica Aztecs.* Austin: University of Texas Press, 1972. A careful chronicle of the Aztecs, based on intensive study of the codices. Brundage concludes that Montezuma was insecure, bloodthirsty, and morbidly religious.

Burland, C. A. *Montezuma: Lord of the Aztecs.* New York: G. P. Putnam's Sons, 1973. This biography, richly illustrated with photographs of Mexico and the Aztec codices, is somewhat melodramatic and error prone.

Collis, Maurice. *Cortés and Montezuma.* New York: New Directions, 1999. Extensively researched and highly accessible account of the meeting between Cortés and Montezuma provides many details to make the points of view of both men, and their followers, come to life. Includes illustrations, map, and index.

Díaz del Castillo, Bernal. *The Discovery and Conquest of Mexico.* Translated by A. P. Maudslay. Introduction by Hugh Thomas. New York: Da Capo Press, 1996. First written in the 1560's and first published in 1632, Díaz documented in this work his vivid memories of the conquest of Mexico and his observations of the Aztecs and of Montezuma.

Fagan, Brian M. *The Aztecs.* New York: W. H. Freeman, 1984. This copiously illustrated work is a topical examination of Aztec society that updates older studies by George C. Vaillant, Jacques Soustelle, and Nigel Davies.

Madariaga, Salvador de. *Hernán Cortés: Conqueror of Mexico.* Garden City, N.Y.: Doubleday, 1969. A lively work that is much more than a biography of the Spanish conqueror. Gives extensive, sympathetic treatment to Montezuma.

Padden, R. C. *The Hummingbird and the Hawk: Conquest and Sovereignty in the Valley of Mexico, 1503-1541.* Columbus: Ohio State University Press, 1967. One of the narratives of the conquest of Mexico. Padden concludes that Montezuma was reaching for divinity and lost his grip on humanity and reality.

Thomas, Hugh. *Conquest: Cortés, Montezuma, and the Fall of Old Mexico.* New York: Touchstone, 1995. Simultaneous intimate study of Montezuma and Cortés, sociological analysis of their two cultures, and dramatic retelling of the clashes between both personalities and empires. Includes photographic plates, illustrations, maps, bibliographic references, and index.

White, Jon Manchip. *Cortés and the Downfall of the Aztec Empire.* 2d ed. New York: Carroll & Graf, 1996. A psychological and analytical portrait of Cortés and Montezuma that places both leaders in their religious and cultural milieus.

SEE ALSO: Hernán Cortés; Cuauhtémoc; Doña Marina; Nezahualcóyotl.

RELATED ARTICLES in *Great Events from History: The Renaissance & Early Modern Era, 1454-1600:* 1502-1520: Reign of Montezuma II; Beginning 1519: Smallpox Kills Thousands of Indigenous Americans; April, 1519-August, 1521: Cortés Conquers Aztecs in Mexico.

SIR THOMAS MORE
English statesman, scholar, and author

Devoted to his faith and to Renaissance learning, More was the first layman to serve as Lord Chancellor of England. He opposed Henry VIII's break with Rome and forfeited his exalted position and his life rather than swear allegiance to the king as the supreme head of the Church of England.

BORN: February 7, 1478; London, England
DIED: July 6, 1535; London, England
AREAS OF ACHIEVEMENT: Literature, government and politics, religion and theology

EARLY LIFE

Thomas More was born in the Cripplegate neighborhood of London. He was the second of five children born to John More and Agnes Granger. Three siblings apparently died in childhood, and Thomas was the only surviving son. An ambitious and talented man, John More had succeeded his father as butler of Lincoln's Inn but aspired to be a barrister. The benchers of Lincoln's Inn liked the young fellow who managed their meals and approved him for membership; he subsequently was admitted to the bar. His marriage to Agnes Granger advanced his career, for she was the daughter of a prosperous merchant and sheriff of London. John More was appointed judge in the Court of Common Pleas, then promoted to the Court of King's Bench, and was even knighted by the king. Having risen from the working class himself, he had great expectations for his son.

Young More learned Latin at St. Anthony's School in London. He was much influenced by headmaster Nicholas Holt, who had taught John Colet and William Lattimer, both of whom became English Humanists and friends of More. At thirteen, More was placed in the household of Thomas Morton, archbishop of Canterbury and Lord Chancellor, who immediately took a liking to the intelligent boy. In 1492, at Morton's urging, More entered Canterbury Hall (later absorbed by Christ College), Oxford University, where he met and began lasting friendships with Thomas Linacre and William Grocyn, two scholars who had studied in Italy and drunk deeply of the Renaissance literature. Along with the classics, More studied mathematics and history and learned to play the flute and viol. His lifelong love of Humanistic learning had been kindled.

Convinced that his son should pursue a legal career, John More recalled Thomas to London in 1494 and enrolled him as a law student at New Inn. Thomas moved to Lincoln's Inn in 1496, began lecturing on the law, and came to be known as an eloquent and insightful student of law. He did not, however, forsake literature. He wrote Latin and English verse, immersed himself in the Humanistic writings of Giovanni Pico della Mirandola, and joined the intellectual circle that included Grocyn, Linacre, William Lily, and John Colet. He especially looked to Colet for direction in both life and learning. He and Lily published epigrams rendered from the Greek anthology into Latin prose. More met and began an enduring friendship with the remarkable Desiderius Erasmus of Rotterdam, undoubtedly the leading Christian Humanist. As Erasmus later recounted, More seriously considered devoting his life to the Church. For almost four years, he lived near the Charterhouse in London and followed the discipline of the Carthusian order. Spending much of his time in prayer and fasting, he regularly scourged himself and began a lifelong habit of wearing a hair shirt. He came near to joining the Franciscan order. During this time, he also lectured, at the request of his friend Grocyn, on Saint Augustine's *De civitate Dei* (413-427; *The City of God*, 1610).

After four years of living much like a monk, More apparently resolved his doubts about what he should do. Although he remained a pious Catholic, he threw himself into the practice of law. Various reasons have been suggested for this abrupt shift to the secular. The corruption of the Church, his own intellectual and material ambitions, and his unwillingness to remain celibate may all have contributed to his decision; he soon gained a reputation as a just and knowledgeable barrister. He also studied politics, adding to what he had learned from his father and Archbishop Morton. At twenty-six, he was elected to Parliament (apparently from the City of London) and quickly emerged as a primary critic of government inefficiency and heavy taxation.

More played a major role in frustrating Henry VII's efforts to extract one hundred thousand pounds from Parliament on the marriage of his daughter Margaret to the king of Scotland. Henry was so angry with young More that he trumped up charges against his father, John More, had him imprisoned in the Tower of London, and released him only after he had paid a large fine. This lesson on sovereign power was not lost on Thomas, whose thoughts were concerned with much more than politics. In 1505, More married Jane Colte, the eldest daughter of a landed gentleman, and together they had four children.

An engraved depiction of Sir Thomas More bidding his daughter farewell upon his arrest. (F. R. Niglutsch)

On her death in 1511, More wasted little time in marrying Alice Middleton, an affable but rather unattractive and unlettered woman who proved to be a fine mother for his children.

LIFE'S WORK

By the time of his second marriage, More was emerging as a leading London barrister. In 1509, the same year that Henry VIII ascended the throne, More was elected to Lincoln's Inn, where he became a reader in 1511. The year before, he was appointed undersheriff of London, a position of considerable responsibility in the sheriff's court. Especially well liked by London merchants, More was chosen by King Henry as a member of an English delegation sent to Flanders in 1514 to negotiate a commercial treaty. His contribution was minor, but during those six months abroad, he delighted in the company of Peter Giles, a renowned Humanist and friend of Erasmus, and began work on his *De optimo reipublicae statu, deque nova insula utopia* (1516; better known as *Utopia*; English translation, 1551).

His most significant work, *Utopia* was a skillful satire that condemned the poverty, intolerance, ignorance, and brutality of English society by juxtaposing it to the economic communism and political democracy that prevailed among the tolerant and peace-loving Utopians. Although surely attracted by the idealism of *Utopia*, More was always the realist, as his *History of King Richard III*, written about the same time, makes clear. Disturbed by the ineptitude and avarice in both church and state, he wanted change for the better, but not revolutionary change.

Over the next few years, More became a favorite of Henry VIII and his Lord Chancellor, Cardinal Thomas Wolsey. They sent him on several diplomatic missions dealing with commercial matters critical to the interests of London merchants. More's skill in arguing the law convinced Henry that he should be an officer of the Crown. In 1517, he was appointed master of requests, the official through whom all petitions were passed to the king, and he was elevated to the Privy Council the next year. King Henry appreciated Humanist learning and found in More a delightful intellectual companion. He encouraged More to defend Greek studies against the obscurantist attacks of conservative critics. In his turn, More joined Henry in denouncing the Lutheran heresy. On Wolsey's recommendation, More was appointed speaker of the House of Commons in 1532 and generally worked smoothly with the powerful cardinal. More surely learned from Wolsey, as he had from Archbishop Morton, and proved to be a fair and effective official, respected by the people as well as his peers. Henry rewarded him with both sinecures and landed estates.

More bought more land in Chelsea in 1523 and built a mansion there with an orchard and spacious garden. It was a happy place, where More delighted in entertaining his many friends and relatives. Illuminati such as Erasmus were frequent guests, and the king himself regularly visited More at Chelsea. As Erasmus portrayed him, More was the epitome of Christian Humanism, a wonderfully enlightened public official who nurtured intellectual and scholarly pursuits. More's idyllic existence, however, was not to last. The king's "Great Matter"—his desire to divorce Queen Catherine and marry Anne Boleyn—threatened the kind of revolutionary change that was repugnant to More's conservative temperament. When Pope Clement VII denied Henry's request for an annulment, Wolsey was the first to feel his sovereign's wrath, being deprived of his position as Lord Chancellor, dismissed from the court, and accused of treason. Although Henry knew that More disapproved of his plans for divorce, he nevertheless made him Lord Chancellor, the first layman to hold that august office. Yet the real power in the Privy Council was exercised not by More but by the duke of Norfolk, Anne Boleyn's uncle.

If Henry thought that in the role of Lord Chancellor More would be more pliable, the king was mistaken. More performed his duties admirably enough, but he was increasingly on the fringes of the religious revolution that Henry and Parliament were undertaking. Even as Henry made overtures to leading English Protestants, More was trying his best to root out heresy. He even approved of torture for those who defied Catholic orthodoxy. Ironically, his own day of reckoning was coming. Between 1530 and 1532, Henry gradually extended royal authority over the Church of England, and More was at last compelled to resign as Lord Chancellor when Henry suggested relaxing the laws against her-esy. More wanted to withdraw to his Chelsea estate and be left alone, but Henry demanded his assent to the laws taking England out of the Church of Rome. More resisted. He was motivated not by love for the Papacy but by reverence for the unity of the Church. Stripped of his office and stipends, he was confined to the Tower of London in 1534. After more than a year of increasingly harsh treatment, he still refused to yield. In July, 1535, More was convicted of defying the Supremacy Act of November, 1534, and executed. Instantly proclaimed a martyr to the cause of Catholicism, More was beatified in 1886 and canonized in 1935.

SIGNIFICANCE

Sir Thomas More was pulled in several directions at once. He was a talented royal official, a learned and intelligent Humanist, and a devout Catholic. As a lawyer and a judge, he gained a reputation for fairness. As the first lay Lord Chancellor, he personified the growing secularization of both society and government in the sixteenth century. Yet like the prelates who had preceded him, More understood the practical limitations of politics, and as Lord Chancellor, he was not about to embrace the religious and political toleration so idealized in *Utopia*. Indeed, More was basically conservative when it came to religion and politics. He did not hesitate to prosecute religious heretics, regarding them as a threat to both the church and the state.

On the other hand, More found great satisfaction in intellectual and scholarly pursuits. Christian Humanism shaped his writings and his relationships with friends and family alike. *Utopia* at once established his international reputation as a leading literary figure. Among his early works were poems, Latin epigrams, and an English translation and adaptation of the biography in Latin of Pico della Mirandola, the brilliant young Italian Humanist whose writings More deeply admired. Like Pico, More prized the life of the mind. He carried on a prolific corre-

MORE'S MAJOR WORKS	
1510	*The Life of John Picus, Earl of Myrandula* (translation of Giovanni Pico della Mirandola)
1516	*De optimo Reipublicae Statu, deque nova insula utopia* (*Utopia,* 1551)
1529	*A Dyaloge of Sir Thomas More*
1533	*An Apologye of Syr Thomas More, Knight*
1543	*History of King Richard III*
1553	*A Dialoge of Comfort Against Tribulacion*

spondence with fellow intellectuals, performed numerous tasks for friends such as Erasmus, and defended Humanist literatures from obscurantist criticism.

More was happiest when his family and friends were with him. The children of his household, whether male or female, were educated under More's personal supervision. Friends such as Erasmus celebrated the intellectual exchange and hospitality that they always enjoyed with More. He had a modern devotion to intellectual curiosity.

Yet for all his reaching toward modernity, More remained tied to the religious faith of the Middle Ages. A part of him always yearned for the monastery. He was a pious man, and his piety was grounded in a fundamental distrust of the human animal. The spiritual realm was very real to him, and very difficult to reach, and in that quest for spiritual understanding, the Church was crucial. It was not the pope, but the Church—its saints, its sacraments, and its history—that More loved and revered. Despite the sordidness of individual priests or even popes, he believed that the Church was pure and spiritual and must not be corrupted by either Martin Luther or Henry VIII. In the end, it was his spiritual side that prevailed. He defied his sovereign and paid for that defiance with his life. He cared more for his king than for any pope, but he truly loved his Church best of all.

—*Ronald William Howard*

FURTHER READING

Baker-Smith, Dominic. *More's "Utopia."* Toronto, Canada: University of Toronto Press, 2000. Places More's *Utopia* in its cultural context, explaining its connections to Humanism and Christian political theory. Argues for its treatment as a literary reflection on the nature of political idealism, rather than as an example of such idealism. Includes bibliographic references and index.

Chambers, Raymond Wilson. *Thomas More.* New York: Harcourt, Brace, 1935. Reprint. London: J. Cape, 1962. A Pulitzer Prize-winning biography published in the same year that More was canonized, this scholarly and thoroughly sympathetic study presents More as truly the one for all seasons—the Christian Humanist and statesman who opposed the tyrannical Henry VIII.

Fox, Alistair. *Thomas More: History and Providence.* New Haven, Conn.: Yale University Press, 1983. An intellectual biography of More, this work details the evolution of More's thought, delving deep into his views of God and humankind. Emphasizes More's contradictions and makes him more of a tragic figure.

Guy, John. *Thomas More.* New York: Oxford University Press, 2000. This is both a biography of More and a survey of the various other biographical portrayals that have emerged over the centuries. Attempts to adjudicate between the different versions of More, and uses newly discovered evidence to explain what he really believed and the real reasons for his execution. Includes genealogical table, bibliographic references, and index.

Marius, Richard. *Thomas More.* New York: Alfred A. Knopf, 1984. A comprehensive study of More's life and thought. It is distinguished by its felicitous prose and its brilliant analysis of a man, torn between the medieval world of faith and the modern world of reason, who ultimately chooses the spirit over the flesh.

More, Thomas. *Saint Thomas More: Selected Letters.* Edited by Elizabeth Frances Rogers. New Haven, Conn.: Yale University Press, 1961. Contains sixty-six letters revealing the many sides of More—his literary friendships, his concern with politics, his religious views, and especially his concern for his children.

Moynahan, Brian. *God's Bestseller: William Tyndale, Thomas More, and the Writing of the English Bible—A Story of Martyrdom and Betrayal.* New York: St. Martin's Press, 2003. Chronicles Tyndale's struggle to translate the Bible into vernacular English and More's efforts to stop Tyndale and to try him as a heretic. Includes illustrations, bibliographic references, and index.

Reynolds, E. E. *Thomas More and Erasmus.* New York: Fordham University Press, 1965. A careful study of the relationship between these two dynamic men, so similar in many ways and yet so very different. Besides explaining the influence that Erasmus had on More, Reynolds illuminates the nature of northern European Humanism.

Routh, Enid M. *Sir Thomas More and His Friends.* New York: Russell and Russell, 1963. An interesting study that portrays More as a transitional figure between the Renaissance and the Reformation. Gives insight into the intellectual life of More and other English Humanists as well as political and religious figures. Demonstrates the connections between English and Continental Humanism.

Wilson, Derek. *In the Lion's Court: Power, Ambition, and Sudden Death in the Reign of Henry VIII.* New York: St. Martin's Press, 2002. Vivid study of the perils of Henry VIII's court details the fates of six members of the court, including More and five other men named Thomas. Details More's background and education, as well as thoroughly surveying his activities in the court and the events leading up to his execution. Includes illustrations, maps, sixteen pages of plates, bibliographic references, and index.

SEE ALSO: Anne Boleyn; Catherine of Aragon; Clement VII; John Colet; Desiderius Erasmus; Henry VII; Henry VIII; Martin Luther; Giovanni Pico della Mirandola; Cardinal Thomas Wolsey.

RELATED ARTICLES in *Great Events from History: The Renaissance & Early Modern Era, 1454-1600:* Beginning 1485: The Tudors Rule England; 1499-1517: Erasmus Advances Humanism in England; 1516: Sir Thomas More Publishes *Utopia*; June 5-24, 1520: Field of Cloth of Gold; 1531-1540: Cromwell Reforms British Government; 1532: Holbein Settles in London.

THOMAS MORLEY
English composer and musician

Morley is often credited with the invention of the English madrigal, adapted from Italian musical forms and translated into English idioms. He also was a pioneer in music publishing in England, and his treatise on musical practice and composition—A Plaine and Easie Introduction to Practicall Musicke—remains perhaps the most influential musical treatise in English.

BORN: 1557 or 1558; Norwich, England
DIED: October, 1602; London, England
AREAS OF ACHIEVEMENT: Music, scholarship, education

EARLY LIFE

The early years of Thomas Morley are exceedingly vague, although it is known that he was the son of a brewer, Francis Morley. The town in which he was born, Norwich, became something of a haven for European Protestant refugees in the 1560's, and the town's establishment was itself associated with a strongly Protestant, puritanical culture.

This fact may have prompted Morley's departure from his hometown, since Morley appears to have had Roman Catholic leanings. His dedication to a tradition of elaborate, polyphonic church music would not have been well received in a Protestant culture that was often inimical to such music.

Morley served as an organist and choral master for the cathedral at Norwich at some point between 1574 and 1583, although it is extremely likely that during this time he also studied with William Byrd, at that time the preeminent composer in England. It was from Byrd that Morley learned much about the tradition of Anglican church music, particularly the composition of motets

(the most important form of polyphonic music in the Renaissance).

Morley earned a bachelor of music degree from Oxford University in 1588. Although it is not precisely clear when Morley left Norwich for good, he was certainly established in London by 1591, the same time that he was employed as church organist in St. Paul's Cathedral.

LIFE'S WORK

Morley's contribution to the English musical tradition is generally considered to be his adaptation of the Italian madrigal within an English context. His early sacred music was very much in the tradition of English works, however, most notably the tradition developed by the sixteenth century English composers Byrd and Thomas Tallis. These works include motets, psalm settings, anthems, and services, and Morley's handling of these forms, which are notable for their weightiness and complex harmonic texture, very much betrays the influence of Byrd and Tallis's earlier examples.

Morley published several collections of music in the early 1590's that demonstrate his fascination with Italian forms and styles, most notably the madrigal, a type of musical piece in which a poetic text is set to an elaborate, polyphonic score of four to six parts. The form that Morley was most directly imitating had as its greatest proponents the Italian composers Andrea Gabrieli, Orlando di Lasso, and Giovanni Pierluigi da Palestrina. Morley's *Madrigalls to Foure Voyces* (1594) demonstrates a remarkable combination of the Italian madrigal form with the type of English polyphonic writing he had learned from Byrd. Morley's development, or "Englishing," of Italian forms is found in his *Canzonets to Three Voyces* (1593), his *Canzonets to Five and Six Voices* (1597), and *The Triumphes of Oriana* (1601).

In addition to his copious compositional output, Morley was active in the burgeoning field of music publication, a relatively new phenomenon in sixteenth century England. Publication of music at that time was strictly controlled by a court-appointed monopoly, and it was not until 1598 that Morley was granted a patent to publish (as a result of the expiration in 1596 of a monopoly that had originally been granted to Byrd). In addition to the publication of metrical psalms, Morley's patent allowed him to print part books (ensemble, or polyphonic, music in which each part appears in a separate book) and ruled paper.

Morley's *A Plaine and Easie Introduction to Practicall Musicke* (1597) was the most popular text devoted to the instruction of singing and composing music in Renaissance England. Although Morley's book was not the first of its kind (a shorter book on practical music had been published a few years earlier), it was more widely distributed, going through a second edition in a relatively short time, and was regularly read in England throughout the seventeenth century. It remains a famous musical treatise into the twenty-first century.

The first part of the work, "Teaching to Sing," outlines a method for learning to sight-sing (i.e., to sing directly from a printed musical score), while the second and third parts, "Treating of Descant" and "Treating of Composing or Setting of Songs," outline rules of musical composition.

In addition to his contributions to the madrigal tradition and music publication, Morley enjoyed an immensely successful professional career. In 1592, he was appointed to the position of gentleman of the Chapel Royal, a select group of paid musicians that normally consisted of male choristers (gentlemen) and boy singers. His *First Booke of Songs or Ayres* (1600) shows his experience with the lute-song tradition, a form that was being popularized by figures such as English composer John Dowland and that would overtake the madrigal in popularity in the early seventeenth century.

Morley seems to have suffered from ongoing illness as early as 1597, as he mentions in *A Plaine and Easie Introduction to Practicall Musicke*, and he died in October of 1602.

SIGNIFICANCE

The importance of the publication of Morley's *A Plaine and Easie Introduction to Practicall Musicke* in 1597 cannot be overestimated. Music publication in England was still fairly new, and the idea that one could learn how to perform and compose music (or at least learn aspects

of performance), such as sight-singing, directly from a text must have been strikingly original; musical instruction was almost always a one-on-one personal affair in sixteenth century England. Morley's text thus helped to usher in the dissemination of practical music (i.e., the study of musical performance and composition) to a wider audience, as well as helping to formalize and regularize the system of musical notation.

Although modern scholars have tended to downplay the traditional notion that England did not have a substantial musical tradition in the Renaissance independent of Italian influences, there is little doubt that Morley's adaptation of Italian madrigals and his publication of English madrigals were indispensable in introducing the most prominent European musical innovations to a wide, English-speaking public. Before Morley, most innovations had been introduced through the much more limited sphere of the royal court.

—*Joseph M. Ortiz*

FURTHER READING

Jacobson, David Christopher. "Thomas Morley and the Italian Madrigal Tradition: A New Perspective." *Journal of Musicology* 14 (1996): 80-91. Discusses Morley's classification of his own compositions in relation to the Italian forms he was adapting, paying special attention to the discussion of music in Morley's *Plaine and Easie Introduction to Practicall Musicke*.

Kerman, Joseph. *The Elizabethan Madrigal.* New York: American Musicological Society, 1962. A book-length study of the madrigal tradition in Renaissance England, focusing on the late sixteenth and early seventeenth centuries. Morley's contributions to the genre are treated at length. Includes several musical examples.

Morley, Thomas. *A Plain and Easy Introduction to Practical Music.* Edited by R. Alec Harmon. Introduced by Thurston Dart. New York: Norton, 1973. Dart's introduction is one of the very few articles that address comprehensively the historical and biographical context for the publication to Morley's treatise, although it must be noted that the introduction's historical accuracy is occasionally sloppy. The treatise itself is presented with copious annotations and helpful editorial notes, and all of the original musical examples are retained (in a much more readable type).

Perkins, Leeman L. *Music in the Age of the Renaissance.* New York: Norton, 1999. Discusses the Italian madri-

Mornay, Philippe de

gal tradition in England and English madrigals. Examines Morley's composition and publication of madrigals and canzonets. Bibliography, illustrations, and musical examples (including a lengthy excerpt from Morley's "April Is In My Mistress' Face," from the first book of *Madrigalls to Foure Voyces* of 1594).

SEE ALSO: William Byrd; John Dowland; Andrea Gabrieli; Giovanni Gabrieli; Orlando di Lasso; Luca Marenzio; Giovanni Pierluigi da Palestrina; Thomas Tallis.

RELATED ARTICLES in *Great Events from History: The Renaissance & Early Modern Era, 1454-1600:* 1567: Palestrina Publishes the *Pope Marcellus Mass*; 1575: Tallis and Byrd Publish *Cantiones Sacrae*; 1588-1602: Rise of the English Madrigal; 1590's: Birth of Opera; October 31, 1597: John Dowland Publishes *Ayres*; 1599: Castrati Sing in the Sistine Chapel Choir.

PHILIPPE DE MORNAY
French scholar, diplomat, and military leader

Mornay was one of the formative influences within the early Protestant Huguenot movement in France. As the author of numerous religious and political tracts, he has had a lasting impact on liberal political theory. As a military leader and diplomat, he performed invaluable service toward securing the succession to the French throne for King Henry IV.

BORN: November 5, 1549; Buhy, Normandy, France
DIED: November 11, 1623; La Forêt-sur-Sèvre, France
ALSO KNOWN AS: Seigneur du Plessis-Marly
AREAS OF ACHIEVEMENT: Diplomacy, government and politics, military, religion and theology

EARLY LIFE

Philippe de Mornay (fee-leep deh mohr-neh) was born into a minor aristocratic family. He converted to Calvinist Protestantism at the age of eighteen, largely, it would appear, through the influence of his mother. He was sent abroad for his education, embarking on the study of law, jurisprudence, and German at the University of Heidelberg in Germany; he also studied Hebrew and history at the University of Padua in Italy. Prior to 1572, he had traveled extensively through Britain, western Germany, and the Netherlands, and he was fluent in six languages other than French.

Mornay began his career in letters while at Cologne, Germany, in 1571 and 1572, writing a theological tract, *Dissertation sur l'église visible* (thesis on the visible church) and two well-publicized remonstrances justifying and advocating further resistance to Spanish rule among Protestants in the Netherlands. The Spanish Netherlands had been a seething cauldron of conspiracy, subversion, and repression throughout the 1560's and early 1570's. The alienation of the nobility of the Nether-

lands, under the leadership of William the Silent, the outbreaks of vandalism and destroying of images and statues by Protestant mobs, and the chronic ineffectiveness of the government of the regent, Duchess Margaret of Parma, led to the replacement of Margaret with the Spanish duke of Alva in 1567. Alva soon unleashed a campaign of terror that resulted in the execution or imprisonment of some twelve thousand (mainly Protestant) dissidents. By April, 1572, the Dutch, or northern, Netherlands had erupted into open rebellion against Spain when a band of Dutch seamen dubbed "sea beggars" seized the port city of Brill.

Mornay thus came to the notice of the Huguenot leader, Admiral Gaspard de Coligny. Coligny's skillful handling of French Protestant armies during the Third French War of Religion (1568-1570) had forced the royal government to grant a cease-fire (the Edict of Pacification of St. Germain, 1570), and he had subsequently gained great influence over the young king, Charles IX. By June, 1572, Mornay had been called back to France and taken into Coligny's entourage. At the request of the admiral, Mornay composed a memorial to the king urging France to intervene militarily against Spain in support of the Dutch Protestants. The queen mother, Catherine de Médicis, resentful of Coligny's sway over her son and alarmed at the possible disastrous consequences of open conflict with Spain, used the occasion of a royal marriage in Paris during the month of August to eliminate the threat posed by the Huguenot Party. Mornay witnessed an abortive attempt on Coligny's life on August 22, 1572; two days later, he narrowly escaped death during the St. Bartholomew's Day Massacre, in which agents of the queen mother and Catholic followers of the duke of Guise killed the admiral and much of the Huguenot leadership. Mornay sought refuge in England and did not return to France until the following year.

LIFE'S WORK

From 1572 to 1574, Mornay acted in support of another prominent Huguenot, François La Noue, at whose request he sailed from England to the port of La Rochelle in 1573. There he composed the first in a series of pamphlets denouncing both the royal Valois family and the Guise family; he returned to England for a few weeks at the end of 1573 on a diplomatic mission for La Noue. In 1574, Mornay broke with La Noue, incensed by the latter's cooperation with the Politiques, a moderate Catholic faction sponsored by the queen mother.

He became radical in his views, entering military service in support of the Protestant king Henry of Navarre, a royal cousin whose family (the Bourbons) stood next in line to the French throne after the Valois. In 1575, he was captured by Catholic forces, but he managed to conceal his true identity, and he was quickly ransomed and released into the custody of Henry de la Tour d'Auvergne, duke of Bouillon, at Sedan. It was while he was at the duke's household that he met Charlotte Arbaleste, whom he married the following year.

During the next five years, Mornay went through his most radical phase, advocating the overthrow of the Valois and rejecting compromise with both the Catholics and the Politiques. This phase culminated in his purported writing of *Vindiciae contra tyrannos* (1579; a defense of liberty against tyrants). Some scholars call into question Mornay's authorship, attributing *Vindiciae contra tyrannos* to either Hubert Languet or Johan Junius de Jonge, or to Mornay and Languet in a collaborative effort. It is certain, however, that *Vindiciae contra tyrannos* uncannily mirrors both Mornay's style and what is known about his views at the time. *Vindiciae contra tyrannos* is widely considered the most significant and influential work of political theory arising out of the French Wars of Religion.

Building on the theories of Theodore Beza and François Hotman, *Vindiciae contra tyrannos* developed the idea of government as a contractual agreement between a people and their sovereign. In the event of a monarch's violation of popular liberties under this unwritten contract, resistance to, rebellion against, and deposition of the tyrannical ruler were justified. *Vindiciae contra tyrannos*, however, fell short of advocating total popular revolution by reserving this power for the lower magistrates (the nobility, judges, and justices) in their representative capacities; this group could include the magistracy

from foreign states. It is of significance that the leadership of the Huguenot Party consisted of the lower magistracy, as defined by the author, and that the door was left open for foreign intervention (the assistance of Queen Elizabeth I of England and the German Protestant princes was actively solicited by the Huguenot Party, and Mornay's diplomatic missions played a crucial role in these efforts). During the 1570's, Mornay also published *Discours sur le roi Charles* (1572; debate concerning King Charles), *Remonstrances aux estats pour la paix* (1576; on the conditions necessary to achieve peace), and *Excellent discours sur la vie et la mort* (1577; deep discussion on life and death).

From 1578 to 1580, Mornay was dispatched on missions to the Netherlands and England several times for Henry of Navarre. He had risen so high in the king's confidence that, in 1581, Henry named him as his chief adviser. Mornay's prestige within the Huguenot community as a philosopher, activist, negotiator, and propagandist had been so enhanced by this time that his opponents labeled him the Huguenot pope. In the 1580's, Mornay seems to have moderated his political stance to the extent that he could reach agreement and work with the Politique element on Henry's behalf.

Much of Mornay's time was spent on diplomatic missions, preparing briefs for Henry of Navarre and speaking to various estates and parliaments on his master's behalf. His first administrative appointment, as governor of

Philippe de Mornay. (Hulton|Archive by Getty Images)

the Huguenot stronghold of Montauban in the Languedoc, 1585-1586, ended in failure. After fifteen months of being frustrated by the independent-minded Montaubanois, who resented Mornay as a northerner, he resigned. The final break occurred after Mornay's wife had been publicly humiliated at church when the pastor and elders refused to allow her to take Holy Communion, citing as the cause her frivolous attire and hairstyle.

The death in 1584 of the heir to the French throne, François, duke of Anjou, placed Henry of Navarre next in succession to his childless cousin, King Henry III. From 1585 to 1589, Henry III engaged in armed conflict with both Navarre and his Huguenot forces, and with those of Henry I of Lorraine, duke of Guise, leader of the ultra-Catholic League (the conflict is often referred to as the War of the Three Henrys). Mornay directed and composed most of the pro-Navarre propaganda of the period, choosing to concentrate his attacks on the Guise faction in the hope of leaving the door open to accommodation with Henry III.

On December 23, 1588, Henry III connived at Guise's assassination, an act that placed the king in a desperate state of political isolation. In July, 1589, in the greatest diplomatic coup of his career, Mornay negotiated an alliance between Henry III and Navarre. On August 1, 1589, Henry III was fatally stabbed by a fanatical monk, Jacques Clément; on his deathbed, he acknowledged Navarre to be his successor as King Henry IV. Mornay was awarded the governorship of Saumur, and the Huguenot University he founded there became a great seat of Calvinist scholarship.

Henry IV's conversion to Catholicism in 1593 deeply mortified Mornay, who three times refused his sovereign's request to come to Paris and remained at Saumur, though his loyalty was never in question. The estrangement became complete after the publication of Mornay's 1598 work *De l'institution, usage, et doctrine du saint sacrament de l'Eucharistie* (on the founding, practice, and doctrine of the holy sacrament of the Eucharist). Mornay intended to prove that the Protestant Eucharist more closely resembled the original Eucharist, as instituted by Jesus Christ and perpetuated within the early Christian church, than did the version practiced by the Catholic Church. When challenged, he rashly accepted to debate a skilled theologian, Jacques Davy Du Perron, bishop of Evreux. The debate, approved by the king, took place from May 2 to May 4, 1600, at Fontainebleau. The event proved a disaster for Mornay, who lost on every point; as a result, he blamed the king for engineering his entrapment.

After Henry IV's assassination in 1610 and the succession of his son Louis XIII, the political situation of the Huguenots deteriorated. Mornay had to fight to maintain his influence within the Huguenot community against the young, militantly antiroyalist Henry, duke of Rohan. Though successful in fending off Rohan's attempts to precipitate a crisis at the Assembly of Saumur in 1612, Mornay was unable to prevent his rival from launching the Huguenot War against the government in 1621. Reaffirming his loyalty to the crown, he welcomed Louis XIII into Saumur. The mistrustful Louis, however, relieved him of the governorship, and Mornay retired to his estate at La Forêt-sur-Sèvre, where he died on November 11, 1623.

SIGNIFICANCE

Mornay held the Huguenot Party together and molded it during a pivotal stage in its history, mapping out most of its major initiatives during the 1580's. His assistance to Navarre in facilitating his ascension to the throne was perhaps indispensable, and he certainly participated in the formulation of the Edict of Nantes in 1598, although the extent of his role is the subject of conjecture. It is certain that his polemical skills and command of the written and spoken word publicized and placed in context the issues of obedience and resistance to authority in the name of freedom, and he thus merits recognition as a significant figure in the development of Western political thought.

Mornay, however, failed to gain a firm political base. His censorious moralizing tended to isolate him, and his public berating of Henry IV over the king's sexual promiscuity contributed to their ultimate alienation. Had Mornay shown greater tact in the matters of faith and morals, he might not have been supplanted by the duke of Sully.

—*Raymond Pierre Hylton*

FURTHER READING

Buisseret, David. *Henry IV*. London: Allen & Unwin, 1984. Uses the life of the king to shed light on the times and the interaction of personalities, including Mornay. Provides the most complete account of the Mornay-Du Perron debate.

Conner, Philip. *Huguenot Heartland: Montauban and Southern French Calvinism During the Wars of Religion*. Burlington, Vt.: Ashgate, 2002. Study of the Wars of Religion, especially of the differences between the experiences of Southern and Northern France during the wars. Focuses on the southern town of Montauban as a case study of the larger religious, cultural, and political upheaval during Mornay's time. Includes maps, bibliographic references, and index.

Greengrass, Mark. *France in the Age of Henry IV: The Struggle for Stability.* New York: Longman, 1984. Scholarly background treatment that tries to explain Henry's achievement as the restorer of equilibrium as a personal phenomenon, and thus tends to downplay or obscure the role of nonregal participants.

Heller, Henry. *Iron and Blood: Civil Wars in Sixteenth Century France.* Montreal: McGill-Queen's University Press, 1991. Provides interesting insights on Calvinist/Huguenot constitutional theory and acknowledges Mornay's crucial behind-the-scenes contributions—as confidant, ghostwriter, and go-between—to the eventual eclipse of the Catholic League.

Koenigsberger, H. G., George L. Mosse, and G. Q. Bowker. *Europe in the Sixteenth Century.* New York: Longman, 1989. Detailed overview that includes maps, genealogical tables, chronology, bibliography, an excellent treatment of *Vindiciae contra tyrannos*, and a creditable attempt to place the entire French Calvinist movement in its Continental perspective.

Mentzer, Raymond A., and Andrew Spicer, eds. *Society and Culture in the Huguenot World, 1559-1685.* New York: Cambridge University Press, 2002. Anthology of essays investigating various aspects of Mornay's culture, from the role of religious polemics in the Huguenots' self-perceptions to Huguenot academic institutions to the Edict of Nantes. Includes illustrations, bibliographic references, and index.

Racaut, Luc. *Hatred in Print: Catholic Propaganda and Protestant Identity During the French Wars of Religion.* Burlington, Vt.: Ashgate, 2002. Study of the pamphlets and propaganda distributed by Catholics during the Wars of Religion. Analyzes the strategies, production, and impact of pro-Catholic propaganda of the period. Includes bibliographic references and index.

Sutherland, N. M. *Henry IV of France and the Politics of Religion, 1572-1596.* 2 vols. Bristol, Avon, England: Elm Bank, 2002. Extremely detailed account of the role of religion in France's monarchy and political sphere during the late sixteenth century. Each chapter discusses a specific political event or issue from the point of view of the conflict between Protestants and Catholics. Includes illustrations, map, bibliographic references, and index.

Thompson, Jack Westfall. *The Wars of Religion in France, 1559-1576: The Huguenots, Catherine de Medici, and Philip II.* Reprint. New York: Frederick Ungar, 1957. Discusses events from the death of Henry II to the end of the fifth civil war. Cites significant details on Mornay's early career and associations with Coligny and La Noue.

SEE ALSO: John Calvin; Catherine de Médicis; Charles IX; Elizabeth I; Henry III; Henry IV; François Hotman; Martin Luther; Margaret of Parma; William the Silent.

RELATED ARTICLES in *Great Events from History: The Renaissance & Early Modern Era, 1454-1600:* March, 1536: Calvin Publishes *Institutes of the Christian Religion*; March, 1562-May 2, 1598: French Wars of Religion; August 24-25, 1572: St. Bartholomew's Day Massacre.

NĀNAK
Indian religious leader

Nānak was a religious reformer who synthesized the fundamental principles of Islam and the tradition of Hinduism into a new universal religion called Sikhism. His teaching emphasized the equality of all human beings and regarded responsible social action as integral to true spiritual practice. Monism and the rejection of excessive ritual are the basic tenets of this religion.

BORN: April 15, 1469; Rāi Bhoi dī Talvaṇḍī, Punjab
    (now in Nankana Sahib, Pakistan)
DIED: 1539; Kartārpur, Punjab, Mongol Empire (now
    in Pakistan)
ALSO KNOWN AS: Guru Nānak Dev
AREAS OF ACHIEVEMENT: Religion and theology,
    education

EARLY LIFE

The historical facts concerning the life of Nānak (NAHN-ahk) can be gleaned only by sifting them carefully from the embellishments of myth and legend. The essential story of his life, however, seems fairly clear. Nānak's father, Kalu, was a relatively well-to-do person and commanded local influence.

Nānak was a precocious and gifted child possessing unusual intelligence and an extraordinarily pronounced concern for the well-being of everyone with whom he came into contact. He had a contemplative nature with a strong inclination toward otherworldly preoccupations. Stories about his childhood and the years toward adulthood indicate these qualities. It is said that even when Nānak was an infant, his heart would melt at the sight of others' suffering. At play, he would devise games imitating holy men and involving mental concentration to achieve a perception of God.

Nānak's intellectual abilities and spiritual insights had already developed phenomenally before he was old enough to start school, although the story of his questioning the teacher on the first day of school about the significance of the letters of the alphabet and his composing on that occasion an acrostic on each letter is almost certainly apocryphal. The same must be said about his discussion with the family Brahmin when the latter came to invest him with the sacred thread. Nānak rejected the thread, thus refuting the importance of the external trappings of religion. A hymn by Nānak ascribed to this occasion must be of later date.

Nānak was married at a very young age and soon had children, but to his father's dismay he did not settle down to a regular occupation. If Kalu sent him on a trip to buy merchandise for business, Nānak gave away the money to holy mendicants and called it a "true transaction." Asked to work at the family farm, he left things unattended. Stories about this period of his life relate several supernatural occurrences. For example, one hot, sunny day while herding cattle, he fell asleep under the shade of a tree. The shade did not move with the sun's movement. Another time, a cobra was seen shading his head with its hood while he slept in the sun.

LIFE'S WORK

At the age of eighteen, Nānak moved to Sultanpur, where his father and brother-in-law procured for him employment as storekeeper and accountant at a government store. He stayed there for about ten years, settling down to a well-regulated life. He maintained his family with only a small portion of his salary, giving the rest away to the poor. He spent his spare time meditating or discussing metaphysics with holy men and continued thus to progress steadily in his spiritual search. One morning, when he went for his daily bath in the Bein, a nearby stream, he disappeared, some thought in the Bein. During his disappearance, he had a spiritual experience. Soon after he reappeared, he proclaimed that he was neither Hindu nor Muslim, left his family and all other worldly belongings, and set out on worldwide travels.

Popular accounts of Nānak's travels are filled with fantastic occurrences. He is described as traveling to distant places, often by a supernatural process of instant self-transportation. These stories do have a basis in history, however, and they are also quite meaningful in another way, for they convey in a veiled manner aspects of his teaching. Primary biographical sources, such as they are, claim that he went as far as Assam in the east, Ceylon (modern Sri Lanka) in the south, Tibet and China in the north, and the Middle Eastern countries and Turkey in the west. On many of these journeys, he was accompanied by his Muslim disciple, Mardana. Wherever Nānak went, many people became his followers. Hindus regarded him as their guru and Muslims as their *Pir*, and eventually his followers came to be known as Sikhs, meaning disciples. Thus started Sikhism, a new religion transcending the boundaries of Hinduism and Islam.

The religion that Nānak preached emphasized a monistic metaphysics and the importance of social and moral responsibility. The elements of his teaching are illustrated by various incidents during his peregrinations. According to one account, Nānak pointed out the difference between the wholesomeness of honest living and the corruption of ill-gotten wealth by squeezing in separate hands two morsels of food, one from a hard-working carpenter with whom he stayed and the other from a rich man whose banquet he had refused. From his host's food poured milk and from the rich man's food poured blood.

In another story, Nānak reformed a highway thug whose name, Sajjan, meant friend. With his hospitality and show of piety, Sajjan enticed travelers to stay with him and robbed them while they slept. Nānak shocked Sajjan into realizing the true meaning of his name and the karmic consequences of evil deeds. Sajjan mended his ways. At Hardwar, on the banks of the Ganges, Nānak stood in the river and started to splash water toward the west. Asked by the Hindu pilgrims what he was doing, he said that he was watering his fields in the Punjab. When they laughed, he asked how they expected the water they threw toward the sun to reach the sun, thus pointing out the futility of rituals. Similarly, in a dialogue with a pundit, he expounded on the vanity of learning devoid of the inner experience of true reality. Inner peace, he insisted, is obtained by contemplation, not mere reading. During his sojourn in the Himalayas, he met some yogis. He reprimanded them for hiding from the social and political turmoil of the time, saying that it was their duty to guide and help oppressed humanity.

The best-remembered story about Nānak's travels is one about his visit to Mecca. It is said that on reaching the Kaaba, Nānak lay down with his feet toward the shrine, the holiest in Islam. Outraged, the keepers of the shrine admonished him to move his feet away from the Kaaba. He refused and told them to turn his feet to where there was no God. As they dragged him around, the Kaaba moved in the same direction as his feet, the moral being that God is everywhere. In the turmoil caused by Bābur's invasion of India, Nānak was taken prisoner. It is believed that Bābur, whose interest in religion was deep, heard about Nānak and met with him. Nānak is said to have given him instruction and conveyed to him his concern for people's suffering.

In about 1526, Nānak ended his travels and settled down at Kartarpur, on the bank of the river Ravi in central Punjab. There he consolidated his life's work and laid down the essential organizational bases of the Sikh religion—the institutions of guruship, prayer, *sangat* (congregation), *langar* (communal meal and sharing), and family. He returned to the life of a regular householder,

considering it far superior to renunciation as a means of spiritual realization. Before his death, in 1539, he chose his best disciple, Angad, as the next guru in preference to his own sons.

Throughout his life, Nānak regularly recorded his observations about life in poetical compositions that over time added up to a large volume. These compositions, or hymns, articulate with intense feeling Nānak's views on theology and ethics, and on social, political, and economic issues. Used as recitations for prayer from the very time of their creation, Nānak's hymns comprise the nucleus to which the verses of the later Sikh gurus and other saints were added to make the Sikh scripture, the *Ādi Granth*. Nānak's verses contain the essence of the Sikh religion. They are gathered in various sequences. Most important among these sequences is the *Japji*, meaning recitation, the daily morning prayer. Its recitation is also central to prayers for many other occasions. In a sense, *Japji* contains the gist of the whole scripture. The root mantra of the Sikh religion is *Japji*'s opening verse. Because of its quintessential character, the verse is also a complete prayer by itself and figures at the start of other major compositions. It reads,

> There is one God
> Whose name is Truth
> He is the Creator
> Devoid of fear
> Without rancour
> Of eternal form
> Beyond birth and death.
> Self-existent,
> By the Guru's grace He is obtained.

The root mantra has its further summation in "There is one God" (*Ek Onkar*)—oneness including all other attributes of divinity. In Nānak's teachings, as Creator, the divine Self produces creation from within Itself. Creation, therefore, is part of the divine reality, emerging from and merging back into the eternal oneness of Being. There is no duality between the Creator and the created. As creatures, however, human beings suffer from the illusion that they have an existence of their own as separate individuals. This separateness from the source, regardless of whether they know it, causes grief and suffering for them. The state of being an all-encompassing unity is alone a state of unqualified happiness. God is that state; God is perfect bliss.

Nānak explained that to free themselves from the sorrows of the endless cycle of birth, death, and rebirth, human beings must regain union with God. One cannot achieve this goal only by the performance of outward acts of piety or by learning. Spiritual realization requires sincere devotion to God and detachment from worldly desires. One must bring to this devotion complete self-surrender to God's will and a total renunciation of the ego. Nānak often described the relation between God and the human soul as one between the bride and the bridegroom. He prescribes the recitation (*simran*) of God's name (*nam*) as a necessary means for expressing as well as winning the love of God. *Nam* comprehends all compositions (*bani*), such as Nānak's hymns, so that *simran* involves not mere mechanical repetition of words but concentration on their meaning and application of this meaning in one's daily conduct.

The process by which, with *simran*, one overcomes the ego, achieves mental calm, and becomes disciplined in action is slow and gentle (*sahaj*). Nānak rejected extreme asceticism as a means to spiritual development. He rather recommended a life of moderation—one that includes normal worldly activities but shuns attachment to the world. One should be like the lotus, which stays dry amid water. Progress on this path of spiritual growth requires personal guidance by a teacher (guru), the true guru being one who has realized truth. Also necessary for progress is the company (*sangat*) of others who are on the same quest. *Sangat* not only provides mutual mental reinforcement but also is the arena for right social action, without which there can be no spiritual life. It represents the equality, community, and mutual interdependence of all humanity. In Nānak's teaching, God, guru, and humans are one. The road to God realization lies squarely in the human world. A loving acceptance of this world fills Nānak's compositions with such enchanting poetry and music as make the face of the earth a window on the divine.

SIGNIFICANCE

Nānak's teaching was part of the religious reform that swept India during the fifteenth and sixteenth centuries. By that time, Muslims had ruled the country for about three hundred years and made a deep impact on it. On one hand, Islam and its social egalitarianism had spread widely, but on the other, the strictly defined character of the Muslim religion and the Muslim state's discriminatory policy toward Hindus caused extreme religious conflicts and social strife. Communal antagonism bred bigotry and an excessive preoccupation with the external forms of religion, leading to frequent oppression of non-Muslims. That tended to tear asunder the fabric of society. There was a dire need for a resolution of this conflict, for the creation of unity and harmony.

Sufis, the mystics of Islam, who emphasized love of God instead of works of religion, many of whom were active in India, helped prepare the way toward such a resolution. The full answer to the problem came with the rise of the *bhakti* movement, which spontaneously overwhelmed India on all sides toward the fifteenth century. *Bhakti*, which means love of God, rejected all outward forms of religion and found the universal meaning of religion in intense devotion to God. It considered the love of God inseparable from the love of humanity and the rest of creation, thus combining the quest for the divine with active involvement in the world.

Indian Sufism and the *bhakti* movement reached a culmination in Nānak's teaching. He preached a universal religion based on the oneness of God and the sameness of human beings everywhere. Because of the force his message had for unifying people of widely divergent backgrounds, he left a deep imprint on Indian civilization. His picture, which shows him with a long, white, perfectly rounded beard, with large eyes half closed in quiet bliss, and with his whole aspect exuding a deep friendliness and tranquillity, hangs prominently in the homes of Indians, and his image lives in their minds.

—*Surjit S. Dulai*

FURTHER READING

Anand, Balwant Singh. *Guru Nānak: His Life Was His Message*. New Delhi, India: Guru Nānak Foundation, 1983. A lucid biographical account.

Banerjee, Anil Chandra. *Guru Nānak and His Times*. Patiala, India: Punjabi University, 1971. About half of the volume is devoted to the historical context of Nānak's life and work.

McLeod, W. H. *Guru Nānak and the Sikh Religion*. Reprinted in *Sikhs and Sikhism*. New York: Oxford University Press, 2004. A major work by a non-Indian. The focus of this volume is on Nānak rather than on Sikhism as a whole, but three other volumes explore the religion itself in greater detail. The book has aroused some controversy.

Nānak. *Hymns of Guru Nānak*. Translated by Khushwant Singh. New Delhi, India: Orient Longmans, 1969. A judicious selection of hymns from Nānak's works. Translated with literary sensitivity.

_____. *Hymns of Guru Nānak*. Translated by S. Manmohan Singh. Patiala, India: Language Department,

Punjab, 1972. Contains all of Nānak's compositions. Gives the original in Punjabi, an English translation, and an explanation of the meaning in Punjabi prose.

Ralhan, O. P., ed. *Guru Nanak Dev.* Vol. 1 in *Great Gurus of the Sikhs.* New Delhi, India: Anmol, 1998. Combines a biography of Nānak with social, theological, political, and economic analysis of his career and teachings.

Singh, Daljeet, and Kharak Singh, eds. *Sikhism: Its Philosophy and History.* Introduction by Choor Singh. Chandigarh, India: Institute of Sikh Studies, 1997. Comprehensive anthology of essays on all aspects of Sikhism; delves into the history of the religion and the role of Nānak in its founding. Includes color illustrations and bibliographic references.

Singh, Ganda, ed. *Sources of the Life and Teachings of Guru Nānak.* Patiala, India: Punjabi University, Department of Punjab Historical Studies, 1969. Compiled by a foremost scholar of Sikh history, it is a basic work.

Singh, Harbans. *Guru Nānak and Origins of the Sikh Faith.* New York: Asia Publishing House, 1969. Examines Nānak's work as the foundation of Sikhism.

Singh, Kartar. *Guru Nānak Dev: Life and Teachings.* Ludhiana, India: Lahore Book Shop, 1969. Tells the story of the guru's life and concludes with a review of his teachings.

Singh, Trilochan. *Guru Nānak, Founder of Sikhism: A Biography.* Delhi, India: Gurdwara Parbandhak Committee, 1969. This book is a standard, well-documented work.

Talib, Gurbachan Singh. *Guru Nānak: His Personality and Vision.* Delhi, India: Gur Das Kapur, 1969. A comprehensive and analytical survey of Nānak's thought.

SEE ALSO: Akbar; Ibrāhīm Lodī.

RELATED ARTICLE in *Great Events from History: The Renaissance & Early Modern Era, 1454-1600:* Early 16th century: Devotional Bhakti Traditions Emerge.

JOHN NAPIER
Scottish mathematician, inventor, and theologian

Working alone, without the benefit of earlier work and the encouragement of mentors, Napier invented logarithms, which revolutionized arithmetic calculation and was the greatest boon to experimental science produced during the Renaissance.

BORN: 1550; Merchiston Castle, near Edinburgh, Scotland
DIED: April 4, 1617; Merchiston Castle
ALSO KNOWN AS: John Neper
AREAS OF ACHIEVEMENT: Mathematics, science and technology, military, religion and theology

EARLY LIFE

John Napier (NAY-pyuhr), eighth lord of Merchiston, was born at Merchiston Castle, the son of Sir Archibald Napier by his first wife, Janet Bothwell. He was born into a family notable for several famous soldiers at a time when religious controversy was rife in Scotland.

Little is known of his childhood, but when Napier was thirteen, his mother died. He was subsequently sent to St. Salvator's College, St. Andrews University, a school not noted for its quiet academic environment. Although Napier remained at St. Andrews for only one year, he developed two intense interests that were to continue for the remainder of his life: theology and arithmetic. Because of the nonacademic environment, the bishop of Orkney advised that young John could better pursue an academic career at schools on the Continent. Although no direct evidence remains to confirm this, it is highly probable that he followed this course.

As young Napier traveled through a Europe divided into warring factions by the Protestant Reformation, he became a strong adherent of the Calvinist movement then sweeping Scotland. He was to remain a fervent and uncompromising believer, active in Protestant politics throughout his life, much of which was spent embroiled in bitter religious dissension aggravated by the embarrassing political activities of his papist father-in-law, Sir James Chisholm.

By 1571, he had returned to Scotland. The following year, he married Elizabeth Stirling and occupied a castle at Gartnes. In 1579, his wife died, leaving two children. Subsequently, Napier married Agnes Chisholm and fathered ten additional children. On the death of his father in 1608, Napier moved into Merchiston Castle, where he remained for the rest of his life.

As a member of the Scottish landed aristocracy, he

had the time and resources to pursue his many interests. These included theology, agricultural improvements, and military science. In the latter field, he anticipated inventions three centuries before they were actually fabricated, and he invented an artillery so powerfully destructive that he refused, in horror, to develop or even to publicize it. Napier also experimented with fertilizers for crops and invented a mechanical device to pump water out of coal pits.

LIFE'S WORK

Napier's first literary work, *A Plaine Discovery of the Whole Revelation of St. John*, published in 1593 after five years of toil, was the first important work of biblical interpretation written in Scotland. In the book's introduction, the Scottish king James VI (the future James I of England) is entreated to safeguard the Scottish Protestant church and to purge and punish the Roman Catholic nobility. The body of this bitterly anti-Catholic exposition, among other things, identifies the pope as the anti-Christ described in the biblical Book of Revelations. Although from the perspective of history this enterprise may appear to be little more than fruitless theological supposition, it established Napier's reputation as both scholar and theologian. His theological interpretations followed the Greek form of mathematical argument, a form of theological reasoning that would not become popular for several centuries.

Although Napier's public life during these tumultuous times has been amply documented, the development of his mathematical work, conducted alone and almost in secret, is more difficult to trace. It seems as though mathematics was for Napier a solitary pursuit of leisure, while his highly visible public life focused on anti-Catholic proclamations meant to keep Catholicism out of Scotland.

An early treatise concerned with arithmetic and algebra was apparently assembled during his first marriage but remained unpublished until 1839. About 1590, he set out to make arithmetic easier; the task required twenty years of labor, but he succeeded by inventing logarithms, a system that simplified the computation of products, quotients, and roots. His fanatical dedication to Calvinist Protestantism shows the same obsessive persistence that enabled him to finish the grueling task of producing a usable set of logarithmic tables.

Logarithms, or "logs," are the exponents of a stated number, the "base," and are used to represent powers (exponents) of the base. Consider, for example, the powers of 2: 2^1, 2^2, 2^3, 2^4, 2^5, and so on. These correspond to 2, 4,

John Napier. (Hulton|Archive by Getty Images)

8, 16, 32, and so on. The exponents 1, 2, 3, 4, and 5 are the logs of these numbers to the base 2. To multiply any two numbers in the series, it is necessary only to add the exponents (or logs) of the numbers and then find to the antilog of the result, which corresponds to the sum desired. Thus, to multiply 32 by 4, take the log of 32, which is 5, and add it to the log of 4, which is 2, to get 7. The antilog of 7 (that is, the number with a log of 7) is 128, the desired result. Division is performed by subtracting logs.

By extension, numbers not found in the above series can be used if a noninteger number can be found such that when 2 is raised to this power the desired number is produced. For example, since $2 = 2^1$ and $4 = 2^2$, it follows that $3 = 2^x$, where x must be a number greater than 1 but less than 2. In fact, x is approximately equal to 1.585. Since any number can be expressed to a good approximation as a power of 2, any arithmetic operations can be performed provided a table of powers of 2 is provided.

Although Napier did not use 2 as the base of his logarithms, the principle is the same. Whereas logs make arithmetic computation considerably easier, Napier set himself the grueling task of computing, by various mathematical means, a complete set of log tables, that is, sufficient powers of the base to generate a complete set of numbers, including decimal fractions. The calculation of the tables occupied Napier for almost twenty years. While not entirely error-free, the calculations were basically accurate, forming the foundation for all subsequent log tables.

In 1614, Napier published the description of his logarithms together with a set of log tables, several uses for them, and rules for the solution of both plane and spherical triangles using the tables. This work, titled *Mirifici Logarithmorum Canonis Descriptio* (*Description of a Marvelous Canon of Logarithms*, 1857), omitted any explanation of his methods of calculation. Although the common folk who were Napier's neighbors had always suspected him of being a warlock who delved into the black arts behind his thick castle walls, his miraculous technique of logarithms, presented unexpectedly without explanation or rationale, seemed like black magic even to the relatively sophisticated people who had the occasion to use them.

A later work, published posthumously in 1619, *Mirifici Logarithmorum Canonis Constructio* (*Construction of a Marvelous Canon of Logarithms*, 1889), provides the explanation of his calculations, an outline of the steps leading to his invention, and the properties of his logarithmic function.

Napier sent a copy of his 1614 work to Henry Briggs, a professor at Gresham College. Briggs had the idea of making the base of the log tables 10, an innovation of which Napier approved because it simplified calculations. In 1624, Briggs published his tables of common logs (base 10 logarithms), but he gave full credit to Napier for the original idea.

Napier also invested considerable time in deriving complicated equations and exponential forms of trigonometric functions, since these played such important roles in astronomical computations. By mathematical manipulation, he was able to reduce the requisite number of spherical trigonometry equations from ten to just two general statements.

Napier's tables of logarithms were greeted with great enthusiasm by astronomers, since they simplified computations and removed some of the drudgery from analyzing data. Johannes Kepler (1571-1630), who inherited several decades of extremely accurate data on planetary motions from the great Danish astronomer Tycho Brahe, used Napier's logarithms to simplify the analysis. The results of his work led to Kepler's three laws of planetary motion, the first correct and accurate

statement of planetary motion. Later, Isaac Newton (1642-1727) used Kepler's laws in formulating his theory of gravity.

In 1617, Napier published the results of his work on a mechanical system to simplify arithmetic computation, *Rabdologiae, seu numerationis per virgulas libri duo* (*Study of Divining Rods: Or, Two Books of Numbering by Means of Rods*, 1667). This involved manipulating a set of small counting rods (later termed "Napier's Bones") to multiply and divide numbers. This device could be considered the precursor of the slide rule (a set of sliding logarithmic scales that enabled rapid multiplication and division), a device widely used by scientists and students until the latter half of the twentieth century. Last but not least, Napier standardized and popularized the system now universally used for decimal notation, in which a decimal point is used to separate the integer from the fractional part of a number.

SIGNIFICANCE

The 1614 publication of Napier's canon of logarithms is one of those extraordinary and exceptional events in the history of science whereby a new invention of great importance appears, seemingly out of thin air, with no obvious precursors foreshadowing its creation. Napier's invention removed much of the drudgery from reducing scientific data, particularly for astronomers attempting to use accurate measurements to predict planetary motions. When Johann Kepler used Tycho Brahe's accurate data to deduce his laws of planetary motion, Napier's logarithms helped make the arduous task possible.

In the centuries following their invention, log tables grew more detailed and more accurate, culminating in 1964 with the publication of a table of logarithms accurate to 110 decimal places. Until the 1970's, when inexpensive hand-held calculators and personal computers rendered them obsolete, log tables formed an essential component of college-preparatory secondary education, and no reputable engineer would be without his slide rule, a portable version of the log tables.

As a titled landowner, Napier, lord of Merchiston, devoted considerable energy to agricultural products to improve his crops and cattle. He tinkered with inventions and was granted a patent for a hydraulic screw to pump water from coal pits, and he outlined plans for (but never constructed) four new weapons of war, including an artillery piece that was designed to kill anything within a one-mile radius. Napier's first literary work, an interpretation of the Book of Revelation, secured his reputation as a scholar and as a theologian, although outside Scotland this work no longer commands high regard.

—*George R. Plitnik*

FURTHER READING

Burton, David M. *The History of Mathematics: An Introduction*. 5th ed. Boston: McGraw-Hill, 2003. Survey of important developments in math and the people behind those developments. This edition adds broader coverage of important mathematicians, including women in math. Includes illustrations, bibliographic references, and index.

Gladstone-Millar, Lynne. *John Napier: Logarithm John*. Edinburgh: National Museums of Scotland, 2003. Biography of Napier emphasizes his importance, not just to mathematics, but to astronomy as well. Includes illustrations and bibliographic references.

Hobson, E. W. *John Napier and the Invention of Logarithms*. Cambridge, England: Cambridge University Press, 1914. This lecture is the most useful of the various reconstructions of Napier's invention of logarithms. Highly recommended.

Knott, C. G., ed. *Napier Tercentenary Memorial Volume*. London: Dawson's of Pall Mall, 1966. A reprint of a 1915 original. Contains a set of articles detailing different aspects of Napier's accomplishments by experts in various fields of mathematics, as well as some considerable detail on the historical background to his work. Also included is a complete bibliography of books exhibited at the July, 1914, Napier Tercentenary Celebration.

McLeish, John. *Number*. New York: Fawcett Columbine, 1991. Chapter 12, "John Napier: The Rationalization of Arithmetic," details his work on logarithms and Napier's Bones. Included are examples detailing the construction and use of both these inventions.

Napier, John. *Napier's Mathematical Works*. Translated by William F. Hawkins. 3 vols. Auckland, New Zealand: University of Auckland Press, 1982. A translation from Latin of all of Napier's writings on mathematics, including those published posthumously. Volumes 2 and 3 include a commentary on Napier's work and how it fits into the history of mathematics.

Napier, Mark. *Memoirs of John Napier of Merchiston: His Lineage, Life, and Times*. Edinburgh: W. Blackwood, 1834. Written by a direct descendant of John Napier with access to the family's private papers, this carefully researched work provides the original source material from which most later books were derived.

Neal, Katherine. *From Discrete to Continuous: The Broadening of Number Concepts in Early Modern England*. Boston: Kluwer Academic, 2002. Places Napier's invention of logarithms in the context of other changes in number theory in early modern England. Discusses Napier alongside such contemporaries and successors as Isaac Barrow and John Wallis. Includes illustrations, bibliographic references, and index.

SEE ALSO: Tycho Brahe; John Calvin; Nicolaus Copernicus; John Dee; Georg von Peuerbach; Rheticus.

RELATED ARTICLES in *Great Events from History: The Renaissance & Early Modern Era, 1454-1600:* 1462: Regiomontanus Completes the *Epitome* of Ptolemy's *Almagest*; 1550's: Tartaglia Publishes *The New Science*.

THOMAS NASHE
English writer

A versatile writer of satiric pamphlets, plays, lyric poetry, and a novel, Nashe had a marked influence on many of his contemporaries, including William Shakespeare and Ben Jonson, who admired his powers of wit and observation and his inventive use of language.

BORN: November, 1567; Lowestoft, Suffolk, England
DIED: 1601; Yarmouth?, England
ALSO KNOWN AS: Thomas Nash
AREAS OF ACHIEVEMENT: Literature, theater

EARLY LIFE

Thomas Nashe was born the third son of William Nashe, a clergyman. In 1573, when Thomas was six, the family moved to West Harling, Norfolk, where Thomas's father took up a position as rector. Since the nearest school was seven miles away, it is likely that Nashe received his early schooling from his father.

In October, 1582, Nashe matriculated as a sizar scholar of St. Johns College, Cambridge University, although he may have been in residence at St. Johns for two terms before this. A sizar was a poor student who performed menial tasks such as making beds and serving at table in return for free food rations.

Student life at Cambridge was strict. The academic day began at dawn; students were expected to attend college for all but three weeks a year and were allowed to leave the college only twice a week. Punishments were severe, including whippings and fines; lodgings were crowded, and in winter were damp and cold.

In spite of these privations, Nashe seemed to flourish at Cambridge, and in 1584, he was appointed as a scholar of the Lady Margaret Foundation of the University. In Nashe's later writings, he praised St. John's College highly, although he did lament the strong Puritan influence there, which gave him a lifetime aversion to Puritanism.

While at Cambridge, Nashe was a close friend of the dramatist Christopher Marlowe, and he probably had a hand in producing some satirical plays during his student years. In 1586, Nashe was awarded the degree of bachelor of arts. He continued at St. Johns to work on a master of arts degree, but he never completed it, leaving Cambridge for London in the early fall of 1588. The reason for his departure is not known, but it may have been because his father, who had helped to support him at the university, died the previous year, leaving Nashe without the financial means to continue. Nashe's intention in London was to follow his fellow Cambridge graduate Robert Greene and make a living as a writer. In Elizabethan England, the idea of pursuing a career as a professional writer was a novel one, but Nashe, full of youthful confidence, was prepared to give it a try.

LIFE'S WORK

Once Nashe reached London, he registered his first literary piece, a dull pamphlet entitled *The Anatomie of Absurditie*, which he had written during a vacation in 1587. Not published until 1589, it received almost no attention. Shortly thereafter, Nashe wrote a preface to Robert Greene's *Menaphon* (1589); that he was commissioned to write such a piece for an established author suggests that he already had something of a reputation in literary London. Yet it was not until the publication of his pamphlet *An Almond for a Parrat* in the spring of 1590 that Nashe found his true voice: a satirical, colloquial, vivid, journalistic style that was to make him the most popular of the Elizabethan pamphleteers. *An Almond for a Parrat* was Nashe's contribution to the controversy surrounding the Puritan pamphlets of "Martin Marprelate," which were attacks on the Church of England written in colloquial language to appeal to public opinion. Nashe's reply successfully imitated the style of the Martin pamphlets and also identified for the first time in print the name of their author.

Armed with his new style, Nashe produced his greatest popular success, the social satire *Pierce Penniless, His Supplication to the Divell* (1592), which went through at least five editions between 1592 and 1595. In this book, Nashe's persona, Pierce Penilesse, grumbles that his talents go unrewarded and that in the society in which he lives, money goes to those least deserving of it. He therefore decides to send a supplication to the devil, asking him for a loan. The supplication takes up most of the book, in which contemporary social abuses are described in terms of the seven deadly sins. Nashe's purpose appears to have been to entertain rather than to moralize, however, and *Pierce Penniless* is memorable for its lively anecdotes, the feeling of spontaneity it conveys, the poetic imagery, and the realistic detail taken from the streets of the Elizabethan London that Nashe walked every day. It is notable also for its defense of literature and of the theater.

Thin and long-haired, with a boyish appearance, Nashe was a well-known figure in London, and his self-cultivated notoriety was only increased by a long-running literary quarrel between himself and Cambridge scholar Gabriel Harvey. It was Harvey who had first attacked Nashe in print, and Nashe responded later in the same year with *Strange Newes of the Intercepting of Certain Letters* (1592). So began an exchange of slanderous pamphlets that showed Nashe at his most boisterous and vituperative.

Strange Newes of the Intercepting of Certain Letters was written in the country at Croydon, where Nashe, eager to escape the plague that was sweeping London, took refuge as guest of the Archbishop John Whitgift. While in Croydon, he also wrote his only surviving play, *Summer's Last Will and Testament*, which was probably performed in Croydon in 1592 but was not published until 1600. After returning to London, Nashe wrote the long *Christ's Tears over Jerusalem* (1593), in which he made a comparison between the sins of the Jews that led to the destruction of Jerusalem and the decayed morals of contemporary London, which, he argued, would bring a similar calamity. A born controversialist, Nashe had much to say about greedy merchants and corrupt public officials, and the outcry was such that he was forced to issue a denial that he was attacking any particular individual. This did not stop the London city council from taking action against him in December; Nashe was extricated from his ensuing difficulties only by the intervention of his influential acquaintance, Sir George Carey. Nashe stayed at the Carey family castle on the Isle of Wight until early 1594.

Returning to London once again, he published *The Unfortunate Traveller: Or, The Life of Jack Wilton* (1594), which he had completed the previous year. Describing the picaresque adventures of its protagonist, this book is sometimes called the first English novel. Later that year Nashe published *The Terrors of the Night* (1594), which he described as an "incredible narration" of a series of visions that came to a man in his last illness. Intended as an attack on superstition, the work discusses dreams and spirits in a rambling and digressive style that is typical of Nashe generally.

During 1595, Nashe worked on his final reply to Harvey, *Have with You to Saffron-Walden* (1596). In this period, he was also trying to write plays, but on his own admission with little success. In 1597, Nashe was again involved in a dangerous controversy when he collaborated with Ben Jonson and others on a satirical play, *The Isle of Dogs*, now lost. When performed in July, the play was declared seditious by the authorities. Nashe's lodgings were searched and his papers confiscated. Nashe claimed to have written only the induction and the first act, the remaining four acts being supplied by the players without his consent. Several of those involved in the play, including Jonson, were imprisoned, a fate Nashe avoided by fleeing to the coastal town of Yarmouth, in Norfolk. He arrived probably in December and remained there for six weeks.

After leaving Yarmouth, Nashe wrote his last pamphlet, *Nashe's Lenten Stuffe* (1599), during Lent. The book arose out of his desire to thank the town of Yarmouth for its hospitality to him. It is not known where Nashe was living at the time, although he does comment that the book was written "in the country." Nashe was certainly back in London by February, 1599, when he wrote the preface to *Nashe's Lenten Stuffe*.

Several months later, in June, 1599, another disaster struck Nashe. The authorities issued an order confiscating Nashe's books wherever they might be found and banning any further printing of them. The order also applied to Nashe's adversary, Gabriel Harvey, as well as a number of other satirical writers. After the

NASHE'S MAJOR WORKS	
c. 1586-1587	*Dido, Queen of Carthage* (with Christopher Marlowe)
1589	*The Anatomie of Absurditie*
1589	Preface to Robert Greene's *Menaphon*
1590	*An Almond for a Parrat*
1591	Preface to Sir Philip Sidney's *Astrophel and Stella*
1592	Preface to Robert Greene's *A Quip for an Upstart Courtier*
1592	*Strange News of the Intercepting of Certain Letters* (also known as *The Four Letters Confuted*)
1592	*Summer's Last Will and Testament*
1592	*Pierce Penilesse, His Supplication to the Divell*
1593	*Christ's Tears over Jerusalem*
1594	*The Unfortunate Traveller: Or, The Life of Jack Wilton*
1594	*The Terrors of the Night*
1596	*Have with You to Saffron-Walden*
1597	*The Isle of Dogs* (with Ben Jonson; no longer extant)
1599	*Nashe's Lenten Stuffe*
1899	*The Choise of Valentines*, pb. 1899

edict, little more was heard of Nashe, and in Charles Fitzgefrey's *Affaniae* (1601), he is referred to as already deceased. No other facts about his death or place of burial are known.

SIGNIFICANCE

Perhaps more than any other Elizabethan writer, Thomas Nashe had his finger on the pulse of the times. He kept his eyes and ears close to the chatter and bustle of the London streets, and his writings catch the rawness of life as it was lived in the 1590's.

Although Nashe is usually described as a pamphleteer, the term gives little indication of the range of his work; the form in which his writing would have flourished best, journalism, had not yet been invented. Many of his pieces would qualify today as investigative reports or magazine feature articles. Not only did Nashe have a nose for news, he also possessed the ability to write quickly, with a helter-skelter style (which he called his "extemporall veine") that was easily recognizable. Such a rapid style seemed to come naturally to him, but it was also necessitated by the conditions under which he lived. Lacking a wealthy patron, he chose to make a living from the popular press, which yielded small financial rewards and demanded a quick output.

Harassed by poverty and government censors and dying young, Nashe did not achieve all that his talents merited. As a satirist however, he influenced other Elizabethan writers such as Ben Jonson and William Shakespeare. For example, Nashe's distinctive use of language finds an echo in Shakespeare's *The Taming of the Shrew* (pr. c. 1593-1594); the character Moth in *Love's Labour's Lost* (pr. c. 1594-1595) is widely believed to be based on Nashe; and Shakespeare also drew extensively, in *Henry IV, Part I* (pr. c. 1597-1598), on Nashe's observations of the idiosyncrasies of speech and behavior.

—Bryan Aubrey

FURTHER READING

Hibbard, G. R. *Thomas Nashe: A Critical Introduction.* Cambridge, Mass.: Harvard University Press, 1962. The most detailed critical study of Nashe, written with the intention of rescuing him from critical neglect. Contains some errors of chronology regarding Nashe's writings, which are corrected in McGinn. Concludes that there was a gap between Nashe's talents and what he was able to achieve with them.

Lewis, C. S. *English Literature in the Sixteenth Century, Excluding Drama.* London: Oxford University Press, 1954. Describes Nashe as the greatest of the Elizabethan pamphleteers and one of the most original writers in the English language. Lewis portrays Nashe as a literary showman who could keep a crowd entertained by his sheer virtuosity.

McGinn, Donald J. *Thomas Nashe.* Boston: Twayne, 1981. Probably the best place to start for an overall understanding of Nashe's life and work. McGinn analyzes the works in chronological order and, in a concluding chapter about Nashe's place in English literature, describes him as a sixteenth century H. L. Mencken. Includes a chronology of Nashe's life and an annotated bibliography.

Moulton, Ian Frederick. *Before Pornography: Erotic Writing in Early Modern England.* New York: Oxford University Press, 2000. Looks at the relationship between masculinity and English national identity in the erotic writings of Nashe, Ben Jonson, and several other Renaissance authors.

Nicholl, Charles. *A Cup of News: The Life of Thomas Nashe.* London: Routledge & Kegan Paul, 1984. The only full-length biography of Nashe, this work is so comprehensive it is unlikely to be superseded. Meticulous research sheds new light on many episodes in Nashe's life and also gives a picture of London literary life in the last decade of the sixteenth century. Includes ten illustrations and twelve reproductions of documents.

Nielson, James. *Unread Herrings: Thomas Nashe and the Prosaics of the Real.* New York: P. Lang, 1993. An examination of the relationship between rhetoric and the real in Nashe's pamphlets. Written in an extremely dense and playful style meant at once to mimic and to contest deconstructionist readings of Nashe. Includes bibliographic references.

Wells, Stanley, ed. *Thomas Nashe: Selected Writings.* Cambridge, Mass.: Harvard University Press, 1965. Contains four of Nashe's books in their entirety (with spelling modernized) and extracts from five others. Also contains a glossary and an introductory critical essay.

Wheeler, Laura Scavuzzo. "The Development of an Englishman: Thomas Nashe's *The Unfortunate Traveler.*" In *Historicizing Christian Encounters with the Other,* edited by John C. Hawley. Washington Square: New York: New York University Press, 1998. Study of Nashe's representation of conversion to Christianity in *The Unfortunate Traveler.* Includes bibliographic references and index.

Yates, Julian. *Error, Misuse, Failure: Object Lessons from the English Renaissance.* Minneapolis: University of Minnesota Press, 2003. This study of the misuse and outright failure of Renaissance objects includes a chapter on Nashe's use of the printing press. Discusses both the rise of Renaissance printing and the effects of typographical errors on Nashe's work. Includes illustrations, bibliographic references, and index.

SEE ALSO: Sir Thomas Malory; Christopher Marlowe; William Shakespeare; Edmund Spenser.
RELATED ARTICLES in *Great Events from History: The Renaissance & Early Modern Era, 1454-1600:* 1576: James Burbage Builds The Theatre; c. 1589-1613: Shakespeare Writes His Dramas; December, 1598-May, 1599: The Globe Theatre Is Built.

SAINT PHILIP NERI
Italian religious leader

As a priest living in Rome during the Counter-Reformation, Saint Philip Neri stood apart from the religious politics of his time and influenced countless Catholics to reform their lives and return to traditional spirituality. Called the Apostle of Rome, he founded the Congregation of the Oratory, which inspired laypersons and clergy to lead lives of holiness and charity.

BORN: July 21, 1515; Florence (now in Italy)
DIED: May 26, 1595; Rome (now in Italy)
AREAS OF ACHIEVEMENT: Religion and theology, church reform

EARLY LIFE

Saint Philip Neri (NAY-ree) was born in a poor section of Florence, ruled at that time by the Medicis. His father, Francesco Neri, was unsuccessful in his career as a notary and thus turned to alchemy, losing the family's financial security through his improvidence. When Philip was five years old, his mother, Lucrezia da Mosciano, died shortly after giving birth to her fourth child. The household, by all reports a happy one, was thereafter managed by a woman who was either the mother-in-law of Francesco or his second wife.

Young Philip, unlike many other saints, showed no evidence of a precocious interest in religion. Yet even as a child he was noted for his charm and sweetness of disposition, personal qualities that would characterize his relationships with others throughout his life. His nickname was Pippo Buono (good little Philip). His formal schooling with the Dominican fathers probably ended when he was about sixteen, and thereafter he was self-educated. In 1532, he went to San Germano to work for his father's cousin Romolo Neri, with the understanding that he would eventually take over the family business. Instead, during a period of intense prayer and meditation, he decided to give his life to God. He had no plans to enter the priesthood but intended to live in poverty and offer his service to humankind. Accordingly, in 1533 he left San Germano and traveled to Rome, where he lived in the home of Galeotto Caccia, a customs official from Florence, serving as tutor to Caccia's two young sons.

LIFE'S WORK

Although Philip would not be ordained a priest until he was thirty-six years old, he quietly began the work to which he would dedicate the rest of his life. Philip lived during the Counter-Reformation, thus called by those who consider it to have been a response to the Protestant movement; it is also known as the Catholic Revival by those who consider it to have been an internal revitalization of the Church begun in the previous century in Spain.

Rome, sacked during an invasion in 1527, was noted for its atmosphere of licentiousness and low moral standards, and was ripe for reform. To Catholic observers, the influence of classical, or pagan, authors was responsible for the weakness of faith in the Church. Abuses within the Church were flagrant, with the Medicis using their political power to control church elections and corrupt clergymen neglecting the spiritual needs of the people. The Council of Trent, meeting from 1545 to 1563, would reform the abuses and clarify church teaching but would be unsuccessful in the attempt to reunite with the Protestants.

Philip, his life newly dedicated to God, became one of the many hermits of the streets of Rome, preaching informally to anyone who would listen. At night, however, he went to the catacombs outside the city to pray and meditate in solitude, beginning his life as a mystic. He also took courses in philosophy and theology at the university but, realizing that he had no calling to the scholarly life, sold his books and gave the money to the poor. He contin-

Saint Philip Neri. (Hulton|Archive by Getty Images)

ued to live with the Caccia family, in a small attic room, eating a meager diet of bread and olives.

Soon Philip's gift for influencing others came to public attention. With his good humor, he succeeded in converting many young men who had come at first to mock his preaching. He also took up charitable work in the public hospitals, offering spiritual comfort to the dying. Although he met Saint Ignatius of Loyola during this time, Philip was not attracted to the Jesuit priesthood and had no intention of seeking ordination himself, even though many of the young men he converted became priests.

In 1544, on the eve of Pentecost, Philip underwent an unusual experience while praying in the catacombs. He reported that a ball of fire entered his mouth and lodged in his heart, creating a swelling or malformation that was visible to others. The autopsy report of his death showed an enlarged heart that had broken several ribs. Whatever the explanation for this phenomenon, observers noticed throughout his life that his heartbeat could be heard across a room and that he would tremble violently when overcome by a mystical experience.

In 1548, Philip laid the foundation for the organization that would eventually become the Congregation of the Oratory. With Father Persiano Rossi, he formed a confraternity of laymen that met at the Church of San Girolomo to pray, read the Scriptures, and discuss the lives of the saints and Church history. In 1551, at the insistence of Father Rossi (and probably because the Church disapproved of lay preachers), Philip was ordained. At that time, no special education was required for ordination, although the Council of Trent was to found the system of seminaries that would educate priests in the future.

Given the power to hear confessions, Philip, contrary to the custom of the time, insisted that his followers receive this sacrament frequently. He was noted for his insights as a spiritual adviser, reportedly knowing what the penitent was thinking before any words were spoken. Despite his need for solitude, he made himself available at all hours, even during the night, to those who asked for his guidance.

Philip's meetings became famous in Rome, attracting many followers. After the spiritual exercises, the followers would make the pilgrimage to the Seven Churches, a special devotion in Rome, stopping to eat and drink with the enthusiasm of picnickers. Among his followers were the historian Cesare Baronio, Cardinal (later Saint) Carlo Borromeo of Milan, Giovanni Pierluigi da Palestrina, and Giovanni Animuccia. These last two composed sacred music for the prayer meetings, originating the musical form of the oratorio, which takes its name from this group.

In 1575, Pope Gregory XIII formally recognized the Congregation of the Oratory. Although Philip had not intended to found a religious congregation, his movement spread to several other cities in Italy. The Congregation of the Oratory differed significantly from other religious organizations in that, although the priests lived in community, they took no vows, kept their personal property, and were free to leave at any time. The pope gave Philip the property of Santa Maria in Vallicella, where he had a new church constructed and lived for the rest of his life. Since he had no wealth of his own, he apparently depended on contributions from the faithful to carry out his work.

Philip's reputation for clownish behavior might seem at first to contradict his saintly vocation. He often ordered strange penances, such as requiring a follower to sing or dance in the streets or perform humiliating work such as sweeping the church steps while dressed in an outlandish costume. Once, when a penitent asked permission to wear a hair shirt, Philip commanded him to wear it outside his clothing, visible to all. With his belief in the virtue of humility, Philip saw these penances as a way of puncturing the egos of sinners full of self-love. Although he was personally fastidious, his appearance was sometimes laughable. Once he appeared in the streets with half his beard shaved, and sometimes he wore his clothes inside out. When the pope offered him the red hat of a cardinal, Philip took this honor as a joke and tossed the hat around like a ball. This good-humored mockery of his own dignity was taken by Romans as evidence of his saintliness and increased their affection for him.

Throughout his life, Philip wrote poetry, although little remains, as he destroyed his papers before death. As his reputation for sanctity grew, so did stories about his mystical experiences while celebrating Mass. He would often lose himself in contemplation and go into a trancelike state, reportedly rising in the air, then collapse in a state of exhaustion. His followers increased, including not only ordinary people but also cardinals and even several popes.

In his old age, Philip had a luxuriant white beard and bright, childlike blue eyes. His frail appearance became more pronounced; always an ascetic, he ate barely enough to sustain life and in his last years withdrew entirely to a life of contemplation. Philip died in 1595. Popularly acclaimed as a saint during his lifetime, he was canonized by Pope Gregory XV in 1622.

SIGNIFICANCE

Saint Philip Neri is an example of the power of a humble man, devoid of any desire for public acclaim or political power, to exert a significant influence on the events of his time. A priest of the Roman Catholic Church during the turbulent years of the Counter-Reformation, his example of personal holiness, balanced with a whimsical (at times eccentric) sense of humor, persuaded countless Romans, from ordinary workers to highly placed churchmen, to reform their lives.

The most significant event during Philip's lifetime was the Council of Trent, which clarified the doctrines of the Catholic Church, set down the rules for the reform of the clergy, and called on the faithful to lead disciplined lives under the spiritual direction of the Church. Although Philip took no part in the deliberations of the council, he founded the Congregation of the Oratory (Oratorians), a loosely organized group of laymen and priests who gathered to pray, read and discuss the Scriptures, and exhort others to a life of holiness. Some of Rome's most notable clerics, public figures, and musicians attended these meetings. The Oratorians, unlike members of other religious orders, took no vows.

As is often the case in reports of saints' lives, controversy arises over the contemporary biographers' records of miraculous occurrences (ecstasies, prophecies, medical cures) as manifestations of Philip's holiness. Interpretation of the meaning of these phenomena is a matter of faith. Yet there can be no question that, in a time when the Church produced both illustrious and notorious public figures, Philip stands out as one who, through his considerable personal magnetism and holiness, became a model for personal reform for the countless people who sought his spiritual guidance.

—*Marjorie J. Podolsky*

FURTHER READING

Bouyer, Louis. *The Roman Socrates: A Portrait of St. Philip Neri.* Translated by Michael Day. Westminster, Md.: Newman Press, 1958. Offers insight into Philip's spiritual life from the viewpoint of a modern French priest who belongs to the Congregation of the Oratory.

Burke, Peter. "How to Become a Counter-Reformation Saint." In *The Counter-Reformation: The Essential Readings*, edited by David M. Luebke. Malden, Mass.: Blackwell, 1999. This study of the canonization of Philip and others is one of nine essays on the state of Counter-Reformation studies since 1945. Includes bibliographic references and index.

Butler, Samuel. "St. Philip Neri." In *Butler's Lives of the Saints*, edited by Herbert Thurston and Donald Atwater. New York: P. J. Kenedy and Sons, 1956. An indispensable reference work, which gives a concise overview of Philip's life and contributions to the history of the Catholic Church.

Daniel-Rops, Henry. *The History of the Church of Christ.* Vol. 5 in *The Catholic Reformation*. Translated by John Warrington. London: J. M. Dent & Sons, 1962. A detailed scholarly study, especially useful in placing Philip's life and work within the framework of the Catholic Revival, which influenced him and was influenced by him, because so many of his followers were church officials.

Harney, Martin P. "Religious Orders, Old and New." In *The Catholic Church Through the Ages*. Boston: Daughters of St. Paul, 1974. A good account of church history for those without scholarly knowledge of the times. Valuable in describing the Congregation of the Oratory against the background of the Council of Trent.

McGinness, Frederick J. *Right Thinking and Sacred Oratory in Counter-Reformation Rome.* Princeton, N.J.: Princeton University Press, 1995. Exhaustive analysis of the theory and practice of preaching in Rome during the Counter-Reformation. Covers everything from the general strategy of Catholic sermonizing to the physical conditions of the sermon audience. Includes illustrations, bibliographic references, and index.

Maynard, Theodore. *Mystic in Motley: The Life of St. Philip Neri.* Milwaukee, Wis.: Bruce Publishing, 1946. A lucid biography that draws on sources from Philip's own time as well as earlier biographies not generally available. Sifts through the technical accounts of canonization procedures and miracles to provide a balanced explanation for many events in Philip's life.

Schamoni, Wilhelm. "Philip Neri, the Apostle of Rome." In *Face of the Saints,* translated by Anne Freemantle. New York: Pantheon Books, 1947. Reprint. Freeport, N.Y.: Books for Libraries Press, 1972. A fascinating collection of images of death masks and portraits of the saints painted during their lives, along with brief biographies. The introduction has a useful explanation of the canonization process for the general reader.

Türks, Paul. *Philip Neri: The Fire of Joy.* Translated by Daniel Utrecht. Edinburgh: T&T Clark, 1995. This biography of Philip emphasizes the human qualities, such as sense of humor, that helped him to win back followers of Catholicism by convincing them that the religion had more to do with loving worship than with self-denial and asceticism. Includes bibliographic references and index.

SEE ALSO: Barbe Acari; John Calvin; Vittoria Colonna; Gregory XIII; Saint Ignatius of Loyola; Saint John of the Cross; Martin Luther; Marguerite de Navarre; Paul III; Giovanni Pierluigi da Palestrina; Pius V; Girolamo Savonarola; Sixtus V; Saint Teresa of Ávila.

RELATED ARTICLES in *Great Events from History: The Renaissance & Early Modern Era, 1454-1600:* March, 1536: Calvin Publishes *Institutes of the Christian Religion;* July 22, 1566: Pius V Expels the Prostitutes from Rome; 1567: Palestrina Publishes the *Pope Marcellus Mass.*

NEZAHUALCÓYOTL
Aztec ruler (r. 1431-1472)

Nezahualcóyotl, who was primarily responsible for the creation of the Aztec Empire, was a proponent of a religious vision that, if it had prevailed, might have made possible that empire's survival.

BORN: 1402; probably Texcoco (now in Mexico)
DIED: 1472; Texcoco
AREAS OF ACHIEVEMENT: Religion and theology, government and politics, diplomacy

EARLY LIFE

Nezahualcóyotl (nehz-zah-wahl-KOY-yoh-tuhl), which means "hungry coyote," was the son of Ixtlilxóchitl, king of Texcoco, and therefore a descendant of Xólotl, who led a Chichimec tribe into the northern part of the Valley of Mexico in the mid-thirteenth century and established the kingdom of Alcolhuacán. Quinatzin, who established his Alcolhuacán capital at Texcoco in 1318, was the great-grandson of Xólotl and the great-grandfather of Nezahualcóyotl, who also had connection with the Mexica Aztecs of Tenochtitlán through his mother,

Matlalcihuatzin, who was the daughter of a Tenochtitlán king.

The childhood of Nezahualcóyotl was a time of great peril for the royal house of Alcolhuacán because of the wars fought in the valley in the period before the rise of the Mexica Aztecs of Tenochtitlán. The arena of these wars was a relatively small area in the vicinity of what is now called Mexico City, and the powers engaged were all cities on or near the shores of Lake Texcoco or on its islands. Because the various codices on which one depends for knowledge of these events were written from memory after the Spanish Conquest, they do not agree in detail, but their description of the wars that tore apart the Valley of Mexico in the years before Nezahualcóyotl came to the throne of Texcoco are in agreement on the basic events.

The dominant power on the western shore of the lake was the Tepanecans of Azcapotzalco, whose great King Tezozómoc, though he was himself a grandson of Xólotl, was determined to extend his control over the valley by conquering Texcoco, which dominated the country between the lake and the mountains to the east. In 1412, Tezozómoc launched a three-pronged attack, sending armies against Alcolhuacán around the north and south ends of the lake and sending his Mexican allies from Tenochtitlán directly across the lake in their war canoes. Ixtlilxóchitl repulsed the southern attack and drove off the war canoes; then, in a war that lasted three years, he defeated the armies of Tezozómoc in every battle in the country north of the lake and laid siege to Azcapotzalco itself.

At this point, Tezozómoc sued for peace, and Ixtlilxóchitl, who had virtually won the war, magnanimously chose not to demand unconditional surrender. This stance ensured his own downfall, because Tezozómoc chose not to abide by the terms of the peace treaty, which called for both sides to disarm. In 1418, he launched a treacherous attack, and Ixtlilxóchitl was defeated and forced to flee to the mountains with Nezahualcóyotl. There, hiding in the branches of a tree, the boy saw his father make his last stand before he was cut down by the pursuing Tepanecans. From that moment, apparently, Nezahualcóyotl was determined to have his vengeance on Azcapotzalco.

Though the chronicles may rely only on popular legend, they all suggest that after fleeing across the mountains to Tlaxcala, where he found refuge with relatives, Nezahualcóyotl spent the next few years traveling incognito in Alcolhuacán, preparing his people for the day when he would lead them in a war of liberation against Azcapotzalco. In any case, during this period, he was in great peril as a result of a reward posted by Tezozómoc, and he eventually was captured at Chalco, a city on the southeast shore of the lake subject to Tezozómoc. According to the chronicles, Tezozómoc ordered him caged and starved to death, but his guards, remembering the greatness of his father, secretly fed him. Later, when he was to be put to death, one of his guards permitted him to escape and was killed in his place.

Eventually—in 1425 according to one account—two of his aunts, related to the royal houses of both Texcoco and Azcapotzalco, persuaded Tezozómoc to permit the young prince to return, and he was allowed to live in Texcoco and with his mother's relatives in Tenochtitlán. In his last days, however, Tezozómoc regretted giving the

---

A POEM BY NEZAHUALCÓYOTL, OR HUNGRY COYOTE

All the earth is a grave and nothing escapes it, nothing is so perfect that it does not descend to its tomb. Rivers, rivulets, fountains and waters flow, but never return to their joyful beginnings; anxiously they hasten on the vast realms of the rain god. As they widen their banks, they also fashion the sad urn of their burial.

Filled are the bowels of the earth with pestilential dust once flesh and bone, once animate bodies of men who sat upon thrones, decided cases, presided in council, commanded armies, conquered provinces, possessed treasure, destroyed temples, exulted in their pride, majesty, fortune, praise and power. Vanished are these glories, just as the fearful smoke vanishes that belches forth from the infernal fires of Popocatepetl. Nothing recalls them but the written page.

Source: Indigenous Peoples' Literature, http://www.indigenouspeople.net/ aztpoem.htm. Accessed September 23, 2004.

---

prince even this limited freedom and sent an assassin to kill him. Again, Nezahualcóyotl survived as a result of the prestige he enjoyed as the son of Ixtlilxóchitl; the assassin warned him of the plot.

In 1426, Tezozómoc died. Nezahualcóyotl, as an Aztec prince related by blood or marriage to all the royal houses of the valley, attended the funeral, apparently keeping his own counsel as he observed the final rites performed for the tyrant against whom he had sworn vengeance. Even then the sons of Tezozómoc were arguing about the succession, and Nezahualcóyotl, whose political instincts were strong, must have been planning the conspiracy by which he would destroy them and their city. The accession of Maxtla to the throne of Azcapotzalco in 1426 set in motion the events that led eventually to the destruction of Azcapotzalco, the rise of Tenochtitlán to prominence, and the return of Nezahualcóyotl to his rightful place on the throne of Texcoco.

LIFE'S WORK

In 1420, Tezozómoc had rewarded his allies in Tenochtitlán with suzerainty over Texcoco. Now with Tezozómoc's death, Chimalpopoca, the king of Tenochtitlán, granted the rule of Texcoco to Nezahualcóyotl, who immediately conspired with Chimalpopoca against Azcapotzalco's new king, Maxtla. The plot was a failure, and Nezahualcóyotl was again forced to flee. In 1427, however, Chimalpopoca was killed—either by agents of Maxtla or by the most aggressive elements in Tenochtitlán itself—and Ixtcóatl (or Itzcóatl, as the name is also transliterated) succeeded him on the throne of Tenochtitlán. The way was now prepared for the alliance that would bring Maxtla down.

Though Maxtla's henchmen ruled in Texcoco, Nezahualcóyotl was able to call on the goodwill he had earned among the people in the other cities east of the lake during his exile. The alliance of these cities now became part of a grander alliance of all those city-states that had grievances against Azcapotzalco. They were a mixed lot. Besides Nezahualcóyotl's cities, the alliance included his allies in Huexotzinco and Tlaxcala beyond the mountains east of the lake, Cuauhtitlán on the northwest shore of the lake, and Tlacopán on the west shore. Above all, it included Tenochtitlán. These Mexica Aztecs had fought against Nezahualcóyotl's father, they had opposed Nezahualcóyotl himself, and they had reduced him for a time to the status of a tribute-paying prince. He knew that the alliance against Azcapotzalco would not succeed without their warriors, however, and the alliance that resulted was primarily the result of his recognition of the political realities of the valley. Tenochtitlán, more or less imprisoned on its island in the lake, needed land, and Nezahualcóyotl used this land-hunger as a means of wreaking vengeance on Azcapotzalco.

As a result, he took a force of his best warriors to Tenochtitlán to aid in its defense. Maxtla's Tepanecans attacked across the causeways that linked Tenochtitlán to the western shore, and the Mexica and Nezahualcóyotl's Acolhua repulsed it. Meanwhile, armies from Huexotzinco and Tlaxcala were advancing on Azcapotzalco from the north. In 1428, the allies laid siege to Azcapotzalco and eventually destroyed it. The primary result of the victory was the ascendancy of Tenochtitlán in the political and military life of the valley and the rise to dominance of the most warlike and aggressive elements in that city.

Nezahualcóyotl remained in Tenochtitlán for several years, even building a palace there, while planning his campaign to regain the throne of Texcoco from the henchmen of Maxtla. The Mexica, keeping their part of the bargain, assisted him from 1429 to 1430 in the recovery of Texcoco. Now firmly allied with Tenochtitlán, he assisted them in their campaigns against the other cities on the shores of the lake, including Coyoacán and Xochimilco. In 1433, the fall of Cuitláhuac ended the Tepaneca War.

In 1431, Nezahualcóyotl was crowned emperor of the three-city league of Texcoco, Tenochtitlán, and Tlacopán, which he, more than anyone, had created. He realized that the kind of empire his ancestor Xólotl had achieved, a single state ruled by a single overlord, was no

longer possible. Peace in the Valley of Mexico, therefore, depended on the maintenance of a loose confederation of the Acolhua of Texcoco, the Mexica of Tenochtitlán, and the Tepaneca of Tlacopán. Whatever the faults of this "empire," it endured until the Spanish Conquest.

In 1433, Nezahualcóyotl returned to Texcoco and embarked on a program that inaugurated that city's golden age and made it the most beautiful city in the Valley of Mexico and its intellectual and cultural center. He was a patron of science, industry, art, and literature; he was himself a poet of considerable renown; and he encouraged the creation of historical archives that at the time of the Spanish Conquest were the most extensive in Mexico.

In 1440, when King Itzcóatl of Tenochtitlán died, Nezahualcóyotl rededicated himself to the friendship of the three cities and gave his support in the election of a new king to Montezuma I. Apparently he believed that Montezuma would be a less ambitious threat than any other candidate to the integrity of Alcolhuacán and was willing to make concessions to ensure this election, which in time proved to be disastrous. The Mexica under Montezuma's leadership became the dominant power in the valley, though Nezahualcóyotl continued as emperor.

In 1450, when torrential rains raised the level of the lake and flooded Tenochtitlán, Nezahualcóyotl, who was perhaps the most distinguished engineer and builder in Mexico before the conquest, proposed the great dike that stretched nine miles north to south down the lake and isolated Tenochtitlán from the east side of the lake, which received the heaviest runoff from the mountains. In the next few years, however, the Valley of Mexico was afflicted with a long drought. Nezahualcóyotl distributed food from his own supplies and resisted the charge of some of his subjects that the gods had withheld the rain because Nezahualcóyotl had neglected to maintain the rites of human sacrifice. Characteristically, he preferred to build an extensive irrigation system to bring water from the mountains.

Nezahualcóyotl's antipathy to human sacrifice, which is in itself enough to make him the most remarkable political figure of his time and place, apparently derived from his sympathy with the cult of Tloque Nahuaque. This god, who was assumed to be unfathomable, all-present, and formless, was the one god in the pantheon that did not demand human sacrifice, and in the encouragement of his cult, Nezahualcóyotl seems clearly to have been attempting to lead his people toward a religion based on a benevolent monotheism.

One of Nezahualcóyotl's concessions to Montezuma

was his agreement to assist his ally in future wars of aggression. From 1455 to 1458, therefore, he contributed to the success of Tenochtitlán's war against the Mixtecs, and in 1464 he sent an army that helped Tenochtitlán destroy Chalco.

In 1467, Nezahualcóyotl completed in Texcoco the temple to the war god Huitzilopochtli, which was required as a further concession to the Mexica of Tenochtitlán. In the same year he completed a temple to the peaceful, benevolent Tloque Nahuaque. The coincidence of these two events must be considered an indication of the tragedy inherent both in the life of Nezahualcóyotl and in the history of Mexico. In the next half century, that tragedy would play itself out to its inevitable conclusion as the adherents of Huitzilopochtli, with their doctrine of war, aggression, and human sacrifice, would triumph over the cult of peace and benevolence of which Nezahualcóyotl had been the champion.

SIGNIFICANCE

Nezahualcóyotl was a supreme example of the Aztec knight, but he was also a poet, a lawgiver, a skillful politician and diplomat often called on to mediate disputes, a builder and engineer, and a great patron of culture and learning. When he dedicated the temple to Huitzilopochtli in 1467—which in the Aztec calendar was called One Reed—he predicted that when One Reed returned in fifty-two years, the Aztec Empire would be destroyed. This prediction, along with the popular assumption that the benevolent god Quetzalcóatl would return in One Reed, was part of a complex of fears that haunted the last years of Aztec supremacy in Mexico with visions of the end of their civilization.

The demands of the Aztec war god for ever-increasing gifts of blood caused wars waged to capture sacrificial victims and ultimately dissension within the empire, which an astute conqueror would find easy to exploit. For this reason, Nezahualcóyotl's political decision to make concessions to Tenochtitlán—and thus to the cult of Huitzilopochtli—for the sake of peace within the empire must be considered an unfortunate development in the religious history of Mexico. If he had been able to unite the empire under the protection of a god of brotherhood and benevolence, the Spanish Conquest would undoubtedly have been more difficult. As it happened, however, when One Reed came around again (in 1519), it brought the Spanish and, as Nezahualcóyotl had predicted, the destruction of the civilization of which he was the outstanding representative.

—*Robert L. Berner*

FURTHER READING

Brundage, Burr C. *A Rain of Darts: The Mexica Aztecs.* Austin: University of Texas Press, 1973. Based on thorough scholarship, this book is the single most important work in English on Aztec history, with a thorough and well-balanced account of the kingdom of Alcolhuacán and the life and achievements of Nezahualcóyotl.

Gillmor, Frances. *Flute of the Smoking Mirror: A Portrait of Nezahualcoyotl, Poet-King of the Aztecs.* Tucson: University of Arizona Press, 1949. Reprint. Salt Lake City: University of Utah Press, 1983. A biography of Nezahualcóyotl, based on extensive scholarship but written in a novelistic style that requires the reader to check the narrative against the thoroughly documented end notes.

Longhena, Maria. *Ancient Mexico: The History and Culture of the Maya, Aztecs, and Other Pre-Columbian Peoples.* New York: Stewart, Tabori & Chang, 1998. Examination of Aztec history and culture, alongside the cultures of the Maya, the Olmecs, and other ancient civilizations, which emphasizes the importance of religion in every aspect of early people's behavior and experience. Includes photographic plates, illustrations, maps, diagrams, and bibliographic references.

Padden, R. C. *The Hummingbird and the Hawk: Conquest and Sovereignty in the Valley of Mexico, 1503-1541.* Columbus: Ohio State University Press, 1967. Padden treats primarily Aztec affairs during the reign of the last Aztec emperor and the early colonial period, but his book also includes a useful account of the religious conflicts in Mexico during Nezahualcóyotl's lifetime.

Peterson, Frederick A. *Ancient Mexico.* New York: Capricorn Books, 1962. A splendid survey of Mexican history and culture before the Spanish Conquest, with a useful discussion of Nezahualcóyotl's achievements and their historical background.

Radin, Paul. "The Sources and Authenticity of the History of the Ancient Mexicans." *University of California Publications in American Anthropology and Ethnology* 17 (1920-1926): 1-150. Includes the text of the Codex Xólotl, the most important original chronicle to discuss Nezahualcóyotl and the history of Texcoco.

Smith, Michael E. *The Aztecs.* 2d ed. Malden, Mass.: Blackwell, 2003. Survey of every aspect of life in the Aztec Empire, based primarily on archaeological research of the late twentieth century. Discusses religion, politics, science, the arts, and the everyday life of ordinary people. Includes illustrations, maps, genealogical tables, bibliographic references, and index.

Townsend, Richard F. *The Aztecs*. Rev. ed. New York: Thames & Hudson, 2000. This survey of Aztec history begins with the conquest and fall of the empire, then goes back in time to chart the beginnings of Aztec society and its growth into an imperial power. Nezhualcóyotl is discussed throughout, and special attention is paid to his system of law. Includes illustra-

tions, calendar of annual Aztec ceremonies, bibliography, and index.

SEE ALSO: Pedro de Alvarado; Hernán Cortés; Cuauhtémoc; Doña Marina; Montezuma II.

RELATED ARTICLES in *Great Events from History: The Renaissance & Early Modern Era, 1454-1600:* 1502-1520: Reign of Montezuma II; April, 1519-August, 1521: Cortés Conquers Aztecs in Mexico.

NICHOLAS OF CUSA
German philosopher and theologian

Nicholas of Cusa contributed to preserving the hierarchical authority and unity of the Catholic Church while at the same time advocating Humanism and lay participation in both sacred and secular government during the early years of the Renaissance. His most lasting contribution has been to Western philosophy.

BORN: 1401; Kues, Upper Lorraine (now Bernkastel-Kues, Germany)

DIED: August 11, 1464; Todi, Papal States (now in Italy)

ALSO KNOWN AS: Nicholas Krebs; Nicholas Kryfts (given name); Nicolaus Cusanus (Latin name)

AREAS OF ACHIEVEMENT: Philosophy, religion and theology, government and politics

EARLY LIFE

Nicholas of Cusa (KYEW-sah) was born in the village of Kues on the Mosel River in the German Rhineland. His moderately prosperous father operated a barge on the busy river, which served as a major commercial waterway in Northern Europe. Young Nicholas was first sent to a school administered by the Brothers of the Common Life at Deventer on the Lower Rhine. Nicholas was inspired by the new learning that the brothers emphasized, and they also encouraged him in a spirit of church reform centered on the idea of the Roman church as a community of clergy and the faithful.

In 1416, at the age of fifteen, Nicholas registered at the University of Heidelberg. Although Nicholas remained at Heidelberg for only one year, here, too, he was exposed to modern learning. Nominalistic philosophy—rejection of universals as myths and a turn toward philosophizing based on individualism—left its mark on young Nicholas. He began to question truths arrived at through pure deduction and based on traditional authority. The

Scholasticism of the late Middle Ages was giving way to a Humanistic thinking in both theology and philosophy.

Nicholas of Cusa next enrolled at the University of Padua in Italy. Padua was a major center for the study of canon law in Europe. In its lecture halls, scholars of science, mathematics, astronomy, and the humanities rigorously challenged established sacred and secular dogma. Yet the revival of Neoplatonism—envisioning a hierarchy of knowledge extending from a perfect and infinite God to an imperfect and finite world—also played a crucial role in Nicholas's education. It was at Padua that young Nicholas had an opportunity to observe the government of Roman city-states, many of which inherited the idea of citizen participation from Greek antiquity. Nicholas studied at Padua for six years, earning a doctorate in canon law in 1423.

Nicholas's early education shaped his later life's work within the Roman Catholic Church; it reflected the change in worldview in the transition years from the late Middle Ages to the early Renaissance years. The medieval notion that God governed the world through unchallenged hierarchical authority was tempered by growing acknowledgment that the Creator provided all his creatures with freedom and responsibility, subject to divine judgment. The dialectic of God's transcendence and his immanence in the world dominated the thought and life of Nicholas of Cusa; he sought in his philosophy and in his daily life to reconcile these views of God and world.

LIFE'S WORK

Nicholas of Cusa returned to Germany in 1425 to embark on his life's work as papal diplomat, theologian, and philosopher. At first he enrolled at the University of Cologne to lecture and to continue his research. There he attracted the attention of Cardinal Giordano Orsini, who was impressed by a legal document prepared by Nicholas at his request. Cardinal Orsini was a noted Humanist and progressive within the Roman church; he played an important role in Nicholas's ordination as a priest in 1426. Orsini's influence was also instrumental in securing an appointment for Nicholas as a legal adviser to the Council of Basel in 1432.

Nicholas's career in church politics began in earnest at the Council of Basel. The debate centered on the issue of the pope's authority. Nicholas sided with those who believed that the Roman church ought to be governed by a general council representing clergy and congregations. The council was to be superior to the pope, who would remain the Church's religious and administrative head but who could be discharged by the council. Nicholas's conviction was that it was through conciliar government that church unity would be best preserved. The congregation ought to be the source of church law, with pope and hierarchy serving the general council.

Nicholas expanded his thinking on church government in a philosophical treatise. This work, *De concordantia Catholica* (1433; *The Catholic Concordance*, 1991), sets forth what has been called the conciliar theory of government, based on Nicholas's belief that authority of the ruler must rest on consent granted by the ruled. His main thesis was that this governmental form would bring about unity within the Church.

The controversy over conciliar government continued after the Council of Basel. Subsequently, Nicholas of Cusa modified his antipapal stance. Three reasons have been offered to explain this turnabout. First, Nicholas was displeased with the turmoil between members of the council and the Holy See. Second, Nicholas's highest priority was church unity. Finally, Nicholas was motivated by the opportunities for his own career within the church hierarchy.

Nicholas was rewarded with a papal appointment. In 1437, he was a delegate to a meeting between the Roman and Eastern Orthodox Christians in Constantinople. There he invited Greek representatives to attend a scheduled council in Italy on reunification of the Greek and Roman churches. Although his efforts failed, Christian unity and reform continued to motivate Nicholas throughout his life, in his dealings with church politics as well as in his philosophical writings.

Nicholas continued to accept diplomatic posts from the Vatican. From 1438 to 1448, he was a papal delegate to Germany, where he worked for both reform and unity within the Church. As a reward, in 1449 Pope Nicholas V made Nicholas of Cusa a cardinal of the titular Church of Saint Peter in Chains in Rome. In 1450, he was named bishop of Brixen, in Austria. During his tenure as bishop, Nicholas encountered the growing conflict between the Church and secular politics. It was a difficult phase in his life.

His later years were spent in a bitter struggle with the secular ruler of Austria, Archduke Sigismund. Nicholas

---

NICHOLAS OF CUSA ON LEARNED IGNORANCE

Nicholas of Cusa was on the cusp of the late medieval, early Renaissance rebirth of thought that acknowledged not only the significance of human reason but also the continuing relevance of religious ideals to that rebirth. In this excerpt from Of Learned Ignorance, *he tells the reader that if one accepts that not all things can be known by humans and accepts that God is all-knowing, then one can attain a "learned ignorance" through faith in God. Faith in God is the only true way one can know anything at all.*

Pythagoras judged with vigour that everything was constituted and understood through the force of numbers. But the precision of combinations in material things and the exact adaptation of the known to the unknown so far surpass human reason that it seemed to Socrates that he knew nothing expect his ignorance, and the very wise Solomon affirmed that all things are difficult and inexplicable in language. . . . If, therefore, it is true, as Aristotle affirms in his *First Philosophy*, that such a difficulty befalls us in the things most manifest in nature, like owls trying to see the sun, since the divine in us is certainly not vain, we need to know that we are ignorant. If we can attain this end completely, we shall attain "learned ignorance." . . . Every man who wishes to raise himself to knowledge must necessarily believe in the things without which he cannot raise himself. . . . Faith [in God], therefore, comprises in herself all that is intelligible. Understanding is the explication of faith. . . . For the greatest and most profound mysteries of God, hidden from those who go about in the world, however wise they may be, have been revealed to the small and humble in the faith of Jesus, because Jesus is the one in whom all the treasures of wisdom and science are enclosed, and without whom no one can do anything.

Source: From *De docta ignorantia*, in *The Portable Medieval Reader*, edited by James Bruce Ross and Mary Martin McLaughlin (New York: Penguin Books, 1977), pp. 668, 672, 673.

set out to reform corrupt practices among the priests and monks of his diocese, but his efforts met with apathy and hostility among the clergy. At one point, he sought to reform a convent at Sonneburg, and there Bishop Nicholas ran into bitter opposition from secular authorities because many of the nuns had been recruited from noble families. Archduke Sigismund assumed the role of protector of the nuns.

Added to this controversy was one that concerned ecclesiastical appointments. Sigismund was unhappy over several of Nicholas's choices for church posts; the bishop had bypassed candidates supported by the duke. Open conflict between the bishop and the duke resulted in negotiations, appeals to the Vatican, and, ultimately, compromise. Nicholas was recalled in 1459 to Rome.

As a reward for his services to the Holy See, Nicholas was appointed to the high post of vicar-general for temporal affairs; he was governor of Rome and the papal territories. It was Nicholas of Cusa's last and highest office. Unfortunately, Cardinal Cusa was not freed from conflict with the Austrian duke. Now the controversy turned into a dispute between Sigismund and the Church over certain property rights in Austria. Claims and counterclaims intensified.

On one occasion, the duke's soldiers surrounded and fired their guns on a castle in Austria in which Nicholas was temporarily residing as the pope's representative in the dispute. The cardinal surrendered and was put under house arrest. Pope Pius II, humiliated by this treatment of his representative, intervened directly and sought to punish the duke. Nicholas was extricated from the affair. He returned to Italy to live his final days in relative peace and contemplation.

During his many years of church diplomacy, Nicholas of Cusa continued his theological and philosophical research and writing. He wrote about forty-six books and manuscripts. In addition, he was an enthusiastic collector of literary and philosophical works. His two most influential works are *De docta ignorantia* (1440; *Of Learned Ignorance*, 1954) and *De coniecturis* (1442; on conjecture); together they make up a complete outline of his philosophy.

In *Of Learned Ignorance*, Nicholas sets forth the doctrine that humans know God through whatever God chooses to reveal and through human experience. Human reason reaches its limitations in its knowledge of God, for humans are finite and God is infinite. Reason is applicable to this finite world, but it is a stumbling block to knowing God. Humans will be the more learned the more they grasp their own ignorance of the unknown

God. The infinite God is not accessible through reason, but his awareness is present in the minds of individuals. Through human recognition of reason's limits, a realization that is itself reached through reason, the wisdom of learned ignorance is achieved. For Nicholas's speculative metaphysics, the highest stage of knowledge for humans is the recognition that humans cannot attain a comprehensive knowledge of God.

In *De coniecturis*, Nicholas expands his philosophy of learned ignorance. Here Nicholas argues that God is prior to the opposition of being and nonbeing. God is unity transcending the coincidence of all opposites; he transcends and confines in himself all distinctions and oppositions. God is thus the unity of opposites, of the finite and the infinite. He transcends human understanding, and thus humans cannot form a full and accurate concept of his nature. God transcends the world, but the world is his mirror. God is the unity of world and cosmos. These statements lead into Nicholas's theology, which concludes that because God is beyond human intellect, learned ignorance opens the way to Christian faith.

Nicholas of Cusa died in 1464. He is buried in the Church of Saint Peter in Chains in Rome. Inside the church there is a statue of Nicholas kneeling before Saint Peter. His best monument, however, is the home and hospital for the poor that he and his family founded in his native Kues. The attached library contains many of Nicholas's original manuscripts and his collection of books. It remains a center for scholarly research.

SIGNIFICANCE

Nicholas of Cusa is an outstanding example of a philosopher who was active in practical affairs; he combined a life of contemplation with one of action. Throughout his life, Nicholas attempted to resolve the conflict between old and new views of God and humankind while he remained an obedient member of the Church hierarchy. His later writings and practical work reflected his moderation: He sought reform within the context of order and continuation. In philosophy and ecclesiastical politics, Nicholas advocated gradual development and progress, not rebellion and revolution. Nicholas lived his life according to the fundamental principles of his thought; he remains an exemplar of the unity of thought and practice in a person's life. As such, his life captured the spirit of the Golden Rule. Above all, Nicholas's life reflected his deep devotion to the ideal of the unity of all being in God, of harmony between reason and faith, theology and philosophy, and church and state.

Scholars do not agree on whether Nicholas of Cusa was the first modern thinker or a transitional figure standing between the Middle Ages and the Renaissance. It is clear that he combined traditional elements of Neoplatonism and the Scholastic tradition with postmedieval nominalism and Humanism. Evidence is inconclusive as to whether Nicholas contributed original ideas or dressed the thought of Plato, Saint Augustine, and others in the modes of his era. It is certain, however, that Nicholas of Cusa must be included in any list of the world's great philosophers. He forged a speculative metaphysics that influenced Gottfried Wilhelm Leibniz, George Wilhelm Friedrich Hegel, Martin Heidegger, and the existential philosophers. Nicholas's philosophical legacy remains his enduring contribution to Western civilization.

—Gil L. Gunderson

FURTHER READING

Bett, Henry. *Nicholas of Cusa.* London: Methuen, 1932. Reprint. Merrick, N.Y.: Richwood, 1976. Standard biography, presenting a detailed account of Nicholas's life coupled with a discussion of his writings and a critique of his philosophy. Stresses Nicholas's consistent thought throughout his political, philosophical, and theological writings; this thought culminates in the unity of all existence in the hidden God.

Cassirer, Ernst. *The Individual and the Cosmos in Renaissance Philosophy.* Translated with an introduction by Mario Domandi. Oxford, England: Basil Blackwell, 1963. An advanced critique of Nicholas's philosophy. Argues that he was a systematic thinker who presented a totally new philosophical orientation and that the beginning of modern philosophy cannot be understood without a consideration of Nicholas's work. Nicholas offered the foundations for a new theory of knowledge and history; his greatness is enhanced because he achieved this major contribution to Renaissance philosophy from within the religious ideas of the Middle Ages.

Copleston, Frederick Charles. "Nicholas of Cusa." In *A History of Philosophy.* 3d ed. Vol. 3. Garden City, N.Y.: Doubleday, 1985. Concise treatment of Nicholas of Cusa's philosophy from the perspective of the contemporary Roman Catholic Church. Author's theme is that Nicholas's work and writings aimed at reconciliation, harmony, and unity in difference.

Harries, Karsten. *Infinity and Perspective.* Cambridge, Mass.: MIT Press, 2001. This controversial philosophical text reviews the history of theories of perspective in an attempt to argue in favor of objective truth. Engages in close reading of Nicholas's work on the infinity of God as a basis for objectivity. Includes illustrations, index, bibliographic references.

Hopkins, Jasper. *A Concise Introduction to the Philosophy of Nicholas of Cusa.* 3d ed. Minneapolis, Minn.: A. J. Banning Press, 1986. Includes a text in Latin and English of Nicholas's *De possest* (1460; *On Actualized-Possibility,* 1978). Hopkins contends that this short essay contains an excellent summation of Nicholas of Cusa's philosophy; he recommends that first-time students begin here. The long introductory interpretation serves as a useful reader's guide. Excellent bibliography containing a list of the English translations of Nicholas's works as well as a list of secondary interpretations.

Izbicki, Thomas M., and Christopher M. Bellitto, eds. *Nicholas of Cusa and His Age—Intellect and Spirituality: Essays Dedicated to the Memory of F. Edward Cranz, Thomas P. McTighe, and Charles Trinkaus.* Boston: Brill, 2002. These essays cover many aspects of Nicholas's work, his legacy, and his culture, from his contributions to astronomy to his sermons to the meaning of excommunication in fifteenth century Germany. Includes bibliographic references and index.

Jaspers, Karl. "Nicholas of Cusa." In *The Great Philosophers,* edited by Hannah Arendt and translated by Ralph Manheim. Vol. 2. New York: Harcourt, Brace and World, 1966. A detailed critique of the metaphysics of Nicholas of Cusa. Jaspers considers Nicholas's philosophical writings from the perspective of his own existentialist philosophy. He finds Nicholas's major contribution to have been keeping alive the idea of individual freedom in human relations and in relation to God.

Nicholas of Cusa. *Unity and Reform: Selected Writings of Nicholas de Cusa.* Edited with an introduction by John P. Dolan. Notre Dame, Ind.: University of Notre Dame Press, 1962. Selected excerpts from Nicholas's major philosophical and theological writings. Text is supplemented by editor's informative introduction, which serves as an excellent reader's guide.

Sigmund, Paul E. *Nicholas of Cusa and Medieval Political Thought.* Cambridge, Mass.: Harvard University Press, 1963. Concentrates on Nicholas's political theory, emphasizing the foundational principle of government by consent. The philosophical and legal antecedents of Nicholas's political philosophy are traced. Good bibliography of secondary sources from the political philosophy perspective.

Yamaki, Kazuhiko, ed. *Nicholas of Cusa: A Medieval Thinker for the Modern Age.* Richmond, Surrey, England: Curzon Press, 2002. Collection of essays first presented at a conference held in Tokyo in October, 2000. Covers Nicholas's relationships to tradition and to religion, as well as the contemporary importance of his contributions to philosophy. Includes bibliographic references and index.

SEE ALSO: Marsilio Ficino; Giovanni Pico della Mirandola; Pius II.
RELATED ARTICLES in *Great Events from History: The Renaissance & Early Modern Era, 1454-1600:* 1462: Regiomontanus Completes the *Epitome* of Ptolemy's *Almagest*; 1583-1600: Bruno's Theory of the Infinite Universe.

NOSTRADAMUS
French astrologer, physician, and writer

A prominent physician and political adviser, Nostradamus achieved widest fame with collections of veiled prophecies in poetical form.

BORN: December 14, 1503; St. Rémy de Provence, France
DIED: July 1 or 2, 1566; Salon de Provence, France
ALSO KNOWN AS: Michel Notredame (birth name); Michel Nostredame; Michel de Nostredame; Michel de Notredame
AREAS OF ACHIEVEMENT: Literature, astronomy, medicine, government and politics

EARLY LIFE

Nostradamus (nohs-truh-dah-muhs) was born Michel Notredame in southern France. Although he would later claim that his father and grandfather were physicians, it appears more likely that they were prosperous grain merchants. What is certain is that the family had converted from Judaism to Christianity and dropped its original name in order to remain in Catholic France.

The young Michel received his earliest education from his grandfathers, who found him a promising student. He was able to continue his studies at two nearby cities renowned for their intellectual and cultural life, Avignon and Montpellier. Michel began secondary school at the former in 1517, where the prescribed course of study included grammar, rhetoric, logic, music, mathematics, and astronomy (which encompassed astrology as well). At the time, Avignon was under direct control of the Catholic Church; there, as in all seats of learning, classes were taught in Latin.

Michel went on to study medicine at the University of Montpellier in 1522, where once again astrology played a role alongside such subjects as anatomy and surgery. Tradition has it that he concentrated on pharmacology and various methods of treating the plague. When he graduated in 1525 at the age of twenty-two, he followed the custom of signaling his accomplishment by Latinizing his last name to Nostradamus, thus adopting the form by which he is best known today.

LIFE'S WORK

Nostradamus was now fully qualified to practice medicine and did so for several years, but he undertook further study and teaching at the University of Montpellier, from which he received an advanced medical degree. He eventually apprenticed himself to eminent physician and scholar Jules-César Scaliger of Agen in 1532. Soon afterward, he married, and the couple had two children.

Nostradamus's family, however, died of the plague in 1537 while he was traveling to treat other victims. He subsequently quarreled with the notoriously irascible Scaliger and was accused of making heretical remarks, events that were to lead to his quitting Agen. After ten more years of travel, practice, and teaching in France and Italy, Nostradamus met and married Anna Ponce Gemelle of Salon de Provence, a town not far from his birthplace. The couple eventually had six children.

Nostradamus began compiling astrological almanacs—popular and highly salable publications—in 1550. He followed with two collections of medical and cosmetic formulas in 1552, *Traicté des fardemens* and *Vray et parfaict embellissement de la face.* These were combined in 1555 as *Excellent et moult utile Opuscule à touts necessaire qui desirent auoir cognoissance de plusiers exquises Receptes* (excellent and very useful treatise necessary for all those who desire to have knowledge of several exquisite recipes). Nostradamus also published *Orus Apollo, fils de Osiris, roi de Ægipte niliacque* (the book of Orus Apollo, son of Osiris, king of Egypt), a collection of maxims of dubious origin. More important was his translation from Galen, the classical Greek physician, *Paraphrase de C. Galen sur l'exortation de Menodote*, in 1557. This translation was criticized as inaccurate, although Nostradamus may have been working from an imperfect manuscript.

Nostradamus's most famous works, however, were his *Centuries*, originally published in French as *Les Prophéties de M. Michel Nostradamus*, a series of ambiguously worded prophecies. Unlike his almanacs, which forecast events one year at a time, these new works predicted events to the year 3797, although in no particular order. The first three series appeared in 1555; by 1558, seven more had been published, although their exact dates are not certain. Referred to as "centuries" because each ostensibly included one hundred verses, their total actually comes to somewhat less than one thousand. A complete collection seems to have been published in 1558, but no copies of this edition are known to survive.

Cast in quatrains (stanzas of four lines), the *Centuries* are notoriously obscure. They mix local allusions, references to France's unsettled political situation, and generalized predictions of disasters and calamities—as cynics have noted, always a safe bet. Although claims have been made for Nostradamus's skills as a poet, his work is oddly punctuated and his grammar and syntax wayward. It has never been clearly established what Nostradamus intended to express in these writings, nor whether profit was his motive in publishing them.

Public reaction to the *Centuries* varied, with the wide range of responses illustrating the intellectual and social ferment of the times. Wealthier readers found the verses' daunting obscurity both a compliment and a challenge to their erudition. The masses, on the other hand, seem to have disliked and distrusted Nostradamus, partly because of his growing wealth and partly because of his presumed league with supernatural powers. Two other groups openly ridiculed him: those who dismissed astrology as nonsense and, ironically enough, astrologers themselves, who protested that the astrological content of the *Centuries* was defective. Despite—or, more likely, because of—such opposition, Nostra-

---

NOSTRADAMUS'S PREDICTIONS

Nostradamus predicted cataclysmic events at the end of the second millennium. Here is one such prediction, foretelling war and the rise of a powerful ruler. It remains a matter of debate whether this prophecy was in fact fulfilled.

In the year 1999 and seven months,
From the sky will come a great king of terror,
Reviving the great King of Angolmois.
Before and after, luckily, Mars will reign.

Here is a more typically nebulous prediction by Nostradamus. It could apply equally to a covert terrorist leader, a duplicitous government minister, or a dishonest employee.

[He] gnaws long, dry, playing the good little servant,
In the end shall have nothing but his dismissal.
Piercing poison and letters in his collar
will be seized, escape, in danger.

Source: From *The Complete Prophecies of Nostradamus*, translated, edited, and interpreted by Henry C. Roberts (Oyster Bay, N.Y.: Nostradamus, 1982), pp. 336, 269. Translations modified by Andy Perry.

---

damus's works sold well and were routinely reprinted and pirated.

In any case, Nostradamus's fame spread quickly, and he soon found an important and suitably superstitious reader in the French court. So impressed was Catherine de Médicis, the queen of France, that she invited Nostradamus to Paris. He subsequently visited the city in mid-1556 (a trip of a month in those days) and was asked by the queen to cast the horoscopes of her sons. He seems to have remarked in guarded terms that her sons would be kings—a prediction both gratifying and not, after all, unlikely—and returned to Salon more famous still. When the French court visited southern France nearly a decade later, they made a point of visiting Nostradamus and bestowing official honors on him.

Throughout the latter part of his life, Nostradamus seems to have increased his income by moneylending, which in at least one instance had long-lasting consequences. Approached by an entrepreneur anxious to link the Rhône and Durance Rivers with a canal and thus irrigate the surrounding region, Nostradamus helped finance the project, which was completed in 1559.

Nostradamus has routinely been portrayed as both an astrologer and an orthodox Catholic, roles not regarded as necessarily contradictory during his lifetime. A cache of letters discovered by scholar Jean Dupèbe has revealed, though, that Nostradamus's sympathies were Protestant—which could easily have led to his execution in passionately Catholic France had the letters fallen into the wrong hands.

Nostradamus was described in his prime by an apprentice as being slightly shorter and stockier than average, heavily bearded, energetic, and short-tempered. The same source praised his quick intelligence, keen memory, and outstanding generosity, although the ascription of such qualities may strike modern readers as being somewhat generalized and formulaic. He is traditionally pictured wearing the four-cornered cap typical of a medical doctor of his time.

Nostradamus suffered from arthritis, gout, and dropsy toward the end of his life and by 1566 was confined to his house, where he died in early July. One of his predictions had suggested that his body would be found near his bed and bench. Nostradamus had placed a bench in such a way as to help himself into bed, and he was indeed found sprawled near or on it after death—another example of a prophecy both tantalizingly suggestive and yet far from unlikely.

SIGNIFICANCE

Nostradamus lived during a period in Western civilization torn between two divergent systems of thought. One was the occult, which strove to interpret the world supernaturally and which was even then falling out of favor. The other was the scientific, which had increasingly but never totally predominated.

It was a time of enormous upheaval. France's political situation was chaotic, and Protestantism vied with Catholicism for supremacy throughout Europe. The plague ravaged southwestern Europe several times during Nostradamus's lifetime, and although he seems to have established a reputation as an effective plague doctor, he lost his own family to the dreadful disease. Thus his preoccupation as expressed throughout the *Centuries* with disaster of all kinds is easy to understand and may have been fueled by fears for his own safety as a Protestant sympathizer.

Neither is it difficult to understand the keen interest that subsequent generations have taken in Nostradamus. Although Europe has experienced periods of stability since his day, the desire to know the future seems to be a constant. Scholars have demonstrated that Nostradamus filled his many prophecies with topical and contemporary references—a great many of them lost to modern readers—but the poet's allusive style lends his work mystery and ambiguity. Thanks to these characteristics,

later readers have discovered "references" to such leaders and tyrants as Napoleon and Adolf Hitler and have been able to make persuasive arguments for their discoveries. The mirror that Nostradamus holds up to his readers is so clouded, it seems, that almost anything for which one looks may be found there.

—*Grove Koger*

FURTHER READING

Dumézil, Georges. *The Riddle of Nostradamus: A Critical Dialogue.* Translated by Betty Wing. Baltimore: Johns Hopkins University Press, 1999. A serious academic study of Nostradamus written in dialogue form. Seeks to understand the function of riddles in prophecy and society. Asks if it is possible that Nostradamus could have predicted the future without understanding it. Includes bibliographic references.

Gould, Rupert T. "Nostradamus." In *Oddities: A Book of Unexplained Facts.* 3d ed. New York: Bell, 1965. A noted but skeptical student of anomalies, Gould compares Nostradamus with other "prophets" and astrologers. He concludes that Nostradamus produced puzzlingly accurate prophecies in a few cases.

Laver, James. *Nostradamus: Or, The Future Foretold.* London: Collins, 1942. Reprint. Maidstone, Kent, England: George Mann, 1973. An influential historian of art and fashion, Laver summarizes Nostradamus's life and devotes most of his attention to the prophecies, which he argues are valid.

Leoni, Edgar. *Nostradamus: Life and Literature.* New York: Exposition Press, 1961. Still the most thorough study of the *Centuries* to have appeared in English. Leoni's book contains complete texts and translations of the *Centuries* and a survey of pertinent literature. Reprinted as *Nostradamus and His Prophecies* in 1982.

LeVert, Liberté E. *The Prophecies and Enigmas of Nostradamus.* Glen Rock, N.J.: Firebell Books, 1979. Written under a pseudonym by acknowledged speculative fiction expert Everett Bleiler. Bleiler argues that Nostradamus was a fascinating personality and a skillful, though not great, poet, and that the *Centuries* repay careful study for these reasons alone. Objective and evenhanded.

Randi, James. *The Mask of Nostradamus: The Prophecies of the World's Most Famous Seer.* Buffalo, N.Y.: Prometheus Books, 1993. Intensely skeptical and at times sarcastic, Randi surveys Nostradamus's life, examines the early editions of his works, analyzes the mind-set of those he calls the "Nostradamians," and places the *Centuries* within a framework of similar prophecies.

Shumaker, Wayne. *The Occult Sciences in the Renaissance: A Study in Intellectual Patterns.* Berkeley: University of California Press, 1972. Shumaker outlines five occult systems of thought and practice common to the Renaissance, including astrology. The works of Shumaker and Lynn Thorndike are the best sources for locating Nostradamus and his writings within the intellectual context of his time. Good bibliography.

Thorndike, Lynn. *A History of Magic and Experimental Science.* New York: Macmillan; Columbia University Press, 1923-1958. Thorndike's vast survey complements Shumaker's narrower study. Especially pertinent are Volumes 5 and 6 (*The Sixteenth Century*) and Volumes 7 and 8 (*The Seventeenth Century*), all of which discuss Nostradamus. Extensive bibliographical references.

Ward, Charles A. *Oracles of Nostradamus.* New York: C. Scribner & Welford, 1891. Reprint. New York: Dorsett Press, 1986. Ward opens with a biography of Nostradamus drawn from the first translator of the writer into English. Arguing that Nostradamus foresaw the future, he explicates the prophecies that he believes relate to subsequent events. A good example of the involved literature produced by believers in Nostradamus's occult powers.

Wilson, Colin. "The World of the Kabbalists." In *The Occult: A History.* New York: Random House, 1971. This chapter from a standard work on the subject compares Nostradamus with two roughly contemporary figures in the occult tradition, Cornelius Agrippa and Paracelsus.

Wilson, Damon. *The Mammoth Book of Nostradamus and Other Prophets.* Introduction by Colin Wilson. New York: Carroll & Graf, 1999. Study of prophets and oracles through the ages, from the Delphic Oracle through the twentieth century. Places Nostradamus in the context of other possible prophets and seers, including fellow sixteenth century occult figure Mother Shipton. Includes index.

Wilson, Ian. *Nostradamus: The Man Behind the Prophecies.* New York: St. Martin's Press, 2002. Straight biography of Nostradamus, attempting to bracket off the question of whether he was really a prophet and instead produce a fully realized profile. Includes illustrations, bibliographic references, and index.

See also: Catherine de Médicis; Paracelsus.

Related articles in *Great Events from History: The Renaissance & Early Modern Era, 1454-1600:* 1530's-1540's: Paracelsus Presents His Theory of Disease; 1531-1585: Antwerp Becomes the Commercial Capital of Europe.

ODA NOBUNAGA
Japanese general

The greatest soldier of his time, Oda Nobunaga started a process through diplomacy and war that put an end to political fragmentation in Japan and paved the way for the unique feudal system that governed Japan during the 265-year Tokugawa period. His policies also altered the role of Buddhism in Japanese society.

BORN: June, 1534; Owari Province, Japan
DIED: June 21, 1582; Kyōto, Japan
ALSO KNOWN AS: Kichihōshi (given name); Saburō; Kippōshi
AREAS OF ACHIEVEMENT: Military, diplomacy, government and politics

EARLY LIFE

Oda Nobunaga (oh-dah noh-bew-nah-gah) lived during the Sengoku Jidai, or Warring States period, when both the shogun and the emperor were figureheads and a multitude of warlords, known as daimyo, held sway over the provinces. In addition to the secular warlords, there were militant Buddhist organizations with standing armies often allied to some of the daimyo. The country may thus be viewed as a patchwork quilt of power centers.

Oda was born in Nagoya Castle in Owari Province. His father, Oda Nobuhide, was a lower-ranked official of the Shiba family serving in Owari. Oda Nobunaga's original name was Kichihōshi, but it was changed at age thirteen. While still a teenager, Oda began to adopt eccentric dress and behavior, which earned for him the nicknames Great Fool and Idiot. It has been suggested by some scholars that he chose to play the fool as part of a ploy for surviving the pending fratricidal struggle that ensued on the death of his father in 1551, when Oda was seventeen years old. Despite his learning to use firearms from a very early age and although much of his military reputation hinged on guns, he was alleged to have favored the spear.

LIFE'S WORK

Among those who served the young Oda Nobunaga was his sandal-bearer Kinoshita Tokichiro, who is more popularly remembered as Toyotomi Hideyoshi and who became Oda's most valuable military follower; ultimately Toyotomi took over the reins of power. From 1551 until 1560, Oda fought a series of campaigns to gain control of his home province of Owari. As many members of the Oda clan were reluctant to follow him because of his youth, he used a band of one thousand low-ranking sol-

diers to gain a foothold in the initial period of clan infighting. In 1556, Oda managed to displace a number of his rivals in Kiyosu, which became his first "capital." Oda's younger brother posed a challenge when he gained support from some of his father's retainers. The rivalry ended with the death of the younger brother. In 1560, Oda became daimyo of Owari Province.

Oda was quite adept at splitting his opponents' defensive efforts. For example, he would try to make an alliance with daimyo whose territory bordered on that of an enemy of Oda. In that manner, the enemy was then compelled to divide his forces to deal with an attack on two fronts. One of the most expedient tools for cementing diplomatic and political alliances was the arranged marriage. Marriages were often used to facilitate alliances, but they remained fragile agreements at the best of times. Oda himself married the daughter of Saitō Dōsan, the daimyo of neighboring Mino Province, which lay between Owari and the capital. In 1556, while Oda was still trying to consolidate his own power in Owari, Saitō was killed by his son Tatsuoki, Oda's brother-in-law. The murder gave Oda the pretext for invasion on the grounds of avenging his father-in-law's death.

During June of 1560, Oda had a chance to prove his mettle to other daimyo. Imagawa Yoshimoto, the daimyo of Suruga, Totomi, and Mikawa Provinces, was on his way through Owari to Kyōto at the head of a vast army of twenty-five thousand. Although Oda could muster no more than eighteen hundred men, he nevertheless decided to give battle. His opportunity came when his enemy was encamped in a narrow sheltered valley. Taking advantage of a violent rainstorm, he launched a surprise attack, routing his enemy in the furious but brief Battle of Okehazama.

In contrast, the operations against Saitō Tatsuoki, for control of Mino, dragged on for years. Nevertheless, by 1564, Oda had reduced Saitō's fortress of Inabayama, and by 1567, at the age of thirty-three, he had finally defeated Saitō. He decided to use Inabayama as his own capital and renamed it Gifu. At the same time, he adopted the motto *Tenka fubu*, incorporating it into his personal seal. *Tenka fubu* is translated variously as "the realm covered in military glory," "the realm subjected to the military," or "rule the realm by force." Alarmed by Oda's increasing strength, his enemies banded together to form an anti-Oda league. To bolster his position, Oda decided to espouse the cause of Ashikaga Yoshiaki, heir to the

Ashikaga shogunate. After defeating limited opposition, Oda entered Kyōto with Ashikaga on November 9, 1568. The latter was installed as the shogun, the last of the Ashikaga line. The stormy relationship between Oda and the shogun was to last five years.

Much of Oda's energy during the last ten years of his life was absorbed in attempts to suppress the military power of the Buddhists. Various Buddhist groups had evolved powers that paralleled those of the daimyo, and their temples became centers of political, economic, and military activity. First, Oda dealt with the Enryakuji, the temple of the Heian school on Mount Hiei, which had been labeled The Indestructible Light of the [Buddhist] Law. In 1571, Oda's forces stormed their stronghold, and the mountainside became a killing ground as men, women, and children were slain, and the temple complex put to the torch. Between three and four thousand priests were killed; the orgy of bloodletting lasted a week.

Then Oda turned his attention to the Shinshu Buddhists (also known as Ikkō), whose sectarian strongholds were strewn across the land. Their headquarters was located at Honganji, an impregnable fortress situated on highly defensible terrain and ringed by more than fifty forts and outposts. In seeking to reduce the Honganji, Oda found that he had first to dispose of the threat of the shogun and the powerful daimyo Takeda Shingen. In July, 1574, Oda laid siege to the Ikkō stronghold of Nagashima, located on an estuary of the Kisogawa. The captive population tried to surrender but to no avail. Oda ordered the fortress to be burned to the ground, and anyone who sought to escape was shot. It is estimated that as many as twenty thousand people died inside the burning fort.

The Battle of Nagashino, against Takeda Katsuyori (Shingen's son), in 1575, demonstrated Oda's military insight. The battle grew out of Oda's efforts to relieve the Siege of Nagashino Castle in Mikawa Province. The Takeda forces had surrounded the castle, which was within the territory of Oda's trusted follower Tokugawa Ieyasu. Oda had a combined force of up to thirty-eight thousand troops, of which ten thousand were armed with matchlocks. From those troops, three thousand of the best sharpshooters were selected for deployment. The Takeda clan relied on mounted samurai, which epitomized the art of the cavalry, but Oda denied the enemy a chance to utilize his horsemen effectively. Oda's men were arranged behind wooden barriers, or a palisade, which served to channel the Takeda attack. The lack of a single clear-cut objective meant that the horsemen had to thread their way through the deadly obstacles that con-cealed the sharpshooters. The peasant foot soldiers, or *ashigaru*, were trained to fire in ranks, which allowed a steady rate of fire as the weapons were fired and loaded in sequence.

Although the majority of sixteenth century Japanese wars were the domain of the samurai, there were also naval operations involved in Oda's rise to power. The siege of the Honganji fortress was prolonged for years, because Kennyo Kōsa, who commanded the Honganji force, had arranged for resupply to be provided by the Mōri clan, who shipped men and supplies from Ōsaka up the Inland Sea. Oda ordered his vassal daimyo to prepare a fleet to intercept the Mōri navy. The three-hundred-ship force assembled for Oda was outnumbered by more than two to one by the Mōri vessels. The destruction of Oda's fleet in August, 1576, compelled him to build a new navy. This naval reconstruction program resulted in the delivery of seven ironclads, complete with cannons, in July, 1578. The new navy sailed into Ōsaka and effectively cut Honganji from its supply line when it destroyed the six-hundred-vessel Mōri fleet on December 4, 1578. Despite all the time and effort to reduce the Honganji, the affair ended in a rather anticlimactic fashion, when the emperor negotiated a peace to end the Ishiyama Honganji war in 1580.

Toyotomi, who had been assigned to pacify western Japan, had become bogged down, and he was compelled to request assistance from his superior. Oda dispatched the bulk of his troops to Toyotomi's aid. With a small band of only two hundred to three hundred men, Oda took shelter at the Honnōji temple in Kyōto before joining the main force. While there, he was attacked by thirteen thousand troops led by one of his most trusted vassal daimyo, Akechi Mitsuhide. The death of Oda on June 21, 1582, at the hands of the renegade Akechi is known as the Honnōji Incident. Toyotomi made peace with his opponents almost immediately, and thirteen days later, he avenged his master's death by defeating Akechi at the Battle of Yamazaki. Akechi is referred to in some texts as the Thirteen Day Shogun. Toyotomi eventually prevailed as the heir to Oda's efforts, and he also inherited the conquest of the Buddhist armies.

SIGNIFICANCE

Despite Oda Nobunaga's reputation as a warlord, he did make contributions to other aspects of Japanese life and culture. Oda declared a number of free trade centers, which helped to break up the economic stagnation of a tradition-bound economy. He also sought to alter the role played by guilds in market centers. There was no blanket policy but rather a series of adjustments made to derive greater economic benefit. In some cases, guilds were abolished, while in other circumstances they were established. Oda also sought to modernize the economy by banning barter trade and replacing it with currency exchange to promote a true money economy. To prevent unfair practice, he also established currency regulations that set official standards for exchange and for the value of copper, silver, and gold. Oda took steps to simplify land ownership and encourage single-party control of estates. That went hand in hand with his implementation of cadastral surveys, which were designed to expedite administration, taxation, and assessment of land productivity.

Oda's policies had the effect of altering the role of Buddhism in Japanese society. The changes evoke include the elimination of military power, the limitation of economic power, and the subjugation of religious authorities to the central administration. Despite the tremendous amount of energy and resources expended against the Buddhists, Oda was not anti-Buddhist. Oda patronized certain temples, had Buddhist military allies, and had even relied on Zen priests as military advisers on occasion.

The Sengoku period was dominated by a warlord society, and even Oda's followers feuded. On occasion, there was treachery, and Oda had to execute some of those daimyo who sought to betray him. Yet such action was not particularly abnormal in a warlord society. That Oda indulged in such behavior did not prove that he was more bloodthirsty than any other daimyo. Oda was responsible for the initial military operations that altered the balance of power and led to the centralization of power in Japan. Eventually, the process culminated in the Tokugawa shogunate (1602-1867), followed by a period of Japanese modernization known as the Meiji Restoration.

—*Randolf G. S. Cooper*

FURTHER READING

Hall, John Whitney. *Government and Local Power in Japan, 500 to 1700: A Study Based on the Bizen Province*. Princeton, N.J.: Princeton University Press, 1966. This study focuses on Bizen Province, yet chapter 10 has relevant information on Oda. This book establishes Oda's efforts within the realm of the evolving political scene and is useful as a brief overview for those new to the subject.

Hall, John Whitney, Nagahara Keiji, and Kozo Yamamura, eds. *Japan Before Tokugawa: Political Consolidation in Economic Growth, 1500 to 1600*. Princeton, N.J.: Princeton University Press, 1981. Although the entire volume is worthwhile from the standpoint of historical context, one chapter is of special interest: chapter 5, "The Political Posture of Oda Nobunaga and Toyotomi Hideyoshi." The work focuses on the nonmilitary side of the warlord.

Lamers, Jeroen P. *Japonius Tyrannus: The Japanese Warlord, Oda Nobunaga Reconsidered*. Leiden, the Netherlands: Hotei, 2000. The first modern biography of Oda in English, which seeks to provide a comprehensive chronology of his political and military career. Includes illustrations, maps, bibliographic references, and index.

McMullin, Neil. *Buddhism and the State in Sixteenth Century Japan*. Princeton, N.J.: Princeton University Press, 1984. An advanced examination of the relationship between Oda and the Buddhists. Despite the omission of Oda's name from the title, the work is to a large degree centered on him. This volume uses by far the greatest number of original documents from which to draw information. Central to the thesis is the concept that Oda does not deserve the heinous reputation he has received.

Perrin, Noel. *Giving Up the Gun: Japan's Reversion to the Sword, 1543-1879*. Boston: David R. Godine, 1979. Primarily concerned with Japan's adoption and then later rejection of firearms. Although the chapters concerning Oda are few, this book is excellent for those seeking to understand the cultural implications of Oda's use of firearms. The author also used a number of historic Japanese texts for his research, so his bibliography is noteworthy for those studying the history of technology.

Sansom, George. *A History of Japan, 1334-1615*. Stanford, Calif.: Stanford University Press, 1961. Still one of the standard works in the field. The chapters devoted to Oda are 17, 18, and 19. The author, however, remains firm in his conviction that Oda was a brute. An effective balance between chronology and analysis.

Sato, Hiroaki. *Legends of the Samurai*. Woodstock, N.Y.: Overlook Press, 1995. Oda is one of the warlords covered in this survey of famous samurai and other warriors of Japan. Includes illustrations, maps, bibliographic references, and index.

Souyri, Pierre. *The World Turned Upside Down: Medieval Japanese Society*. Translated by Käthe Roth. New York: Columbia University Press, 2001. This history of medieval Japan culminates in Oda's unification and transformation of Japanese society. Includes maps, bibliographic references, and index.

Turnbull, Stephen. *Samurai Warriors*. London: Bland-
ford Press, 1987. Chapter 5 is the most relevant. A
study of Oda the warlord, with an emphasis on military achievements, and the chronology of battles,
combined with technical information. The illustrations serve to make this the most colorful of the works
listed.

SEE ALSO: Hosokawa Gracia; Ōgimachi; Oichi; Toyotomi Hideyoshi.

RELATED ARTICLES in *Great Events from History: The
Renaissance & Early Modern Era, 1454-1600:* c.
1473: Ashikaga Yoshimasa Builds the Silver Pavilion; 16th century: Proliferation of Firearms; Autumn,
1543: Europeans Begin Trade with Japan; 1550's-
1567: Japanese Pirates Pillage the Chinese Coast;
1550-1593: Japanese Wars of Unification; June 12,
1560: Battle of Okehazama; 1568: Oda Nobunaga
Seizes Kyōto; 1594-1595: Taikō Kenchi Survey; October, 1596-February, 1597: *San Felipe* Incident.

ŌGIMACHI
Emperor of Japan (r. 1557-1586)

*Ascending the throne at the height of the Warring
States or Sengoku period (1467-1600), when the
fortunes of Japan's imperial dynasty were arguably at
their lowest ebb, Ōgimachi succeeded in reclaiming
part of the prestige and authority that the Japanese
imperial institution had lost. By refusing to be reduced
to a mere pawn in the hands of powerful warlords, he
revived and redefined the political position of the
imperial court in a feudal society controlled by
samurai.*

BORN: 1517; Kyōto, Japan
DIED: 1593; Kyōto
ALSO KNOWN AS: Michihito
AREA OF ACHIEVEMENT: Government and politics

EARLY LIFE

Prince Michihito, the future Emperor Ōgimachi (oh-gee-
mah-chih), was the son of Crown Prince Tomohito and
Fujiwara Shigeko. His grandfather had reigned as Emperor Go-Kashiwabara since 1500, but the official enthronement ceremonies were postponed for lack of funds
until 1521, when Michihito was four years old. Although
this particular situation resulted largely from the fact that
Japan had disintegrated into a patchwork of autonomous
fiefdoms ruled by warlords (daimyo) in the half century
preceding Michihito's birth, the Japanese imperial institution had ceased to play an active political role centuries
earlier.

Believed to be direct descendants of the sun goddess
Amaterasu, Japanese emperors traditionally played a
role that was sacerdotal rather than political, with real
power resting in the hands of regents and, since the thirteenth century, of the shogun. By the time of Michihito's
birth, the shogun's powers had been reduced to almost

nothing by the civil wars. Tellingly, the position of shogun remained officially vacant from 1508 until 1522, and
it was a former shogun, Ashikaga Yoshitane (r. 1490-
1493), who provided the funds for the enthronement ceremonies for Go-Kashiwabara in 1521.

Michihito was thus born into illustrious but impoverished circumstances. This remained unchanged after the succession of his father to the throne in 1526.
Reigning as Emperor Go-Nara for thirty-one years, he
became famous for "peddling his calligraphy in the
streets of Kyōto" to earn a living, as contemporary observers remarked. While this is almost certainly an over-
statement, that the calligraphy of Emperor Go-Nara was
for sale is undisputed. That there was a market for his
artwork hints at the continued prestige the imperial institution held even at that point. Go-Nara had to wait for
ten years for his official enthronement ceremonies, financed by the powerful daimyo houses of Imagawa,
Hōjō, Asakura, and Ōuchi. Again, the willingness of
powerful warlords to finance the seemingly empty rituals
of a politically insignificant institution shows that political capital could be gained by making such an investment.

At the time of Go-Nara's official enthronement, his
son and heir apparent Michihito was a young adult of
nineteen, but he would have to wait for another twenty-
one years before ascending the throne himself. He thus
had ample time to devote both to classical learning and to
the observation of the political realities in Warring States
Japan, an era of turmoil when, as the saying went, "those
below overthrow those above."

LIFE'S WORK

On the death of Go-Nara, Michihito took the throne as
Emperor Ōgimachi in 1557, at the age of forty. Not since

the eighth century had a person of such relatively advanced age become emperor. Officially he was the 106th in a line of rulers stretching back to antiquity, in actuality a direct descendant in the male line from the likely dynastic founder Keitai (r. 507-531). He formally took possession of the imperial regalia (a sacred mirror, a sword, and a jade jewel) but, like his father and grandfather before him, lacked the funds for the ceremony of communion with the sun goddess that officially marked an emperor's enthronement.

Kyōto, seat of the courts of both emperor and shogun, was effectively ruled by a daimyo who had forced the shogun to flee the capital in 1549. The shogun was allowed to return in 1558 but was in no position to support the imperial court financially.

The year 1560 brought two events that would be significant for Emperor Ōgimachi. In the first month of the new lunar year, his official enthronement ceremonies could finally be conducted, thanks to the financial support of a powerful daimyo from western Japan. Later that year, in the Battle of Okehazama, a relatively little-known daimyo by the name of Oda Nobunaga eliminated the house of Imagawa, a traditional supporter of the imperial court. Known as one of the three "Great Unifiers" of Japan after a century of civil war, Oda is portrayed by historians as a cunning politician who made shrewd use of traditional sources of legitimacy. Yet he did find the emperor somewhat less pliable than expected. By working with Oda, Ōgimachi intended to restore at least some measure of autonomy to the imperial institution, instead of becoming a mere legitimizing figurehead for Oda's military actions.

Although he lent some financial support to the court in 1563, Oda did not respond to an official missive from the emperor about a year later. As the political situation in the capital had deteriorated once again, Ōgimachi was looking for military and political support, especially with regard to recovering the estates from which the court derived its income.

More tumultuous times were to come before Oda would make his entry to the capital. Shogun Ashikaga Yoshiteru was assassinated in 1565. Ashikaga Yoshiaki, the slain Yoshiteru's younger brother, succeeded in claiming the vacant position of shogun in 1568 with the help of Oda, entering Kyōto and deposing his cousin, the fourteenth shogun, Yoshihide. Yoshiaki had tried to enlist the support of several other daimyo before settling on Oda. Ōgimachi, however, had been endorsing Oda all along; he even sent an official approval when Oda conquered Mino Province in 1567.

The investiture of Ashikaga Yoshiaki as shogun in late 1568 was perhaps the best example of political deal making in the capital. Oda legitimized what was in essence a *coup d'état* by posing as the protector of traditional order as embodied by the shogun. Yoshiaki could not have staked his claim without Oda. Most important, however, was that the emperor formally invested the shogun. Ōgimachi used the occasion to issue an order to both Oda and the shogun to restore the imperial estates to his control.

In the ensuing conflict between Shogun Yoshiaki and his erstwhile champion Oda, the emperor was apparently not afraid to take the side of the former. In 1569, he urged Oda to accept the post of vice shogun offered to him by Yoshiaki, an offer that Oda refused to consider. Even when relations between the shogun and Oda deteriorated to the point of open warfare in 1573, with Oda's forces torching large sections of the capital, Ōgimachi initially saved Yoshiaki but could not prevent his ouster later the same year.

After effectively ending the Ashikaga shogunate, Oda took the unprecedented step of petitioning the emperor to abdicate, offering to pay for the considerable expense of the ceremonies. After initially consenting to the petition, the emperor postponed his abdication indefinitely and offered a high-level court appointment to Oda. The acceptance of this appointment by Oda can be construed as a political victory for Ōgimachi, since it bound the warlord into the court hierarchy. Oda was being promoted through the ranks for several years, but he abruptly resigned all his court appointments in 1578, freeing himself from formal obligations to Ōgimachi. The emperor had no choice but to accept this resignation, but he adamantly refused to transfer Oda's rank and title to his son.

This peculiar tug-of-war continued in 1581. After attending a splendid parade of Oda and his vassals in the capital, the emperor offered Oda the title of grand minister of the left, the second highest in the imperial government. Oda, in turn, accepted, on the condition that the emperor make good on his earlier promise and abdicate in favor of Crown Prince Sanehito. The court retorted that times were singularly inauspicious for such a transfer, and the matter became moot with the assassination of Oda in 1582.

Ōgimachi finally abdicated in 1586, several months after the death of his son, in favor of his grandson, who ruled as Go-Yōzei for the next twenty-five years. Already of advanced age, Ōgimachi lived for seven more years and died in 1593.

SIGNIFICANCE

From the pages of diaries, chronicles, and his own writings, Ōgimachi emerges as an astute politician who stood his ground against vastly superior forces. Historians will continue to debate his moves and the motivation behind them for some time, but in the final analysis his reign put the imperial court back onto the political stage of Japan. Refusing merely to reflect the glory of great warlords, he managed to rescue the imperial institution from obscurity and to prevent it from slipping into obsolescence.

—*Ronald K. Frank*

FURTHER READING

Hall, John W., et al., eds. *Japan Before Tokugawa: Political Consolidation and Economic Growth, 1500 to 1650*. Princeton, N.J.: Princeton University Press, 1981. A collection of scholarly essays on the Sengoku period.

_____. *Sengoku and Edo*. Vol. 4 in *The Cambridge History of Japan*. New York: Cambridge University Press, 1991. Contains a comprehensive account of the Sengoku period.

Lamers, Jeroen. *Japonius Tyrannus: The Japanese Warlord Oda Nobunaga Reconsidered*. Leiden, the Netherlands: Hotei, 2000. A detailed scholarly account with ample quotations from primary sources, informative on the relationship between Ōgimachi and Oda.

Martin, Peter. *The Chrysanthemum Throne: A History of the Emperors of Japan*. Honolulu: University of Hawaii Press, 1997. A collection of short biographical sketches of all emperors and empresses.

SEE ALSO: Hōjō Ujimasa; Hosokawa Gracia; Oda Nobunaga; Oichi; Sesshū; Toyotomi Hideyoshi; Saint Francis Xavier.

RELATED ARTICLE in *Great Events from History: The Renaissance & Early Modern Era, 1454-1600:* June 12, 1560: Battle of Okehazama.

OICHI

Japanese noblewoman

The sister of Oda Nobunaga, the powerful Japanese warlord who attempted to unify Japan by conquest, Oichi was thrown into civil wars that were engulfing her country. As a noblewoman, her fate was tied to that of her two husbands, and she is remembered for her tragic loyalty, which led to her suicide at Kitanosho Castle.

BORN: 1548; Nagoya Castle, Japan
DIED: June 14, 1583; Kitanosho Castle, Japan
ALSO KNOWN AS: Odani no Kata (Lady of Odani Castle)
AREAS OF ACHIEVEMENT: Government and politics, warfare and conquest

EARLY LIFE

Oichi (oh-ee-chee) was born to Oda Nobuhide, the lord of Nagoya Castle in the cultural heartland of medieval Japan, near Kyōto. Oichi's father was a daimyo, a lord over samurai, and she grew up in an aristocratic and ambitious household.

When her father died, Oichi was three, and her much older brother Oda Nobunaga (1534-1582) became head of the family. Helped by an uncle, Oda conquered Kiyosu Castle in 1555 and moved into it, taking along seven-year-old Oichi. Two years later, Oda had his younger brother Nobuyuki killed there, accusing him of betrayal.

As a teenager, Oichi became famous for her great beauty. Her skin was extremely fair, and her luscious black hair enchanted even her female friends. Clothed in silk garments, she was considered a dazzling sight. At fifteen, Oda betrothed Oichi to a fellow daimyo, Asai Nagamasa (1545-1573). In 1559, Nagamasa had been married to the daughter of a samurai chosen by his father. Considering that bride his social inferior, he had divorced her. Meeting Oda at Odani Castle, he became allies with him, and Oda sent his sister to marry Nagamasa in 1563.

LIFE'S WORK

Oichi became Odani no Kata, Lady of Odani Castle. Contemporary accounts speak of a happy marriage. As wife of the daimyo, Oichi had high social standing but spent most of her time in the castle. There, she entertained her husband and her guests playing the koto, a Japanese string instrument, and was considered a hostess of radiant beauty.

Oichi had five children with Nagamasa. Her first daughter, Chacha, was born in 1567, and two more daughters and two sons followed. Mother and children were close, and Nagamasa adored his family.

In 1570, conflict erupted between Oichi's husband and her brother. Oda invaded Echizen Province next to

Odani Castle on the grounds that its daimyo had slighted him. As a result, Nagamasa was placed in an awkward position. During his marriage negotiations over Oichi, her brother had guaranteed not to touch Echizen. Now, Oichi's father-in-law insisted that his son attack Oda.

Disregarding his ties to Oichi's brother, Nagamasa broke with Oda. He was defeated in the summer of 1570 at the Battle of Anegawa. In September, 1573, Oda was ready to attack Odani Castle. He asked his brother-in-law to surrender, but Nagamasa refused.

Early on September 26, 1573, Nagamasa called together his family. At twenty-five, Oichi had just given birth to the youngest of her five children, a baby boy. Her contemporaries were still startled by her beauty and worried about her fate. Now, Nagamasa asked his wife and his children to burn incense and pray for him.

Oichi initially refused, preferring to die with him. However, Nagamasa ordered her to live and take care of their children. Oichi obeyed. Their two sons were smuggled out on September 28. That night, Oichi shared her last cups of sake with her husband. In the morning, she left with her three daughters. Oda welcomed Oichi and his nieces and resumed his attack. On the morning of September 30, defeated in battle, Nagamasa committed *seppuku*, ritual suicide.

On October 3, her brother tricked Oichi into revealing the hiding place of her eldest son, Mampukumaru, promising to treat him well. Instead, he ordered the man whom he gave Odani Castle to rule and who would take the name Toyotomi Hideyoshi (1537-1598) to fetch and kill the boy. Hideyoshi refused, but Oda did not relent. The boy was killed and his head publicly displayed on a spike.

After she learned that he had killed her son, Oichi refused the romantic advances of Hideyoshi. Instead, she withdrew with her three daughters to Kiyosu Castle, where she had been reared. On the way, Oichi stopped at Lake Biwa and prayed where her husband's tombstone had been dropped into the water. For the next nine years, Oichi lived in isolation at Kiyosu with her daughters, her baby son having been killed as well. At the castle, Oichi preferred to stay in her half-darkened chambers, hidden from the sun by screens and paper walls. For the first three years, Oichi lost much weight, but then she recovered.

On June 19, 1582, Oda Nobunaga was betrayed by one of his generals. Fighting to the end in the burning Honnōji temple, the mortally wounded Oda committed suicide by *seppuku*. Word of her brother's death reached Oichi as his followers converged on Kiyosu Castle.

Toyotomi Hideyoshi arrived as well. He had killed the traitor and resumed wooing Oichi, who hated him for having killed her son.

Oichi's nephew Nobutaka, a son of Oda by a concubine, approached her with another marriage request. Shibata Katsuie, now sixty, desired Oichi. He had been an ally of her younger brother (whom Oda had killed in 1557), switching over to Oda just in time. He had been among the attackers at Odani Castle in 1573 and had seen the vermilion-lacquered skull of Oichi's first husband, which Oda displayed on a tabletop on New Year's Day 1574.

Oichi wanted to stay loyal to her dead husband, yet she also sought protection for her daughters. While she forgave her brother, her hatred of Hideyoshi remained. His proposal came with the added insult that she would only become his concubine. Katsuie, even though he was twenty-six years older than Oichi, enjoyed the support of Oichi's nephew. November of 1582, Oichi married Katsuie at Gifu Castle. Afterward, they traveled through the falling snow to Katsuie's castle at Kitanosho. There Oichi blossomed under her new husband's love. After nine years of loneliness and seclusion, she embraced social life.

Within one month of their marriage, Katsuie found himself at war with Hideyoshi, ready to start fighting after winter. In February, 1583, fugitive lord Kyōgoku Takatsugu appeared and begged Oichi to protect him. He was one of Oda's samurai who had betrayed his lord. Oichi persuaded Katsuie to forgive her nephew by her first marriage. As a teenager, Takatsugu had visited Oichi and her daughters at Kiyosu Castle. Now, he romanced Chacha, who rejected him as an outcast. He turned his affection to Oichi's second daughter, Ohatsu, and they were married.

With spring, warfare began. Oichi said farewell to her husband, who was decisively defeated at the Battle of Shizugatake on June 11, 1583. When he fled to his castle, Hideyoshi quickly encircled it. Takatsugu slipped out, leaving his wife with Oichi. Hideyoshi offered Katsuie life for surrender, but everybody suspected this was a trick to catch Oichi. The old samurai angrily refused. At thirty-five, Oichi had been married to Katsuie for only seven months, and he was still full of vigor. However, the prospect of a second widowhood and her hatred of Hideyoshi influenced her decision to end her life together with Katsuie.

In the evening of June 13, 1583—raised on a dais and dressed in her most precious clothes, surrounded by her daughters and her husband—Oichi helped preside over a final banquet in the castle hall. The aristocrats drank sake, sang, danced, and remembered their lives together. On the morning of June 14, 1583, Oichi wrote her farewell poem, answered by one from Katsuie, before both retired to die. Hideyoshi had made plans to save Oichi, but his men managed only to abduct her daughters. Setting fire to their castle tower, Oichi and Katsuie ritually killed themselves, and the flames consumed their bodies.

Shortly afterward, Hideyoshi won the heart of Oichi's surviving daughter Chacha. She became his concubine and mother of his only two sons. Made lady of Yodo Castle, she took the name of Yodogimi. She saved her sister Ohatsu's husband when she made Hideyoshi forgive the fugitive Takatsugu.

After Hideyoshi died in 1598, Takatsugu would turn against his heir, Toyotomi Hideyori (1593-1615), son of Yodogimi and Hideyoshi, and therefore a grandson of Oichi. On June 4, 1615, Yodogimi and her son found themselves defeated at Ōsaka Castle. Like their mother and grandmother Oichi, they committed *seppuku* together as their castle burned to the ground.

Oichi's youngest daughter, Sūgen In, became the wife of the shogun Tokugawa Hidetada. Thus Oichi's daughters achieved considerable success in their noble society.

SIGNIFICANCE

Oichi lived for only thirty-five years, but she had a profound influence on the way Japanese noblewomen were perceived. The extremes of her innocent suffering, her obedience to her husband, and her final suicide provided a moral and philosophical model for her society. Her decisions were considered extremely brave and worthy of respect and imitation. Her intelligence, beauty, and noble birth linked her to the most powerful warlords of her time and made her especially fascinating. Her fate was held up as an illustration of the Japanese Buddhist belief that earthly life was apt to heap undeserved pain on even the kindest and best people.

In Japan, the fascination with Oichi continues. Her life became the subject of poetry, drama, and fiction. She is widely recognized in Japan as a woman who perfectly rose to the standards of her time. Although role models for women are being critically reexamined, especially in the light of feminist and antifeudal thinking, Oichi's significance remains: She was a Japanese Renaissance woman struggling to survive in an extremely hostile and vicious world, and she ultimately remained true to her society's high code of honor.

—*R. C. Lutz*

FURTHER READING

Jansen, Marius. *The Making of Modern Japan.* Cambridge, Mass.: Harvard University Press, 2000. Discusses the role of the Oda family in Japan's transition to modern times. Bibliography, index.

Tanizaki, Jun'ichiro. "A Blind Man's Tale." In *Seven Japanese Tales,* translated by Howard Hibbett. New York: Vintage Books, 1996. Fictional account of Oichi's life that is based on historical facts and brings her to life as a tragic person.

Tocco, Martha C. "Norms and Texts for Women's Education in Tokugawa Japan." In *Women and Confucian Cultures in Premodern China, Korea, and Japan,* edited by Dorothy Ko. Berkeley: University of California Press, 2003. An in-depth account of the education of noblewomen such as Oichi. Illustrations, glossary, index.

Weston, Mark. *Giants of Japan: The Lives of Japan's Greatest Men and Women.* New York: Kodansha International, 1999. Chapters 17 and 18 deal with Oda Nobunaga and Toyotomi Hideyoshi and include a discussion of Oichi's life. Bibliography, index.

JOHAN VAN OLDENBARNEVELT
Dutch statesman and diplomat

Oldenbarnevelt was the founder-lawgiver of the United Provinces of the Netherlands, whose statesmanship set the constitutional libertarian course that the modern Netherlands has followed. He was one of the greatest statesmen and diplomats in early modern Europe and in all Dutch history.

BORN: September 14, 1547; Amersfoort, bishopric of Utrecht (now in the Netherlands)

DIED: May 13, 1619; The Hague, United Provinces (now in the Netherlands)

AREAS OF ACHIEVEMENT: Government and politics, diplomacy, law

EARLY LIFE

Johan van Oldenbarnevelt (YOH-hahn fahn ahl-dehn-BAHR-neh-vehlt) given the name Johan Gerrit Reyerszoon van Oldenbarnevelt, was born in the bishopric of Utrecht, one of seventeen Netherlandic provinces in the possession of the Habsburg Dynasty; thus, he was born a subject of Emperor Charles V.

Johan belonged to the regent class, the burgher-oligarchy and provincial nobility of the Netherlands who governed locally by hereditary right on town councils and provincial representative assemblies that were called the states, or estates. The regent class was jealous of its position and privileges, and defended them against both the general populace and the Habsburgs and their lieutenants, called stadtholders.

Johan inherited the traditions of both his father's family and his mother's, the Weedes, traditions of burgher-oligarchy and provincial nobility, but he would not proceed directly to eminence. His father appears to have suffered mental incapacitation, and therefore he never served on the Amersfoort town council let alone on a council of the states of Utrecht, Holland, and Zealand, which were in very close political relations, or for the States-General of the Netherlands, the representative assembly of all the provinces. Because of this family crisis, Johan did not go directly from the Amersfoort Latin school to university studies or on the customary grand tour of France, Germany, and Italy. Instead, in 1563, Johan served a sort of apprenticeship with a lawyer in The Hague. Between 1566 and 1570, Johan combined university study and grand tour and traveled through Louvain, Bourges, Cologne, Heidelberg, Italy, and perhaps Padua, studying arts and the law.

When Oldenbarnevelt returned to The Hague in 1570, the duke of Alva for the Spanish Habsburgs tyrannized the Netherlands, which had begun the Dutch Wars of Independence in 1568. Oldenbarnevelt established law practice in the courts at The Hague, where he specialized in feudal law and law concerning dikes, drainage, and land reclamation. Because much of the Netherlands, the polders, had been reclaimed from the sea, and questions about title, responsibility for maintaining dikes, and similar matters were many, Oldenbarnevelt's practice grew quickly and soon became very lucrative. The Revolt of the Netherlands swept up Oldenbarnevelt. Though he had become a moderate Calvinist while a university student in Heidelberg, in The Hague he became a partisan of William the Silent.

War interrupted Oldenbarnevelt's legal practice and brought him onto the battlefield in the cause of Netherlandic independence. He saw action as a soldier in the disastrous attempt to relieve the Siege of Haarlem in 1573 and as supervisor of breaching the dikes in order to flood the polders for the celebrated relief of the Siege of Leiden in 1574. He also served William the Silent and his family in a legal capacity.

In 1575, Oldenbarnevelt was married to Maria van Utrecht, the illegitimate daughter of a noble family, who had become a wealthy heiress when Oldenbarnevelt's legal shrewdness secured her legitimation. His courtship of Maria seems not to have been entirely mercenary, for they remained happily married for forty-three years, until his execution, and had two daughters, two sons, and grandchildren. Meanwhile, Oldenbarnevelt had regained his rightful place in the regent class, demonstrated considerable legal ability, gained a fortune by his law practice and marriage, and made important friends in the House of Orange.

LIFE'S WORK

In 1576, Oldenbarnevelt became pensionary of Rotterdam, the legal representative and political secretary of the town, and entered the politics of Holland. Because Holland was the leading province, he thus became prominent in Netherlandic politics. Oldenbarnevelt promoted the Union of Utrecht of 1579 and the Act of Abjuration of 1581, which together became the declaration of independence and the constitution of the seven United Provinces of the Netherlands. Tensions between centralism and particularism remained, and at first the States-General thought to confer the sovereignty, which Spain had forfeited by its bloody tyranny, on the duke of Anjou and then the earl of Leicester, an action that would have made the United Provinces a satellite of France or England. Oldenbarnevelt led the states of Holland in opposition to such centralizing policies and in 1585 secured the appointment of Maurice of Nassau, son of William the Silent, who had been assassinated in 1584, as stadtholder and captain general. So long as the war against Spain continued, the advocate and the stadtholder collaborated in harmony—Oldenbarnevelt strengthened the United Provinces politically and diplomatically, and supported Maurice with revenue and political cooperation, and Maurice won military victories.

Oldenbarnevelt led the United Provinces during the celebrated Ten Years (1588-1598), when the provinces achieved full self-government, balancing centralism among the States-General, the stadtholder and captain-general, and the councils, with particularism in the provincial states and the town councils, thus transforming the loose defensive alliance of seven sovereign provinces into the United Provinces of the Netherlands. It was in

Johan van Oldenbarnevelt. (Library of Congress)

this that Oldenbarnevelt's leadership proved decisive. He scored the diplomatic triumph of the Triple Alliance in 1596 with France and England against Spain and thus gained international recognition of the independent United Provinces.

In 1598, France made peace with Spain, and in 1604, England did the same, so in 1605, Oldenbarnevelt decided to make peace. Spain was exhausted and wanted peace, and Oldenbarnevelt knew that a peace treaty would mean at least de facto recognition by Spain and the Spanish Netherlands (the ten provinces not part of the Union of Utrecht) of the independence of the United Provinces. Oldenbarnevelt's peace policy was opposed by Maurice and by his war party, which distrusted Spain's intentions, by the orthodox Calvinists who saw the war in apocalyptic terms, and by commercial interests who wanted economically to penetrate the West Indies. Oldenbarnevelt himself had an energetic commercial policy. He had in 1602 chartered the Dutch East India Company, but he was reluctant to charter a Dutch West India Company, which would jeopardize the peace with Spain. In the face of such opposition to make peace with Spain, Oldenbarnevelt characteristically compromised and negotiated the Twelve Years' Truce.

Yet the truce was disturbed by religious conflict within the United Provinces. This conflict had originated in an academic theological debate between two professors at the University of Leiden, the strict Calvinist Franciscus Gomarus and the revisionist Jacobus Arminius, over the Calvinist doctrine of predestination. The orthodox Calvinist Gomarists regarded the moderate Arminians, whom Oldenbarnevelt favored, as religious traitors worse than papists.

In 1617, Maurice declared for the Gomarists and rallied all parties that opposed Oldenbarnevelt over the Twelve Years' Truce. Oldenbarnevelt responded with the Sharp Resolution of August 4, 1617, which attempted to remove the military in Holland from the stadtholder and captain-general and to place it under control of the states of Holland and towns of the province. Maurice mobilized the other six provinces in the union against Holland and moved quickly and decisively. On August 28, 1618, the States-General conferred dictatorial powers on Maurice, and on August 29, 1618, Maurice ordered the arrest of Oldenbarnevelt and a few of his followers. In February, 1619, the States-General created an extraordinary tribunal to try Oldenbarnevelt and three codefendants, who included his protégé the great jurist and political philosopher Hugo Grotius.

Oldenbarnevelt's trial lasted from November, 1618, to May, 1619, but he was given neither writing materials nor access to books, documents, witnesses, or counsel. Yet he conducted an eloquent and dignified defense. The judges that were picked were his personal and political enemies, and the tribunal found Oldenbarnevelt guilty of vaguely defined capital crimes, despite his age and long service to the United Provinces. From the scaffold on May 13, 1619, Oldenbarnevelt addressed the crowd, "Men, do not think me a traitor; I have acted honestly and religiously, like a good patriot, and as such I die." After the headsman had done his work, the crowd pressed forward and, for relics of the martyred Oldenbarnevelt, dipped handkerchiefs in his blood.

SIGNIFICANCE

Oldenbarnevelt founded the United Provinces of the Netherlands and its traditions of constitutionalism and libertarianism. While William the Silent and his sons won Dutch independence on the battlefields of the Eighty Years' War against Spain, Oldenbarnevelt preserved independence through lawgiving, statesmanship, and diplomacy. He spent his long life serving his country, and he died an old man beheaded in 1619 by a Dutch special tribunal, a martyr for his vision of Dutch republican liberty.

As pensionary of Rotterdam and advocate of Holland, Oldenbarnevelt was architect of the United Provinces of the Netherlands, which lasted until 1795, and the Dutch libertarianism that has thrived since. His leadership fostered moderation, freedom, enterprise, toleration, peace, and prosperity, and began the great cultural florescence of the United Provinces during the seventeenth century. The United Provinces became a refuge for intellectual freedom in an age of persecution.

Oldenbarnevelt's diplomatic triumphs were the Triple Alliance with France and England in 1596 and the Twelve Years' Truce with Spain and the Spanish Netherlands, which gave the new United Provinces both a respite from war and international recognition. Ironically, it was Oldenbarnevelt's peace policy and religious moderation that led to his fall in 1618, and in 1619, his Dutch political enemies sentenced him to execution on very vague and unfounded charges of official misconduct and treason.

Oldenbarnevelt was a moderate in religion and politics, a believer in liberty of conscience, and a constitutionalist who saw the necessity of balancing particularism and centralism in order to secure freedoms. He shared William the Silent's vision of an independent, united Netherlands. On the scaffold at The Hague, the venerable statesman died as he had lived—brave and proud for the cause of liberty.

—*Terence R. Murphy*

FURTHER READING

Darby, Graham, ed. *The Origins and Development of the Dutch Revolt.* New York: Routledge, 2001. Anthology of scholarship on the causes and consequences of the sixteenth century Dutch rebellion against Spanish rule. Includes illustrations, maps, bibliographic references, and index.

Geyl, Pieter. *History of the Low Countries: Episodes and Problems.* London: Macmillan, 1964. An important collection of essays, several of which supply very useful background on Oldenbarnevelt; contentious in tone.

_____. *The Revolt of the Netherlands, 1555-1609.* Reprint. London: Cassell, 1988. An admirably clear and cogent narrative, somewhat tendentious about the historical contingency of the divided Netherlands and hence inevitably ambivalent about Oldenbarnevelt's founding of the United Provinces.

Koenigsberger, H. G. *Monarchies, States Generals, and Parliaments: The Netherlands in the Fifteenth and Sixteenth Centuries.* New York: Cambridge University Press, 2001. History of the States-General of the Netherlands, its internal and external strife, and its division into the United Provinces and the Spanish Netherlands. Includes illustrations, maps, bibliographic refernces, index.

Motley, John Lothrop. *The Life and Death of John of Barneveld.* 2 vols. New York: Harper & Brothers, 1874. A classic history, with a strong Protestant and liberal bias, that is still well worth reading for its drama, eloquence, and insights into Oldenbarnevelt.

Rowen, Herbert H., ed. *The Low Countries in Early Modern Times.* New York: Walker, 1972. Includes well-selected key documents that are edited, translated, and commented on judiciously. Sections 4 and 6 present such texts as the Union of Utrecht, the Act of Abjuration, the Treaty of the Twelve Years' Truce, and several of Oldenbarnevelt's letters.

Swart, K. W. *William of Orange and the Revolt of the Netherlands, 1572-1584.* Edited by R. P. Fagel, M. E. H. N. Mout, and H. F. K. van Nierop. Translated by J. C. Grayson. Burlington, Vt.: Ashgate, 2003. Authoritative, comprehensive biography of William, the first stadtholder of the United Provinces. Includes illustrations, maps, bibliographic references, and index.

Tex, Jan den. *Oldenbarnevelt*. Translated by R. B. Powell. 2 vols. Cambridge, England: Cambridge University Press, 1973. The standard scholarly biography, this work is appreciative of the great statesman but not uncritically so. Better on his public life than on his private life. The book makes a peculiar defense of the special court that condemned Oldenbarnevelt.

See also: Duke of Alva; Jacobus Arminius; John Calvin; Alessandro Farnese; Kenau Hasselaer; Philip II; William the Silent.

Related articles in *Great Events from History: The Renaissance & Early Modern Era, 1454-1600:* 1568-1648: Dutch Wars of Independence; July 26, 1581: The United Provinces Declare Independence from Spain.

Grace O'Malley
Irish pirate and noblewoman

O'Malley, a Gaelic noblewoman and notorious "pirate queen," is remembered for her command of a fleet of Irish galleys and for the leading roles she played in the politics of rebellion and war during the decades of England's final conquest of Ireland.

Born: 1530; Clew Bay, County Mayo, Ireland
Died: 1603; Rockfleet Castle, Clew Bay
Also known as: Granuaile; Granny Imallye; Grany Ni Maly; Gráinne Ni Mháille
Areas of achievement: Military, government and politics, warfare and conquest

Early Life
The O'Malley clans descended from the eldest son of the high king of Ireland from the fourth century. The men of Grace O'Malley's family were hereditary lords of Umhalls, part of the Connaught territory on Ireland's west coast. Grace O'Malley was born into this noble Gaelic clan. She was called by the unusual nickname of Graniuale, which most likely is a corruption of the Gaelic for "Grace of the Umhalls." The British anglicized Graniuale to "Granny."

O'Malley's mother was Margaret of clan Moher O'Malley, a branch of the O'Malley clan. Her father was Owen O'Malley, also named Black Oak (Dubhdarra). He was chieftain of Umhall Uachtarach, the Barony of Murrisk. According to the traditions and laws of the Gaelic Irish, Black Oak O'Malley was king of his territory and swore no allegiance to higher monarchs. He remained one of the few Gaelic chiefs never to acknowledge allegiance to the English crown. It is fair to assume that growing up in the political heart of her clan taught Grace the nuances, subtleties, and violence of sixteenth century Irish politics.

When not at sea, young Grace lived in one of several family castles around Clew Bay in northwestern Ireland.

Most of her early childhood centered in the castle at Belclare, the clan seat, or on Clare Island, a favored summer castle. Few facts are available about her life as a child.

Life's Work
Grace O'Malley lived in an age that saw the end of an era; an age that saw the bloody and brutal conversion of the Irish political system of Brehon law overseen by elected Gaelic lords to an emulation of Great Britain's system of common law and inherited rule.

In 1546, sixteen-year-old O'Malley made a political marriage to Donal O'Flaherty, the chieftain of Connemara and heir to the O'Flaherty clan. The marriage was not a love match but produced two sons and a daughter. Donal was reckless and ill-tempered, one whose inconsistent and volatile rule likely played a formative role in the intrigue, piracy, and rebellion that filled O'Malley's adult years. Historical record shows that—forced (or perhaps allowed) by Donal's irresponsibility—Grace assumed clan leadership in action if not in name. This was unusual since Gaelic law banned women as chieftains. In addition to her "wifely" duties of rearing children and serving as mistress to two castles, O'Malley gradually superseded Donal's rule. Throughout twenty-plus years of marriage, she settled tribal disputes, handled peaceful trading missions to Ulster, Scotland, Spain, and Portugal, and led pirate attacks on merchant ships.

Both the O'Malley and O'Flaherty clans boasted skilled seamen, a significant factor to clan well-being, wealth, and success. Trading, be it for fish or goods, was the primary source of O'Malley and O'Flaherty income. Piracy also was one of several profitable choices for Grace O'Malley. When a ship entered her territory, Grace could charge a toll, pilot them to safe passage, enter into trade, or steal their cargo. Pillage and plunder was

---

A POEM AND SONG FOR GRACE O'MALLEY

The life of Grace O'Malley (here Grainne Mhaol) is known mostly from myths, legends, poems, and songs. The following excerpt, part of a poem written to remember O'Malley's homecoming from battle, was originally composed in Gaelic by the Irish Republican leader and poet Pádraig Pearse (1879-1916). Irish folksinger Sinead O'Connor (b. 1967) included the piece, in its entirety, as a song on her album Sean Nos-Nua *(2002).*

You Are Welcome Home
Welcome Oh woman who was so afflicted,
It was our ruin that you were in bondage,
Our fine land in the possession of thieves,
And sold to the foreigners

Grainne Mhaol is coming over the sea,
Armed warriors along with her as guard,
They are Irishmen, not English or Spanish,
And they will rout the foreigners

Source: The Celtic Lyrics Collection, 2000-2004, http://celtic-lyrics.com. Accessed September 23, 2004.

---

not unusual nor was it considered an evil pursuit. Piracy was deemed a fact of doing business on the high seas.

By the time her husband was murdered by a rival clan sometime in the early 1560's, O'Malley had a strong following within the clan. One of many legends surrounding her involves Cock's castle, named for Donal's ferocity in defending it. O'Malley and a few followers were supposedly trapped on the island fortress by an English force from Galway. Under siege and understaffed, O'Malley ordered the castle's lead roof removed, melted, and poured over the turrets onto the English below. With the English soldiers removed to a safe distance, O'Malley and her retinue escaped by sea. The fortress was thereafter called Hen's castle in honor of her ingenuity and resourcefulness.

Another legend that has basis in fact is the Howlth incident. Tradition suggests that O'Malley landed her ship at Howlth for resupply and, as is the Gaelic custom, went to the castle of the lord for hospitality. The lord, being at dinner, refused admittance. O'Malley was reportedly so incensed by this breach of polite behavior that she kidnapped the lord's son. When Lord Howlth followed and begged for his son's release, O'Malley demanded that the gates of Howlth castle never be closed to anyone who requested hospitality and that an extra plate always be laid at his table. Reportedly, Howlth castle follows the custom to this day.

O'Malley was near forty years old, her husband was dead, her sons and daughter were grown, and she faced a grim future in O'Flaherty territory. She gathered her followers aboard a flotilla of galleys and returned to the O'Malley territory. Sixteenth century Ireland was rife with violent rebellions by the Gaelic lords against the rule of England's Queen Elizabeth I. Amid political turmoil and clan war, O'Malley and her followers flourished in Clew Bay, especially after she married Richard Burke in a bid to gain his castle, Rockfleet, which controlled the inland harbor.

Theobald, her youngest son, was born in 1567 at sea. Legend claims that Turkish pirates attacked the galley a day after his birth. The battle was going against the Irish crew when O'Malley's captain implored her to come on deck to motivate the men. After a brief speech, she launched herself into the battle, rallied her crew, and sailed the captured Turkish ships home to Clew Bay.

In 1584, the English lord Sir Richard Bingham was given charge of the administration of Connaught. His governorship marked the end of forty years of prosperity for O'Malley. Bingham brought the previously distant power of Queen Elizabeth I to western Ireland. He was a brutal overlord who hated Granny O'Malley. Ten years of his vicious administration of British law drove O'Malley into poverty.

Another famous legend about O'Malley is also the best source about her life. Bingham's campaign appropriated her wealth and holdings and blocked her sea ventures, even legitimate voyages. In desperation, O'Malley decided to challenge his authority. Early in 1593, she petitioned Queen Elizabeth for relief from Bingham's reign of terror. In a daring and clever letter, O'Malley described her dismal circumstances and asked the queen for maintenance from her late husbands' estates. In a brilliant twist, O'Malley ended her letter with an offer to use her seafaring skills and fleet of galleys to fight enemies of the queen, a bold bid to resume piracy under the queen's name.

In July of 1593, Queen Elizabeth responded with a letter of her own in which she asked eighteen questions about O'Malley and her life. Called the "Articles of Interrogatory," the questions and O'Malley's answers provide a factual telling of her unusual life and a reflection of Irish society and politics. Bingham's vicious crusade increased, however. When her son Owen was murdered in Bingham's custody and her youngest son, Theobald, was arrested, O'Malley set sail for England to have a face-to-face audience with the queen. The meeting, which has sparked the imagination of many fiction writers, would have been an astonishing event, since Elizabeth sent written orders to Bingham granting all O'Malley's requests.

The legends surrounding Grace O'Malley are among the most colorful to come from the tumultuous sixteenth century. Ireland's pirate queen died in 1603 at Rockfleet Castle. She was laid to rest beside the sea that gave her enduring support and enrichment.

SIGNIFICANCE

The record-keeping practices of the sixteenth century ignored Grace O'Malley. Except for the "Articles of Interrogatory," historical record has little direct information about her. It has fallen to the world of fiction and myth to pay tribute to Ireland's pirate queen. Legend describes a colorful and romantic figure whose deeds were splendid and larger than life. Many historical facts about Graniuale lend credence to the legend—in a time when women had little power, Grace O'Malley carved a kingdom on land and on sea for herself, her family, and her followers.

—C. K. Zulkosky

FURTHER READING

Boylan, Henry, and C. O. Niwot. *A Dictionary of Irish Biography*. 3d ed. New York: Rinehart, 1998. Provides a biographical entry about Grace O'Malley.

Chambers, Anne. *Granuaile: Life and Times of Grace O'Malley c. 1530-1603*. Rev. ed. Dublin: Wolfhound Press, 1998. Exploration of the legend and true circumstances surrounding the life of Grace O'Malley within the context of the eventful age to which she belonged.

McCully, Emily Arnold. *The Pirate Queen*. New York: G. P. Putnam's Sons, 1995. An account of O'Malley's life written for younger readers.

Netzley, Patricia D. *The Encyclopedia of Women's Travel and Exploration*. Phoenix, Ariz.: Oryx Press, 2001. Provides a biographical entry about Grace O'Malley.

Wagner, John A. *Historical Dictionary of the Elizabethan World: Britain, Ireland, Europe, and America*. Phoenix, Ariz.: Oryx Press, 1999. A chapter on Ireland contains informative entries profiling O'Malley and her contemporaries.

SEE ALSO: Elizabeth I.
RELATED ARTICLES in *Great Events from History: The Renaissance & Early Modern Era, 1454-1600:* 1558-1603: Reign of Elizabeth I; 1597-September, 1601: Tyrone Rebellion.

PACHACUTI
Emperor of the Inca Empire (r. 1438-1471)

Pachacuti, through personal courage, brilliant political sense, and administrative genius, was primarily responsible for the creation of the Inca Empire in its final form.

BORN: c. 1391; probably Cuzco, Inca Empire (now in Peru)

DIED: 1471; near Cuzco

ALSO KNOWN AS: Pachacutec Inca Yupanqui; Cusi Inca Yupanqui

AREAS OF ACHIEVEMENT: Government and politics, warfare and conquest, military

EARLY LIFE

Pachacuti (pah-chah-KEW-tee), the ninth emperor of the Inca in a direct line from the perhaps legendary Manco Capac, who founded the dynasty about the year 1200, was, with his son Topa Inca Yupanqui and his grandson Huayna Capac, one of the three greatest Inca emperors. Since he was said to have been about eighty years of age when he died in 1471, he presumably was born in Cuzco, the capital, about 1391, the son of Viracocha Inca and Runtu Coya. As the son of the emperor, Pachacuti was thoroughly educated in military science and the art of administration, but almost nothing is known about his life before the dramatic events of 1437-1438 brought him to the throne.

The Inca had no written historical records, and what is known of their origins is to be found in chronicles written after the Spanish Conquest. These were based on the memory of native historians, however, who used the *quipu*, knotted ropes that served as memory devices, to recall the events of Inca history. Certainly, from the beginnings of Pachacuti's reign, the chronicles must be considered generally reliable, though it is possible that he may have dictated an account of his accession in order to justify the legitimacy of his claim to the throne.

During the reign of Viracocha, the Inca Empire, an area from the country north of Cuzco to the shores of Lake Titicaca, was threatened by various tribes on its borders to the north and west. In 1437, the Chanca, a warrior tribe in the Apurimac Valley northwest of Cuzco, defeated the Quechua, thus upsetting the balance of power the Inca had maintained among their enemies, and pushed through the Quechua country to the Inca frontier. Viracocha, apparently assuming that Cuzco could not be held, fled the city, while Pachacuti became the leader of a cabal that was determined to defend Cuzco and to put

Pachacuti on the throne. He organized the city's defenses, and, even though the Chanca actually broke into the city itself, he drove them out. In one account, he is described as wearing a lionskin as he personally led his troops in battle. Later he won a great victory over the Chanca at their stronghold of Ichupampa, west of Cuzco, virtually destroying them as a tribe, and in 1438 he became emperor. At this time, by one account, his father gave him the name Pachacuti, translated variously as cataclysm or Earth upside down, which suggests that even at that time he was determined to change the Inca Empire completely.

LIFE'S WORK

The chronicles do not agree on the exact nature of Pachacuti's claim to the throne. According to some, he was Viracocha's eldest son and thus his legitimate heir but was, in effect, disinherited by his father on behalf of Inca Urcon, a younger brother. By another account, he was a younger son, and when Viracocha resigned the throne to Inca Urcon, the latter made Pachacuti governor of Cuzco while he retired to the enjoyment of his vices. What is certain is that Pachacuti, after his victory in the Chanca War, made Viracocha his virtual prisoner, was given his blessing, and by methods that are not clear, brought about the death of Inca Urcon. Viracocha died soon after.

Pachacuti spent the first three years of his reign in Cuzco, consolidating power and creating an entirely new leadership; then, in 1441, he embarked on a three-year tour of inspection of the empire and the reconquest of the territory of those tribes that had rebelled against Inca rule during the Chanca incursion. Only then did he undertake the military campaigns that made him the most remarkable conqueror of any South American Indian leader.

His first campaign, in 1444, took him into the Urupampa Valley, in an area now called Vilcapampa, north of Cuzco, and then west into Vilcas. Later he conquered the Huanca tribe in Huanmanca (the modern areas of Junín and Huancavelica) and the provinces of Tarma, Pumpu, Yauyu, and Huarochiri. When Hastu Huaraca, the defeated Chanca leader, organized opposition to the Inca in the Apurimac Valley, Pachacuti again defeated him in battle and achieved his submission and a grant of warriors for the Inca army. Later he won a great victory at Corampa, and in a campaign against the Soras, which culminated in a successful two-year Siege of Challomarca, their capital, he achieved virtual control of all central Peru south of Ecuador. He then sent his Chanca auxiliaries south into Collao, followed with his main army, defeated the Canas at Ayavire, at the end of Lake Titicaca, and in a decisive battle at Pucara eliminated Collao power. This military victory was probably in 1450.

Pachacuti's firm control of the imperial administration and of the armies by which it was maintained is indicated by the fact that when he dispatched his general Capac Yapanqui into the province of Chucurpu and then learned that Capac had exceeded his orders and had advanced farther into the lands beyond Chucurpu, he ordered him back to Cuzco and had him executed for disobedience, even though the expedition had added more land to the empire than he had anticipated.

By 1457, Pachacuti had conquered all the territory between the coastal range of Peru and the valley of the Marañón. In 1463, he gave command of the army to his son (and heir), Topa Inca. This force of forty thousand men began in 1464 the subjugation of Chimor, an advanced civilization on the northern Peruvian coast that was, in a sense, Greece to Cuzco's Rome. By 1470, with the fall of the Chimor capital of Chanchan (modern-day Trujillo), this conquest was complete. Other commanders under Pachacuti's orders conquered the territory beyond Lake Titicaca and as far south as the Atacama Desert in northern Chile. In all, these conquests created an empire of sixteen million people, extending from Ecuador to northern Chile and Bolivia.

If Pachacuti were only a conqueror, he would be less remarkable. In fact, his supreme achievement was the creation of a political structure that survived with great stability until the civil war that broke out over the question of imperial succession shortly before the arrival of the Spanish. It was Pachacuti who inaugurated the system of populating conquered lands with colonists who eventually intermarried with the local population and gave them identity as Inca, and he created the *mitimaes* system, by which dissident elements in a conquered territory would be moved as colonists to another region where Inca rule had been accepted. He also instituted a system of runners to carry royal messages, which gave the empire the kind of coherence that only rapid communication could make possible.

In religious matters, Pachacuti simplified and redefined the rites of the Incas and incorporated the deities of conquered peoples into the Inca pantheon. Above all, he was determined to make each conquered nation an organic part of a larger whole. Often after conquering a nation, he would take its king to Cuzco, bestow on him lavish gifts and hospitality, and then send him home to rule as his proconsul. He also completely reorganized the imperial school in Cuzco, where not only the sons of the Inca caste but also those of conquered lords studied economics, government, military science, the arts and sciences of the Inca, and Quechua, the language of the empire.

Many of the engineering achievements of Pachacuti are still seen in Peru. In 1440, he began the complete rebuilding of Cuzco, and at about the same time the great fortress of Sacsahuaman, the house of the sun north of the city, was begun by twenty thousand laborers, a monument so massive that it was not completed until 1508, during the reign of his grandson. Though scholars no longer agree whether Pachacuti ordered the construction of Machu Picchu, it is probable that he was responsible for its later development as a bastion of Inca defense. He also encouraged terracing to take advantage of the steep Andean terrain for agriculture and is credited with the development of the greatest Inca irrigation systems.

When Topa Inca returned from his conquest of Chimor and Ecuador, Pachacuti partially resigned the throne to him, serving until his death in 1471 as a kind of coregent. This arrangement ensured a smooth transfer of power and enabled Topa to embark on more conquests when he became emperor, though some accounts suggest that as a result of Pachacuti's declining physical powers, he had no choice but to share power with his son.

SIGNIFICANCE

Pachacuti was not only a valiant warrior but also a statesman with a clear understanding of the requirements of imperial administration. The laws and the political structure he created survived almost a century until his descendants, forgetting the need for imperial unity in their quarrels over the succession to the throne, weakened the empire at precisely the moment that the soldiers of Spanish explorer and conquistador Francisco Pizarro landed on the Peruvian coast in 1532. It seems unlikely, in fact, that the Spanish conquest of Peru would have been possible, at least with Pizarro's small force, if it had been attempted when Pachacuti was at the height of his power.

Though Pachacuti's wars with those immediate neighbors who had conspired against the Inca were fought to the death and often culminated in massacre, his conquests through the rest of his empire were followed by liberal treatment of his subjects. For Pachacuti, war was a necessary evil, the last application of political methods to achieve Inca hegemony and the order that, under his leadership, accompanied it. If war in the reigns of his predecessors was a means of personal aggrandizement not unlike hunting or sport, it was for Pachacuti the work of trained professionals and an instrument of public policy. His armies fought aggressively, but their success was in large part a result of Pachacuti's attention to logistic detail. When their victories had been achieved, he directed their energies to the administration of the conquered territory and the creation of those public works that would make them more productive.

For these reasons, Pachacuti must be considered not only the greatest conqueror among all South American Indian leaders but also the most brilliant ruler.

—Robert L. Berner

FURTHER RYEADING

Brundage, Burr Cartwright. *Empire of the Inca.* Norman: University of Oklahoma Press, 1963. A thorough discussion of Inca civilization from its origins until the arrival of the Spanish, this study synthesizes the chronicles and scholarship to provide the most probable account of these events.

Cieza de León, Pedro de. *The Incas.* Edited and translated by Harriet de Onis. Norman: University of Oklahoma Press, 1959. Cieza's account, first published in 1553, is the most objective early account of the Incas. This objectivity and annotations by Victor Wolfgang von Hagen make it a basic text for understanding Inca history.

Cobo, Bernabé. *History of the Inca Empire.* Edited and translated by Roland Hamilton. Austin: University of Texas Press, 1979. Cobo was a Jesuit priest who went to Peru in 1599 as a missionary to the Indians. Most of his manuscript was lost; what remained, published in 1653, was largely concerned with pre-Columbian America. This work is based on Cobo's archival research in Mexico City and Lima and on interviews with descendants of the Inca royal dynasty.

D'Altroy, Terence N. *The Incas.* Malden, Mass.: Blackwell, 2002. Study of the Inca Empire from its beginnings to its fall. Reconsiders the social, political, and economic structure of the empire in the light of recent scholarship and archaeological discoveries. Includes illustrations, maps, bibliographic references, index.

Davies, Nigel. *The Incas.* Niwot: University Press of Colorado, 1995. A close analysis of the Spanish sources of Incan history, the archaeological evidence, and scholars' interpretations. Davies argues that little is known with certainty about the Inca rulers.

Garcilaso de la Vega. *Royal Commentaries of the Incas and General History of Peru.* Translated by Harold V. Livermore. 2 vols. Austin: University of Texas Press, 1966. Completed in 1604 and first published in 1609 as *Primera parte de los comentarios reales,* Garcilaso's history of Peru cannot be ignored but must be used with caution and corrected by reference to Cobo and Cieza de León.

Hyams, Edward, and George Ordish. *The Last of the Incas.* London: Longman, 1963. This work is concerned primarily with the Spanish conquest of Peru and the events that immediately preceded it, but its second chapter is a thorough discussion of Inca civilization and the events of the reign of Pachacuti.

Malpass, Michael A. *Daily Life in the Inca Empire.* Westport, Conn.: Greenwood Press, 1996. Written for complete newcomers to pre-Columbian history, the text carefully defines Inca terms and anthropological concepts as it describes Inca culture and history. Includes illustrations and a handy glossary.

Means, Philip Ainsworth. *Ancient Civilizations of the Andes.* New York: Gordian Press, 1964. A thorough study, originally published in 1931, of all the cultures and civilizations of Peru from the earliest prehistoric times to the Spanish Conquest. Means devotes two chapters to Inca history that are valuable, though partially superseded by later scholarship.

Rowe, John Howland. "Inca Culture at the Time of the Spanish Conquest." In *Handbook of South American Indians,* edited by Julian H. Steward. Vol. 2. Washington, D.C.: Government Printing Office, 1949-1959. Rowe's seven-volume study is primarily concerned with social and cultural aspects of Inca civilization, but it is important for the dating of pre-Conquest events generally accepted by later scholars.

SEE ALSO: Atahualpa; Huáscar; Francisco Pizarro.

SOPHIA PALAEOLOGUS
Princess of Russia

Sophia Palaeologus's marriage to Ivan the Great helped establish Russian princes as protectors of Orthodox Christianity in the East. The marriage also gave the princes a connection with the Byzantine Dynasty and claims to higher social status than that derived from their descent from the semilegendary Viking leader Rurik.

BORN: c. 1449; Constantinople, Byzantine Empire (now Istanbul, Turkey)

DIED: April 7, 1503; Moscow (now in Russia)

ALSO KNOWN AS: Zoe; Sophia Paleologus; Sophia Palaiologus

AREAS OF ACHIEVEMENT: Government and politics, religion and theology

EARLY LIFE

Sophia Palaeologus (SOH-fee-ah pay-lee-AHL-oh-guhs) was the daughter of Thomas, despot of Morea, the younger brother of Constantine XI, the last emperor of the Byzantine Empire. When Constantine died fighting the Turks on the walls of Constantinople in 1453, Thomas and his family fled to Italy. Thomas died there, and Pope Paul II took his daughter and two sons as wards and placed them under the guardianship of Cardinal Bessarion, a Greek scholar who had converted from Greek Orthodoxy to Roman Catholicism and attained high rank in the Church.

Sophia was fourteen years old when her father died, and she remained in Rome for ten years. There is evidence, however, that these were not happy years. Although she received a good education, it was always as an act of charity. Cardinal Bessarion insisted that she and her brothers consider themselves paupers and be humbly grateful for papal generosity. This did not sit well with the scions of an ancient and noble house, but they realized that their dependence on others for bed and board kept them from refusing the cardinal's insistence. In any case, under Cardinal Bessarion's tutelage, Sophia became an intelligent woman, skilled in intrigue. Some writers considered her beautiful, while others described her as grotesquely obese.

LIFE'S WORK

In 1469, Pope Paul began negotiations to marry Sophia to Ivan the Great, grand prince of Moscow. Little is known about Ivan's personal life, since the chroniclers of the time were churchmen concerned with, primarily, the moral significance of a ruler's actions. Some records recognize him as Ivan the Hunchbacked; this may not have indicated a true deformity but instead that he had the rounded shoulders of a scholar rather than the broad chest of a fighter.

Ivan seems to have been shrewd, reflective, and one who preferred to lay his plans within the Kremlin rather than ride forth in dramatic charges against enemy forces. At that time, Russia was still surrounded and dominated by the Tatars, and Ivan hoped that this royal match would gain him a military alliance against the Tatars along with the obvious prestige. The pope hoped to gain Russian support against the Muslims Turks, who threatened Christendom from the east, and to pave the way for a reunion of the Eastern and Western churches.

Sophia left Rome in June of 1472 and arrived in Moscow on November 12. On that day, she was received into the Orthodox church and wed Ivan. According to one story, her enormous weight broke the great bed of the grand princesses on her first night in Moscow. There was resentment of her almost from the beginning, and many Russian aristocrats considered her to be wielding a sinister influence on Ivan. Her education and worldly wisdom placed her in stark contrast to the illiterate wives of the Russian noblemen, who were kept in seclusion, an Asiatic custom. This practice of secluding high-ranking women, known as the *terem*, would continue until the 1700's, when Peter the Great formally abolished it and commanded that noblewomen must appear at public functions in accordance with Western customs.

To a woman such as Sophia, a child of Constantinople brought up in ancient and cultured Rome, Moscow of the time could only appear crude and rustic. The Kremlin of that day was not yet the red brick walls and stone palaces familiar to modern minds from Cold War news clips, but instead a wooden palisade sheltering a few buildings constructed of logs. Only during Sophia's life did the first stone building, the Uspensky Cathedral, go up within the Kremlin's walls. During this time, Ivan steadily expanded his titles and the rituals surrounding his activities, and he began to use the title czar, the Russian version of "caesar." Chroniclers who desired to curry the monarch's favor began to produce various legends glorifying him, including a fabricated genealogy that traced his descent from an imagined kinsman of the emperor Augustus.

Although Sophia had formally embraced Orthodoxy upon her marriage, returning to the faith of her Byzantine childhood after years as a convert to Catholicism, she was continually suspected of adhering to Roman ways. She also was the subject of intense jealousy by Ivan Molodoi (*molodoi* means "the younger"), the son of Ivan the Great by his previous marriage. Ivan Molodoi feared that Sophia's children might supplant him and his heirs, not an unreasonable concern in a time and place in which inheritance laws were fluid. Her first two children were daughters, who posed no dynastic threat, but in 1479, she gave birth to a son, Vasily (the future Grand Prince Vasily III), whom she clearly hoped to make Ivan's heir in place of Ivan Molodoi.

In 1483, Ivan Molodoi fathered a son of his own, Dmitry, by his wife, Yelena Stepanova of Moldavia. As a result, his concern about his half brother's possible ambitions toward the throne grew steadily stronger, and he sought his father's assurances that he and his descendants would indeed inherit the throne of Muscovy. In 1490, Ivan Molodoi died, leaving his young son vulnerable to Sophia's intrigues. These came to a head in 1497 with a plot to have Dmitry murdered, apparently by poison. Ivan discovered the scheme just in time to foil it, and although he did not punish Sophia or her son Vasily, he executed a number of Sophia's supporters. Among them were several women accused of being poisoners, whom he had thrown into the river Muskva in view of the Kremlin.

On February 4, 1498, Ivan formally blessed Dmitry as his heir. In the absence of a clear law of primogeniture to make the inheritance right of the eldest son's line automatic, such promises, however, remained mutable. With Sophia's aid, Vasily continued to intrigue for his father's favor, and in April of 1502, Ivan reversed his earlier decision. Dmitry was disgraced and sent into exile, along with his mother Yelena. Vasily was formally proclaimed heir.

In the following year, Sophia died, but she had secured the right of her son to inherit the throne. Ivan the Great died in 1505 and was succeeded by Vasily. Dmitry remained in exile on an estate well away from Moscow, and he died there three years later without once trying to wrest the throne from his uncle. Vasily's son, Ivan the Terrible, grandson of Sophia Palaeologus, was the first Muscovite grand prince to incorporate the title czar into his coronation rituals, and as such he is often reckoned to have been the first true czar of Russia. He earned the sobriquet *grozny*, the terrible, as a result of his harsh and often brutal rule.

SIGNIFICANCE

The marriage of Sophia Palaeologus to Ivan the Great permanently secured Moscow's ascendancy as the primary principality of Russia. By providing a blood tie, however tenuous, with the emperors of Byzantium, the marriage enabled the grand princes of Moscow to style themselves as czars of Russia, using a Russified form of the Italian word caesar, which had come to be synonymous with the term emperor.

This dynastic link also led to the tradition of Moscow as the Third Rome, replacing Constantinople as the seat of Eastern Christendom. According to this tradition, Constantinople had become the Second Rome after Rome proper fell to the barbarians in the late fifth and early sixth centuries and was deemed by the Eastern Church to no longer maintain headship over the Church.

Although the Rurikid Dynasty to which Ivan belonged came to an end with his grandson Ivan the Terrible, the use of the title czar and the Byzantine double-headed eagle persisted and were adopted by the Romanovs, the second and last great dynasty of Russian monarchs. With the fall of the Soviet Union in 1991 and the abolition of Soviet symbols such as the red star and the hammer and sickle, the double-headed eagle has returned as the emblem of the Russian Federation, although without dynastic significance in a republican government.

—*Leigh Husband Kimmel*

FURTHER READING

Nicol, Donald M. *The Immortal Emperor: The Life and Legend of Constantine Palaiologus, Last Emperor of the Romans.* New York: Cambridge University Press, 1994. Background information on Sophia's childhood and escape to Rome.

Payne, Robert, and Nikita Romanoff. *Ivan the Terrible.* Lanham, Md.: Cooper Square Press, 2002. Includes background information on Ivan's ancestors, including Sophia and Ivan the Great.

Warnes, David. *Chronicle of the Russian Tsars: The Reign-by-Reign Record of the Rulers of Imperial Russia.* London: Thames and Hudson, 1999. Good overview of each czar's reign, from Ivan the Great to Nicholas II.

SEE ALSO: Ivan the Great; Ivan the Terrible; Vasily III.

RELATED ARTICLES in *Great Events from History: The Renaissance & Early Modern Era, 1454-1600:* 1478: Muscovite Conquest of Novgorod; After 1480: Ivan the Great Organizes the "Third Rome."

GIOVANNI PIERLUIGI DA PALESTRINA
Italian composer

Palestrina, a leading, prolific composer of masses and motets for the Roman Catholic Church during the Counter-Reformation, brought the musical art of Renaissance counterpoint to its full perfection.

BORN: c. 1525; Palestrina, near Rome, Papal States (now in Italy)
DIED: February 2, 1594; Rome
AREA OF ACHIEVEMENT: Music

EARLY LIFE

Giovanni Pierluigi da Palestrina (joh-VAHN-nee pyehr-lew-EE-jee dah pah-lay-STREE-nah) is known by the name Palestrina from the place of his birth. His early music training began as a choirboy at Santa Maria Maggiore in Rome in 1537. Most of his career was spent in Rome in the service of the Roman Catholic Church. Between 1544 and 1551, he returned to the city of Palestrina as organist, singer, and music teacher at its cathedral. Here he married Lucrezia Gori and began a family with three sons.

LIFE'S WORK

Palestrina must have immersed himself in the great Renaissance masses and motets of his predecessors and begun composing his own masses and motets while in Palestrina. Masses are musical settings of the liturgy of the Eucharist. Motets are sacred polyphonic compositions sung in Latin.

Palestrina's compositions are in the Renaissance polyphonic or contrapuntal style. Usually unaccompanied by instruments, the four or more voices sing independent melodic lines simultaneously; compositions usually begin with voices entering one after another until all voices are singing together. Frequently, the voices merge into a homophonic (or chordal) texture, where they sing the same words note against note, creating chordal passages.

In 1551, Palestrina returned to Rome, where he was appointed, by Pope Julius III, *maestro di cappella* (choir master) of the Cappella Giulia (Julian Choir) at the Basilica of San Pietro (St. Peter's) in the Vatican, where his duties included teaching singing to the choirboys. In 1554, he dedicated his first published book of masses to Pope Julius. The wood-cut illustration on its title page shows Palestrina kneeling and presenting the book to the pope.

Perhaps as a result of the dedication, on January 13, 1555, Palestrina was appointed a member of the Cappella Sistina (choir of the Sistine Chapel), even though he was married. Three months later, Julius died and was succeeded by Pope Marcellus II, who was pope for three weeks only. Palestrina's most famous mass was later to be named after Marcellus. The next pope, Paul IV, was so strict about the Sistine Chapel's rule on celibacy that Palestrina was dismissed in September. The following month, he became *maestro di cappella* of San Giovanni Laterano (Saint John Lateran) but left suddenly in 1560 because of a dispute over needed funds for the musicians. The following year, Palestrina returned to Santa Maria Maggiore for four years, and then took a post in 1566 at the new Seminario Romano (the Roman Seminary). During this appointment, he also directed concerts at Cardinal Ippolito II d'Este's famous Villa d'Este at Tivoli until 1571.

By the 1560's, Palestrina's reputation had spread. In 1568, Holy Roman Emperor Maximilian II offered him a post in Vienna as imperial choirmaster, but Palestrina's salary demands were too high, and the offer fell through. He also was corresponding with and writing masses for some of Italy's great noblemen and published additional books of masses and motets. His second book of masses, published in 1567, included his famous *Missa Papae Marcelli* (*Pope Marcellus Mass*).

In 1571, Palestrina returned to his previous post as choirmaster at the Capella Giulia; he also had resumed a post at the Sistine Chapel. In these positions, he remained secure for the rest of life. The years, though, brought him some personal losses. The plague took his brother and two sons in 1572 and 1575; he was seriously ill in 1578; and two years later, his wife died. He began steps to join the priesthood, but in 1581, he married a wealthy widow of a fur merchant, which provided financial security. He combined productive years as a composer with activities as a businessman and investor.

As a church musician, he still had the duties of his fixed appointments, but he also received numerous commissions for other churches or confraternities (devotional societies). These commissions included music for Lenten devotions on Good Friday, special processions, and special holy days. The output of his compositions is staggering, even in an age of prolific composers. He wrote more than 100 Latin masses, more than 300 motets and 200 other sacred pieces, and more than 140 madrigals (sacred or secular polyphonic vocal compositions).

Giovanni Pierluigi da Palestrina. (Hulton|Archive by Getty Images)

In his compositions, Palestrina avoided some of the arid, complex canons and part writing of his predecessors and achieved smooth vocal lines with clear rhythms and melodies that matched the text effortlessly. His music contains less dissonance, more homophonic passages, and rich sonorities.

Even before his death in 1594, Palestrina was being praised as the greatest composer of his age. In 1575, he had been described as "the very first musician in the world." Although his music circulated in manuscript copies during his lifetime, his music was widely known through his published music, which especially increased with the financial security of his marriage.

A great part of Palestrina's reputation as "the savior of Church music" comes from the place of his work in the reforms of Catholic Church music in the wake of the Council of Trent. Much of this reputation has, unfortunately, been shown to be myth or exaggeration. The Council of Trent met intermittently between 1545 and 1563 and set off the Counter-Reformation. In response to challenges of the Protestant Reformation, the council enacted a series of sweeping self-reforms to purge the Catholic Church of those abuses that motivated the Protestant Reformation. The council clarified Church

doctrine and practices and developed guidelines about proper Church music. They sought to purge it of anything that seemed lascivious, impure, or similar to secular music, or that appeared to be Church music performed merely for pleasure. Music for church services had to show clarity, simplicity, and an element or realism and emotion, and the words had to be intelligible to the listener. This meant that composers had to avoid long florid lines (where a syllable or word was stretched out over many notes) or different voices singing different words simultaneously.

It is unlikely, as a seventeenth century legend tells it, that Palestrina's composing of *Pope Marcellus Mass* proved that Catholic Church music could avoid the excesses and abuses condemned by the Protestants and the Council of Trent, thereby saving polyphonic music from official prohibition. There is, though, a more likely possibility that the mass (though published in 1567) does have a connection with Pope Marcellus. On the third day of his papacy, Good Friday in 1555, the pope called together the singers of his private chapel to tell them that the music for the following Holy Week must be more in keeping with the solemn character of the occasion and that the words of the music must be understood clearly. The mass might then refer to this event.

The mass, however, was most likely written later (in about 1562, when it was copied into a choirbook at Santa Maria Maggiore). After the Council of Trent, two cardinals were to oversee musical reform, Carlo Borromeo and Vitellozzo Vitelli. Borromeo was archpriest of Santa Maria Maggiore, where Palestrina was serving, and Vitelli had a private musical establishment. It is recorded that on April 28, 1565, Vitelli assembled the singers of the papal chapel at his home to sing some masses as a test to see whether the words could be understood. Since Palestrina served under Borromeo, it is highly likely that some of Palestrina's music, and perhaps the *Pope Marcellus Mass*, was sung on that occasion.

SIGNIFICANCE

Palestrina's music, with its pure textures, rich sonorities, full harmonies, smooth melodic lines, careful treatment of dissonance, and intelligibility of words, did meet the new Church demands for clear text declamation and music.

Palestrina took the Renaissance vocal polyphony of the previous generation of Franco-Flemish masters and refined, purified, and polished the style. With smooth vocal lines, full harmony, and careful setting of texts, he brought the vocal polyphony of the Renaissance

Counter-Reformation to that state of perfection, which has remained a model of counterpoint ever since.

—*Thomas McGeary*

Further Reading

Coates, Henry. *Palestrina*. London: J. M. Dent, 1948. A classic and very readable account of Palestrina's life and works.

Grout, Donald J., and Claude V. Palisca. *A History of Western Music*. 6th ed. New York: W. W. Norton, 2001. Standard textbook account of Palestrina and his place in Western music history.

Palestrina. *Pope Marcellus Mass*. Edited by Lewis Lockwood. New York: W. W. Norton, 1975. Contains the score of Palestrina's most famous mass, with contemporary documents and modern essays about the mass.

Reese, Gustave, et al., eds. *The New Grove High Renaissance Masters: Josquin, Palestrina, Lassus, Byrd, Victoria*. New York: W. W. Norton, 1984. Presents a biography of Palestrina and discussion of his works from an authoritative English-language music encyclopedia.

Roche, Jerome. *Palestrina*. London: Oxford University Press, 1971. Concise discussion of Palestrina's musical style, with numerous musical examples.

Sadie, Stanley, ed. *The New Grove Dictionary of Music and Musicians*. 20 vols. London: Macmillan, 1980. 2d. ed. 29 vols. London: Macmillan, 2001. Excellent articles on Palestrina, mass, motet, and other related topics in an excellent English-language music encyclopedia.

See also: William Byrd; Andrea Gabrieli; Giovanni Gabrieli; Orlando di Lasso; Luca Marenzio; Maximilian II; Thomas Morley; Saint Philip Neri; Michael Servetus; Saint Teresa of Ávila.

Related article in *Great Events from History: The Renaissance & Early Modern Era, 1454-1600:* 1567: Palestrina Publishes the *Pope Marcellus Mass*.

Andrea Palladio
Italian architect

Palladio was the first great professional architect, one of the most influential the world has ever known, and possibly the most imitated architect in history. He fused Classical proportions and harmony with Renaissance exuberance, thus creating an architectural manner that has endured through the centuries.

Born: November 30, 1508; Padua, Republic of Venice (now in Italy)
Died: August, 1580; Vicenza, Republic of Venice (now in Italy)
Also known as: Andrea di Pietro della Gondola
Area of achievement: Architecture

Early Life

Andrea Palladio (ahn-DRAY-ah pah-LAHD-yoh) was born to Piero, a miller, and Donna Marta, called the cripple. Very little is known of his early years; the record of his activities begins with his apprenticeship in 1521 to a stone carver in the local trade corporation of bricklayers and stonemasons. His master at the corporation of Mount Berico has been identified as Bartolomeo Cavazza de Sossano, the artist responsible for the altar in the Church of Santa Maria dei Carmini in Padua. In 1523, Andrea ran away to Vicenza, where he was followed by Cavazza, who forced him to return to Padua to serve out the rest of his apprenticeship. A year later, the sixteen-year-old Andrea broke his bond and returned to Vicenza, where for the next fourteen years, he was first apprentice and then assistant to two sculptors, Giovanni da Porlezza and Girolamo Pittoni, both of the Pedemuro workshop, who had a near-monopoly on commissions, both private and public, to create many of Vicenza's monuments and ornamental sculptures in the then-popular mannerist style.

Records show that in 1534 Andrea married Allegradonna, the daughter of a carpenter; the union produced five children. Working with the Pedemuro masters gave Andrea a thorough grounding in the techniques of stonework and sculpture, and he might have remained a craftsperson for the rest of his life had he not, at age thirty, met Count Gian Giorgio Trissino.

Trissino hired the young stonecarver to work on a new loggia and a few additions he had designed for his Villa Cricoli on the outskirts of Vicenza. Trissino took Andrea under his wing, housing and educating him with a group of young aristocrats who studied mathematics, philosophy, music, and classical literature. During this period, Andrea was given the appropriately classical name of

Palladio by Trissino. Under Trissino's tutelage, the newly christened Palladio embarked on a far-reaching study of architecture—especially that of Vitruvius—and engineering, as well as ancient topography.

Palladio may have joined Trissino on an extended stay in Padua in the late 1530's; perhaps it was then that Palladio encountered the work of Alvise Cornaro, whose influence is evident in Palladio's elegantly simple and clear writing style and in the economy of ornamentation in his designs. In 1541 and in 1545, Palladio visited Rome with Trissino. During these journeys, Palladio acquired a firsthand knowledge of classical architecture by sketching and measuring the ancient buildings—baths, arches, bridges, temples—whose remains could be seen above ground, and by studying and copying from the sketchbooks of other architects.

Shortly after Palladio returned to Vicenza, he won a commission to refurbish the Palazzo della Ragione, a vast Gothic structure that served as the meeting hall of Vicenza's Council of the Four Hundred. Whatever the council's reasons, their choice of Palladio in 1549 brought him instant recognition, and thereafter he was kept busy with commissions for palaces, villas, and churches.

Trissino died in 1550—a loss not only to Palladio but also to Vicenza's intellectual and artistic community— but by then Palladio was firmly established as an architect with several villas and public buildings under commission. Furthermore, in 1554, he published the results of his study tours in *L'antichità di Roma* (the antiquities of Rome), a small but reliable guidebook to the ancient ruins of Rome that became the standard guidebook to Roman antiquities for two centuries.

LIFE'S WORK

Ever an active student of architecture, Palladio published his ideas and theories in several works issued throughout his career. In 1556, he collaborated with Daniele Barbaro in an edition of Vitruvius. Palladio's greatest piece of writing, *I quattro libri dell'architettura* (1570; *The Four Books of Architecture*, 1738), was published late in his career, after he had devoted two decades to design and building. Using many drawings of his own buildings to exemplify the principles of design to which he tried to adhere, Palladio created an architectural pattern book that dictated building practice throughout Western civilization for four centuries. His last book, *I commentari di C. Givlio Cesare* (1575), is an edition of Julius Caesar's *Commentaries*, with illustrations by Palladio's sons Leonida and Orazio.

Andrea Palladio. (Library of Congress)

Palladio's architectural legacy can be classified loosely into three categories: villas, palaces and public buildings, and ecclesiastical buildings. Contrary to a popular misconception, there is no such thing as a typical Palladian villa. Palladio was far too innovative an architect to rely on one standard design, and his villas display the variety and inventiveness of his work. All the villas, however, share, as James Ackerman wrote, "a common conception of architectural harmony and composition" and a fusion of the practical and the ornamental, the commonplace and the luxurious, modernity and antiquity. Unlike the typical villas of the day, Palladio's villas were nearly all built for gentlemen farmers—men of wealth, culture, and sophistication. In the mid-sixteenth century, many of the great families moved inland to their vast estates to supervise their new ventures. These families needed homes for themselves and for their workers, shelter for their livestock, and storage for their crops. Palladio, already committed to the blending of the utilitarian and the majestic, was the perfect architect to create the new style that had no single architectural ancestry but a style that would integrate the traditional, the classical, and the innovative.

Palladio believed in a hierarchy of functions in design and architecture, and in one of his most famous metaphors, he compared a well-designed building to the human body: In both, the noble and beautiful parts are exposed and the unattractive but essential portions are hidden. Accordingly, his villas are completely functional structures or structural complexes, created both to accommodate the day-to-day business of a large agricultural venture and to disguise that practicality with a grand design drawn from classical architecture. In another departure from common practice, these villas were situated not in walled gardens but central to the activities of the great estates. Palladio's signature element, which appeared on all the villas except Sarego (c. 1568-1569), is a pedimented temple front that appears in some buildings as a porch, in others as a relief. Although this feature appeared in classical architecture only on religious structures, Palladio incorporated it into nearly all his domestic buildings.

None of the palaces for which Palladio created designs was completed; in some cases, only the façades and entrances were built. Only one public building was ever completed. The Veneto region in the mid-sixteenth century was subject to much financial and political instability, which hampered the building of the grand structures envisioned by Palladio's patrons in Vicenza. Modern knowledge of Palladio's intentions comes from the finished façades and sections and from the detailed illustrations of specific designs in *The Four Books of Architecture*. Produced between about 1540 and the early 1570's—with a break of a few years in the late 1560's—the palace designs share with the villas Palladio's distinctive combination of mannerist elements with classical proportion and repose; indeed, four of the palace designs in *The Four Books of Architecture*, of which only the Palazzo Antonini (c. 1556) was even partially built, resemble nothing so much as Palladian villas adapted to narrow city building sites and already crowded streets.

While Palladio's villas and palaces are all in the Veneto region, his churches are all in Venice, in which he was increasingly spending much of his time. It is clear that he traveled often in the 1560's: to Turin, to Provence, to Florence, where he became a member of the Academy of De-

sign, and to Venice, where he met Giorgio Vasari, who became his friend. In 1568, Palladio was so busy that he was forced to decline an invitation to visit the Imperial Court of Vienna.

In his fifties by the time he began to design churches, Palladio believed strongly that church architecture should both glorify God and ornament the city. His commissions—private or civic or monastic, rather than from the Church—reflected his belief that religious architecture, like secular design, should surpass the achievement of earlier builders. Palladio, as well as two contemporaries, Galeazzo Alessi and Giacomo Barozzi da Vignola, developed a church design that took into account both the needs of the liturgical revival and the demands of architectural unity. This new ecclesiastical space combined a substantial nave with large side chapels, all joined but not restricted or blocked by a majestic central space that rose to a dome.

In 1558, Palladio's first ecclesiastical commission (which does not survive) was a design for the façade of San Pietro di Castello in Venice. During the next decade, he worked on a cloister for Santa Maria della Carita; the refectory and cloister and then the Church of San Giorgio Maggiore; and the façade of San Francesco della Vigna, all in Venice. In the decade before his death, Palladio produced four more designs: the Zitelle church (c. 1570) in

---

PALLADIO ON THE PERSISTENCE OF RUINS

Andrea Palladio, in The Four Books of Architecture, *is concerned with the lastingness of the great buildings of the ancient world, namely the Mediterranean region. Here he discusses what makes architecture good and what makes ancient buildings survive through the ages. He remarks also on the beauty of it all, evident even in ruins.*

Whereas it happens sometimes that Buildings are made, the whole, or a good part of Marble, or of some other great Stones; I think it very proper here to explain what the Ancients did on such occasions; because it is to be observ'd in their Works, that they were so nice [precise] in the joining of their Stones together, that sometimes the Joints are difficult to be perceiv'd: which every one ought carefully to consider, who, besides the Beauty, desires also the solidity and lastingness of the Work. . . . Every Person who is not altogether depriv'd of Judgment, may very manifestly perceive, how excellent the manner was, which the Ancients used in the Buildings; seeing that after so long a space of time, after so many destructions and mutations of Empires, there still remain in *Italy*, and out of it, vestiges or ruins of so great a number. . . .

Source: Michelangelo and the Mannerists: The Baroque and the Eighteenth Century. Vol. 2 in A Documentary History of Art, *edited by Elizabeth G. Holt (New York: Anchor Books, 1958), pp. 51, 55.*

Venice, considerably altered by the architects who finished it after Palladio's death; a chapel for the Villa Valmarana in Vicenza (c. 1576); Il Redentore in Venice (c. 1576-1577); and the Tempietto at the Villa Maser (c. 1579-1580). In the Tempietto, Palladio found his opportunity to design a central-plan church, modeled on his ideas for reconstructing the Pantheon in a modern idiom. The Tempietto retains the symbolic cross structure, which is integrated with a unified interior space enclosed by wall masses that support a dome. Palladio's last project was the Teatro Olimpico in Vicenza. Commissioned by the members of the Accademia Olimpica for their regular and elaborate stage performances, the theater is an interpretive reconstruction of an ancient Roman theater in France. Palladio did not live to see the theater completed, although most of the construction was done by the time he died in August, 1580.

SIGNIFICANCE

Appealing more to austere Protestant sensibilities than to Catholic preferences, which favored the exuberance of the Baroque, the restrained Palladian style enjoyed its greatest popularity in the northern European cultural centers. Palladio's ideas and designs first traveled to England through the work of English architect Inigo Jones in the seventeenth century, although the true flowering of the Palladian style had to wait for the eighteenth century and Lord Burlington, who was responsible for the popularization of Palladianism in England. The style spread to Ireland and then to the American colonies, where the simple lines and harmonic proportions of Palladianism dominated in both domestic and public architecture. Not until the classical and Gothic revivals of the nineteenth century would the Palladian style be challenged, but its popularity has remained high even today.

Palladianism has been interpreted variously. To some, it means restraint and simplicity; to others, it signals correct proportions and cool detachment; to the great majority, it denotes a pediment plus a portico on a public building. Basically, the Palladian style is symmetrical, harmonically proportioned, majestic, and based on reason. At the same time, it is classical in its form and in its use of ornamentation. It conforms to Palladio's goals of composition: hierarchy, or the movement of subordinate elements to a dominant focal point; integration of part to part, and part to the whole; coordination between the exterior design and interior structure; and consistency of proportion.

—*Edelma Huntley*

FURTHER READING

Ackerman, James S. *Palladio*. Harmondsworth, England: Penguin Books, 1966. A good general study detailing both Palladio's uniqueness and his borrowings from the past and from his contemporaries. Describes his education, his era, and the physical and cultural environment in which he worked. Provides brief critical introductions to Palladio's major buildings. The text is copiously illustrated with photographs and line drawings.

Boucher, Bruce. *Andrea Palladio: The Architect in His Time*. Rev. and updated ed. New York: Abbeville Press, 1998. Study of Palladio's career and development, tracing the differences between his early, mature, and late works. Incorporates the major research done in the thirty years following the publication of Ackerman's text. Includes illustrations, bibliographic references, and index.

Constant, Caroline. *The Palladio Guide*. 2d ed. New York: Princeton Architectural Press, 1993. Although technically belonging to the genre of the architectural guidebook, this volume theorizes that Palladio's buildings share an integral relationship with and a spatial attitude to the site. Begins with a brief biography and introduction, followed by a chronological listing of the buildings. The body of the book is a series of articles, each devoted to a single villa and arranged chronologically. Features a selected bibliography and maps. Probably too confusing to be used as a guidebook, but the interpretive commentary is most informative.

Guinness, Desmond, and Julius Torusdale Sadler, Jr. *Palladio: A Western Progress*. New York: Viking Press, 1976. A brief account of Palladio's life and achievement, followed by several chapters describing the influence of Palladianism on architecture in England, Ireland, North America, and the West Indies. Very informative; profusely illustrated, primarily with photographs.

Kaufmann, Emil. *Architecture in the Age of Reason: Baroque and Post-Baroque in England, Italy, and France*. Cambridge, Mass.: Harvard University Press, 1955. The first chapter, "English Baroque and English Palladianism," offers a good introduction to Palladio's principles of design and their application in the architecture of eighteenth century England. An extensive bibliography is provided for each chapter.

Puppi, Lionello. *Andrea Palladio*. Boston: New York Graphic Society, 1975. An extensive, exhaustive, and profusely illustrated critical study of Palladio's life and work. The detailed and well-documented catalog of works makes up half of the volume and provides a thorough introduction to Palladio's achievement. An excellent bibliography includes works by Palladio and commentators on his work and covers material from the sixteenth century to the 1970's.

Rybczynski, Witold. *The Perfect House: A Journey with the Renaissance Master Andrea Palladio*. New York: Scribner, 2002. Part architectural treatise, part travel journal, this book recounts an architect's visits to the seventeen surviving Palladio villas and his observations about each one. Includes illustrations, bibliographic references, and index.

Williams, Kim, and Giovanni Giaconi. *The Villas of Palladio*. New York: Princeton Architectural Press, 2003. A collection of pen-and-ink watercolor renderings of all thirty-two of the villas originally designed by Palladio. Also includes sketches, Palladio's original woodcut plans, a color map, and bibliographic references.

Wittkower, Rudolf. *Architectural Principles in the Age of Humanism*. 5th ed. Chichester, West Sussex, England: Academy Editions, 1998. An essential work that laid the foundations of modern Palladian criticism. Discusses Palladio's cultural development, analyzes style in the villas and the ecclesiastical buildings, and provides analyses of Palladian principles.

SEE ALSO: Leon Battista Alberti; Donato Bramante; Jacopo Sansovino; Giorgio Vasari.

RELATED ARTICLES in *Great Events from History: The Renaissance & Early Modern Era, 1454-1600:* c. 1500: Revival of Classical Themes in Art; December 23, 1534-1540: Parmigianino Paints *Madonna with the Long Neck.*

PARACELSUS
Swiss scientist, physician, and scholar

Paracelsus has been hailed as the founder of biochemistry. He also made major contributions to the development of modern chemistry and made revolutionary changes in Renaissance medical theory and practice.

BORN: November 11 or December 17, 1493; Einsiedeln, Swiss Confederation (now in Switzerland)
DIED: September 24, 1541; Salzburg (now in Austria)
ALSO KNOWN AS: Philippus Aureolus Theophrastus Bombast von Hohenheim
AREAS OF ACHIEVEMENT: Chemistry, medicine, philosophy

EARLY LIFE

Philippus Aureolus Theophrastus Bombast von Hohenheim, known as Paracelsus (par-ah-SEHL-sehs), was the only son of a physician, Wilhelm of Hohenheim, who came from a noble Swabian family whose original seat was at Hohenheim, near Stuttgart in northern Germany. Paracelsus's mother, Els Ochsner, came from a family of peasants living on land belonging to the local Benedictine abbey, and she worked as a nurse's aid. Because his illegitimate father had no legal right to the family heritage, Paracelsus was reared in poverty. Yet he said that his home environment was quiet and peaceful, although his mother apparently suffered from manic depression (bipolar disorder) and committed suicide when he was nine.

Following his wife's death, Wilhelm and his son moved to Villach, Austria. Paracelsus probably attended the mining school of the Fuggers at nearby Hutenberg, where his father was a tutor. In Paracelsus's writings, he pays generous tribute to his father, who played a large part in his son's education. Paracelsus also states that he learned from experts, including bishops and an abbot. It is therefore likely that he received what was considered to be a universal education, including Kabbalistic, alchemical, and magical traditions, as well as orthodox religion and philosophy. It is clear, however, that Paracelsus neglected many of the formal aspects of his education. His Latin was not good, nor did he acquire elegance in speech and writing.

In 1507, at the age of fourteen, Paracelsus became a traveling student, attending universities in Germany, Italy, France, and Spain. He studied for a bachelor's degree at Vienna between 1509 and 1511, and between 1513 and 1516, he traveled and studied medicine in Italy, notably at Ferrara. Yet he was a restless, pugnacious, and rebellious student, and he soon found himself completely dissatisfied with the education that was offered by the universities he attended. From 1517 to 1524, he again traveled extensively throughout Europe. He was employed as a military surgeon in Venice and was involved in three wars of the period. He traveled to Moscow when the grand duke Basil invited Western physicians and Humanists to the Russian court, accompanied a Tatar prince on a diplomatic mission to Constantinople, and visited the Holy Land and Alexandria. In all his journeys, Paracelsus was building the knowledge that would enable him to revolutionize many aspects of Renaissance medicine.

LIFE'S WORK

With his fame spreading rapidly and many of his cures being regarded as miraculous, Paracelsus reached Salzburg in 1524. Yet the following year, he was arrested for siding with the peasants in the Peasants' War of 1524-1526 and was forced to flee. In 1526, he arrived in Strasbourg and was entered in the city register as a surgeon. He apparently enjoyed great popularity there and was consulted by many prominent men. Yet he left after less than a year, for unknown reasons. During this period, he wrote eleven treatises on various diseases, ranging from tuberculosis to gout.

Paracelsus. (Library of Congress)

From Strasbourg, he traveled to Basel, where he cured the famous and influential printer Johann Froben. Through Froben, he was introduced to the intellectual elite of Basel, the result being his appointment as municipal physician and professor of medicine at Basel in March, 1527. This influential position proved to be the highlight of Paracelsus's professional life. Yet he made no attempt to moderate his habitually aggressive and combative manner. He challenged the established medical system by saying that he would not accept the authority of Hippocrates or Galen. Instead, he would form his theories from his direct experience in dealing with the sick. In a famous incident, he put Avicenna's classical works on medicine to the bonfire. The authorities retaliated by refusing him the right to lecture and disputing his medical qualifications. Yet Paracelsus continued his work. Defying all tradition, he lectured in German rather than Latin, and he drew large and appreciative audiences. Many were attracted by his credo: "The patients are your textbook, the sickbed is your study."

Perhaps because Paracelsus had made so many enemies, his fortunes soon took a turn for the worse. His benefactor, Froben, died suddenly in October, and shortly afterward a malicious lampoon of Paracelsus appeared. He counterattacked in typical fashion, denouncing past authorities and his colleagues in extreme language: They were all liars, cheats, and fakes, according to him. The situation came to a head when Paracelsus accused the town magistrate of ignorance and bias after a legal suit in which Paracelsus had attempted to collect a promised fee from a patient he had cured. Facing arrest and severe punishment for insulting a high official and with most of the town against him, Paracelsus fled in February, 1528.

After this debacle, he embarked on a new set of journeys, to Alsace, Germany, Switzerland, Bohemia, and Austria, rarely staying more than a few months in one place. In 1529, he was in Nürnberg, but professional doors were closed to him. He responded by proposing to cure any patient who had been declared incurable, and he is reported to have succeeded in nine out of fifteen cases involving lepers. In Nürnberg, he also wrote much, particularly on the disease of syphilis, the most pressing medical problem of the day.

In 1530, he was in Beratzhausen, where he again wrote copiously, including one of his best-known works, the brief *Das Buch Paragranum* (1530; *Against the Grain*, 1894), in which he claimed that medicine should be based on four pillars: natural philosophy, astronomy, alchemy, and virtue. In 1531, he reached Saint Gall, where he wrote *Opus paramirum* (1531), which contains the fundamentals of his medical doctrine. During this period, he also focused strongly on the inner life, writing more than one hundred religious tracts, and he also took to religious preaching.

Facing poverty and adversity wherever he went, he came in 1533 to Appenzell, Switzerland, and to the mining districts of Hall and Schwaz, where he wrote a treatise on the miner's disease—the first ever written on an occupational disease. From Switzerland, he went again to Austria and in 1534 to Sterzing and Meran, living all the time like a beggar and rarely sleeping two nights in the same bed. In 1536, he was in Ulm and Augsburg, where his book on surgery, *Grosse Wundarzney* (1536; *Great Surgery Book*, 1894), was first printed; it said far more about how to avoid surgery than about surgery itself. In 1537, Paracelsus reached Munich and Bohemia, where he began work on his philosophical magnum opus, the *Astronomia magna* (1537-1538; *Great Astronomy*, 1894), which was an attempt to write a comprehensive system of natural philosophy. Highly eclectic but disorderly and inconsistent, it covers a vast range of topics, including humans and the universe, salvation, magical lore, such as the healing power of stones, physiognomy, phrenology, meteorology, and Paracelsus's vision of the development of new technologies.

The best-known and most reliable likeness of Paracelsus, in a portrait by Augustin Hirschvogel, dates from 1537. It shows him clean-shaven and bald on the top of his head, with long unruly hair at the sides. Stern-faced, with deep-set eyes, his solemn expression tells the story of a hard but determined life. Of Paracelsus's last three years, little is known. From August, 1540, he was again in Salzburg, summoned by Archbishop Prince Ernst of Bavaria. On September 21, 1541, he suffered a stroke and died three days later.

SIGNIFICANCE

From Paracelsus's own day to the present, a fierce debate has raged about his contribution to the development of Western science. Some people in his time denounced him as a charlatan, and his modern detractors have argued that his fame is more the result of his colorful and controversial life than any original contributions he made to human thought. On the other hand, his supporters argue that he was a great medical reformer who made substantial achievements in the development of modern chemistry, that he was the founder of biochemistry, and that he also made contributions to gynecology, psychiatry, and even psychotherapy.

In chemistry, it can certainly be said that he worked toward a systematic classification of all known chemical substances and that he devised a method of detoxifying dangerous chemical compounds, which he was then able to use for therapeutic purposes. He also introduced new laboratory methods. The methods of early chemists such as Andreas Libavius, Oswald Croll, and Jan Baptista van Helmont are clearly linked to those of Paracelsus. In medicine, he left accurate descriptions of diseases and had much success in the treating of wounds and chronic ulcers.

Yet if his contributions to modern knowledge are overemphasized, the picture of his work as a whole becomes distorted. He belongs firmly in the Renaissance. His belief in the correspondence between the microcosm and the macrocosm was a commonplace of the period, but it has been rejected by the modern world. Without it, however, much of Paracelsus's work would become unintelligible. He always viewed humans in terms of their relationship with nature and the cosmos as a whole, believing that everything in the inner world corresponded to something in the outer world and that knowledge of this relationship was vital for the healer. The philosophical bases of his views were the esoteric systems of Gnosticism and Neoplatonism. It is this unique coexistence of contradictory elements in his thought, the ancient and the modern, that makes Paracelsus enduringly fascinating.

—*Bryan Aubrey*

FURTHER READING

Debus, Allen G. *The Chemical Philosophy: Paracelsian Science and Medicine in the Sixteenth and Seventeenth Centuries*. Rev. ed. Mineola, N.Y.: Dover, 2002. Corrected edition of a seminal work in the study of Paracelsus, as a scientist and a philosopher of science who put his particular theoretical understanding of nature into scientific practice. Includes illustrations, bibliographic references, and index.

Grell, Ole Peter, ed. *Paracelsus: The Man and His Reputation, His Ideas and Their Transformation*. Boston: Brill, 1998. Collection of essays on the legacy and historical judgments of Paracelsus. Discusses his importance for medicine and science, his political appropriations, and the ways in which historians have variously interpreted his life. Includes illustrations, bibliographic references, and index.

Jung, Carl G. "Paracelsus" and "Paracelsus the Physician." In *The Spirit in Man, Art, and Literature*. Translated by R. F. C. Hull. New York: Pantheon Books,

1966. The first essay is the text of an address delivered by Jung in 1929 at the house in Einsiedeln where Paracelsus was born. Some of the biographical information is inaccurate, but Jung's insights into the essence of Paracelsus, although full of broad generalizations, remain valuable. The second, longer essay, originally given as a lecture in 1941, is one of the best short introductions in English to Paracelsus's thought.

Pachter, Henry M. *Magic into Science: The Story of Paracelsus.* New York: Henry Schuman, 1951. A lively and very readable biography. Pachter tries to rescue Paracelsus from what he sees as an attempt by esoteric groups, including faith healers, mystics, occultists, and homeopaths, to claim Paracelsus as one of their own. Instead, Pachter gives most prominence to those aspects of Paracelsus's work that show his contribution to the development of modern science, including chemistry, chemotherapy, biochemistry, gynecology, and psychiatry.

Pagel, Walter. *Paracelsus: An Introduction to Philosophical Medicine in the Era of the Renaissance.* New York: S. Karger, 1958. One of the best and most comprehensive examinations in English of Paracelsus's work. Excellent on his philosophy, his medical theories and practice, and his sources. Resists viewing Paracelsus exclusively as a forerunner of modern science and medicine, and as a result serves as a useful corrective to Pachter. Instead, shows how Paracelsus forged mystical, magical, and scientific elements into a new synthesis based on personal experience.

Paracelsus. *Selected Writings.* 2d rev. ed. Edited with an introduction by Jolande Jacobi. Translated by Norbert Guterman. Reprint. Princeton, N.J.: Princeton University Press, 1988. One of the best anthologies in English of Paracelsus's writings. Extracts from his works are arranged under thematic headings; references are comprehensive, although only German titles of the works are given. Jacobi's introduction to Paracelsus's life and work, from a Jungian point of view, contains valuable insights. The detailed glossary of Paracelsan terms is an exceptionally valuable aid to study. Includes many illustrations and a bibliography of primary and secondary sources.

Shumaker, Wayne. *The Occult Sciences in the Renaissance: A Study in Intellectual Patterns.* Berkeley: University of California Press, 1972. Extremely useful for understanding the intellectual and cultural milieu in which Paracelsus lived. Shumaker examines five areas of Renaissance thought: astrology, natural or white magic, witchcraft, alchemy, and the body of occult writings associated with the name Hermes Trismegistus. Includes extensive quotations from primary sources, many of which are unavailable in translation elsewhere, illustrations, and an annotated bibliography.

Weeks, Andrew. *Paracelsus: Speculative Theory and the Crisis of the Early Reformation.* Albany: State University of New York Press, 1997. This revisionist account of Paracelsus argues that he must be understood as much in terms of religion as in science. Places his scientific thought as a response to Reformation sectarian conflicts. Includes illustrations, bibliographic references, and index.

Williams, Gerhild Scholz, and Charles D. Gunnoe, Jr., eds. *Paracelsian Moments: Science, Medicine, and Astrology in Early Modern Europe.* Kirksville, Mo.: Truman State University Press, 2002. Wide-ranging anthology of essays on Paracelsus includes a study of his biography as written by his detractors, the role of gender in Paracelsus's model of truth, and a study of Renaissance representations of magic and demonology. Illustrations, bibliographic references, and index.

SEE ALSO: Georgius Agricola; Andrea Cesalpino; Girolamo Fracastoro; Leonhard Fuchs; William Gilbert; Nostradamus; Michael Servetus; Andreas Vesalius.

RELATED ARTICLE in *Great Events from History: The Renaissance & Early Modern Era, 1454-1600:* 1530's-1540's: Paracelsus Presents His Theory of Disease.

MATTHEW PARKER
English church reformer and archbishop of Canterbury (1559-1575)

As the first archbishop of Canterbury under Elizabeth I, Matthew Parker helped the queen achieve a truly national church, whose doctrine, ritual, and organization would be determined by Scripture, church tradition, and royal supremacy. Under Parker's archbishopric, the Anglican church continued as a reformed branch of the Catholic Church rather than as a separate Protestant sect, maintaining religious peace in England.

BORN: August 6, 1504; Norwich, Norfolk, England
DIED: May 17, 1575; London, England
AREAS OF ACHIEVEMENT: Religion and theology, church reform

EARLY LIFE

Matthew Parker was born in the parish of St. Saviour. He was the eldest son of William Parker, a merchant, and his wife, Alice (née Monins). When Matthew Parker was twelve years old, his father died; his mother then married John Baker, a wealthy gentleman who became an excellent stepfather to Parker. Parker was close to all his siblings, especially his brother Thomas, later a mayor of Norwich, and his stepbrother, John, a future benefactor to Corpus Christi College, Cambridge.

Parker was educated at the local grammar school, and in September, 1522, he entered Corpus Christi College, where, in 1525, he earned a bachelor of arts degree. On December 22, 1526, he became a subdeacon; on April 20, 1527, a deacon; and on June 15, 1527, a priest. In 1528, he earned a master of arts degree, and he was soon singled out as a promising theologian and scholar, although of a moderately reforming interest. He was a member of the Cambridge Reformers, a group that included such notable reformation figures as Hugh Latimer. Parker was even charged with heresy in 1539, although the charges were dismissed as being "frivolous."

Parker's popular and dynamic preaching style, however, brought him favor. In 1533, he was licensed to preach through the southern province of England, and on March 30, 1533, he agreed to be chaplain to Anne Boleyn. With this chaplaincy came a deanery at the college of St. John the Baptist at Stoke in Suffolk. In 1535, he received a bachelor of divinity degree at Cambridge and, in 1538, a doctor of divinity degree. In March, 1537, he had also been appointed chaplain to Henry VIII. On December 4, 1544, he was elected master of Corpus Christi College, Cambridge, and a short time later, he became vice-chancellor of the university. On June 24, 1547, he was married to Margaret Harlestone, the daughter of Robert Harlestone of Mattis Hall, Norfolk. Throughout the reign of Edward VI, Parker was valued for his moderate reforms, and on October 7, 1552, he received the rich deanery of Lincoln.

On the accession of Mary Tudor (Queen Mary I), Parker supported the cause of Lady Jane Grey. This support, along with his marriage and earlier friendships with reformers, resulted in the loss of his church preferments. Throughout Mary's reign, Parker lived in fear and concealment. His health, never good, deteriorated even more rapidly after a fall from a horse. He thus devoted his time to theological studies and writing. On the accession of Elizabeth I, his continued poor health prevented him from working on a revision of the prayer book (in 1558), and although Parker preferred a quiet theological life, his virtues recommended him to Elizabeth I. Despite protests because of his poor health, he became archbishop of Canterbury in 1559. For Elizabeth, Parker combined scholarship, administrative experience, loyalty, and moderation; he was free of any taint of Calvinism or continental exile.

LIFE'S WORK

As the archbishop of Canterbury, Parker faced tremendous difficulties. The negotiation of the Elizabethan church settlement had involved unwilling concessions by both the queen and the more radical Protestant reformers. Elizabeth's liturgy contained as wide a selection of sixteenth century doctrinal matter as possible, but for Anglican doctrine to be so comprehensive it necessarily had to remain vague rather than explicit. The emphasis on the Church of England's continuity with the medieval church, the deletion of black rubric on kneeling, the maintenance of vestments, and the inclusion of sentences within the Communion service (implying a belief in real presence) only alienated many Protestant reformers.

In addition, clerical ignorance, minor corruption, and liturgical irregularities abounded. It is, therefore, much to Parker's credit that he so diligently sought to establish this fledgling Anglican church on a firm foundation of Scripture, tradition, and reason.

Deeply conscious of the importance of his own consecration as archbishop to the whole question of episcopal succession in the Church of England, Parker caused an

Matthew Parker. (Library of Congress)

account of the rites and ceremonies to be drawn up and deposited at Corpus Christi College. This account was essential because the Roman ritual was not observed. Indeed, on March 26, 1560, in answer to a letter from deprived bishops denouncing the theory of the new episcopate as subversive of papal authority, Parker drew up a statement declaring the equality of all bishops since the time of the Apostles. This statement has remained a cornerstone of Anglican theology.

After England's refusal to attend the Council of Trent, the Roman Catholic party believed that England's breach with Rome was irreparable. Meanwhile, the more radical British groups expanded their reforms to include the removal of bishops, the elimination of the prayer book, vestments, saints' days, and wedding rings.

Faced with these difficulties and with a queen who would not tolerate any changes, Parker followed a path of what he called, not innovation, but restoration to the times of the more primitive Catholic Church. He reduced the Forty-two Articles of Religion to thirty-nine articles while continuing a policy of no explicit definitions. For use in the universities, he issued a new edition of the prayer book that had large numbers of traditional feasts and saints' days. He saw to it that a new translation of the Bible, which became known as the Bishop's Bible, was undertaken in order that the Geneva Bible's Calvinist influence would be reduced.

By 1563, however, disorders concerning ceremonies and vestments so concerned Elizabeth I that Parker was ordered to exact uniformity. In 1566, Parker's *Advertisements* laid down fixed rules for public service and vestments. Elizabeth urged Parker to use his church courts and rites of visitation more. Much to Parker's horror, his moderate statement only inflamed the Puritan reformers backed by the powerful earl of Leicester. Thirty-seven percent of the London clergy refused to conform and left the church to form the foundation of English Nonconformity.

Meanwhile, at Cambridge University, the assertiveness of the Puritans led by Thomas Cartwright grew. Cartwright represented undiluted Calvinism. A brilliant and determined leader, he advocated sweeping reforms stating that Anglicanism, like Roman Catholicism, was in error for its dependence on church tradition and the early church fathers. Cartwright favored abolishing the episcopal system in favor of Presbyterianism, the election of ministers by congregations, and the elimination of the prayer book along with vestments, crosses, statues, painted glass windows, and organs. Both William Cecil and Parker agreed, however, that no concessions could be made. In 1570, Parker was deprived of his professorship, in 1574, he lost his fellowship at Trinity College, and as a result of a summons by the ecclesiastical commission for his arrest, he fled abroad. Cartwright's writings became the foundation of Presbyterian Nonconformity and represented the most comprehensive attack on everything for which the Anglican church stood.

As a result of all these controversies, a new code was compiled for the universities that modified their constitutions in order to prevent future innovations. In his later years, therefore, though Parker was personally and financially dedicated to the universities, his relations with them were not cordial.

Parker's defense of the Anglican church against the Puritans earned for him the title "the pope of Lambeth." Parker persisted against the Puritans. He removed the Puritan Thomas Aldrich from the mastership of Corpus Christi College, prohibited prophesying on biblical texts in the diocese of Norwich, and saw to it that church patronage and appointments, previously impartial, were now aimed at advancing the careers of those opposed to the Puritan-Calvinist doctrine.

After 1573, Parker withdrew to a more scholarly life. The death of his wife on August 17, 1570, had deeply troubled him. The church controversies made him withdraw from court despite Elizabeth's support. Then in December of 1574, his son Matthew died at the age of twenty-three. Thereafter, Parker's health declined rapidly. He died on May 17, 1575, from kidney disease. He was buried in his private chapel at Lambeth. The Puritans' resentment against him was long-lived, and in 1648, his body was disinterred and buried under a dunghill. At the Restoration, in 1660, his remains and a monument were restored.

Parker died wealthy; many of his bequests were to Corpus Christi College and its library. The library received numerous manuscripts from the monasteries, Anglo-Saxon documents, and thousands of volumes on theology. His preservation of such documents was an invaluable service to future Anglican theologians.

SIGNIFICANCE

Despite Parker's own hesitation about accepting the appointment as archbishop of Canterbury, he proved to be an excellent leader for the foundation of the Church of England under Elizabeth I. With his own preference for moderation and tolerance, he stood firm against the early Puritan attack and oversaw the establishment of an Anglican church that would eventually view itself as absolute and infallible in its interpretations of tradition, Scripture, and history, as did Rome. The importance of Parker's years as archbishop are emphasized even more by the fact that the church was to survive despite the difficulties of its next archbishop, Edmund Grindal. Grindal, who favored Puritan ideas, was sequestered from office in May, 1577, leaving the church without a primate until his death in July, 1583. Grindal's successor, Archbishop John Whitgift, for the most part followed Parker's policies.

Parker's legacy is most visible in that the Anglican church he helped to establish remained uniquely English in its rites, rituals, traditions, and doctrine of a clerical hierarchy. His firm stance against the Puritans, combined with his own broad views, led to the survival of a Church of England accommodating both a High and a Low Church view in one church body on a relatively peaceful basis. The magnitude of this accomplishment becomes clear when England's religious peace is compared with the Continent's religious upheavals and wars.

—Rose Ethel Althaus Meza

FURTHER READING

Brook, V. J. K. *A Life of Archbishop Parker.* Oxford, England: Clarendon Press, 1962. This detailed biography provides a careful if not minute examination of events in which Parker was even marginally involved.

Dickens, A. G. *The English Reformation.* 2d ed. University Park: Pennsylvania State University Press, 1991. Dickens's book stresses the creation of an Anglican church poised between Protestant and Catholic ideals. It shows the complexity and difficulty of working out a compromise between the contending forces. In its emphasis on the unique accomplishments of Anglicanism, it reveals—if unconsciously—that inherent feeling of superiority that Anglicanism came to possess.

Graham, Timothy. "Changing the Context of Medieval Manuscript Art: The Case of Matthew Parker." In *Medieval Art—Recent Perspectives: A Memorial Tribute to C. R. Dodwell*, edited by Gale R. Owen-Crocker and Timothy Graham. New York: Manchester University Press, 1998. An analysis of Parker's role in influencing the conventions of religious manuscript art during his tenure as archbishop of Canterbury. Includes illustrations, bibliographic references, and index.

Graham, Timothy, and Andrew G. Watson, eds. *The Recovery of the Past in Early Elizabethan England: Documents by John Bale and John Joscelyn from the Circle of Matthew Parker.* Cambridge, England: Cambridge Bibliographical Society, 1998. This volume comments on three primary documents from Parker's time: a letter and two bibliographies. All three concern collections of medieval historical and ecclesiastical texts. They demonstrate the kinds of religious scholarship in which Parker was engaged. Includes bibliographic references and indexes.

Grim, Harold J. *The Reformation Era, 1500-1650.* New York: Macmillan, 1964. A standard account of the Continental Reformation, the English Reformation, and the Catholic Counter-Reformation. Excellent for the factual record but not an interpretive history.

Kennedy, William Paul McClure. *Archbishop Parker.* London: Sir Isaac Pitman and Sons, 1908. This biography is still useful; biographies of Parker are in short supply. The emphasis of this book, which is supported by current works in the field, is that Parker played a crucial role in laying the foundation for Anglicanism.

Perry, Edith Weir. *Under Four Tudors: Being the Story of Matthew Parker, Sometime Archbishop of Canterbury.* 2d ed. London: Allen & Unwin, 1964. Perry sees Parker as the vital figure in the creation of an Anglican church. She attributes to Parker's influence, backed by Elizabeth I, the fact that the Church of England continued as a branch of the Catholic Church instead of becoming a separate Protestant sect. Perry also is very revealing on Parker's wife.

Reardon, Bernard M. G. *Religious Thought in the Reformation*. 2d ed. New York: Longman, 1995. This is a detailed theological examination of the Reformation period. Chapters 10 and 11 discuss the complex theological issues of the English Reformation; a reading of these chapters gives an understanding of why problems developed in the Church of England with Puritans, Separatists, and others.

Williams, Neville. *Elizabeth the First, Queen of England*. New York: E. P. Dutton, 1968. This biography provides a vivid portrait of Elizabeth I as a woman of strong opinions. Unlike many biographies of Eliza-beth, it is informative concerning the relationship between Parker and the queen.

SEE ALSO: Anne Boleyn; John Calvin; William Cecil; Miles Coverdale; Edward VI; Elizabeth I; Saint John Fisher; Lady Jane Grey; Henry VIII; John Knox; Hugh Latimer; William Tyndale.

RELATED ARTICLE in *Great Events from History: The Renaissance & Early Modern Era, 1454-1600:* January, 1563: Thirty-nine Articles of the Church of England.

CATHERINE PARR
Queen of England (r. 1543-1547)

Parr, the sixth and last wife of King Henry VIII, wrote about the need to translate the Scriptures so that all people could read and interpret them without the help of priests.

BORN: c. 1512; London, England

DIED: September 5, 1548; Sudeley Castle, Gloucestershire, England

ALSO KNOWN AS: Katherine Parr; Katharine Parr; Catharine Parr

AREAS OF ACHIEVEMENT: Literature, government and politics

EARLY LIFE

Catherine Parr was the daughter of the socially prominent Sir Thomas Parr, who served Britain's royal family. Catherine, Maud Greene, was an heiress from Northamptonshire. The exact date of Catherine's birth remains uncertain. In all likelihood, she was born in 1512. She was married twice before her union with King Henry VIII on July 12, 1543. Henry had already been king of England for some years before Catherine's birth, having ascended to the throne in 1509 to begin his thirty-eight-year reign.

Catherine's first marriage was to Edward Borough, who died in 1529, about a year after their marriage. Catherine next married John Neville, Lord Latimer, who died on March 2, 1543. Neither marriage produced children. Edward Borough, about Catherine's age, was the son of Thomas, Lord Borough, chamberlain to Queen Anne Boleyn, Henry VIII's second wife, who was beheaded as an adulterer. During her marriage to Borough, Catherine resided mostly on the family estates in Lincolnshire. Following her husband's death, Catherine lived on a small income derived from some estates in Kent. She was only twenty years old and living at a time when widows had little status; thus her remarriage, which occurred in 1533, was inevitable.

When Catherine married Lord Latimer, he was about forty years old, twice Catherine's age. He had lost two previous wives and was left with two children, John and Margaret. The marriage took place at about the time of Anne Boleyn's coronation. Catherine, through her husband's official connection with the queen, began to form strong social and political connections at court.

Catherine was highly competent and unquestionably intelligent, although she lacked the coveted classical education available to members of the nobility who became an increasing part of her life. At twenty-one, she was a stepmother and mistress of a large household.

A sensitive person, well attuned to the feelings of those around her, Catherine quickly gained the admiration and love of Margaret Neville, who more than a decade later wrote an encomium to her stepmother in her last will and testament. Catherine's most salient personal characteristic was tact. She had an unerring ability to put people at ease and to understand implicitly their points of view.

Living through England's rift with the Roman Catholic Church, Catherine was a committed Humanist who valued the sentiments of the evangelical Protestant reformers. Respected not only for her tact and compassion, Catherine was also valued for her practical intelligence and devoutness.

Catherine Parr. (Library of Congress)

Catherine gained a further connection with the court when her sister Anne became a lady-in-waiting for Queen Catherine Howard, the king's fifth wife. The king knew Catherine Parr and apparently had designs on her even before her husband died. He gave her a gift on February 16, 1543. Catherine, who was due to come into a great deal of money on Lord Latimer's death, had fallen in love with Thomas Seymour in the preceding year, during which she faithfully attended her dying husband. Despite her attentions to Lord Latimer, Catherine planned to marry Thomas, for whom she felt considerable passion, when Lord Latimer died.

LIFE'S WORK

Catherine Parr is remembered chiefly as the sixth and last wife of King Henry VIII. Her marriage to him lasted for the last three and a half years of the king's life.

Despite his prominence as king of England, Henry VIII had gained an unsavory reputation by the time he was ready to marry for the sixth time. He had shed by divorce or annulment two of his wives, Catherine of Aragon and Anne of Cleves, whose marriage to him was never consummated and lasted less than six months. Two other of his wives, Anne Boleyn and Catherine Howard,

were beheaded after being convicted of adultery, and one wife, Jane Seymour, died from complications twelve days after bearing Henry's son, Edward.

The king was devastated by Jane Seymour's death after only a year of marriage. Despite his devastation, Henry knew that he would be expected to remarry, and he soon took Catherine Howard as his fifth wife. When her adultery was uncovered, he had her beheaded, but hopelessness engulfed him. Ill and overweight, overbearing and dangerously imperious, Henry was far from the sort of person one would choose to marry. He faced the prospect of living his remaining years without a mate.

Shortly before Catherine Howard's execution, Henry had enacted the 1542 Act of Attainder. The act stipulated that if anyone presented a prospective bride to the king and, on marrying her, the king deemed her not to be a virgin, the bride, her family, and the person who first presented her to the king would be guilty of treason, an offense punishable by death. Understandably, the king, seeking to remarry, received few recommendations of prospective brides.

Catherine Parr emerged as one of the few viable candidates to marry Henry VIII and become queen of England. Because she had been married twice before, the question of her virginity was moot. The only obstacle was that Catherine was in love with someone else whom she hoped to marry.

As the king intensified his pursuit of Catherine, however, Catherine was more responsive to the call of duty than to the inclinations of her heart. Therefore, on July 12, 1543, four months after the death of her husband, Lord Latimer, Catherine married the ailing king and became much the sort of wife/nurse she had been to Lord Latimer.

Catherine did everything she could to make Henry happy and comfortable. She sought out medicines that she could apply to his painfully swollen, gout-ravished legs. She was diligent in being a good stepmother to his three children, all of whom responded well to her. From all accounts, it was difficult for people not to like the new queen.

A year after Catherine married him, Henry went on a campaign to France. Having earlier arranged for his daughters, Mary and Elizabeth, to be in line for the throne after Prince Edward and his male offspring, Henry arranged officially for any male child he might have by Catherine to come before Mary and Elizabeth in the line of succession. On July 7, 1544, the minutes of the Privy Council declared Catherine Parr regent to serve in the king's stead during his absence, a responsibility that had been granted previously only to Catherine of Aragon.

During Henry's three months in France, with guidance from Thomas Cranmer, archbishop of Canterbury, Catherine reigned over England. She was the model of a conscientious regent and faithful wife, writing frequently to Henry with proclamations of how much she and England missed him. During his absence, Catherine's signature appeared on all official documents.

As a result of her close association with Thomas Cranmer during her husband's absence, Catherine began to refine some of her own religious views, which had always been slightly subversive. At about this time, Catherine also formed a close relationship with Katherine, duchess of Suffolk, a woman not yet thirty, the death of whose sixty-five-year-old husband left her with considerable wealth and prestige.

The duchess had close ties with religious reformers of her day and sided emphatically with those who wanted everyone to be able to read Scripture rather than have it interpreted for them through a priest. Catherine shared this view, although it is doubtful that Henry agreed with it. She is known to have read and been influenced by Thomas à Kempis's *The Imitation of Christ* (c. 1526) and by Marguerite de Navarre's *Le Miroir de l'âme pércheresse* (c. 1540; *The Mirror of the Sinful Soul*), which her eleven-year-old stepdaughter, Elizabeth, had translated into English for her as a New Year's gift in 1544.

Partly as a result of these readings, Catherine published her *Prayers and Meditations* (1545), which went through nineteen editions in the next half century. Catherine was one of only eight women to publish during the reigns of Henry VII and Henry VIII. Her book was derivative and obviously was published largely because she was queen. That it reached an audience as large as it did and remained popular for as long as it did clearly suggests that it was well received.

Catherine also published *A Lamentation or Complaynt of a Sinner* (1547) shortly after Henry's death. This book was in part an antipapist attack on the Roman Catholic Church, something that would have disturbed Henry. Its most salient plea was for biblical translation so that people could be their own interpreters of Scripture. Henry's daughter Elizabeth, later queen of England, translated Catherine's first book into French, Latin, and Italian when she was a mere eleven years old.

During the king's final year, Catherine frequently entertained the religious reformers of her day in the royal residence. Although Henry was unsympathetic to their cause, he endured their presence because of his regard for Catherine. Some of Henry's conservative followers tried to undermine the queen and went so far as to attempt to

arrest her, but the king struck out against the forty guards who tried to carry out the arrest, and the queen's position was assured.

The king's health declined precipitously in December of 1546. On January 28, 1547, he died. By the end of May in the same year, Catherine, her passion for Thomas Seymour reignited, married him. On August 30, 1548, Catherine bore a daughter, Mary. Barely a week afterward, on September 7, she died from complications associated with childbirth. Catherine, considered unable to conceive because she had remained childless through three marriages, proved herself capable of motherhood but did not survive it.

SIGNIFICANCE

Living in an era when men ruled and women obeyed, Catherine Parr, although compassionate and acquiescent, was a complex woman capable of considerable passion and independence. She embraced many of the Humanistic elements of the New Life, considered quite radical by the conservative ruling class in England during her lifetime.

King Henry VIII seemed truly to have appreciated Catherine, although it was clear that his first love was Jane Seymour, beside whom he is buried. Catherine's first real love after three marriages appears to have been Thomas Seymour, whom she wed shortly after Henry's death.

Catherine in her day was an emancipated woman. That she published set her apart, but the sentiments in her second book, *A Lamentation or Complaynt of a Sinner*, were extremely radical for her day.

—*R. Baird Shuman*

FURTHER READING

Beilen, Elaine. *Redeeming Eve: Women Writers of the English Renaissance*. Princeton, N.J.: Princeton University Press, 1987. This study presents Parr in the context of her writing.

Fraser, Antonia. *The Wives of Henry VIII*. New York: Alfred A. Knopf, 1992. Fraser's book is thorough, carefully researched, and eminently readable, devoting some sixty fact-filled pages to Parr.

James, Susan E. *Kateryn Parr: The Making of a Queen*. Brookfield, Vt.: Ashgate, 1999. Study argues that Parr was a more important figure in English history than is commonly acknowledged. Looks at her influence on Henry's court, and on Elizabeth I, both as a model to the queen and as someone who protected Elizabeth's life and made it possible for her to become queen in the first place. Includes photographic plates, illustrations, bibliographic references, and index.

Lindsey, Karen. *Divorced, Beheaded, Survived: A Feminist Reinterpretation of the Wives of Henry VIII*. New York: Addison-Wesley, 1995. Lindsey's feminist assessment of Henry's wives is particularly lucid in its discussion of the plot in Henry's court to discredit Parr shortly before Henry's death. Also contains good discussions of Elizabeth's love for Parr and of Parr's emotional involvement with Thomas Seymour.

Loades, David. *Henry VIII and His Queens*. Stroud, Gloucestershire, England: Sutton, 2000. This short and highly readable work by a respected British historian provides a useful introduction to the topic.

Martienssen, Anthony. *Queen Katherine Parr*. New York: McGraw-Hill, 1974. Dated and in some particulars inaccurate, as new information has been unearthed since its publication. Nevertheless, as the only modern full-length study of Parr, it makes a significant contribution to the scholarship on her.

Parr, Katherine. *Katherine Parr*. Vol. 3 in *The Early Modern Englishwoman: A Facsimile Library of Essential Works*, edited by Betty S. Travitsky and Patrick Cullen. Brookfield, Vt.: Ashgate, 1996. Collected volume of Parr's essential writings, demonstrating her skill and breadth as an author. Includes illustrations and bibliographic references.

Plowden, Allison. *Tudor Women: Queens and Commoners*. New York: Atheneum, 1979. Despite its age, this book places Parr in an interesting context that reveals much about the social standing of women in the sixteenth century.

Starkey, David. *Six Wives: The Queens of Henry VIII*. New York: HarperCollins, 2003. Emphasizes the religious and political complexities of Henry's court, and fleshes out many of the significant players in that milieu, in order better to understand the lives, careers, and deaths of each of Henry's wives.

Weir, Alison. *The Six Wives of Henry VIII*. London: Pimlico, 1991. Weir offers succinct and penetrating insights into Parr and her ability to manage a marriage relationship with a man whose marital record was questionable.

SEE ALSO: Anne of Cleves; Anne Boleyn; Catherine of Aragon; Clement VII; Thomas Cranmer; Thomas Cromwell; Elizabeth I; Henry VIII; Catherine Howard; Marguerite de Navarre; Mary I; Sir Thomas More; Jane Seymour; The Tudor Family; Cardinal Thomas Wolsey.

RELATED ARTICLE in *Great Events from History: The Renaissance & Early Modern Era, 1454-1600:* May, 1539: Six Articles of Henry VIII.

PAUL III
Italian pope (1534-1549)

Pope Paul III was the last of the Renaissance popes, aristocratic, educated in the classics, with the concerns of his family often paramount. Yet he was also the first pope of the Catholic or Counter-Reformation, and it was he who summoned the Council of Trent, whose decisions governed the Church in subsequent centuries.

BORN: February 29, 1468; Canino, Papal States (now in Italy)
DIED: November 10, 1549; Rome, Papal States (now in Italy)
ALSO KNOWN AS: Alessandro Farnese
AREAS OF ACHIEVEMENT: Religion and theology, church reform

EARLY LIFE
Paul III, born Alessandro Farnese, was part of an old aristocratic family whose lands in central Italy were located between Rome and Florence. Generally supportive of the Papacy in its struggles with the Holy Roman Empire, over time the family owned a large amount of land. Yet it was not until early in the fifteenth century that the Farneses succeeded in becoming important in Rome, an event occasioned by a successful marriage. Educated in classical studies in Florence in the establishment of Lorenzo de' Medici, Farnese entered the Church, and inasmuch as it was the era of Renaissance Humanism, the choice was probably more for social than for spiritual reasons.

His sister Giulia, the favorite mistress of Alexander VI, head of the Borgia family, was able to advance Farnese's career, and when he became a cardinal in the Church at the age of twenty-five, many claimed that it was a result of her influence. He well might have succeeded anyway; members of his class often rose to the highest positions in the Church during that era. He was properly educated, intelligent and shrewd, and had a pleasing manner. After becoming a cardinal, he maintained one of the most opulent palaces in Rome. Although as a cleric he could not marry, he did father several children out of wedlock, which was not unusual among the clergy at that time. He subsequently supervised their upbringing and furthered their careers.

Although Farnese had been a cardinal for many years, it was not until he was about fifty that he took holy orders and became a priest. His abilities and ambition had long been recognized. In 1521, he was one of the alternative candidates to Clement VII, and afterward Farnese became Clement's chief adviser. It was predicted that he would succeed to the papal throne after Clement, and he did so in 1534, against little opposition, at the advanced age of sixty-seven. He took the name Paul III.

LIFE'S WORK

Paul's accession was acclaimed among most factions in Christendom. Because of his age, many believed that his reign would be brief and his impact on events slight. As a Roman, he was popular among the city's populace. As he was an aristocrat, his selection was no threat to the hierarchical social order. Because of his Humanistic education, many felt assured that those values would be maintained. Unlike many previous popes, Paul was not tainted with much of the corruption associated with the papal office, this in spite of his own illegitimate children.

It was a complex and difficult time. Paul would probably have preferred to continue in the tradition of most then-recent popes, focusing mainly on secular concerns and pleasures. In 1517, however, Martin Luther began his public criticism of the Catholic Church, and by 1534, the demands of the Protestant Reformers were threatening to tear apart the fabric of the Church and the unity of Christendom. In addition, there were military and political struggles that often impinged on the security of Italy and the Papal States and even, it seemed, the survival of the Church itself. In 1527, the forces of Emperor Charles V had captured and sacked Rome, a traumatic event not only for the Romans but also for the Papacy.

It is probable that Paul was chosen pope as much for his diplomatic and political abilities as for his spiritual commitments. If so, it was a good choice; in the years that followed, Paul succeeded in maintaining his, and the Church's, independence, and the Papacy did not become merely a pawn in the game of power politics, a possibility that seemed likely at the time of his accession.

Paul believed that, in order to resist the various religious and political threats to the Catholic Church, it was necessary to make changes in the papal court itself. The

transitional nature of Paul's reign can be seen by his choice of new cardinals. Two were his teenage grandsons, but others, such as John Fisher, Reginald Pole, Gasparo Contarini, and Gian Pietro Caraffa, proved to be significant selections. Pope Paul also appointed a commission of cardinals to make recommendations regarding possible reforms. When the report was submitted in 1537, it was critical of many past clerical appointments. The buying and selling of church offices and legal decisions from the various church courts was condemned, as were the abuses in the sale of indulgences. It was argued that even the absolute authority of the popes needed to be changed and that Rome itself should be cleansed of corruption. Paul refused to have the report published, but soon unauthorized editions were circulating throughout Europe. Most Protestants were in the process of weakening the authority of the clergy, but the cardinals, and Paul, were more concerned with strengthening the clergy through reform.

Paul III. (Library of Congress)

Progress was slow. Paul, cautious and conservative, was unwilling to alter the existing system radically, but in 1540, he ordered the banishment of numerous church officials who were improperly residing in Rome. Paul also entertained the possibility of summoning a general church council to reform the Catholic Church, but he was opposed to any weakening of papal authority, and in the past councils had often attempted to place limits on the Papacy. There was no unity on the matter of a council outside the Church. The Protestants were as reluctant to accept a council's authority and its decisions as to follow papal demands. Various European rulers, in an age of rising nationalism, were unwilling to compromise their freedom of action to any supranational body such as the Church had been in the Middle Ages. Charles V was especially in a difficult position. He was a loyal Catholic, but by the 1530's many of his German subjects had become fervent Protestants. His need for peace within Germany and for support against both Francis I of France and the invasion by Muslim Turks, however, meant that he had to make peace with his Protestant citizens. He desired compromise in a world of increasing polarization. An attempt was made in 1541, at Ratisbon, but little was accomplished. The differences between the two factions were already too great.

Many doubted Paul's own commitment to reform. He had, against considerable opposition, made his illegitimate son a duke from lands of the Papal States, and he continued to help with the private interests of his own family, including negotiating the marriage of a grandson to the illegitimate daughter of Charles V. Could such a figure of Renaissance Rome be taken seriously as a religious reformer? He was committed, but only under the condition that the council remain under the firm leadership of the Papacy. Finally, Paul called for a general council to meet in northern Italy at Trent, a compromise location not too far from Rome but also within the lands of the Holy Roman Empire. For a number of reasons—military, political, diplomatic, and personal—the council was postponed and did not formally begin until December, 1545. Although meeting only sporadically over many years, it proved to be a momentous event in the furthering of the religious reformation of the Catholic Church itself as well as countering the accomplishments and appeals of Luther, John Calvin, and other Protestants.

Paul also gave his support to two other significant events of the Counter-Reformation. In 1540, he gave his consent to the formation of a new religious order, the Society of Jesus, under the leadership of Ignatius of Loyola. Loyola had been a controversial figure and had been im-

prisoned by Catholic officials in Spain before moving to Paris and then to Rome in 1538. Initially, Paul was reluctant to grant Loyola's request: Too much fanatical enthusiasm was suspect by the Farnese aristocrat. Yet one of his own cardinals, Gasparo Contarini, convinced him to charter the Jesuits, who then owed allegiance directly to the Papacy. Under Loyola and his successors, the order, in its commitment to missionary activity and to the teaching of approved Catholic doctrine, became one of the most important elements in the Counter-Reformation.

In 1542, Paul granted to Cardinal Gian Pietro Caraffa, another of his appointments to the curia, the office of inquisitor-general of the Inquisition, giving Caraffa full authority in Italy. Influenced by the earlier Spanish Inquisition, Caraffa soon made his mark in rooting out Lutherans and other heretics within and without the clergy. Under Paul, a person of the Renaissance, Caraffa's Inquisition was somewhat limited, but when Caraffa was elected pope as Paul IV in 1554, the Inquisition became more threatening to the unorthodox in religious belief and practice.

Paul III reigned as pope for fifteen years in spite of his advanced age. In 1545, somewhat reluctantly, he gave Parma and Piacenza to his illegitimate son, Pier Luigi. The lands belonged to the Papal States, but it was argued that they could be better defended by their own ruler. It was an extravagant example of papal nepotism. Pier Luigi became the first duke. The decision was not popular, and Pier Luigi was assassinated in 1547. Emperor Charles V demanded the cession of Parma, and when Paul considered instead making a member of the Orsini family the new duke of Parma, his own grandchildren, fearing a loss of their recently achieved patrimony, began negotiations with the emperor. The rebellion of his family was too much for the eighty-one-year-old pope, and he died in Rome on November 10, 1549.

SIGNIFICANCE

In 1543, Titian painted the portrait of Paul III. The pope was then in his mid-seventies, a formidable age. In the artist's rendition, however, Paul still shows his qualities of authority and perseverance. His white beard and aged wrinkles are countered by the focus of his eyes, which appear to be concentrating on one of his many concerns—Charles V, Francis I, Loyola, or Caraffa. His years as pope were as momentous as any in the long history of the Catholic Church. An individual of the Renaissance, he was forced to confront an era of spiritual renewal that was perhaps foreign to his essential nature. As leader of the Church universal, he faced a world of rising nationalism. Nevertheless, Paul, while remaining a product of his immediate past, also transcended it.

By cautiously committing himself to the reform of the Church, he helped pave the way for its rehabilitation. At one time, it seemed as if the Protestants would totally replace the Roman church with a reformed church, or churches, but that was not to be. For his support of change within the papal curia, his willingness to countenance the activities of new Catholic reformers such as Loyola, his support of the Inquisition under Caraffa, and most of all his summoning of the Church council that met at Trent, Paul, in spite of his secular background, his family concerns, and his conservative nature, must rank among the most important of the popes during the early modern period.

—Eugene Larson

FURTHER READING

Burns, Edward McNall. *The Counter Reformation.* Princeton, N.J.: D. Van Nostrand, 1964. The author has combined a brief narrative of the events and figures of the era with a selection of documents. There is no full biography of Paul III in English, but Burns gives a succinct account of his life and activities.

Dickens, A. G. *The Counter Reformation.* New York: Harcourt, Brace & World, 1969. Dickens, an English academic, is one of the most influential historians of sixteenth century religion. This volume is an excellent survey, with many illustrations, of the era of the Counter-Reformation.

Freedman, Luba. *Titian's Portraits Through Aretino's Lens.* University Park: Pennsylvania State University Press, 1995. This study of painterly and poetic portraiture contains a chapter on Pope Paul III and his relationship to his portraits. Includes illustrations, bibliographic references, and index.

Luebke, David M., ed. *The Counter-Reformation: The Essential Readings.* Malden, Mass.: Blackwell, 1999. Collection of essays surveying Counter-Reformation scholarship in the second half of the twentieth century from the points of view of a variety of disciplines. Includes bibliographic references and index.

Mullett, Michael A. *The Catholic Reformation.* New York: Routledge, 1999. Building on his earlier scholarship, Mullett traces the entire history of the Catholic Reformation, beginning with its roots in the Middle Ages, as well as the impact of the movement on the arts and on the daily lives of ordinary people. One chapter details the mutual influence of the Papacy on the Counter-Reformation and of the Counter-Reformation on the Papacy. Includes bibliographic references and index.

_____. *The Counter-Reformation and the Catholic Reformation in Early Modern Europe.* London: Methuen, 1984. This brief pamphlet not only covers the major events but also provides a bibliographical account of the various interpretations by historians of the Catholic reformation and the era of Paul III.

Ranke, Leopold von. *The History of the Popes During the Last Four Centuries.* Translated by E. Foster. London: George Bell & Sons, 1907. Ranke, the great German historian of the nineteenth century and the father of scientific history, portrays Paul III as a secular figure, diplomatically and politically astute, whose support for the religious reform of the Catholic Church had little to do with any deeply felt spiritual concerns.

Solari, Giovanna R. *The House of Farnese.* Translated by Simona Morini and Frederic Tuten. Garden City, N.Y.: Doubleday, 1968. The author has written a popular history of the Farnese family, beginning with the life of Alessandro Farnese, Paul III. The volume focuses primarily on personalities and family activities.

Pemisapan
Chief of Roanoc and Secotan nations

Pemisapan was the first North American Indian to be confronted by English explorers of the New World, and he was one of the first victims of the hostility that developed between the English and the American Indians during Sir Walter Ralegh's attempt to establish the first English colony.

Born: Date unknown; place unknown
Died: June 1, 1586; Dasamonquepeuc (now in North Carolina)
Also known as: Wingina
Areas of achievement: Government and politics, warfare and conquest

Early Life

Nothing is known for certain about the early years of the life of Pemisapan (peh-mee-SAH-pahn). He was a son of Ensinore and was known originally as Wingina. At some point, his father became *manamatowick*, or king, of the tribes inhabiting what is now called Roanoke Island, North Carolina, and the western neighboring mainland to the Neuse River. As ruler of the Roanoc or Secotan nation, Ensinore exercised his power through local sub-kings and warriors called *weroances*.

As a young male of that class, in an Algonkian-speaking Eastern Woodlands culture, Wingina's upbringing and training would have centered on military and political leadership and hunting skills and would have probably included an initiation ritual into manhood called the *huskanaw*. Initiates between ten and fifteen years of age would be taken into the woods for months, given hallucinogenic drugs fashioned from roots, occasionally beaten, and usually caged.

Prior to 1582, Ensinore retired as *manamatowick* in favor of Wingina, and his other son Granganimeo became a *weroance* of Roanoke Island. Competition for resources in what was a subsistence economy that centered on hunting, fishing, and the cultivation of corn, squash, beans, gourds, and pumpkins was keen, and warfare with neighboring Neiosioke and Pamlico nations occurred quite frequently. In 1582, the Neiosiokes allegedly fell on some Roanocs while at a peaceful get-together, murdering the men and taking some thirty women and children as slaves. At the time of the first reconnaissance expedition by the English in 1584, Wingina was recuperating from severe wounds sustained in battle with either the Neiosiokes or Pamlico at his mainland town of Secotan. (He had reportedly sustained two wounds to his body, one going straight through his thigh.) It was his brother Granganimeo who made the initial contact with the English explorers, Philip Amadas and Arthur Barlowe.

Life's Work

Initial contact proved friendly, and Amadas and Barlowe, who had been dispatched to the New World by Sir Walter Ralegh, took back to England with them (undoubtedly with Wingina's consent) two younger Indians: Manteo and Wanchese.

The following year, however, the English returned and brought back Manteo and Wanchese, but they also established a military colony under command of Captain Ralph Lane, who built a redoubt on Roanoke Island, which he called Fort Ralegh. Relations began to deteriorate after Lane's superior, Sir Richard Grenville, before returning to England, massacred the Roanocs at the village of Aquascogoc in retaliation for the theft of a silver cup. The English awed the Indians with their firearms, armor, and steel weapons, but they did not grow their own food; the English depended on the Roanocs and other Indians to supply them with food, which strained the resources of an already fragile economy. The imperious and arrogant attitude of some Englishmen, Lane among them, and cultural miscommunications contributed to an increased atmosphere of mistrust.

Despite requests by the Roanocs for the English to assist them in waging war against their Neiosioke and Pamlico enemies, Lane refused to get involved, and this may have been interpreted as a sign of gross ingratitude on the part of the newcomers. As European diseases such as smallpox began taking a toll on the indigenous population and Roanoc society began to unravel, an anti-English party (that included Wanchese) began to emerge. Wingina himself seemed to vacillate, but for the time being appeared to listen to the *weroances* who favored cooperating with the English. Notable among them were Ensinore and Granganimeo, who believed that Lane and his men were actually long-dead ancestors who had returned to life.

Changes occurred early in 1586. In March, Granganimeo succumbed to what was probably smallpox or measles. Wingina changed his name to Pemisapan. Then, on April 20, 1586, the aged Ensinore sickened and died—also most likely because of smallpox or measles—and the last effective pro-English voice was eliminated from the ruling council, a fact that was not lost on Lane, who gathered information from Indians such as Manteo, who remained friendly to the English.

Having long suspected Pemisapan's true intentions, Lane was convinced that the chieftain was concocting a plot to annihilate Fort Ralegh's garrison. Lane had heard that Pemisapan was going to attempt to assemble at least seven hundred warriors from the Roanoc, Weampemeoc, Chawanoac, and other adjacent nations to burn the fortress on June 10, 1586. Lane later said the story was based on intelligence passed on to him by Skyco, a young *weroance* of the Chawanoac nation (allied to Pemisapan) whom Lane was holding hostage.

There had been debate as to whether the plot actually existed or whether, at best, Lane was breaking under the strain and had become delusional. Thomas Hariot, a scientist who accompanied the expedition, of which he would write his own account, was highly skeptical and had always asserted that Pemisapan had acted honorably.

Lane was determined to make a preemptive strike, an ambush, and on June 1, 1586, sailed from Roanoke Island to the mainland town of Dasamonquepeuc, where Pemisapan was known to be staying. On encountering Pemisapan and his *weroances* in the village, Lane ordered his men to fire by uttering the prearranged command "Christ, our victory!" Pemisapan was among those who fell, but within a few moments he got up again and ran toward the woods. Shot again before he reached the underbrush, he was pursued and eventually slain by a soldier named Edward Nugent, who returned to Dasamonquepeuc to present Lane with Pemisapan's severed head.

SIGNIFICANCE

Pemisapan's fate might be seen as a prototype of the antagonism that still haunts American Indians and Europeans. Though Pemisapan's assassination might have eased the threat to Lane's colony temporarily, the English left with Sir Francis Drake's fleet three weeks later. It is probable that Lane's actions made it more difficult for the second Roanoke Island settlement (the Lost Colony) of 1587-1588 and even to have ensured its ultimate failure.

—Raymond Pierre Hylton

FURTHER READING

Durant, David N. *Ralegh's Lost Colony: The Story of the First English Settlement in America*. New York: Atheneum, 1981. Strongly slanted toward Lane's version of events, to the point of granting him heroic stature,

and supportive of the theory of duplicity on Pemisapan's part.

Hulton, Paul. *America 1585: The Complete Drawings of John White*. Chapel Hill: University of North Carolina Press, 1984. The best visual account of the Roanoke settlement. Includes depictions of Secotan, life among the Roanocs, and perhaps the only pictorial likeness of Pemisapan.

Miller, Lee. *Roanoke: Solving the Mystery of the Lost Colony*. New York: Penguin, 2002. An iconoclastic work that takes a radically different view, arguing that Lane was paranoid and becoming mentally ill and that Pemisapan's plot was nonexistent.

Morison, Samuel Eliot. *The European Discovery of America: The Northern Voyages, A.D. 500-1600*. New York: Oxford University Press, 1971. Believes in the conspiracy but blames Grenville rather than Lane for having poisoned intercultural relations between American Indians and Europeans.

Quinn, David Beers. *Set Fair for Roanoke: Voyages and Colonies, 1584-1606*. Chapel Hill: University of North Carolina Press, 1985. Gives a matter-of-fact narration that attempts to place the Roanoke colonies into a larger perspective.

Rountree, Helen C. *The Powhatan Indians of Virginia: Their Traditional Culture*. Norman: University of Oklahoma Press, 1989. A detailed depiction of Eastern Algonkian society, with a particularly thorough analysis of the *huskanaw* ceremony.

Rountree, Helen C., and E. Randolph Turner, III. *Before and After Jamestown: Virginia's Powhatans and Their Predecessors*. Gainesville: University of Florida Press, 2002. In the absence of substantial material on the Outer Banks Algonkians, this detailed account of a similar, neighboring society is highly useful.

Stick, David. *Roanoke Island: The Beginnings of English America*. Chapel Hill: University of North Carolina Press, 1986. The most balanced and impartial attempt to discern Pemisapan's motives. Leaves it open to question as to whether there was a true conspiracy.

SEE ALSO: Thomas Cavendish; Deganawida; Sir Francis Drake; Sir Humphrey Gilbert; Sir Richard Grenville; Hiawatha; Kalicho; Sir Walter Ralegh; Tascalusa.

RELATED ARTICLE in *Great Events from History: The Renaissance & Early Modern Era, 1454-1600:* July 4, 1584-1590: Lost Colony of Roanoke.

GEORG VON PEUERBACH
Austrian mathematician and astronomer

A pre-Copernican astronomer, Peuerbach accepted, reintroduced, and extended the ideas of Ptolemy and made original astronomical observations. His published works include a look at new theories of the planets, which became a standard astronomy textbook, and an aid for the calculation of eclipses.

BORN: May 30, 1423; Peuerbach, Austria
DIED: April 8, 1461; Vienna, Austria
ALSO KNOWN AS: Georg von Purbach; Georg von Peurbach; Georgius Aunpekh de Pewrbach
AREAS OF ACHIEVEMENT: Mathematics, astronomy

EARLY LIFE

Georg von Peuerbach (gay-awrg fawn PEWR-bahk) was born in Upper Austria. Other than his father's name, Ulrich, nothing is known about his early years. In 1446, he entered the University of Vienna with the name Georgius Aunpekh de Pewrbach, and earned a bachelor's degree in 1448. By this time, he had probably already begun the study of astronomy under the followers of John of Gmunden (d. 1442).

Between 1448 and 1453, Peuerbach traveled to several countries, including France, Germany, and Italy, and lectured in Padua and Ferrara. In Ferrara, he met the most important contemporary Italian astronomer, Giovanni Bianchini, who tried to convince him to teach at an Italian university; Peuerbach had been given offers to teach at Bologna and Padua. In his later years, Peuerbach knew Nicholas of Cusa, and it is possible that he met him in Rome during this period. Peuerbach received a master's degree from the University of Vienna in 1453. Around this time, he became the teacher and colleague of Johann Müller, known as Regiomontanus.

From 1453 to 1456, Peuerbach corresponded with the imperial astrologer to Holy Roman Emperor Frederick III, in Wiener Neustadt. With the astrologer's encouragement, the impoverished Peuerbach accepted in 1454 the position of court astrologer to King László V of Hungary, and later became the imperial astrologer.

While Peuerbach's service to king and emperor employed his knowledge of astronomy and astrology, his contribution to the University of Vienna involved Humanistic studies. He was among the scholars who brought the revival of classical learning to the University of Vienna by lecturing on Vergil's *Aeneid* (c. 29-19 B.C.E.), on Juvenal, and possibly on Horace, and by participating in a disputation on the art of oratory and poetics in 1458. Scholars believe that Peuerbach was the author of a treatise on letter writing. He also wrote poetry in Latin.

LIFE'S WORK

Peuerbach's correspondence with Nihil reveals that during the 1450's, Peuerbach engaged in the construction of horseshoe-shaped sundials with magnetic needles, the making of almanacs—necessary for his astrological work—and the interpretation of comets. For his almanacs, Peuerbach revealed that he had mastered the use of the thirteenth century Alfonsine tables, the first set of astronomical tables in Europe, to determine planetary positions and movement and that he was learning to use the newer tables of Bianchini. Twenty works by Peuerbach are known.

With the 1456 appearance of Halley's comet, Peuerbach became the first to attempt to calculate the length of a comet's tail and a comet's diameter. His results—4 German miles (one German mile equals 25,000 feet, or 7,620 kilometers) for the diameter and 80 German miles for the tail—were erroneous, however, because he based them on the doubtful values for the diameter of Earth and the distance of the Moon computed by Ptolemy (c. 100-c. 178) and Archimedes (c. 287-212 B.C.E.). This work provided inspiration for Regiomontanus and sixteenth century astronomers to produce additional important works about comets.

Peuerbach contributed also to the measurement of space and time. Among the instruments on which he wrote papers were the astrolabe quadrant, the astrolabe, a sundial with gnomon, and the geometric square, a device to measure the heights of constellations and other distant terrestrial objects. The geometric square had rods forming a square, with 1,200 gradations on two of the rods and movable points with a sighting hole. He also invented an instrument to represent the true new moon.

Much of Peuerbach's work involved direct observations. He revised the latitude of Vienna, setting it at 48.22°, closer to the modern value of 48.12°. With Regiomontanus, he observed a lunar eclipse in 1457 and two in 1460. As calculations based on the Alfonsine tables gave an incorrect midpoint for the 1457 eclipse, Peuerbach reorganized and expanded the tables to facilitate computations greatly. Finished around 1459 and available in manuscript form, the work was edited and published in 1514 as *Tabulae eclipsium super meridiano*

Viennensi (tables of eclipses above the Viennese meridian). Astronomers throughout the sixteenth century recognized the monumental efforts put into the work. Peuerbach and Regiomontanus used the *Tabulae eclipsium super meridiano Viennensi* to determine the eclipses of 1460.

Peuerbach was the author of an extremely important textbook based on Ptolemy's second century Earth-centered astronomy, *Theoricae novae planetarum* (English translation, 1987), published by Regiomontanus in 1474. The standard text until this time had been the anonymously written *Theorica planetarum communis* (thirteenth century; theory of the planets). The topics covered in Peuerbach's text covering new theories of the planets include the Sun, Moon, superior planets, Venus, Mercury, eclipses, the theory of latitude, and the motion of the eighth sphere based on the Alfonsine tables. As an elementary work, it provided many definitions of technical terms. In this work, Peuerbach attempted to reconcile two conceptions explaining the motion of the planets: the planet-bearing crystalline spheres, which Ptolemy accepted in *Hypotheseis ton planomenon* (planetary hypotheses) and the epicycle/deferent system of Ptolemy. He presented a model of the solid spheres based on the work of the Arab mathematician and astronomer, Alhazan (965-1039). These spheres remained part of the astronomical tradition until disproved by Tycho Brahe.

Peuerbach also explained the particular motions of the planets according to Ptolemy's epicycles. It may also be pointed out the Peuerbach suggested that the Sun controlled the motions of the planets and thus anticipated the new role the Sun acquired during the scientific revolution.

Another major work was Peuerbach's abridgment of Ptolemy's *Mathēmatikē suntaxis* (c. 150; better known as *Almagest*, 1952). In 1460, Cardinal Bessarion, a Greek scholar and Catholic Church official, invited Peuerbach to prepare an epitome of the *Almagest*, that is, a short, understandable translation with explanatory comments, which was called *Epitoma magesti Ptolemaei* (1496). Peuerbach knew Gerard's Latin translation almost by memory, but insisted on the aid of Regiomontanus, who knew Greek and could work with the original. Peuerbach had finished six of the thirteen books when he died at age thirty-seven, having obtained a promise from Regiomontanus to complete the translation. Regiomontanus completed it by 1463 and died in 1476. The epitome was first published in 1496 with many errors, but better editions appeared in 1543 and 1550.

Other contributions include Peuerbach's work in mathematics. He wrote a short treatise on the computation of sines and chords. In another work, he presented computations of sines at intervals of ten minutes. Following the work of Arab scholars, he recognized for astronomical calculations the superiority of using sines rather than chords, which Ptolemy had used. Finally, he produced a popular elementary mathematical book on computation using integers and fractions, a book that was printed several times in the late fifteenth and early sixteenth centuries. Peuerbach is also noted for using Arabic numerals, which were still not universally employed in the fifteenth century.

SIGNIFICANCE

Peuerbach's work clarified Ptolemy's astronomy and helped to bring consistency to the work of Peuerbach's contemporaries. His influence continued until after Copernicus began the revolution that overturned Ptolemaic, Earth-centered astronomy.

His *Theoricae novae planetarum* and *Epitoma magesti Ptolemaei* provided contemporary scholars with definitions of technical terms employed until the early seventeenth century. *Theoricae novae planetarum* went through fifty-six editions by 1650 and was the subject of numerous commentaries.

To the time of Galileo and Kepler, scholars, including Copernicus, relied on the *Epitoma magesti Ptolemaei* as the basic treatise on Ptolemy's astronomy. Finally, astronomers used his tabulae well into the sixteenth century, when new astronomical tables were prepared.

Peuerbach represents the use of Arabic learning in the West because he worked with Arabic numerals in computing sines, and he adopted the crystalline spheres of the Alfonsine tables.

—Kristen L. Zacharias

FURTHER READING

Aiton, E. J. "Pürbach's *Theoricae novae planetarum:* A Translation with Commentary." *Osiris* (2d series) 3 (1987): 4-43. A short description of Peuerbach's life that introduces the translation of his important theory of the planets, including drawings of planetary motions.

Dobrzycki, J., and R. L. Kremer. "Pürbach and Maragha Astronomy? The Ephemerides of Johannes Angelus and Their Implications." *Journal of the History of Astronomy* 27, no. 3 (1996): 187-237. Argues that Peuerbach was familiar with Arab astronomy and that it influenced his work.

Margolis, Howard. *It Started with Copernicus: How Turning the World Inside Out Led to the Scientific*

Revolution. New York: McGraw-Hill, 2002. Chapter 1 covers pre-Copernican astronomy, based on Ptolemy, on which Peuerbach's new theory of the planets was highly influential.

North, John. *The Norton History of Astronomy and Cosmology*. New York: W. W. Norton, 1995. An excellent history of astronomy, useful again for a discussion of Peuerbach's influence.

Zinner, Ernst. *Regiomontanus: His Life and Work*. Translated by Ezra Brown. New York: North-Holland, 1990. A biography of Peuerbach's teacher, Johannes

Müller, also known as Regiomontanus, which provides details about Peuerbach's life and work as well.

SEE ALSO: Tycho Brahe; Giordano Bruno; Gerolamo Cardano; Nicolaus Copernicus; John Dee; John Napier; Nicholas of Cusa; Rheticus; Niccolò Fontana Tartaglia.

RELATED ARTICLE in *Great Events from History: The Renaissance & Early Modern Era, 1454-1600:* 1462: Regiomontanus Completes the *Epitome* of Ptolemy's *Almagest*.

PHILIP THE MAGNANIMOUS
Count of Hesse (r. 1509-1567)

Philip the Magnanimous was perhaps the most significant single political supporter of the Protestant Reformation during the critical early years of the movement in the sixteenth century.

BORN: November 13, 1504; Marburg, Hesse (now in Germany)
DIED: March 31, 1567; Cassel (now Kassel), Hesse
ALSO KNOWN AS: Philip of Hesse; Philipp der Grossmütige
AREAS OF ACHIEVEMENT: Government and politics, church reform, religion and theology

EARLY LIFE

Philip the Magnanimous succeeded his father, Landgrave (Count) William II, on the throne of Hesse in 1509, when he was not yet five years of age. For half a century, the principality of Hesse had been riven by dynastic feuds and minority administrations, which had allowed the estates to obtain considerable influence. In 1509, a conflict for control of the regency erupted between the mother of young Philip, Anne of Mecklenburg, and the estates, which resulted in civil war and the intervention of neighboring princes, especially the rival Ernestine and Albertine branches of the House of Saxony.

These conflicts continued throughout the minority of Philip, providing an extremely strife-filled youth for the prince, who was often the object of contention and was shuffled about from one faction to another. Anne was supported by the Albertine duke George the Bearded of Saxony and arranged for the marriage of Philip to George's daughter, Christine. The Ernestine elector Frederick the Wise of Saxony, on the other hand, supported Anne's opposition. In 1518, when Philip was but four-

teen years old, Emperor Maximilian I proclaimed Philip of age in an effort to restore peace, but the landgrave's mother continued to dominate the government, and civil conflict would continue until Philip assumed personal control of the Hesse throne in the mid-1520's.

In 1521, Philip attended the Diet of Worms, at which Martin Luther's teachings were condemned, and left with a strong attachment to the Wittenberg professor. During the following years, he took part in suppressing the uprising of imperial knights led by Franz von Sickingen and Ulrich von Hutten, and the peasant uprising led by Thomas Münzer.

Philip was a prince of considerable personal charm, with a handsome physique. At least during his youth, he was dynamic and outspoken, even to a fault. At the Diet of Speyer in 1526, for example, he was so eager to testify publicly to his new faith that he dined on an ox on a Friday. His activist nature, joined to the caution of his Saxon allies, often led to divided command in the Protestant camp. Despite the obvious sincerity of his adherence to the Reformation, Philip had strong sensual desires that would lead him into bigamy in 1540. On May 12, 1525, his mother died, and Philip became, for the first time, master of his own house.

LIFE'S WORK

By the time of his mother's death, Philip was effectively master of his principality and was committed to the Lutheran Reformation. During the winter of 1525-1526, Philip reached an agreement with the elector John of Saxony, cousin and rival of his mother's supporter, to pursue a common policy in defense of the Reformation at the upcoming Diet of Speyer. At that meeting, the princes, led by John and Philip, were able to prevent the enforcement of the decrees against Lutheranism, obtaining instead an agreement that each prince would act in his own lands "in such a way as everyone trusted to justify before God and the Imperial Majesty." This gave the princes a free hand in their own territories, setting the precedent for the later principle of state supremacy—*cuius regio, eius religio*—adopted by the Peace of Augsburg in 1555.

With this mandate, Philip called a synod of the Hessian church at Homburg in October, 1526, which adopted the *Reformatio ecclesiarum Hassiae*. This plan, primarily the work of François Lambert of Avignon, a Franciscan friar trained at Wittenberg, would have provided the Hessian church with a democratic structure, consisting of elected clergy and annual synods. On the advice of Luther, this model was rejected in favor of that being developed in neighboring Saxony, under which Philip became the effective head of the new church administration.

Twelve months later, Philip summoned the estates of Hesse for the first time in nine years to consider the disposition to be made of the confiscated monastic properties. This Parliament agreed that 41 percent of these revenues were to be used by the prince, while the remaining 59 percent were to serve pious, educational, and ecclesiastical purposes, including the foundation of the University of Marburg to train future clergymen and officials. It was Philip's liberal endowment of the new university and various pious and charitable institutions that earned for him the sobriquet "the Magnanimous."

In the atmosphere of mutual suspicion following the rapprochement between Emperor Charles V and Pope Clement VII in 1528, Philip fell prey to the forgeries of Otto von Pack, a discredited councillor of Duke George. Pack persuaded him that Catholic forces were assembling to exterminate the new heresy, whereupon Philip formed an alliance with John, sent feelers to the emperor's enemies in France and Hungary, and assembled a significant armed force. Although no actual fighting ensued, Philip's precipitate action in appealing to the enemies of the emperor weakened the Protestant cause at the next diet, also held at Speyer, where in April, 1529, a new law revoked the concessions made three years earlier, halting all ecclesiastical innovations and restoring the jurisdiction of Catholic bishops. Philip joined with six other princes and fourteen cities in the Protest of Speyer in rejecting this decision, from which the adherents of Luther were known as "Protestants."

By this time, voices other than Luther's had been raised demanding the reform of the Church, resulting in divided councils among the Protestants. The major con-

Philip the Magnanimous. (Hulton|Archive by Getty Images)

troversy was between Luther and Huldrych Zwingli over the doctrine of the Eucharist. Believing that a common front was necessary to defend the Protestant cause, Philip sponsored the Marburg Colloquy from October 1 to 3, 1529, in an effort to promote harmony. The disputants agreed on fourteen points, but their failure to achieve full agreement on the fifteenth article, on the Lord's Supper, was also the failure of the Protestant movement to achieve unity.

In 1530, Philip took part in the Diet of Augsburg, where an attempt was made to reach agreement between the Lutherans and the Catholics, and was one of the seven princes to subscribe to the Augsburg Confession presented there. With the failure of these negotiations, the emperor ordered the complete restoration of Catholicism. To defend themselves against this threat, the Protestant princes and the cities of Magdeburg and Bremen formed the military Schmalkaldic League in February, 1531. This league became the major political expression of German Protestantism for a generation.

Philip became the leading spirit in the Schmalkaldic League, overshadowing his more cautious cousin Elector John Frederick of Saxony. With French support, in 1534, Philip made the first significant territorial gain for Lutheranism in southern Germany when he conquered

Württemberg from the Habsburgs, restoring the previous ruler, the Lutheran duke Ulrich. Philip then gave support to the prince-bishop of Münster in his conflict with the radical Anabaptists, assisting in the siege of the city, which fell on June 25, 1535. Thus, during the 1530's, Philip was at the height of his influence.

At the age of nineteen, Philip had married Christine of Saxony, a daughter of his mother's ally, Duke George. The marriage was not successful. Influenced by Luther's statement that bigamy was not as serious an offense as divorce, he entered into a second union with Margaret von der Saal, which was soon made public. This not only caused dissension among the members of the league but also, because bigamy was a crime against imperial law as well, gave the emperor considerable leverage with Philip.

A confrontation in Germany had been avoided since 1530, largely because of the emperor's desire to obtain the support of the princes in his wars with the French and the Turks and because of disagreements with the Papacy. In 1544, with the Treaty of Crépy, peace was concluded with France, and in 1545, the Council of Trent began its deliberations. After failing to convince the Lutherans to attend the council, Charles determined on war. At the Diet of Regensburg in 1546, Philip and John Frederick were placed under the ban of the empire.

In the War of the Schmalkaldic League, the dynamic Philip and the cautious John Frederick shared the command with other allies, which was the major cause of their defeat at Mühlberg on April 24, 1547. John Frederick was captured, and Philip was summoned to surrender, with the promise that his life would be spared; he would not suffer perpetual imprisonment, but he would have to pay a substantial fine of 150,000 guilders. Philip consulted his estates, which advised accepting, and they pledged their loyalty to their prince. A regency under Philip's eldest son was established, which governed during his five-year imprisonment. Taken to the Netherlands, he was not released until after the Truce of Passau in 1552.

The Peace of Augsburg (1555) ended the wars of religion in Germany for this generation. Chief among its provisions was the principle of *cuius regio, eius religio*, confirming the authority of the German princes over the Church in their lands. During the remaining years of his life, Philip devoted himself primarily to the governance of Hesse, but he strove to promote unity among the Protestants of Germany and to support the Huguenots of France. After his death in 1567, his lands were partitioned among the four sons of his first marriage.

SIGNIFICANCE

Philip the Magnanimous, building on the foundations laid during the regency of his mother, broke the power of the estates of Hesse, creating the strong princely authority that would allow his descendants to play an important role in German affairs into the nineteenth century. More important, his early, ardent, and consistent support for the Protestant cause contributed to its spread and eventual acceptance in large parts of Germany.

Although the sincerity of his religious convictions is manifest, so also are the limitations placed on his contributions by the strength of his emotions. His precipitate action in the Pack affair contributed to the Protestant setback at the Diet of Speyer in 1529. His bigamous marriage in 1540 caused scandal for and within the Protestant forces, while politically neutralizing him for a time. His inability to work in harmony with the more cautious John Frederick contributed to the Protestant defeat in 1547.

Despite these failures, Philip undoubtedly contributed significantly to the success of the Lutheran movement. The Protest of Speyer of 1529, the Augsburg Confession of 1530, and the Schmalkaldic League of 1531 were signed by only seven princes. Other than Philip, the only significant signatory was John Frederick. Without Philip's support, the Lutheran movement in Germany might have been overwhelmed at this critical time in its development. This, alone, is sufficient to justify the inclusion of Philip the Magnanimous among the leading figures of the Reformation.

—*William C. Schrader*

FURTHER READING

Bainton, Roland H. *The Reformation of the Sixteenth Century.* Boston: Beacon Press, 1952. This work by one of the premier scholars of the Reformation is a significant contribution to the interpretation of the Protestant movement. It contains a brief but insightful discussion of the impact of Philip's actions on the Diet of Speyer in 1529 and of his bigamy.

Cahill, Richard Andrew. *Philip of Hesse and the Reformation.* Mainz, Germany: P. von Zabern, 2001. Study of Philip's rule and his effects on both the Reformation in particular and Protestantism in general. Includes bibliographic references and index.

Carsten, Francis Ludwig. *Princes and Parliaments in Germany, from the Fifteenth to the Eighteenth Century.* Oxford, England: Clarendon Press, 1959. This seminal work on the estates of the lesser German principalities contains an extremely useful discussion of the troubled regency period in Hesse, of the relations of Philip with his subjects, and of the unilateral actions of the landgrave in introducing the Reformation into his principality.

Grimm, Harold J. *The Reformation Era, 1500-1650.* 2d ed. New York: Macmillan, 1973. Grimm's masterful study of the Reformation remains unsurpassed among traditional interpretations for its breadth and objectivity. Contains excellent analyses of the character of Philip, his role in the political events of the age, the Sacramentarian controversy and Marburg Colloquy, and the impact of his bigamous marriage.

Holborn, Hajo. *The Reformation.* Vol. 1 in *A History of Modern Germany.* New York: Alfred A. Knopf, 1959. Reprint. Princeton, N.J.: Princeton University Press, 1982. This classical study of German history is especially useful in placing Philip in his historical context and in developing the influence of individual political actions on the course of the Reformation.

Rittgers, Ronald K. *The Reformation of the Keys: Confession, Conscience, and Authority in Sixteenth-Century Germany.* Cambridge, Mass.: Harvard University Press, 2004. In-depth study of Lutheran reforms in the practice of private confession and their consequences for the Reformation as a whole. Includes illustrations, map, bibliographic references, and index.

Scribner, R. W., and C. Scott Dixon. *The German Reformation.* 2d ed. New York: Palgrave Macmillan, 2003. Classic reconsideration of the social and cultural genesis and consequences of the Reformation in Germany, revised and updated to take into account early twenty-first century scholarship. Includes two bibliographies and an index.

Wright, William John. *Capitalism, the State, and the Lutheran Reformation: Sixteenth Century Hesse.* Athens: Ohio University Press, 1988. This work utilizes developments in modern historiography to place both the individual prince and the Protestant movement as a whole securely in their socioeconomic setting.

See also: Martin Bucer; Charles V; Clement VII; Balthasar Hubmaier; Martin Luther; Maximilian I; Menno Simons; Huldrych Zwingli.

Related articles in *Great Events from History: The Renaissance & Early Modern Era, 1454-1600:* June, 1524-July, 1526: German Peasants' War; February 27, 1531: Formation of the Schmalkaldic League; September 25, 1555: Peace of Augsburg.

Philip II
King of Spain (r. 1556-1598)

Philip II was one of the most dominant monarchs in Europe during the late sixteenth century. Guided by his deep religious faith, Philip was involved in virtually every major European historical event in the last half of the sixteenth century.

Born: May 21, 1527; Valladolid, Spain
Died: September 13, 1598; El Escorial Palace, Spain
Also known as: Philip of Habsburg
Areas of achievement: Government and politics, religion and theology

Early Life

Philip was born into the most influential family in sixteenth century Europe—the Habsburgs. His father, Charles V (Charles I of Spain), was the most powerful Holy Roman Emperor to that date. Philip's first years were spent under the guidance of his mother, Isabel of Portugal, as Charles traveled on imperial business. Isabel's religious and serious nature had a pronounced effect on her son. In 1535, Charles established a separate household for Philip, who was taught such arts as riding and hunting. In addition, Philip received a formal education, excelling in language skills. He could speak and write Latin, understand French and Italian, and speak French, but he was most comfortable with the language of his homeland.

Philip's physical appearance was similar to that of his ancestors. Having the famous Habsburg jaw, a large protruding under jaw and lip, he wore a short and pointed beard early in life and allowed it to grow longer and wider as he grew older.

Philip had an unusual married life. He had four wives, and he outlived each of them. At age eighteen, he married Maria of Portugal, the mother of a son who died later under questionable circumstances. Philip's next wife was the English queen Mary I. In 1558, Mary died without heirs, and that broke all connections Philip had with England. His third wife was Elizabeth of Valois, who bore him two daughters before dying in 1568. His last marriage was to Anne of Austria, the daughter of his cousin, Emperor Maximilian II. Anne bore Philip four sons and one daughter before she died in 1580.

LIFE'S WORK

Philip ruled many lands. Although Charles V gave the Austrian lands to his brother, Ferdinand, he reserved for Philip the Spanish lands in the New World and Europe. The New World lands were most important as sources of revenue. Among his holdings, however, Philip loved Spain best. Indeed, he never left his homeland after his return from Northern Europe in 1559. He built for himself a palace, El Escorial, which became a monument to his reign; some called it a monastery.

One of the most disturbing problems Philip faced throughout his rule was the Protestant Reformation. Indeed, the fight against the heretics colored almost every aspect of his reign. He had been reared as a Catholic and was devoted to the Church. When the Council of Trent finished its work, he attempted to enforce its decisions. He believed that it was his duty to restore Europe to the true Church. He did not always agree, however, with the popes and often fought with them over authority in church-state issues. In turn, the popes resented Philip's control over the Spanish church. The Spanish clergy, however, supported Philip.

Philip's reign was usually dominated by affairs outside the Iberian Peninsula. The situation in the Netherlands created much difficulty. The Dutch were growing wealthy and were gaining a sizable Protestant population. Although they had been restless under Charles V, they did not create major problems for him; they paid their taxes and, as a result, were low in funds when Philip assumed control. Philip expected the Dutch not only to pay their taxes but also to maintain a defense against his northern enemies, while promoting the Roman Catholic Church.

Philip attempted several different approaches to the Netherlands. He first tried to rule through a regent, his half sister Margaret, and a close adviser, Antoine Perrenot de Granvelle, bishop of Arras (after 1561, Cardinal Granvelle). The cardinal actually controlled the government and attempted to carry out Philip's orders. The Dutch Protestants, led by William the Silent, insisted that they had certain privileges that had to be respected. William finally forced Philip's recall of Granvelle, only to discover that Granvelle had been following orders. When the Protestant militants began to destroy churches and other property, Philip sent troops to end the rebellion. Several thousand people were executed for heresy.

Philip II. (Library of Congress)

Taking control of the northern provinces, William demanded religious freedom, along with the removal of troops and restoration of rights. Philip could never allow religious freedom, so this civil war continued throughout his reign. While there were a few periods of Spanish success, the northern provinces gained their independence, although Spain refused to recognize the loss until 1648.

England prevented Philip from pursuing the revolt in the Netherlands as actively as he might have wished. Throughout the sixteenth century, Anglo-Spanish relations had seen peaks and valleys. When Philip married Mary in 1554, it had only been after careful consideration. Many in the English Parliament opposed the marriage and relented only after ensuring that Philip would have little to do with English government. Philip was unhappy about the situation but accepted his father's advice to rule England through Mary. Unfortunately for this goal, Mary died soon after the marriage.

Problems constantly beset the two countries during the Elizabethan years. One of the most vexing was the English Sea Dogs (privateers), who preyed on Spanish

New World trade. Although Philip beseeched Elizabeth to control her sea captains, she never did. She also angered Philip by providing English troops to aid the Protestant cause in the Netherlands.

Convinced that diplomacy was not going to control the English, Philip plotted an invasion. His plans originally called for assembling a large armada and sending it to the Netherlands, where it would board troops and cross the Channel to capture England. This Spanish Armada quickly ran into problems. In 1587, an English sea captain, Francis Drake, surprised the Spanish fleet in port and inflicted considerable damage. Determined, even at great financial costs and administrative difficulties, Philip repaired the Armada and sent it to sea in 1588. As it arrived in the Channel, a combination of English ships and Channel weather seriously crippled the fleet, and only a small portion managed to limp back to Spain. While Philip never gave up the idea of conquering England, the idea remained only a dream.

Spain was in the middle of a war with France when Philip assumed the mantle of leadership from his father in 1555-1556. It was not until 1559 that the Treaty of Cateau-Cambrésis was negotiated with the king of France, Henry II, ending the conflict. After the death of Henry II, there was a struggle for control of the French throne. The French Huguenots demanded their religious rights as well as certain political ones. Wars frequently raged between the Catholic and Huguenot factions. Philip carefully watched the situation and in December, 1584, signed the secret Treaty of Joinville with the Catholic League. The goals of the treaty were to keep a Huguenot off the throne and to suppress heresy in France. When the next in line to the throne seemed to be Henry of Navarre, a Huguenot, Philip forced the reigning King Henry III to proclaim an elderly uncle, Charles, cardinal of Bourbon, as his successor. When Charles died in 1591, Philip advanced his daughter, Isabella Clara Eugenia, by Elizabeth of Valois, the eldest daughter of Henry II's eldest daughter. These claims failed, and Henry of Navarre assumed his place on the French throne; Philip could not dislodge him.

During the last few years of his life, Philip suffered from crippling arthritis and usually had to be carried from place to place. He accepted what comfort he could from his religion. He had faith, and his religious beliefs, which carried him throughout his life, were with him when he died.

SIGNIFICANCE

Philip II was one of the most dominant forces in the second half of the sixteenth century. He touched the lives of many both in the New World and in Europe. In his own fashion, he established a Spanish colonial governance that lasted well into the nineteenth century. In Europe, he fought with his fellow monarchs for control, even seizing the Portuguese crown when it became vacant in 1580. He rarely retreated from any position because he was usually convinced that God had ordained him to undertake a mission.

Philip would not make decisions quickly. Some argue that he was being prudent, while others say that he was timid. Perhaps his procrastination was caused by his lack of funds. Despite the riches of the New World, Philip had such staggering debts that his reign was bankrupt in 1557, 1575, and 1596. He collected money from every possible source to meet his needs. Another reason for his procrastination could have been his habit of employing ministers with widely varying views, even ones opposed to his own, and then demanding that they express themselves. Council meetings, such as the Council of State, often became battlegrounds for rival factions.

Because of his absolute faith and strong convictions, Philip became part of the Black Legend, or anti-Spanish view, that surfaced in the English-speaking world. Philip's connection with the legend began when William the Silent, deep in battle over the Netherlands, branded Philip a murderer. Two major contributions to the Black Legend's growth were books by Antonio Pérez and John Lothrop Motley. Perez, who had been close to Philip and had fallen from power, tried to destroy Philip's name to avenge himself. Motley, a noted Protestant historian, used the distorted documents of Perez and others to paint Philip as evil. More balanced accounts have since emerged, and Philip has been placed in a more appropriate perspective.

—*Eric L. Wake*

FURTHER READING

Kamen, Henry. *Philip of Spain*. New Haven, Conn.: Yale University Press, 1997. A massive and detailed biography of Philip, documenting almost every aspect of his life, but somewhat light on his legacy and influence on future events. Includes photographic plates, illustrations, maps, bibliographic references, and index.

Mattingly, Garrett. *The Armada*. 1959. Reprint. Boston: Houghton Mifflin, 1987. A readable book about one of the major issues of Philip's reign—the defeat of the Spanish Armada. Contains a good, but outdated, bibliography. This work is considered a classic.

Merriman, Roger Bigelow. *Philip the Prudent*. Vol. 4 in *The Rise of the Spanish Empire in the Old World and the New*. New York: Macmillan, 1918. Reprint. New York: Cooper Square, 1962. While Merriman's work might be considered an old source, it is still excellent for information on Philip's life. This is a balanced account and a good starting point for a serious study of Philip. Contains bibliographic information.

Parker, Geoffrey. *The Grand Strategy of Philip II*. New Haven, Conn.: Yale University Press, 1998. Contests the traditional view of Philip as conducting his empire by reacting to events as they occurred without any grand plan to guide him. Uses correspondence and other historical documents to delineate a "strategic culture" informing Philip's decisions and his reign. Includes illustrations, maps, bibliographic references, and index.

_____. *Philip II*. 4th ed. Chicago: Open Court, 2002. A good overview of Philip's reign, this edition is updated with a new bibliographic essay. Also includes a map, portraits, genealogical table, bibliography, and an index.

_____. "Philip II of Spain: A Reappraisal." *History Today* 19 (1979): 800-847. Parker provides the reader with a close examination of Philip in this article. Contains comments on the physical problems that Philip had toward the end of his life and addresses the problem of the Black Legend, briefly explaining Philip's role in it.

Pierson, Peter. *Philip II of Spain*. London: Thames and Hudson, 1975. A superb short biography. Pierson covers each major section of Philip's life and work. He tries to make the point that Philip thought in terms of dynasty and religion and not of nation state.

Rule, John C., and John J. TePaske, eds. *The Character of Philip II*. Boston: D. C. Heath, 1963. An excellent source for trying to determine what Philip was really like. Includes selections from authors representing several nationalities.

Williams, Patrick. *Armada*. Charleston, S.C.: Tempus, 2000. Monograph on the English defeat of the Spanish Armada. Details the causes of the attempted invasion, the battle itself, and its aftermath. Includes illustrations, maps, bibliographic references, and index.

_____. *Philip II*. New York: Palgrave, 2001. Biography that attempts to capture the complexities of Philip's public and private lives and of the evolution of both his private persona and his royal career over time. Includes maps, bibliographic references, and index.

SEE ALSO: Duke of Alva; Charles V; Sir Francis Drake; Elizabeth I; Alessandro Farnese; El Greco; Henry II; Henry III; Margaret of Parma; Mary of Hungary; Mary I; Maximilian II; Pedro Menéndez de Avilés; Pius V; Sixtus V; William the Silent.

RELATED ARTICLES in *Great Events from History: The Renaissance & Early Modern Era, 1454-1600:* July 16, 1465-April, 1559: French-Burgundian and French-Austrian Wars; c. 1500: Netherlandish School of Painting; 16th century: Evolution of the Galleon; 16th century: Worldwide Inflation; 1521-1559: Valois-Habsburg Wars; July, 1553: Coronation of Mary Tudor; 1555-1556: Charles V Abdicates; April 3, 1559: Treaty of Cateau-Cambrésis; March, 1562-May 2, 1598: French Wars of Religion; 1563-1584: Construction of the Escorial; 1565: Spain Seizes the Philippines; 1568-1648: Dutch Wars of Independence; February 25, 1570: Pius V Excommunicates Elizabeth I; October 7, 1571: Battle of Lepanto; August 24-25, 1572: St. Bartholomew's Day Massacre; June 17, 1579: Drake Lands in Northern California; 1580-1581: Spain Annexes Portugal; July 26, 1581: The United Provinces Declare Independence from Spain; July 7, 1585-December 23, 1588: War of the Three Henrys; September 14, 1585-July 27, 1586: Drake's Expedition to the West Indies; April, 1587-c. 1600: Anglo-Spanish War; July 31-August 8, 1588: Defeat of the Spanish Armada; August 2, 1589: Henry IV Ascends the Throne of France; April 13, 1598: Edict of Nantes; May 2, 1598: Treaty of Vervins.

GIOVANNI PICO DELLA MIRANDOLA
Italian philosopher

Pico della Mirandola, a brilliant synthesizer of Humanist thought, articulated the concept of self-determination, which helped extend the idea of humans as individuals. His work extols the intrinsic godliness of humans and their responsibility toward society, commitment to learning, and, most important, control over their own destiny.

BORN: February 24, 1463; Mirandola, duchy of Ferrara (now in Italy)
DIED: November 17, 1494; Florence (now in Italy)
AREAS OF ACHIEVEMENT: Philosophy, religion and theology

EARLY LIFE

Giovanni Pico della Mirandola (joh-VAHN-nee PEE-koh DAYL-lah-mee-rahn-doh-lah), a precocious child endowed with a prodigious memory, was raised in an exclusive environment at a time when there was growing cultural and political turmoil in most parts of Italy. Before he was twenty years old, he was acquainted with some of the leading minds and powerful politicians that marked the era known as early Renaissance Humanism.

He was educated mostly in the great learning centers of northern Italy. He studied in Mantua, where he met Leon Battista Alberti and Angelo Poliziano, who became a lifelong friend. In 1477, he studied canon law in Bologna. Two years later, he sojourned briefly in Florence and met poet Girolamo Benivieni, and then traveled in Pavia, a haven for logicians and scientists. He then spent time in Ferrara, where he studied the *litterae humaniores* (liberal arts), including philosophy. He met also the visionary religious leader Girolamo Savonarola.

In 1480, he relocated to Padua for two crucial years and began the systematic study of Aristotle. A voracious reader, Pico took full advantage of the arrival in Italy of some of the great teachers and translators from Greece, Byzantium, and the Middle East, who in many cases were fleeing the spread of the Ottoman Empire into southeastern Europe. While in Padua, he encoun-

tered Elias de Medigo, who introduced him to the Hebrew and Arabic languages and cultures and who translated for Pico Arabic texts by Averröes. He also requested that Marsilio Ficino, head of the Florentine Academy, send him his book, *Theologia platonica* (1482; *Platonic Theology*, 2001-2003).

LIFE'S WORK

In the open intellectual atmosphere of the Florentine Academy, to which Pico was by then associated, a growing passion grew into the desire to find a way to make all the different schools of thought cohere in one general understanding of the human condition. He entered into a respectful epistolary dispute with Ermolao Barbaro in *Epistola ad Hermolao Barbaro* (wr. 1485; "The Correspondence of G. Pico della Mirandola and Ermolao Barbaro Concerning the Relation of Philosophy and Rhetoric," 1952), which attacked the excessive rhetoric of scholars. Excessive rhetoric, Pico argued, made philosophy, or the search for truth, not simple and direct, as it ought to be, but complex and convoluted.

Pico also spent nearly one year in Paris studying theology, but ultimately found the Parisian approach unsophisticated and "barbarous." He returned to Florence charged with new enthusiasm and resumed the study of

---

PICO DELLA MIRANDOLA ON HUMAN FREE WILL AND SELF-DETERMINATION

Giovanni Pico della Mirandola came to understand that humans, unlike other living things, are given the freedom to determine not only what they shall do with their lives but also their very nature. In the following passage, his "Great Artisan," God, that is, speaks to the human individual about free will and self-determination.

Neither an established place, nor a form [belongs] to you alone, O Adam, and for this reason, that you may have and possess, according to your desire and judgment, whatever place, whatever form, and whatever functions you shall desire. . . . The nature of other creatures, which has been determined, is confined within the bounds prescribed by Us. You, who are confined by no limits, shall determine for yourself your own nature, in accordance with your own free will.

Source: From *Oration on the Dignity of Man*, excerpted in *The Portable Renaissance Reader*, edited by James Bruce Ross and Mary Martin McLaughlin (New York: Viking Press, 1968), pp. 477, 478.

Hebrew, Arabic, and Chaldean. Soon, he was able to read the Qur'ān, the Kabbalah, and the Chaldean Oracles in the original and read the works of other critics and commentators who preceded him in this effort.

Pico was ready to try the supreme mediation, an approach to philosophy in which the knowledge and wisdom gathered from different and often contradictory sources can be unified in one general theory. He thus devised a way of showing to an international group of the most learned men of his day what he had in mind: He organized a public disputation (debate) on a set of nine hundred theses, to be held in Rome in early 1487.

Rich, noble, handsome, and brilliant, Pico was not solely a bookworm. Accounts by his contemporaries reveal that he did not disdain socializing; he participated in feasts and banquets as the occasion arose. In May of 1486, while in Arezzo, he attempted to kidnap Margherita, the beautiful and rich wife of Giuliano de' Medici, a relative of Lorenzo de' Medici. The scandal would cost him dearly, as Giuliano, the country's aristocracy, and the Church demanded justice. His reputation was forever tarnished. Through Lorenzo's intervention, however, Pico did not suffer dire consequences. He repented and expiated his sin by dedicating himself to a life of research and meditation.

The importance of Pico's work and ideas cannot be overestimated. Contemporary scholars and thinkers of the rank of Desiderius Erasmus and Thomas More spoke about and integrated some of Pico's ideas into their work. In the theses and in *De hominis dignitate oratio* (wr. 1486-1487; *Oration on the Dignity of Man*, 1956), which introduced the theses and reflected his idea of combining his work with the philosophies of others, Pico intended to resolve, among other things, the dispute on the differences between Aristotle and a "Christianized" Plato through syncreticism. According to his contemporaries, he was *princeps concordiae*, the prince of harmony, a syncretic thinker who could find similarities between opposing tendencies.

Pico argued that if God is one and the same, then a way exists to demonstrate that Plato and Aristotle must be saying the same thing, albeit in different ways. From this came Pico's desire to find in the different language and style of Aristotle and Plato the signs of a common aspiration. With the growing availability of other exoteric texts from Arabic and Jewish traditions, Pico opened Humanism to comparable discussions from the East, and rather than rejecting them, he was determined to find an even deeper and common wisdom to the understanding of God and to humanity's position in the cosmos.

Giovanni Pico della Mirandola. (Hulton|Archive by Getty Images)

Pico's theses were printed in Rome on December 7, 1486, and were supposed to circulate in the schools for a month before the beginning of his defense, slated for the day after the Feast of the Epiphany. In preparation for his defense, he wrote the short work *Oration on the Dignity of Man*, which was not published until after his death, however. It is part of the collection *Commentationes Joannis Pici Mirandulea* in 1495-1496.

The debate was interrupted by Pope Innocent VIII on suspicion that thirteen of the theses were heretical. Pico reacted to this accusation by writing his passionate *Apologia*, which defended his work; on August 5, all of the theses were condemned. Pico fled to France but was arrested then released through the intervention of King Charles VIII. He was invited back to the academy, under the protection of Lorenzo, who never stopped requesting a pardon from the pope. The absolution did come, finally, in June of 1493, but from another pope, Alexander VI. It arrived about one year before Pico's death.

Oration on the Dignity of Man contains references to the Phythagoreans, the pre-Socratics, the Agnostics, the

PICO DELLA MIRANDOLA'S MAJOR WORKS

1486	*Conclusiones* (*Syncretism in the West: Pico's "900 Theses,"* 1998)
1486-1487	*De hominis dignitate oratio* (pb. 1496; *Oration on the Dignity of Man*, 1956)
1487	*Apologia*
1488	*Heptaplus* (English translation, 1967)
1496	*Disputationes adversus astrologos*
1492	*De ente et uno* (*Of Being and the One*, 1943)

Kabbalists, Orphic and Hermetic theosophies, pseudo-Dionysius the Aeropagite, Zoroaster, certain aspects of astrology, and the Bible, in which Moses is considered the greatest philosopher. Pico's attempt at synthesis could be considered superhuman in that he tried to balance the One, the supreme Being, with the human predisposition toward multiplicity, toward the endless variety present in creation. Pico developed the notion that humans, though created by God, are "work[s] of indeterminate form" who have been placed at the center of creation and can sculpt themselves "into whatever shape" they prefer (*Oration on the Dignity of Man*). His more mature works are scholarly attempts at working out the complexity of this assumption. These works include *Heptaplus* (1488; English translation, 1967), which concerned the seven days of creation, and *De ente et uno* (1492; *Of Being and the One*, 1943). He died before completing an even more thorough work titled *Concordia Platonis et Aristotelis* (on the agreement between Plato and Aristotle).

SIGNIFICANCE

Pico's work was revolutionary because it placed the responsibility for human life and actions squarely on human shoulders. He wanted to be inclusive rather than selective of the contributions from different schools of thought, and above all, he opened the discussion on free will and self-determination, which became foundational concepts for Renaissance and later thought.

—*Peter Carravetta*

FURTHER READING

Cassirer, Ernst, Paul Oskar Kristeller, and John Hermann Randall, Jr., eds. *The Renaissance Philosophy of Man.* Chicago: University of Chicago Press, 1948. One of the best introductions on Humanism in general, which contextualizes Pico in reference to his great contemporaries. Contains a slightly different translation of Pico's oration.

Craven, William G. *Giovanni Pico della Mirandola, Symbol of His Age: Modern Interpretations of a Renaissance Philosopher.* Geneva, Switzerland: Librairie Droz, 1981. One of the most thorough works on the complexity of Pico's life and writings.

Grafton, Anthony. *Commerce with the Classics: Ancient Books and Renaissance Readers.* Ann Arbor: University of Michigan Press, 1997. Important for the role Pico played in shaping the reading of the classics and his promotion of translations from the Middle East.

Pico della Mirandola, Giovanni. *Commentary On a Canzone of Benivieni.* Translated by Sears Jayne. New York: Peter Lang, 1984. Written just before the defense of his theses, Pico's analysis reveals the depth of his Platonism.

_____. *On the Dignity of Man, On Being and the One, Heptaplus.* Introduction by J. W. Miller. Indianapolis, Ind.: Bobbs-Merrill, 1965. Contains Pico's major works, with a good introduction.

Wirszubski, Chaim. *Pico della Mirandola's Encounter with Jewish Mysticism.* Cambridge, Mass.: Harvard University Press, 1989. Very detailed and illuminating work on the key role played by Pico in the development of Kabbalah in the west.

SEE ALSO: Leon Battista Alberti; Charles VIII; Desiderius Erasmus; Marsilio Ficino; Francesco Guicciardini; Leo X; Lorenzo de Medici; Sir Thomas More; Nicholas of Cusa; Peter Ramus; Girolamo Savonarola.

RELATED ARTICLES in *Great Events from History: The Renaissance & Early Modern Era, 1454-1600:* 1462: Founding of the Platonic Academy; 1486-1487: Pico della Mirandola Writes *Oration on the Dignity of Man*; c. 1500: Revival of Classical Themes in Art.

PIERO DELLA FRANCESCA
Italian painter

Though admired selectively for centuries, Piero's paintings were not placed among the world's masterpieces until the twentieth century. His works are now seen as crucial to the development of the characteristic forms and methods of Italian Renaissance painting. Also, Piero wrote the first Renaissance treatise on perspective.

BORN: c. 1420; Borgo San Sepulcro, Republic of Florence (now Sansepolcro, Italy)
DIED: October 12, 1492; Borgo San Sepulcro
AREAS OF ACHIEVEMENT: Art, mathematics

EARLY LIFE

Partly because of his being born and reared—and later choosing largely to remain—in a provincial Tuscan market town, almost nothing is known of the life of Piero della Francesca (pyehr-oh dehl-lah frahn-CHAY-skah) to the age of about twenty. For this reason, the date of his birth, and consequently his age at the time of his dated works, have been subjects of considerable debate. This debate is more significant than such things normally are, for Piero was active during the formative period of the high Italian Renaissance. For a long time, his role in this development was obscured by ignorance, and influences originating in him were attributed to others; later, the pendulum swung the other way. Now his genius is firmly established.

He was born into the Dei Franceschi family (della Francesca is a feminine variant of the name), locally prominent leather merchants, dyers, and farm owners. The first notice of him appears on September 7, 1439, as an assistant to Domenico Veneziano in a series of now-ruined frescoes in the Church of Sant'Egidio in Florence. Later, in 1442, Piero became one of the priori (town councilmen) of San Sepulcro, an office he kept for the remainder of his life, though he did leave the town periodically to work in Florence, Milan, and Urbino.

This provincial, rustic upbringing supplied an essential element in Piero's mature technique, for the arid, desolate masses of the Apennine foothills provide the brooding, static backgrounds of his scenes of secular and religious history. In this respect, he adapted the scene-framing techniques of Fra Angelico and his master Domenico Veneziano, going beyond them in using natural settings to shape the emotional and iconological contexts of the foreground subjects. That is, he was one of the first to create thematically integrated compositions,

in which every detail contributed to the dominant effect. He undoubtedly received the initial impetus toward this totally unified vision during his apprenticeship to Veneziano in Florence, at a time when the dominant artists were, besides his master, Leon Battista Alberti, Luca della Robbia, Lorenzo Ghiberti, Fra Angelico, Masaccio, and Andrea del Castagno. Piero had the good fortune to mature at the very moment that advances in perspective theory, form, light, and color seemed to call for fusion in a new technique. In the course of his career, Piero forged that technique.

LIFE'S WORK

Piero's first known work, an altarpiece commissioned in 1445 for the charitable company known as the Misericordia in his hometown, at first seems to show little evidence of this fusion. This commission, intended to replace an existing work in several segments of different sizes, required him to use the existing panels and frames, thus limiting him to what was by then an antique format. This format dominates the work; at first viewing, the observer is likely to believe that the painting dates from the preceding century, so stiff and compartmentalized do the figures represented appear. Fire damage and overpainting during attempted restorations do not correct the impression. Further study, however, reveals that Piero is here experimenting with novel treatments of light as a means of defining and disclosing form. His light is flushed with color, subtly varied from surface to surface, pervading even the shadows from which it emerges. This is the light of Angelico and Veneziano, but immensely refined in that it takes on and projects texture, in the process inhabiting form. His figures, the clothes they wear, and the volumes they create become tactile, almost palpable. Further, the whole breathes an appropriate, and characteristic, solemnity.

Around 1450, Piero created his first masterwork, *Baptism of Christ*, for a priory in San Sepulcro. The large panel centers on Christ standing in the ankle-deep flow of a translucent stream winding its way down a Tuscan hillside; John strides out from the right to perform his ministry, while three angels watch from the left, under the arch of a small poplar springing improbably from the very bank of the stream, and a postulant in the middle distance pulls off his tunic to become the next candidate. The painting is an arresting combination of strength and subtlety. The Christ is severe, stark, almost repulsive; his features are harsh, peasantlike, rather brutal, certainly common. He stands resolute, firm, determined to take what is coming to him, even if against or beyond his will. The angels lounge idly yet ceremonially, as if they were paid attendants, early altar boys. The event may inaugurate a revolutionary mission, yet no one is paying much attention to it; it is simply another baptism, and even John seems to be merely resigned to it, going through a formality.

Still, this Christ is as vulnerable as he is determined. His contours swell softly: His skin would quiver to the touch, and his transparent loincloth reveals his essential humanity. Further, his white, columnar body precisely parallels the trunk of the poplar, as if the two were of one kind, two manifestations of the same spirit, sprung from the same root. Similarly, the dove centered above the vessel from which John pours, representing the Third Person of the Trinity, is almost indistinguishable from the adjacent clouds. More remarkable, and in defiance of artistic tradition, God the Father does not appear, not even by disembodied hand. Piero seems to suggest that the Father, nevertheless, is there, as much as Son and Holy Spirit. He is simply more immanent than they, as the Son is also in the tree and the Spirit in the clouds. This revela-

Piero della Francesca. (Library of Congress)

tion of theme in seemingly accidental yet completely integrated detail is the signature of Piero. Typically, every naturalistic detail—like the inverted reflection of landscape in the stream—is rendered with the utmost fidelity to the natural phenomena.

The *Resurrection* fresco (c. 1453) is Piero's best-known work. The subject was the official symbol of the town—hence its name—and Piero deliberately represents the event as taking place while the sun rises in the rocky hills above the town. Christ mounts the sarcophagus with his left foot, grasping a red-cross standard that unfolds above him. His pale rose-colored robe opens to expose the spear wound. The face is as compelling as that in the *Baptism of Christ*, but these eyes are simultaneously harrowing—they have experienced everything—and compassionate, probing into the soul of the viewer. Four soldiers sprawl in front of the tomb, dozing, the back of one resting against the frontal plane of the painting. Though apparently disposed at random, the figures combine with that of the risen Christ in a pattern of interlocking and embedded triangles, creating an impression of great strength and endurance.

In the middle background, the landscape on the left—luminous in the shimmering light of dawn—is withered and barren, while that on the right is in full leaf. This is the iconographic equivalent of Christ's remark on the way to Calvary: "If they do these things in a green tree, what shall be done in the dry?" (Luke 23:31), referring to the persecution that would follow on his execution. There was a further association of green and withered trees with the Trees of Life and of Knowledge in the Garden of Eden, the second of which in legend became both symbolically and actually the agent of human redemption, by furnishing the wood for Christ's cross. In this painting, Piero created an image in which all the details fuse in a vision of total integrity, in which psychological intensity and doctrinal content reinforce each other.

Piero's only major fresco cycle, the *Legend of the True Cross* (1452-1457), is the most ambitious project he attempted: a series of twelve frescoes setting forth a pious medieval legend of complex, and improbable, fantasy. Unfortunately, the entire chancel, on which the frescoes were done, has suffered from water seepage over the ensuing centuries, and much of the surface has been lost and ineptly restored. These restorations were removed, so that what remains of the original can now be seen.

What is there is astonishing. The panels narrate major episodes in the legend, from the fetching of a branch from Eden by Seth to cure his father Adam through Solomon's burying of a beam and Helena's discovery of the cross fashioned from it to its recovery from Chosroes by the Emperor Heraclius. Piero arranged them not chronologically but in order to focus on visual, symbolic, and thematic resonances. Thus, for example, scenes dominated by women are set on opposite walls, as are those of battles and those involving visions of the Cross. Further, each panel consists of two paired scenes representing two incidents within a single episode. Independently, these paintings serve as illustrations of rhythmic group composition, Albertian perspective, and visual and thematic integration; together, they constitute one of the most magnificent sequences of painting ever composed, truly remarkable especially for the fidelity of its coloring, so that the landscapes and people represented take on tangible reality.

In the middle of his career, Piero occasionally left San Sepulcro to do some of his most significant work at Urbino, Milan, and Florence. In Urbino, for example, he painted a mysterious *Flagellation of Christ* (probably 1463-1464), the thematic content of which has been convincingly interpreted. The dignity of his figures, however, the delicacy of light and color, and the austere sincerity of the work have never been in doubt. Also in Urbino, Piero composed complementary portraits of *Count Federico da Montefeltro* and his wife, *Battista Sforza* (after 1474), which bear allegorical triumph scenes on their reverses. The portraits show to the highest degree Piero's fusion of austerity of vision and revelation of character, and the triumphs disclose a blend of imaginative landscape with mythological content. His last known painting, *Nativity* (1480), reveals modulations of color and light that have never been surpassed; Piero almost makes the air visible.

Though he lived on for some twenty years, he seems not to have returned to painting, busying himself instead in theoretical studies, which included the treatise on perspective and a book on geometry. According to legend, he became blind in the last years of his life.

SIGNIFICANCE

Through to the twentieth century, Piero and his work were believed to be remote and somewhat primitive; at best, he was considered a "provincial master" and treated somewhat condescendingly. At this point, it is difficult to understand that neglect. His work is always compelling, particularly in his rare union of force and subtlety. Even when disfigured by time or made to appear crude by clumsy overpainting, his scenes are honest, direct, forthright, and sincere. Further study always reveals what can

only be called marvelous hidden harmonies underlying fully integrated compositions. It is almost as if Piero thought out each painting completely and then executed what he saw in his mind's eye. Every detail falls into its necessary place, supporting and subordinated to the whole.

Probably the most striking aspect of Piero's painting is a quality not immediately perceptible, since the underlying unity and harmony of his work is accomplished by means of subtle geometric patterns; abstract shapes—triangles, parallelograms, rhomboids—emerge through the living figures of the surface. These anchor his compositions, creating weight and mass, imparting a solid dignity rivaled only by Masaccio and Castagno. These geometrical patterns contribute to the formal emphasis of his work, giving it almost palpable substance, as if his scenes have more body than real life. It is easy to understand why the abstract painters and formalists of the early twentieth century should have made a hero out of Piero; he anticipated many of their interests.

Other qualities of his work also had to wait until the twentieth century for proper appreciation. Among them is his creation of human characters who, though outwardly commonplace, even crude, are absolutely convincing in their individuality and humanity. For this reason, reproductions of his incidental figures became favorites of painters and art students during the ascendancy of French painter Georges Braque (1882-1963) and Spanish painter Pablo Picasso (1881-1973). Still, there are elements in Piero's work that stand independent of such fashionable revivals. The lyricism of his colors, for example, is a pure joy, transcending the accomplishments of everyone before Leonardo da Vinci. Coincident with that is his use of light, especially in the way he combines the two to bring out the solidity and mass of his figures. Finally, there is his use of landscape to integrate the composition of his paintings and to unify them thematically. No one had done this kind of thing before him; no one ever did it better.

—*James Livingston*

FURTHER READING

Battisti, Eugenio. *Piero della Francesca.* University Park: Pennsylvania State University Press, 1972. This text is the standard academic study of Piero, fully documented, with excellent reproductions, a complete bibliography, and thorough discussions of the paintings and their artistic and historical contexts. The explanations of the paintings are outstanding, particularly because the quality of the plates is so high.

Baxandall, Michael. *Painting and Experience in Fifteenth-Century Italy: A Primer in the Social History of Pictorial Style*. New York: Oxford University Press, 1974. One of the standard reference works for Quattrocento art, this offers a particularly incisive account of Piero's pivotal role in the development of painting. Also contains useful insights into his failure to attract general appreciation until the twentieth century.

Clark, Kenneth. *Piero della Francesca*. 2d ed. Reprint. Ithaca, N.Y.: Cornell University Press, 1981. An early account of Piero's work and development, this is perhaps the most accessible study of the paintings. Some of the material and the plates are dated, requiring correction and amplification in later studies.

Gilbert, Creighton. *Change in Piero della Francesca*. Locust Valley, N.Y.: J. J. Augustin, 1968. This is a groundbreaking account of Piero's stylistic development, offering a more thorough technical analysis of his methods than any other source. Some of the arguments seem forced, but in general this is an indispensable work for an appreciation of what Piero really accomplished.

Ginzburg, Carlo. *The Enigma of Piero: Piero della Francesca*. Translated by Martin Ryle and Kate Soper. New ed. London: Verso, 2000. In-depth historical investigation of the culture and events surrounding Piero's work, explicates the political intrigues captured in his paintings and the effects of Piero's patrons on his art. Includes eighty pages of photographic plates, illustrations, bibliographic references, and index.

Hartt, Frederick. *History of Italian Renaissance Art: Painting, Sculpture, Architecture*. 5th ed. New York: H. N. Abrams, 2003. Hartt gives an excellent account of Piero's position in the development of Italian Renaissance art; in short space, he sketches the essential qualities of his work, focusing on formal and thematic integrity. His writing is eminently readable, making this the best available introduction.

Lavin, Marilyn Aronberg. *Piero della Francesca*. New York: Phaidon, 2002. Comprehensive survey of Piero's work, including the newly restored Arezzo frescoes. Discusses the intersections of religion and politics in Piero's art. Includes illustrations, map, bibliographic references, and index.

Longhi, Roberto. *Piero della Francesca*. 3d ed. Translated by David Tabbat. Lebanon, N.H.: University Press of New England, 2002. A new translation of one of the first revisionist studies of Piero's formal qualities and of his role in the evolution of Italian painting. Includes photographic plates, illustrations, bibliographic references, and index.

Vasari, Giorgio. *Lives of the Most Eminent Painters, Sculptors, and Architects*. Translated by Gaston du C. de Vere. Reprint. New York: Abrams, 1979. In this edition of a famous volume of biographical sketches by a near-contemporary of Piero, Vasari includes many details that would otherwise have been unrecorded; he is thus the source of most of what is known, though much is based on hearsay. Vasari also shows what was thought of Piero during the sixteenth century.

Wood, Jeryldene M., ed. *The Cambridge Companion to Piero della Francesca*. New York: Cambridge University Press, 2002. Collection of essays covering such topics as Piero's mathematical treatises, the spiritual aspects of his paintings, his portraits of rulers, and his use of perspective to represent the ideal city. Includes illustrations, bibliographic references, and index.

SEE ALSO: Leon Battista Alberti; Andrea del Sarto; Sandro Botticelli; Donato Bramante; Leonardo da Vinci; Andrea Mantegna; Raphael; Tintoretto; Giorgio Vasari; Paolo Veronese.

RELATED ARTICLE in *Great Events from History: The Renaissance & Early Modern Era, 1454-1600:* c. 1500: Revival of Classical Themes in Art.

The Pinzón Brothers
Spanish explorers

The two Pinzón brothers provided crucial assistance for Christopher Columbus's first voyage to the New World. The brothers helped Columbus obtain and outfit his three ships and served as captains of the Pinta *and the* Niña.

Martín Alonso Pinzón

Born: c. 1440; Palos (now in Spain)
Died: March, 20, 1493; Palos

Vicente Yáñez Pinzón

Born: c. 1462; Palos
Died: c. 1523; probably Spain
Area of achievement: Exploration

Early Lives

Martín Alonso (mahr-TEEN ah-LAWN-soh) and Vicente Yáñez Pinzón (bee-SAYN-tay YAHN-yays peen-SAWN) were brothers in a family of wealthy shipowners and navigators in the Spanish port city of Palos. Martín, the elder of the two men, had spent most of his life since the age of fifteen at sea. He had sailed throughout the Mediterranean and along the northwest coast of Africa, serving Spain in a war against Portugal. He was widely recognized as an expert seaman, navigator, and captain. His younger brother, Vicente, about whom less is known, also spent most of his life at sea, learning the practical arts of seamanship and navigation.

The Pinzón family was one of the three leading shipping families in the important port city of Palos, on Spain's southwest coast. The enthusiastic support of the Pinzóns for Christopher Columbus's first voyage to the New World greatly helped Columbus to secure the skilled seamen, ships, material, and leaders necessary for success. In the summer of 1491, Columbus arrived in Palos to consult with a Franciscan friar and astronomer who supported his claims of the possibility of a trans-Atlantic trade route to Asia. This friar, Fray Antonio de Marchena, introduced Columbus to the leading families of Palos, including Martín Alonso of the Pinzóns.

Following the initial visit of Columbus, de Marchena and others communicated their support to the Spanish royal court. Columbus was then called to meet with Queen Isabella. When she decided to support Columbus's voyage, Martín Alonso Pinzón and his family in Palos helped Columbus to obtain the use of two ships, the *Pinta* and the *Niña*, for the voyage. Martín Pinzón also assisted Columbus in recruiting the necessary skilled hands for the expedition's three vessels, helped to calm fears of a voyage into the unknown, and offered his services and that of his brother as captains of the two ships provided by the city of Palos. Columbus himself captained the third ship, the *Santa Maria*. By the late summer of 1492, the small fleet had finished preparations for the historic journey.

Lives' Work

On Friday, August 3, 1492, the three ships departed Palos, heading south toward the Canary Islands off the northwest coast of Africa. The fleet left the Canaries in early September and set a course due west in search of a trade route to Asia. Columbus had chosen a more southern course to avoid difficult and heavy seas in the North Atlantic. He hoped to find the mythical island of Antilla halfway to Japan where he could restock his ships with water, and possibly food. Martín and Vicente Pinzón, captains of the *Pinta* and the *Niña*, followed this course diligently. The fleet made more than 1,100 miles in its first nine days, pushed onward by easterly winds.

In the last week of September, the fleet made less than 400 miles. Columbus never found the island of Antilla, and the ships' water began to go bad. Under this stress, the crews of all three ships began to grumble. No man in any crew had been so distant from land before. Grievances formed, fights had to be broken up, and the men began to fear for their lives. There were rumors of mutiny. Then, in October, things turned better for Columbus and the Pinzóns. Rainstorms replenished the ships' water supplies, and the wind increased. By October 6, the fleet had traveled more than 2,400 miles. That day, Martín Pinzón told Columbus that the ships should alter their course to the southwest, because he feared that they had missed Japan. Columbus, though, held true to his westerly course.

The next day, great flocks of birds passed over the ships, heading to the southwest. Columbus decided to follow Martín Pinzón's advice and changed course. This was fortunate for the fleet, because this was the shortest course to the nearest land. Yet mutiny reared its head again, as the crewmen began to once more question Columbus; they had sailed much farther west than anyone had expected. Columbus's resolve was heartened by the complete support of both Martín and Vicente Pinzón.

On October 11, signs of land began to appear, as tree branches and flowers drifted by on the ocean. The mutterings of mutiny died away as all expected a quick landfall.

At two o'clock in the morning of October 12, a lookout on the *Pinta* spotted what looked like white cliffs shining in the moonlight. Martín Pinzón checked and verified the landfall, firing a gun as the agreed signal. Columbus, in the *Santa Maria*, caught up to Pinzón and shouted across the water that he would pay a large bonus to his captain. The fleet had found one of the islands of the Bahamas in the Caribbean Sea. The next afternoon, the expedition found a shallow bay and anchored offshore. Columbus and the Pinzóns went ashore, and Columbus gave the island the name San Salvador, or "holy savior."

In the next month, the fleet cruised about the eastern Caribbean Sea, exploring about the Bahamas and discovering Cuba and the island of Hispaniola. Columbus found fine harbors, beautiful beaches, and virgin forests, excellent for the construction of ships, but there was no gold. He could not find Japan or China either. The fever for gold was so great that Martín Pinzón left the fleet on November 21 and sailed for the mythical island of Babeque without asking Columbus for permission. The *Santa Maria* and *Niña*, captained by the more loyal Vicente Pinzón, continued on without him. They found generally friendly Indians, ripe for exploitation, as Columbus wrote in his journal.

Very early on December 25, 1492, disaster struck. The *Santa Maria* ran into a coral reef off the north coast of the island of Hispaniola. Despite Columbus's best efforts, the ship's hull filled with water, and the *Santa Maria* had to be abandoned. Columbus and his crew moved to join Vicente Pinzón on the *Niña*. On January 2, 1493, the *Niña* departed for home. Sixteen men were left behind to build a fort, look for gold, and explore the area. Two days later, Columbus sighted the *Pinta*. Martín Pinzón explained his six-week absence as a successful one of both exploration and a search for gold. Columbus, glad to have company on the long voyage back to Spain, decided to forgive Martín Pinzón.

The return trip was rough, as the two ships ran into contrary winds and made little headway eastward. In mid-February, the *Pinta* and the *Niña* encountered a tremendous storm that almost sank both vessels. The two ships were separated sometime during the night of February 13-14, and the *Niña*'s crew almost gave up hope on Valentine's Day. Fearing that both ships would be lost, Columbus threw a summary of his journey overboard in a

bottle. The *Niña* survived and finally beat its way back to Spain after surviving another great tempest that almost drove the ship onto Portugal's rocky western coast.

On March 15, 1493, the *Niña* reached Palos. Finally back home, Columbus discovered that the *Pinta* had survived and that Martín Pinzón had sent a message to Queen Isabella announcing his arrival. Pinzón had reached Spain's northwest coast in February. He had then begged for permission to tell the Spanish queen about the voyage, but she told him to wait. The *Pinta* arrived in Palos shortly after Columbus on March 15. Martín Pinzón, older than Columbus, exhausted from his journey and snubbed by the Spanish royalty, went directly to his home near Palos and died there on March 20.

Vicente Pinzón made important discoveries on his own after his return with Columbus in 1493. In late 1499, he sailed from Spain and discovered South America on February 7, 1500, three months before the first Portuguese discovery. He also discovered the Amazon River and continued northwest along the South American coast at least as far north as present-day Costa Rica. In 1507, he returned again to explore the coast of Central America. Two years later, Vicente Pinzón explored southward along the Argentinean coast. All traces of Vicente Pinzón's life after 1523 are lost.

SIGNIFICANCE

While the support of the Pinzóns and other families in Palos proved critical to the successes of Columbus's voyage, the exploration could most likely have continued without their support, if necessary. It is quite possible, however, that without the assistance of the Pinzóns, Columbus first voyage would not have been as successful as it was.

The loyalty and material assistance provided by the Pinzóns allowed Columbus to proceed with his first voyage as planned. Despite Martín's insubordination in November and his attempt to steal Columbus's glory on his return to Spain in 1493, Martín's assistance greatly helped the expedition. His suggestion to change to a southwesterly course on October 6 allowed Columbus to make a landfall earlier than expected and may have helped to avert further difficulties with their crews. His death on March 20, 1493, was a major loss to history, for there has never been a reliable account of the first voyage other than that of Columbus.

Vicente Pinzón's role in history is also nearly forgotten. His primary importance to the early exploration of the New World lies with his discovery of South America and with his explorations in Central America and of the

Amazon River. Unfortunately for Vicente, the Portuguese explorer Pedro Cabral, who actually arrived in South America later, has been given historical credit for the European discovery of the continent.

While it would be a historical fallacy to claim that the assistance of the Pinzóns ensured Columbus's successes, their importance should be neither overlooked nor forgotten. Men such as the Pinzóns provided the foundation for the accomplishments of explorers such as Christopher Columbus.

—Jeff R. Bremer

FURTHER READING

Bradford, Ernie. *Christopher Columbus*. New York: Viking Press, 1973. Gives the best explanation of how Columbus first encountered Martín Pinzón but does not provide much biographical information on the two brothers. Surpassed by Samuel Eliot Morison's work on Columbus.

Collis, John Stewart. *Christopher Columbus*. New York: Stein & Day, 1976. This biography includes good information on preparations and plans for the voyage, as well as some brief background on the two Pinzóns.

De Madariaga, Salvador. *Christopher Columbus*. Reprint. New York: Frederick Unger, 1967. An outdated and overly enthusiastic endorsement of Columbus and his historical role; however, this book does provide one of the best biographical outlines of Martín Alonso's early life.

Fernadez-Armesio, Felipe. *Columbus*. New York: Oxford University Press, 1991. An excellent overview of Columbus's life, with an especially good treatment of the role of both Pinzóns in the first voyage. The work is rather broad in its scope, however, and it dedicates less than thirty pages to the first voyage.

Fyre, John. *Los Otros: Columbus and the Three Who Made His Enterprise of the Indies Succeed*. Lewiston, N.Y.: Mellen Press, 1992. The only biography that provides a detailed history of the Pinzóns. A short but accurate work that summarizes what is known about Martín Alonso and Vicente Yáñez Pinzón.

Heat-Moon, William Least. *Columbus in the Americas*. Hoboken, N.J.: John Wiley, 2002. Careful reappraisal of Columbus as explorer, colonizer, and man, by a best-selling Native American author. Heat-Moon uses many quotations from Columbus's journals to provide insight into the thoughts and motives of the explorer. Includes maps.

McKee, Alexander. *A World Too Vast: The Four Voyages of Columbus*. London: Souvenir Press, 1990. A well-written and thorough summary of Columbus's voyages that, however, contains little biographical material on either Pinzón.

Morison, Samuel Eliot. *Admiral of the Ocean Sea: A Life of Christopher Columbus*. Rev. ed. New York: Book-of-the-Month Club, 1992. One of the best biographies of Columbus, with new illustrations by Joan Paterson Kerr. The tenth chapter, on officers and men, contains brief but useful biographical information on both Pinzóns.

_____. *The Great Explorers: The European Discovery of America*. New York: Oxford University Press, 1978. Morison is one of the greatest of maritime historians, and his chapters on Columbus's voyage and the roles of Martín Alonso and Vicente Yáñez Pinzón are unmatched.

SEE ALSO: Pedro de Alvarado; Vasco Núñez de Balboa; Álvar Núñez Cabeza de Vaca; Christopher Columbus; Francisco Vásquez de Coronado; Hernán Cortés; Juan Sebastián de Elcano; Ferdinand II and Isabella I; Guacanagarí; Pedro Menéndez de Avilés; Francisco Pizarro; Juan Ponce de León.

RELATED ARTICLE in *Great Events from History: The Renaissance & Early Modern Era, 1454-1600:* October 12, 1492: Columbus Lands in the Americas.

TOMÉ PIRES
Portuguese pharmacist, diplomat, writer

Pires traveled through Southeast Asia between 1512 and 1516 and wrote a famous treatise, Suma Oriental *(sum of the things of the Orient), which contributed much knowledge of the region for the time.*

BORN: c. 1468; Portugal
DIED: c. 1540; Jiangsu Province, China
AREAS OF ACHIEVEMENT: Geography, scholarship

EARLY LIFE

Little information is available on the details of the life of Tomé Pires (toh-MAY PEE-resh). He was the son of an apothecary, and was a pharmacist for the short-lived prince Afonso (1475-1491) before he sailed for India in 1511. He was, however, initially of greater service to his king as scribe and accountant for the Portuguese trading factory in Melaka (Malacca). During these years, he also traveled to such destinations as Java.

LIFE'S WORK

Despite his desire to return to Europe, Pires was instead sent on a sensitive diplomatic mission to China in 1516. The chronicler Fernão Lopes de Castanheda (d. 1559) suggested that Pires was nominated for the mission on the understanding that he was "discreet and eager to learn, and because he would know better than anyone else the drugs there were in China." With great ceremony, the ambassador went ashore with a retinue of sixty-seven companions, bearing presents and letters for the emperor in Beijing. Only after a three-year delay, however, could he proceed from Guangzhou (Canton) to Beijing. Once there, he was ill received for many reasons: the misbehavior of Portuguese traders and sailors who had preceded him; denunciations of the Portuguese seizure of Melaka in 1511 by the ousted sultan, one of the Chinese tributary rulers; breaches of protocol in the letters that Pires bore; and reports of unscrupulous Portuguese business practices. Pires, ultimately, was refused an audience with the emperor.

Returning to Guangzhou, he was imprisoned together with three or four compatriots. This situation resulted from the Portuguese refusal to leave China on the death of Ming Dynasty emperor Zhengde (Zhu Houzhao) in 1521 and the Portuguese military presence in Guangzhou and on islands in the Pearl River Estuary. It is not clear from circumstantial accounts—such as a report given by the Portuguese traveler Fernão Mendes Pinto—whether he was liberated (as the Portuguese historian

Luís de Albuquerque maintained) or remained incarcerated. Some accounts hold that he remained in China until his death in 1540, others suggest that he died in 1524 after prolonged suffering, privations, and probably torture.

Pires's legacy is most comprehensively and impressively contained within his great *Suma Oriental* (wr. 1512-1515; English translation, 1944), an encyclopedic work that he probably started to write in Melaka and finished in Cochin during the years 1512 to 1515. The work served as a report to be sent to King Manuel and was divided into six books dealing with different geographical areas: Egypt to Cambay, Cambay to Ceylon (Sri Lanka), Bengal to Indochina, China to Borneo, the Indian archipelago (Indonesia), and Malacca (Melaka). The work is particularly detailed on what is now Malaysia, Java, and Sumatra, areas Pires knew from experience. It was also particularly valuable to historians for the last four books, which shed light on areas hitherto little, if at all, known in western Europe.

The text frequently supports the importance that Pires places on information gathered from experience and firsthand encounters. Regarding a story about the kings of Cambay being "brought up on poison," for example, he remarks, "But I do not believe this, although they say it is so." Where it was not possible to confirm information from firsthand experience, Pires relied on informants. In China, for example, these informants were not only mariners, such as Pedro Álvares Cabral, but also traditional Chinese and Malay merchants.

Pires was particularly interested in trading matters, but his work was more often cited for its potted (dull) history of Asian trading cities. The *Suma Oriental* reads like a report and is not written with great style. Despite this flaw, certain observations that Pires makes on wider concerns, such as the geopolitical realities of the Eurasian spice trade, have gone down in history for their acuteness and vision. "Whoever is Lord of Malacca," he observed, "has his hand on the throat of Venice." Elsewhere, he reminds readers of the importance of trade with Asia, stating, for example, that "the world could not otherwise sustain itself: it ennobles cities and kingdoms and makes men; it decides on the destiny of war and peace in the world."

Although manuscript copies of the *Suma Oriental* circulated in Portugal, Pires's work was not published until 1551, when it appeared anonymously, incompletely, and in Italian translation as part of the first volume of Giovanni Battista Ramusio's compilation *Delle navigationi et viaggi* (1550-1559; of voyages and travels). The Portuguese text was not published until 1944 in an edition with English translation by Armando Cortesão, exhaustive annotations, and a biographic and bibliographic introduction. In one of his letters, Pires refers to another book on measures and weights used in the Orient that he wrote or was thinking of writing. It has, however, been lost.

Beyond this, Pires may be the author of some letters of 1524 that the envoy smuggled out from his Guangzhou jail, which urged the Portuguese king to mount a military expedition against China. In the *Suma Oriental*, Pires advanced the preposterous claim that the Chinese war junks and coastal defenses were so weak that the dispatch of ten Portuguese ships from Melaka could subjugate the entire Chinese coast. Although his recommendation was wisely never undertaken, it nevertheless had far-reaching consequences. The conquest of China was an idea entertained not only by the Portuguese but also by the Spanish, through the sixteenth century.

Beyond the impact of his written legacy, many of the opinions voiced by Pires spread, such as his belief that Chinese clothing gave them the appearance of Germans. The spread of these rumors was probably the result of Pires's stay in Cochin in 1515; it was an opinion reiterated by other Portuguese travelers of the era.

Significance

Pires is to be remembered far more for his book than his failed diplomatic mission. The *Suma Oriental*, which in its most complete version lay forgotten in manuscript form in Paris until first published in 1944, is probably the most important and complete account of the East produced in the first half of the sixteenth century. It stands as testament to the great sweep of Portuguese navigation across the Indian Ocean and charts its territory with directness and honesty. This straightforward approach clearly differentiates the text from the fables of fifteenth century writers on the East. It is written with a tremendous curiosity for places and products of trade, is quick to use indigenous sources, and overturns the long-held body of Anglo-Saxon historical opinion that, since William Marsden's *The History of Sumatra* came out in

1783, the Portuguese "were more eager to conquer nations than to explore their manners and antiquities."
—*Stefan C. A. Halikowski Smith*

Further Reading

Cortesão, Armando. *The "Suma Oriental" of Tomé Pires . . . and "The Book" of Francisco Rodrigues*. 2 vols. London: Hakluyt Society, 1944. The definitive edition of the text for English readers, together with lengthy introduction. The edition comes together with Francisco Rodrigues's *The Book*, consisting of a selection of rutters of the East, which Cortesão found together with the *Suma Oriental* in the same Paris Codex. The full title reads *The "Suma Oriental" of Tomé Pires, an Account of the East, from the Red Sea to Japan, Written in Malacca and India in 1512-1515, and "The Book" of Francisco Rodrigues, Rutter of a Voyage in the Red Sea, Nautical Rules, Almanack and Maps, Written and Drawn in the East Before 1515*.

Ptak, Roderich. "Sino-Portuguese Contacts to the Foundation of Macao." In *Portugal the Pathfinder: Journeys from the Medieval Toward the Modern World, 1300-ca. 1600*, edited by G. Winius. Madison, Wis.: Hispanic Seminary of Medieval Studies, 1995. Chapter 14 explores the circumstances surrounding Pires's diplomatic mission to China and the state of affairs between the two nations, especially in the Pearl River Delta.

Tracy, James D. *The Rise of Merchant Empires: Long-Distance Trade in the Early Modern World, 1350-1750*. New York: Cambridge University Press, 1990. Contains discussions of Pires and his place in European trade with Asia. Includes illustrations and maps.

Willis, Clive, ed. *China and Macau*. Burlington, Vt.: Ashgate, 2002. Extracts relating to Pires's embassy to Beijing are translated from the Portuguese chroniclers Barros and Correia, as is the purported letter of Cristóvão Vieira. Further references to Pires can be found in Castanheda's account of the expedition of Fernão Peres de Andrade, also translated here.

See also: Manuel I; Zhengde.
Related article in *Great Events from History: The Renaissance & Early Modern Era, 1454-1600:* 1514-1598: Portuguese Reach the Swahili Coast.

PIUS II
Italian pope (1458-1464)

Through his elegant rhetoric and skilled diplomacy,
Pius II reconciled differences among Christians to
bring some peace to Western Christendom and tried
vainly to mobilize a Crusade to liberate
Constantinople from the Turks.

BORN: October 18, 1405; Corsignano (now Pienza,
Italy), Republic of Siena

DIED: August 14/15, 1464; Ancona, Papal States (now
in Italy)

ALSO KNOWN AS: Enea Silvio Piccolomini (given
name); Aeneas Silvius Piccolomini (Latin name)

AREAS OF ACHIEVEMENT: Religion and theology,
government and politics, literature

EARLY LIFE

Pius (PI-uhs) II was born Enea Silvio Piccolomini in the
village of Corsignano (which changed its name to Pienza
when its most famous son was elected to the Papacy) of a
noble but poor family. Piccolomini left home to begin his
studies at the University of Siena in 1423, but he really
began his career in 1431, when he accompanied Domenico Capranica to the Council of Basel. For the next four
years, Enea learned his trade, polishing his rhetorical
skills in speaking and writing and earning the trust of others, for whom he conducted many diplomatic errands.
On one of his missions to Scotland, he fulfilled a vow to
walk barefoot for ten miles to a shrine; as a result, he
froze his feet so badly that he was disabled for the rest of
his life.

In 1436, he obtained a seat on the Council of Basel,
which soon moved to Florence. At Florence, he participated in the election of Amadeus VIII of Savoy as Pope
Felix V. As ecclesiastical conflicts raged and Felix was declared an antipope, Piccolomini left Rome in 1442 to enter into the diplomatic service of Holy Roman Emperor
Frederick III of Habsburg. Welcomed by Frederick, who
promptly named him poet laureate, Piccolomini wrote
most of his pagan poetry and prose during this time. Writing in the style of Giovanni Boccaccio's *Decameron: O,*
Prencipe Galeotto (1349-1351; *The Decameron*, 1620),
Piccolomini wrote a play, *Chrysis* (1444), and a more substantial prose romance, *De duobus amantibus Eurialo et*
Lucresia (1444; *The Tale of Two Lovers*, 1560), which endeared him to the literary Humanists of the Italian Renaissance.

All this activity ended, to the skepticism of his peers,
when in 1446 Piccolomini announced that he was "for-

saking Venus for Bacchus," by which he meant that
he was renouncing sexual license for the wine of the
Eucharist. He took holy orders as a deacon and was reconciled to the church hierarchy by Pope Eugene IV. After that, ascent was swift. Pope Nicholas V appointed
him bishop of Trieste in 1447 and promoted him to the
bishopric of Siena in 1449. Callistus III made him cardinal in 1456. Finally, on August 19, 1458, a sharply divided College of Cardinals looked for a peacemaker and
elected Piccolomini pope; he boldly chose the name of a
second century saint, Pius, to be "reminiscent of pious
Aeneas."

LIFE'S WORK

Pius II faced an enormous challenge. Surrounded on all
sides by rivals and enemies, he would need all his diplomatic skills to play his enemies against one another.
From the northeast there was the Papacy's oldest rival,
the Holy Roman Empire—which people had long since
declared to be neither "holy" nor "Roman" nor an "empire," but which remained powerful. Pius relied on his
previously congenial diplomatic service with Frederick
to defuse this threat. From the northwest there was the
Papacy's most dangerous enemy, the kingdom of France,
which nearly fifty years earlier had been forced to give up
its Avignon antipope and which, a half century hence,
would invade Italy. Pius would fight his fiercest battle
with King Louis XI.

On the Italian peninsula itself, in the north, the commercial city-state republics of Venice, Florence, and others defied papal pretensions; in the south, the shaky
throne of Naples was attracting the covetous attention of
both Spanish Aragon and French Anjou. Pius could ignore the northern threat; he tried to mediate between the
latter claimants. Overriding all other threats for the
leader of Western Christendom, however, were two supreme challenges: one from within—conciliarism—and
one from without—the calamitous fall of the capital of
Eastern Christianity, Constantinople, to the Turks in
1453.

During the first four years of his reign, Pius persuaded
France's new king, Louis XI, to withdraw his support for
the Pragmatic Sanction in order to gain papal support for
the French claim to the kingdom of Naples. This diplomatic coup was designed to nullify simultaneously the
conciliarism and the enmity of France. The Pragmatic
Sanction of 1438 represented the high point of the

conciliar movement, the ecclesiastical movement to subordinate the pope to the church councils. The French kings and most French clergy had supported the sanction because they hated the clerical power of Rome. Pius had inherited his predecessors' policy, which supported the Aragonese claim to Naples, but he suggested to the French king that he could back the Angevin claim in exchange for some concessions. This diplomatic feat was Pius's only political success, and he was unable to capitalize on it.

The diplomatic situation was complicated because there were other players in the game. In fact, Louis's repudiation of the conciliar movement stemmed more from his fear of his own clergy in France (called Gallicans) than from any foreign policy consideration. The Gallican clergy opposed many aspects of monarchical rule. Louis was also fighting the Burgundian duke who claimed the French throne. Unfortunately, Pius was unable to follow through on his bargain with Louis. Finding that he needed Spanish support for his greater enterprise, the pope was compelled to turn to Burgundy, making concessions that solidified French hostility. The conciliar movement, however, was mortally wounded, and Pius deserves partial credit for administering its coup de grâce.

For the last two years of his reign, Pius prepared for the Crusade to liberate Constantinople from the Ottoman Turks. Eight centuries of fighting had culminated in the

Pius II. (Hulton|Archive by Getty Images)

city's capture in 1453, only five years before Pius's election. In his eyes, a crusade was essential to vindicate his life, his career, and his faith. At the personal level, a crusade was the only way that Pius could prove to his public, to his skeptical Humanist peers—who were angry at his desertion—and to the anxious religious constituents who were not yet convinced of his piety and faith, that he was what he professed to be: a true Christian. At the political level, this was the best way that Pius could protect the Papacy from its internal enemies.

In *Commentarii* (1464; *The Commentaries of Pius II*, 1936-1937), which he wrote in the last years of his life, Pius had four themes, which were largely political. On the Italian peninsula, to recover papal territory and support the anti-French candidate to the throne of Naples, Sigismondo Malasta of Rimini had to be fought. On the Continent, the pope had to curb France, but he also had to intervene judiciously in the turmoil of the empire, where Frederick III was embattled. In the moral realm, there was the nonreligious materialism of the Venetians, Florentines, and even Sienese—as dangerous as the outright heresy of the Hussites in Bohemia. Finally, there was what many considered the greatest menace of all: the Turks.

Pope Pius's Crusade was a failure. Providentially finding alum mines in Italy to help raise money, he decided to lead the Crusade himself. Carried on a litter because of his ruined feet, he embarked on June 18, 1464. Accompanied by a handful of loyal troops from Rome, Pius crossed to the shores of the Adriatic Sea. At the rendezvous, there were virtually no Italians. Louis XI from France did not come; the Aragonese from Spain and Naples, the Burgundians, and Emperor Frederick III did not come. During the night of August 14/15, at Ancona on the Adriatic Sea, far from Constantinople, Pius died.

SIGNIFICANCE

The question still lingers: Who was dominant? Enea Silvio Piccolomini, Renaissance Humanist and man of letters, or Pope Pius II, Crusader and would-be martyr? Pius was not a mystic like Joan of Arc, whose accomplishments and martyrdom streaked across the European landscape when Piccolomini was in his twenties. He was not a poet or scholar like his idols and peers, whose literary achievements were transforming Europe throughout his lifetime. He was not a charismatic reformer capable of cleansing the Church from the inside. All he had learned from his formal education was to write elegantly and speak persuasively to educated people. All he had inherited from his medieval profession was the desire to protect the papal office and to start a crusade.

History has remembered neither the Humanist nor the pope, and scholars who study him in the context of other pursuits have not been kind. In a speech to a group of cardinals, Pius frankly observed that the Europe of his day had rejected the medieval concept of a crusade without having yet awakened to the Turkish threat to Western civilization. When he said this in 1462 (before he was committed to his futile project), he was aware of his own variety of motives, both practical and idealistic. Nevertheless, he did decide to mobilize the gigantic defense operation necessary to save Christian Europe from the Turks—although he did not know how to proceed. All he could manage was to be carried in the direction of the battle and wait for either natural or supernatural intervention. He waited in vain.

What remains, then, are his writings. Although he ranks as a second-rate writer of the Italian Renaissance, being neither as good a storyteller as Boccaccio nor as incisive politically as Niccolò Machiavelli nor as philosophically profound as Giovanni Pico della Mirandola, he was adept enough to rise from poverty in a world of elegant Humanists. In addition, he was concerned enough to perceive that the greatest peril of the day emanated not from antipopes but from materialism in the West and the Turks from the East. He was brave enough to act on his observations with courage and commitment to the very end.

—David R. Stevenson

FURTHER READING

Abulafia, David. "Ferrante I of Naples, Pope Pius II, and the Congress of Mantua (1459)." In *Montjoie: Studies in Crusade History in Honour of Hans Eberhard Mayer*, edited by Benjamin Z. Kedar, Jonathan Riley-Smith, and Rudolf Hiestand. Brookfield, Vt.: Variorum, 1997. Essay discussing Ferrante I, who Pius had preferred for the throne of Naples over the claims of the French House of Anjou, and the consequences of that preference for the pope's attempts to mount a crusade in 1459. Includes bibliographic references and index.

Ady, Cecilia M. *Pius II (Aeneas Silvius Piccolomini) the Humanist Pope*. London: Methuen, 1913. This older study was written by an authority on late medieval and Renaissance Italy. It is favorable and sympathetic to someone caught in the predicament of being both a Humanist intellectual and a political leader of an insti-

tution not respected by Humanist intellectuals. Outdated.

Gragg, Florence A., and Leona C. Gabel. *Memoirs of a Renaissance Pope*. New York: Putnam, 1959. Gragg and Gabel delineate four major themes in the introduction to this abridged translation of *The Commentaries of Pius II:* Italian political conflicts, both between the pope and secular opponents and between two factions for the throne of Naples; France's malevolent presence; the disintegration of the amorphous Holy Roman Empire; and the planned Crusade against the Ottoman Turks, who had conquered Constantinople in 1453.

Kallendorf, Craig W., ed. and trans. *Humanist Educational Treatises*. Cambridge, Mass.: Harvard University Press, 2002. Collects three significant fifteenth century Humanist treatises, including Pius II's "The Education of Boys," as well as writings by Pier Paolo Vergerio and Battista Guarino. Useful, not only for Pius's primary text, but also for the juxtaposition of two competing contemporary visions of Humanist education that help to place the pope's thought in its larger context. Includes bibliographic references and index.

Martels, Zweder von, and Arjo Vanderjagt, eds. *Pius II, "el Più Expeditivo Pontifice": Selected Studies on Aeneas Silvius Piccolomini, 1405-1464.* Boston: Brill, 2003. Collection of papers presented at an academic workshop on Pius II in the Netherlands. Essays discuss the pope's educational program, his ethics, his historical and geographical publications, and court culture. Includes bibliographic references and index.

Pius II. *Commentaries*. Edited by Margaret Meserve and Macello Simonetta. Cambridge, Mass.: Harvard University Press, 2003. Volume 1 only. A new and comprehensive collection of Pius's autobiographical writings. Includes maps, bibliographic references, and index.

Rowe, John Gordon. "The Tragedy of Aeneas Silvius Piccolomini." *Church History* 30 (1961): 288-313. A savage critique of Pius as a Humanist and as a pope. This review is valuable to balance the usually positive view of Pius II. Unless a pope was spectacularly villainous—as many were in this period—most are sympathetically treated by both popular and academic critics. Since the literature in English on Pius is limited, this critique must serve. Ample bibliography.

Woodward, William Harrison. *Vittorino da Feltre and*

Other Humanist Educators. 1897. Reprint. New York: Bureau of Publications, Teachers College, Columbia University, 1964. Woodward devotes most of his attention to Vittorino da Feltre. Although Pius is placed in his historical context, he is portrayed as not very important. No bibliography.

See also: Leon Battista Alberti; Alexander VI; Frederick III; Louis XI; Niccolò Machiavelli; Nicholas of Cusa; Giovanni Pico della Mirandola.

Related article in *Great Events from History: The Renaissance & Early Modern Era, 1454-1600:* 1463-1479: Ottoman-Venetian War.

Pius V
Italian pope (1566-1572)

Pius V effected the Catholic reforms dictated by the Council of Trent, attempted to stem the spread of Protestantism, participated in the Inquisition, and was largely responsible for the naval defeat of the Ottoman Empire at Lepanto. His piety, religious zeal, and dedication led to his canonization.

Born: January 17, 1504; Bosco, duchy of Milan (now in Italy)
Died: May 1, 1572; Rome, Papal States (now in Italy)
Also known as: Antonio Ghislieri
Areas of achievement: Religion and theology, church reform

Early Life

Antonio Ghislieri, who would become Pope Pius (PI-uhs) V, was born in the small town of Bosco. His parents, Paolo and Dominica (née Augeria), were poor, and the future pope worked as a shepherd as a youth. Through the generosity of a more prosperous neighbor, he was put under the tutelage of the Dominican friars at Bosco; two years later, at fourteen, he was sent to the Dominican convent at Voghera. After beginning his novitiate at the Convent of Vigevano, he received his Dominican habit in 1520 and assumed his religious name, Michael, the following year. During this time, he developed his scholarly talent and practiced the monastic ideals of austerity, simplicity, and self-denial. His character and conduct as a pope were shaped in large part by his early life in the monastery.

An avid student, Ghislieri attended the University of Bologna, and he later became an equally successful teacher of philosophy and theology, which he taught at several Dominican friaries. In 1528, he was raised to the priesthood at Genoa and for the next several years served at various Dominican convents, where his piety, humility, and dedication won for him the respect of his colleagues—he was elected prior at four of the friaries. During this time, he also became confessor to many important people, among them the governor of Milan, yet he remained humble and, unlike many of his clerical peers, traveled everywhere by foot.

In 1542, the humble priest's life was changed by an act that ultimately led to his elevation to the Papacy. As a result of religious schism, notably the spread of Martin Luther's doctrine, a papal bull instituted the Roman Inquisition. Because of Ghislieri's skill at refuting the so-called Lutheran heresies—he had been summoned to Parma in 1543 to combat Lutheran doctrine and attacks on pontifical authority—he became inquisitor in the diocese of Patvia in 1543. It was his zealous role in the Inquisition that brought him to the attention of church leaders and his eventual election as Pope Pius V.

Life's Work

Although he was almost forty years old when he began his inquisitorial career, Pius's life's work and place in history are inextricably related not only to his pontificate but also to the Inquisition. In the relentless pursuit of his duties, he was often embroiled in disputes with a populace, including clergy, that was sympathetic to Luther. After he confiscated twelve bales of "heretical" books and excommunicated the guilty parties in Como, he barely escaped an enraged crowd. He was vindicated in Rome and, as inquisitor of Bergamo, dealt severely with a Luther supporter, Bishop Vittorio Soranzo, who was subsequently imprisoned, convicted, deposed as bishop, and exiled to Venice.

In 1551, he became, despite his objections, prefect of the Palace of the Inquisition, and in 1558, he became the first and the only grand inquisitor of the Roman Catholic Church. Ecclesiastical advancement accompanied his increasing role in the Inquisition. In 1556, he became bishop of Sutri and Nepi, then bishop of Mondovi; in 1557, he was named Cardinal Alessandrino (after the large city near his birthplace). So secure was his position that the 1559 election of Pope Pius IV, which adversely affected other cardinals, left him untouched. In fact, he demonstrated that his principles were more important than politics when he opposed Pius IV's elevation of a relative youngster to a position of authority in the Church.

On Pius IV's death, Cardinal Alessandrino became, through the efforts of Cardinal Borromeo, Pope Pius V. While his papacy lasted only six years, he presided over a church under siege from without and undermined from within. The Turks of the Ottoman Empire were a constant threat, and the Reformation sects in Germany, France, England, and the Lowlands were rapidly gaining converts, a disturbing development since church and state were one in the sixteenth century. Unfortunately, the Catholic princes—Philip II of Spain, Maximilian II of Germany, and Sigismund Augustus of Poland—were protective of their own power, unwilling to offend powerful Protestants, or bent on achieving their own ends. Pius also had to contend with clergy who did not share his enthusiasm for the reforms of the concluded Council of Trent (1545-1563) and with clergy who had been tainted by Lutheran doctrine.

Pius moved quickly to effect the reforms dictated by the Council of Trent, reforms that were consistent with his monastic life, his idealism, and his piety. During his papacy, the *Catechismus Romanus* (for pastoral use) appeared, the reform of the Breviary was completed, the *Missale Romanum* was printed, and three new masses were composed. Besides the liturgical reforms, he brought about an improvement in public morals in a Rome accustomed to the luxury-loving Renaissance popes. His internal reforms, which can be seen as a Counter-Reformation or reaction to Reformation inroads, can also be regarded as the Church's efforts to reform itself, efforts that had begun before Luther's break with the Church.

In Germany, where the Reformation was solidly established, Pius's efforts to influence Maximilian II (who was also the Holy Roman Emperor) were unsuccessful, for the emperor pursued a policy of conciliating the Catholics without alienating the Protestants. Despite the efforts of Commendone, the pope's nuncio (representative) to Germany, Maximilian was unwilling to move beyond the Augsburg Confession of 1530, which was unacceptable to the pontiff, and the emperor continued to let his Protestant subjects practice their religion. When his numerous concessions to Maximilian proved fruitless, Pius responded with an action that angered the emperor because it encroached on political matters. In an attempt to recapture the ancient rights of papal authority,

which had been diminished by his predecessors, Pius crowned Cosimo I de' Medici as grand duke of Tuscany in 1569.

The same erosion of papal authority had occurred in Spain, where Philip II shared Maximilian's concern about the threat to Caesaropapistical rights, rights that political rulers had gained at the expense of the Papacy. Philip II was reluctant to have the imprisoned archbishop Carranza moved to Rome for his heresy trial, and Pius succeeded in moving Carranza only after making financial concessions and conducting protracted negotiations with Philip. Though, like Maximilian II, Philip vowed his support of Pius, the Spanish king was equally reluctant to grant the pope's request that he send his troops to subdue the rebellious Netherlanders. The political/ecclesiastical conflict was heightened by Pius's unpopular papal bull prohibiting bullfighting and cruelty to animals in general, but Philip was also guilty of making civil inroads on papal authority. When Pius attempted to curb civil authority in his papal bull of 1568, *In Coena Domini*, Philip essentially ignored it and never really relinquished his regal rights to Pius V.

Even in Poland, a Catholic stronghold, there were problems. Although the Catholics were able to prevail over the Protestants at the 1570 diet in Warsaw, Pius's nuncio to Poland could not persuade Sigismund Augustus to reform the monasteries or to join the league against the Turkish threat. The Polish monarch's recalcitrance was caused in part by the pope's unwillingness to grant him a divorce from Queen Catherine of Habsburg.

England's king Henry VIII had divorced Catherine of Aragon in 1534, which caused England's break with Rome and the Catholic Church. Pius later failed in his attempt to return the country to the Catholic faith, however. Unsuccessful in gaining support for Mary, Queen of Scots, from Philip or from the duke of Alva, Pius excommunicated Queen Elizabeth I, a Protestant, in 1570. His *Regnans in Excelsis*, which also freed Catholics from the obligation to obey her, was countered by Elizabeth's repressive anti-Catholic measures. Elizabeth was the last monarch to be excommunicated by a pope.

Only in the Netherlands and in France did Pius win convincing victories for the Church. Philip finally dispatched the duke of Alva to crush the revolt in the Netherlands; the duke was only partly successful, and his brutality was notable even when judged by sixteenth century standards. In France, the civil war was ended in 1569 at Jarnac, where the Catholics won a decisive victory.

The pope's greatest achievement, however, was the defeat of the Turkish forces at Lepanto in 1571. Although the Ottoman Empire had invaded Hungary and threatened not only Venice but also Italy, only Pius seemed aware of the danger. Through the pope's negotiating skills and his financial commitment to the cause, Philip was persuaded to join Venice against the Turks. Under the command of Don Juan of Austria, the Christian fleet sailed to battle against the Ottoman forces, which had already overrun Nicosia and Famagusta in Cyprus. The Christian victory at Lepanto marked the high point of Pius's efforts for the Catholic Church.

Soon after the battle, the pope's health, which had never been good, deteriorated, and he died on May 1, 1572. One hundred years later, Pope Clement X beatified Pius V, and on May 22, 1712, he was canonized by Pope Clement XI.

SIGNIFICANCE

That no pope had been canonized in the 350 years that preceded Pius's canonization vividly demonstrates the esteem that he enjoyed within the Catholic Church. His efforts to effect the reforms dictated by the Council of Trent, his own monastic piety, his missionary zeal (during his papacy many missionaries were sent to South America, especially Brazil), and his lack of personal ambition—these traits reflect the saintliness of the pope known as the Pope of the Holy Rosary. History, however, has not been kind to Pius V, whose redemption of Sixtus of Siena must be measured against the strict censorship and the brutal torture of the Inquisition he endorsed and supported.

Pius was motivated by his ambition for the Catholic Church, threatened by the Turks and the Protestant Reformers, beset by internal apathy, and undermined by the political ambitions of rulers whose expanding powers eroded traditional papal authority. From the Church's perspective, church and state were the same, and political threats were religious threats (England, the Ottoman Empire, the Protestant German states) that ultimately threatened a civilization synonymous with the Church. Given the besieged condition of such an integrated world, Pius's extreme measures can be understood, if not justified.

The Western world was, however, irrevocably fragmented politically and theologically, and Pius's attempts to return to an earlier unified age were futile. In fact, his efforts to restore lost papal authority were not realistic, given the religious ferment and the political ambitions of rulers. Philip ignored Pius's papal bull of 1568, and Elizabeth's response to her excommunication revealed that weapon to be futile and obsolete. The world was effectively divided between the temporal and spiritual realms, and even the glorious victory at Lepanto was followed by apathy and dissension among the Catholic allies. Although he did not restore the Church's power and did not prevent the spread of Protestantism, Pius did achieve some success at reforming the Church and did enhance the image of the Papacy, which had been in decline.

—*Thomas L. Erskine*

FURTHER READING

Antony, C. M. *Saint Pius V: Pope of the Holy Rosary.* New York: Longmans, Green, 1911. A short biography from a Roman Catholic perspective, the book was one of the sources for Browne-Olf's *The Sword of Saint Michael* (1943). The book is rich in anecdotes and provides information about the details of the pope's canonization.

Browne-Olf, Lillian. *The Sword of Saint Michael: Saint Pius V, 1504-1572.* Milwaukee, Wis.: Bruce, 1943. One of the few biographies in English, the book vindicates Pius and suffers from such a Roman Catholic bias that it equates World War II with the Reformation and Adolf Hitler with Martin Luther. Nevertheless, the book is helpful at showing the Reformation in context. Contains a select bibliography.

Collins, Michael. *The Fisherman's Net: The Influence of the Papacy on History.* Chester Springs, Pa.: Dufour Editions, 2003. A survey of the influence of the office of the Papacy and of specific popes on the course of world history, from Saint Peter through John Paul II.

Daniel-Rops, H. *The Catholic Reformation.* Translated by John Warrington. New York: E. P. Dutton, 1962. An evenhanded evaluation of Pius that praises his reforms, summarizes his relations with Maximilian and Elizabeth, and discusses his "draconian orders for the hunting down of heresy, free thinking, and the faintest scent of Protestant sympathies." Daniel-Rops describes Pius's outlook as "largely medieval."

Rendina, Claudio. *The Popes: Histories and Secrets.* Translated by Paul D. McCusker. Santa Ana, Calif.: Seven Locks Press, 2002. Massive, comprehensive study of the biographies, historical significance, personal experiences, political and religious milieus, and controversies surrounding each of the popes from Saint Peter to John Paul II. Includes bibliographic references and index.

Seppelt, Francis X., and Clement Löffler. *A Short History of the Popes: Based on the Latest Researches.* St. Louis, Mo.: B. Herder, 1932. A short overview of the pope's most important achievements, which are seen as church reform and monastic life. His role in the Inquisition is virtually ignored except for an observation that he could be "harsh and severe when offenses were committed against ecclesiastical discipline."

Von Ranke, Leopold. *The History of the Popes During the Last Four Centuries.* 3 vols. London: G. Bell & Sons, 1913. The first volume contains an overview of Pius from the perspective of a German Protestant. While granting the pope's achievements, the author does portray Pius as an obstinate zealot who insisted on obedience and as a persecutor of innocence and purity. Consequently, Pius's role in the Inquisition is stressed, and his sainthood is not mentioned.

Walsh, William Thomas. *Characters of the Inquisition.* Reprint. Port Washington, N.Y.: Kennikat Press, 1969. Examines the inquisitorial spirit from the time of Moses to the twentieth century. Walsh focuses on the relationship between Philip and Pius, discusses the Carranza affair, and concludes that Spain ruthlessly trampled on the rights of the Catholic Church.

Wright, A. D. *The Early Modern Papacy: From the Council of Trent to the French Revolution, 1564-1789.* New York: Longman, 2000. Examination of both the scope and the limitations of the powers of the popes after the Council of Trent. Emphasizes the multiple, potentially conflicting obligations of the popes to the city of Rome, the Italian church, the transnational Catholic Church, the Papal States, and other specific religious and political entities.

SEE ALSO: Catherine of Aragon; Elizabeth I; Henry VIII; Martin Luther; Mary, Queen of Scots; Maximilian I; Cosimo I de' Medici; Mehmed II; Mehmed III; Saint Philip Neri; Philip II; Sigismund II August; Sixtus V; Süleyman the Magnificent; Tomás de Torquemada.

RELATED ARTICLES in *Great Events from History: The Renaissance & Early Modern Era, 1454-1600:* July 15, 1542-1559: Paul III Establishes the *Index of Prohibited Books*; July 22, 1566: Pius V Expels the Prostitutes from Rome; February 25, 1570: Pius V Excommunicates Elizabeth I; October 7, 1571: Battle of Lepanto.

FRANCISCO PIZARRO
Spanish conquistador

Pizarro experienced many frustrating years in the New World in search of fame and fortune before discovering and conquering the Inca Empire of Peru.

BORN: c. 1478; Trujillo, Extremadura, Castile (now in Spain)
DIED: June 26, 1541; Lima (now in Peru)
AREAS OF ACHIEVEMENT: Exploration, warfare and conquest

EARLY LIFE
The early life of Francisco Pizarro (frahn-CHAY-skoh pee-ZAH-roh) is poorly documented. He was born probably around 1478 in Trujillo, a city in the province of Extremadura, Spain, from which came many of the famous conquistadores. Pizarro was one of several illegitimate sons of Gonzalo Pizarro, an infantry officer. His mother, Francisca Morales, was a woman of plebeian origin about whom little is known. He received little attention from his parents and was, apparently, abandoned in his early years. He could neither read nor write, so he became a swineherd and was so destitute that, like the prodigal son, he was reduced to eating the swill thrown out for the pigs. He probably needed little encouragement to abandon this ignoble profession to go to Seville, gateway to the New World and fame and fortune.

In his thirties, Pizarro was in his prime, yet his most productive years lay ahead. Contemporary portraits depict him as tall and well built with broad shoulders and the characteristic forked beard of the period. He possessed a noble countenance, was an expert swordsman, and had great physical strength.

LIFE'S WORK
The circumstances under which Pizarro made his way across the Atlantic Ocean to the island of Hispaniola in the early years of the sixteenth century are not known. In 1510, he joined Alonso de Ojeda's expedition to Uraba in Terra Firma, where, at the new colony of San Sebastian, Pizarro gained knowledge of jungle warfare. When the colony foundered and Ojeda was forced to return for supplies to the islands, Pizarro was left in charge. He remained in the doomed colony for two months before death thinned the ranks sufficiently to allow the survivors to make their way back to civilization on the one remaining vessel.

Shortly thereafter, Pizarro entered the service of Vasco Núñez de Balboa and shared in the glory of founding a settlement at Darien and the subsequent discovery of the Pacific Ocean in 1513. Yet when Balboa fell from favor and was accused of treason by the governor of Panama, Pedrarias, Pizarro was the arresting officer. In the service of Pedrarias, there were new adventures, but, approaching fifty, old for that day, Pizarro had only a little land and a few South American Indians to show for his years of labor in the New World.

In 1515, Pizarro crossed the Isthmus and traded with the indigenous peoples on the Pacific coast. There he probably heard tales of a mysterious land to the south rich beyond belief in gold and silver. The subsequent exploits of Hernán Cortés in 1519-1521 and an expedition by Pascual de Andagoya in 1522, which brought news of wealthy kingdoms, gave impetus to further exploration and greatly excited the cupidity of the Spaniards. To finance an expedition, Pizarro formed a business triumvirate with Diego de Almagro, a solider of fortune, and Hernando de Luque, a learned ecclesiastic.

Pizarro's first foray, launched in December, 1524, took him down the coast of modern Colombia, where he encountered every hardship imaginable and soon returned quietly to Panama. Under the guidance of Bartolomé Ruiz, a famous navigator and explorer, Pizarro's second expedition set sail in early 1526. The voyage took them beyond modern-day Ecuador into the waters south of the equator, where they found evidence of an advanced South American Indian civilization. An inadequate number of men, dwindling provisions, and resistant Native Americans forced Pizarro and part of the company to take refuge first on the island of Gallo and later on Gorgona while Almagro returned to Panama to seek assistance. The governor, however, refused further help and sent a ship to collect the survivors. Audaciously, Pizarro and thirteen others refused to return. They endured seven months of starvation, foul weather, and ravenous insects until Almagro returned with provisions and the expedition was resumed. At length, they discovered the great and wealthy Incan city of Tumbes on the fringes of the Peruvian Empire. After a cordial stay, Pizarro returned to Panama with some gold, llamas, and Indians to gain support for an even greater expedition. The governor remained uninterested, so the business partners decided to send Pizarro to Spain to plead their case.

Charles V and his queen were sufficiently impressed with Pizarro's exploits and gifts to underwrite another expedition. In July, 1529, Pizarro was given extensive powers and privileges in the new lands, among them the titles of governor and captain-general with a generous salary. Almagro received substantially less, which caused

Francisco Pizarro. (Library of Congress)

a rift between the two friends. Before leaving Spain, Pizarro recruited his four brothers from Extremadura for the adventures ahead.

In January, 1531, Pizarro embarked on his third and last expedition to Peru. With no more than 180 men and three vessels, the expedition charted a course to Tumbes, which, because of a great civil war in the country, they found much less hospitable. Even so, the Spaniards' arrival was fortuitous in that the victor, Atahualpa, had not yet consolidated his conquests and was now recuperating at the ancient city of Cajamarca. In September, 1532, Pizarro began his march into the heart of the Inca Empire. After a difficult trek through the Andes, during which they encountered little resistance, they entered Cajamarca on November 15, 1532. Finding the Incan king at rest with only a portion of his army, Pizarro, pretending friendship, seized Atahualpa after a great slaughter of Indians. Atahualpa struck a bargain with his captors. In return for his release, he promised to fill a large room with gold. A second, smaller room was to be filled with silver. Fearing revolt, however, the captors carried out a summary trial, and the Inca was condemned to death.

Meanwhile, Almagro and his men had arrived in February, 1533, and loudly demanded a share of the wealth. The gold and silver vessels were melted down and distributed among the conquerors, while Almagro's men received a smaller amount and the promise of riches to come. Hernando Pizarro, Francisco's only legitimate brother, was sent to Spain with the royal one-fifth portion. From Cajamarca, Pizarro and his company pushed on to Cuzco. After encountering some resistance in the countryside, the conquistadores entered the city on November 15, 1533, where the scenes of rapine were repeated again.

After the conquest of Cuzco, Pizarro settled down to consolidate and rule his new dominion, now given legitimacy and the name of New Castile in royal documents brought back from Spain by Hernando Pizarro. A new Inca, Manco Capac II, was placed on the throne, and a municipal government was organized after the fashion of those in Iberia. Most of Pizarro's time, however, was consumed with the founding of a new capital, Lima, which was closer to the coast and had greater economic potential. These were difficult years. In 1536, Manco Capac grew tired of his ignominious status as a puppet emperor and led the Peruvians in a great revolt. For more than a year, the Incas besieged Cuzco. After great loss of life and much destruction throughout the country, the siege ended, although the Incas would remain restive for most of the sixteenth century.

In the meantime, a power struggle had developed between Almagro, who had returned from a fruitless expedition into New Toledo, the lands assigned him by the Crown, and Pizarro for control of Cuzco. On April 6, 1538, Almagro's forces were defeated in a great battle at Las Salinas. Almagro was condemned to death. In the three years that followed, Pizarro became something of a tyrant. On June 26, 1541, the Almagrists broke into Pizarro's palace in Lima and slew the venturesome conquistador.

SIGNIFICANCE

There are, perhaps, two possible ways in which the career of Francisco Pizarro might be evaluated. On the one hand, it is easy to regard him as one of many sixteenth century Spaniards, called conquistadores, whose cupidity sent them in search of fame and fortune, specifically gold and silver, in the New World.

In a relatively short period of time, Incas everywhere were conquered, tortured, murdered, and systematically stripped of their lands, families, and provisions. Pizarro played a major role in the rapacious conduct of the Castilians. Although this view is not without some merit, it must be understood within the context of Pizarro's world. He was not unlike a medieval Crusader who sallied forth against the enemy with the blessings of Crown and Church. The Crown was interested in precious metals and new territorial possessions, while the Church was concerned about lost souls. When his opportunity for fame and fortune finally presented itself, Pizarro had to overcome seemingly insurmountable odds—financial difficulties, hostile indigenous peoples, harsh weather and terrain, and later the enmity of other conquistadores—to create a Spanish empire in South America. Although his methods cannot be condoned, the empires of Alexander the Great, Charlemagne, and other conquerors were fashioned in much the same way.

—*Larry W. Usilton*

FURTHER READING

Abercrombie, Thomas A. *Pathways of Memory and Power: Ethnography and History Among an Andean People*. Madison: University of Wisconsin Press, 1998. Groundbreaking interdisciplinary combination of history and anthropology details the social memory and inherited rituals, hybrids of indigenous and European custom, of the Andean people. Discusses Pizarro's conquest of the region, and includes an appendix detailing his grant of Acho and Guarache to Hernando de Aldana. Illustrations, maps, bibliographic references, glossary, and index.

Adams, Charles. "How Cortes and Pizarro Found That Taxes Were the Chink in the Armor of the Aztec and Inca Rulers." In *For Good and Evil: The Impact of Taxes on the Course of Civilization*. 2d ed. Lanham, Md.: Madison Books, 1999. Study of one of the factors that enabled Pizarro to defeat the Incas and take control of their civilization. Includes bibliographic references and index.

Beardsell, Peter. *Europe and Latin America: Returning the Gaze*. New York: Manchester University Press, 2000. Collection of indigenous reactions to Latin American encounters with Europe, including Inca perspectives on Pizarro. Includes illustrations, bibliographic references, and index.

Birney, Hoffman. *Brothers of Doom: The Story of the Pizarros of Peru*. New York: G. P. Putnam's Sons, 1942. A well-written study of Pizarro and his brothers from the opening of the age of exploration to the death of Gonzalo Pizarro in 1548. The author purposely eschews footnotes and lengthy bibliographical references. A good introductory work.

Hemming, John. "Atahualpa and Pizarro." In *The Peru Reader: History, Culture, and Politics*, edited by Orin Starn, Carlos Iván Degregori, and Robin Kirk. Durham, N.C.: Duke University Press, 1995. Account of the meeting between Pizarro and Atahualpa at Cajamarca, attempting to evaluate the success or failure of attempts at communication and mutual understanding. Illustrations, map, bibliographic references, index.

_____. *The Conquest of the Incas.* New York: Harcourt Brace Jovanovich, 1970. A history of the conquest from Balboa's "discovery" of the Pacific Ocean in 1513 through the disintegration of the Inca Empire, with reference to the life of Pizarro. Includes chronological and genealogical tables plus an excellent bibliography.

Howard, Cecil, and J. H. Perry. *Pizarro and the Conquest of Peru.* New York: American Heritage, 1968. A well-illustrated history of the conquest and the civil wars that followed. Excellent for younger readers.

Kirkpatrick, F. A. *The Spanish Conquistadores.* 2d ed. Reprint. New York: Barnes & Noble Books, 1967. A survey of Spanish exploration, conquest, and settlement of the New World beginning with the voyages of Christopher Columbus. Provides a good overview of Pizarro's career.

Means, Philip Ainsworth. *Fall of the Inca Empire and the Spanish Rule in Peru, 1530-1780.* New York: Charles Scribner's Sons, 1932. Reprint. New York: Gordian Press, 1964. A history of the last years of the Inca Empire and Spanish dominion to 1780. Most of the important events of Pizarro's life are mentioned. Includes a scholarly bibliography plus a helpful index and glossary.

Prescott, William H. *History of the Conquest of Peru.* Rev. ed. New York: Modern Library, 1998. After more than a century and many editions, still one of the best works on the subject. Prescott's style will appeal to readers at all levels.

Varón Gabai, Rafael. *Francisco Pizarro and His Brothers: The Illusion of Power in Sixteenth-Century Peru.* Translated by Javier Flores Espinoza. Norman: University of Oklahoma Press, 1997. Study of the short-lived dominance of Pizarro and his family in Peru. Interprets the Pizarros' project as essentially a private business enterprise, and examines the relationship of the business both to the government and public funds of Spain and to indigenous groups in South America. Includes illustrations, bibliography, and index.

SEE ALSO: Pedro de Alvarado; Atahualpa; Vasco Núñez de Balboa; Álvar Núñez Cabeza de Vaca; Charles V; Christopher Columbus; Francisco Vásquez de Coronado; Hernán Cortés; Juan Sebastián de Elcano; Ferdinand II and Isabella I; Huáscar; Pedro Menéndez de Avilés; Montezuma II; Pachacuti; The Pinzón Brothers; Juan Ponce de León.

RELATED ARTICLES in *Great Events from History: The Renaissance & Early Modern Era, 1454-1600:* 16th century: Worldwide Inflation; 1525-1532: Huáscar and Atahualpa Share Inca Rule; 1532-1537: Pizarro Conquers the Incas in Peru.

JUAN PONCE DE LEÓN
Spanish explorer

Ponce de León was the first European discoverer of Florida and, more important, the Bahama Channel and the Gulf Stream, which proved invaluable to Spanish treasure ships making the passage from Mexico to Spain.

BORN: c. 1460; Tierra de Campos, Palencia, Leon (now in Spain)
DIED: July, 1521; Havana (now in Cuba)
AREA OF ACHIEVEMENT: Exploration

EARLY LIFE

Historical facts about the early life of Juan Ponce de León (WAHN ponts day lee-OHN) are limited. Born of uncertain parentage, Ponce may have been one of twenty-one illegitimate children acknowledged by Count Juan Ponce de León, a noble of Seville. Ponce probably served as a page to the knight Pedro Núñez de Guzmán, mastering sword and combat skills, the social graces, and religious instructions.

During the late 1480's, Ponce probably participated in the campaign to drive the Moors out of Spain, which succeeded in 1492. With the wars over, Ponce would have been at loose ends when Christopher Columbus returned triumphantly to Spain in the spring of 1493, boldly claiming the discovery of a New World filled with spices and gold, exhibiting its gold-ornamented Indians and exotic animals, and promising quick fortunes. When Columbus organized his second voyage to colonize the new lands in late 1493, foot-soldier Ponce was among the eager volunteers.

LIFE'S WORK

On September 25, 1493, according to Fernández de Oviedo's *Historia general de las Indias* (c. 1535-1557), Ponce left with Columbus's expeditionary force of seventeen ships, twelve hundred men, and six priests, bound for the island of Hispaniola (now called Haiti and the Dominican Republic). Arriving in late October or early November, Ponce and the other volunteers followed Columbus's orders of establishing the new settlement of Isabella. Ponce survived the bad food and drink, the malarial swamps, and the unfamiliar climate that afflicted the volunteers. He and the others were expected to press the Caribbean Indians into slavery, forcing them under threat of torture to clear and plant fields, tend cattle, or mine for gold.

Between 1494 and 1502, Ponce most likely returned to Spain but came back to Hispaniola, living in Santo Domingo from 1502 to 1504 and in Salvaléon from 1505 to 1508. During these years, Ponce's soldiering abilities and his rising social status on the island made him a favorite of Governor Nicolás de Ovando. He married a prominent innkeeper's daughter named Leonor, secured an impressive dowry from his father-in-law, and fathered three daughters and a son. When the Indians of the eastern province of Hispaniola rebelled and massacred Spaniards in 1504 because of cruel Spanish treatment, Ponce helped put down the rebellion and hanged its leader. Governor Ovando then appointed Ponce as deputy governor of the rebel province.

Finding little gold in the rebel province, Ponce developed farms, equitably distributing land grants and Indian slaves, building permanent stone buildings for defense, and creating a long-term commitment to developing the island's economy. Now in his thirties, the dauntless conquistador was also a devout Christian and an honest administrator, with a pleasing, ruddy-hued face. Still, he wanted more than financial success from agricultural endeavors. He looked eastward, toward the nearby island of Borinquén, a legendary cache of gold.

Between 1506 and 1508, Ponce sent Governor Ovando coded information about the possibility of gold on Borinquén (now called Puerto Rico) and secretly led a preliminary exploration of the island. Ponce, as captain of the militia, made friendly contact with the native Indians of Borinquén, who helped him to find gold deposits and led him to an excellent harbor for his ships. In 1508, Ponce claimed Borinquén for the Spanish Crown, establishing farms that later produced casava bread and other staples.

In 1509, King Ferdinand II appointed Ponce acting governor of Borinquén. Ponce became a wealthy and powerful man, encouraging Spanish settlers and gold seekers to make their fortunes on the island. He controlled the distribution of land grants, licensed the native Indian-slave trade, and mined for gold. At the harbor near Caparra (now called San Juan), he built warehouses, a causeway, docks, roads, and some fortifications. On October 26, 1510, he opened a foundry for smelting and refining precious metals.

Ponce's island became increasingly popular with Spanish settlers from 1509 to 1511 because of his administration, the abundant food supply, and the availability of Indian slaves. Yet the native Indians suffered terrible abuses and torture. Some Indians resigned themselves to a hopeless future; others did not resist because they believed the Spanish were immortal and godlike. This belief persisted until the Indians drowned a lone Spaniard and allowed his body to decompose. Once convinced that the Spaniards were mortal, the Indians planned a bloody uprising. While Ponce was away from the island in early 1511, rebel Indians wiped out the most notorious abuser of Indians, Cristóbal de Sotomayor, and his settlement. Ponce, commanded to put down the spreading rebellion, gathered an army that fell on the rebellious Indians, killing many in a series of skirmishes and returning others to slavery. Although Ponce was more lenient in his treatment of the indigenous than most Spaniards of his time, he did not hesitate to destroy Indian rebels or to kidnap them from other islands to serve as laborers.

Juan Ponce de León. (Library of Congress)

Also in 1511, political enemies in Spain forced an ailing King Ferdinand to replace Ponce as governor of Borinquén with Diego Columbus, nephew of the discoverer of the Americas. For a time, Ponce and his supporters found themselves under house arrest, and their properties were confiscated by the Columbus faction. On hearing what had happened, Ferdinand insisted that restitution be made to Ponce and his followers. After dismissing Ponce as governor, the king curiously sent messages to Ponce in June or July, 1511, urging him to negotiate a contract to discover and settle new lands to the north, such as the legendary island of Bimini, which promised much gold and a fabulous fountain that made the old young again.

No historical evidence exists that Ponce actually sought the "fountain of youth" during his voyage to discover Bimini in 1513. The first mention of the marvelous fountain in Bimini may be found in Antonio de Herrera's account of Ponce's voyage, *Historia general de los hechos de los castellanos* (c. 1549-1625). Historians have speculated that perhaps Ponce simply reported the Indian legends, that he may have wished to inflame the passions of those whose support he needed to make his voyage successful, and that perhaps the aged Ferdinand wanted the fountain's curative powers to restore his health and enable him to father a son. At any rate, Ferdinand issued a contract on February 23, 1512, appointing Ponce *adelantado*, or governor, over all lands he discovered. Ponce agreed to pay all expenses of the venture, build a settlement, and provide the king his usual one-fifth share of the proceeds.

On March 3, 1513, Ponce and his followers sailed to what is now called the Bahama Islands, finding the Bahama Channel but not Bimini or its fabled riches. They reached the eastern coast of present-day Florida on April 2, probably going ashore the next week somewhere between Saint Augustine and the St. Johns River to claim possession of the land for Spain. Believing his discovery an island, Ponce named it *La Florida* (meaning "land of flowers") to honor the Catholic observance of Easter. By late April, Ponce's ships sailed southward until they ran into the strong current of the Gulf Stream, which forced them back toward land. Landing, the voyagers encountered several ferocious attacks by Indians. Proceeding to the tip of Florida, Ponce's ships moved through the Florida Keys, then sailed up the west shore, doing some trading with North American Indians.

By late May or early June, Ponce and his voyagers anchored probably near present-day Charlotte Bay, only to be driven off by a hissing cloud of arrows and hordes of Indians in canoes. Ponce ordered his other ship to continue the exploration while he returned to Puerto Rico by mid-October, 1513. While Ponce failed to find the promised gold or the fountain of youth, he had discovered Florida and, more important, the Bahama Channel and the Gulf Stream, which later expedited the movement of Spanish treasures from the Caribbean to Spain.

During the early part of 1514, Ponce sailed to Spain, reporting his discoveries to Ferdinand and seeking approval for his colonization plans. After giving the king five thousand gold pesos, Ponce on September 27, 1514, received his contract, which called for him to colonize the lands, convert the indigenous population to Catholicism, captain an armada to destroy the cannibalistic Carib Indians, and pay all expenses for the venture.

From 1515 to 1521, Ponce spent much of his time and energy in wiping out the marauding Caribs, who threatened Spanish dominance in the Caribbean by preying on Spaniards and their Indian allies. During the interim, Ponce also busied himself with domestic matters, such as arranging the marriages of his daughters to prominent men on Borinquén; remarrying on his first wife's death and then burying his second wife; and devoting much of his increasing wealth to religious and charitable purposes. As an influential politician, Ponce became involved in the intense power struggle after the death of Ferdinand in 1516 and the accession of Charles I of Spain.

Ponce postponed his earlier plans for settling Florida until late February, 1521. Little is known about his second expedition other than he took equipment and supplies for establishing a self-sufficient colony. Somewhere on the west coast of Florida, probably on one of the islands in Charlotte Harbor, he and his followers unloaded their gear and constructed some dwellings and a chapel. Unfortunately for the Spaniards, they misjudged the reception of the indomitable Caloosa Indians and went ashore with too small a force of soldiers. In the ensuing battle, the Indians used fire-hardened reed arrows to pierce the Spaniards' chain armor, causing many deaths. Ponce received a severe arrow wound in the thigh and bled heavily. He and the other battered survivors made their way to Havana, Cuba, where Ponce died of his infected wounds. He was buried at San Juan, Puerto Rico. Ponce's heirs did not seek to continue his efforts in settling Florida. His son became a friar, while his daughters' descendants became prominent in Puerto Rico and Central America.

SIGNIFICANCE

After his death, Ponce de León's achievements tended to be forgotten in the wake of public acclaim for other conquistadores' exploits and their fabulous discoveries of gold and treasure in the New World. Ponce's name mistakenly became associated with the fruitless search for the fountain of youth. Yet Ponce's exploration of the Caribbean resulted in the colonization of and creation of economic prosperity on the islands. As a noted farmer, he became instrumental in raising self-sufficient food supplies for all Spanish-maintained islands in the Caribbean. As a negotiator skilled in working with various Indian chieftains, Ponce left a legacy of relatively humane treatment of the Indians, a legacy the priests on the islands continued by pressuring Spaniards who treated the Indians cruelly to mend their ways.

Although other explorers such as John Cabot and Amerigo Vespucci claimed to have discovered Florida earlier, Ponce de León received official credit because his 1513 voyage was made under Spanish auspices and officially recorded. Ponce's discovery of Florida laid the foundation of a Spanish heritage in Florida, linking it culturally to the Caribbean and Latin America. More important, Ponce's exploration of Florida's coastlines resulted in his marking both the Gulf Stream and the Bahama Channel, allowing expedient passage of Spanish treasure ships from Mexico to Cuba to Spain itself. Ponce de León's discoveries helped Spain maintain its dominance over other European powers during the ensuing era of conquest.

—*Richard Whitworth*

FURTHER READING

Bolton, Herbert E. *The Spanish Borderlands: A Chronicle of Old Florida and the Southwest.* Reprint. Albuquerque: University of New Mexico Press, 1996. Surveys the history of the discovery, exploration, and development of Florida and the Southwest by the Spanish. Includes bibliographic references and index.

Devereux, Anthony Q. *Juan Ponce de León, King Ferdinand, and the Fountain of Youth.* Spartanburg, S.C.: Reprint Company, 1993. Draws on Spanish archival information about Ponce's life, filling in the historical gaps.

Dolan, Sean. *Juan Ponce de Léon.* New York: Chelsea House, 1995. A highly readable biography with vivid illustrations of life in the New World.

Fuson, Robert H. *Juan Ponce de Léon and the Spanish Discovery of Puerto Rico and Florida.* Blacksburg, Va.: McDonald & Woodward, 2000. Seeks to counter the traditional accounts of Ponce de Léon as a naive and ineffective explorer searching for the fountain of youth. Emphasizes his honesty, trustworthiness, basic competence, and relatively humane treatment of indigenous peoples. Includes illustrations, maps, bibliographic references, and index.

Kenny, Michael. *The Romance of the Floridas: The Finding and the Founding.* New York: AMS Press, 1970. Part 1 covers Ponce's contributions to later Spanish settlements in Florida. Defends the Catholic Church's role in the Spaniards' enslavement of the Indians.

Kerby, Elizabeth P. *The Conquistadors.* New York: Putnam, 1969. Compares Ponce de Léon's contributions to those of such conquistadores as Hernán Cortés, Francisco Pizarro, and others.

Pérez de Ribas, Andrés. *History of the Triumphs of Our Holy Faith Amongst the Most Barbarous and Fierce Peoples of the New World.* Translated by Daniel T. Reff, Maureen Ahern, and Richard K. Danford. Tucson: University of Arizona Press, 1999. First published in 1645, this history of the Spanish missions in northern New Spain from 1591 to 1643 begins with an "Approval of Fray Juan Ponce de Léon." Includes maps, bibliographic references, and index.

Rienits, Rex, and Thea Rienits. *The Voyages of Columbus.* London: Hamlin, 1970. Provides information on the political times in which Ponce lived. Richly illustrated.

SEE ALSO: Pedro de Alvarado; Vasco Núñez de Balboa; Álvar Núñez Cabeza de Vaca; John Cabot; Christopher Columbus; Francisco Vásquez de Coronado; Hernán Cortés; Juan Sebastián de Elcano; Ferdinand II and Isabella I; Guacanagarí; Pedro Menéndez de Avilés; The Pinzón Brothers; Francisco Pizarro; Hernando de Soto; Amerigo Vespucci.

RELATED ARTICLE in *Great Events from History: The Renaissance & Early Modern Era, 1454-1600:* 1493-1521: Ponce de León's Voyages.

QĀYTBĀY
Sultan of the Mamlūk Dynasty (r. 1468-1496)

Qāytbāy, a military leader, diplomat, and prolific builder who considered architectural grandeur politically expedient, was the last powerful sultan of the Mamlūk Dynasty in Egypt.

BORN: 1414; Circassia (now in Russia)
DIED: August 8, 1496; Cairo, Egypt
ALSO KNOWN AS: al-Ashrāf Sayf al-Dīn Qāʾit Bāy; Qait Bey; Qaʾit Bay; Qaitbay; Qayitbey
AREAS OF ACHIEVEMENT: Military, warfare and conquest, government and politics, architecture, patronage of the arts

EARLY LIFE

Qāytbāy (KAYT-bay) was born among the Circassian peoples of what is today southern Russia. Like all Mamlūks, his parents sold him as a *mamlūk* (slave-soldier) for service in Egypt. He arrived in 1435, and because of his expertise with lance and bow, was purchased by Sultan al-Ashrāf Barsbay to become a royal *mamlūk*. The next sultan, Jaqmaq, promoted Qāytbāy to the elite of elites, the *khassaki*, or bodyguards. By the mid-1450's, he attained the highest rank, the so-called emir of one thousand.

A notable feature of Qāytbāy's formative years was his steadfast loyalty. This was a rare commodity in Mamlūk politics, which were notorious for cabals, cliques, betrayal, and in-fighting. Indeed, after going through three sultans in the 1460's, his fellow emirs saw Qāytbāy as a model *khushdash* (companion) and the ideal ruler. On January 31, 1468, he was proclaimed the forty-first Mamlūk sultan.

LIFE'S WORK

Arab historian Ibn Iyas, Qāytbāy's contemporary, wrote that "Although tainted by greed," Qāytbāy "was the noblest of the Circassian rulers, their finest." Reputation, personality, political skills, and charisma all played a part in this record. Indeed, one could argue it was exceptional because challenges faced him from the start.

Qāytbāy ruled an empire in decline. A hallmark of his reign was a decline in revenue juxtaposed with increased expenses. Although Qāytbāy was adroit at finding new sources of cash, the empire's economy had almost collapsed, and it failed to revive even with his attempts to improve trade relations with entrepreneur states such as Venice or Genoa. Money problems beset his regime every year and sometimes created disastrous consequences during war time.

All *mamlūks*, from lowly cadet through the highest emir, expected lavish compensation for their martial skills. When expectations did not meet reality, riots and revolutions occurred frequently. Qāytbāy faced continual disorders in Cairo, even among his own royal soldiers, as angry *mamlūks* robbed merchants, murdered government officials, and sometimes staged miniature wars over protection rackets and other extralegal activities.

Qāytbāy contributed to the financial dilemma. His power and longevity were based on building up a retinue of royal *mamlūks*. Qāytbāy purchased nearly eight thousand during his long reign, the largest number of any fifteenth century sultan. These men represented a tremendous outlay of cash, and once purchased, their expense continued with training, arming, and support.

Another drain on Qāytbāy's hard-pressed treasury was a public works program that included mosques, fountains, caravansaries, fortresses, and a magnificent mausoleum. Like previous sultans, Qāytbāy believed architecture served as a statement to his subjects and foreigners that he was powerful and wealthy. Qāytbāy left eighty-five significant structures in Syria, Palestine, Mecca, Alexandria, and Cairo.

Many of these buildings reflected Qāytbāy's pious support for Islam. Others were more mundane but very necessary, such as his forts at Rosetta and Alexandria (built over the site of the ancient Pharos lighthouse). They were necessary because Mamlūk coastal possessions were subject to continual raids by Christian corsairs (pirates), which interrupted the Asia-Europe spice trade, for which Egypt was a nexus until the Portuguese discovered an alternative route around Africa in the 1490's.

Pirate raids hurt the economy, but rebellion presented an even greater threat. Syria had been part of the Mamlūk realm for more than two hundred years. Important for strategic and economic reasons, sultans worked hard to keep Syria under their domination. Mamlūk Syria's defenses included a string of vassal states along the frontier. These dominated mountain passes that funneled north-south traffic from Anatolia to Syria.

By the 1470's, regional powers like the Ottoman Turks and Aq-Quyunlu (White Sheep) Confederation sought ways to take over these buffer states. A good example was Dulkadir, where a member of the local royal family was encouraged by Ottoman agents to end his fealty to Qāytbāy. Between 1466 and 1472, three expeditions left Cairo to crush the rebel leader. Although the rebel was a good general, his several victories over larger Mamlūk forces occurred partly because of the Mamlūks' poor discipline and leadership—endemic problems for the late Mamlūk armed forces. Finally, Qāytbāy's companion and *dawadar* (chancellor) Yashbak min Mahdi, was sent with a large army, which defeated the rebel leader in 1472.

Twelve years later, Dulkadir again figured in Qāytbāy's foreign policy, when Ottoman sultan Bayezid II attempted to supplant Mamlūk authority. Mamlūk-Ottoman relations had turned sour since a 1481 succession crisis between Bayezid and his brother Cem (or Jem). Cem lost a short war and fled south with a considerable entourage. Qāytbāy sheltered Cem for a year but did little to halt efforts to build an army of Turkish dissidents. After Cem's second effort to overthrow Bayezid failed, the Ottoman sultan viewed Qāytbāy as an enemy.

In 1483, Ottoman intrigue detached Dulkadir's new ruler from his Mamlūk suzerain. After spending so much blood and treasure to fight the rebel leader, Qāytbāy was unwilling to accept this fait accompli and opted for war. Beginning in 1485, Ottoman and Mamlūk forces fought for six years along their Syrian borders. Although Mamlūk soldiers won most of the battles, the cost of these campaigns ruined the treasury. Thus, in 1491, Qāytbāy was satisfied with peace and a return to the status quo.

The war's conclusion did little to alter the precarious state of Mamlūk finances. Inflation, spurred by a debased currency, competed with Mamlūk riots to shut down much of Cairo's once-vibrant markets. During the 1490's, Qāytbāy kept some control over his fellow Mamlūks by allowing them to loot what remained of the civilian economy through extraordinary taxes and outright theft. Although this allowed a semblance of power, it bankrupted the state, divorced most Egyptians from any sense of regime loyalty, and placed future sultans in a perilous position.

In addition, a virulent plague hit Egypt in 1492. This was a particular problem for Mamlūks, who, unaccustomed to Egypt's climate, food, and water, were more susceptible to disease than native-born Egyptians. It was not unusual for death rates to approach 33 percent among the soldier immigrants. The outbreak of 1492 killed only thousands, but these included many royal *mamlūks* and some of Qāytbāy's senior advisers. These losses increased tensions as outsiders saw the opportunity for a new sultan and a new *mamlūk* force.

Although the plague passed over Qāytbāy, his age and general health were major political factors. Every time he

was ill, rumors of his impending demise created cabals poised for revolution. This happened in 1477 and 1486. In the latter case, Qāytbāy ordered his doctors to put off their resetting of his badly fractured leg so he would have time to write personal letters to Syrian governors about his good health. No amount of letter writing could disguise his age, and Qāytbāy's authority waned in the 1490's. Indeed, rival factions were already fighting in his Cairo palace, when Qāytbāy, racked by dysentery, died on August 8, 1496.

SIGNIFICANCE

Qāytbāy was the last great Mamlūk sultan. His reign was memorable for defeating local rebels and Ottoman armies who attempted to seize vital Anatolian buffer states. He was a patron of the arts who also supported scholars and the construction of many public building projects.

Egypt's one-pound banknote provides perhaps the best image, however, of Qāytbāy's place in history. It features his mausoleum in Cairo's "city of the dead," an appropriate rendering, as the sultan's wars and buildings bankrupted the nation and led to its collapse and destruction in 1517.

—*John P. Dunn*

FURTHER READING

Har-El, Shai. *Struggle for Domination in the Middle East: The Ottoman-Mamlūk War, 1485-91.* Leiden, the Netherlands: Brill, 1995. The best authority on the most important conflict during Qāytbāy's reign.

Hattox, Ralph S. "Qāytbāy's Diplomatic Dilemma Concerning the Flight of Cem Sultan (1481-82)." *Mamlūk Studies Review* 6 (2002): 177-190. Good details on the first major dispute between Ottoman and Mamlūk leaders.

Petry, Carl F. *Protectors or Praetorians? The Last Mamlūk Sultans and Egypt's Waning As a Great Power.* Albany: State University of New York Press, 1994. Examines the many problems of the Mamlūk state during the fourteenth to fifteenth centuries. Petry is a leading authority on Qāytbāy.

_____. *Twilight of Majesty: The Reigns of Mamlūk Sultans al-Ashrāf Qāytbāy and Qansuh al-Ghawri in Egypt.* Seattle: University of Washington Press, 1993. A fine, authoritative biography of Qāytbāy.

SEE ALSO: Barbarossa; Bayezid II; Mehmed II.

RELATED ARTICLE in *Great Events from History: The Renaissance & Early Modern Era, 1454-1600:* May, 1485-April 13, 1517: Mamlūk-Ottoman Wars.

FRANÇOIS RABELAIS
French writer and physician

Rabelais, although a physician by trade, is best known for his writings, which satirize the Catholic Church and its officials while capturing the spirit of the Renaissance through grandiose characters who have an insatiable thirst for knowledge. Rabelais's strong challenge to spiritual authority is representative of a new period in literary thought and action.

BORN: c. 1494; La Devinière, near Chinon, France
DIED: April, 1553; Paris, France
ALSO KNOWN AS: Alcofribas Nasier (pseudonym)
AREAS OF ACHIEVEMENT: Literature, medicine

EARLY LIFE

François Rabelais (frah-swaw rab-eh-lay) was most likely born in the Loire Valley of France. His father was a lawyer, a prominent member of the landowning middle class. Little is known of his youth and, in fact, scarcely a date in his biography is beyond dispute. At some point, he entered the Franciscan monastery of La Baumette at Angers as a novice.

Since his subsequent actions and especially his writings suggest the opposite of the stereotypical monastic temperament, Rabelais, scholars surmise, entered the order so that he might study ancient texts. By the age of twenty-seven, Rabelais is known to have been a monk in the monastery of Puy-Saint-Martin at Fontenay-le-Comte, where he was immersed in Greek and other Humanistic studies. The faculty of theology at the Sorbonne was opposed to the study of Greek (eventually proscribing such study in France), and the head of the monastery was hostile to it as well. As a result, Rabelais petitioned Pope Clement VII for a transfer to the more liberal and scholarly Benedictine order. His request was granted in 1524, and the rest of his life was a step-by-step return to a secular status.

Little is known about the next six years of Rabelais's life. He must have found even the Benedictine monastery unsatisfactory, for he left it in 1527 or 1528. It is believed that he did considerable traveling over the next three years or so, principally because his books would later show evidence of wide travel. In September, 1530, he entered the University of Montpellier as a medical student and earned a bachelor's degree in medicine; the extreme brevity of his residence and his knowledge of Parisian student types, as exhibited in his writings, suggest that he had previously studied medicine in Paris. Early the next year, Rabelais was giving public lectures on Galen and Hippocrates, the ancient Greek physicians. In 1532, he moved to Lyons and was appointed a physician in the city hospital of the Pont-du-Rhône. Henceforward, medicine was Rabelais's trade. The Church did not object, so long as he retained his priestly garb and abstained from the practice of surgery.

LIFE'S WORK

Rabelais was an outstanding Greek scholar. He was a lecturer on anatomy, using the original Greek treatises. He received his doctorate of medicine at Montpellier in 1537 and for the last two decades of his life was highly regarded as a skilled physician. He was an intimate of the learned and powerful. It was not until he began his literary career at almost forty years of age, however, that he won lasting fame.

In 1532, Rabelais was working for a Lyons printer, editing Greek medical texts. During that summer, he read *Grandes et inestimables cronicques du grant et énorme géant Gargantua* (1532; great and inestimable chronicles of the great and enormous giant Gargantua), a newly published book by an anonymous author. This crude tale was an adjunct to the Arthurian legends, employing a character who had been present in French folklore for centuries. Rabelais was moved to write a sequel, greatly superior to the original in both style and content. *Pantagruel* (English translation, 1653), the literal meaning of which is "all-thirsty," was published in the autumn of 1532. It is the story of Gargantua's son, a boisterous and jovial drunkard, who is the gross personification of the tippler's burning thirst. A visit by Rabelais to his home province during a time of severe drought also may have been an inspiration for the book. *Pantagruel*'s author was

RABELAIS'S MAJOR WORKS	
1532	*Pantagruéline prognostication*
1532	*Aphorisms*
1532	*Ars medicinalis*
1532	*Pantagruel* (English translation, 1653)
1534	*Gargantua* (English translation, 1653)
1534	*Topographia antiquae Romae*
1541	*Gargantua and Pantagruel* (new ed.)
1546	*Tiers livre* (*Third Book*, 1693)
1548	*Le Quart livre* (rev. 1552; *Fourth Book*, 1694)
1549	*La Sciomachie et festins*
1564	*Le Cinquième livre* (*Fifth Book*, 1694)

identified as Alcofribas Nasier, which was an anagram of François Rabelais. The book was an immediate success with the public but was censured by the theological faculty of the Sorbonne as obscene. Also in 1532, Rabelais published a tongue-in-cheek almanac, *Pantagruéline prognostication*, which survives only in fragments.

Rabelais met Jean du Bellay, bishop of Paris and subsequently a cardinal, in 1533. By the next year, Rabelais was the bishop's personal physician and was attending him during a trip to Rome. In Rome, Rabelais requested absolution for leaving the Benedictine monastery without permission, but the pope declined to grant it. Later in 1534, back in France and still under the protection of his powerful patron, he published *Gargantua* (English translation, 1653), the main episode of which (concerning the Picrocholine War) was based on his father's dispute with a neighbor over fishing rights. The events of *Gargantua* precede those of *Pantagruel*; *Gargantua* would eventually become book 1 of the combined work. This volume was more satiric than the first, and Rabelais made his enemies, the theologians at the Sorbonne, the objects of scorn and derision.

Rabelais's satire of Scholasticism, the Church's official intellectual system for the previous two hundred years, roused such prejudice against him that he went into hiding for a time. By 1536, however, he was back in Rome, again traveling as a member of Jean du Bellay's party. This time, his petition was successful. The pope granted him absolution, and later in the year, after his return to France, he gained the status of a secular priest.

For the rest of his life, Rabelais avoided the official censure of the Church. He continued to travel during the years that followed, and he acquired further protection from his academic enemies by winning a minor post at the court of King Francis I. In all, Rabelais made four documented visits to Italy, under the protection either of Jean du Bellay or Jean's older brother Guillaume. The third sojourn in Rome lasted until 1541 and put Rabelais in frequent contact with the most learned and powerful men at the courts of the French ambassador and the pope. During these years, Rabelais was regarded as a greater physician than writer—he was famed for his dissection of cadavers and for the number of amazing cures he had effected.

Also in 1541, a new edition of Rabelais's work, *Gargantua and Pantagruel* (which combined the two earlier publications), appeared. Rabelais edited the work so as to soften somewhat its satirical treatment of theologians. The Sorbonne was not, however, in the least mollified; it forbade the sale or possession of the book.

During the 1540's, relations between the temporal and spiritual authorities were severely strained in France as elsewhere, so Rabelais maintained a low profile. Eventually, Rabelais used his court connections to publish the next installment of the giants' adventures. Book 3 of *Gargantua and Pantagruel*, called *Tiers livre* (1546) was dedicated to Queen Marguerite de Navarre, sister to the king. In fact, in 1545, Rabelais had secured official permission from the king to publish the book. Still, the faculty of theology at the Sorbonne condemned book 3. In this volume, the central character is really Panurge. In the loose narrative of the earlier works, Gargantua has sent Pantagruel to Paris to be educated. There the giant falls into the company of Panurge, who is about thirty-five years of age at the time they meet. Panurge

---

RABELAIS'S UTOPIA AT THE ABBEY OF THÉLÈME

*Few examples of the Humanist ideal can match Rabelais's utopian Abbey of Thélème (*Gargantua and Pantagruel*, book 1). The rule of Thélème is the obverse of that of Saint Benedict, which Rabelais had finally fled. Only the brightest and most beautiful are admitted to the abbey. There, members of both genders freely mingle, wear beautiful clothes, and engage in exhilarating conversation. Their behavior is virtuous not because of codes and admonitions but because of their natural high-mindedness. The only rule at Thélème could serve as the motto of the Renaissance:* Fay ce que vou dras *(do what you wish).*

Thélème in Greek means free will. . . . Here indeed he [Friar John] could institute a religious order contrary to all others. . . . Accordingly, they decided to admit into the new order only such women as were beautiful, shapely, pleasing of form and nature, and such men as were handsome, athletic and personable. . . . Moreover, since both men in monasteries and women in convents were forced after their noviciate [*sic*] to stay there perpetually, Gargantua and Friar John decided that the Thélèmites, men or women, might come and go whenever they saw fit. . . . Further, since the religious usually made the triple vow of chastity, poverty and obedience, at Thélème all had full leave to marry honestly, to enjoy wealth and to live in perfect freedom.

Source: The Norton Anthology of World Masterpieces, vol. 1, edited by Maynard Mack (New York: W. W. Norton, 1980), pp. 1253, 1254.

François Rabelais. (Library of Congress)

(literally "all-doer" or "knave") is the stereotypical perennial college student: He lives by his wits and is sly, mischievous, lascivious, and debauched.

Rabelais made his fourth and final visit to Rome in 1548, and in his absence opposition to *Gargantua and Pantagruel* grew steadily. Nevertheless, in 1550, he again obtained the king's permission to publish. In 1552, he brought out book 4 (wr. 1548), as well as revised and corrected versions of the first three books. Not unexpectedly, the Sorbonne banned book 4 immediately on its publication. In 1551, Rabelais had been appointed to the two curacies of Saint-Martin-de-Meudon and Saint-Cristophe-de-Jambet. He resigned both appointments early in 1553. Some scholars believe that he was forced to give up the curacies as a result of having published book 4; others speculate that poor health was his motivation. According to tradition, Rabelais died in April, 1553, in the rue des Jardins, Paris.

From 1562 through 1564, a fifth book was assembled. Few accept book 5 as being totally the work of Rabelais,

especially given that he was dead by this time. Critical opinion ranges from the belief that it includes only sketches and fragments by Rabelais to the belief that it is essentially his work, edited and expanded by the hand of another.

SIGNIFICANCE

Rabelais has been afforded the greatest honor that can be bestowed on any literary man or woman—his name has become an adjective. The term Rabelaisian is often applied too narrowly, to mean simply a story that graphically features copulation and the bodily functions. It more broadly means extravagance of caricature or robust humor. Still, the origination of that adjective is an acknowledgment that Rabelais's work is so singular as to be described only on its own terms.

It has been suggested that no writer better captures the spirit of the Renaissance. His giants represent the grandiosity of his age. Their appetite for life is as huge as their bodies, and they thirst for knowledge as well as wine. Few passages in literature contrast the medieval and the Renaissance attitudes so strikingly as do chapters 21 through 24 of book 1. Gargantua's tutor, Ponocrates, an advocate of the "new learning," saves the giant from the slothful and ineffective instruction of his former teachers, the worst of whom is the Sophist and Scholastic master, Tubal Holofernes. The demanding regimen of Ponocrates turns Gargantua into a complete man, physically, mentally, and spiritually—what the moderns have come to call the Renaissance man.

—*Patrick Adcock*

FURTHER READING

Bakhtin, Mikhail. *Rabelais and His World.* Reprint. Translated by Hélène Iswolsky. Bloomington: University of Indiana Press, 1985. A reprint of the English translation first published by the Massachusetts Institute of Technology Press in 1968; the Russian edition was published in 1965. Bakhtin's widely influential study considers Rabelais in the context of the "carnival" tradition: a rich and subversive vein of folk humor and comic festivities evident throughout the Middle Ages and the Renaissance.

Bowen, Barbara C. *Enter Rabelais, Laughing.* Nashville, Tenn.: Vanderbilt University Press, 1998. An account of Rabelais's humor and what made it funny to his contemporaries. Provides general coverage of French Renaissance culture in addition to an original and contentious reading of Rabelais and his work. Includes bibliographic references and index.

Brown, Huntington. *Rabelais in English Literature.* Reprint. New York: Octagon Books, 1967. A reprint of Brown's study, first published by Harvard University Press in 1933. Argues that since the Renaissance, Rabelais has been better appreciated in England than in his own country and that his influence on English literature has been very marked. Brown traces this influence in Ben Jonson, Sir Thomas Browne, Jonathan Swift, Laurence Stern, Tobias Smollett, and others.

Coleman, Dorothy Gabe. *Rabelais: A Critical Study in Prose Fiction.* Cambridge, England: Cambridge University Press, 1971. This study examines the first four books of *Gargantua and Pantagruel* in nine chapters and some 230 pages of text. The author excludes discussion of book 5 on the grounds that its authenticity has not been established in four hundred years and may never be. She has used the English version (a very free interpretation) of Sir Thomas Urquhart of Cromarty (1611-1660) for the first three books and that of Peter le Motteux for the fourth. She quotes Rabelais directly when a more accurate rendering is required. Contains a chronology and a select bibliography.

Duval, Edwin M. *The Design of Rabelais's "Tiers Livre de Pantagruel."* Geneva: Librairie Droz, 1997. Argues that Rabelais has been consistently misunderstood by those who fail to notice, or are unable to negotiate, the extreme erudition of his work. Includes bibliographic references and index.

Kaisar, Walter. *Praisers of Folly: Erasmus, Rabelais, Shakespeare.* Cambridge, Mass.: Harvard University Press, 1963. Begins with a prologue, discussing the fool in Renaissance literature. Part 2 is devoted to Rabelais's Panurge. He is compared to Desiderius Erasmus's Stultitia (part 1) and to William Shakespeare's Falstaff (part 3). Includes an extensive bibliography.

Parkin, John. *Interpretations of Rabelais.* Lewiston, N.Y.: E. Mellen Press, 2002. Survey of Rabelais's work and critical reactions to it, up to and including Bakhtin. Includes bibliographic references and index.

Rabelais, François. *Rabelais: A Dramatic Game in Two Parts.* Edited by Jean-Louis Barrault. Translated by Robert Baldick. New York: Hill & Wang, 1971. A play adapted from the five books of Rabelais. The playwright attempts to capture and project Rabelais's essential psychic health and love of life. Part (act) 1 is devoted to Gargantua and Pantagruel; part (act) 2 is devoted largely to Panurge. Each of the famous incidents is dramatized: part 1, scene 5, "Medieval Education"; part 1, scene 6, "Humanist Education"; part 1, scene 7, "Picrochole"; part 1, scene 8, "The Abbey of Thélème"; and the epilogue, "The Death of Rabelais." Includes nine photographs from the play in performance.

Tilley, Arthur Augustus. *Studies in the French Renaissance.* New York: Barnes & Noble Books, 1968. A reprint of a work first published by Cambridge University Press in 1922. Three chapters are devoted exclusively to Rabelais: chapter 3, "Rabelais and Geographical Discovery," chapter 4, "Rabelais and Henry II," and chapter 5, "Rabelais and the Fifth Book." Fully indexed.

SEE ALSO: Pietro de Aretino; Desiderius Erasmus; Francis I; Marguerite de Navarre; Michel Eyquem de Montaigne; William Shakespeare.

RELATED ARTICLES in *Great Events from History: The Renaissance & Early Modern Era, 1454-1600:* 1499-1517: Erasmus Advances Humanism in England; 1580-1595: Montaigne Publishes His *Essays.*

SIR WALTER RALEGH
English explorer and poet

Ralegh's vision and enterprise paved the way for English settlement in North America and prevented the northward expansion of the Spanish Empire.

BORN: c. 1552; Hayes Barton, Devon, England
DIED: October 29, 1618; London, England
ALSO KNOWN AS: Sir Walter Raleigh
AREAS OF ACHIEVEMENT: Exploration, government and politics, literature, military

EARLY LIFE

The birth date of Walter Ralegh (RAWL-ee) is even more uncertain than that of his contemporary William Shakespeare, but the dates of their deaths are precisely recorded, because by then they were among the most famous men of their time. Similarly, their family names are spelled in various ways. More than seventy spellings are recorded for Ralegh, the form he preferred in the second half of his life.

Ralegh is often designated as having been born in 1552, though 1554 accords with depositions he made in lawsuits. In any case, his birth occurred on the farm, or Barton, of Hayes, near East Budleigh on the south coast of Devon. His father was a gentleman farmer, who, like some of his relatives and other adventurous men of southwestern England, made money from maritime ventures, including privateering. Young Walter assuredly learned much about seafaring, as imaginatively depicted in Sir John Everett Millais's famous painting of Walter and another boy sitting on the beach, listening enthralled to a sailor's tale.

Famous as he was to become by seafaring, however, Walter first made his mark as a soldier on land. At the end of the 1560's, he was campaigning in France as one of the volunteers fighting for the Protestant Huguenots against the Catholics, an experience that helped to shape his anti-Catholic attitude for the rest of his life. By 1572, he was an undergraduate at Oriel College in Oxford University, but within two years he left without taking a degree, a common practice then. In 1575, he enrolled in the Middle Temple, one of the Inns of Court in London, though he did not complete his legal education. No doubt he acquired knowledge of city and court ways.

LIFE'S WORK

In 1578, Ralegh sailed from Plymouth in Devon as captain of one of the ships under the command of his half brother, Sir Humphrey Gilbert, who held the charter to settle new lands for the Crown. The expedition aimed to explore and colonize the coast of North America. Bad weather drove the other ships back to England, but Ralegh persevered and reached the Cape Verde Islands, four hundred miles west of Africa.

After obtaining a minor post at court, in 1580, he was given command of a company of soldiers sent to help suppress rebellion in Ireland. He was involved in savage fighting, he befriended the poet Edmund Spenser, and had a child with Alice Gould. (He provided in his will for their illegitimate daughter and found Alice a well-to-do husband.) According to one account, "Ralegh coming out of Ireland to the English Court in good habit (his clothes then being a considerable part of his estate) found the Queen walking [in] a plashy place." He immediately "spread his new plush cloak on the ground, whereon the Queen trod gently, rewarding him afterward." This story, reported some eighty years later in Thomas Fuller's *The History of the Worthies of England* (1662), may be apocryphal, but it contains two indisputable truths: paintings and miniatures of Ralegh show that he dressed in the most opulent styles of the period, and he quickly became one of Queen Elizabeth I's favorite courtiers.

In 1583, Elizabeth gave him Durham House, a mansion on the north bank of the Thames, east of Westminster Abbey, and in 1584 the profitable monopolies of "the farm of wines" (by which he was authorized to charge every vintner in the realm one pound a year to sell wine) and the license to export woolen broadcloths. Also in 1584, he became a member of Parliament for Devon and soon afterward vice admiral of Devon and Cornwall, lord lieutenant of Cornwall, and lord warden of the Stannaries (the tin mines of Cornwall). In January, 1585, the queen bestowed a knighthood on him and later made him captain of her guard.

Ralegh was adept at flattering the queen in Petrarchan poems praising her beauty, power, and influence. More tangibly, he would present to her the new lands of "Virginia," now North Carolina, where the expedition he equipped had landed in 1584. The following year, he sent about one hundred men to Roanoke Island on its coast, but they returned after the hardships of the first winter proved too severe for them. In 1587, a third expedition brought more than one hundred men and women to the site. The first child was born to the colonists on August 18 and christened Virginia Dare. Dealing with the Spanish Armada prevented a relief expedition from coming

Sir Walter Ralegh. (Library of Congress)

out until 1590, by which time the colonists had vanished. Although this lost colony was Ralegh's last colonizing attempt in North America, his efforts paved the way for the establishment there of an English-speaking empire in the early seventeenth century and prevented the northward spread of the Spanish Empire.

By the end of the 1580's, Ralegh could have been more than satisfied both by his personal advancement and by England's success at Spain's expense. Yet his fortunes were being undermined. The dashing and ambitious Robert Devereux, earl of Essex, arrived at court and soon became the aging queen's latest favorite. Meanwhile, Ralegh became involved with one of her ladies-in-waiting, Elizabeth Throckmorton, who was a dozen years younger than he and some thirty years younger than the queen. By November, 1591, if not earlier, Ralegh was secretly married to Throckmorton. A son was born in March, 1592, but seems not to have survived for long. A second son, Walter, was born in 1593 and a third, Carew, in 1604.

In 1592, Queen Elizabeth had put Ralegh in command of an expedition against Panama, though forbidding him to sail beyond Spain. While he was at sea, she learned of

his secret marriage, and on his return, she had him and his wife imprisoned separately in the Tower of London. When the expedition returned with a captured Portuguese galleon laden with riches from the East Indies, Ralegh was sent to Dartmouth to make sure that the queen's share of the booty—and his share, which she appropriated—were not looted. In effect, he was obliged to buy his pardon. Released from prison but banished from court, Ralegh and his wife withdrew to the Dorset estate of Sherborne, which he had begged from the queen while still in favor and which he now set about rebuilding. This activity, however, did not satisfy his ambitions.

After Sir Humphrey Gilbert drowned on the voyage home from Newfoundland in 1583, Ralegh had acquired Gilbert's charter to explore and settle new lands. He now focused on South America, source of the wealth carried to Spain in the ships that Sir Francis Drake, Ralegh, and others captured at sea. In one such action, Sir Richard Grenville lost his life in a heroic (though perhaps ill-judged) rearguard action at the Azores in 1591; Ralegh glorified this event in *A Report of the Truth of the Fight About the Isles of Açores This Last Summer* (1591; also known as *The Last Fight of the Revenge*), his first published book. (Individual poems by or attributed to him were published from 1576 onward, but he never published a collection of his poems.) Ralegh was convinced that in the hinterlands of Guiana, now Venezuela, lay the fabulously rich empire of El Dorado. In 1595, he led an expedition to Guiana and on his return promptly wrote and published *The Discovery of the Large, Rich, and Beautiful Empire of Guiana . . .*(1596), in which he argued that abundant gold could be found there, and that friendly South American Indians were eager to overthrow their cruel Spanish oppressors and welcome the benign rule of Elizabeth.

Whatever the queen thought of this argument, Ralegh was soon employed on a different venture. He was given command of a squadron in the 1596 expedition against Cádiz, under the leadership of Lord Admiral Howard and Essex. Ralegh boldly led his ships against the harbor defenses and suffered a leg wound that left him using a cane for the rest of his life. His spirited initiative was not shared by the commanders, whose temporizing failed to secure the fullest spoils possible.

The following year, he and Essex led another expedition to seize a Spanish treasure fleet off the Azores. Again, Essex's inadequacies and Ralegh's courage were revealed, the only gain being the temporary capture of the port of Fayal, which Ralegh achieved by leading his men ashore under fire. These events did nothing to assuage the rivalry between the two courtiers. When the irrationally ambitious Essex raised his abortive rebellion against the queen in 1601 and was executed for doing so, suspicion that Ralegh had contributed to his doom was widespread.

While Essex was ruining himself, Ralegh was improving the trade and fortifications of the isle of Jersey, of which the queen made him governor in 1600. This was to be his last advancement, however, because with her death in 1603 his fortunes plummeted. The new sovereign, James I, was strongly biased against Ralegh, reportedly greeting him with the words, "I have heard rawly of thee" and soon depriving him of his positions. Rumored to be discontented, as he might well have been, Ralegh was suspected of treasonous conspiracies against the new king from Scotland. In 1593, he had been exonerated when tried for atheism for his association with the "School of Night," a group of skeptics and freethinkers that included Christopher Marlowe. In 1603, the charges were to be even more implausible but more far-reaching. Ralegh was accused of being in Spanish pay to seek a new policy of peace toward Spain and to be part of a conspiracy to depose James and replace him with his cousin Arabella Stuart. Though Ralegh's position on these matters is not entirely clear, his trial was conducted with appalling injustice and venom, and in spite of the splendid speeches he made in his defense, a rigged jury guaranteed that he would be found guilty and sentenced to death.

Perhaps because executing the "last Elizabethan" hero was deemed to be impolitic, Ralegh was not put to death but imprisoned in the Tower of London again, this time for almost thirteen years. Again refusing simply to languish in royal disfavor, Ralegh wrote letters containing exaggerated professions of regard for James and humiliating pleas for pardon. He had hundreds of books brought in and embarked on writing *The History of the World* (1614). This monumental undertaking went as far as 133 B.C.E., and although Ralegh does not refer to the sovereigns he served, James denounced the book as "too saucy in censuring princes" and tried to suppress its publication. James's enmity was not shared by his queen, Anne of Denmark, and their son Prince Henry, both of whom often visited Ralegh in the Tower. Ralegh served as tutor to Prince Henry, for whom he wrote *The History of the World* and whose premature death in 1612 at the age of eighteen caused Ralegh to stop work on the book. The death was a double blow to Ralegh, not only because of the prince's announcement that "No one but my father would keep such a bird in a cage," but also because the manly and chivalric prince seemed likely to be the inspiring monarch that James was not.

James's attempts to secure a substantial dowry from a proposed marriage between his younger son Charles and a Spanish princess had been frustrated by 1616. Hearkening to Ralegh's continual claim that gold could be extracted from Guiana, James released Ralegh to organize and lead an expedition there. At the same time, James secretly assured the Spaniards that if Ralegh came into conflict with them, his life would be forfeit. Ralegh was now in his sixties and had suffered several strokes. By the time the expedition neared Guiana in late 1617, he was so ill with fever that he had to delegate command of the party that went up the river Orinoco to his trusted second-in-command, Lawrence Keymis. At the fort of San Thomé, the party got into a fight with the Spaniards, during which Ralegh's son Walter was killed. No gold was found; after returning to the ships, Keymis committed suicide.

Ralegh returned to England shattered and was soon imprisoned yet again in the Tower. After having been condemned to death in 1603 on the charge of conspiring to make peace with Spain, he was now to be executed for making war with Spain. The sentence of fifteen years earlier was carried out on October 29, 1618. A huge crowd gathered in the Old Palace Yard at Westminster and Ralegh, elegantly dressed, delivered a speech of nearly one hour in which he defended himself against the charges brought against him and committed himself to the mercy of God. Declining a blindfold, he laid his head on the block and told the hesitant executioner, "What dost thou fear? Strike man, strike!" The headsman needed two blows to sever Ralegh's head, which was carried away by his widow, while his body was buried in the nearby church of St. Margaret's, Westminster.

SIGNIFICANCE

Often disliked as a proud, ambitious upstart during his rise, Sir Walter Ralegh, by the courage and grace with which he faced his end, won widespread sympathy as a political martyr. Among those who witnessed his execution were some of the men who would lead the Great Rebellion of the 1640's against the autocratic despotism of the Stuart monarchy. Ironically, therefore, the beheaded victim of King James became an influence on those who would behead James's son King Charles I thirty years and three months later.

Ralegh's vision of the possibilities of empire for England in the Americas, although persuasively supported by his gift as a writer and his daring as an explorer and

soldier, would not be realized in his lifetime. Still, he captured the imagination of the English people, and his enterprises and plans were brought to completion by others.
— *Christopher Armitage*

FURTHER READING

Adamson, J. H., and H. F. Folland. *The Shepherd of the Ocean: An Account of Sir Walter Ralegh and His Times.* Boston: Gambit, 1969. Sets Ralegh's life in its historical and political contexts and devotes ample space to summarizing his literary work and relationships.

Armitage, Christopher M. *Sir Walter Ralegh: An Annotated Bibliography.* Chapel Hill: University of North Carolina Press, 1987. Lists nearly two thousand items by and about Ralegh, from 1576 to 1986.

Hammond, Peter. *Sir Walter Ralegh.* London: Pitkin Books, 1978. A concise biography, with abundant pictures of people and places of significance in Ralegh's life.

Jones, H. G., ed. *Raleigh and Quinn: The Explorer and His Boswell.* Chapel Hill: North Caroliniana Society, 1987. A wide-ranging set of papers from the 1987 International Conference on Ralegh, at which David Beers Quinn, emeritus professor at the University of Liverpool, was honored for his many publications in the field.

Miller, Lee. *Roanoke: Solving the Mystery of the Lost Colony.* New York: Penguin Books, 2002. Miller attempts to determine the real causes of the colonists' disappearance. Includes illustrations, maps, bibliographic references, and index.

Miller, Shannon. *Invested with Meaning: The Ralegh Circle in the New World.* Philadelphia: University of Pennsylvania Press, 1998. Study of the failed New World colonies attempted by Ralegh and his circle. Explains the links between these projects and changes in England's economy and social structure. Includes illustrations, bibliographic references, and index.

Raleigh, Sir Walter. *The History of the World.* Edited by C. A. Patrides. London: Macmillan, 1971. The most substantial modern selection from this huge work, with an analysis of Ralegh's achievement as a writer of history.

_____. *Selected Prose and Poetry.* Edited by Agnes M. C. Latham. London: University of London, Athlone Press, 1965. A selection by the editor of the standard edition of *The Poems of Sir Walter Ralegh* (1929).

_____. *Selected Writings.* Edited by Gerald Hammond. Harmondsworth: Penguin Books, 1986. A convenient modern selection of Ralegh's poems, prose works, and letters.

_____. *The Works of Sir Walter Raleigh.* New York: Oxford University Press, 1829. 8 vols. Reprint. New York: Burt Franklin, 1965. Volume 1 contains the early biographies of Ralegh by W. Oldys and T. Birch; volumes 2-7 contain *The History of the World*; and volume 8 contains miscellaneous essays, poems, and letters, many now considered to have been foisted on Ralegh after his death.

Trevelyan, Raleigh. *Sir Walter Raleigh.* New York: H. Holt, 2004. Exhaustive biography of Ralegh, written by a direct descendant. Includes illustrations, maps, bibliographic references, and index.

Wallace, Willard M. *Sir Walter Ralegh.* Princeton, N.J.: Princeton University Press, 1959. Covers Ralegh's life and pays considerable attention to his literary work.

SEE ALSO: Thomas Cavendish; John Davis; Sir Francis Drake; Elizabeth I; Sir Martin Frobisher; Sir Humphrey Gilbert; Sir Richard Grenville; Christopher Marlowe; Pemisapan; First Earl of Salisbury; William Shakespeare; Edmund Spenser.

RELATED ARTICLES in *Great Events from History: The Renaissance & Early Modern Era, 1454-1600:* July 4, 1584-1590: Lost Colony of Roanoke; 1596: Ralegh Arrives in Guiana.

PETER RAMUS
French philosopher and rhetorician

Ramus rethought and reorganized Aristotle's logic and devised what he called a simplified system of rhetoric based on method, observation, daily speech, and usefulness. He was highly influential on Puritan thinkers of the early seventeenth century, and he advocated the redesign of university curricula according to Humanist principles.

BORN: 1515; Cuts, near Noyon, Vermandois, Picardy, France
DIED: August 26, 1572; Paris, France
ALSO KNOWN AS: Pierre de la Ramée (given name); Petrus Ramus
AREAS OF ACHIEVEMENT: Philosophy, literature, education, scholarship

EARLY LIFE

Peter Ramus (PAY-tehr RAY-muhs) was one of the most widely read and influential rhetoricians of the European Renaissance. Born Pierre de la Ramée to poor parents, he later latinized his name to Petrus Ramus. He entered the Collège de Navarre in Paris in 1527, earning his master of arts degree nine years later. In 1537, he began giving well-received lectures at the Collège du Mans. Despite his popularity among students, however, his strongly anti-Aristotelian opinions angered faculty and administrators, who disagreed with his energetic plans to redesign the university curriculum by eliminating its reliance on courses of study dating from the Middle Ages.

LIFE'S WORK

In 1544, Ramus was relieved of his teaching duties, but in 1545, he was appointed director of the Collège de Presles, and a ban against his teaching was waived in 1547. In 1551, he became the first head of the Collège de France. Despite his Roman Catholic upbringing, Ramus became a Protestant convert in 1561, an action that alienated his former advocate Cardinal Charles de Lorraine. He embarked on a plan to reorganize the University of Paris by arguing for a reduction of the teaching staff, the eradication of student tuition, the use of monies drawn from bishops and monasteries, and the inclusion of new professorships in physics, mathematics, botany, Hebrew, Greek, and other subjects.

Calvinists were expelled from Paris in 1562, forcing Ramus to leave for Fontainebleau. He returned to Paris in 1563 but spent only four years there, fleeing again after an academic controversy. In his absence, his library had been burned. The mounting religious conflict caused him to depart for Protestant Germany and Switzerland in 1568-1570. Though his Calvinism found him friends, his opposition to Aristotle continued to earn him criticism. He returned to Paris in 1570 but was denied again a teaching post, and in 1572, he was condemned by the synod of Nîmes for advocating a congregational form of Church rule.

On August 26, 1572, Ramus was murdered, becoming one of the three thousand Huguenots killed by Parisian Catholics in what became known as the St. Bartholomew's Day Massacre, a religious persecution that claimed eventually seventy thousand French Protestants. It is possible that Ramus was executed at the order of an embittered faculty member at his own college.

In spite of his life of frequent travel, bitter controversy, and hard study (he reputedly slept only three hours per night), Ramus published more than sixty works in rhetoric, logic, languages, and religion, as well as collections of his lectures and commentaries and editions of the classics. Thirteen additional works were completed with the aid of Omer Talon (Audomarus Talaeus), a fellow academic with whom he worked at the Collège de Presles. Collected editions of all their works number well more than one thousand, testimony to the broad influence of this reformer during the later sixteenth and early seventeenth centuries. Ramus's first major works, *Dialecticae partitiones* (structure in dialectic) and *Aristotelicae animadversions* (remarks on Aristotle) appeared in 1543. *Brutinae quaestiones in Oratorem Ciceronis* (questions of Brutus against Cicero's orator) was published in 1547, followed in 1549 by *Rhetoricae distinctiones in Quintilianum* (*Arguments in Rhetoric Against Quintilian*, 1986). Twenty years later, *Scholae in liberales artes* (lectures on the liberal arts) was published. A work on religion, *Commentariorum de religione Christiana libri quatuor* (commentary on the Christian religion in four books), was published four years after his death.

Ramus is not known for the sheer originality of his thought; rather, he is noteworthy for having attempted to revise the art of rhetoric (written and oral persuasion) as it had been practiced prior to the Renaissance and for his efforts to revamp the college curricula of his time. His scholarly energy and later conversion to Calvinism made him very popular among Puritans, yet his efforts to overturn the centuries-old academic methods of the universities met with hostility in England and on the Continent.

Ramus's opposition to the ancient methods of Aristotelian rhetoric was clear as early as 1536 in the title of his master's thesis, "Whatever Aristotle Has Said Is a Fabrication."

Rhetoric had been traditionally a part of the *trivium*, the academic course of study that included grammar, rhetoric, and logic. Aristotelian rhetoric consisted of invention (the finding of content material to support the argument), arrangement (the order or structure of the parts of the argument), style (the manner of expression), memory (to eliminate the need for notes), and delivery (effective oral presentation). Ramus was influenced in his renovation of this structure by the fifteenth century Dutch Humanist Rodolphus Agricola (Roelof Huysman), who, like other Humanists of the period, was dismayed by the voluminous medieval discussions that had complicated a clear understanding of Aristotle. Ramus had declared in his master's thesis that even Aristotle did not follow his own rules of organization, and in his *Dialectique* (1555; *Dialectics*, 1574) Ramus chose to simplify rhetoric by teaching invention and arrangement as branches of logic, leaving only style (which included memory and delivery) as the basis for what had been a five-part subject. This simplification would also be understood by students more easily, making his rhetorical renovation also a pedagogical one.

In Ramus and Talon's *Rhetorica* (1548), rhetoric was essentially limited to the use of ornamental poetic figures. Because invention and arrangement were fundamental ways of *thinking* about a topic, not merely writing or speaking about it, Ramus regarded them as logical, not rhetorical, functions.

Ramist logic was presented not primarily in terms of Aristotle's favorite method, the syllogism, but mostly in terms of self-evidently true statements or axioms. Ramist educational practice focused not on the intricacy of the three-part syllogism, but on specific statements from actual speeches or various works of literature. Education in logic thus proceeded from specific examples that were regarded as universally true, demonstrable, and general, not from confusing, intricate arguments. Ramus's method of simplification went further: Statements were divided into two contrasting, binary elements, each of which could again be subdivided into an opposing pair of ideas. This bipartite or dichotomous analysis of axioms was often portrayed pictorially as a kind of tree-diagram, with branching subordinate headings displayed across a page. Ramus had in this way also succeeded in appealing to students who might now be called visual learners.

SIGNIFICANCE

Although Ramus's influence faded in the eighteenth century, he was widely read and debated during and after his life. His rejection of the medieval scholastic reliance on Aristotle made him especially appealing to the emerging Puritan intellectuals of the seventeenth century. He was a shaping influence on the Puritan culture of the American colonies, as seen in the theology of Thomas Hooker and Thomas Shepard. In England, his work affected many, including the Cambridge preacher William Perkins, whose sermons were an example of the new plain-style expression. The more famous Cambridge graduate, John Milton, author of *Paradise Lost* (1667, 1674), adhered to Ramist principles in his Latin grammar of 1669. In 1672, Milton published *Artis logicae plenior institutio ad Petri Rami methodum concinnata* (a fuller course in the art of logic conformed to the method of Peter Ramus), his compilation of Ramus's *Dialectics*. Ramus's binary method for organizing knowledge would influence book 2 of Francis Bacon's *Advancement of Learning* (1605) and influence Robert Burton's *Anatomy of Melancholy* (1621), two works of importance in the scientific revolution that flourished after Ramus's death.

—*Christopher Baker*

FURTHER READING

McKim, Donald K. *Ramism in William Perkins' Theology.* New York: Peter Lang, 1987. Studies the impact of Ramus on the theology of one of the most prominent English Puritans.

Miller, Perry. *The New England Mind: The Seventeenth Century.* 1939. Reprint. Cambridge, Mass.: Harvard University Press, 1963. An important study that considers the impact of Ramus and other intellectual forces affecting New England Puritan culture.

Ong, Walter J. *Ramus and Talon Inventory.* Cambridge, Mass.: Harvard University Press, 1983. A complete listing of the works by Ramus and Talon.

————. *Ramus, Method, and the Decay of Dialogue.* 1958. Reprint. Cambridge, Mass.: Harvard University Press, 1983. The most detailed examination of the origins and practice of Ramism.

Parker, David L. "Petrus Ramus and the Puritans: The 'Logic' of Preparationist Conversion Doctrine." *Early American Literature* 8 (1973): 140-162. Discusses how the American Puritans Thomas Hooker and Thomas Shepard might have employed Ramist logic in their theology.

Sharratt, Peter. "Ramus 2000." *Rhetorica* 18, no. 4 (Autumn, 2000): 399-455. An extensive review of scholarly studies on Ramus and Ramism appearing between 1987 and 2000.

Skalnik, James Veazie. *Ramus and Reform: University and Church at the End of the Renaissance.* Kirksville, Mo.: Truman State University Press, 2002. Examines Ramus as a reformer of university programs and as a Protestant rebel within the Church.

SEE ALSO: Francis Bacon; Giordano Bruno; Giovanni Pico della Mirandola.

RELATED ARTICLES in *Great Events from History: The Renaissance & Early Modern Era, 1454-1600:* 1486-1487: Pico della Mirandola Writes *Oration on the Dignity of Man*; August 24-25, 1572: St. Bartholomew's Day Massacre.

RAPHAEL
Italian painter

With Leonardo da Vinci and Michelangelo, Raphael was part of the great trio of High Renaissance masters. He became the most prolific and most widely celebrated painter of his time.

BORN: April 6, 1483; Urbino, duchy of Urbino (now in Italy)
DIED: April 6, 1520; Rome, Papal States (now in Italy)
ALSO KNOWN AS: Raffaello Sanzio
AREAS OF ACHIEVEMENT: Art, architecture

EARLY LIFE

Raffaello Sanzio, known as Raphael (RAF-ee-ehl), had the good fortune to be born in the mountain town of Urbino, where Federico da Montefeltro maintained a ducal court manifesting splendor, pomp, elegance, and the new learning. Raphael's father, Giovanni, a minor painter and versifier, had access to the court; from his youth, Raphael was introduced to the ongoing works of Piero della Francesca, Sandro Botticelli, Paolo Uccello, and other contemporary masters. Giovanni died, however, when Raphael was eleven; at this age, he may already have been apprenticed to Pietro Perugino in Perugia. There he rapidly moved to the head of that artist's busy workshop, which won so many commissions that the master had to develop an elaborate atelier system, in which assistants did much of the preliminary work on projects. By the age of sixteen, Raphael was already influencing local artists, and from this time his hand is detectable in Perugino's works.

Raphael's earliest independent paintings both date from 1504. The first, *Marriage of the Virgin*, shows both his indebtedness to Perugino—the disposal of figures, the use of a temple as background, and an array of colors are all drawn from him—and the introduction of what are to become signature characteristics—the supple, resilient posture of the figures, their unearthly serenity of expression, and the rhythmic organization of the composition. The second, *Saint George and the Dragon*, is a small panel that was commissioned by the duke of Urbino to present to Henry VII of England. The influence of Leonardo da Vinci's *Battle of Anghiari* (1503) is evident here, as it is in all subsequent mounted battle paintings. Again the dominant element is rhythmic organization: The mounted knight on his diagonally placed steed intersects the massed landscape, so that all the tension of the painting drives through the lance, pinning the wriggling monster to the earth. The spiral coil of the horse's body generates much of the accumulated tension; yet the animal itself is surprisingly static, betraying the artist's inexperience. The painting abounds in finely observed, meticulously rendered details; the young artist seems to be showing off the facility of his technique. These two paintings constitute the auspicious beginning of an ambitious career.

LIFE'S WORK

Raphael's fifteen-year career falls into two phases, Florence and Rome. He settled in Florence in 1505, stepping into a void created by the withdrawal of both Leonardo and Michelangelo, at a time when the appetite for painting had been stimulated by their examples. Raphael's facility soon proved prosperous. Within three years, he finished seventeen still-extant Madonnas and Holy Families, besides several other major works. That kind of activity makes both Michelangelo, productive as he was, and Leonardo, who failed to complete one painting during that period, look like monuments of indolence. Part of the reason for this difference derives from Raphael's method of working. Unlike either of his fellow giants, Raphael did not approach painting as a series of solutions to technical problems of representation. Instead, he made preliminary sketches—many of them preserved—which show him testing variables in the relationship of forms. Only in the painting itself would he settle on one moment in the flow of forms. That allowed him to produce paintings that merely glossed over problems that would have hamstrung either of the other two. That is, Raphael painted for his patrons, not for his peers.

The *Madonna of the Meadows* (1505) is one of the best of the markedly similar items in the series. As before, much of the design and the framing landscape derives from Leonardo's examples and much of the iconography from Michelangelo's. Yet the rhythmical organization, the sinuous upward coiling, is distinctly Raphael, as is the countermovement in the downward glance of the Virgin. Yet the truly astonishing feature is the Virgin's face. Though both Fra Angelico and Fra Filippo Lippi had anticipated this clarity of line and simplicity of form, the viewer is still struck almost dumb by this representation of incarnate grace and superhuman serenity.

Raphael also produced for his patrons a remarkable series of portraits, in the process raising the portrait to a new level. At the same time that he was idealizing the features of his sacred work, he reversed the practice with his portraits. With them, he became the dispassionate observer, coolly recording the essential character of his subjects. The result is a gallery of distinct personalities, caught in moments of self-revelation. In doing this, he became the most successful portraitist of all time.

Around 1509, the twenty-six-year-old Raphael was called to Rome by Pope Julius II to embark on the major phase of his career, which would last for eleven years. His first commission from the pope was to take over the official decorations of the Vatican apartments (called Stanze, or rooms) from Sodoma. He started with the Stanza della Segnatura; in it, he determined to depict the ideals of the new pope's regime and, in the act, create frescoes of unprecedented refinement and harmony of form. His plan included two major wall frescoes facing each other and a complementary lunette: the *Dispute over the Sacrament* (1510-1511), the misnamed *School of Athens* (1510-1511), and the *Cardinal Virtues* (1511). The first is an attempt to represent the entire doctrine of the Eucharist, from its origin in Heaven to its veneration by the people. In the cloud scene above, Raphael portrays the ordered harmony of divine Providence, in sharp contrast to the fierce contention of theologians from various disciplines on Earth below. The grandeur and rhythmic energy of the composition surpass anything yet attempted in art—or would, if Michelangelo were not simultaneously at work on the Sistine Chapel ceiling a few barricaded corridors away. Even so, the scene is colossal.

The medallion inset above the *Dispute over the Sacrament* depicts Theology; opposite it is that for Philosophy.

The fresco below, the *School of Athens*, attempts to do for that field what the *Dispute over the Sacrament* does for theology—that is, represent all the leading figures in classical philosophy engaged in debate. This painting is Raphael's best-known work; it provides the textbook example of the High Renaissance ideals of integral unity and spatial harmony. The figures circulate in depth around the central figures of Plato and Aristotle, all set within a great vaulted dome in the classical manner, impractical but magnificently proportioned. This beautifully rational frame establishes the perfect setting for the debate of abstract problems; the figures surge beneath the stable, solid dome. The philosophers themselves are wonderfully individualized, yet each is playing an ensemble role in the total composition. The only modern figure slumps prominently in the foreground, dressed in stonecutter's work clothes: He turns out to be Michelangelo, the single man alive whom Raphael considered worthy of a place in the company of the ancients. The painting thus constitutes Raphael's statement of the relationship of the Renaissance to antiquity. Furthermore, the lunette of the *Cardinal Virtues* demonstrates what

Raphael. (Library of Congress)

Raphael had learned from Michelangelo; for his figures there suddenly take on the monumentality of that master, though transformed by Raphael's characteristic sweetness, organic rhythm, and grace.

This transition in style, from balanced serenity to dramatic expressiveness, culminates in the second apartment, the Stanza d'Eliodoro, which contains two full-wall frescoes and two window surrounds: the *Expulsion of Heliodorus* (1512), the *Expulsion of Attila* (1513-1514), the *Mass of Bolsena* (1512), and the *Liberation of Saint Peter from Prison* (1512). These combine harmony of organization with new, vibrant coloring and dramatic tension, so that the images seem almost to seethe with motion and sing with color. They show Raphael raising his unique style of spiral rhythmic organization to a new height: His figures gain weight and tension, and energy explodes in their dynamic interconnection. The artist seems to be moving toward a mode of representation beyond the capacity of the High Renaissance. His work here has been termed proto-Baroque for this reason. The *Expulsion of Heliodorus* is typical of this new sense of the dramatic. In it Raphael shows that he was secure enough in his habits of rational organization to test them to their limits. His figures take on the mass and muscle of Michelangelo's; they vibrate with energies that threaten to tear apart his rationally organized scheme. Everything still harmonizes, but only barely.

Raphael's *Sistine Madonna* (1513) created a vision of the Madonna that totally eclipsed all his former efforts. If any painting crystallizes the essence of the High Renaissance, this one does. This work defines rhythmic organization: Its broad spiral curves and delicately balanced masses, counterpointed by the two often-excerpted putti at the bottom of the frame, almost look like a demonstration piece for a painting class. Furthermore, the Virgin is the quintessential Virgin, perhaps the loveliest woman ever painted. Among other portraits of this period that confirm his reputation as a portraitist are those of *Baldassare Castiglione* and *Pope Leo X with Cardinals*. They have never been excelled.

Raphael's most ambitious pictorial project was to design ten massive tapestries, for which he produced full-size watercolor cartoons as models. These were intended to continue the iconographic cycle on Christian religious history begun by Michelangelo. This is Raphael's largest work, and it exhibits his dramatic intensity raised to its highest power. At the same time, Raphael was busy with architectural projects, the grandest of which is the Villa Madama in Rome; though unfinished at his death and never completed, the fragment is exqui-site in design and proportion and elegant in its imaginative detail.

His final great painting, completed by assistants, is the *Transfiguration of Christ* (1517). Here Raphael matches the level he had reached in the *Expulsion of Heliodorus*; color, design, and rhythm fuse in a drama that swirls off the canvas, and the figures pulse with real breath and warmth. Moreover, this painting generates a religious intensity far removed from the serene, rational indifference of the early Madonnas. Unfortunately, Raphael had little time to develop this mystical strain, for he died after a brief illness on April 6, 1520.

SIGNIFICANCE

Raphael is the Renaissance artist ideal, or at least the embodiment of one half of the Renaissance standard of excellence. In *Il libro del cortegiano* (1528; *The Book of the Courtier*, 1561), Raphael's friend Baldassare Castiglione had defined the essential quality of the refined gentleman as *sprezzatura*, an untranslatable term that means something like making difficult things look easy. Raphael certainly had the technical facility for that. Perhaps no other painter possessed equal talent. Raphael could do things effortlessly with brush or pen that artists of normal ability could produce only with monumental labor. Moreover, this effortlessness comes through in his work: Everything he does looks easy, natural, right; his figures seem not to be figures but simply themselves. In many ways, he taught his viewers what it meant to see. In the paintings, this ease of technique translates itself into ineffable grace.

Yet in his early works, Raphael pays a price for this facility. He produced so much so easily that it is possible to accuse him of creating by mechanical formula. Furthermore, instead of solving technical problems, he merely brushes by them; in this respect, he falls short of another Renaissance ideal, to make human intelligence the norm by which everything knowable was to be measured. As a result, a premium was placed on meeting the difficult head-on; problems were meant to be solved, and the individual of true genius used reason to find a solution. Raphael's talent was so great that he ran the risk of becoming merely facile.

His encounters with Leonardo and Michelangelo changed that. Not that he became a great innovator, though much of his work did establish formal precedents, especially in portraits and in group narratives. Rembrandt, for example, copied Raphael's canvases with care and imitated his poses, and Nicolas Poussin and Jean-Auguste-Dominique Ingres are almost unimaginable without his examples.

His work for the Vatican, however, clearly ranks with the greatest paintings of all time. In them, the early grace and serenity take on weight, mass, and energy, and a dynamic intelligence informs the whole. In these respects, Raphael becomes the incarnation of the High Renaissance ideal.

As a portraitist he is supreme; his perfectly balanced, perfectly poised figures seem to occupy a moment in time, so that one can imagine a gallery of them carrying on civilized conversation when no one is in the room. His real genius, however, appears in the Vatican group compositions, in which he seems to create his own heroic universe, electric with its own energy and populated with entirely plausible though larger-than-life characters. There Raphael seems to reach the limits of the natural. It is small wonder that painters succeeding him were forced to grotesque distortions to represent superabundant energy; only Raphael could cage such forces within his cosmos of radiant and dynamic calm.

—*James Livingston*

FURTHER READING

Beck, James. *Raphael*. New York: Harry N. Abrams, 1976. This is an excellent, thorough study of Raphael and his times, with much technical information. Intended mainly for specialists, it is surprisingly approachable and packed with a wealth of detail and good reproductions.

De Vecchi, Pierluigi. *Raphael*. New York: Abbeville Press, 2002. Major study of the life and work of Raphael, including his paintings, drawings, etchings, interior design, and architecture. Reads the work largely as a function of the need to express the relationship between earthly love and divine love. Includes three hundred color illustrations, chronology, bibliography, and index.

Fischel, Oskar. *Raphael*. Translated by B. Rackham. 2 vols. London: Kegan Paul, 1948. Reprint. London: Spring Books, 1964. Fischel presents the authoritative, old-fashioned account of Raphael's life and works. Though somewhat dated, Fischel is indispensable, partly because critical opinion on Raphael has not changed much since the publication of this work.

Freedberg, Sydney J. *Painting in Italy, 1500-1600*. 3d ed. New Haven, Conn.: Yale University Press, 1993. The reproductions in this small-format book do little justice to Raphael's large-scale works, but then no reproductions can. The text, intended for the general reader, is appealingly informative and nontechnical, making this a useful general reference.

Hall, Marcia, ed. *Raphael's "School of Athens."* New York: Cambridge University Press, 1997. Anthology of criticism of Raphael's most famous fresco. Collects two classic essays by Giovanni Pietro Bellori and Heinrich Wolfflin, together with four previously unpublished articles. Includes illustrations, bibliographic references, and index.

Hartt, Frederick. *History of Italian Renaissance Art: Painting, Sculpture, Architecture*. 5th ed. New York: Harry N. Abrams, 2003. Hartt provides the most accessible brief introduction to the work of Raphael, in clear, nontechnical language and with good reproductions, though mostly in black and white. He is particularly good at summarizing iconography and analyzing formal qualities.

Jones, Roger, and Nicholas Penny. *Raphael*. New London, Conn.: Yale University Press, 1983. This nonspecialist text is a fine source for the general reader, placing Raphael squarely in his historical and social setting and including brilliant reproductions of entire works as well as enlargements of details.

Meyer zur Capellen, Jürg. *Raphael in Florence*. Translated by Stefan B. Polter. Edited by Jane Havell. London: Azimuth Books, 1996. A study of Raphael's formative years in Florence from 1500 to 1508 and the influence of Florentine culture on his career. Includes illustrations and bibliographic references.

Pon, Lisa. *Raphael, Dürer, and MarcAntonio Raimondi: Copying and the Italian Renaissance Print*. New Haven, Conn.: Yale University Press, 2004. An important study of the meaning of art and the figure of the artist in Renaissance Italy. Argues that the notion of the individual genius expressing his distinctive self through his images comes into being at almost the same time that new engraving technologies were invented that involved collaborative artistry and the dissemination of multiple copies of previously unique images. Looks at the cultural tension between these two novel models of art in the work of Raphael and Albrecht Dürer with engraver Marcantonio. Includes illustrations, bibliographic references, and index.

Raphael. *The Complete Works of Raphael*. Edited by Mario Salmi et al. New York: Reynal, 1969. As the title indicates, this is the only work available that attempts to catalog and reproduce everything that Raphael accomplished. This volume offers more than any other, and the documentation is thorough.

Vasari, Giorgio. *Lives of the Most Eminent Painters, Sculptors, and Architects*. Translated by Gaston du

C. de Vere. Reprint. New York: Harry N. Abrams, 1979. Though not always accurate, Vasari is the best near-contemporary source for Raphael's life and his contemporary reception and reputation. Vasari's work is full of entertaining anecdotes and much miscellaneous information, all gathered at second hand. He is better on Raphael than on some, perhaps because he identified so closely with him.

See also: Andrea del Sarto; Sandro Botticelli; The Carracci Family; Baldassare Castiglione; Correggio; Lavinia Fontana; Julius II; Leonardo da Vinci; Michelangelo; Piero della Francesca; Jacopo Sansovino; Titian.
Related article in *Great Events from History: The Renaissance & Early Modern Era, 1454-1600:* 1508-1520: Raphael Paints His Frescoes.

Rheticus
Austrian astronomer and mathematician

Rheticus was instrumental in spreading the heliocentric theory of Nicolaus Copernicus, which argued that the sun rotated around the earth. Rheticus also prepared the first set of mathematical tables with all six trigonometric functions.

Born: February 16, 1514; Feldkirch, Austria
Died: December 5, 1574; Kassa, Hungary (now Košice, Slovakia)
Also known as: Georg Joachim von Lauchen; Georg Joachim von Lauchen Rheticus; Georg Joachim de Porris; Georg Joachim Iserin (given name); Rhäticus
Areas of achievement: Astronomy, mathematics

Early Life

Rheticus was the son of Georg Iserin, a town physician, and Thomasina de Porris, an Italian. When Iserin was beheaded for sorcery in 1528, it became illegal to use his name. Rheticus's mother changed the family name, Iserin, to de Porris, which means "of the leeks." Rheticus translated the Italian name into the German von Lauchen, and added Rheticus, after Rhætia, the ancient Roman name for his birthplace. Later, he dropped the name von Lauchen and assumed Rheticus as his last name.

Rheticus's father was his first teacher. He continued his schooling at the Feldkirch Latin school and the Frauenmünsterschule in Zürich. Achilles Gasser, who had become the town physician of Feldkirch after the death of Rheticus's father, provided him with a letter of introduction to Philipp Melanchthon, who was both a noted Protestant (Lutheran) reformer and an educational reformer at the University of Wittenberg. In 1532, Rheticus entered the university, from which he earned a master's degree in 1536. His thesis argued that Roman law did not prohibit astrological predictions if they were based on physical causes.

Rheticus taught mathematics—arithmetic and geometry—and astronomy at the University of Wittenberg from 1536 to 1538. In 1538, he took a leave of absence to visit leading astronomers, including Nicolaus Copernicus, and he returned to the University of Wittenberg in 1541, when he was elected the dean of the arts faculty. Rheticus then secured a position as professor of higher mathematics at the University of Leipzig in 1542. The positions at the two universities, and the leave-of-absence, were facilitated by Melanchthon.

Life's Work

The first part of Rheticus's work is connected with the Melanchthon circle, a group of young Wittenberg University astronomers, including Erasmus Reinhold, who gathered under the intellectually charismatic Melanchthon. While remaining neutral concerning the truth of geocentrism versus heliocentrism, Reinhold and others focused on the elimination of mathematical errors and the use of Copernican data to construct new planetary tables and to calculate astronomical events and distances more accurately.

Rheticus, in contrast, accepted heliocentrism and emphasized the harmony underlying the Copernican system. In 1539, Rheticus had sought Copernicus at Frombork in Poland to discuss rumors of a revolutionary form of astronomy. Copernicus had resisted publishing his heliocentric theory and saw in Rheticus a means to spread his ideas privately. Rheticus adopted the theory immediately and enthusiastically, and he secured permission from Copernicus to prepare *De libris revolutionum Nicolai Copernici narratio prima* (1540; *The Narratio Prima of Rheticus*, 1939; better known as *Narratio prima*), an introduction to Copernicus's *De revolutionibus orbium coelestium* (1543; *On the Revolutions of the Heavenly Spheres*, 1952; better known as *De revolutionibus*).

Written in ten weeks, *Narratio prima* was the first printed announcement of a challenge to Ptolemy's geocentric astronomy. It was not a mere report, though, for it contained material not found in any of Copernicus's writings and concentrated on the determination of the relative distances and periodicity of the planets, an emphasis not present in the Copernican treatise. It also contained a few errors.

Rheticus convinced Copernicus to publish *De revolutionibus*, becoming its first editor. He found a publisher in Nuremberg but had to leave the city before the printing was completed to attend to academic duties. The town theologian, Andreas Osiander, who had experience getting books on mathematics published, then assumed book's printing and also authored the infamous preface that warned that the book need not be taken seriously, for a hypothesis need not be true. Copernicus had hoped that *Narratio prima* would have quelled outrage against his theory, but he was wrong.

Rheticus made important contributions to mathematics, particularly trigonometry. In early 1542, he published separately a section on plane and spherical geometry from *De revolutionibus* entitled *De lateribus et anguli triangulorum* (on the sides and angles of triangles). The tables of sines employed radii different from those in Copernicus's tables, however, and, moreover, the table included values for what are now called cosines. Cosines were the work of Rheticus alone. Later, he wrote "Canon of the Doctrine of Triangles" (1551), the first table to provide all six trigonometric functions. This work contained the first extensive table of tangents and the first table of secants ever printed. Here Rheticus defined the trigonometric functions in terms of the sides of triangles, in contrast to earlier definitions based on chords or arcs. He also realized that the functions of angles greater than 45° equaled the cofunctions of the complementary angles of less than 45°. This insight allowed him to halve the length of his tables.

Taking a leave from the University of Leipzig in 1545, Rheticus traveled throughout Italy, but he also suffered a severe mental disorder in early 1547. He recovered sufficiently to teach at Constance later that year. Then he studied medicine in Zürich with Conrad Gesner, from 1547 to 1548, before returning to Leipzig, where he was chosen dean of the faculty of arts.

In 1551, Rheticus had to flee from Leipzig because of a homosexual relationship with a male student, homosexuality being illegal at the time. He first left for Chemnitz, then to Prague, where he resumed medical studies, and he settled finally in Krákow in 1554. The authorities in Leipzig tried him in absentia, sentenced him to 101 years of exile, and impounded all his possessions. At this point, Melanchthon and the members of his circle stopped their association with him.

In Krákow, Rheticus practiced medicine for twenty years. During this period, he rekindled his interest in astrology, following up on his master's thesis. In 1562, he was still contemplating the possibility of constructing a chronology of the world from its creation to its end. In 1571, he correctly predicted that King Sigismund II Augustus of Poland would have a short reign, thus attaining a reputation as a great seer. He also constructed instruments, made astronomical observations, and performed experiments in alchemy.

During these last years of his life, Rheticus continued the painstaking work on trigonometric tables. Holy Roman Emperor Maximilian II's funding of his work enabled Rheticus to employ six assistants. In 1574, a young student of mathematics at the University of Wittenberg, Valentin Otto, visited Rheticus. Recalling his service to Copernicus, Rheticus hoped to see him arrange for the publication of his tables. Unfortunately, Rheticus died, and Otto, after some difficulties, found a patron in Palatinate elector Frederick IV, for whom he became the official mathematician. Otto finished the tables and named them in honor of his backer *Opus palatinum de triangulis* (the palatine work on triangles) (1596).

SIGNIFICANCE

There was deep enmity between science and religion during Rheticus's time. Copernicus feared that people would reject his heliocentric system because it contradicted Scripture. As a member of Melanchthon's circle, Rheticus—a Lutheran and a Copernican—wrote an anonymous treatise on the Holy Scripture and the motion of Earth, published only a century later. On one hand, Rheticus had argued that the Bible is authoritative only in matters of ethics and salvation, but not in science; while on the other hand, he attempted to find evidence in Scripture suggesting that Earth does move. Such attempts to reconcile science and religion appeared much more frequently after the arrest of Galileo.

Rheticus has had a lasting significance in mathematics because of his preparation of trigonometric-functions tables and the painstaking efforts he took to the end of his life to refine them further. The first trigonometry textbook appeared soon thereafter, and Rheticus's tables helped lay the foundation for the discovery of logarithms.

—Kristen L. Zacharias

FURTHER READING

Barker, Peter. "The Role of Religion in the Lutheran Response to Copernicus." In *Rethinking the Scientific Revolution*, edited by Margaret J. Osler. New York: Cambridge University Press, 2002. Describes Rheticus's role in the publication of Copernicus's work and reevaluates the Lutheran response to it.

Blumenberg, Hans. *The Genesis of the Copernican World*. Translated by Robert M. Wallace. Cambridge, Mass.: MIT Press, 1987. A massive work on the Copernican revolution and its significance for understanding modernity. Places Rheticus in the context of its supporters.

Hooykaas, R. *G. J. Rheticus's Treatise on Holy Scripture and the Motion of the Earth, with Translation, Annotations, Commentary, and Additional Chapters on Ramus-Rheticus and the Development of the Problem Before 1650*. New York: North Holland, 1984. Includes a discussion of religious issues created by scientific developments in the sixteenth century, especially among Copernicus's circle.

Motz, Lloyd, and Jefferson Hane Weaver. *The Story of Astronomy*. New York: Plenum Press, 1995. A short history of astronomy from the time of antiquity, useful for understanding the issues surrounding Copernicus.

Westman, Robert S. "The Melanchthon Circle, Rheticus, and the Wittenberg Interpretation of the Copernican Theory." *Isis* 66 (1975): 165-193. Examines the social context of the early reaction to Copernican astronomy and explains the appeal of Copernican theory in terms of Rheticus's personal history.

SEE ALSO: Tyco Brahe; Giordano Bruno; Gerolamo Cardano; Nicolaus Copernicus; Conrad Gesner; William Gilbert; Martin Luther; Maximilian II; Philipp Melanchthon; John Napier; Sigismund II Augustus; Niccolò Fontana Tartaglia.

RELATED ARTICLE in *Great Events from History: The Renaissance & Early Modern Era, 1454-1600:* 1543: Copernicus Publishes *De Revolutionibus*.

MATTEO RICCI
Italian missionary, geographer, and mathematician

As a pioneer of cultural relations between China and Europe, Ricci introduced China to Western mathematics and introduced the West to China's ancient civilization. During his long and colorful career as a Jesuit missionary, Ricci developed the first map of China in the West, which correctly situated China geographically.

BORN: October 6, 1552; Macerata, Papal States (now in Italy)
DIED: May 11, 1610; Beijing, China
ALSO KNOWN AS: Li Madou (Pinyin); Li Ma-tou (Wade-Giles); Li-ma-teou; Hsi-t'ai
AREAS OF ACHIEVEMENT: Astronomy, mathematics, geography, religion and theology

EARLY LIFE

Matteo Ricci (REE-chee) entered the Jesuit school in his hometown of Macerata in 1561. Although he had the inclination to join a religious order early in life, in 1568, he went to Rome to study law at the Roman College. Despite his father's strident orders to the contrary, he joined the Roman Catholic Jesuit Order, also known as the Society of Jesus, in 1571. Remaining in Rome, Ricci studied

mathematics, cosmology, and astronomy under the direction of Father Stephan Clavius, the prominent German mathematician who was influential in instituting the Gregorian calendar in 1582.

Ricci next studied for the priesthood at the University of Coimbra in Portugal, and from there he sailed to the Portuguese city of Goa in western India, where he was ordained in 1580. The Jesuits, following in the footsteps of their missionary founder Saint Ignatius Loyola, maintained distant missionary outposts in India, Japan, Canada, Central and South America, and China. Shortly after his ordination, at the request of Father Alessandro Valignani, Ricci sailed for China, where he was to live for the next twenty-seven years. Arriving at Macau on China's east coast in 1582, he settled in Guangdong Province and began his lifework by studying, in addition to in-depth work on the Chinese language, the philosophy, art, literature, and myriad other aspects of China's ancient society.

LIFE'S WORK

Before Ricci's arrival, it was still unclear in Europe whether Cathay, the country described by the Italian explorer Marco Polo in the late thirteenth century, was in fact the same country as China. Ricci's overland journey from India confirmed this as fact. Before leaving Guangdong Province for Shaozhou in 1589, Ricci produced his extraordinary map of the world, the *Yudi shanhai quantu* (1584; complete map of the Earth's mountains and seas), which is no longer extant, and the third edition, *Kunyu wanguo quantu* (1602; map of the ten thousand countries), which has survived. In Shaozhou, he gained popularity among the city's Chinese intellectuals to whom he taught mathematics, especially the Euclidian mathematical systems that he had earlier studied under Clavius. Ricci's mathematical and astronomical treatises demonstrated his fine intelligence and high learning to the Chinese mandarins who tended to look on missionaries, and all foreigners for that matter, as primitive barbarians with nothing to teach the Chinese.

From the beginning, Ricci was intent on making himself, and his work, known to the emperor, but foreigners were forbidden entrance to Beijing, the capital. It was hoped that by winning the support of the emperor, Ricci could also win large numbers of Chinese converts to Christianity, his ultimate goal. His attempt to enter Beijing in 1595 resulted in failure, so he settled instead in Nanjing in 1599, where he formed a Christian church and came to be accepted by the city's scholars.

An illustration from a Chinese manuscript depicting Jesuit missionary Matteo Ricci (left) and his first convert. (Hulton|Archive by Getty Images)

He became noted for his remarkable memory and renowned for his ability to educate and train young Chinese men in the art of memory, a trait essential for high scores in the country's civil service examinations. It was not until 1601, after waiting twenty-one years, that he was summoned by the reclusive emperor Wanli and allowed to live in Beijing. Thanks to Ricci's map of the world, the Chinese emperor, and the Ming elite, came to see their country's location in the world for the first time and learned of the existence of so many other kingdoms. Soon Ricci became the court mathematician. While in Beijing, he managed to publish several books in Chinese: *Jiaoyou lun* (1595; treatise on friendship), *Ershiwu yan* (1605; the twenty-five sayings), *Jihe yuanben* (1607; Chinese translation of the first six books of the elements of Euclid), and *Jiren shipian* (1608; ten discourses by a paradoxical man).

To gain acceptance in missionary outposts, Jesuit missionaries would often dress and act like the local popula-

tion in host countries, because to declare openly their intention to preach Christianity would have resulted in expulsion. This Jesuit missionary practice, which took great care to adapt to the special conditions of the host country and not to criticize traditional customs, was referred to as accommodation. So, in his efforts to gain respect and acceptance in China, Ricci gave up his Jesuit clerical habit, dressing instead in the style of a Chinese scholar. He also adopted a Chinese name, Li Madou. Another aspect of the Jesuits method to infiltrate China was to have the members of their missionaries in China declare their intention to remain in that country permanently.

Ricci whetted the Chinese appetite for knowledge and, in his desire to gain acceptance and respect, brought with him valuable gifts of clocks, mathematical and astronomical instruments, musical instruments, religious oil paintings, and maps and books, elaborately bound Bibles in particular. Chinese mandarins and the educated were enormously impressed, especially by his map of the world, and they began to take on a different view of Europe as a civilized nation. In short, Ricci opened the door to China. He played the chief role as missionary, in time translating and spreading Chinese copies of the Ten Commandments and composing a Chinese catechism.

Taking care not to offend the Chinese, he also composed various moral treatises in Chinese. In particular, the *Tianzhu shiyi* (wr. 1579-1584, pb. 1603; *The True Meaning of the Lord in Heaven*, 1985, first complete translation) used Christian scriptures, supported by ancient Chinese philosophical tracts, to teach moral values. Although he had earlier persecuted Christians, the emperor granted Ricci the right to preach the Gospel in 1592. By this time his mission included, in addition to Beijing, three residences of Nanjing, Nanchang, and Shaozhou, and eventually Shanghai in 1608.

SIGNIFICANCE

Ricci's contributions to geography include his calculations on the actual size of China. He also introduced trigonometry to China, which laid the groundwork for his successors to make great advances in astronomy, mapmaking, and the design of accurate calendars. The respect Ricci achieved as a mathematical and astronomical scholar overflowed eventually into high regard for his Christian teachings, but it was Ricci's extraordinary memory and his knowledge of astronomy that gained him the most recognition. No doubt, the work he began as a devout Jesuit missionary also had far reaching economic, political, and social consequences.

Through his willingness to share his vast knowledge, and by his demonstrations of intense respect for Chinese society and traditions, Ricci introduced the West to China and led the isolated country to a better understanding of Europe.

—*M. Casey Diana*

FURTHER REAING

Cronin, Vincent. *The Wise Man from the West*. Reprint. London: Harvill Press, 1999. Covers Ricci's early years in Rome, his ordination in India, his disheartening attempts for acceptance among the Ming Dynasty elite, his subsequent successes as a scholar in astronomy and mathematics, his many converts to Christianity, and his role in bringing the reclusive China into the modern world.

Gernet, Jacques. *A History of Chinese Civilization*. Translated by J. R. Foster and Charles Hartman. New York: Cambridge University Press, 1996. Examines the historical evolution of the Chinese world from early nomadic antiquity through the unification of China during the medieval area, the great upsurge of Buddhism, and the Mandarin and Mongol influence leading to Ricci's arrival. Also discusses Ricci's and other Catholic missionaries' influence and places Ricci and his work in historical perspective.

Neill, Stephen. *A History of Christian Missions*. 1964. Reprint. New York: Penguin Books, 1990. Chapter 5, "The Age of Discovery, 1500-1600," traces the expansion of Roman Catholic missionaries throughout Europe, India, North and South America, and China, with many references to Ricci's impact on astronomy and mathematics in China.

Ricci, Matteo. *China in the Sixteenth Century: The Journals of Matteo Ricci, 1583-1610*. New York: Random House, 1953. Illustrates in particular China's isolation from the rest of the world in this era. Provides a historical framework within which to read Ricci's successes as a Jesuit missionary in the fields of astronomy and mathematics and to learn how he gained the Ming elite's respect and trust.

Spence, Jonathan D. *The Memory Palace of Matteo Ricci*. 1984. Reprint. New York: Penguin Books, 1985. This scholarly work examines much of the cultural history of both Europe and China during the sixteenth century. Presents in great depth Ricci's memory techniques and, especially, his use of religious paintings and icons to help scholars navigate his memory palace while simultaneously impressing on them Christian values.

_____. *The Search for Modern China*. Reprint. New York: W. W. Norton, 2001. Written in an informative, but not overly scholarly style. Covers Chinese history beginning with the sixteenth century Ming Dynasty, when Ricci made his influential mark on China. Contains more than two hundred illustrations, including maps.

SEE ALSO: Saint Ignatius of Loyola.

RELATED ARTICLES in *Great Events from History: The Renaissance & Early Modern Era, 1454-1600:* 1514-1598: Portuguese Reach the Swahili Coast; August 15, 1534: Founding of the Jesuit Order; 1583-1610: Matteo Ricci Travels to Beijing.

RICHARD III
King of England (r. 1483-1485)

England's most maligned monarch, Richard III, attempted to restore order and dynastic stability to a nation torn by three decades of civil war, but he fell victim to the intrigues of those who were jealous of his loyalty and abilities and who coveted the Crown.

BORN: October 2, 1452; Fotheringhay Castle,
     Northamptonshire, England
DIED: August 22, 1485; Bosworth Field,
     Leicestershire, England
ALSO KNOWN AS: Richard Plantagenet; Richard, duke
     of Gloucester
AREA OF ACHIEVEMENT: Government and politics

EARLY LIFE

Richard III (Richard Plantagenet) was born the youngest of nine children of Richard, duke of York, and Cicely (née Neville), duchess of York. He had two sisters— Anne, duchess of Exeter, and Margaret (later duchess of Burgundy)—and three brothers—Edmund, earl of Rutland, Edward (later Edward IV), and George (later duke of Clarence)—who survived to adulthood. Young Richard's father had a claim to the throne, which was then occupied by the third king of the House of Lancaster, Henry VI. Although Richard, duke of York, secretly aspired to the throne, he made no formal claim until 1459, four years after the outbreak of the dynastic struggle between the houses of York and Lancaster known as the Wars of the Roses. In the 1450's, young Richard was nothing more than a junior cadet of a leading aristocratic family. None would have anticipated that within three decades he would become England's most controversial monarch.

Richard's attitudes and actions throughout his life were determined by the violence and chaos that became endemic among the great noble families during the Wars of the Roses, lasting from 1455 until Richard's death thirty years later. The immediate background of the wars can be traced to the mental incapacitation of Henry VI in the summer of 1453. Henry's wife, Margaret of Anjou, to whom a son, the future Edward, prince of Wales, was born in October, 1453, desired a regency for herself. Richard of York was named protector, however, and served capably until Henry regained his sanity in 1455. Then, under the influence of York's enemies, the restored king not only demanded and secured the duke's resignation but also threatened his life. It was at this time that the duke of York and his supporters, chiefly his

cousin Richard Neville, earl of Warwick, rose in rebellion.

The first phase of the Wars of the Roses was decided at the Battle of St. Albans. Henry was defeated and taken prisoner by Richard, but the duke of York did not take the throne, remaining temporarily satisfied to control the government indirectly. Queen Margaret was displeased, however, with York's unofficial supremacy. Determined that her son should eventually succeed his father, she made her move in late 1460. At the Battle of Wakefield, on December 30, 1460, the Yorkists suffered a seemingly disastrous defeat. The duke of York and his oldest surviving son, Edmund, earl of Rutland, were killed. Warwick did not arrive from France fast enough to save his cousin, and the Lancastrians had regained unchallenged control.

The revival of Lancastrian power did not, however, last long. The leadership of the Yorkist cause was now assumed by the dead duke's oldest surviving son and Richard's oldest brother, Edward. Joining his forces with those of Warwick, Edward defeated the Lancastrian forces at Towton Moor on March 29, 1461. Henry VI and Queen Margaret fled, and Edward of York marched on London, claiming the throne as Edward IV by right of descent from Edward III. Soon after his coronation in June, 1461, his brothers George and Richard were admitted to the Order of the Garter. At this time also, George was created duke of Clarence and Richard duke of Gloucester.

The first years of Edward's reign went well, and primarily with the aid of Warwick, he succeeded in restoring order to the realm. In 1463, Queen Margaret again raised the standard of revolt for the House of Lancaster. Again defeated, she fled with her son Edward into exile in France. Henry VI was captured and imprisoned in the Tower of London. At this point, Richard was only eleven years old. Already in his short life, he had witnessed extreme violence and had been its indirect victim. His father and brother and various relatives and friends had been killed in battle or executed, and he had been forced into exile with his mother. The impressionable boy had learned that immorality and duplicity were rewarded often with success. Soon, he himself was to play a leading role in the tumultuous course of events.

Little is known about Richard's life during the 1460's. He, his brother Clarence, and his unmarried sister Margaret probably were quartered at the royal palace at Greenwich from 1461 to 1465. From 1465 until at least

1468, Richard alone was placed in the custody of the earl of Warwick, then the most powerful magnate in England with extensive landholdings throughout England and especially in the north. Richard spent those years at Warwick's castles of Middleham and Sheriff Hutton, where he became acquainted with his future wife, Warwick's younger daughter, Anne Neville (the duke of Clarence married Warwick's older daughter, Isabel), and with one of his closest lifelong friends and supporters, Francis, Lord Lovell. Richard also became acquainted at this time with many of the northern noblemen and gentry who were attached to Warwick. Through marriage, Richard would later become Warwick's principal heir in the north, and this region became his base of popularity and power. His connections there were later helpful in his securing the throne and in his brief reign.

During the 1460's, relations between Edward IV and Warwick began to sour. Warwick, who had played a key role in advancing the Yorkist cause, assumed the right to advise the king unofficially and direct his policy. One of his major goals was to arrange a fortuitous marriage alliance for the young Edward in order to establish greater stability for the House of York's dynastic future. Several royal alliances were considered, but Edward, strong-willed, impetuous, and amorous, secretly married an Englishwoman of his own choosing, Elizabeth Woodville, the daughter of Richard Woodville, Baron Rivers, a former Lancastrian ally, and the widow of Sir John Grey, a Lancastrian retainer who had been killed at St. Albans. Edward kept his marriage, which was to doom his dynasty, secret for several months. When he was finally forced to reveal it to Warwick, the latter was incensed, as were many of Edward's other supporters who resented his marriage into a Lancastrian family, and who were especially alienated by the preferments the king showed to members of his wife's family.

In 1468, Warwick and his supporters, which a year later came to include his new son-in-law, Edward's brother the duke of Clarence, struck against the king. Taken by surprise at Northampton, Edward was imprisoned at Middleham. Warwick thus acquired the nickname "the kingmaker," for he had two kings as prisoner: Edward at Middleham and Henry in the Tower. Although Warwick soon restored Edward to his throne, the king, infuriated by Warwick's execution of his wife's father and brother, refused to accept permanent subservience to the earl. In March, 1470, Warwick was accused of treason. The earl escaped to France, taking Clarence with him. Joining forces with Queen Margaret and her son Edward of Lancaster, and aided by a subsidy from Louis XI

of France, Warwick planned to return to England, restore Henry VI to the throne, and marry his daughter Anne (later Richard III's wife) to Edward of Lancaster. They then crossed the Channel to England in September, 1470, raised the banner of rebellion against Edward, and forced him to flee across the Channel to his ally, his brother-in-law the duke of Burgundy, taking with him his loyal younger brother, Richard of Gloucester.

Life's Work

While abroad, Richard began to play an active role in the affairs of his family and the realm. In his late teens, those physical features distorted by later pro-Tudor detractors, especially by William Shakespeare, had developed. Physically, he resembled his father. Darker and shorter than Edward and George, who had inherited the Neville fairness and height, Richard was not the deformed "crookback" as he was later portrayed in order to enhance his villainy. Perhaps one arm and shoulder were larger than the other, but this was probably more because of its use with a sword in the practice of the martial arts than because of a deformity. Richard was held in exceptionally high regard by his brother Edward because of his loyalty, martial abilities, and intelligence.

Richard III. (Library of Congress)

In March, 1471, Edward and Richard set sail for England. Within three months, the king and his younger brother had met Warwick in battle at Barnet, where the mighty earl was killed, and had defeated the main Lancastrian army at Tewkesbury, where Edward of Lancaster was slain. Most of the Lancastrians were killed at Tewkesbury. A few escaped, however, including the young Henry Tudor, earl of Richmond, who was later to become Richard's most inveterate foe as King Henry VII. Edward IV resumed the throne, and soon after, Henry VI died in the Tower under mysterious circumstances. In the summer of 1471, it appeared that the last Lancastrian threat had been removed, and England looked forward to many years of peace and enlightened rule by its young king. The duke of Clarence had been temporarily reconciled with the king, and Richard was rewarded by the king for his loyalty and services at Barnet and Tewkesbury. Richard received large grants of land and offices and was married in 1472 to Edward of Lancaster's young widow and the companion of his youth, Warwick's daughter Anne Neville.

The marriage to Anne brought to Richard half of the Warwick inheritance. The duke of Clarence, however, resented having to split the inheritance with his brother. The estrangement that had already developed between the brothers as a result of Clarence's treachery toward Edward widened and was never to be resolved. As a result, historians have been unable to determine the extent of Richard's involvement in Clarence's conviction on the charge of treason in 1478 and his subsequent private execution, according to tradition in a butt of Malmsey wine. Certainly, Clarence's fall was primarily the work of the Woodvilles, whom he continued to resent. Nevertheless, although some defenders of Richard have argued that Richard intervened unsuccessfully to save his brother's life, certainly they were on very poor terms personally by 1478, and Richard was not overly saddened by his duplicitous brother's demise.

Richard spent the remaining years of Edward's reign primarily in the north, where he had his base of power and wealth. Eventually, in 1480, he was made Edward's lieutenant general in the north and, in 1483, hereditary warden of the western marches. In his viceregal position, he exercised his authority effectively and scrupulously and became much loved in that section. In 1482, he also undertook a successful military expedition to recapture Berwick-upon-Tweed from the Scots. Most important, after 1478 Richard was seldom at court and thus not directly involved in the intrigues that revolved around the feud over the succession between the king's closest friend and adviser, Lord Chamberlain William Lord Hastings, and the queen, her two sons by her first marriage (the marquess of Dorset and Lord Richard Gray), and their ally John Morton, bishop of Ely.

Edward, with Hastings's support, decided that in the event of his premature death, his brother Richard should head a regency for his oldest son, Prince Edward. The Woodvilles opposed a protectorate by Richard, fearing that they would be supplanted in positions of importance by Richard's supporters. They wanted a Woodville regency, or at least the authority to hold the young king and thus control his actions, both of which were vehemently opposed by many of the most powerful families, who regarded the Woodvilles as dangerously ambitious upstarts. Although Edward IV succeeded in effecting a reconciliation between Hastings and the Woodville faction at the time of his death in April, 1483, the succession question arose again immediately thereafter.

Richard, motivated by both personal ambition and a desire to avert a return to the factionalism of the 1450's and 1460's, then made his move and became intimately involved in a series of events that formed the foundation of the later Tudor defamation of the last Yorkist king. In a letter from Hastings, Richard (still in the north) received the news of his brother's death and his appointment as lord protector. He then wrote the proper letters of condolence and set out for London. During the course of his journey, he received additional letters from Hastings telling of the Woodville machinations. At Stony Stratford, Richard joined forces with his main ally, Henry, duke of Buckingham, took the young king, Edward V, away from his uncles and half brothers, and placed Edward under his own protection. Richard Woodville (the young king's uncle) and his half brother Richard Grey were executed soon after, the queen mother sought sanctuary with her younger son, Richard, and her daughters at Westminster, and Dorset fled to France.

The Woodville's attempted coup had been thwarted, and the young king and the lord protector arrived in London on May 4, 1483. By the middle of May, Edward V had taken up residence in the Tower of London, where he was joined in mid-June by his brother Richard. This was by no means unusual during the period before a coronation. What happened at this point is unclear. Apparently, the queen mother was continuing her intrigues against Richard and was accused of conspiring with one of her husband's former mistresses and Hastings's mistress at the time, Jane Shore. Whatever the case, during a council meeting in the Tower on June 13, Richard accused his old friend Hastings, as well as John Morton, bishop of Ely, and Thomas, Lord Stanley, the stepfather of Henry Tudor, of plotting against his authority and life. Hastings was beheaded immediately on Tower Green, Stanley was briefly imprisoned, and Morton was placed in Buckingham's custody.

Although the coronation of Edward was postponed, it was becoming clear that Richard's position as lord protector was precarious. Increasingly, he became convinced that he must take the throne. Several more years of divided loyalties and conspiracies under a regency was politically untenable. On June 22, one Dr. Shaw in a sermon at St. Paul's Cross accused Edward IV of bigamy, thus questioning the legitimacy of his children by Elizabeth Woodville. Four days later, with the assistance and prodding of Buckingham, a petition was drafted that set aside the claims of Edward IV's children, reduced their mother from queen and wife to Dame Elizabeth Grey, mistress of the late king, and prevailed on Richard, as Edward IV's nearest legitimate heir, to take the crown. Richard agreed and, in so doing, regardless of his motives, undoubtedly helped to avert another civil war. On July 6, 1483, Richard was crowned king and his wife, Anne, queen.

Richard's coronation proved to be the personal apex of his reign. Although he attempted to govern well by enacting financial reforms, reducing taxes, building churches, patronizing learning, and instituting reforms to aid petitioners, he was plagued almost from the beginning by rumors and plottings. To discredit him, the Woodville faction complained that Edward IV's sons were in danger, thus laying the foundations for the most vicious accusation soon leveled against Richard: that he had ordered the murder of the little princes in the Tower. Ostensibly sickened by these rumors, Richard undertook a royal progress to York and was most enthusiastically received wherever he stopped. Buckingham accompanied him as far as Gloucester, where he left the royal train to go to his castle of Brecknock, where he met with Morton, the crypto-Lancastrian he had been holding captive since the crucial meeting in the Tower. Richard, who had made a fatal mistake by temporarily abandoning his capital and the south, was enthusiastically welcomed at York, where he knighted his nine-year-old son, Edward. When he left York in mid-September to return south, he soon received word that his most trusted supporter, Buckingham, had assumed the leadership of an uprising against him.

The motive for the duke's defection has never been clear, but the prime movers in the plot appear to have been Morton, Lord Stanley, and his wife, Lady Margaret Beaufort, who advanced a dubious claim to the throne through the Lancastrian line for her son Henry Tudor, earl of Richmond. Morton, who held great influence over Buckingham, was apparently convinced to support the Stanley-Tudor connection because of the fall of the Woodville faction that had originally provided his hope for advancement. Although Richard defeated and captured Buckingham and had him executed, he failed to deal sufficiently harshly with the other rebels. Most portentously, Lady Stanley's life was spared, and Morton escaped to join Henry Tudor. In April, 1484, Richard's only son and heir, Edward, prince of Wales, died at Middleham. A year later, in March, 1485, Richard's wife, Anne, succumbed to tuberculosis.

Within a period of less than two years, Richard had had his royal authority seriously challenged and had lost his wife and only child. Within less than six months, he was to lose his crown and his life. In August, 1484, Henry Tudor crossed from Brittany and landed at Milford Haven with a motley army composed primarily of mercenaries paid for by his mother, Lady Stanley. Although Lord Stanley and his brother Sir William Stanley professed their loyalty to Richard, they, along with the equally duplicitous earl of Northumberland, on whom Richard had depended, defected at the beginning of the Battle of Bosworth, where the armies of Richard and Henry Tudor met on August 22, 1485. Abandoned by most of his friends, with the notable exception of Lord Lovell, who had remained a faithful friend since childhood, Richard fought valiantly but was finally killed. Stripped naked and thrown across the back of a pack horse, his body was taken to nearby Leicester, where it was buried in the church of the Grey Friars. With the dissolution of the monasteries during Henry VIII's reign, the grave was opened and the remains were scattered. Henry Tudor, the last indirect remnant of the Lancastrian line, then took the throne as Henry VII and inaugurated the Tudor Dynasty. The Yorkist line and the Wars of the Roses were effectively ended.

SIGNIFICANCE

Although the historical Richard III died on the battlefield of Bosworth, the legendary Richard was born there with Henry Tudor's assumption of a throne to which he had a highly dubious claim. Immediately, Henry found it necessary to blacken the name and reputation of his predecessor as a means of enhancing his own and to provide a justification for his usurpation. He and his son, Henry VIII, remained acutely insecure about the stability of the Tudor Dynasty and as a result welcomed accounts critical of the last Plantagenet. Unfortunately, many of Richard's actions, regardless of their motivation, made him suspect.

Two individuals were particularly responsible for the creation of the myth that has made Richard III the most controversial English monarch. The first, Polydore Vergil, was an Italian Humanist who came to England in 1502 as a deputy of his Italian patron and collector of papal taxes, Cardinal Adriano Castelli. Under Henry VII's encouragement, Vergil wrote a history of England, his *Anglicae Historia Libri XXVI*, completed in 1513 but not published until 1534. Vergil was not rewarded by the king for his labors; thus, he was not a lackey of Henry. It was nevertheless he who first portrayed Richard as the consummate villain. The second, and best-known, creator of the Tudor tradition of Richard III historiography was Sir Thomas More, whose *History of King Richard III* first appeared in 1543. More's history may have been influenced, or some have suggested even written, by John Morton, bishop of Ely, the traitor to Richard in whose household More served as a page in his youth. Vergil's and More's histories portray Richard as a monster in physical appearance and deeds.

It is the image of Richard that has come down to the present through two of Shakespeare's historical plays, *Henry VI, Part III* (pr. c. 1590-1591) and *Richard III* (pr. c. 1592-1593). This is the Richard who has been accused of a catalog of crimes of gargantuan proportions. It was Shakespeare's Richard who not only murdered the little princes in the Tower but also slew Henry VI in that same mysterious building and his son, Edward, prince of Wales, at Tewkesbury. It was this Richard who tricked his brother Edward IV into ordering the execution of the duke of Clarence. Shakespeare's Richard even gloated over the death of his own wife, Anne, and perhaps even ordered it to enable himself to effect a more beneficial marriage alliance with his niece and Henry Tudor's later bride. Although Shakespeare intended his play to be good theater rather than sound history, the popularity of his dramatic works, especially *Richard III*, and the appeal of the Bard's Richard to actors, who revel in his cleverness and villainy, have assured that Shakespeare's portrayal of Richard will remain foremost in the popular imagination.

Fortunately, Richard's defenders and supporters have also vigorously advanced their argument that he was the innocent victim of Tudor vilification. The first major exponent of the revisionist school of Richard historiography was the man of letters Horace Walpole, whose *Historic Doubts on the Life and Reign of Richard III* was published in 1768. Since then, the debate has raged on unabated. Indeed, it has been suggested that something has been written about Richard in every single generation since his death. The Richard III Society, an international organization dedicated to his rehabilitation, remains very active. Although most of the questions about Richard's actions will never be definitively answered, the continuation of the great debate about the last Plantagenet promises to attract curious and passionate detractors and defenders long into the future.

—J. Stewart Alverson

FURTHER READING

Cunningham, Sean. *Richard III: A Royal Enigma*. Richmond, England: National Archives, 2003. This new attempt to solve the mysteries of Richard III makes use of, and reproduces, surviving documents from Richard's life and reign, including letters written in his own hand. Structured to lay out all the evidence and then let readers decide for themselves. Includes color illustrations, bibliographic references, and index.

Gill, Louise. *Richard III and Buckingham's Rebellion*. Stroud, Gloucestershire, England: Sutton, 1999. Close study of the events, the personalities, and the alliances of the rebellion against Richard in 1483. Includes illustrations, maps, bibliographic references, and index.

Kendall, Paul Murray. *Richard III*. New York: W. W. Norton, 1955. This account was the definitive biography of Richard III until Charles Ross's publication. Although Kendall occasionally romanticizes his subject, his biography is still valuable to the scholar and the best-written of all, thus providing an ideal introduction to this fascinating subject.

_____. *Richard III: The Great Debate*. New York: W. W. Norton, 1965. This volume includes the texts of the two key conflicting arguments in the great debate over Richard III's character and deeds: More's *History of King Richard III* and Walpole's *Historic Doubts on the Life and Reign of King Richard III*. Edited and introduced by one of the two leading twentieth century authorities on the subject.

_____. *The Yorkist Age: Daily Life During the Wars of the Roses*. New York: W. W. Norton, 1962. An extremely evocative social history of the era in which Richard lived by a scholar who has immersed himself in the period he has chosen for study. This is a marvelously detailed, eminently readable companion piece to Kendall's biography of Richard.

Lamb, Vivien B. *The Betrayal of Richard III*. Rev. ed. Wolfeboro Falls, N.H.: A. Sutton, 1991. This small volume has been included as a good example of the continued intensity of the great debate over Richard. This book, as its title indicates, is a defense of the maligned king and discounts, or at least seriously questions, most of the charges of Richard's detractors.

Pollard, A. J. *Richard III and the Princes in the Tower*. 1991. Reprint. Stroud, Gloucestershire, England: Sutton. 2002. Seeks to answer what for many is the central question of Richard's reign: Did he or did he not cause the deaths of the young princes imprisoned in the Tower of London? Includes illustrations, bibliographic references, and index.

_____. *The Worlds of Richard III*. Charleston, S.C.: Tempus, 2001. A study of a neglected part of Richard's world: his loyal supporters in Northern England. Looks at the relationship between Richard's northern strongholds and the vicissitudes of his career. Includes illustrations, maps, bibliographic references, and index.

Ross, Charles. *Richard III*. Berkeley: University of California Press, 1981. This is the indispensable study of Richard and of the historic debate that has arisen about him. Exhaustively researched and scholarly, yet well written and readable, Ross's biography is scrupulously objective. It is one of the few books on the subject that deals fairly, but critically, with both Richard's detractors and his defenders.

Tey, Josephine. *The Daughter of Time*. New York: Macmillan, 1952. Reprint. New York: Collier Books, 1988. This novel by one of England's best-known mystery writers centers on an amateur sleuth's attempt to solve the mysteries associated with Richard III while temporarily confined to a hospital. Although the work is fictional, the material dealing with Richard is sound history. There is no better introduction to the subject for the curious but superficially informed reader.

Wilson, Derek. *The Tower: The Tumultuous History of the Tower of London from 1078*. New York: Charles Scribner's Sons, 1979. Although the historical time frame covered by this volume is far broader than the era of Richard III, it is nevertheless a fascinating study and provides interesting insights into those dark events associated with the Tower during the Wars of the Roses, especially the fate of the little princes, Edward and Richard.

SEE ALSO: Lady Margaret Beaufort; Edward IV; Henry VI; Henry VII; Henry VIII; Louis XI; Sir Thomas More; William Shakespeare; The Tudor Family; Earl of Warwick.

RELATED ARTICLES in *Great Events from History: The Renaissance & Early Modern Era, 1454-1600:* 1455-1485: Wars of the Roses; 1483-1485: Richard III Rules England; Beginning 1485: The Tudors Rule England; December 1, 1494: Poynings' Law.

NICHOLAS RIDLEY
English bishop, church reformer, and martyr

English bishop and Protestant reformer Nicholas Ridley worked closely with Archbishop Thomas Cranmer to consolidate the reformation of the Church of England. Through his theological writings and by his martyrdom under Queen Mary I, Ridley helped to further the development of the Anglican Church.

BORN: c. 1500; probably at Willimotiswick Castle, South Tynedale, Northumberland, England
DIED: October 16, 1555; Oxford, England
AREAS OF ACHIEVEMENT: Church reform, religion and theology

EARLY LIFE
Nicholas Ridley was born in Northumberland (now called Northumbria). He was the younger son of Christopher Ridley of Unthank Hall and Ann Blenkinsop. Nicholas had an older brother, Hugh, and two sisters, Elizabeth and Alice. The Ridley family had lived in the South Tynedale area, near the Scottish border, for three centuries prior to Nicholas's birth. In addition to Willimotiswick Castle, the Ridley family possessed several family homes in northern England, including that of Nicholas's father. When Nicholas was born, Tynedale was a dangerous and backward area, and the residents were subjected to frequent raids by the Scots as well as by numerous local bandits.

Nicholas's uncle, Robert Ridley, a priest and conservative Humanist scholar at Cambridge University, most likely urged his nephew Nicholas to enter the church. Considering the role that Nicholas was to play in the Reformation of the English church, it is interesting to note that his uncle not only worked against the English translation of the Bible by William Tyndale but also publicly supported the condemnation of the German reformer Martin Luther in 1521. At Cambridge, moreover, Robert Ridley was a teacher who helped to shape the philosophical outlook of Thomas Cranmer, the future archbishop of Canterbury, who, together with Nicholas, would later help to move the English church into the Reformation.

Nicholas was first educated at Newcastle; in 1518, at his uncle Robert's expense, he went to Cambridge to study at Pembroke Hall. There, in addition to his other studies, he read Greek and Latin.

In 1522, he received his bachelor's degree. His uncle provided for his further study at Pembroke, where he read philosophy and theology. Nicholas was ordained a priest sometime prior to April, 1524, and he then received a fellowship at Pembroke Hall. In July, 1525, Nicholas received his master's degree. At his uncle's expense, Nicholas continued his studies at the Sorbonne in Paris and later at Louvain in Brabant. By 1530, Nicholas had returned to Cambridge, where in 1533 he was elected senior proctor of Cambridge University. There, he would soon be drawn into the work of the English Reformation.

LIFE'S WORK
In order to facilitate his divorce from Catherine of Aragon, the English king Henry VIII appointed the reform-minded Thomas Cranmer as archbishop of Canterbury and primate of all England. The pope, unaware of Henry's plan, agreed to Cranmer's appointment in 1533. After Henry's excommunication in the fall of 1533, Henry enlisted the help of the English universities to uphold his position that the pope had no ecclesiastical jurisdiction in England. In May, 1534, Cambridge University officially approved Henry VIII's position on the Papacy. The pope was to be recognized only as the bishop of Rome, with no right to interfere in the ecclesiastical affairs of England. Along with his Cambridge colleagues, Nicholas Ridley approved of Henry's break with Rome. This was not a hard decision, for by 1534, Ridley had become a convinced Protestant.

Beginning in 1534, the Oaths of Succession and Supremacy were required of the clergy and those in the political sphere. By these oaths, Henry consolidated his leadership in matters political and ecclesiastical. Henry's reform of the church was somewhat along Lutheran lines and was conservative in nature. Monasteries were dissolved, and an English Bible based on Tyndale's

Nicholas Ridley. (Library of Congress)

translation was published by royal order. A large number of relics and shrines of saints were destroyed or removed from churches and sold. Still, the traditional ordering of bishops, priests, and deacons continued. The traditional vestments, language (Latin), and even understanding of the mass (transubstantiation) were retained.

As the English Reformation progressed, so did Ridley's ecclesiastical career. In 1537, he received the bachelor of divinity degree and became chaplain for Archbishop Cranmer. The next year, Cranmer appointed Ridley vicar of Herne, in Kent. By that time, Ridley had come to more radical Protestant views, holding that confession was not necessary for salvation and that the services of the church should be sung in English rather than Latin. By the end of 1546, Ridley had given up his belief in transubstantiation and in any form of corporal presence of Jesus Christ in the holy communion, coming to this position through his reading of the ninth century eucharistic controversy and the work of Ratramnus of Corbie. Shortly before his death, in his 1554 *Treatise Against the Error of Transubstantiation*, Ridley articulated his developed views on the holy communion in a definite Reformed manner, holding that holy communion is only a memorial of Christ's suffering. It was specifically for these views on holy communion that he was burned at Oxford in 1555.

In 1539, the movement of the English Reformation was slowed with the publication of Henry VIII's Six Articles, which among other things set forth transubstantiation as the official understanding of holy communion. The Catholic party within the English church was now in the ascendancy. Publicly preaching or teaching contrary to the articles was made a capital offense. The king allowed Archbishop Cranmer and those such as Ridley with Protestant leanings to continue their livings as long as they supported the Six Articles.

In July, 1540, Ridley became a doctor of divinity at Pembroke. Later that year, he was elected master of Pembroke. He soon received another honor: He was appointed a royal chaplain. In this capacity, he would have presided at a number of royal masses and heard the private confession of the king. Even though he had to fend off charges of heresy from the Catholic party, Ridley's preferments continued. In April, 1541, Cranmer appointed him as a prebendary of Canterbury Cathedral, and in October, 1545, Ridley was appointed a prebendary of Westminster.

In 1547, Henry VIII died. Shortly before his death, Henry had turned the ecclesiastical tide back toward the Protestants. With the accession of Henry's son Edward VI as king, the English Reformation picked up where it had left off. In that same year, Ridley was made bishop of Rochester, and in February, 1550, after the deposition of Bishop Bonner, Ridley was appointed bishop of London. A brief physical description of Ridley at this period was made by John Foxe in his 1563 *Actes and Monuments of These Latter and Perillous Dayes* (often known as *Foxe's Book of Martyrs*): "He was a man right comely and well proportioned in all points, both in complexion and lineaments of the body." In terms of his personal life, Ridley was recognized by all sides as possessing a morally upright character. Furthermore, his generosity was widely acknowledged. While he defended the marriage of the clergy, Ridley never married.

Ridley influenced the development of both the 1548 and 1552 editions of the Book of Common Prayer. He had more impact on the production of the 1552 version, as by then he had persuaded Cranmer into coming to a more Reformed understanding of the eucharist. As bishop of London, Ridley rapidly spread Protestant practices throughout his diocese. He caused controversy by removing altars and replacing them with unadorned communion tables. He also wrote *A Treatise on the Worship of Images*, which condemned the use of religious images in churches.

On July 6, 1553, Edward VI died; shortly thereafter, the Catholic Mary Tudor became Queen Mary I. Later that month, Ridley and other Protestants were placed in prison in the Tower of London. In March, 1554, Ridley was sent to Oxford with Cranmer and Bishop Hugh Latimer for a disputation with Catholic theologians on the presence of Christ's body in holy communion. They were imprisoned in the Bocardo jail, above Oxford's North Gate, and eventually kept in separate quarters. Ridley and the others refused to give up their faith, despite numerous attempts to convert them. After being ceremonially degraded from their clerical status, Ridley and Latimer were burned together on October 16, 1555. They were led in chains outside what was then the city wall and were martyred on a spot that today is on Oxford's Broad Street. As the fire was lit, Latimer reportedly said to Ridley: "Be of good comfort, Master Ridley, and play the man; we shall this day by God's grace light such a candle in England, as I trust shall never be put out." Latimer, being a good deal older than Ridley, died quickly, but Ridley took some time to die, suffering greatly. He finally succumbed only when a bag of gunpowder, tied round his neck by his brother-in-law in an effort to shorten Ridley's suffering, exploded.

SIGNIFICANCE

The Protestant reforms for which Ridley worked and died were soon restored when Elizabeth I became queen in 1558. Supporters of the established Church of England and those dissenters who formed the Puritan party both looked on the Oxford martyrs as martyrs for their cause. Ridley's legacy was remembered in different ways by his ecclesiastical heirs. His work with Cranmer in consolidating the Anglican Reformation was upheld within the established church, while his protest unto death against the Catholic party was upheld by the Puritan party.

The spot where Ridley died is marked today in the road with a black cross and a wall plaque nearby. Around the corner from this spot, on St. Giles Street, stands the 1841 Martyrs Memorial honoring Cranmer, Ridley, and Latimer. This monument was erected by the evangelical wing of the Church of England and caused embarrassment to the Anglo-Catholics of the Oxford Movement, who sought to defend the theological and liturgical connectedness of the Anglican Reformation with the Anglican Church's Catholic past.

Despite the sixteenth and nineteenth century controversies over Ridley's ecclesiastical legacy, he was able to rise above the barbarity of his native Tyndale to become both a respected scholar and an able and dedicated churchman. As a bishop and as a theologian, he played an important role in the development of the Anglican tradition.

—*J. Francis Watson*

FURTHER READING

Ayris, Paul, and David Selwyn, eds. *Thomas Cranmer: Churchman and Scholar.* Rochester, N.Y.: Boydell Press, 1999. Anthology of essays on all aspects of Cranmer's thought and career, including his facility with the English language, his stint as ambassador, his revisions of ecclesiastical canon law, and the relationship of his ideas to those of Erasmus and Luther. Includes illustrations, bibliographic references, index.

Foxe, John. *The Acts and Monuments of John Foxe.* 8 vols. New York: AMS Press, 1965. Popularly known as *Foxe's Book of Martyrs*, this work, originally published in 1563, has been reprinted numerous times, frequently in abbreviated form. It provides a significant sixteenth century account of the events surrounding the English Reformation and the life and work of Bishop Ridley.

MacCulloch, Diarmaid. *Thomas Cranmer.* New Haven, Conn.: Yale University Press, 1996. A useful account of the development of the English Reformation, offering insight into Ridley's collaboration with Cranmer in shaping the Anglican tradition as well as the social and political implications of the Reformation in England.

Marshall, Peter. *Reformation England, 1480-1642.* New York: Oxford University Press, 2003. Extremely detailed, meticulously supported argument that the English Reformation should be understood to begin in the late fifteenth century and to last well into the seventeenth century. Grapples with and explicates the specific meanings of Protestantism and Catholicism to the major players and to laypeople during the Renaissance. Includes bibliographic references and index.

Ridley, Glocester. *The Life of Dr. Nicholas Ridley.* London: 1763. A helpful source of information on Ridley's family history by one of Ridley's descendants. The volume offers particulars of Ridley's personal de-

velopment as well as details of his role as a church reformer.

Ridley, Jasper. *Nicholas Ridley: A Biography.* London: Longmans, Green, 1957. The most complete biography, also by one of Ridley's descendants. Contains details of his personal and intellectual development. Treats his life and work primarily from a historical perspective yet offers insight into the religious dimensions of his thought. Includes a detailed bibliography of secondary sources.

Ridley, Nicholas. *The Works of Nicholas Ridley.* Edited by Henry Christmas. Cambridge, England: Cambridge University Press, 1841. Reprint. New York: Johnson Reprint, 1968. A collection of Ridley's major and minor writings, covering a wide range of theological and practical issues. Includes accounts of his disputation at Oxford and other correspondence demonstrating Ridley's perspective on the development of the English Reformation.

Ryle, J. C. *Five English Reformers.* London: Banner of Truth Trust, 1960. A brief popular account of Ridley's life and work from a decidedly Protestant perspective. Offers brief excerpts from Ridley's writings plus a shortened version from Foxe's account of Ridley's death.

Shagan, Ethan H. *Popular Politics and the English Reformation.* New York: Cambridge University Press, 2003. Study of the way in which ordinary English subjects interpreted and reacted to Protestantism. Argues that religious history cannot be understood independently of political history, because commoners no less than royals understood religion and politics as utterly intertwined. Includes bibliographic references and index.

SEE ALSO: Anne Askew; Catherine of Aragon; Thomas Cranmer; Edward VI; Elizabeth I; Saint John Fisher; Stephen Gardiner; Henry VIII; John Knox; Hugh Latimer; Martin Luther; Mary I; William Tyndale.

RELATED ARTICLES in *Great Events from History: The Renaissance & Early Modern Era, 1454-1600:* 1473-1600: Witch-Hunts and Witch Trials; January 28, 1547-July 6, 1553: Reign of Edward VI; July, 1553: Coronation of Mary Tudor.

Pierre de Ronsard
French poet

Ronsard enriched French poetry by adapting classical genres and styles to his native language. He wrote historically significant odes, hymns, and lyrics and one of the most important sonnet sequences in the history of literature.

Born: September 11, 1524; Château de la Possonnière, near Couture, Vendômois, France
Died: December 27, 1585; Saint-Cosme, near Tours, France
Area of achievement: Literature

Early Life

Pierre de Ronsard (rohn-sawr) was born into a noble family in the Vendômois area of France. His father, Louis, was made a chevalier by Louis XII a few years before the poet was born. At the age of twelve, Ronsard was placed as a page in the French court, which put him in a position to become an important courtier or functionary in the royal household. His father wanted him to pursue a legal career, then the path to preferment, but Ronsard performed poorly at each school he attended. He was bored with the subjects that were taught but fascinated by the Latin poetry he read, and he nurtured the ambition of becoming a poet.

After the death of his father in 1544, Ronsard took a crucial step in becoming a poet. He placed himself under the tutelage of Jean Dorat, an early French Humanist. He studied Latin and Greek language and literature under Dorat with his friend Jean-Antoine de Baïf. This rigorous training provided him with classical models in form, genre, and style that he believed were superior to the existing medieval models, which were primarily romances and religious works. Ronsard and his friends Joachim du Bellay, Baïf, and others, formed a group that supported the aims of the new poetry and became known as La Pléiade. Ronsard was determined to become not merely another poet but also the poet who would change the tradition by incorporating classical models, elegance, and rigor into French literature. In 1550, three years after completing his studies with Dorat, he published *Odes* and was hailed as the French Pindar.

Life's Work

Ronsard's *Odes* were well received at the time, but later criticism has tended to disparage them, and a nineteenth century critic, Charles-Augustin Sainte-Beuve, called them unreadable. They were historically important in in-troducing classical forms and myths into French literature, and some can still affect readers. One of the problems later readers faced was that Ronsard followed the metrical and stanzaic patterns of Pindar—primarily a short poetic line and stanzas grouped into triads—and he transferred some of the subject matter from Pindar directly into poems that seemed distant from sixteenth century France. The odes that imitated Horace were more successful; Horace's structure was looser, the style more urbane, and the world they represented had some analogies to those of Ronsard.

The first poem of the third book of odes, in which he announces his vocation as a poet, is a good example of Ronsard's celebration of his classical models. After announcing that he has become "the gods' mortal companion" because the Greek Muse of poetry, Euterpe, has lifted him up to that state, he now can scorn common pretenders since the "Muse loves me. . . ." At the end of the poem, he describes his poetic position as directly linked to Greece and Rome: "Making me part of high Athens' glory,/ Part of the ancient wisdom of the Romans." The common pretenders would be those still mired in the older forms of poetry or those writing merely love lyrics, while Ronsard has become one of the ancients.

Ronsard's next major work was *Les Amours* (1552). Petrarch, who was Ronsard's poetic model for this work, was closer in time. Ronsard wrote sonnets that followed and varied the Petrarchan structure and metaphors. These poems have remained popular through the years and to most people are the quintessential Ronsard. The first part of *Les Amours* deals with the poet's love for Cassandra. In poem 20, he desires to be rain that falls "one golden drop after another/ Into Cassandra's lovely lap. . . ." He then metamorphoses into a white bull who will take her when she passes. Finally, he becomes a narcissus and she a spring so he can plunge into her. After suggesting metaphorical and mythical ways to unite, the last three lines speak of a union at night with a desire to suspend the approach of dawn. The poem varies slightly from Petrarchan conventions, since it speaks directly about the union with the beloved.

In 1554, Ronsard offered a less ambitious but delightful collection, *Le Bocage*. These poems deal more directly with the countryside, nature, and contemporary events. There is, for example, a poem on the frog "La Grenouille"; Ronsard celebrates the ordinary frog above other animals and even calls her a goddess. In addition, the frog is not subject, as humans are, to hard times. He also asks, in a personal touch, that the frog not disturb "the bed or study/ Of my good friend Remy Belleau." The tone is playful and clearly different from the *Odes*. The most interesting poem from that collection, however, is on famine. It asks God to relieve his people and compares the situation of the French to the Israelites. Near the end, he asks that this hardship be visited on barbarians, Scyths, Tatars, and Turks. The last request is the only classical allusion in the poem; the poet asks for a return to the age of precious gold, a common allusion in Ronsard, where people lived naturally and freely.

Also in 1554, Ronsard began the frustrating attempt to produce a national epic of France, *La Franciade* (1572). The poem was to be modeled after Vergil's *Aeneid* (c. 29-19 B.C.E.) and deal with the legendary founding of France. He published fragments of the poem over the years and one book for the royal family; however, even though he wished to master all poetic forms including the epic, as the greatest poets did, the ambitious work was never

Pierre de Ronsard. (Hulton|Archive by Getty Images)

completed and seems to have been alien to Ronsard's genius. His gift was for the lyric, not the epic.

In 1555, Ronsard found a form midway between the lyric and the epic in the first book of *Les Hymnes* (1555-1556). The subjects for these poems were lofty and general. For example, there is a hymn to eternity and one on philosophy. Later, he wrote a sequence on the four seasons. The most interesting poem in this collection is, perhaps, "Hymne des astres," a long poem on the mythic history of the stars.

In 1556, he published the *Nouvelle Continuation des amours* and the second book of hymns. In the new *Nouvelle Continuation des amours*, Ronsard wrote poems on a mysterious rural woman called Marie. These poems use many of the familiar strategies of the sonnet tradition, including the *carpe diem* motif. They are, however, more immediate and intense in their approach to the beloved. For example, in one poem Ronsard urges Marie to rise and join nature, which is already active. At the end, the poet states that he will teach her through kisses on her eyes and breast. There is no Petrarchan coyness here.

In 1559, Ronsard finally achieved the preferment for which he had wished in order to make his life less precarious. He was appointed *counseiller* to King Henry II, and he dropped *Nouvelle Continuation des amours* for poems on political and religious subjects. He defended the royal cause and the Catholics against the Protestants. In 1562, he published *Discours des misères de ce temps*, appealing to Catherine de Médicis to heal the division within the country. Yet the religious conflict continued, and, although Ronsard defended the Catholic cause, he was moderate and always counseled peace and toleration. In 1563, he wrote *Remonstrance au peuple de France*, scolding his country folk for their failure to be reasonable and preserve peace. He also tried to influence the new king Charles IX by writing a plan for his education and training. Ronsard's strong desire for harmony is a reflection of the structure and themes of his poems.

Ronsard also continued his sonnet writing during this period and created one of his finest works, *Sonnets pour Hélène* (1578; *Sonnets for Helen*, 1932). The poems have an intensity and feeling about the experience of love that goes beyond the mythic approach of the Cassandra sonnets. In "Quand vous serez bien veille" ("When You Are Old"), he warns Hélène that she will grow old and live only in the memory and blessing Ronsard's poems will give, an important theme in William Shakespeare's sonnets. The final lines turn from a warning to a plea, "take me, living, now."

RONSARD'S MAJOR WORKS

1549	*L'Hymne de France*
1550	*Odes*
1552	*Cinquième livre des odes*
1552	*Les Amours*
1554	*Le Bocage*
1555-1556	*Les Hymnes*
1555	*Continuation des amours*
1556	*Nouvelle Continuation des amours*
1562	*Discours des misères de ce temps*
1562	*Remonstrance au peuple de France*
1563	*Résponce aux injures et calomnies de je ne sçay quels prédicans et ministres de Genève*
1565	*Abbregé de l'art poëtique français*
1572	*La Franciade*
1578	*Sonnets pour Hélène (Sonnets for Helen, 1932)*
1578	*Les Amours sur la mort de Marie*
1586	*Les Derniers vers*

After the triumph of *Sonnets for Helen*, Ronsard completed *Les Derniers vers*, which marked a change in tone and approach. It was published the year after his death. The poems do not speak of love but of a rejection of the body. Appropriately, one of his last poems is to his soul; his soul, which had been his body's host, at death will be purged of remorse and rancor. The last lines are a farewell: "Ladies and gentlemen, my talk/ Is finished: follow your/ Fortune. Don't trouble/ My rest. I will sleep now."

In his last years, Ronsard's health failed. He suffered from a variety of ailments, including gout. He died at Saint-Cosme in 1585, at the age of sixty-one.

SIGNIFICANCE

Ronsard remains an important historical figure in the development of European literature. He transformed the rediscovered texts and myths of the Greeks and Romans into new French poems. The poetic tradition and the range of allusion and reference could not be the same after his poems. He wrote extensively in every available poetic genre of his time. In addition, he wrote some of the finest lyrics and one of the most influential sonnet sequences of the period. French and European poetry would not have been the same without Ronsard.

There is no doubt that Ronsard wrote too much; there are a huge number of poems, and many are of interest only to students of the period. In addition, he tended to lean on classical mythology to do the work of structuring many of his poems. The job of a critic or reader is to separate the poems that are permanent and valuable from those that are ephemeral or dated, so that one might see the value of a poet who was exalted in his own lifetime and who still deserves careful and proper attention.

—*James Sullivan*

FURTHER READING

Bishop, Morris. *Ronsard, Prince of Poets*. New York: Oxford University Press, 1940. Reprint. Ann Arbor: University of Michigan Press, 1959. An old but readable biography of the poet. The author claims knowledge of Ronsard's inmost thoughts and provides some important background information.

Cave, Terence, ed. *Ronsard the Poet*. London: Methuen, 1973. An excellent collection of essays on Ronsard's poetic art. Cave's essay "Ronsard's Mythological Universe" is especially good. There are useful essays on Ronsard's conception of beauty and on the last poems.

Jones, K. R. W. *Pierre de Ronsard*. New York: Twayne, 1970. An excellent introduction to the life and works of Ronsard. Jones places more emphasis on the poems than the life, but he does give the necessary facts. Contains a chronology and a bibliography.

McGowan, Margaret M. *Ideal Forms in the Age of Ronsard*. Berkeley: University of California Press, 1985. McGowan connects the poetry of Ronsard to structures found in the art of the period. This is an excellent interdisciplinary study with illustrations of paintings and sculpture. The book is learned but not leaden.

Shapiro, Norman R., ed. and trans. *Lyrics of the French Renaissance: Marot, Du Bellay, Ronsard*. New Haven, Conn.: Yale University Press, 2002. English translations of Ronsard's poetry, together with one of his fellow La Pléiade poets and their major precursor. Includes illustrations and bibliographic references.

Silver, Isadore. *The Intellectual Evolution of Ronsard*. St. Louis, Mo.: Washington University Press, 1969. A good study of the early years of Ronsard's intellectual life and how his association with Dorat and the accompanying introduction to the classics of ancient Greece prepared him for a life as a poet.

Smith, Malcolm C. *Renaissance Studies: Articles 1966-1994*. Edited by Ruth Calder. Geneva: Librairie Droz,

1999. Smith was a major Ronsard scholar, and thirteen of the twenty-eight articles collected in this posthumous anthology are devoted to Ronsard's work. Includes illustrations, bibliographic references, and index.

_____. *Ronsard and Du Bellay Versus Bèze: Allusiveness in Renaissance Literary Texts*. Geneva: Librairie Droz, 1995. Study of the war of words carried out by Ronsard and Du Bellay against another French poet, Théodore de Bèze, through allusions hidden within their poems. Provides insight into the social and literary context of La Pléiade, as well as the social function of Renaissance poetry. Includes bibliographic references and index.

Willett, Laura, ed. and trans. *Poetry and Language in Sixteenth-Century France: Du Bellay, Ronsard, Sébillet*. Toronto, Canada: Centre for Reformation and Renaissance Studies, 2004. Translations of four works of criticism and poetic theory, including one by Ronsard and two by Du Bellay. A valuable source of insight into the poetics of La Pléiade. Includes bibliographic references.

Wilson, D. B. *Ronsard: Poet of Nature*. Manchester, England: Manchester University Press, 1961. Deals fully with one of the most important subjects of Ronsard and connects the poet to the tradition of the descriptive poem in that period. Good discussion of Ronsard's use of landscape and his typical strategies in using nature as subject and context.

SEE ALSO: Ludovico Ariosto; Catherine de Médicis; Joachim du Bellay; Henry II; Marguerite de Navarre; Torquato Tasso; François Villon.

RELATED ARTICLE in *Great Events from History: The Renaissance & Early Modern Era, 1454-1600*: 1549-1570's: La Pléiade Promotes French Poetry.

RUDOLF II
King of Hungary (r. 1572-1608), king of Bohemia (r. 1575-1611), and Holy Roman Emperor (r. 1576-1612)

The eccentric, impolitic, and unstable Rudolf became one of the sixteenth century's most renowned patrons of science and mannerist painting at his relocated imperial court in Prague.

BORN: July 18, 1552; Vienna, Habsburg domains (now in Austria)

DIED: January 20, 1612; Prague, Bohemia (now in the Czech Republic)

ALSO KNOWN AS: Rudolf V, archduke of Austria; Rudolf

AREAS OF ACHIEVEMENT: Government and politics, patronage of the arts

EARLY LIFE

The Holy Roman Emperor Rudolf II was groomed for exalted rank from early childhood. He was reportedly cultured, erudite, and able to speak five languages besides his native German. Like his father, Maximilian II, Rudolf was well acquainted with Humanist literature and many of the still-respected Hermetic texts. A lengthy sojourn (1563-1571) at the Spanish court of his uncle, Philip II, endowed him with a broad understanding of world affairs and an enduring fascination for many things Spanish; for the rest of his life, Rudolf favored Spanish dress and frequently relied on advisers with Spanish experience or wives.

Rudolf wrote little, so historians rely on the accounts of others for limited insight into his personality. Even in his youth, the future emperor was described as melancholic and withdrawn. Rudolf's aloofness generated an enduring fog of uncertainty; he was alternately depicted as engaging and distant, friendly and rancorous, judicious and intemperate, measured and mad. In light of his erratic behavior as emperor, it has been suggested that Rudolf may have suffered from schizophrenia, a heritable disease that plagued some near relations, including his illegitimate son Don Giulio. Several contemporary and later writers attributed the emperor's increasingly intemperate behavior in his later years to syphilis, but the evidence for this thesis is tenuous. It is more likely that the frustrations of imperial rule merely exacerbated an already mistrustful and solitary disposition.

LIFE'S WORK

To maintain the Austrian Habsburgs' precarious hold on their imperial and other elective crowns, Rudolf was recalled from Madrid and crowned king of Hungary, of Bohemia, and of the Romans (the accepted prelude to coronation as Holy Roman Emperor) before his father's death. On his imperial accession, Rudolf began to relocate his court to Prague; the move was completed by 1583.

Vienna's vulnerability to Ottoman Turkish attack may have played a role in the emperor's decision, but Prague also seemed a logical choice as capital. The extensive "lands of the Bohemian crown" were the richest of Rudolf's domains, and Bohemia's king was one of seven electors who would decide Germany's next Holy Roman Emperor. By residing in the Hrad (or Hradschin, Prague's castle complex) amongst a predominantly Czech population, the young emperor and king strengthened his family's hereditary claim to the imperial title and seated himself firmly on the throne of a key territory.

The move to Prague also accorded well with Rudolf's desire to be a cosmopolitan, and not merely Germanic, ruler. The Habsburg Empire of his day was not an integrated national state in any case; it included an almost bewildering array of inchoate nationalities, contending faiths, and neofeudal jurisdictions. Rudolf exercised his greatest authority in the Habsburgs' German-speaking ancestral lands (the Erblande, which comprised most of modern Austria), Bohemia, and Hungary, but even in these core regions, he was constrained by a plethora of confessional, local, and noble privileges. Within Germany itself, deepening hostility among the Lutheran, Calvinist, and Roman Catholic minor rulers and between individual Protestant princes and the Catholic Habsburgs, diminished Rudolf's already limited role as Holy Roman Emperor. Always reluctant to leave the artificial paradise of his castle, an increasingly frustrated Rudolf attended no meetings of the Reichstag (imperial legislature) after 1594.

Rudolf attempted to consolidate and legitimize his rule over a realm that lacked an economic, geographic, or national focus by emphasizing the majesty of the imperial ideal. To this end, Rudolf lavishly patronized learning and the arts at his court in Prague. He welcomed Humanist literati and numerous botanists, chemists, and astronomers. Johannes Kepler completed his work on celestial mechanics there; he and Tycho Brahe both held the title of imperial astronomer. Empiricism had not yet supplanted traditional modes of investigation, however, so the inquisitive Rudolf sponsored also many alchemists, astrologers, and devotees of the occult arts.

Like his father and many contemporary rulers, Rudolf developed a passion for collecting. Although few outsiders were privileged to view it, the emperor assembled possibly the greatest private art and antiquarian collec-

Rudolf II. (Hulton|Archive by Getty Images)

tions of the late Renaissance. Rudolf also became a leading patron of mannerist art. This post-Renaissance style, which emphasized allegorical themes and artistic virtuosity, attained striking levels of refinement at Rudolf's court. The Italian painter Giuseppe Arcimboldo and Dutch painter Bartholomaus Spranger were the emperor's acknowledged favorites, but other noted protégés included the painters Hans von Aachen and Roelandt Savery, the Flemish illustrator Joris Hoefnagel, the Dutch sculptor Adriaen de Vries, and the goldsmith Hans Vermeyen, who produced Rudolf's celebrated Bohemian crown.

Although the spectacular Rudolfine court sought to present an idealized, even utopian, vision of universal monarchy, Habsburg politics during the late sixteenth century were increasingly overshadowed by the realities of a divisive confessional crisis. To the dismay of successive papal nuncios, the nondogmatic Rudolf for many years gave only nominal support to the Counter-

Reformation. The emperor paid lip service to the Tridentine decrees, but he never sanctioned introduction of the Inquisition into his territories. Despite Jesuit efforts among the aristocratic and educated, more than 90 percent of Bohemia's inhabitants remained Protestant. Furthermore, the traditional Austrian, Bohemian, and Hungarian noble estates all contained powerful, potentially dominant Protestant factions.

Renewed warfare against the Ottoman Turks (1593-1606) temporarily enhanced the Habsburgs' prestige as traditional defenders of all Christendom, yet military bungling and fiscal insolvency deprived Rudolf of any chance for a decisive victory. Widespread disillusion with an exhausting and inconclusive war eventually merged with dismay at Rudolf's growing indecisiveness and reputed mental instability to precipitate a series of destabilizing crises during the last full decade of his reign.

Rudolf endured the most severe of several mental collapses in 1599-1600, during which he may have attempted suicide; other collapses occurred in 1578-1580 and 1606. Distrusting papal and rival Spanish Habsburg ambitions, Rudolf had relied for many years on moderate Catholic and Protestant advisers who shared his Humanist outlook and doctrinal indifference. Most of the emperor's moderate Catholic confidants died during the 1590's, however, and Rudolf cashiered his remaining Protestant counselors in 1599 for reasons that remain unclear. Rudolf subsequently depended on zealous Catholic courtiers who were determined to recover the empire for the Roman faith. Intemperate religious policies in Hungary soon provoked rebellion (1604-1606) by a once-loyal general, István Bocskay. Confronted by Bocskay, the Hungarian nobility, and his hated younger brother Matthias (Holy Roman Emperor, r. 1612-1619), the emperor was forced to accept a compromise settlement with the Turks (Peace of Zsitvatorok, 1606) and to grant concessions to Bocskay (henceforth, prince of Transylvania) and the Hungarian Protestants (Peace of Vienna, 1606).

The emperor's defeat in Hungary precipitated his downfall. Seeking powerful allies against his elder brother, Matthias aligned himself with the Protestant-dominated estates of Austria, Bohemia, and Hungary. In 1608, Matthias secured election as king of Hungary by guaranteeing the Protestant nobility's right to unhindered worship. The following year, in 1609, Rudolf was forced to grant a concessionary Letter of Majesty to the Protestant-controlled Bohemian estates in order to retain the electoral crown of that land. The embittered emperor

then conspired with his cousin Leopold, bishop of Passau, to support the latter's assault on Bohemia in 1610-1611. How Rudolf expected this bizarre adventure to restore his fortunes remains a mystery. The failure of the Passau invasion led to Rudolf's deposal and confinement within the Hrad until his death.

SIGNIFICANCE

Rudolf reigned during a transitional period in Central Europe's political history. By the late sixteenth century, Habsburg pretensions in Germany were already weak. Although Habsburg authority in Austria, Bohemia, and Hungary was more tangible, its rulers had not yet developed the bureaucratic machinery needed to mobilize the resources of those lands. Rudolf was therefore insecure in his monarchical role and unable to exercise power consistently or effectively; the weakness of the emperor's position may have contributed as much as his enigmatic personality to the eventual rash policies that undermined his reign. All Rudolf's successors would confront these same fundamental problems of identity, purpose, and means during the following centuries; none decisively resolved them.

The emperor also stood at a crossroads in European cultural history. Rudolf embraced a waning Humanist ethos whose adherents still hoped to bring about an all-embracing artistic, intellectual, and moral synthesis. His court attracted the best artisans of this cosmopolitan spirit, providing a refuge from rising dogmatism in Germany and other European lands. Once Rudolf's patronage was removed, however, this late flowering of the Renaissance faded quickly. Within a few short decades, both Humanism and mannerism were submerged by the vigorous Baroque world of the Counter-Reformation.

—*Michael Wayne Guillory*

FURTHER READING

Evans, Robert John Weston. *Rudolf II and His World: A Study in Intellectual History, 1576-1612*. New York: Oxford University Press, 1984. The only English biography of Rudolf, which examines his worldview and provides vignettes of contemporary court and Bohemian notables. Includes illustrations and a bibliography.

Fichtner, Paula Sutter. *The Habsburg Monarchy, 1490-1848: Attributes of Empire*. New York: Palgrave Macmillan, 2003. An institutional study that places Rudolf within the context of Habsburg and Central European history. Includes illustrations, maps, genealogical table, bibliography, and index.

Fučíková, Eliška, Lubomír Konecný, and Jaroslava Hausenblasová, eds. *Rudolf II and Prague: The Court and the City.* New York: Thames and Hudson, 1997. Addresses Rudolfine architectural and artistic influences on Bohemia's capital. Includes illustrations, bibliography, and index.

Kaufmann, Thomas DaCosta. *The School of Prague: Painting at the Court of Rudolf II.* Chicago: University of Chicago Press, 1988. Discusses the development of mannerism under imperial patronage. Includes illustrations, bibliography, and index.

SEE ALSO: Tycho Brahe; Maximilian II; Philip II.
RELATED ARTICLES in *Great Events from History: The Renaissance & Early Modern Era, 1454-1600:* September 25, 1555: Peace of Augsburg; 1576-1612: Reign of Rudolf II; 1594-1600: King Michael's Uprising.

FIRST EARL OF SALISBURY
English earl, statesman, and diplomat

As the principal secretary to both Queen Elizabeth and King James I, the first earl of Salisbury, Robert Cecil, managed Parliament, supervised the peaceful transition from Tudor to Stuart rule, and negotiated a peace treaty with Spain.

BORN: June 1, 1563; Westminster, England
DIED: May 24, 1612; Marlborough, Wiltshire, England
ALSO KNOWN AS: Robert Cecil
AREAS OF ACHIEVEMENT: Government and politics, diplomacy

EARLY LIFE

Robert Cecil (SEE-sihl) was the second son born to Queen Elizabeth's lord treasurer, William Cecil (the later Lord Burghley), by his second wife, Mildred, the daughter of Sir Anthony Cooke. A frail child, Cecil grew up with a twisted foot, a bent back, a short stature, and a keen mind. His education was closely supervised by his father, who recognized in his younger son qualities lacking in his heir, Thomas. He provided Robert with a number of fine tutors who cultivated in him the skills needed for a career in public life. The young Cecil won a degree of affection and support from his parents that they never gave to his older brother, and his father took time to teach Robert some of the valuable political skills and lessons he had learned at court.

Robert Cecil's formal education is not well recorded. He entered St. John's College, Cambridge, in 1579 or 1580, several years later in life than did most of his contemporaries. In 1580, he was among those "specially admitted" to study law at Gray's Inn, London, though he seems to have returned to Cambridge later that fall. In 1580, he sat in Parliament (the third session of 1576) through his father's patronage. He continued his studies, and in 1581, Vice Chancellor Perne wrote to his father and commended Cecil for his piety, diligence, and industry. Cecil appeared to have learned the importance of hard work, prudence, and caution and to have gained a mastery of foreign languages, which served him well throughout his career. Despite his success as an undergraduate, Cecil was prepared for a career in public life and sent abroad to expand his education.

After the parliamentary session of 1584, Cecil traveled to France, where he spent the greater part of the next two years, returning in 1586 to represent Westminster as he had in 1584. While on the Continent, Cecil accompa-nied Lord Derby's mission to the Netherlands to negotiate peace terms with the Spanish. He was chosen for several tasks because of his excellent facility with foreign languages as well as his growing reputation for handling matters with tact and prudence.

Cecil returned to England before the victory over the Spanish Armada, and he may have been employed by Queen Elizabeth to write a pamphlet in her defense. He was elected to Parliament as a knight of the shire for Hertford in the February, 1589, session and was appointed high sheriff of the county later in that year.

On August 31, 1589, four months after his mother's death, Cecil married Elizabeth Brook, the daughter of Lord Cobbam. She died on January 24, 1596, from complications delivering her third child, Catherine, having provided Cecil with an heir, William, and another daughter, Frances.

LIFE'S WORK

In the aftermath of the execution of Mary, Queen of Scots and the defeat of the Spanish Armada, as the rivalry between the factions led by Robert Devereux, second earl of Essex, and Lord Burghley intensified, Cecil began to gain influence and experience at court. After the death of Secretary Walsingham in 1590, Burghley convinced Elizabeth to allow him to assume the duties of the secretary's office, which he then delegated to his son Cecil. On May 20, 1591, while Elizabeth was visiting Burghley at Theobalds, Burghley was made chief secretary and Cecil was knighted. Three months later, Cecil was made a member of the Privy Council, but he was not made secretary until July, 1596, though he increasingly exercised the duties of the office as a result of his father's declining health.

As a member of the council, Cecil helped to convict Sir John Perrot, sat in the parliaments of 1592, 1597, and 1601, and served the queen in a variety of ways. In 1593, he became the functional leader of the Crown's supporters in the Commons, with little prior speaking experience. Despite some initial difficulties, Cecil quickly learned to manage the government's business with great effectiveness. In one session, he secured a large bounty for the queen and assistance for the poor despite a severe economic depression.

As he worked to gain the trust and confidence of the queen, Cecil experienced a period of personal and political difficulties. His wife's death in 1596 left him depressed, gray-haired, and heavily burdened. Despite his wife's advice to remarry, Cecil remained a widower and devoted himself to the service of his royal mistress to a degree that left little room for shared affections. Cecil's isolation increased when his cousins, Francis and Anthony Bacon, joined his rival, Essex, and even further intensified with the death of his father in July, 1698, shortly after Cecil's return from a diplomatic mission to France.

While Thomas received his father's title and the bulk of his estate, Robert received Theobalds, land in Hertfordshire and Middlesex, and a network of political associates who had served his father. In 1608, Cecil exchanged Theobalds with King James VI of Scotland and received Hatfield House, which still survives as one of the better examples of early Stuart interior decoration. He also succeeded his father as master of the Court of Wards, a lucrative position that he supervised with unusual skillfulness.

First Earl of Salisbury (Robert Cecil). (Library of Congress)

In the final years of the queen's reign, Cecil replaced his father as one of the queen's most trusted councillors. His sagacity, prudence, and leadership were severely tested by the political difficulties in Parliament, the troubles in Ireland, Essex's rebellion, and the misadventures of Sir Walter Ralegh. Through all these difficult trials, conspiracies, and rivalries, Cecil effectively safeguarded the Crown's interests and his own. He skillfully defended himself against Essex's slanders, maintained his control of the machinery of government, and kept the esteem of the queen, who called him her little "elf."

Only after Essex's execution did Cecil initiate a secret correspondence with King James VI of Scotland that helped James gain Elizabeth's favor and Privy Council support for his ascension to the English throne after Elizabeth's death on March 24, 1603. Cecil dispelled the doubts that his rivals had planted and gained James's confidence by his good advice, which spared Elizabeth from embarrassment and allowed James to ascend the throne unopposed.

In appreciation for Cecil's management of the peaceful transition, King James I of England kept Cecil as his principal secretary of state. The government discovered a conspiracy led by Henry, Lord Cobbam, his brother George, and Sir Walter Ralegh, in 1603, known as the Bye and Main Plots. As a reward for his efficacious handling of the conspirators, Cecil was made lord of Essendine, Rutland, on May 13, 1603. In October, he was appointed lord high steward to Queen Anne, whose interests he also supervised with notable success.

After negotiating a peace with Spain in 1604, Cecil was made Viscount Cranborne in August of that year, and on May 4, 1605, he was elevated to become the first earl of Salisbury. A year later, he was made a knight of the Garter after becoming lord-lieutenant of Hertfordshire. On May 6, 1608, after the death of Thomas, earl of Dorset, Cecil became lord treasurer, an office once held by his father.

Cecil served King James I with the same devotion and sagacity with which he had served Queen Elizabeth I. He urged moderation in the treatment of Puritan ministers and supported conciliation efforts that resulted in the Hampton Court Conference and the King James version of the Bible, published in 1611. He supervised a series of negotiations with France and played a small role in the diplomacy that ended hostilities in the Netherlands in 1609.

While King James poked fun at his "little beagle" who labored at home while all the good hounds were at the hunt, the king recognized Cecil's immense talents and left most domestic and foreign affairs in his capable hands. From his seat in the House of Lords, James had difficulties managing business in the House of Commons.

Cecil was able to frustrate Puritan initiatives in all five sessions of James's first Parliament, secure new tax revenues, and guide the government through the dangerous Gunpowder plot of 1605, without allowing it to become an anti-Catholic crusade. The event is celebrated as Guy Fawkes Day, a holiday named after the chief conspirator in this plot to kill the king and destroy Parliament.

Cecil expanded tariff revenues with the imposition of a new book of rates in 1608, despite parliamentary opposition, which had earlier defeated his effort to unify England and Scotland. In the fourth session, Cecil worked diligently to stabilize and restructure royal finances by negotiating the Great Contract of 1610. While royal extravagance, the king's unwillingness to compromise, and the suspicions of the Commons combined to frustrate the negotiations in the fall of 1610, Cecil's long hours of hard work and dedicated service took their toll on his frail constitution. Despite Cecil's increasing medical problems and the king's disappointment with the failure of the Great Contract, James continued to grant favors to Cecil's friends and solicit Cecil's advice on all major government business in the following two years.

Cecil not only supervised the administration of government in England but also was chiefly responsible for supervising Scottish affairs from London. If James ruled Scotland "by pen," as one historian asserts, then it is clear that the penmanship was Cecil's. Despite his strong efforts and the work of a commission to settle disputes, Cecil was not able to secure passage in Parliament of an Act of Union to unite James's two kingdoms. Given their long history of animosity, Cecil wisely abandoned the project as harmony existed without it.

The unsuccessful effort to unite the two realms, the rise of a royal favorite, Robert Carr, and the failure of the Great Contract were events that, to some degree, worked to limit Cecil's effectiveness. As he became ill and weary in the last years of his life, it seemed to some that he lost political control and royal favor after 1610. Scholarship has shown that he maintained his influence, the support of the king, and his ability to aid office seekers, including Carr. He was given new honors in August, 1611, and all the members of the royal family visited him when he suffered his final illness, a stomach tumor.

SIGNIFICANCE

Cecil was an immensely hardworking politician and statesman who successfully served two monarchs with great wisdom and effectiveness. While he was not always correct in his political assessments or an advocate of reform, he survived and kept the confidence and support of his monarch despite many challenges and crises. In a hectic and economically troubled era, Cecil provided the domestic stability and external peace that enabled Queen Elizabeth I to retire gracefully and allowed King James I to establish a new dynasty with popular support.

—Sheldon Hanft

FURTHER READING

Cecil, Algernon. *A Life of Robert Cecil, First Earl of Salisbury.* London: John Murray, 1915. Reprint. Westport, Conn.: Greenwood Press, 1971. A dated, apologetic, and occasionally inaccurate biography, it is still the best picture of the "public" man.

Cecil, David. *The Cecils of Hatfield House.* Boston: Houghton Mifflin, 1973. A popular portrayal of the family's founder by a descendant; includes an account of the house that Cecil spent five years and thirty-eight thousand pounds to restore.

Coakley, Thomas M. "Robert Cecil in Power: Elizabethan Politics in Two Reigns." In *Early Stuart Studies: Essays in Honor of David Harris Willson.* Edited by Howard S. Reinmuth. Minneapolis: University of Minnesota Press, 1970. A balanced assessment of the style and consequences of Cecil's managerial and political activities.

Croft, Pauline. "Brussels and London: The Archdukes, Robert Cecil, and James I." In *Albert and Isabella, 1598-1621: Essays,* edited by Werner Thomas and Luc Duerloo. Turnhout, Belgium: Brepols, 1998. Explores Cecil's diplomatic activities in Brussels on behalf of the king. Includes bibliographic references.

_____, ed. *Patronage, Culture, and Power: The Early Cecils.* New Haven, Conn.: Yale University Press, 2002. Interdisciplinary anthology of essays about the patronage activities of Robert Cecil and his father. Discusses the Cecils effects on painting, music, architecture, and other arts, as well as the relationship between their patronage and their political goals. Includes illustrations, maps, bibliographic references, index.

Handover, P. M. *The Second Cecil.* London: Eyre and Spottiswoode, 1959. A detailed biography of Cecil's rise to power that corrects factual errors in Algernon Cecil's account. Contains a weak assessment of Cecil's career.

Hurstfield, Joel. *The Queen's Wards: Wardship and Marriage Under Elizabeth I.* Rev. ed. London: Cass, 1973.

A valuable description of the activities of the court with a defense of Cecil's activities as its master.

_____. "The Succession Struggle in Late Elizabethan England." In *Freedom, Corruption, and Government in Elizabethan England.* Cambridge, Mass.: Harvard University Press, 1973. A realistic evaluation of Cecil's contribution to the negotiations that produced an orderly transition of power.

Lindquist, Eric N. "The Last Years of the First Earl of Salisbury, 1610-1612." *Albion* 18 (Spring, 1986): 33-41. A solid refutation of the assertion that Cecil fell from favor after the failure of the Great Contract of 1610.

Loomie, Albert J. *Spain and the Early Stuarts, 1585-1655.* Brookfield, Vt.: Variorum, 1996. Study of Stuart-Spanish diplomacy, with a chapter on Salis-bury's diplomatic service. Includes illustrations, bibliographic references, and index.

Wilson, David Harris. *King James VI and I.* New York: Oxford University Press, 1956. A definitive biography; includes a detailed account of Cecil's activities during James's reign.

SEE ALSO: Sir Thomas Bodley; William Cecil; Elizabeth I; Guy Fawkes; Mary, Queen of Scots; Sir Walter Ralegh.

RELATED ARTICLES in *Great Events from History: The Renaissance & Early Modern Era, 1454-1600:* July 29, 1567: James VI Becomes King of Scotland; July 31-August 8, 1588: Defeat of the Spanish Armada; May 2, 1598: Treaty of Vervins.

JACOPO SANSOVINO
Italian architect

Sansovino was the first architect to bring Renaissance classical ideas of architecture into a successful conjunction with the Venetian Byzantine-Gothic style, resulting in buildings in the Piazza San Marco that were to confirm its reputation as one of the greatest architectural developments in the world.

BORN: July 2, 1486; Florence (now in Italy)
DIED: November 27, 1570; Venice, Republic of Venice (now in Italy)
ALSO KNOWN AS: Jacopo Tatti
AREA OF ACHIEVEMENT: Architecture

EARLY LIFE

Jacopo Sansovino (JAHK-oh-poh sahn-soh-VEE-noh) was born in Florence. His original name was Jacopo Tatti, but he later took the name Sansovino in honor of his master, the sculptor Andrea Sansovino, whose wall tombs were deeply admired and imitated throughout the sixteenth century. Jacopo Sansovino's early training was, therefore, as a sculptor, and his early reputation was confined to that discipline. He worked in Florence and, particularly, in Rome and was a close associate of many of the great artists of the high Renaissance, many of whom were adept in more than one artistic discipline.

It was not, in fact, unusual at the time for an artist to work with considerable distinction at painting, sculpture, and architecture, and Sansovino's contemporaries, who included Raphael, Michelangelo, and Donato Bramante, would provide the model for a young sculptor eager to try his hand at other forms of artistic expression.

Sansovino had done some architectural work in Florence at the Duomo in 1515, but it was only for a temporary, decorative façade to mark the visit of Pope Leo X to the city. In Rome, he began two churches, San Marcello al Corso and San Giovanni di Fiorentini, but he did not finish either of them. He completed one important private residence, the Palazzo Gaddi, and showed considerable skill in handling Renaissance architectural ideas. The site for the Palazzo was not an easy one with which to work, but Sansovino solved the problems with elegance and style, anticipating the way in which he would deal with architectural troubles in his Venetian career.

In 1527, at the time of the sack of Rome, Sansovino went to Venice, intending to return to the south when political turmoil had eased. He was forty-one years old, and his reputation was mainly as a sculptor. He gained a commission to restore the domes of St. Mark's Basilica, and he did so with marked competence. His appointment as the *proto*, the supervising architect for the procurators of Saint Mark, a body of prominent Venetian citizens responsible for the maintenance of the buildings in Saint Mark's Square, was the factor that kept him in Venice. He joined them on April 7, 1529, and held that office until his death in 1570.

LIFE'S WORK

Architecture is, perhaps, the least independent kind of art form, and Sansovino's work as the *proto* was not confined to keeping existing structures repaired; he was to provide a complete renewal of one side of the Piazza San Marco to extend around the corner of the piazza into the smaller piazzetta facing the doge's palace, immediately to the south of the basilica. This was a task of major urban renewal, all the more important because the piazza, the piazzetta, the basilica, and the doge's palace were, together, the center of Venetian religious and political life. Any changes or additions had to reflect that sense of importance. It was decided that the buildings on the south side of the square were to be razed and a library built to house the world-famous Venetian collection of Greek and Latin manuscripts; the building would also house the procurators.

This project continued throughout Sansovino's life, and parts of it were not finished until after his death. It was the major test of his skill, not only as an architect but also as a negotiator, compromiser, and manager. The main difficulty was designing a building that would be both a visual exemplification of Venetian power and grandeur and a residence for important local politicians, while remaining commercially viable. Long-term leases with merchants in the existing buildings had to be renegotiated, and the new structure had to be able to accommodate shops that would provide income for the procuracy.

Sansovino managed to overcome all the complications to produce what Giorgio Vasari called a building without parallel; Andrea Palladio, the greatest architect of the period, proclaimed it the richest and most ornate building since antiquity. Venice had longed to make the piazza something that Rome would envy. Sansovino gave it to them in a building that makes ample use of Renaissance architectural ideas but lightens them and opens them up to the Venetian tradition of lavish encrustation and lively sculptural decoration. The use of the local Istrian stone, easy to carve, responding in its bright whiteness to the sparkling light flashing off the lagoon, makes the building typically Venetian, while the use of the classical orders, Doric below, Ionic on the second floor, topped by a balustrade on which sculptural figures seem to float in the air, gives it a sense of both majestic solidity and ethereal lightness. The library was to be Sansovino's greatest work.

Sansovino completed two other projects in the San Marco complex. The campanile had, until Sansovino's time, been tucked into a corner of the buildings, losing much of its visual power in a jumble of shops and commercial structures. Sansovino adjusted the line of the library to allow space around the tower, giving it the sight line from all sides that makes it one of the major points of interest in the piazza. He also rebuilt the loggia, a small meeting house at the base of the campanile. Prior to his work, the building had no particular aesthetic appeal; when Sansovino was done, it had become a tiny gem of rich red-and-white marble, appropriate for its place at the base of the tower. It is, as Deborah Howard has suggested, not so much a building as a piece of sculpture.

On the lagoon side of the library, Sansovino had another problem, the rebuilding of the Venetian Mint, or Zecca, and again he displayed a capacity for compromise that allowed him to make art out of impossible situations. Something had to be provided for the cheese merchants who had always had shops immediately in front of the proposed site. The multiple bays of the ground floor, heavily rusticated in the Renaissance tradition of acknowledging the classical heritage of Italian architecture, provide an appropriate fortresslike base for a building in which the coin of the realm was cast and stored. The Zecca has become part of the library; in its time, the bays led into the separate shops of the cheese sellers without compromising visually the importance or aesthetic unity of the structure. The upper stories, Doric on the second floor, Ionic on the third, are formidable in their use of column, lintel, and window surround. The Zecca reflects the practice of mirroring a building's function in its façade—the lower floor suggesting its impregnability, the upper levels, particularly the second floor, with its massive protruding lintels, exaggerating the same idea of sudden closure.

Sansovino's career was not confined to the piazza. He was allowed to take private commissions, and he provided an interesting building for the Rialto market area, still extant and still used today. The Fabbriche Nuove again incorporates the Renaissance use of the orders into the long, three-storied building. Sansovino also undertook the more modest problem of a residence for destitute women; the success of the inexpensive stucco building lies in its tasteful proportions and some very witty chimney pots.

Sansovino also designed several churches, probably six in all, but only three of them survive, one of them with a façade by Palladio. The façades of the other two, San Martino and San Giuliano, have interesting mannerist inclinations. San Giuliano in particular manifests the mannerist tendency to eccentric manipulation of architectural motifs. Sansovino usually eschewed variations that were too idiosyncratic in his use of the Renaissance architectural vocabulary, but the narrow site of San Giuliano, and the determination of his patron to be publicly recognized, led to the mounting of a statue of the patron, seated on a sarcophagus, on the front of the church. The statue reminds one of Sansovino's beginnings as a pupil of Andrea Sansovino, the master of tomb sculpture (sculptures usually only mounted on the interior of a church). It is a stunning façade, clearly original in conception and execution.

Sansovino also designed two palazzos of considerable distinction. The Venetian palazzo was used not only as a residence but also as a place of business, since so many of the great Venetian families were traders. Their palazzos were proof of business success, but they were also used as warehouses and offices and often sheltered several generations of the family at once. The first floor was, therefore, designed not only to store goods but also to take in and distribute the goods from the door facing immediately onto the canals. Other floors housed the extended family, and the façades of the buildings, often right on the canal, were required to be as handsome as money could make them. Palazzos were usually in an established style that was partly Byzantine, partly Gothic.

Sansovino's Palazzo Dolfin was built to serve in the old way as a home and place of business, but there was no need for a large central entrance on the canal, since there was a small stream down one side of the building that could be used to enter the residential areas of the palace. That allowed Sansovino to use on the ground level six Doric arches in a regularized Renaissance pattern leading to six separate warehouses. The second and third floors made use of Ionic and Corinthian decoration, but Sansovino kept the common Venetian arrangement of windows to achieve another successful mix of the old and the new.

Sansovino's second, grander commission was for a family of political consequence, and again, on a much larger scale, Sansovino put the classical orders into play, especially in a generous inner courtyard. Vasari called it the finest palace in Italy in its time, and it displayed the sense of amplitude and richness of design that Sansovino seemed peculiarly able to manipulate without vulgarity.

Sansovino remained active until his death. Vasari writes that he was a handsome and charming young man, well-built and red-bearded. In his old age, he retained his charm, but the beard was white. Tintoretto painted him, bright-eyed and wary, and Vasari notes that in old age, he dressed elegantly and kept himself well-groomed.

SIGNIFICANCE

Sansovino was not a great architect, but he was a very good one, and he produced a handful of major projects that are as good as anything produced in Venice. He was able to break the hold that the Byzantine-Gothic tradition had on Venetian architecture and develop a new kind of style that was thoroughly modern and committed to the dignity and calm weight of Renaissance classicism, yet also retained the lively, decorative lightness of the island mode. He showed other architects how to bring Venice forward into the Renaissance without repudiating the peculiar history or virtues of the old style.

Sansovino was also able to make architectural compromise work without debasement of standards; he worked with the complicated Venetian committees, demanding a certain amount of tradition within a mercurial political and economic climate. He was, in a sense, the ideal architect—learned, modestly imaginative, sensitive to local prejudices, capable of playing the game, able to nurse major projects along despite constant threats of setbacks and changes of mind. His contributions to the Piazza San Marco alone entitle him to be considered one of the finest architects of urban renewal.

—Charles Pullen

FURTHER READING

Boucher, Bruce. *The Sculpture of Jacopo Sansovino*. 2 vols. New Haven, Conn.: Yale University Press, 1992. The best single source on Sansovino in English. Volume 1 is a biography and analysis of his artistic, political, and philosophical influences. Volume 2 is a photographic catalog of his sculptures. Includes bibliographies and index.

Fletcher, Sir Banister. *Sir Banister Fletcher's "A History of Architecture."* 19th ed. Edited by John Musgrove. Boston: Butterworths, 1987. The architecture student's basic reference text. Provides good illustrations and puts Venetian architecture, Renaissance Italian architecture, and Sansovino's version of both in context.

Hopkins, Andrew. *Santa Maria della Salute: Architecture and Ceremony in Baroque Venice*. New York: Cambridge University Press, 2000. This study of Baldassare Longhena's great Venetian church discusses the impact of Sansovino on Longhena and his influence on the design of the baroque masterpiece.

Howard, Deborah. *Jacopo Sansovino: Architecture and Patronage in Renaissance Venice*. New Haven, Conn.:

Yale University Press, 1975. A very sensible and easily understood study of how Sansovino went about making art in the context of a social and political structure that foiled many men. Howard is good on the history of Venice and its architecture and shows how Sansovino adjusted its "rules."

Lotz, Wolfgang. *Architecture in Italy, 1500-1600*. Translated by Marty Hottinger. Introduction by Deborah Howard. New Haven, Conn.: Yale University Press, 1995. Detailed study of both major and minor architects, working in the well-known artistic centers and in less-discussed areas such as Piedmont. Includes illustrations, maps, bibliographic references, index.

Lowry, Bates. *Renaissance Architecture*. New York: George Braziller, 1962. A substantial essay on the subject of Renaissance architecture. Includes a generous selection of photographs.

McCarthy, Mary. *Venice Observed*. New York: Reynal, 1956. A famous essay by one of America's finest writers. Venice is a work of art and should be understood as such. McCarthy and other literary figures, such as Hugh Honour, Jan Morris, and Henry James, are able to make that phenomenon sensible.

Norberg-Schulz, Christian. *Meaning in Western Architecture*. Rev. ed. New York: Rizzoli, 1980. This text does not speak directly of Sansovino but examines how architects make buildings illustrate the ideals of a society, a skill at which Sansovino was particularly good.

Rowe, Colin, and Leon Satkowski. *Italian Architecture of the Sixteenth Century*. New York: Princeton Architectural Press, 2002. Survey of the major figures and works of the sixteenth century in Italy, with a chapter on Sansovino and Sanmicheli. Includes illustrations, bibliographic references, index.

SEE ALSO: Leon Battista Alberti; Donato Bramante; Michelangelo; Andrea Palladio; Raphael; Tintoretto; Giorgio Vasari.

RELATED ARTICLES in *Great Events from History: The Renaissance & Early Modern Era, 1454-1600:* 1508-1520: Raphael Paints His Frescoes; June, 1564: Tintoretto Paints for the Scuola di San Rocco.

GIROLAMO SAVONAROLA
Italian church reformer

Savonarola set in motion the greatest religious revival of his day, turning a materialistic and worldly city—Florence—into a democratic theocracy. He inspired many Florentines with a new, simple faith, and he began the tide of Reformation soon to sweep over Europe.

BORN: September 21, 1452; Ferrara, duchy of Ferrara (now in Italy)
DIED: May 23, 1498; Florence (now in Italy)
AREAS OF ACHIEVEMENT: Church reform, religion and theology, government and politics

EARLY LIFE

Girolamo Savonarola (jee-ROHL-ahm-oh sav-eh-neh-ROH-leh) was the third son of Niccolò di Michele della Savonarola and Elena Bonacossi. His mother was a descendant of the Bonacossi family who had been lords of Mantua. The Savonarolas were a merchant family with an aristocratic-military background. The boy's grandfather, Michele, had been a well-known physician and teacher at the University of Padua, and had become personal physician to Niccolò III d'Este. This grandfather was the primary influence on the boy—a pious, ascetic, aged, and scholarly man, he had much of the medieval schoolman in him and passed this characteristic along to his grandson, who became, partly because of this influence, somewhat out of his time.

Savonarola's family intended that he become a doctor, but he studied many disciplines, including art, music, poetry, and philosophy (Aristotelian and Thomist). Savonarola did study the sciences and medicine, but he eventually turned instead to theology and close study of the Bible.

Pious and inflexible, from a very early age, Savonarola seemed wounded by the corruption of the time. On April 24, 1475, he left home and his medical studies, which he had begun after taking his degree in the liberal arts, and entered the Dominican Order at Bologna, which had a famous school of theology. At the monastery, Savonarola wished to live humbly as one of the brothers, to rid himself of his philosophy, and to be obedient and at peace. The superiors of the order, however, did not wish to waste such a fine education and wanted him to become a priest. His theological studies began in 1476. In 1479, he was sent to complete his studies in Ferrara. Sustaining a disputation there, Savonarola impressed his superiors sufficiently to be elected to the office of lecturer at the Convent of San Marco in Florence. He first arrived in that city on foot that May. Florence was at that time in the hands of Lorenzo de' Medici, patron and poet of the Humanism so hated by Savonarola.

LIFE'S WORK

Arriving at Florence in 1482, Savonarola took up his post of lecturer at San Marco. A great biblical scholar, he taught the Bible to novices at the monastery. The Old Testament was his specialty, especially the canonical books. He was a very learned teacher but was primarily concerned to move his students. He inspired a quiet religious revival at San Marco during his tenure there. His first sermons in Florence, preached at small churches such as the Murate and Orsanmichele, were not successful. His sermons were not to the sophisticated taste of the Florentines, who admired the art of rhetoric, and they also found his Ferrarese accent laughable. Nevertheless, in 1484, he preached at one of the main churches in the city, San Lorenzo, the parish church of the Medicis. He had no more success there.

It was not until he began preaching sermons based on his apocalyptic revelations, at the Church of San Gimignano during Lent of 1485 and 1486, that he began to wield influence as a preacher. Perhaps the reason for his success then was that the theme of his sermons—the need for church reform, his prophecy that the Church would be scourged and renewed—struck an urgent chord after the election of the pope with the ironical name of Innocent VIII. On August 12, 1484, Sixtus IV had died. He had not been a virtuous pope, but his successor was far worse.

In 1487, Savonarola left Florence, having been appointed master of studies at the Studium Generale of San Domenico in Bologna, his own illustrious school. After the year of his appointment was over, he was sent to preach in various cities. In 1488, he went to Ferrara to see his mother and sisters (his father had died during Lent in 1485); he stayed two years at the convent of Santa Maria degli Angeli in that city and traveled to other towns on foot preaching. By this time, Giovanni Pico della Mirandola, a famed scholar and linguist, had become a great admirer of Savonarola and requested of his patron and friend Lorenzo de' Medici that he use his influence to bring Savonarola back to Florence. This Lorenzo did, and in 1490, Savonarola was back again in Florence, at the request of the very family to whom he was to be such a scourge.

In August of that year, Savonarola began preaching his sermons on the Apocalypse, which continued until 1491. His rough style began to gain favor with the people, though his adherents were the pious, the poor, and the malcontents, not the city's elite. His themes were based on real abuses: the confiscatory taxes and corruption of the Medicis, and their looting of the dowry foundations (the *monte del doti*) set up for the marriages of poor girls. In 1491, he preached the Lenten sermons at Santa Maria del Fiori, the principal church of the city.

Lorenzo began to awake to the danger that these revolutionary sermons posed and warned Savonarola not to prophesy or stir up unrest. Savonarola did not take this advice and continued to vilify Lorenzo and the city government for abuses. His popularity continued to increase as Lorenzo's health failed. In 1491, Savonarola was elected prior of San Marco. He began to be seen as a saint. Poets, philosophers, and artists became his adherents at about this time. His Lenten sermons of 1492 had a more markedly prophetic tone than ever before. Soon after this, Lorenzo lay dying and sent for Savonarola to ask his blessing. Contrary to an apocryphal story, eyewitness accounts have it that Savonarola did indeed give his blessing to the dying man and that Lorenzo was greatly consoled by it. Medici rule did not long survive Lorenzo, largely because his son and successor, Piero, was not a competent leader.

In 1492, Pope Innocent VIII died, fulfilling one of Savonarola's prophecies. His successor was the notorious Borgia pope Alexander VI, who was almost certainly an atheist, had droves of children whose fortunes he aggrandized, had reportedly committed incest with two of his daughters, and had openly purchased the Papacy. At this time, Savonarola had a vision: An arm with a sword appeared to him. A voice spoke, inviting conversion, speaking with "holy love," and warning that a time was coming when conversion would no longer be possible. Clouds of angels appeared, dressed in white, carrying red crosses, offering the same accoutrements to all. Some accepted, some did not, and some prevented others from accepting. The sword then turned down, and thunder, lightning, darkness, plague, war, and famine began.

During this time, Savonarola had been engaged in the reform of cloistered life. He told his monks of San Marco that he had had a vision wherein it had been revealed to him that of the twenty-eight monks who had died in the last few years, twenty-five were eternally damned for love of possessions. The monks then brought him all

Girolamo Savonarola preaching in Florence. (F. R. Niglutsch)

their private goods, which were sold for the benefit of the poor. He changed the dress and diet of the monks, and wanted to found a new, very austere convent outside Florence. He also battled to separate San Marco from the Lombard Congregation and to start a new congregation along with the Convents of Fiesole and Pisa. Savonarola eventually accomplished this goal.

The French invasion of Italy, the event that proved the end, for the time, of Medici administration in Florence, occurred in 1494. The French were opposed by the Aragonese of Naples and the pope; Piero de' Medici sided with them against Florence's traditional ally, France. In 1492, Savonarola had predicted the French invasion and its success; now, with the approach of King Charles VIII and his army, Piero's administration was imperiled. It did not help that he was arrogant, openly tyrannical, and a less-than-clever politician. Piero panicked when it became obvious that he could not raise funds for the defense of the city, and he went to treat directly, on his own authority and not that of the Signoria (the Florentine Senate), with the French king. He con-

ceded all the Florentine strong points to the French, and the French entered the city and began to mark houses for the billeting of troops. The citizens were angry, and a group was appointed, among them Savonarola, to negotiate with Charles. All during this time, Savonarola had been preaching apocalyptic sermons on the theme of Noah's Ark and invoking his earlier prophecy. He now played an important part in negotiations with Charles, hailing Charles as a prophesied deliverer, but warning him to be careful of Florence and admonishing him not to abuse the city.

When Piero de' Medici returned to Florence after his disastrous private embassy, he was baited and ridiculed. He fled; Florence became a republic once more, with Savonarola as its de facto ruler. Savonarola advocated the republican form of government and was not personally ambitious. His goal was to found the City of God in Florence that would then act as a model for reform throughout Italy. In the difficult days after the end of Medici rule, with the French occupying the city and the citizens beginning to align along traditional factional lines, Savonarola's constant preaching of moderation, forgiveness, and calm prevented any outbreaks that could have set off civil war. He rejected vengeance against Medici adherents and rebuked the people for executing a particularly hated tool of the Medicis, Antonio Bernardo. There were no more executions, and Savonarola's government grew in popularity.

Nevertheless, there were opponents. The Arrabbiata (the enraged), the opposition faction, began to ally themselves with the opponents of the king of France: the duke of Milan, the pope, and the other members of the Holy League, the Italian anti-French alliance. The Holy League saw Savonarola as the main obstacle preventing Florence's joining them, and the pope began to use his authority over Savonarola as head of the Church to bring him to heel. He summoned Savonarola to Rome, praising him for his wonderful works; Savonarola was justly suspicious and pleaded illness as an excuse for not going. Alexander sent a second brief vilifying him and ordered him to Bologna under threat of excommunication. Savonarola replied respectfully to this brief but did not comply, pointing out mistakes in its formulation. A third brief arrived a month later, forbidding him to preach. Several months later, admitting the political reason behind the ban on Savonarola's preaching, which Savonarola had obeyed, Alexander gave a Florentine embassy a verbal revocation of the ban. Savonarola then preached his 1496 Lenten sermons on Amos, in which he continued to criticize the Church and vilified Alexander's private life. Despite this impolitic behavior, a college of theologians convened to examine the propriety of Savonarola's preaching found nothing to criticize in it. He was allowed to continue.

The pope, however, tried other angles: He offered a cardinal's hat as a bribe and tried to incorporate San Marco into another congregation, in which Savonarola would have no authority. The incorporation was ordered on pain of excommunication. Savonarola protested but obeyed—and the order was not put into effect; he could continue his course. Just before Lent in 1497, during carnival season, Savonarola's authority and popularity reached a kind of peak with "the burning of the vanities," when bonfires were made of those possessions deemed sinful by the new regime. Bands of children went about the city encouraging the destruction of these "vain things." Soon afterward, Savonarola's grip on the city began to fail. His own faction, the Frateschi, or brothers (termed pejoratively the Piagnoni or the weepers), lost control of the government to the Arrabbiata, who bought a bull of excommunication from Alexander VI. It was se-

cret, and marred by errors; the pope himself disowned it. Nevertheless, it was not withdrawn. The Arrabbiata began to foment riots against Savonarola. The Florentine government tried to get the bull of excommunication revoked; Rome offered to do it if Florence joined the Holy League. At this point, Savonarola took a hand in his own defense and began to preach on Exodus; these Lenten sermons of 1498 were to be his last. The city was threatened with an interdict, and Savonarola was forced to stop preaching.

His final downfall was caused, indirectly, by one of his own supporters in a rather ludicrous episode of failed heroism. A Franciscan monk had challenged to an ordeal by fire anyone who maintained that the pope was not correct in excommunicating Savonarola. A loyal adherent, Fra Domenico da Pescia, took up this challenge. The Franciscan did not show up. Even though, by the terms of the trial, this meant that Savonarola's team had won, the city was disappointed in the lack of a miracle, and the following day, Savonarola and two followers were arrested.

His trial for heresy was marked by confessions extracted under torture. His testimony is very touching in its frankness, and it is evident that the verdict was unjust. He was found guilty by the papal commissioners and was hanged and burned by the civil authorities. He received the pope's absolution and plenary indulgence before his death. A cult soon grew up around him, and until the nineteenth century, flowers were found on the spot of his execution every May 23, left by devotees in the night. Miracles that he performed were recorded, and occasionally his name was brought up as a candidate for sainthood.

SIGNIFICANCE

Savonarola's primary importance was as a reformer. In a time that had become corrupt, he reawakened the possibility of virtue, both in religion and in civic life. His remarkably direct and simple approach to right action brought together the life of the spirit and the life of the body, religious life and civil life, in a time when these aspects of life were becoming more separate—when life was becoming, actually, what one would recognize as modern.

That, after all, is the oddity of his life. He was a reformer, a voice of the new, a revolutionary even; yet the source of his ideas was archaic. In living out perhaps the last medieval life in Renaissance Italy, in resisting the alienation of personal life from the eternal that marked the beginning of the modern, he opened the door to attacks on the centralized authority of the Church.

Reared in the aura of his grandfather's fourteenth century education and finding his own time too relativistic, too "advanced," he revolutionized his society in the attempt to archaize it. The life of Savonarola shows the difficulty, for interpreters of history, in the consistent application of the idea of progress. He is remembered now for his incorruptibility and for his championing of the humble against the great, for his devotion to the Church and his opposition to its human incarnation, and for his effect on certain of the thinkers and artists of his day, such as Michelangelo and Pico della Mirandola.

—Ann Klefstad

FURTHER READING

Butters, H. C. *Governors and Government in Early Sixteenth-Century Florence, 1502-1519*. Oxford, England: Clarendon Press, 1985. A thorough examination of the political aftermath of Savonarola's rule of Florence. Chapter 1, "Florentine Politics and Society at the End of the Fifteenth Century," covers the period of transition and reorganization. The details of political and economic life ignored by nineteenth century Romantic historians are included. Good index and an appendix of principal actors in the various aspects of the state.

Fletcher, Stella, and Christine Shaw, eds. *The World of Savonarola: Italian Elites and Perceptions of Crisis*. Burlington, Vt.: Ashgate, 2000. Anthology of essays presented at a conference in Warwick to mark the five hundredth anniversary of Savonarola's death. Contains sections on Savonarola and Florence, the crisis of the church at the end of the fifteenth century, Italian states and their elites, and the cultural changes following Savonarola's execution. Includes illustrations, bibliographic references, and index.

Kottman, Karl A., ed. *Catholic Millenarianism: From Savonarola to the Abbé Grégoire*. Vol. 2 in *Millenarianism and Messianism in Early Modern European Culture*. Boston: Kluwer, 2001. Discusses Savonarola's contributions to Millenarianism and to messianic thought. Includes bibliographic references and index.

Lucas, Herbert. *Fra Girolamo Savonarola*. 2d rev. ed. St. Louis, Mo.: B. Herder, 1906. An account of Savonarola's life, copious but rather dry, in which special attention is paid by its Jesuit author to points of theology and canon law. The author takes great pains to present a balanced view of both Savonarola and his enemies. Contains an index.

Macey, Patrick. *Bonfire Songs: Savonarola's Musical Legacy*. New York: Oxford University Press, 1998. Detailed study of the underground sacred music (laude) composed by Savonarola as an alternative to what he saw as the elitist tradition of the formal motet. This is followed by an analysis of the many musical compositions created by others after Savonarola's death to provide backgrounds for his meditations on Psalms 30 and 50. Includes a compact disc with more than seventy-five minutes of music, illustrations, bibliographic references, and index.

Popkin, Richard. *The History of Skepticism: From Savonarola to Bayle*. Rev. and expanded ed. New York: Oxford University Press, 2003. Analyzes Savonarola's thought and his relationship to the skeptical tradition. Includes bibliographic references and index.

Ridolfi, Roberto. *The Life of Girolamo Savonarola*. Translated by Cecil Grayson. London: Routledge & Kegan Paul, 1959. Probably the best general biography of Savonarola, written with grace and scope, and an account that strives for balance. The author has a wide, cultured grasp of the Florentine spirit and Florentine history.

Rowdon, Maurice. *Lorenzo the Magnificent*. Chicago: Henry Regnery, 1974. A heavily illustrated look at the Florence of Lorenzo, which includes material on Savonarola's career. His earlier life as a prophet and reformer of influence in the days of Lorenzo is fairly well covered, but his three-year period of rule is cursorily dismissed. Offers a sound introduction to the period. An index is provided, as well as a bibliography for further study, a list of illustrations, and maps, paintings, and photographs.

Savonarola, Girolamo. *A Guide to Righteous Living, and Other Works*. Translated by Konrad Eisenbichler. Toronto, Canada: Centre for Restoration and Renaissance Studies, 2003. Collection of a broad range of Savonarola's writings, designed to provide an introduction to his thought and work. Includes sermons, poetry, pastoral works, and correspondence. Illustrated, with bibliographic references and index.

Villari, Pasquale. *Life and Times of Girolamo Savonarola*. Translated by Linda Villari. New York: Charles Scribner's Sons, 1888. This is the commonly cited authoritative biography before the Ridolfi work. A copious treatment but outdated. A sort of apology for Savonarola, and the classic account of his life, heroicizing it in opposition to the wickedness of the times. A thorough index is provided.

Weinstein, Donald. "The Prophet as Physician of Souls: Savonarola's Manual for Confessors." In *Society and Individual in Renaissance Florence*, edited by William J. Connell. Berkeley: University of California Press, 2002. Discussion of Savonarola's understanding of confession and his theoretical and practical influence on other theologians. Includes bibliographic references and index.

SEE ALSO: Alexander VI; Charles VIII; Leo X; Niccolò Machiavelli; Lorenzo de' Medici; Michelangelo; Saint Philip Neri; Giovanni Pico della Mirandola; Sixtus IV.
RELATED ARTICLES in *Great Events from History: The Renaissance & Early Modern Era, 1454-1600:* 1469-1492: Rule of Lorenzo de' Medici; September, 1494-October, 1495: Charles VIII of France Invades Italy.

JOSEPH JUSTUS SCALIGER
French historian and scholar

Scaliger was the foremost scholar of Greek and Latin in his time. His editions of Latin authors set high critical standards and his research on ancient chronology established the study of ancient history, introducing to Europe the literature and history of Byzantium.

BORN: August 5, 1540; Agen, France
DIED: January 21, 1609; Leiden, Holland, United Provinces (now in the Netherlands)
AREAS OF ACHIEVEMENT: Historiography, scholarship, literature

EARLY LIFE

In 1525, the father of Joseph Justus Scaliger (SCAHL-ih-guhr), physician Julius Caesar Scaliger, accompanied the Italian nobleman M. A. de la Rovère to Agen, a small town in western France, where the nobleman would serve as bishop. The physician claimed a remarkable record. Julius Caesar Scaliger was descended from the family (the della Scala) that once had ruled Verona. He had studied art (with Albrecht Dürer), medicine, theology, natural history, and classical literature. He had earned military distinction during seventeen years of service under his kinsman the Holy Roman Emperor Maximilian I. Now the physician devoted himself to other pursuits. His medical practice at Agen flourished, and in 1528, he married an adolescent orphan of a noble family, Andiette de Roques Lobejac. From this union came fifteen children.

The physician studied Greek and Latin in his leisure. He circulated a brilliant (if misguided) polemic against Desiderius Erasmus's criticism of contemporary Latin in 1531, from 1533 to 1547 wrote volumes of his own Latin verse, which would be critically disparaged but read widely and reprinted often, and composed his own Latin

grammar in 1540 and a notable treatise on Latin poetry (published in 1561 after his death). His major work was a massive commentary on the ancient Greek tradition of natural history as understood by Hippocrates, Aristotle, and Theophrastus. This great study was completed in 1538 but not published until after the author's death, when Gottfried Wilhelm Leibniz praised it as the best contemporary guide to Aristotle.

Julius Caesar Scaliger's love of classical learning bore its greatest fruit in his third son (and tenth child), Joseph Justus. Educated at home to age twelve, Joseph was then sent, with his brothers Leonard and John, to the College of Guyenne at Bordeaux. There they read standard Latin authors and learned Greek by using the fashionable new grammar of the Protestant educator Philipp Melanchthon. Plague erupted in Bordeaux in 1555, and the three boys returned to Agen to be educated again by their father. The elder Scaliger required of his sons daily composition and declamation in Latin—studies in which Joseph excelled: By age seventeen, he had composed an original Latin drama (*Oedipus*), of which his father approved and of which he himself remained proud in his old age.

His father, however, did not instruct his son in Greek. Therefore, after his father's death in 1558, Joseph Scaliger set out for the University of Paris. There he attended the lectures of a contemporary master of Greek, Adrian Turnèbe, but soon realized that he knew insufficient Greek to profit from the course. Scaliger thereupon dedicated two years to reading basic Greek authors and, in the process, compiled his own Greek grammar. He then went on to study Hebrew and Arabic to a good level of proficiency. Scaliger's formal education at Paris ended in 1563, when another Greek professor, Jean Dorat, was sufficiently impressed by Scaliger's learning to recommend him successfully as companion to the young nobleman Louis de Chastaigner.

LIFE'S WORK

Scaliger's position as companion to Chastaigner provided secure employment and other advantages: extensive travel, access to learned men and to scholarly collections throughout Europe, and, what was of especial importance in an age of turmoil (for these were the years of religious and dynastic wars in France), freedom to study and write. Thus, in 1564, Scaliger published his first work, *Coniectanea in M. Terentium Varronem de lingua latina*, a wide-ranging discussion of textual problems and the etymologies of Latin words in the *De lingua latina* (first century B.C.E.; *On the Latin Language*, 1938) by the Roman scholar Marcus Terentius Varro. The book attracted scholarly attention, because in it Scaliger demonstrated his profound knowledge of classical and Near Eastern languages and revealed what would become a deep interest in archaic (before 100 B.C.E.) Latin. Thus, as well, Scaliger accompanied Chastaigner on several journeys to Italy, where he met the great French Humanist and textual critic Marc-Antoine Muret, who introduced Scaliger to Italian scholars and their libraries.

Chastaigner and his companion next traveled to England and Scotland, where Scaliger disliked the insularity, ignorance, and vulgarity of the scholars he encountered but found time to continue his studies on Varro and record his negative impressions of Mary, Queen of Scots, and his positive impressions of Queen Elizabeth I. The years from 1567 through 1570 Scaliger spent with the Chastaigner family, moving from place to place in France to avoid the ravages of civil war.

From 1570, Scaliger lived for two and a half years at Valence with the great scholar of Roman law Jacques Cujas. Cujas provided an introduction to a wide range of scholars (with whom Scaliger would correspond in years to come), expert instruction in the study of Roman legal texts, and a library of more than two hundred Greek and Latin manuscripts and instruction in how to discriminate among them. Cujas's influence and the texts he placed at Scaliger's disposal encouraged Scaliger to concentrate his energies on the manuscript sources for individual ancient authors and the ancient sources for specific topics. Thus, in 1573, Scaliger published an edition of the late, difficult Latin poet Ausonius, based on his own scrutiny of an important ninth century manuscript that Cujas possessed.

The St. Bartholomew's Day Massacre—the slaughter of Huguenots in France in 1572—caught Scaliger en route to Poland on a diplomatic mission. Scaliger had been reared as a Roman Catholic, but in Paris he had taken instruction from Calvinists and, by the time of his

Joseph Justus Scaliger. (Hulton|Archive by Getty Images)

sojourn in England, had declared himself a Protestant. He therefore fled to Calvinist Geneva, where he was given a professorship of philosophy. He lectured on Aristotle and Cicero but did not enjoy his subjects. His private tutorials were more successful.

At the first opportunity, in 1574, Scaliger returned to France to live with Chastaigner. Intermittent wars made the next twenty years far from comfortable; Scaliger several times had to serve in the military. Nevertheless, with the financial support of Chastaigner, Scaliger produced important studies of individual Latin authors in which he demonstrated his skill at textual emendation (the correction of the received text of an author). Scaliger's breadth of knowledge and technical skill at evaluating manuscripts changed emendation from a common and popular practice of haphazard guesses to a rational procedure founded on consistently applied principles.

In this same period (1574-1594), Scaliger produced works that established the study of ancient chronology on a solid basis. Scaliger's 1579 edition of the poetry of the Latin astrologer Manilius was in fact a treatise on astronomy as understood by the ancients and served as preface to Scaliger's *De emendatione temporum* (1583; on the correction of chronologies), in which Scaliger argued that a correct understanding of ancient history must be based on a comparative, critical, and analytic study of the surviving fragments of ancient chronological systems (king lists, calendars, and the like) and a correct understanding of how the ancients reckoned the passage of time. Furthermore, Scaliger in a sense here created a new discipline, ancient history, by establishing comparative chronologies not only for Greek and Roman civilization but also for the societies of the ancient Near East (Egypt, Mesopotamia, Judæa). These studies were the foundations of Scaliger's most important work: *Thesaurus temporum* (1606; treasure of chronologies), a collection of the known Greek and Latin fragments on chronology and a reconstruction of the great *Chronicon* (fourth century) of Eusebius. Eusebius had compiled a comparative chronology of Greek, Roman, Christian, and Jewish events back to the time of Abraham, but his chronicle was known only from Saint Jerome's and other Latin versions. Scaliger's reconstruction of Eusebius was so good that some later scholars have mistaken Scaliger's work for Eusebius's own text. Later study and discovery of other manuscripts confirmed the accuracy of Scaliger's reconstruction.

In 1594, Scaliger accepted a position at the University of Leiden, where, with no teaching responsibilities, he dedicated his time to scholarly correspondence and encouraging a new generation of scholars who, in their own ways, would carry on his work. He enjoyed complaining of his accommodations and the climate at Leiden but enjoyed even more the honor in which he was held at this Protestant university. His energies, however, were sapped by dispute. Leiden recognized his claim of descent from the princes of Verona. Assorted Jesuits and lay scholars, for whom Scaliger's historical and textual criticism was perceived as a threat, did not. They attacked Scaliger's scholarship and religious beliefs by questioning his ancestral pedigree. A few months after completing a pamphlet in his own defense, the embittered scholar died at Leiden, on January 21, 1609, in the company of his colleague and student Daniel Heinz. Scaliger was buried four days later in Saint Mary's, the church of the Huguenots in Leiden.

SIGNIFICANCE

A typical scholarly production of Scaliger's time was the *Adversaria*, a miscellany volume wherein an author offered his observations, argued his criticism, and proposed his emendations on a variety of classical texts. Scaliger often affirmed that, while he could have written volumes of *Adversaria*, he preferred to work on complete scholarly editions of classical authors. Indeed, when his

contemporaries saluted Scaliger as among the most learned of any age, they cited as evidence his skill at emendation exhibited in his editions of, for example, Catullus and Manilius.

Later generations acknowledged the worth of those editions but recognized that Scaliger's studies of ancient chronology were more significant. Furthermore, the breadth of his chronological studies was the manifestation of Scaliger's firm belief that as broad a knowledge of antiquity as possible was the prerequisite for a proper understanding of ancient texts. Scaliger thus anticipated the nineteenth century German scholarly ideal of *Altertumswissenschaft*—a science of antiquity. In addition, Scaliger's study of the sources for ancient chronology drew attention to an entire field of history and literature previously unrecognized in Western Europe. In the nineteenth century, students of Byzantine history and literature looked back to Scaliger as their master and as the founder of their discipline.

In retrospect, Scaliger may be recognized as the first of a new breed of scholar. That scholarship ought to impart skills and values was a basic principle of Renaissance Humanism. That principle, in turn, was founded on a tradition stretching back to the Greek historian Polybius and beyond: The ideal historian was involved politically and brought to his studies the experience of life; those studies would then instruct others to lead more effective lives. Scaliger's father was of this mold. Scaliger, however, thought otherwise: "Scholars should not teach practical politics." The scholar should, in Scaliger's estimate, devote himself to scientific study; knowledge should be pursued for purely intellectual, not practical, ends. In this emphasis on "value-free" studies, Scaliger asserted an educational and academic principle that would not be widely recognized until two centuries later and still remains a topic of considerable debate.

—*Paul B. Harvey, Jr.*

FURTHER READING

Bietenholz, Peter G. *Historia and Fabula: Myths and Legends in Historical Thought from Antiquity to the Modern Age.* New York: E. J. Brill, 1994. Discusses the ideas of Scaliger and Richard Simon about Old Testament scholarship and objectivity. Includes photographic plates, illustrations, bibliographic references, and index.

Grafton, Anthony. *Joseph Scaliger: A Study in the History of Classical Scholarship.* 2 vols. New York: Oxford University Press, 1983-1994. Volume 1 takes its subject up to 1579. Grafton treats well Scaliger's early education and assesses Scaliger's early writings in their contemporary context. The second volume, more than twice the length of the first, discusses Scaliger's later life, concentrating especially on the work he did to determine accurate dates for the major events of ancient and medieval history. Includes bibliographic references and index.

Grafton, Anthony, and Lisa Jardine. *From Humanism to the Humanities*. Cambridge, Mass.: Harvard University Press, 1986. A fine study of education and the emergence of scholarly disciplines in Europe during the fifteenth and sixteenth centuries. Documents and discusses the education that Scaliger and his brothers received at Bordeaux. An excellent index and full bibliographic footnotes compensate for the lack of a bibliography.

Hall, Vernon, Jr. *Life of Julius Caesar Scaliger (1484-1558)*. Philadelphia: American Philosophical Society, 1950. This is the best single discussion of the elder Scaliger's life and literary works. Contains information on the education the Scaliger sons received at home and at Bordeaux. Includes reference notes, a bibliography, and a full index. Hall's discussion of the elder Scaliger's early (pre-1525) career should be supplemented with Paul Oskar Kristeller's discussion in *American Historical Review* 57 (1952): 394-396.

Pattison, Mark. *Essays by the Late Mark Pattison*. 2 vols. Edited by Henry Nettleship. Reprint. New York: Burt Franklin, 1978. Volume 1 contains two essays that constitute an excellent sketch of Scaliger. Pattison emphasizes both Scaliger's scholarly work and the circumstances of his life. Volume 2 contains a brief index.

Pfeiffer, Rudolf. *History of Classical Scholarship from 1300 to 1850*. New York: Oxford University Press, 1976. A standard discussion, with emphasis on Scaliger's place in the history of classical philology. Pfeiffer offers sound critical judgments on Scaliger's scholarly works and places those works in their contemporary intellectual context. Contains bibliographic footnotes and a full index.

Sandys, John Edwin. *From the Revival of Learning to the End of the Eighteenth Century*. Vol. 2 in *History of Classical Scholarship*. Cambridge, England: Cambridge University Press, 1908. Reprint. New York: Hafner, 1964. Features a straightforward, brief literary biography of Scaliger, with little analysis. Contains bibliographic footnotes and a full index.

Scaliger, Joseph Justus. *Autobiography of Joseph Scaliger with Autobiographical Selections from His Letters, His Testament, and the Funeral Orations by Daniel Heinsius and Dominicus Baudius*. Edited and translated by George W. Robinson. Cambridge, Mass.: Harvard University Press, 1927. The brief (five-page) autobiography takes Scaliger to Leiden in 1594; the selection of letters illustrates Scaliger's personality; the will offers information on the scholar's family, library, and other worldly goods. Contains an adequate index, a fine bibliographical introduction by Robinson, and two contemporary portraits of Scaliger.

Smitskamp, R. *The Scaliger Collection: A Collection of over Two Hundred Antiquarian Books by and About Josephus Justus Scaliger, with Full Descriptions*. Leiden, the Netherlands: Smitskamp Oriental Antiquarium, 1993. In addition to the detailed descriptions of books for sale by the author, this catalog includes a checklist of all known publications by and about Joseph Scaliger through 1993, a list of annotations made by Scaliger, and an index to a nineteenth century biography of Scaliger.

SEE ALSO: Francis Bacon; Pierre Belon; John Calvin; Elizabeth I; Conrad Gesner; Francesco Guicciardini; François Hotman; Mary, Queen of Scots; Philipp Melanchthon; Giorgio Vasari.

RELATED ARTICLES in *Great Events from History: The Renaissance & Early Modern Era, 1454-1600:* 1499-1517: Erasmus Advances Humanism in England; 1549-1570's: La Pléiade Promotes French Poetry; August 24-25, 1572: St. Bartholomew's Day Massacre.

SEBASTIAN
King of Portugal (r. 1557-1578)

Sebastian's dreams of invading North Africa and extending Portuguese territories there culminated in disaster, when the young king was killed along with nearly all his men in Morocco, thus extinguishing the reigning Portuguese Avis Dynasty. His name, however, lingered in Portuguese popular consciousness as a king who would return to usher in a better age.

BORN: January 20, 1554; Lisbon, Portugal
DIED: August 4, 1578; Ksar el Kebir, Morocco
ALSO KNOWN AS: Sebastiäo
AREAS OF ACHIEVEMENT: Law, warfare and conquest, exploration

EARLY LIFE

Historians consider the rule of Sebastian, sixteenth king of Portugal, as falling into two periods. The first—from his immediate accession to the throne on June 16, 1557, at the age of three and in circumstances of great jubilation since the Crown risked falling to Spain—was a period of regency. The first regent was Sebastian's grandmother Catherine, the widowed queen of John III and sister of Charles V, Holy Roman Emperor, and the second regent, from 1562, was Cardinal Henry. Of these two regencies, the former is accredited conscientiousness, the second incompetence. The second period of Sebastian's rule followed his coronation on January 20, 1568, celebrated on the occasion of his coming of age at fourteen years.

Sebastian, despite a good physique, was of fragile health. He was subject to dizziness and fits of shivers and, in an age of high infant mortality, was not widely expected to survive. From early in life, however, he demonstrated two great passions: war and religious zeal, which his milieu only exacerbated. He grew up in the conviction that his future reserved great things for him, though his mysticism and fanaticism made of him a difficult and unwise leader of men.

He had little interest in study, despite having instructors as famed as the mathematician Pedro Nunes; he preferred jousting and horse riding. Sebastian's religious proclivity manifested itself in his active support of missionary activity in the East and, especially, in his court, which came to resemble more a school of religious observation than a court of individual courtiers. His fundamentalism was reflected in his glee at attending the autos-da-fé of the Holy Office and his approval of the St. Bartholomew's Day Massacre in France.

Growing up amid two courtly regencies of opposing interests, Don Sebastian avoided both, championing instead a group of favorites, young men of his age with martial interests and keen to push the young king for the sake of self-advancement. Despite a number of possible brides, Sebastian showed only the greatest repugnance to the idea of marriage. Sebastian was also not much interested in affairs of state, nor did he have the patience or prudence to be very effective. These charges and responsibilities he happily passed to Martim Gonçalves da Câmara, erstwhile rector of the University of Coimbra, and Martinho Pereira. This allowed Sebastian the liberty of living his dream of crusade: subjecting the lands of Barbary, razing the walls of Constantinople, making himself lord of the Egyptian caliphate, and bringing Palestine into his sovereignty.

LIFE'S WORK

Sebastian thus lived in his dreams, keeping him far not only from the affairs of state but also from his people, for whose sake he did not summon the Cortes (parliament) even once, and he refrained from traveling the countryside dispensing justice as his forebears had done. The regime remained far from his hands and became an object of detestation in the eyes of the people.

His reign did, however, see a fair amount of legislation (seventeen decrees, twenty-three laws, and fifty-two provisions) which, for the most part, were enacted before 1573, after which royal grants were more the norm. Legislative boundaries were redrawn, creating two jurisdictions (*alçadas*) for the counties north of the Tagus and another for the south. Otherwise, the royal monopoly on spices was abandoned in 1570 in favor of a system of contracts, which came into effect in 1576. The problem of piracy was addressed with legislation insisting on the accompaniment of a stipulated number of crew according to the ship's tonnage. Military squadrons were dispatched to confront the corsairs off the rivers of Guinea and São Tomé.

Sebastian's African policy began with exhortations to his governor Rodrigo de Sousa de Carvalho to enlarge the territories of the Portuguese military footholds in Tangier. After a personal visit in August, 1574, during which Sebastian saw for himself the impossibility of conquering seaports in Morocco, the idea of African crusades nevertheless continued to fascinate him. The excuse he sought to intervene more forcefully was found in a dispute within the Sa'di Dynasty surrounding a struggle for leadership following the death of al-Ghalib (r. 1557-1574). Sebastian tried to convince the Spanish to join an alliance, reasoning that once a successor to al-Ghalib succeeded in conquering Morocco, the peninsula would be easy prey to the Turks. Philip II of Spain remained unconvinced. Sebastian similarly tried to involve England in his Moorish plans, but the lord high treasurer and counselor to Queen Elizabeth I, William Cecil, first Baron Burghley, would have no part in the plan.

Undaunted, various measures were adopted to fill the royal treasury and pay for Sebastian's campaigns in North Africa. The pope was prevailed on to announce the African expedition a crusade and to force the holders of ecclesiastical benefices to contribute a certain tax to the state. Prelates, officeholders, wealthy merchants, and principal towns of the realm were asked to make a voluntary contribution to the royal treasury. Even the special funds for orphans and of the "dead and absent" (*defuntos e ausentes*) were raided with the promise that they would be promptly replenished on the king's return from Africa. Rights to salt and pepper were contracted out, while the New Christians were offered a ten-year amnesty in return for 240,000 cruzados.

Armed and supplied, Sebastian's forces landed in Tangier, Morocco, and moved on to Arzila. From there on July 29, 1578, a small and ill-equipped Portuguese expeditionary force, led by the king himself, set out for Larache on an overland march. On August 4, 1578, it was engaged in battle at Ksar el Kebir (also known as the Battle of the Three Kings or, in the Arab tradition, the Wad el-Mekhazen). It was a disaster for the Portuguese. More than eight thousand Portuguese died, while fifteen thousand of the Portuguese and their allied forces became prisoners in Morocco. Sebastian was killed along with the flower of the Portuguese nobility. The Moroccan leader was drowned while fording a river. Only one hundred people from the Portuguese host managed to avoid death or capture and to make their way back to the fleet anchored off the coast.

SIGNIFICANCE

The aftermath of defeat at Ksar el Kebir in Portugal was upheaval and domestic chaos akin to that of the 1383-1385 dynastic revolution, chiefly because of the lack of an obvious successor. In 1580, Spain annexed Portugal.

In another development, Sebastian became associated with a particular strain of Portuguese messianism, which was fed by rumors that the body that had been handed over to the governor of Ceuta (a Spanish enclave in Mo-

rocco) in December, 1578, was not Sebastian's. The belief persisted that the king had survived and would return again one morning to make Portugal great again. The belief that Sebastian still lived received encouragement from a story published in France. It claimed that a wounded noble arrived in Tangier soon after the battle and won admittance to the fortress by declaring himself to be the king. Other versions rumored Sebastian to be living with the mythical priest-king Prester John in Persia or incognito somewhere in Europe. Indeed, pretenders presented themselves sporadically at the Portuguese court and elsewhere, only to be unmasked and executed. None of these executions, however, quelled belief in the Rei Encuberto, or hidden king, whose cult persisted often in semiofficial circles into the nineteenth century.

—*Stefan C. A. Halikowski Smith*

FURTHER READING

Birmingham, David. *A Concise History of Portugal.* 2d ed. New York: Cambridge University Press, 2003. A good and accessible overview that includes discussion of Sebastian. Also includes bibliographical references.

Bovill, E. W. *The Battle of Alcazar: An Account of the Defeat of Don Sebastian of Portugal at El-Ksar el-Kebir.* London: Batchworth Press, 1952. A full if somewhat old-fashioned narrative account of the train of events leading to the battle, as well as a description of the deadly battle itself.

Bowen, Marjorie. "Dom Sebastião, King of Portugal and Algarve (1554-1578)." In *Sundry Great Gentlemen: Some Essays in Historical Biography.* London: Lane, 1928. Very much a biographical panegyric and written in a romantic style but based on sound bibliographic research. The idea sustained is that Sebastian was one of the last gleams of medieval chivalry.

Olsen, H. Eric R. *The Calabrian Charlatan, 1598-1603: Messianic Nationalism in Early Modern Europe.* New York: Palgrave Macmillan, 2003. The microstudy of one of the many pretenders to come forward and claim to be the Portuguese king Sebastian, in this instance twenty years after his death among a community of Portuguese exiles in Venice. Olsen describes the political and millenarist context of the day as he traces the charlatan's rapid demise at the hands of the Spanish authorities.

SEE ALSO: William Cecil; Philip II.

RELATED ARTICLES in *Great Events from History: The Renaissance & Early Modern Era, 1454-1600:* August 4, 1578: Battle of Ksar el-Kebir; 1580-1581: Spain Annexes Portugal.

MICHAEL SERVETUS
Spanish church reformer and physician

Servetus was the first to provide a systematic account of Unitarian ideas. As a doctor, Servetus's greatest achievement was the discovery of the pulmonary circulation of the blood.

BORN: 1511; Villanueva de Sixena, Spain
DIED: October 27, 1553; Geneva Champel (now in Switzerland)
ALSO KNOWN AS: Miguel Serveto
AREAS OF ACHIEVEMENT: Medicine, religion and theology, science and technology

EARLY LIFE

Michael Servetus (MI-kuhl suhr-VEET-uhs) was the son of Antonio Serveto, alias Reves, and Catalina Conesa, locally prominent community members; his father was raised to the nobility in 1529. Little, however, is known about Servetus's childhood. It is evident, however, that the young Michael was given a good education. During the years of his youth, Spain was in a period of relative toleration and admiration of Renaissance learning. The works of Humanists such as Thomas More and Desiderius Erasmus were in circulation. The mixed heritage of Spain meant that both Jewish and Islamic literatures were also available, and Servetus had become well acquainted with the Qur'ān before reaching maturity. His writing suggests that Jewish and Muslim criticisms of the Trinity as polytheistic influenced his own opinion.

On completing his primary education, Servetus studied law at Toulouse in 1528-1529. It was here, in all probability, that he first saw a complete copy of the Bible (the Catholic tradition was that priests studied the Bible and then told communicants about it). Eagerly perusing the Scriptures, he concluded that there was no biblical basis for the doctrine of the Trinity.

Meanwhile, his academic talents led to a position in the service of Juan de Quintana, confessor to Charles V, king of Spain and Holy Roman Emperor. As a servant of Quintana, Servetus was taken to Italy, where emperor and pope were meeting to settle their differences. His observation of the veneration and obeisance paid to the pope and other Church officials during the ceremony in Bologna left a deeply negative impression on the young Servetus.

After leaving Quintana's employ in late 1529 or early 1530, Servetus visited Johannes Oecolampadius in Basel. Although Servetus was inclined toward the Protestant movement, Reformers such as Oecolampadius, fighting desperately to establish their own sects, were little more tolerant of deviation than were papal authorities. The newcomer's forthrightness about his Unitarian beliefs led to agreement among the leading Reformers in Switzerland—including Huldrych Zwingli, Martin Bucer, and Oecolampadius—that if he would not convert to the true faith, he should be suppressed.

LIFE'S WORK

During his time in Switzerland, Servetus wrote his first book, *De trinitatis erroribus libri septem* (1531). Although his Latin was crude, Servetus's discussion of the Trinity was erudite, and the work's publication marked his emergence from obscurity. Later, wishing to respond to some of his critics, Servetus revised and expanded his views in *Dialogorum de trinitate libri duo, de justicia regni Christi capitual quatuor* (1532).

Trinitarian doctrine, which the Church had adopted as orthodox, was far from simple. God, it stated, had a single essence but existed in three coequal, eternal forms: Father, Word or Son, and Holy Spirit. The Son had both human and divine natures, each of which had all the properties of the other. Despite all these forms and natures, God—that is, the single essence—was One.

Servetus, who believed that the Church's teachings should be understandable to all the faithful, regarded Trinitarian thought as a disguised polytheism with no scriptural warrant. Father, Son, and Holy Spirit, according to Servetus, were simply the various manifestations of God and not separate entities at all. The Holy Spirit was God's spirit, which enters all humans and has no independent existence. The biblical Jesus was purely human, though specially infused with the Holy Spirit, as shown by his supernatural origins. He was sent by God, as the prophets had been. Although Servetus never made a clear distinction between the human Jesus and Logos, the Word (he applied the term "Christ" to both), some might judge his Unitarian doctrine simpler and easier to understand than Trinitarian orthodoxy.

Although some Protestants of Servetus's time were apparently troubled by Trinitarian ideas, they preferred to avoid debate on that point, and Servetus's assertion that God as the Holy Spirit was in all things sounded too much like pantheism. Accordingly, in 1532 Oecolampadius and Bucer repudiated him, and he fled to France. He was welcomed to his new country by an arrest order from the Inquisition. Warned of the danger, he flirted with the idea of emigrating to the New World, but instead enrolled at the University of Paris as Michel de Villeneuve. Though he made himself unpopular with his haughty behavior and even challenged John Calvin, himself a fugitive, to a debate (Servetus did not appear), Villeneuve was not unmasked. Increasing hostility toward heretics, however, made discretion the better part of valor, and in 1534, still as Villeneuve, Servetus moved to Vienne, just outside Lyons.

Many people around Lyons favored religious reform, and the leading cleric, Archbishop Pierre Palmier, was as liberal as any ecclesiastic of the time. Publishing flourished in the area, and Servetus was quickly employed as editor and corrector for the firm of Trechsel. His first project was a new edition of Ptolemy's study of geography; he was to correct errors made by previous editors and to update the work, incorporating new discoveries. The 1535 edition was so successful that he was commissioned to do an even more completely revised version that was published in 1541.

Michael Servetus. (National Library of Medicine)

Servetus quickly developed a friendship with Symphorien Champier, a local Humanist and doctor. In 1537, presumably on Champier's advice, Servetus returned to the University of Paris to study medicine. He supported himself by publishing medical pamphlets and lecturing on geography, but when he added astrology, he was soon in trouble. Because of a remark by Saint Augustine that the stars influence the body but not the will, the Church had permitted the use of astrology in medical treatment. It did, however, condemn efforts to foretell the future. Although apparently moderate in his espousal of astrological influence, Servetus was greatly annoyed by criticism of his ideas and wrote *Apologetica disceptatio pro astrologia* (1538) in response. He was brought before the Parlement of Paris to answer charges that included heresy. Although the court ordered confiscation of all copies of his apology for astrological study, it went no further than to read him a lecture on respect for his university's faculty. Soon Servetus left Paris, apparently without taking a degree.

Although he did not publish the information until 1553, it was probably in Paris that Servetus made the medical discovery that is most commonly associated with his name: the concept of the pulmonary circulation of the blood. Galen, the second century Greek physician whose ideas still dominated Western medicine, had asserted that blood was created in the liver and consumed as part of the body's nutritive process. Servetus accepted these ideas but also recognized the blood's purification in the lungs and return to the heart. The fact that this discovery was published in a theological tract is explained by Servetus's adoption of the idea that the soul is in the blood. Galen spoke of a vital spirit that flowed through and vivified humans; for Servetus, that spirit was clearly the Holy Spirit. Although Matteo Realdo Colombo is known to have made the same discovery during this period, an unpublished manuscript of Servetus seems to predate Colombo's work, and it is certain that Servetus published first.

After two or three years at Charlieu, in late 1540 or early 1541, Servetus returned to Vienne; he spent the next twelve years working as physician and editor. He had the patronage of Palmier and aristocratic friends and patients. His second edition on Ptolemy appeared in 1541. The next four years were spent editing the Bible.

Perhaps hoping that Calvin might still be induced to reconsider his doctrine, Servetus initiated a correspondence, but he was haughty and didactic. He enclosed copies of his earlier works on theology, and in 1546, a draft of what would become *Christianismi restitutio*

(1553). Calvin, increasingly exasperated, eventually stopped replying and, despite requests, did not return the books and manuscripts to their author. He did send a copy of his own book, *Christianae religionis institutio* (1536; *Institutes of the Christian Religion*, 1561), which Servetus inscribed with sarcastic and critical annotations and returned. Whether out of rage at being ignored or simply out of excessive zeal, Servetus drifted off into apocalyptic prophecy.

In *Christianismi restitutio*, Servetus attempts to restore the Church to its original nature—a common theme for him and most Christian Reformers. Although the Protestants had made a beginning on one of the central tenets that had to be reformed—the means of redemption—they had done nothing to improve Church doctrine concerning the Incarnation. Servetus expanded his earlier idea that God is manifest in all things, skirting but not quite embracing pantheism. He called for adult baptism, suggesting that the ritual represented a process of redemption and spiritual rebirth that could not occur until the individual was mature in his or her knowledge of good and evil; such maturity was not possible before age twenty. After all, Servetus noted, Jesus deferred baptism until the age of thirty. His position on baptism was much like that of the Anabaptists, but he rejected the social radicalism that marked that group.

Soon after the anonymous publication of *Christianismi restitutio* in January, 1553, Servetus was betrayed to the Inquisition. Although he did not write the letters of betrayal, Calvin supplied evidence from the correspondence of a few years earlier. Arrested and questioned, Servetus escaped. His whereabouts were unknown until he was arrested by Genevan authorities in August.

Calvin, who argued that Protestants should be no less ruthless than Catholics in the fight against heresy, worked to have Servetus prosecuted. The trial, which was highlighted by direct, though mostly written, confrontation between the two theologians, was also a battleground in the confrontation between Calvin and the Libertine Party for control of the city. The outcome was a triumph for Calvin. Servetus was condemned for heresy and sentenced to the stake. He was burned, dying in agony, on October 27, 1553. Two months later, the Catholic authorities in Vienne burned his effigy. Calvin was never again challenged for control of Geneva.

SIGNIFICANCE

Servetus's intellect penetrated divergent areas of thought. He knew classical and modern languages, theology, mathematics, and medical science. His discovery of the pulmonary circulation of the blood was a significant advance in physiology, and he practiced successfully as a physician. Although not the first to advance a Unitarian theory, Servetus was a key figure in pulling such ideas together and stating them systematically. As such, he is an important forerunner of modern Unitarianism.

Servetus's failures came in the areas of politics and human relations. He was so convinced that his views were correct that he had no patience with those who disagreed. He died a martyr not only to his faith but also to tolerance and free speech, yet he probably could have avoided that martyrdom by leaving Calvin alone. His ego drove him to proselytize and to become infuriated when his ideas were rejected. His career, then, reflects the best and worst of the Renaissance and Reformation era. As Humanist and scientist, he had great breadth and depth of knowledge. His condemnation to a hideous death by both Protestants and Catholics exemplifies the tension and fear produced by the zealously held religious convictions of the Reformation.

—*Fred R. van Hartesveldt*

FURTHER READING

Bainton, Roland H. *Hunted Heretic: The Life and Death of Michael Servetus, 1511-1553*. Boston: Beacon Press, 1953. Reprint. Gloucester, Mass.: Peter Smith, 1978. A valuable biography, containing a thorough description of Servetus's life as well as an analysis of his theology. The account is balanced, well documented, and easy to read. An extensive bibliography is also included.

_____. "Michael Servetus and the Pulmonary Transit." *Bulletin of the History of Medicine* 7 (1938): 1-7. A short but helpful discussion of the major medical discovery made by Servetus. This article will be most useful for those interested in Servetus as a doctor.

Durant, Will. *The Reformation*. Vol. 6 in *The Story of Civilization*. New York: Simon & Schuster, 1957. Colorful writing and effective storytelling are the hallmarks of Durant's monumental series about civilization. This volume and its concise biography of Servetus are no exceptions. For the general reader seeking information about Servetus and his era, Durant is a delight. Unfortunately, his work is marked by rather too-frequent factual errors and should be used with care.

Friedman, Jerome. *Michael Servetus: A Case Study in Total Heresy*. Geneva: Droz, 1978. A biography with an emphasis on the religious elements in Servetus's career and a tendency to be hostile toward its subject.

The analysis of Servetus's theology and his problems with the Church is interesting but not always convincing.

Fulton, John F., and Madeline E. Stanton. *Michael Servetus: Humanist and Martyr*. New York: H. Reichner, 1953. A biography that is rather favorable to Servetus. The authors make an effort to establish Servetus's place in Renaissance Humanism, and the book is most useful for setting that context.

Goldstone, Lawrence, and Nancy Goldstone. *Out of the Flames: The Remarkable Story of a Fearless Scholar, a Fatal Heresy, and One of the Rarest Books in the World*. New York: Broadway Books, 2002. At once a study of Servetus and a study of the power of books, this text discusses Servetus's life and ideas, the religious and cultural upheavals of his time, and the role of the printing press in those upheavals. The authors then follow Servetus's legacy by charting the fates of each of the three copies of *Christianismi restitutio* that survived the Inquisition. Includes illustrations, maps, bibliographic references, and index.

Hillar, Marian. *The Case of Michael Servetus, 1511-1553: The Turning Point in the Struggle for Freedom of Conscience*. Lewiston, N.Y.: E. Mellen Press, 1997. This massive study of freedom of conscience devotes its middle third to a biography of Servetus. It begins with a survey of the history of conscience and religious persecution, and it concludes with an extended look at the legacy and intellectual and spiritual descendants of Servetus. Includes bibliographic references and index.

Hillar, Marian, with Claire S. Allen. *Michael Servetus: Intellectual Giant, Humanist, and Martyr*. Lanham, Md.: University Press of America, 2002. Briefer and more focused than Hillar's previous book, this text serves as an introduction to the life, influence, and ideas of Servetus, especially his doctrine of justification. With illustrations, map, index of names, and bibliographic references, including a bibliography in chronological order of all works published by Servetus and their translations.

Wilbur, Earl Morse. *Socinianism and Its Antecedents*. Vol. 1 in *A History of Unitarianism*. Cambridge, Mass.: Harvard University Press, 1947. This standard work on Unitarianism devotes five chapters to the career of Servetus. The focus is on theology and Servetus's importance in the development of the Unitarian position. Much biographical information is included.

Wilcox, Donald J. *In Search of God and Self: Renaissance and Reformation Thought*. Boston: Houghton Mifflin, 1975. Servetus is discussed at length in this book, which provides an excellent background for an understanding of his life and theology. The emphasis is on intellectual history, particularly religion, and the major themes of the era are clearly presented.

SEE ALSO: Georgius Agricola; Martin Bucer; John Calvin; Andrea Cesalpino; Charles V; Desiderius Erasmus; Girolamo Fracastoro; Balthasar Hubmaier; Menno Simons; Sir Thomas More; Nostradamus; Paracelsus; Andreas Vesalius; Huldrych Zwingli.

RELATED ARTICLES in *Great Events from History: The Renaissance & Early Modern Era, 1454-1600*: 1530's-1540's: Paracelsus Presents His Theory of Disease; March, 1536: Calvin Publishes *Institutes of the Christian Religion*; 1543: Vesalius Publishes *On the Fabric of the Human Body*; 1546: Fracastoro Discovers That Contagion Spreads Disease; 1553: Michael Servetus Describes the Circulatory System.

SESSHŪ
Japanese painter

Sesshū is considered the greatest of Japanese landscape painters and a major ink painter whose genius pushed Japanese art toward its apex at the beginning of the sixteenth century.

BORN: 1420; Akahama, Bitchū Province (now Okayama Prefecture), Japan
DIED: 1506; Yamaguchi, Suho Province, Japan
ALSO KNOWN AS: Sesshū Oda (given name); Tōyō
AREA OF ACHIEVEMENT: Art

EARLY LIFE

Sesshū (sehs-shoo) was born in a rural village and was placed while very young in the Hōfukuji, a large temple in the city of Soja nearby, to undergo religious training. Still in his early years, Sesshū entered a monastery in Kyōto as a novice. He acted as attendant to a priest, Shunrin Shuto, who eventually became chief abbot.

He also studied painting with the monk-painter Ten-shō Shūbun, who later was welcomed by the Ashikaga shogunate as a master of the official academy. Both Shunrin and Shūbun had a tremendous influence on Sesshū's life. Sesshū became a monk and practiced Zen discipline under the tutelage of the Zen master Shunrin, who was highly respected for his piety and truthfulness. Sesshū's career was determined by Shūbun, whom Sesshū called "my painting master," and who was the first Japanese artist to rise to the full power and grasp of Chinese art.

LIFE'S WORK

Already enjoying great renown as a painter and past the age of forty, Sesshū left the monastery in 1462, for nothing could satisfy him short of studying in China. He moved west in the hope of making his way to China and established himself in a studio in Yamaguchi, which was under the control and patronage of the Ōuchi family. Japan was going through a time of civil disturbance that culminated in the Ōnin Wars (1467-1477), which devastated Kyōto and dispersed its culture to the provinces; Yamaguchi thrived as a Little Kyōto.

In 1467, Sesshū traveled to China with a shogunal commercial fleet to study Chinese ink painting at first hand. His trip, which took him by land from Ningbo to Beijing, gave him numerous opportunities to see not only some famous Chinese scenery but also many Chinese paintings, including those by Ming Dynasty painters still unknown in Japan. Sesshū had gone to China in search of a good painting master and found only mediocre ones who were weighed down with academic formalism. The grandiose landscape of the continent, however, revealed to him the secret composition in Chinese painting. Wherever he went, he drew landscapes and scenes of popular life that display the essential qualities of his art: solid construction and concise brushwork. He traveled especially to all the famous scenes where the great Sung landscapists had painted from nature. His style of sketching was so rapid and incisive that he brought back to Japan in 1469 thousands of fresh impressions of all the most noted places in Chinese scenery and history, along with accurate studies of costumes worn by famous individuals and of portrait types.

After returning to Japan in 1469 with his invaluable raw materials from China, Sesshū moved from place to place in northern Kyūshū in order to avoid the disorder of civil war. He finally settled in Ōita, under the patronage of the Ōtomo family. There he opened a studio he named Tenkai Togaro, situated high on the side of a hill overlooking town, water, and mountains. Sesshū would often begin his work by gazing out on the beautiful broad landscape that lay beneath his window. After a drink of sake, he would pick up his bamboo flute and play a sonorous, lingering melody to establish the right mood. Only then would he take up his brush and begin to paint. He was truly prolific; his floor was constantly covered with scattered pieces of used and unused paper. His monk friend Bofu Ryoshin, after visiting him in 1476, commented that everyone in the town, from the nobility to the common people, admired Sesshū's art and asked for a piece of his work. It seems that Sesshū never grew weary of depicting his private world, communing from time to time with the great world of nature outstretched beneath his balcony.

His practice of *zazen* (meditation) and his custom of making leisurely pilgrimages to various Buddhist temples and monasteries seem to have given him a strong body and robust health; he was able to travel on foot to various parts of the country, painting realistic pictures of the places he visited along the way. Sesshū always kept his clerical name and his Buddhist robe, which allowed him to travel through districts that were dangerous or that were barred to others.

Between 1481 and 1484, Sesshū made a long journey throughout Japan, making landscape drawings along the way. This artistic pilgrimage deepened his ability to capture the essential features of Japanese landscapes in his wash drawings. The Sung tradition of Chinese wash drawing had been fully assimilated in Japan, thanks to Shūbun's talents and common sense, but it was Sesshū who first succeeded in giving a deeply personal and national expression to the new technique. Moreover, Sesshū's style is remarkable for its clear departure from the lyrical mode associated with his teacher Shūbun. Dynamic brushwork and structured composition dominate Sesshū's works. He thoroughly developed and perfected a style of his own, and throughout his career, he pushed back the limits of expression. Sesshū was completely wrapped up in his art. On returning to the west, he set up his Tenkai Togaro studio in Yamaguchi.

Sesshū's studio became a place of pilgrimage as people requested a token from his brush. He painted the walls of many monasteries (unfortunately long-since destroyed) and hundreds of sixfold screens, of which many have moldered away or been burned. An enormous amount of his work remains, however, though it is so zealously prized and guarded that few have seen many of his great masterpieces.

Among his compositions that are available to public view and representative of his work are *Autumn and Winter Landscapes* (c. 1470-1490), a pair of hanging scrolls that must have belonged to a sequence of four seasons, a traditional theme for a set of landscapes, and *Landscapes of the Four Seasons* (1486), a long picture sequence illustrating the transition from spring to winter, done in a horizontal hand scroll format and representing the synthesis of his art. *Haboku Landscape* (1495), his best-known work, is a landscape in cursive style. It was given to his disciple Josui Soen, a painter-monk of the Enkakuji, when he took leave of Sesshū to return to Kamakura after a long course of study in his studio. The landscape, with a few rapid wash strokes accentuated with dark black lines, skillfully represents a tiny segment of nature lacking neither grandeur nor stability. *Amanohashidate* (1502-1505; bridge of heaven), drawn on the spot during a visit to the famous place on the Sea of Japan, represents the climax of his art. In this panoramic view of a pilgrimage site, all the details are represented with clean-cut lines, accompanied even by the names of the localities. Sesshū succeeded in capturing the innermost qualities of the famous place; to the technique of wash painting, he gave a highly personal expression.

Sesshū's versatility extended to other genres such as bird and flower painting—numerous sets of screens on this subject have been attributed to him. Moreover, note-worthy examples of portraits and other figure subjects including *Huike Severing His Arm*, a large, deeply moving composition executed in 1496 in which Huike (Huiko) is cutting off his arm to show his will power to Bodhidharma.

Sesshū died shortly after painting *Amanohashidate*; he was vigorously healthy right to the end of his life. During his lifetime, Sesshū was the host of many pupils, mostly Zen priests, of whom the greatest is Sesson Shūkei. Among other acknowledged masters of this Sesshū school were Shugetsu Tokan, Umpo Toetsu, Kaiho Yusho, and Soga Chokuan. The Sesshū school continued on into the seventeenth century before melding with other schools. Its decline and death was not surprising, for no school of Japanese pictorial art so entirely depended on the skill of its delineator.

SIGNIFICANCE

The style of Sesshū is central in the whole range of Asian art. Its primary vigor lies in its line—Sesshū's conceptions are thought out in terms of dominant lines. The line is hard, rough, and splintery, as if his brush were intentionally made of hog bristles irregularly set. Sesshū is a great master of straight line and angle. Moreover, he perfected the Chinese *suiboku* style of painting, making it typically Japanese by using the *haboku* technique, literally meaning flung ink, which employs a freely handled wash. *Suiboku* was monochrome work using black ink on a brush, which emphasized skilled brush work in place of a balance of color. Sesshū was the master of this style.

Sesshū loved painting landscapes because the landscape remains personal. It is the individual who selects its elements, stamps them with a seal, and infuses them with strength and will. The genius clings throughout to human values, imposes them on the world, and victoriously refashions a world of his or her own.

Sesshū's primary achievements can be easily categorized. He was preeminently skillful in landscape and figure painting. He excelled in the portrayal of birds, animals, and flowers. His manner was distinguished by the rapidity and certainty of its brushwork. He cultivated the habit of capturing as much of the subject as possible with one stroke. The effects of details such as leaves, feathers, and the like were almost invariably done at the single application of the brush, controlled by an unerring but perfectly free hand.

Many of the finest artists of the sixteenth century claimed to be his successor. The competition became so fierce that Unkoku Togan and Hasegawa Tohaku became embroiled in a legal dispute over the right to claim artistic descent from Sesshū.

—*Edwin L. Neville, Jr.*

FURTHER READING

Akiyama, Terukaza. *Japanese Painting*. Cleveland, Ohio: World Publishing, 1961. A beautiful volume with illustrations covering the whole range of Japanese painting according to their genre. Chapter 6 emphasizes the influence of Chinese art and the development of monochrome painting, at the heart of which is Sesshū.

Binyon, Laurence. *Painting in the Far East*. 3d ed., rev. Reprint. New York: Dover, 1959. An interesting analysis of Sesshū's paintings appears in chapter 11.

Brinker, Helmut, and Hiroshi Kanazawa. *Zen: Masters of Meditation in Images and Writings*. Translated by Andreas Leisinger. Zürich, Switzerland: Museum Reitberg, 1996. This catalog of a museum exhibition places a study of major Zen artists alongside legendary figures and clergymen. It is meant to emphasize the philosophical component and the spiritual function of Zen art. Includes illustrations, bibliographic references, and index.

Fenollosa, Ernest F. *Epochs of Chinese and Japanese Art*. 2 vols. New and rev. ed. Reprint. New York: Dover, 1963. One of the first interpreters of note on Japanese and Chinese art. Reviews Sesshū's accomplishments and their significance. Provides a unique perspective of Sesshū.

Paine, Robert Treat, and Alexander Soper. *The Art and Architecture of Japan*. 3d ed. New Haven, Conn.: Yale University Press, 1981. Part 1 deals with the broad sweep of Japanese painting through history. Chapters 9 and 10 emphasize Sesshū, his compatriots, and his influence on successors. This revised edition contains an invaluable bibliography by W. D. Waterhouse.

Philips, Quitman E. *The Practices of Painting in Japan, 1475-1500*. Stanford, Calif.: Stanford University Press, 2000. Close study of Japanese painting and society, arguing that the painting should be seen as a body of social practices that forms one component of the larger body of social practices. Combines art historical analysis with sociology and social history of the period. Includes illustrations, appendices, bibliographic references, and index.

Sadao, Tsuneko S., and Stephanie Wada. *Discovering the Arts of Japan: A Historical Overview*. New York: Kodansha International, 2003. General survey of the evolution of the forms and functions of Japanese art through history. Places Sesshū within his broad cultural context. Includes illustrations, bibliographic references, and index.

Tanaka, Ichimatsu. *Japanese Ink Painting: Shūbun to Sesshū*. Translated by Bruce Darling. New York: Weatherhill, 1972. A standard work on Sesshū and his master Shūbun that places them in historic perspective in the development of Japanese painting. Chapter 4 is devoted exclusively to Sesshū.

Warner, Langdon. *The Enduring Art of Japan*. New York: Grove Press, 1952. A classic analysis of Japanese art trends in a historical perspective. Chapter 5 emphasizes the Ashikaga period, into which fit Sesshū and ink painting.

SEE ALSO: Giovanni Bellini; Pieter Bruegel, the Elder.
RELATED ARTICLES in *Great Events from History: The Renaissance & Early Modern Era, 1454-1600:* 1457-1480's: Spread of Jōdo Shinshū Buddhism; 1467-1477: Ōnin War; c. 1473: Ashikaga Yoshimasa Builds the Silver Pavilion; 1477-1576: Japan's "Age of the Country at War"; March 5, 1488: Composition of the *Renga* Masterpiece *Minase sangin hyakuin*; Beginning 1513: Kanō School Flourishes.

JANE SEYMOUR
Queen consort of England (r. 1536-1537)

The third wife of King Henry VIII, Jane Seymour gave birth to Henry's only son, the future King Edward VI. Although Jane did not long survive Edward's birth, the connection she established between her family and the throne would play a crucial role in England becoming a predominantly Protestant country.

BORN: c. 1509; Wolf Hall, Wiltshire, England
DIED: October 24, 1537; Hampton Court, London, England
AREAS OF ACHIEVEMENT: Government and politics, religion and theology

EARLY LIFE

Jane Seymour was the daughter of Sir John Seymour and Lady Margery Wentworth, who had ten children, of whom six—three boys and three girls—lived to maturity, a rare feat of survival for the early sixteenth century. Jane's parents were members of the minor English aristocracy who had important connections to the royal court, and Jane's mother could trace her descent to King Edward III.

Jane grew up in the family home, Wolf Hall. Her education was probably the typical one for a girl of her station in life: She learned to read and write, to do needlework, and to manage a household. There would also have been an emphasis on the development of religious devotion and modest behavior, since Jane's era believed the model woman was chaste, silent, and obedient. The evidence from Jane's life as queen indicates she took these instructions to heart: her motto was "bound to serve and obey."

Jane's family connections earned her a place at court in the service of Henry VIII's first wife, Catherine of Aragon. Jane was there by at least 1529 and, after Catherine had been replaced by Anne Boleyn, Jane moved to Anne's service, no later than the end of 1533. Thus, Henry would have known Jane for several years before he developed an interest in her, most likely toward the end of 1535.

LIFE'S WORK

When she first attracted Henry's attention, Jane was around twenty-six or twenty-seven years old. It was unusual for a young woman of her class to be unmarried at that age. She was known at court more for propriety than beauty, and it may have been her quiet calmness that attracted a king who was rapidly growing weary of a vola-

tile and demanding queen. Yet at the start of 1536, Anne's position seemed secure, as she was pregnant with what everyone assumed was the future male heir Henry so desperately desired. Anne's miscarriage of that child at the end of January—her second miscarriage of a male fetus—changed the situation entirely.

Had Jane not been open to the king's attentions before, she certainly was after Anne's miscarriage. Whether by her own inclination, or her brother Edward's advice, or both, however, Jane made it clear that she would not compromise her virtue. She accepted Henry's gifts, but when he was careless and crass enough to send money, she respectfully but firmly refused it, on the grounds that to accept would harm her honor. Far from being angry, Henry praised her modesty, and from that April on, as their relationship was becoming more widely known, the king visited Jane only in the company of her brother Edward and his wife. Clearly, Henry was thinking of Jane as more than a mistress. On May 2, Anne was arrested on charges of adultery and incest, and she was executed May 19. The next day, Henry and Jane Seymour were formally betrothed, and they married May 30, 1536.

Clearly, the most important job for the new queen was to conceive and bear a son. While waiting for that to happen, however, Jane had other tasks she wished to accomplish. Perhaps the most important, in her view, was to reconcile the king with his eldest daughter, Mary, the future Queen Mary I. Mary's mother, Henry's first wife Catherine, had died late in 1535, so the young princess had no resentment against Jane, as she had with Anne. Jane managed to persuade Mary to submit to her father. Jane then persuaded Henry to accept the girl's submission and restore her to a proper place at court by the end of the year.

Jane also wanted a devout and dignified court. Reflecting her own strong sense of decorum, she insisted that the ladies in her service conduct themselves virtuously and dress modestly. Henry and the nation approved of this. He was less approving, however, when she attempted to influence him on policy; he pointedly and publicly rebuked her for it on at least one occasion. Jane understood the place she was to take. If there were other attempts by her to influence the king, they were done discreetly and privately.

In most ways, though, Jane pleased her husband, and no more so than when, early in 1537, it became apparent that she was pregnant. Henry did everything in his power to make his expectant wife comfortable and happy. She made no public appearances, and prayers for her and the unborn child were offered in churches throughout England. When Jane began to crave quail, the king went to a great deal of trouble and expense to keep her well-supplied with them. Henry had already made Jane's brother Edward Viscount Beauchamp shortly after their wedding; to please her even more, the king made Beauchamp a member of the Privy Council.

Jane passed her pregnancy pleasantly, "entirely beloved" of her royal spouse. On October 12, 1537, after three days of labor, Jane cemented her place in Henry's affections by giving birth to a baby boy, and so the king had, at long last, a son and heir.

The boy was christened Edward in a lavish ceremony on October 15, and three days later the boy's uncle, Edward Seymour, was created earl of Hertford. Jane seemed to have come through the difficult birth well, and she received visitors after the christening, as was customary. The next day, however, she began to show signs of puerperal, or "childbed" fever, a virulent infection that progressed quickly. On October 24, 1537, Jane Seymour

died. She was buried in St. George's Chapel, Windsor, where Henry was eventually laid to rest beside his "sweet Jane" in 1547.

SIGNIFICANCE

Jane Seymour gave Henry VIII what two previous wives over twenty-five years could not: a surviving son. By this she also created a connection between her family and the throne, which became important when Edward, while still a child, succeeded his father in 1547. Edward's maternal uncle, Edward Seymour, then became England's lord protector, acting as regent for his nephew between 1547 and 1549, which began the process by which the Church of England became Protestant in its doctrine and worship.

Jane also helped to reconcile Henry VIII with his estranged eldest daughter Mary, and she helped maintain an atmosphere of decorum and piety at the royal court. Although she was in a position to influence the king on political and religious matters and, in fact, might have attempted to do so, she was not significant in this regard. As mother to Edward, the heir to the throne, she might have become more influential had she not died prematurely.

—Sharon Arnoult

FURTHER READING

Fraser, Antonia. *The Wives of Henry VIII*. New York: Alfred A. Knopf, 1992. More scholarly than most works covering Henry's wives, this already classic book is nonetheless written in a lively style by a noted historian.

Gross, Pamela M. *Jane, the Quene, Third Consort of King Henry VIII*. New York: Edwin Mellen Press, 1999. This is the only book devoted entirely to Jane Seymour.

Lindsey, Karen. *Divorced, Beheaded, Survived: A Feminist Reinterpretation of the Wives of Henry VIII*. New York: Addison-Wesley, 1995. This work seeks to define Henry's wives, including Jane, on their own terms and within the context of their times.

Loades, David. *The Politics of Marriage: Henry VIII and His Queens*. Dover, N.H.: Sutton, 1994. This book is concerned with the political contexts that led to, and created, Henry's marriages, including that with Jane Seymour.

MacCulloch, Diarmaid. *The Boy King: Edward VI and the Protestant Reformation*. New York: Palgrave, 1999. This is a scholarly work covering the reign of Jane's son Edward and the impact of Jane's brother, Edward Seymour.

Jane Seymour. (Hulton|Archive by Getty Images)

Weir, Alison. *The Six Wives of Henry VIII*. New York: Grove Weidenfeld, 1991. One of many works that includes Jane Seymour, by a popular and prolific author.

SEE ALSO: Anne of Cleves; Anne Boleyn; Catherine of Aragon; Thomas Cranmer; Thomas Cromwell; Edward VI; Henry VIII; Catherine Howard; Mary I; Catherine Parr; First Duke of Somerset; The Tudor Family.

RELATED ARTICLES in *Great Events from History: The Renaissance & Early Modern Era, 1454-1600:* 1531-1540: Cromwell Reforms British Government; 1532: Holbein Settles in London; May, 1539: Six Articles of Henry VIII.

CATERINA SFORZA
Italian noblewoman

Caterina was a strong, dynamic, and intelligent woman who governed well in the Romagna region of Italy. Her political career was exemplary in demonstrating that virtue, in Machiavellian terms, was not reserved for men only.

BORN: 1462 or 1463; Duchy of Milan (now in Italy)
DIED: May 20, 1509; convent of Annalena, Florence, Republic of Florence (now in Italy)
ALSO KNOWN AS: Virago; Tiger of Romagna
AREA OF ACHIEVEMENT: Government and politics

EARLY LIFE

Caterina Sforza (SFAWRT-sah) was an illegitimate daughter of Galeazzo Maria Sforza, born before he became duke of Milan in 1466. She was reared in the Milanese court and given an excellent education. She preferred the active life over the study of books, however. In 1473, she was married to count Gerolamo Riario, the nephew of Pope Sixtus IV (Francesco Della Rovere). Riario was to become lord of the small but strategically important city of Imola in the Romagna region northeast of Rome.

LIFE'S WORK

After being blessed by the pope in Rome, Caterina and her husband triumphantly entered Imola in 1477. In the following years, while living mostly at the Vatican, she gave birth to four children: Bianca, Ottaviano, Cesare, and Giovanni Livio. The young couple ruled the cities of Forlì and Imola, and they prospered because of their political and familial ties. Riario participated in several plots (notably, the Pazzi conspiracy, the goal of which was to remove the Medici brothers from Florence) and wars (namely the war against Ferrara, the aim of which was to destroy the Este Dynasty). Riario's intentions with these activities was to enhance and enlarge his and Caterina's sphere of power and influence in central Italy.

In August, 1484, the death of Sixtus IV changed their fortunes dramatically. Caterina, leading a small group of soldiers, held the greatest Roman fortress, Castel Sant'Angelo, for her husband until he reached a deal with the new pope, Innocent VIII (Giovanni Battista Cibò). Eventually, the couple moved to Romagna. The enemies of Count Riario, however, did not stay idle. In 1488, after a series of unsettling uprisings, some plotters secretly inspired by Lorenzo de' Medici—who wanted to avenge the death of his brother Giuliano—managed to assassinate Gerolamo Riario. Caterina and her children were supposed to be their next victims, but she convinced the aggressors to release her, leaving the children as hostages. As soon as she reached the fortress of Forlì, according to the political philosopher Niccolò Machiavelli, she mockingly raised her skirts, exposed herself, and declared that she could have as many other children as she wanted. The plotters eventually surrendered and fled. With the help of her uncle Ludovico Sforza, who was acting as duke of Milan, and not her stepbrother Gian Galeazzo, she regained control over all the Romagna territories.

Caterina was then twenty-eight years old and a relatively independent ruler of a small but solid kingdom. She fell in love with the nineteen-year-old Giacomo Feo, the younger brother of one of her loyal military commanders. He was energetic but very arrogant and made a lot of enemies among the local aristocrats. Caterina and he became increasingly unpopular, especially after they raised taxes in order to maintain the army and their expensive lifestyle. In 1495, while the couple was riding in the streets of Forlì, Giacomo was attacked and stabbed to death. Caterina reacted violently and unleashed her fury onto the killers and their families.

The next year, the grain harvest was poor in the Tuscan lands. The Florentines sent an envoy to buy grain from Forlì and Imola. The envoy was the handsome and intelligent Giovanni de' Medici. He was born into a minor branch of the great Medici family, which ruled Florence. Soon Caterina was in love again, and Giovanni loved her in return. A marriage between people from two such powerful dynasties, however, was likely to provoke opposition. Hence, they were wed in secret. Then, at age thirty-six, Caterina bore a son whom she named Giovanni, the last and most beloved of her children. Caterina's eldest son, Ottaviano Riario, had grown into a lazy young man with great ambition and few abilities.

In 1498, Giovanni de' Medici died of natural causes. The timing was unfortunate because Caterina was about to face the greatest threat of her life: the ambitions of Cesare Borgia, the son of Pope Alexander VI (Rodrigo Borgia). Cesare Borgia, duke of Valentinois, made famous by Machiavelli's account of his deeds as the "model prince," conquered all the major and minor cities in central Italy—a plan that Caterina's first husband had failed to realize. When Cesare finally captured Caterina, who had dared to mount some resistance to him, he took her to Rome as a trophy, abused her privately, shamed her publicly, and threw her into the dungeons of Castel Sant'Angelo, the same fortress she had once commanded and defended.

Eventually, the Borgia family fortune collapsed, and Caterina was freed, but she never was able to recover control of her cities in Romagna. She moved to Florence and took residence in the Convent of Annalena, where she died in May, 1509, at the age of forty-seven. She did not have the chance to see her last son, Giovanni, become one of the last and most celebrated Italian captains of arms, under the nickname of Giovanni delle Bande Nere (John of the Black Bands). He died in 1526, after having fathered Cosimo, who was eventually to become Cosimo I, or Cosimo the Great, the youngest duke of Florence (1537) and the first grand duke of Tuscany (1569).

SIGNIFICANCE

Caterina Sforza, throughout her adventurous life, always gave proof of being a courageous, independent, and strong woman. Some contemporaries considered her "the first lady of our times," and rightly so. She stood up against the killers of two of her companions and also against the most ruthless of all Renaissance princes, Cesare Borgia.

Her reputation as a virago (women warrior) did not prevent her from cultivating feminine interests, specifically in the make up and "magic" of rejuvenating potions. She avidly collected herbal recipes, in particular those that might preserve her health and beauty. Some of her balms and remedies are still recommended by doctors and studied by historians of medicine. She also enjoyed dancing, hunting, and all forms of physical activity. Finally, she was a patron of architecture. She enriched her cities with new buildings, creating beautiful gardens and public palaces.

Caterina's offspring on the Medici side would lead very successful lives, especially her grandson Cosimo I de' Medici, first grand duke of Tuscany. Her blood combined the fighting spirit of the Sforza Dynasty with the leadership skills of the Medici family. Ironically, the sons from her first marriage with Riario, who had tried to eliminate the Florentine rulers, ended up nameless and powerless.

—*Marcello Simonetta*

FURTHER READING

Breisach, Ernst. *Caterina Sforza: A Renaissance Virago*. Chicago: University of Chicago Press, 1967. A fine biographical study, based on original sources and pleasantly narrated.

Hairston, Julia. "Skirting the Issue: Machiavelli's Caterina Sforza." *Renaissance Quarterly* 53, no. 3 (2000): 687-712. A reading of Machiavelli's passages devoted to Caterina's deeds.

Pasolini, Pietro Desiderio. *Catherine Sforza*. Translated by Paul Sylvester. London: W. Heinemann, 1893. The original full-length work on Sforza. A romantic vision of Sforza rich in documentation though overdramatized in tone.

SEE ALSO: Cesare Borgia; Niccolò Machiavelli; Cosimo I de' Medici; Lorenzo de' Medici; Ludovico Sforza.

RELATED ARTICLE in *Great Events from History: The Renaissance & Early Modern Era, 1454-1600:* 1481-1499: Ludovico Sforza Rules Milan.

LUDOVICO SFORZA
Duke of Milan (r. 1481-1499)

One of the most spectacular and significant statesmen and political manipulators of the High Renaissance in Italy, Sforza directed the duchy of Milan during a crucial period of European history. His political maneuvers determined the following century of Italian affairs.

BORN: July 27, 1452; Vigevano, duchy of Milan (now in Italy)
DIED: May 27, 1508; Loches, Toubrenne, France
ALSO KNOWN AS: Il Moro; The Moor
AREAS OF ACHIEVEMENT: Government and politics, patronage of the arts

EARLY LIFE

The fourth legitimate son of Francesco Sforza, first duke of Milan, and Bianca Maria Visconti, Ludovico Sforza (lood-oh-VEECH-oh SFAWRT-sah) was born into two of the most powerful families of the fourteenth century. At birth, his mother gave him the surname Maurus, which she later changed to Maria. By that time, however, "Maurus" had evolved into the nickname Il Moro (the Moor), which Ludovico liked, not only because it suited his dark complexion but also because it conjured up images of romance and adventure. Thereafter, the name stuck; Ludovico even used puns on that name to provide the metaphorical basis of some of his favorite personal devices and symbols, a Moor's head (*moro*) and a mulberry tree (*mora*).

He became his mother's favorite while still young, remaining devoted to her his entire life. Discovering that he was bright, she directed his early education and eventually hired the Humanist Francesco Filelfo as his tutor. Sforza received a thorough grounding in the new learning of the Renaissance, becoming adept in both ancient languages and literature and the intellectual and technical innovations of the time. As a result of this background, he would later take his responsibilities as patron of the arts and literature and as commissioner of public buildings seriously, though he apparently had little confidence in the consistency or accuracy of his taste and judgment.

When the twenty-four-year-old Sforza was visiting France, his brother Galeazzo Maria, who had succeeded their father as duke of Milan ten years earlier, was assassinated on December 24, 1476, leaving the seven-year-old Gian Galeazzo as heir. The child's mother, Bona of Savoy, assumed the regency, with Cicco Simonetta as principal adviser. Intrigues seemed to occur overnight, prompted chiefly by older Sforza relatives. When a plot implicated Ludovico and his brothers, all three were exiled. Eventually, however, Ludovico persuaded Bona to pardon him. On his return to Milan, he learned that Bona had taken a young servant, Tamino, as her lover. He used both his privileged position and his inside knowledge to gain control, having Simonetta murdered, driving Tamino away, discrediting Bona, and getting the nominal duke to appoint him chief counselor. From that time— November, 1480—he was on his way to becoming duke.

LIFE'S WORK

Sforza's life was the governing of Milan. At first, that meant making his rule legitimate, but eventually it would mean making it both legitimate and secure; neither was easy. Sforza's opening move was to ally himself with Ferdinand I, king of Naples. This eventually led to a marriage arrangement between Isabella of Aragon, granddaughter of Ferdinand, and the teenage Gian Galeazzo; in confirming the marriage, Sforza probably outsmarted himself, failing to realize that this articulate and ambitious woman would not accept the title of duchess without the power. At any rate, he refused to relinquish control after the wedding, thereby precipitating his ultimate downfall. Isabella immediately began conspiring to turn her Aragonese kinsmen against him, especially after January, 1491, when he married the young and equally spirited Beatrice d'Este of Ferrara, who was also of the family of Aragon. The Aragonese listened to Isabella.

Desperate for allies, Sforza turned to Charles VIII of France, establishing a mutual defense compact with him in 1492. Later that year, Alexander VI became pope with the support of Sforza's brother, Cardinal Ascanio; this gave Sforza hope of papal support. Temporarily safe, Sforza attempted to maintain security by constructing a tenuous web of secret alliances and counteralliances. Once again he was too subtle for his own good: Charles VIII, who claimed the throne of Naples in his own right, and who had become obsessed with establishing a base in Italy for mounting a crusade, seized on a pretext of perceived danger to invade Italy in 1494. During this campaign, Charles visited Gian Galeazzo at Pavia; the next day, the young man became ill and died, in circumstances that looked suspiciously like poisoning.

Meanwhile, Sforza was also carrying on surreptitious negotiations with Emperor Maximilian I, who needed both money and a wife. In exchange for accepting a well-dowried niece of Sforza, Maximilian agreed to legitimate him as duke of Milan. Gian Galeazzo's death occurred before this could happen. To divert public accusation, Sforza immediately summoned the Milanese Council, proposing that the duke's infant son be named his successor. Since he had packed the council, he knew in advance that its recommendation would be in favor of strength and experience, not rule by children. Thus, Sforza finally became duke of Milan in name as well as in fact.

In the meantime, Charles pushed on through Italy and subjugated Naples. His success unsettled the states of Italy; Sforza feared that he had given Charles a foothold from which he would not budge—a fear intensified by the presence in Charles's army of the Duc d'Orléans, himself a claimant to the throne of Milan through his mother. Quickly Sforza withdrew his troops from the alliance and opened talks with Venice. The various Italian states joined forces to trap Charles in the peninsula, but he evaded them, withdrawing from Italy in October, 1495. Sforza took credit for forcing the retreat; he bragged at the time that the pope was his chaplain, the emperor his condotierre (military commander), Venice his chamberlain, and the king of France his courier. This was at best wishful thinking; Sforza was more likely a master in the art of self-deception.

He did not have much leisure to indulge such delusions. Maximilian came for a visit but proved too poor and vacillating to provide any real assistance. Shortly thereafter, the pope changed his strategy, Venice asserted its independence, the Aragonese recovered Naples, and Charles VIII died, to be succeeded by Sforza's antagonist, the duc d'Orléans, now Louis XII, who had himself crowned both king of France and duke of Milan. Far from manipulating his enemies, Sforza was now hemmed in on all sides. Sforza tried the desperate expedient of urging the Turks to invade Venice. Instead, Maximilian abandoned him, and the pope, France, and Venice formed a common league. Louis XII invaded the outlying districts, seizing the mountain strongholds. Sforza had no recourse but to flee. With his fortress at Milan in the hands of his chosen commandant, he packed his treasury in an immense mule train and escaped to Maximilian's court at Innsbruck. The emperor had probably never dreamed of such a windfall; Sforza's coffers went a long way toward solving Maximilian's financial problems.

In the meantime, rather than defending the castle to the death as instructed, in September, 1499, Sforza's commandant surrendered it to the French for 150,000 ducats. Sforza's cause was almost lost. He used what remained of his treasure to hire an army of Swiss and Burgundian mercenaries. At first, his campaign was successful; the people rallied behind him, since the high-handed methods of the French had alienated them. Yet Sforza did not have the opportunity to bring his opponents to battle. The Swiss were bribed to surrender him to the French, which they did on April 5, 1500. Taken to France as a prisoner, he was confined to the fortress at Loches in Touraine, where he remained in captivity until his death eight years later.

Sforza's lifetime marked the high point of Italy's greatness. At the beginning of his life, Italy was the paragon of Europe, the leader in the new civilization of the Renaissance, setting the pace of innovation in painting, music, sculpture, literature, philosophy, and all the arts of civilization. At the beginning of Sforza's career, Italy was considered a superior civilization, impregnable, almost sacrosanct, a region populated by a higher race. By his end, it had become a playground for petty princes and their mercenaries, stamped with fraud, corruption, greed, and venality. Worse, its vulnerability to external aggression had been exposed. Henceforth, it would become merely a collection of victims for plundering.

Ludovico Sforza. (Library of Congress)

A SFORZA "PERFORMANCE BANQUET" MENU

The Sforza court of Milan was marked by an ostentatiousness reminiscent of the best of Renaissance court life, and this included its banquets. The "performance banquet" was more than an outpouring of food; it also was an art, where food and its display became both theatrical and sculptural. In a twist of irony, Ludovico Sforza commissioned Leonardo da Vinci's masterpiece The Last Supper. *One Sforza banquet menu—and not the "last supper"—includes the following foods and forms of presentation, from a menu of some two hundred items.*

Food: Large boiled pikes covered with black pepper sauce; one large whole boiled *tori* [likely a kind of fish] without sauce per plate, with bowls of blue sauce on the side; and salted fish, i.e. two large *dentali* [another kind of fish] per plate.
Presentation: The covers of the plates holding the salted fish should consist of a model of the Colosseum lavishly decorated with gold and mottoes.

Food: A course of large boiled meats: two whole calves; four whole heifers; . . . eight hares; pigs, and two wild boar. . . . On large platters should be served six large capons; six geese; six pheasants; six ducks; twelve pigeons, and ten partridges.
Presentation: A centrepiece with a laurel tree which is cut open and spurts blood; a small boy comes out on horseback reciting apposite verses and mottoes with much grace and skill.

Food: Oysters in large basins with little bowls of pepper on the side; truffles in little plates or cups; giant roast chestnuts with fennel and pepper.
Presentation: A galleon full of oysters presented with other marine creatures adorned with mottoes.

Source: Sforza archives, Milan, excerpted in *The Renaissance in Europe: An Anthology*, edited by Peter Elmer, Nick Webb, and Roberta Wood (New Haven, Conn.: Yale University Press, 2000), pp. 174, 175.

tion, though there was plenty of that. It did mean that general prosperity and enlightened regulation were fundamental to his plan—ideals that unfortunately often conflicted with his political and military operations. Along these lines, he built a model farm to test new agricultural methods; for it and others near it, he devised a new system of irrigation by canal. He had his hometown and favorite retreat of Vigevano completely rebuilt. He promoted art, literature, science, and trade.

Yet his reputation for courtly living derived more from his dreams and plans than from what he actually was able to bring into being. Sympathetic contemporary biographers contributed largely to his legend. Thus Sforza is widely credited with patronage of Leonardo da Vinci and Donato Bramante. Yet the encouragement he gave them was often more verbal than financial. Ludovico commissioned the astonishing *Last Supper* (1495), which he also had almost completely reconstructed; he also did much to make both art and learning more available to the community. The final judgment on his patronage is aptly symbolized in the fate of the great statue of Francesco Sforza, which, like so many of Ludovico's dreams, never materialized. The brass for its casting was diverted during the French invasion to be made into cannons, and the model itself was shattered by French soldiers, who used it for target practice, after the fall of the castle.

Finally, Sforza is perhaps best seen as one who dreamed grandly but could not control the forces, social and political, in which he found himself. It is hard to imagine what might have happened had he not seized power when he did. He failed to accomplish what he intended. The temporary security he provided made the destruction following him seem that much more devastating. In his subtlety, he outmaneuvered himself. His extravagance was financed by increasing and unpopular taxation. Yet for his time, he was magnificent. If he, with his intensity, intelligence, and force, failed, what would

SIGNIFICANCE

Like many other notable Renaissance princes, Sforza has not been given the attention by contemporary historians that he received from previous generations.

Yet Sforza was celebrated in his time for the splendor of his court and his patronage of the arts. He set a standard of living that has rarely been equaled for style and taste. His center lacked the strenuous intellectualism and the learned grace of his great predecessor, Federico da Montefeltro of Urbino; yet that gathering of learning, beauty, and wit, the fantasy of all academics since, could never be duplicated, and Sforza did not try. He wanted to build not a haven for intellectuals but a model of harmonious living for all his citizens. This did not mean conspicuous consumption of luxury for the sake of ostenta-

have happened under Gian Galeazzo? He has been blamed for the dissolution of Italian self-rule that followed him, but it is likely that it would have taken place anyway. His career is ultimately tragic, for he tried much and failed grandly. His attempt remains impressive.

—*James Livingston*

FURTHER READING

Abulafia, David, ed. *The French Descent into Renaissance Italy, 1494-95: Antecedents and Effects*. Brookfield, Vt.: Ashgate, 1995. Anthology of essays contesting the traditional view that Italy was largely internally harmonious for the forty years leading up to the French, peace-shattering invasion of Charles VIII. Essays delve into the internal strife and rivalries of the Italian states; political, military, and technological aspects of the invasion itself; and the effects of the invasion on both the Italians and the French. Includes illustrations, maps, bibliographic references, index.

Breisach, Ernst. *Caterina Sforza: A Renaissance Virago*. Chicago: University of Chicago Press, 1967. In this scholarly biography of one of the most remarkable women of the fifteenth century, Breisach includes much incidental information about Sforza since his focus is properly on his subject. He does emphasize the interrelationship of the two, which was not of primary importance for Sforza. The bibliography is helpful in locating material on Sforza, most of which is in Italian.

Burckhardt, Jacob. *The Civilization of the Renaissance in Italy*. Translated by S. G. C. Middlemore. 2 vols. New York: Harper & Row, 1958. In this classic study, Burckhardt may be said to have invented the idea of the Renaissance as a cultural entity. Since one of his focal points is the development of the individual personality, he shows insight into all the major personalities of the period, as he does with Sforza.

Cole, Alison. *Virtue and Magnificence: Art of the Italian Renaissance Courts*. New York: H. N. Abrams, 1995. A study of two related values in Renaissance culture: the virtue of the artist, and the magnificence of the ruler who commissions the art. Includes a chapter on Sforza's patronage of the arts in Milan and Pavia. With illustrations, map, bibliographic references, and index.

Larner, Joseph. *The Lords of Romagna: Romagnol Society and the Origins of the Signorie*. Ithaca, N.Y.: Cornell University Press, 1965. Larner presents a balanced view of Sforza with extensive information and provocative points of view. His portrait is somewhat revisionist, in that he rejects the once-conventional notion that Sforza was simply a subtle schemer with dreams of glory. He presents Sforza as a progressive for his time, concerned with the welfare of the state as a whole.

Plumb, J. H. *The Italian Renaissance: A Concise Survey of Its History and Culture*. New York: Harper & Row, 1965. Though not known as an authority on the Italian Renaissance, Plumb here presents a brilliant synthesis of the basis of that culture. His account of Sforza is lucid, readable, and packed with detail. This is easily the best source for the general reader.

Potter, G. R., ed. *The Renaissance*. Vol. 1 in *The New Cambridge Modern History*. Cambridge, England: Cambridge University Press, 1967. Includes a general account of Sforza in relation to the historical events of his time.

Pyle, Cynthia M. *Milan and Lombardy in the Renaissance: Essays in Cultural History*. Rome: La Fenice, 1997. Study of the culture that produced Sforza, and of the culture that Sforza produced. Includes illustrations, bibliographic references, and index.

Shaw, Christine. *The Politics of Exile in Renaissance Italy*. New York: Cambridge University Press, 2000. Study of the practice of political exile in Renaissance Italy—both of the importance of the practice itself to political life and of the role played by exiles who then intervened in the politics of the nation that had banished them. Includes bibliographic references and index.

Welch, Evelyn S. *Art and Authority in Renaissance Milan*. New Haven, Conn.: Yale University Press, 1995. Study of three specific fourteenth and fifteenth century Milanese monuments and the structures of patronage and political power underlying them. Looks at Sforza's use of art to legitimize his rule and represent it as benevolent, and at the importance of his hospital as a political, rather than a social or medical, construct. Includes illustrations, maps, bibliographic references, index.

SEE ALSO: Alexander VI; Donato Bramante; Charles VIII; Leonardo da Vinci; Louis XII; Maximilian I; Caterina Sforza.

RELATED ARTICLES in *Great Events from History: The Renaissance & Early Modern Era, 1454-1600:* c. 1478-1519: Leonardo da Vinci Compiles His Notebooks; 1481-1499: Ludovico Sforza Rules Milan; September, 1494-October, 1495: Charles VIII of France Invades Italy; 1495-1497: Leonardo da Vinci Paints *The Last Supper*; 1499: Louis XII of France Seizes Milan.

WILLIAM SHAKESPEARE
English playwright, dramatist, and poet

The leading playwright in the great flowering of Renaissance English drama, Shakespeare created some of the world's most enduring literary and dramatic masterpieces.

BORN: April 23, 1564; Stratford-upon-Avon, Warwickshire, England
DIED: April 23, 1616; Stratford-upon-Avon
AREAS OF ACHIEVEMENT: Literature, theater

EARLY LIFE

William Shakespeare was descended from tenant farmers and landed gentry. One of his grandfathers, Richard Shakespeare of Snitterfield, rented land from the other, Robert Arden of Wilmcote. Shakespeare's father, John, moved to nearby Stratford-upon-Avon, became a prosperous shop owner (dealing in leather goods) and municipal officeholder, and married his former landlord's youngest daughter, Mary Arden. Thus Shakespeare—the third of eight children, but the first to survive infancy—was born into a solidly middle-class family in a provincial market town.

During Shakespeare's infancy, his father was one of the town's leading citizens. In 1557, John Shakespeare had become a member of the town council and subsequently held such offices as constable, affeeror, and chamberlain; in 1568, he became bailiff (mayor) and justice of the peace. As the son of a municipal officer, the young Shakespeare was entitled to a free education in the town's grammar school, which he probably entered around the age of seven. The school's main subject was Latin studies—grammar and readings drilled into the schoolboys year after year. The Avon River, the surrounding farmlands, and the nearby Forest of Arden offered plenty of opportunities for childhood recreations.

When Shakespeare was a teenager, his family fell on hard times. His father stopped attending town council meetings in 1577, and the family's fortunes began declining. Matters were not improved in 1582 when Shakespeare, at the age of eighteen, hastily married Anne Hathaway, the twenty-six-year-old daughter of a farmer from the nearby village of Shottery; she presented him with a daughter, named Susanna, approximately five months later. In 1585, the couple also became the parents of twins, Hamnet and Judith. As was then customary, the young couple probably lived in his parents' home, which must have seemed increasingly crowded.

The next mention of Shakespeare is in 1592, when he was an actor and playwright in London. His actions during the seven-year interim have been a matter of much curious speculation, including unproved stories of deer poaching, soldiering, and teaching. It may have taken him those seven years simply to break into and advance in the London theater. His early connections with the theater are unknown, although he was an actor before he became a playwright. He might have joined one of the touring companies that occasionally performed in Stratford-upon-Avon, or he might have gone directly to London to make his fortune, in either the theater or some other trade. Shakespeare was venturesome and able, and had good reasons to travel—his confining family circumstances, tinged with just enough disgrace to qualify him to join the disreputable players. The theater was his escape to freedom; he therefore had strong motivation to succeed.

LIFE'S WORK

The London theater, in Shakespeare's day, was composed of companies of men and boys (women were not allowed on the Renaissance English stage but were played by young men or boys) who performed in public playhouses roughly modeled on old innyards. The theaters were open to the air, had balconies surrounding the pit and stage, and held from two thousand to three thousand people. A group known as the University Wits—John Lyly, George Peele, Thomas Lodge, Robert Greene, Thomas Nashe, and Christopher Marlowe—dominated the drama. Shakespeare learned his art by imitating these Oxford and Cambridge men, but for him they were a difficult group to join. They looked down on most actors and on playwrights, such as Thomas Kyd, who had not attended a university. Shakespeare offended on both counts, and Robert Greene expressed his resentment in the posthumously published book *Greene's Groatsworth of Wit* (1592), which included the following famous warning to three fellow "gentlemen" playwrights:

> Yes, trust them [the players] not: for there is an upstart crow, beautified with our feathers, that with his *Tiger's heart wrapt in a player's hide*, supposes he is as well able to bombast out a blank verse as the best of you: and being an absolute *Johannes Factotum*, is in his own conceit the only Shake-scene in a country.

Greene's literary executor, Henry Chettle, later printed an apology for this slur on Shakespeare, with its pun on his name and its parody of a line from *Henry VI, Part III* (pr. c. 1590-1591). On meeting him, Chettle found Shakespeare's "demeanor no less civil than he, excellent in the quality he professes. Besides, divers of worship have reported his uprightness of dealing, which argues his honesty, and his facetious grace in writing, that approves his art."

Actually, Greene's judgment of Shakespeare's early work is more accurate. The early plays are far from excellent; they include some of the most slavish imitations in Renaissance English drama, as Shakespeare tried his hand at the various popular modes. The interminable three-part history play *Henry VI* (wr. c. 1589-c. 1591) makes, as Greene notes, bombastic attempts at Marlowe's powerful blank verse. In *The Comedy of Errors* (pr. c. 1592-1594), based on Plautus's *Menaechmi*, and in the Senecan tragedy *Titus Andronicus* (pr., pb. 1594), Shakespeare showed his ability to copy Roman models down to the smallest detail, even if he did lack a university degree. Apparently, he also lacked confidence in his own imagination and learned slowly. *Richard III* (pr. c. 1592-1593), however, showed promise in the malignant character of King Richard III, while *The Taming of the*

William Shakespeare. (Library of Congress)

Shrew (pr. c. 1593-1594) offered its rambunctious lovefight.

Despite their imitative nature and many other faults, Shakespeare's early plays—notably *Henry VI*—were popular onstage, but his greatest early popularity came from two long narrative poems, *Venus and Adonis* (1593) and *The Rape of Lucrece* (1594). Shakespeare wrote these two poems during the two years that the plague closed down the London theaters. He dedicated the poems to a patron, the young Henry Wriothesley, third earl of Southampton, who may have granted him a substantial monetary reward in return. In any event, when the theaters reopened in 1594, the acting companies were almost decimated financially, but Shakespeare was in a position to buy or otherwise acquire a partnership in one of the newly reorganized companies, the Lord Chamberlain's Men. Henceforth, Shakespeare earned money not only from the plays he had written or in which he acted but also from a share of the profits of every company performance. The financial arrangement seemed to inspire his creative efforts, for he set about writing the plays that made him famous, beginning with *Romeo and Juliet* (pr. c. 1595-1596) and going on to the great history plays and comedies, including *Richard II* (pr. c. 1595-1596), the two-part *Henry IV* (pr. c. 1597-1598), *Henry V* (pr. c. 1598-1599), *A Midsummer Night's Dream* (pr. c. 1595-1596), *The Merchant of Venice* (pr. c. 1596-1597), *Much Ado About Nothing* (pr. c. 1598-1599), *As You Like It* (pr. c. 1599-1600), and *Twelfth Night: Or, What You Will* (pr. c. 1600-1602).

At about the time Shakespeare wrote *Romeo and Juliet* and *Richard II*, he probably also began his great sonnet sequence, not published until 1609. The 154 sonnets, tracing a friendship with a young man and a romance with a "dark lady," raise the question of how Shakespeare lived when he was away from Stratford, where his wife and children presumably remained. The young man might be a patron—perhaps Wriothesley, though other names have also been proposed—and the "dark lady" strictly imaginary, created to overturn the sonnets' trite Petrarchan conventions. Other speculations favor a more personal interpretation, seeing an actual ménage à trois of the poet, the young man, and the "dark lady." All the questions raised by the sonnets remain open, and the only evidence about how Shakespeare spent his spare time in London indicates that he sometimes frequented taverns (notably the Mermaid) with his fellow playwrights and players.

Evidence also indicates that he remained in close contact with Stratford-upon-Avon, to which he probably returned as frequently as possible. He used his earnings from the theater to install himself as the town's leading citizen, buying New Place as a family residence in 1597 and thereafter steadily amassing other land and property. In 1596, his father was granted a hereditary coat of arms and thus became a gentleman, a status he had never achieved on his own. Unfortunately, also in 1596, Shakespeare suffered a setback when his son, Hamnet, died at the age of eleven. His affection for his two remaining children, Susanna and Judith, may be reflected in the witty, saucy, but lovable heroines of his great comedies.

Shakespeare's company in London prospered. In 1599, it stopped renting theaters and built its own, the Globe, which increased company profits. The company was a favorite of the reigning monarchs, who paid well for special performances at court—first Elizabeth I, then after 1603, James I, who loved the theater even more and renamed Shakespeare's company the King's Men. The company also began performing most of the plays of Ben Jonson, who ranked second only to Shakespeare and who excelled at satiric comedy. Shakespeare turned to tragedy, first writing *Julius Caesar* (pr. c. 1599-1600) and *Hamlet, Prince of Denmark* (pr. c. 1600-1601) and then— one after another–*Othello, the Moor of Venice* (pr. 1604), *King Lear* (pr. c. 1605-1606), *Macbeth* (pr. 1606), and *Antony and Cleopatra* (pr. c. 1606-1607).

Yet even during this period—perhaps the high point in the history of world drama—Shakespeare's company had its problems. One was the competition of the boys' companies that performed in the private theaters—small indoor theaters that charged higher admission and appealed to a more exclusive audience than the public theaters. In 1608, the

King's Men acquired one of the private theaters, the Blackfriars, plus the services of two playwrights who wrote for it, the collaborators Francis Beaumont and John Fletcher. With their light, witty comedy and melo-

SHAKESPEARE'S MAJOR WORKS	
1589-1590	*Henry VI, Part I* (pr. 1592)
c. 1589-1595	*Edward III*
c. 1590-1591	*Henry VI, Part III*
c. 1590-1591	*Henry VI, Part II*
c. 1592-1593	*Richard III* (rev. 1623)
c. 1592-1594	*The Comedy of Errors*
1593	*Venus and Adonis*
c. 1593- 1594	*The Taming of the Shrew*
1594	*Titus Andronicus*
1594	*The Rape of Lucrece*
c. 1594-1595	*Love's Labour's Lost* (rev. 1597 for court performance)
c. 1594-1595	*The Two Gentlemen of Verona*
c. 1595-1596	*Romeo and Juliet*
c. 1595-1596	*A Midsummer Night's Dream*
c. 1595-1596	*Richard II*
c. 1596-1597	*The Merchant of Venice*
c. 1596-1597	*King John*
1597	*The Merry Wives of Windsor* (rev. c. 1600-1601)
c. 1597-1598	*Henry IV, Part I*
1598	*Henry IV, Part II*
c. 1598-1599	*Henry V*
c. 1598-1599	*Much Ado About Nothing*
1599	*The Passionate Pilgrim* (miscellany with poems by Shakespeare and others)
c. 1599-1600	*Julius Caesar*
c. 1599-1600	*As You Like It*
c. 1600-1601	*Hamlet, Prince of Denmark*
c. 1600-1602	*Twelfth Night: Or, What You Will*
1601	*The Phoenix and the Turtle*
c. 1601-1602	*Troilus and Cressida*
c. 1602-1603	*All's Well That Ends Well*
1604	*Measure for Measure*
1604	*Othello, the Moor of Venice* (rev. 1623)
c. 1605-1606	*King Lear*
1606	*Macbeth*
c. 1606-1607	*Antony and Cleopatra*
c. 1607-1608	*Coriolanus*
c. 1607-1608	*Timon of Athens*
c. 1607-1608	*Pericles, Prince of Tyre*
1609	*Sonnets*
1609	*A Lover's Complaint*
c. 1609-1610	*Cymbeline*
c. 1610-1611	*The Winter's Tale*
1611	*The Tempest*
c. 1612-1613	*The Two Noble Kinsmen* (with John Fletcher)
1613	*Henry VIII* (with Fletcher)

dramatic tragicomedy, represented by such plays as *The Knight of the Burning Pestle* (pr. 1607), *Philaster: Or, Love Lies A-Bleeding* (pr. c. 1609), and *A King and No King* (pr. 1611), Beaumont and Fletcher introduced a new cavalier style into Renaissance English drama that ultimately eclipsed even Shakespeare's popularity and perhaps hurried his retirement. It is uncertain whether they or Shakespeare introduced tragicomedy, but Shakespeare's final complete plays are in this fashionable new mode: *Pericles, Prince of Tyre* (pr. c. 1607-1608), *Cymbeline* (pr. c. 1609-1610), *The Winter's Tale* (pr. c. 1610-1611), and *The Tempest* (pr. 1611). After Beaumont married an heiress and stopped writing plays in 1612 or 1613, Shakespeare collaborated with Fletcher, and possibly others, on *Henry VIII, The Two Noble Kinsmen*, and *Cardenio* (now lost), all performed around 1612-1613.

By 1608, when his productivity dropped to one play per year, Shakespeare may have spent part of each year in Stratford-upon-Avon. In 1607, his elder daughter had married John Hall, the local physician, and in 1608, with the birth of their daughter, Elizabeth, Shakespeare became a grandfather. Around 1613, he retired completely to Stratford-upon-Avon, though he also joined John Heminge, a partner in the King's Men, and William Johnson, the host of the Mermaid Tavern, in purchasing the gatehouse of the Blackfriars priory, probably for London visits. On February 10, 1616, his younger daughter, Judith, at the age of thirty-one, married Thomas Quiney, a member of another prominent Stratford family. On March 25, 1616, Shakespeare made out his last will and testament, leaving most of his estate to Susanna, a substantial amount of money to Judith, and his "second best bed" to Anne. He died on April 23, 1616, and was buried in Holy Trinity Church, Stratford-upon-Avon.

In 1623, Shakespeare's surviving partners in the King's Men, John Hemings and Henry Condell, published the First Folio collection of his plays. The portrait included in the First Folio depicts Shakespeare with a short mustache, large staring eyes, and an oval face accentuated by his high, balding forehead and the remaining hair that almost covers his ears. The bust erected above his grave is similar, except that he has a goatee and the balding has progressed further. The First Folio portrait resembles a soulful intellectual, while the Stratford bust suggests a prominent burgher.

SIGNIFICANCE

The two portraits of Shakespeare portray the two parts of his nature. On the one hand, he possessed immense intel-

lectual curiosity about the motives and actions of people. This curiosity, plus his facility with language, enabled him to write his masterpieces and to create characters who are better known than some important figures in world history. On the other hand, reflecting his middle-class background, Shakespeare was himself motivated by strictly bourgeois instincts; he was more concerned with acquiring property and cementing his social position in Stratford than he was with preserving his plays for posterity. If his partners had not published the First Folio, there would be no Shakespeare as he is known today: still acted and enjoyed, the most widely studied and translated writer, the greatest poet and dramatist in the English and perhaps any language.

Besides his ability to create a variety of unforgettable characters, there are at least two other qualities that account for Shakespeare's achievement. One of these is his love of play with language, ranging from the lowest pun to some of the world's best poetry. His love of language sometimes makes him difficult to read, particularly for young students, but frequently the meaning becomes clear in a well-acted version. The second quality is his openness, his lack of any restrictive point of view, ideology, or morality. Shakespeare was able to embrace, identify with, and depict an enormous range of human behavior, from the good to the bad to the indifferent. The capaciousness of his language and vision thus help account for the universality of his appeal.

Shakespeare's lack of commitment to any didactic point of view has often been deplored. Yet he is not entirely uncommitted; rather, he is committed to what is human. Underlying his broad outlook is Renaissance Humanism, a synthesis of Christianity and classicism that is perhaps the best development of the Western mind and finds its best expression in his work. This same generous outlook was apparently expressed in Shakespeare's personality, which, like his bourgeois instincts, defies the Romantic myth of the artist. He was often praised by his fellows, but friendly rival and ferocious satirist Ben Jonson said it best: "He was, indeed, honest, and of an open and free nature," and "He was not of an age, but for all time."

—*Harold Branam*

FURTHER READING

Alexander, Peter. *Shakespeare's Life and Art*. Reprint. London: Nisbet, 1961. A short but much-admired critical biography, treating Shakespeare's life in relation to his work.

Bloom, Harold, ed. *Elizabethan Drama*. Philadelphia: Chelsea House, 2004. Anthology of essays that place Shakespeare and his plays in their cultural context, evaluating both his originality and his indebtedness to tradition. Includes bibliographic references and index.

Bradbrook, Muriel C. *Shakespeare, the Poet in His World*. London: Weidenfeld and Nicolson, 1978. An excellent study by one of the leading scholars and critics of Renaissance English drama.

Chute, Marchette. *Shakespeare of London*. New York: E. P. Dutton, 1949. A readable popular biography, based on documents contemporary to Shakespeare.

De Grazia, Margreta, and Stanley Wells, eds. *The Cambridge Companion to Shakespeare*. New York: Cambridge University Press, 2001. Anthology of commissioned essays on the life and work of the Bard. Includes a survey of Shakespeare criticism in the seventeenth through the nineteenth centuries, a survey of performances from 1660 to 1900, an overview of Shakespeare on film, an essay on genre, and an exploration of Shakespeare's reading habits, among others. With illustrations, bibliographic references, and index.

Frye, Roland Mushat. *Shakespeare's Life and Times: A Pictorial Record*. Princeton, N.J.: Princeton University Press, 1967. Introduces the most important information about Shakespeare through 114 illustrations and captions of one to three paragraphs each.

Halliday, F. E. *Shakespeare and His World*. New York: Charles Scribner's Sons, 1956. Another short introduction containing the essential facts and 151 illustrations.

McDonald, Russ, ed. *Shakespeare: An Anthology of Criticism and Theory, 1945-2000*. Malden, Mass.: Blackwell, 2004. Collects approximately fifty of the most influential essays and book chapters on Shakespeare from the second half of the twentieth century. Organized on the basis of the school of criticism represented into fourteen sections, such as "New Criticism," "Psychoanalytic Readings," and "Race and Post-colonialism." Includes illustrations, bibliographic references, and index.

Quennell, Peter. *Shakespeare: A Biography*. New York: World, 1963. Another fine critical biography, scholarly and readable.

Reese, M. M. *Shakespeare: His World and His Work*. Rev. ed. New York: St. Martin's Press, 1980. A full, well-written introduction to Shakespeare's life, the drama that preceded his, the Elizabethan stage, and his art.

Schoenbaum, Samuel. *Shakespeare's Lives*. New York: Oxford University Press, 1970. Not a biography per se, but rather an evaluation of the portraits of Shakespeare, the contemporary references, the legends, and the many biographies written about him up to 1970. Fascinating but dense reading. An important scholarly reference work.

_____. *William Shakespeare: A Compact Documentary Life*. New York: Oxford University Press, 1977. A scholarly biography that scrupulously examines the facts, documents, and myths of Shakespeare's life, supported by the author's considerable knowledge of previous biographies.

Wells, Stanley. *Shakespeare: For All Time*. New York: Oxford University Press, 2003. Survey of Shakespeare reception and criticism, from the Renaissance through the twentieth century. Includes illustrations, bibliographic references, and index.

SEE ALSO: Pietro Aretino; Francis Bacon; Francis Beaumont and John Fletcher; George Chapman; Elizabeth I; Henry IV; Henry VI; Aemilia Lanyer; Niccolò Machiavelli; Sir Thomas Malory; Marguerite de Navarre; Christopher Marlowe; Thomas Nashe; Richard III; Sir Philip Sidney.

RELATED ARTICLES in *Great Events from History: The Renaissance & Early Modern Era, 1454-1600:* 1576: James Burbage Builds The Theatre; c. 1589-1613: Shakespeare Writes His Dramas; December, 1598-May, 1599: The Globe Theatre Is Built.

SIR PHILIP SIDNEY
English poet and statesman

Known during his lifetime as the perfect example of a Renaissance courtier because of his learning, nobility, and chivalry, Sidney was also a poet of the first rank whose sonnet sequence Astrophel and Stella *is a classic of English literature.*

BORN: November 30, 1554; Penshurst, Kent, England
DIED: October 17, 1586; Arnhem, the Netherlands
AREAS OF ACHIEVEMENT: Literature, government and politics, military

EARLY LIFE

From his birth, Philip Sidney was associated with the court of England. His godfather was Philip II of Spain, husband of Queen Mary I, and his godmother (his grandmother) was the duchess of Northumberland. Philip's father, Sir Henry Sidney, was active in government affairs in Wales and Ireland. Sidney's early years were spent at Penshurst, the family estate. In 1564, he began attending Shrewsbury School, where he met the future writer Fulke Greville, who would later compose the first biography of Sidney.

In 1568, Sidney entered Christ Church, Oxford, where he impressed his teachers and fellows with his intelligence and character. His circle of friends grew to include such notables as Richard Carew, who would become known as a poet, and Richard Hakluyt, who would win fame as an explorer and writer.

His stay at Oxford was cut short in 1571 when he left the university because of the plague; Sidney never received a degree. In 1572, he began a two-year tour of the Continent, ostensibly to improve his knowledge of foreign languages, but also to serve in a quasi-diplomatic function for Elizabeth I. It was during this visit that Sidney met a number of Protestant leaders in Europe and became a firm and vocal champion of their cause. This belief was strengthened during his stay in France by the St. Bartholomew's Day Massacre of Protestants on August 23, 1572.

During his extensive travels, Sidney met and befriended Hubert Languet, who accompanied Sidney to Vienna and the court of Maximilian II, and later to Poland. Languet had a great influence on Sidney and further confirmed for the young Englishman the truth of the Protestant cause. Sidney also visited Hungary, spent time in Venice studying astronomy, music, and Italian literature, and, on his return to Vienna, learned horsemanship under John Peter Pugliano, the foremost equestrian of the age. Later, in his *Defence of Poesie* (1580), published in another edition as *An Apologie for Poetry*, Sidney gave a vivid description of these lessons.

In June, 1575, Sidney returned to England. His education was now complete, and he was ready to embark on his service to England and the court of Elizabeth. He was already known for his intelligence and his serious nature, and his contemporaries universally acknowledged him as a paragon of virtues. In appearance, he was quite handsome, with light hair, a fair complexion, and fine features. The numerous portraits that survive testify to his refined but not overly elegant presence.

LIFE'S WORK

As a member of the court, Sidney met Walter Devereaux, first earl of Essex, and his daughter, Penelope, who would later become the "Stella" of Sidney's sonnet sequence. Although there was discussion of marriage, the death of Essex in 1576 and Sidney's attention to political matters at court allowed the desultory courtship to lapse. At the time, Sidney composed verses inspired more by literary models than Penelope herself; his earlier sonnets are clearly patterned after those of the earl of Surrey to his love, Geraldine. It was only after 1581, when Penelope had married Lord Rich, that Sidney seemed to have been moved by real passion toward her. By then, he could only vent his feelings in the sonnets of *Astrophel and Stella* (1591).

In the meantime, however, Sidney was occupied with political and diplomatic affairs at court. In 1577, he was dispatched with messages for the newly crowned elector palatine and to Emperor Rudolf II, who had also earlier succeeded to the throne. While in Prague, Sidney boldly lectured the new emperor on the need to combat the threat of Spanish domination of Europe. While returning to England, he traveled through the Low Countries, where he met and was captivated by William the Silent, leader of the Protestant cause in northern Europe.

Back in England, Sidney wrote a defense of his father's conduct of Irish affairs to counter criticism. Sidney also turned to more creative work, composing a masque called *The Lady of May* (1578) to celebrate Elizabeth's May Day visit to one of her subjects. Such visits were, under Elizabeth, elaborate state occasions of considerable importance, and their ceremonies were often expressions of political significance. Increasingly, Sidney was to be found in association with scholars and writers such as Gabriel Harvey and Edmund Spenser. Sidney and Spenser met in 1578; the next year, Spenser dedicated to Sidney his important work, *The Shepheardes Calendar.*

Sidney recognized Spenser's talent and contribution, but another work dedicated to him that year pleased him not at all: Stephen Gosson's *The Schoole of Abuse* (1579), a virulent attack on the theater and the quickly developing English drama. Sidney composed and circulated in manuscript his *Defence of Poesie* as a reply to Gosson's charges.

The *Defence of Poesie* is one of the earliest and most important pieces of English literary theory, and formed the standard defense of literature that would be used against Puritans and others who decried the art as being at best trivial and at worst sinful. In his spirited and vigorous defense, Sidney used the argument that poetry (by which he meant all forms of literature, including drama) teaches virtue more vividly, and therefore more profoundly, than do history or philosophy. Through its creative powers, poetry instills in its audience a lasting love of proper actions, and so makes them better persons. To bolster his argument, Sidney used as examples such English writers as Geoffrey Chaucer, the earl of Surrey, and Edmund Spenser.

Sidney published none of his literary works during his lifetime, but he was much less discreet with the distribution of his political writings. In January, 1580, he dared to send Queen Elizabeth a lengthy, well-reasoned, but highly improper essay that argued against her possible marriage to the duke of Anjou, the Roman Catholic heir to the French throne. Sidney's reproach to his sovereign was based on the grounds of loyal patriotism and Protestantism, but the queen was so angered that she banished Sidney from her presence for months. During this inter-

lude, Sidney wrote his romance, *Arcadia* (1590), to amuse his sister.

Sidney's talents and abilities, as well as his reputation and his many admirers, regained him favor at court. In 1581, he was elected to Parliament; that spring he took a major part in a festive tournament and other ceremonies honoring a French embassy; and on January 13, 1583, he was knighted. He was also given a more practical post as joint master of the queen's ordnance.

The income from the ordnance position and other funds he had been granted from fines paid to the Crown were necessary, for a marriage had been arranged by Sidney's father and Sir Francis Walsingham, whose daughter Frances was then only fourteen. The two were married on September 20, 1593. Although Sidney seems to have felt genuine affection for his wife, he continued his devotion to Penelope. These emotions, deep as they appear to have been, found expression only in his collection of sonnets that were given the title *Astrophel and Stella* ("star lover" and "star," the poetical names Sidney devised for himself and Penelope).

By far the most important of Sidney's literary creations, *Astrophel and Stella* chronicles his long, passionate, and ultimately unhappy relationship with Penelope Rich. The collection consists of 108 sonnets, which use the familiar "Shakespearean" form of three quatrains and a concluding couplet. There are also eleven songs in the sequence.

Sidney's powers as a poet grew as he composed the series; the earlier poems often seem flat or contrived, but the later sonnets are both technically proficient and poetically powerful. He made particularly good use of metaphors and allusions from military and political affairs, as was fitting for a courtier poet. The influence of these poems on other writers, including Shakespeare, is clear.

Because of Sidney's personal appeal, and the success of the *Arcadia*, unauthorized editions of *Astrophel and Stella* began appearing in the early 1590's, with the first being prepared by the noted Elizabethan writer, Thomas Nashe (1591). The 1598 edition of *Arcadia* contains the most complete version of the sequence, and presents it in an order probably close to that which Sidney intended.

Sidney's desire for service found little outlet during the months he served as joint master of the queen's

---

SIDNEY'S MAJOR WORKS

1578	*The Lady of May*
1581	*Fortress of Perfect Beauty* (with Fulke Greville, Lord Brooke; Phillip Howard, the earl of Arundel; and Baron Windsor of Stanwell)
1590	*Arcadia* (rev. 1593, 1598; also known as *The Countess of Pembroke's Arcadia*)
1591	*Astrophel and Stella* (1591: pirated edition printed by Thomas Newman; 1598: first authorized edition)
1595	*Defence of Poesie* (also published as *An Apologie for Poetry*)
1598	*Certaine Sonnets*
1823	*The Psalmes of David, Translated into Divers and Sundry Kindes of Verse* (pb. 1823; with Mary Sidney Herbert, Countess of Pembroke)

Sir Philip Sidney. (Library of Congress)

ordnance. Frustrated, he considered joining voyages of exploration or colonization. In Parliament, he sat on a committee setting boundaries for the projected Virginia colony, and his interest in this topic was well enough known that Hakluyt, his friend from Oxford, dedicated his own celebrated work, *Divers Voyages, Touching the Discovery of America* (1582), to Sidney.

A more urgent call to action lay closer to home. In 1584, the assassination of William the Silent shocked Protestant Europe and made Sidney more determined than ever to insist on England's resistance to Spanish actions in the Low Countries. Elizabeth, anxious to avoid open conflict with the powerful Spanish, was finally convinced to send an army to the Netherlands in the summer of 1585, but her commitment was tentative and hesitant.

Sidney, craving a more active part, attempted to join Sir Francis Drake, who was then preparing a raid on the Spanish coast. Sidney's arrival at Plymouth was secret, but Drake promptly and prudently informed Elizabeth, who summoned Sidney to court. Once again, however, peace was restored between monarch and subject, and on November 7, Sidney was appointed governor of Flushing, a town in the Low Countries garrisoned by the English. He sailed on November 16, 1585.

The English army was small and its supplies poor. Operations with the Dutch were hampered by language barriers and mutual suspicion. Contact with the Spanish forces consisted mainly of raids and skirmishes, rather than full battles, which the English could not afford and the Dutch did not desire. On July 6, 1586, Sidney was part of a daring raid on Axel, a small village 20 miles (32 kilometers) from Flushing. Conducted at night and by boat, the assault took the town's garrison by surprise. Later that year, Sidney participated in the assault of Doesburg, a small citadel near the town of Arnhem.

The English commander, the earl of Leicester, was embarked on a policy of systematically reducing the Spanish strong points. The next one he attacked was at Zutphen. Leicester brought his army to Zutphen on September 13 and was soon engaged in a running series of skirmishes with the defenders. On September 22, Sidney joined the earl with about five hundred English cavalry in an attack on the Spanish lines. Meeting a friend who was wearing no leg armor, Sidney gallantly but rashly removed his own.

In the battle, Sidney had one horse killed under him, mounted another, and charged through the enemy line. On his return to the English forces, a bullet struck him in the left leg just above the knee. He was able to ride back to camp and was carried by barge to Arnhem. His wife had joined him earlier, in March, and, although pregnant, remained to care for him. The wound became infected, and on October 17, Sidney died.

The grief that was felt throughout England at Sidney's death was profound and sincere. His funeral brought mourners from all social classes to St. Paul's Cathedral. Both Oxford and Cambridge published collections of elegies in his honor, and more than two hundred other poetic memorials were printed, among them eight elegies in Spenser's *Colin Clout's Come Home Again* (1595).

SIGNIFICANCE

It was appropriate that Sidney's passing be marked by poetic tributes, because he himself is best known as a poet and writer. His three major works were important influences on English literature, and one has attained the status of a classic.

Sidney's *Arcadia*—composed primarily to amuse his sister, and therefore sometimes called *The Countess of Pembroke's Arcadia*—is an elaborate chivalric romance, with verse interludes. The language, highly patterned and deliberately ornate, is typical of the genre, which was established by John Lyly's *Euphues: The Anatomy of Wit*

(1578) and which captivated an entire generation of Renaissance readers.

The plot is a rambling account of two princes' pursuit of their two princesses, and there are numerous episodes of disguises, mistaken identities, battles, tournaments, and philosophical speeches. Pastoral eclogues are scattered throughout the work. *Arcadia* was first published in 1590, but the edition of 1593, which was prepared by Sidney's sister, provides the first reliable text. Although very popular during the sixteenth and seventeenth centuries, the romance has since declined in reputation and influence.

The *Defence of Poesie*, which was widely circulated in manuscript during the author's life, remains an important document of the English Renaissance and provides an interesting insight into the critical views of the time. When Gosson dedicated his work, *The Schoole of Abuse*, to Sidney without permission, Sidney was moved to prepare his rebuttal. Gosson attacked plays, poems, and all other forms of fiction as being vain and sinful. Sidney sought to refute these charges in his reply, which consists of three parts. The first justifies poetry as a source of virtue; the second reviews the forms of poetry; and the third offers an optimistic prediction of the future of English writing. Interestingly, Sidney seems to have been unaware of the forthcoming achievements English drama was about to make.

Although he was loved and admired in his own time as an outstanding individual, a defender of the Protestant cause, and an English patriot, Sidney's enduring legacy consists of his place among the first rank of poets who created the English Renaissance.

—Michael Witkoski

Further Reading

Buxton, John. *Sir Philip Sidney and the English Renaissance*. 3d ed. London: Macmillan, 1987. A solid study of Sidney and his place within the Elizabethan period, concentrating on his literary works, but also providing background on his life and activities as a courtier and soldier.

Greville, Sir Fulke (First Baron Brooke). *The Life of the Renowned Sir Philip Sidney*. In *The Prose of Fulke Greville, Lord Brooke*, edited by Mark Caldwell. New York: Garland, 1987. The original biography, written by Sidney's longtime friend. First published in 1652, this work is the primary source for Sidney's life. It also sheds light on the thoughts and perspectives of his contemporaries.

Hamilton, A. C. *Sir Philip Sidney: A Study of His Life and Works*. Cambridge, England: Cambridge University Press, 1977. A well-written, well-balanced overview of Sidney's life and writings, especially helpful for showing how the two relate in many areas.

Howell, Roger. *Sir Philip Sidney: The Shepherd Knight*. Boston: Little, Brown, 1968. Concentrates on Sidney's political and diplomatic activities, placing his writings within the historical context of the times, particularly his patriotism and intense devotion to the Protestant cause.

Kimbrough, Robert. *Sir Philip Sidney*. New York: Twayne, 1971. Good introductory overview of Sidney's life and his work as a writer. Kimbrough takes special care to provide a quick but adequate sketch of the turbulent period of the late sixteenth century. A good starting place for the beginning student.

Klein, Lisa M. *The Exemplary Sidney and the Elizabethan Sonneteer*. Newark: University of Delaware Press, 1998. Examination of the extent to which Sidney's contemporaries and immediate successors both created and criticized his reputation as a legendary writer of sonnets. Explores the function of the sonnet in Elizabethan society and the importance of Sidney and his followers and respondents in shaping that function. Includes illustrations, bibliographic references, and index.

Mazzola, Elizabeth. *Favorite Sons: The Politics and Poetics of the Sidney Family*. New York: Palgrave Macmillan, 2003. Looks not only at the poetic practice of the Sidney family (Philip, Robert, Mary Sidney Herbert, and Mary Wroth) but also at the interconnections between poetry and the early modern family as such. Reads both poetry and family history as similar cultural projects founded on similar types of cultural logic. Includes bibliographic references and index.

Sidney, Sir Philip. *The Poems of Sir Philip Sidney*. Edited by William A. Ringler, Jr. Oxford, England: Clarendon Press, 1962. Since Sidney is best known today for his sonnets, a thorough study of him must include *Astrophel and Stella*. This edition is textually impeccable and contains a fine introduction useful to literary and nonliterary readers alike.

_____. *Selected Prose and Poetry*. Edited by Robert Kimbrough. New York: Holt, Rinehart and Winston, 1969. A handy one-volume collection of Sidney's major writings, very helpful for those readers who want at least a sample of the *Arcadia* or *Defence of Poesie*. Kimbrough's introduction is useful in placing Sidney within the context of his times.

Stewart, Alan. *Philip Sidney: A Double Life*. New York:

St. Martin's Press, 2001. Thorough study of the vicissitudes of Sidney's life, especially his success on the European continent in contrast with his denigration at the hands of Queen Elizabeth at home. Portrays Sidney as ironically harmed by his noble birth, because all of his family connections were to aristocrats who were out of favor with the queen and other powerful political figures. Includes photographic plates, illustrations, maps, bibliographic references, and index.

SEE ALSO: Chevalier de Bayard; Sir Francis Drake; Elizabeth I; Richard Hakluyt; Mary I; Maximilian II; Thomas Nashe; Philip II; Rudolf II; Edmund Spenser; William the Silent.

RELATED ARTICLES in *Great Events from History: The Renaissance & Early Modern Era, 1454-1600:* 1528: Castiglione's *Book of the Courtier* Is Published; 1558-1603: Reign of Elizabeth I; August 24-25, 1572: St. Bartholomew's Day Massacre.

SIGISMUND I, THE OLD
King of Poland (r. 1506-1548)

Sigismund I defended Poland's eastern front from invading forces, had his army disempower and secularize the Teutonic Order, and incorporated the duchy of Mazovia, now the province of Warsaw. He provided protection for Jews and promoted tolerance of Orthodox Christians, and he is often associated with Poland's golden age for his arts patronage.

BORN: January 1, 1467; place unknown
DIED: April 1, 1548; Kraków, Poland
ALSO KNOWN AS: Zygmunt Stary; Zygmunt I Stary; Sigismund the Old; Sigismund I, the Elder
AREAS OF ACHIEVEMENT: Government and politics, patronage of the arts, warfare and conquest

EARLY LIFE

Sigismund (SEE-gihs-muhnt) was the son of Casimir IV, king of Poland, and Elizabeth of Habsburg. Nothing indicated that Sigismund would ascend the Polish throne, as he had four elder brothers; one of them died prematurely. All the brothers received excellent educations. The eldest brother, Vladislav II, became the king of Bohemia in 1471 and king of Hungary in 1490. The second brother, John I Albert, succeeded the Crown of Poland after his father's death in 1492. The third brother, Alexander I, became grand duke of Lithuania.

Without a better prospect, Sigismund stayed at his brother Vladislav's court in Buda from 1498 to 1501. This sojourn permitted him to imbibe Renaissance culture and art. Living in Buda Castle, the prince held a miniature court. Although unmarried at the time, Sigismund had a concubine, with whom he had three children.

Vladislav had been endowing his brother with several Silesian duchies since 1498. Finally, in 1501, Sigismund moved to Silesia. The prince, as governor of Silesia and Lusatia, undertook monetary reform and managed to unify Silesian money in 1505.

In 1501, King John I Albert was succeeded by Alexander, who died unexpectedly in 1506. Sigismund immediately hastened toward Lithuania. Proclaimed the grand duke there, he hoped to be elevated to the Polish throne, which was legally elective. In fact, he was elected in December of 1506 and solemnly crowned in January of 1507 in the Wawel Cathedral. He commenced his reign as a mature forty year old.

He accentuated his reign by marrying Barbara Zápolya, the daughter of a Hungarian prince. Barbara bore him two daughters, but she soon died (1515).

LIFE'S WORK

Having ascended the Polish throne, Sigismund resigned his rights to the Silesian duchies. The situation in his kingdom was complex. The king often had to give up his pacifist tendencies and throw himself into the whirlpool of international conflicts. During the first years of his reign, his policy was strongly anti-Habsburg.

The kingdom's treasury was almost empty, so Sigismund tried to augment his revenue through enlarging the salt mines in Wieliczka and Bochnia and through annual taxes; he also tried to impose a tax for the army. He also avoided bestowing the royal estates and tried unsuccessfully to repurchase those that had been leased. Yet most of his projects went unrealized.

Among international problems, what seemed most critical was the threat of the Teutonic Order, a religious order of knights, which, in 1309, had established a military principality in East Prussia (now in Poland). The grand masters, taking advantage of the Holy Roman Emperor's mandate to protect the Church, consistently refused to swear allegiance to the king. Sigismund tended

Sigismund I, the Old. (Hulton|Archive by Getty Images)

to a compromise with the Habsburgs in order to find a solution to the problem of the Teutonic Order. During the congress of Vienna (1515), the emperor promised to stop inciting Muscovy and the Teutonic Order against Poland, but in return he expected several dynastic advantages in Bohemia and Hungary. Finally, the grand master, Albert von Hohenzollern, after a short war with Poland, declared that he would adopt Lutheranism and swear the oath to the Polish king as his secular vassal, duke in Prussia. Albert paid his homage in Kraków Main Square in 1525. In the nineteenth century, this scene inspired the Polish artist, Jan Matejko, to create the well-known work *Hołd Pruski* (the Prussian homage).

In 1526, after the death of the last piast of Mazovia, which was a hereditary fief subordinated to the Crown, Sigismund incorporated this province into Poland. In the same year, the young Hungarian king, Louis II, Vladislav's son, was killed in the Battle of Mohács. Also, the Bohemian throne, formerly Jagiellonian, became empty.

The situation in Hungary grew complex in face of the Ottoman Turkish threat. Sigismund sought neither the Hungarian nor the Bohemian throne. When Holy Roman Emperor Ferdinand I and John Zápolya, the *vaivode* (governor) of Transylvania, rivaled for the Hungarian crown, Sigismund supported Ferdinand in hopes of keeping the Turks far from Poland. Hungary as an Austrian dominion might be the best barrier against the Turks, and Sigismund was anxious to keep the peace.

Even after the famous victory at Obertyn (1531), where the grand hetman (chief army commander) of the Crown, Jan Tarnowski, had crushed the Moldavians and their *hospodar* (prince) Petrylo, Sigismund did not allow him to invade Moldavia, which was paying homage to the Ottomans. Instead, in 1533, a treaty with the Turks was signed.

In 1518, Sigismund married the niece of Holy Roman Emperor Maximilian I, Italian princess Bona Sforza, with whom he had five children (but only one son), and who also became a personification of new cultural models. Bona strengthened the position of the dynasty and suggested that Sigismund elect his son grand duke of Lithuania and then also king of Poland *vivente rege* (while the king is still alive). In 1530, she achieved the coronation of Sigismund II Augustus, then ten years old, who became coruler with his father. Sigismund I became known as the *old* king. Bona led anti-Habsburg policy. She opposed the decision of marriage between the young king and the archduchess Elisabeth of Austria, which concluded in 1543.

Sigismund was the main protector of Renaissance art in Poland. Between 1507 and 1537, he rebuilt and extended his Wawel Royal Castle, and he commissioned many Italian artists. The courtyard of the castle, with its arcaded cloisters, and the Sigismund Chapel in the Wawel Cathedral, are pearls of Renaissance architecture. Sigismund commissioned the largest church bell in Poland (the Sigismund Bell), made by Johan Behem in 1520.

Toward the end of his long reign, Sigismund grew increasingly passive. He was easily influenced by senators and by his wife, Bona, who, in fact, reigned in his stead and replaced the old, unruly senators with new ones. The last days of Sigismund's life were adumbrated by a sad message: The young king, Sigismund II Augustus, secretly married his mistress, Barbara Radziwill. This decision caused opposition in many political circles and discord between the young king and Bona, who suspected some intrigue on the Radziwills' side. The offended queen retired to Mazovia and then left for Italy, taking a large fortune with her. Thus, the end of the old Jagiellonian reign was sealed.

SIGNIFICANCE

Scholarly assessment of Sigismund's reign varies: Immediately after his death, many panegyrics were printed, conveying a luminous and idealized portrait of the king. This might be due to the hatred of the gentry for Bona and the young king. Nineteenth century scholars criticized

Sigismund as the "king of senators" and emphasized his passivity. Twentieth century scholars tried to rehabilitate his legacy by showing his thriftiness and political realism. Paweł Jasienica rather disdained him, considering him an improper man in an improper place, who, with his limited horizons and scant energy, was suited rather to be a treasurer or an administrator of some province.

Generally, Sigismund ruled dynamically, especially during the first half of his reign. He tried to reform diplomatic service, to update the currency, and to codify law. In the realm of international policy, he demonstrated shortsightedness but also common sense. He enjoyed the sympathy of his subjects and enjoyed prominent people in his midst. He protected Renaissance art and architecture, and his name will always be linked with the threshold of the Renaissance and Poland's golden age.

—*Elwira Buszewicz*

FURTHER READING

Halecki, Oscar. *Borderlands of Western Civilization: A History of East-Central Europe.* San Diego, Calif.: Simon Publications, 2000. Presents the history of the Jagiellonian state from a political point of view in a large cultural and international context. Readers are led through a labyrinth of sociopolitical dependencies and complications. Originally published in 1952.

Jasienica, Pawel. *Jagiellonian Poland.* Translated by Alexander T. Jordan. Miami, Fla.: American Institute of Polish Culture, 1978. A vivid historical narrative, full of facts and details, yet ravishing reading; a journey through the entire Jagiellonian era. The author's evaluation of the successive kings is strongly subjective, yet enriched with numerous anecdotes.

Stone, Daniel Z. *The Polish-Lithuanian State, 1386-1795.* History of East Central Europe 4. Seattle: University of Washington Press, 2001. This book facilitates a deeper understanding of the specifics of the Polish-Lithuanian union.

SEE ALSO: Sigismund II Augustus; Vladislav II.

RELATED ARTICLE in *Great Events from History: The Renaissance & Early Modern Era, 1454-1600:* c. 1500: Rise of Sarmatism in Poland.

SIGISMUND II AUGUSTUS
King of Poland (r. 1548-1572)

Sigismund II Augustus's reign saw a Polish-Lithuanian union, which established that both nations shall elect the king of the commonwealth but shall retain their own territories, laws, treasuries, and armies. Also during Sigismund's reign, the gentry played an important part in political life, urging, through the "execution movement," the return of the royal domains to the Crown.

BORN: August 1, 1520; Kraków, Poland
DIED: July 7, 1572; Knyszyn, Poland
ALSO KNOWN AS: Sigismund August; Zygmunt August; Zygmunt II August
AREAS OF ACHIEVEMENT: Government and politics, patronage of the arts, warfare and conquest

EARLY LIFE

Sigismund II Augustus (SEE-gihs-muhnt AW-guhs-tuhs) was born at the Wawel Royal Castle in Kraków, the second child—and the only son—of the marriage between Sigismund I, king of Poland, and the Italian princess, Bona Sforza. He obtained his cognomen "August" from the month of his birth and also in remembrance of the great Roman emperor Augustus.

His career was decided early in his life by his mother, who stressed his election to the Polish throne before his father's death. In fact, she effected his elevation as grand duke of Lithuania in 1529 and, in 1530, his coronation *vivente rege* (while the king as still alive) as the king of Poland, ruling with his father until his father's death in 1548.

The prince grew up at his mother's court, mostly among Italians, so he learned Italian quickly. His first governess was Bona herself, but by 1529, Sigismund was being educated by a morally ambiguous man of notable learning. Governed by him and by several other courtiers, the prince learned Latin and German, knew both the oratory and epistolary art, and took interest in architecture and the fine arts.

Before the commencement of his independent rule, Sigismund II Augustus married the archduchess Elisabeth of Austria in 1543. This marriage, accepted by his father but disapproved by his mother, was short and unfortunate. The young king, disgusted, avoided his wife during her epileptic strokes. In 1544, Sigismund I yielded the rule of Lithuania and sent Sigismund II Augustus there. Elisabeth had died in 1545, and soon the young king commenced a love affair with Barbara Radziwill, the daughter of his castellan (castle warden), whom he married secretly in 1547. He tried to legalize the marriage, which was strongly opposed by his mother and which caused public ferment. With King Sigismund I's death in 1548 came the beginning of Sigismund II Augustus's reign.

LIFE'S WORK

Sigismund II Augustus devoted the first years of his rule to the struggle to legalize his marriage and to crown Barbara. He had to choose, however, between promises for several social groups or threatening abdication. Finally, he chose an alliance with the Habsburgs to prevent the rebellion of his subjects. The struggle to crown Barbara was actually a political game with his mother and her accomplices. In 1550, at the diet of Piotrków, the king forced Barbara's coronation, which took place the same year, but Barbara died the very next year and was buried in Vilnius. Afterward, the king wore black clothes, avoided people and amusements, and stayed mostly in Lithuania.

Sigismund's presence in Vilnius animated and enlivened the city, which was rebuilt and took on a European refinement. Sigismund established the first art gallery there; he collected books and jewels and protected the literati; his patronage of the arts and architecture was significant not only in Vilnius but also in Warsaw and even in Kraków, a city where he spent only three years of his rule. He enriched the royal chambers at Wawel Castle with a collection of Flemish tapestries that mainly represented biblical scenes.

In 1553, Sigismund married Catherine Habsburg, his first wife's sister, in face of a threat of an alliance between Muscovy and the Habsburgs, which was actually less fearful than he believed. This marriage was rather unhappy, and the king consequently avoided his wife, especially since any hope for an heir had been extinguished.

The king, although he had previously ignored the execution movement of the gentry, changed his policy when faced with the problem of Livonia. This region was an object of interest of Muscovy, Sweden, Denmark, Poland, and Lithuania. In 1561, Sigismund dissolved the Livonian Order and subordinated a part of Livonia to his state. When Russian czar Ivan the Terrible proclaimed war against him, the king had to try to win the support of the gentry and to support the execution movement.

Sigismund II Augustus. (Hulton|Archive by Getty Images)

"The execution of laws" was proclaimed at the diet of Piotrków in 1562-1563. In 1563, Ivan the Terrible occupied Płock, which resulted in Polish-Lithuanian negotiations about the "real" union (the Lithuanian gentry aspired to obtain the same privileges as the Polish). The union was concluded in 1569 at the diet of Lublin. Poland and Lithuania became a commonwealth with a common king, elected by both nations, and common Sejm (parliament). The treasury, army, and several offices remained separate. Royal Prussia was incorporated into the Crown. As early as 1563, the Brandenburg line of the Hohenzollerns was allowed to inherit the duchy of Prussia, the Polish fief, which was soon to be separated from Poland.

In 1560, in connection with the Livonian war, Sigismund organized the royal navy and then established a maritime commission. After several protests in Gdansk, he issued statutes that defended royal laws regarding navigation. The Livonian War ended with a truce in Moscow in 1570. The king did not take advantage of Ivan's defeat by the Tatars nor did he claim more territories.

The king accepted the resolutions of the Catholic Church's Council of Trent (1545-1563), a council formed to reply to the doctrinal challenges of Protestant reformers, but he respected religious tolerance, declaring that he was a king of conscience. Religious freedom was guaranteed to all Protestants.

Sigismund II Augustus spent the last years of his life mostly in Warsaw, afflicted with disease and lonely among untrustworthy people. He was desperately trying to father a male heir with his concubines. Finally, he made his testament in 1571. Then, fearing an epidemic, he left Warsaw for Knyszyn, where he died in 1572, without an heir, a bit later than his wife, Catherine, who resided in Linz. Thus, the Jagiellonian era came to an end.

SIGNIFICANCE

Sigismund II Augustus's rule coincided with the golden age of the Renaissance in Poland. It was an era of flourishing arts, architecture, literature, and learning. Mikołaj Rej, called the father of Polish literature, and Jan Kochanowski, the Polish Orpheus, were contemporary writers. Sigismund even established the first regular mail service between Kraków and Venice.

His contemporaries rarely called him a great king. His enemies wrote several pasquinades (satires), which described him as improperly educated, false, and tyrannizing and one who died indecently. Several annalists, though, defended him as a prudent and consistent ruler.

Today's historians are still uncertain how to describe his character. Paweł Jasienica has criticized him as too submissive to the Catholic hierarchy and undecided in his politics. From Jasienica's point of view, the death of the last Jagiellon caused political emptiness and public disgust. He considered the entire dynasty remiss politically, but he respected the dynamism of Queen Bona.

Most historians esteem Sigismund II Augustus as a tragic and interesting character. He did not create a political school. He consulted his senators, but he ruled independently and made his own decisions; he was also a procrastinator. Nevertheless, his prudence prevented any violent religious conflicts. The last Jagiellon was typical of his time, collecting art, books, jewels, and weapons, which enriched the heritage of Renaissance culture in Poland.

—*Elwira Buszewicz*

FURTHER READING

Halecki, Oscar. *Borderlands of Western Civilization: A History of East-Central Europe.* San Diego, Calif.: Simon Publications, 2000. Presents the history of the Jagiellonian state from a political point of view and in cultural and international context. Readers are led through a labyrinth of sociopolitical dependencies and complications. Originally published in 1952.

Jasienica, Pawel. *Jagiellonian Poland.* Translated by Alexander T. Jordan. Miami, Fla.: American Institute of Polish Culture, 1978. A vivid historical narrative, full of facts and details, yet ravishing reading; a journey through the entire Jagiellonian era. The author's evaluation of the successive kings is strongly subjective, yet enriched with numerous anecdotes.

Stone, Daniel Z. *The Polish-Lithuanian State, 1386-1795.* History of East Central Europe 4. Seattle: University of Washington Press, 2001. This book facilitates a deeper understanding of the specificity of the Polish-Lithuanian union and of the multinational and multicultural state of the Polish-Lithuanian Commonwealth.

Tazbir, Janusz. *A State Without Stakes: Polish Religious Toleration in the Sixteenth and Seventeenth Centuries.* Translated by A. T. Jordan. New York: Kosciuszko Foundation, 1973. Discusses Sigismund II Augustus's reign from a wide temporal, political, and cultural perspective.

SEE ALSO: Pius V; Rheticus; Sigismund I, the Old; Vladislav II.

RELATED ARTICLES in *Great Events from History: The Renaissance & Early Modern Era, 1454-1600:* 1499-c. 1600: Russo-Polish Wars; 1557-1582: Livonian War.

DIEGO DE SILOÉ
Spanish architect and sculptor

Siloé ranks as one of Spain's greatest architects for his exquisite translations and combinations of Roman, Moorish, and High Renaissance Italian style into a Spanish idiom, most evident, despite his many other works, in the great Cathedral of Granada.

BORN: c. 1495; Burgos, Castile (now in Spain)
DIED: October 22, 1563; Granada, Spain
AREAS OF ACHIEVEMENT: Architecture, art

EARLY LIFE

While the artistic and intellectual achievements of fifteenth and sixteenth century Renaissance figures are often well documented, this is rarely true of their early lives. Of Diego de Siloé (DYAY-goh day see-loh-AY), it is known that he was born in Burgos, Castile. Founded in the eighth century, Burgos had served as an important commercial center, as the seat of the monarch for many years, and more important for Siloé, as a town famed for its architects and architecture, all markedly influenced by northern Gothic styles and very little by those of Mediterranean origins.

Burgos was also the home of the wealthy and cultivated Bartholome Ordóñez, who, breaking with local tradition, between 1490 and 1500 studied with the great Florentine and Neapolitan sculptors and artists, absorbing the best of his Italian masters and becoming familiar with Michelangelo's work.

In Naples, Ordóñez befriended Diego, the son of Gil de Siloé. Apparently a migrant from Orléans, France, to Burgos, Gil had earned esteem in his adopted town as a specialist in late Gothic carving. Diego and Ordóñez collaborated to perfect their craftsmanship. Given his Catholic artistic convictions, Ordóñez, like Siloé, was a devotee of Michelangelo's Florentine style and a spiritual disciple of Donatello. Each man's influence on the other was beneficial. Siloé's sculpture of *Saint George Slaying the Dragon* (c. 1514-1515) for the renowned Caraccioli Altar and his *Virgin and Child*, a relief for a chapel of the Naples Cathedral, amply demonstrate this stylistic affinity.

LIFE'S WORK

Siloé returned to Burgos in 1519 and immediately was selected by the cathedral to design an alabaster monument to a bishop. With restrained, High Renaissance, three-dimensional realism, the monument's face was made from the bishop's death mask and was soon recog-

nized as the most convincing of Spain's integrated effigies, even exceeding similar works by Ordóñez. Only twenty-four years old, Siloé next designed a masterpiece in the Escalera Dorado's iron balustrade, with painted and gilded bas-reliefs, varied grotesques, and delightful nudes. Between 1523 and 1526, he collaborated on the Constable Chapel at Burgos Cathedral. There his mastery of polychrome wood sculpture, the *Presentation* in particular, as well as his *Pietà* at Saint Anne's Altar, represented the best of Renaissance elements, establishing him as Burgos's undisputed master of his field.

Such creativity led in 1528 to his completion of an unfinished church in Granada, marking it with traditional heraldic devices evocative of proud Spanish lineages and with heroic figures, both ancient and biblical. For a Granadan bishop, he designed a monument of Almería marble, while in the late 1520's, he carved for San Jeronimo the choir stalls and the prior's seat. In that same church, the bust of the Virgin and Child beneath a bust of God is comparable to the finest Italian Renaissance work of its genre.

Collectively, such commissions expressed the maturing characteristics of Siloé's youthful style: joyous and passionate yet restrained Catholicity, meticulous and imaginative execution, and lively and gently rhythmic lines. With remarkable chasteness and clarity, Siloé combined the vestiges of Spanish Gothic with *mudéjar*, a style developed during the Moors' domination of Spain. These stylistic signatures and his eclecticism uniquely identified him with the best of High Renaissance art.

Siloé's crowning efforts were invested from approximately 1528 until the late 1530's in the design, erection, and embellishment of the great Cathedral of Granada. Siloé's role in the cathedral's origins for years divided architectural and art historians, blurring an accurate understanding of the cathedral's architectural evolution and a full appreciation of Siloé's contributions. Modern scholarship generally acknowledges that the credit for the cathedral belongs more to Siloé than to anyone else. He did employ the peripheral walls of the original foundations, but within that arc the foundations for the chevet (the apse or termination of the apse—that upper portion of a church, which usually consists of several smaller, secondary apses radiating from the main apse) were of Siloé's design. Moreover, the nave's proportions are solely attributable to him.

Contrary to allegations that he enclosed the cathedral's rotunda sanctuary by copying a fashion common in other Spanish churches, Siloé opened it not only to the transept but also to the ambulatory. Most such criticisms reflected efforts to place the cathedral's development entirely within the Spanish architectural tradition, while in fact, Siloé's experiences were broader. Because of his years of working in Italy, more of his inspiration and stylistic conceptions flowed from the Tuscan-Roman Italy of the High Renaissance than from northern Europe. Siloé, however, did not employ pure Italian Renaissance architecture in the vocabulary of the Cathedral of Granada. No Italian church featured a prototype of the rotunda of the Granada Cathedral. Granada's dome roofed a high, cylindrical shaft of space, opened by tunnels as its base. The normal Latin cross that characterized Italian churches was replaced by Siloé's siting the choir in the central aisle as well as by a cruciform arrangement of the nave around a central lantern. Unlike Italian architectural idioms, the Granadan dome did not dominate. Siloé's conjunction of a domed rotunda with a basilican nave was unprecedented in late medieval, early Renaissance Europe.

Though Siloé's design was always under the scrutiny of communal and Church officials and though it was without traditional models, whether from the Gothic, *mudéjar*, or Italian Renaissance, Siloé's cathedral was very much a distinctive hybrid. It owes perhaps more to ancient Roman architecture and Vitruvius than to the modern Roman style, which he imitated in many other designs.

Siloé's combination of the mausoleum with the cathedral's ambulatory was also novel. Other Renaissance churches had been planned to include the mausoleum with ambulatory, but they were never constructed. Nor did earlier European models of the apse have such central openness as Siloé's did. The cathedral's huge rotunda rises from two stages of Corinthian columns with a Roman grandeur, but it is well proportioned to its space. Siloé made the chevet, the cathedral's spiritual center, the cynosure of his design.

As Siloé designed the cathedral, he planned to have more than one hundred windows and whitewashed walls to create a luminous interior; the church was to be capped by a lantern of glass located over the nave's central bay. Such a light-flooded interior comported fully with a general Renaissance ideal. Unfortunately, this effect was never achieved.

In 1559, Siloé carefully designed a floor plan in which each section of the pavement was to be distinguished from other units by different colors and patterns. This practice was as ancient as buildings in Pompeii and Herculaneum and was even relatively common in classical households. It remained spectacularly effective. Black-and-white marble squares were to cover the sanctuary; black marble would floor the transept; and white marble was to cover the ambulatory pavement. Siloé probably also sought to accentuate the central aisle with a cross of black marble within the white flooring of the square nave, emphasizing the cruciform shape dramatically.

The cathedral's upper structure was supported by multiple cruciform piers: Gothic vaults with well-proportioned Roman ribs rose from Roman piers. Construction of basilican churches during the Renaissance—structures consisting of naves and aisles with a clerestory and a large, high transept from which an apse projected—had presented previous architects with almost insurmountable problems. Siloé managed with his combination of ancient orders of columns with barrel vaults to resolve these problems with great ingenuity. No less ingenuity was demonstrated in his distinctive styling and decoration of the cathedral's four portals. A finishing touch, a twin-towered façade that was to rise above the roof, was never completed. Nevertheless, the Cathedral of Granada stands as one of Renaissance Europe's great processional churches.

SIGNIFICANCE

The liberation of Spain following centuries of Moorish domination, along with the restoration of both secular and Christian authority, lent special inspiration to national religious celebration. This fact helps to explain the communal and religious support that drew Diego de Siloé and other artists, sculptors, and architects to Granada as well as to numerous other Spanish communities during the first sixty years of the sixteenth century. His association with Ordóñez in Italy and his collaboration with him and others in Spain as well as his many commissions filled a substantial catalog by the time he had reached his mid-twenties, establishing him as a master who seems to have been in constant demand.

Despite years of confusion and critical debate about his role in designing, building, and embellishing the Cathedral of Granada, modern scholarship appears to confirm that while he deserves less credit than once was accorded him on minor points, the great cathedral is nevertheless his premier achievement. Siloé ingeniously, joyously hybridized elements of Gothic, Moorish, and Renaissance architecture with the essentials of ancient Roman structures. Siloé's extraordinary, versatile talent produced what has since been exalted as a unique architectural-artistic monument. Principal elements of its design and construction reached across to Spain's overseas empire and cultural enclaves in the sixteenth and seventeenth centuries.

—*Clifton K. Yearley*

FURTHER READING

Barral i Altet, Xavier, ed. *Art and Architecture of Spain*. Boston: Little, Brown, 1998. This general survey places Siloé's work and Renaissance Spanish architecture within its larger historical context. Includes chronology, maps, illustrations, glossary, bibliography, and index.

Benevolo, Leonardo. *The Architecture of the Renaissance*. 2 vols. Reprint. New York: Routledge, 2002. Comprehensive study of European architecture beginning in fifteenth century Florence and expanding to cover the entire continent through the early 1700's. Includes illustrations, bibliographic references, and index.

Byne, Arthur, and Mildred Stapley. *Spanish Architecture of the Sixteenth Century*. New York: G. P. Putnam's Sons, 1917. An informative work. Though somewhat technical, the writing is clear and sufficiently authoritative to inform general readers. It has good photographs, schematics, and plates, as well as notes, a bibliography, and an index.

Hamlin, Talbot. *Architecture Through the Ages*. New York: G. P. Putnam's Sons, 1940. A well-written, richly illustrated survey for the general reader. Superb photographs, numerous schematic drawings, and an extensive, useful index.

Kubler, George, and Martin Soria. *Art and Architecture in Spain and Portugal and Their American Dominions, 1500 to 1800*. Harmondsworth, England: Penguin Books, 1959. This authoritative and ambitious work is superb for an understanding of Siloé's achievements. The writing is scholarly and somewhat uncompromising, but there are extensive chapter notes and scores of excellent photographs, schematics, and plates. Also includes a superb index.

Markschies, Alexander. *Icons of Renaissance Architecture*. New York: Prestel, 2003. This brief but wide-ranging survey of the effects of Italian innovations on the rest of Europe includes a study of Renaissance Spain's Moorish cathedrals. Illustrations, bibliographic references, and index.

Rosenthal, Earl. *The Cathedral of Granada: A Study in the Spanish Renaissance*. Princeton, N.J.: Princeton University Press, 1961. This is perhaps the definitive work on the cathedral. Covers all that is known about Siloé, his colleagues, the debates about the evolution of the cathedral, its technical construction, its setting, and its meaning. The terminology is scholarly, but the work is immensely informative. There are hundreds of photographs, illustrations, schematics, and plates. Contains a lengthy appendix, a very extensive bibliography, and an excellent index.

_____. "Changing Interpretations of the Renaissance in Art History." In *The Renaissance: A Reconsideration of Theories and Interpretations of the Age*, edited by Tinsley Helton. Madison: University of Wisconsin Press, 1961. Rosenthal is a preeminent authority on Spanish Renaissance architecture, particularly on Ordóñez, Siloé, and the Cathedral of Granada. Essential reading for an understanding of Siloé. The book has plates, notes, and a useful index.

SEE ALSO: Leon Battista Alberti; Donato Bramante; Benvenuto Cellini; Pierre Lescot; Michelangelo; Andrea Palladio; Piero della Francesca; Raphael; Jacopo Sansovino; Giorgio Vasari; Andrea del Verrocchio.

RELATED ARTICLES in *Great Events from History: The Renaissance & Early Modern Era, 1454-1600:* 1508-1512 and 1534-1541: Michelangelo Paints the Sistine Chapel; 1563-1584: Construction of the Escorial.

Sixtus IV
Italian pope (1471-1484)

A Franciscan friar from a humble background, Sixtus IV is best known for his extensive patronage of the arts, his nepotism, and his high taxation. He commissioned more art and architectural projects than any other fifteenth century pope, monuments that include the Sistine Chapel, the Vatican Library, the Hospital of Santo Spirito, and the Ponte Sisto.

Born: July 21, 1414; Celle Ligure, near Savona, Republic of Genoa (now in Italy)

Died: August 12, 1484; Rome, Papal States (now in Italy)

Also known as: Francesco della Rovere (given name)

Areas of achievement: Patronage of the arts, architecture, religion and theology

Early Life

Sixtus IV, a devout Franciscan admired for his understanding of complicated theological issues, came from an obscure family. He was born Francesco della Rovere, but the early events of his life remain unclear. According to some sources, he was the second of seven children of Leonardo della Rovere and Luchina Monleone. Other scholars maintain that he was separated from his birth parents and adopted by Leonardo and Luchina.

Despite these different accounts, it is clear that Sixtus joined the Franciscan order at the age of nine. He studied in Chieri, near Turin, and then at the University of Padua. After he received his doctorate in theology in 1444, Sixtus lectured in Padua, Perugia, Bologna, Siena, Pavia, and Florence. Between 1462 and 1471, he wrote three theological treatises. These treatises were based on debates in which he had argued the Franciscan position on God's will (*de futuris contingentibus*; on future contingencies), God's power (*de potentia Dei*), and the sanctity of Christ's blood (*de sanguine Christi*) before the Resurrection. Earning wide acclaim for his intellect, he rose in the ranks of the Franciscan order.

Sixtus served as dean of the Franciscan house at Padua in 1449. In 1460, he was elected minister of the Franciscan order in Genoa and was appointed to the positions of vicar to the minister general of the Franciscans and procurator general of the Franciscans in Rome. He became the minister of the Roman province in 1462. Two years later, in 1464, he attained the highest rank in the Franciscan order, minister general, where he re-ceived praise as a reformer. His distinguished career led Pope Paul II to elevate him to cardinal in September, 1467.

Life's Work

After a short tenure as cardinal, Francesco della Rovere was elected pope on August 9, 1471. With his modest upbringing and long, dedicated career in the Franciscan order, the newly elected Sixtus IV lacked influence in European politics and at the Papal court. To compensate, he filled the College of Cardinals with family members and is known today for his blatant nepotism. He elevated his nephews Giuliano della Rovere, the future Pope Julius II, and Pietro Riario to the cardinalate in 1471. Sixtus also nominated Girolamo Basso della Rovere, Raffaele Sansoni Riario, and Cristoforo della Rovere for the cardinalate. Eventually, the pope selected a total of six nephews as cardinals, married three into eminent families, and employed other relatives in the curia.

As pope, Sixtus focused his attention on threats to Rome and the Papal States, such as that of the Turks. In an effort to extend his authority and to expand the territory of the Papal States to Florence, Sixtus and his nephew, Cardinal Raffaele Riario, along with members of a wealthy Florentine family, the Pazzi, devised a plan to destabilize the influential Medici family. On April 26, 1478, Giuliano de' Medici was stabbed to death during services at the Florence cathedral, and his brother, the powerful Lorenzo de' Medici, was wounded. Despite the death of Giuliano, the plan ultimately failed and the Medici retained their power. The infamous incident is now known as the Pazzi Conspiracy.

Sixtus is also recognized for his promotion of Franciscan interests and for his ardent devotion to the Virgin Mary. He promoted the cult of the Madonna by establishing the feast of the Presentation of the Virgin in the Temple, by encouraging devotion to the Rosary, and, most important, by promoting the controversial doctrine of the Immaculate Conception and recognizing it as a feast day (December 8). Although not interested in antiquity personally, Sixtus nevertheless supported Humanist scholars and reopened the Roman Academy, a circle of Humanists devoted to studying and celebrating Rome's classical past. The Roman Academy had been considered dangerous and its members had been imprisoned during the reign of the previous pope, Paul II.

Sixtus IV. (Hulton|Archive by Getty Images)

In 1475, Sixtus presided over the Holy Year, or Jubilee, in which pilgrims received special indulgences for visiting churches in Rome. The Jubilee of 1475 created the impetus for Sixtus to refurbish Rome. His art and architectural projects were ambitious. He established the Capitoline Museum, the first public collection of antiquities in Europe, which opened on December 14, 1471. Sixtus's urban renovations included the improvement of the streets of Rome and the city's main aqueduct, the Aqua Vergine, and the construction of a bridge across the Tiber. The bridge, called the Ponte Sisto, was the first bridge built over the Tiber since antiquity.

Although Pope Nicholas V founded the Vatican Library, Sixtus was responsible for enlarging and decorating the library and increasing the holdings of the institution. He also ordered the building and decoration of the Hospital of Santo Spirito, which featured an extensive fresco cycle of the pope's life. Additionally, Sixtus founded, restored, or rebuilt more than thirty churches in the Christian capital, including Santa Maria del Popolo, Santa Maria della Pace, and SS. Quirico e Giulitta.

The Sistine Chapel is Sixtus's most famous commission. Completed in 1482, the chapel was decorated with sixteen frescoed narrative scenes that contained twenty-five biblical episodes. A team of artists, including Pietro Perugino, Ghirlandaio, Sandro Botticelli, Cosimo Rosselli, and Luca Signorelli completed the wall decoration. Sixtus's art and architectural patronage extended outside the city of Rome and included projects in Savona and Assisi. He died on August 12, 1484.

SIGNIFICANCE

Unlike many Renaissance popes, Sixtus IV ascended the Papacy not through noble birth and family connections, but through his monastic career. As pope, Sixtus tried to expand the Papal States, to stave off the Turkish threat, and to champion the interests of the Franciscan order.

The most significant contribution of his papacy, though, is his ambitious art and architectural patronage. The sheer breadth of Sixtus's commissions had never been seen in Rome. Unlike his predecessors, Sixtus completed many of his impressive architectural monuments during his tenure as pope, and many were finished before the 1475 Jubilee.

Moreover, Sixtus's extensive patronage inspired his nephew, Julius II. Julius II learned the power of art from his uncle. Nearly thirty years after Sixtus had commissioned the building of the Sistine Chapel, Julius II hired Michelangelo to paint the now-famous ceiling.

—*Jill Elizabeth Blondin*

FURTHER READING

Ettlinger, Leopold S. *The Sistine Chapel Before Michelangelo.* New York: Oxford University Press, 1965. Demonstrates how the frescoes commissioned by Sixtus for the Sistine Chapel represent the legitimization of papal power.

Howe, Eunice D. *The Hospital of Santo Spirito and Pope Sixtus IV.* New York: Garland Press, 1978. This investigation, in which the author establishes the autobiographical nature and sources of the fresco cycle at the Hospital of Santo Spirito, remains the most complete examination of this ambitious project.

Lee, Egmont. *Sixtus IV and Men of Letters.* Rome: Edizioni di Storia e Letteratura, 1978. This book focuses on the Humanists and the intellectual atmosphere in Rome during Sixtus's reign. The first chapter provides excellent biographical information about Sixtus.

Partridge, Loren. *The Art of Renaissance Rome, 1400-1600.* New York: Harry N. Abrams, 1996. Discusses several of Sixtus's projects, including the Vatican Library and Santa Maria del Popolo.

Stinger, Charles L. *The Renaissance in Rome.* Bloomington: Indiana University Press, 1998. Provides general information about Sixtus's papacy, including his art and architectural patronage and his relationship with his cardinal nephews.

Weiss, Roberto. *The Medals of Pope Sixtus IV (1471-1484)*. Rome: Edizioni di Storia e Letteratura, 1961. Documents and reproduces the medals commissioned during Sixtus's reign, medals that celebrate his coronation as well as urban improvements. Also discusses medal portraits of Sixtus as the visual sources for other images of the pope.

See also: Sandro Botticelli; Julius II; Lorenzo de' Medici; Michelangelo; Girolamo Savonarola; Sixtus V; Tomás de Torquemada.
Related articles in *Great Events from History: The Renaissance & Early Modern Era, 1454-1600:* 1469-1492: Rule of Lorenzo de' Medici; 1473-1600: Witch-Hunts and Witch Trials; 1477-1482: Work Begins on the Sistine Chapel; April 26, 1478: Pazzi Conspiracy; November 1, 1478: Establishment of the Spanish Inquisition; 1508-1512 and 1534-1541: Michelangelo Paints the Sistine Chapel.

Sixtus V
Italian pope (1585-1590)

Sixtus V reorganized the curia, increased the efficiency of the Vatican's administrative offices, made improvements to the urban fabric of Rome, and brought law and order to the Papal States. These achievements, along with significant additions to St. Peter's and the Vatican, Lateran, and Quirinal Palaces, enhanced the Papacy's prestige.

Born: December 13, 1521; Grottamare, Ancona, Papal States (now in Italy)
Died: August 27, 1590; Rome, Papal States (now in Italy)
Also known as: Felice Peretti (given name); Felice Peretti di Montalto
Areas of achievement: Religion and theology, architecture, government and politics

Early Life

Sixtus V was born Felice Peretti in a small village on Italy's Adriatic coast. Two generations earlier, his family had emigrated from Dalmatia because of the threat of Turkish invasion and settled in Montalto. They were dislocated further when the duke of Urbino's troops sacked the town in 1518 during war with Leo X, forcing Felice's father, Piergentile Peretto, to flee to the nearby borough of Grottamare, where Peretti was born.

The refugee family was of humble circumstances. Piergentile worked as a gardener or peasant farmer, and among other chores, Peretti tended the pigs as a young boy. Peretti's uncle, Fra Salvatore, however, belonged to the (Franciscan) Minorite convent in Montalto, and the nine-year-old child was taken there to be educated.

At the age of twelve, Peretti became a novice in the order. Continuing his studies in Bologna and Ferrara, he earned a doctorate in theology. He was ordained at Siena in 1547, where he became rector of his convent three years later. Impressing those around him with his eloquence and administrative talents, he was soon patronized by a circle of powerful Counter-Reformationist clerics, including Cardinal Carafa (the future Paul IV), Cardinal Antonio Ghislieri (later Pope Pius V), Saint Philip Neri, and Saint Ignatius of Loyola. A high point in his early career as a preacher came in 1552, when he delivered the Lenten sermons in Rome. In 1553, he was named rector of the convent of San Lorenzo in Naples, and rector of the Frari in Venice in 1556. The next year, he was appointed as an inquisitor in Venice but proved so harsh that civic leaders succeeded in having him recalled from that post in 1560.

Life's Work

For better or worse, rigor and autocratic severity remained Peretti's hallmarks throughout his career. In 1565, he served as a papal legate accompanying Cardinal Ugo Buoncompagni (who would become Pope Gregory XIII) on a mission to investigate charges of heresy against Archbishop Bartolomé de Carranza of Toledo, but he alienated Buoncompagni and the two remained lifelong enemies. Nevertheless, Peretti retained his circle of powerful benefactors and received the bishopric of Sant' Agata dei Goti in the Kingdom on Naples (1566) after his friend Ghislieri ascended to the throne of Saint Peter as Pius V. Pius named Peretti vicar-general of the Franciscans, and on May 17, 1570, he made him a cardinal with the titular church of San Simeone.

During the years of Gregory XIII's pontificate, which followed Pius's death in May, 1572, Cardinal Peretti, or

Felice Peretti di Montalto, as he was known at that time, wisely distanced himself from public affairs, devoting himself to art collecting and study, most notably the works of Gratian and Saint Ambrose. During this period, he first employed Domenico Fontana in 1576 as architect for his Villa Montalto (now Villa Massimi) near Santa Maria Maggiore in Rome.

Despite Peretti's long absence from the counsels of state, the conclave that elected him pope on April 24, 1585, was relatively short, lasting only two weeks. During Gregory XIII's last years, the treasury had languished on the verge of depletion, while the Papal States and Rome itself were rife with banditry, violence, and corruption. Indeed, the circumstances seemed to call for the fierce energies of a disciplinarian such as Peretti, who took the name Sixtus after his Franciscan predecessor, Sixtus IV. The new pope, Sixtus V, had little reason to love the Roman barons whose lawlessness had helped create the current conditions. His own nephew, Francesco, had been murdered in 1581 because one of them, Giordano Orsini, coveted Francesco's famously beautiful wife. Not only did Sixtus confront and intimidate Orsini, but in order to suppress bands of armed brigands, often retainers of aristocratic clans, he began to enforce the prohibition against carrying deadly weapons. Vowing that "while I live, every criminal must die," he ordered four young men hanged for such offenses in Rome on the day before his coronation.

By vigorous prosecution, Sixtus made his territories the safest in Christendom. Gaining the cooperation of neighboring states, he prevented outlaw armies from finding refuge across those borders. Then he began to exterminate them ruthlessly. At the same time, Sixtus rebuilt the Papacy's wealth by confiscating lands held by dubious claims, by heavy taxation with strict collection methods, by debasing the coinage, by floating loans, and by perfecting the art of selling appointments to ecclesiastical office. Despite huge engineering and architectural expenditures, he left the papal treasury the wealthiest in Europe, with an estimated 4.6 million gold and silver crowns. Shortly before his death, he disbursed 500,000 crowns for the relief of the Roman poor, but his treasure kept so much local money out of circulation that it caused a deep recession. Along with his severity, this made him so hated that after his death, the Roman people pulled down his commemorative statue.

Within the Vatican, Sixtus's love of order led him to reform the College of Cardinals into a more efficient administrative body. On December 3, 1586, he issued the bull *Postquam verus*, limiting the administration to a maximum of seventy persons and dividing them into fifteen congregations, each overseeing some aspect of faith, instruction, and observance, or charged with supervising some temporal matter within the Papal States. Other clerical measures included regularly inspecting monasteries and requiring bishops to appear periodically at the Vatican to account for their administration. The only exception to Sixtus's stringency was his indulgence of his own family, especially his granting cardinalship to his grandnephew Alessandro Damasceni Peretti, then just fifteen years old, which angered many.

Sixtus's construction projects rivaled his administrative achievements. Employing Fontana, Giacomo della Porta, and others, he commissioned aqueducts and fountains that brought water to Rome's undeveloped districts, set about draining the Pontine marshes near the city, laid out a network of straight thoroughfares connecting several of the most important churches in Rome, built a new Vatican Library, completed the dome of St. Peter's to the lantern, and relocated ancient obelisks to adorn Christian sites, most notably in the piazza of St. Peter's.

Sixtus V. (Hulton|Archive by Getty Images)

Rebuilding Rome as the glorious capital of Christendom was part of Sixtus's international policy, a way of responding to the dual challenges posed by the power of Protestantism and Islam. His family having suffered from Turkish expansion, he dreamed of recapturing the Holy Land but was unable to interest King Philip II of Spain in a crusade. Cautiously, he supported Philip's Spanish Armada, which was sent to invade Queen Elizabeth I's Protestant England in 1588. Whereas France was torn by religious strife, however, Sixtus's final act was to resist Philip's plans for replacing the Protestant king Henry IV of France (whom had previously been declared a heretic), with a Spanish partisan.

SIGNIFICANCE

The loss of France to Protestantism would have been a grave blow to the Catholic Church, but Sixtus clung to the hope that the capable Henry would embrace the Roman faith, which he did after the pope's death in 1590. Sixtus's final opposition to Philip II helped to save Europe from eventual Habsburg domination, since an independent France remained to check the overweening power of Spain.

At home, by curbing the power of local barons, standardizing the rule of law, and imposing uniform observance of ordinances, weights, measures, and trade practices throughout the Papal States, he undermined the feudal mentality by introducing the concept of unified, centralized state authority. Indeed Sixtus's curia, organized rationally and operating with consistency and relative speed, provided a model for bureaucratic administration in the newly emerging secular nation-states.

Although Sixtus's urban plans were only partly realized, they established a prototype for the layout of grand capital cities such as Paris and Washington, D.C., with broad avenues creating impressive vistas and converging on important focal points.

—*James Carlton Hughes*

FURTHER READING

Anker, Andrew. "Il Papa e Il Duce: Sixtus V's and Mussolini's Plans for Rome, Capital of the World." *Journal of Urban Design* 1, no. 2 (June, 1996): 165-178. Examines the ideological strategy behind Sixtus's alterations and relocations of ancient monuments. Compares this with Mussolini's urban interventions.

Giedion, Sigfried. "Sixtus V and the Planning of Baroque Rome." *Architectural Review* 111 (April, 1952): 217-226. Concise overview stressing Sixtus's awareness of Rome as a "complex organism in which aesthetic and social factors were inseparably interlocked."

Hall, Marcia. "Sixtus V." In *After Raphael*. New York: Cambridge University Press, 1999. Focuses on Sixtus's approach to using ancient remains and classicizing art for asserting the primacy of Christian Rome and the popes.

Mandel, Corinne. *Sixtus V and the Lateran Palace*. Rome: Istituto Poligrafico e Zecca dello Stato, 1994. Gives careful analysis to the frescoes Sixtus commissioned for the Lateran, arguing that they refer to his ideals as pope and to his own "good works."

Pastor, Ludwig. *History of the Popes from the Close of the Middle Ages*. 40 vols. Edited and translated by Ralph Kerr. London: Kegan Paul, Trench, Trubner, 1932. Volume 21 remains the most thorough, richly annotated biography of Sixtus.

Polverini Fosi, Irene. "Justice and Its Image: Political Propaganda and Judicial Reality in the Pontificate of Sixtus V." *Sixteenth Century Journal* 24, no. 1 (1993): 75-95. Questions the real effectiveness of Sixtus's juridical measures and examines the internal contradictions in his policies.

SEE ALSO: Elizabeth I; Gregory XIII; Henry IV; Saint Ignatius of Loyola; Saint Philip Neri; Philip II; Pius V; Sixtus IV.

RELATED ARTICLE in *Great Events from History: The Renaissance & Early Modern Era, 1454-1600:* 1599: Castrati Sing in the Sistine Chapel Choir.

FIRST DUKE OF SOMERSET
English duke and lord protector

*Edward Seymour, first duke of Somerset, was an
ambitious nobleman of Tudor England who became
governor of his nephew, the young king Edward VI. His
appointment as lord protector of England initiated
Protestant religious practice that sparked rebellions
and led to his overthrow.*

BORN: c. 1506; England
DIED: January 22, 1552; London, England
ALSO KNOWN AS: the Protector; Sir Edward Seymour;
  Viscount Beauchamp of Hache; Earl of Hertford;
  Edward Seymour (given name)
AREAS OF ACHIEVEMENT: Government and politics,
  religion and theology

EARLY LIFE

One of ten children born to Sir John Seymour and his
wife, Lady Margery Wentworth, Edward Seymour, his
younger brother Thomas, and younger sister Jane were
significant figures during the reign of Henry VIII.

Because of his father's connections, young Edward
was attached to the court of Henry VIII's sister, Mary I,
and attended Oxford and Cambridge Universities. In
1523, he accompanied Charles Brandon, the first duke of
Suffolk, to France, where he was knighted. He had married Katherine Fillol, whom he later abandoned on
grounds of adultery, and then married Anne Stanhope, a
woman of radical reformist (or Protestant) religious
views, before Fillol's death.

As one of Henry VIII's favorites, Seymour played
sports and cards with Henry and benefitted from loans
and grants of land from him, but his rise in influence accompanied the fall of Henry's second queen, Anne
Boleyn, and the king's marriage to Jane Seymour on May
30, 1536. Seymour was elevated to viscount beauchamp
of Hache, which was followed in 1537 with the title earl
of Hertford. He was connected to Henry's powerful minister, Thomas Cromwell, through the marriage of Cromwell's son Gregory and Seymour's sister Elizabeth. The
birth of Prince Edward (Edward VI) on October 12,
1537, increased Seymour's prestige because of his status
as the prince's oldest uncle; his prestige did not lessen as
a result of Queen Jane's death on October 24, 1537. In
1539, he journeyed to France to oversee the defense of
Guisne (now Guînes) and Calais, where he met Henry
V's future and fourth wife, Anne of Cleves, and returned
with her to London.

LIFE'S WORK

Additional honors flowed Seymour's way during the latter years of Henry VIII's reign, as Seymour became a
Knight of the Garter in January, 1541, and lord high admiral and warder of the Scottish Marches in 1542. He
participated in military campaigns against Scotland and
France (1544-1546) and was present with the king at the
defense of Boulogne in France (1545). Seymour's forces
burned Edinburgh in May, 1545.

In March, 1546, Seymour once again supervised the
strengthening of Guisne and Calais, but Henry's deterio-
rating health brought Seymour back to England, where he
became involved in the complex power struggle during
the final months of the king's life. The exact workings of
these maneuvers are still the subject of scholarly debate.

Several factions were involved in these intrigues: a
Conservative Catholic group headed by Bishop Stephen
Gardiner and the Howard family, and a Reformist Protestant group composed of Seymour's supporters and
Archbishop Thomas Cranmer. As the oldest uncle of Edward, prince of Wales, Seymour wielded considerable
influence, and he had been instrumental in the trial and
execution of Henry Howard, earl of Surrey. Henry's will
designated sixteen executors and councillors for Edward
VI; Seymour was one of the sixteen, and Henry had given
Seymour the will on December 30, 1546.

Along with his chief ally William Paget, a secretary of
state, Seymour made a bid for power by concealing news
of Henry's death on January 28, 1547, for three days. On
January 31, 1547, the councillors named Seymour lord
protector of England and governor of the young king.
Even greater authority was granted Seymour on February 4, 1547, when Edward VI and thirteen councillors
confirmed these powers through Edward VI's minority.
Shortly thereafter, he became lord high treasurer on February 10, 1547, and was elevated to duke of Somerset on
February 16, 1547.

Disregarding the instructions of Henry's will, Seymour expanded membership of the council and procured
titles and grants of land for himself and his supporters.
Symbolic of his tremendous power, Seymour had a
prominent role in Edward VI's coronation procession
and ceremony on February 19, 1547, as he and Archbishop Cranmer jointly placed the crown on the nine-
year-old king's head.

Early scholarly works characterized Seymour as the
"good duke" who held enlightened views on social is-

sues, patronized education, literature, and drama, and was a pious Protestant in his private religious views. Scholarship since the mid-1970's, however, has focused on three main topics: religious change, military engagements with Scotland and France, and the rebellions of 1549, demonstrating that Seymour was a grasping, materialistic man.

During Seymour's period as protector (1547-1549), no individual was burned for heresy, but greater control was exercised over the English church, which moved toward Protestantism. Visible changes promulgated by Seymour and Cranmer involved removal of images from churches and the declaration that practices such as lighting candles were superstitious. Also, the number of holy days was reduced and the clergy were allowed to marry. The first Book of Common Prayer (1549) and the Act of Uniformity (1549) mandated that the entire worship service be in English, and many aspects of baptismal and marriage services were abrogated.

Military involvement with France centered on retaining Boulogne and Calais and on issues surrounding the 1543 betrothal of Prince Edward and Mary, Queen of Scots. During the summer of 1547, Seymour invaded Scotland and defeated its troops at the Battle of Pinkie. The Scots had disavowed the betrothal of 1543 and initiated discussions for an alliance and marriage between Mary, Queen of Scots and the French dauphin. French troops sent to Scotland attacked Somerset's army, and by July 7, 1548, the Franco-Scottish marriage negotiations were completed and Mary, Queen of Scots was sent to France. On August 8, 1549, France declared war on England, and because England was racked by internal rebellions, the French had success and acquired Boulogne on March 28, 1550, through a treaty. The costly military operations led Seymour to continue to debase the coinage of the realm, as had Henry in order to cover the costs.

The extension of Seymour's status as protector—a position that could be terminated by Edward VI only and not automatically on the king's eighteenth birthday—caused Seymour's jealous brother Thomas Seymour to plot against him. The protector moved against Thomas, who was arrested on January 17, 1549, condemned by an act of attainder, and executed March 19, 1549.

Other problems emerged, as population increases put pressure on land and resources, which in July and August led to rural disturbances and outright rebellions in Oxfordshire and Buckinghamshire, including Kett's Rebellion. These disturbances were subdued by government forces; similar disturbances in Norfolk and Suffolk were ended by negotiations and military actions. Rebellion in Devon and Cornwall was sparked by protests against the use of the new Prayer Book and the English language in worship services. Troops that Seymour had intended for use in Scotland were used to put down that rebellion.

In early October of 1549, members of the council in London moved against Seymour because of his handling of the rebellions and his rejections of their advice. Seymour was arrested on October 11, 1549, and placed in the Tower of London, where he confessed to twenty-nine articles critical of his rule. The leader of the opposition, John Dudley, earl of Warwick and lord president of the council, began to consolidate power, but he needed support against the Catholic faction, so Seymour was released from the Tower on February 6, 1550, and pardoned by Edward VI on February 18, 1550. After he returned to the council on April 10, 1550, rivalry developed between Dudley, who had become duke of Northumberland, and Seymour, who sought to regain power. Seymour was arrested on October 11, 1551, tried in December, 1551, and convicted of a felony for assembling men for the purpose of creating a riot. He was executed on January 22, 1552, and his body was buried in St. Peter's Chapel in the Tower of London.

SIGNIFICANCE

Seymour's religious policies, a sharp break from those of Henry VIII, initiated a distinctively Protestant influence, which encouraged iconoclasm's destruction of a substantial amount of religious art. After Seymour's fall, the duke of Northumberland continued these policies until their reversal under the Catholic queen Mary I.

In foreign policy, Seymour's focus on the traditional rivalries with Scotland and France resulted in military conflict, crushing debt, the strengthening of the French influence in Scotland, and loss of Boulogne to the French. This forced Northumberland to pursue a foreign policy of peace and economic retrenchment. The 1549 rebellion caused by economic problems and radical religious change exposed Seymour's weakness as a politician. Suspected of being too sympathetic with the "lower orders" of society and granting inappropriate concessions to the rebels in the east, his rivals managed to strip him of power. Although briefly restored to the circles of power, his overweening ambition to reacquire his old status caused his final downfall and execution.

—Mark C. Herman

FURTHER READING

Bush, M. L. *The Government Policy of Protector Somerset*. Montreal: McGill-Queen's University Press, 1975. The first major revision of the view of Seymour as the "good duke," which focuses on the Scottish war and religious change.

Hoak, D. E. *The King's Council in the Reign of Edward VI*. Cambridge, England: Cambridge University Press, 1976. An extensive analysis of the council and the policy of Seymour as Protector Somerset.

Loach, Jennifer. *Edward VI*. Edited by George Bernard and Penry Williams. New Haven, Conn.: Yale University Press, 1999. Not strictly a biography, this work examines Seymour's policies and his relationship with Edward VI.

MacCulloch, Diarmaid. *Tudor Church Militant: Edward VI and the Protestant Reformation*. London: Allen Lane, 1999. This work examines the key personalities and policies connected with the extensive religious changes of Edward VI's church in which Seymour played a prominent part.

Shagan, Ethan. "Protector Somerset and the 1549 Rebellions: New Sources and New Perspectives." *English Historical Review* 114, no. 455 (February, 1999): 34-63. An analysis of Seymour's handling of the Kett's Rebellion, along with copies of nine letters related to negotiations with rebel leaders.

SEE ALSO: Anne of Cleves; Anne Boleyn; Thomas Cranmer; Edward VI; Elizabeth I; Stephen Gardiner; Lady Jane Grey; Henry VIII; Jane Seymour.
RELATED ARTICLES in *Great Events from History: The Renaissance & Early Modern Era, 1454-1600:* 1544-1628: Anglo-French Wars; 1549: Kett's Rebellion.

SONNI ʿALĪ
King of Songhai Empire (r. 1464-1492)

Sonni ʿAlī, a ruthless ruler but also an effective military strategist, laid the foundation for the expansion of the Songhai Empire into the last great state of the western Sudan. The empire would control major trade routes in the region through the sixteenth century.

BORN: c. early fifteenth century; Songhai Empire (now in Mali)
DIED: November 6, 1492; Gurma (now in Mali)
ALSO KNOWN AS: Sonni ʿAlī Ber; The Chi (Shi); ʿAlī the Great; Sunni Ali
AREAS OF ACHIEVEMENT: Warfare and conquest, military, government and politics

EARLY LIFE

Little is known about the early life of Sonni ʿAlī (sawn-EE-ah-LEE), who would rule over the Songhai Empire, an ancient state that developed during the first millennium on the eastern bend of the Niger River. In the thirteenth century, the Songhai people were incorporated into the Mali Empire, but Malian power faded at the close of the fourteenth century, leaving the Songhai to expand their own empire. Sonni ʿAlī's father earlier had raided and sacked the Malian capital.

LIFE'S WORK

Sonni ʿAlī's entire reign was devoted to warfare. He was an excellent strategist and tactician and had a gift for selecting capable officers to carry out his will. His martial abilities, combined with his reputation as a magician, gave him an aura of invincibility, an immense advantage in western Africa, where psychological warfare was often more decisive than having many warriors. He is said to have never lost a battle.

Sonni ʿAlī's strategy of conquest centered on control of the Niger River and its banks, from which he made incursions inland. The key to Sonni ʿAlī's success was mobility, and his most important battles took place usually on land that bordered the river. Songhai's riverain navy consisted of warriors in large dugout canoes who served as marines, attacking from the water or on land as ferried infantrymen.

Sonni ʿAlī also used cavalry as part of his strategy of mobility. The cavalry provided land support for water-borne marine assaults and also made quick sorties inland. Cavalrymen were drawn from the Songhai nobility, with reckless bravery the surest avenue for advancement up the ranks of the officer corps. The king himself led the cavalry.

Sonni ʿAlī's earliest campaigns were directed southward from the right bank of the Niger bend. Between 1464 and 1468, he attacked along a wide front, defeating the Dogon, Mossi, and Fulbe. Beyond its immediate rim, the southern front was raided more than it was conquered. Sonni ʿAlī struck deep into Mossi country (what is now Burkina Faso) on two occasions, returning with rich spoils. He could not hold land far from the powerful arm of the canoes, however.

The region to the southwest, upriver on the Niger, was vulnerable to conquest. Moving through the inland delta region, Sonni ʿAlī took the city of Jenne (Djenné) in 1473, a city that had controlled the interior trade routes for gold. Tradition states that the siege began seven years, seven months, and seven days before the fall of the city. After famine had ravaged both sides and the Songhai were preparing to withdraw, the starving city capitulated. Its people were accorded honors, and no massacre took place. Sonni ʿAlī married the mother of the city's chief as a sign of respect.

Beyond Jenne lay the remnants of Mali, which Sonni ʿAlī attacked twice with mixed results. Songhai power proved overwhelming on the savanna, but in the tropical-forest region, Songhai cavalry could not be deployed effectively against the deadly Malian archers. Also, the canoes were hindered by a rough river. Ultimately, the Songhai annexed the area downriver of what is now called Ségou, which became an uneasy border between the two empires.

Sonni ʿAlī's conquests on the north side of the Niger began in 1468, when he took the city of Timbuktu. In these battles, his major adversaries were the Tuareg, the tribal nomads of the Sahara. The Songhai military was not equipped to fight in the desert, as were the Tuareg, but in the cities, the Songhai prevailed and the Tuareg were vulnerable. Of the great cities that the Tuareg controlled, namely Timbuktu, Tadmekka, and Walata, Sonni ʿAlī was able to sack Timbuktu and destroy the ancient city of Tadmekka, scattering its inhabitants.

Sonni ʿAlī is best remembered for his conquest of Timbuktu. A large section of the city's ulema, the ruling oligarchy of religious functionaries and scholars, left for self-imposed exile to Walata before the Songhai arrived. Sonni ʿAlī considered this a personal affront, and he vented his wrath on those who stayed behind, particularly the remaining ulema. Although the city offered no resistance, Timbuktu was put to the sword, pillaged, and partially burned.

During subsequent years, the breach Sonni ʿAlī had opened with the intellectuals of Timbuktu broadened, and the king continued to persecute the ulema. In this lopsided conflict, the ulema nevertheless had time on their side, so they defamed Sonni ʿAlī. Among the allegations recorded by chroniclers was that he castrated venerable old men and disemboweled pregnant women. In one anecdote, Sonni ʿAlī threw a baby into a grain mortar, forced the baby's mother to grind her child to death with a pestle, and then fed the child's remains to horses.

The devout Muslims of Timbuktu resented Sonni ʿAlī in another way. Although nominally Muslim, Sonni ʿAlī was one of the most famous magicians in African history, with charms as his specialty. He was thought to be able to turn himself into a vulture and to make his soldiers invisible. Much of his political power was based on his reputation both for magic and for being an intermediary between the corporeal and spiritual worlds.

In 1477, thousands of men dug a canal for the Songhai canoes to navigate to Walata. This was a huge undertaking, an effort that would have dwarfed the building of the Suez and Panama Canals had it been completed. Work continued until 1483, but when a Mossi raid distracted Sonni ʿAlī, he hurried off to meet the invaders. Work on the canal ended.

Significance

Sonni ʿAlī spent the last few years of his reign fighting in Gurma, south of the Niger bend. On November 6, 1492, as he was returning from a campaign against the Fulbe, he is reported to have drowned after falling from his horse while crossing a swollen river. Another account states that he was assassinated by one of his lieutenants, Mohammed Ture, who would become Songhai king Mohammed I Askia in 1493. Subsequently, Muhammed Ture overthrew Sonni ʿAlī's son and established the Askia Dynasty by using the base established by Sonni ʿAlī, making the Songhai Empire the greatest state in sixteenth century Africa and one of the century's largest empires not only in Africa but also in the world.

—*Richard L. Smith*

Further Reading

Hunwick, John. *Shariʿa in Songhay.* New York: Oxford University Press, 1985. Some years after Muhammad Ture assumed power, he interviewed a noted North African cleric with the intention of justifying his usurpation of the kingship. Embedded in Muhammad Ture's questions is valuable information on Sonni ʿAlī's life and reign.

_____. *Timbuktu and the Songhay Empire: Al-Sadi's Ta'rikh al-Sudan Down to 1613 and Other Contemporary Documents.* New York: E. J. Brill, 1999. From the don of Songhai studies, this work includes a lengthy interpretative essay and a fully annotated translation of the most important chronicle on the history of the Songhai. Sonni ʿAlī gets his own chapter. The place to start for research on this subject.

Kaba, Lansime. "The Pen, the Sword, and the Crown: Islam and Revolution in Songhay Reconsidered, 1464-1493." *Journal of African History* 25 (1984): 241-

256. Helpful analysis of Sonni ʿAlī's reign, focusing on the rise of militant Islam and the resulting stress within the Songhai military that led to the end of Sunni Islam in Songhai.

Saad, Elias N. *Social History of Timbuktu: The Role of Muslim Scholars and Notables, 1400-1900.* New York: Cambridge University Press, 1983. Assesses Sonni ʿAlī's infamous struggle with the Timbuktu ulema.

Thornton, John K. *Warfare in Atlantic Africa, 1500-1800.* London: UCL Press, 1999. Provides a good overview of West African warfare and a helpful description of the Songhai military.

SEE ALSO: Amina Sarauniya Zazzua; Askia Daud; Leo Africanus; Muḥammad ibn ʿAbd al-Karīm al-Maghīlī; Mohammed I Askia.

RELATED ARTICLES in *Great Events from History: The Renaissance & Early Modern Era, 1454-1600:* c. 1464-1591: Songhai Empire Dominates the Western Sudan; 1493-1528: Reign of Mohammed I Askia.

HERNANDO DE SOTO
Spanish conquistador

After playing a prominent role in the conquest of Nicaragua and Peru, de Soto led the 1539-1542 expedition that explored what became the southeastern United States. He also was the first European discoverer of the Mississippi River.

BORN: c. 1496; Jérez de los Caballeros?, Spain
DIED: May 21, 1542; along the Mississippi River (now near Ferriday, Louisiana)
AREAS OF ACHIEVEMENT: Exploration, warfare and conquest

EARLY LIFE

Hernando de Soto (ehr-NAHN-doh day SOH-toh) was the second son of Francisco Méndez de Soto and Leonor Arias Tinoco (the proper family name is Soto but the English-speaking world calls him de Soto). The family was lower nobility, and Hernando received some education, although he was always by temperament a soldier and adventurer.

De Soto could expect to inherit little from his father's small estate and thus sailed to Central America in 1513-1514 with Don Pedro Arias Dávila (called Pedrarias), the new governor of Panama. Pedrarias allowed his followers to ravage Central America as long as they respected his authority. In these lawless conditions, de Soto flourished. Above average in height, bearded, and darkly handsome, he was vigorous, brave, and aggressive, always in the vanguard. His spoils in land and Central American Indian workers made him wealthy.

By 1517, de Soto was a captain. He soon formed a partnership with Hernán Ponce de León and Francisco Campañón to share equally in the booty that fortune might bring them. They helped conquer Nicaragua in 1524. Campañón died in 1527, but de Soto and Ponce de León stayed on in Nicaragua. De Soto served a year as magistrate of León, although temperamentally unsuited to administration. He also became ambitious for his own governorship, but Pedrarias blocked those aspirations in Nicaragua.

LIFE'S WORK

In 1530, de Soto agreed to join forces with Francisco Pizarro in the conquest of Peru. When he met Pizarro at Puná Island in late 1531, de Soto had two ships, one hundred men, and some horses. He expected to be Pizarro's second in command and to receive an independent governorship. Pizarro gave de Soto charge of the vanguard. On a scouting foray inland to Cajas, de Soto seized several hundred Indian women and turned them over to his men. The Spaniards also learned at Cajas that the Inca Empire had been torn apart by a great civil war and that Atahualpa, leader of the victorious faction, was encamped with his army at Cajamarca not too far away.

When the Spaniards arrived at Cajamarca, Pizarro sent de Soto with a small detachment to greet Atahualpa. A great horseman, de Soto tried unsuccessfully to frighten the emperor, who had never seen a horse before, by riding right up to him: Atahualpa accepted Pizarro's invitation to visit the Spaniards in Cajamarca the next day. Once he was inside the city walls, they took him captive. While a hostage, Atahualpa became close to de Soto and gave him valuable gifts. De Soto was on a scouting expedition when Pizarro executed Atahualpa. On his return, de Soto criticized the execution, arguing that Atahualpa should have been sent to Spain as a prisoner rather than killed. Always punctilious about keeping bargains, de Soto was also upset that Pizarro had killed the emperor after Atahualpa had filled rooms with gold and silver, as his agreed-on ransom.

On the march from Cajamarca to the Inca capital, Cuzco, during the second half of 1533, de Soto again led the vanguard. As they neared Cuzco, he disregarded orders and rushed ahead with his small force to claim credit for occupying the city. The Indians ambushed his party at Vilcaconga, however, and only the timely arrival of reinforcements saved him. Pizarro appointed de Soto lieutenant governor of Cuzco in 1534 but replaced him by that year's end. Convinced that Pizarro would never give him an independent command in Peru, de Soto headed for Spain. He left behind Leonor Curuilloi, an Inca princess and his mistress, and their daughter Leonor. Ponce de León came from Nicaragua to manage de Soto's property.

In Spain by 1536, de Soto had 100,000 pesos with him, a reputation as a great conqueror and explorer, and a hunger to lead a new expedition. He petitioned the king. On April 20, 1537, Charles V made him governor and captain general of Cuba and Florida and gave him authority to explore and conquer the New Land at his own expense. Álvar Núñez Cabeza de Vaca, a survivor of the disastrous Panfilo de Narváez expedition to Florida, had come to Spain with tales of great riches in the New Land. De Soto tried but failed to persuade him to join the expedition. Hundreds of young adventurers rushed to enlist, however, assuming that Florida would make them rich and famous. His wife, Doña Isabel de Bobadilla (Pedrarias's daughter, whom he had married in 1536), and about seven hundred carefully chosen soldiers of fortune sailed with him to Cuba in 1538.

De Soto spent a year in Cuba to train his men and gather provisions. The expedition departed for Florida in May, 1539, with de Soto's wife remaining behind to govern Cuba. It landed at Espiritu Santo (Tampa) Bay on May 30. At the outset, de Soto discovered Juan Ortiz, a survivor of the Narváez expedition who had lived with the Indians for twelve years. Ortiz became de Soto's interpreter.

De Soto had made his fortune in Central America and Peru by plundering the Indians. He intended to do the same in Florida. When the expedition came to an Indian settlement, de Soto took the chief hostage so that the Indians would serve the Spaniards while they ravaged the village. When the expedition was ready to move on, de Soto forced the hostage chieftain to provide porters (he took neck irons and chains to Florida with this aim in mind). De Soto released the porters and chief at the next

Hernando de Soto. (Library of Congress)

village, where new hostages where seized. Those who resisted were mutilated, burned alive, or thrown to the dogs.

The Spaniards wandered through what later became Florida, Georgia, South Carolina, North Carolina, Tennessee, Alabama, Mississippi, Arkansas, Louisiana, and Texas. De Soto knew nothing of the land, nor did he have a destination in mind. He simply assumed that the Indians of the New Land would have riches to plunder. The expedition proceeded north from Tampa Bay and soon exhausted its supplies. From then on, the explorers lived off the land and Indian agriculture, plus a herd of swine that de Soto had brought in the fleet. Turning west, they reached the rich agricultural lands of the Apalachees in the Florida panhandle and stayed from October to March, 1540.

Then they marched northeast toward Cofitachequi, on the Savannah River near what became Augusta, Georgia. Their porters had died during the winter, and the Apalachees had run away before they could be enslaved. Thus, the Spaniards had to carry their own food and equipment. At Cofitachequi, they found large quantities of freshwater pearls, and de Soto himself obtained a chestful after plundering the village and burial grounds. Taking the queen hostage and thus provided with porters, de Soto headed northwest through Cherokee land in the Carolina piedmont and then turned west toward the Tennessee River. The Spanish learned about tribes rich in gold somewhere farther on but could never find them. De Soto cared nothing about mining; only plunder interested him.

In July, 1540, de Soto marched south, having learned of a rich people called Coosa (Creek territory). They were moving through Alabama, toward Mobile Bay. Disappointed by Coosa, they continued southwest and came to the Mabilas (Choctaws). At Mabila, the Indians revolted, killed twenty-two Spaniards, and burned much of the equipment, including de Soto's pearls. By then, more than one hundred of the men who had started with de Soto at Tampa Bay were dead. Although not too far north of Mobile Bay, de Soto refused to push on to the coast, fearful that his men would desert. Instead, he turned north again and occupied a Chickasaw village for winter quarters. After enduring the Spaniards for several months, the Chickasaws revolted on March 4, 1541. They set fire to the village and killed a dozen Spaniards, fifty horses, and many of the pigs. The Spanish escaped annihilation only because a sudden storm prevented the Indians from immediately renewing their attack.

Pushing westward, de Soto discovered the Rio Grande (Mississippi) on May 8, 1541, built barges, and crossed the mighty river on June 18 a little above its junction with the Arkansas. The Spaniards wandered for two months through central Arkansas. De Soto sent a scouting party to the Ozarks after rumors of gold there. They spent the severe winter of 1541-1542 at Utiangue in south-central Arkansas.

Battered and discouraged, the expedition left Utiangue on March 6, 1542, and followed the Ouachita River south through Louisiana to the Mississippi. De Soto fell ill with a fever. Realizing that his end was near, he named Luis de Moscoso, another veteran of Peru, to succeed him. The explorer died on May 21, 1542, to the relief of those who wanted to abandon the quest. His men sank his body in the Mississippi to hide it from the Indians.

The men decided to march overland to Mexico and traveled several hundred miles into Texas. After four months and no sign of Mexico, they turned back. They spent their last winter near the Mississippi at Aminoya (northwest of Natchez). In the spring of 1543, they built barges, and floating down the river to the Gulf of Mexico in July, they then sailed west. Clad in rags and animal skins when they arrived in Mexico in September, 1543,

about one-third survived of those who had started at Tampa Bay.

SIGNIFICANCE

De Soto evokes conflicting impressions. On one hand, he was certainly one of the bravest Spaniards of his time. He was gallant and courageous, the epitome of the explorer and conquistador. On any expedition, he was always in the vanguard; in any battle, he was in the front ranks. He amassed a huge fortune in Nicaragua and Peru, and he failed to do so in North America only because there were no rich Indian cities to plunder. Yet adventure, danger, and the unknown seemed to attract him more than riches. His expedition was extremely well organized. He recruited not only soldiers but also artisans, who could build boats and bridges. He raised a herd of pigs on the march so that the expedition would have meat later. Despite rugged terrain and many attacks from Indians, he held the expedition together.

On the other hand, de Soto was a plunderer, not a builder. His expedition made no effort to settle or colonize; nor did it even attempt to exploit the natural resources of the region. De Soto had learned too well the lessons under Pedrarias, and the experiences in Peru reinforced them. Perhaps he took less delight in butchery than some Spaniards, but he was ready to torture and kill in his quest for the riches of Florida. Indians' lives were worth little to him. Although he considered Christianization of the Indians one of his expedition's responsibilities, he did little to achieve it. Moreover, he was too stubborn and proud to end the foray despite its obvious failure to find the booty for which the Spaniards hunted.

The Spanish atrocities should not, however, obscure the achievements of the expedition. It was the first major European exploration of the North American interior and left valuable information about the North American Indians and the geography of the region. De Soto and his men left a legacy of courage, ambition, and perseverance rarely equaled as they opened the region to European expansion. The great river they discovered eventually proved to be a natural treasure more valuable than the booty de Soto sought.

—Kendall W. Brown

FURTHER READING

Bourne, Edward Gaylord, ed. *Narratives of the Career of Hernando de Soto.* Translated by Buckingham Smith. 2 vols. New York: Allerton, 1904. Reprint. New York: AMS Press, 1973. Contains English translations of the three most important chronicles of de Soto's expedition by Luis Hernández de Biedma, factor of the expedition, Rodrigo Ranjel, de Soto's secretary, and an unidentified Portuguese man from Elva.

Ewen, Charles R., and John H. Hann. *Hernando de Soto Among the Apalachee: The Archaeology of the First Winter Encampment.* Gainesville: University Press of Florida, 1998. Narrative of the discovery, excavation, and interpretation of the only known de Soto camp site. Provides historical background, detailed description of the site and what was learned from it, and new translations of the portions of the sixteenth century travel narratives relating to this camp. Includes illustrations, maps, bibliographic references, and index.

Galloway, Patricia, ed. *The Hernando de Soto Expedition: History, Historiography, and "Discovery" in the Southeast.* Lincoln: University of Nebraska Press, 1997. Anthology of essays that seeks to expand traditional studies of de Soto's expedition to discuss its broad cultural implications, as well as focus on specific details such as the daily routine and health of its members. Includes bibliographic references and index.

Hemming, John. *The Conquest of the Incas.* New York: Harcourt Brace Jovanovich, 1970. An excellent, well-written account of the conquest of Peru, with information about de Soto's role in it.

Hudson, Charles. *Knights of Spain, Warriors of the Sun: Hernando de Soto and the South's Ancient Chiefdoms.* Athens: University of Georgia Press, 1997. Study of the disastrous impact of de Soto's expedition on the Native American civilizations he encountered. Includes illustrations, maps, bibliographic references, and index.

Maynard, Theodore. *De Soto and the Conquistadores.* New York: Longmans, Green, 1930. The best biography of de Soto, although marred by some inaccuracies and omissions.

Ober, Frederick A. *Ferdinand de Soto and the Invasion of Florida.* New York: Harper and Brothers, 1906.

Based extensively on Garcilaso's narrative and aimed primarily at younger readers.

Sauer, Carl Ortwin. *Sixteenth Century North America: The Land and the People as Seen by the Europeans.* Berkeley: University of California Press, 1971. Contains a chapter on de Soto's expedition by the leading historical geographer of sixteenth century North America. Critical of de Soto's motives and behavior.

Sola y Taboada, Antonio del, and José de Rújula y de Ochotorena. *El Adelantado Hernando de Soto: Breves noticias, nuevos documentos para su biografía.* Badajoz, Spain: Ediciones Arqueros, 1929. Particularly important for its documentary appendices, that include the agreement between de Soto and Ponce de León, de Soto's capitulation for the conquest of Florida, the information about his background that he submitted to enter the Order of St. James, his will, and an inventory of his property.

United States de Soto Expedition Commission. *Final Report of the United States De Soto Expedition Commission.* Washington, D.C.: Government Printing Office, 1939. A scholarly, definitive study of the route followed by the de Soto expedition.

Vega, Garcilaso de la. *The Florida of the Inca.* Translated and edited by John Grier Varner and Jeannette Johnson Varner. Austin: University of Texas Press, 1951. The most famous of the four early chronicles of de Soto's expedition. Unlike the others, it was not written by an eyewitness and is thus more problematical.

SEE ALSO: Atahualpa; Álvar Núñez Cabeza de Vaca; Charles V; Francisco Vásquez de Coronado; Pedro Menéndez de Avilés; Pemisapan; Francisco Pizarro; Juan Ponce de León; Tascalusa.

RELATED ARTICLES in *Great Events from History: The Renaissance & Early Modern Era, 1454-1600:* 16th century: Decline of Moundville; 1532-1537: Pizarro Conquers the Incas in Peru; May 28, 1539-September 10, 1543: De Soto's North American Expedition.

EDMUND SPENSER
English writer and poet

Reflecting both Renaissance and Reformation ideals in his Christian Humanism, Spenser incorporated classical, continental, and native English poetic traditions to create in his epic The Faerie Queene, *the quintessential statement of Elizabethan national and moral consciousness.*

BORN: c. 1552; London, England
DIED: January 13, 1599; London
AREA OF ACHIEVEMENT: Literature

EARLY LIFE

Little is known about Edmund Spenser's life. He was born one of the three children of Elizabeth and John Spenser (a Lancashire gentleman by birth who had settled in London and become a free journeyman of the Merchant Taylors' Company). The family's income must have been limited, because a wealthy Lancashire family assisted with Edmund's education. At the Merchant Taylors' School from 1561 to 1569, he was influenced by the famous Humanist educator Richard Mulcaster, who imparted to Spenser the notion that a man must use his learning in the service of the public good (usually as a courtier advising his prince). During this period, Spenser demonstrated his Reformation sympathies by contributing several verse translations to *A Theater for Worldlings* (1569), a strongly anti-Catholic work.

Spenser matriculated at Pembroke Hall, Cambridge University, in 1569 as a sizar, or poor scholar; there he continued his study of the Greek and Latin classics and contemporary French and Italian literature. Spenser was also fascinated by the mystical elements in Plato and the writings of the Italian Neoplatonists Pietro Bembo and Marsilio Ficino. Spenser's Neoplatonism was always blended with staunch Protestantism, which was strengthened by Cambridge's Puritan environment. While at Cambridge, Spenser formed a friendship with Gabriel Harvey, a university don; the two shared a concern with poetic theory and hoped for a revival of English verse.

After receiving his bachelor of arts degree in 1573 and his master of arts degree in 1576, Spenser, in true Renaissance fashion, became both active and scholarly. He served as secretary to John Young, bishop of Rochester, and was later employed by Robert Dudley, the earl of Leicester, whose nephew Sir Philip Sidney was well known for his promotion of English poetry (his famous *Defence of Poesie* was published in 1580).

It is to Sidney that Spenser's first major work, *The Shepheardes Calender* (1579), is dedicated. Heralding a new movement in English verse, *The Shepheardes Calender* consists of twelve pastoral eclogues, one for each month. The classical eclogue records shepherds' songs and conversations about their simple lives. Vergil had established the form as a preparation for the greater genre of epic, dealing with war instead of love and with the founding of a great civilization. Spenser thus identified himself as England's epic poet, who would sing the praises of the nation and its sovereign: In the April Eclogue, Colin Clout (Spenser's shepherd persona) sings the beauties of the shepherdess Elisa (Elizabeth I).

Moreover, Colin Clout is a shepherd (*pastor* in Latin) in the spiritual sense; the eclogues can be read as a satiric critique of contemporary ecclesiastical practices, and the poet-shepherd, like Moses and Christ, is also a prophet. Spenser thus established himself within both classical and Christian contexts. He also proclaimed himself truly English by deliberately using archaic language, which provides a rustic "native English" tone and, more important, identifies Spenser as the heir of Geoffrey Chaucer.

Spenser was eminently qualified for this role: *The Shepheardes Calender* displays both his Humanist learning and his technical skill (he experimented with thirteen different meters in the work). In an age that encouraged self-fashioning, Spenser firmly established himself as Elizabeth's "poet laureate."

LIFE'S WORK

In 1580, Spenser was appointed secretary to Lord Grey of Wilton, the lord deputy of Ireland; with the exception of a few visits to England, Spenser lived the rest of his life in Ireland, and his love of the Irish countryside is evident in his poetry. In 1588, Spenser was granted a three-thousand-acre estate, Kilcolman, between Limerick and Cork in Munster. There, while serving in various official capacities, he practiced his poetic craft.

Most Elizabethan poets engaged in the fashionable practice of sonnet writing, and Spenser was no exception: His sonnet sequence *Amoretti* was published in 1595. Always the innovator who transformed his models, Spenser combined the Italian and English sonnet forms to create the Spenserian sonnet: three linked quatrains and a couplet, rhyming *abab bcbc cdcd ee*. Spenser also imbued the Petrarchan sonnet with his own Christian, Neoplatonic sensibility. Sonnet 79, for example, celebrates the "true beautie" of his mistress, which is not physical but spiritual and proceeds from God, the source of beauty. It is thus "free from frayle corruption." The sequence's structure is loosely based on the Christian liturgical cycle (reflecting the concern with time's movement introduced in *The Shepheardes Calender*).

Spenser had married Elizabeth Boyle in 1594; by publishing his *Epithalamion* (a poem celebrating the wedding day) at the conclusion of the *Amoretti* in 1595, he reverses the Petrarchan tradition: His courtship, unlike the never-ending frustrated yearning of Petrarchan lovers, would be consummated in a fruitful marriage. The *Epithalamion* is one of Spenser's most beautiful and intricate works. Typically eclectic, it combines the Italian *canzone* form with numerous allusions to classical mythology and descriptive details drawn from the Irish countryside. The poem is numerologically significant in that it contains twenty-four stanzas and 365 long lines, symbolizing not only the wedding day and night but also the year and ultimately man's entire life in its movement from birth through death to heaven. Highly formal and intensely personal, the poem cre-

Edmund Spenser. (Library of Congress)

ates an "endlesse moniment" to love and the power of poetry.

Spenser's syncretism culminated in his greatest work, *The Faerie Queene*, first published in 1590, with an introductory letter to Sir Walter Ralegh. Fortunately, Spenser's letter to Ralegh provides readers with clues to interpret his "continued Allegory, or dark conceit." The work's purpose, according to Spenser, is "to fashion a gentleman or noble person in vertuous and gentle discipline." *The Faerie Queene* thus functions as a courtesy or conduct book used to train a perfect courtier. Each of the six books is devoted to the exploits of a knight who represents a particular virtue: holiness, temperance, chastity, friendship, justice, and courtesy.

In writing this courtesy book, Spenser drew on several literary sources: the classical epics of Homer and Vergil (the poem began in medias res with the well-known line, "A Gentle Knight was pricking on the plaine. . . ."); the medieval tradition of allegory; the "matter of Britain," or Arthurian legend; sixteenth century Italian epic romance (such as Ludovico Ariosto's *Orlando furioso*, 1532, and Torquato Tasso's *Gerusalemme liberata*, 1581; *Jerusalem Delivered*, 1600); and the Bible. The use of allegory was typical of Elizabethan thought, given the fourfold method of biblical exegesis inherited from the medieval period and the common habit of allegorizing classical authors such as Homer, Vergil, and Ovid. *The Faerie Queene* operates on several allegorical levels, though not always simultaneously. Narrative events can be interpreted literally, historically (the character Sir Calidore, for example, was modeled on Sir Philip Sidney), morally, or theologically.

The work's verse form, the Spenserian stanza (eight lines of iambic pentameter followed by an iambic line of six feet rhyming *ababbcbcc*), is both unique and challenging. The demanding rhyme scheme gives Spenser an opportunity to show off the poetic suppleness of vernacular English, as well as establish a stanzaic unity of thought. Simultaneously active and static, the stanza continues the narrative flow of events (and Spenser uses inversion to create rhythmical effects that imitate the canter of a horse or the seductive charm of an enchantress) while also standing as a discrete unit. In this sense, the stanza operates as a stationary picture or emblem, which the Alexandrine at its end explains or summarizes. The reader is thus forced to be active and contemplative, involved and detached, simultaneously.

Read as the great English epic of the Elizabethan age, *The Faerie Queene* is an intensely nationalistic poem, celebrating the person of Gloriana, the fairy queen (Eliz-

SPENSER'S MAJOR WORKS	
1579	*The Shepheardes Calender*
1580	*Three Proper, and Wittie, Familiar Letters*
1586	*Foure Letters and Certaine Sonnets*
1590	*The Faerie Queene* (rev. 1596)
1591	*Daphnaïda*
1591	*Complaints*
1595	*Epithalamion*
1595	*Astrophel*
1595	*Colin Clouts Come Home Againe*
1595	*Amoretti*
1596	*Fowre Hymnes*
1596	*A View of the Present State of Ireland* (pb. 1633)
1596	*Prothalamion*

abeth I). The poem is not, however, merely an effusive compliment that Spenser wrote to gain patronage; it was intended to reflect Elizabethan England in its idealized form, so that in reading or gazing into the textual mirror and imitating the vision, the sovereign, her courtiers, and ultimately the country would be transformed. Spenser recreated England's past, present, and future in an intricate overlapping of plot and life; he unites the fairy-tale world—replete with knights, ladies, magicians, castles, giants, and dragons—with the temptations and emotions of everyday experience.

Except for an annual pension of fifty pounds granted in 1591, Spenser was not rewarded by his queen for singing England's praises. When Kilcolman was sacked in 1598 by Irish forces rebelling against English domination, Spenser and his wife fled to London. Spenser died in 1599 in forlorn and diminished, if not penurious, circumstances and was buried, appropriately, near Geoffrey Chaucer in what is now known as the Poets' Corner of Westminster Abbey. Always fascinated by time's cyclical ability to move forward and yet stay the same, Spenser ended his life very much as he began it.

SIGNIFICANCE

Spenser was perhaps the most articulate spokesperson for the values and attitudes of the Elizabethan age. His life reflects the dual Renaissance commitment to action and thought, and his works reflect the exuberant eclecticism of Humanist learning.

Manifesting the period's eagerness to discover new worlds, Spenser's imagination simply created them and, in so doing, forged a national identity and revitalized English prosody. His technical innovations attested the powers of the English language in an age that cele-

brated the vernacular. The Spenserian stanza was used by Percy Bysshe Shelley, John Keats, and George Gordon, Lord Byron. Spenser also profoundly influenced John Milton, who considered himself a descendant of Spenser as a Christian Humanist poet-prophet to the English nation.

As the father of English pastoral, Spenser united classical and native traditions to celebrate a past, present, and future golden age. Concerned with the transience of life's beauty and the devastating effects of time, Spenser reflected the Elizabethan vogue for pleasurable, cultivated melancholy yet affirmed the permanence of Christian glory. His poetry exemplifies Elizabethan literary theory in its endeavor to teach and delight, but at the same time it possesses an unfading psychological relevance. *The Faerie Queene*'s episodic structure and its vast narrative scope, its portrayal of determined questing interrupted by moments of vision, directly reflect human experience. Though rooted unmistakably in the Elizabethan age, Spenser's poetry is, paradoxically, "eterne in mutabilitie."

—*Caroline McManus*

FURTHER READING

Alpers, Paul J. *The Poetry of "The Faerie Queene."* Princeton, N.J.: Princeton University Press, 1967. Alpers's goal is to "bring *The Faerie Queene* into focus." He analyzes verse and narrative, emphasizing Spenser's manipulation of reader response; he also considers historical and iconographical sources and provides a detailed reading of books I and III.

Frye, Northrop. "The Structure of Imagery in *The Faerie Queene*." *University of Toronto Quarterly* 30 (1961): 109-127. Frye focuses on imagery rather than allegory to demonstrate the work's unity and sees the six books as a unified structure. Private and public education are discussed as central themes.

Hadfield, Andrew, ed. *The Cambridge Companion to Spenser*. New York: Cambridge University Press, 2001. Anthology of essays on Spenser by major scholars. Discusses his life and career, his use of language, and his religion, and provides extended readings of his poetic works. Includes bibliographic references and index.

Hamilton, A. C. *The Structure of Allegory in "The Faerie Queene."* Oxford, England: Clarendon Press, 1961. One of the foremost Spenser critics, Hamilton argues for reading the poem simultaneously on the literal and allegorical levels and shows how book I prefigures the remaining books. Hamilton has also edited an excellent annotated edition of *The Faerie Queene*, published by Longman.

Hankins, John Erskine. *Source and Meaning in Spenser's Allegory: A Study of "The Faerie Queene."* Oxford, England: Clarendon Press, 1971. As the title suggests, Hankins focuses on a possible source in a work by Francesco Piccolomini. Emphasizes internal allegory as *psychomachia*. An informative discussion of all six books follows his analysis of the poem's allegorical basis, method, quest, and landscape.

Lewis, C. S. *Spenser's Images of Life*. Edited by Alastair Fowler. Cambridge, England: Cambridge University Press, 1967. A brief 144 pages, the work expands Lewis's Cambridge lecture notes. Views *The Faerie Queene* as a series of masques, pageants, and emblems, which results in simple fairy-tale pleasure made sophisticated by polyphonic technique. Somewhat disjointed (Lewis died before completing the book) but delightfully written, it conveys a genuine love of Spenser.

MacCaffrey, Isabel G. "Allegory and Pastoral in *The Shepheardes Calender*." *English Literary History* 36 (1969): 88-109. Shows how *The Shepheardes Calender* prefigures the technique and theme of *The Faerie Queene* in its encyclopedic nature, concern with the nature of human life, and simultaneously linear and cyclical structures.

Morrison, Jennifer Klein, and Matthew Greenfield Aldershot, eds. *Edmund Spenser: Essays on Culture and Allegory*. Burlington, Vt.: Ashgate, 2000. A collection of critical essays dealing with the works of Spenser. Includes bibliographical references and an index.

Nohrnberg, James. *The Analogy of "The Faerie Queene."* Princeton, N.J.: Princeton University Press, 1976. An incredibly detailed commentary (791 pages) on Spenser's allegory, mythography, and sources. Citations not always accurate.

Oram, William A. *Edmund Spenser*. New York: Twayne, 1997. An introductory biography and critical study of selected works by Spencer. Includes bibliographic references and an index.

Owens, Judith. *Enabling Engagements: Edmund Spenser and the Poetics of Patronage*. Ithaca, N.Y.: McGill-Queen's University Press, 2002. Study of the relationship between Spenser's poetry and various institutions of Elizabethan patronage of the arts. Argues that Spenser boldly resisted the potential artistic dominance of the royal court. Includes bibliographic references and index.

Woodhouse, A. S. P. "Nature and Grace in *The Faerie Queene*." *English Literary History* 16 (1949): 194-228. Analyzes major characters and key incidents in the light of grace's superiority to nature. Good comparison of books 1 and 2.

SEE ALSO: Ludovico Ariosto; Elizabeth I; Marsilio Ficino; Sir Thomas Malory; Christopher Marlowe; Thomas Nashe; Sir Walter Ralegh; William Shakespeare; Sir Philip Sidney; Torquato Tasso.

RELATED ARTICLES in *Great Events from History: The Renaissance & Early Modern Era, 1454-1600:* Early 16th century: Fuzuli Writes Poetry in Three Languages; 1558-1603: Reign of Elizabeth I; April or May, 1560: Publication of the Geneva Bible; October 31, 1597: John Dowland Publishes *Ayres*.

STEPHEN BÁTHORY
Prince of Transylvania (r. 1571-1575) and king of Poland (r. 1575-1586)

Stephen Báthory enjoyed remarkable success, first, as prince of an autonomous Transylvania and, second, as king of Poland. He stabilized both countries and defended them from their external foes.

BORN: September 27, 1533; Szilágysomlyó, Transylvania (now Simleul Silvaniei, Romania)
DIED: December 12, 1586; Grodno, grand duchy of Lithuania (now Hrodno, Belarus)
ALSO KNOWN AS: István Báthory; Stefan Batory
AREA OF ACHIEVEMENT: Government and politics

EARLY LIFE

Stephen Báthory (BAH-tawr-ee) was the son of a former *vajda* (royal governor) and a member of one of the most powerful families in late medieval and early modern Hungary. He was born soon after a significant moment in the history of the region.

On August 29, 1526, at Mohács, the Ottoman sultan, Süleyman the Magnificent, defeated the Hungarians and dismembered the sprawling medieval kingdom. Thereafter, Hungary was divided into three components: an Ottoman province, governed by the pasha of Buda; "Royal Hungary," a truncated northern section, ruled by the Habsburgs from Pozsony (Bratislava, Slovakia); and the autonomous principality of Transylvania, with its capital at Gyulafehérvár (Alba Iulia, Romania).

The *vajda* of Transylvania enjoyed an ambiguous status as vassal of both the Ottoman sultan and the Habsburg emperor, but if he were politically deft, he could be virtually autonomous. John Zápolya, scion of a powerful family of local magnates, ruled Transylvania from 1526 to 1540. After his death, his wife, Isabella, governed intermittently on behalf of her son (1540-1559), John Sigismund, who ruled from 1559 to 1571, and died childless. The Transylvanian Estates then elected Stephen (István) Báthory as *vajda* on May 25, 1571.

Báthory had served as a page to the Hungarian primate, Archbishop Pál Várday of Esztergom, visited the Habsburg court in Vienna, and was a student in Padua. Returning to Transylvania, he entered the service of Isabella and her son, beginning as castellan of Nagyvárad (Oradea, Romania) and acquiring a reputation as a formidable military leader. In 1565, on a mission to the Habsburg court, he was arrested under obscure circumstances and spent the next two and a half years as a prisoner of Maximilian II in Prague.

Experience confirmed him as a lifelong Catholic and as implacably anti-Habsburg. Well-educated, prudent, and intelligent, he was widely acclaimed for his military prowess; when John Sigismund died, the Estates enthusiastically elected him *vajda*. A longtime rivalry with Gáspár Bekes (1520-1579), whom Maximilian supported with German mercenaries, led to civil war. Báthory won a decisive victory over his rival on July 10, 1575, at Kerelöszentpál (Sinpaul, Romania), and Bekes fled to Habsburg territory. Kerelöszentpál contributed substantially to Báthory's reputation and his subsequent election as Polish king.

As prince of Transylvania, Báthory proved a strong, independent-minded ruler. His determination, however, to keep the Habsburgs out of Transylvania forced him to pursue a pro-Ottoman program. Under him, the principality enjoyed considerable prosperity and his court at Gyulafehérvár brought a measure of Renaissance Humanism to Transylvania. However, the extinction of the male line of the Polish Jagiellon dynasty offered a larger stage for his talents.

LIFE'S WORK

In 1576, the year in which Stephen Báthory became king of Poland, the Polish-Lithuanian Commonwealth was the largest state in Christendom west of Muscovy, extending from the Baltic almost to the Black Sea. The Union of Lublin (1569) had united the two components, but profound tensions remained unresolved: between Poles and Lithuanians, between a king who sought to rule and a nobility that desired him only to reign, between magnates and gentry (comprising between 5 percent and 10 percent of the population), and between Catholics and non-Catholics.

In 1572, the last Jagiellonian king, Sigismund II Augustus, died without issue. It fell, therefore, to the Sejm (parliament) to elect a new sovereign. The first choice, Henry of Valois, younger brother of the French king, Charles XI, proved a disaster, for on learning of his brother's death, he fled to France to claim the throne as Henry III. The election of another king hardly a year after the previous one unleashed a crisis. Rival candidates included Stephen Báthory, Emperor Maximilian II, Ivan IV (the Terrible) of Muscovy, Alfonso II of Ferrara, and John III, the Vasa king of Sweden. The senate, composed of the great officers of state and the leading magnates, urged on by the papal nuncio, formally elected Maximilian II, while the gentry, bitterly anti-Habsburg and anti-German, chose Báthory, impressed with his warlike reputation.

Báthory's bid was further helped by the support of the Ottoman sultan Murad III (r. 1574-1595), who underscored his preference by ordering the pashas of Buda and Temesvar to mobilize 100,000 men along the Habsburg frontier. Maximilian II procrastinated; Báthory did not. He appointed his brother, Christopher, viceregent of Transylvania, and with twenty-five hundred Transylvanian troops, he rode hard for the border. On March 23, 1576, he made his state entry into Kraków, and on May 1, 1576, he was crowned in the cathedral along side his fifty-three-year-old bride, Anna Jagiellonka, sister of the late Sigismund II Augustus. Civil war and foreign invasion had barely been averted.

Báthory's triumph was partly due to one of the most remarkable figures in Polish history: Jan Zamoyski (1542-1605). He helped Báthory to power and was subsequently made crown chancellor (1578-1605) and grand crown hetman (head of the army, 1581-1602). He thereby controlled both domestic and foreign policy. Spokesperson of the middle-ranking gentry against the great magnates, Zamoyski himself amassed great wealth. Báthory's well-placed confidence in him exemplified a notable trait in the king's character: However implacable to opponents, he knew well how to select first-rate men for his service and then give them his full confidence. This was also the case for the Lithuanian Palatine Mikołaj Radziwill and his son, Christopher, and most remarkably, his old adversary from Transylvanian days, Gáspár Bekes, who joined him in Poland to become one of his most loyal and successful generals.

Báthory proved one of the most impressive Polish monarchs. In particular, he brought to a victorious conclusion the long, costly and destructive Livonian War (1558-1583), originally embarked on by Ivan the Terrible to acquire Livonia and give Muscovy an outlet to the sea. Initially, the czar's forces had met with great success, but as the years passed, the conflict ground to a stalemate. Between 1578 and 1582, however, Báthory pressed ahead with ruthless energy to reform the army, forming an impressive body of infantry. These were to face the Muscovite *streltsy*, or musketeers. Light cavalry were provided mainly by Ukrainian Cossacks, for the first time formally integrated into the Polish service under their own hetmans. A formidable artillery arm was also developed.

Preeminently practical and politically astute, Báthory brought with him on campaign skilled mapmakers and a field printing press. His cartographer, Stanisław Pachlowiecki, was later rewarded for his services by ennoblement, as was Reinhold Heidenstein (1556-1620), a chancery clerk turned historian, who wrote a laudatory history of the reign, as well as an account of the war. The new formed army had to be paid, but the Sejm was not inclined to be generous. Báthory, however, proved as formidable a fiscal reformer as a military organizer. He nearly doubled the royal revenues between 1576-1577 and 1585-1586, doing almost as well for the public revenues.

With his new army, he soon saw the tide turn in Livonia, although the campaigning was exceptionally savage and fought in harsh conditions. Notable successes were the capture of Düneburg on the Western Dvina in 1577; the Polish storming of Wenden in 1578; and the capture of Polotsk in 1579 and of Velikiye Luki in 1580. The Siege of Pskov, which cut the lines of communication between Moscow and Livonia, was Báthory's gamble to assert military superiority before financial support from the Sejm ran out. Fortunately, Muscovy was even more exhausted, and at Yam Zapolski (1582), Ivan the Terrible agreed to a ten-year truce: Poland kept Livonia and Polotsk. Despite his achievement in securing the commonwealth's frontiers, Báthory earned little gratitude from his subjects. By the time of his death at Grodno in 1586, he had become a figure more feared than loved and, in the eyes of some, a tyrant.

SIGNIFICANCE

Stephen Báthory, one of the most effective rulers of Counter-Reformation Europe, established the Principality of Transylvania, which under later rulers Gábor Bethlen (r. 1613-1629) and György Rákóczi (r. 1630-1648) enjoyed a golden age of independence. In Poland, he proved the most formidable of the commonwealth's elected kings, strengthening monarchical institutions in the face of aristocratic faction, reforming the army, and beating back the Muscovites.

—*Gavin R. G. Hambly*

FURTHER READING

Butterwick, Richard, ed. *The Polish-Lithuanian Monarchy in European Context, c. 1500-1795.* New York: Palgrave, 2001. A useful anthology reflecting current scholarly thought. Includes bibliographical references and an index.

Davies, Norman. *God's Playground: A History of Poland.* 2 vols. New York: Columbia University Press, 1982. An excellent general history. Volume 1 specifically deals with Polish history from ancient times to 1795. Includes illustrations, bibliography, and an index.

Fedorowicz, J. K., ed. and trans. *A Republic of Nobles: Studies in Polish History to 1864*. New York: Cambridge University Press, 1982. Useful collection of scholarly essays. Includes illustrations and an index.

Jasienica, Paweł. *The Commonwealth of Both Nations: The Silver Age*. Translated by Alexander Jordan. New York: Hippocrene Books, 1987. The first volume of a three-volume series completed in 1992. A leisurely narrative of Báthory's period.

Köpeczi, Béla, ed. *History of Transylvania*. Translated by Péter Szaffkó et al. Translation edited by Bennett Kovrig. 3 vols. Boulder, Colo.: Social Science Mono-graphs, 2001-2002. Volume 1, "From the Beginnings to 1606," provides excellent coverage of Báthory's early career. Includes bibliographical references and indexes.

SEE ALSO: Elizabeth Báthory; Henry III; Ivan the Terrible; Maximilian II; Süleyman the Magnificent; Vlad III the Impaler.

RELATED ARTICLES in *Great Events from History: The Renaissance & Early Modern Era, 1454-1600*: 1499-c. 1600: Russo-Polish Wars; 1557-1582: Livonian War; November, 1575: Stephen Báthory Becomes King of Poland.

SIMON STEVIN
Flemish mathematician, scientist, and engineer

Stevin is best known for his advocacy of the decimal system, his discoveries in hydrostatics, his work on the inclined plane, and his musical theory of consonance. His many and varied contributions have merited him a place in histories of mathematics, accounting, science, engineering, and music.

BORN: 1548; Brugge, Flanders (now in Belgium)
DIED: February, 1620; The Hague, Holland, United Provinces (now in the Netherlands)
ALSO KNOWN AS: Simon Stevinus
AREAS OF ACHIEVEMENT: Mathematics, architecture, astronomy, geography, government and politics, music, science and technology, warfare and conquest

EARLY LIFE

Simon Stevin (steh-VIHN) lived through an age of turbulent change that would eventually divide his homeland. He was born in Brugge, a former port in the southern Netherlands that, because of silting, had lost its access to the sea. Although Antheunis Stevin and Cathelijne van de Poort, Simon's parents, were wealthy, Simon was born out of wedlock (his mother had earlier borne two illegitimate daughters with Brugge's burgomaster).

Because of his later expertise in languages, including Latin and Greek, and his knowledge of ancient mathematics and science, Stevin must have received an excellent education, but not much is known about the details. Some scholars think that he learned bookkeeping at a private school, whereas others believe that he may have attended the Catholic university at Louvain.

His first position was in bookkeeping and tax collecting for Brugge's city administration. He later moved to the commercial city of Antwerp, where he worked as an accountant for a rich merchant. During this time, revolution erupted in the Netherlands, destroying the union of the Catholic south and Protestant north. Stevin left the Netherlands and traveled to Prussia, Poland, and Norway. When he returned to his divided country in 1581, he settled in Leiden. He attended the University of Leiden, which was recently founded to train jurists, physicians, and Protestant theologians for the new Dutch Republic. Unlike Louvain, which emphasized traditional Humanistic studies, Leiden became a center for the study of new scientific ideas. Stevin made excellent use of both his classical and modern education in his career.

LIFE'S WORK

Stevin published his first book in 1582. Its subject was simple and compound interest, and he computed tables for the rapid calculation of annuities. This and his later work were based on the writings of Luca Pacioli, the Italian "father of accounting," who took a pragmatic approach to bookkeeping. Stevin understood the long history of accounting, but he built on this understanding to help create several modern accounting practices. For example, accounting historians consider him to be the inventor of the income statement, a summary of revenues and expenses for a given period.

After his work in business mathematics, Stevin turned to geometry, decimal fractions, and algebra. In 1583, he published a book on geometrical problems, which grew out of his fascination with the works of the ancient mathematician Archimedes. Although he was not the first to use decimal fractions, his book on this subject was the stimulus for their widespread use by bookkeepers. He also encouraged the use of decimals in coinage and in weights and measures. In algebra, he invented a powerful and widely used exponential notation that conveniently designated ordinary, fractional, and negative powers.

While working on these books, and as a citizen of the Low Countries, he became interested in the control of water. In 1588, the States-General granted him a patent for a high-capacity drainage mill that was able to lift four times as much water as old mills, and several of these wind-driven mills were built. He also invented a system of sluices, the floodgates of which could be opened to inundate lands before an enemy could occupy them.

The year 1586 is considered Stevin's *annus mirabilis*, or wonderful year, because of the amount of significant work he produced. One of Stevin's most important books was on hydrostatics, the science that deals with liquids at rest and under pressure, and was published that year. For some, this work warranted him the title of "founder of modern hydrostatics." In it, he clearly stated the hydrostatic law that a liquid's pressure depends only on its vertical height, not on the shape of its container.

Also published in 1586 was an influential book on the art of weighing. As in his work on mathematics and hydrostatics, this Flemish book built on the earlier studies of Archimedes, in particular on the problem of the equilibrium of a stationary object under the influence of a vertical force such as gravity. In fact, he is most famous for the *clootcrans* theorem, his clever derivation of the law of the inclined plane through a device called the wreath of spheres. Using a triangle with unequal sides and a string of evenly weighted beads, he proved the law that "two bodies on two different, inclined planes are in balance if their weights are proportional to the lengths of the two planes."

A further discovery in 1586 was Stevin's experimental demonstration that the velocity of two freely falling lead spheres, one ten times heavier than the other, was independent of this weight difference. Galileo is often given credit for refuting Aristotle's claim that heavy objects fall faster than light ones, but he most likely never did the actual experiment, and even if he did, it would have taken place after Stevin's well-evidenced demonstration.

During the late sixteenth and early seventeenth centuries, the religious and political turmoil in the Netherlands intensified, and the Dutch prince Maurice of Nassau played an important role in helping to establish the Dutch Republic. Prince Maurice had met Stevin when they were both students at Leiden, and in 1604, Stevin became quartermaster in the Dutch army under the prince. Stevin's knowledge of practical mechanics made him extremely useful. For example, he wrote a treatise on the art of fortification that Prince Maurice used during his military campaigns. Stevin also studied how to best train, equip, and make use of troops in war, and how to effectively finance these tasks. He was one of the first to write a book on governmental accounting, and "Bookkeeping for War and Other Extraordinary Finances" was an important part of this treatise. For the Dutch navy, he figured how to use magnetic declinations and a Mercator map to accurately guide ships.

In addition to his official work for the Dutch military, Stevin also tutored Prince Maurice in science and mathematics. He often wrote out the prince's lessons in great detail, and the prince, deeply impressed, had them published between 1605 and 1608. This massive work of fifteen hundred pages contained a comprehensive account of Stevin's accomplishments in mathematics, accounting, mechanics, and astronomy. His chief book on astronomy was also published during this time (1608), and it contained his analysis of the Copernican heliocentric system, which he strongly supported.

While he was engaged in his military work, Stevin amazingly found time for the scientific study of music. In particular, he devised an influential theory of consonance to explain which combinations of musical sounds are pleasant. He was unique in rejecting the ancient Pythagorean idea that pleasing sounds coincided with simple integral ratios. He argued that geometric, not arithmetic, division of the octave yielded genuine consonantal ratios. Though some have criticized Stevin's theory for its insensitivity to the practices of actual musicians, others have seen his work as anticipating the later development of a scale of equal temperament.

Despite marrying late in life (he was sixty-two), he and his wife, Catherine Gray, had two boys and two girls. During his final years, he was deeply admired for his many contributions to the Dutch Republic. He lectured in Dutch at the University of Leiden and helped organize its engineering school. His belief that the Dutch language was particularly suitable for mathematical and scientific works probably contributed to their lack of influence in foreign countries, where Latin was still the language preferred by most scholars.

SIGNIFICANCE

Stevin was very much a Renaissance man, accomplished in such Humanistic fields and political and musical theory, such technical fields as military science and engineering, and such scientific fields as mechanics and astronomy. Because of his deep understanding of both ancient and modern science, he helped bridge the gap between the two approaches. Because he was both a theoretical scientist and a practical engineer, he was able to use his theories in mechanics to develop improved windmills, lifting devices, and military fortifications.

His many published books exhibit his versatility and curiosity, his ability to combine theory and practice, and his skill in crafting clear and creative arguments to support his many original ideas. A major figure in the scientific revolution, he exhibited the movement's confidence in reason to solve the many puzzles of a natural world, a world he believed was governed by beautiful mathematical laws.

—*Robert J. Paradowski*

FURTHER READING

Boyer, Carl B. *A History of Mathematics.* Revised by Uta C. Merzbach. 2d ed. New York: John Wiley & Sons, 1991. This classic textbook, expanded and updated by Merzbach, contains an analysis of Stevin's contributions to mathematics. Includes bibliographies with each chapter, a general bibliography, and an index.

Chatfield, Michael, and Richard Vangermeersch, eds. *The History of Accounting: An International Encyclopedia.* New York: Garland, 1996. This pioneering book contains a biographical article on Stevin that analyzes his contributions to such topics as balance sheets and compounds entries. Bibliographies at the ends of articles. Comprehensive index.

Dijksterhuis, E. J. *Simon Stevin: Science in the Netherlands Around 1600.* The Hague, the Netherlands: Martinus Nijhoff, 1970. This English translation of a work originally published in Dutch in 1943 has been abridged and edited by R. Hooykaas and M. G. J. Minnaert. It remains the best English account of Stevin's life and work.

Grout, Donald J., Claude V. Palisca, and Peter J. Burkholder. *A History of Western Music.* 7th ed. New York: W. W. Norton, 2004. This textbook contains an analysis of Stevin's contributions to music theory. Bibliographies at the ends of each chapter. Comprehensive index.

SEE ALSO: Gerolamo Cardano; John Napier; Johan van Oldenbarnevelt; Georg von Peuerbach; Rheticus; Niccolò Fontana Tartaglia.

RELATED ARTICLES in *Great Events from History: The Renaissance & Early Modern Era, 1454-1600:* 1531-1585: Antwerp Becomes the Commercial Capital of Europe; December 23, 1534-1540: Parmigianino Paints *Madonna with the Long Neck.*

SÜLEYMAN THE MAGNIFICENT
Sultan of the Ottoman Empire (r. 1520-1566)

Süleyman is undoubtedly the best-known Ottoman Turkish sultan. He extended the domains of the empire eastward, establishing a long-lasting border between the Islamic Sunni Turks and the Islamic Shīʿite realm under the Ṣafavid shahs. His reign marked a period of internal stability, primarily through an ordered system of laws.

BORN: 1494 or 1495; probably in Istanbul, Ottoman Empire (now in Turkey)

DIED: September 5 or 6, 1566; near Szigetvár, Hungary

ALSO KNOWN AS: Süleyman I; Süleyman Kanuni; Suleiman I; Suleiman the Magnificent; Suleiman the Lawgiver; Suleiman the Great

AREAS OF ACHIEVEMENT: Government and politics, law

EARLY LIFE

Süleyman (sew-lay-MAHN) the Magnificent, tenth in the line of Ottoman Turkish sultans, was the son of Sultan Selim I (r. 1512-1520) by his wife, Aisha Sultan. Aisha Sultan was herself the daughter of a prestigious Islamic ruler, Menghli Giray, the head of the Black Sea Crimean khanate. Little is known about Süleyman's early education in the palace environment of Istanbul. The young prince received practical training, first as governor of the district, or *sancak*, of Kaffa, during the sultanate of his grandfather Bayezid II, and later, under Selim, as governor of the province of Manisa (ancient Lydia, in Asia Minor).

Possibly because Selim was such a dominant sultanic authority, his son's succession at the time of Selim's death seems to have come automatically, without the necessity of advance preparation to avert internal intrigues between rival pretenders. Once on the Ottoman throne, Süleyman proved that he was more than worthy of Selim's confidence in his administrative as well as his military capacities.

LIFE'S WORK

The Ottoman sultan whose reputation is symbolized by the Western epithet, the Magnificent, carried a different title in Ottoman tradition. The nearly half-century rule of Süleyman earned for him the Ottoman epithet *qanuni*, or lawgiver. This honor resulted largely from the fact that he systematized imperial Turkish rule over diverse provinces conquered by his predecessors in Christian Europe and in the Arab Islamic zone. Süleyman's reign was also marked by repeatedly spectacular demonstrations of Turkish strength. Süleyman personally commanded thirteen major Ottoman military campaigns, ten against European adversaries and three in Asia against Islamic rivals.

Süleyman's reputation for military leadership began in the first two years of his reign, when he captured the city of Belgrade (1521) and the island fortress of Rhodes (1522). From then on, Ottoman armies would play an important role in the international game of influence between the French Valois king Francis I and the Austrian Habsburg emperor and Spanish king Charles V. The latter was a natural rival of Süleyman because the Habsburg and Ottoman empires were both tempted to expand claims over the territory of weaker Danubian neighbors.

First, at the Battle of Mohács in 1526, when the Ottomans toppled the last medieval Hungarian dynasty, killing King Louis II, and again in the spectacular campaign of 1529, the future of Hungary was the object of Habsburg-Ottoman struggles. These ended, at least temporarily, when Süleyman laid siege to Vienna itself in September, 1529. After this extraordinary show of force, Süleyman was able to ensure recognition of his protégé-king John Zápolya in Buda.

From the Danubian valley, the focus of Ottoman imperial pretensions spread to North Africa. Here again, despite Habsburg efforts to stop the sultan's expansionist diplomacy, Ottoman domination would become increasingly imminent in the 1530's. An important sign of Süleyman's intention to bring the North African areas into closer dependence on the Ottoman Empire was his appointment of Barbarossa, perhaps the dominant renegade corsair leader along the North African coast, to the post of *kapudan pasha* (Ottoman high admiral) in 1533.

In 1534, Süleyman also succeeded in annexing Iraq to

Süleyman the Magnificent. (Library of Congress)

the empire—defeating the Ṣafavid Persian shah's claims. From their southernmost bases in Iraq, the Ottoman navy could proceed to dominate the Persian Gulf, entering the Indian Ocean at the height of Süleyman's reign. Süleyman took great interest in the newly annexed Ottoman province of Iraq. He built an important mausoleum in Baghdad for Abu Hanifah, founder of the Hanifite school of Islamic law (the "official" school followed by the Ottomans). He also personally visited the most important Islamic shrines of Iraq, including the holy Shia sites of Nedjef and Karbala.

By the 1540's and 1550's, it was quite clear that, with the exception of the westernmost area of North Africa (the independent sultanate of Morocco), all major Arab zones of the eastern and southern Mediterranean would fall under the suzerainty of Süleyman or his immediate successors. Only the borders of the Danubian west and eastern Anatolia, where the struggle with the Ṣafavid shah went on until the Treaty of Amasia in 1555, were still in question. It might have been possible to gain a comparable treaty with Süleyman's Habsburg rival, Emperor Ferdinand I, who had never abandoned hopes of dominating Hungary. Apparently Süleyman's Grand Vizier Rustem (who was also his son-in-law) made this impossible until his death in 1561. No sooner had Süleyman signed a treaty (1561) than, with the advent of a new Habsburg monarch (Emperor Maximilian), new hostilities erupted.

The last five years of Süleyman's long reign seemed to be marked with signs of both personal and political decline. The death of his wife, Khurram, demoralized the sultan. Two of his sons, Princes Bayezid and Selim, began a bitter rivalry. The tragic outcome of this split, which ended with the execution of Bayezid, not only shook the sultanic family itself but also affected the interests of contending political groups who could no longer be certain how to organize support for the future sultan, Selim II. Nevertheless, Süleyman's visible strength was enhanced by his choice of a new grand vizier, Mehmed Sokollu. Süleyman accompanied his armies, now virtually under Sokollu's command, one more time, to the Hungarian battlefield of Szigetköz. Although the Ottomans were successful in this confrontation with their perennial Christian enemies, Süleyman died during the campaign, presumably without knowledge of his army's victory.

SIGNIFICANCE

The reign of Süleyman the Magnificent can be considered representative of the golden age of the Ottoman Empire, which ran roughly from 1450 to about 1600: The empire at that time was politically, militarily, and culturally strong. Probably the outstanding example of the strength of Ottoman political and military organization was the Janissary (literally, new army) corps. Although this military corps had arisen at least a century before Süleyman's sultanate, it seems to have reached the zenith of its efficiency in the first half of the sixteenth century. What the Janissaries represented militarily was characteristic of the entire structure of Ottoman rule under Süleyman: absolute loyalty and individual subservience to the sultan.

Süleyman was careful to maintain and control the Ottoman institution that could provide for such a system of unquestionable loyalty; this was the *devshirme*, or levy of non-Turkish conscripts, who were mainly Christian youths "contributed" by subjects populations in the Balkan zone or raided areas beyond Ottoman frontiers. Such conscripts, called *kapi kullar* (slaves of the imperial gate), were brought into the special schools of Istanbul and trained for very select service, either as military elites or bureaucratic officials—such high-ranking officers as the grand vizier could be drawn from these men. Since their sole source of sponsorship was the palace at Istanbul, such elites could be sent to any area of the empire at the sultan's will.

In Süleyman's time, the practical results of such centralization were still quite visible: There were very few acts of insubordination, either within the formal imperial administration or on the part of provincial populations under Ottoman rule. In this respect, Ottoman governing institutions under Süleyman represented a considerably more efficient substructure for monarchical authority than could be found anywhere else, either in Europe or in the immediately adjacent areas of western Asia under the Ottomans' neighbors, the Ṣafavid shahs of Iran. The unquestioned authority of the sultanate probably contributed to other symbols of self-assurance in the Ottoman Empire under Süleyman I. There are suggestions, in the form of the great *ganunnahmes*, or "books of law" prepared under the sultan's supervision for each major province of the empire, of a pervading sense of social and economic order that would have affected not only elite but also all classes of governed populations, whether Christian, Jewish, or Islamic. One may still observe, in the splendid architectural monuments (especially mosques and schools, or *madrasas*) erected by Süleyman's chief architect, Sinan Pasha, models of structural support and harmony which, in purely aesthetic terms, ensured imperial supremacy.

—*Byron Cannon*

FURTHER READING

Ahmed, S. Z. *The Zenith of an Empire: The Glory of the Suleiman the Magnificent and the Law Giver.* Trumbull, Conn.: Weatherhill, 2001. Biography of Süleyman, emphasizing the creative and dynamic aspects of his rule and his empire. Includes illustrations.

Fisher, Sydney Nettleton, and William Ochsenwald. *The Middle East: A History.* 6th ed. Boston: McGraw-Hill, 2004. Chapter 18 of this well-known general history is entitled "The Ottoman Empire as a World Power." In addition to providing a comprehensive review of the major events of Süleyman's reign, Fisher covers a number of cultural topics including Ottoman literature and architecture of the period.

Gibb, H. A. R., and Harold Bowen. *Islamic Society in the Eighteenth Century.* Vol. 1 in *Islamic Society and the West: A Study of the Impact of Western Civilization on Moslem Culture in the Near East.* New York: Oxford University Press, 1960. Although the joint authors of this work dedicate the majority of their analysis to Islamic society in the eighteenth century, chapters 2 and 3 ("Caliphate and Sultanate" and "The Ruling Institution") provide essential details of the internal organization of the Ottoman Empire in the age of Süleyman I. These include discussions of the army and central administration, both originally recruited by means of the *devshirme* system.

Goffman, Daniel. *The Ottoman Empire and Early Modern Europe.* New York: Cambridge University Press, 2002. Reconsideration of the Ottoman Empire, arguing that it should be understood as part of Renaissance Europe, rather than as a "world apart," isolated and exotic. Includes illustrations, maps, bibliographic references, and index.

Hodgson, Marshall G. S. *The Gunpowder Empires and Modern Times.* Vol. 3 in *The Venture of Islam: Conscience and History in a World Civilization.* Chicago: University of Chicago Press, 1974. Chapter 3 of this volume is entitled "The Ottoman Empire: *Shari'ah*—Military Alliance, 1517-1718." In this section dealing with the strongest period of Ottoman history, the author provides an analytical framework for comparing prototypes of government and society in several geographical areas of Islamic civilization. The Ottoman model represented by Süleyman is compared with that of the Ṣafavid shahs in Iran and the "Indo-Timuri" (Mughal) empire of India.

Inalcik, Halil. "The Heyday and Decline of the Ottoman Empire." In *The Further Islamic Lands, Islamic Society and Civilizations.* Vol. 2 in *The Cambridge History of Islam,* edited by P. M. Holt, Ann K. S. Lambton, and Bernard Lewis. Cambridge, England: Cambridge University Press, 1970. This is the most concise history of the Ottoman Empire in the age of Süleyman. Like most other political histories dealing with the reign of Süleyman, it turns very quickly to a discussion of decline under his immediate successors, particularly under Selim.

Kunt, Metin, and Christine Woodhead, eds. *Süleyman the Magnificent and His Age: The Ottoman Empire in the Early Modern World.* New York: Longman, 1995. Anthology of essays covering the genesis of the Ottoman Empire, the policies and problems faced by the Empire in the sixteenth century, and Süleyman's reign in the context of those problems. Includes illustrations, maps, bibliographic references, and index.

Lybyer, Albert H. *The Government of the Ottoman Empire in the Time of Suleiman the Magnificent.* Cambridge, Mass.: Harvard University Press, 1913. Reprint. New York: AMS Press, 1978. This is one of the earliest attempts by a Western historian to provide a comprehensive history of Süleyman's reign. Nevertheless, it provides basic facts and the beginnings of an analytical framework for discussing the structures of the Ottoman "ruling institution," a term and concept taken over and developed in much greater detail by H. A. R. Gibb and Harold Bowen in the 1950's.

THOMAS TALLIS
English composer

Thomas Tallis is considered one of the greatest composers in English history. He is noted for his quality sacred music that incorporates continental polyphony with the English choral tradition. Although a Catholic during the Reformation, Tallis's talent earned him royal respect and tolerance. He was a leading composer of the new Anglican Church music.

BORN: c. 1505; probably Kent County, England
DIED: November 20 or 23, 1585; Greenwich, England
ALSO KNOWN AS: Thomas Tallys; Thomas Talles
AREA OF ACHIEVEMENT: Music

EARLY LIFE

Little is known of the early years of Thomas Tallis (TEH-lus). His family had longtime connections in Kent County, and, thus, this is probably where he was born. He is listed in 1530-1531 as an organist for the Dover priory, and in this modest Benedictine religious house he may have been the sole professional musician. In 1537-1538, he was employed in London at the church of St. Mary-at-Hill, where some of the finest musicians in England performed. In late 1538, he went to Essex to work in the likewise musical Waltham Abbey. This monastery was dissolved in 1540, at which time Tallis returned to Kent. By 1541, he had taken a post as a singer (although he no doubt was still active as an organist) at the Canterbury Cathedral, which was then secular. In 1543, Tallis probably became a member of the Chapel Royal, and thus he began to serve full-time at the court, beginning with the reign of Henry VIII.

LIFE'S WORK

For most of his adult life, Tallis was a significant member of the Chapel Royal, a long-standing institution comprising thirty-two men and twelve boys who performed sacred pieces and offered divine service for the sovereign. The Chapel was not stationed at a single place but instead traveled with the royal household; consequently, its members had an opportunity to become more readily noticed by the king or queen. Tallis's career with the Chapel was extraordinary, for he was so well liked that he continually served under four monarchs: Henry VIII, Edward VI, Mary I, and Elizabeth I for more than half of her reign. More remarkable was the fact that Tallis, a Catholic composer of sacred works, was able to thrive during the volatile and dynamic culture of the English Reformation. Except for Mary I, all of the sovereigns he served were Protestant.

Tallis worked as a singer and organist. He no doubt also led choral rehearsals and trained boys in composition and keyboard performance. One of Tallis's students was probably William Byrd, a fellow Roman Catholic who would officially join the Chapel Royal in 1572 and become a leading composer of the next generation. Byrd and Tallis were both dearly admired by Elizabeth I, and in 1575, the queen granted them an exclusive license to print and sell music, bestowing on the musicians a unique monopoly. The pair published their *Cantiones sacrae* (sacred pieces), an anthology of Latin motets, later that year, each contributing seventeen pieces, perhaps in honor of Elizabeth's seventeenth year on the throne. The publication was a commercial failure: It is believed that amateurs who may have purchased the book were dissuaded by its polyphony (individual lines of sound performed simultaneously), which was perceived to be difficult.

Throughout the many decades that Tallis was a musician, styles and tastes changed dramatically, as did religious liturgy, prescribed practices, and cultural attitudes. Tallis continually adapted himself as a composer and was able to produce a variety of successful works in almost every genre of the sixteenth century English church. Moreover, while staying alert to the circumstances in his own nation, Tallis also absorbed modern continental music threads (for instance, using imitation of musical lines more structurally), which kept his works current.

During the beginning years of the Anglican Church (c. 1547), Tallis was one of the first composers to write music for English words rather than Latin. His early anthems, such as "Hear the Voice and Prayer" and "Remember Not," address a concern of the Reformers, who sought text in songs to be clear and understandable. Thus, these works are syllabic (having one note per syllable) and chordal (all voices moved in similar rhythm) and, consequently, textually clear. Of course, Latin Church music was not abandoned by either Catholics or Protestants, and Tallis continued composing for the traditional language. However, some of his Latin pieces were later fitted with English words.

During the reign of the Catholic queen Mary I, Tallis enthusiastically revived older forms, such as the large-scale Latin Mass and grand antiphons, known for their rich polyphonic style and at times indecipherable texts. Tallis's massive six-voice votive antiphon *Gaude gloriosa*

Dei Mater, which was most likely written for Queen Mary, was probably one of the last antiphons he composed. In 1554, during Philip II of Spain's residence in London, Tallis probably penned the seven-voice *Mass Puer natus est nobis*, which was most likely to be performed by the combined English and Spanish royal chapels. This is Tallis's longest polyphonic setting and one of the most elaborate Masses in English history.

One of Tallis's most celebrated works is the monumental motet *Spem in Alium*, composed around 1570 during the reign of Elizabeth I. It was probably written as an English competitive response to the forty-voice motet *Ecce beatam lucem*, by the Italian composer Alessandro Striggio. Striggio's work was performed in London in 1567, stirring much excitement. *Spem in Alium*, likewise for forty voices, was apparently to show that English composers were just as gifted as those of the Continent, if not more so. The work met the challenge, becoming one of the treasures of Elizabethan music.

The opening of is dramatic and moving. The forty individual parts are divided into eight choirs of five voices each. The main theme is first introduced by four of the choirs: Each of the twenty voices enters one by one, so the texture progressively thickens and the volume slowing increases. As these voices conclude their entrances, the remaining four choirs, the twenty other voices, respond, again imitatively, until all are sounded together in a climax in the fortieth measure. The work is noted for its evocative character combined with simple, heartfelt text from the Book of Judith: "I have never put my hope in any other than you God of Israel."

Tallis's *Lamentations of Jeremiah*, composed in the 1560's, is one of his most highly acclaimed works. The piece may have been used as part of the Protestant liturgy, or, it has been speculated, for private Catholic gatherings. Tallis incorporates a variety of compositional techniques to produce his dramatic lament. Indeed, the work is somewhat a microcosm of Tallis's compositional skills: It includes lyric melodies, antiphony, chordal texture, expressive imitation and counterpoint, tasteful dissonances, and creative modulation. Yet, because of its serene essence, beyond technical mastery, *Lamentations of Jeremiah* is considered one of Tallis's most soulful works.

SIGNIFICANCE

Tallis is often called the father of English church music. As a Catholic, he was well versed in traditional Latin styles, and with the coming of the English Reformation, he used his knowledge to help create a new sound for the Anglican Church. He provided works in the old Latin manner, many of which were given English texts, and works in the new English anthem style, with singable melodies and chordal texture. Moreover, he presented grand compositions of great magnitude that represented the sacred spirit of England. Tallis did this during a time of immense religious turmoil, for more than fifty years and during the reign of four monarchs, yet he succeeded—indeed flourished—as a Catholic musician in a Protestant land.

—*Lisa Urkevich*

FURTHER READING

Caldwell, John. *Oxford History of English Music*. Vol. 1. Oxford, England: Clarendon Press, 1991. Survey of English music to about 1715. Includes a discussion of the development of sixteenth century choral music, featuring Tallis's *Spem in Alium*.

Doe, Paul. *Tallis*. Oxford Studies of Composers 4. London: Oxford University Press, 1968. The only book devoted exclusively to Tallis's music.

Harley, John. *William Byrd: Gentleman of the Chapel Royal*. Brookfield, Vt.: Ashgate, 1997. Contains informative sections on Tallis and discusses the relationship between Byrd and his teacher.

Le Huray, Peter. *Music and the Reformation in England, 1549-1660*. Cambridge, England: Cambridge University Press, 1978. Discusses composers and historical events alongside music.

Morehen, John. *English Choral Practice, c. 1400-c. 1650*. New York: Cambridge University Press, 1995. Essays written by specialists discuss techniques of performance, including methods of performing Tallis's music.

Phillips, Peter. *English Sacred Music, 1549-1649*. Oxford, England: Gimell, 1991. Written by the director of The Tallis Scholars, a famous Renaissance music performing group. An encyclopedic account of the history of sacred music with English words.

SEE ALSO: William Byrd; Sir Thomas Morley.

RELATED ARTICLES in *Great Events from History: The Renaissance & Early Modern Era, 1454-1600:* 1567: Palestrina Publishes the *Pope Marcellus Mass*; 1575: Tallis and Byrd Publish *Cantiones Sacrae*; 1588-1602: Rise of the English Madrigal; 1590's: Birth of Opera; October 31, 1597: John Dowland Publishes *Ayres*; 1599: Castrati Sing in the Sistine Chapel Choir.

NICCOLÒ FONTANA TARTAGLIA
Italian mathematician

Tartaglia helped create the field of algebra, once considered a branch of geometry, by using the wisdom of ancient Greek mathematics in unforeseen ways. His discovery of the cubic formula in algebra was one of the first distinctive advances in theoretical mathematics beyond the accomplishments of the Greeks.

BORN: c. 1500; Brescia, Republic of Venice (now in Italy)
DIED: December 13, 1557; Venice, Republic of Venice (now in Italy)
ALSO KNOWN AS: Niccolò Fontana; Niccolò Tartalea
AREAS OF ACHIEVEMENT: Mathematics, science and technology, military

EARLY LIFE

Niccolò Fontana Tartaglia (nee-kohl-LAW fohn-TAH-nah tahr-TAHL-yah) was the son of a postal carrier named Michele, who died in 1506. It is not known what his family's name was, although a brother of Tartaglia used the name "Fontana." The name "Tartaglia," which is connected with the Italian verb for stammering, was assumed after Niccolò was attacked by a French soldier during France's military activities in Brescia in 1512; only the assiduous attention of Tartaglia's mother kept him alive. Tartaglia was the name he used for all his publications.

Early efforts at education were frustrated by the family's inability to cover the costs, so Tartaglia was almost entirely self-taught. When he went to Verona in 1516, he was already capable of teaching calculation. He was never able to keep his family in the best of financial conditions, compared with his contemporaries with similar familial backgrounds. Nevertheless, he persevered in his own studies, which included the text of Euclid's *Stoicheia* (c. 300 B.C.E.; *Elements*). It has been suggested that part of Tartaglia's originality stemmed from his not having followed the more traditional pattern of education available to his wealthier fellow citizens.

In 1534, Tartaglia moved to Venice to take up a professorship in mathematics and to give public lessons, and he remained there for the rest of his life.

LIFE'S WORK

When Tartaglia was in Venice, he also took part in public disputations. In mathematics, such disputations involved challenges to solve problems of various degrees of diffi-

culty and provided a kind of excitement more familiar in sporting competitions. In Italy, one of the most challenging disputations was the solving of equations. An equation in which the variable occurs to the second power is called a "quadratic equation," and methods for solving those had been known to several ancient civilizations. There had been no general technique for solving equations in which the variable occurred to a third power (called "cubic"). The reason, in part, was that the influence of Euclid's geometry encouraged those tackling equations to think in geometric terms. In addition, there was no system for translating a problem into the kind of shorthand that an algebraic equation represents.

Tartaglia was not the first to approach the problem of solving cubic equations. Ancient mathematicians tried to extract cube roots, and so even the Greeks considered the issue of whether they could handle such calculations with Euclidean methods.

In medieval Islamic mathematics, trigonometry afforded a new set of techniques for looking at algebraic equations. It was not clear how much Islamic material was brought back to Europe, along with the text of Euclid used by mathematicians in the Near East. The mathematician Scipione del Ferro had come up with a method for solving cubic equations in which there was no quadratic term.

In the highly competitive atmosphere of intellectual competitions, it was worth keeping methods secret, and del Ferro passed his along to a student named Antonio Fiore. Fiore challenged Tartaglia to a mathematical duel, and Tartaglia's reputation depended on the result of the competition. Tartaglia, however, had managed to go beyond the technique of del Ferro and could solve cubic equations even when they included a quadratic term. As a result, Tartaglia emerged victorious, the "star" among mathematicians of the time.

Tartaglia also was reluctant to let the details of his method enter the public realm. He had discussed them with mathematician Gerolamo Cardano, but Tartaglia swore him to secrecy. Cardano subsequently claimed to have found a way to solve a quartic equation (solving with a fourth power of the variable) that used but went beyond the cubic equation of Tartaglia and so felt that he was released from his vow of secrecy. The controversy that resulted when Cardano published Tartaglia's method, even though he gave Tartaglia credit by name, is an indication of the extent to which intellectual property was an important issue in the Italy of the Renaissance. It also shows that Tartaglia had no shortage of strong language to use when he was indulging in acrimonious debate. Tartaglia was not always able to make the same impression in public confrontations as he had done with Fiore, and that probably contributed to his relative isolation later in life. He died with relatively little to show for his success in solving cubic equations.

In addition to his work in algebra, Tartaglia produced in 1543 the first printed translation of the text of Euclid into any modern language. The influence of Euclid had remained strong in mathematics throughout the medieval period, and Tartaglia argued that some of the foundations of Euclidean mathematics could be jettisoned without having to abandon the results gathered by Euclid. As an example, Euclid did not include the number one among his list of numbers and, instead, assigned it a special place as the "root" of all numbers. Tartaglia argued that mathematicians could make more sense out of their calculations by including one as a number. The inclusion of one as a number helped to cast off some of the restrictions that the Euclidean formulation of mathematics had imposed more than eighteen centuries before.

Of greater contemporary interest was Tartaglia's work on gunnery. Just as he had not been inhibited by Euclidean precedent from striking out in new directions, so he did not let the dominance of Aristotle in the study of motion get in his way. Trying to describe the trajectory of cannon shells was an important matter for the many military forces involved in sieges of walled cities during Tartaglia's lifetime. Tartaglia studied the work of Archimedes, the third century B.C.E. Greek mathematician who had done much after Euclid to make applied mathematics a respectable field. His work on the parabolic shape of the trajectories of projectiles was not entirely theoretical, but it gave subsequent generations of students of ballistics a sense of freedom from the kinds of explanation that Aristotle had proposed.

SIGNIFICANCE

Tartaglia's accomplishments in the field of mathematics helped to create the field of algebra as an autonomous discipline rather than as a branch of geometry. His willingness to deviate from the text of Euclid on matters that were not primarily geometrical enabled subsequent mathematicians to look at algebraic questions in their own right.

Contemporary mathematician François Viète established a system for equations that would have been impossible without the work of Tartaglia. The introduction of analytic geometry by René Descartes, which enabled both geometers and algebraists to benefit from each other's work, would have been senseless if algebra had not been made to stand on its own as a method.

It is difficult to know what Tartaglia could have accomplished with a notation better suited to describe algebraic manipulations, but those who did create that notation were inspired by Tartaglia's accomplishments.

—*Thomas Drucker*

Niccolò Fontana Tartaglia. (Library of Congress)

FURTHER READING

Bergamini, David. *Mathematics*. New York: Time, 1967. A lively narration of the public confrontation, with illustrations intended to capture the flavor of the period.

Dauben, Joseph W., and Christoph J. Scriba, eds. *Writing the History of Mathematics: Its Historical Development*. Basel, Switzerland: Birkhauser, 2002. Scholarly assessment of some of the legends associated with Tartaglia and his contemporaries, arranged by region.

Drake, Stillman, and I. E. Drabkin, eds. *Mechanics in Sixteenth-Century Italy*. Madison: University of Wisconsin Press, 1969. Still the best collection of material on the innovations that Tartaglia and his students introduced in transforming the study of projectiles from a theoretical and philosophical discipline to a practical and mathematical one.

Dunham, William. *Journey Through Genius*. New York: John Wiley and Sons, 1990. Looking at Tartaglia primarily through the lens of Cardano, a more-thorough presentation of the algebraic details than the presentation of strictly biographical accounts.

Mahoney, Michael Sean. *The Mathematical Career of Pierre de Fermat*. 2d ed. Princeton, N.J.: Princeton University Press, 1998. Simply the best account of the influence of Tartaglia on the subsequent development of algebra, not just for specific achievements but also for his transforming algebra into a separate discipline.

Mankiewicz, Richard. *The Story of Mathematics*. Princeton, N.J.: Princeton University Press, 2000. Further details about the later years of Tartaglia's career after

Cardano had given him fame but taken away his proprietary interest in the cubic formula.

Stillwell, John. *Mathematics and Its History*. New York: Springer, 2002. Presents the familiar biographical narrative but indicates the algebraic details of Tartaglia's advances.

SEE ALSO: Gerolamo Cardano; Georg von Peuerbach; Rheticus.

RELATED ARTICLES in *Great Events from History: The Renaissance & Early Modern Era, 1454-1600:* 16th century: Proliferation of Firearms; 1550's: Tartaglia Publishes *The New Science*.

TASCALUSA
Choctaw chief

Tascalusa was the paramount chief of the Mobile Indians, who led his people first in diplomacy with Spanish explorer Hernando de Soto and then in opposition. The first-contact experience ended for the Mobile with a valiant but deadly battle, the largest and deadliest in sixteenth century North America between American Indians and Europeans, but it did stop de Soto's advance.

BORN: c. 1500; Mabila (now in Alabama)
DIED: October 18, 1540; Mabila
ALSO KNOWN AS: Tuskaloosa; Tuscaluza; Tuscaloosa; Tuscaluca; Tazaluza; Tastaluca; Black Warrior
AREAS OF ACHIEVEMENT: Government and politics, diplomacy, warfare and conquest

EARLY LIFE

Not much is known of the early life of Tascalusa (taw-skah-LOO-saw). The legendary parameters of Tascalusa's spare biography never entered the folk storehouse of southeast Indian stories for a number of reasons. First, the Mobile Indians began to disappear as a tribe after 1540, eventually being absorbed into the Choctaw Nation in the early eighteenth century. Second, the North American Indian cultures in the path of Hernando de Soto's expedition suffered almost complete cultural annihilation, wiping out any form of oral history that might have been passed on about Tascalusa and his tribe. Third, Spanish versions of Tascalusa's life focus solely on his final days serving as the worthy counterpart to de Soto.

Tascalusa, whose name means "black warrior" in the Choctaw language, governed one of the most developed and complex of the Mississippian Indian cultures at the end of what had been an approximately eight-hundred-year period of growth and development before the first European contact in the sixteenth century. The hunter-gatherer society had metamorphosed into a more complex farming society that included one of the southernmost examples of mound building. The Mobile Indians, in their daily religious practices, paid religious honor to the sun, a behavior de Soto himself attempted to exploit by introducing himself to the Southeast Indians as the "child of the sun."

Tascalusa appears to have been married, though there is no specific mention of him having a wife. There are, however, multiple references to groups of tribal women expressing both their homage to and their concern for him as he fought in the nine-hour Battle of Mabila. Tascalusa had a namesake son who was old enough to fight at Mabila and whose grisly death in combat is recounted by several different Spanish eyewitnesses. Interestingly enough, although all the Mobile men and virtually all the women were reported to have been dead or dying by nightfall on October 18, 1540, there is a single transcribed report of captured Indian women by a Spanish lieutenant that claims that Tascalusa was encouraged to leave the fortress walls of Mabila, repeatedly refused to do so, but finally relented and left with thirty men. This report, however, might simply be flawed understanding. The report assumed that many Indians, presumably twenty-five hundred or more, died outside the fortress walls of living trees and daub, even as another three thousand died inside the walls by the sword or lance; another thirty-five hundred died horrible deaths, either burned or suffocated in the huge structures to which de Soto and his men set fire and often blocked egress of the mostly women and children inside.

LIFE'S WORK

Tascalusa, as the leader of the largest village among North American Indian tribes of the southeast of his day, made every attempt to remain a diplomat rather than become a warrior-leader. Indeed, he seems to have been well-prepared to play both roles. Tascalusa had welcomed de Soto initially and sent amicable, if somewhat cryptic and reserved, messages by courier to de Soto as the expedition moved west and north toward Tascalusa and his people.

On October 11, 1540, the two men finally met face-to-face. De Soto asked for several hundred men to serve as guides and carriers and seems to have asked for at least one hundred women as well, presumably for sexual favors. Tascalusa apparently provided a significant number of burden carriers but told de Soto that the women would be provided at the next town to the north, the fortress town of Mabila. Over the next few days, Tascalusa traveled with de Soto toward Mabila. Extremely tall, Tascalusa's stature was such that one of de Soto's lieutenants noted that only a pack horse would be large enough to support his impressive frame.

De Soto seems to have become suspicious as he approached the walled fortress of Mabila, since houses that were outside the tree-and-mud-walls had been dismantled, which would have provided a more open plain for fighting. De Soto also seems to have received some information from a Christian missionary at Mabila, who reported to de Soto that the Indians were acting suspiciously and that an inordinate number of armed men were collecting within the huts and meeting halls of the town, including Tascalusa, who by this time had been in one of the larger houses near the central plaza and had refused to emerge from the structure. The largest and bloodiest battle of the century on the North American continent soon ensued during all nine sunlight hours of October 18, 1540.

The Spaniards were not ready for the scope or organization of the Indian attack, so they gathered outside the gates of the city to regroup. The Spaniards fought for hours, then launched a four-pronged attack on both gates and two points of the wall of the city, entering the fortress to kill the remaining soldiers and set fire to all the houses inside the walls of Mabila.

Despite the extent of the battle, the ferocity of the ensuing firestorm was so complete that to this day, scholars debate the exact location of the battle, though it was most likely at what is now known as Choctaw Bluff in Clarke County, Alabama. Somewhere in south-central Alabama, there is an archaeological library of information embedded in the swampy earth, containing at minimum more than ten thousand skeletal remains, pottery, arrowheads, and the remnants of a remarkable village, palisaded with live (most likely, pine) trees daubed into city walls.

Tascalusa and his entire retinue of subordinate chiefs died that day, but so did a number of significant officers on the Spanish side, notably de Soto's two nephews, Don Carlos Enriquez and Diego de Soto. De Soto died two years later of a fever, and his men hurriedly buried him in the Mississippi River so that his demigod stature would not be mitigated. Therefore, the Battle of Mabila and de Soto's confrontation with Tascalusa constitute the critical points not only in the lives of these two leaders but also in the history of their cultures in North America as well.

SIGNIFICANCE

Tascalusa was the paramount chief of forces who engaged in the largest and most significant sixteenth century battle involving North American Indians and Europeans. His name has been given to both a city and a county in Alabama (Tuscaloosa), and his life is emblematic and representative of first-contact experiences with Europeans: With diplomacy, guile, and pitched and valorous battle, the Spaniards followed through by annihilating and then essentially ending the chiefdom-level leadership within tribal cultures that faced colonialist Europeans.

—*Richard Sax*

FURTHER READING

Clayton, Lawrence A., et al., eds. *The De Soto Chronicles: The Expedition of Hernando De Soto to North America in 1539-1543*. Tuscaloosa: University of Alabama Press, 1996. Widespread use of primary sources detail the scope of de Soto's four-year expedition from Florida to Texas and its impact on the indigenous tribes of the Southwest.

Duncan, David Ewing. *Hernando De Soto: A Savage Quest in the Americas*. Norman: University of Oklahoma Press, 1997. Revisionist biography of de Soto, which uses expedition logs, colonial archival manuscripts, and eyewitness accounts to describe de Soto as a gambler and megalomaniac, not a genial bearer of Western civilization.

Higginbotham, Jay. *Mauvila*. Mobile, Ala.: A. B. Bahr/ Factor Press, 2000. The only full-length book about the Battle of Mabila (also known as Mauvila).

Hudson, Charles. *Knights of Spain, Warriors of the Sun: Hernando De Soto and the South's Ancient Chiefdoms*. Athens: University of Georgia Press, 1997. Uses archaeological and documentary evidence to establish the route of de Soto's *entrada* and its impact on the indigenous tribal communities.

Josephy, Alvin M., Jr. *Five Hundred Nations: An Illustrated History of North American Indians*. New York: Alfred A. Knopf, 1994. Revised edition of a seminal text that includes brief but relevant discussions on Mississippi Indian civilizations, Tascalusa, Mabila, and de Soto.

Mancall, Peter C., and James Merrell, eds. *American Encounters: Natives and Newcomers from European Contact to Indian Removal, 1500-1850*. New York: Routledge, 1999. Republished academic essays, mostly from scholarly journals, describing first-contact encounters throughout North America.

Swanton, John R. *Final Report of the United States De Soto Expedition Commission*. 76th Congress, 1st Session, House Document no. 71. Washington, D.C.: Government Printing Office, 1939. Swanton established an initial route for de Soto's *entrada*, which has been revised numerous times by subsequent scholars.

Trigger, Bruce G., and Wilcomb E. Washburn, eds. *The Cambridge History of the Native Peoples of the Americas*, vol. 1, pt. 1. New York: Cambridge University Press, 1996. Comprehensive survey of indigenous North America, with passages on precontact Mississippian Indian cultures and their rapid sociopolitical decline after initial contact.

Wilson, James. *The Earth Shall Weep: A History of Native America*. New York: Grove Press, 1998. Historical survey that includes descriptions of hunter-gatherer and farming cultures as well as mound-building traditions of Mississippian Indian tribes at the time of the de Soto expedition.

SEE ALSO: Pemisapan; Hernando de Soto.
RELATED ARTICLE in *Great Events from History: The Renaissance & Early Modern Era, 1454-1600:* May 28, 1539-September 10, 1543: De Soto's North American Expedition.

TORQUATO TASSO
Italian poet

Tasso was one of the greatest Italian poets, who sought to reconcile classical ideals with the renewed religious fervor arising from the Counter-Reformation. The significance of his major works lies in his attempt to synthesize the vision of perfection and human dignity of the classics with Christian spiritual values.

BORN: March 11, 1544; Sorrento, Kingdom of Naples (now in Italy)
DIED: April 25, 1595; Rome, Papal States (now in Italy)
AREA OF ACHIEVEMENT: Literature

EARLY LIFE
Torquato Tasso (tawr-KAWT-oh TAHS-oh) was born in the coastal village of Sorrento, just south of Naples. His mother came from a noble Neapolitan family, while his father, originally from the northern town of Bergamo, was a diplomat and an accomplished man of letters who wrote a well-known chivalric poem entitled *Amadigi* in 1560.

Although Tasso's first years were spent in the serene and idyllic atmosphere of the Mediterranean Sea, they were soon disturbed by a sudden and unexpected turbulence: His father, caught in the political misfortunes of his protector, the prince of Salerno, was forced into exile, and all his goods were confiscated. At the age of ten, Tasso was taken from the Jesuit school in Naples, where for two years he had studied Latin and Greek and had received a thorough religious training, and sent to Rome to be with his father. Thus began the agitated and roaming existence that was to mark his entire life, first by necessity and later as a tormented vocation. This abrupt separation from his mother, whom he was never to see again (she died prematurely a year later in 1556), left in the young Tasso an indelible impression that was to influence his lyrical production and reinforce his pessimistic view of the human condition.

In 1557, he was at the court of Urbino; his father had just entered in the service of the duke, who was aware of Torquato's penchant for poetry and wanted the precocious young man to be a study companion to his own son. It was at Urbino that Torquato first came into contact with the splendid yet treacherous courtly environment that was to influence his life and writings deeply. At the age of fifteen, he relocated to Venice, and it was there, where the presence of the Turks was most felt and feared, that he began a rough draft of his famous epic poem on the First Crusade (1095-1099). The next five years were spent studying at the University of Padua, first law, according to his father's wishes, and then his own chosen fields of philosophy and letters. There, he met and frequented one of the most celebrated literary figures of the Renaissance, Sperone Speroni, and other famous scholars who stirred in him the ardent desire for lyrical expression.

At Padua, Tasso joined the Accademia degli Eterei and in 1562 published a chivalric poem in octaves, *Rinaldo* (English translation, 1792). This is a significant work in that it contains many of the themes that were to characterize his later production: the thirst for glory, adventure, and love and the yearning for chivalric ideals. It was during this time that Tasso's first doubts on religious matters surfaced—a lifelong spiritual struggle that would culminate in his later years in a complete revision of his famous epic, using orthodox religious teachings, and a dedication of the final years of his life to religious didactic works. Finally, it was at Padua that his love for Lucrezia Bendidio blossomed, and it was to her that many of his love poems would be dedicated.

LIFE'S WORK

In 1565, Tasso entered the service of Cardinal Luigi d'Este at the court of Ferrara and began the happiest and most fruitful period of his career; for the next ten years, he lived the ideal life of the man of letters for which he had longed. In 1567, he was given a literary stipend by Duke Alfonso II, and in this serene and refined courtly environment, he was able to cultivate his genius and produce his most important works. Ferrara had been the home of the famous Renaissance poet, Ludovico Ariosto, and this for Tasso was both a source of inspiration and a spur to competition. Although the court of Ferrara was flourishing only in appearance and in reality was following Italy toward its political downfall, Tasso saw in its pomp and false grandeur the last vestiges of the ideals of the Renaissance, and he felt compelled to sing its praises.

Torquato Tasso. (Library of Congress)

Even though he composed many of his most beautiful poems during this period, dedicated to the ladies of the court, it was with the *Aminta* (1573; English translation, 1591) that Tasso established his reputation as a poet and playwright. This pastoral drama in five acts was first represented in the presence of Alfonso II on the island of Belvedere, the lovely summer residence of the Estensi, and was an immediate success. In his depiction of the world of the classical shepherd-poets, so rich in literary tradition, Tasso projected his ideals of a genteel and serene existence devoid in its primordial innocence of the sense of evil and sin. It also becomes for the poet an allegory of courtly life seen as a point of encounter for poets, sensitive souls, and fervent lovers. Although there are elements of tragedy in *Aminta*, all negativism is dissolved in the atmosphere of myth in which the drama evolves, and Tasso arrives at a perfect Renaissance unity of tone, rhythm, and style.

Only two years later, Tasso completed his most famous work and the one that established his poetic immortality, *Gerusalemme liberata* (1581; *Jerusalem Delivered*, 1600). The poem is divided into twenty cantos, in octaves, and follows the traditional hendecasyllabic scheme. While the subject matter is the historical conquest of Jerusalem by the First Crusade and therefore conforms to the rules of the epic, which Tasso had intended to follow as he states in *Discorsi del poema eroico* (1594; *Discourses on the Heroic Poem*, 1973), within the narration there are numerous secondary episodes that betray the poet's ambivalent feelings. It is in *Jerusalem Delivered* that the crisis of the Counter-Reformation is most strongly reflected. It is clear, especially in the love stories of Erminia, Clorinda, and Tancredi, that Tasso

	TASSO'S MAJOR WORKS
1562	*Rinaldo* (English translation, 1792)
1573	*Aminta* (English translation, 1591)
1581	*Rime* (rev. 1591, 1593; *From the Italian of Tasso's Sonnets*, 1867)
1581	*Dialoghi*
1581	*Gerusalemme liberata* (*Jerusalem Delivered*, 1600)
1581	*Allegoria del poema*
1586	*Apologia*
1587	*Il re Torrismondo*
1587	*Discorsi dell'arte poetica*
1587	*Lettere* (rev. 1588, 1616-1617)
1593	*Gerusalemme conquistata* (*Jerusalem Conquered*, 1907)
1594	*Discorsi del poema eroico* (*Discourses on the Heroic Poem*, 1973)
1607	*Le sette giornate del mondo creato* (*Creation of the World*, 1982)

tries to recuperate the ideals of the Renaissance. Yet in the depiction of the struggle between good and evil, in the veiled sensuality and the sense of guilt found in the description of the garden of Armida, and in the tragic deaths of Solimano and Clorinda, a melancholy and pessimistic mood becomes apparent that reflects the crisis of the Baroque era.

Technically, *Jerusalem Delivered* tries to solve the debate concerning the relative merits of the chivalric and epic traditions. To the multiform variety of Ludovico Ariosto's chivalric poem, Tasso opposes the Aristotelian unity of action, and to the use of classical mythology, he opposes the Christian supernatural. Yet the true value of the work lies in its depiction of the human condition; the main characters appear to be victims of a cruel fate that places them in utter solitude and renders them incapable of appeasing their desires. Even the surroundings are arid and desolate and seem to symbolize humankind's frailty and impotence.

This sense of tragic isolation was also felt in Tasso's personal experiences. Immediately after the completion of the epic, Tasso was haunted by religious scruples and personal self-doubt. On a literary plane, he revised the work along orthodox lines, culminating in the appearance of *Gerusalemme conquistata* (1593; *Jerusalem Conquered*, 1907), and he dedicated the rest of his life to religious writings such as *Le sette giornate del mondo creato* (1607; *Creation of the World*, 1982), in which he was able to meditate on Christian mysteries. On a personal level, he began a life of roaming marked by bizarre behavior and psychic disequilibrium. Torn by religious doubts (on more than one occasion he asked to be examined by the Inquisition) and haunted by a sense of perse-

cution, he traveled throughout Italy only to return to Ferrara in 1579 on the occasion of the duke's marriage. Believing that he was slighted since little note was taken of his return, Tasso provoked a scandal by criticizing the duke, was declared mad, and was incarcerated in Sant' Anna.

After seven years of incarceration (much has been written concerning his presumed madness during this period), Tasso was freed through the intercession of the prince of Mantua, but he could not find peace and continued to wander throughout Italy until his death on April 25, 1595.

SIGNIFICANCE

Tasso is a prime example of a genius caught up in a period of transition, of change and upheaval. His major works reflect the conflict of the age of the Counter-Reformation and betray a nostalgic homage to the splendid literary revival of the Renaissance. Critics disagree as to whether Tasso was the last major poet of the Renaissance or the first great poet of the Baroque. Many consider him to be a transitional figure between the two periods, and indeed characteristic elements of both can be found in his writings.

There is no disagreement, however, that Tasso belongs on the list of the world's greatest poets—from John Milton to Voltaire, from Lord Byron to T. S. Eliot, the poetry of Tasso has been praised and imitated, contemplated and enjoyed.

The melancholy and pessimistic mood that pervades much of his literary production can be attributed to the rapid changes that were taking place during his lifetime in the areas of religion, science, and politics. Amid such changes, Tasso attempted to reconcile the classical ideals that he cherished with contemporary reality. It is not surprising, therefore, that he was a favorite of the Romantic poets and still has much to offer to the modern reader.

—Victor A. Santi

FURTHER READING

Boulting, William. *Tasso and His Times*. London: Methuen, 1907. Reprint. New York: Haskell House, 1968. The classic biography of Tasso. Details the life of the author from both a factual and, at times, romantic point of view, with little critical analysis of his works. Although later scholarship has rejected its romanticized view of Tasso's life, Boulting's book is still fascinating reading and offers valuable insights into the author's age and the courtly environment that influenced his writings. Includes illustrations.

Brand, C. P. *Torquato Tasso*. Cambridge, England: Cambridge University Press, 1965. The standard English biographical and critical work on Tasso. Discusses the author's use of historical sources, gives a detailed account of his life, and analyzes his major works. Includes an interesting essay on the legend of Tasso's life and presumed madness, and ends with a lengthy chapter on the poet's contribution to English literature. Bibliographic references are included in the notes.

Cody, Richard. *The Landscape of the Mind*. Oxford, England: Clarendon Press, 1969. The first half of the book discusses the pastoral and Platonic theories in Tasso's *Aminta*. Also studies the play from the point of view of theater and makes references to it in the second half, where William Shakespeare's early comedies are analyzed.

Eriksen, Roy. "Designing Epic Rooms: Ariosto, Tasso, and Milton." In *The Building in the Text: Alberti to Shakespeare and Milton*. University Park: Pennsylvania State University Press, 2001. Reads Tasso's poetry as composed in accordance with Renaissance principles of architecture and Humanism. Includes illustrations, bibliographic references, and index.

Giamatti, A. Bartlett. *The Earthly Paradise and the Renaissance Epic*. Princeton, N.J.: Princeton University Press, 1966. Contains an interesting chapter on Armida's garden, with references to classical antecedents. Argues that *Jerusalem Delivered* was one of the most concentrated efforts of the sixteenth century to incorporate classical and chivalric materials into a Christian view of the world.

Greene, Thomas. *The Descent from Heaven: A Study in Epic Continuity*. New Haven, Conn.: Yale University Press, 1963. Presents a concise introduction to the epic from Homer to Vergil to Ludovico Ariosto's failed attempt. Proposes that Tasso does not produce a true epic since *Jerusalem Delivered* is too close to the romance tradition and much of the tragic potential is subordinated to the calls of the Counter-Reformation. Work includes a thorough bibliography.

Günsberg, Maggie. *The Epic Rhetoric of Tasso: Theory and Practice*. Oxford, England: European Humanities Research Centre, Modern Humanities Research Association, 1998. Extended discussion of Tasso's poetics, both from the point of view of sixteenth century theories of poetic language and from the point of view of twentieth century theories of language and the body. Includes bibliographic references and indexes.

Kates, Judith A. *Tasso and Milton: The Problem of Christian Epic*. Lewisburg, Pa.: Bucknell University Press, 1983. Following a discussion of the critical content of *Jerusalem Delivered*, this work analyzes *Discorsi dell' arte poetica* (1587), which is seen as a primer for the epic poem. The central chapter discusses *Jerusalem Delivered* in terms of the classical heroic and the modern romance. Concludes with Tasso's influence on John Milton's *Paradise Lost* (1667) and a lengthy bibliography.

Looney, Dennis. *Compromising the Classics: Romance Epic Narrative in the Italian Renaissance*. Detroit, Mich.: Wayne State University Press, 1996. A study of three Renaissance Italian epic poets: Tasso, Ludovico Ariosto, and Matteo Maria Boiardo. Looks at the way their works both imitate and reinterpret classical epics, and at the importance of this imitation for their contemporaries. Argues that classical influences not only shaped Tasso's work, but that his work in turn changed the way the classics were read and interpreted. Includes bibliographic references and index.

Saez, Richard. *Theodicy in Baroque Literature*. New York: Garland, 1985. Places Tasso's work within a Baroque framework and uses religion as a critical guide. Of major importance is the bibliography that follows the text.

Tasso, Torquato. *Jerusalem Delivered*. Translated and edited by Ralph Nash. Detroit, Mich.: Wayne State University Press, 1987. Easily the most readable translation in prose of *Gerusalemme liberata*. Includes a very useful glossary of names and places and an index of characters.

Zlatar, Zdenko. *The Epic Circle: Allegoresis and the Western Tradition, from Homer to Tasso.* Lewiston, N.Y.: E. Mellen Press, 1997. Discusses Tasso's use of epic allegory and compares it to the work of his predecessors. Includes illustrations, bibliographic references, and index.

SEE ALSO: Ludovico Ariosto; Andrea Gabrieli; Luca Marenzio; Marguerite de Navarre; Pierre de Ronsard; Edmund Spenser; François Villon.

RELATED ARTICLES in *Great Events from History: The Renaissance & Early Modern Era, 1454-1600:* 1545-1563: Council of Trent; July 22, 1566: Pius V Expels the Prostitutes from Rome.

SAINT TERESA OF ÁVILA
Spanish church reformer

Teresa of Ávila, a patron saint of Spain and a doctor of the Church, was active in reforming monasticism in Spain. She also is known for her mystic writings, which describe how mental prayer can bring the soul through successive stages to union with God.

BORN: March 28, 1515; Ávila, Spain
DIED: October 4, 1582; Alba de Tormes, Spain
ALSO KNOWN AS: Teresa de Cepeda y Ahumada (given name); Saint Teresa of Jesus
AREAS OF ACHIEVEMENT: Church reform, religion and theology

EARLY LIFE

Teresa of Ávila (tay-RAY-sah uhv AH-bee-lah) was born during a time of religious fervor, controversy, and fanaticism in Spain. The Inquisition was established to impose purity of thought on the peninsula. In this atmosphere of religious zeal, the Inquisition forced Teresa's grandfather, Juan Sánchez, along with his two sons (including Teresa's father) to accept public humiliation to prove that they were sincere converts to Christianity. Such demonstrations did not necessarily preserve converted Jews from future abuse, so Sánchez took his wife's name, de Cepeda, and left his home in Toledo to begin a new life free from the scrutiny of the Inquisition. Teresa's father, Alonso de Cepeda, settled in Ávila, where he worked as a merchant and tax collector. There he married his second wife, Beatriz Ahumada, Teresa's mother.

Teresa was a cheerful, vivacious child who loved friends and conversation. She was very pretty, plump with white skin and curly black hair. Her looks and personality made her a favorite of her father and her nine siblings, and throughout her life she continued to charm all who knew her. As a child, she enjoyed reading, from her father's serious books to her mother's light romances.

The carefree childhood years ended when Teresa was thirteen and her mother died. For three years, Teresa indulged in behavior that could have damaged her reputation. Her father removed her from danger by sending her to study at the Augustinian convent. In 1536, she overcame her father's objections and entered the Carmelite Convent of the Incarnation in Ávila, where she took her vows the following year.

The Convent of the Incarnation observed a mitigated Rule of Mount Carmel, which meant that it was not very strict. For almost twenty years in the convent, Teresa was torn between her conflicting desires. She yearned for a spiritual life, reading mystic books and practicing mental prayer. At the same time, she desired a secular life, enjoying the admiration of her many visitors. In later years, Teresa wrote against lax convents that permitted nuns to indulge in such vanities, and her experience as a young nun shaped her reform movement. During this time, perhaps partly because of her internal turmoil, she became ill and suffered pain and temporary partial paralysis. For the rest of her life, she endured recurring illness. When she was thirty-nine years old, she had a vision of Christ and then began to have other mystic experiences that finally let her free herself from her worldly temptations and begin her spiritual life as a mystic and church reformer.

LIFE'S WORK

Teresa's first visible manifestations of spirituality were raptures, during which she became rigid and cold with no discernible pulse. During these raptures, Teresa also was reputed to have experienced levitation, floating up uncontrollably, much to her embarrassment. These external manifestations of her spiritual state did not end her struggles with the Spanish hierarchy. Her grandfather's Jewish past was not forgotten, and it made some religious leaders look at her experiences with suspicion.

By 1557, the Catholic Reformation was well under way. The Council of Trent was meeting to defend doctrine against the challenge of Protestants. Spanish Catholics such as Teresa seemed to fear Lutherans as much as they feared appearances of the Devil. As part of the Church's rigorous reform, Pope Paul IV issued a new *Index librorum prohibitorum*, or Index of Prohibited Books, that censored many of the mystical writings that had guided Teresa's mental prayers. Religious authorities searched convents and confiscated books.

In 1559, the Inquisition increased its efforts to protect the peninsula from unorthodox thought, often focusing on converted Jews, whom they believed were susceptible to secret nonconformity often expressed through mystic theology. Church authorities assigned Teresa a series of confessors to examine her raptures, and her confessors' doubts caused her much turmoil. In 1559, she received her most famous vision, seeing and feeling an angel piercing her heart with a spear. This vision settled her doubts; she no longer feared confessors or inquisitors. Thus spiritually at ease, she began her active life as a reformer of the Carmelite Order.

In 1560, Teresa and a small group of nuns at the Convent of the Incarnation made a vow to follow the more rigorous unmitigated rule of the original Carmelites. Her desire to move out of her unreformed convent into a new one in Ávila raised an outcry. Many monks and nuns objected to Teresa's dedication, because such a reform represented an implicit criticism of their own lives. Further objection came from the population of Ávila. In the mid-sixteenth century, almost one-fourth of the population in Spain was ecclesiastical, either clerical or monastic. The lay public had to finance this religious population, and the people of Ávila were reluctant to support another convent within their city walls. Opposition from both of these groups, monastic and lay, plagued the reform movement that represented much of Teresa's life's work.

Two years after Teresa began her efforts at reform, she received permission to establish a new convent in Ávila. In August of 1562, she founded the reform convent of San José, and became its prioress the following year. As a symbolic gesture of her new reform, she and the novices removed their shoes to wear rough sandals. This act gave her reform movement the name Discalced (without shoes), and writers describe the subsequent struggles within the Carmelite movement as between the Calced and Discalced groups.

Teresa's notoriety brought her again to the attention of the Inquisition, which ordered her to write an account of her life for its review. In 1562, Teresa completed the first version of her autobiography, which she later expanded. The Inquisition found this *Libro de su vida* (wr. 1565, pb. 1611; *The Life of the Mother Teresa of Jesus*, 1611) acceptable. This work is a major source of information about the saint's early life. It also opens a new and influential side of Teresa's active life: her writings. In addition to her autobiography, Teresa wrote four books, six shorter works (including a collection of verses), and many letters, of which 458 survive. Her most famous mystical works are *El camino de perfección* (wr. 1565, pb. 1583; *The Way of Perfection*, 1852), written to guide the nuns in her newly reformed convents, and *El castillo interior: O, Tratado de las moradas* (wr. 1577, pb. 1588; *The Interior Castle: Or, The Mansions*, 1852). In these and other works, Teresa described her techniques of mental prayer, which had been so important in her own spiritual growth.

From 1567 to 1576, Teresa expanded the Discalced Reform by establishing new convents throughout most of Spain. Teresa, frequently ill, traveled throughout the countryside to bring enclosed convents, erected in poverty, to many parts of the kingdom. The indefatigable founder overcame problems of opposition and financing

Saint Teresa of Ávila. (Library of Congress)

to found seventeen reform convents for women. During her travels, Teresa met John of the Cross, a Carmelite and priest, who became her confessor, friend, and supporter in establishing two Discalced monasteries for men.

Between 1576 and 1578, the expansion of the reform movement was stopped by increasing pressure from the opposition. The Calced Carmelites kidnapped leaders of the Discalceds to force them back into observance of the Mitigated Rule of Carmel. Calced monks imprisoned John of the Cross in Toledo for eight months during these times of troubles. The turmoil reached Teresa herself; once again, the Inquisition summoned her to respond to its interrogations. Throughout this period, Teresa wrote many letters to gather support for her movement and was able to win the support of influential patrons, including King Philip II of Spain.

Finally, in 1580, her reform movement was victorious. Pope Gregory XIII officially separated the Calced from the Discalced Carmelites, sanctioning the reform and creating its independent administration. Teresa's favorite, Jerome Gracián, was made the first leader of the Discalceds, and John of the Cross became an administrator of the movement. Teresa was content that papal authority had safeguarded her reform, and she spent the last two years of her life establishing three more foundations and writing many letters. She became ill as she journeyed to the reform convent in Alba and died there on October 4, 1582. (The day after her death, the Gregorian reform calendar was adopted, and her feast day is celebrated on October 15 because of the changed calendar.)

SIGNIFICANCE

Nine months after Teresa of Ávila's death, her followers exhumed her body and allegedly found that it had not decayed. Her supporters used this discovery to forward her cause for sanctity, and her immediate popularity led to repeated dismemberments of the body and distribution of her relics to many churches. In 1614, Pope Paul V declared her blessed, and the Spanish parliament proclaimed her the patroness of Spain in 1617. In 1622, Pope Gregory XV pronounced Teresa a saint.

One of Teresa's enduring accomplishments was her reform of Spanish monasticism, which was part of the Catholic Reformation's response to the growth of Protestantism. The Discalced Reform she began continued and spread after her death to remain a force in Spanish life. Teresa is probably most widely remembered for her mystical experiences and for her written articulation of spiritual doctrine. The sculptor Gian Lorenzo Bernini popularized the piercing of Teresa's heart in his statue *The Ecstasy*

of Saint Teresa, made in 1645 for the Church of Santa Maria della Vittoria in Rome. Reverence for this ecstasy grew in the eighteenth century, when churchmen examined Teresa's heart and reported that it bore a hole as evidence of the angel's piercing arrow. In 1726, Pope Benedict XIII instituted the Feast of the Transverberation of Teresa's heart to commemorate this mystical event.

In 1970, Pope Paul VI declared Teresa to be a doctor of the church and her works worthy of study. All Teresa's major spiritual writings include discussions of her mystic theology, but the most sophisticated expression of her theology is found in *The Interior Castle*. Teresa wrote this book while in a trance, and it discusses the soul's capacity to move progressively through the rooms of itself to reach God, who dwells at the center. By locating God at the center of the soul, Teresa expressed God's presence and accessibility to searching believers.

The Interior Castle mirrors the life of the saint herself. Teresa had to cut herself off from her past, which in Counter-Reformation Spain marked her as a converted Jew; she called herself Teresa of Jesus, renouncing her family name. She had to transcend the temptations that bound her for twenty years in feelings of sin, and she fought against a monastic system that she believed had grown too lax for spiritual safety. She did all these things by retreating to a strength inside herself, where she found God. Through this strength, she changed her world and wrote to tell others how to change theirs.

—*Joyce E. Salisbury*

FURTHER READING

Clissold, Stephen. *St. Teresa of Ávila*. New York: Harper & Row, 1982. A fine, easy-to-read short biography that brings Teresa's world and accomplishments to life. Provides a sensitive balance between the reputation of the saint, with her raptures and levitations, and the woman, who worked hard in her reform movement. Contains an index.

Howells, Edward. *John of the Cross and Teresa of Ávila: Mystical Knowing and Selfhood*. New York: Crossroad, 2002. Study of the theology and philosophy of mind put forward by John and Teresa, demonstrating and analyzing their notion that the dynamic nature of the Holy Trinity bridges the gap between interior subjective experience and exterior objective reality. Includes bibliographic references and index.

Lincoln, Victoria. *Teresa: A Woman*. Albany: State University of New York Press, 1984. A thorough, well-researched, and readable biography of Teresa with details on all aspects of her life and work. Stresses the woman rather than the saint. Contains a useful index and a brief bibliography.

May, Gerald G. *The Dark Night of the Soul: A Psychiatrist Explores the Connection Between Darkness and Spiritual Growth*. New York: HarperSanFrancisco, 2004. Psychological study of Saint John of the Cross and Teresa of Ávila, illuminating the positive and transformative aspects of spiritual darkness. Includes map, bibliographic references, and index.

O'Brien, Kate. *Teresa of Ávila*. London: Max Parrish, 1951. A short book describing Teresa's life and work. Rambling at times, but provides background on the Carmelite Order and Teresa's reform work.

Peers, E. Allison. *Saint Teresa of Jesus, and Other Essays and Addresses*. London: Faber & Faber, 1953. A collection of essays by the preeminent Teresan scholar. Contains an index.

Sackville-West, Victoria. *The Eagle and the Dove*. Garden City, N.Y.: Doubleday, Doran, 1944. A comparison of the life of Saint Teresa with that of Thérèse de Lisieux. The section on Teresa of Ávila offers a short account of her mystic experiences, written from within the Catholic tradition.

Whalen, James. *The Spiritual Teachings of Teresa of Ávila and Adrian Van Kaam: Formative Spirituality*. New York: University Press of America, 1984. Offers a sophisticated description of Teresa's theology and compares it with a twentieth century existential philosopher. Useful especially for those who want to explore the complexities of Teresa's thought and its relevance for modern times. Contains a full annotated bibliography.

Williams, Rowan. *Teresa of Ávila*. New York: Continuum, 2000. Written by an archbishop, this biography of Teresa emphasizes her belief that Christianity is defined by the belief in a God who sacrificed dignity and status to become incarnated for the sake of humanity. Traces the theme of incarnation in all of Teresa's major writings. Includes bibliographic references and index.

SEE ALSO: Isaac ben Judah Abravanel; Barbe Acarie; Saint Angela Merici; Saint Catherine of Genoa; Vittoria Colonna; Gregory XIII; Saint John of the Cross; Saint Philip Neri; Philip II; Tomás de Torquemada.

RELATED ARTICLES in *Great Events from History: The Renaissance & Early Modern Era, 1454-1600:* Beginning c. 1495: Reform of the Spanish Church; August 15, 1534: Founding of the Jesuit Order.

TINTORETTO
Italian painter

Tintoretto was a leading exponent of the mannerist movement in painting, a style that parted with the rational symmetry of the Renaissance and moved toward dramatic imbalance and tension and the creation of mysterious moods by means of chiaroscuro, radical foreshortening, and unorthodox brushwork.

BORN: c. 1518; Venice, Republic of Venice (now in Italy)
DIED: May 31, 1594; Venice
ALSO KNOWN AS: Jacopo Robusti
AREA OF ACHIEVEMENT: Art

EARLY LIFE

Jacopo Robusti derived his artistic pseudonym Tintoretto (teen-toh-RAYT-toh) from his father's trade as a dyer (*tintore*). He left Venice only once or twice in his lifetime, for a visit to Mantua and the Gonzaga court in 1580 and a probable trip to Rome in 1547. His marriage at age thirty-six produced eight children, of whom four, most notably Domenico and Marietta, were painters.

Tintoretto may have studied under Bonifazio de' Pitati (Bonifazio Veronese). Almost uniquely among Renaissance artists, however, he was largely self-taught, copying available models of Michelangelo's works and devising his own clay or wax models, dressing them, arranging them in different attitudes in cardboard houses, and introducing light through tiny windows in order to study the effect of lights and shadow on the figures. He also suspended the models from above to learn their chiaroscuro effects and foreshortenings when seen from below. As early as 1545, the letters of Pietro Aretino, Tintoretto's first important patron (for whom he painted *Apollo and Marsyas* in 1545), criticize his arrogance and apparent hasty sketchiness (which stemmed from the artist's early work in fresco but was also a genuine factor in his inventive style).

In his own lifetime, Tintoretto's biography was written by Giorgio Vasari. In 1642, Carlo Ridolfi's adulatory biography reported that Tintoretto had served an apprenticeship with Titian that ended within days because of Titian's jealousy of his pupil's talent coupled with Tintoretto's youthful pride. The real reason for the dismissal, however, may have been Tintoretto's careless style. The combined judgment of Titian and Aretino were, in any case, costly in terms of artistic patronage, as they were the arbiters of taste in Venice. Nevertheless, Tintoretto reputedly hung in his studio the motto (coined by Paolo Pino in his *Dialogo della pittura*, 1548), "The drawing of Michelangelo, the color of Titian."

As Tintoretto began his career, however, the Tuscano-Roman style and the colorful, horizontal Venetian style of these two masters were locked in a losing struggle with the new mannerist impulse throughout Italy; in Venice, the carriers were Andrea Schiavone, Veronese, and, eventually, Tintoretto.

Tintoretto's earliest works (1539-1540) are standard *sacre conversazioni* (Virgin and Child with saints), in the warm reds, golds, and whites expected of a painter of a Venice dominated by Titian. They contain almost nothing of the conscious artificialities of emergent mannerism. His early *The Last Supper* (1545-1547) is marked by emotional restraint and horizontal symmetry; only the violent foreshortening of the floor is a mannerist device. Tintoretto's reputed visit to Rome and his first masterpiece culminate this early period of laborious experimentation. His *Saint Mark Rescuing a Slave* (1548) indeed evinces the muscular forms of Michelangelo and the rich color of Titian. The large monument forecasts the dramatic use of light so prominent in Tintoretto's narrative style.

LIFE'S WORK

During the 1550's, the chief elements of Tintoretto's unique style found their place in his voluminous output. *Susanna and the Elders* (1550) manifests the use of strong diagonals. In the Genesis scenes for the Scuola della Trinitá (1550-1553), the colors are less brilliant as Tintoretto first joined color, light, and form to create the mood dictated by the subject matter. The Old Testament scenes (1554-1555) brought to Madrid by Diego Velázquez mark an important moment in Tintoretto's evolving mannerism: The six ceiling paintings feature color that is subtle but sparkling with light and an almost improvisational sketchiness. In the later 1550's, the artist began to use crowds in procession to accentuate space. In *Saint Ursula and Her Virgins* and the *Miracle of the Loaves*

Tintoretto. (Library of Congress)

and Fishes, the processions fade away into the depths of the paintings, dissolving in the distance in a *non finito* (unfinished) diaphanous sketchiness.

Between 1552 and 1562, Tintoretto contributed, for the cost of materials alone (he was disliked in the artistic community for frequently underpricing his art or working free), several paintings to his beloved parish church, Madonna dell' Orto. One was his famous *Presentation of the Virgin in the Temple*. On either side of the high altar, his *Laws and Golden Calf* and *The Last Judgment* rose fifty feet high.

During the 1560's, Tintoretto's work became increasingly dramatic, psychological, and artistically sophisticated. He achieved these effects by using a less diffuse, more immediate light source allowing more pronounced chiaroscuro, increased use of diagonal composition, and vast panoramic scenes. He continued to be prolific. In the *Finding of the Body of Saint Mark*, the radically oblique, sharply receding vault of the church and the stark chiaroscuro enhance the miraculous event taking place in the foreground. Similarly, the ominous storm lightening the edge of the clouds is the focus of the *Translation of the Body of Saint Mark* (both were painted for the Scuola di

S. Marco in 1562-1566). Tintoretto concurrently painted for S. Trovaso Church a *Crucifixion* with massive diagonals and a *The Last Supper.*

In 1564, Tintoretto started his work in the Scuola di S. Rocco, which was to span twenty-three years. The Scuola was an asymmetrical building, worthy of Tintoretto's bold designs. There followed a series of large scenes of Christ's Passion, including an immense and profoundly moving *Crucifixion*, which the nineteenth century English art critic and historian John Ruskin pronounced "above all praise." Tintoretto was made a member of the Scuola, a sort of civic-service lodge, and later a lifetime officer.

Contemporaneously (1564-1568), Tintoretto produced a *Crucifixion*, a *Resurrection*, and a *Descent of Christ into Limbo* for S. Cassiano Church, a *The Last Judgment* for the Sala del Scrutinio in the doges' palace, and for the Church of S. Rocco, a great *Saint Roche in Prison*. Between 1576 and 1581, Tintoretto resumed his work in the upper hall of the Scuola di S. Rocco. There, the ceiling received twenty-one Old Testament scenes, while the walls were decorated with ten events from the life of Christ, of which the *Baptism* and *Ascension* are noteworthy.

Meanwhile, Tintoretto's trip to Mantua in 1580 bore fruit in the eight battle scenes completed with the help of assistants. From 1577 to 1584, too, the artist painted, with less enthusiasm, the four small allegories of classical mythology in the Sala del' Anticollegio of the doges' palace. He also executed important scenes from Venice's history in the Sala del Senato, and in the imposing Sala del Maggior Consiglio, an enormous *Paradise* occupying the years 1584-1587. It was the largest oil painting ever done until that time.

In 1583, Tintoretto returned to the Scuola di S. Rocco, this time producing scenes from the life of the Madonna in the lower hall. His conception was consummate: His space opens out dynamically in all directions and his perspectives are limitless; light dominates and dissolves volume and color, rendering his figures incorporeal and unfinished. The entire project in Scuola di S. Rocco has been compared to the Sistine Chapel and the Raphael stanze. Tintoretto finally put down his brush in 1587 and painted no more for the Scuola di S. Rocco.

Among Tintoretto's approximately three hundred paintings are dozens of portraits. In these, he aimed to capture the inner spirit or personality of the subject more than his clothing or background. Notable is his self-portrait at age seventy. Additionally, about one hundred drawings survive; they are mainly practice sets by

which Tintoretto perfected his chiaroscuro and foreshortening skills and cartoons for mosaics in San Marco Church.

His last works include two large oils for the presbytery of S. Giorgio Maggiore. Of these, *The Last Supper* epitomized all his earlier achievements and effects and attained a new level of psychological impact: The darkened room is lit by a lamp striking the disciples from behind and by an unnatural glow radiating from the halo of Christ, who intently administers communion; the table thrusts diagonally into the canvas; angels hovering above add their mystical presence. All this is in stark contrast to the realism of the Venetian pitchers on the table, a cat drinking from the water cistern, and the everyday activities of servants taking place in the same room.

Tintoretto's last work, the *Entombment* for the chapel of S. Giorgio Maggiore (1594), also employs a double illumination, one the natural sunset, the other artificial, or rather spiritual, which divides the groups of figures by their separate lighting.

SIGNIFICANCE

The legendary rivalry between the older Titian and Tintoretto has occasioned an ongoing division among art critics. Both artists are truly representative of Venetian artistic tradition, but Titian had known the glorious time of Venice; his art reflects the sensuous richness of the city. Tintoretto, however, was born in a Venice humbled by the League of Cambrai (1508); he grew up in a Counter-Reformation atmosphere of religious revival. Thus, a religious mysticism pervades his art.

Contemporaries also took sides. Vasari and Aretino favored Titian. In the seventeenth century, the age of the Baroque, the tide moved to Tintoretto, who was much admired by El Greco and Ridolfi. The eighteenth century saw Tintoretto unfavorably, through the neoclassical eyes of the Age of Reason. Ruskin represents the nineteenth century preference for Tintoretto over Titian and even over Michelangelo. The nineteenth century Swiss art historian Jakob Burckhardt, however, regarded Tintoretto as crude, barbaric, and artistically immoral, "abandoning himself to the most shameless superficiality."

Today, Tintoretto remains a giant; he has been regarded variously as one who succeeded in spiritualizing reality, a forerunner of modern illusionism or of German Expressionism. The theatrical quality of his later works comports well with modern artistic sensibilities, which share his delight in foreshortening, his artificial use of lighting to emphasize action or suggest spirituality, his penchant for oblique composition, his use of subdued subaqueous color, his *non finito* sketchiness, and his pre-occupation with the human body caught unfolding and poised in mid-action.

—*Daniel C. Scavone*

FURTHER READING

Berenson, Bernhard. *Italian Pictures of the Renaissance: A List of the Principal Artists and Their Works, with an Index of Places, Venetian School.* 2 vols. London: Phaidon Press, 1957. Volume 1 includes a complete list of Tintoretto's works and their locations; volume 2 contains seventy-six black-and-white plates. Both volumes present a list of all the principal Venetian artists, their works and their locations, and 1,334 representative plates.

Honour, Hugh. *The Companion Guide to Venice.* London: Fontana Books, 1970. Tintoretto's art is affectionately discussed as discovered by the author in the churches and galleries of Venice. En route, the reader is exposed to the cultural and political history of Venice in its living stones and works of art and in its relationship to the rest of Italy. Street plans and museum layouts bring the world of Tintoretto into clarity.

Krischel, Roland. *Jacopo Tintoretto, 1519-1594.* Translated by Anthea Bell. Cologne, Germany: Könemann, 2000. Short but detailed study of Tintoretto's life and work, emphasizing the influence of Venetian culture and ideals on his painting. Includes illustrations, chronology, glossary, and bibliography.

Newton, Eric. *Tintoretto.* New York: Longmans, Green, 1952. A superlative biography with details not found elsewhere. Throughout, Newton draws from Ridolfi and urges caution in accepting Ridolfi's interpretations. Includes a chronological list of Tintoretto's paintings and seventy-six black-and-white plates.

Nichols, Tom. *Tintoretto: Tradition and Identity.* London: Reaktion Books, 1999. Emphasizes the originality, and indeed the radicality, of Tintoretto's works and their difference from the traditional Venetian School of Titian. Includes illustrations, bibliographic references, and index.

Ridolfi, Carlo. *The Life of Tintoretto, and of His Children Domenico and Marietta.* Translated and introduced by Catherine Enggass and Robert Enggass. University Park: Pennsylvania State University Press, 1984. A translation of volume 2 of Ridolfi's 1642 classic work. Ridolfi, the preeminent art historian of his day, provides an account from a time nearly contemporaneous with that of his subjects.

Rosand, David. *Painting in Sixteenth-Century Venice: Titian, Veronese, Tintoretto.* Rev. ed. New York: Cambridge University Press, 1997. Wide-ranging study of Renaissance Venice's most famous painters, discussing the formal qualities characteristic of the Venetian School, the techniques of painting employed by Tintoretto and his fellows, and the social, economic, and political factors influencing the art they produced. Includes thirty-two pages of plates, illustrations, appendix of primary documents, bibliographic references, and index.

Tintoretto. *Tintoretto: The Paintings and Drawings.* Edited by Hans Tietze. London: Phaidon Press, 1948. A short biography and appreciation of Tintoretto. Especially useful for its three hundred black-and-white illustrations and excellent detailed commentary on each plate.

SEE ALSO: Andrea del Sarto; Pietro Aretino; The Carracci Family; Giorgione; El Greco; Leonardo da Vinci; Michelangelo; Piero della Francesca; Raphael; Jacopo Sansovino; Titian; Giorgio Vasari; Paolo Veronese.

RELATED ARTICLES in *Great Events from History: The Renaissance & Early Modern Era, 1454-1600:* November 3, 1522-November 17, 1530: Correggio Paints the *Assumption of the Virgin*; c. 1500: Revival of Classical Themes in Art; June, 1564: Tintoretto Paints for the Scuola di San Rocco.

Marietta Robusti Tintoretto
Italian painter

Tintoretto is one of the few women painters to emerge in the late sixteenth century. She was known as a portrait painter who also assisted her father, the painter Jacopo Tintoretto, with his commissions.

Born: c. 1554; Venice, Republic of Venice (now in Italy)

Died: c. 1590; Venice

Also known as: Marietta Robusti (given name); La Tintoretto

Area of achievement: Art

Early Life

Marietta Robusti Tintoretto (teen-toh-RAYT-toh) learned painting in her father's workshop. This training was like a number of her female contemporaries, who studied in their family studios, such as Lavinia Fontana. Given the gender restrictions of guild practice and late Renaissance society, this familial instruction was the only way women could develop their artistic talents.

Marietta was the child of the famous Venetian painter Jacopo Robusti, known as Tintoretto. She was the eldest of eight children, which included her painter brothers Domenico (1560-1635) and Marco (1561-1637). She was apparently her father's favorite, at least until her younger brothers matured, and he personally oversaw much of her education. Tintoretto not only taught her to paint but also, according to the seventeenth century biographer of Venetian artists Carlo Ridolfi, had her dress as a boy to accompany him to his many projects. She was frequently at his side and thus learned a great deal more than strict studio training could have given her. Marietta also assisted him on many of his projects. Tintoretto arranged her marriage to a local jeweler, Mario Augusto, so she could continue to have access to his studio and her work there.

Life's Work

Marietta never received large commissions of frescoes or altar panels but instead engaged herself as a portraitist. This apparently was the limiting genre for artists of her gender in the late Renaissance. It is thought that Marietta's painting technique was almost indistinguishable from her father's, and she was given the name La Tintoretto in honor of this fact. It is believed that, in most working studios at the time, the hands of many talented assistants were involved in paintings attributed to the master artist. Historians speculate that Marietta's contributions to her father's studio and work were significant.

A single *Self-Portrait* in the Uffizi, Florence, is the only painting that can be assigned to Marietta Tintoretto with certainty. However, *Portrait of Two Men*, in Dresden, Germany—originally considered one of her father's best—was found to have the initials "MR" (Marietta Robusti) and is the only known work signed by her. Three other portraits—in the Prado in Madrid, Spain—are also attributed to her, one of which is thought to be a self-portrait.

The location of the portraits in Spain helps confirm Ridolfi's report that Emperor Maximilian II and Philip II of Spain expressed interest in her paintings. Some historians suggest that both rulers invited her to paint at their courts. She either refused in order to stay close to her father and home studio or was not allowed to go by her father, who wanted her close to him. Although Marietta's hand is thought to be evident in her father's painting of 1578, *St. Agnes Reviving Licinio*, in Santa Maria dell' Orto, this is largely speculative. Two drawings in a private collection in Milan have also been attributed to her.

La Tintoretto died during childbirth at the age of thirty, around 1590. Some claim that her father's grief over her death hastened his death a few years later. Her loss would have been keenly felt since not only did she die young, but she also was an exceptional painter in a family of famous artists, and she was a gifted musician and singer.

Significance

Marietta's short life, lack of major commissions, a brief career possibly inhibited by marriage and certainly inhibited by the status of women in the late Renaissance, and no secure paintings have resulted in a speculative corpus of fewer than six works. However, many believe that she was a major factor in the quality and quantity of work produced in her father's studio and name.

Details of Marietta's life remain obscure, and the few examples of paintings associated with her are not well documented. She never claimed the success of her contemporary among women painters in Italy, Sofonisba Anguissola, or of her successor Artemesia Gentileschi (1593-1652/1653), both of whom received commissions for altar panels and whose independent activities extended beyond portraiture. Marietta pre-deceased her father and, thus, was unable to inherit his studio with her brothers Domenico and Marco, who continued Tintoretto's shop for four more decades after his death.

—*Edward J. Olszewski*

FURTHER READING

Chadwick, Whitney. *Women, Art, and Society.* 3d ed. New York: Thames and Hudson, 2002. A popular reference book that includes several pages on La Tintoretto.

Jacopo Tintoretto, Portraits. Milan, Italy: Electa, 1994. An exhibition catalog with entries and essays on forty-one portraits and self-portraits displayed at the Accademia, Venice, touching peripherally on Marietta.

Krischel, Roland. *Jacopo Tintoretto, 1519-1594.* Translated by Anthea Bell. Cologne, Germany: Könemann, 2000. A study on Tintoretto that includes references to Marietta. Bibliographical references.

Nichols, Tom. *Tintoretto, Tradition, and Identity.* London: Reaktion Books, 1999. A comprehensive study of the artist's life, career, and major paintings, with reference to Marietta.

Ridolfi, Carlo. *The Life of Tintoretto, and of His Children Domenico and Marietta.* Translated and introduced by Catherine Enggass and Robert Enggass. University Park: Pennsylvania State University Press, 1984. A translation of volume 2 of Ridolfi's 1642 classic work. Ridolfi, the preeminent art historian of his day, provides an account from a time nearly contemporaneous with that of his subjects.

Rosand, David. *Painting in Sixteenth-Century Venice: Titian, Veronese, Tintoretto.* Rev. ed. New York: Cambridge University Press, 1997. A standard study on late Renaissance Italian and specifically Venetian painting. Provides a good background to the historical and social situations of artists. Includes plates, extensive bibliography, and index.

SEE ALSO: Sofonisba Anguissola; Lavinia Fontana; Tintoretto; Titian.

RELATED ARTICLE in *Great Events from History: The Renaissance & Early Modern Era, 1454-1600:* June, 1564: Tintoretto Paints for the Scuola di San Rocco.

TITIAN
Italian painter

Titian is considered one of the greatest artists of the Italian High Renaissance. During his long and prolific career, he developed an oil-painting technique of successive glazes and broad paint application that influenced generations of artists.

BORN: c. 1490; Pieve di Cadore, Republic of Venice (now in Italy)
DIED: August 27, 1576; Venice (now in Italy)
ALSO KNOWN AS: Tiziano Vecellio; Tiziano Vecelli
AREA OF ACHIEVEMENT: Art

EARLY LIFE

Titian (TISH-ehn) was born Tiziano Vecellio. Over the centuries, there has been considerable confusion concerning his birth date, as a result of a misprint in his biography by sixteenth century art historian Giorgio Vasari, who recorded it as 1480. The progress of Titian's career, along with other documentary evidence, indicates instead that Titian was born sometime between 1488 and 1490.

According to the 1557 biography of Titian's life written by his friend Lodovico Dolce, it is known that Titian arrived in Venice, in the company of his brother Francesco, when he was only eight years old. He first worked for the mosaicist Sebastiano Zuccato but soon entered the workshop of the aging painter Gentile Bellini. Unhappy with Gentile's old-fashioned style, he moved to the studio of Gentile's brother, Giovanni, and it is there that Titian learned the current Venetian style and techniques. He also met the short-lived but magnificent painter Giorgione. By 1508, Titian had left Bellini's studio and was working with Giorgione, perhaps as his assistant, on exterior frescoes for the Fondaco dei Tedeschi (German commercial headquarters) in Venice.

Until around 1515, Titian's style would remain very close to that of Giorgione. In fact, scholars have difficulty distinguishing between the two hands when their paintings from this period are unsigned. The most famous example of this attribution problem is the so-called *Fête Champêtre* of around 1510, now in the Louvre. The lush pastoral setting, soft lighting, and strong atmospheric qualities characterize the styles of both artists at this time.

Titian. (Hulton|Archive by Getty Images)

In 1511, Titian completed his first dated work, a series of three frescoes in the Scuola di San Antonio at Padua. This commission established his career. Within the next decade, his independent, mature style found expression.

LIFE'S WORK

In 1518, Titian's *Assumption of the Virgin* was unveiled at the Church of the Frari in Venice. In this dynamic, monumental composition, Titian seemed suddenly to assimilate the achievements of the Roman High Renaissance style. Since there is no evidence that he had yet traveled beyond the region near Venice, it is assumed that he learned these stylistic lessons through visiting artists, drawings, and reproductive engravings. The painting reflects the harmony and delineation of forms typical of High Renaissance classicism, and an energetic movement similar to that found in Raphael's Vatican murals and Michelangelo's Sistine Chapel ceiling. To this, Titian added his distinctive brilliant colors, unified by successive layers of glazes.

During the succeeding decades, Titian's reputation grew until he was, along with Michelangelo, the most famous artist in Europe. His patrons included some of the most powerful men and families of the age. For Alfonso I d'Este of Ferrara he created, among other works, three famous mythological paintings, *The Bacchanal of the Andrians* (c. 1520), *The Worship of Venus* (1518-1519), and *Bacchus and Ariadne* (1522-1523), which were installed in Alfonso's alabaster *studiolo*. He also worked for Gonzaga of Mantua and several popes. His most important patrons, however, were the Spanish Habsburgs. In 1533, Titian was summoned to Bologna for the first of several meetings with the emperor Charles V, who became one of his greatest admirers. The emperor made him a count and brought him to Augsburg two times as court painter. When Charles died in 1558, his son Philip II continued the relationship.

These prestigious patrons brought Titian fame, wealth, and social position. A shrewd businessman, he invested wisely and by the 1530's was living in luxury. Sometime in the early 1520's, he began a relationship with a woman named Cecilia, by whom he had four children, two before they married in 1525. Cecilia died in 1530, and the next year, Titian moved his family to a palace that came to be known as the Casa Grande. There he lived a princely existence far removed from the craftsperson status artists had held only one hundred years earlier.

Titian's compositions were often revolutionary as he freed Renaissance classicism from its planar symmetry. He exploited the dramatic possibilities of diagonal placings and perspectives, and set up unusual spectator viewpoints. In this way, he could give traditional subjects a fresh look. This predisposition to creative compositions was evident very early in his career. *The Gypsy Madonna* (1510-1515) is a variation of the half-length Madonna and Child popular with Giovanni Bellini. Yet Titian has moved all the major forms off center and encouraged the viewer to look diagonally into a landscape to the left of the Madonna. *The Madonna of the Pesaro Family* (1519-1526) shows a more radical alteration of a traditional subject. The pyramidal grouping of figures, with the enthroned Madonna at the apex, has been shifted so that it is placed diagonally to the frontal plane.

Titian's style never stagnated. Over the years, his brushwork loosened and forms were increasingly defined by color and light instead of line. In 1546, he returned from an eight-month visit to Rome, and from this point on, his broad handling of paint increased. The result was a type of optical realism, in which the structures of objects were built up through a free application of paint. Details that the human eye does not see without close inspection were not delineated with precise drawing but rather indicated with freely manipulated color and light. In the hands of a master such as Titian, the result was one of startling reality since he had essentially reproduced with paint the reality that the human eye actually absorbs. An example of this loosely painted style was *The Rape of Europa* (1559-1562), in which textures of fur, skin, cloth, and water were faithfully rendered through broad relationships of color and light. Titian's development of this technique, which would influence artists throughout forthcoming centuries, played no small part in his fame.

Toward the end of his long career, Titian's technique loosened still further, and a certain dematerialization of form took place in his paintings. Especially in his religious works, which reflected his own growing awareness of mortality, physicality was overcome by mystical light and emotional expression. Like the late works of Michelangelo, Titian's final paintings seemed more concerned with spirituality than with the substance of the natural world.

SIGNIFICANCE

Titian's career was a watershed in the evolution of artistic status within society. Well traveled and well respected, he was a friend of princes and intellectuals. Collectors clamored for his works and, despite a large workshop and numerous assistants, he could not satisfy them all. The laws of supply and demand were in his favor and provided a degree of freedom for artistic development rarely seen before. He became the first artist to achieve the status of gentleman.

As early as the middle of the sixteenth century, artists and intellectuals argued over whether Titian or Michelangelo was the greater painter. At the center of this discussion was Titian's emphasis on color, versus Michelangelo's preference for line, in creating forms. Some art historians see a dualism of technique and expression beginning with these two artists that can be traced through Baroque art to the theories and practices of the later European art academies. To be sure, sixteenth century Italian painters formulated a tradition that would serve as a reference point for art until the middle of the nineteenth century. Titian's style was an essential option within that tradition.

—Madeline Cirillo Archer

FURTHER READING

Freedberg, Sidney J. *Painting in Italy: 1500-1600.* Baltimore: Penguin Books, 1975. An extensive chronological survey of painting in sixteenth century Italy, this volume discusses the various stages of Titian's career as they relate to contemporary artistic developments in Venice and the rest of Italy. A solid introduction to Titian's art, with an emphasis on stylistic issues. Contains limited but pertinent photographs and a basic bibliography.

Hope, Charles, et al. *Titian: Essays.* London: National Gallery, 2003. This collection of essays by world-class Titian scholars was produced to accompany a major exhibition of the artist's work at the National Gallery in London. Includes lavish illustrations, bibliographic references, and index.

Meilman, Patricia, ed. *The Cambridge Companion to Titian.* New York: Cambridge University Press, 2004. Collects interpretive essays on Titian's works by major scholars. Essays are grouped into three sections: "Titian's Diverse Genres," "Titian and His Art," and "Titian Interpreted." Includes twenty-eight pages of plates, illustrations, bibliographic references, and index.

Panofsky, Erwin. *Problems in Titian, Mostly Iconographic.* New York: New York University Press, 1969. Examines the subjects of a number of Titian's paintings and how they connect with medieval and Renaissance iconographic traditions. Shows how Titian drew on both popular imagery and high philosophical ideas in devising his symbolism. Contains numerous photographs. There is no bibliography, but as with all Panofsky's work, the extensive citations in the footnotes serve as the equivalent.

Pedrocco, Filippo, and Maria Agnese Chiari Moretto Wiel. *Titian.* Translated by Corrado Federici. New York: Rizzoli, 2001. A complete catalogue raisonné, designed to replace that of Wethey, taking into account both research and restoration work done in the final quarter of the twentieth century. In addition to color reproductions of every painting attributed to the artist, critical essays discuss Titian's life, work, critical reception, and artistic, social, and political milieu. Includes bibliographic references and index.

Rosand, David. *Painting in Sixteenth-Century Venice: Titian, Veronese, Tintoretto.* Rev. ed. New York: Cambridge University Press, 1997. Contains several innovative articles that place Titian's compositions within the pictorial and theatrical traditions of Venice. Lengthy analysis of *The Madonna of the Pesaro Family* and *The Presentation of the Virgin.* Contains excellent illustrations, photographs, and bibliography.

Rosand, David, and Michelangelo Muraro. *Titian and the Venetian Woodcut.* Washington, D.C.: International Exhibitions Foundation, 1976. Discusses Titian's involvement with the graphic media, especially woodcuts. Extensive illustrations of woodcuts by Titian and other artists influenced by his imagery or technique. Expansive catalog entries on the prints, with excellent illustrations and insightful art historical analysis. Includes a topically limited bibliography.

Wethey, Harold E. *The Paintings of Titian.* 3 vols. New York: Phaidon, 1969-1975. The standard reference in English and the most recent catalogue raisonné of Titian's paintings. Each volume contains general essays surveying the artist's biography, chronology, stylistic development, and handling of themes. Extensive catalog entries on every known or attributed painting, with photographic reproductions (black-and-white) of the complete works. Wethey's attributions of some early and minor works are not universally accepted, yet this remains one of the most complete sources on Titian.

Zuffi, Stephano. *Titian.* Edited by Stephano Zuffi and Stefano Peccatori. New York: DK Publishing, 1999. Brief biographical study of Titian, followed by reproduction of the major works. Includes indexes.

SEE ALSO: Pietro Aretino; Giovanni Bellini; The Carracci Family; Charles V; Vittoria Colonna; Giorgione; El Greco; Isabella d'Este; Michelangelo; Paul III; Philip II; Raphael; Tintoretto; Giorgio Vasari; Paolo Veronese; Andreas Vesalius.

RELATED ARTICLES in *Great Events from History: The Renaissance & Early Modern Era, 1454-1600:* c. 1500: Revival of Classical Themes in Art; November 3, 1522-November 17, 1530: Correggio Paints the *Assumption of the Virgin;* 1543: Vesalius Publishes *On the Fabric of the Human Body;* June, 1564: Tintoretto Paints for the Scuola di San Rocco.

TOMÁS DE TORQUEMADA
Spanish religious leader

Torquemada was the most prominent religious leader in shaping the Spanish Inquisition, which led ultimately to the expulsion of Jews from Spain in 1492.

BORN: 1420; Torquemada, near Valladolid, Castile (now in Spain)

DIED: September 16, 1498; Ávila, Castile (now in Spain)

AREAS OF ACHIEVEMENT: Church reform, religion and theology, government and politics

EARLY LIFE

Tomás de Torquemada (toh-MAHS day tawr-kay-MAH-dah) was born in the small town of Torquemada (a name derived from the Latin phrase *torre cremata*, burnt tower), in northern Castile. The only son of the nobleman Pero Fernández de Torquemada, Tomás was a nephew of Juan de Torquemada, cardinal of San Sisto, who had gained a reputation among his contemporaries for his theological works, including early defenses of the doctrines of papal infallibility and the Immaculate Conception.

Little is known of Tomás's early life. While still a boy, he entered the Dominican order, later taking his vows at the Convent of St. Paul in Valladolid. He completed a doctorate in philosophy and divinity, soon gaining a reputation both for his scholarship and for the extreme austerity in which he lived. For the rest of his life, Torquemada never ate meat or permitted linen to be used in

either his clothing or bedding. As a means of mortifying his flesh, he wore a rough hair shirt against his skin regardless of the weather and denied himself even the slightest appearance of luxury. This asceticism was extended even to other members of his family. After his father died and his sister came of age, Torquemada limited her, his sole surviving close relative, to a dowry no larger than that sufficient to permit entrance into the Tertiary Order of Dominican nuns.

The grave and austere young Torquemada soon came to the attention of his superiors, and in 1452, he became prior of the Dominican monastery of Santa Cruz in Segovia. It is possible that this would have been the extent of his rise to power had he not been given the opportunity to serve as confessor to the Castilian monarch Isabella I in 1474. Five years earlier, Isabella had married Ferdinand of Aragon, and together these two monarchs ruled kingdoms that would become the core of the modern nation of Spain. As confessor to Isabella, and soon to Ferdinand as well, Torquemada obtained precisely the right position in which to have a profound impact on the direction that Spanish religion would take throughout the early years of the Renaissance.

LIFE'S WORK

In 1482, as Torquemada was supervising the construction of a new monastery of Saint Thomas Aquinas in the city of Ávila, he was informed that Ferdinand's campaign against the Moors near the city of Loja was about to fail. The king's army was suffering from disease, and supplies of both food and weapons were running low. Torquemada immediately ordered that twenty-four pitchers be filled with gold he had painstakingly acquired to pay for the fabric and vestments of his new monastery. These pitchers were then covered with a layer of cloth and leaves and carried by mule to Isabella. Torquemada's instructions were that the queen should use the gold in whatever way might best assist the king in his siege of Loja. Torquemada's gold arrived too late to be of much use; the siege had to be lifted and the army recalled. Nevertheless, the young priest's swift action proved his loyalty to the crown in a manner that would soon be repaid by Ferdinand and Isabella.

In 1483, conservative elements of the Church, alarmed by tales (many of them false) of Jewish converts to Chris-

tianity who had reverted to their ancestral faith or lapsed into heretical doctrines, persuaded Pope Sixtus IV to reorganize a board of inquisition that had been established in Spain five years earlier. This original board had taken a largely passive role, lending support to a plan of Cardinal Mendoza, the archbishop of Seville, to combat instances of heresy through the issuance of a new catechism. Now, with papal blessing—and the strong support of Isabella— the conservative faction saw to it that Torquemada was appointed the first inquisitor general of Castile on October 2, 1483. Fifteen days later, Torquemada's appointment was also extended into Aragon. Torquemada's Dominican order, the Order of Preachers most fervently devoted to combating heresy, remained in charge of the Inquisition for the rest of its history. In 1487, Pope Innocent VIII expanded Torquemada's position still further by appointing him grand inquisitor of all Spain.

In theory, the newly reorganized Inquisition was charged only with investigating Christians who were accused of unorthodox views. It was never intended to prosecute unconverted Jews or even to punish Christians who were guilty of heresy. The stated goal of the Inquisition was to return sinners to the "true faith" and, if this proved impossible, to surrender them to the Spanish government for "condign punishment" (a phrase used for "appropriate penalties" that were supposed to be merciful and to stop short of injury, torture, or death). In reality, however, the Spanish Inquisition was responsible for as many as two thousand deaths by fire, the imprisonment of at least one hundred thousand people, countless acts of torture and, indirectly, the expulsion of all Jews from Spain.

Torquemada's procedure was to investigate any charge of heresy made by two or more witnesses. The accused were informed of the charges against them and, if they were reluctant to confess, threatened with torture. Often this threat alone was enough to compel a confession; if the defendant refused to cooperate, however, Torquemada permitted the use of force. The most common tor-

---

CONDEMNED BY THE SPANISH INQUISITION

Inquisitor general Tomás de Torquemada was part of a system of accusations, condemnations, public proclamations, imprisonments, and tortures of "heretics." Ceremonious death processions were followed by the burning of heretics in the auto-da-fé. Outlined here is the series of punishments made upon the condemned by secular authorities, not the Church itself.

The punishments meted out by the Inquisition were of four kinds according to the official enumeration:

1. Citation before the Inquisition;
2. the performance of pious deeds;
3. public pilgrimages, flagellations, and the wearing of large crosses; and
4. confiscation of goods, perpetual imprisonment, and death.

All those found guilty at the trial were led back again in the same solemn procession; the heretic penitent and relapsed, the heretic impenitent and not relapsed, the heretic "impenitent and relapsed," the heretic negative (who denied his crime), and the heretic contumacious, were all delivered over to the secular arm, as the Inquisition itself technically refused to carry out the death-sentence on the principle "ecclesia non sitit sanguinem" (the Church thirsts not for blood). The various sentences of death always ended with some such formula as "For these reasons we declare you relapsed, we cast you out of the forum of the church, we deliver you over to the secular justices; praying them, however, energetically, to moderate the sentence in such wise that there be in your case no shedding of blood nor danger of death."

Source: The Jewish Encyclopedia: A Descriptive Record of the History, Religion, Literature, and Customs of the Jewish People from the Earliest Times to the Present Day, edited by Cyrus Adler et al., eds. (New York: Funk & Wagnalls, 1903-1906), p. 340.

ture used by the Spanish Inquisition was the rack and water torture, in which a long cloth was forced down the throat of the accused person and then drenched in water, which led to choking and near drowning.

Those who were found guilty of the charges brought against them could be fined, have their property confiscated, or be forced to undergo a public penance before being surrendered to the government for further punishment. True to his ascetic habits, Torquemada kept none of the goods confiscated for himself but used them both to advance his religious order and to enrich the government's coffers. Ferdinand, whose religious zealotry seems to have been less intense than Isabella's, was attracted to the Inquisition at least as much for its economic advantages as for its suppression of heresy.

Once in the hands of the state, the most recalcitrant of the convicted—largely former Jews found guilty of false conversion—were subjected to a highly public final punishment. Though the Inquisition always kept true to its charge by making a perfunctory request that the state show mercy, the convicted were usually executed. In a public spectacle known as the auto-da-fé (Portuguese for act of the faith), victims were subjected to a lengthy sermon detailing their faults, led in a procession to the place of execution (during which they were often dressed in the sanbenito, a yellow tunic specially revived by Torquemada that was emblazoned with images of infernal torment), bound, and burned at the stake, with the burning wood occasionally dampened to prolong their agony. In extreme cases, before the fires were lit, the bodies of the victims were torn by pincers or otherwise mutilated. Those convicted in absentia were sometimes burned in effigy, a symbol of the fate awaiting them if they ever returned to Spanish territory.

Torquemada's first auto-da-fé (burning of a heretic) took place in May, 1485, with a second following in June. Later that same year, the deaths of Torquemada's fellow inquisitors, Pedro Arbues and Gaspar Juglar—Arbues was assassinated and Juglar died of illness, though his death widely suspected at the time to be the result of poisoning—led the Inquisition to be even more severe in its oppression of Jewish converts to Christianity. In 1486, Saragossa was the site of no fewer than fourteen autos-da-fé, with forty-two victims executed and an additional 134 imprisoned, flogged, or subjected to public penance. Those who were convicted of Arbues's murder were castrated and had their hands cut off before they were hung; while still alive, they were cut down from the gibbet and killed by having their bodies quartered and burned.

Torquemada's reputation as a religious figure grew after he predicted a dire fate for the king of Naples. The grand inquisitor had been attempting to prosecute a political appointee of Ferrantino, king of Naples, when the pope agreed to a special dispensation protecting the accused. A Neapolitan ambassador presented Torquemada with the documents, which he accepted only after remarking that he would now need to contact Rome so as to be certain that the papers were genuine. When the ambassador expressed shock at such an insult, Torquemada replied that he had a greater right to be amazed, as the king of Naples wished to protect a heretic. "In any case," Torquemada is reported to have continued, "it matters little, since Ferrantino will soon die without an heir." Remarkably, Ferrantino's only son did die soon thereafter, and, at the king's death, the throne of Naples passed to his uncle.

Perhaps the most infamous prosecution undertaken by Torquemada was the so-called La Gardia (or La Guardia) Trial of 1490-1491. Torquemada was informed that, in a travesty of Good Friday, a four-year-old Christian boy had been crucified by false Jewish converts to Christianity. A lengthy investigation began, and it is unclear whether the confessions that were finally received resulted from exhaustion following extensive torture or an actual instance of necromantic rite. In any case, eight converted Jews were burned. Three who repented at the last moment were strangled as a sign of mercy. Three others who had cheated the executioner by their earlier deaths were burned in effigy. Two Jews implicated in the plot were tortured and then burned. The crucified four-year-old boy, who may never have existed at all, was later canonized as San Cristobal, or the *santo niño* (holy infant) of La Gardia.

The public outcry resulting from the La Gardia Trial led to the expulsion of Jews from Spain in 1492. Shortly thereafter, Torquemada resigned his positions as grand inquisitor and royal confessor. He spent the rest of his life overseeing the monastery of Saint Thomas Aquinas in Ávila, and he died peacefully after receiving the last rites of the Catholic Church in September, 1498.

SIGNIFICANCE

Without the persistence of Torquemada, the Spanish Inquisition might never have occurred. At the very least, Torquemada must be held accountable for the brutality of many of the prosecutions undertaken by the Inquisition. Although many have argued that other courts of the day, whether religious or secular, resorted to torture and summary judgment even more frequently than that established by Torquemada, the grand inquisitor's single-minded hatred of Jews and Jewish converts to Christianity was responsible for the deaths of hundreds, the torture of thousands, and the impoverishment of numerous others.

So completely did the Inquisition rid Torquemada's country of opposition to Catholic orthodoxy that Spain was almost the only nation in Europe unaffected by the Reformation during the 1500's. Torquemada's legacy was to leave Spain arguably the most homogeneously Catholic country in Europe, a status that may have led to later conflicts, including the launch of the unsuccessful Spanish Armada against England in the summer of 1588.

—Jeffrey L. Buller

FURTHER READING

Anderson, James M. *Daily Life During the Spanish Inquisition*. Westport, Conn.: Greenwood Press, 2002. Part of the Daily Life Through History series, this book surveys the effects of the Inquisition on every aspect of mundane existence, from the royal court to rural farming communities, from military life to the daily experience of students. Includes illustrations, bibliographic references, and index.

Hope, Thomas. *Torquemada: Scourge of the Jews*. London: Allen & Unwin, 1939. A concise introduction for the general reader. Marred by a few strained comparisons of Torquemada and the Inquisition to Hitler and Nazism.

Kamen, Henry. *The Spanish Inquisition: A Historical Revision*. New Haven, Conn.: Yale University Press, 1998. Attempts to argue that the Inquisition was neither as widely accepted nor as cruel as is generally believed. While accepting the judgment that the Inquisition had disastrous and brutal effects on the Jewish population, Kamen argues that it was not an all-powerful instrument of terror and domination, and that other nations of the time in fact used torture more frequently and malevolently. Includes illustrations, maps, bibliographic references, and index.

Longhurst, John Edward. *The Age of Torquemada*. Lawrence, Kans.: Coronado Press, 1964. A short survey both of Torquemada's life and of the principal events of his period.

Paris, Erna. *The End of Days: A Story of Tolerance, Tyranny, and the Expulsion of the Jews from Spain*. Amherst, N.Y.: Prometheus Books, 1995. This history of the Inquisition discusses Torquemada's use of the Holy Child of La Gardia Trial to motivate the expulsion of the Jews. Includes illustrations, maps, bibliographic references, and index.

Pérez Galdós, Benito. *Torquemada*. Translated by Frances M. Lopez-Morillas. New York: Columbia University Press, 1986. Unquestionably the most thorough source on Torquemada. Suited primarily to the advanced academic reader.

Roth, Norman. *Conversos, Inquisition, and the Expulsion of the Jews from Spain*. Madison: University of Wisconsin Press, 2002. Study of the experience of the Jews under the Inquisition, especially those who attempted to convert to Catholicism. Includes bibliographic references and index.

Sabatini, Rafael. *Torquemada and the Spanish Inquisition: A History*. New York: Houghton Mifflin, 1924. A still-useful source that has the advantage of providing information on the history of the Inquisition both before and after Torquemada and the disadvantage of a flowery, tendentious style.

Whitechapel, Simon. *Flesh Inferno: Atrocities of Torquemada and the Spanish Inquisition*. London: Creation, 2003. A somewhat sensational and one-sided but informative portrayal of Torquemada and the horrors of the Inquisition. Includes bibliographic references.

SEE ALSO: Ferdinand II and Isabella I; John III; Manuel I; Pius V; Sixtus IV; Saint Teresa of Ávila.

RELATED ARTICLES in *Great Events from History: The Renaissance & Early Modern Era, 1454-1600:* November 1, 1478: Establishment of the Spanish Inquisition; 1492: Jews Are Expelled from Spain.

TOYOTOMI HIDEYOSHI
Japanese politician and military leader

Hideyoshi was one of the pivotal figures in the unification of Japan out of a welter of competing feudal domains at the end of the sixteenth century. As an astute general and canny power broker and lawgiver, Hideyoshi was to go a long way toward establishing the political foundations that brought Japan from the Middle Ages into its early modern period.

BORN: February 6, 1537; Nakamura, Owari Province (now Aichi Prefecture), Japan

DIED: September 18, 1598; Fushimi, Yamashiro Prefecture, Japan

ALSO KNOWN AS: Hiyoshimaru (original name)

AREAS OF ACHIEVEMENT: Government and politics, military

EARLY LIFE

Toyotomi Hideyoshi (toh-yoh-toh-mee hee-deh-yoh-shee) was born to a father who was a retired foot soldier in the service of Oda Nobuhide, the father of General Oda Nobunaga, who was to be Hideyoshi's overlord during the early phases of his military career. Legends surrounding Hideyoshi's birth recount that his mother dreamed that a ray of sunshine entered her womb and he was thus conceived. Hideyoshi perhaps himself perpetrated this fable to embellish his otherwise humble beginnings.

The only picture extant of Hideyoshi shows a deeply lined, narrow, ascetic face with cold haughty eyes and a sour mouth set atop a squat body. Singularly ugly, he was later jokingly referred to by Oda as a bald rat or a monkey.

Hideyoshi came of age in the latter part of Japan's Warring States period, during which local lords jockeyed constantly for advantage with growing armies of samurai and musket-wielding foot soldiers. The Ashikaga family of shoguns maintained only nominal sovereignty over this patchwork of local power centers, able to exert influence only through shifting military alliances. It is small wonder, therefore, that Hideyoshi chose a military career. A family tradition, it was also virtually the only means of advancement for those of humble birth.

LIFE'S WORK

In 1558, Hideyoshi, having already served in the army of another lord, presented himself to Oda Nobunaga, a fast-rising military star who was master of Hideyoshi's home area. Oda quickly took a liking to Hideyoshi, whose mili-

tary talents began to bloom as Oda began the campaigns that were to conquer the heartland of Japan around the ancient imperial capital of Kyōto. Through military conquest, Oda was to set in motion the process of pacification of contending power blocs known in Japanese history as the unification. Fundamentally more ruthless than Hideyoshi in his approach to military matters, Oda moved to defeat feudal coalitions in central Japan and also besieged and laid waste to armed Buddhist monasteries with a cruelty reminiscent of Mongol conqueror and ruler Genghis Khan (between 1155 and 1162-1227).

As Hideyoshi demonstrated his military talents, his position in Oda's command structure rose. It was Hideyoshi who, in 1566-1567, secured a victory over Saitō Tatsuoki at Inabayama by constructing at night a fortress facing the enemy. Hideyoshi was rewarded with lands seized from Oda's enemies. In these lands, Hideyoshi exercised an enlightened administrative policy of easing taxation in order to encourage economic development.

In 1575, Oda, with Hideyoshi leading one of two wings of his army, pushed westward to challenge the formidable Mōri clan. Hideyoshi here made siege craft his specialty by taking the massive and strategic Himeji Castle and two other fortresses by imaginative engineering (including flooding) and by clever psychological warfare. In 1582, Oda was treacherously assassinated. Hideyoshi hastily made peace with the Mōri clan, then returned to confront and defeat Oda's murderer. At the council of vassals, Hideyoshi successfully presented himself as Oda's avenger and overrode opposition to sponsor the infant grandson of Oda as heir. He thus became, at age forty-five, the master of five provinces and primary councillor at the head of the mightiest military coalition yet seen in Japan.

Hideyoshi had now inherited the mission of completing unification, and he embarked on a carrot-and-stick strategy of combining massive attacks on those who actively opposed him with generous land rewards to win over potential rivals as well as keep faithful supporters. In 1582, he defeated the Shibata family, who had opposed him within the coalition, then used Shibata lands to reward his supporters. By 1584, he came to an uneasy settlement with Tokugawa Ieyasu (who was later to complete the unification after Hideyoshi's death). In 1587, he undertook a difficult campaign to subdue the southern island of Kyūshū. The defeated were treated generously, but loyal supporters were placed strategically, in the center, and his erstwhile opponents, the Mōri, were given generous tracts in the north.

At the conclusion of the Kyūshū campaign, he issued his famous eleven-point edict against Christianity, denouncing it as subversive and calling for expulsion of Jesuit missionaries. Although the edict was not enforced for some years, it was clear that Hideyoshi was interested in European contact only for trade. It is possible that he used this as a gesture in support of his hegemony, since he issued the ban on behalf of the entire nation.

Military force was not the only implement used by Hideyoshi in his creation of a national hegemony. Any combination of forces could always undo any purely military arrangement. Therefore, he started to build political power out of his military position. First, he amplified his status as military hegemon through oaths of allegiance and the requiring of hostages from nominal subordinates. In 1585, he secured an appointment from the figurehead emperor to the office of imperial regent as a means of bolstering his legitimacy as a national leader. Realizing that the most solid basis for national power was the capacity to control the right to land proprietorships, Hideyoshi undertook a systematic program of redistributing landholdings aimed at reducing the powers of some lords, placing trustworthy ones in strategic locations, and appeasing potential rivals. It was mainly the smaller lords who were moved around, but gradually the idea solidified that the lords held their land in trust and not absolutely. Acceptance of this growth of central power might have been difficult except that it was recognized that Hideyoshi was merely doing at a national level what the lords had to do locally to hold their territory. They were willing to give up some autonomy to safeguard their domains under Hideyoshi's seal of approval. Never again after 1590 could individual lords acquire land rights not permitted by a national hegemon.

Between 1587 and 1590, Hideyoshi instituted administrative measures that were to be his most far-reaching legacies. He ordered the land survey begun by Oda to be extended and improved. Uniform units of measurement were used. For the first time, Japan's leadership, both local and national, had an accurate plot-by-plot estimate of the productive capacity. This allowed a tax base to be determined, and it revolutionized the tax structure by allowing the lords greater access to the taxable product and standardized accounting. Once Hideyoshi determined the feudal lord's status in relation to productive capacity, he could more easily shift the lords around, since they were tied more to status than to a particular geographic

place. In 1588, he ordered a mass confiscation of all weapons from peasants. That had the double aim of reducing the likelihood of armed rebellion and of separating the warrior classes from all unarmed commoners. In 1590, an accurate population census froze the social classes into samurai, farmers, artisans, and merchants and bound peasants to their land. Samurai were gradually pulled into castle garrisons and, rather than collecting their own taxes, were paid by fixed stipends.

In 1590-1591, Hideyoshi crushed his final remaining challengers in the east of Japan. Now that he was the undisputed master of Japan, he considered the conquest of Korea and China. The first Korean expedition in 1592 ended in a draw after the Japanese encountered determined resistance from the Koreans. The second, in 1597, ended with Hideyoshi's death. Surrounded by magnificent gardens and artworks, pleading for loyalty to his heir from his coalition vassals, he died on September 18, 1598.

SIGNIFICANCE

Hideyoshi's military unification of Japan represents only one facet of a diverse life. In his own time, his primary impact seemed to be that he, more than any other individual, acted the role of central figure. He restored the imperial dignity, rebuilt the capital and other cities, and enforced peaceful symbols on the popular mind by parades, theatricals, and tea ceremonies for thousands of commoners. He encouraged new building and patronized new, flamboyant, and colorful artistic fashions. Ostentation became a tool of statecraft. Even the megalomania of the Korean expeditions seemed to bring personal destiny together with national destiny.

Hideyoshi's last appeals for loyalty to his five-year-old son failed. His plans for succession were aborted by the wily Ieyasu, who asserted his supremacy in one final battle, took the title of shogun, and went on to complete Japan's unification by taming feudalism into a stable, peaceful system for the next 250 years. He did so by making full use of the existing legal and administrative structure of census roles, frozen class structure, surveys, and tax procedures and by shifting lords around, assuring loyalty through hostages, closing off Japan from the outside, and the like. That Ieyasu built on the existing legal, political, and social foundations is proof of Hideyoshi's enduring legacy.

—*David G. Egler*

FURTHER READING

Beasley, W. G. *The Japanese Experience: A Short History of Japan.* Berkeley: University of California

Press, 1999. Survey of the entirety of Japanese history. Hideyoshi is covered in the chapter on the unification of Japan. Includes photographic plates, illustrations, maps, bibliographic references, and index.

Berry, Mary Elizabeth. *Hideyoshi*. Cambridge, Mass.: Harvard University Press, 1989. Clearly the primary biographical source in English on Hideyoshi's life and a thoroughly modern treatment. Save for artistic matters, Berry is comprehensive in her coverage. Gives a complete background and then exhaustively analyzes developments in economics, military affairs, and administrative and political arrangements. Based almost entirely on Japanese sources but, surprisingly, lacks a bibliography.

Dening, Walter. *The Life of Toyotomi Hideyoshi*. 3d ed. Kobe, Japan: J. L. Thompson, 1930. Reprint. New York: AMS Press, 1971. The first edition of this biography was published in 1888 and not much was added in later editions. A classic Victorian biography, rich with anecdotes and extensive detail about Hideyoshi's life. Contains extensive quotes of conversations without footnote citation; while it is true that Hideyoshi left much correspondence, it is probable that most is the product of the imagination of an author overanxious to paint a vivid personal picture.

Elison, George. "Hideyoshi, the Bountiful Master." In *Warlords, Artists, and Commoners: Japan in the Sixteenth Century*, edited by George Elison and Bardwell Smith. Honolulu: University of Hawaii Press, 1981. This essay sheds some light on Hideyoshi's genealogy by focusing on his search for legitimacy as a leader. Elison draws a theoretical comparison between Hideyoshi as a charismatic leader—drawing legitimacy from his accomplishments and through invented mythology about a supernatural birth and miraculous deeds—and Hideyoshi as one who sought traditional legitimacy by inventing a conventional pedigree and taking on court titles.

Hall, John W. *Government and Local Power in Japan, 500 to 1700: A Study Based on Bizen Province*. Princeton, N.J.: Princeton University Press, 1966. Reprint. Ann Arbor: University of Michigan Press, 1999. Hall offers many general historical comments and insights. His powers of summary are acute, so the book is valuable as an overview. His treatment of Hideyoshi in chapters 9, 10, and 11 shows the impact of some of the central decisions on this one region in western Honshu.

Hall, John W., Nagahara Keiji, and Kozo Yamamura, eds. *Japan Before Tokugawa: Political Consolidation*

and Economic Growth, 1500-1650. Princeton, N.J.: Princeton University Press, 1981. This collection is the product of a binational conference on the Warring States and gives an overview of the whole period, focusing on historiographical questions. Hall's chapter on Hideyoshi's domestic policies attempts to draw out his contribution to the political scene as Japan moved out of its middle ages into its early modern condition. Hall summarizes specific measures devised by Hideyoshi, most of which were to survive as the basis for government for the next 250 years.

Kang, Etsuko Hae-jin. *Diplomacy and Ideology in Japanese-Korean Relations: From the Fifteenth to the Eighteenth Century*. New York: St. Martin's Press, 1997. Details Hideyoshi's diplomatic relations and break with Korea and the Korean embassy of 1590. Includes illustrations, maps, bibliographic references, and index.

McWilliams, Wayne C. "Tototomi Hideyoshi, 1536-1598: Supreme Daimyo of Japan." In *Great Leaders, Great Tyrants? Contemporary Views of World Rulers Who Made History*, edited by Arnold Blumberg. Westport, Conn.: Greenwood Press, 1995. Reassessment of the political and military career of Hideyoshi from a contemporary perspective. Includes bibliographic references and index.

Murdoch, James. *A History of Japan During the Century of Early Foreign Intercourse, 1542-1651*. Vol. 2 in *A History of Japan*. Maps by Isoh Yamagata. Reprint. New York: Routledge, 1996. The second of a massive three-volume history. Murdoch, a Scot who spent many years teaching in Japan, is rather stilted in his prose and idiosyncratic in his approach. Still, this work is valuable. Modern works seldom offer such lavish detail. Hideyoshi is covered in chapters 8, 9, 12, and 13. Murdoch, who is ordinarily disdainful of feudalism as such, is more positive in his treatment of Hideyoshi. Although he ignores economic considerations, he offers a fuller picture of the range of administrative problems addressed by Hideyoshi.

Sansom, George B. *A History of Japan, 1334-1615*. Stanford, Calif.: Stanford University Press, 1961. This is the second volume in a three-volume history of Japan that is arguably the most complete general history of premodern Japan available in English. This well-illustrated and readable work, based entirely on Japanese sources, is indispensable as a reference work. Hideyoshi's life and career are covered in chapters 19 through 24, including a chapter on the artistic scene. Although less adequate for economic matters than more modern works, Sansom's history as a whole comes close to striking the perfect balance between lively prose and a wealth of detail. His bibliography is annotated, his appendices pertinent, his index meticulous. This is a full-service history to which all students of pre-1867 Japan should come first.

Toyotomi Hideyoshi. *101 Letters of Hideyoshi: The Private Correspondence of Toyotomi Hideyoshi.* Edited and translated by Adriana Boscaro. Tokyo: Sophia University Press, 1975. Boscaro gives an extensive introduction and then intersperses the graceful translations with editorial comment and explanation of the letters. She explains some of the problems of dealing with this kind of documentation. Contains appendi-

ces, a catalog of letters with a photoreproduction of a sample letter, and notes on people and places.

SEE ALSO: Hosokawa Gracia; Oda Nobunaga; Ōgimachi; Saint Francis Xavier.

RELATED ARTICLES in *Great Events from History: The Renaissance & Early Modern Era, 1454-1600:* 1550's-1567: Japanese Pirates Pillage the Chinese Coast; 1550-1593: Japanese Wars of Unification; 1587: Toyotomi Hideyoshi Hosts a Ten-Day Tea Ceremony; 1590: Odawara Campaign; 1592-1599: Japan Invades Korea; 1594-1595: Taikō Kenchi Survey; October, 1596-February, 1597: *San Felipe* Incident; October 21, 1600: Battle of Sekigahara.

THE TUDOR FAMILY
English kings and queens (r. 1485-1603)

The Tudor monarchs dominated the politics of their time, moving England into the modern era.

REIGNED: 1485-1603
AREA OF ACHIEVEMENT: Government and politics

EARLY LIVES

The accomplishments of the Tudor (TEWD-ur) Family must be measured against the challenges occurring during the late Middle Ages and the Renaissance era. The disaster of the Black Death, the decline of the Roman Catholic Church and the breakdown of Christian unity resulting from the Protestant Reformation, the Hundred Years' War between England and France, the development of the printing press, and the voyages of discovery to Asia and the Western Hemisphere were factors that weakened the medieval fabric of earlier centuries.

England suffered during the 1400's. The forced abdication of Richard II in 1399 placed the throne under a cloud. Henry V arguably hurt rather than helped his kingdom with his military victories over the French, which resulted in the unification of the French and English thrones. England was overextended on the Continent. When Henry V died in 1422, his son, Henry VI, was only a year old; when he came of age, moreover, he showed that he had inherited the mental instability of his French grandfather, Charles VI. After England's defeat and withdrawal from France in 1453, various factions in England turned on each other in the so-called Wars of the Roses, and with a weak king, anarchy and violence was the result, particularly at the upper levels of society. By

the 1470's, stability seemed to have returned under the leadership of Edward IV, but during the reign of Richard III, the Crown was under siege again, ending only at the Battle of Bosworth. The victor and new king, the first of the Tudor dynasty, was Henry VII.

The Tudors were impoverished Welsh nobility. Owen ap Meredith ap Tudor, a minor member of Henry V's court, married Henry's widow, Catherine of France, after the king's death. Through this marriage, the children of Owen Tudor were by blood tied to the rule of the unstable Henry VI, their half brother. During the Wars of the Roses, the Tudors sided with the Crown. Owen Tudor was captured and beheaded in 1461. Owen's son, Edmund, earl of Richmond, died in 1456; Edmund's only son, Henry, was born three months later, in January, 1457. After the deaths of Henry VI and his heir in 1471, Henry Tudor became the Red Rose faction's candidate for the throne; he was supported by the opponents of Edward IV and the White Rose faction, which endorsed the House of York. Henry Tudor was an opportunistic survivor; with French assistance, he landed a small army in south Wales in August, 1485, and three weeks later defeated Richard III at Bosworth.

LIVES' WORK

Victory did not guarantee survival. During the rest of Henry VII's reign, there were various claimants to the throne, but the stratagems and plots against him failed. Consolidating his rule was paramount, and he married Elizabeth of York, sister to Edward IV and Richard III, in an attempt of reconcile the Yorkists. In often controversial ways, Henry VII increased the financial resources of the crown, and he left a surplus in the royal treasury when he died, an unusual accomplishment in those times. His concern for money gave him the reputation of a miser, governed by avarice only, but he spent money generously on his court, believing that royal pomp not only was his due but also reinforced his royal authority.

Concerned with the survival of his dynasty, Henry often focused his diplomacy on matrimonial matters. After the death of his queen, he offered himself as a groom to prospective royal candidates from the Continent. In addition, his eldest son, Arthur, was married to Catherine of Aragon, a princess from one of the most powerful royal families in Europe. Arthur died shortly after the marriage, but with Catherine already in England, Henry VII arranged that Catherine marry his remaining son, Henry. When the king died in 1509, the survival of the dynasty seemed ensured. Henry VII was not loved by many, but he was respected.

Henry VIII epitomized the Renaissance prince. Young, athletic, charismatic, he was well read, not least in religious matters. His marriage to Catherine was consummated, and in 1516, she gave birth to their only child, Mary. Henry attempted to establish his fame, and English power, through military actions, but in the rivalries between the Valois monarchs of France and the Habsburgs of Spain, Henry VIII was unable to achieve parity with his continental rivals. Instead, his dynastic concerns and the accompanying religious issues made him the larger-than-life figure he desired to be.

Catherine of Aragon was several years older than Henry, so Henry found solace with younger, more attractive women. Compounding his lack of sexual interest in Catherine was the inability of the two to produce a male heir to the throne, necessary in a society that assumed male superiority, in part because of the military valor associated with monarchy. By the end of the 1520's, Henry had fallen in love with Anne Boleyn and wished to be legally rid of Catherine in order to remarry. In the Catholic Church, marriage was a sacrament. Marriages, particularly among royalty, could be dissolved, but only through the Church's auspices. Pope Clement VII was probably willing to annul the marriage, but he and Rome were under the control of Charles V, ruler of Spain and the Germanies, and Catherine's nephew. Yet Henry found another alternative.

In 1517, Martin Luther had set off the spark that led to the Protestant Reformation and the division of Christendom. With Thomas Cromwell as chancellor, the English Parliament, claiming that there was no higher authority than national sovereignty, passed legislation ending Henry's marriage to Catherine. Henry immediately married Anne, who soon gave birth—but to a daughter, Elizabeth. Although Henry was well into middle age, his romantic eye continued to wander, and he contrived to have Anne executed. Henry then married again, this time to Jane Seymour, who did her royal "duty" by presenting Henry a son, Edward, but who died soon after giving birth. Three more royal marriages followed: Anne of Cleves, whom Henry divorced, Catherine Howard, who was executed for adultery, and Catherine Parr, who survived his death.

More important than Henry's matrimonial failures was the impact he had on government and religion. Using Parliament, Henry and Cromwell engineered a revolution in increasing the powers of Parliament as the fount of law. Because of his divorce, Henry inadvertently became the founder of the Protestant Church of England, or the Anglican Church. His own religious beliefs have been described as being essentially Catholic but without veneration of the Papacy, although he veered at times in a Protestant direction.

With Henry VIII's death in 1547, Protestantism quickly triumphed in England, at least temporarily. The new king, Edward VI, Henry's youngest child but sole son, was only nine years of age; however, he was precocious. Surrounded by royal uncles, Edward was a convinced Protestant. He could hardly have been anything else, in that his own legitimacy depended on the legality of Henry's divorce from Catherine of Aragon. Edward's reign was brief, however, and he died at the age of fifteen in 1553. During those years, however, the Anglican Church established deep roots, particularly under the leadership of Thomas Cranmer, the archbishop of Canterbury.

Edward's oldest half sister, Mary, ascended the throne. Ignored by her father and believing that she had the obligation to restore her mother's reputation and religion, Mary was a staunch Catholic. Not alone in the violent sixteenth century, she was willing to use force to achieve her religious aims, which were to bring England back to Catholicism. Her reign was a disaster. Her religious persecutions gained her the nickname "Bloody Mary," and, in an era of rising national consciousness, her marriage to Philip II of Spain was equally controversial. The mourners were few when she died in 1558.

Elizabeth, the second of Henry VIII's three children, was twenty-five when she became queen, and she exhibited the survival qualities of the earlier Tudors. Historians have debated her motives, some claiming that her actions were determined by her psychological experiences under her father and her sister, and some arguing that it was her intellect that guided her decisions. She moved cautiously, and given that she was Anne Boleyn's daughter, had little alternative but to keep England Protestant. She stated that she was not interested in looking into her subjects' souls, but she did demand outward adherence to the Anglican faith. Well-educated, she had her father's charisma, and she used both her mind and her charm to good effect, steering a middle way between the Catholic monarchs on the Continent and the radical Protestants—the Puritans—in England.

To the north ruled Mary, Queen of Scots, distantly related to Elizabeth. Scotland was riven by religious concerns, with Mary representing the Catholic interest and John Knox the Protestant cause. Mary fled Scotland for England, where she was placed under close confinement. The eternal schemer, Mary hoped to eliminate Elizabeth, become queen of England, and restore Catholicism; nevertheless, it was with considerable reluctance that Elizabeth ordered Mary executed in 1587. With Mary's death, Philip II of Spain launched a great naval armada against England. When it failed in 1588, the English surmised that God must truly be a Protestant.

Elizabeth never married, perhaps associating marriage with death and possibly unwilling to share her position with a male who might, because of the times, become the dominant figure; as a result, she was referred to as the "virgin queen." With her death in 1603, the Tudor Dynasty came to an end; ironically, it was James, the son of Mary, Queen of Scots, who became the next English monarch.

SIGNIFICANCE

The Tudors are the most famous dynasty in English history, both for their accomplishments and for their powerful personalities. Henry VIII and Elizabeth I were larger-than-life figures. "Bloody Mary," because of her religion and marriage, became one of the chief villains in English history. Even the young Edward VI was memorable, perhaps because of his youthful death. The monarch who left the least mark on subsequent historical imagination was Henry VII, arguably the most able of the Tudors.

This was an important era in English history, and the Tudors were at the center. Henry VII restored the position of the monarchy, ending the endemic ruling-class violence. Henry VIII, intentionally or not, strengthened Parliament and established the Anglican Church. Even Edward and Mary affected the politics and religion of the

time. Furthermore, Elizabeth—hailed as "Gloriana" and "Good Queen Bess"—also successfully ruled England for a long time, ending in the Age of Shakespeare and the English Renaissance.

The Tudor accomplishments can be contrasted with those of the monarchs who preceded them and those of the dynasty that followed. Between 1399 and 1485, the throne was frequently in dispute. The Stuart Dynasty of the seventeenth century was also a story of royal failure. The Tudors have been defined as despotic rulers, but "Tudor despotism" incorporated Parliament into the decision- and law-making process, even if only as a secondary factor. By making use of Parliament to advance their own aims, moreover, the Tudors so strengthened Parliament that within a century of their passing, England had become a constitutional monarchy, with Parliament more powerful than the monarchs.

—Eugene Larson

FURTHER READING

Chimes, S. B. *Henry VII*. Berkeley: University of California Press, 1972. Scholarly but readable, this is an excellent biography of perhaps the most important but least known Tudor.

Elton, G. R. *England Under the Tudors*. 3d ed. New York: Routledge, 1991. An excellent survey of Tudor England by a premier historian. Especially good on Henry VIII's revolution in government.

Erickson, Carolly. *Bloody Mary*. Garden City, N.Y.: Doubleday, 1978. A sympathetic and entertaining account of Mary. Erickson is a popular biographer of many historical characters.

Loades, David. *The Tudor Court*. 3d ed. Oxford, England: Davenant, 2003. Comprehensive account of the courts of the Tudor monarchs. Discusses both the external trappings and the internal politics of the court, and the often labyrinthine nature of the relationship between appearance and political reality. Includes illustrations, bibliographic references, and index.

Rex, Richard. *The Tudors*. Stroud, Gloucestershire, England: Tempus, 2003. A study of the relationship between the public persona and the private life of each of the Tudors. Emphasizes the common characteristics of the monarchs, especially their mixture of charisma with the threat of violent action. Includes photographic plates, illustrations, bibliographic references, and index.

Ridley, Jasper. *A Brief History of the Tudor Age*. New York: Carroll & Graf, 2002. Brief but comprehensive survey of English culture under the Tudors. The focus on both London and rural England is especially useful, given the tendency of other sources to look primarily at the royal court. Includes photographic plates, illustrations, bibliographic references, and index.

Scarisbrick, J. J. *Henry VIII*. Berkeley: University of California Press, 1968. The best biography of Henry VIII, both critical and sympathetic to England's most famous king.

Slavin, Arthur Joseph. *The Precarious Balance*. New York: Alfred A. Knopf, 1973. Energetically written, this volume is challenging and insightful, with the additional value that includes a discussion of both the pre- and post-Tudor centuries.

Smith, Lacey Baldwin. *Elizabeth Tudor: Portrait of a Queen*. Boston: Little, Brown, 1975. Written by a distinguished authority of the Tudor era, this is a brief, exciting, and readable biography.

SEE ALSO: Anne of Cleves; Anne Boleyn; Catherine of Aragon; Clement VII; Thomas Cranmer; Thomas Cromwell; Edward VI; Elizabeth I; Lady Jane Grey; Henry VI; Henry VII; Henry VIII; Catherine Howard; John Knox; Martin Luther; Mary, Queen of Scots; Mary I; Catherine Parr; Philip II; Richard III; Jane Seymour.

RELATED ARTICLES in *Great Events from History: The Renaissance & Early Modern Era, 1454-1600:* 1455-1485: Wars of the Roses; August 29, 1475: Peace of Picquigny; 1483-1485: Richard III Rules England; Beginning 1485: The Tudors Rule England; 1489: Yorkshire Rebellion; August 22, 1513-July 6, 1560: Anglo-Scottish Wars; 1515-1529: Wolsey Serves as Lord Chancellor and Cardinal; 1531-1540: Cromwell Reforms British Government; December 18, 1534: Act of Supremacy; July, 1535-March, 1540: Henry VIII Dissolves the Monasteries; 1536 and 1543: Acts of Union Between England and Wales; May, 1539: Six Articles of Henry VIII; 1544-1628: Anglo-French Wars; January 28, 1547-July 6, 1553: Reign of Edward VI; July, 1553: Coronation of Mary Tudor; 1558-1603: Reign of Elizabeth I.

WILLIAM TYNDALE
English translator and church reformer

During the Reformation, Tyndale translated the New Testament and the first five books of the Old Testament into English.

BORN: c. 1494; probably Gloucestershire, England
DIED: October 6, 1536; Vilvorde, near Brussels, Brabant (now in Belgium)
ALSO KNOWN AS: William Tindal; William Tindale; William Hutchins
AREAS OF ACHIEVEMENT: Religion and theology, literature

EARLY LIFE

William Tyndale (TIHN-dihl) was born near the border between Wales and England. He was also known as William Hutchins; the family moved from the north and took the name Hutchins to avoid detection during an unsettled period of war. Nothing is known about either his childhood or his family except that he had a brother named John and possibly another one named Edward.

Tyndale entered the University of Oxford around 1508. While there, he abandoned the teachings of the Church and instructed students in scriptural truths. About 1516, after receiving his master's degree, Tyndale entered the University of Cambridge, where he remained until 1521. Tyndale's friends loved and respected him, and even his enemies acknowledged his learning and his irreproachable integrity. Neither proud nor selfish, he was zealous in his work, courageous, and faithful throughout his life.

LIFE'S WORK

From 1521 to 1523, Tyndale served as schoolmaster to the children of Sir John Walsh, a knight of Gloucestershire, at the manor house of Little Sodbury. He also began to preach in nearby villages and to crowds that gathered around him in Bristol. When Thomas Parker, who had a violent temper and who vigorously prosecuted accusations of heresy, was appointed chancellor of the district, Tyndale was accused of heretical teaching and summoned to appear before him. He was threatened and reviled, but because no witnesses would testify against him, he was given no punishment. This was the only time, aside from his last trial, that Tyndale was brought before any church officer on charges of heresy.

Tyndale realized that the clergy of his day opposed his doctrine because they did not know Latin, the language of their Bible, and consequently could not know what

Scripture actually taught. Concerned more with ritual than with truth, their ignorance was indicative of the spirit of the church rulers. When a friend told him that the pope was the antichrist of Scripture, Tyndale concluded that, as antichrist, the pope would strive to keep the Holy Writ from the people. Tyndale had come to know Christ through his study of Scripture, and he believed that if others had that opportunity they would also choose Christ over the church. He decided that the only remedy would be an English translation of the Bible distributed to the people so that they could study it for themselves.

Tyndale resolved that he would be the translator. While still at Little Sodbury, he began translating the New Testament, working from the original Greek and not from the Latin Vulgate as John Wyclif had done in the 1300's. Because of his sympathy with the religious reformers, Gloucestershire was unsafe for him, and he moved to London in 1523. He had hoped that Cuthbert Tunstall, the new bishop, would grant him patronage, which would support him while he studied and wrote. This was not to be the case; when Tyndale was granted an interview, Tunstall coldly refused to help.

Fortunately, while preaching at St. Dunstan's-in-the-West in London, Tyndale met Humphrey Monmouth, a wealthy cloth merchant and patron of needy scholars. Monmouth invited Tyndale to stay with him and paid him to pray for his parents and other saints. In Monmouth's home, Tyndale was free to work on his translation, and he heard men discuss the history of King Henry VIII's reign and the progress of the Reformation in Germany, France, and Switzerland.

Deciding that the English version of the New Testament would be impossible to print in England, Tyndale sailed for Germany in May of 1524, never to set foot in his native land again. On his arrival in Hamburg, he visited Martin Luther in Wittenberg and remained there until April, 1525. While at Wittenberg, he worked on his translation with the help of a secretary, William Roye. In the spring of 1525, Tyndale returned to Hamburg to collect some money he had left with Monmouth. He and Roye then traveled to Cologne and arranged for the printing of the New Testament. Johannes Cochlaeus, dean of St. Mary's Church at Frankfurt, discovered the plan and obtained an order from the Cologne senate that prohibited the printers from proceeding with the work. In addition, Cochlaeus warned Henry VIII to watch the British seaports in order to prevent the translation's arrival in England.

Before Cochlaeus could confiscate the papers, Tyndale and Roye escaped to Worms in October of 1525, tak-

ing the already printed sheets with them. They hired Peter Schoeffer, a printer with Lutheran sympathies, to complete a new printing of the New Testament. In spite of the precautions taken by the king and the bishops, the copies of the Testament were smuggled into England early in 1526 by enterprising merchants and were widely circulated and sold.

When the translation was discovered in London in the early fall of 1526, the church authorities met to discuss possible courses of action. Tunstall recommended prohibition, and the prelates unanimously agreed to burn all copies of the book that were found. Acting on their decision, Tunstall denounced and burned the work at Paul's Cross. People were warned to rid themselves of all copies of the Testament or face excommunication. The prelates' goal was to cleanse England of all Tyndale's translations; the archbishop of Canterbury bought copies simply to destroy them. After the bishops learned that Tyndale was the source of the translation, he was forced to leave Worms to escape arrest. Roye had left earlier for Strasbourg, so Tyndale went alone to Marburg in 1527. He was able to write there under the protection of the landgrave of Hesse-Cassel and probably visited other cities as well. Near the end of 1529, he moved to Antwerp.

During this same period, Tyndale published *The Par-*

William Tyndale. (Library of Congress)

able of the Wicked Mammon (1527), which discusses the parable of the unjust steward and justification by faith, and *The Obedience of a Christian Man, and How Christian Rulers Ought to Govern* (1528), his most important original work, intended as a defense of the reformers against charges of encouraging disobedience of the government. He also finished translating the first five books of the Old Testament, and the Pentateuch was printed in January, 1530, probably at Marburg. This edition of the Pentateuch included a general preface, a preface to each book, a glossary, and marginal notes.

The Practice of Prelates, printed in 1530, criticized both the English government and the church's practices; unfortunately, however, Tyndale could not accurately judge the political revolution in England from his place of refuge on the Continent. Nevertheless, the book described the ways in which the pope and clergy had gone from poverty and humility to universal supremacy, a topic with which Tyndale was most familiar. In *The Practice of Prelates*, Tyndale also spoke out against the king's attempts to obtain a divorce from Catherine of Aragon, and Tyndale's fierce stand on this controversial issue made for him many enemies. Displeased with Tyndale's criticism of the Church, Sir Thomas More, a layman and member of Parliament, wrote an essay in 1529, defending the doctrines and practices of the Church. In 1531, Tyndale's answer appeared as a clear argument for reform and a sharp criticism of More's work. This controversy continued for several years; More asserted the authority of the Church, and Tyndale replied by quoting Scripture; their discussion defined the issues but brought no agreement.

In 1531, Thomas Cromwell became a privy councillor, and he sent Stephen Vaughan, an English envoy in the Netherlands, to find Tyndale and offer him safe conduct back to England. Cromwell advocated a "one king, one law" policy, which Tyndale also recommended; Cromwell probably wanted Tyndale to help him wage a literary war in support of this policy. Tyndale, however, refused to return, as he feared for his safety. This proved to be a wise decision; during the following year, Henry commissioned Sir Thomas Elyot to find and apprehend Tyndale. Tyndale left Antwerp as a consequence, returning in 1533 when the situation again seemed safe. In 1534, he moved into the home of Thomas Poyntz, an English merchant, and worked on his revised translations of the Pentateuch and the New Testament, which were issued in 1534.

In 1535, Tyndale met a young Englishman, Henry Phillips, who falsely declared himself a supporter of religious reform. Phillips posed as an admirer and friend of Tyndale and then betrayed him to the Belgian imperial officers. Tyndale was arrested in May, 1535, and imprisoned at the castle of Vilvorde. Poyntz zealously worked for his release but failed and was also imprisoned. In 1536, Tyndale was tried for heresy, condemned, and sentenced to death. On October 6, 1536, at Vilvorde, Tyndale was strangled and burned at the stake.

SIGNIFICANCE

Although Tyndale left England and lived in exile for twelve years before his death, his name became well known in his native land because of his work on the Bible. His translations of the New Testament and Pentateuch from their original languages into English were endorsed by the translators of the King James Version in 1611 for their accuracy and style. His work set the standard for later versions because of its simplicity, forcefulness, and lack of Latinized expressions. His literary style also influenced future English writers encouraging the use of simple, ordinary language and idioms.

Tyndale was one of the most important English reformers. Although Tyndale was not a public figure, his writings are scholarly expositions of the reformist views. His Bible translations and treatises were important factors in promoting the Reformation in England, and his writings give the reformist perceptions of the ecclesiastical and royal governments.

Before Tyndale was executed, he prayed aloud that God would open the eyes of the king of England. Within a year, a version of the English Bible, based largely on Tyndale's work, circulated in England with the king's permission. Within two years, the English Bible was set up in every English church so that all could come and read it for themselves. Thus, Tyndale's vision of a Bible for the people was realized.

—Elaine Mathiasen

FURTHER READING

Bainton, Ronald H. *Here I Stand: A Life of Martin Luther.* New York: New American Library 1977. The most popular biography of Luther, comprehensive in its details. Useful in understanding the individual who was so highly esteemed by Tyndale.

Bruce, F. F. *History of the Bible in English.* 3d ed. New York: Oxford University Press, 1978. A scholarly work that traces the English Bible from its beginnings in picture form to the many versions available in the 1970's. Includes some English history, biography, and comparisons of excerpts from different translations.

Daniell, David. *William Tyndale: A Biography.* New Haven, Conn.: Yale University Press, 2001. In addition to Tyndale's life, this work studies his skills as a linguist and literary stylist. Details the development of Tyndale's linguistic prowess, and provides a detailed study of the style and rhetoric of his biblical translation. Includes photographic plates, illustrations, bibliographic references, and index.

Demaus, Robert. *William Tyndale.* Revised by Richard Lovett. Amsterdam: J. C. Gieben, 1971. A reprint of the London edition of 1886. Considered to be the standard authority on Tyndale. Gives an accurate account of his life and works as well as the historical details of that era.

Durant, Will. *The Reformation: A History of European Civilization from Wyclif to Calvin, 1300-1564.* New York: Simon & Schuster, 1957. Considers religion in general and explores the problems and conditions of the Catholic Church, particularly after 1300. Discusses the Reformation in relation to politics, economics, art, and the social revolution.

Elton, G. R. *Reform and Reformation: England, 1509-1558.* Cambridge, Mass.: Harvard University Press, 1977. A study of the reigns of Tudor rulers Henry VIII, Edward VI, and Mary I and the ways in which reform shaped English politics, religion, and behavior. Gives no facts on Tyndale, but the background information on this period is helpful.

Long, John D. *The Bible in English: John Wycliffe and William Tyndale.* Lanham, Md.: University Press of America, 1998. Biography of Tyndale and Wyclif, together with a study of the translation of the Bible. Details the portions of Tyndale's translation that appear in later English editions such as the King James Bible and the American Standard Bible. Includes portraits, bibliographic references, and indexes.

Moynahan, Brian. *God's Bestseller: William Tyndale, Thomas More, and the Writing of the English Bible—A Story of Martyrdom and Betrayal.* New York: St. Martin's Press, 2003. Chronicles Tyndale's struggle to translate the Bible into vernacular English and More's efforts to stop Tyndale and to try him as a heretic. Includes illustrations, bibliographic references, and index.

Mozley, J.F. *William Tyndale.* New York: Macmillan, 1937. A good biography that covers some material not included in Demaus's original work. Includes a chapter on Tyndale's translation of the New Testament.

Spitz, Lewis W. *The Protestant Reformation: 1517-1559.* New York: Harper & Row, 1985. Emphasizes the Reformation as the outstanding achievement of the age but includes the significant developments in other areas of life throughout Europe. Argues that the Reformation was of even more critical importance to history than the Renaissance.

SEE ALSO: Catherine of Aragon; William Caxton; Miles Coverdale; Thomas Cranmer; Thomas Cromwell; Saint John Fisher; Henry VIII; John Knox; Hugh Latimer; Martin Luther; Philipp Melanchthon; Sir Thomas More; Matthew Parker; Nicholas Ridley.

RELATED ARTICLE in *Great Events from History: The Renaissance & Early Modern Era, 1454-1600:* April or May, 1560: Publication of the Geneva Bible.

GIORGIO VASARI
Italian historian, painter, and architect

Vasari's Lives of the Most Eminent Painters, Sculptors, and Architects *is an almost singular source on what is known of the lives and works of artists of the Renaissance. Vasari, who has been called the first art historian, was also a painter and architect.*

BORN: July 30, 1511; Arezzo, Republic of Florence (now in Italy)
DIED: June 27, 1574; Florence, Republic of Florence
AREAS OF ACHIEVEMENT: Literature, art, architecture

EARLY LIFE

Giorgio Vasari (JYOHR-jyoh vah-ZAHR-ee), from ancient Arezzo, a hill town dating from Etruscan times and rich in mementos of the Middle Ages and the early Renaissance, was born into a family numbering several local artists among its antecedents. His father, Antonio, a tradesman, compensated for his own lack of creativity and financial success by maintaining close contact with men of consequence within the church and in artistic circles and was particularly proud of his kinship with Luca Signorelli, a major figure in mid-Renaissance art, who provided the young Vasari with his first lessons in drawing. Giorgio's formal training, however, began under the guidance of a Frenchman resident in Arezzo, Guglielmo di Marsillac, now remembered as a major stained-glass artist. Yet it is likely that Giorgio learned much more from his daily exposure to local art treasures; he claimed, in fact, to have spent his early youth copying "all the good pictures to be found in the churches of Arezzo."

At age fifteen, as a result of his father's splendid contacts, Vasari was taken to Florence by Cardinal Silvio Passerini of Cortona, who brought him to the studios of Andrea del Sarto and Michelangelo. This initial contact with Michelangelo marked the beginning of a close relationship destined to last for forty years, and no single artist in Vasari's vast knowledge of Renaissance creativity was more admired by him than Michelangelo: "I courted Michelangelo assiduously and consulted him about all my affairs, and he was good enough to show me great friendship."

Cardinal Passerini also introduced him to members of the Medici family, in whose favor Vasari would remain for the duration of his career. At this particular time, however, such contact was of little consequence, for the Medicis were soon driven from the city, and Vasari, fearful for his own safety in the ensuing anti-Medici atmosphere, fled back to Arezzo, only to find his hometown ridden with a plague that had already taken his father's life. His uncle, as guardian of the family, advised him not to go home and expose himself to such peril and instead arranged for him to live in nearby villages, where he made a meager living doing decorative work in small churches. The following year, the plague having run its course, he joined his family in Arezzo, once more relishing the opportunity to observe and copy local artworks and also finishing his first commission, a painting for the Church of San Piero.

Yet, when Florence again appeared safe for a Medici protégé, he returned, this time in the hope of making a reasonable living for his family, whose welfare was now his responsibility. He entered into an apprenticeship with a goldsmith. Once more his plans were disrupted by political upheaval, now in the form of the 1529 Siege of Florence. Vasari, never one to court danger, made his way to Pisa, where he abandoned his new craft and returned to painting, quickly making a name for himself as a reliable, competent, hardworking artist. His patrons were not Pisans but exiled Florentines, members of the distinguished Pitti and Guicciardini families.

Still not yet twenty years old and driven by the restlessness of youth, Vasari soon left Pisa, traveling a circuitous route via Modena and Bologna back to Arezzo, where he completed his first fresco, a representation of the four evangelists with God the Father and some life-size figures. From that time on, he was never lacking in distinguished patronage. Working on commissions for local rulers, princes of the Church, and the pope, he completed, always in record time, major fresco projects in Siena, Rome, Arezzo, and Florence. His works in this medium, most notably those in Rome's Palazza della Cancelleria, the interior of Filippo Brunelleschi's monumental dome in Florence's cathedral, and the splendidly reconstructed rooms in the Palazzo Vecchio, were viewed as masterpieces in their day, and Vasari was richly rewarded. Yet despite their great contemporary appeal, posterity has dealt harshly with Vasari's decorative works, viewing his efforts as superficial and flamboyant, devoid of intellectual clarity and spiritual depth.

LIFE'S WORK

Although Vasari described himself as a painter and architect and clearly exerted a major portion of his time and energy on works in these fields, he made his principal contribution with *Le vite de' più eccellenti architetti, pittori, et scultori italiani, da cimabue insino a' tempi nostri* (1550; *Lives of the Most Eminent Painters, Sculptors, and Architects*, 1855-1885), a prodigious compendium of information on art and artists gradually accumulated throughout his mature years. Wherever he happened to be—and he traveled widely—and whatever the primary purpose of his journey, he always devoted a significant portion of his time to the observation of works by other artists, making sketches and taking notes and, whenever the opportunity was there, acquiring original sketches and drawings for his steadily mounting collection to which in his work he refers time and again, invariably with great pride.

It is quite possible that without the prodding of others, in particular his Rome patron Cardinal Farnese, the *Lives of the Most Eminent Painters, Sculptors, and Architects* would have remained the writer's private, unpublished notes on the arts of the Renaissance. The subject of compiling all his material into a published account, Vasari reports, was brought up at a dinner party in the home of the cardinal in 1546, when Paolo Giovio, already a renowned collector of portraits and a biographer but not an artist, expressed the wish for having available "a treatise discussing all illustrious artists from the time of Cimabue to the present." Considering that the first manuscript was ready for the scribe in 1548, it stands to reason that Vasari must have had most of the material on hand by the time the subject of a book was broached, and that the two ensuing years must have been spent organizing the vast body of notes into a logical entity.

Not everything in the work represents the writer's original thoughts. Vasari borrowed liberally from all available sources—written observations by Brunelleschi, Lorenzo Ghiberti, Ghirlandajo, Raphael, and many others—as a rule acknowledging his indebtedness. Such secondary aspects of the work, however, are far less important than Vasari's own meticulous, often pedantic, descriptions of thousands of works of art in terms of structure, form, color, and purpose.

To facilitate the reader's comprehension and establish a degree of unity in his flood of observations, he puts forth a set of criteria that in his opinion form the basis on which a work of art should be judged. First in this hierarchy of values is *disegno*, by which Vasari implies not only the total conceptual layout of a particular work but also the actual skill of drawing that must precede the finished product. With *natura*, true to the Renaissance spirit, he claims that excellence in art derives from careful observation and faithful re-creation of nature, or even, in the Neoplatonic consciousness so prevalent at the time, an improvement on nature. *Decoro* refers to the appropriateness, the decorum, or dignity, that should always be part of all visual creativity, stressing that the representation must befit the subject at hand. *Iudizio*, a less tangible term, is a criterion applied to the evaluation of an artist's sense of sound judgment relative to his combining all the separate elements that go into the evolvement and completion of his work. Last in Vasari's listing is *maniera*, an overall consideration referring either to a single artist's unique style and approach or to the style, the manner, of an entire school, for example, the Sienese or the Florentine.

Vasari's personal style of writing ranges from the matter-of-fact listing of data and descriptive details to a florid gushing of superlatives. In his discussion of the Italian painter Masaccio (1401-1428), he describes the *Pisa Madonna* in this straightforward way:

VASARI ON MICHELANGELO

Giorgio Vasari, considered to be the first art historian and also a painter, believed art to be progressive. Art is perfected through the generations, as artists use and then build upon methods from the past. Here Vasari gives high praise to the transcendent artistic skills of Michelangelo, especially as his work surpasses the art of others.

But he who bears the palm of both the living and the dead, transcending and eclipsing all others, is the divine Michelagniolo Buonarroti, who holds the sovereignty not merely of one of these arts [painting, sculpture, and architecture], but of all three together. This master surpasses and excels not only all those moderns who have almost vanquished nature, but even those most famous ancients who without a doubt did so gloriously surpass her; and in his own self he triumphs over moderns, ancients, and nature, who could scarcely conceive anything so strange and so difficult that he would not be able, by the force of his most divine intellect and by means of his industry, draughtsmanship, art, judgment, and grace, to excel it be a great measure.

Source: Michelangelo and the Mannerists: The Baroque and the Eighteenth Century. Vol. 2 in *A Documentary History of Art*, edited by Elizabeth G. Holt (New York: Anchor Books, 1958), p. 30.

In the Carmelite church at Pisa, inside a chapel in the transept, there is a panel painting by Masaccio showing the Virgin and Child, and some little angels at her feet, who are playing instruments and one of whom is sounding a lute and inclining his ear very attentively to listen to the music he is making. Surrounding Our Lady are St. Peter, St. John the Baptist, St. Julian, St. Nicholas, all very vivacious and animated.

Entirely different and far more elevated are his comments on Leonardo da Vinci.

The excellent productions of this divine artist had so greatly increased and extended his fame that all men who delighted in the arts (nay, the whole city of Florence) were anxious that he should leave behind him some memorial of himself; and there was much discussion everywhere in respect to some great and important work to be executed by him, to the end that the commonwealth might have glory, and the city the ornament, imparted by the genius, grace, and judgment of Leonardo to all that he did.

While the weight and importance placed on Vasari's descriptions and evaluations in subsequent times have shifted, his approach to artistic biography remained the unchallenged standard for the next three hundred years. Even in modern times any study of the artists of the Italian Renaissance tends to have Vasari's *Lives of the Most Eminent Painters, Sculptors, and Architects* as its point of departure. It is to a considerable extent to his particular credit that neglect was not to be the destiny of the multitude of artists active on the Italian peninsula in those two hundred years he designated as the Renaissance.

SIGNIFICANCE

In *Lives of the Most Eminent Painters, Sculptors, and Architects*, Vasari devotes much space to a detailed description of his own numerous works carried out on commission in various parts of Italy, and to the lofty sociocultural standings of the many who sought to employ his talent and fame. It is therefore quite evident that he would have preferred to be remembered as a significant painter. Even so, he never succeeded in making a lasting impact in that field. Even his major commission, the challenging decorations in the most auspicious rooms in the Palazzo Vacchio, did not in retrospect come up to the standards set by his Florentine predecessors in the art of fresco painting, let alone those by artists much closer to his own time, Michelangelo and Raphael, whom he so deeply admired and whose works he so eloquently described.

In the final analysis, he failed by his own standards as

Giorgio Vasari. (Library of Congress)

well, for most of his frescoes are hopelessly congested, pompously rhetorical, wearisome to the eye, and clearly lacking the visual mellowness, the decorum, and the sound judgment set forth in his work as prerequisites for true artistic accomplishment.

None of this detracts in the least from the pioneering importance of his written work. Modern research carried out under circumstances far more favorable than those under which Vasari labored may have brought to light certain inaccuracies in his findings, and some of his evaluations have not withstood the test of time. More often than not, however, new research has simply resulted in a validation of his findings and observations. Furthermore, his minute descriptions of works of art not only constitute the basis on which the field of art history has been built but also provide the pattern for the process of attribution of works of art of the past, so important for the development of collections, private and public.

—*Reidar Dittmann*

FURTHER READING

Burckhardt, Jacob. *The Altarpiece in Renaissance Italy.* Edited and translated by Peter Humfrey. New York: Cambridge University Press, 1988. Swiss scholar Burckhardt's nineteenth century works on the Italian

Renaissance are considered classics in the field. Originally published in 1894 with two other essays, "The Collectors" and "The Portrait," the original edition was entirely without illustrations, whereas in this first English edition the accompanying illustrations, in color and black and white, greatly enhance the discussion. While Burckhardt based his studies on personal probing of the subject, his principal documentation is rooted in Vasari's *Lives of the Most Eminent Painters, Sculptors, and Architects.*

Decker, Heinrich. *The Renaissance in Italy: Architecture, Sculpture, Frescoes.* New York: Viking Press, 1969. A profusely illustrated volume containing meaningful references to Vasari. Although this and other statements tend to reinforce some of the negative criticism so often aimed at Vasari, Decker also stresses the importance of his contribution and actually judges his frescoes more favorably than do other writers.

Jacks, Philip, ed. *Vasari's Florence: Artists and Literati at the Medicean Court.* New York: Cambridge University Press, 1998. Collection of essays on Vasari's art, his criticism, his cultural milieu, and his representation of that milieu. Includes illustrations, bibliographic references, and index.

Pon, Lisa. *Raphael, Dürer, and MarcAntonio Raimondi: Copying and the Italian Renaissance Print.* New Haven, Conn.: Yale University Press, 2004. An important study of the meaning of art and the figure of the artist in Renaissance Italy. Argues that the notion of the individual genius expressing his distinctive self through his images comes into being at almost the same time that new engraving technologies were invented that involved collaborative artistry and the dissemination of multiple copies of previously unique images. Looks at the cultural tension between these two novel models of art in the work of Vasari, Raphael, and Dürer with engraver Raimondi. Includes illustrations, bibliographic references, and index.

Robert, Carden W. *The Life of Giorgio Vasari: A Study of the Later Renaissance in Italy.* New York: Henry Holt, 1911. Drawing on Vasari's own accounts and on other sources, the author discusses Vasari's contribution as an artist and a writer in the perspective of the creative spirit of the waning years of the Renaissance and the early period of mannerism. Because Vasari's own detailed description of his life and activities has made it less urgent to write on that subject, Robert's work still remains the only comprehensive study available in English.

Rubin, Patricia Lee. *Giorgio Vasari: Art and History.*
New Haven, Conn.: Yale University Press, 1995. Detailed study of Vasari's *Lives of the Most Eminent Painters, Sculptors, and Architects* reveals both the concepts of art and artistry and the biographical man that stand behind the text. Includes illustrations, bibliographic references, and index.

Tarchi, Rossella, ed. *The Rediscovery of "The Last Judgement": The Restoration of the Frescoes in the Dome of Santa Maria del Fiore.* Firenze, Italy: Cooperativa Firenze, 2000. Brief study of the discovery and restoration of a fresco by Vasari and Federico Zuccari. Includes illustrations and bibliographic references.

Wackernagel, Martin. *The World of the Florentine Renaissance Artist: Projects and Patrons, Workshop and Art Market.* Translated by Alison Luchs. Princeton, N.J.: Princeton University Press, 1980. Wackernagel's book, a pioneering study originally published in 1938, examines the relationship between the arts and the immediate sociopolitical and economic conditions under which artists worked. Vasari's documentations and judgment, as well as his relationship with patrons, receive good coverage.

Wittkower, Rudolf. *Idea and Image: Studies in the Italian Renaissance.* London: Thames and Hudson, 1978. The last volume in the author's collected essays contains extensive references to *Lives of the Most Eminent Painters, Sculptors, and Architects,* always cited with great respect for the authority of the document. Particularly interesting is Wittkower's discussion of the evolvement of Michelangelo's dome of St. Peter's in the Vatican, of which, Wittkower states, Vasari provided "detailed and reliable description," whereas it was totally ignored by subsequent builders. Equally positive is Wittkower's estimation of Vasari's perspicacity relative to the development of Raphael's talent.

SEE ALSO: Andrea del Sarto; Sofonisba Anguissola; Giovanni Bellini; Correggio; Giorgione; Francesco Guicciardini; Leonardo da Vinci; Cosimo I de' Medici; Michelangelo; Andrea Palladio; Raphael; Jacopo Sansovino; Joseph Justus Scaliger; Tintoretto; Titian; Andrea del Verrocchio.

RELATED ARTICLES in *Great Events from History: The Renaissance & Early Modern Era, 1454-1600:* 1477-1482: Work Begins on the Sistine Chapel; 1495-1497: Leonardo da Vinci Paints *The Last Supper*; 1508-1512 and 1534-1541: Michelangelo Paints the Sistine Chapel; December 23, 1534-1540: Parmigianino Paints *Madonna with the Long Neck*; June, 1564: Tintoretto Paints for the Scuola di San Rocco.

Vasily III

Grand prince of Moscow (r. 1505-1533)

Vasily III successfully continued the process of expanding and centralizing political power in Moscow, building on the efforts of his predecessors to bring together independent Russian principalities. He increased Russia's territorial size through economic pressure, diplomacy, and wars, and he left a strong state to his son Ivan the Terrible.

Born: Possibly March 25 or 26, 1479; Moscow (now in Russia)

Died: December 3, 1533; Moscow

Also known as: Vasily Ivanovich; Vasili Ivanovich; Vasili III; Vasili III Ivanovich; Basil III

Areas of achievement: Government and politics, military, warfare and conquest, religion and theology

Early Life

Vasily (vehs-YEEL-yi) was the son of Ivan the Great and Sophia Palaeologus, Ivan's second wife. Vasily was not expected to become the ruling prince of Moscow, but family disputes and the premature death of his step-brother, who was next in line of succession, gave Vasily the opportunity to vie successfully for power. In 1502, Ivan designated Vasily next in line as grand prince of Moscow.

Information is limited about Vasily's personal life, but he could read and write, a talent unusual for that period. He is described as able and intelligent but also willing to use violence and intimidation against domestic opponents. His firmness denied marriage rights to his brothers, but Vasily married twice. His first marriage, to Solomonia Saburova, which lasted more than two decades, did not produce a son, so he divorced Solomonia in 1525. In 1526, he married Elena Glinskaya, and they had two sons: Ivan and Yuri. The older son became Czar Ivan IV, who ruled Russia with an iron hand, earning him the epithet "Ivan the Terrible."

Life's Work

The focus of Vasily III's foreign policy continued his father's efforts to expand the borders of the principality of Muscovy to a size that justified changing the country's name from Muscovy to Russia. Competition with Russia's western neighbors, Lithuania and Poland, was a common feature during Vasily's reign. A Russian victory annexed in 1514 the important Lithuanian city of Smolensk to the west. Another territorial goal was to reach the Baltic Sea to the northwest.

Vasily opposed rival Russian princes who ruled small regional principalities, which had given nominal allegiance to Moscow but still maintained a degree of economic and foreign policy independence. Through intimidation and diplomacy, Vasily succeeded in absorbing several outlying regions.

Farther to the south, Vasily faced the Tatars in the Crimea region, but he failed to decisively defeat them, as they later reached the environs of Moscow on two occasions and caused considerable chaos in the center of the Russian state. On the eastern border, he faced the Tatars in the Kazan area on the Volga River, fighting three campaigns to bring it under Moscow's control. On other occasions, he used diplomacy and money to obtain Tatar support for his military campaigns against other opponents.

Vasily's primary objective was to strengthen Moscow and consolidate its authority over all territories within the Russian domain. In addition, he wanted to establish a credible military force to deal with his enemies to the west, south, and east.

Throughout his rule, Vasily continued Moscow's contacts with Europe, with the goal of borrowing and utilizing the technical skills of the more advanced West to modernize his nation. He recruited Europeans to live in Moscow and to share their expertise.

Like his father, Vasily sought to increase his ruling power and to reduce the influence of the feudal and powerful land-owning nobles, the boyars. He had to undercut their authority and reduce their influence without creating unified opposition against him. The boyar (noble) Duma, an advisory council, still existed to offer advice to the ruler, but Vasily relied on the council less and less.

As the Russian nation expanded in size, he also provided land and authority to his followers in the *pomestie* system, which bound them closer to the national ruler. These loyal members of his administration steadily increased in power as boyar authority gradually declined.

During this period, as in prior centuries, the Russian Orthodox Church was an important source of influence and guidance for the nation and its population. Moscow's rulers used this institution to unify and centralize the state further. Vasily, even before assuming power, defended and supported the Russian Orthodox Church as an essential bulwark that helped to hold Russia together. He cooperated with religious leaders who opposed rival

Vasily III. (Hulton|Archive by Getty Images)

and Constantinople as centers of the faith in prior centuries. This theological argument portrayed the Russian rulers as the most important defenders of Christianity, and hence the Russian Orthodox Church favored the increase of Moscow's political authority. Vasily took advantage of this theory to extend his influence.

Vasily, though, never became subservient to the Orthodox Church. Visitors described life at the royal court at the Kremlin in Moscow as cultured and impressive, even with secular overtones. Occasionally, Vasily would don Western-style clothing, and he trimmed his beard, radical departures that offended social and religious traditionalists.

Despite Vasily's achievements, Russia under his rule was not a just and democratic nation and society. His extensive and autocratic government, the continued power of the boyar class, and the overwhelming role of the Orthodox Church dominated millions of poor Russians whose quality of life could only be marginal at best. Serfdom, made more legally binding over several centuries (especially expanded during the reign of Vasily's father, Ivan the Great), added to the oppressive social conditions in this period.

religious movements, and their support aided Vasily's efforts to create a more autocratic state under his rule in Moscow.

Religious opponents to the traditional Orthodox leadership, and consequently to Vasily as the Russian ruler, included the Trans-Volga Elders, who criticized the extensive wealth of the established church as being incompatible with Christian doctrine and behavior. The traditional religious leaders understandably opposed relinquishing their massive authority and extensive possessions. Joseph of Volokolamsk was a prominent Orthodox theologian who asserted that the church needed these economic resources to carry out its Christian mission; he led the Orthodox Church's opposition to the Trans-Volga Elders. Vasily supported Joseph and his followers (the Josephites) in this bitter religious confrontation, which maintained the status quo.

Another significant element drawing state and church closer together in this period was the concept of the Third Rome. This theory asserted that Moscow was the leader of the true Christian faith, after the fall of ancient Rome

SIGNIFICANCE

Nation building in Russia replicated a similar process taking place in England, France, and Spain at about the same time. Ruling between a famous father (Ivan the Great) and a powerful son (Ivan the Terrible), Vasily III is given less attention than his illustrious relatives. Nonetheless, his leadership significantly increased Russia's territorial growth. It also continued the important trend toward consolidating power in the hands of autocratic Russian rulers.

Vasily's diplomatic and economic contacts with Europe helped to modernize his administration, and the contacts led to greater efficiency in guiding the Russian state.

As grand prince of Muscovy, with Moscow as its capital, Vasily III ruled Russia with energy and success. He occasionally used the word "czar" (from the Latin "caesar") to describe his political position and power. This title became a source of authority that his son Ivan the Terrible institutionalized within fifteen years of his father's death and lasted until the abolition of the Russian monarchy in the 1917 revolution.

—*Taylor Stults*

FURTHER READING

Crummey, Robert O. *The Formation of Muscovy, 1304-1613*. New York: Longman, 1987. Traces Moscow's emergence as the nucleus of the growing Russian state.

Duffy, James P., and Vincent L. Ricci. *Czars: Russia's Rulers for over One Thousand Years*. New York: Facts on File, 1995. This comprehensive reference work describes Russia's rulers from the tenth to the twentieth century.

Herberstein, Sigmund von. *Description of Moscow and Muscovy*. New York: Barnes and Noble Books, 1969. English translation of an important contemporary source, written by a German diplomat who served in Moscow during Vasily's rule.

Kollmann, Nancy. S. *Kinship and Politics: The Making of the Muscovite Political System, 1345-1547*. Stanford, Calif.: Stanford University Press, 1987. Examines changes in the Russian administrative and governing system, tracing the interplay of boyar power with efforts to achieve more-centralized authority.

Payne, Robert, and Nikita Romanoff. *Ivan the Terrible*. New York: Cooper Square Press, 2002. Paperback reprint of a 1975 biography of Ivan the Terrible that includes coverage of Vasily's impact on Russian government and daily life, which he passed on to his son.

Solovev, Sergei M. *The Age of Vasili III*. Gulf Breeze, Fla.: Academic International Press, 1976. English translation of a noted Russian historian's extensive description and analysis of Russia during Vasily's years in power.

Troyat, Henri. *Ivan the Terrible*. London: Phoenix Press, 2002. Paperback reprint of a 1984 biography of Ivan the Terrible. Includes an assessment of Vasily's impact on the Russian government and nation.

Vernadsky, George. *Russia at the Dawn of the Modern Age*. New Haven, Conn.: Yale University Press, 1959. Covers the fifteenth and early sixteenth centuries to the end of Vasily's reign. Includes discussion of domestic and foreign policies and the changes taking place in the growing Russian state.

SEE ALSO: Ivan the Great; Ivan the Terrible; Sophia Palaeologus.

RELATED ARTICLES in *Great Events from History: The Renaissance & Early Modern Era, 1454-1600:* 1478: Muscovite Conquest of Novgorod; 1499-c. 1600: Russo-Polish Wars.

PAOLO VERONESE
Italian painter

Veronese was one of the greatest painters in sixteenth century Venice and, along with Titian and Tintoretto, was responsible for the countermannerist style of art. Veronese's luminous colors and dynamic, decorative compositions foreshadow the artistic concerns of the painters of the seventeenth century.

BORN: 1528; Verona, Republic of Venice (now in Italy)
DIED: April 19, 1588; Venice, Republic of Venice
ALSO KNOWN AS: Paolo Caliari
AREA OF ACHIEVEMENT: Art

EARLY LIFE

Paolo Veronese (PAH-loh vay-roh-NAY-zay) was born Paolo Caliari. His father, Gabriele di Piero Caliari, was a sculptor and stonecutter in that city, and in all likelihood Veronese received his earliest artistic instruction in his father's studio, perhaps learning to model in clay. Further training came in the painting workshop of his uncle, Antonio Badile, and he may also have worked for a time with the painter and architect Giovanni Caroto.

Veronese appears to have remained in Verona until around 1552, when he left to execute commissions in various northern Italian cities, including Mantua, where he worked on an altarpiece for the cathedral with several other painters. It is not clear exactly when he first settled in Venice, but in 1553, he was given work at the Venetian Ducal Palace. This important commission, also a collaboration, involved painting the ceiling of the room where the Council of Ten met for deliberations (Sala del Consiglio dei Dieci).

Veronese's style during his earliest period was in line with the sophisticated mannerism popular in Italy during the middle of the sixteenth century. In particular, his early work shows the influence of Emilian artists such as Parmigianino. As he matured, however, his style evolved into a more classical handling of space and form. A natural predisposition for pictorial compositions, along with the influence of Titian's style, seemed to account for this countermannerist development.

LIFE'S WORK

Veronese is generally considered, along with Titian and Tintoretto, one of the greatest painters of sixteenth century Venice. His paintings, frequently of immense size and crowded with figures, are like tapestries filled with color and light. The sumptuous textures, details, and colors create patterns that emphasize the decorative qualities of what is, emphatically, a joyful, aristocratic art. Veronese's colors are pure and clear, a combination of pale and vivid tones, unsubdued by shadows or glazes such as those of Titian and Tintoretto.

Within a few years of his arrival in Venice, Veronese was given a commission that, along with his work in the Ducal Palace, established his reputation as one of Venice's preeminent painters. For the Church of San Sebastiano, he executed, around 1556, a series of frescoed murals and canvas ceiling paintings. The ceiling paintings in particular demonstrate dramatic compositional arrangements. Exploiting the position of the paintings above the viewer's head, Veronese employed perspective to create the illusion that the ceiling had opened up and that the scenes being depicted were in fact happening while the viewer looked up from below. In *The Triumph of Mordecai*, horses shy at the edge of an abyss in which, spatially speaking, the viewer stands. Lords and ladies look directly down from a balcony. Veronese was not the first artist to use this illusionistic device (called *di sotto in su*). Andrea Mantegna had employed it in the fifteenth century, and Correggio had explored its possibilities. Veronese, however, developed its full pictorial and atmospheric potential and served as a reference for Baroque artists of the seventeenth century.

Veronese appears to have spent most of his mature career in and around Venice. He did visit Rome sometime between 1555 and 1560, where he saw the work of the High Renaissance masters, but most of his travels took him to cities near Venice. Around 1561, he executed a series of frescoes at the Villa Barbaro in Maser, and in 1575, he is documented as working in Padua on a *Martyrdom of Saint Justina* and *An Ascension of Christ*. In the late 1570's, Veronese received one of his most important commissions. A 1577 fire had destroyed the painted decorations in the Hall of the Great Council (Sala del Maggior Consiglio) of the Ducal Palace, and Veronese was hired to repaint the ceiling. His central allegorical scene, *The Triumph of Venice*, combines the illusionism of the San Sebastiano ceiling paintings with a new spatial ex-

Paolo Veronese. (Library of Congress)

pansiveness full of strong, almost unearthly highlights and pure color.

Veronese's personal life was fairly uneventful. He married Elena Badile, the daughter of his teacher, in 1566 and had two sons. By all accounts, he was religious and morally strict. It is ironic, then, that his name has been immortalized not only for his art but also because he was called before the Inquisition to defend one of his paintings.

In April of 1573, Veronese completed a painting depicting the Last Supper for the refectory of Saints Giovanni and Paolo in Venice, to replace a work of the same subject by Titian that had been destroyed by fire in 1571. Three months later, he was summoned to appear before the Holy Tribunal, or Inquisition, to answer complaints against the work. Specifically, the Church hierarchy was concerned by what it perceived as a lack of decorum in the composition. The crowded painting showed, in addition to the traditional Christ and apostles, dwarfs, buffoons, drunkards, and Germans. These superfluous figures, added for picturesque and decorative effects, violated the decrees of the Council of Trent, which, in its codification of the tenets of the Counter-Reformation, had stated that religious paintings should contain no distortions or distractions that might interfere with the moral message. The transcript of Veronese's interview with the tribunal survives and shows him deflecting the criticism with naïveté, claiming that he added the excess figures for compositional, or artistic, purposes. The tribunal decided that Veronese was to make corrections at his own expense. Instead, he changed the title of the painting to *The Feast in the House of Levi* and left it mostly as he had painted it, with only the most minor alterations.

SIGNIFICANCE

Veronese is sometimes described by art historians as a proto-Baroque artist. His essentially naturalistic and illusionistic handling of form and space was certainly not in keeping with the mannerist taste that dominated Italian painting during the middle of the sixteenth century. Some of his mature works do, in fact, demonstrate expansive views of space, theatrical compositions, and decorative arrangements of color and light that point to the styles of the next two centuries. At the same time, other of his paintings look back to the pictorial traditions of fifteenth century Venice. In particular, his use of the old tableau composition, with figures lined along a shallow plane before a descriptive Venetian backdrop, hark back to the works of Vittore Carpaccio and Gentile Bellini.

Of the three great masters of sixteenth century Venetian painting (Titian, Tintoretto, and Veronese), the reputation of Veronese has suffered the most. Critics often find his decorative compositions lacking in profundity. The perceived deficiencies are not those of talent or technique, but rather in the area of expression. This attitude may say more about the expectations of art in the modern world than about Veronese's intentions and accomplishments.

—Madeline Cirillo Archer

FURTHER READING

Cocke, Richard. "The Development of Veronese's Critical Reputation." *Arte Veneta* 34 (1980): 96-111. Discusses the critical attitudes toward Veronese over the centuries and the extent of his influence in each period of art. Especially valuable in describing Veronese's influence on Baroque artists.

_____. *Paolo Veronese: Piety and Display in an Age of Religious Reform.* Burlington, Vt.: Ashgate, 2001. Details the decisive effects of Veronese's many religious paintings on Venetian ideas about piety. Argues that critics have failed to notice Veronese's skill with paint-

erly narrative. Includes twenty-four pages of plates, illustrations, bibliographic references, and index.

_____. *Veronese.* London: Jupiter Books, 1980. A monographic overview of Veronese's life and career, this book is a useful introduction to the artist. Particular emphasis is placed on stylistic issues, although biographic information is also included. Contains one hundred illustrations, with some in color, and a bibliography.

_____. *Veronese's Drawings, with a "Catalogue Raisonné."* Ithaca, N.Y.: Cornell University Press, 1984. A thorough analysis of Veronese's drawings and how they relate stylistically and programatically to their related paintings. Includes a chronology of documentable activities, a bibliography, and illustrations and catalog entries for each drawing. Useful as a supplement to Cocke's work.

Fehl, Philipp. "Veronese and the Inquisition: A Study of the Subject Matter of the So-Called *Feast in the House of Levi.*" *Gazette des Beaux-Arts* 58 (1961): 325-354. Discusses the iconography of Veronese's famous painting and the events surrounding the confrontation with the Inquisition.

Goldwater, Robert, and Marco Treves, eds. *Artists on Art.* New York: Pantheon Books, 1972. A translation of the examination of Veronese by the Holy Tribunal regarding his *Last Supper*, later retitled *The Feast in the House of Levi.* The original record is preserved in the archives in Venice. Most other anthologies of art-historical documents also include this transcript.

Pedrocco, Filippo. *Veronese.* Translated by Christopher Evans. Antella, Florence, Italy: Scala, 1998. Brief monograph covering the major works of Veronese, discussing their meaning and importance. Includes color illustrations, bibliographic references, and index.

Priever, Andreas. *Paolo Caliari, Called Veronese, 1528-1588.* Translated by Paul Aston and Fiona Hulse. Cologne, Germany: Könemann, 2000. In addition to a study of Veronese's life and art, this work contains a discussion of the revival of the artist's reputation in the twentieth century. Includes illustrations and bibliographic references.

Rosand, David. *Painting in Sixteenth-Century Venice: Titian, Veronese, Tintoretto.* Rev. ed. New York: Cambridge University Press, 1997. This work contains readable, scholarly articles investigating the sources of and influences on Veronese's compositions, including fifteenth century traditions and contemporary theater designs. Also provides an analysis of Veronese's waning reputation and a synopsis of the examination by the Inquisition. Contains excellent black-and-white photographs and a bibliography.

SEE ALSO: Andrea del Sarto; The Carracci Family; Correggio; Andrea Mantegna; Piero della Francesca; Tintoretto; Titian.

RELATED ARTICLES in *Great Events from History: The Renaissance & Early Modern Era, 1454-1600:* December 23, 1534-1540: Parmigianino Paints *Madonna with the Long Neck*; June, 1564: Tintoretto Paints for the Scuola di San Rocco.

ANDREA DEL VERROCCHIO
Italian sculptor

Verrocchio was one of the best sculptors of the later part of the fifteenth century and a great favorite of the Medici family. He was able to work in silver, bronze, and terra-cotta as well as marble and was also active as a painter. It was in Verrocchio's workshop that Leonardo da Vinci received his first training.

BORN: 1435; Florence (now in Italy)
DIED: October 7, 1488; Venice, Republic of Venice (now in Italy)
ALSO KNOWN AS: Andrea di Michele Cione
AREA OF ACHIEVEMENT: Art

EARLY LIFE

Andrea del Verrocchio (ahn-DRAY-ah dehl vayr-RAWK-kyoh) was the son of Michele Cione and his first wife, Gemma. He grew up in and spent most of his life in Florence. His father, who was in his fifties when Andrea, his first child, was born, worked as a tilemaker or brickmaker and was a member of the Stoneworkers' Guild. He owned a home on the Via dell'Angolo in the parish of San Ambrogio as well as some land outside the city. Andrea's mother evidently died while he was young, for his father remarried and Andrea was reared by his stepmother. In 1452, his father died.

The following year, the eighteen-year-old Verrocchio was involved in an incident in which a man was killed in a scuffle outside the walls of the city. Verrocchio had thrown a stone that hit a young wool worker, who subsequently died of his injuries. Verrocchio was brought before the authorities and charged with homicide, but he was acquitted and the cause of the death was determined to be accidental.

According to his sixteenth century biographer, Giorgio Vasari, Verrocchio was largely self-taught; historians have no certain knowledge of when he received his early training or who his teachers may have been. From 1467 onward, his name appears in the surviving contemporary documents as "del Verrocchio," and while a seventeenth century source reports that he received his first training in the shop of a goldsmith named Giuliano da Verrocchi, it is now known that he owed his nickname to the fact that in his youth he was a protégé of an ecclesiastic named Verrocchio. In the tax return that he and his younger brother Tommaso filed for the year 1457, he does state that he has been working as a goldsmith but complains that there is no work in this craft and that he has been forced to abandon it. One early source implies that he was trained by Donatello, and while that is possible, modern critics have also suggested that he may have studied or worked with Desiderio da Settignano or Bernardo Rossellino. In 1461, Verrocchio was one of a number of Florentine artists who were asked to furnish designs for the construction of a chapel in the cathedral at Orvieto, but none of the Florentines received the commission.

LIFE'S WORK

Verrocchio emerged as an important artist only in the late 1460's. His earliest authenticated works are decorative or architectural, and two of them were commissioned by the Medicis, marking the beginning of his long association with that family. The marble, brass, and porphery tombstone for Cosimo de' Medici in the Church of S. Lorenzo, Florence, was completed in 1467. By 1472, the year in which he was listed as a painter and carver in the records of the Florentine artists' professional association, the Guild of Saint Luke, he had completed his first major work and one of his most important ones: the tomb of Piero and Giovanni de' Medici in the Church of S. Lorenzo. Verrocchio employed virtually no figural decoration and no Christian symbolism, but the tomb has a solemn majesty that derives from his characteristic combination of simplicity of design and great richness of detail.

Verrocchio's famous bronze *David* in the Museo Nazionale di Bargello in Florence was probably commissioned in the early 1470's and is certainly one of the earliest of his figural compositions. Like Donatello's bronze *David*, it was a Medici commission, but there is an embellishment of the forms that signals the change in Florentine taste toward the richer and more sumptuous taste that marks the late fifteenth century. At about the same time, Verrocchio completed his most popular work, the wonderful bronze *Putto with a Dolphin* that was part of a fountain in the Medici villa at Careggi. This is a work of great importance for the history of Renaissance sculpture, for it is the first sculpture since antiquity to present equally pleasing views from all sides.

In January of 1467, Verrocchio received the first payments for one of his finest works, the bronze group of *Christ and Saint Thomas* in the central niche on the east front of the Or San Michele in Florence. The niche had originally been designed for a single figure, and the creation of a two-figure, more than life-size group for the narrow space presented unusual difficulties. Verrocchio was able to solve these problems by making the figures very shallow, a fact of which the spectator is unaware, and by letting the figure of Saint Thomas extend out of the niche toward the viewer. It is possible that the creation and execution of these figures may have occupied

Andrea del Verrocchio. (Library of Congress)

him for as long as eighteen years, for they were not placed in the niche until June of 1483.

Verrocchio also carried out several important commissions in marble, of which one of his finest is the half-length *Portrait of a Woman*, a work that bears a strong resemblance to Leonardo's *Portrait of Ginevra dei Benci*. None of his monumental marble works, though, remains in its original condition. The earliest of these was the monument to Francesca Tornabuoni, which was set up in the Church of S. Maria sopra Minerva in Rome, where the Tornabuoni family of Florence had a chapel. It may have been executed in the late 1470's, but very little of it remains. Of the monument to Cardinal Niccolò Forteguerri, there are at least some substantial remains, and the original appearance of the work can be partially reconstructed from the large terra-cotta sketch held in the Victoria and Albert Museum in London. In May of 1476, Verrocchio's model was chosen from among five competitors by the council of Pistoia, the cardinal's native city. The monument was to be erected in the Cathedral of Pistoia, but the execution dragged on, and several figures and some of the architectural framework were still not finished when Verrocchio died. The monument was given its present form in the mid-eighteenth century. Verrocchio also was responsible for some of the decoration of the huge silver altar frontal for the altar in the Florentine Baptistery. This masterpiece of the goldsmith's art was begun in the fourteenth century, and generations of artists had contributed to it. In 1480, Verrocchio completed the silver relief representing *The Beheading of Saint John the Baptist*, which was placed on the lower right side of the altar.

Verrocchio and his studio regularly produced paintings as well as sculpture, but very few paintings can now be identified as his with any certainty. Of the many half-length Madonnas attributed to him, there is little agreement as to which, if any, are actually by him. The *Madonna Enthroned with Saints John the Baptist and Donatus* was commissioned from Verrocchio not long before 1478, but much of the execution seems to be by Lorenzo di Credi, who worked with Verrocchio and often collaborated with him. Verrocchio's best painting, and the only one universally agreed to be his, is the *Baptism of Christ*, which probably dates from the mid-1470's. Vasari's statement that one of the kneeling angels is by Leonardo, who was in Verrocchio's studio in 1476, is generally accepted. What is clear is that Verrocchio depended heavily on pupils, members of his workshop, and collaborators to produce the paintings that were commissioned from him.

The last years of Verrocchio's life were devoted to the design of what was to become his masterpiece: the larger-than-life-size *Equestrian Statue of Colleoni* in Venice. The noted Renaissance soldier Bartolommeo Colleoni of Bergamo had died in 1475 and in his will left funds for a commemorative equestrian statue to be erected in his honor in Venice. Verrocchio's full-scale model was completed in the summer of 1481, and in 1483 Verrocchio moved to Venice, where he remained until his death in 1488. At the time of his death, no parts of the work had yet been cast, and it was not until 1496 that the work was completed and installed on a high pedestal in the Piazza of SS. Giovanni e Paolo. Although he never lived to see its completion, it is in every way the supreme achievement of his artistic genius.

SIGNIFICANCE

Verrocchio's contribution to the development of monumental sculpture during the Renaissance is a major one. Only Donatello ranks with him. Verrocchio's workshop was one of the largest and most active in Florence, and in his mastery of all facets of the visual arts he provided a role model for his greatest pupil, Leonardo da Vinci. Leonardo's conception of the artist as a man of science, versed in all aspects of engineering and anatomy as well as design, owes much to Verrocchio's example. It would be unfair, however, to see Verrocchio's achievement primarily in terms of the accomplishments of his best pupil. In his own right, he is one of the most characteristic artists of the Florentine Renaissance. The naturalistic element in his work is very strong, and in this he reflects the dominant ideal of the Florentine artist of his day: fidelity to nature. All aspects of the natural were to be studied and understood, but for Verrocchio this naturalism was never an end in itself. Instead, it was the means by which he could create a perfect and untarnished world of forms and ideal types.

Verrocchio's contemporaries fully appreciated this aspect of his work. One of them noted that his head of Christ in the group of *Christ and Saint Thomas* was thought to be "the most beautiful head of the Saviour that has yet been made."

His masterpiece, the monument to Colleoni, shows how effectively he was able to balance these two tendencies. It is a work of enormous power, and the violent and aggressive twist of the rider's body gives a sense of tremendous energy waiting to be unleashed. To achieve this effect, Verrocchio has twisted the figure to the limits of human possibility. Similarly, the brutal face is an un-

flinching delineation of a type, not an individual, but it is rendered so plausibly that it seems more vital than any portrait. No fifteenth century artist better exemplified the artistic ideals of the era.

—Eric Van Schaack

FURTHER READING

Brown, David Alan. *Leonardo da Vinci: Origins of a Genius*. New Haven, Conn.: Yale University Press, 1998. The first two chapters of this study of Leonardo deal directly with Verrocchio, his workshop, and his influence on Leonardo. Includes illustrations, bibliographic references, and index.

Bule, Steven, Alan Phipps Darr, and Fiorella Superbi Gioffredi, eds. *Verrocchio and Late Quattrocento Italian Sculpture*. Firenze, Italy: Le Lettre, 1992. Collection of papers presented at two conferences marking the quincentenary of Verrocchio's death. Includes illustrations, bibliographic references, and index.

Butterfield, Andrew. *The Sculptures of Andrea del Verrocchio*. New Haven, Conn.: Yale University Press, 1997. Comprehensive study of the sculpture, utilizing sources and technical data not previously available. Discusses the practical aspects of Verrocchio's creations, both technical and financial, as well as his style and iconography. Includes color illustrations, bibliographic references, and index.

Covi, Dario A. "Four New Documents Concerning Andrea del Verrocchio." *Art Bulletin* 48 (1966): 97-103. New and important documents dealing with the life of the artist and his work.

Passavant, Günter. *Verrocchio: Sculptures, Paintings, and Drawings, Complete Edition*. Translated by Katherine Watson. London: Phaidon Press, 1969. The best general modern survey. The text covers all aspects of Verrocchio's work, and there is a catalog of the sculptures, paintings, and drawings, which the author believes to be authentic, as well as information on rejected works.

Pope-Hennessy, John. *Italian Renaissance Sculpture*. London: Phaidon Press, 1958. The best general introduction to the field of Italian Renaissance sculpture, with extensive coverage of the major masters. The short article on Verrocchio is an excellent summary of his work as a sculptor, and there are catalog entries of his major works.

Seymour, Charles, Jr. *The Sculpture of Verrocchio*. Greenwich, Conn.: New York Graphic Society, 1971. The best catalog of Verrocchio's sculpture. Contains notes on the principal works, an appendix of documents with translations, and a partial translation, with some explanatory notes, of Vasari's biography of the artist.

Vasari, Giorgio. *Lives of the Most Eminent Painters, Sculptors, and Architects.* Translated by Gaston du C. de Vere. Vol. 3. Reprint. New York: Abrams, 1979. The standard translation of the second edition of Vasari's biography of the artist, published in 1568. This is the only nearly contemporary biography of the artist, written twenty years after the death of Verrocchio. While it is not a reliable source for dates or attributions, it contains a wealth of information available in no other source.

Verrocchio, Andrea del. *Verrocchio and the Renaissance Atelier.* Translated by Susan Herbstritt. Firenze, Italy: Pagliai Polistampa, 2001. This exhibition catalog is part of the Leonardo and Surroundings series. It contains photographs of Verrocchio's works exhibited in Arezzo in 2001, along with other Renaissance pieces from Tuscany, and includes a discussion of the artist's relation to the culture of the Tuscan workshops. Bibliographic references.

Wilder, Elizabeth. *The Unfinished Monument by Andrea del Verrocchio to the Cardinal Niccolò Forteguerri at Pistoia.* Vol. 7 in *Studies in the History and Criticism of Sculpture.* Northampton, Mass.: Smith College, 1932. Photographs by Clarence Kennedy and appendix of documents by Peleo Bacci. The most thorough study of any of Verrocchio's works. Includes complete documentation and excellent photographs.

SEE ALSO: Donato Bramante; Benvenuto Cellini; Leonardo da Vinci; Lorenzo de' Medici; Michelangelo; Jacopo Sansovino; Giorgio Vasari.

RELATED ARTICLE in *Great Events from History: The Renaissance & Early Modern Era, 1454-1600:* c. 1478-1519: Leonardo da Vinci Compiles His Notebooks.

ANDREAS VESALIUS
Flemish physician and historian

Vesalius published the first modern comprehensive text of human anatomy, and his accurate description of the structure of the human body, the result of firsthand dissection, is the basis of the modern scientific study of human anatomy.

BORN: December 31, 1514; Brussels (now in Belgium)
DIED: October 15, 1564; Zacynthus, Republic of Venice (now in Zákinthos, Greece)
AREAS OF ACHIEVEMENT: Medicine, science and technology, historiography

EARLY LIFE

Andreas Vesalius (ahn-DRAY-ahs veh-SAY-lee-uhs) belonged to the fifth-generation family of a long line of physicians, a family line that combined scholarly and Humanistic interests (several had written medical treatises or commentaries on Arabic and Hippocratic works) with medical ability and ambition, having served the courts of Burgundy and the Habsburgs. Although the family had long lived in Flanders, it had come originally from Wesel on the lower Rhine River, hence the family's name, of which Vesalius is the Latin form. Vesalius's father was apothecary to the court of the Habsburg emperor Charles V.

As a boy, Vesalius dissected dogs, cats, moles, mice, and rats. He attended the University of Louvain from 1529 to 1533, where he studied Latin and Greek. He then went to the University of Paris to study medicine, remaining there from 1533 to 1536. The medical faculty at Paris was under the influence of Galen, the great second century Greek medical writer, whose authority in anatomical matters was unchallenged. Vesalius found that there was little practical teaching of anatomy. Human corpses were dissected only twice a year, and Vesalius found the procedure disappointing. The professor of anatomy never performed the dissection himself but merely read passages from Galen as an assistant dissected the cadaver. In most cases, pigs or dogs were dissected. Eager to obtain human skeletons, Vesalius sought them from cemeteries and gallows outside the city, where he obtained corpses of criminals in various states of decay. He became skilled at dissection and gained a firsthand knowledge of human anatomy. He began to acquire a reputation as an anatomist and even conducted a public dissection.

Vesalius left Paris in 1536 on the outbreak of war between France and the Holy Roman Empire. He returned to Louvain, where he completed his baccalaureate degree in the following year. Thereupon, he traveled to Italy and

Andreas Vesalius. (Library of Congress)

enrolled in the University of Padua, which enjoyed an outstanding reputation. On December 5, 1537, Vesalius received his medical degree with highest distinction. On the following day, he was appointed professor of surgery, which entailed the teaching of anatomy as well. He was only twenty-three years of age.

LIFE'S WORK

The young professor was enormously successful at Padua, where he lectured to some five hundred students, professors, and physicians. Dispensing with an assistant, he personally descended from his academic chair to dissect cadavers. He prepared four large anatomical charts to illustrate his lectures. In 1538, he published three of them and three skeletal views, which have come to be known as *Tabulae anatomicae sex* (*Six Anatomical Tables*, 1874). The publication of these accurate and detailed plates marked a major advance in anatomical illustration. In the same year, he published a dissection manual based on Galen, *Institutiones anatomicae* (1538), and in the following year he published *Epistola, docens venam axillarem dextri cubiti in dolore laterali secandam* (1539; *The Bloodletting Letter of 1539*, 1946),

in which he argued for the importance of the direct observation of the body.

As a result of his publications and success in teaching, Vesalius began to acquire more than an ordinary reputation. He was reappointed to the medical faculty in 1539 at an increase in salary. In his lectures on anatomy, Vesalius had, as was then customary, expounded the views of Galen, whose authority was accepted in virtually every medical faculty in Europe. In dissections he performed, however, he began to notice discrepancies between what he observed and what Galen had described. At first, so few cadavers were available that there was only limited opportunity for dissection. Beginning in 1539, however, corpses of executed criminals were made available to him. Repeated dissections made it increasingly apparent to Vesalius that Galen's descriptions were erroneous and that Galen had based his descriptions on the anatomy of animals, primarily apes, pigs, and dogs. He expounded his discoveries first at Padua (in his fourth public dissection, at which he ceased to use Galen as a text), then, in 1540, at Bologna, where he was invited to lecture.

As early as 1538, Vesalius had apparently contemplated a major work on anatomy. As his dissections revealed many discrepancies between Galen's anatomy and his own discoveries, he recognized the need for a new and comprehensive text to replace Galen. After his return to Padua from Bologna, he commenced work on one in earnest. Vesalius had woodcut illustrations for the work prepared in Venice, probably in the artist Titian's studio. To produce at least some of the illustrations, he chose a compatriot, Jan Steven van Calcar, who belonged to the school of Titian and had drawn the skeletal figures for the plates in *Six Anatomical Tables*. Other painters associated with the school of Titian almost certainly had a hand in the illustrations as well. Vesalius selected a firm in Basel to print the work, and the woodblocks for the illustrations were transported by donkey.

In the summer of 1542, Vesalius went to Basel to oversee the printing of *De humani corporis fabrica libri septem* (*On the Fabric of the Human Body*, books I-IV, 1998; better known as *De fabrica*), which was published in August, 1543. In *De fabrica*, Vesalius corrected more than two hundred errors of Galenic anatomy and described certain features that either were previously unknown or had been described only partially. He was not the first to find mistakes in Galen, but he went beyond mere correction by insisting that the only reliable basis of anatomical study was dissection and personal observation. *De fabrica* was the first modern treatise on human anatomy that was not based on Galen or drawn from dissected animals. The most extensive and accurate description of human anatomy that had yet appeared, it surpassed all previous books on the subject. Its publication revolutionized the study of anatomy, not least of all by its outstanding use of illustrations. Vesalius was only twenty-eight years of age when the book appeared, less than a week after the publication of Nicolaus Copernicus's *De revolutionibus orbium coelestium* (1543; *On the Revolutions of the Heavenly Spheres*, 1952; better known as *De revolutionibus*), which challenged the dominant geocentric theory of Ptolemy as *De fabrica* challenged the anatomy of Galen. Both books aroused violent controversy.

De fabrica also was one of the most outstanding examples of the bookmaker's art in the sixteenth century. Every detail had been personally supervised by Vesalius: the paper, woodcuts, typography, and famous frontispiece. The woodcuts, showing skeletons and flayed human figures, represented the culmination of Italian painting and the scientific study of human anatomy. They were meant to be studied closely with the text and were so successful that they were frequently plagiarized; they set the standard for all subsequent anatomical illustrators.

Vesalius's fame spread rapidly, and many Italian physicians came to accept his views. Yet Galen's supporters reacted with strong attacks. Jacobus Sylvius, the leading authority on anatomy in Europe and Vesalius's former teacher, published a vitriolic pamphlet against Vesalius,

perhaps angered at his attacks on the deficiencies of training in anatomy. Disappointed by the opposition of the Galenists, he abandoned his anatomical studies, burned all his manuscripts, resigned his chair at Padua, and left Italy to accept the position of third court physician to the Holy Roman Emperor Charles V.

Vesalius was to spend some thirteen years in the service of the emperor, following a family tradition of service to titled houses. In 1544, his father, who had been an apothecary to Charles, died and left a substantial inheritance to Vesalius, who then was married to Anne van Hamme. About a year later, a daughter, his only child, was born. Vesalius spent much of his time traveling with the emperor, who suffered from gout and gastrointestinal disorders. He served as a military surgeon as well, during which time he introduced several new procedures, the most notable of which was the surgical drainage of the chest in empyema. Vesalius enjoyed the full confidence of the emperor, and his professional reputation continued to grow. On Charles's abdication from the Spanish throne in 1556 (he had abdicated as Holy Roman Emperor in 1555), he granted Vesalius a pension for life.

In 1546, Vesalius found time to write a short work, *Epistola, rationem modumque propinandi radicis Chynae* (*Vesalius on China-root*, partial translation 1935), in response to a friend who sought his opinion of a fashionable remedy called the China root. In 1552, he began work on a second edition of *De fabrica*, which was issued a few months after Charles's abdication in 1555, though, like the first edition, it was dedicated to the emperor. The new edition was even more sumptuous than the first. Vesalius took the opportunity to revise and correct the text and make a number of additions. In 1556, he took up residence in Madrid as one of the physicians in the service of Philip II, who had succeeded his father, Charles, as king of Spain. Vesalius's reputation was sufficiently outstanding that in 1559, when King Henry II of France was severely wounded in the head during a tournament, Vesalius was summoned to Paris, where he joined the distinguished French surgeon Ambroise Paré in treating the king. The wound proved fatal, however, and the king died ten days later. Vesalius's reputation as one of the greatest physicians

---

FROM VESALIUS'S
ON THE FABRIC OF THE HUMAN BODY

Andreas Vesalius is best remembered for his foundational work in anatomy, specifically the dissection of the body. Here he states, briefly and directly, that dissection is the best way for medical students to learn the details and makeup of the human body.

I thought that this branch of natural philosophy [anatomy] should be recalled from the dead, so that if it did not achieve with us a greater perfection than at any other place or time among the old teachers of anatomy, it might at least reach such a point that one could with confidence assert that our modern science of anatomy was equal to that of the old.... [M]y practice has ... been to encourage students of medicine ... to perform dissections with their own hands.... Dissection of dead bodies gives accurate instruction in the number, position, and shape of each part, and its particular substance and composition.

Source: Excerpted in *The Portable Renaissance Reader*, edited by James Bruce Ross and Mary Martin McLaughlin. (New York: Viking Press, 1968), pp. 565, 567.

of the age was secure, and his opinion was repeatedly sought. In 1562, Don Carlos, heir to the throne of Spain, received a severe head injury as the result of a fall. As his condition grew worse, the king summoned Vesalius to join several Spanish physicians in attendance on the infant. Although they distrusted him from the beginning, the Spanish physicians eventually allowed Vesalius to administer a treatment that resulted in a rapid improvement of the prince, who recovered.

In the spring of 1564, Vesalius embarked on a trip to the Holy Land by way of Venice. There is reason to believe that he did not intend to return to Spain. He seems to have been regarded with hostility by the Spanish physicians at court. He was probably motivated as well by a desire to return to an academic position, inspired by reading Gabriello Fallopio's *Observationes anatomicae*, which had been published in 1561. He was offered the vacant chair at Padua of his pupil Fallopio, who had died, and he signified his intention to take the position on his return. He proceeded to Palestine by way of Cyprus, but he became ill on the return journey and died on October 15, 1564. He was buried on the island of Zacynthus.

SIGNIFICANCE

The product of a long line of distinguished physicians and Humanists, Vesalius received a fine Renaissance education, had an excellent Latin style, and excelled in philological scholarship. He was trained in the Galenic system, which was taught in all European medical faculties. Only gradually did he come to see why Galen's anatomical descriptions, based on the dissection of animals, needed correction. Even then he was not wholly able to escape Galen's influence, for he sometimes reproduced his errors. His great contribution to medicine was his insistence that anatomical study be based on repeated dissection and firsthand observation of the human body.

The personality of Vesalius remains somewhat enigmatic. He appears to have had considerable dynastic and personal ambition, and he possessed great energy and desire to succeed. A genius, he enjoyed an enviable reputation in his own time but was nevertheless sensitive; he resented the attacks that were made on him by former teachers and jealous colleagues. Independent, unafraid of challenging authority, and confident of his own opinions, he combined great powers of observation with a reputation for remarkably accurate prognosis. He defended himself and his opinions when attacked but was willing to accept correction of his own errors.

Vesalius may be called the founder of modern anatomy. The importance that he placed on the systematic in-vestigation of the human body led to dissection becoming a routine part of the medical curriculum. His *De fabrica* revolutionized the study of anatomy, and its anatomical illustrations became the model for subsequent medical illustrators. Its publication marked the beginning of modern observational science and encouraged the work of other anatomists. Vesalius's ideas spread rapidly throughout Italy and Europe and came to be widely accepted within a half century, in spite of the continuing influence of Galen. In his remarkable genius and his influence, Vesalius deserves to be ranked among the most distinguished contributors to medical science.

—Gary B. Ferngren

FURTHER READING

Cockx-Indestege, Elly. *Andreas Veselius—A Belgian Census: Contribution Towards a New Edition of H. W. Cushing's Bibliography.* Brussels, Belgium: Royal Library Albert I, 1994. An update and emendation of the Cushing volume. Includes illustrations and indexes.

Cunningham, Andrew. *The Anatomical Renaissance: The Resurrection of the Anatomical Projects of the Ancients.* Brookfield, Vt.: Ashgate, 1997. This important study of the history of anatomy emphasizes Vesalius's indebtedness to Galenic anatomy, as well as the importance of ancient science to Renaissance thinkers generally. Includes illustrations, bibliographic references, and index.

Cushing, Harvey. *A Bio-Bibliography of Andreas Vesalius.* 2d ed. Hamden, Conn.: Archon Books, 1962. Contains an excellent bibliography of the various editions of Vesalius's writings and secondary literature about him.

Friedman, Meyer, and Gerald W. Friedland. *Medicine's Ten Greatest Discoveries.* New Haven, Conn.: Yale University Press, 2000. Vesalius's invention of the modern science of anatomy is the first of the ten discoveries discussed in this book. Includes illustrations, bibliographic references, and index.

Lambert, Samuel W., Willy Wiegand, and William M. Ivins, Jr. *Three Vesalian Essays.* New York: Macmillan, 1952. These essays deal with aspects of the printing and illustrations of *De fabrica*.

O'Malley, C. D. *Andreas Vesalius of Brussels, 1514-1564.* Berkeley: University of California Press, 1964. The definitive biography of Vesalius, which replaces that of Moritz Roth (1892).

Persaud, T. V. N. *A History of Anatomy: The Post-*

Vesalian Era. Springfield, Ill.: Charles C Thomas, 1997. Study of Vesalius's legacy and the development of the science of anatomy. Includes illustrations, bibliographic references, and index.

Simmons, John. *The Scientific Hundred: A Ranking of the Most Influential Scientists, Past and Present.* Secaucus, N.J.: Carol, 1996. Simmons ranks Vesalius as the twenty-first most important scientist in world history and explains how he has influenced anatomical science up to the present day. Includes illustrations, bibliographic references, and index.

Singer, Charles, and C. Rabin. *A Prelude to Modern Science.* Cambridge, England: Cambridge University Press, 1946. A discussion of the history of *Six Anatomical Tables* and its sources.

Vesalius, Andreas. *The Illustrations from the Works of Andreas Vesalius of Brussels.* Introduction and annotations by J. B. de C. M. Saunders and Charles D. O'Malley. Cleveland, Ohio: World, 1950. Contains a lengthy introduction describing the life and career of Vesalius and reproduces the woodcuts from *De fabrica* and other works of Vesalius.

SEE ALSO: Georgius Agricola; Charles V; Nicolaus Copernicus; Girolamo Fracastoro; Henry II; Nostradamus; Paracelsus; Philip II; Michael Servetus.

RELATED ARTICLES in *Great Events from History: The Renaissance & Early Modern Era, 1454-1600:* 1543: Vesalius Publishes *On the Fabric of the Human Body*; 1553: Servetus Describes the Circulatory System.

AMERIGO VESPUCCI
Italian explorer

The first European credited with persuading his contemporaries that what Christopher Columbus had discovered was a New World, Vespucci revolutionized geographic thinking when he argued that the region now bearing his name (America) was a continent distinct from Asia.

BORN: March 9, 1454; Florence (now in Italy)
DIED: February 22, 1512; Seville, Spain
ALSO KNOWN AS: Americus Vespucius (Latin name)
AREAS OF ACHIEVEMENT: Exploration, geography, cartography

EARLY LIFE

Amerigo Vespucci (ah-MEHR-ee-goh vay-SPEWT-chee) was the third son of a Florentine family of five children. His father, Stagio Vespucci, was a modestly prosperous notary and a member of a respected and learned clan that cultivated good relations with Florence's intellectual and artistic elite. The fortunes of the family improved during Amerigo's lifetime, and his father would twice occupy positions of fiscal responsibility in the Florentine government.

Unlike his older brothers, who attended the University of Pisa, Amerigo received his education at home under the tutelage of a paternal uncle, Giorgio Antonio, a Dominican friar. The youth became proficient in Latin and developed interests in mathematics and geography, interests he was able to indulge in his tutor's extensive library. In his uncle's circle, Amerigo also became acquainted with the theories of Paolo Toscanelli dal Pozzo, a Florentine physician and cosmographer who first suggested the possibility of a westward voyage as an alternative route to the Orient, an idea that Christopher Columbus and others eventually borrowed.

The study of geography was considered useful for anyone interested in a career in commerce, the profession chosen for Amerigo by his parents. Travel was also considered suitable training for businessmen, and Amerigo accepted the first opportunity when another uncle, Guido Antonio Vespucci, a lawyer, invited the twenty-four-year-old to Paris. The elder Vespucci had been appointed Florentine ambassador to the court of Louis XI in 1478 and had asked his young relative to join him as his private secretary.

In 1482, two years after Amerigo's return to Florence from France, his father died, making Amerigo responsible for the support of the family. The following year, Amerigo became manager of the household of one of the branches of the ruling Medici family, and he performed his task loyally for the next sixteen years. In this capacity, he traveled to Spain at least once to look after the financial interests of the Medicis. He was in Spain again toward the end of 1491 and settled permanently in the city of Seville, where he established financial relations with the city's active Italian merchant community. He would eventually marry María Cerezo, a native of Seville. The couple had no children.

At the close of the fifteenth century, the port city of Seville was the hub of commercial activity and the center of overseas travel and exploration. The Portuguese had taken the lead in the search for a new route to India by circumnavigating Africa. Confirmation of the accuracy of their vision came with news that Bartolomeu Dias's expedition had reached the Cape of Good Hope (the southernmost tip of Africa) in 1488. The Spanish lagged behind their Portuguese neighbors until Columbus's triumphant return from his first voyage. The Crown had paid Columbus's expenses, and he was expected to search for yet another alternate route to the East. Following the theories of Toscanelli, Columbus sailed in 1492 and returned to Spain early the following year.

Columbus's initial optimistic reports that he had found a new route to Asia ensured greater interest and opportunities for investment on the part of all who knew of his trip, and Vespucci would soon be involved in several of the many maritime enterprises that mushroomed in Seville in the wake of Columbus's success. Vespucci, as a subaltern of the Italian merchant Giannetto Berardi, assisted Columbus in financing and outfitting a second voyage of discovery, which sailed in 1493. Berardi died before the provisioning of the fleet was complete, and Vespucci assumed the task. It is highly likely that

Amerigo Vespucci. (Library of Congress)

Vespucci and Columbus had many opportunities to meet during this period and that the Florentine's early interest in geography and cosmography was revived as a result of these contacts. The lure of the sea and the prospects of discovery would soon prove irresistible. By 1499, Vespucci had decided to change professions from businessman to explorer.

LIFE'S WORK

Much controversy surrounds certain facts about Vespucci's life between the years 1497 and 1499—the period immediately prior to his first generally acknowledged ocean voyage—especially because some of his biographers assert that he, not Columbus, was the first European to discover the American mainland along the coast of northern South America. In order for this assertion to be valid, Vespucci would have had to undertake this voyage before Columbus's third—during which Columbus sailed along the coast of Venezuela—that is, before June, 1498.

Vespucci was an inveterate letter writer. The most compelling evidence that he might have gone on this trip appears in a document of dubious authenticity attributed to Vespucci himself, the *Lettera di Amerigo Vespucci delle isole nouvamente trovate in quattro suoi viaggi* (c. 1505; *The First Four Voyages of Amerigo Vespucci,* 1885). This long letter is addressed to the head of the Florentine republic, the gonfalonier Piero Soderini. In this document, the author purports to have made four voyages overseas, the first of which, around 1497, took him along the Caribbean coast of the American mainland—that is, to Venezuela, Central America, the Yucatán Peninsula, and the Gulf of Mexico—well in advance of Columbus. Since there is little independent evidence to corroborate information about this voyage, many scholars dismiss this episode as a fiction propagated by the letter, which could have been a forgery published by an overzealous and unscrupulous printer eager to cash in on a reading public thirsty for news of and reports from the New World. The fourth voyage described in the letter is also believed to be apocryphal.

What is universally accepted is that Vespucci sailed for the New World as a member of a three-ship expedition under the command of the Spaniard Alonso de Ojeda in the spring of 1499. Two of the ships had been outfitted by Vespucci, at his own expense, in the hope of reaching India. Vespucci's expectations were founded on a set of maps drawn from the calculations of Ptolemy, the Egyptian mathematician and astronomer of the second century, whose work *Geōgraphikē hyphēgēsis* (*Geography,*

1932) was the foremost authority to fifteenth century Europeans on matters related to the size and shape of the world.

Ptolemy had concluded that the world was made up of three continents: Europe, Africa, and Asia. When Vespucci set out on his voyage in 1499, he expected to reach the Cape of Cattigara, the southernmost point of Asia on Ptolemy's map. Instead, his expedition reached the northern coast of Brazil and the mouth of the Amazon River. From there, Vespucci's ship proceeded southward to the equatorial zone, after which it turned northward to the Caribbean, navigating along the northeastern coast of South America. Seeing houses on stilts that reminded the crew of Venice, they named the area Venezuela, meaning little Venice. The entire expedition returned to Spain, with a cargo of pearls and slaves and not the hoped-for Asian spices.

Back in Seville, Vespucci planned a second expedition that would take him farther south along the Brazilian coastal route, but his license to travel was suddenly revoked, on the grounds that he was a foreigner, when the Spanish crown, in competition with the Portuguese, began to treat geographical knowledge as secrets of state. When the ships that made up the expedition sailed in August, 1500, they carried only Spaniards. A Portuguese explorer, Pedro Álvars Cabral, had already claimed Brazil for the Portuguese crown in 1500 and, perhaps because of this fact, Vespucci's knowledge of its northern coast might have been of interest to Portugal. He was summoned to appear before King Manuel I. The monarch commissioned the Florentine to undertake a new voyage of discovery along the coast of Brazil, following Cabral's and Vespucci's own original intentions. Vespucci sailed from Lisbon in the spring of 1501.

This second independently verifiable voyage of Vespucci followed the coast of Brazil, crossed the equator, and proceeded south to Patagonia. Experiences during this last stage convinced Vespucci that Ptolemy's calculations had been mistaken, that the Cape of Cattigara and Asia were not where they were expected to be, and that the landmass before his eyes was more likely a new continent, separate and distinct from Asia. On his return to Lisbon, Vespucci, along with geographers and mapmakers, began to redraw and redesign Ptolemy's world to accommodate this new insight. The Atlantic coast of this region began to be detailed in maps that circulated throughout Europe, the first of which appeared in 1502.

Vespucci's employment by the Portuguese did not last long. He returned to Seville in 1502, disappointed that his plans for the exploitation of the new lands were not accepted by Manuel. In Spain, Vespucci's efforts and considerable geographical and navigational knowledge were finally recognized, and in 1505, he was granted citizenship by King Ferdinand II, who appointed him pilot major of the country's board of trade, the Casa de Contratación de las Indias. Vespucci held this position until his death in 1512.

Vespucci is believed to have been short of stature, with an aquiline nose, brown eyes, and wavy hair. This description comes from a family portrait painted by the Florentine muralist Ghirlandajo. Vespucci has also been described as deceitful, self-promoting, and cunning. His reputation suffered after the publication of two letters attributed to him, *The First Four Voyages of Amerigo Vespucci*, mentioned earlier, and *Mundus novus* (c. 1503; English translation, 1916), an account of Vespucci's 1501 expedition addressed to Lorenzo de' Medici, his Florentine employer. In this second letter, the author argues that the lands he had earlier visited (the Atlantic coast of South America) could only be part of a new world.

The ideas contained in the disputed letters, published in many editions and languages shortly after their initial printing, inspired a German mapmaker, Martin Waldseemüller, at Saint-Dié in Lorraine, to draw a new map to accompany narrative descriptions of this new world. The map, which was published in 1507, more closely resembles the geography of the South American continent than earlier efforts, separates South America from Asia, and assigns to the new land the name America in honor of its presumed discoverer Americus (Amerigo). The feminine version of Amerigo was selected to be consistent with the feminine names of the other continents, Europe, Africa, and Asia. This is the first known example of the use of America as the name of the new continent. The word was quickly accepted by northern Europeans as the rightful name for South America, but it would take some fifty years before southern Europe adopted the name and applied it to the entire American landmass, north and south.

Vespucci's complicity in this matter has never been fully established; some believe that he contributed to his own mythology by making himself the center of attention in all his correspondence, never mentioning others in his circle under whose direction he might have worked. He is accused of taking credit for the deeds of his collaborators. Defenders of Columbus, the bulk of Vespucci's critics, argue that the new continent should have been named for Columbus rather than for Vespucci the impostor. Columbus, however, was never quite convinced that the lands he had reached were not in Asia and did not live long enough to experience the historical slight in favor of Vespucci.

SIGNIFICANCE

Vespucci, in spite of his being seriously criticized by a number of eminent and revered figures, deserves much of the credit for revolutionizing geographic thinking in Europe. His travels, especially his vain search for Asia following a Ptolemaic map, convinced him that the accepted authority on things geographical was mistaken. To challenge Ptolemy and a scientific tradition of such long standing in sixteenth century Europe was an act of great intellectual and moral courage.

While Europeans were slow in accepting the full implications of Vespucci's discoveries, his insights nevertheless received much immediate publicity. Vespucci's ideas captivated the imagination of cartographers and publishers, and a steady stream of historical literature filled the minds of Europe's growing reading public. These accounts fired readers' imaginations. Vespucci's conclusions stimulated the growing community of cartographers, navigators, and geographers. He described his experiences in detail, kept careful records of astronomical, navigational, and geographical observations, and made it possible for his contemporaries to accept the idea of America long before additional eyewitness evidence would confirm the wisdom of his insights.

—*Clara Estow*

FURTHER READING

Arciniegas, Germán. *Why America? Five Hundred Years of a Name: The Life and Times of Amerigo Vespucci.* Translated by Harriet de Onís. 2d ed. Bogotá, Colombia: Villegas Editores, 2002. New edition of the classic, if perhaps overly admiring, biography. Argues vehemently in favor of the authenticity of Vespucci's four voyages. The author dismisses some of the criticism of Vespucci as nationalistic propaganda.

Branch, Michael P., ed. *Reading the Roots: American Nature Writing Before Walden.* Athens: University of Georgia Press, 2004. Provides an excerpt from Vespucci's descriptions of America, along with commentary placing this text as one of the earliest examples of the genre of American nature writing. Looks at the way Vespucci's understanding of nature in the New World compares to later authors. Includes bibliographic references and index.

Masini, Giancarlo, with Iacopo Gori. *How Florence Invented America: Vespucci, Verrazzano, and Mazzei and Their Contribution to the Conception of the New World.* New York: Marsilio, 1998. Argues that Vespucci and his fellow Florentines not only helped convince people that the continents of America existed but also contributed to the ideals of democratic republicanism that eventually shaped the government of the United States.

Parry, J. H. *The Discovery of South America.* New York: Taplinger, 1979. An informative and panoramic account of European expansion in the Americas by one of North America's most respected historians. This work is filled with replicas of contemporary maps and charts and is a serious and objective treatment of the period. Parry disputes the authenticity of *The First Four Voyages of Amerigo Vespucci* but credits Vespucci with having contributed to Europe's knowledge of geography and navigation.

Pohl, Frederick J. *Amerigo Vespucci, Pilot Major.* 2d ed. New York: Octagon Books, 1966. The author devotes much attention to Vespucci's mature years, the period of his life that coincides with his voyages overseas. Pohl believes that Vespucci was a most deserving individual and that his fame was legitimately earned. Contains a complete English version of two of Vespucci's letters and two informative appendices.

Vespucci, Amerigo. *Letters from a New World: Amerigo Vespucci's Discovery of America.* Edited by Luciano Formisano. Translated by David Jacobson. New York: Marsilio, 1992. Collects the letters of Vespucci recounting his travels and discoveries in the New World. Several appendices contain important historical documents, such as Vespucci's letter of naturalization, a letter about Vespucci written by Christopher Columbus to his son, and excerpts from Bartolomé de Las Casas's *History of the Indies.* Includes eight pages of plates, illustrations, maps, bibliography, and index.

Vigneras, Louis-André. *The Discovery of South America and the Andalusian Voyages.* Chicago: University of Chicago Press, 1976. A carefully constructed survey of the separate expeditions from Spain to the Americas beginning with Columbus's first voyage in 1492. A separate appendix is devoted to Vespucci's Portuguese voyage. The author's treatment of Vespucci echoes the consensus of contemporary scholarship about him by doubting the authenticity of two of the four voyages.

Zweig, Stefan. *Amerigo: A Comedy of Errors in History.* Translated by Andrew St. James. New York: Viking Press, 1942. An account by the popular Austrian writer who at one point resided in Brazil. Zweig believes that the Americas were so named because of an error, and he argues that Vespucci's letters are filled with serious factual mistakes and coincidences. For Zweig, Vespucci's great fame rests on a false foundation.

See also: John Cabot; Christopher Columbus; Bartolomeu Dias; Ferdinand II and Isabella I; Louis XI; Manuel I; Lorenzo de' Medici; Ponce de León.

Related articles in *Great Events from History: The Renaissance & Early Modern Era, 1454-1600:* 1462: Regiomontanus Completes the *Epitome* of Ptolemy's *Almagest*; October 12, 1492: Columbus Lands in the Americas; 1493-1521: Ponce de León's Voyages; 1519-1522: Magellan Expedition Circumnavigates the Globe.

FRANÇOIS VILLON
French poet

In his intensely personal, forthright verse, which was sordidly realistic yet devout, Villon was the greatest poet of late medieval-early Renaissance France.

Born: 1431; Paris, France
Died: 1463?; place unknown
Also known as: François de Montcorbier; François des Loges
Area of achievement: Literature

Early Life
Born in Paris in 1431, François Villon (frah-swaw vee-yohn) was originally named François de Montcorbier. Apparently his father died when the child was quite young, for François was sent to live with Guillaume de Villon, a priest who was chaplain to the church of Saint-Benoît-le-Bientourné, near the University of Paris. His protector gave the boy a home and an education; the grateful François adopted his name, Villon, and several times wrote fondly of him in his verse, calling him "more than father . . . who has been to me more tender than a mother and raised me from swaddling-clothes." Nothing is known of his real father, not even his first name; Villon called himself "of poor and obscure extraction." His mother, for whom he wrote "Ballade to Our Lady," he describes at the time as a poor old woman who knew nothing of letters.

Nothing is known of Villon's boyhood. Joan of Arc was burned at the stake the year he was born, and for the first five years of his life, Paris was in the hands of the English conquerors, while the ineffectual Charles VII nominally ruled the unoccupied part of France. Most of the country had been ravaged by the Hundred Years' War, and bands of freebooters were plundering whatever of value remained in the countryside or the capital. In 1434, there was the coldest winter in memory, followed in 1436 by a famine, which was succeeded in 1438 by an epidemic of smallpox that claimed some fifty thousand victims. Starving wolves invaded Paris and preyed on children and the weak. It was a grim, harsh era, and as a child, Villon must have seen violence and famine and been surrounded by death.

When he was about twelve, Villon was enrolled at the University of Paris, from which he was graduated in March, 1449, with a bachelor of arts degree. He was tonsured and received minor holy orders, affording him some protection from the police—which he needed, as he was involved in student escapades that were typical of the medieval conflict between town and gown, including stealing boundary stones and house signs that were then carried off to the student quarter, which in turn was raided by the police. Despite his peccadilloes, Villon received a master of arts degree in August of 1452.

Life's Work
Despite his education and the opportunities that it might have provided him, Villon fell in with a group of criminals known as Coquillards and began a life of crime. Among his cronies, who are featured in his poems, were Colin des Cayeulx, described by the authorities as a thief and picklock, and Regnier de Montigny, a thief, murderer, and church robber. Both of them were hanged, and Villon wrote their epitaphs. Villon also prowled around Paris with Guy Tabarie, Jehan the Wolf, and Casin Cholet, all thieves, and spent much time at brothels and taverns such as the Mule and the Pomme de Pin, whose proprietor, Robin Turgis, was often a target of Villon's humor.

According to a poem of the time entitled "Repues Franches," thought to be by Friar Baulde de la Mare, Villon and his rascally friends had a genius for conning free fish, meat, bread, and wine from gullible victims. Soon Villon's picaresque career became more sinister. In the evening of June 5, 1455, the Feast of Corpus Christi, Villon was seated under the clock of Saint-Benoît-le-Bientourné, in company with a priest and a woman named Ysabeau, when another priest, Philip Chermoye, who had apparently been harboring a grudge, started a quarrel with Villon, drew a dagger, and slashed his upper lip. Bleeding copiously, Villon drew his own dagger and stabbed Chermoye in the groin; when Chermoye still attempted to injure him, Villon threw a rock that struck him in the face. After having his wound dressed, Villon fled from the city. Chermoye was taken to the Hôtel-Dieu, where he died after a few days.

According to one account, Chermoye on his deathbed confessed that he had started the fight and forgave Villon. Thus Villon's friends were able to get him a pardon in January of 1456, and he then returned to Paris. There, he fell in love with Katherine de Vausselles, who may have been a kinswoman of a colleague of Guillaume de Villon. At any rate, she teased and tormented Villon and eventually left him for Noël Joliz, who beat him in her presence. Heartsick and purse poor, Villon resolved to leave Paris at the end of 1456 and wrote for the occasion his first important work of poetry, *Le Lais* (1489; *The Legacy*, 1878, also known as *Le Petit Testament*, *The Little Testament*), in which he bids an ironic farewell to his friends and mockingly bequeaths them his worldly goods.

Before departing, he and four of his Coquillard cronies, probably on Christmas Eve, climbed over the wall into the College of Navarre, broke into the sacristy, and stole five hundred gold crowns from the faculty of theology. With his one-fifth share, Villon left the city, going first to Angers and thence wandering for the next four and a half years. In the meantime, Guy Tabarie boasted of the crime, was arrested and tortured, and confessed the details. A wanted man, Villon stayed on the run, going at one time to the court of Blois, where he associated with the courtly poet Charles d'Orléans, to whose daughter Marie he wrote a poetic epistle. Otherwise, except for a few clues that he drops in his verse, his activities are unknown until the summer of 1460, when he was in a dungeon at Orléans under sentence of death, from which he was pardoned during the passage through the city of the princess Marie.

A year later, at Meung-sur-Loire, he was tried at the ecclesiastical court of Thibault d'Aussigny, bishop of Orléans, who chained him in a dungeon under the moat and inflicted the water torture on him. Villon's health was broken, but he once more received a pardon when King Louis XI made a royal progress through the town and freed the prisoners.

Hiding near Paris, during the winter of 1461, Villon wrote his major work, aside from some of the ballades, *Le Grand Testament* (1489; *The Great Testament*, 1878), which follows the form of the earlier *The Legacy* but has far more depth and texture and which also incorporates a number of ballades, chansons, and rondeaux. Back in Paris itself, he was arrested in November, 1462, for petty theft; before he was released, the authorities made him sign a bond promising to repay the money that was stolen from the College of Navarre. Shortly thereafter, following an evening of revelry, one of Villon's companions got into a brawl with a papal scribe and wounded the man with a dagger thrust. Though Villon had left at the first sign of trouble, he was identified, arrested as an accomplice, and imprisoned in the Châtelet, where he was tortured and sentenced to the gallows. While awaiting execution, he wrote an ironic "Quatrain" and his great "L'Épitaphe Villon," otherwise known as "Ballade of the Hanged," in which he imagines himself and six others rotting on the gibbet and prays to God to absolve them all.

Yet once more Villon cheated the gallows. He appealed to Parliament, and since he had not taken part in the fight and the victim had not died, his sentence was annulled and changed to ten years' exile from Paris. In response, Villon wrote his "Panegyric to the Court of Parliament," requesting three days to prepare for his departure, and his sardonic "Question to the Clerk of the Prison Gate." In January, 1463, he left Paris and vanished from history and into legend. Though only thirty-two years old, he may have died from the lasting effects of imprisonment and torture. In *The Great Testament*, he speaks of having the worn-out body of an old man and of "spitting white"—a hint that he may have had a lung disease, perhaps tuberculosis. A century later, François Rabelais recounts Villon's having gone to England and received the protection of Edward V; Rabelais also tells of Villon's having retired in his old age to Poitou. Without any corroborating evidence, however, Rabelais's accounts are probably fiction. At any rate, no more of Villon's poetry is recorded after he left Paris.

The Legacy is made up of forty octaves or *huitains* of octosyllabic lines; *The Great Testament* has 175 such octaves, among which are interspersed sixteen ballades, a triple ballade, three rondels, and *Belle Leçon*; in addition, there is Villon's codicil, containing other ballades, the quatrain written after his being sentenced to death, and a number of poems in thieves' jargon. The standard ballade consists of three stanzas of eight octosyllabic lines each, followed by a four-line *envoi* generally beginning with

François Villon. (Library of Congress)

the vocative "Prince!"—though Villon's may be addressed to Fortune, a mistress, a fellow poet, or God. The rhyme scheme is invariably *ababbcbc* in the octave and *bcbc* in the *envoi*. A difficult verse form with only three rhymes, the ballade went out of favor after Villon's time and was not revived until nineteenth century imitations of Villon.

The Legacy is minor apprentice work, but after his career of crime, five years of vagabondage, and several ordeals under torture, Villon emerged as a great poet in *The Great Testament*. In it, he re-creates with vivid intensity the underworld of medieval Paris—the same setting as Victor Hugo's *Nôtre-Dame de Paris* (1831; *The Hunchback of Notre Dame*, 1833). Writing sometimes in thieves' jargon, Villon takes the reader through the taverns, brothels, thieves' dens, and prisons. His is a world of ribald bawdry, crime, revelry, profanity, prostitution, disease, and the dance of death, but it is redeemed by sardonic wit, by an intense relish for life, and, despite Villon's sacrilege, by a devout reverence for medieval Christianity and an awareness of the vanity of his riotous life. Outstanding among his poems are his "Ballade of Fat Margot"; "Lament of the Belle Heaulmière" (the beautiful armoress), about an aging prostitute; the

ballades to the ladies and lords of bygone times, the first with its haunting refrain, "But where are the snows of yesteryear?"; the "Ballade of the Hanged"; the "Ballade as a Prayer to Our Lady," which he put into the mouth of his aged mother; the "Ballade Against the Enemies of France"; and "The Dialogue Between the Heart and Body of Villon."

SIGNIFICANCE

The first critical edition of Villon's poems was made in 1533 by Clément Marot, himself a major poet of the Renaissance. Thereafter, Villon's life and works fell into obscurity for the next three centuries. Not until the 1830's did Villon resurface, when Théophile Gautier began to write about him as a precursor to the Romantics and bohemians and to praise Villon's defiance of bourgeois values. In England, Villon was quite unknown until the 1860's, but during the rest of the century, he received a considerable amount of attention, his work appearing in numerous translations, most notably by Dante Gabriel Rossetti and Algernon Charles Swinburne, both of whom tried to make the French poet fit into their Pre-Raphaelite aesthetic and who portrayed him as a rebel against middle-class morality. Following them, a number of other poets—Andrew Lang, Edmund Gosse, Walter Besant—did routine translations of some of Villon's poems as well as imitations of him.

In 1878, John Payne published the first complete translation of Villon's work, issued to subscribers called "The Villon Society" to circumvent Victorian censorship. An edition for the public three years later was bowdlerized and expurgated of Villon's frank realism.

In 1877, Auguste Longnon published the first biography of Villon, following which a number of articles appeared in British periodicals providing a condensed account of Villon's life and exploiting the sensationalism of Longnon's discoveries. Several used Villon as a cautionary example to condemn bohemianism and aestheticism. Despite his own genteel bohemianism, Robert Louis Stevenson, in an article in 1877, presented Villon as an example of dissipation and degradation, one lacking the dignity of a Victorian gentleman, and condemned his "way of looking upon the sordid and ugly aspects of life," which he found becoming prominent in the work of such nineteenth century French writers as Émile Zola. Stevenson believed that one should bear one's sufferings stoically and complained that "Villon, who had not the courage to be poor with honesty, now whiningly implores our sympathy, now shows his teeth upon the dungheap with an ugly snarl." In the same year, Stevenson published his first short story, "A Lodging for the Night," about Villon's supposedly whining, cowardly behavior after his friend de Montigny murdered a priest. All the nineteenth century writers who saw in Villon a reflection of certain features of their own time oversimplify his life and his works and ignore the complexity of the medieval Christian not only indulging in debauchery, theft, murder, and sacrilege but also repenting and expressing a profound faith.

Reversing the portrayal by Stevenson and other nineteenth century writers, twentieth century fiction transformed Villon into the dashing and noble hero of swashbuckling romance. In 1901, Justin Huntly McCarthy's novel and play *If I Were King* turned Villon into a king of vagabonds who becomes grand constable of France for a week and saves Paris from the invading Burgundians. The narrative is melodramatic and posturing; the characters speak what W. S. Gilbert called "platitudes in stained-glass attitudes." The title poem, the best-known "verses" of Villon, are not by Villon at all but by McCarthy. *If I Were King* was turned into the popular operetta *The Vagabond King* (1925), with music by Rudolf Friml, which has been filmed twice, and a variation on the novel has been filmed three times, with William Farnum, John Barrymore, and Ronald Colman, respectively, playing Villon. It sounds an essentially false note but has colored the popular impression of Villon.

In a more serious vein, Villon influenced Ezra Pound, who wrote an opera about him, *The Testament of François Villon* (1926); an appreciative essay, "Montcorbier, alias Villon"; and several "Villonaud" poems. Pound and T. S. Eliot also borrow for their own work the opening line of *The Great Testament*. Among Villon's other modern admirers was poet William Carlos Williams, who praised Villon's "intensity of consciousness," his psychological forthrightness and artistic integrity, his wit and daring realism, and the immediacy and modernism of his personal note. Of all the poets of the Middle Ages, Villon speaks most forthrightly to modern readers.

—Robert E. Morsberger

FURTHER READING

Anacker, Robert H. *François Villon*. New York: Twayne, 1968. A critical survey in the Twayne World Authors series, Anacker's work follows the standard format for that series, with a chronology; a brief account of Villon's world and of his life; chapters analyzing *The Legacy*, *The Great Testament*, and other works; and an annotated bibliography. Dismisses the simplistic view of Villon as a "carefree vagabond," a "tavern minstrel," a bohemian, a Romantic lover, and a forerunner of beatniks and hippies; tries to see him in the context of his times.

Burl, Aubrey. *Danse Macabre: François Villon—Poetry and Murder in Medieval France.*, Stroud, Gloucestershire, England: Sutton, 2000. This detailed biography emphasizes the contrast between Villon's chaotic life of crime and depravity and the extremely controlled and technically dazzling poetry. Includes illustrations, bibliographic references, and index.

Daniel, Robert R. *The Poetry of Villon and Baudelaire: Two Worlds, One Human Condition*. New York: P. Lang, 1997. Comparison of Villon with one of the great poets of the nineteenth century. Emphasizes the fundamental thematic and metaphysical similarities between the two, despite the very different eras in which they lived. Includes bibliographic references and index.

Fein, David A. *François Villon Revisited*. New York: Twayne, 1997. Emphasizes that many of the references in Villon's poems are to specific persons and events that are beyond recovery by modern scholarship. Argues that the best way for a contemporary reader to understand Villon's work is therefore to take note of its internal structure: patterns of imagery, recurring themes, the relationship between different narrative voices, and so on. Includes one illustration, bibliographic references, and index.

_____. *A Reading of Villon's Testament*. Birmingham, Ala.: Summa, 1984. Fein reads the poetry on three levels: surface value, "that which Villon appears to be saying"; travesty, when Villon praises or blesses his enemies; and symbolic meaning. Quotes extensively from Villon.

Freeman, Michael. *François Villon in His Works: The Villain's Tale*. Amsterdam: Rodopi, 2000. Reads Villon's poetry as a direct, self-conscious attempt to gain acceptance from his peers and to convince them that he was rehabilitated and deserved to return to French society. Also provides an account of the way in which the poetry was actually received at the time. Includes bibliographic references and index.

Lewis, D. B. Wyndham. *François Villon: A Documented Survey*. New York: Coward-McCann, 1928. The best biographical and critical study in English, Lewis's volume reconstructs in vivid detail the life of fifteenth century Paris. The biographical section is sometimes conjectural, as the author, writing in the first person, imagines the character of some of Villon's associates and dramatizes some of his escapades. Lewis also provides commentary on the works, followed by a variety of translations and an extensive bibliography of French sources.

Morsberger, Robert E. "Villon and the Victorians." *Bulletin of the Rocky Mountain Modern Language Association* 23 (December, 1969): 189-196. A study of the rediscovery of Villon; his influence on such nineteenth century writers as Dante Gabriel Rossetti, Charles Algernon Swinburne, and Robert Louis Stevenson; the interpretations and misinterpretations of him by the Victorian decadents and aesthetes; and his transformation in twentieth century fiction and films into a noble hero of romance.

Stevenson, Robert Louis. "François Villon, Student, Poet, and Housebreaker." In *Familiar Studies of Men and Books*. London: Collins, 1956. A sometimes biased study, Stevenson's article condemns Villon for not having the traits of a Victorian gentleman but is important for showing the reaction of a leading Victorian writer. The article led to and parallels Stevenson's first short story, "A Lodging for the Night."

Taylor, Jane H. M. *The Poetry of François Villon: Text and Context*. New York: Cambridge University Press, 2001. Where other scholars have tended to represent Villon's verse as simultaneously derivative and divorced from the poetry of his time, Taylor attempts to demonstrate that his work was in fact both original and brilliantly responsive to the verse of his contemporaries. Includes illustrations, bibliographic references, and index.

Villon, François. *The Complete Works of François Villon*. Translated by Anthony Bonner. New York: Bantam Books, 1960. This edition gives the works in their original French, with Bonner's unrhymed translation on the facing page. The introductory material includes an appreciative essay by poet William Carlos Williams and a brief biography. The thirty-seven pages of notes are extremely thorough, identifying all the poems' characters, allusions, and historical details. A brief bibliography refers the reader chiefly to sources in French.

_____. *Poems*. Translated by John Heron Lepper. New York: Horace Liveright, 1926. A complete translation, following Villon's rhyme scheme, with an introduction by Lepper. Includes as well the first complete and unabridged translation by John Payne (also in Villon's rhyme scheme), as well as Payne's introduction to his 1883 edition and translations by Swinburne, Rossetti, Arthur Symons, and Ezra Pound.

Vitz, Evelyn Birge. *The Crossroads of Intention: A Study of Symbolic Expression in the Poetry of François Villon*. The Hague, the Netherlands: Mouton, 1974. Vitz studies the symbolic expression in Villon's poetry—the process by which places, people, and things become symbolic. Considers the sexual symbolism, the symbolism in writing a will, and the contrast between Villon's self and the symbolic persona he assumes. Analyzes the medieval concept of psychology and cosmography.

SEE ALSO: Ludovico Ariosto; Marguerite de Navarre; François Rabelais; Pierre de Ronsard; Torquato Tasso.

RELATED ARTICLE in *Great Events from History: The Renaissance & Early Modern Era, 1454-1600:* 1549-1570's: La Pléiade Promotes French Poetry.

FRANCISCO DE VITORIA
Spanish theologian and legal scholar

Vitoria, a theologian, was a pioneer in the field of international law. He is credited with the idea that the nations of the world constitute a community based on natural law.

BORN: c. 1483; Vitoria, Álava, Castile (now in Spain)
DIED: August 12, 1546; Salamanca, Spain
AREAS OF ACHIEVEMENT: Law, religion and theology, philosophy

EARLY LIFE

Francisco de Vitoria (fran-SIHS-koh day vee-TOH-yah) was born in a small town in the Basque province of Álava. The exact date of his birth is uncertain. When still very young, Vitoria entered the Dominican Order, of which his elder brother Diego was also a member. He went to San Pablo in Burgos for his education, and, because he showed promise as a scholar in the classics, he was sent to the College of the Dominicans in Paris for further study. While in Paris, he also attended classes at the Sorbonne. His education equipped him as a Humanist versed in Greek and Latin texts, and Vitoria is also said to have met the great Humanist Desiderius Erasmus during those years.

Vitoria arrived in Paris around 1506 and studied first at the Dominican College of Saint Jacques, becoming well versed in the classics before occupying the chair of theology there. He was influenced by nominalist teachers, who helped revive the study of Saint Thomas Aquinas's *Summa theologiae* (c. 1265-1273; *Summa Theologica*, 1911-1921) in addition to, or sometimes instead of, the previous standard Dominican text, Peter Lombard's *Sententiarum libri IV* (1148-1151; *The Books of Opinions of Peter Lombard*, 1970; better known as *Sentences*). He even became involved in the preparations of editions of Aquinas's work that appeared in the period of 1514-1519. Before returning to Spain, he completed his degree of licentiate in theology at the Sorbonne on March 24, 1522.

LIFE'S WORK

Vitoria embarked on his life's work on his return to Spain after earning his degree in theology. He had attained a good reputation among his colleagues and was able to serve at the College of Saint Gregory in Valladolid from 1523 to 1526 before being appointed to the chair of theology at the University of Salamanca. He would remain at the university until his death.

Vitoria made his first mark on history as he lectured on theology. He impressed a new character on this field of study, as his discussions were full of ideas and drew other areas of learning into the consideration of theological questions. Such questions were to be considered not intellectual exercises but rather areas of legitimate practical concern in the real world. That such discussions and proposed solutions could actually produce serious consequences was shown in many lectures, notably those discussions on the rights and treatment of Native American Indians in the newly discovered hemisphere and those on the question of what constitutes a just war. His teaching incorporated a desire for justice in world affairs and a strong belief that moral questions have an impact on all phases of life.

One of the greatest influences on Vitoria was his contact with the great Humanists, including Erasmus. Vitoria's defense of the American Indians and his humanitarian principles in relation to war bear the stamp of this influence. Vitoria distinguished himself as a professor and helped increase the reputation of the University of Salamanca. At first he was compelled to lecture on the *Sentences* of Peter Lombard while he preferred Saint Thomas Aquinas, but it later became the rule to discuss the *Summa theologiae* with references to Lombard—a practice that better suited Vitoria's thinking. His courses soon met with favorable reactions as he combined solid doctrine with a clear, elegant style of exposition. Among his students were Melchor Cano, Domingo Soto, and Bartolomé de Medina. Although Vitoria did not publish his lectures, his students gathered many of them and published them after his death, as a tribute to him. Vitoria's reputation for applying theology to practical matters and his broad knowledge were such that Charles V consulted him on a number of questions, including the arguments by Henry VIII of England for annulling his marriage to Catherine of Aragon.

In 1532, Vitoria discussed the justifications for Spanish domination in the New World. In 1539 and 1540, Charles V consulted him about several matters relating to the conquest of the Indies. Then, in 1541, Vitoria was consulted on the question of baptizing Native Americans without religious instruction, a question brought to the Council of the Indies by Bartolomé de Las Casas, in whose favor Vitoria argued. In 1545, Vitoria was invited to attend the Council of Trent; however, because of illness, other representatives were sent instead.

Vitoria's tenure at Salamanca lasted from 1526 to 1546. The last two years of his life, he suffered from rheumatic pain, and a substitute lecturer, Juan Gil Fernández de Nava, had to be called in. Vitoria died on August 12, 1546. The efforts of his students ensured that his influence continued long after that.

Some of Vitoria's lectures were collected for publication by his former students in *Relectiones theologicae* (1557; English translation, 1934). Vitoria's guiding premise was that theology or questions of morality extend over the entire field of human activity. He particularly believed that the question of the treatment of Native Americans as a barbarian race, not subject to an established human law, must be viewed from the point of view of divine law. The Native Americans had been reduced to servitude on the large landholdings or to slavery in the mines. Compulsory labor and separation of families was the norm. Bartolomé de Las Casas became a famous defender of the Native Americans at this time, and Vitoria himself defended a humanitarian view. Using his considerable skill in reasoning and argumentation, he contradicted proposed theories that allowed for the subjugation of Native Americans based on the right to convert them to Christianity, on the right to punish idolatry, or on the (supposed) superiority of Christians over so-called barbarians.

Vitoria also refuted the argument that Spain had title to the land based on discovery. He resorted to the Law of Nations, which allows such title only if the regions are uninhabited—which these clearly were not. He also argued that Spaniards could travel in these new lands on condition that they did not harm the inhabitants and that, where there was common property, Spaniards might also profit. Vitoria's concept of a just war included the idea that it was lawful for the Spaniards to defend themselves against Native American attacks, while always showing generosity and moderation to the defeated. If the Native Americans persisted with their attacks, however, the Spaniards were allowed recourse to the rights of war, including plunder and captivity, which were seen as the right to punish wrongdoing according to law.

Because of his many students and his participation in the important discussions of his time, Vitoria's influence was widespread. With the publication of his lectures, that influence continued after his death.

SIGNIFICANCE

During the period when the rules of international law were being formulated, the two main schools of thought included positivists and naturalists. Hugo Grotius, the leading Dutch naturalist writer, is often regarded as the founder of modern international law. For other scholars, however, this title should go to Vitoria, who based his arguments as well on natural law. Vitoria's argument was that the basic principles of all laws are derived from principles of justice with universal validity. He believed that such principles were part of a natural, divine law, not a human-made one.

Vitoria spoke often on the question of war. To Vitoria, war was justified to ensure free trade and communication when other means of persuasion had failed. The violation of a right was the essential condition for a just war. Defensive wars protected the individual or nation from tyranny; offensive wars might punish a nation guilty of injustice. In any case, he believed that the defeated should always be treated with moderation once the purpose has been achieved. Furthermore, a just war must always promote the common good of the world community over the advantage of an individual state.

When Vitoria has been called the founder of modern international law by scholars, that assessment has been based particularly on *De Indis* and *De jure belli relectiones*, lectures given in 1532, published in 1557, and translated into English in 1917. In *De Indis*, he first defined international law as a natural law binding all states of the world, and he applied it to the treatment of the Native Americans in the New World. In visualizing an international society, he applied Saint Thomas Aquinas's principles to the concept of state and built a theory of international society as well on his principles. His guiding principle was that an international society was based on a natural association of equal states. In the areas of philosophy and theology, his contributions were recognized within his lifetime; his contributions in the area of law, especially international law, are equally indisputable.

—*Susan L. Piepke*

FURTHER READING

Anghie, Antony. "Francisco de Vitoria and the Colonial Origins of International Law." In *Laws of the Postcolonial*, edited by Eve Darian-Smith and Peter Fitzpatrick. Ann Arbor: University of Michigan Press, 1999. Study of Vitoria's contribution to the founding of international law from a postcolonial perspective. Includes bibliographic references and index.

Benkert, Gerald Francis. *The Thomistic Conception of an International Society*. Washington, D.C.: Catholic University of America Press, 1942. Examines the writings of Thomas Aquinas and, from his philosophical principles, delineates the basis for constructing an international society. Particular emphasis is given to the views of Vitoria in the Spanish revival of Thomistic thought. Includes an extensive bibliography.

Delos, Joseph Thomas. *International Relations from a Catholic Standpoint*. Edited and translated by Stephen J. Brown. Dublin: Browne and Nolan, 1932. Contains a discussion of the Catholic viewpoint on natural law and international relations. Particularly useful in defining the Catholic attitude and contributions to peaceful international relations throughout history and particularly the contributions of various theologians, Vitoria among them.

Grewe, Wilhelm G. *The Epochs of International Law*. Translated and revised by Michael Byers. New York: Walter de Gruyter, 2000. Comprehensive survey of the history of international law from the Middle Ages through 1998. Includes illustrations, bibliographic references, and index.

Hamilton, Bernice. *Political Thought in Sixteenth Century Spain: A Study of the Political Ideas of Vitoria, De Soto, Suárez, and Molina*. Oxford, England: Clarendon Press, 1963. A discussion of the political ideas of four Spanish thinkers on natural-law theory, political communities, war, New World colonization, the law of nations, and relative powers of church and state. Contains bibliographies.

O'Donovan, Oliver, and Joan Lockwood O'Donovan, eds. *From Irenaeus to Grotius: A Sourcebook in Christian Political Thought, 100-1625*. Grand Rapids, Mich.: William B. Eerdmans, 1999. Provides excerpts from Vitoria's writings, along with commentary placing him in the context of the history of Christian political thought. Includes bibliographic references and index.

Reidy, Stephen J. *Civil Authority According to Francis de Vitoria*. River Forest, Ill.: Aquinas Library, 1959. A specialized study of Vitoria's teaching on the nature and causes of civil authority, with a discussion of his position on the ancient Scholastic teaching. Contains a bibliography of books and periodicals in several languages.

Scott, James Brown. *The Spanish Origin of International Law: Francisco de Vitoria and His Law of Nations*. Oxford, England: Clarendon Press, 1934. A thorough discussion of Vitoria's life, putting his accomplishments in the context of the "era of discoveries" and the thinking of the Spanish School. Appendices include translations of six important *relectiones*.

Vitoria, Francisco de. *De Indis et De Ivre Belli: Relectiones*. Edited by Ernest Nys. Reprint. New York: Oceana, 1964. Includes a translation by John Pawley Bate of the two *Relectiones theologicae* by Vitoria, along with the full Latin text. Marginal notes and summary of the major points are maintained from the original. Helpful introduction by Ernest Nys includes biographical information and a discussion of some of Vitoria's principal arguments.

SEE ALSO: Catherine of Aragon; Charles V; Alberico Gentili; Henry VIII; Bartolomé de Las Casas; Niccolò Machiavelli.

RELATED ARTICLE in *Great Events from History: The Renaissance & Early Modern Era, 1454-1600*: 1552: Las Casas Publishes *The Tears of the Indians*.

VLAD III THE IMPALER
Walachian prince (r. 1448, 1456-1462, 1476)

Vlad III is remembered for his brutality and for his struggle for independence from the Turks. He was ruthless with his enemies and with the people of his own country who did not meet his strict moral standards. Vlad III is believed to have killed up to 100,000 people, with impalement as his preferred means of execution. Along with the life of Hungarian countess Elizabeth Báthory, his life is considered to have partly inspired the Dracula legends.

BORN: Late 1431; Sighisoara, Transylvania (now in Romania)

DIED: December, 1476; near Bucharest, Walachia (now in Romania)

ALSO KNOWN AS: Vlad Tepes; Vlad Dracula; Vlad the Impaler; Vlad Tepesch; Vlad Tzepes

AREAS OF ACHIEVEMENT: Government and politics, warfare and conquest

EARLY LIFE

Vlad III was the middle son of the military governor of Transylvania, who seized power in neighboring Walachia in 1436. He had an older brother named Mircea and a younger brother, Radu (later known as Radu the Handsome). Little is known of his mother beyond that she was a Transylvanian noblewoman. During his early years, Vlad III became an apprentice to a knight, learning the skills necessary to become a knight himself: fencing, jousting, archery, and court etiquette.

Vlad III's father, Vlad II, was a knight in the Order of the Dragon, founded by King Sigismund of Hungary to defend Christianity against the Ottoman Turks. As "drac" means both dragon and devil in Romanian, Vlad II became known as Vlad Dracul, or Vlad the Dragon. The suffix "ula" means "son of," so Vlad III became known as Vlad Dracula. "Tepes" is from *tse-pesh* or *teapa*, meaning "the stake" in Romanian, and was appended to Vlad II's name shortly after his death.

Walachia was in a strategically difficult position, being located between the Muslim Turks and the Christians in Hungary. Though a vassal of the king of Hungary, Vlad II was forced to pay tribute to the powerful Ottomans. His attempt to remain neutral when the Ottomans invaded Transylvania in 1442 enraged the Hungarians, who later forced him from power. With the support of the Turks, Vlad II regained the throne in 1443, but in return he was forced to surrender his two youngest sons, Vlad III and Radu, as hostages to ensure his loyalty.

The pair remained with the Turks for four years, and scholars credit this imprisonment during Vlad III's formative years as a possible cause for his lack of humanity and coldhearted tendencies. During his captivity, he learned the methods of the Turks, specifically their use of terror as a weapon. Vlad III and Radu were treated as guests of the sultan initially, but as relations between the two groups deteriorated, the boys' situation worsened.

In 1944, the Hungarians launched a campaign to force the Turks from Europe. Still technically a vassal of the Hungarian king, Vlad II once more attempted to remain neutral. The Hungarians were soundly defeated and, blaming Vlad II, had both him and his oldest son, Mircea, assassinated in 1447.

LIFE'S WORK

With the death of their father, the young hostages were released by the Turks. The Turks even supported Vlad III as their own candidate for the throne. With their support, he held it briefly in 1448 but was quickly deposed by the Hungarians, and he fled to Moldavia.

It was not until he switched his allegiance back to Hungary that Vlad III was able to advance his political career. He made an alliance with János Hunyadi (known as the White Knight of Hungary) and was allowed to assume control of his father's former lands in Transylvania. When Hunyadi made his final push against the Turks in Serbia in 1456, Vlad III invaded Walachia and retook his throne, which he would hold for the next six years.

Vlad III established Tîrgovişte as the capital of Walachia and set out to rebuild a castle for himself near the Argeş River. To solidify his power, he invited the most powerful families to an Easter feast, many of whom were the same people who had his father and older brother assassinated. All were arrested. Those too old to work were impaled, while the rest were sent as slaves to work on his castle.

Subsequently, no one was exempt from Vlad III's cruelty; however, his main targets were the merchants and boyars (nobles) of Walachia and Transylvania, most of whom were German Saxons. His attempts to eliminate the disloyal boyars and promote the middle class and peasants, whom he knew would be loyal, lead some historians to view Vlad III as a sort of Robin Hood figure.

Vlad III used cruelty to enforce morality among the people as well. Women were particular targets, espe-

Vlad III the Impaler. (Hulton|Archive by Getty Images)

of respect, Vlad III had the turbans nailed to their heads. His dismay over the number of indigent people in his realm led him to invite all the poor, infirm, beggars, and lame to a massive feast, proclaiming that none should go hungry. The grateful guests were permitted all they could eat and drink, and the feast lasted well into the night. Vlad III asked them, "What else do you desire? . . . Do you want to be without cares, lacking nothing in this world?" When they answered yes, he ordered the building boarded up, and he burned them alive.

Vlad III was driven from the throne by the Turks in 1462. When the Turks arrived, his wife, Elizabeth, leapt into the Argeş River and committed suicide rather than allow herself to be captured. Vlad III escaped to Transylvania, where he was placed under house arrest by Matthias I Corvinus, the Hungarian king. The duration of his imprisonment is disputed. During the next twelve years, however, he converted to Catholicism, married into the royal family, and fathered two sons. Vlad III's successor to the Walachia throne was his younger brother, Radu the Handsome, who had remained with the Turks after Vlad II's death.

Vlad III and the Transylvanian prince Stephen Báthory invaded Walachia in 1476. Radu had since died, replaced by Basarab the Old, who fled as they approached. Vlad III retook the throne but lacked the support to hold it. He died in a battle against the Turks at the end of the year. The victorious Turks decapitated his body and sent his head, preserved in honey, to Constantinople. The sultan displayed it on a stake as proof that Vlad III the Impaler was finally dead. The rest of Vlad III's body was reportedly buried at the island monastery of Snagov, near Bucharest.

SIGNIFICANCE

Horror novels were very popular in late nineteenth century England, so when novelist Bram Stoker searched for a subject, his research led him to Romania. Belief in vampires and other superstitions was strong in Eastern Europe, and much of the traditional vampire lore emerged from that region. While there is no evidence that Vlad III was an actual vampire, his bloody legacy contained enough horror—real and imagined—to inspire Stoker to write his 1897 novel, *Dracula*. Furthermore, Vlad III is reported to have provided inspiration for such notorious historical leaders as Ivan the Terrible and for twentieth century despots, including Romanian president Nicolae Ceauşescu.

Despite his cruelty, Vlad III is remembered differently in his homeland of Romania. Many Romanians

cially those he viewed as unchaste. Dishonest merchants and thieves suffered the same gruesome fate. Vlad III would have stakes arranged in geometric patterns outside the city, and the impaled corpses would remain on the stakes for months. According to some reports, a Turkish invasion met an abrupt end when the Turkish army encountered twenty thousand impaled Turkish prisoners outside the capital. This was known as the Forest of the Impaled.

In 1459, thirty thousand merchants and landowners were impaled in Braşov. A famous image of that period shows Vlad III feasting while the executioner does his work. Ten thousand victims were impaled in Sibiu, Transylvania, in 1460.

Many of the storie of Vlad III's authority and cruelty are anecdotal. He was reported to have ordered a golden cup displayed without guard in the center of Tîrgovişte. Thieves, fearful of the stake, dared not touch it, and it remained untouched throughout his reign. Another famous story has him receiving some Turkish noblemen in his court, but when they refused to remove their turbans out

view him as a hero who both withstood invading foreigners and supported the peasant class against the merchants and wealthy landowners.

—*P. S. Ramsey*

FURTHER READING

Boia, Lucian. *Romania: Borderland of Europe.* Translated by James Christian Brown. London: Reaktion Books, 2002. A history of Romania from the Middle Ages to 2002, including the reign of Vlad III and his struggles against the Turks.

Florescu, Radu, and Raymond T. McNally. *Dracula: A Biography of Vlad the Impaler, 1431-1476.* New York: Hawthorne Books, 1973. The first complete biography of Vlad III.

McNally, Raymond T., and Radu Florescu. *In Search of Dracula: The History of Dracula and Vampires.* 1972. Rev. ed. New York: Houghton Mifflin, 1994. Focuses on the vampire legends in general and those that trace back to Vlad III.

Treptow, Kurt W., ed. *Dracula: Essays on the Life and Times of Vlad Tepes.* New York: Columbia University Press, 1991. From the East European Monographs series, these essays provide a different scholarly view of Vlad III. Includes a chronology and a bibliography.

Wolf, Leonard. *Dracula: The Connoisseur's Guide.* New York: Bantam Books, 1997. A collection of essays on the mythology of Dracula and vampire legends in general.

SEE ALSO: Elizabeth Báthory; Matthias I Corvinus; Stephen Báthory.

RELATED ARTICLES in *Great Events from History: The Renaissance & Early Modern Era, 1454-1600:* April 14, 1457-July 2, 1504: Reign of Stephen the Great; 1463-1479: Ottoman-Venetian War.

VLADISLAV II
King of Bohemia (r. 1471-1516) and king of Hungary (r. 1490-1516)

Vladislav II allowed the Hungarian nobility to undermine the monarchy, strengthen the nobility's hold over their own serfs, weaken the armed forces, and exempt the nobility from military service. His reign combined the Hungarian and Bohemian national territories.

BORN: March 1, 1456; place unknown
DIED: March 13, 1516; Buda, Hungary (now Budapest, Hungary)
ALSO KNOWN AS: Vladislav Jagiełło (given name); Władysław II; Vladislas II Jagiellon; Ulászló II
AREA OF ACHIEVEMENT: Government and politics

EARLY LIFE

The early life of Vladislav (VLAHJ-ihs-lahv) II was one of a future ruler preparing for his turn at the throne. His mother was a member of the Habsburg family, which made Vladislav a potential heir to the vast Habsburg lands throughout Europe. His father was Polish king Casimir IV. Vladislav was also a member of Poland's ruling Jagiellonian Dynasty, and he sought to expand its influence throughout Eastern Europe.

The dynasty, however, would be continued not by Vladislav but rather by his three brothers, all of whom would reign over their Polish homeland. John I Albert was king from 1492 to 1501, Alexander ruled from 1501 to 1506, and Sigismund I the Old ruled from 1506 to 1548. Vladislav, though, would not rule his homeland. Instead, he would extend Jagiellonian control to central Europe, as he was chosen at the age of fifteen, after Bohemian king Jirí's (George's) death in 1471, to assume the monarchy of the neighboring state of Bohemia. The death of Jirí left a power vacuum in the Bohemian state. The nobility took control and held an assembly in Kutna Hora in May of that year. Vladislav was chosen by the Bohemian nobility to serve as a figurehead king who would allow Bohemia to regain the power it had lost during the reign of his predecessors.

LIFE'S WORK

Vladislav remained docile as the nobility used two institutions, the royal council and the diet, to shift authority to the nobles. The royal council was an advisory body filled with the king's handpicked advisers. Vladislav, however, allowed the nobility to pack it with their supporters, who in turn advised the young king to surrender his power. The nobility also seized control of the Bohemian legislature, with the king acting only as a rubber stamp to approve the fundamental changes to the government passed by the nobles.

Vladislav was also weak when it came to foreign affairs. Bohemia was being threatened by its Hungarian neighbor to the south. The Hungarian king Matthias I Corvinus was bent on conquering much of central Europe using his large army of mercenaries. Matthias attacked Bohemia in 1469 and for the next decade was successful at conquering many of the provinces surrounding Bohemia, including Silesia to the north and Moravia to the east.

Matthias's death saved Bohemia from years of further war and likely defeat at the hands of the Hungarian army. Also, his death left a political vacuum in Hungary. Fearful of an activist king such as Matthias, who would challenge their authority, the nobles decided that Vladislav would be the type of monarch they could use to regain their authority. Vladislav obtained his name on ascending the Hungarian throne. His dual role as king of Bohemia and king of Hungary placed the much-valued province of Bohemia within Hungarian borders.

Vladislav proved to be the type of pliable ruler desired by the Hungarian nobility. He inherited a large, well-trained, and well-financed army of mercenaries from Matthias. Instead of continuing Matthias's aggressive policies against his neighbors, however, Vladislav allowed the nobility to eliminate the army and the monarch's ability to construct a new one.

The Hungarian legislature, or diet, had been weak under Matthias, who preferred ruling on his own. Vladislav, however, allowed the nobility to pass laws, and he signed them without much discussion. The new laws exempted the nobility from the taxes Matthias had used to build his army. In addition, the nobility was exempted from military service. Vladislav also signed a law eliminating much of the labor that the nobles' serfs were required to perform for the monarch. Under Matthias, serfs would perform tasks for the monarch three days per week, but under Vladislav, serfs would be limited to working for the nobility.

Vladislav spent much of his reign grooming his son Louis to be his successor. In 1515, Vladislav met with the Habsburg emperor Maximilian I. The two leaders signed an agreement in which the Austrian king agreed that Vladislav's son, Louis II, would succeed him as king. On Louis's death, the Hungarian and Bohemian lands would become part of the Habsburg empire. This ensured that the Jagiellonian Dynasty would be extended beyond Vladislav's reign.

While securing the future of his son, Vladislav allowed the Hungarian army to deteriorate, making the king vulnerable to internal and external enemies. One of those internal threats was the peasant revolt that Vladislav was forced to crush during the last years of his reign.

The changes in the legal status of serfs during Vladislav II's reign ran counter to the economic and political changes sweeping Europe at that time. Hungary's nobility asserted greater control over the serfs, removing some of the protections and freedoms offered by Matthias. Throughout Europe, feudalism had been disintegrating, as more people sought prosperity in the cities and towns. In Hungary, the nobility limited the movement of serfs, which limited the available workforce for urban areas and the new middle class. Hungarian laborers could not leave the land and work in the towns and cities.

The revolt began as a call for another crusade against the Ottoman Empire. Gathering angry, disaffected peasants and arming them for war was a miscalculation by the nobility. The religious crusade quickly transformed into a political revolt against the Hungarian nobles. Under the leadership of György Dózsa, the peasant army went on a rampage through Hungary, beginning in May of 1514. It targeted the very nobles who had kept them tied to the land. Vladislav, prompted by the horrified nobility, formed an army to quash the revolt. The turning point in the rebellion occurred when the peasant army attempted to storm the Castle Temasvár, where several nobles had dug in for defense. The nobles' army attacked the peasants, defeated them, captured Dózsa, and executed him.

To prevent any further revolts, the diet rewrote the laws into a system known as the Tripartitum (1514). One of Hungary's greatest judicial authorities, István Werboczi, composed a law code that prevented serfs from moving from estate to estate and that increased taxes and the overall burden on the common people. The code remained the basis of Hungarian law into the nineteenth century and maintained feudalism in Hungary longer than in any other country in western Europe. Vladislav II signed the Tripartitum, seemingly unaware that it had reduced even further the authority of the monarchy.

Vladislav was successful at continuing the Jagiellonian Dynasty, even if for a short time. On his death, the throne was taken by his son Louis. Louis's reign, however, was shortened by the threat of the Ottoman Turks to the south and by the lack of an effective military. When the Ottomans attacked, Louis led the Hungarian army, and in the Battle of Mohács (1526), the Hungarians were crushed and Louis was killed.

SIGNIFICANCE

Vladislav II's reign in Bohemia and Hungary followed the reigns of powerful kings who had seized power from their countries' nobility. In Bohemia, Vladislav was limited by the country's religious divisions after the Hussite (Protestant) revolt, which began in the early fifteenth century, and the desire of the nobility to divert power from the king and give it to the newly forming cities.

In Hungary, the nobility imposed an even stricter feudal system on the country, exempting all nobles from taxes and military service. Vladislav agreed to these changes, tempering his rule in order to extend the Jagiellonian Dynasty to his son. The result of his passivity was a weakening of the Hungarian state, just as military pressure from the south in the forms of the Ottomans was beginning to build. Vladislav left Hungary in a state of unpreparedness that led to the demise of the kingdom and the death of his son.

—Douglas Clouatre

FURTHER READING

Lendvai, Paul. *The Hungarians: A Thousand Years of Victory in Defeat*. Princeton, N.J.: Princeton University Press, 2003. This work examines the key role played by Hungary in eastern Europe through the Renaissance and the Enlightenment and into modern times. The book details the wars between the Hungarians and the Ottomans and the eventual combination of the Hungarian kingdom with the Habsburg empire.

Molnar, Miklos. *A Concise History of Hungary*. New York: Cambridge University Press, 2001. This book discusses the history of Hungary from medieval to modern times. It examines the various rulers of the independent Hungarian kingdom and how they handled their Ottoman and Austrian neighbors.

Sayer, Derek. *The Coasts of Bohemia*. Princeton, N.J.: Princeton University Press, 2000. The book looks at Bohemia as an independent kingdom and as a province within other empires. It discusses the political and religious turmoil that affected Bohemia after the Hussite rebellion and the kingdom's wars with Hungary.

Teich, Mikulas, ed. *Bohemia in History*. New York: Cambridge University Press, 1998. This detailed work describes Bohemia during its independence and the rulers and people of the Renaissance and Enlightenment periods. The book focuses on the religious problems of the region, including the Hussite movement, and the monarchs who ruled over the region in central Europe.

SEE ALSO: Bayezid II; Frederick III; İbrahim Paşa; Matthias I Corvinus; Maximilian I; Sigismund I, the Old; Sigismund II Augustus; Süleyman the Magnificent.

RELATED ARTICLES in *Great Events from History: The Renaissance & Early Modern Era, 1454-1600:* 1458-1490: Hungarian Renaissance; June 12, 1477-August 17, 1487: Hungarian War with the Holy Roman Empire; 1514: Hungarian Peasants' Revolt.

WANG YANGMING
Chinese scholar-official

As a high official, holding many governmental offices from magistrate to governor, Wang suppressed rebellions and created a reign of peace in China that lasted a century. His Neo-Confucian philosophy exercised tremendous influence in both China and Japan for 150 years.

BORN: November 30, 1472; Youyao, Zhejiang, China
DIED: January 9, 1529; Nanen, Jiangxi, China
ALSO KNOWN AS: Wang Yang-ming (Wade-Giles); Shouren; Shou-jen (Wade-Giles); Boan; Po-an (Wade-Giles)
AREAS OF ACHIEVEMENT: Philosophy, government and politics

EARLY LIFE

Wang Yangming (wayng yayng-mihn) was the son of a minister of civil personnel in Nanjing. He was renamed Wang Yangming by his students, but his private name was Shouren and his courtesy name was Boan. According to legend, he could not speak until he was given a name at the age of five. He soon began reading his grandfather's books and reciting their contents. When he was eleven years old, he went to live with his father at Beijing. At the age of twelve, Wang announced to a fortune-teller that the greatest occupation was that of a sage, not that of a government official. His mother, Madame Zheng (Cheng), died when he was thirteen. At fifteen, he visited the Zhuyong Mountain passes, where he first became interested both in archery and in the frontier.

Wang was married at the age of seventeen, but he was so absorbed in a conversation he was having with a Daoist priest on his wedding night that he forgot to go home until he was sent for the next morning. As he and his wife were passing through Guangxin the next year, he had another important discussion, this time with a prominent scholar named Lou Liang. Lou was so impressed with Wang that he predicted that Wang could become a sage if he studied diligently. Wang, however, devoted his nineteenth year to the study of archery and military tactics.

During the next ten years, Wang was torn between pursuing a career in the military, in politics, in literature, or in philosophy. After receiving his civil service degree, he delved deeply into the works of Zhu Xi (Chu Hsi). While visiting his father in Beijing, he spent seven days sitting quietly in front of some bamboos in an attempt to discern the principles of Zhu Xi embodied within them. The stress was too much for Wang, however, and he became very ill. Thoroughly disillusioned with philosophy, he spent his time writing flowery compositions instead of studying for his civil service examinations. Consequently, he failed his examinations in 1493 and again in 1496, and he shifted his interest back to military crafts and to the Daoist philosophy.

Wang finally settled on one career choice after passing his civil service examinations in 1499, at the age of twenty-seven. He was appointed to the Ministry of Public Works, where he impressed his superiors with a method for defending China against invasion. Though his proposal was rejected, Wang was made minister of justice in Yunnan in the following year. In 1501, Wang reversed the convictions of many prisoners after checking the prison records near Nanjing. Ill health forced Wang to retreat to the Yangming ravine to recuperate. He built a house in the ravine and began calling himself Philosopher of Yangming. Wang soon became very skeptical of some of the teachings of Daoism and Buddhism and of his own literary pursuits.

Having fully recovered from his illness, Wang returned to Beijing in 1504, where he was appointed director of the provincial examinations in Shandong. That same year, he became a secretary in the Ministry of War. In 1505, members of his large student following convinced him that he was better suited as a philosopher, and he began lecturing on the importance of becoming a sage. His practice of reciting classics and writing flowery compositions alienated him from the more conservative scholars, who accused him of trying to build a reputation for himself. Only one scholar, the honored academician Zhan Ruoshui (Chan Jo-shui), appreciated his merits. Not only did he befriend Wang, but he also helped him spread the true doctrine of Confucius.

A year later, Wang's career as a lecturer was dramatically interrupted. In 1506, he came to the defense of a group of supervising censors who had been imprisoned by a corrupt eunuch, Liu Jin (Liu Chin). Wang wrote a memorial that so angered Liu Jin that he ordered Wang to be beaten, imprisoned, and banished to Longchang, a place inhabited primarily by barbarian tribes. Wang was demoted to head of a dispatch station. He began his journey in 1507 and arrived at Longchang a year later. During his trip, he barely escaped an assassination attempt by Liu's agents.

LIFE'S WORK

The three years that he spent living among the aborigines marked the turning point of his life. Having to scavenge for food and water for himself and his subordinates in a desolate land and to build houses for the Miao aborigines took its toll on Wang's health. Yet the isolation was beneficial, for his privations forced him to look inward. One night, he suddenly realized that one need only look into one's own mind to find the eternal principles of life, instead of searching for these principles in objects. In 1509, he developed a theory that held that knowledge and action are one. Monogamy, for example, can be fully understood only when it is practiced. With these theories, Wang was revising Idealist Neo-Confucianism, as it had been pronounced by Lu Xiangshan (Lu Hsiang-shan). In addition, Wang was directly opposing the rationalistic Neo-Confucianism of Zhu Xi.

As soon as Wang's term as head of the dispatch station had ended in 1510, he was made magistrate of Luling. During his seven-month stay in office, he carried out a number of reforms. As the result of an audience with the emperor, Wang was promoted to secretary of the Ministry of Justice and director of the Ministry of Personnel in 1511, vice minister of imperial stables in 1512, and minister of state ceremonials in 1514.

Wang enjoyed his greatest military successes at Jiangxi (Kiangsi). When he first arrived there in 1517 as the new senior censor and governor, Jiangxi was the scene of repeated insurrections by rebels and bandits. Two months after his arrival, he suppressed the rebellion and initiated the rehabilitation of the rebels. In 1518, he conducted tax reform, established schools, carried out reconstruction, and instituted the Community Compact, which improved unity as well as community morals.

Wang reached the pinnacle of his political career in 1519. On his way to suppress a rebellion in Fujian, he discovered that the prince of Ning, Chenhao (Ch'en-hao), had declared himself head of state. Wang surrounded the prince's base, Nanchang, and captured him. Rumors had surfaced as a result of his contact with Chenhao, and Wang was accused by a jealous official of conspiring with the prince, resulting in the imprisonment of one of Wang's pupils. Nevertheless, Wang was appointed governor of Jiangxi by the end of the year. In 1520, he instituted more reforms.

Wang's achievements were not viewed as a cause for celebration by everyone in the kingdom. The emperor tried to claim credit for the victory at Nanjing by leading the expedition himself. Wang also embarrassed the emperor, first by capturing the prince and then by giving credit to the department of military affairs. Most damaging of all, though, was that Wang and the prince had exchanged messengers before the rebellion took place. Wang's political enemies were so incensed by his correspondence with the prince that Wang's messenger, Ji Yuanheng, was tortured to death.

Wang was exonerated of all charges in 1521 when the Jiajing emperor ascended the throne. After his father died in 1522, Wang went into virtual retirement at Yuyao for five years, where he attracted hundreds of disciples from all over China, even though his critics escalated their attacks against him. During this period, he developed his philosophy to full maturity with his doctrine of the extension of innate knowledge. With this theory, Wang turned psychology into ethics, suggesting that the human mind possesses an innate capacity for distinguishing between good and evil. Wang's conversations with his students were collected in his major work, *Chuanxi lu* (1572; *Instructions for Practical Living*, 1963).

In 1522, Wang was called on to suppress a rebellion in Jiangxi, a feat he accomplished in only six months. The

Wang Yangming. (Library of Congress)

coughing that had bothered him for years became so pronounced during the fighting that he had to conduct the battles from carriages. On his return home, he died in Nanen, Jiangxi, on January 9, 1529. After his death, a political enemy of Wang, senior academician Gui E (Kuei O), vented his anger against Wang by revoking his earldom and all his hereditary privileges, thereby disinheriting Wang's sons. In 1567, though, a new emperor bestowed on Wang the posthumous title of marquis of Xinjian. In 1584, he was accorded the highest honor of all by the offering of sacrifice to him in the Confucian temple.

SIGNIFICANCE

Wang Yangming will be remembered as the scholar-official who brought a lasting peace to China. Under the leadership of such corrupt eunuchs as Liu Jin, fifteenth century China was a chaotic country, overrun with rebels and bandits. Wang rose to power through the civil service examination system, which had been the traditional avenue to fame and political authority for more than one thousand years. Although he had many political enemies, Wang used his various offices to quell the rebellions. Consequently, a large portion of China enjoyed a century of peace.

Wang's contributions to Neo-Confucian philosophy also had a tremendous effect on China. In the fifteenth century, the Confucian classics, such as the works of Zhu Xi, were being used by the rulers to restrict freedom of thought. Wang arrived at this conclusion through a three-step learning process that began with the writing of flowery compositions, proceeded to intense study of Zhu Xi's works, and culminated in his revolutionary pronouncements. His doctrine of unity of action and knowledge and his doctrine of innate knowledge invigorated the Confucian system. After his death, Wang's philosophy would become a potent force in China and Japan for 150 years, producing a number of brilliant reformers.

—Alan Brown

FURTHER READING

Berthrong, John H. *Transformations of the Confucian Way*. Boulder, Colo.: Westview Press, 1998. History of the evolution of Confucian thought, emphasizing the struggle of individual philosophers to find their own version of the Way and analyzing Wang's particular contribution to Neo-Confucianism. Includes bibliographic references and index.

Chang, Carsun. "Wang Yang-ming's Philosophy." *Philosophy East and West* 5, no. 1 (1955): 3-18. A short introduction to Wang's life and work. Useful primarily for its clear, concise explanation of Wang's philosophy.

Feng, Yu-lan. *The Period of Classical Learning*. Vol. 2 in *A History of Chinese Philosophy*. Translated by Derk Bodde. Princeton, N.J.: Princeton University Press, 1983. Contains an introduction to Wang's philosophy. Although the introduction relies heavily on quotations from Wang's works, it does offer commentary at the beginning and ending of each section.

Hauf, Kandice. "'Goodness Unbound': Wang Yangming and the Redrawing of the Boundary of Confucianism." In *Imagining Boundaries: Changing Confucian Doctrines, Texts, and Hermeneutics*, edited by Kai-wing Chow, On-cho Ng, and John B. Henderson. Albany: State University of New York Press, 1999. Argues that Wang essentially altered the very definition of Confucianism, changing what did and did not count as authentically Confucian thought. Includes bibliographic references and index.

Ivanhoe, Philip J. *Ethics in the Confucian Tradition: The Thought of Mengzi and Wang Yangming*. 2d ed. Indianapolis, Ind.: Hackett, 2002. An introduction to the thought of both Wang and Mencius, which seeks to demonstrate both the continuity between Wang and earlier Confucian philosophy and the important modifications he made in the Confucian system. Includes bibliographic references and index.

Kim, Heup Young. *Wang Yang-ming and Karl Barth: A Confucian-Christian Dialogue*. Lanham, Md.: University Press of America, 1996. A comparison of Confucianism and Christianity, placing Wang in dialogue with a Christian thinker. Attempts to demonstrate the radical Humanism of both thinkers and both systems of thought. Includes bibliographic references.

Wang Yang-ming. *Instructions for Practical Living and Other Neo-Confucian Writings*. Translated by Wing-tsit Chan. New York: Columbia University Press, 1963. The introduction is a comprehensive account of Wang's achievements as a politician and as a philosopher, based on standard Chinese sources. This text is an indispensable biography for the English-speaking reader.

_____. *The Philosophy of Wang Yang-ming*. Translated by Frederick Goodrich Henke. 2d ed. New York: Paragon, 1964. An uncritical translation, based largely on such legends as Wang's escape by boat from assassins. Omits some essential material but provides a good overview of Wang's early life.

Zehou, Li. "Thoughts on Ming-Quing Neo-Confucianism." In *Chu Hsi and Neo-Confucianism*, edited by Wing-tsit Chan. Honolulu: University of Hawaii Press, 1986. Clarifies Wang's philosophy by contrasting it with the work of Wang's precursor, Chu Hsi.

SEE ALSO: Wuzong.
RELATED ARTICLES in *Great Events from History: The Renaissance & Early Modern Era, 1454-1600:* 1505-1521: Reign of Zhengde and Liu Jin; 1521-1567: Reign of Jiajing.

EARL OF WARWICK
English earl, military leader, and diplomat

The earl of Warwick's activities during the Wars of the Roses proved that the accumulation of wealth and power in the hands of the nobles led only to chaos and destruction. New techniques of government—nationalism and diplomacy—were needed in a more modern world.

BORN: November 22, 1428; probably Wessex, England
DIED: April 14, 1471; Barnet, Hertfordshire, England
ALSO KNOWN AS: Richard Neville; the Kingmaker; second earl of Salisbury
AREAS OF ACHIEVEMENT: Military, government and politics

EARLY LIFE

Richard Neville was born the eldest son of Richard Neville, the fifth earl of Salisbury, and his wife, Alice (née Montacute). The Nevilles were one of the oldest, most important, and wealthiest families in England and were descended from and related to kings. Cecily Neville, Neville's aunt, was married to Richard, the duke of York, who was heir to the English throne. Shortly before Neville's birth, his mother's father, the fourth earl of Salisbury, had been killed while fighting in France. In his wife's name, Neville's father inherited Salisbury's lands and title. As a consequence, Neville was reared to wealth and power.

As a child, Richard was married to Anne Beauchamp, the only daughter of the earl of Warwick. In June, 1449, following the death of his wife's brother, Richard inherited his father-in-law's title and lands, making him the most powerful earl in England, with precedence over even his father. Not that his father minded; both his father and his grandfather had provided astutely for their numerous children. (Richard's father had twenty-two full or half siblings.) They intended to make their family the most powerful in England, and for a short while they were successful. Of thirty-five members of the House of Lords, eleven were Nevilles. Richard Neville expected to play an important role in his country's politics.

The influence of this small number of very powerful nobles was one reason mid-fifteenth century England was both prosperous and chaotic. Henry VI, born during the Hundred Years' War while England was victorious, ruled both England and France. Governed by others, he never learned to rule well and was a weak king. When the war with France was lost, the English people blamed Henry's ministers, especially those responsible for the king's marriage to Margaret of Anjou, the niece of Charles VII of France. The war's end brought not only popular discontent but also hosts of disbanded mercenaries. These soldiers swelled the private armies of the powerful barons, including the Nevilles.

Fifteenth century England was not isolated from international politics. Richard's childhood was spent in the shadow of these events, as the country negotiated with France and continued its friendship with France's enemy, Burgundy. Scotland, Ireland, and Wales were also areas of concern; Neville's father was Henry VI's warden of the West Marches near Scotland.

In 1450, these national and international influences resulted in the Wars of the Roses. The duke of York, supported by popular agitation to punish the ministers responsible for the mismanagement of the French war, began to demand reforms in government. Supporting those ministers, Queen Margaret excluded York from the King's Council. The populace protested, and the barons began to choose sides. In August, 1453, when Henry VI was declared insane, the duke of York, as heir, was named regent in spite of Margaret's animosity. The earl of Salisbury went to London to serve on the Council of Regency, and Warwick went with him. It was not until 1455, however, that Richard Neville, earl of Warwick, began his own life's work.

LIFE'S WORK

Having regained his senses, Henry VI summoned a Royal Council in 1455 and once again excluded the duke of York and his followers. York, Salisbury, and Warwick,

Earl of Warwick. (Library of Congress)

with their thousands of retainers, rode to meet the king and his army at St. Albans. Discussion failed to settle the matter, and the opening battle of the Wars of the Roses between Henry's Lancastrians and the Yorkists was fought there on May 22, 1455. York and Warwick were victorious; they captured the king, only to release him when he agreed to appoint Yorkists to government positions.

Warwick gained a military reputation at St. Albans. His chief talent, however, was administrative, and, when he was named governor of Calais in 1455, he was given the perfect setting for his talents. On the coast of France, adjacent to both Burgundy and Flanders, Calais was constantly threatened by the French because of its strategic importance. Calais also controlled the trade route between Flanders and Burgundy. Even though Calais was an important continental outpost, the garrison was seldom paid adequately or on time. Consequently, Warwick's creativity and talent for management made him a popular commander, as he became a pirate to pay his soldiers. Seizing Spanish, French, Burgundian, and even some Hanseatic vessels en route to London, Warwick plundered them for his men, regardless of the king's policy. All the men serving at Calais wore the Warwick badge out of admiration for their swashbuckling leader.

In 1459, at the moment when Margaret of Anjou believed herself secure enough to challenge the Yorkists, Warwick made a lightning raid on England to rescue his cousin, Edward, and his father. When Margaret's representative attempted to seize Calais, Warwick was in control, and when the queen sent arms to her men, they fell into Warwick's hands. To retrieve his ships from royal control, Warwick and his men slipped into the borough of Sandwich, seized them, and returned to Calais. In 1460, Warwick sailed to Ireland, conferred with the duke of York, and returned to Calais. Margaret's naval forces offered battle; Warwick, without hesitating, bore down directly on the English fleet as it turned and fled. Mutinous English sailors refused to fight Warwick.

These years before 1460 may well have been some of Warwick's best. Calais gave him the necessary scope for his courage, love of action, administrative skill, and vanity. Young, strong, friendly, generous, and fair, Warwick was well loved by the Calais garrison. He punished only those men who had turned against him and those nobles who had wronged him. The common people he spared. This ability to manage men and to excite their loyalty, first apparent at Calais, appeared again and again in Warwick's dealings with individuals, Parliament, military retainers, and foreign rulers.

Calais held for Warwick in spirit, if not in fact, until he died. He returned often to Calais between battles, but after 1460, the earl's attention shifted to England. In June, 1460, Warwick and his father landed at Sandwich after distributing throughout the country a proclamation of grievances against the king. Joining the duke of York, they defeated the Lancastrians at Northampton and again captured the king. The duke of York with difficulty resisted the temptation to claim the throne and resumed his place as regent.

In January, 1461, Margaret momentarily reclaimed the initiative at the second Battle of St. Albans—a battle that cost the duke of York and Warwick's father their lives. By the end of February, Edward of York, succeeding to his father's title and ambition, had won the Battle of Mortimer's Cross, claimed the throne as Edward IV, and routed the Lancastrians at Towton at a cost of thirty thousand lives, though only eight thousand of them were Yorkists. On May 1, 1461, Edward IV, Warwick's cousin and protégé, entered London. Warwick "the kingmaker" remained in the north to pacify the English and Scottish rebels.

Wary of Margaret's negotiations to secure French or Burgundian assistance and of her efforts to stir up Scottish and Lancastrian rebellion, the Yorkists fought sporadically until May, 1464, when the Lancastrians were finally subdued and the civil wars temporarily ended. In September, Warwick appeared before Parliament to propose a treaty with the French that would permanently prevent aid to Margaret and her supporters. To seal the treaty, he urged a marriage between the sister-in-law of Louis XI of France and Edward, only to be told that Edward had secretly married Elizabeth Woodville, a widow with a family as prolific, if not as noble, as the Nevilles.

During the spring of 1465, Warwick traveled to Burgundy and France to negotiate a truce. Burgundy vowed to continue its aid to Margaret; France quickly agreed to a truce. In 1467, Warwick returned to France to make that peace permanent. Diplomatic negotiation, like the command at Calais, was work that suited Warwick well. In England, between 1465 and 1467, Warwick spent more time on his own estates than he had during the previous ten years. The Nevilles were being replaced by Woodvilles. Edward's dependence on Warwick waned, and the cousins grew apart. The king refused to allow his brother, the duke of Clarence, to marry Warwick's daughter, Isabella, and dismissed Warwick's friends and kinsmen from office. When Warwick brought the French delegates to London to conclude the peace with Edward, the king treated them coldly, having already concluded an agreement with Burgundy. The French were humiliated; more important for England, Warwick, who had placed Edward on the throne, was humiliated. These actions demonstrated foolish ingratitude on Edward's part: Warwick was popular and seen as a friend of the people; the Woodvilles, on the other hand, were disliked as renegade Lancastrians.

At Christmas, 1467, Warwick refused to attend a Royal Council while his enemies surrounded the king. In January, 1468, popular leaders threatened to rise against the king and called on Warwick for leadership, but Warwick sent them home. In the spring, Edward attempted to reconcile with Warwick by consulting him about a planned attack against France. Warwick hid his dissatisfaction and waited. In April, 1469, he took his wife and daughters to Calais, where the duke of Clarence married Isabella. Meanwhile, riots broke out again in York. Clarence and Warwick landed in Kent with the Calais guard after the ritual demand for reforms. At Olney, Edward was outfought and captured. His capture provided the opportunity for an outbreak of private wars and the resurgence of Lancastrian rebellions. In order to restore order to the realm, Warwick was forced to bargain with Edward.

A cautious peace continued between the two, with Warwick supporters in office and Woodvilles out, until March, 1470, when Edward claimed that rebels in Lincolnshire had implicated Warwick and Clarence in their rebellion. Branded as traitors, Warwick, his family, and his son-in-law fled south to Kent, where the seafaring people helped them acquire ships. The Warwick party sailed to Calais, where the garrison reluctantly refused to admit them. Having captured a Burgundian fleet en route to France, Warwick was welcomed by Louis XI. Happy to avenge himself against Edward's threat, Louis encouraged Warwick to reconcile with Margaret of Anjou, sealing the bargain with a marriage between Warwick's daughter and Margaret's son.

In September, Warwick again landed in England and declared himself for Henry VI. Quickly defeated by Warwick's forces, Edward fled to Burgundy. From October, 1470, to February, 1471, Henry VI ruled with Warwick—kingmaker for the second time—as his chief minister. Through Parliament, Warwick inaugurated a new reign of tolerance and amnesty, and he concluded a treaty with France against Burgundy. Popular with some, Warwick had acquired enemies: the London merchants, the Yorkist nobles allied to the Woodvilles, and the duke of Clarence.

By March, 1471, Edward had gathered support in Burgundy and landed at Ravenspur in the north. By strategy and guile, proclaiming his loyalty to King Henry VI, Edward was able to marshal his troops, reach his wife and son in London, and reclaim the throne. Warwick, unable to unite his own forces, met Edward at Barnet on a foggy Easter morning. Warwick's army could not defeat Edward's troops, and the kingmaker fell in battle, at the age of forty-two. Soon after, Margaret of Anjou's son Edward fell at Tewkesbury.

SIGNIFICANCE

Richard Neville, earl of Warwick and Salisbury, was the last of the great English nobles to oppose the Crown. His death ended the possibility that any noble family would ever again be able to dominate the throne. The Lancastrians were killed, as were many of the Woodvilles. By the end of the fifteenth century, Henry VII, a king neither Yorkist nor Lancastrian, ruled. His primary goal was to be wealthier and more powerful than all his nobles put together. He fought few wars, balanced the budget, and strengthened the gentry and merchant classes. A new world was dawning.

Warwick was the last of a dying breed. He was also, by his ability and interest, the first of a new kind of government manager, much like those who later served Henry VIII. As a leader, he realized the importance of popularity with the ordinary man and soldier. As a statesman, he was a skillful speaker and diplomat. His negotiations with France and Burgundy were for England as a nation rather than for himself. In this sense, Warwick was future-thinking, committed more to solving problems than to fighting wars.

—Loretta Turner Johnson

FURTHER READING

Gillingham, John. *The Wars of the Roses: Peace and Conflict in Fifteenth-Century England.* London: Weidenfeld and Nicolson, 1981. Debunks the Shakespearean myth of the Wars of the Roses as characterized by bloodshed and long-term conflict. A military history.

Hicks, Michael. *The Wars of the Roses, 1455-1485.* New York: Routledge, 2004. Detailed history of the military campaigns of the Wars of the Roses and the reasons behind them. Includes nine strategic maps, illustrations, bibliography, and index.

_____. *Warwick the Kingmaker.* Malden, Mass.: Blackwell, 1998. Study of the life of Warwick and the political climate that shaped him. Includes illustrations, bibliographic references, and index.

Jacob, E. F. *The Fifteenth Century, 1399-1485.* Oxford, England: Clarendon Press, 1961. The sixth volume of the Oxford History of England series presents the traditional view of the Kingmaker and his king. Portrays the problem between them as one of policy: Warwick wanted to control foreign policy with a French alliance, while Edward wanted to recover the French lands lost in 1450.

Kendall, Paul Murray. *Warwick the Kingmaker.* Reprint. New York: Norton, 1970. A well-written, dramatic biography enlivened by inferences and reconstructions. Portrays Warwick as a precursor of sixteenth century statesmen.

Lander, J. R. *Government and Community: England, 1450-1509.* London: Edward Arnold, 1980. Identifies the Yorkist party only in 1460; sees no conspiracy against Henry VI. Depicts Warwick as greedy and Edward as a more competent ruler than usually portrayed.

Oman, Charles W. *Warwick the Kingmaker.* New York: Books for Libraries Press, 1891. A standard laudatory biography by a military historian. Emphasizes battles and generalship.

Ross, Charles. *Edward IV.* London: Eyre, Methuen, 1974. Adds to the traditional assessment that the Woodvilles had kin in Burgundy to help to explain Edward's insistence on the Burgundian alliance.

Wolffe, Bertram. *Henry VI.* London: Methuen, 1981. This view of Henry downplays the role of Margaret of Anjou and concedes that Edward was restored without opposition in 1471. A standard biography.

Young, Charles R. *The Making of the Neville Family in England, 1166-1400.* Rochester, N.Y.: Boydell Press, 1996. A study of the evolution of the power and influence of the Neville family. Provides essential background to understanding both the source of Warwick's power and his motives in using that power. Includes genealogical tables, bibliographic references, and index.

SEE ALSO: Charles VII; Edward IV; Henry VI; Henry VII; Henry VIII; Louis XI; Richard III.

RELATED ARTICLE in *Great Events from History: The Renaissance & Early Modern Era, 1454-1600:* 1455-1485: Wars of the Roses.

WILLIAM THE SILENT
Prince of Orange (r. 1544-1584) and count of Nassau (r. 1559-1584)

William led the revolt of the Netherlands against Spain despite overwhelming difficulties. His leadership proved decisive to the Dutch independence movement at its crucial beginnings in the late sixteenth century.

BORN: April 24, 1533; Dillenburg Castle, Nassau (now in the Netherlands)

DIED: July 10, 1584; Delft, Holland (now in the Netherlands)

ALSO KNOWN AS: William I; William of Orange; William of Nassau

AREAS OF ACHIEVEMENT: Government and politics, military

EARLY LIFE

William the Silent, the eldest son of Count William of Nassau-Dillenburg and his second wife, Juliana von Stolberg, was born at Dillenburg Castle. The family was large, and the young heir's prospects were particularly remarkable until 1544, when, at the age of eleven, he inherited the titles and possessions of an elder cousin, René of Orange, who was killed during the Siege of Saint Dizier. Because of the wealth and importance of his new estates, and because William's parents had become Lutherans, the Habsburg emperor Charles V determined that the boy should be brought up at his court and educated in the Roman Catholic faith.

William's pleasant manners and appearance and his genial personality soon made him a general favorite at court. The aging emperor became very fond of the young man and arranged an advantageous marriage for him with a pretty heiress, Anne of Egmond-Buren; this union would produce a son, Philip William, and a daughter. Anne died in 1558.

William had fulfilled a number of social and military duties at the court before the abdication of Charles V in 1555 in favor of his son Philip II. It was perhaps ironic that the emperor chose to lean on the shoulder of the young prince of Orange as he passed the sovereignty of Spain and his Burgundian territories to the man who would become Orange's most bitter enemy. Yet for a while the relationship between William and Philip was amicable, if not warm. Philip was godfather to Philip William, and William would be given new responsibilities. Now in his middle twenties, William's career as a loyal servant of the new monarch seemed assured.

LIFE'S WORK

There is a traditional story that Philip and William disliked each other on sight; if that were so, their mutual antagonism took time to mature. William was named a councillor of state and a Knight of the Golden Fleece by the new king. In 1559, William was chosen to be one of three chief negotiators concluding the Treaty of Cateau-Cambrésis between France and Spain. His associates, Antoine Perrenot de Granvelle, bishop of Arras, and Fernando Álvarez de Toledo, duke of Alva, would also play crucial roles in the revolt of the Netherlands. It was during this stay in France that William began to acquire his reputation for being discreet, but "taciturn" or even "sly" are better descriptive terms than the misleading nickname "silent." William was a career diplomat, fond of company and never at a loss for words.

With the conclusion of this diplomatic mission, William was appointed stadtholder (governor and military commander) in Zeeland, Utrecht, Holland, and, later (1561), Franche-Comté. On the eve of Philip's departure for Spain in August, 1559, however, the nobility and people of the Netherlands were beginning to complain. Spanish troops had not been withdrawn despite the peace, Spanish courtiers were being made councillors of state, and sterner measures were being authorized against Protestants. William and other important nobles protested, and Philip seemed willing to make concessions regarding Spanish troops and politicians—but not heretics. He appointed his half sister Margaret, duchess of Parma, as regent, with Granvelle (now a cardinal) as her adviser.

William was eager to marry again, but his choice of wives was not a fortunate one. Anne of Saxony, a well-born heiress, was erratic and quarrelsome, her family had traditionally opposed the Habsburgs, and, worse, she was a Lutheran. William made vague promises about his wife's conformity when they were married in 1561, but Philip was not pleased.

As Granvelle's influence increased (he created more than a dozen new bishoprics), the nobility of the Netherlands felt their traditional leadership threatened. Snobbery also played a role in the nobility's dislike for Granvelle, who was said to be the grandson of a blacksmith. Toleration of Calvinists was initially less important than the replacement of the hated minister with one more to their liking. In letters to Philip, however, the nobles, led by William and the counts of Egmond and Hoorne, were careful to avoid direct criticism of royal policies.

In the spring of 1564, it seemed that the anti-Granvelle faction had won; Margaret had also decided that Granvelle was a political liability, and he was withdrawn. Yet Philip, however preoccupied with the Turks and the administration of his vast empire, was unyielding in matters of faith. Catholicism was to be imposed on the Netherlands and Protestant heresy rooted out.

William and his associates tried to support Margaret while attempting to promote a policy that would allow liberty of conscience, if not public worship, for Protestants. Efforts at a reasonable compromise were doomed to failure by both sides. A number of the lower nobility and their supporters advocated violence to intimidate the regent and the Catholics. These men became known as Les Gueux (the Beggars), from a slighting reference made about them by one of Margaret's advisers. Riots erupted in the summer of 1566. Calvinist mobs sacked churches, even turning some of them into Protestant meetinghouses. By the end of the year, an angry Philip appointed the duke of Alva as his general to pacify the Netherlands at any cost.

William the Silent. (Library of Congress)

William hesitated; he refused to command the rebels, protested his loyalty to the king, and then declined to take the oath of unconditional obedience that Margaret demanded. In April, 1567, he retired to his family estates at Dillenburg. Other prudent men fled the country, but Hoorne and Egmond remained, only to be betrayed, arrested, and executed. The duke of Alva's methods for maintaining order were so brutal that eventually Margaret resigned. A reign of terror instituted by a special commission, the Council of Troubles—soon nicknamed the Council of Blood—filled the land with fear, as thousands of victims were arrested and executed. When William refused to return, he was declared a rebel, his property in the Netherlands was sequestered, and his son, a student at the University of Louvain, was carried off to Spain, never again to see his father.

With few choices remaining save armed rebellion, William and his brothers raised an army to expel the duke of Alva. Two invasions were launched in April, 1568, but the people did not rise; both attempts were badly defeated. William and his few supporters took refuge in France. William was entering the most difficult period of his life. Impoverished, outlawed, and peripatetic, he was made miserable by Anne of Saxony's irrational behavior. She was flagrantly unfaithful, and at last he divorced her in 1571.

Meanwhile, William continued to look for allies. Elizabeth I of England was not encouraging. The German Protestant princes had provided little support. His best hopes seemed to lie with the Calvinists, whose faith he would adopt in 1573. Another area of resistance lay with the Sea Beggars, an irregular band of nobles, merchants, patriots, and pirates. In April, 1572, they seized the town of Brielle, which triggered a popular uprising, and soon most of Holland, Zeeland, and Friesland declared William their stadtholder.

To strengthen William's advantage, William's brother Louis of Nassau launched an attack from France but was eventually blockaded at Mons. As William moved to aid him, his support among the French Huguenots was undercut by the St. Bartholomew's Day Massacre on August 24, 1572. Again William's forces were obliged to disband, and he retreated to Holland to lead the resistance there for four more frustrating years between 1572 and 1576.

In June, 1575, William married his third wife, Charlotte de Bourbon, a former nun who had fled her convent, escaped to Germany, and converted to Calvinism. Catholics were outraged at this union, but it proved to be both happy and successful, as Charlotte won the trust and affection of her husband's countryfolk by her devotion to their cause.

By 1576, even Philip was becoming aware of the costs of this seemingly endless war. The rebellion was not crushed, and his own troops began to mutiny for lack of pay. William's status rose with the Pacification of Ghent (November 8, 1576), in which the seventeen provinces agreed to a common cause against Spain. This was followed in January, 1577, by the short-lived Union of Brussels, in which both Catholics and Protestants joined in demanding the withdrawal of Spanish troops, the southerners reserving the right to remain Catholics. At this point, William was at the height of his power and influence, but he was unable to maintain this fragile alliance, despite his natural toleration and his talents as a diplomat.

Believing that he must have the support of another ruling dynasty against Spain, William again turned to France and proposed the unlikely candidacy of the feckless duke of Anjou, brother of Henry III of France, as sovereign of the Netherlands. Philip riposted in March, 1581, with a ban proclaiming William a traitor and offering a considerable reward for his assassination. The first attempt on his life a year later failed, but his wife died of a fever and the strain of nursing her husband.

The duke of Anjou's double-dealing and ambitions made him unacceptable to his new subjects, few of whom would mourn his death in June, 1583. Two months before, William had married Louise de Coligny, a daughter of the famous Huguenot leader Gaspard II de Coligny, killed on St. Bartholomew's Day. Of his twelve children, it would be her son Frederick Henry who would leave heirs to carry on the Nassau name. With Louise, William lived simply and quietly in Delft, a father figure beloved by the people, until July 10, 1584, when he was fatally shot by a Catholic fanatic. William's dying words were a prayer for his poor country. He was given a state funeral by the city and buried in the New Church at Delft.

SIGNIFICANCE

The sequence of events following the murder of William the Silent was a study in vengeance and intolerance by all parties. William's friends and supporters relieved their outraged feelings by torturing and slowly executing the young assassin Balthazar Gérard. When the murder became known, William's enemies, who included Philip and Granvelle, expressed triumphant satisfaction at what they considered to be divine justice. The reconquest of the entire Netherlands appeared a certainty, but such was not to be.

Philip's dream of a Catholic Netherlands as the obedient handmaiden of Spain faded before the realities of Dutch determination, his own financial mismanagement, and the defeat of his grand armada by England in 1588. Yet William's dream of a united Netherlands would not become a reality. The depths of distrust between Protestants and Catholics, middle-class merchants and the nobility, and north and south were too great to be bridged. William invested his fortune, his family (three of his brothers would die on campaigns), and finally his own life for the cause in which he so strongly believed. Yet not even his personal popularity and his diplomatic skills could hold the provinces together for long. William's cause failed, but he had dared greatly and became the heart and symbol of the Dutch independence movement.

—*Dorothy Turner Potter*

FURTHER READING

Darby, Graham, ed. *The Origins and Development of the Dutch Revolt.* New York: Routledge, 2001. Anthology of scholarship on the causes and consequences of the sixteenth century Dutch rebellion against Spanish rule. Includes illustrations, maps, bibliographic references, and index.

Geyl, Pieter. *The Revolt of the Netherlands, 1555-1609.* Reprint. London: Cassell, 1988. This is the first in a series of three books by Geyl that deals with the Netherlands from 1555 to 1715. As a Dutch historian, Geyl has a special perspective on the revolt. This book places William in his historical context. Includes maps, an extensive index, and a short bibliography.

Harrison, Frederic. *William the Silent.* Reprint. Port Washington, N.Y.: Kennikat Press, 1970. The style and interpretation of this biography are of necessity somewhat dated, but the lack of a standard biography of William in English makes it useful. Contains a bibliography and useful information on William's family and descendants.

Koenigsberger, H. G. *Monarchies, States, Generals, and Parliaments: The Netherlands in the Fifteenth and Sixteenth Centuries.* New York: Cambridge University Press, 2001. History of the States-General of the Netherlands, the region's internal and external strife, and the Netherland's division into the United Provinces and the Spanish Netherlands. Includes illustrations, maps, bibliographic references, index.

Kossman, E. H., and A. F. Mellink, eds. *Texts Concerning the Revolt of the Netherlands.* New York: Cambridge University Press, 1974. This book introduces the reader to letters and documents related to the revolt. Several letters by William are included. Contains a short bibliography and an index.

Parker, Geoffrey. *The Dutch Revolt.* Ithaca, N.Y.: Cornell University Press, 1977. Parker makes the valid point that there was not one Dutch revolt but several. This study attempts to balance the majority of treatments, which are pro-Dutch, with attention to the Spanish viewpoint. Contains maps, diagrams, tables, and an extensive bibliography.

Putnam, Ruth. *William the Silent, Prince of Orange, 1533-1584, and the Revolt of the Netherlands.* New York: G. P. Putnam's Sons, 1911. The character of William the Silent is at times overly idealized, but this book is a useful beginning to a study of William and his times. Pictures, maps, and facsimiles of letters make it interesting to the general reader. Includes a detailed bibliography and an index.

Swart, K. W. *William of Orange and the Revolt of the Netherlands, 1572-84.* Translated by J. C. Grayson. Edited by R. P. Fagel, M. E. H. N. Mout, and H. F. K. van Nierop. Burlington, Vt.: Ashgate, 2003. A major and authoritative biography, published posthumously, with introductory essays and commentary by other noted scholars of William's reign. Includes illustrations, maps, bibliographic references, and index.

Wedgwood, C. V. *William the Silent, William of Nassau, Prince of Orange.* New Haven, Conn.: Yale University Press, 1944. Reprint. New York: Norton, 1968. Well written and detailed but continues the trend of older studies in idealizing William's motives and character. For the general reader.

Wilson, Charles. *Queen Elizabeth and the Revolt of the Netherlands.* London: Macmillan, 1970. The English view of the Netherlands as well as the role played by Elizabeth I is the focus of this useful study, but it also includes good background material on William. Contains detailed notes on sources.

SEE ALSO: Duke of Alva; John Calvin; William Cecil; Charles V; Elizabeth I; Alessandro Farnese; Kenau Hasselaer; Martin Luther; Margaret of Austria; Margaret of Parma; Philippe de Mornay; Johan van Oldenbarnevelt; Philip II; Sir Philip Sidney.

RELATED ARTICLES in *Great Events from History: The Renaissance & Early Modern Era, 1454-1600:* 16th century: Worldwide Inflation; April 3, 1559: Treaty of Cateau-Cambrésis; 1568-1648: Dutch Wars of Independence; July 26, 1581: The United Provinces Declare Independence from Spain.

CARDINAL THOMAS WOLSEY
English religious leader and politician

By combining for himself the highest lay administrative post of chancellor and the religious position of papal legate a latere, *Wolsey paved the way for the combining of church and state under Henry VIII.*

BORN: 1471 or 1472; Ipswich, Suffolk, England
DIED: November 29, 1530; Leicester Abbey, Leicester, England
AREAS OF ACHIEVEMENT: Government and politics, religion and theology

EARLY LIFE

Thomas Wolsey (WOOL-zee) was the child of Robert Wulcy, a butcher, from Ipswich, Suffolk, and his wife, Joan. Sent at an early age to Oxford, he received his bachelor of arts degree at the age of fifteen. He became a fellow at Magdalen College in 1497, soon after receiving his master of arts degree and becoming first junior and then senior bursar there. Forced to resign as bursar for using funds without authorization in order to complete the building of the great tower at the college, he became a priest in 1498.

Subsequently, Wolsey became chaplain to Sir Richard Nanfan, the deputy lieutenant of Calais, and Nanfan recommended him to Henry VII. The king appointed Wolsey as one of his chaplains and occasionally used him on royal business. With the accession of Henry VIII in April, 1509, and the death of his grandmother, who did not like Wolsey, Wolsey came into his own. He became Henry's almoner in November and was advanced to councillor in late 1511.

LIFE'S WORK

From 1512 until his fall from power in 1529, Wolsey controlled the government of England, by acquiescing to the desires of his sovereign. Wolsey satisfied Henry's appetite for glory with the successful French campaign of 1513, in which Henry's forces won the Battle of Spurs and captured the French towns of Tournai and Thérouanne. In return for this success, Henry rewarded Wolsey by securing for him several clerical appointments—the bishopric of Tournai, the bishopric of Lincoln, the archbishopric of York, and the cardinalate. Later, Wolsey would add legate *a latere*, the bishopric of Bath and Wells, the abbacy of St. Albans, the bishopric of Durham, and the bishopric of Winchester to his titles. Though only archbishop of York and thus theoretically under the archbishop of Canterbury, Thomas Warham, Wolsey surpassed Warham and the entire English church by virtue of his status as papal legate *a latere*. Moreover, when Warham resigned as chancellor in December, 1515, Henry appointed Wolsey to the post. Thus, Wolsey united in himself the supreme lay post of chancellor and the supreme clerical post of legate *a latere*, making him the second most important person in the kingdom, only below the king. As Henry's chief minister, Wolsey expended most of his energies on diplomacy. Whenever he saw either Charles V, the Holy Roman Emperor, or Francis I, the king of France, growing stronger, Wolsey sided with the other, trying to maintain a balance of power on the Continent. His greatest successes included the 1513 campaign against the French; the Anglo-French treaty of 1514; the 1518 peace treaty of Noyon, which involved England, France, and the Holy Roman Empire; and the magnificent Field of Cloth of Gold of 1520, when Henry and Francis met in a glorious spectacle of amity. His failures included the refusal of the East Anglians to agree to the Amicable Grant of 1525 and the pope's refusal to annul Henry's marriage to Catherine of Aragon so that he could marry Anne Boleyn.

In 1527, Henry began to worry about his lack of a male heir and about the legality of his marriage to Catherine, who had previously been married for nearly five months to his elder brother, Arthur. Wolsey, with Warham, in May, 1527, examined the king about the marriage but came to no conclusion. Instead, Wolsey decided to use his influence to secure a decree of nullity from Pope Clement VII. Clement was unwilling to antagonize Charles V, whose troops had sacked Rome in 1527 and briefly imprisoned the pope. Charles was Catherine's nephew, and he had sworn to help her.

Nevertheless, the pope sent his legate to England but instructed him to do nothing without papal permission. Wolsey and the papal legate heard the marriage case from June 18 to July 23, 1529, when the case was called back to Rome because the planned Treaty of Cambrai between Charles and Francis soon made it unnecessary for Clement to give Henry what he wanted. Earlier in the year, when Clement had been gravely ill, Wolsey had desper-

Cardinal Thomas Wolsey. (Library of Congress)

ately tried to accumulate enough votes in the college of cardinals for his own candidacy, in the event of Clement's death. Twice before, in 1522 and in 1523, Wolsey had thought of himself as a papal candidate, but in 1522, Charles's tutor became Adrian VI, and in 1523, Giulio de' Medici became Clement VII. Perhaps it was unrealistic for a man such as Wolsey, who had never been to Rome and had not developed his Italian contacts, to think of himself as a viable candidate. Wolsey expended most of his energies on serving Henry and advancing his own interests.

Failure to secure the decree of nullity led to Wolsey's fall from power. He was indicted on October 9, 1529, under the statute of *praemunire*, which said that no ecclesiastical causes could be taken outside England for settlement, for his having overstepped his authority as legate. Wolsey lost his post as chancellor on October 18, 1529, to Sir Thomas More and signed a confession of his wrongdoing three days later. On November 3, he answered forty-six parliamentary charges against him (he was ably defended by Thomas Cromwell). In February, 1530, Henry restored him as archbishop of York, and

Wolsey went to that city in the spring. Once there, he endeared himself to the people by singing masses in parish churches and adopting a more religious way of life, even to the wearing of a hair shirt. Questions, however, arose about his correspondence with foreign powers after his fall, and the king had him arrested for treason. As Wolsey made his way to London, he stopped at Leicester Abbey, where he died on November 29, 1530. He was buried in the abbey chapel, next to Richard III.

SIGNIFICANCE

Money from Wolsey's various ecclesiastical posts, combined with his fees from chancery and foreign pensions, made him the wealthiest man in the kingdom, wealthier even than the king in personal income. Wolsey was a great builder. He constructed York Place; his palace in Westminster, which later became the palace of Whitehall when Henry took it over; and Hampton Court, which Wolsey gave to Henry in 1525 to appease the king's jealousy.

Although Wolsey was given the power as papal legate to reform the English church, he failed to do so. He was anti-Lutheran and, in 1521, had presided over the burning of Martin Luther's books. Nevertheless, Wolsey had a reputation for fairness in his dealings in the Court of the King's Council and in the Star Chamber.

Wolsey's private life, arrogance, and pluralism made for him many enemies, including the poets William Roy and John Skelton, who viciously satirized him in their poetry. Possibly Wolsey's example fed the anticlericalism that enabled Henry and Thomas Cromwell to reform the English church in the Reformation Parliament of 1529-1536. Moreover, Wolsey's practice of dissolving decaying monasteries in order to use the revenue to found colleges at Ipswich and Oxford was not lost on Cromwell, who dissolved all the English monasteries and nunneries to feed Henry's coffers. Thus, Wolsey's example of uniting lay and clerical power in himself paved the way for the extension of Henry's power over the church as well as the state. Wolsey served Henry well, but financially, he served himself better. At his death he was scarcely mourned, except by the good people of York, who, in the few months that he spent with them, saw him as their spiritual father.

—*M. J. Tucker*

FURTHER READING

Cavendish, George. *The Life and Death of Cardinal Wolsey.* Reprinted in *Two Early Tudor Lives*, edited by Richard S. Sylvester and Davis P. Harding. New Haven, Conn.: Yale University Press, 1962. One of the earliest of English biographies, written in 1557 by Wolsey's gentleman usher.

Elton, G. R. *Reform and Reformation: England, 1509-1558.* Cambridge, Mass.: Harvard University Press, 1979. Notes the ephemeral nature of Wolsey's achievements. The real administrative revolution awaited the energy, efficiency, and work of Thomas Cromwell.

Erickson, Carolly. *Great Harry: The Extravagant Life of Henry VIII.* New York: Summit Books, 1980. Fascinating insights into both Wolsey and Henry VIII.

Ferguson, Charles W. *Naked to Mine Enemies: The Life of Cardinal Wolsey.* New York: Time, 1965. Dramatic, readable retelling of Wolsey's life by the former editor of *Reader's Digest*.

Gunn, S. J., and P. G. Lindley, eds. *Cardinal Wolsey: Church, State, and Art.* New York: Cambridge University Press, 1991. Anthology of essays assessing all aspects of Wolsey's career, from his patronage of the arts to his handling of the church to his involvement in foreign affairs. Includes thirty-six pages of plates, illustrations, sheet music, bibliographic references, and index.

Guy, J. A. *The Cardinal's Court: The Impact of Thomas Wolsey in Star Chamber.* Totowa, N.J.: Rowman and Littlefield, 1977. Based extensively on documents in England's Public Record Office, this study notes Wolsey's innovative use of the Court of Star Chamber but concludes that the court was used more extensively and more practically by Thomas Cromwell. Challenging, but well worth reading.

Harvey, Nancy Lenz. *Thomas Cardinal Wolsey.* New York: Macmillan, 1980. A brief, readable account. Follows the judgments of Wolsey's gentleman usher and Wolsey's other contemporaries.

Loades, David. *Politics and Nation: England, 1450-1660.* 5th ed. Malden, Mass.: Blackwell, 1999. Includes a chapter on Wolsey's administration and his role in the establishment of the Tudor Dynasty. Includes bibliographic references and index.

Pollard, A. F. *Wolsey.* New York: Longmans, Green, 1953. Originally issued in 1929, this is Pollard's masterpiece. Revised by works of Erickson, Williams, and Elton, but still worth reading.

Smith, Lacey Baldwin. *This Realm of England, 1399 to 1688.* Vol. 2 in *A History of England*, edited by Lacey Baldwin Smith. 7th ed. Lexington, Mass.: D. C. Heath, 1996. A wonderfully written tour de force. The sort of history that cannot fail to excite the reader.

Strong, Roy. *The Spirit of Britain: A Narrative History of the Arts.* New York: Fromm International, 2000. Examines Wolsey's role in shaping the course of the history of British art and music. Includes illustrations, map, sheet music, bibliographic references, and index.

Williams, Neville. *The Cardinal and the Secretary: Thomas Wolsey and Thomas Cromwell.* New York: Macmillan, 1975. A fascinating dual biography of two men, Wolsey and Cromwell, who were at the center of English public events for nearly thirty years. Shrewd insights from a master historian.

Wilson, Derek. *In the Lion's Court: Power, Ambition, and Sudden Death in the Reign of Henry VIII.* New York: St. Martin's Press, 2002. Vivid study of the perils of Henry VIII's court that details the fates of six members of the court, including Wolsey and five other men named Thomas. Examines Wolsey's background and education, and provides a thorough survey of his activities in the court and the events leading up to his arrest for treason. Includes illustrations, maps, sixteen pages of plates, bibliographic references, and index.

SEE ALSO: Adrian V; Anne Boleyn; Catherine of Aragon; Charles V; Clement VII; Miles Coverdale; Thomas Cromwell; Saint John Fisher; Stephen Gardiner; Henry VIII; Martin Luther; Sir Thomas More; Catherine Parr.

RELATED ARTICLES in *Great Events from History: The Renaissance & Early Modern Era, 1454-1600:* Beginning 1485: The Tudors Rule England; 1515-1529: Wolsey Serves as Lord Chancellor and Cardinal; June 5-24, 1520: Field of Cloth of Gold; 1531-1540: Cromwell Reforms British Government; December 18, 1534: Act of Supremacy.

SAINT FRANCIS XAVIER
Spanish religious leader

Francis, who suffered many physical and mental hardships in order to bring the Christian message to countries of the Far East, was one of the first seven members of the Roman Catholic Church's Jesuit Order as well as its most successful missionary.

BORN: April 7, 1506; the castle of Xavier, Navarre (now in Spain)

DIED: December 3, 1552; island of Sancian, China

ALSO KNOWN AS: Francisco de Yasu y Javier (given name); Francisco Javier

AREA OF ACHIEVEMENT: Religion and theology

EARLY LIFE

The youngest of a family of several children, Francis Xavier (FRAHN-sehs ZAY-vyuhr) was born to a prosperous nobleman, Don Juan de Jasso of Navarre, and a mother whose connection with the Xavier family brought property into her marriage. Francis's parents focused on his education early in his life, and, since they determined he had a real love for learning, he was allowed to go to the College of Saint Barbara at the University of Paris, where, in 1530, he received a master of arts degree.

After graduating, Francis taught Aristotelian philosophy at the same institution. Francis was known to be a generous, helpful, and stirring lecturer, having a thorough knowledge of his subject. Yet it was his sense of adventure, combined with a serious, searching, and scholarly nature, that drew students to him and made him ready to embark on daring journeys to little-known or unknown lands.

It was Ignatius of Loyola, a fellow student of Francis at the University of Paris, who helped Francis find his calling—that of Christian missionary work. For three years, Ignatius prodded Francis to dedicate his life to God rather than to the vain pursuits of the worldly minded, yet Francis ignored the summons. Finally, however, Francis's resistance broke down, and he decided to serve God rather than scholarship. Together, Francis and Ignatius, along with five other idealistic youths, pledged themselves to church service at Montmartre in Paris, their group becoming the Society of Jesus (Jesuits). Six of the original seven members went on to become ordained into the priesthood at Venice.

Francis and Ignatius then went to Rome and informed Pope Paul III that they would do whatever he asked of them. The pope, impressed by their youthful vigor and intellectual gifts, eventually gave official approval to the Society of Jesus. When the time came, the young men—Ignatius, Francis, Peter Faber, Nicholas Bobadilla, Diego Laínez, Alfonso Salmeron, and Simon Rodriguez—not only took traditional monastic vows of perpetual poverty and chastity but also pledged total obedience to the pope's wishes, going wherever he might find it necessary to send them.

From inauspicious beginnings in 1534, the society would help evangelize many nations and bring countless converts to the Church, while performing humanitarian deeds for the people converted and battling any heresy, vice, and spiritual lethargy they might encounter. Francis's name would become forever intertwined with that of the society, for he came to exemplify all that was positive in it.

LIFE'S WORK

After being ordained in the priesthood in 1537, Francis, in the company of Ignatius and the other Jesuits, worked long days to make the society into a successful venture, enthusiastically spreading the news about it to potential recruits. In 1540, the Portuguese king, John III, instructed his Vatican emissary to petition the pope to allow Jesuits the right to propagate the Christian faith within the new Portuguese possessions overseas. An opportunity for missionary work came after a vision of Ignatius, in which God told him to ask the pope a second time for a chance to do missionary tasks. In Ignatius's vision, God said that he would make certain that the permission would be granted.

With Ignatius elected the general of the society and with orders from Paul to convert pagans in Portugal's expanding empire, Francis joined fellow priest Rodriguez in Lisbon; then, with two trusted aides, he sailed on to Goa, a Portuguese colony in India, situated on the coast. While on board the ship taking him to Goa, Francis showed characteristic love for his fellow passengers by assisting those sickened by scurvy and other diseases, by saying Mass regularly, and by arbitrating arguments among the sailors. Once in Goa, which had been a Portuguese possession for only thirty years, Francis noted with dismay that the Europeans within the colony were dissipated by debauchery of all kinds and thus provided the indigenous people with a terrible example of Christian conduct.

Taking on himself the same selfless activities that he had performed on ship—caring for the sick, comforting the dying, advising those in difficult situations, teaching the catechism, and saying Masses—Francis slowly created order out of the Goan chaos, giving by precept as well as example a measure of self-discipline to the unruly inhabitants. Because he taught the residents of Goa the principles of the Catholic religion and put those principles directly into practice, Francis gained the residents' complete trust and high regard.

In 1542, having done much for Goa, Francis decided to journey to Cape Cormorin in southern India in order to teach a group of half-converted native Indians, called the Paravas, Christian values and beliefs; his message was well received by the poorest Paravas, who gathered in large numbers to hear him deliver his inspiring sermons. The love Francis had for the people of India was evident to almost everyone, even if his message sometimes became garbled or was incomprehensible. Once more, Francis's actions did more persuading than did his eloquent words.

Saint Francis Xavier. (Hulton|Archive by Getty Images)

After working with the Paravas, Francis decided to return to Goa in order to find new priests for the Society of Jesus. Again he was forced to deal with the immoral behavior and often outright hostility of Portuguese traders, who found his preaching an affront to a libertine way of life. This time, he worked alongside two Goanese priests and a lay catechist, helping the Goanese people by protecting them from European harassment.

At Travancore, Francis founded many churches, but at the same time he tore down the native Indians' ancestral places of worship and idols. He was said to have brought the dead back to life in the manner of Jesus Christ. Francis's exploits and his miracles led to his being hated by the Hindu Brahmans as well as local Muslims, who on occasion massacred Christian converts. As for his mission at Goa, Francis often wrote in letters to John III about how difficult an endeavor the mission had been for him and his followers. Fighting the immorality of the Portuguese residents at Goa demanded so much of Francis's time that he admitted to chronic weariness and, on more than one occasion, a sense of defeat.

It may well have been his exasperation with fellow Europeans that led to Francis's departure from Goa in 1545, when he sailed to a city on the Malaysian peninsula called Malacca. People there, who had previously been hostile to Christianity, converted enthusiastically after Francis worked his miracles. He journeyed on to the southern Pacific Ocean, where he spent time on the Molucca Islands. There Francis once more battled the hardened, sinning Portuguese traders, some of whom would have liked to kill him.

From the Moluccas, Francis returned to Goa, this time by way of Ceylon, but he wanted to journey on to the little-known country of Japan. He traveled to Kagoshima on the island of Kyūshū, where he and his band were given permission to learn the Japanese language and to preach Christian doctrine to the city's inhabitants; unfortunately, this budding mission was almost destroyed when the prince who gave permission for Francis's evangelistic efforts became irate with him over the fact that Francis had dared use a base of Japanese operations other than his own city of Kagoshima.

Nevertheless, the converts that Francis had made remained faithful to the Church established in Japan. He made still more converts when he moved to the town of Hirado near Kagoshima. Other attempts at reaching the Japanese at the port city of Yamaguchi in 1549 were unsuccessful. At Kyōto, the imperial city itself, Francis found himself at another impasse, this time because he was so poorly dressed that the emperor believed that he could not possibly be an important Western dignitary and thus would not deign to see him. Francis, ever able to rise to a challenge, decided to purchase luxurious clothing for himself and for his fellow adventurers. Dressing as extravagantly as he could, he presented himself to Oshindono, prince of Nagote, who, after having been impressed by the splendor of Francis's party, decided to allow him to preach the Gospel in his realm. This opening allowed Francis to baptize many in the Christian faith.

Still other missionary ventures opened at Bungo in Kyūshū province, where the ruler was friendly to Francis and his followers and friends. When Francis left Japan in 1551, he could look back on a considerable achievement: He had single-handedly converted more than seven hundred Japanese people to the Christian faith without bloodshed or turmoil, which often in the past had come with attempts to convert populations to Christianity.

Francis's last major challenge was to find a way to establish a mission in the forbidding country of China, long closed to all outsiders on the pain of death. Encouraged solely by the fact that so many missions had already been established in places once thought to be totally inhospitable to Christianity, Francis believed that God wanted him to open China to his faith and gain many converts there. Yet from the outset, the venture proved impossible. Francis dreamed of being the first priest to enter China. After he had done much exhausting work for the lepers at Malacca, he asked the new governor, Don Alvaro d'Ataide, to provide him with a ship and supplies so that he might sail to China. The governor, knowing well that China remained closed to outsiders, at first refused the request but then, after reconsidering, grudgingly allowed it.

Francis's plan was to sail to Japan in company with a Christian brother and a Chinese Christian, and then to travel secretly to China in the hope of somehow gaining entry. In the late summer of 1552, he landed at the port of Sancian, where he hired a merchant to take him by night into Canton province. At a time when he needed all the strength he could find, Francis fell ill with a raging fever and was summarily left alone by most of the Portuguese on the island, who made a precarious living trading with mainlanders. Although one ship would have taken him home to Europe, Francis could not bear the ship's motion as it made its way out to sea, and he begged the captain to take him back to Sancian, where he died asking God's forgiveness and praising him.

SIGNIFICANCE

Saint Francis Xavier, canonized by Pope Gregory XV in 1622 at the same time as was his great friend Ignatius,

was one of the Catholic Church's most daring, astute, and productive leaders. He used his fine intellectual gifts and his ability to deliver powerful speeches and sermons to glorify God when he very well might have pursued far less arduous and far more lucrative careers than that of a missionary.

Francis was fortunate to have been born during Spain and Portugal's Golden Age of the sixteenth century, when empire building was the pursuit of the Hispanic nations and their kings. Both countries, out to counter the Reformation brought on by followers of Martin Luther and to add to national coffers, needed able priests to subdue, through converting, the indigenous peoples of conquered lands. Thus, Francis found the kind of support he needed for his missionary efforts.

Without Francis and his fellow Jesuits, India, Japan, and other places in Asia would have remained untouched by the Church's message and, without Francis's support, Ignatius might not have been able to found and properly organize the Jesuit Order. Today, with a debt owed to its founders, the society remains the preeminent scholarly order of the Catholic Church as well as its greatest supplier of educators, who teach children in secondary schools, colleges, and universities around the world. Appropriately, Francis remains the patron saint of all involved in missionary work and the guiding influence of multitudes of priests who have served their God in foreign places.

—*John D. Raymer*

FURTHER READING

Aveling, J. C. H. "The Dangerous Missions." In *The Jesuits*. Briarcliff Manor, N.Y.: Stein & Day, 1981. This superb study of the Society of Jesus and its dynamic of faith, though it chooses not to dwell for long on Francis, does a fine job of discussing the magnitude of his opening the Far East to the Christian faith.

Barthel, Manfred. "The Light of the World: The Jesuit as Missionary." In *The Jesuits: History and Legend of the Society of Jesus*. Translated by Mark Howson. New York: William Morrow, 1984. Explains Francis's contribution to the founding of the Society of Jesus and to its early mission work, and how he is to be remembered. Good for those readers wishing to have a grounding in the Jesuit Order's history and Francis's place in it. The general bibliography is useful.

Bartoli, Daniello, and J. P. Maffei. *The Life of St. Francis Xavier, Apostle of the Indies and Japan*. Baltimore: John Murphy, 1862. This account is one of the handful of studies of the saint in English translation. Serves as a basic guide to the subject of Francis's travels.

Bermejo, Luis M. *Unto the Indies: Life of St. Francis Xavier.* Anand, Gujarat, India: Gujarat Sahitya Prakash, 2000. A life of the saint that seeks to reveal the real Francis behind the various myths that have accumulated about him. Includes maps and bibliographic references.

Clarke, C. P. S. "St. Francis Xavier." In *Everyman's Book of Saints.* Revised by Rosemary Edisford. New York: Philosophical Society, 1969. Elementary but helpful introduction to Francis's place in the canon of saints.

D'Costa, Anthony. *The Call of the Orient: A Response by Jesuits in the Sixteenth Century.* Mumbai, India: Heras Institute of Indian History and Culture, 1999. A study of fifteen of St. Francis Xavier's companions and their missionary work in South Asia. Includes illustrations, maps, bibliographic references, and index.

Foss, Michael. "Reform of the Church and the Life of Renewal." In *The Founding of the Jesuits, 1540.* New York: Weybright and Talley, 1969. Foss traces the society from its inception to the modern era. Francis is given credit for his pioneering work.

Lacouture, Jean. *Jesuits: A Multibiography.* Translated by Jeremy Leggatt. Washington, D.C.: Counterpoint, 1995. Provides biographies of the most important and influential Jesuits, including St. Francis Xavier. Includes illustrations, map, bibliographic references, and index.

Maynard, Theodore. *The Odyssey of Francis Xavier.* Westminster, Md.: Newman Press, 1950. Compelling study of Francis and his importance to the Catholic Church's missionary outreach.

SEE ALSO: José de Acosta; Hosokawa Gracia; Saint Ignatius of Loyola; John III; Martin Luther; Paul III; Toyotomi Hideyoshi.

RELATED ARTICLES in *Great Events from History: The Renaissance & Early Modern Era, 1454-1600:* August 15, 1534: Founding of the Jesuit Order; 1549-1552: Father Xavier Introduces Christianity to Japan; 1583-1610: Matteo Ricci Travels to Beijing.

XIAOZONG
Emperor of China (r. 1488-1505)

The ninth emperor of China during the Ming Dynasty, Xiaozong ruled China for seventeen years. He is considered the most benevolent of the Ming emperors and was admired for his honesty, virtue, and frugality, as well as for the reforms he instituted to correct the excesses of the prior emperor.

BORN: July 30, 1470; Beijing, China
DIED: June 8, 1505; Beijing
ALSO KNOWN AS: Hsiao-tsung (temple name, Wade-Giles); Zhu Youtang (personal name, Pinyin); Chu Yu-t'ang (personal name, Wade-Giles); Hongzhi (reign name, Pinyin); Hung-chih (reign name, Wade-Giles)
AREA OF ACHIEVEMENT: Government and politics

EARLY LIFE

Xiaozong (sheeaw-tsung) was born Zhu Youtang in the northern city of Beijing, the capital of China. He was the eldest of three sons of the Emperor Zhu Jianshen (r. 1465-1487 as Xianzong). There is little information about his mother, including her family name. This gap would later indirectly lead to one of the few scandals associated with him. What is known is that she belonged to a minority group (possibly the aboriginal Yao) in Guanxi and that when she was a child, she was captured during a local uprising and brought to Beijing by a court eunuch. She then became a maid in the Forbidden City in charge of a storeroom. Her relationship with Zhu Jianshen was kept secret.

When she became pregnant in 1469, she was swiftly hidden because Empress Guifei, Zhu Jianshen's second wife, was a very jealous and vindictive woman, who, it was widely believed, had been involved in the death of a son whom the emperor had had with another consort. Xiaozong's existence was not acknowledged until June, 1475, when a eunuch finally informed a surprised but pleased Zhu Jianshen, who had been grieving because he did not have an heir, that he in fact had a son. One month after this recognition, Xiaozong's mother died under suspicious circumstances. Months later, on December 5, 1475, Xiaozong was declared heir apparent.

He received a traditional Chinese education, studying the famous Confucian Four Books: Confucius's *Lunyu* (late sixth-early fifth centuries B.C.E.; *The Analects*, 1861), Mencius's *Mengzi* (first transcribed in the early third century B.C.E.; English translation in *The Confucian Classics*, 1861; commonly known as *Mencius*), the *Da Xue* (fifth-first century B.C.E.; *The Great Learning*, 1861), and the *Zhong yong* (written c. 500 B.C.E.; *The Doctrine of the Mean*, 1861), as well as a special work that was compiled for him in 1482 on admirable heirs in Chinese history. These books and the teachings of his first teacher, the scholarly eunuch Tan Ji (T'an Chi), had a major influence on him. Xiaozong especially took seriously the Confucian idea that a ruler must lead by virtue and not by force, for only if one governs by being a proper moral exemplum will the people follow and emulate.

In February of 1487, Zhu Youtang married Zhang Luan (known as Lady Zhang), the daughter of Zhang Luan (Chang Luan), a minor government official. Their relationship was very close, so much so that Zhu was the only monogamous emperor in Chinese history. Zhang Luan bore him three daughters and two sons. On September 17, 1487, at the age of seventeen, on the death of his father, Zhu Youtang became Xiaozong, the ninth Ming emperor.

LIFE'S WORK

The seventeen years of Xiaozong's reign were relatively tranquil, politically stable, and prosperous. Only three significant events disturbed the period. In 1494, China's second biggest river, the Yellow River, changed its direction, breaking dikes and preventing the movement of grain to Beijing. This potential disaster was effectively handled by the famous statesman Liu Daxia, who built a new channel, repaired the dikes, and directed the river into its southern course. Several small-scale rebellions also sporadically occurred throughout his reign in some parts of the country, including one on Heinan island, but these uprisings were all quickly put down. In 1495, the army retook the northeast-central Asian city of Hamil from the Turfan khanate Ahmed, who had captured it from the Chinese in 1488.

Unlike other Ming rulers, Xiaozong displayed little interest in military matters. Ming military power had begun a slow decline since 1449, when Emperor Zhu Qizhen (1427-1464) was captured by Esen, a Mongolian chieftain. By the time of Xiaozong's rule, Chinese military policy was defensive in nature, no attempts were made to gain new territory, and the army was used only to quash rebellions or to protect the country if it was invaded. In the area of foreign relations, Xiaozong continued the Ming policy of xenophobic isolationism, based on the traditional idea that China was the Middle King-

dom of the world, the only real center of world civilization, and all other nations were accordingly inferior.

While Xiaozong was not a great innovator or reformer like the first Ming emperor, Zhu Yuanzhang (r. 1368-1398 as Hongwu), or the third, Zhu Di (r. 1402-1424 as Yonglo), he did received much acclaim during his time for the quick and efficient way in which he dealt with the excesses of his father's reign. During Zhu Jianshen's rule, Empress Guifei—along with her chief eunuch, Liang Fang, and the infamous Wang Zhi, the eunuch in charge of the powerful Beijing secret service—for many years sold high titles, offices, and ranks. This corruption occurred with the tacit approval of Emperor Zhu Jianshen. As a result, many disreputable and incompetent individuals were promoted to high government positions. Soon after Xiaozong assumed office, he corrected this long-standing practice by quickly replacing many of the high officials who had been involved in the matter. He also brought in several honest and highly capable men who had been forced into retirement by his father. Another important change that Xiaozong made was to demote several thousand people who had purchased promotions. These included Tibetan magicians, astrologers, Lama and Daoist priests, and Buddhist monks.

Perhaps the greatest contribution that Xiaozong made was to set an example of governance: Of all the Ming emperors, he is considered to have been the most humane. He was personally honest, very hardworking, and serious about his demanding duties. An example of this dedication occurred in 1498, when he practically begged his senior grand secretary to cancel his daily early-morning audience for one day because the night before a fire in the Forbidden City had kept him awake most of the night.

In addition, Xiaozong was the only Chinese emperor who was monogamous, perhaps in part in reaction to the numerous problems his father had with his wives and concubines. Xiaozong was also a tolerant, even-tempered emperor, widely known for his self-restraint and for his kind treatment of officials, which was rare in a period where many Ming emperors commonly had their officials beaten in the public courtyard when they displeased them and treated their advisers cruelly as a matter of course. He also had a deep interest in the arts, especially calligraphy and painting. Several works survive which are said to have been painted by him.

On the negative side, his reign was slightly tarnished by one scandal, an outgrowth of the early death of his mother and the lack of information about her. Her sudden death when he was five strongly affected him. Tellingly, one of his first acts when he became emperor was to give her the posthumous title of empress-dowager and build a special shrine in honor of her. Xiaozong also put out a search for her family, but nothing was discovered. Because he was the sole survivor of his mother's side, he became protective of his wife's family. As a result, he ignored many of the excesses her two brothers committed.

Overall, Xiaozong's rule was viewed positively by his contemporaries, and several early Chinese historians characterized his early years of reign as a golden period. The famous *Ming shi* (1739; history of the Ming), written by several renowned Chinese historians and edited by Zhang Tingyu, listed Xiaozong as one of only five Ming emperors who deserved mention.

Xiaozong died in 1505, having not quite reached the age of thirty-five. He was succeeded by his son, Zhu Houzhao (r. 1506-1521 as Zhengde). Portraits of Xiaozong show him to have been worn a beard and display a sensitive and reserved countenance.

SIGNIFICANCE

Today, Xiaozong is generally considered to have been a conscientious and capable ruler. Some historians criticize him for his conservative, at times timid and reclusive, nature, which prevented him from properly addressing pressing problems, such as the rising power of the eunuch bureaucracy and the growing economic gap between the classes, which were both slowly weakening the Ming.

Several historians however, including Edward Dreyer, have argued that the greatest contribution of the Ming Dynasty from the period beginning in 1436 was to restore the Confucian state and the social order associated with it, thereby providing the stability that enabled China to withstand the alien rule of the Manchus (Qing) from 1644 to 1911.

The ultimate significance of Xiaozong is that he, more than any other Ming emperor, contributed to this restoration, by best exemplifying the moral qualities that the Chinese philosopher Confucius believed a good ruler needed to possess in order to rule well: personal honesty, self-restraint, a strong sense of propriety, and tolerance.

—*Ronald R. Gray*

FURTHER READING

Dreyer, Edward. *Early Ming China, 1355-1435*. Stanford, Calif.: Stanford University Press, 1982. Although this book is devoted to the early Ming emperors, it provides a good context for understanding Xiaozong's reign.

Fairbank, John K., and Merle Goldman. *China: A New History*. Enlarged ed. Cambridge, Mass.: Harvard University Press, 1998. An overview by the dean of American scholars of China.

Goodrich, L. Carrington, and Chaoying Fang, eds. *Dictionary of Ming Biography*. 2 vols. New York: Columbia University Press, 1976. A good source for information about Xiaozong and the people associated with him.

Mote, Fredrick W. *Imperial China, 900-1800*. Cambridge, Mass.: Harvard University Press, 2000. A useful discussion of the Ming period.

SEE ALSO: Wang Yangming; Zhengde.
RELATED ARTICLE in *Great Events from History: The Renaissance & Early Modern Era, 1454-1600:* 1488: Reign of Xiaozong.

ZARA YAQOB
Emperor of Ethiopia (r. 1434-1468)

With an authoritarian hand, Zara Yaqob instituted religious reform, centralized imperial powers, encouraged Ethiopic literature, and maintained ties with Europe. His life was devoted to the institution of Christianity and the conversion of pagans within his realm.

BORN: 1399; Telq, Ethiopia
DIED: 1468; Aksum, Ethiopia
ALSO KNOWN AS: Zara Yakob; Zara Yakub; Constantine I Zara Yaqob; Constantine I of Ethiopia; Qwastantinos I
AREAS OF ACHIEVEMENT: Government and politics, religion and theology, literature, diplomacy

EARLY LIFE

Ethiopia's greatest medieval emperor, Zara Yaqob (ZAH-rah YAH-kob) was born Constantine I Zara Yaqob (seed of Jacob) to Emperor Dawit I and Empress Egzi Kebra. At the time, bitter upheavals divided Coptic (Egyptian Orthodox) Christianity deeply, to which Ethiopia had adhered since 331. Threatening to shatter the empire, these controversies concerned Old Testament regulations, particularly dietary laws, male circumcision, and, above all, the observance of Sabbath on Saturdays as well as Sundays.

The chief advocate of strict observance, Ewostatewos, had been forced into exile in 1337. Following his 1352 death, his sympathizers were permitted to establish a monastery in Hamasien. Gaining great prestige and many converts throughout northern Ethiopia, they challenged church authorities. Dawit organized a theological debate on the Sabbath question around 1400 and, influenced by followers of Ewostatewos, decreed religious toleration in 1404, a move seen as subversive by many.

Following Dawit's death in 1412, his sons and grandsons succeeded one another in rapid succession. Hence Zara Yaqob's childhood was subjected to much intrigue. A widely revealed prophecy predicted future greatness for him. The resulting jealousy of his brothers, especially Tewodros (r. 1412-1413), led his mother to remove him from the royal court and have him secretly educated in a monastery in the ancient religious and political capital of Aksum. Remaining incognito, he later joined the monastery of Debre Abbi in Shire. This intimate exposure to Christian learning and to Aksum proved highly significant throughout his life.

LIFE'S WORK

On the death of Yetshak, the last of Zara Yaqob's brothers, in 1430, troops were dispatched to search for the hidden prince. Some accounts claim that he was forcibly returned to court and crowned. He later claimed he was an active contender for the Crown and was brought from the royal prison at Amba Gishen on the eve of his accession in 1434.

Ethiopian monarchs were usually crowned at the most important church wherever they were when they came to power. Zara Yaqob, however, reinstated the ancient tradition of being crowned in Aksum, thereby investing the monarchy with the historic city's prestige. Subsequent rulers continued this tradition. He later granted land to Aksum's cathedral, Maryam Seyon (Mary of Zion), where, according to Ethiopian tradition, the Hebraic Ark of the Covenant reposes.

Ethiopia's monarchy had profoundly changed since Aksumite times, when monarchs ruled as feudal lords over loosely controlled provinces where only hints of Christian influence were evident in their courts. Some exceptional early rulers, such as Ezana, Lalibela, and Amda Tseyon, were able to increase their control. By Zara Yaqob's time, emperors had consolidated their power and Christianity had become extremely important. The centralized rule of a single emperor ran parallel to the Christian emphasis on a single god.

Strengthening these trends throughout his thirty-four-year reign, Zara Yaqob expanded the imperial bureaucracy. He frequently appointed daughters or sisters as provincial governors. At one point, his administration was mostly female. Choosing whom his female kin married and which of their male heirs would eventually be governors, he was able to control his realm's provinces for many years to come. In the expanding empire's distant regions, however, newly conquered populations remained barely touched by Christianity. Language differences and the limited education of most clergy rendered priests incapable of effectively transmitting their faith, beyond officiating at routine ceremonies. Ge'ez, the Ethiopian Church's liturgical language, was incomprehensible to most. Pagan practices flourished in this atmosphere, and many Christians consulted pagan priests and evoked magic to ward off evil spirits.

As theologian-emperor, Zara Yaqob energetically pursued a relentless religious agenda with often oppressive results. Not hiding his sympathies, he found Ewostatewos's ideas both personally inspiring and politically convenient at a time when Ethiopia had gone twenty-three years without an *abuna*, its primate or spiritual head. Passionately interested in religious education, he required all churches to establish libraries and all priests to preach on the essentials of the faith. Numerous churches were built, and monastic education was improved. A staunch defender of Orthodoxy, Zara Yaqob introduced dramatic reforms in church practices and policies, including changes in the liturgical cycle. Following a Christmas Day victory over an invading Muslim army greatly outnumbering his own, he decreed that henceforth Christmas would be celebrated every month. Devoted to the Virgin Mary and inspired by reports of her miraculous appearance at Metmaq in Egypt, he ordered all churches to dedicate altars to her and commanded that all thirty-three of her feast days be observed as Sabbaths, regardless of when they fell.

Backed by imperial troops, monks enforced the strict observance of fasts and feasts, including compulsory church attendance on the now two official Sabbaths. Every Christian was to have a priestly confessor whose recommendation was necessary for receiving Holy Communion. Every believer's forehead was to be tattooed with the Trinity, and the sign of the cross was to be affixed to all belongings. Two Egyptian bishops, who arrived in 1438, bolstered these reforms and oversaw the ordination of new priests. To enforce measures regulating clergy behavior, provincial governors were ordered to confiscate the property of disobedient priests.

Zara Yaqob tried to stamp out paganism, mysticism, and mixed forms of Christianity. Offering sacrifices to spirits and using magical prayers were equated with devil worship and became punishable by death. Pagan priests were flogged and their homes burned. The emperor ordered the destruction of all talismans and writings associated with the *tebab*, Ethiopia's esoteric tradition. Based on neo-Pythagorean and Neoplatonic sources, the *tebab* was a body of mystical wisdom, spells, and cures, which ran parallel to alchemy and the Jewish Kabbalah.

Writing numerous works in Ge'ez, Zara Yaqob was part of a literary renaissance that began in the thirteenth century. Freer, more poetic, and richer in description, metaphor, and alliteration than its earlier Aksumite form, Ge'ez flowered in royal chronicles, accounts of the lives of saints, original compositions, and translations from Greek, Arabic, and Latin. Most of the homilies and other religious writings attributed to Zara Yaqob contain admonitions and regulations related to his reforms. In particular, his *Meshafa Berhan* (book of light) expounds on his ideas and attacks paganism and heresies. Many classic works of Ge'ez literature dating from his reign, and influenced by

him, are connected with the veneration of the Theotokos (mother of God). Despite royal opposition, mystical writings also appeared, including the *Lefafa Tsedeq* (decree of righteousness), a scroll containing magical names buried with the dead to aid their entry into heaven.

Zara Yaqob is noted for fostering ties with the Catholic West, whose contacts with Ethiopia date from the 1300's. The appearance of translations from Latin, in particular the *Miracles of the Virgin*, demonstrate his interest in Western Christianity and Europe, which he saw as potential allies against Islam. He allied Ethiopia with Aragon and initiated contacts with Pope Eugenius IV. Hoping to help mend the rift between Catholicism and Orthodoxy, he sent delegates to the Council of Florence (1431-1445) and sponsored a meeting between Orthodox theologians and the Venetian monk Francisco de Branca-Leone. In 1443, his representatives in Cairo protested the persecution of Christians there. Convening a council at Debra Metmaq in 1450, he took a leading role in deciding the Sabbath issue in favor of Ewostatewos's followers, who in turn agreed to be ordained by Egyptian bishops. Venetian Niccolò de' Conti, Spaniard Pero Tafur, and other European visitors believed him to be the legendary ruler Prester John, the object of numerous searches by Christians in the West.

Zara Yaqob's religious reforms were unpopular, even among the staunchly Orthodox. A Western-style Madonna painted by Branca-Leone provoked riots. The monks of Debre Libanos condemned his two-day Sabbath as Judaizing. Saint Takla Hawaryat and other noted church figures opposed his harsh measures. Revealing a hypocritical side, Zara Yaqob feared magic and, though forbidding polygamy, had many wives and concubines. His ruthless punishments led many to conform outwardly to Christianity while continuing pagan practices in secret. His despotism promoted increasing unrest, forcing him to repeatedly dismiss officials after 1450.

Fear of coups, particularly after an attempt to depose him in 1453, and a desire to appear implacably impartial in the enforcement of his decrees led him to execute members of his family, including three of his daughters and one of his empresses. Though his son Be'eda succeeded him on his death in 1468, his favorite empress, Elleni, effectively ruled until her son Lebna Dengel came to power in 1508.

SIGNIFICANCE

Despite his authoritarianism, Zara Yaqob became a popular figure in Ethiopian history. His formidable personality, strengthening of imperial authority, promotion of monasteries, and encouragement of Ethiopic literature all proved to be lasting achievements, even if his attempt to transform Christianity failed. Chroniclers recorded him as a second Solomon.

—*Randall Fegley*

FURTHER READING

Mercier, Jacques. *Art That Heals: The Image as Medicine in Ethiopia*. New York: Prestel Books and the Museum for African Art, 1997. A good work on Ethiopia's esoteric tradition of *tebab*.

Munro-Hay, Stuart. *Aksum*. Edinburgh, Scotland: Edinburgh University Press, 1991. An excellent look at Ethiopia's ancient capital, including much about Zara Yaqob.

Pankhurst, Richard, ed. "Zara Yaqob." In *The Ethiopian Royal Chronicles*. Addis Ababa, Ethiopia: Oxford University Press, 1967. Contemporary accounts of Zara Yaqob's life.

Silverberg, Robert. *The Realm of Prester John*. Athens: Ohio University Press, 1972. A thorough examination of the Prester John legends, including that surrounding Zara Yaqob.

Sumner, Claude. *The Treatise of Zara Yaqob and of Wolde Heywot: An Analysis*. Addis Ababa, Ethiopia: University of Addis Ababa, 1978. Detailed work, with the title below, on Zara Yaqob's writing.

_____. *The Treatise of Zara Yaqob and of Wolde Heywot: Text and Authorship*. Addis Ababa, Ethiopia: University of Addis Ababa, 1976.

SEE ALSO: Pêro da Covilhã.

RELATED ARTICLE in *Great Events from History: The Renaissance & Early Modern Era, 1454-1600*: 1527-1543: Ethiopia's Early Solomonic Period Ends.

ZHENGDE
Emperor of China (r. 1505-1521)

Zhengde's pursuit of pleasure, his reliance on eunuchs as advisors, and his neglect of imperial governance led to an increase in power and prestige of local scholar-officials and a decline of central government authority.

BORN: 1491; China
DIED: 1521; China
ALSO KNOWN AS: Cheng-te (reign name, Wade-Giles); Zhu Houzhao (personal name, Pinyin); Chu Houchao (personal name, Wade-Giles); Wuzong (temple name, Pinyin); Wu-tsung (temple name, Wade-Giles); Yidi (posthumous name, Wade-Giles); I-ti (posthumous name, Pinyin)
AREA OF ACHIEVEMENT: Government and politics

EARLY LIFE

Zhengde (jehng-deh) was born in 1491. His given name was Zhu Houzhao. Zhengde's father, the Ming emperor Xiaozong (Hongzhi, r. 1488-1505), had ascended the Chinese throne in 1488. Having received the traditional Confucian-based education, Xiaozong instituted a number of reforms, including weakening the avaricious ambitions of the many eunuchs who were traditionally in charge of the royal wives and concubines but who too often exerted influence outside the harem, gaining power and wealth beyond their prescribed duties. Xiaozong was the only Ming emperor who was monogamous. His wife, and Zhengde's mother, was Empress Zhang. In addition to Zhengde, Xiaozong fathered one other son and two daughters. Not a strong emperor personally but hardworking and well-meaning, he oversaw a relatively uneventful reign. The same would not be said of his eldest son and heir.

LIFE'S WORK

Xiaozong deeply loved Zhengde but was doubtful about both his son's ability and his dedication to ruling China's vast empire. On the eve of his death in 1505 at the age of thirty-four, Xiaozong advised the high court officials, the Grand Secretaries, to keep close control of the young Zhengde, who was only fourteen when he ascended the throne. Unlike his father, Zhengde had little interest in government and quickly abandoned any Confucian precepts that he had been taught or that his father had so faithfully followed. Court ritual, so important to the Confucian philosophy and practice, held no interest for Zhengde. His teachers were dismissed, as were many of the officials whom his father had instructed to guide the young Zhengde, and he relied instead on many of the palace eunuchs who were more than willing to do the emperor's bidding. Self-indulgent to a fault, Zhengde pursued hunting and horsemanship as well as even the less acceptable pleasures of wine, women, and song.

An attempt was made early in Zhengde's reign to separate the emperor from his corrupt eunuch clique, but it failed, and by 1506, the eunuchs dominated the court and would continue to exert power and control until Zhengde's death fifteen years later. Zhengde's wife was Empress

Xia (who died long after her husband, in 1535), but the royal couple had no children. Unlike his father, however, Zhengde was far from monogamous. Prostitutes were brought to the royal palace and inspected by the emperor, and his guards seized beautiful women for Zhengde's pleasure. Even the concubines of his own military commanders were not above being commandeered by the dissolute emperor. Zhengde frequented Beijing's brothels, and although usually disguised, in reality, his presence was widely known throughout the city and beyond. It was reported that the emperor's fondness for wine was carried to such an extreme that he would remain drunk for days on end. The conservative Confucian officials were appalled, but in the general population Zhengde's foibles and his reputation as a lover and a drinker were better tolerated.

The eunuch who dominated the court was Liu Jin, who was given responsibility for defense of China's Great Wall, China's most famous symbol. Built to protect civilized China from the nomadic barbarians to the north, parts of the wall were originally constructed at least as early as the third century B.C.E. during the reign of China's first emperor, Qin Shi Huangdi, and various portions had been added during subsequent dynasties. The Ming emperors were the greatest builders of the wall, or walls, and work continued on the Great Wall throughout the Ming years (1368-1644).

Liu Jin had many officials and military commanders removed and often persecuted on trumped-up accusations. Even senior generals were not exempt; Yan Yiqing was convicted of embezzlement and imprisoned, and while he was imprisoned, little work was done on the section of the wall for which he was responsible. Zhengde's reign proved disastrous for the integrity of the wall and northern defenses. Some government funds were redirected away from defensive matters to construct the so-called Panther House near Beijing's Forbidden City. A large palace, the Panther House was Zhengde's own private brothel.

Liu Jin was the empire's de facto ruler for several years. To intimidate and destroy any possible opposition, he established a secret intelligence unit, the Net Chang, to ferret out potential foes. Many were tortured and murdered whether such punishments were justified or not. Eventually, after being accused of plotting to kill Zhengde and seize the throne for himself, Liu Jin was executed in 1510, but one vicious favorite was simply replaced by another corrupt courtier, Jiang Bin, who continued to indulge the emperor's appetites.

Zhengde was convinced that he had a talent for military affairs. A rebellion in the province of Ningxia, east of Beijing, in 1510, and an uprising in Sichuan, in China's south, in 1512, sparked the emperor's enthusiasm for combat. He organized eunuchs as troops and personally trained them, and he adopted more than one hundred young officers as his sons. Zhengde ordered new uniforms for his commanders, and it became fashionable to wear military costumes at court. From 1517 to 1519, the emperor pursued his military endeavors in the north, along the Great Wall, where he claimed he had personally killed and beheaded a barbarian. In 1520, after hearing of still another rebellion, Zhengde journeyed south, traveling with a large entourage along the Grand Canal. The expense was considerable, but those who objected were flogged and beaten, and many died of their injuries. After reaching the city of Nanjing, one account reports, Zhengde ordered the inhabitants to refrain from raising hogs because in Chinese, "hog" was similar to the emperor's family name of Zhu.

More significant for China's future, the emperor while in Nanjing gave an audience to a Portuguese naval officer, Tomé Pires. The Portuguese had first arrived in China in 1514, landing in Guangdong Province in the far south. They returned in 1517 with eight warships and a letter from the king of Portugal. After numerous delays and undoubtedly resorting to bribes, in 1520, Pires was able to converse with the emperor. It was even claimed that Pires taught Zhengde some Portuguese, a most unlikely occurrence. Shortly after Zhengde's death, war broke out between the Chinese and the Portuguese, but ultimately a later Chinese government leased the island of Macao to Portugal. This was the beginning of Western relations with China, relations that often boded ill for China in the centuries to come.

In 1521, after leaving Nanjing, the emperor was fishing when his boat accidentally sank at Qingjiangpu. Zhengde survived, but he soon became ill, and he died three months later.

SIGNIFICANCE

Zhengde was not the worst emperor in China's long history, but by every measurement his reign was a failure. His alienation of his Confucian advisors and his willingness to grant power and prestige to the court eunuchs brought the regime into disrepute, particularly among the traditional scholar-gentry class, which was so important to the stability of any imperial regime. With the central government's authority weakened, the local gentry class added to their lands and evaded taxes, thus worsening the plight of the peasants.

Only a strong imperial government had the ability to cope with the ever-threatening invasions from northern nomads and from regional uprisings. The Ming Dynasty lasted another century before it fell to the non-Chinese Manchus (Qing Dynasty), but the seeds of the Ming decline are reflected in Zhengde's years of rule.

Because of his amorous adventures and his dissolute life, however, Zhengde has remained notorious for his exploits and continues to be a popular character in Asian movies and television shows—vice always being a more attractive subject than virtue.

—*Eugene Larson*

FURTHER READING

Ebrey, Patricia Buckley. *Cambridge Illustrated History of China*. New York: Cambridge University Press, 1996. Good coverage of the Ming period.
Paludan, Ann. *Chronicle of the Chinese Emperors*. New York: Thames and Hudson, 1998. A reign-by-reign account of all the Chinese emperors from the Qin through the Qing, including a discussion of Zhengde.
Roberts, J. A. G. *A History of China*. Vol. 1. London: Alan Sutton, 1996. Includes a chapter on Ming China and references to Zhengde.
Twitchett, Denis, and John. K. Fairbank. *The Cambridge History of China*. New York: Cambridge University Press, 1978. The major work of scholarship on Chinese history. Volumes 7 and 8 focus on the Ming Dynasty, including the era of the reign of Zhengde.
Waldron, Arthur. *The Great Wall of China: From History to Myth*. New York: Cambridge University Press, 1990. The standard account of the Great Wall, including a considerable discussion of the Ming era.

SEE ALSO: Wang Yangming; Xiaozong.
RELATED ARTICLE in *Great Events from History: The Renaissance & Early Modern Era, 1454-1600:* 1505-1521: Reign of Zhengde and Liu Jin.

HULDRYCH ZWINGLI
Swiss theologian and church reformer

Zwingli led the Swiss Reformation against Roman Catholic ecclesiastical abuses and shared the rhetoric and theology of Martin Luther, but the two disagreed over the nature of the Eucharist. Overshadowed by both Luther and John Calvin, Zwingli's most lasting contribution is his incipient Reformed theology and his recognition of the role that secular government might play in ecclesiastical matters.

BORN: January 1, 1484; Wildhaus, Swiss Confederation (now in Switzerland)
DIED: October 11, 1531; near Kappel, Swiss Confederation (now in Switzerland)
ALSO KNOWN AS: Ulrich Zwingli; Master Ulrich
AREAS OF ACHIEVEMENT: Church reform, religion and theology, government and politics

EARLY LIFE

Huldrych Zwingli (HOOL-drihk TSVING-lee) was born to wealthy, devout parents. Zwingli's father served as a village magistrate and sought early to train his son in the ways of his Catholic faith—a Catholic faith invigorated by the new Humanism, which recognized and bestowed on humankind more human responsibility and involvement in divine affairs. His father earnestly desired that Zwingli be educated as a priest and sent the boy at age ten to a Latin school in Basel, where he excelled in grammar, music, and dialectics.

In 1498, Zwingli entered college study at Berne, where he came under the tutelage of Heinrich Wölflin, an influential Humanist scholar, who planted the initial seeds of intellectual independence in Zwingli. At Berne, Zwingli, at the time called Ulrich, distinguished himself as a musician and singer and was urged by the Dominican Order in Berne to join their choir and study music further. Zwingli initially accepted their invitation but abruptly withdrew. He chose instead to continue his theological education and entered in 1500 the University of Vienna, where he spent two years studying Scholastic philosophy, astronomy, and physics.

In 1502, Zwingli returned to the University of Basel, where he continued his classical studies while teaching Latin in the school of Saint Martin. He completed his bachelor's degree in 1504 and his master of arts degree in 1506 and became known officially as Master Ulrich. At Basel, he became friends with Leo Jud, who would later become a chief associate in the Reformation efforts in Zurich. Both studied under the famous Thomas Wyttenbach, professor of theology at Basel, whom Zwingli credits with opening his eyes to evils and abuses of the contemporary Church, especially its trafficking in indulgences—the sale of divine favors, such as forgiveness of or license to sin, or immediate entrance into heaven on death.

Zwingli was ordained in the priesthood by the bishop of Constance in 1506 and appointed pastor of Glarus, the capital city of the canton of the same name. Zwingli spent ten years in Glarus, occupied by preaching and pastoral duties as well as continuing to advance his knowledge of biblical languages, Greek and Roman philosophy, and the church fathers. Unlike Martin Luther, Zwingli did not in this fallow period seek a doctor of divinity degree, content with work in local pastorates and aiming at no higher church office. In the spring of 1515, Zwingli met the great Humanist scholar Desiderius Erasmus, whose writings he had been studying, and was deeply impressed by both his learning and his moderate theological views on inherited sin and his emerging symbolic reinterpretation of the Lord's Supper. Both Wyttenbach and Erasmus had helped remove the theological naïveté from Zwingli, infusing the spirit of Humanism into his own understanding and response to traditional Catholic teaching and a spirit of skepticism in his relationship with the Church hierarchy.

During this time, Zwingli also served as chaplain to the Glarus mercenaries who served the pope—devout men who he believed were being exploited by an illegitimate foreign power. This experience fueled his Swiss patriotism and compelled him to oppose publicly the mercenary system itself so vociferously that he was forced out of his pastorate in 1516. He subsequently moved to Einsiedeln, where he served as parish priest for three years, continuing his inquiry into the Greek New Testament and the church fathers. There Zwingli crystallized his views on salvation by faith, memorizing the New Testament letters of the apostle Paul and meshing his patriotic fervor with Erasmus's radical pacifism to take both a theological and a political stance against Rome. In his preaching, Zwingli began to oppose the use of relics in worship and pilgrimages to holy shrines as acts of devotion, regarding them as needless and idolatrous concessions to a religion that had left its eternal moorings.

LIFE'S WORK

Zwingli thus emerged from his early adult life as a clergyman emancipated from blind trust in the wisdom and infallibility of the Church hierarchy and its magisterium—the accumulated body of interpretation of Scripture used as an authority in disputes over the meaning of the Bible. In his slow but inexorable independence from established Christendom, he began to place great value on his classical learning and great emphasis on the need for individuals to exercise their faith in God directly—without the help of intermediaries such as relics and images, priests, and departed saints. This intellectual ferment prepared him for the greatest task of his life: the reformation of Swiss Catholicism.

In the biographies of all the activists within the

Huldrych Zwingli. (Library of Congress)

Protestant Reformation, the most important aspects of their lives rest as much on their intellectual efforts as on their dramatic deeds. This is the case with Zwingli, although his willingness to engage in armed warfare on behalf of his faith distinguishes him from some of his fellows. Nevertheless, Zwingli is most prominent for his contribution to the theological ferment of his times as well as to the realignments and associations forged in his native land of Switzerland and his adopted city, Zurich. As Luther had Wittenberg and Calvin had Geneva, so Zwingli had Zurich, a city in which his great ideals would find incarnation not only in its cathedrals but also in its government structures. His beliefs eventually led him into local and canton politics, as he sought to move the secular city and the city of God into a more symbiotic, merciful status with each other.

In 1518, Zwingli was nominated for the position of people's priest at the Great Minister Church in Zurich, a prestigious and powerful pastorate. His candidacy was at first opposed in view of Zwingli's admittedly broken vow of celibacy; a friend intervened, however, and Zwingli assumed his new post on January 1, 1519. His early sermons were practical and ethical rather than doctrinal and divisive. From an unassuming beginning, Zwingli's pulpit became famous and extremely popular in Zurich; his down-to-earth expositions of biblical texts—as opposed to the dense, allegorical sermons common to the time—opened up the Scriptures to his flock and made Christianity seem present and vital rather than otherworldly and detached. This fresh emphasis on the Bible as an authoritative document that could speak directly to the hearts of people became the scaffolding for the Reformation everywhere, including Switzerland.

As Luther's reform movement began to shake the Church in Germany, Zwingli could not help but take notice. The war over indulgences that Luther had valiantly won in the German church became only a minor skirmish in Zurich, as the Roman church moved quickly to rectify abuses in Switzerland in an effort to stall the wholesale revolution it feared. Zwingli would engage the war on a different front: the authority of the Bible against the authority of the papal hierarchy. Zwingli's active involvement in the reform movement may well be located in August, 1519, when a plague broke out in Zurich and swept away one-third of the population and nearly took Zwingli's life. His experience in ministry to the sick and bereaved brought him renewed faith in God and emboldened him to speak out about the responsibility of the Church to offer grace, not law, to its members. Zwingli suggested that this would be accomplished by restoring Scripture to its rightful place in the authority of the Church and by dismantling the elaborate liturgy of the Mass, replacing it with a more homely and accessible kind of personal worship that would focus on God, not humans.

Zwingli also began to see the civil government as an ally in his reform effort. Actively campaigning in the city council, Zwingli persuaded its members to take action against preaching in Zurich that was not centered on the Bible. In December, 1520, the council ordered the priests in the city and country to preach only from the Bible—the first time a secular authority had intervened in the affairs of the Church. Zwingli himself was elected to the council in 1521, and, within a month, the council repudiated its citizens' participation in the mercenary system he had long opposed. Renouncing his papal salary, Zwingli parlayed his alliance with local government into greater dominion and influence, as his pulpit became a sharp weapon against Rome. During the season of Lent in 1522, Zwingli openly called for his parishioners to ignore prohibitions against eating meat and to practice their liberty. In addition, he called for the end of forced celibacy for clergy, having entered the same year into a secret marriage himself with Anna Reinhard, a widow with three children.

These radical demands brought on direct opposition from Rome, and the civil authorities called for two public debates on the matter. Threatened with assassination, Zwingli defended his stance vigorously both in public and

in print. His *Artikel* (1523; *Luther's and Zwingli's Propositions for Debate*, 1963)—parallel to the famous Ninety-five Theses that Luther nailed to the Wittenberg Cathedral door—boldly repudiated papal authority, forced celibacy, the veneration of the saints, the transubstantiation view of the Eucharist, the existence of purgatory, and the necessity of fasting. In January, 1523, the Council of Zurich declared Zwingli the victor in the disputation, and Zurich became a firm canton of the Reformation.

Most of Zwingli's writings were born of conflict, including his *De vera et falsa religione commentarius* (*Commentary on True and False Religion*, 1929), published in 1525, which may be regarded as the first Protestant systematic theology—a thoroughgoing treatise explaining the Protestant view of key doctrines such as salvation, the nature of Christ, the authority of the Scriptures, and the role of the church. With his co-Reformer, Leo Jud, he also translated the Scriptures into German-Swiss as the Swiss reform quickly spread to other German and Italian cantons. Zwingli's radical departure from received Catholic doctrine reached its zenith in 1525. Preceding it were months of organized purges of pictures, crucifixes, altars, candles, and any other images from the churches of the city—all on the principle that the Second Commandment forbade the making of any artistic image of God or Christ as idolatry. Then, during Holy Week of April, 1525, Zwingli formally displaced the traditional Catholic Mass with the first great Reformed communion service in the Great Minister Church, the bread and the wine celebrated as representations and not the "real presence" of Christ.

The reformation of Zwingli's Zurich was substantially complete by 1525, as both secular and ecclesiastical institutions united in iconoclastic spirit to create a uniquely Swiss Protestant church. Yet the controversy over the roles of each institution in the lives of Christians continued from a right flank, as a group of Reformers known as the Anabaptists, or re-baptizers, began to oppose Zwingli's accommodations with Rome and the council. A split had occurred in 1523 during an intense debate over the Zurich city council's refusal to bring about certain religious changes called for by Anabaptist theologians. Zwingli's view that the civil authorities should be persuaded by patient preaching rather than violent social action differed from the even more radical Anabaptists, who believed that Scripture alone—not the wisdom or political machinations of a secular government—should determine the course of the Reformation.

Over two years, the gap widened, as the Anabaptists pressed their opposition to the baptism of infants and to any jurisdiction of the civil government in their church life. In spring, 1525, a complete rupture occurred when the Zurich city council, led by Zwingli, forbade the Anabaptists to assemble or to disseminate their views. Those who refused the order were tortured, incarcerated, and, in a few prominent instances, put to death by drowning. There is no indication that Zwingli opposed the latter.

From 1526 to 1531, the Reformation spread to other cantons, and intolerance of opposing views accompanied it as Protestant Switzerland was internally beset by both military and theological challenges from Rome and by doctrinal challenges from Lutheran comrades in the Reformation. In October, 1529, the Colloquy of Marburg occurred, bringing together Zwingli and Luther, and their colleagues, to reconcile their differing views on the Lord's Supper. Zwingli held firmly to his view that the transubstantiation taking place at the Lord's Supper was not in the bread and wine but in the living saints who are gathered in the congregation to celebrate it. Unable to find common ground, the Reformers and their followers went their separate ways.

Meanwhile, tensions continued to build between those cantons that had joined the Reformation, notably Basel, Berne, and Zurich, and those that remained staunchly Catholic. In 1529, a modest peace had been negotiated at Kappel that would allow for mutual toleration and the freedom of a canton to be either Catholic or Protestant. By 1531, relationships had again deteriorated as a Catholic alliance, fearing the eventual domination of Protestant Christianity over them, launched a virtual civil war, an offensive designed to bring them final relief from their aggressors. In October 9, 1531, a Catholic militia, aided by papal mercenaries, marched to the borders of Zurich at Kappel, which was unprepared. Zwingli, who had warned the city council of the impending danger that the Catholic cantons presented, accompanied the small army gathered for defense and was himself killed. His body was recovered by the victorious Catholic militia and then quartered for treason and burnt for heresy, his ashes scattered to the winds. Zwingli's mantle of leadership then fell on Heinrich Bullinger, a friend of John Calvin, who continued to fight for Zwingli's theological and political principles.

SIGNIFICANCE

Zwingli's legacy to history takes the form of his unique contribution to Protestantism, particularly his dissenting views on the Lord's Supper and the proper relationship between the church and civil authority. Zwingli had much in common with Luther and Calvin, particularly with their high view of Scriptural authority and their op-

position to the legalistic theology of salvation commonly preached by contemporary Roman Catholic clerics. The Reformers, however, parted company significantly in their views of the church, the nature of the Lord's Supper, and the relationship between the church and civil authority. While Lutheran and Calvinistic Protestantism emphasized the church's responsibility to preach the Word and its authority to administer the Sacraments, Zwingli understood the church less as an institution than as a relationship called into being by Christ, a relationship resting on the loyalty of the members of a local body of Christ to one another. What binds them together in his view is not hierarchical authority but commitment to the Bible as sole spiritual authority and to one another as functioning members of the body of Christ. Thus, Zwingli promoted the Lord's Supper as an activity to unite the church in recognition of a common calling, not as a reenactment of the death of Christ proffered by an authoritative church hierarchy.

Zwingli thus emerges from the sixteenth century as a much more modern, even liberal, theologian when compared with Luther and Calvin. His advocacy of an activist role in church matters by a godly civil state sets him apart from his fellow Protestants in Germany, France, and Britain, who bitterly opposed secular intrusion into their theological and ecclesiastical dealings. Believing that God ordained the civil government as a coequal community with the church to provide peace and order so that Christians could minister grace and salvation to the world, Zwingli offered a compromise position that established the kingdom of God in the politics of humankind. Despite the flaws of intolerance that crept into his own social and theological practice in times of tension, Zwingli's beliefs serve as a precursor to much liberation theology of the late twentieth and early twenty-first centuries and certainly foreshadow the Civil Rights movement headed by Martin Luther King, Jr., in the United States of the 1950's, 1960's, and 1970's.

—*Bruce L. Edwards*

FURTHER READING

Bromiley, Geoffrey W., ed. *Zwingli and Bullinger.* Philadelphia: Westminster Press, 1953. Contains selected texts of Zwingli—and his successor Bullinger—translated into English with a good, short introduction to Zwingli's life, writings, and Reformed theology. This is the most accessible English source for Zwingli's primary texts.

Davies, Rupert E. *The Problem of Authority in the Continental Reformers: A Study in Luther, Zwingli, and Calvin.* Westport, Conn.: Greenwood Press, 1978. This monograph has a single focus: How did the Reformers resolve issues of religious authority in their efforts to reform Roman Christianity? Davies documents with admirable clarity—in a lengthy chapter devoted entirely to Zwingli—Zwingli's attempt to place biblical authority at the center of the Reformation, while recognizing a proper sphere for ecclesiastical authority within the life of an individual Christian. The author's comparative study of the three Reformers illuminates the answers of each to this vexing question.

Elton, G. R. *Reformation Europe, 1517-1559.* 2d ed. Malden, Mass.: Blackwell, 1999. Places Zwingli and the Swiss Reformation within the context of the larger movement throughout Europe. Includes maps, bibliographic references, and index.

Farner, Oskar. *Zwingli the Reformer: His Life and Work.* Translated by D. G. Sear. New York: Philosophical Library, 1952. A brief, very readable overview of the life, times, and theology of Zwingli by the most prominent German scholar of Zwingli in the twentieth century. Farner's main intention is to acquaint the general reader with the broad outlines of Zwingli's thought.

Furcha, E. J., and H. Wayne Pipkin, eds. *Prophet, Pastor, Protestant: The World of Huldrych Zwingli After Five Hundred Years.* Pittsburgh, Pa: Pickwick, 1984. An anthology of essays by ten prominent, contemporary Zwingli scholars, who have evaluated the historical impact of his Reformation efforts on Church history. A compendium of wise scholarship on various aspects of his political and theological thought, valuable for its corrective reassessment of earlier Zwingli scholarship.

Garside, Charles, Jr. *Zwingli and the Arts.* New Haven, Conn.: Yale University Press, 1966. A unique work of Zwingli scholarship that attempts to assess the nature and impact of his views of art and creativity on sixteenth century Christian worship, particularly in the visual and musical arts. Skillfully juxtaposing Zwingli's views to those of Calvin and Luther, Garside reveals Zwingli's austere devotion to an "invisible" God who could not and should not be represented in art.

Gordon, Bruce. *The Swiss Reformation.* New York: Manchester University Press, 2002. A comprehensive study of the distinctive features of the Swiss Reformation in comparison to other national reformations. Emphasizes Zwingli's role in the movement, as well as the influences of the unique political structure of the Swiss Confederation, of Switzerland's distinctive theology, and of mercantilism. Includes maps, bibliographic references, and index.

Lindberg, Carter. *The European Reformations.* Cambridge, Mass.: Blackwell, 1996. Compares Zwingli's work in Zurich to Reformation movements in other cultural centers. Includes illustrations, maps, bibliographic references, and index.

Potter, G. R. *Zwingli.* Cambridge, England: Cambridge University Press, 1976. This volume is the standard scholarly work on Zwingli, breathtaking in its scope and coverage of his personality, theology, and politics. Its author sets a high standard for readable scholarly biography in this work, which should be the first volume consulted for serious inquiry into Zwingli's impact on Swiss culture and European Church history.

Rilliet, Jean. *Zwingli: Third Man of the Reformation.* Translated by Harold Knight. Philadelphia: Westminster Press, 1964. Regards Zwingli as the least known and appreciated of the three famous reformers. Rilliet highlights both the unique emphases and truths Zwingli discovered and the errors he unwittingly promoted. The book's chief value lies in its extensive treatment of the Eucharistic controversy and of Zwingli's denial of the common Catholic and Lutheran understanding of transubstantiation.

Schaff, Philip. *The Swiss Reformation.* Vol. 8 in *History of the Christian Church.* 3d ed. Peabody, Mass.: Hendrickson, 1996. This volume focuses entirely on the Swiss Reformation and Zwingli's dominant contribution to it. The main advantage of Schaff's text, as an earlier—and formerly standard—Church history, is that it presents with its wider angle a holistic, comprehensive overview of Church history through the centuries and labors to present a less-provincial treatment of the isues raised by the Swiss version of the Reformation.

Walton, Robert C. *Zwingli's Theocracy.* Toronto, Canada: University of Toronto Press, 1967. This work helpfully clarifies a long-standing controversy regarding Zwingli's conception of the role and relationship of the clergy and royalty in the governance of a Christian state. Walton argues that, when one attends to Zwingli's later writings in comparison with his more often quoted, better-known earlier works, one finds that Zwingli did not, in fact, advocate a "theocracy" but rather a state in which authority is shared in a cooperative government operated by both sacred and secular officials.

SEE ALSO: Martin Bucer; John Calvin; Thomas Cranmer; Desiderius Erasmus; Conrad Gesner; Balthasar Hubmaier; Martin Luther; Philipp Melanchthon; Menno Simons; Philip the Magnanimous; Michael Servetus.

RELATED ARTICLES in *Great Events from History: The Renaissance & Early Modern Era, 1454-1600:* September 13-14, 1515: Battle of Marignano; March, 1536: Calvin Publishes *Institutes of the Christian Religion.*

Appendices

RULERS AND DYNASTIES

Major world leaders during and beyond the period covered in *Great Lives from History: Renaissance & Early Modern Era, 1454-1600* are listed below, beginning with the Roman Catholic popes and followed by rulers of major nations or dynasties, alphabetically by country. Within each country section, rulers are listed chronologically. It is important to note that name spellings and regnal dates vary among sources, and that variations do not necessarily suggest inaccuracy. For example, dates when leaders took power may not match dates of coronation, and the names by which leaders have been recorded in history may represent given names, epithets, or regnal names. Date ranges and geographical borders of nations and dynasties vary, given the complexities of politics and warfare, and the mere fact that "nations" (a concept just beginning to be defined during the early modern era) evolved over time from competing and allied principalities, particularly in the post-Roman Empire millennium conventionally called the "Middle" Ages. Hence, not every civilization, dynasty, principality, or region can be covered here; we have, however, attempted to provide lists of those rulers for those countries most likely to be studied in general and area history courses.

CONTENTS

POPES AND ANTIPOPES

Asterisked (*) names indicate popes who have been sainted by the Church. Names appearing in square brackets [ ] are antipopes.

Term	Pope
440-461	*Leo I the Great
461-468	*Hilarius
468-483	*Simplicius
483-492	*Felix III
492-496	*Gelasius I
496-498	Anastasius II
498-514	*Symmachus
498-505	[Laurentius]
514-523	*Hormisdas
523-526	*John I
526-530	*Felix IV
530-532	Boniface II
530	[Dioscursus]
533-535	John II
535-536	*Agapetus I
536-537	*Silverius
537-555	Vigilius
556-561	Pelagius I
561-574	John III
575-579	Benedict I
579-590	Pelagius II

Term	Pope	Term	Pope
590-604	*Gregory I the Great	884-885	*Adrian III
604-606	Sabinian	885-891	Stephen V
607	Boniface III	891-896	Formosus
608-615	*Boniface IV (Adeodatus I)	896	Boniface VI
615-618	*Deusdedit	896-897	Stephen VI
619-625	Boniface V	897	Romanus
625-638	Honorius I	897	Theodore II
638-640	Vacant	898-900	John IX
640	Severinus	900-903	Benedict IV
640-642	John IV	903	Leo V
642-649	Theodore I	903-904	Christopher
649-655	*Martin I	904-911	Sergius III
655-657	*Eugene I	911-913	Anastasius III
657-672	*Vitalian	913-914	Lando
672-676	Adeodatus II	914-928	John X
676-678	Donus	928	Leo VI
678-681	*Agatho	929-931	Stephen VII
682-683	*Leo II	931-935	John XI
684-685	*Benedict II	936-939	Leo VII
685-686	John V	939-942	Stephen IX (VIII)
686-687	Conon	942-946	Marinus II
687	[Theodore II]	946-955	Agapetus II
687-692	[Paschal I]	955-963	John XII
687-701	*Saint Sergius I	963-964	Leo VIII
701-705	John VI	964	Benedict V
705-707	John VII	965-972	John XIII
708	Sisinnius	973-974	Benedict VI
708-715	Constantine	974-983	Benedict VII
715-731	*Gregory II	983-984	John XIV
731-741	*Gregory III	983-984	Boniface VII
741-752	*Zachary	985-996	John XV
752-757	Stephen II	996-999	Gregory V
757-767	*Paul I	996-998	[John XVI]
767	[Constantine]	999-1003	Sylvester II
767	[Philip]	1003	John XVII
767-772	Stephen III	1003-1009	John XVIII
772-795	Adrian I	1009-1012	Sergius IV
795-816	*Leo III	1012-1024	Benedict VIII
816-817	Stephen IV	1012	[Gregory VI]
817-824	*Paschal I	1024-1033	John XIX
824-827	Eugene II	1033-1045	Benedict IX
827	Valentine	1045	Sylvester III
827-844	Gregory IV	1045-1046	Gregory VI (John Gratian Pierleoni)
844	[John VIII]	1046-1047	Clement II (Suitgar, count of Morslegen)
844-847	Sergius II	1048	Damasus II (Count Poppo)
847-855	*Leo IV	1049-1054	*Leo IX (Bruno of Egisheim)
855-858	Benedict III	1055-1057	Victor II (Gebhard, count of Hirschberg)
855	[Anastasius III]	1057-1058	Stephen IX (Frederick of Lorraine)
858-867	*Nicholas I the Great	1058	Benedict X (John, count of Tusculum)
867-872	Adrian II	1058-1061	Nicholas II (Gerhard of Burgundy)
872-882	John VIII	1061-1073	Alexander II (Anselmo da Baggio)
882-884	Marinus I	1061-1064	[Honorius II]

Term	Pope
1073-1085	*Gregory VII (Hildebrand)
1080-1100	[Clement III]
1086-1087	Victor III (Desiderius, prince of Beneventum)
1088-1099	Urban II (Odo of Lagery)
1099-1118	Paschal II (Ranieri da Bieda)
1100-1102	[Theodoric]
1102	[Albert]
1105	[Sylvester IV]
1118-1119	Gelasius II (John Coniolo)
1118-1121	[Gregory VIII]
1119-1124	Callixtus II (Guido, count of Burgundy)
1124-1130	Honorius II (Lamberto dei Fagnani)
1124-1130	[Celestine II]
1130-1143	Innocent II (Gregorio Papareschi)
1130-1138	[Anacletus II (Cardinal Pierleone)]
1138	[Victor IV]
1143-1144	Celestine II (Guido di Castello)
1144-1145	Lucius II (Gherardo Caccianemici)
1145-1153	Eugene III (Bernardo Paganelli)
1153-1154	Anastasius IV (Corrado della Subarra)
1154-1159	Adrian IV (Nicolas Breakspear)
1159-1181	Alexander III (Roland Bandinelli)
1159-1164	[Victor IV]
1164-1168	[Paschal III]
1168-1178	[Calixtus III]
1179-1180	[Innocent III (Lando da Sessa)]
1181-1185	Lucius III (Ubaldo Allucingoli)
1185-1187	Urban III (Uberto Crivelli)
1187	Gregory VIII (Alberto del Morra)
1187-1191	Clement III (Paolo Scolari)
1191-1198	Celestine III (Giacinto Boboni-Orsini)
1198-1216	Innocent III (Lothario of Segni)
1216-1227	Honorius III (Cencio Savelli)
1227-1241	Gregory IX (Ugo of Segni)
1241	Celestine IV (Goffredo Castiglione)
1243-1254	Innocent IV (Sinibaldo Fieschi)
1254-1261	Alexander IV (Rinaldo di Segni)
1261-1264	Urban IV (Jacques Pantaléon)
1265-1268	Clement IV (Guy le Gros Foulques)
1268-1271	Vacant
1271-1276	Gregory X (Tebaldo Visconti)
1276	Innocent V (Pierre de Champagni)
1276	Adrian V (Ottobono Fieschi)
1276-1277	John XXI (Pietro Rebuli-Giuliani)
1277-1280	Nicholas III (Giovanni Gaetano Orsini)
1281-1285	Martin IV (Simon Mompitie)
1285-1287	Honorius IV (Giacomo Savelli)
1288-1292	Nicholas IV (Girolamo Masci)
1294	*Celestine V (Pietro Angelari da Murrone)
1294-1303	Boniface VIII (Benedict Caetani)
1303-1304	Benedict XI (Niccolò Boccasini)
1305-1314	Clement V (Raimond Bertrand de Got)

Term	Pope
1316-1334	John XXII (Jacques Duèse)
1328-1330	[Nicholas V (Pietro di Corbara)]
1334-1342	Benedict XII (Jacques Fournier)
1342-1352	Clement VI (Pierre Roger de Beaufort)
1352-1362	Innocent VI (Étienne Aubert)
1362-1370	Urban V (Guillaume de Grimord)
1370-1378	Gregory XI (Pierre Roger de Beaufort, the Younger)
1378-1389	Urban VI (Bartolomeo Prignano)
1378-1394	[Clement VII (Robert of Geneva)]
1389-1404	Boniface IX (Pietro Tomacelli)
1394-1423	[Benedict XIII (Pedro de Luna)]
1404-1406	Innocent VII (Cosmto de' Migliorati)
1406-1415	Gregory XII (Angelo Correr)
1409-1410	[Alexander V (Petros Philargi)]
1410-1415	[John XXIII (Baldassare Cossa)]
1415-1417	Vacant
1417-1431	Martin V (Ottone Colonna)
1423-1429	[Clement VIII]
1424	[Benedict XIV]
1431-1447	Eugene IV (Gabriele Condulmero)
1439-1449	[Felix V (Amadeus of Savoy)]
1447-1455	Nicholas V (Tommaso Parentucelli)
1455-1458	Calixtus III (Alfonso de Borgia)
1458-1464	Pius II (Enea Silvio Piccolomini)
1464-1471	Paul II (Pietro Barbo)
1471-1484	Sixtus IV (Francesco della Rovere)
1484-1492	Innocent VIII (Giovanni Battista Cibò)
1492-1503	Alexander VI (Rodrigo Borgia)
1503	Pius III (Francesco Todeschini Piccolomini)
1503-1513	Julius II (Giuliano della Rovere)
1513-1521	Leo X (Giovanni de' Medici)
1522-1523	Adrian VI (Adrian Florensz Boeyens)
1523-1534	Clement VII (Giulio de' Medici)
1534-1549	Paul III (Alessandro Farnese)
1550-1555	Julius III (Giovanni Maria Ciocchi del Monte)
1555	Marcellus II (Marcello Cervini)
1555-1559	Paul IV (Gian Pietro Carafa)
1559-1565	Pius IV (Giovanni Angelo de' Medici)
1566-1572	Pius V (Antonio Ghislieri)
1572-1585	Gregory XIII (Ugo Buoncompagni)
1585-1590	Sixtus V (Felice Peretti)
1590	Urban VII (Giambattista Castagna)
1590-1591	Gregory XIV (Niccolò Sfondrato)
1591	Innocent IX (Giovanni Antonio Facchinetti)
1592-1605	Clement VIII (Ippolito Aldobrandini)
1605	Leo XI (Alessandro de' Medici)
1605-1621	Paul V (Camillo Borghese)
1621-1623	Gregory XV (Alessandro Ludovisi)
1623-1644	Urban VIII (Maffeo Barberini)
1644-1655	Innocent X (Giovanni Battista Pamphili)
1655-1667	Alexander VII (Fabio Chigi)

Term	Pope
1667-1669	Clement IX (Giulio Rospigliosi)
1670-1676	Clement X (Emilio Altieri)
1676-1689	Innocent XI (Benedetto Odescalchi)
1689-1691	Alexander VIII (Pietro Ottoboni)
1691-1700	Innocent XII (Antonio Pignatelli)
1700-1721	Clement XI (Giovanni Francesco Albani)
1721-1724	Innocent XIII (Michelangelo Conti)
1724-1730	Benedict XIII (Pierfrancesco Orsini)
1730-1740	Clement XII (Lorenzo Corsini)
1740-1758	Benedict XIV (Prospero Lambertini)
1758-1769	Clement XIII (Carlo Rezzonico)
1769-1774	Clement XIV (Giovanni Ganganelli)
1775-1799	Pius VI (Giovanni Angelo Braschi)
1800-1823	Pius VII (Barnaba Gregorio Chiaramonti)
1823-1829	Leo XII (Annibale della Genga)
1829-1830	Pius VIII (Francesco Saverio Castiglioni)
1831-1846	Gregory XVI (Bartolomeo Cappellari)
1846-1878	Pius IX (Giovanni Mastai-Ferretti)
1878-1903	Leo XIII (Gioacchino Pecci)
1903-1914	Pius X (Giuseppe Sarto)
1914-1922	Benedict XV (Giacomo della Chiesa)
1922-1939	Pius XI (Achille Ratti)
1939-1958	Pius XII (Eugenio Pacelli)
1958-1963	John XXIII (Angelo Roncalli)
1963-1978	Paul VI (Giovanni Battista Montini)
1978	John Paul I (Albino Luciani)
1978-	John Paul II (Karol Wojtyla)

AFRICA. *See also* EGYPT

BENIN

Reign	Ruler
1200-1235	Eweke I
1235-1243	Uwakhuanhen
1243-1255	Ehenmihen
1255-1280	Ewedo
1280-1295	Oguola
1295-1299	Edoni
1299-1334	Udagbedo
1334-1370	Ohen
1370-1400	Egbeka
1400-1430	Orobiru
1430-1440	Uwaifiokun
c. 1440-1473	Ewuare the Great
1473	Ezoti (14 days)
1473-1480	Olua
1481-1504	Ozolua
c. 1504-1550	Esigie
1550-1578	Orhogbua
1578-1606	Ehengbuda
1606-1641	Ohuan

Reign	Ruler
1641-1661	Ahenzae
1661-1669	Ahenzae
1669-1675	Akengboi
1675-1684	Akenkpaye
1684-1689	Akengbedo
1689-1700	Oroghene
1700-1712	Ewuakpe
1712-1713	Ozuaere
1713-1735	Akenzua I
1735-1750	Eresonyen
1750-1804	Akengbuda
1804-1816	Obanosa

ETHIOPIA

The evidence for the succession of Ethiopian rulers is debated by scholars; here, the regnal dates reflect primarily the order of succession and vary widely among sources.

Early Kings

Reign	Ruler
c. 320-350	Ezana
c. 328-370	Shizana
c. 356	Ella Abreha
?	Ella Asfeha
?	Ella Shahel
474-475	Agabe
474-475	Levi
475-486	Ella Amida (IV?)
486-489	Jacob I
486-489	David
489-504	Armah I
504-505	Zitana
505-514	Jacob II
c. 500-542	Ella Asbeha (Caled)
542-c. 550	Beta Israel
c. 550-564	Gabra Masqal
?	Anaeb
?	Alamiris
?	Joel
?	Israel
?	Gersem I
?	Ella Gabaz
?	Ella Saham
c. 625	Armah II
?	Iathlia
?	Hataz I
?	Wazena
?	Za Ya'abiyo
?	Armah III
?	Hataz II
?	Gersem II
?	Hataz III

Zagwe Dynasty

Reign	Ruler
c. 1137-1152	Mara Tekle Haimanot
c. 1152-1181	Yimrehane-Kristos
c. 1181-1221	Lalibela
c. 1221-1260	Na 'akuto La 'ab
c. 1260-1270	Yitbarek (Yetbarek)
1270	Solomonid Dynasty begins; reign of Yekuno Amlak

Solomonid Dynasty

Reign	Ruler
1270-1285	Yekuno Amlak
1285-1294	Solomon I
1294-1297	Bahr Asgad
1294-1297	Senfa Asgad
1297-1299	Qedma Asgad
1297-1299	Jin Asgad
1297-1299	Saba Asgad
1299-1314	Wedem Arad
1314-1344	Amade Tseyon I
1344-1372	Newaya Krestos
1372-1382	Newaya Maryam
1382-1411	Dawit (David) I
1411-1414	Tewodros (Theodore) I
1414-1429	Isaac
1429-1430	Andrew
1430-1433	Takla Maryam
1433	Sarwe Iyasus
1433-1434	Amda Iyasus
1434-1468	Zara Yacob (Constantine I)
1468-1478	Baeda Mariam I
1478-1484	Constantine II
1494	Amade Tseyon II
1494-1508	Naod
1508-1540	Lebna Dengel (David II)
1529	Battle of Shimbre-Kune
1540-1559	Galawedos (Claudius)
1543	Battle of Lake Tana (defeat of Muslims)

Later Rulers

Reign	Ruler
1560-1564	Menas
1564-1597	Sarsa Dengel
1597-1603	Jacob
1603-1604	Za Dengel
1604-1607	Jacob
1607-1632	Susneyos (Sissinios)
1632-1667	Fasilidas (Basilides)
1667-1682	Yohannes (John) I
1682-1706	Iyasu (Jesus) I the Great
1706-1708	Tekle Haimanot I
1708-1711	Tewoflos (Theophilus)
1711-1716	Yostos (Justus)

Reign	Ruler
1716-1721	Dawit (David) III
1721-1730	Bekaffa
1730-1755	Iyasu II
1755-1769	Iyoas (Joas) I
1769	Yohannes II
1769-1777	Tekle Haimanot II
1777-1779	Salomon (Solomon) II
1779-1784	Tekle Giorgis I (first)
1784-1788	Jesus III
1788	Ba'eda Maryam I
1788-1789	Tekle Giorgis I (second)
1789-1794	Hezekiah
1794-1795	Tekle Giorgis I (third)
1795	Ba'eda Maryam II
1795-1796	Tekle Giorgis I (fourth)
1796-1797	Solomon III
1797-1799	Tekle Giorgis I (fifth)
1799	Solomon III
1799-1800	Demetrius
1800	Tekle Giorgis I (sixth)
1800-1801	Demetrius

KONGO

Reign	Ruler
Before 1482-c. 1506	João I (Nzinga Nkuwu)
c. 1506-1543	Afonso I (Nzinga Mbemba)
1543-1545	Peter I
1545-1545	Francis I
1545-1561	Diogo I
1561-1561	Affonso II
1561-1566	Bernard I
1566-1567	Henry I
1568-1587	Alvare I
1587-1614	Alvare II
1614-1615	Bernard II
1615-1622	Alvare III
1622-1624	Peter II
1624-1626	Garcia I
1626-1631	Ambrosio
1631-1636	Alvaro IV
1636-1636	Alvaro V
1636-1642	Alvaro VI
1642-1661	Garcia II
1661-1665	Antonio I
1665	Battle of Mbwila, decline of independent Kingdom of Kongo

MOROCCO

Almoravids

Reign	Ruler
1061-1106	Yūsuf ibn Tāshufīn
1107-1142	'Alī ibn Yūsuf

Reign	Ruler
1142-1146	Tāshufīn ibn ʿAlī
1146	Ibrāhīm ibn Tāshufīn
1146-1147	Isḥāq ibn ʿAlī

Almohads

Reign	Ruler
To 1130	Ibn Tūmart
1130-1163	ʿAbd al-Muʾmin
1163-1184	Yūsuf I Abū Yaʿqūb
1184-1199	Yaʿqūb Yūsuf al-Manṣūr
1199-1213	Muḥammad ibn Yaʿqūb
1213-1224	Yūsuf II Abū Yaʿqūb
1224	ʿAbdul Wāḥid I
1224-1227	ʿAbdallah Abū Muḥammad
1227-1235	Yaḥyā Abū Zakariyyāʾ
1227-1232	Idrīs I ibn Yaʿqūb
1232-1242	ʿAbd al-Wāḥid ibn Idrīs I
1242-1248	ʿAlī ibn Idrīs I
1248-1266	ʿUmar ibn Isḥāq
1266-1269	Idrīs II ibn Muḥammad
After 1269	Dissolution; power divided among Marīnids, Ḥafṣids, and Zayyānids

Marīnids

Reign	Ruler
1269-1286	Abū Yūsuf Yaʿqūb
1286-1307	Abū Yaʿqūb Yūsuf al-Nasīr
1307-1308	Abū Tabit
1308-1310	Abū Rabia
1310-1331	Abū Said Othman (Osman ibn Yaʿqūb)
1331-1348	Abū al-Hasan
1348-1358	Abū Inan Faris
1358-1361	Vacant
1361-1366	Moḥammad ibn Yaʿqūb
1366-1372	ʿAbd al-Aziz I
1372-1384	Vacant
1384-1387	Mūsā ibn al-Fers
1387-1393	ʿAbu al-ʿAbbās
1393-1396	ʿAbd al-Aziz II
1396-1398	Abdallah
1398-1421	Osman III
1421-1465	ʿAbd al-Haqq

Wattasides

Reign	Ruler
1472-1504	Moḥammad al-Saih al-Mahdi
1505-1524	Abū Abdallah Moḥammad
1524-1550	Abul ʿAbbās Aḥmad

Saʿdīs (Cherifians)

Reign	Ruler
1510-1517	Muḥammad al-Qāʾim
1517-1544	Aḥmad al-Aʿraj
1544-1557	Muḥammad I al-Shaykh

Reign	Ruler
1557-1574	Abdallah al-Ghālib
1574-1576	Muḥammad al-Mutawakkil
1576-1578	ʿAbd al-Malik
1578	Battle of the Three Kings
1578-1603	Aḥmad al-Manṣūr
1603-1607	ʿAbd al ʿAbd Allah Moḥammad III
1607-1628	Zaidan al-Nāṣir
1628-1631	Abū Marwan ʿAbd al-Malik II
1631-1636	al-Walīd
1636-1654	Moḥammad IV
1654-1659	Aḥmad II
1659-1665	War

Alawis

Reign	Ruler
1666-1672	Rashid ben Ali Cherif (founder)
1672-1727	Ismael ben Ali Cherif
1727-1729	Civil war
1729-1757	Abdallah
1757-1790	Mohamed III
1790-1792	Yazid
1792-1822	Suleiman
1822-1859	Abdelrahman
1859-1873	Mohamed IV
1873-1894	Hassan I
1894-1908	Aziz
1908-1912	Hafid

SONGHAI

Reign	Ruler
c. 1464-1492	Sonni ʿAlī
1493	Sonni Baru
1493-1528	Mohammed I Askia (Mohammed Ture)
1528-1531	Askia Mūsā
1549-1582	Askia Daud
1588-1591	Askia Ishak II

AMERICAS

MAYA KINGS OF TIKAL

The Maya, who occupied the region of Central America from the Yucatán to Guatemala, maintained several centers in the region, but one, Tikal, recorded in Mayan glyphs a line of kings for nearly eight hundred years, roughly corresponding to the Classic Period now considered by scholars to be the height of Mayan civilization. The list below is from Chronicle of the Maya Kings and Queens, *by Simon Martin and Nikolai Grube (New York: Thames and Hudson, 2000).*

Reign	Ruler
c. 90-150	Yax Ehb Xook (First Step Shark)
c. 307	Siyaj Chan K'awiil I

Reign	Ruler
d. 317	Ix Une Balam (Baby Jaguar)
d. 359	K'inich Muwaan Jol
360-378	Chak Tok Ichaak I (Great Jaguar Paw)
378-404	Nuun Yax Ayiin I (Curl Snout)
411-456	Siyaj Chan K'awiil II (Stormy Sky)
458-c. 486	K'an Chitam
c. 486-508	Chak Tok Ich'aak II
c. 511-527	Kaloomte' B'alam
537-562	Wak Chan Ka'awiil
c. 593-628	Animal Skull
c. 657-679	Nuun Ujol Chaak
682-734	Jasaw Chan K'awiil I
734-746	Yik'in Chan K'awiil
768-794	Yax Nuun Ayiin II
c. 800	Nuun Ujol K'inich
c. 810	Dark Sun
c. 849	Jewel K'awiil
c. 869	Jasaw Chan K'awiil II
c. 900	End of Mayan Classic Period

AZTEC KINGS OF TENOCHTITLÁN (MEXICO)

Reign	Ruler
Legendary	Ténoch (founder)
1375-1395	Acamapichtili
1395-1417	Huitzilíhuitl
1417-1427	Chimalpopoca
1427-1440	Itzcóatl
1440-1469	Montezuma (Moctezuma) I
1469-1481	Axayacatl
1481-1486	Tízoc
1486-1502	Ahuitzotl (Auítzotl)
1502-1520	Montezuma (Moctezuma) II
1520	Cuitláhuac
1520-1521	Cuauhtémoc

INCAS (PERU)

Reign	Ruler
c. 1200	Manco Capac I
?	Sinchi Roca
?	Lloque Yupanqui
?	Mayta Capac
?	Capac Yupanqui
?	Inca Roca
?	Yahuar Huacac
?	Viracocha
1438-1471	Pachacuti
1471-1493	Topa
1493-1525	Huayna Capac
1525-1532	Huáscar
1525-1533	Atahualpa
1532-1533	Spanish conquest (Pizzaro)
1533	Manco Capac II

Reign	Ruler
1544-1561	Sayri Tupac
1561-1571	Titu Cusi
1571	Tupac Amaru I

AUSTRIA. *See* HOLY ROMAN EMPIRE

BOHEMIA. *See also* HUNGARY, POLAND

PŘEMYSLIDS

Reign	Ruler
c. 870-888/889	Borivoj I
894/895-915	Spytihnev I
915-921	Vratislav I
921-935	Duke Wenceslaus I
935-972	Boleslaus I the Cruel
972-999	Boleslaus II the Pious
999-1002	Boleslaus III
1002-1003	Vladivoj
1003	Boleslaus III
1003	Jaromir
1003	Boleslaus III
1003-1004	Boleslaus I (nondynastic Piast)
1004-1012	Jaromir
1012-1033	Oldrich
1033-1034	Jaromir
1034	Oldrich
1035-1055	Bretislav I
1055-1061	Spytihnev II
1061-1092	Vratislav II
1092	Konrad I
1092-1100	Bretislav II
1101-1107	Borivoj II
1107-1109	Svatopluk
1109-1117	Vladislav I
1117-1120	Borivoj II
1120-1125	Vladislav I
1125-1140	Sobeslav I
1140-1172	Vladislav II
1172-1173	Bedrich
1173-1178	Sobeslav II
1178-1189	Bedrich
1189-1191	Konrad II Ota
1191-1192	Duke Wenceslaus II
1192-1193	Ottokar I
1193-1197	Jindrich Bretislav
1197	Vladislav Jindrich
1197-1230	Ottokar I
1230-1253	King Wenceslaus I
1253-1278	Ottokar II
1278-1305	King Wenceslaus II

Reign	Ruler
1305-1306	King Wenceslaus III
1306	Henry of Carinthia (nondynastic)
1306-1307	Rudolph I of Habsburg (nondynastic)
1307-1310	Henry of Carinthia (nondynastic)

LUXEMBOURGS

Reign	Ruler
1310-1346	John of Luxembourg
1346-1378	Charles I
1378-1419	Wenceslaus IV
1419-1420	Sigismund
1420-1436	Hussite wars
1436-1437	Sigismund

HABSBURGS

Reign	Ruler
1437-1439	Albert of Habsburg
1439-1457	Ladislas I (V of Hungary)
1458-1471	George of Podebrady (nondynastic)
1469-1490	Matthias Corvinus (antiking)

JAGIEŁŁOS

Reign	Ruler
1471-1516	Vladislav (Ladislaus) II
1516-1526	Louis

HABSBURGS

Reign	Ruler
1526-1564	Ferdinand I
1564-1575	Maximilian
1575-1611	Rudolf II
1612-1619	Matthias
1619	Ferdinand II
1619-1620	Frederick, Elector Palatine (Wittelsbach)
1620-1637	Ferdinand II
1627-1657	Ferdinand III
1646-1654	Ferdinand IV
1656-1705	Leopold I
1705-1711	Joseph I
1711-1740	Charles II
1740-1780	Maria Theresa

HABSBURG-LOTHRINGENS

Reign	Ruler
1780-1790	Joseph II
1790-1792	Leopold II
1792-1835	Francis
1835-1848	Ferdinand V
1848-1916	Francis Joseph
1916-1918	Charles III

BULGARIA

EARLY BULGARIA

Reign	Czar
c. 681-701	Asparukh
c. 701-c. 718	Tervel
c. 718-750	Sevar
750-762	Kormesios
762-763	Vinekh
762-763	Teletz
763	Umar
763-765	Baian
765	Tokt
c. 765-777	Telerig
c. 777-c. 803	Kardam
c. 803-814	Krum
814-815	Dukum
814-816	Ditzveg
814-831	Omurtag
831-836	Malamir (Malomir)
836-852	Presijan
852-889	Boris I
865	Boris converts to Christianity
889-893	Vladimir
893-927	Simeon I the Great
927-969	Peter I
969-972	Boris II
971	Bulgaria conquered by John I Tzimisces
971-1018	Dissolution, instability
1018	Basil II annexes Bulgaria to Macedonia

ASEN LINE

Reign	Czar
1186	Bulgarian Independence
1186-1196	John I Asen
1196-1197	Peter II Asen
1197-1207	Kalojan Asen
1207-1218	Boril
1218-1241	John II Asen
1242	Mongol invasion
1242-1246	Kaloman I
1246-1257	Michael II Asen
1257-1258	Kaloman II
1257-1277	Constantine Tich
1277-1279	Ivalio
1278-c. 1264	Ivan Mytzes
1279-1284?	John III Asen
c. 1280	Terter takeover

TERTER LINE

Reign	Czar
1280-1292	George I Terter
1285	Mongol vassal

Reign	Czar
1292-1295/8	Smilech
1295/8-1298/9	Caka (Tshaka)
1298/9-1322	Theodore Svetoslav
1322-1323	George II

SHISHMANS

Reign	Czar
1323-1330	Michael III Shishman
1330-1331	John IV Stephan
1331-1371	John V Alexander
1355-1371	John Sracimir
1360-1393	John VI Shishman
1385-1396	Decline
1396-1879	Ottoman rule

BYZANTINE EMPIRE

Reign	Emperor or Empress
330-337	Constantine I the Great
337-361	Constantius
361-363	Julian the Apostate
363-364	Jovian
364-378	Valens
379-395	Theodosius I the Great
395-408	Arcadius
408-450	Theodosius II
450-457	Marcian
457-474	Leo I the Great
474	Leo II
474-475	Zeno
475-476	Basiliscus
476-491	Zeno (restored)
491-518	Anastasius I
518-527	Justin I
527-548	Theodora
527-565	Justinian I the Great
565-578	Justin II
578-582	Tiberius II Constantinus
582-602	Maurice
602-610	Phocas
610-641	Heraclius
641	Constantine III and Heracleonas
641-668	Constans II Pogonatus
668-685	Constantine IV
685-695	Justinian II Rhinotmetus
695-698	Leontius
698-705	Tiberius III
705-711	Justinian II (restored)
711-713	Philippicus Bardanes
713-715	Anastasius II
716-717	Theodosius III
717-741	Leo III the Isaurian (the Syrian)

Reign	Emperor or Empress
741-775	Constantine V Copronymus
775-780	Leo IV the Khazar
780-797	Constantine VI
797-802	Saint Irene
802-811	Nicephorus I
811	Stauracius
811-813	Michael I
813-820	Leo V the Armenian
820-829	Michael II the Stammerer
829-842	Theophilus
842-867	Michael III the Drunkard
867-886	Basil I the Macedonian
886-912	Leo VI the Wise (the Philosopher)
912-913	Alexander
913-919	Constantine VII Porphyrogenitus (Macedonian)
919-944	Romanus I Lecapenus (Macedonian)
944-959	Constantine VII (restored)
959-963	Romanus II (Macedonian)
963	Basil II Bulgaroktonos (Macedonian)
963-969	Nicephorus II Phocas (Macedonian)
969-976	John I Tzimisces
976-1025	Basil II (restored)
1025-1028	Constantine VIII (Macedonian)
1028-1034	Zoë and Romanus III Argyrus (Macedonian)
1034-1041	Zoë and Michael IV the Paphlagonian (Macedonian)
1041-1042	Zoë and Michael V Calaphates (Macedonian)
1042	Zoë and Theodora (Macedonian)
1042-1050	Zoë, Theodora, and Constantine IX Monomachus (Macedonian)
1050-1055	Theodora and Constantine IX (Macedonian)
1055-1056	Theodora (Macedonian)
1056-1057	Michael VI Stratioticus
1057-1059	Isaac I Comnenus
1059-1067	Constantine X Ducas
1067-1068	Michael VII Ducas (Parapinaces)
1068-1071	Romanus IV Diogenes
1071-1078	Michael VII Ducas (restored)
1078-1081	Nicephorus III Botaniates
1081-1118	Alexius I Comnenus
1118-1143	John II Comnenus
1143-1180	Manuel I Comnenus
1180-1183	Alexius II Comnenus
1183-1185	Andronicus I Comnenus
1185-1195	Isaac II Angelus
1195-1203	Alexius III Angelus
1203-1204	Isaac II (restored) and Alexius IV Angelus
1204	Alexius V Ducas
1204-1205	Baldwin I
1206-1222	Theodore I Lascaris

Reign	Emperor or Empress
1222-1254	John III Vatatzes or Ducas
1254-1258	Theodore II Lascaris
1258-1261	John IV Lascaris
1259-1282	Michael VIII Palaeologus
1282-1328	Andronicus II Palaeologus
1328-1341	Andronicus III Palaeologus
1341-1376	John V Palaeologus
1347-1355	John VI Cantacuzenus (usurper)
1376-1379	Andronicus IV Palaeologus
1379-1391	John V Palaeologus (restored)
1390	John VII Palaeologus (usurper)
1391-1425	Manuel II Palaeologus
1399-1412	John VII Palaeologus (restored as coemperor)
1425-1448	John VIII Palaeologus
1449-1453	Constantine XI Palaeologus
1453	Fall of Constantinople to the Ottomans

CHINA

SUI DYNASTY

Reign	Ruler
581-604	Wendi
604-617	Yangdi
618	Gongdi

TANG DYNASTY

Reign	Ruler
618-626	Gaozu (Li Yuan)
627-649	Taizong
650-683	Gaozong
684	Zhonggong
684-690	Ruizong
690-705	Wu Hou
705-710	Zhongzong
710-712	Ruizong
712-756	Xuanzong
756-762	Suzong
762-779	Daizong
779-805	Dezong
805	Shunzong
805-820	Xianzong
820-824	Muzong
824-827	Jingzong
827-840	Wenzong
840-846	Wuzong
846-859	Xuanzong
859-873	Yizong
873-888	Xizong
888-904	Zhaozong
904-907	Aizong

LIAO DYNASTY

Reign	Ruler
907-926	Abaoji (Taizu)
926-947	Deguang (Taizong)
947-951	Shizong
951-969	Muzong
969-982	Jingzong
982-1031	Shengzong
1031-1055	Xingzong
1055-1101	Daozong
1101-1125	Tianzuodi

WESTERN LIAO DYNASTY

Reign	Ruler
1125-1144	Dezong
1144-1151	Empress Gantian
1151-1164	Renzong
1164-1178	Empress Chengtian
1178-1211	The Last Ruler

JIN DYNASTY

Reign	Ruler
1115-1123	Aguda (Wanyan Min; Taizu)
1123-1135	Taizong (Wanyan Sheng)
1135-1149	Xizong
1150-1161	Wanyan Liang, king of Hailing
1161-1190	Shizong
1190-1209	Zhangzong
1209-1213	Wanyan Yongji, king of Weishao
1213-1224	Xuanzong
1224-1234	Aizong
1234	The Last Emperor

NORTHERN SONG DYNASTY

Reign	Ruler
960-976	Taizu (Zhao Kuangyin)
976-997	Taizong
998-1022	Zhenzong
1022-1063	Renzong
1064-1067	Yingzong
1068-1085	Shenzong
1086-1101	Zhezong
1101-1125	Huizong
1125-1126	Qinzong

SOUTHERN SONG DYNASTY

Reign	Ruler
1127-1162	Gaozong
1163-1190	Xiaozong
1190-1194	Guangzong
1195-1224	Ningzong
1225-1264	Lizong
1265-1274	Duzong

Reign	Ruler
1275-1275	Gongdi
1276-1278	Duanzong
1279	Bing Di

YUAN DYNASTY. *See also* MONGOL EMPIRE

Reign	Ruler
1279-1294	Kublai Khan (Shizu)
1294-1307	Temür Oljeitu (Chengzong)
1308-1311	Khaishan (Wuzong)
1311-1320	Ayurbarwada (Renzong)
1321-1323	Shidelbala (Yingzong)
1323-1328	Yesun Temür (Taiding)
1328-1329	Tugh Temür (Wenzong Tianshundi)
1329	Tugh Khoshila (Mingzong)
1329-1332	Tugh Temür (Wenzong)
1333-1368	Toghon Temür (Shundi)
1368	Ming Dynasty begins: Hongwu

MING DYNASTY

Reign	Ruler
1368-1398	Hongwu (Zhu Yuanzhang)
1399-1402	Jianwen (Zhu Yunwen)
1402-1424	Yonglo (Zhu Di)
1424-1425	Hongxi
1426-1435	Xuande
1436-1449	Zhengtong
1449-1457	Jingtai
1457-1464	Tianshun
1465-1487	Chenghua (Xianzong)
1488-1505	Hongzhi (Xiaozong)
1505-1521	Zhengde
1522-1567	Jiajing
1567-1572	Longqing
1573-1620	Wanli
1620	Taichang
1621-1627	Tianqi
1628-1644	Chongzhen

SOUTHERN MING DYNASTY

Reign	Ruler
1644-1645	Fu (Hongguang)
1645-1646	Tang (Longwu)
1645	Lu (Luh)
1645-1653	Lu (Lou)
1646	Tang (Shaowu)
1646-1662	Gui (Yongli)

QING (MANCHU) DYNASTY

Reign	Ruler
1616-1626	Nurhachi
1626-1643	Hong Taiji
1643-1661	Shunzi

Reign	Ruler
1644	Occupation of China; defeat of the Ming
1661-1722	Kangxi
1722-1735	Yongzheng
1735-1796	Qianlong
1796-1820	Jiaqing
1820-1850	Daoguang
1850-1861	Xianfeng
1861-1875	Tongzhi
1875-1908	Guangxu
1908-1924	Puyi

DENMARK. *See also* NORWAY, SWEDEN

Reign	Ruler
588-647	Ivar Vidfamne
647-735?	Harald I Hildetand
735-750?	Sigurd I Ring (poss. 770-812)
c. 750	Randver
850-854	Horik I
c. 854-?	Horik II
c. 860-865	Ragnar Lobrok
865-873	Sigurd II Snogoje
873-884	Hardeknut I
884-885	Frodo
885-889	Harald II
c. 900-950	Gorm
c. 950-985	Harald III Bluetooth
985-1014	Sweyn I Forkbeard
1014-1019	Harald IV
1019-1035	Canute I (III) the Great
1035-1042	Hardeknut
1042-1047	Magnus the Good
1047-1074	Sweyn II
1074-1080	Harald V Hen
1080-1086	Canute II (IV) the Holy
1086-1095	Olaf IV the Hungry
1095-1103	Eric I the Evergood
1103-1134	Niels Elder
1134-1137	Eric II
1137-1146	Eric III
1146-1157	Sweyn III
1147-1157	Canute III (V) Magnussen
1157-1182	Valdemar I the Great
1182-1202	Canute IV (VI) the Pious
1202-1241	Valdemar II the Victorious
1241-1250	Eric IV
1250-1252	Abel
1252-1259	Christopher I
1259-1286	Eric V
1286-1319	Eric VI
1320-1326	Christopher II
1326-1330	Instability

Reign	Ruler
1330-1332	Christopher II (restored)
1332-1340	Instability
1340-1375	Valdemar III
1376-1387	Olaf V (or II; IV of Norway)
1380	Unification of Denmark and Norway
1376-1412	Margaret I of Denmark, Norway, and Sweden
1397	Unification of Norway, Denmark, and Sweden
1412-1439	Eric VII (III of Norway, XIII of Sweden)
1439-1448	Christopher III

HOUSE OF OLDENBURG

Reign	Ruler
1448-1481	Christian I
1481-1513	John (Hans)
1523	Sweden leaves Kalmar Union
1523-1533	Frederick I
1523-1536	Union with Norway
1534-1559	Christian III
1559-1588	Frederick II
1588-1648	Christian IV
1648-1670	Frederick III
1670-1699	Christian V
1699-1730	Frederick IV
1730-1746	Christian VI
1746-1766	Frederick V
1766-1808	Christian VII
1808-1839	Frederick VI
1839-1848	Christian VIII
1848-1863	Frederick VII

EGYPT

After the rise of Islam in the seventh century, Egypt was Islamicized and came under the control of a succession of emirs and caliphs.

ṬULUNID EMIRS

Reign	Ruler
868-884	Aḥmad ibn Ṭūlūn
884-896	Khumārawayh
896	Jaysh
896-904	Hārūn
904-905	Shaybān
905	Recovered by Abbasids

IKHSHIDID EMIRS

Reign	Ruler
935-946	Muḥammad ibn Ṭughj al-Ikhshīd
946-961	Unūjūr
961-966	ʿAlī
966-968	Kāfūr al-Lābī (regent)

Reign	Ruler
968-969	Aḥmad
969	Fāṭimid conquest

FĀṬIMID CALIPHS IN EGYPT

Reign	Ruler
975-996	al-ʿAzīz
996-1021	al-Ḥākim
1021-1036	al-Zahīr
1036-1094	al-Mustanṣir
1094-1101	al-Mustadī
1101-1130	al-Amīr
1130-1149	al-Ḥāfiz
1149-1154	al-Zafīr
1154-1160	al-Fāʾiz
1160-1171	al-ʿAdīd

AYYŪBID SULTANS

Reign	Ruler
1169-1193	Saladin
1193-1198	al-ʿAzīz Imad al-Dīn
1198-1200	al-Mansūr Naṣīr al-Dīn
1200-1218	al-ʿAdil I Sayf al-Dīn
1202-1204	Fourth Crusade
1217-1221	Fifth Crusade
1218-1238	al-Kāmil I Nāṣir al-Dīn
1227-1230	Sixth Crusade
1238-1240	al-ʿAdil II Sayf al-Dīn
1240-1249	al-Ṣāliḥ II Najm al-Dīn
1249-1250	al-Muʿaẓẓam Tūrān-Shāh Ghiyāt al-Dīn
1248-1254	Seventh (or Eighth) Crusade
1252	Cairo seized by Mamlūks

MAMLŪK SULTANS

Baḥrī Line (Mongol, then Turkish)

Reign	Ruler
1252-1257	Aybak al-Turkumānī
1257-1259	ʿAlī I
1259-1260	Quṭuz al-Muʿizzī
1260-1277	Baybars I (defeats Mongols 1260)
1277-1279	Baraka (Berke) Khān
1279	Salāmish (Süleymish)
1279-1290	Qalāʾūn al-Alfī
1290-1293	Khalīl
1291	Fall of Acre
1293	Baydarā (?)
1293-1294	Muḥammad I
1294-1296	Kitbughā
1296-1299	Lāchīn (Lājīn) al-Ashqar
1299-1309	Muḥammad I
1303	Earthquake destroys Pharos lighthouse
1309-1310	Baybars II al-Jāshnakīr (Burjī)
1310-1341	Muḥammad I

Reign	Ruler
1341	Abū Bakr
1341-1342	Kūjūk (Küchük)
1342	Aḥmad I
1342-1345	Ismā'īl
1345-1346	Sha'bān I
1346-1347	Ḥājjī I
1347-1351	al-Ḥasan
1351-1354	Ṣāliḥ
1354-1361	al-Ḥasan
1361-1363	Muḥammad II
1363-1377	Sha'bān II
1377-1382	'Alī II
1382	Ḥājjī II
1389-1390	Ḥājjī II

Burjī (Circassian) line

Reign	Ruler
1382-1398	Barqūq al-Yalburghāwī
1399-1405	Faraj
1405	'Abd al-'Azīz
1405-1412	Faraj (second rule)
1412	al-Musta'īn
1412-1421	Shaykh al-Maḥmūdī al-Ẓāhirī
1421	Aḥmad II
1421	Ṭāṭār
1421-1422	Muḥammad III
1422-1438	Barsbay
1438	Yūsuf
1438-1453	Chaqmaq (Jaqmaq)
1453	'Uthmān
1453-1461	Ināl al-'Alā'ī al-Ẓāhirī
1461	Aḥmad III
1461-1467	Khushqadam
1467	Yalbay
1467-1468	Timurbughā
1468-1496	Qāyit Bay (Qāytbāy) al-Ẓāhirī
1496-1498	Muḥammad IV
1498-1500	Qānṣawh I
1500-1501	Jānbulāṭ
1501	Ṭūmān Bay I
1501-1516	Qānṣawh II al-Ghawrī
1516-1517	Ṭūmān Bay II
1517	Ottoman conquest

'Abbāsid Caliphs of Egypt

Unlike the earlier 'Abbāsid line (see Islamic Caliphs, below), these were 'Abbāsid figureheads in place under the Mamlūks.

Reign	Ruler
1261	Aḥmad al-Mustanṣir
1261-1302	Aḥmad al-Ḥākim I (Aleppo 1261-1262, Cairo, 1262-1302)
1302-1340	Sulaymān al-Mustakfī I
1340-1341	Ibrāhīm al-Wāthiq I

Reign	Ruler
1341-1352	Aḥmad al-Ḥakīm II
1352-1362	Abū Bakr al-Mu'tadid I
1362-1377	Muḥammad al-Mutawakkil I
1377	Zakariyyā'al-Mu'taṣim
1377-1383	Muḥammad al-Mutawakkil I
1383-1386	'Umar al-Wāthiq II
1386-1389	Zakariyyā'al-Mu'taṣim
1389-1406	Muḥammad al-Mutawakkil I
1406-1414	Sulṭān
1412	'Abbās or Ya'qūb al-Musta'īn
1414-1441	Dāwūd al-Mu'tadid II
1441-1451	Sulaymān al-Mustakfī II
1451-1455	Ḥamza al-Qā'im
1455-1479	Yūsuf al-Mustanjid
1479-1497	'Abd al-'Azīz al-Mutawakkil II
1497-1508	Ya'qūb al-Mustamsik
1508-1516	al-Mutawakkil III
1516-1517	Ya'qūb al-Mustamsik
1517	Ottoman conquest

ENGLAND

ANGLO-SAXONS (HOUSE OF WESSEX)

Reign	Ruler
802-839	Egbert
839-856	Æthelwulf
856-860	Æthelbald
860-866	Æthelbert
866-871	Ethelred (Æthelred) I
871-899	Alfred the Great
899-924	Edward the Elder (with sister Æthelflæd)
924-939	Æthelstan
939-946	Edmund the Magnificent
946-955	Eadred
955-959	Eadwig (Edwy) All-Fair
959-975	Edgar the Peaceable
975-978	Edward the Martyr
978-1016	Ethelred (Æthelred) II the Unready
1016	Edmund II Ironside

DANES

Reign	Ruler
1016-1035	Canute (Knud) the Great
1035-1040	Harold I Harefoot
1040-1042	Harthacnut

WESSEX (RESTORED)

Reign	Ruler
1043-1066	Edward the Confessor
1066	Harold II

NORMANS

Reign	Ruler
1066-1087	William I the Conqueror
1087-1100	William II Rufus
1100-1135	Henry I Beauclerc
1135-1154	Stephen

PLANTAGENETS: ANGEVINS

Reign	Ruler
1154-1189	Henry II (with Eleanor of Aquitaine, r. 1154-1189)
1189-1199	Richard I the Lion-Hearted
1199-1216	John I Lackland
1216-1272	Henry III
1272-1307	Edward I Longshanks
1307-1327	Edward II (with Isabella of France, r. 1308-1330)
1327-1377	Edward III (with Philippa of Hainaut, r. 1327-1369)
1377-1399	Richard II

PLANTAGENETS: LANCASTRIANS

Reign	Ruler
1399-1413	Henry IV
1413-1422	Henry V
1422-1461	Henry VI

PLANTAGENETS: YORKISTS

Reign	Ruler
1461-1470	Edward IV
1470-1471	Henry VI (Lancaster)
1471-1483	Edward IV (York, restored)
1483	Edward V (York)
1483-1485	Richard III Hunchback (York)

TUDORS

Reign	Ruler
1485-1509	Henry VII
1509-1547	Henry VIII
1547-1553	Edward VI
1553	Lady Jane Grey
1553-1558	Mary I
1558-1603	Elizabeth I

STUARTS

Reign	Ruler
1603-1625	James I (VI of Scotland)
1625-1649	Charles I

COMMONWEALTH (LORD PROTECTORS)

Reign	Ruler
1653-1658	Oliver Cromwell
1658-1659	Richard Cromwell

STUARTS (RESTORED)

Reign	Ruler
1660-1685	Charles II
1685-1689	James II (VII of Scotland)
1689-1702	William of Orange (III of England, II of Scotland) and Mary II
1702-1707	Anne
1707	Act of Union (Great Britain and Ireland)
1707-1714	Anne

HANOVERS

Reign	Ruler
1714-1727	George I
1727-1760	George II
1760-1801	George III
1801	Act of Union creates United Kingdom
1801-1820	George III
1820-1830	George IV
1830-1837	William IV

FRANKISH KINGDOM AND FRANCE

The Merovingians and Carolingians ruled different parts of the Frankish kingdom, which accounts for overlapping regnal dates in these tables. The term "emperor" refers to rule over what eventually came to be known as the Holy Roman Empire.

THE MEROVINGIANS

Reign	Ruler (Principality)
447-458	Merovech
458-481	Childeric I
481-511	Clovis I (with Clotilda, r. 493-511)
511	Kingdom split among Clovis's sons
511-524	Chlodomer (Orléans)
511-534	Theodoric I (Metz)
511-558	Childebert I (Paris)
511-561	Lothair I (Soissons 511-561, all Franks 558-561)
534-548	Theudebert I (Metz)
548-555	Theudebald (Metz)
561	Kingdom split among Lothair's sons
561-567	Charibert I (Paris)
561-575	Sigebert I (Austrasia)
561-584	Chilperic I (Soissons)
561-592	Guntram (Burgundy)
575-595	Childebert II (Austrasia 575-595, Burgundy 593-595)
584-629	Lothair II (Neustria 584, all Franks 613-629)
595-612	Theudebert II (Austrasia)
595-613	Theodoric II (Burgundy 595-612, Austrasia 612-613)
613	Sigebert II (Austrasia, Burgundy)

Reign	Ruler (Principality)
623-639	Dagobert I (Austrasia 623-628, all Franks 629-639)
629-632	Charibert II (Aquitaine)
632-656	Sigebert III (Austrasia)
639-657	Clovis II (Neustria and Burgundy)
656-673	Lothair III (Neustria 657-673, all Franks 656-660)
662-675	Childeric (Austrasia 662-675, all Franks 673-675)
673-698	Theodoric III (Neustria 673-698, all Franks 678-691)
674-678	Dagobert II (Austrasia)
691-695	Clovis III (all Franks)
695-711	Childebert III (all Franks)
711-716	Dagobert III (all Franks)
715-721	Chilperic II (Neustria 715-721, all Franks 719-720)
717-719	Lothair IV (Austrasia)
721-737	Theodoric IV (all Franks)
743-751	Childeric III (all Franks)

THE CAROLINGIANS

Reign	Ruler
687-714	Pépin II of Heristal (mayor of Austrasia/Neustria)
714-719	Plectrude (regent for Theudoald)
719-741	Charles Martel (the Hammer; mayor of Austrasia/Neustria)
747-768	Pépin III the Short (mayor of Neustria 741, king of all Franks 747)
768-814	Charlemagne (king of Franks 768, emperor 800)
814-840	Louis the Pious (king of Aquitaine, emperor)
840-855	Lothair I (emperor)
843	Treaty of Verdun divides Carolingian Empire into East Franks (Germany), West Franks (essentially France), and a Middle Kingdom (roughly corresponding to Provence, Burgundy, and Lorraine)
843-876	Louis II the German (king of Germany)
843-877	Charles II the Bald (king of Neustria 843, emperor 875)
855-875	Louis II (emperor)
877-879	Louis II (king of France)
879-882	Louis III (king of France)
879-884	Carloman (king of France)
884-887	Charles III the Fat (king of France, emperor 881)
887-898	Odo (Eudes; king of France)
887-899	Arnulf (king of Germany 887, emperor 896)
891-894	Guy of Spoleto (Wido, Guido; emperor)
892-898	Lambert of Spoleto (emperor)
893-923	Charles III the Simple (king of France)
915-923	Berengar I of Friuli (emperor)
923-929?	Robert I (king of France)

Reign	Ruler
929-936	Rudolf (king of France)
936-954	Louis IV (king of France; Hugh the Great in power)
954-986	Lothair (king of France; Hugh Capet in power 956)
986-987	Louis V (king of France)

THE CAPETIANS

Reign	Ruler
987-996	Hugh Capet
996-1031	Robert II the Pious
1031-1060	Henry I
1060-1108	Philip I the Fair
1108-1137	Louis VI the Fat
1137-1179	Louis VII the Younger (with Eleanor of Aquitaine, r. 1137-1180)
1179-1223	Philip II Augustus
1223-1226	Louis VIII the Lion
1223-1252	Blanche of Castile (both queen and regent)
1226-1270	Louis IX (Saint Louis)
1271-1285	Philip III the Bold
1285-1314	Philip IV the Fair
1314-1316	Louis X the Stubborn
1316	Philip, brother of Louis X (regent before birth of John I and during his short life)
1316	John I the Posthumous
1316-1322	Philip V the Tall
1322-1328	Charles IV the Fair

Valois Dynasty, Main Branch

Reign	Ruler
1328-1350	Philip VI the Fortunate
1350-1364	John II the Good
1364-1380	Charles V the Wise
1380-1382	Louis I of Anjou (regent for Charles VI)
1380-1422	Charles VI the Well-Beloved
1422-1461	Charles VII the Victorious
1461-1483	Louis XI
1483-1484	Anne de Beaujeu (regent for Charles VIII)
1483-1498	Charles VIII the Affable

Valois-Orléans Branch

Reign	Ruler
1498-1515	Louis XII, the Father of His People

Valois-Angoulême Branch

Reign	Ruler
1515-1547	Francis I
1547-1559	Henry II (with Catherine de Médicis)
1559-1560	Francis II
1560-1563	Catherine de Médicis (regent for Charles IX)
1560-1574	Charles IX
1574-1589	Henry III (King of Poland, 1573-1574)

BOURBON DYNASTY

Reign	Ruler
1589-1610	Henry IV (Henry III of Navarre, 1572-1610)
1610-1614	Marie de Médici (regent for Louis XIII)
1610-1643	Louis XIII the Well-Beloved
1643-1651	Anne of Austria (regent for Louis XIV)
1643-1715	Louis XIV the Sun King
1715-1723	Philip II of Orléans (regent for Louis XV)
1715-1774	Louis XV the Well-Beloved
1774-1792	Louis XVI the Beloved
1792-1804	First Republic
1804-1814	First Empire (Napoleon I Bonaparte)
1814-1824	Louis XVIII
1824-1830	Charles X
1830-1848	Louis Philippe of Orléans

GERMANIC TRIBES. *See also* HOLY ROMAN EMPIRE

In the fifth and sixth centuries, Europe was invaded from the east by several "barbarian" tribes from eastern Europe and Central Asia, including the Visigoths, who inflicted the earliest damage on Rome in the late fourth and early fifth centuries; the Burgundians, from central and northeastern Europe; the Vandals, who eventually settled in Spain and North Africa; the Suevi, who made their way to the north of Spain and finally fell to the Visigoths; the Alans, a non-Germanic steppe tribe from Iran who, along with the Suevi and the Visigoths, overran Gaul (France) and the Iberian Peninsula; and the Franks (see Frankish Kingdom and France, above), who occupied most of Gaul during the later Roman Empire and were the only of these early tribes to survive. The Franks would evolve into the Merovingian and Carolingian lines, and by the ninth century they dominated Europe. Below is a list of some of the Germanic tribes and tribal leaders before and during the Frankish period. The region known today as Germany was initially occupied by these tribes and then came under the subjugation of the Frankish Merovingians and Carolingians. In 962, the Holy Roman Empire came into existence and held sway over Germany for nearly a millennium (see Holy Roman Empire, below). Not until the late nineteenth century did the nation-state of Germany come into existence.

ALEMANNI (OR ALAMANNI)

The Alemanni occupied Swabia.

Reign	Ruler
c. 536-554	Leuthari
c. 536-554	Butilin
d. c. 539	Haming

Reign	Ruler
c. 570-587	Leutfred I
588-613	Uncilen
d. 613	Gunzo
c. 615-639	Chrodebert
c. 640-673/95	Leutfred II
c. 700-709	Godefred
d. c. 712	Huocin
d. c. 712	Willehari
c. 720-730	Lanfred I
c. 737-744	Theodobald
d. 746	Nebi
746-749	Lanfred II
791-799	Gerold
799-806	Isenbard
After 806	Annexed by the Franks

BAVARIANS

The Bavarians occupied a region approximating present-day Bavaria.

Reign	Ruler
508-512	Theodo I
512-537	Theodo II
537-565	Theodo III
537-567	Theodobald I
550-590	Garibald I
590-595	Grimwald I
591-609	Tassilo I
609-630	Agilulf
609-640	Garibald II
640-680	Theodo IV
680-702	Theodo V
702-715	Theodobald II
702-723	Grimwald II
702-725	Theodobert
702-730	Tassilo II
725-737	Hubert
737-748	Odilo
748-788	Tassilo III
After 788	Annexed by Franks

BURGUNDIANS

The Burgundians occupied central and southeastern France.

Reign	Ruler
c. 407	Gebicca
407-434	Gundahar/Gondikar/Gunther
434-473	Gundioc/Gunderic
443-c. 480	Chilperic I
473-486	Gundomar I
473-493	Chilperic II
473-501	Godegisel
473-516	Gundobad
516-524	Sigismund

Reign	Ruler
524-532	Gudomar II
532	Frankish conquest

FRANKS

The Franks initially occupied the area now known as the Netherlands and northern France, and they eventually dominated Europe. See Frankish Kingdom and France, above.

LOMBARDS

The Lombards occupied northern Italy.

Reign	Ruler
565-572	Alboin
573-575	Celph
575-584	Unstable
584-590	Authari
590-591	Theodelinda
591-615	Agilulf
615-625	Adaloald
625-636	Arioald
636-652	Rotharis
652-661	Aribert I
661-662	Godipert
662-671	Grimoald
671-674	Garibald
674-688	Bertharit
688-700	Cunibert
700-701	Liutpert
701	Raginpert
701-712	Aribert II
712-744	Liutprand
744-749	Rachis of Friuli
749-756	Aistulf of Friuli
756-774	Desiderius
774	Frankish conquest

OSTROGOTHS

The Ostrogoths migrated from the east into the Balkans and Italian peninsula.

Reign	Ruler
474-526	Theodoric the Great
526-534	Athalaric
534-536	Theodahad (with Amalasuntha)
536-540	Vitiges (Witiges)
540	Theodobald (Heldebadus)
541	Eraric
541-552	Totila (Baduila)
552-553	Teias
553-568	Roman domination (Byzantine emperor Justinian I)
568-774	Lombard domination
774	Frankish conquest

SUEVI

The Suevi migrated from the east into northern Spain.

Reign	Ruler
409-438	Hermeric
428-448	Rechila
439	Mérida
441	Seville
448-456	Rechiar
452	Peace with Romans
456	Visigoths defeat Rechiar
456-457	Aioulf
457-460	Maldras
460-c. 463	Richimund
460-c. 465	Frumar
c. 463-?	Remisund
c. 500-550	Unknown kings
c. 550-559	Carriaric
559-570	Theodemar
561	Catholic
570-582	Miro
582-584	Eboric
584-585	Andeca
After 585	Visigoth conquest

VANDALS

The Vandals migrated west into southern Spain and northern Africa.

Reign	Ruler
c. 406-428	Gunderic
428-477	Gaiseric
477-484	Huneric
484-496	Gunthamund
496-523	Thrasamund
523-530	Hilderic
530-534	Gelimer
After 534	Roman overthrow

VISIGOTHS

The Visigoths migrated west into southwestern France.

Reign	Ruler
395-410	Alaric I
410-415	Athaulf (Ataulfo)
415	Sigeric
415-417	Wallia
417-451	Theodoric I
451-453	Thorismund
453-466	Theodoric II
466-484	Euric I
484-507	Alaric II
508-511	Amalaric
511-526	Theodoric the Great
526-531	Amalaric
531-548	Theudes

Reign	Ruler
548-549	Theudegisel
549-554	Agila
554-567	Athanagild
567-571	Theodomir
571-572	Leuva (Leova) I
572-586	Leuvigild
586-601	Reccared I
601-603	Leova II
603-610	Witterich
610-612	Gundemar
612-621	Sisebut (Sisebur)
621	Reccared II
621-631	Swintilla (Suinthila)
631-636	Sisenand
636-640	Chintila
640-642	Tulga
642-653	Chindaswind
653-672	Recdeswinth
672-680	Wamba
680-687	Euric (Erwig) II
687-702	Egica (Ergica)
702-709	Witiza
709-711	Roderic (Rodrigo)
711	Overthrown by Umayyads
718	Christian Kingdom of Asturias

GERMANY: FIRST REICH. *See* **HOLY ROMAN EMPIRE**

HOLY ROMAN EMPIRE

Although some sources consider the Holy Roman Empire to have begun with Otto I's coronation in 962, others date the Empire's beginning as early as Charlemagne's consolidation of the Franks and his coronation as emperor of the Frankish Empire in 800. The term "Sacrum Romanum Imperium" (Holy Roman Empire) dates to 1254, the use of the term "Holy Empire" to 1157, and the term "Roman Empire" to 1034 (reign of Conrad II). "Roman emperor" was applied to Otto I during his reign; however, Charlemagne also used the term to refer to his own reign. The concept of a "Holy" Roman Empire goes back to the beginning of the Byzantine Empire and the reign of the first Christian Roman emperor, Constantine the Great. Hence, the concept of this political entity can be considered to have evolved incrementally over time. The practice of papal coronation to legitimate the emperor began with Otto I. Regnal dates are therefore often listed as beginning with the date of coronation. However, the German kings who became Holy Roman Emperors fre-

quently asserted their de facto power earlier as rulers of West Frankia (France), East Frankia (essentially Germany), and/or Italy (roughly the northern portion of modern Italy). In the table below, where a date of ascension to the West Frankish (French), East Frankish (German), Middle Frankish (Lorraine south to Italy), or other throne is different from that to Emperor, the former date is set before a slash and the date of assuming the rule of the Empire falls after the slash. Asterisks indicate that the monarch was not formally crowned at Rome by the pope, a practice that officially ended with Frederick II, although Charles V was last to be crowned outside Rome.

Reign	Emperor (House)
768/800-814	Charlemagne (Carolingian)
814/813-840	Louis I the Pious (Carolingian)
840/817-855	Lothair I (Carolingian)
840-876	Louis II the German (Carolingian; first king of East Franks only)
840/875-877	Charles II the Bald (Carolingian)
855/850-875	Louis II of Italy (Carolingian)
877-881	Empire unstable
876/881-888	Charles III the Fat (Carolingian)
888-891	Viking and Arab incursions
891	Italian line begins
888/891-894	Guy (Guido, Wido) of Spoleto (Italian)
894/892-898	Lambert of Spoleto (Italian, co-emperor)
888/896-899	Arnulf (East Frankish)
899/901-905	Louis III of Provence (Carolingian, deposed)
905/915-924	Berengar I of Friuli (Italian)
911-918	*Conrad
919	Saxon line begins
919-936	*Henry I the Fowler (Saxon)
936/962-973	Otto I (Saxon): crowned in 962 by Pope John XII; the Empire no longer lays claim to West Frankish lands (essentially France), but now is basically a union of Germany and northern Italy.
973/967-983	Otto II (Saxon)
983/996-1002	Otto III (Saxon)
1002/14-1024	Henry II the Saint (Saxon)
1024	Franconian/Salian line begins
1024/27-1039	Conrad II (Franconian/Salian)
1039/46-1056	Henry III (Franconian/Salian)
1056/84-1106	Henry IV (Franconian/Salian)
1077-1080	*Rudolf of Swabia
1081-1093	*Hermann (of Luxemburg)
1093-1101	*Conrad (of Franconia)
1106/11-1125	Henry V (Franconian/Salian)
1125	Franconian/Salian line ends
1125/33-1137	Lothair II (duke of Saxony)

Reign	Emperor (House)
1138	Hohenstaufen line begins
1138-1152	*Conrad III (Hohenstaufen)
1152/55-1190	Frederick I Barbarossa (Hohenstaufen)
1190/91-1197	Henry VI (Hohenstaufen)
1198-1208	*Philip of Swabia (Hohenstaufen)
1208/09-1215	Otto IV (married into Hohenstaufens)
1215/20-1250	Frederick II (Hohenstaufen): Last emperor crowned at Rome.
1246-1247	*Henry Raspe
1247-1256	*William of Holland
1250-1254	*Conrad IV
1254-1273	Great Interregnum
1257-1272	*Richard of Cornwall (rival, Plantagenet)
1257-1273	*Alfonso X of Castile (rival)
1273-1291	*Rudolf I (Habsburg)
1292-1298	*Adolf of Nassau
1298-1308	*Albert (Albrecht) I (Habsburg)
1308/11-1313	Henry VII (Luxembourg)
1314/28-1347	Louis IV of Bavaria (Wittelsbach)
1314-1325	*Frederick of Habsburg (co-regent)
1346/55-1378	Charles IV (Luxembourg): Changes the name to the Holy Roman Empire of the German Nation as France begins to assert power; Charles abandons the Empire's French and Italian claims, and the history of the Holy Roman Empire and Germany are now basically the same.
1349	*Günther of Schwarzburg
1378-1400	*Wenceslaus (Luxembourg; deposed)
1400	*Frederick III (of Brunswick)
1400-1410	*Rupert of the Palatinate (Wittelsbach)
1410-1411	*John (of Moravia)
1410/33-1437	Sigismund (Luxembourg)
1438-1439	*Albert II (Habsburg)
1440/52-1493	Frederick III (Habsburg)
1486/93-1519	*Maximilian I (Habsburg)
1499	Peace of Basle; Swiss independence
1513	Swiss Confederation of the Thirteen Cantons
1519-1558	*Charles V (Habsburg, last emperor crowned)
1555	Peace of Augsburg
1558-1564	*Ferdinand I (Habsburg)
1559	Peace of Cateau-Cambrésis
1564-1576	*Maximilian II (Habsburg)
1576-1612	*Rudolf II (Habsburg)
1612-1619	*Matthias (Habsburg)
1619-1637	*Ferdinand II (Habsburg)
1637-1657	*Ferdinand III (Habsburg)
1648	Peace of Westphalia
1658-1705	*Leopold I (Habsburg)
1686-1697	War of the League of Augsburg, conquest of Hungary, Nine Years' War (1688-1697)

Reign	Emperor (House)
1705-1711	*Joseph I (Habsburg)
1711-1740	*Charles VI (Habsburg)
1713	Peace of Utrecht
1740-1742	Interregnum
1742-1745	*Charles VII (Wittelsbach-Habsburg)
1745-1765	*Francis I (Lorraine)
1745-1780	*Maria Theresa (empress consort; queen of Hungary, 1740; empress dowager, 1765)
1756-1763	Seven Years' War
1765-1790	*Joseph II (Habsburg-Lorraine)
1790-1792	*Leopold II (Habsburg-Lorraine)
1792-1806	*Francis II (Habsburg-Lorraine; abdicated)
1806	Holy Roman Empire falls to Napoleon I of France

HUNGARY. *See also* BOHEMIA, POLAND

Reign	Ruler
c. 896-907	Árpád
d. 947	Zsolt
d. 972	Taksony
997	Géza
997-1038	Saint Stephen (István) I
1038-1041	Peter Orseleo
1041-1044	Samuel
1044-1046	Peter (second rule)
1047-1060	Andrew I
1060-1063	Béla I
1063-1074	Salamon
1074-1077	Géza I
1077-1095	Saint László (Ladislas) I
1095-1116	Kalman
1116-1131	Stephen II
1131-1141	Béla II
1141-1162	Géza II
1162-1163	László II
1163-1172	Stephen III
1163-1165	Stephen IV
1172-1196	Béla III
1196-1204	Imre
1204-1205	László III
1205-1235	Andrew II
1235-1270	Béla IV
1270-1272	Stephen V
1272-1290	László IV
1290-1301	Andrew III (end of the Árpád line)
1301-1304	Wenceslaus (Václav) II
1304-1308	Otto I of Bavaria
1305-1306	Wenceslaus (Václav) III
1306	End of the Přemlysid line
1306-1310	Instability
1310-1342	Károly (Charles Robert) I

Reign	Ruler
1342-1382	Lajos (Louis) I
1382-1395	Maria
1387-1437	Sigismund
1438-1439	Albert II of Habsburg
1440-1444	Ulászló I (Władysław III, Poland)
1444-1457	László (Ladislas) V
1458-1490	Matthias (Matyas) I Corvinus
1490-1516	Ulászló II (Vladislav or Władisław Jagiełło)
1516-1526	Louis II
1526-1564	Ferdinand I (Habsburg claims suzerainty)
1526-1540	John I Zápolya (simultaneous claimant)
1540-1571	John II Sigismund
1556-1559	Isabel
1562	Split between Habsburgs, Ottomans, and Ottoman principality Transylvania
1563-1576	Maximilian II (Holy Roman Emperor)
1571-1575	Stephen Báthory
1572-1608	Rudolf II (Holy Roman Emperor)
1575-1581	Christopher (Kristóf) Báthory
1581-1599	Sigismund Báthory
1599	Andrew Cardinal Báthory
1599-1602	Sigismund Báthory
1604-1606	Stephen Bocskay
1607-1608	Sigismund Rákóczy
1608-1619	Matthias (Holy Roman Emperor)
1608-1613	Gabriel (Gábor) Báthory
1613-1629	Gábor Bethlen
1618-1637	Ferdinand II
1625-1657	Ferdinand III
1630-1648	George (György) I Rákóczy
1647-1654	Ferdinand IV
1648-1657	George II Rákóczy
1655-1705	Leopold I
1660-1682	Emeric Thököly (Tökölli)
1687-1711	Joseph I
1703-1711	Francis II Rákóczy leads liberation movement
1711-1740	Charles III
1740-1780	Maria Theresa
1780-1790	Joseph II
1790-1792	Leopold II
1792-1835	Francis
1835-1848	Ferdinand V
1848	Revolutions of 1848

INDIA

FIRST CĀLUKYA DYNASTY

Reign	Ruler
543-566	Pulakeśin I
c. 566-597	Kīrtivarman I
598-610	Maṅgaleśa

Reign	Ruler
610-642	Pulakeśin II
655-680	Vikramāditya I
680-696	Vinayāditya
696-733	Vijayāditya
733-746	Vikramāditya II
747-757	Kīrtivarman II

PALLAVAS

Reign	Ruler
c. 550-575	Simhavarman (some sources give c. 436)
c. 575-600	Simhavishnu
c. 600-630	Mahendravarman I
c. 630-668	Narasiṃhavarman I Mahāmalla
c. 668-670	Mahendravarman II
c. 670-700	Paramesvaravarman I
c. 695-728	Narasiṃhavarman II
c. 728-731	Paramesvaravarman II
c. 731-796	Nandivarman
750-770	Gopāla
770-810	Dharmapāla
810-850	Devapāla
854-908	Narayanpāla
c. 988-1038	Māhipāla I
c. 1077-1120	Rāmapāla
1143-1161	Madanpāla

SECOND WESTERN CĀLUKYA DYNASTY

Reign	Ruler
973-997	Taila II
997-1008	Satyaśraya
1008-1014	Vikramāditya I
1014-1015	Ayyana
1015-1042	Jayasimha I
1043-1068	Someśvara I
1068-1076	Someśvara II
1076-1126	Vikramāditya VI
1127-1135	Someśvara III
1135-1151	Jagadhekamalla II
1151-1154	Taila III
1155-1168	Bijjala
1168-1177	Someśvara IV
1177-1180	Saṇkama II
1180-1183	Āhavamalla
1183-1184	Singhana
1184-1189/90	Someśvara IV

GURJARA-PRATIHĀRA DYNASTY

Reign	Ruler
c. 730-c. 756	Nāgabhaṭa I
n.d.	Devaraja
c. 778-c. 794	Vatsarāja
c. 794-c. 833	Nāgabhaṭa II

Reign	Ruler
c. 836-c. 885	Mihira Bhoja I
c. 890-c. 910	Mahendrapāla I
c. 914-?	Mahipāla
n.d.	Mihira Bhoja II
n.d.	Vinayakapāla
c. 946-c. 948	Mahendrapāla II
c. 948-c. 960	Devapāla
c. 960-?	Vijayapāla
n.d.	Rājyapāla
c. 1018-c. 1027	Trilocanapāla

THE CŌLAS

Reign	Ruler
c. 850-c. 870	Vijayālaya
871-907	Āditya I
907-955	Parāntaka I
956	Arinjayā
956	Parāntaka II
956-969	Āditya II
969-985	Madhurantaka Uttama
985-1014	Rājarāja I
1014-1044	Rājendracōla Deva I
1044-1052	Rājadhirāja I
1052-1060	Rājendracōla Deva II
1060-1063	Ramamahendra
1063-1067	Virarājendra
1067-1070	Adhirājendra
1070-1122	Rājendra III
1122-1135	Vikrama Cōla
1135-1150	Kulottunga II Cōla
1150-1173	Rājarāja II
1173-1179	Rājadhirāja II
1179-1218	Kulottunga III
1218-1246	Rājarāja III
1246-1279	Rājendra IV

DELHI SULTANATE

Mu'izzī Slave Sultans

Reign	Ruler
1206-1210	Qut al-Dīn Aybak
1210-1211	Ārām Shāh
1211-1236	Iltutmish
1236	Ruknuddin Firūz Shāh
1236-1240	Raziya
1240-1242	Bahrām Shāh
1242-1246	Mas'ūd Shāh
1246-1266	Maḥmūd Shāh
1266-1287	Balban Ulugh Khān
1287-1290	Kay Qubādh
1290	Kayūmarth

Khaljī Dynasty

Reign	Ruler
1290-1296	Jalāl-ud-Dīn Fīrūz Khaljī
1296-1316	'Alā'-ud-Dīn Muḥammad Khaljī
1316	'Umar Shāh
1316-1320	Mubārak Shāh
1320	Khusraw Khān Barwārī

Tughluq Dynasty

Reign	Ruler
1320-1325	Tughluq I (Ghiyās-ud-Dīn)
1325-1351	Muḥammad ibn Tughluq
1351-1388	Fīrūz III
1388-1389	Tughluq II (Ghiyās-ud-Dīn)
1389-1390	Abū Bakr
1390-1394	Nāṣir-ud-Dīn
1394	Sikandar I (Humayun Khān)
1394-1395	Maḥmūd II
1395-1399	Nuṣrat
1401-1412	Maḥmūd II (second rule)
1412-1414	Dawlat Khān Lōdī

Sayyid Dynasty

Reign	Ruler
1414-1421	Khiḍr
1421-1434	Mubārak II
1434-1443	Muḥammad IV
1443-1451	'Ālām

Lodī Dynasty

Reign	Ruler
1451-1489	Bahlūl
1489-1517	Sikandar II
1517-1526	Ibrāhīm II

MUGHAL EMPERORS

Reign	Ruler
1526-1530	Bābur
1530-1540	Humāyūn
1540-1545	Shīr Shāh Sūr
1545-1553	Islām Shāh Sūr
1554	Muḥammad V Mubāriz Khān
1554-1555	Ibrāhām III Khān
1555	Aḥmad Khān Sikandar Shāh III
1555-1556	Humāyūn (second rule)
1556-1605	Akbar I
1605-1627	Jahāngīr
1627-1628	Dāwar Bakhsh
1628-1657	Jahān I Khusraw
1658-1707	Aurangzeb (Awrangzīb 'Ālamgīr I)
1707-1712	'Ālam I Bahādur
1712-1713	Jahāndār Mu'izz al-Dīn
1713-1719	Farrukh-siyar
1719	Shams al-Dīn Rāf' al-Darajāt

Reign	Ruler
1719	Jahān II Rāfiʿ al-Dawla
1719	Nīkūsiyar Muḥammad
1719-1720	Muḥammad Shāh Nāṣir al-Dīn
1720	Mohammed Ibrahim
1720-1748	Muḥammad Shāh Nāṣir al-Dīn
1739	Nādir Shāh sacks Delhi
1748-1754	Aḥmad Shāh Bahadur
1754-1779	Alamgir II
1760?	Shāh Jahān III
1779-1806	Shāh Alam II
1806-1837	Akbar Shāh II
1837-1857	Bahadur Shāh II (Bahadur Shāh Zafar)

IRAN (PERSIA). *See also* ISLAMIC CALIPHS, OTTOMAN EMPIRE, SELJUK EMPIRE

LATER SĀSĀNIAN EMPIRE

Reign	Ruler
309-379	Shāpūr II
379-383	Ardashīr II
383-388	Shāpūr III
388-399	Barham (Varahran) IV
399-421	Yazdegerd (Yazdgard) I
421-439	Barham (Varahran) V
439-457	Yazdegerd (Yazdgard) II
457-459	Hormizd III
459-484	Peroz
484-488	Valash
488-496	Kavadh I
496-498	Zamasp
499-531	Kavadh I (restored)
531-579	Khosrow (Khusro or Chosroes) I
579-590	Hormizd IV
590-628	Khosrow (Khusro or Chosroes) II
628	Kavadh II
628-629	Ardashīr III
629-630	Boran
630-632	Hormizd V and Khosrow III
633-651	Yazdegerd (Yazdgard) III
651	Islamic conquest
651-656	ʿUthmān ibn ʿAffān
656-661	Alī ibn Abī Ṭālib
661-750	Umayyad caliphs (*see* Islamic Caliphs)
750-821	ʿAbbāsid caliphs (*see* Islamic Caliphs)

LATER IRANIAN DYNASTIES

Dates	Dynasty
821-873	Tāhirid Dynasty (in Khorāsān, northeastern Persia)
c. 866-c. 900	Ṣafārrid Dynasty
c. 940-1000	Sīmjūrid Dynasty (in Khorāsān)

Dates	Dynasty
945-1055	Būyid Dynasty (western Iran)
977-1186	Ghaznavid Dynasty (in Khorāsān, Afghanistan, northern India)
999-1211	Qarakhanid Dynasty (Transoxania)
c. 1038	Seljuks take power (*see* Seljuk Empire)
1153-1231	Khwārezm-Shāh Dynasty (in Khwārezm, northeastern Iran)
c. 1231	Mongol invasion
1256-1353	Il-Khanid (Mongol) Dynasty
1353-1393	Mozaffarid Dynasty
1393-c. 1467	Timurid Dynasty
c. 1467-1500	Turkmen/Ottoman incursions

ṢAFAVID DYNASTY

Reign	Ruler
1501-1524	Ismāʿīl I
1524-1576	Ṭahmāsp I
1576-1578	Ismāʿīl II
1578-1587	Muḥammad Khudabanda
1587-1629	ʿAbbās I
1629-1642	Safi
1642-1667	ʿAbbās II
1667-1694	Süleyman I
1694-1722	Ḥoseyn I
1722-1732	Ṭahmāsp II
1732-1736	ʿAbbās III
1736-1750	Afshāid shahs
1750	Süleyman II in Mashad
1750-1765	Ismāʿīl III (Karim Khān, regent 1751-1765)

AFSHĀR DYNASTY

Reign	Ruler
1736-1747	Nāder Shāh (regent)
1747	ʿĀdel Shāh
1748	Ibrāhim
1748-1750	Shāh Rukh
1755-1796	Shāh Rukh in Khorāsān
1796-1803	Nāder Mīrza in Mashad

ZAND DYNASTY (WESTERN IRAN)

Reign	Ruler
1750-1779	Karim Khān
1779	Abu'l Fath (Shirāz)
1779	Moḥammad ʿAlī (Shirāz)
1779-1781	Moḥammad Ṣādiq (Shirāz)
1781-1785	ʿAlī Morād (Eṣfahān)
1785-1789	Ja'far (Eṣfahān, later Shirāz)
1789-1794	Luṭf ʿAlī (Shirāz)
1796	Qajar Dynasty begins

IRELAND

THE HIGH-KINGS

Reign	Ruler
379-405	Niall Noígillach of the Nine Hostages
405-428	Dathi (Nath) I
429-463	Lóeguire MacNéill
456-493	Saint Patrick converts Irish
463-483	Ailill Motl MacNath I
483-507	Lugaid MacLóeguiri O'Néill
507-534	Muirchertach MacErcae O'Néill (Muiredach)
534-544	Tuathal Máelgarb MacCorpri Cáech O'Néill
544-565	Diarmait MacCerbaill O'Néill
565-566	Domnall MacMuirchertaig O'Néill and Forggus MacMuirchertaig O'Néill
566-569	Ainmere MacSátnai O'Néill
569-572	Báetán MacMuirchertaig O'Néill and Eochaid MacDomnaill O'Néill
572-581	Báetán MacNinnedo O'Néill
581-598	Aed MacAinmerech O'Néill
598-604	Aed Sláine MacDiarmato O'Néill
598-604	Colmán Rímid MacBáetáin O'Néill (rival)
604-612	Aed Uaridnach MacDomnaill O'Néill
612-615	Máel Cobo MacAedo O'Néill
615-628	Suibne Menn MacFiachnai O'Néill
628-642	Domnall MacAedo O'Néill
642-658	Conall Cóel MacMáele Cobo O'Néill and Cellach MacMáele Cobo O'Néill
656-665	Diarmait MacAedo Sláine O'Néill and Blathmac MacAedo Sláine O'Néill
665-671	Sechnussach MacBlathmaic O'Néill
671-675	Cenn Fáelad MacBlathmaic O'Néill
675-695	Finsnechtae Fledach MacDúnchada O'Néill
695-704	Loingsech MacOengus O'Néill
704-710	Congal Cinn Magir MacFergus Fánat O'Néill
710-722	Fergal MacMáele Dúin O'Néill
722-724	Fogartach MacNéill O'Néill
724-728	Cináed MacIrgalaig
724-734	Flaithbbertach MacLoingsig O'Néill
734-743	Aed Allán MacFergal O'Néill
743-763	Domnall Midi O'Néill
763-770	Niall Frossach MacFergal O'Néill
770-797	Donnchad Midi MacDomnaill Midi O'Néill
797-819	Aed Oirdnide MacNéill Frossach O'Néill
819-833	Conchobar MacDonnchado Midi O'Néill
833-846	Niall Caille MacAedo Oirdnide O'Néill
846-862	Máel Sechnaill MacMáele Ruanaid O'Néill
862-879	Aed Findliath MacNéill Caille O'Néill
879-916	Flann Sionna MacMáele Sechnaill O'Néill
916-919	Niall Glúndubh MacAedo Findliath O'Néill
919-944	Donnchad Donn MacFlann O'Néill
944-950	Ruaidrí ua Canannáin (rival)
944-956	Congalach Cnogba MacMáel Mithig O'Néill

Reign	Ruler
956-980	Domnall MacMuirchertaig O'Néill
980-1002	Máel Sechnaill MacDomnaill O'Néill
1002-1014	Brian Bóruma MacCennétig and Brian Boru
1014-1022	Máel Sechnaill MacDomnaill O'Néill (restored)
1022-1064	Donnchad MacBrian
1064-1072	Diarmait MacMáil na mBó
1072-1086	Toirdelbach O'Brien
1090-1121	Domnall MacArdgar O'Lochlainn O'Néill
1121-1135	Toirrdelbach MacRuaidrí na Saide Buide ua Conchobair (Turlogh)
1141-1150	Toirrdelbach MacRuaidrí na Saide Buide ua Conchobair (Turlogh)
1150-1166	Muirchertach MacNéill MacLochlainn (Murtagh)
1166-1175	Ruaidrí MacToirrdelbaig (Rory O'Connor)
1175-1258	Henry II of England claims title Lord of Ireland
1258-1260	Brian Catha an Duin
1260-1316	English rule restored
1316-1318	Edward de Bruce
1318	English rule restored
1801	Act of Union: Ireland is joined with Britain

KINGDOM OF IRELAND (WITH ENGLAND/GREAT BRITAIN)

Reign	Ruler
1509-1547	Henry VIII
1547-1553	Edward VI
1553-1558	Mary I
1558-1603	Elizabeth I
1603-1625	James (I of England, VI of Scotland)
1625-1649	Charles I
1649-1660	Commonwealth and Restoration
1660-1685	Charles II
1685-1689	James (II of England, VII of Scotland)
1689-1702	William and Mary
1702-1707	Anne
1707	Act of Union (Great Britain and Ireland)
1707-1714	Anne
1714-1727	George I
1727-1760	George II
1760-1801	George III
1801	Act of Union creates United Kingdom

ISLAMIC CALIPHS. *See also* IRAN, OTTOMAN EMPIRE, SELJUK EMPIRE, SPAIN

ORTHODOX (SUNNI) CALIPHS, 632-661

Reign	Caliph
632-634	Abū Bakr
634-644	ʿUmar I

Reign	Caliph
644-656	ʿUthmān ibn ʿAffān
656-661	Alī ibn Abī Ṭālib

UMAYYAD CALIPHS, 661-750

Reign	Caliph
661-680	Muʾāwiyah I (Muʾāwiyah ibn Abī Sufyna)
680-683	Yazīd I
683	Muʾāwiyah II
684-685	Marwān I
685-705	ʿAbd al-Malik
705-715	al-Walīd I
715-717	Sulaimān
717-720	ʿUmar II
720-724	Yazīd II
724-743	Hishām
743-744	al-Walīd II
744	Yazīd III
744	Ibrāhīm
744-750	Marwān II

ʿABBĀSID CALIPHS, 750-1256

Reign	Caliph
750-754	Abū al-ʿAbbās al-Saffāḥ
754-775	al-Manṣūr
775-785	al-Mahdī
785-786	al-Hādī
786-809	Hārūn al-Rashīd
809-813	al-Amīn
813-833	al-Maʾmūn (Maʾmūn the Great)
833-842	al-Muʿtaṣim
842-847	al-Wathīq
847-861	al-Mutawakkil
861-862	al-Muntaṣir
862-866	al-Mustaʿin
866-869	al-Muʿtazz
869-870	al-Muqtadī
870-892	al-Muʿtamid
892-902	al-Muʿtaḍid
902-908	al-Muktafī
908-932	al-Muqtadir
932-934	al-Qāhir
934-940	al-Rāḍī
940-944	al-Mustaqfī
946-974	al-Mutī
974-991	al-Ṭāʾiʿ
991-1031	al-Qadir
1031-1075	al-Qāʾim
1075-1094	al-Muqtadī
1094-1118	al-Mustazhir
1118-1135	al-Mustarshid
1135-1136	al-Rashīd
1136-1160	al-Muqtafī

Reign	Caliph
1160-1170	al-Mustanjid
1170-1180	al-Mustadī
1180-1225	al-Nāṣir
1225-1226	al-Zāhir
1226-1242	al-Mustanṣir
1242-1256	al-Mustaʿṣim

FĀṬIMID CALIPHS, 909-1171

Reign	Caliph
909-934	al-Mahdī
934-945	al-Qāʾim
945-952	al-Manṣūr
952-975	al-Muʿizz
975-996	al-ʿAzīz
996-1021	al-Ḥākim
1021-1036	al-Zahīr
1036-1094	al-Mustanṣir
1094-1101	al-Mustadī
1101-1130	al-Amīr
1130-1149	al-Ḥāfiz
1149-1154	al-Zafīr
1154-1160	al-Fāʾiz
1160-1171	al-ʿAdīd

ITALY

The Italian peninsula was occupied by a number of fiefs and principalities during the better part of the millennium that made up the Middle Ages. These included Lombardy in the north, the Papal States in the center, and various duchies, margavates, and republics, including Sardinia, Benevento, Spoleto, Modena, Milan, Tuscany, Parma, Montferrat, and independent centers of trade such as Venice and Genoa. Only those early rulers who dominated the area are listed below; thereafter, the northern part of the peninsula was primarily under the power of the Carolingians (see Frankish Kingdom and France), the Holy Roman Emperors (see Holy Roman Empire, above), and the Papacy (see Popes and Antipopes, above). In the south, Naples and Sicily dominated. Thus, during the millennium 476-1453, the Italian Peninsula was a complex of ever-shifting jurisdictions, of which only the more prominent rulers are listed below.

BARBARIAN RULERS

Reign	Ruler
476-493	Odoacer
493-526	Theodoric
526-534	Athalaric
534-536	Theodatus (Theodahad)
536-540	Vitiges (Witiges)

Reign	Ruler
540-541	Theodobald (Heldebadus)
541	Eraric
541-552	Totila
552-553	Teias

Byzantine (East Roman) Rule

Reign	Ruler
518-527	Justin I
527-565	Justinian I

Lombards (Northern Italy)

Reign	Ruler
565-572	Alboin
573-575	Celph
575-584	Unstable
584-590	Authari
590-591	Theodelinda
591-615	Agilulf
615-625	Adaloald
625-636	Arioald
636-652	Rotharis
652-661	Aribert I
661-662	Godipert
662-671	Grimoald
671-674	Garibald
674-688	Bertharit
688-700	Cunibert
700-701	Liutpert
701	Raginpert
701-712	Aribert II
712-744	Liutprand
744-749	Rachis of Friuli
749-756	Aistulf of Friuli
756-774	Desiderius
774-888	Frankish conquest, subsumed under Carolingian Empire

Kingdom of Italy

Reign	Ruler
888-891	Berengar I of Friuli
891-894	Guy of Spoleto (Guido, Wido)
894-896	Lambert of Spoleto
896-899	Arnulf, King of Germany
899-905	Louis III
905-922	Berengar I of Friuli (restored)
922-933	Rudolf II
933-947	Hugh of Arles
947-950	Lothair II of Arles
950-961	Berengar II of Ivrea
961	Conquest by Otto I; Italian peninsula divided among Holy Roman Empire, Papacy, and other principalities until unification in 1861

Naples and Sicily

Reign	Ruler (Line)
1042-1046	William Iron Arm (Norman)
1046-1051	Drogo (Norman)
1051-1057	Humphrey (Norman)
1057-1085	Robert Guiscard (Norman)
1071-1101	Roger I (Norman)
1101-1154	Roger II of Sicily (Norman; king in 1130)
1154-1166	William I (Norman)
1166-1189	William II the Good (Norman)
1190-1194	Tancred of Lecce (Norman)
1194	William III (Norman)
1194-1197	Henry VI (Hohenstaufen)
1197-1250	Frederick II (Hohenstaufen)
1250-1254	Conrad IV (Hohenstaufen)
1250-1266	Manfred (Hohenstaufen)
1267-1268	Conradin (rival)
1266-1285	Charles I of Anjou (Angevin)
1282	Sicily and Naples split

Sicily

Reign	Ruler
1282-1285	Pedro III of Aragón
1285-1296	James II of Aragón
1296-1337	Frederick II (or I)
1337-1342	Peter II
1342-1355	Louis
1355-1377	Frederick III (or II) the Simple
1377-1401	Mary
1390-1409	Martin the Younger
1395-1410	Martin (I) the Older Aragón
1412-1416	Ferdinand I Sicily & Aragón
1416-1458	Alfonso (V of Aragón)
1458-1468	John II
1468-1516	Ferdinand II (III of Naples)
1516-1713	United with Spain
1713-1720	Victor Amadeus II (duke of Savoy)
1720	Returned to Spain as part of Kingdom of the Two Sicilies
1720-1735	Austrian rule
1735-1759	Charles (Bourbon king of Spain)
1759-1825	Ferdinand I/IV
1825-1830	Francis I
1830-1859	Ferdinand II/V
1859-1860	Francis II
1861	Annexed to Italy

Naples

Reign	Ruler
1285-1309	Charles II (Angevin)
1309-1343	Robert Ladislas (Angevin)
1343-1382	Joanna I (Angevin)
1382-1386	Charles III (Angevin)

Reign	Ruler
1386-1414	Ladislas (Angevin)
1414-1435	Joanna II (Angevin)
1435-1442	René of Anjou
1442-1458	Alfonso I (V of Aragón)
1458-1494	Ferdinand I
1494-1495	Alfonso II (Naples only)
1495-1496	Ferdinand II (Ferrandino)
1496-1501	Frederick IV (III)
1501-1503	French occupation
1504-1516	Ferdinand III (II of Sicily)
1516-1713	United with Spain
1713	Ceded to Austria
1720	Returned to Spain as part of Kingdom of the Two Sicilies
1799	Parthenopean Republic
1805	Bourbons deposed
1806-1808	Joseph Bonaparte
1808-1815	Joachim Murat
1815	Bourbon restoration
1825-1830	Francis I
1830-1859	Ferdinand II/V
1859-1860	Francis II
1861	Annexed to Italy

VISCONTIS (GENOA)

Reign	Ruler
1310-1322	Matteo Visconti
1322-1328	Galeazzo I
1328-1339	Azzo
1339-1349	Lucchino
1349-1354	Giovanni
1354-1355	Matteo II and Bernabò
1354-1378	Galeazzo II
1378-1402	Gian Galeazzo II
1402-1447	Filippo Maria

SFORZAS (GENOA)

Reign	Ruler
1450-1466	Francesco Sforza
1466-1476	Galeazzo Maria
1476-1481	Gian Galeazzo
1481-1499	Ludovico
1500-1512	[Louis XII of France]
1512-1515	Massimiliano
1521-1535	Francesco Maria

DOGES OF VENICE

Reign	Doge
727-738	Orso (Ursus) Ipato
742, 744-736	Teodato (Deusdedit) Ipato
756	Galla Gaulo
756-765	Domenico Monegaurio

Reign	Doge
765-787	Maurizio I Galbaio
787-802	Giovanni and Maurizio II Galbaio
802-811	Obelerio Antenorio
808-811	Beato
811-827	Angello Partecipazio
827-829	Giustiniano Partecipazio
829-836	Giovanni I Partecipazio
836-864	Pietro Tradonico
864-881	Orso I Badoer (I Partecipazio)
881-888	Giovanni Badoer (II Partecipazio)
887	Pietro I Candiano
888-912	Pietro Tribuno
912-932	Orso II Badoer (II Partecipazio)
932-939	Pietro II Candiano
939-942	Pietro Badoer (Partecipazio)
942-959	Pietro III Candiano
959-976	Pietro IV Candiano
976-978	Pietro I Orseolo
978-979	Vitale Candiano
979-991	Tribuno Menio (Memmo)
991-1009	Pietro II Orseolo
1009-1026	Ottone Orseolo
1026-1030	Pietro Centranico (Barbolano)
1030-1032	Ottone Orseolo (second rule)
1032-1043	Domenico Flabianico
1043-1070	Domenico Contarini
1070-1084	Domenico Silvio (Selvo)
1084-1096	Vitale Falier
1096-1101	Vitale I Michiel (Michel)
1101-1118	Ordelafo Falier
1118-1129	Domenico Michiel
1129-1148	Pietro Polani
1148-1155	Domenico Morosini
1155-1172	Vitale II Michiel
1172-1178	Sebastiano Ziani
1178-1192	Orio Mastropiero (Malipiero)
1192-1205	Enrico Dandolo
1205-1229	Pietro Ziani
1229-1249	Giacomo Tiepolo
1249-1253	Marino Morosini
1253-1268	Reniero Zeno
1268-1275	Lorenzo Tiepolo
1275-1280	Jacopo Contarini
1280-1289	Giovanni Dandolo
1289-1311	Pietro Gradenigo
1311-1312	Marino Zorzi
1312-1328	Giovanni Soranzo
1328-1339	Francesco Dandolo
1339-1342	Bartolomeo Gradenigo
1343-1354	Andrea Dandolo
1354-1355	Marino Falier
1355-1356	Giovanni Gradenigo

Reign	Doge
1356-1361	Giovanni Dolfin
1361-1365	Lorenzo Celsi
1365-1368	Marco Corner
1368-1382	Andrea Contarini
1382	Michele Morosini
1382-1400	Antonio Venier
1400-1413	Michele Steno
1414-1423	Tommaso Mocenigo
1423-1457	Francesco Foscari
1462-1471	Cristoforo Moro
1471-1473	Nicolò Tron
1473-1474	Nicolò Marcello
1474-1476	Pietro Mocenigo
1476-1478	Andrea Vendramin
1478-1485	Giovanni Mocenigo
1485-1486	Marco Barbarigo
1486-1501	Agostino Barbarigo
1501-1521	Leonardo Loredan
1521-1523	Antonio Grimani
1523-1538	Andrea Gritti
1539-1545	Pietro Lando
1545-1553	Francesco Donato
1553-1554	Marcantonio Trevisan
1554-1556	Francesco Venier
1556-1559	Lorenzo Priuli
1559-1567	Girolamo Priuli
1567-1570	Pietro Loredan
1570-1577	Alvise I Mocenigo
1577-1578	Sebastiano Venier
1578-1585	Nicolò da Ponte
1585-1595	Pasquale Cicogna
1595-1605	Marino Grimani
1606-1612	Leonardo Donato
1612-1615	Marcantonio Memmo
1615-1618	Giovanni Bembo
1618	Nicolò Donato
1618-1623	Antonio Priuli
1623-1624	Francesco Contarini
1625-1629	Giovanni Corner
1630-1631	Nicolò Contarini
1631-1646	Francesco Erizzo
1646-1655	Francesco Molin
1655-1656	Carlo Contarini
1656	Francesco Corner
1656-1658	Bertucci (Albertuccio) Valier
1658-1659	Giovanni Pesaro
1659-1675	Domenico Contarini
1675-1676	Nicolò Sagredo
1676-1684	Luigi Contarini
1684-1688	Marcantonio Giustinian
1688-1694	Francesco Morosini
1694-1700	Silvestro Valier

Reign	Doge
1700-1709	Alvise II Mocenigo
1709-1722	Giovanni II Corner
1722-1732	Alvise III Mocenigo
1732-1735	Carlo Ruzzini
1735-1741	Alvise Pisani
1741-1752	Pietro Grimani
1752-1762	Francesco Loredan
1762-1763	Marco Foscarini
1763-1778	Alvise IV Mocenigo
1779-1789	Paolo Renier
1789-1797	Lodovico Manin
1797	Venice Falls to Napoleon Bonaparte

FLORENCE (MEDICIS)

Reign	Ruler
1434-1464	Cosimo the Elder
1464-1469	Piero I
1469-1478	Giuliano
1469-1492	Lorenzo I the Magnificent
1492-1494	Piero II
1494-1512	Charles VIII expels the Medici
1512-1519	Lorenzo II
1519-1527	Giulio (Pope Clement VII)
1527	Sack of Rome
1527-1530	Second expulsion
1530-1537	Alessandro
1537-1574	Cosimo I
1574-1587	Francesco I
1587-1609	Ferdinand I
1609-1621	Cosimo II
1621-1670	Ferdinand II
1670-1723	Cosimo III
1723-1737	Gian Gastone

TUSCANY (AFTER THE MEDICIS)

Reign	Ruler
1738-1745	Francis
1745-1790	Leopold I
1790-1801	Ferdinand III
1801-1803	Louis of Parma (king of Etruria)
1803-1807	Charles Louis of Parma
1803-1807	Maria Louisa of Parma (regent)
1807-1814	Annexed to France
1824-1859	Leopold II
1859-1860	Ferdinand IV
1860	Annexed to Italy

PARMA

Farneses

Reign	Ruler
1545-1547	Pier Luigi
1547-1586	Ottavio

Reign	Ruler
1586-1592	Alessandro
1592-1622	Ranuccio I
1622-1646	Odoardo I
1646-1694	Ranuccio II
1694-1727	Francesco
1727-1731	Antonio

Bourbons

Reign	Ruler
1731-1736	Charles
1738-1748	Habsburg rule
1748-1765	Philip
1765-1802	Ferdinand
1805-1814	French rule
1814-1847	Marie Louise (Habsburg)
1848-1849	Charles II Louis
1849-1854	Charles III
1854-1859	Robert
1859	Annexed to Italy

SARDINIA

Reign	Ruler
1720-1730	Victor Amadeus II (duke of Savoy)
1730-1773	Charles Emanuel III
1773-1796	Victor Amadeus III
1796-1802	Charles Emanuel IV
1802-1821	Victor Emanuel I
1821-1831	Charles Felix
1831-1849	Charles Albert
1849-1861	Victor Emanuel II
1861	Annexed to Italy

JAPAN

ASUKA PERIOD

Reign	Ruler
539-571	Kimmei
572-585	Bidatsu
585-587	Yōmei
587-592	Sushun
593-628	Suiko (empress)
629-641	Jomei
642-645	Kōgyoku (empress)
645-654	Kōtoku
655-661	Saimei (empress)
661-672	Tenji
672	Kōbun
673-686	Temmu
686-697	Jitō (empress)
697-707	Mommu
707-715	Gemmei (empress)

NARA PERIOD

Reign	Ruler
707-715	Gemmei (empress)
715-724	Genshō (empress)
724-749	Shōmu
749-758	Kōken (empress)
758-764	Junnin
764-770	Shōtoku (Kōken, empress)
770-781	Kōnin

HEIAN PERIOD

Reign	Ruler
781-806	Kammu
806-809	Heizei
809-823	Saga
823-833	Junna
833-850	Nimmyō
850-858	Montoku
858-876	Seiwa
876-884	Yōzei
884-887	Kōkō
887-897	Uda
897-930	Daigo
930-946	Suzaku
946-967	Murakami
967-969	Reizei
969-984	En'yu
984-986	Kazan
986-1011	Ichijō
1011-1016	Sanjō
1016-1036	Go-Ichijō
1036-1045	Go-Suzaku
1045-1068	Go-Reizei
1068-1073	Go-Sanjō
1073-1087	Shirakawa (cloistered, 1086-1129)
1087-1107	Horikawa
1107-1123	Toba (cloistered, 1129-1156)
1123-1142	Sutoku
1142-1155	Konoe
1155-1158	Go-Shirakawa (cloistered, 1158-1192)
1158-1165	Nijō
1165-1168	Rokujō
1168-1180	Takakura
1180-1185	Antoku

KAMAKURA PERIOD AND KEMMU RESTORATION

Reign	Ruler
1183-1198	Go-Toba
1198-1210	Tsuchimikado
1210-1221	Jintoku
1221	Chukyo
1221-1232	Go-Horikawa
1232-1242	Shijō

Reign	Ruler
1242-1246	Go-Saga
1246-1260	Go-Fukakusa
1260-1274	Kameyama
1274-1287	Go-Uda
1287-1298	Fushimi
1298-1301	Go-Fushimi
1301-1308	Go-Nijō
1308-1318	Hanazonō
1318-1339	Go-Daigo

KAMAKURA SHOGUNATE

Reign	Shogun
1192-1199	Minamoto Yoritomo
1202-1203	Minamoto Yoriie
1203-1219	Minamoto Sanetomo
1226-1244	Kujo Yoritsune
1244-1252	Kujo Yoritsugu
1252-1266	Prince Munetaka
1266-1289	Prince Koreyasu
1289-1308	Prince Hisaaki
1308-1333	Prince Morikuni

HŌJŌ REGENTS

Reign	Regent
1203-1205	Hōjō Tokimasa
1205-1224	Hōjō Yoshitoki
1224-1242	Hōjō Yasutoki
1242-1246	Hōjō Tsunetoki
1246-1256	Hōjō Tokiyori
1256-1264	Hōjō Nagatoki
1264-1268	Hōjō Masamura
1268-1284	Hōjō Tokimune
1284-1301	Hōjō Sadatoki
1301-1311	Hōjō Morotoki
1311-1312	Hōjō Munenobu
1312-1315	Hōjō Hirotoki
1315	Hōjō Mototoki
1316-1326	Hōjō Takatoki
1326	Hōjō Sadaaki
1327-1333	Hōjō Moritoki

NAMBOKUCHŌ PERIOD

Emperors: Southern Court

Reign	Ruler
1318-1339	Go-Daigo
1339-1368	Go-Murakami
1368-1383	Chōkei
1383-1392	Go-Kameyama

Ashikaga Pretenders: Northern Court

Reign	Ruler
1336-1348	Komyō
1348-1351	Sukō
1351-1371	Go-Kogon
1371-1382	Go-En'yu

MUROMACHI PERIOD

Reign	Ruler
1382-1412	Go-Komatsu
1412-1428	Shōkō
1428-1464	Go-Hanazono
1464-1500	Go-Tsuchimikado
1500-1526	Go-Kashiwabara
1526-1557	Go-Nara
1557-1586	Ōgimachi

ASHIKAGA SHOGUNATE

Reign	Shogun
1338-1358	Ashikaga Takauji
1359-1368	Ashikaga Yoshiakira
1368-1394	Ashikaga Yoshimitsu
1395-1423	Ashikaga Yoshimochi
1423-1425	Ashikaga Yoshikazu
1429-1441	Ashikaga Yoshinori
1442-1443	Ashikaga Yoshikatsu
1449-1473	Ashikaga Yoshimasa
1474-1489	Ashikaga Yoshihisa
1490-1493	Ashikaga Yoshitane
1495-1508	Ashikaga Yoshizumi
1508-1521	Ashikaga Yoshitane (second rule)
1522-1547	Ashikaga Yoshiharu
1547-1565	Ashikaga Yoshiteru
1568	Ashikaga Yoshihide
1568-1573	Ashikaga Yoshiaki

AZUCHI-MOMOYAMA PERIOD

Reign	Ruler
1573-1582	Oda Nobunaga (dictator)
1586-1611	Go-Yōzei (emperor)

EDO PERIOD

Emperors

Reign	Emperor
1612-1629	Go-Mi-no-o
1630-1643	Meishō (Myōshō)
1644-1654	Go-Kōmyō
1655-1662	Go-Saiin
1663-1686	Reigen
1687-1709	Higashiyama
1710-1735	Nakamikado
1736-1746	Sakuramachi
1746-1762	Momozono

Reign	Emperor
1763-1770	Go-Sakuramachi
1771-1779	Go-Momozono
1780-1816	Kōkaku
1817-1846	Ninkō
1847-1866	Kōmei

Tokugawa Shogunate

Reign	Shogun
1603-1605	Tokugawa Ieyasu
1605-1623	Tokugawa Hidetada
1623-1651	Tokugawa Iemitsu
1651-1680	Tokugawa Ietsuna
1680-1709	Tokugawa Tsunayoshi
1709-1712	Tokugawa Ienobu
1713-1716	Tokugawa Ietsugu
1716-1745	Tokugawa Yoshimune
1745-1760	Tokugawa Ieshige
1760-1786	Tokugawa Ieharu
1787-1837	Tokugawa Ienari
1837-1853	Tokugawa Ieyoshi
1853-1858	Tokugawa Iesada
1858-1866	Tokugawa Iemochi
1867-1868	Tokugawa Yoshinobu

KINGDOM OF JERUSALEM

The Christian rulers of Jerusalem were ushered in by the First Crusade and essentially were ushered out after the last Crusade.

Reign	King
1095-1099	First Crusade
1099-1100	Godfrey of Boulogne (or Bouillon)
1100-1118	Baldwin I of Boulogne
1118-1131	Baldwin II of Le Bourg
1131-1153	Melisende
1131-1143	Fulk V of Anjou
1143-1162	Baldwin III
1147-1149	Second Crusade
1162-1174	Amalric I
1174-1183	Baldwin IV the Leper
1183-1186	Baldwin V
1185-1190	Sibylla
1186-1192	Guy of Lusignan
1189-1192	Third Crusade
1190-1192	Conrad of Montferrat
1192-1197	Henry of Champagne
1192-1205	Isabella I
1197-1205	Amalric II
1202-1204	Fourth Crusade
1205-1210	Maria of Montferrat (regent)
1210-1225	John of Brienne
1210-1228	Isabella (Yolanda) II

Reign	King
1217-1221	Fifth Crusade
1225-1228	Frederick II
1227-1230	Sixth Crusade
1228-1254	Conrad IV Hohenstaufen
1244	Fall of Jerusalem
1248-1254	Seventh (or Sixth) Crusade
1254-1268	Conradin Hohenstaufen
1268-1284	Hugh III
1268-1284	Charles of Anjou (rival)
1270	Eighth (or Seventh) Crusade
1284-1285	John I
1285-1306	Henry I of Jerusalem (II of Cyprus)
1291	Fall of Acre to the Mamluks

KOREA

UNIFIED SILLA DYNASTY

Reign	Ruler
661-681	Munmu Wang
681-692	Sinmun Wang
692-702	Hyoso Wang
702-737	Sŏngdŏk Wang
737-742	Hyosŏng Wang
742-765	Kyŏngdŏk Wang
765-780	Hyesong Wang
780-785	Sŏndŏk Wang
785-798	Wŏnsŏng Wang
798-800	Sosŏng Wang
800-809	Aejang Wang
809-826	Hŏndŏk Wang
826-836	Hŭngdŏk Wang
836-838	Hŭigang Wang
838-839	Minae Wang
839	Sinmu Wang
839-857	Munsŏng Wang
857-861	Hŏnan Wang
861-875	Kyŏngmun Wang
875-886	Hŏn'gang Wang
886-887	Chŏnggang Wang
887-896	Queen Chinsŏng
897-912	Hyogong Wang
912-917	Pak Sindŏ Wang
917-924	Kyŏngmyŏng Wang
924-927	Kyŏngae Wang
927-935	Kyŏngsun Wang

KORYŎ DYNASTY

Reign	Ruler
918-943	T'aejo (Wang Kŏn)
944-945	Hyejong
946-949	Chŏngjong

Reign	Ruler
949-975	Kwangjong (Wang So)
975-981	Kyŏngjong (Wang Yu)
981-997	Sŏngjong (Wang Ch'i)
997-1009	Mokshong
1009-1031	Hyŏnjong
1031-1034	Tokjong
1034-1046	Chŏngjong
1046-1083	Munjong (Wang Hwi)
1083	Sunjong
1083-1094	Sŏnjong
1094-1095	Hŏnjong
1095-1105	Sukjong
1105-1122	Yejong I
1122-1146	Injong I (Wang Hae)
1146-1170	Ŭijong
1170-1197	Myŏngjong
1197-1204	Sinjong
1204-1211	Hŭijong
1211-1213	Kangjong
1214-1259	Kojong I
1260-1274	Wŏnjong
1274-1308	Ch'unguyŏl Wang
1308-1313	Ch'ungsŏn Wang
1313-1330	Ch'ungsuk Wang
1330-1332	Ch'unghye Wang
1332-1339	Ch'angsuk Wang
1339-1344	Ch'unghye Wang
1344-1348	Ch'ungmok Wang
1348-1351	Ch'ungjŏng Wang
1351-1374	Kongmin Wang
1374-1388	U (Sin-u)
1389	Sinch'ang
1389-1392	Kongyang Wang

Yi Dynasty

Reign	Ruler
1392-1398	Yi T'aejo
1398-1400	Chŏngjong
1400-1418	T'aejong
1418-1450	Sejong
1450-1452	Munjong
1452-1455	Tanjong
1455-1468	Sejo
1468-1469	Yejong
1469-1494	Sŏngjong
1494-1506	Yŏnsan Gun
1506-1544	Chungjong
1544-1545	Injong
1546-1567	Myŏngjong
1567-1608	Sŏnjo
1608-1623	Kwanghae-gun
1623-1649	Injo

Reign	Ruler
1649-1659	Hyojong
1659-1674	Hyŏnjong
1674-1720	Sukchong
1720-1724	Kyŏngjong
1724-1776	Yŏngjo
1776-1800	Chŏngjo
1800-1834	Sonjo

Mongols. *See also* China: Yuan Dynasty
From his base in Mongolia, founder Genghis Khan conquered a large and diverse region covering much of Asia from the Far East to the steppes of Russia, Turkey and the Middle East, Central Asia, and even parts of Southeast Asia. Although the individual leaders of those who inherited this empire remain unfamiliar to most, Genghis's heirs, among whom are the "great khans" of the immediate generations to follow, would indelibly change and shape the world from Russia to China, the Mideast to India. Genghis divided his empire among four sons. Jochi, the eldest, received the northwestern quadrant of this expanse, and his sons would found the "hordes" (armies) the would become known as the Blue, White, and eventually Golden Hordes; the latter would not meet its match until Russia's founder, Ivan the Great, refused to pay tribute in 1476 and thereafter would dissolve into the various khanates of Kazan, Astrakhan, and the Crimea. Genghis's second son, Chaghatai, would receive the area of Central Asia lying north of India and east of the Caspian and Aral seas, sometimes called Moghulistan or Mughulistan. Genghis's third son, Ogatai, oversaw the southeastern and far east coastal "quadrant" or swathe, which would eventually become part of the huge realm of his nephew Kublai Khan, who in turn was the son of Genghis's youngest, Tolui, heir to the Mongolian homeland. It was Tolui's sons, beginning with Kublai, who would spawn the Chinese emperors of the Yuan Dynasty in the east and, beginning with Hulegu, the great Ilkhans who conquered the Middle East. The Ilkhans' successors, the Jalāyirids, Black Sheep Turks, White Sheep Turks, and ultimately the Timurids (founded by the part-Mongol Timur or Tamerlane), would dominate the Mideast and also give rise to the Mughal Dynasty in India.

Great Khans

Reign	Ruler
1206-1227	Genghis Khan (founder)
1227-1229	Tolui
1229-1241	Ogatai Khan

Reign	Ruler
1241-1246	Toregene (regent, wife of Ogatai)
1246-1248	Güyük
1248-1251	Oghul Qaimish (regent, wife of Güyük)
1251-1259	Mongu
1259-1260	Arigböge (regent, brother of Mongu and Kublai)
1260-1294	Kublai Khan

Khans of China's Yuan Dynasty

Reign	Ruler
1267-1279	Mongols conquer Southern Song
1294-1307	Temür Öljeitü (Chengzong)
1307-1311	Kaishan (Wuzong)
1311-1320	Ayurbarwada (Renzong)
1321-1323	Shidebala (Yingzong)
1323-1328	Yesün Temür (Taiding)
1328	Arigaba (Aragibag)
1328-1329	Tugh Temür (Wenzong)1
1329	Tugh Koshila (Mingzong)
1329-1332	Tugh Temür (restored)
1333-1368	Toghon Temür (Shundi)
1368	Chinese expel Mongols

Later Mongolian Khans

Reign	Ruler
1370-1388	Togus-Temür
1370-1379	Biliktu
1379-1389	Usaqal
1389-1393	Engke Soriktu
1393-1400	Elbek
1400-1403	Gun Timur
1403-1411	Oljei Timur
1411-1415	Delbeg
1415-1425	Eseku
1425-1438	Adai Qa'an
1438-1440	Esen Toghan Tayisi
1440-1452	Tayisung Qa'an
1452-1455	Esen Tayisi
1452-1454	Molon Khan Togus
1454-1463?	Maqa Kurkis
1463?-1467	Mandughuli
1467-1470	Bayan Mongke
1470-c.1485	Civil war
1479-1543	Dayan Khan
1543-1582	Altan Khan
1547-1557	Kudeng Darayisun
1557-1592	Tumen Jasaghtu
1592-1604	Sechen Khan
1604-1634	Ligdan Khan
1628-1759	Manchurian conquest

Middle East (Iraq, Iran, eastern Turkey, Arabia)

Il Khāns

Reign	Ruler
1256-1265	Hülegü (Hülägü)
1255-1260	Invasion of Middle East
1260	Battle of ʿAin Jalut (defeat by Mamlūks)
1265-1282	Abaqa
1282-1284	Aḥmad Tegüder
1284-1291	Arghūn
1291-1295	Gaykhatu
1295	Baydu
1295-1304	Maḥmūd Ghāzān
1304-1316	Muḥammad Khudābanda Öljeytü
1316-1335	Abū Saʿīd ʿAlāʾ ad-Dunyā wa ad-Dīn
1335-1336	Arpa Keʾün
1336-1337	Mūsā
1337-1338	Muḥammad
1338-1353	Conflict among successor states

Jalāyirids

Reign	Ruler
1340-1356	Shaykh Ḥasan-i Buzurg Tāj ad-Dīn
1356-1374	Shaykh Uways
1374-1382	Ḥusayn I Jalāl ad-Dīn
1382-1410	Sulṭān Aḥmad Ghiyāth ad-Dīn
1410-1411	Shāh Walad
1411	Maḥmūd
1411-1421	Uways II
1421-1425	Maḥmūd
1421	Muḥammad
1425-1532	Ḥusayn II
1432	Conquest by Kara Koyunlu

Kara Koyunlu (Black Sheep Turks)

Reign	Ruler
1351-1380	Bayram Khōja (Jalāyirid vassal)
1380-1389	Kara Muḥammad
1382	Independent
c. 1390-1400	Kara Yūsuf
1400-1406	Occupation by Tamerlane
1406-1420	Kara Yūsuf
1420-1438	Iskandar
1439-1467	Jahān Shāh
1467-1469	Ḥasan ʿAlī
1469	Abū Yūsuf
1469	Conquest by Ak Koyunlu

Ak Koyunlu (White Sheep Turks)

Reign	Ruler
1403-1435	Kara Osman (Qara Yoluq ʿUthmān Fakhr ad-Dīn)
1435-1438	ʿAlī Jalāl ad-Dīn
1438-1444	Ḥamza Nūr ad-Dīn
1444-1453	Jahāngīr Muʾizz ad-Dīn
1453-1478	Uzun Ḥasan

Reign	Ruler
1478	Sulṭān Khalīl
1478-1490	Yaʿqūb
1490-1493	Baysonqur
1493-1497	Rustam
1497	Aḥmad Gövde
1497-1502	Alwand (Diyār Bakr and Azerbaijan)
1497-1500	Muḥammad (Iraq and Persia)
1500-1508	Sulṭān Murād (Persia)
1504-1508	Zayn al-ʿAbidīn (Diyār Bakr)
1508	Ṣafawid conquest

SOUTH CENTRAL ASIA

Chaghatayid or Jagataiid (Turkistan and the Tarim Basin)

Reign	Ruler
1227-1244	Chaghatay (Jagatai)
1244-1246	Kara Hülegü
1246-1251	Yesü Möngke
1251-1252	Kara Hülegü
1252-1260	Orqina Khātūn
1260-1266	Alughu
1266	Mubārak Shāh
c. 1266-1271	Baraq Ghiyāth ad-Dīn
1271-1272	Negübey
1272-1282	Buqa/Toqa Temür
c. 1282-1306	Du'a
1306-1308	Könchek
1308-1309	Taliqu
1309	Kebek
1309-1320	Esen Buqa
c. 1320-1326	Kebek
1326	Eljigedey
1326	Du'a Temür
1326-1334	Tarmashīrīn ʿAlā' ad-Dīn
1334	Buzan
1334-1338	Changshi
c. 1338-1342	Yesün Temür
c. 1342-1343	Muḥammad
1343-1346	Kazan
1346-1358	Danishmendji
1358	Buyan Kuli
1359	Shāh Temür
1359-1363	Tughluq Temür
c. 1363	Timurids rule Mughulistan

Timurids

Reign	Ruler
1370-1405	Tamerlane (Timur)
1402	Capture of Bayezid, Battle of Ankara
1405-1407	Pīr Muḥammad (Kandahar)
1405-1409	Khalīl Sulṭān (Samarqand)
1405-1409	Shāh Rukh (Khorāsān)
1409-1447	Shāh Rukh (Transoxania, Iran)

Reign	Ruler
1447-1449	Ulugh Beg (Transoxania, Khorāsān)
1449-1450	ʿAbd al-Laṭīf (Transoxania)
1450-1451	ʿAbdallāh
1451-1469	Abū Saʿīd (Transoxania, Iran)
1469-1494	Sulṭān Aḥmad (Transoxania)
1494-1495	Maḥmūd
1495-1500	Baysonqur, Mas'ūd, ʿAlī (Transoxania)
1500	Özbeg conquest of Transoxania

WESTERN ASIA, RUSSIA, NORTH CENTRAL ASIA

Blue Horde

Reign	Ruler
1227-1256	Batu
1236-1239	Russia conquered
1239-1242	Europe invaded
1256-1257	Sartaq
1257	Ulaghchi
1257-1267	Berke
1267-1280	Möngke Temür
1280-1287	Töde Möngke
1287-1291	Töle Buqa
1291-1313	Toqta
1313-1341	Muḥammad Özbeg
1341-1342	Tīnī Beg
1342-1357	Jānī Beg
1357-1359	Berdi Beg
1357-1380	Period of anarchy
1378	Union with White Horde

White Horde

Reign	Ruler
1226-1280	Orda
1280-1302	Köchü
1302-1309	Buyan
1309-1315	Sāsibuqa?
c. 1315-1320	Ilbasan
1320-1344	Mubārak Khwāja
1344-1374	Chimtay
1374-1376	Urus
1376-1377	Toqtaqiya
1377	Temür Malik
1377-1395	Toqtamïsh
1378	White and Blue Hordes form Golden Horde

Golden Horde

Reign	Ruler
1378-1395	Toqtamïsh
1395-1419	Edigü (vizir)
1395-1401	Temür Qutlugh
1401-1407	Shādī Beg
1407-1410	Pūlād Khān
1410-1412	Temür

Reign	Ruler
1412	Jalāl ad-Dīn
1412-1414	Karīm Berdi
1414-1417	Kebek
1417-1419	Yeremferden?
1419-1422	Ulugh Muḥammad/Dawlat Berdi (rivals)
1422-1433	Baraq
c. 1433-1435	Sayyid Aḥmad I
c. 1435-1465	Küchük Muḥammad
c. 1465-1481	Aḥmad
1476	Ivan refuses to pay tribute
1480	Russian independence
1481-1498	Shaykh Aḥmad
1481-1499	Murtaḍā
1499-1502	Shaykh Aḥmad
1502	Annexed to Crimean khanate

Remnants of the Golden Horde

Reign	Rulers
1437-1552	Kazan khans
1449-1783	Crimean khans
1466-1554	Astrakhan khans

THE NETHERLANDS

Date	Ruler/Government/Event
1559-1567	William I, the Silent, Prince of Orange, Count of Nassau (stadtholder)
1568	Dutch Revolt
1568-1648	Eighty Years' War
1572-1584	William the Silent
1579	Union of Utrecht
1581	Dutch independence declared
1585-1625	Maurice (Maurits)
1609-1621	Twelve Years' Truce
1618-1648	Thirty Years' War
1625-1647	Frederik Hendrik
1647-1650	William II
1648	Peace of Westphalia, Spanish recognition of Dutch independence
1652-1654	First Anglo-Dutch War
1664-1667	Second Anglo-Dutch War
1672-1702	William III
1672-1678	Dutch War with France
1672-1674	Third Anglo-Dutch War
1688-1697	War of the League of Augsburg
1689-1702	England rules
1701-1713	War of the Spanish Succession
1702-1747	Republic
1747-1751	William IV Friso
1751-1795	William V
1780-1784	Fourth Anglo-Dutch War
1795-1806	Batavian Republic

NORWAY. *See also* DENMARK, SWEDEN

Reign	Ruler
680-710	Olaf the Tree Hewer
710-750	Halfdan I
750-780	Oystein (Eystein) I
780-800	Halfdan II White Legs
800-810	Gudrod the Magnificent
810-840	Olaf Geirstade
840-863	Halfdan III the Black
863-872	Civil war
872-930/33	Harald I Fairhair
933-934	Erik I Bloodaxe
934-961	Hákon I the Good
961-970	Harald II Grayfell
970-995	Earl (Jarl) Hákon
995-1000	Olaf I Tryggvason
1000-1015	Erik I
1016-1028	Saint Olaf II Haraldsson
1028-1035	Canute the Great
1035-1047	Magnus I the Good
1047-1066	Harald III Hardrada
1066-1069	Magnus II
1069-1093	Olaf III the Peaceful
1093-1103	Magnus III the Barefoot
1103-1122	Oystein (Eystein) II
1103-1130	Sigurd I the Crusader
1130-1135	Magnus IV the Blinded
1130-1136	Harald IV Gillechrist
1136-1155	Sigurd II
1136-1161	Inge I
1142-1157	Oystein (Eystein) III
1161-1162	Hákon II
1163-1184	Magnus V
1184-1202	Sverre Sigurdsson
1202-1204	Hákon III
1204-1217	Inge II
1217-1263	Hákon IV
1263-1281	Magnus VI
1281-1299	Erik II Magnusson
1299-1319	Hákon V
1320-1343	Magnus VII (II of Sweden)
1343-1380	Hákon VI
1376-1387	Olaf IV (V of Denmark)
1380	Unification of Norway and Denmark
1380-1410	Margaret I of Denmark, Norway, and Sweden
1397	Unification of Norway, Denmark, and Sweden
1412-1439	Erik III (VII of Denmark, XIII of Sweden)
1439-1448	Christopher (III of Denmark)
1448-1481	Christian I of Oldenburg
1481-1513	Hans/John (II of Sweden)
1513-1523	Christian II
1523-1533	Frederick I

Reign	Ruler
1536-1814	Union with Denmark
1534-1559	Christian III
1559-1588	Frederick II
1588-1648	Christian IV
1648-1670	Frederick III
1670-1699	Christian V
1699-1730	Frederick IV
1730-1746	Christian VI
1746-1766	Frederick V
1766-1808	Christian VII
1808-1814	Frederick VI
1814	Christian Frederik
1814-1818	Carl II
1814-1905	Union with Sweden

OTTOMAN EMPIRE. *See also* IRAN, ISLAMIC CALIPHS, SELJUK EMPIRE, SPAIN

Reign	Sultan
1281/88-1326	Osman I
1326-1360	Orhan I
1360-1389	Murad I
1389-1402	Bayezid I
1402-1421	Mehmed I
1421-1444	Murad II
1444-1446	Mehmed II
1446-1451	Murad II (second rule)
1451-1481	Mehmed II (second rule)
1453	Ottomans take Constantinople
1481	Djem I
1481-1512	Bayezid II
1512-1520	Selim I
1520-1566	Süleyman I the Magnificent
1566-1574	Selim II
1574-1595	Murad III
1595-1603	Mehmed III
1603-1617	Ahmed I
1617-1618	Mustafa I
1618-1622	Osman II
1622-1623	Mustafa I
1623-1640	Murad IV
1640-1648	Ibrahim I
1648-1687	Mehmed IV
1687-1691	Süleyman II
1691-1695	Ahmed II
1695-1703	Mustafa II
1703-1730	Ahmed III
1730-1754	Mahmud I
1754-1757	Osman III
1757-1774	Mustafa III
1774-1789	Abd-ul-Hamid I
1789-1807	Selim III

Reign	Sultan
1807-1808	Mustafa IV
1808-1839	Mahmud II
1839-1861	Abd-ul-Mejid
1861-1876	Abd-ul-Aziz
1876	Murad V
1876-1909	Abd-ul-Hamid II
1909-1918	Mehmed V
1918-1922	Mehmed VI

POLAND

Reign	Ruler
962-992	Mieszko I
992-1025	Bolesław I the Brave
1025-1034	Mieszko II
1034-1037	Instability
1037-1058	Casimir I the Restorer
	Instability
1058-1079	Bolesław II
1079-1102	Władysław (Vladislav or Ladislas) I
1102-1106	Zbigniev (rival to brother Bolesław III)
1102-1138	Bolesław III
1138-1146	Instability following Bolesław III's division of Poland into five principalities
1146-1173	Bolesław IV
1173-1177	Mieszko III
1177-1194	Casimir II
1194-1227	Leszek I
1227-1279	Bolesław V
1228-1288	Instability: arrival of Teutonic Knights followed by Mongol incursions
1288-1290	Henry Probus
1290-1296	Przemyslav II (crowned 1295)
1297-1300	Instability
1300-1305	Wenceslaus (Vacław) I
1306-1333	Władysław I (Vladislav IV, Lokietek)
1333-1370	Casimir III the Great
1370	End of the Piast Dynasty
1370-1382	Ludvik I the Great (Louis of Anjou)
1382-1384	Confederation of Radom and civil war
1384-1399	Queen Jadwiga
1386-1434	Władysław II Jagiełło
1410-1411	Battle of Tannenberg and Peace of Thorn
1434-1444	Władysław (Vladislav) III
1444-1447	Instability; Poland united with Lithuania
1447-1492	Casimir IV
1454-1466	Poles defeat Teutonic Order, gain access to the Baltic in the Second Peace of Thorn
1471-1516	Vladislav Jagiełło (son of Casimir IV) king of Bohemia and then Hungary
1492-1501	John I Albert
1496	Statute of Piotrkow (Poland's Magna Carta)

Reign	Ruler
1501-1506	Alexander Jagiełło
1506-1548	Sigismund I, the Old
1548-1572	Sigismund II Augustus
1573-1574	Henry Valois (Henry III)
1575-1586	Stephen Báthory

VASA KINGS OF SWEDEN AND POLAND

Reign	Ruler
1587-1632	Sigismund III Vasa
1632-1648	Vladislaus IV Vasa
1648-1668	Jan Kazimierz Vasa
1669-1673	Michael Korybut Wisniowiecki
1674-1696	John III Sobieski

WETTIN ELECTORS OF SAXONY OF HOLY ROMAN EMPIRE

Reign	Ruler
1697-1706	Augustus II, the Strong (Wettin)
1706-1709	Stanisław Leszczynski
1709-1733	Augustus II, the Strong (Wettin)
1733-1736	Stanisław Leszczynski
1733-1763	August III Wettin
1764-1795	Stanisław August Poniatowski

DUCHY OF WARSAW

Reign	Ruler
1807-1815	Ksiestwo Warszawskie (dependent from France)
1807-1815	Frederick Augustus I of Saxony Wettin

PORTUGAL

Reign	Ruler
1093-1112	Henry of Burgundy, count of Portugal
1112-1185	Afonso I (count of Portugal 1112-1139, king 1139-1185)
1185-1211	Sancho I
1211-1223	Afonso II
1223-1245	Sancho II
1245-1279	Afonso III
1279-1325	Diniz (Denis)
1325-1357	Afonso IV
1357-1367	Peter I
1367-1383	Ferdinand I
1385-1433	John I of Avis
1433-1438	Edward I
1438-1481	Afonso V
1481-1495	John II
1495-1521	Manuel I
1521-1557	John III
1557-1578	Sebastian I
1578-1580	Cardinal Henry

Reign	Ruler
1580-1598	Philip I of Portugal (Philip II of Spain)
1598-1621	Philip II of Portugal (Philip III of Spain)
1621-1640	Philip III of Portugal (Philip IV of Spain)
1640	Revolt of Portugal
1640-1656	João IV (duke of Braganza)
1656-1667	Afonso VI
1667-1706	Pedro II
1706-1750	João V
1750-1777	José I
1777-1786	Pedro III
1777-1816	Maria I Francisca
1799-1816	João VI (regent)
1816-1826	João VI
1826	Pedro IV (I of Brazil)
1826-1828	Maria II da Glória
1828-1834	Miguel I (exiled)
1834-1853	Maria II da Glória
1853-1861	Pedro V
1861-1889	Luis I
1889-1908	Carlos I
1908	Manuel II
Oct. 5, 1910	Republic declared

RUSSIA

PRINCES OF KIEVAN RUS

Reign	Ruler
c. 862-879	Rurik
879-912	Oleg
912-945	Igor
945-964	Saint Olga (regent)
964-972	Svyatoslav I
972-980	Yaropolk
980-1015	Vladimir I (with Anna, Princess of the Byzantine Empire)
1015-1019	Sviatopolk I
1019-1054	Yaroslav
1054-1073	Iziaslav
1073-1076	Svyatoslav II
1076-1078	Iziaslav (restored)
1078-1093	Vsevolod
1093-1113	Sviatopolk II
1113-1125	Vladimir II Monomakh
1125-1132	Mstislav
1132-1139	Yaropolk
1139-1146	Vyacheslav
1146-1154	Iziaslav
1149-1157	Yuri I Dolgoruky
1154-1167	Rostislav

Princes of Vladimir

Reign	Ruler
1169-1174	Andrei I Bogolyubsky
1175-1176	Michael
1176-1212	Vsevolod III
1212-1217	Yuri II
1217-1218	Constantin
1218-1238	Yuri II (restored)
1238-1246	Yaroslav II
1240	Mongol conquest
1246-1247	Svyatoslav III
1248-1249	Michael
1249-1252	Andrei II
1252-1263	Saint Alexander Nevsky
1264-1271	Yaroslav III of Tver
1272-1276	Vasily
1276-1281	Dmitry
1281-1283	Andrei III
1283-1294	Dmitry (restored)
1294-1304	Andrei III (restored)
1304-1319	Saint Michael of Tver
1319-1326	Yuri III of Moscow
1326-1327	Alexander II of Tver
1328-1331	Alexander III

Princes of Moscow

Reign	Ruler
1263-1303	Daniel
1303-1325	Yuri III
1328-1341	Ivan I
1341-1353	Simeon
1353-1359	Ivan II
1359-1389	Dmitry Donskoy
1389-1425	Vasily I
1425-1462	Vasily II
1462-1505	Ivan III the Great
1480	Fall of the Golden Horde
1505-1533	Vasily III

Czars of All Russia

Reign	Ruler
1547-1584	Ivan IV the Terrible
1584-1613	Time of Troubles
1584-1598	Fyodor I
1598-1605	Boris Godunov
1605	Fyodor II
1605-1606	False Dmitri I
1606-1610	Vasily IV Shuysky
1610-1613	Ladislaus IV of Poland
1613-1645	Michael I (first Romanov)
1645-1676	Aleksey I
1676-1682	Fyodor III
1682-1696	Ivan V (with Peter I)
1682-1721	Peter I (with Ivan V)

Emperors of All Russia

Reign	Ruler
1721-1725	Peter I
1725-1727	Catherine I the Great
1727-1730	Peter II
1730-1740	Anne
1740-1741	Ivan VI
1741-1762	Elizabeth
1762	Peter III
1762-1796	Catherine II
1796-1801	Paul
1801-1825	Alexander I
1825-1855	Nicholas I
1855-1881	Alexander II
1881-1894	Alexander III
1894-1917	Nicholas II
1917	Michael II (exiled)
1918	Execution of Romanovs
1917-1921	Revolution

Scotland

Reign	Ruler
404-420	Fergus
420-451	Eugenius II
451-457	Dongardus
457-479	Constantine I
479-501	Congallus
569-606	Aldan
606-621	Eugenius III
646-664	Ferchard II
664-684	Mulduinns
684-688	Eugenius V
688-699	Eugenius VI
699-715	Eugenius VII
715-730	Mordachus
730-761	Etfinus
761-767	Interregnum
767-787	Solvatius
787-819	Achaius
819-824	Dongallus III
824-831	Dongal
831-834	Alpine
834-854	Kenneth
854-858	Donald V
858-874	Constantine II
874-893	Gregory
893-904	Donald VI
904-944	Constantine III
944-953	Malcolm I
953-961	Gondulph
961-965	Duff
965-970	Cullen

Reign	Ruler
970-995	Kenneth II
995-1005	Grimus
1005-1034	Malcolm II
1034-1040	Duncan I
1040-1057	Macbeth
1057-1058	Lulach
1058-1093	Malcolm III
1093-1094	Donaldbane
1094	Duncan II
1094-1097	Donaldbane (second rule)
1097-1107	Edgar
1107-1124	Alexander I
1124-1153	David I
1153-1165	Malcolm IV
1165-1214	William I the Lion
1214-1249	Alexander II
1249-1286	Alexander III
1286-1290	Margaret
1290-1292	Interregnum
1292-1296	John Baliol
1296-1306	Interregnum
1306-1329	Robert I the Bruce
1329-1371	David II
1371	Ascendancy of Robert II, House of Stuart
1371-1390	Robert II
1390-1406	Robert III
1406-1437	James I
1437-1460	James II
1460-1488	James III
1488-1513	James IV
1513-1542	James V
1542-1567	Mary
1567-1625	James VI
1625	Joined with England

SELJUK EMPIRE. *See also* IRAN, ISLAMIC CALIPHS, OTTOMAN EMPIRE, SELJUK EMPIRE

GREAT SULTANS

Reign	Sultan
1037-1063	Toghrïl Beg
1063-1072/73	Alp Arslan
1073-1092	Malik Shāh I
1092-1093	Maḥmūd I
1093-1104	Berk Yaruq (Barkyaruk, Barkiyarok)
1104-1105	Malik Shāh II
1105-1117	Muḥammad Tapar
1117-1157	Aḥmad Sanjar (Sinjar)

SULTANS OF IRAQ

Reign	Sultan
1105-1118	Maḥmūd Tapar
1118-1131	Maḥmūd
1131-1132	Dāʿūd (Dawd)
1132-1135	Toghrïl I
1135-1152	Masʿūd
1152-1153	Malik Shāh
1153-1159	Muḥammad
1159-1161	Sulaimān Shāh
1161-1177	Arslan Shāh
1177-1194	Toghrïl II

SELJUK SULTANS OF ANATOLIA/RUM

Reign	Sultan
1077-1066	Sulaimān Shāh
1092-1107?	Qïlïch (Kilij) Arslan I
1107?-1116	Malik Shāh I
1116-1156	Masʿūd I
1156-1192	Qïlïch (Kilij) Arslan II
1192	Malik Shāh II
1192-1196	Kai Khusrau (Khosrow, Khosru, Khusraw) I
1196-1204	Suleiman II
1203-1204	Qïlïch (Kilij) Arslan III
1204-1210	Kai Khusrau I (second rule)
1210-1219	Kai Kāʾūs I
1219-1236	Kai Qubād (Kobadh) I
1236-1246	Kai Khusrau II
1246-1259	Kai Kāʾūs II
1248-1264	Qïlïch (Kilij) Arslan IV
1249-1257	Kai Qubād (Kobadh) II
1264-1283	Kai Khusrau III
1283-1298	Masʿūd II
1298-1301?	Kai Qubād (Kobadh) III
1303-1308	Masʿūd II (second rule)

SELJUK SULTANS OF SYRIA

Reign	Sultan
1078-1094	Tutush
1095-1113	Riḍwān (Damascus)
1098-1113	Duqaq (Aleppo)
1113-1114	Alp Arslan
1114-1117	Sultan Shāh

SULTANS OF KIRMĀN (KERMAN)

Reign	Sultan
1041-1073	Qāvurt (Qawurd)
1073-1074	Kirmān (Kerman) Shāh

Reign	Sultan
1074-1085	Sultan Shāh
1085-1097	Turān Shāh I
1097-1101	Īrān Shāh
1101-1142	Arslan Shāh I
1142-1156	Muḥammad I
1156-1170	Toghrïl Shāh
1170-1175	Bahrām Shāh
1170-1177	Arslan Shāh II
1175-1186	Muḥammad Shāh II
1177-1183	Turān Shāh II

SPAIN. *See also* PORTUGAL

The Iberian Peninsula now occupied by Spain and Portugal was a turbulent region during the Middle Ages, a place where numerous cultures clashed, notably Christianity and Islam but also a broad and ethnically diverse group of peoples, from the Suevi and Visigoths of the seventh century through the Berbers and Islamic peoples in the south. Through most of the Middle Ages the region saw a succession of fluctuating principalities in the north—primarily Asturias, Galicia, Aragón, Navarre, León, and Castile, while in the south Islam held sway from the eighth century to the time of Columbus's voyage to the Americas in 1492. In that year the Reconquista concluded with the Fall of Granada, and Christianity claimed the peninsula. In 1516, the Kingdom of Spain united all former kingdoms, with the exception of Portugal, into one Kingdom of Spain.

MAJOR ISLAMIC RULERS

Córdoba's Umayyad Caliphs (emirs until 929)

Reign	Ruler
756-788	ʿAbd al-Raḥmān I (emir)
788-796	Hishām I (emir)
796-822	al-Hakam I (emir)
822-852	ʿAbd al-Raḥmān II (emir)
852-886	Muḥammad I (emir)
886-888	al-Mundhir (emir)
888-912	ʿAbd Allāh (emir)
912-961	ʿAbd al-Raḥmān III al-Nāṣir
961-976	al-Hakam II al-Mustanṣir
976-1008	Hishām II al-Muayyad
1008-1009	Muḥammad II al-Mahdī
1009	Sulaimān al-Mustaʿīn
1010-1013	Hishām II (restored)
1013-1016	Sulaimān (restored)
1016-1018	Alī ben Hammud
1018	ʿAbd al-Raḥmān IV
1018-1021	al-Qasim

Reign	Ruler
1021-1022	Yaḥyā
1022-1023	al-Qasim (restored)
1023-1024	ʿAbd al-Raḥmān V
1024-1025	Muḥammad III
1025-1027	Yaḥyā (restored)
1027-1031	Hishām III
1031	End of Umayyads; dissolution of Umayyad Spain into small states

After the Umayyads, Turbulence: Some Major Rulers

Reign	Ruler
1031-1043	Jahwar ibn Muḥammad ibn Jahwar
1043-1058	Muḥammad ar-Rashīd
1058-1069	ʿAbd al-Malik Dhu's-Siyādat al-Manṣur
1069	ʿAbbādid conquest
1085	Toledo falls to León and Castile; Christian Reconquista begins

Almoravid Sultans (Spain and North Africa)

Reign	Ruler
1061-1107	Yūsuf ibn Tāshufīn
1086	Entry into Spain; Alfonso VI defeated at Zallāqa
1107-1142	ʿAlīx ibn Yūsuf
1142-1146	Tāshufīn ibn ʿAlī
1146	Ibrāhīm ibn Tāshufīn
1146-1147	Isḥāq ibn ʿAlī
1147	Almohad conquest

Almohad Caliphs (Spain and North Africa)

Reign	Ruler
1130-1163	ʿAbd al-Muʾmin
1163-1184	Abū Yaʿqūb Yūsuf
1184-1199	Abū Yūsuf Yaʿqūb al-Manṣūr
1199-1213	Muḥammad ibn Yaʿqūb
1212	Christians defeat Almohads at Las Navas de Tolosa
1213-1224	Yūsuf II Abū Yaqūb
1224	ʿAbd al-Wāḥid Abū Muḥammad
1224-1227	ʿAbd Allāh Abū Muḥammad
1227-1232	Idrīs I ibn Yaʿqūb
1227-1235	Yaḥyā Abū Zakariyyāʿ
1228-1229	Retreat from Spain
1232-1242	ʿAbdul-Wāḥid ibn Idrīs I
1242-1248	ʿAlī ibn Idrīs I
1248-1266	ʿUmar ibn Isḥāq
1266-1269	Idrīs II ibn Muḥammad
1269	End of Almohad domination in North Africa

Naṣrid Sultans of Granada

Reign	Ruler
1232-1273	Muḥammad I al-Ghālib (Ibn al-Aḥmar)
1273-1302	Muḥammad II al-Faqīh
1302-1309	Muḥammad III al-Makhlūʿ

Reign	Ruler
1309-1314	Naṣr
1314-1325	Ismāʿīl I
1325-1333	Muḥammad IV
1333-1354	Yūsuf I al-Muʾayyad
1354-1359	Muḥammad V al-Ghani
1359-1360	Ismāʿīl II
1360-1362	Muḥammad VI al-Ghālib (El Bermejo)
1362-1391	Muḥammad V al-Ghani (restored)
1391-1392	Yūsuf II al-Mustahgnī
1392-1408	Muḥammad VII al-Mustaʿīn
1408-1417	Yūsuf III an-Nāṣir
1417-1419	Muḥammad VIII al-Mustamassik (al-Ṣaghīr, El Pequeño)
1419-1427	Muḥammad IX al-Ghālib (al-Aysar, El Zurdo)
1427-1429	Muḥammad VIII al-Mustamassik
1429-1432	Muḥammad IX al-Ghālib
1432	Yūsuf IV, Abenalmao
1432-1445	Muḥammad IX al-Ghālib
1445	Muḥammad X al-Aḥnaf (El Cojo)
1445-1446	Yūsuf V (Aben Ismael)
1446-1447	Muḥammad X al-Aḥnaf
1447-1453	Muḥammad IX al-Ghālib
1451-1455	Muḥammad XI (El Chiquito)
1454-1464	Saʿd al-Mustaʿīn (Ciriza, Muley Zad)
1462	Yūsuf V (Aben Ismael)
1464-1482	ʿAlī (Muley Hácen)
1482-1483	Muḥammad XII al-Zughūbī (Boabdil, El Chico)
1483-1485	ʿAlī (Muley Hácen)
1485-1490	Muḥammad ibn Saʿd al-Zaghal
1482-1492	Muḥammad XII al-Zughūbī (Boabdil, El Chico)
1492	Conquest by Castile and Aragón, end of Islamic Spain

NON-ISLAMIC AND CHRISTIAN RULERS

Asturias and Galicia

Reign	Ruler
718-737	Pelayo
737-739	Favila
739-757	Alfonso I the Catholic
757-768	Fruela I
768-774	Aurelio
774-783	Silo
783-788	Mauregato
788-791	Vermundo I
791-842	Alfonso II the Chaste
842-850	Ramiro I
850-866	Ordoño I
866-910	Alfonso III the Great
910	Subsumed by León

Navarre

Reign	Ruler
840-851	Inigo Arista
905-925	Sancho Garces
925-970	Garcia Sanchez I
970-994	Sancho Abarca
994-1000	Garcia Sanchez II
1000-1035	Sancho III the Great
1035-1054	Garcia IV
1054-1076	Sancho IV
1076-1094	Sancho Ramirez
1094-1134	Subsumed under Aragón, Castile, León; reemerges with reduced territory
1134-1150	Garcia V Ramirez
1150-1194	Sancho VI
1194-1234	Sancho VII
1234-1253	Teobaldo I of Champagne
1253-1270	Teobaldo II
1270-1274	Henry I
1274-1305	Juana I
1305-1316	Luis (Louis)
1316-1322	Philip V the Tall
1322-1328	Charles I
1328-1349	Juana II
1349-1387	Charles II the Bad
1387-1425	Charles III the Noble
1425-1479	Blanca & John
1479	Leonora
1479-1483	Francis Febo
1483-1517	Catalina
1516	Part of Navarre annexed to Spain
1517-1555	Henry II
1555-1572	Jeanne d'Albret
1572-1589	Henry III (IV of France); French rule

León

Reign	Ruler
910-914	Garcia
914-924	Ordoño II
924-925	Fruela II
925-930	Alfonso IV the Monk
930-950	Ramiro II
950-956	Ordoño III
956-967	Sancho I the Fat
967-982	Ramiro III
982-999	Vermundo II
999-1028	Alfonso V the Noble
1028-1037	Vermundo III
1038-1065	Fernando
1065-1070	Sancho II
1070-1072	Sancho III
1072-1109	Alfonso VI (king of Castile)
1109-1126	Urraca (married to Alfonso I of Aragón)
1126-1157	Alfonso VII

Reign	Ruler
1157-1188	Ferdinand II
1188-1230	Alfonso IX
1230-1252	Saint Fernando III
1252	Subsumed under Castile

Castile

Reign	Ruler
1035-1065	Ferdinand I
1065-1072	Sancho II
1072-1109	Alfonso VI
1109-1157	Castile joins with León
1157	Castile restored as separate principality
1157-1158	Sancho III
1158-1214	Alfonso VIII
1214-1217	Henry I
1217-1252	Saint Ferdinand III
1252	Castile rejoins with León
1252-1284	Alfonso X (emperor)
1284-1295	Sancho IV
1295-1312	Ferdinand IV
1312-1350	Alfonso XI
1350-1369	Peter the Cruel
1369-1379	Henry II
1379-1390	John I
1390-1406	Henry III
1406-1454	John II
1454-1474	Henry IV
1474-1504	Ferdinand V (II of Aragon) and Isabella I
1492	Fall of Granada, end of Reconquista
1504-1516	Joan (Juana) the Mad and Philip I of Habsburg
1516	Formation of Kingdom of Spain

Aragon

Reign	Ruler
1035-1063	Ramiro I
1063-1094	Sancho Ramirez
1094-1104	Pedro I
1104-1134	Alfonso I (co-ruled León and Castile, 1109-1126)
1134-1137	Ramiro II
1137	Union with County of Barcelona
1137-1162	Petronilla
1162-1196	Alfonso II
1196-1213	Pedro II
1213-1276	James I the Conqueror (under regency to 1217)
1276-1285	Pedro III
1285-1291	Alfonso III
1291-1327	James II
1327-1336	Alfonso IV
1336-1387	Peter IV
1387-1395	John I
1395-1410	Martin I
1412-1416	Ferdinand I

Reign	Ruler
1416-1458	Alfonso V
1458-1479	John II
1479-1516	Ferdinand II and Isabella I (d. 1504)

KINGDOM OF SPAIN

Reign	Ruler
1516-1556	Carlos (Charles) I (V as Holy Roman Emperor)
1556-1598	Philip (Felipe) II
1598-1621	Philip III
1621-1665	Philip IV
1665-1700	Carlos II

BOURBONS

Reign	Ruler
1700-1724	Philip V
1724	Luis I
1724-1746	Philip V (restored)
1746-1759	Fernando VI
1759-1788	Carlos III
1788-1808	Carlos IV
1808	Fernando VII
1808	Carlos IV (restored)

BONAPARTES

Reign	Ruler
1808-1813	José I Napoleón

SWEDEN. *See also* DENMARK, NORWAY

Reign	Ruler
647-735?	Harald Hildetand
735-750?	Sigurd Ring
750-794?	Ragnar Lodbrok
?	Eystein Beli
794-804	Björn Järnsida
804-808	Erik II (to 870?)
808-820	Erik III
820-859	Edmund I
860?-870	Erik I (poss. Erik II)
870-920	Björn
920-930	Olaf I Ring
?	Erik IV
930-950	Erik V
950-965	Edmund II
965-970	Olaf II
970-995	Erik VI the Victorious
995-1022	Olaf III Skötkonung
1022-1050	Anund Jakob Kolbrenner
1050-1060	Edmund III
1066-1067	Erik VII (VIII)

Reign	Ruler
1066-1070	Halsten
1066-1080	Inge I Elder
1080-1083	Blot-Sven
1083-1110	Inge I Elder
1110-1118	Filip Halstensson
1118-1125	Inge II Younger
1125-1130	Magnus Nielsson
1130-1156	Sverker I Elder
1156-1160	Sain Erik IX
1161-1167	Charles VII
1167-1196	Knut I
1196-1208	Sverker II Younger
1208-1216	Erik X
1216-1222	John I
1222-1229	Erik XI
1229-1234	Knut II the Long
1234-1250	Erik XI
1250-1275	Valdemar
1275-1290	Magnus I
1290-1320	Berger
1320-1365	Magnus II (VII of Norway)
1356-1359	Erik XII
1364-1389	Albert
1389-1412	Margaret I of Denmark, Norway, and Sweden
1397	Unification of Norway, Denmark, and Sweden
1412-1439	Erik XIII (VII of Denmark, III of Norway)
1439-1448	Christopher (III of Denmark)
1448-1481	Christian I of Oldenburg
1481-1513	Hans/John II
1513-1523	Christian II
1523-1560	Gustav I Vasa
1560-1568	Erik XIV
1568-1592	Johan/John III
1592-1604	Sigismund
1604-1611	Carl/Charles IX
1611-1632	Gustav II Adolf
1632-1654	Christina
1654-1660	Charles X
1660-1697	Charles XI
1697-1718	Charles XII (Madman of the North)
1718-1720	Ulrika
1730-1751	Frederick (landgrave of Hesse)
1751-1771	Adolphus Frederick
1771-1792	Gustav III
1792-1809	Gustav IV Adolf
1809-1818	Charles XIII
1814	Sweden and Norway joined
1818-1844	Charles XIV
1844-1859	Oscar I
1859-1872	Charles XI
1872-1907	Oscar II
1905	Norway separates

Reign	Ruler
1907-1950	Gustav V
1950-1973	Gustav VI Adolf
1973-	Karl/Charles XVI Gustaf

VIETNAM

NGO DYNASTY

Reign	Ruler
939-945	Kuyen
945-951	Duong Tam Kha
951-954	Suong Ngap
951-965	Suong Van

DINH DYNASTY

Reign	Ruler
968-979	Dinh Tien
979-981	Dinh De Toan

EARLY LE DYNASTY

Reign	Ruler
981-1005	Hoan
1005-1009	Trung Tong

LATER LI (LY) DYNASTY

Reign	Ruler
1010-1028	Thai To
1028-1054	Thai Tong
1054-1072	Thanh Tong

LATER LE DYNASTY

Reign	Ruler
1072-1127	Nan Ton
1127-1138	Than Tong
1138-1175	Anh Tong
1175-1210	Kao Tong
1210-1224	Hue Tong
1224-1225	Tieu Hoang

EARLY TRAN DYNASTY

Reign	Ruler
1225-1258	Thai Tong
1258-1277	Thanh Tong
1278-1293	Nan Tong
1293-1314	Anh Tong
1314-1329	Minh Tong
1329-1341	Hien Tong
1341-1369	Du Tong
1370-1372	Nghe Tong
1372-1377	Due Tong
1377-1388	De Hien

Reign	Ruler
1388-1398	Tran Thuan Tong
1398-1400	Tran Thieu De

HO DYNASTY

Reign	Ruler
1400	Kui Li
1400-1407	Han Thuong
1407-1428	Ming Chinese occupation

LATER TRAN DYNASTY

Reign	Ruler
1407-1409	Hau Tran Jian Dinh De
1409-1413	Hau Tran
1413-1428	vacant

CHAMPA

Reign	Ruler
1390-1400	Ko Cheng
1400-1441	Jaya Sinhavarman v
1441-1446	Maija Vijaya
1446-1449	Qui Lai
1449-1458	Qui Do (Bi Do)
1458-1460	Ban La Tra Nguyet (Tra Duyet)
1460-1471	Ban La Tra Toan
1471-1478	Bo Tri Tri

LATER LE DYNASTY

Reign	Ruler
1428-1433	Thai To
1433-1442	Thai Tong

Reign	Ruler
1442-1459	Nan Tong
1460-1497	Thanh Tong
1497-1504	Hien Tong
1504-1509	Vi Muc De
1509-1516	Tuong Duc De
1516-1522	Tieu Tong
1522-1527	Kung Hoang
1533-1548	Le Trang Tong (restored)

MAC DYNASTY

Reign	Ruler
1527-1530	Dang Dung
1530-1540	Dang Doanh
1533	Kingdom divides

NGUYEN DYNASTY

Reign	Ruler
1533-1545	Kim
1545-1558	Civil war
1558-1613	Hoang
1613-1635	Phuc Nguyen
1635-1648	Phuc Lan
1648-1687	Phuc Tan
1687-1691	Phuc Tran
1691-1725	Phuc Chu I
1725-1738	Phuc Chu II
1738-1765	Phuc Khoat
1765-1778	Phuc Thuan
1778-1802	Anh
1802	Absorbs other Vietnamese kingdoms

CHRONOLOGICAL LIST OF ENTRIES

The arrangement of personages in this list is chronological on the basis of birth years (where known; other vital years appear where birth year is unknown). All personages appearing in this list are the subjects of articles in *Great Lives from History: The Renaissance & Early Modern Era, 1454-1600*; Francis Beaumont and John Fletcher, The Carracci Family, Ferdinand II and Isabella I, The Pinzón Brothers, and The Tudor Family are the subjects of multi-person essays.

1385-1400

Sir John Fortescue (c. 1385-c. 1479)
Pachacuti (c. 1391-1471)

Zara Yaqob (1399-1468)

1401-1410

Nicholas of Cusa (1401-Aug. 11, 1464)
Nezahualcóyotl (1402-1472)
Charles VII (Feb. 22, 1403-July 22, 1461)

Leon Battista Alberti (Feb. 14, 1404-Apr., 1472)
Pius II (Oct. 18, 1405-Aug. 14/15, 1464)

1411-1420

Qāytbāy (1414-Aug. 8, 1496)
Sixtus IV (July 21, 1414-Aug. 12, 1484)
Frederick III (Sept. 21, 1415-Aug. 19, 1493)

Piero della Francesca (c. 1420-Oct. 12, 1492)
Sesshū (1420-1506)
Tomás de Torquemada (1420-Sept. 16, 1498)

1421-1430

Henry VI (Dec. 6, 1421-May 21, 1471)
William Caxton (c. 1422-c. 1491)
Sir Thomas Littleton (1422-Aug. 23, 1481)
Louis XI (July 3, 1423-Aug. 30, 1483)
Georg von Peuerbach (May 30, 1423-Apr. 8, 1461)

Henry IV of Castile (Jan. 6, 1425-Dec. 11, 1474)
Sir Thomas Malory (early 15th cent.-Mar. 14, 1471)
Sonni ʿAlī (c. early 15th cent.-Nov. 6, 1492)
Earl of Warwick (Nov. 22, 1428-Apr. 14, 1471)
Giovanni Bellini (c. 1430-1516)

1431-1440

Alexander VI (1431-Aug. 18, 1503)
Andrea Mantegna (c. 1431-Sept. 13, 1506)
François Villon (1431-1463?)
Vlad III the Impaler (late 1431-Dec., 1476)
Mehmed II (Mar. 30, 1432-May 3, 1481)
Charles the Bold (Nov. 10, 1433-Jan. 5, 1477)
Marsilio Ficino (Oct. 19, 1433-Oct. 1, 1499)

Andrea del Verrocchio (1435-Oct. 7, 1488)
Francisco Jiménez de Cisneros (1436-Nov. 8, 1517)
Isaac ben Judah Abravanel (1437-Nov., 1508)
Ivan the Great (Jan. 22, 1440-Oct. 27, 1505)
Muḥammad ibn ʿAbd al-Karīm al-Maghīlī (c. 1440-
   Between 1503 and 1506)

1441-1450

Martín Alonso Pinzón (c. 1440-Mar. 20, 1493)
Edward IV (Apr. 28, 1442-Apr. 9, 1483)
Le Thanh Tong (1442-1497)
Mohammed I Askia (c. 1442-1538)
Lady Margaret Beaufort (May 31, 1443-June 29, 1509)
Julius II (Dec. 5, 1443-Feb. 21, 1513)
Matthias I Corvinus (Feb. 24, 1443-Apr. 6, 1490)
Sandro Botticelli (c. 1444-May 17, 1510)
Donato Bramante (1444-Apr. 11, 1514)
Saint Catherine of Genoa (1447-Sept. 15, 1510)

Pêro da Covilhã (c. 1447-After 1526)
Bayezid II (Dec., 1447 or Jan., 1448-May 26, 1512)
Lorenzo de' Medici (Jan. 1, 1449-Apr. 8, 1492)
Sophia Palaeologus (c. 1449-Apr. 7, 1503)
Hieronymus Bosch (c. 1450-Aug. 9, 1516)
John Cabot (c. 1450-c. 1498)
Bartolomeu Dias (c. 1450-May 29, 1500)
Guacanagarí (c. mid-15th cent.-c. early 16th cent.)
Josquin des Prez (c. 1450-1455-Aug. 27, 1521)
Aldus Manutius (c. 1450-Feb. 6, 1515)

1451-1460

Christopher Columbus (Between Aug. 25 and Oct. 31, 1451-May 20, 1506)
Isabella I (Apr. 22, 1451-Nov. 26, 1504; *see* Ferdinand II and Isabella I)
James III (July 10, 1451, or May, 1452-June 11, 1488)
Ferdinand II (Mar. 10, 1452-Jan. 23, 1516)
Leonardo da Vinci (Apr. 15, 1452-May 2, 1519)
Richard III (Oct. 2, 1452-Aug. 22, 1485)
Girolamo Savonarola (Sept. 21, 1452-May 23, 1498)
Ludovico Sforza (July 27, 1452-May 27, 1508)
Afonso de Albuquerque (1453-Dec. 15, 1515)

Amerigo Vespucci (Mar. 9, 1454-Feb. 22, 1512)
John II (Mar. 3, 1455-Oct. 25, 1495)
Vladislav II (Mar. 1, 1456-Mar. 13, 1516)
Henry VII (Jan. 28, 1457-Apr. 21, 1509)
Mary of Burgundy (Feb. 13, 1457-Mar. 27, 1482)
Adrian VI (Mar. 2, 1459-Sept. 14, 1523)
Maximilian I (Mar. 22, 1459-Jan. 12, 1519)
Afonso I (c. late 1450's or early 1460's-1543)
Vasco da Gama (c. 1460-Dec. 24, 1524)
Jacques Lefèvre d'Étaples (c. 1460-1536)
Juan Ponce de León (c. 1460-July, 1521)

1461-1470

Louis XII (June 27, 1462-Jan. 1, 1515)
Vicente Yáñez Pinzón (c. 1462-c. 1523)
Caterina Sforza (1462 or 1463-May 20, 1509)
Giovanni Pico della Mirandola (Feb. 24, 1463-Nov. 17, 1494)
Boabdil (c. 1464-1527 or 1538)
John Colet (Probably 1466-Sept. 16, 1519)
Desiderius Erasmus (Oct. 28, 1466?-July 12, 1536)
Montezuma II (1467-June 30, 1520)

Sigismund I, the Old (Jan. 1, 1467-Apr. 1, 1548)
Paul III (Feb. 29, 1468-Nov. 10, 1549)
Tomé Pires (c. 1468-c. 1540)
Saint John Fisher (1469-June 22, 1535)
Niccolò Machiavelli (May 3, 1469-June 21, 1527)
Manuel I (May 31, 1469-Dec. 13, 1521)
Nānak (Apr. 15, 1469-1539)
Charles VIII (June 30, 1470-Apr. 7, 1498)
Xiaozong (July 30, 1470-June 8, 1505)

1471-1480

Saint Angela Merici (Mar. 21, 1470, or 1474-Jan. 27, 1540)
Albrecht Dürer (May 21, 1471-Apr. 6, 1528)

Cardinal Thomas Wolsey (1471 or 1472-Nov. 29, 1530)
Lucas Cranach, the Elder (1472-Oct. 16, 1553)

Wang Yangming (Nov. 30, 1472-Jan. 9, 1529)
Chevalier de Bayard (c. 1473-Apr. 30, 1524)
Nicolaus Copernicus (Feb. 19, 1473-May 24, 1543)
James IV (Mar. 17, 1473-Sept. 9, 1513)
Ludovico Ariosto (Sept. 8, 1474-July 6, 1533)
Sebastian Cabot (c. 1474-1557)
Isabella d'Este (May 18, 1474-Feb. 13, 1539)
Bartolomé de Las Casas (Aug., 1474-July 17, 1566)
Vasco Núñez de Balboa (1475-Jan., 1519)
Matthias Grünewald (c. 1475-Aug., 1528)
Leo X (Dec. 11, 1475-Dec. 1, 1521)
Michelangelo (Mar. 6, 1475-Feb. 18, 1564)
Cesare Borgia (1475 or 1476-Mar. 12, 1507)

Anne of Brittany (Jan., 25, 1477-Jan., 9, 1514)
Giorgione (c. 1477-1510)
Baldassare Castiglione (Dec. 6, 1478-Feb. 2, 1529)
Clement VII (May 26, 1478-Sept. 25, 1534)
Girolamo Fracastoro (c. 1478-Aug. 6, 1553)
Sir Thomas More (Feb. 7, 1478-July 6, 1535)
Francisco Pizarro (c. 1478-June 26, 1541)
Vasily III (possibly Mar. 25 or 26, 1479-Dec. 3, 1533)
Lucrezia Borgia (Apr. 18, 1480-June 24, 1519)
Balthasar Hubmaier (c. 1480-Mar. 10, 1528)
Ferdinand Magellan (c. 1480-Apr. 27, 1521)
Margaret of Austria (Jan. 10, 1480-Dec. 1, 1530)

1481-1490

Bābur (Feb. 14, 1483-Dec. 26, 1530)
Francesco Guicciardini (Mar. 6, 1483-May 22, 1540)
Martin Luther (Nov. 10, 1483-Feb. 18, 1546)
Raphael (Apr. 6, 1483-Apr. 6, 1520)
Francisco de Vitoria (c. 1483-Aug. 12, 1546)
Huldrych Zwingli (Jan. 1, 1484-Oct. 11, 1531)
Pedro de Alvarado (1485-1541)
Catherine of Aragon (Dec. 16, 1485-Jan. 7, 1536)
Hernán Cortés (1485-Dec. 2, 1547)
Thomas Cromwell (1485?-July 28, 1540)
Charlotte Guillard (c. mid 1480's?-between Apr. 18
   and July 20, 1557)
Leo Africanus (c. 1485-c. 1554)

Hugh Latimer (Between 1485 and 1492-Oct. 16, 1555)
The Tudor Family (Reigned 1485-1603)
Andrea del Sarto (July 16, 1486-Sept. 28, 1530)
Jacopo Sansovino (July 2, 1486-Nov. 27, 1570)
Juan Sebastián de Elcano (c. 1487-Aug. 4, 1526)
Miles Coverdale (c. 1488-Jan. 20, 1568)
Joseph ben Ephraim Karo (1488-Mar. 24, 1575)
Correggio (c. 1489-c. Mar. 5, 1534)
Thomas Cranmer (July 2, 1489-Mar. 21, 1556)
Álvar Núñez Cabeza de Vaca (c. 1490-c. 1560)
Ibrāhīm Lodī (late 15th cent.-Apr. 21, 1526)
Titian (c. 1490-Aug. 27, 1576)

1491-1500

Martin Bucer (Nov. 11, 1491-Feb. 28, 1551)
Jacques Cartier (c. 1491-Sept. 1, 1557)
Henry VIII (June 28, 1491-Jan. 28, 1547)
Saint Ignatius of Loyola (1491-July 31, 1556)
Zhengde (1491-1521)
Pietro Aretino (Apr. 19 or 20, 1492-Oct. 21, 1556)
Vittoria Colonna (1492-Feb. 25, 1547)
Marguerite de Navarre (Apr. 11, 1492-Dec. 21, 1549)
Stephen Gardiner (c. 1493-Nov. 12, 1555)
İbrahim Paşa (1493 or 1494-Mar. 15, 1536)
Paracelsus (Nov. 11 or Dec. 17, 1493-Sept. 24, 1541)
Georgius Agricola (Mar. 24, 1494-Nov. 21, 1555)
Francis I (Sept. 12, 1494-Mar. 31, 1547)
François Rabelais (c. 1494-Apr., 1553)

Süleyman the Magnificent (1494 or 1495-Sept. 5 or 6,
   1566)
William Tyndale (c. 1494-Oct. 6, 1536)
Cuauhtémoc (c. 1495-Feb. 28, 1525)
Huáscar (c. 1495-1532)
Diego de Siloé (c. 1495-Oct. 22, 1563)
Gustav I Vasa (May 12, 1496-Sept. 29, 1560)
Menno Simons (1496-Jan. 31, 1561)
Hernando de Soto (c. 1496-May 21, 1542)
Philipp Melanchthon (Feb. 16, 1497-Apr. 19, 1560)
Hans Holbein, the Younger (1497 or 1498-1543)
Diane de Poitiers (Sept. 3, 1499-Apr. 25, 1566)
Anne Boleyn (c. 1500-1501-May 19, 1536)
Juan Rodríguez Cabrillo (c. 1500-Jan. 3, 1543)

Benvenuto Cellini (Nov. 3, 1500-Feb. 13, 1571)
Charles V (Feb. 24, 1500-Sept. 21, 1556)
Nicholas Ridley (c. 1500-Oct. 16, 1555)

Niccolò Fontana Tartaglia (c. 1500-Dec. 13, 1557)
Tascalusa (c. 1500-Oct. 18, 1540)

1501-1510

Gerolamo Cardano (Sept. 24, 1501-Sept. 21, 1576)
Leonhard Fuchs (Jan. 17, 1501-May 10, 1566)
Atahualpa (c. 1502-Aug. 29, 1533)
Gregory XIII (Jan. 7, 1502-Apr. 10, 1585)
John III (June 6, 1502-June 11, 1557)
Doña Marina (c. 1502-1527 or 1528)
Nostradamus (Dec. 14, 1503-July 1 or 2, 1566)
Matthew Parker (Aug. 6, 1504-May 17, 1575)
Philip the Magnanimous (Nov. 13, 1504-Mar. 31, 1567)
Pius V (Jan. 17, 1504-May 1, 1572)
Michel de L'Hospital (c. 1505-Mar. 13, 1573)
Mary of Hungary (Sept. 17, 1505-Oct. 18, 1558)

Thomas Tallis (c. 1505-Nov. 20 or 23, 1585)
George Buchanan (Feb., 1506-Sept. 29, 1582)
First Duke of Somerset (c. 1506-Jan. 22, 1552)
Saint Francis Xavier (Apr. 7, 1506-Dec. 3, 1552)
Duke of Alva (Oct. 29, 1507-Dec. 11, 1582)
Humāyūn (1508-Jan., 1556)
Andrea Palladio (Nov. 30, 1508-Aug., 1580)
John Calvin (July 10, 1509-May 27, 1564)
Jane Seymour (c. 1509-Oct. 24, 1537)
Francisco Vásquez de Coronado (1510-Sept. 22, 1554)
Miguel López de Legazpi (c. 1510-Aug. 20, 1572)
Pierre Lescot (1510?-Sept. 10, 1578)

1511-1520

Michael Servetus (1511-Oct. 27, 1553)
Giorgio Vasari (July 30, 1511-June 27, 1574)
James V (Apr. 10, 1512-Dec. 14, 1542)
Gerardus Mercator (Mar. 5, 1512-Dec. 2, 1594)
Catherine Parr (c. 1512-Sept. 5, 1548)
John Knox (c. 1514-Nov. 24, 1572)
Rheticus (Feb. 16, 1514-Dec. 5, 1574)
Andreas Vesalius (Dec. 31, 1514-Oct. 15, 1564)
Anne of Cleves (Sept. 22, 1515-July 16, 1557)
Mary of Guise (Nov. 22, 1515-June 11, 1560)
Saint Philip Neri (July 21, 1515-May 26, 1595)
Peter Ramus (1515-Aug. 26, 1572)
Saint Teresa of Ávila (Mar. 28, 1515-Oct. 4, 1582)
Conrad Gesner (Mar. 26, 1516-Dec. 13, 1565)

Mary I (Feb. 18, 1516-Nov. 17, 1558)
Pierre Belon (c. 1517-Apr. 1565 or 1564)
Ōgimachi (1517-1593)
Tintoretto (c. 1518-May 31, 1594)
Catherine de Médicis (Apr. 13, 1519-Jan. 5, 1589)
Edmund Grindal (1519?-July 6, 1583)
Henry II (Mar. 31, 1519-July 10, 1559)
Cosimo I de' Medici (June 12, 1519-Apr. 21, 1574)
Pedro Menéndez de Avilés (Feb. 15, 1519-Sept. 17, 1574)
William Cecil (Sept. 13, 1520-Aug. 4, 1598)
Andrea Gabrieli (c. 1520-1586)
Sigismund II Augustus (Aug. 1, 1520-July 7, 1572)

1521-1530

Anne Askew (c. 1521-July 16, 1546)
Catherine Howard (c. 1521-Feb. 13, 1542)
Sixtus V (Dec. 13, 1521-Aug. 27, 1590)
Joachim du Bellay (1522-Jan. 1, 1560)
Margaret of Parma (1522-Jan. 18, 1586)
Luís de Camões (c. 1524-June 10, 1580)

François Hotman (Aug. 23, 1524-Feb. 12, 1590)
Pierre de Ronsard (Sept. 11, 1524-Dec. 27, 1585)
Askia Daud (c. early 16th cent.-July or Aug., 1582)
Pieter Bruegel, the Elder (c. 1525-Sept. 5, 1569)
Andrea Cesalpino (Probably June 5, 1525-Feb. 23 or Mar. 15, 1603)

Hiawatha (c. 1525-c. 1575)
Giovanni Pierluigi da Palestrina (c. 1525-Feb. 2, 1594)
Kenau Hasselaer (1526-1588)
Bess of Hardwick (c. 1527-Feb. 13, 1608)
John Dee (July 13, 1527-Dec., 1608)
Maximilian II (July 31, 1527-Oct. 12, 1576)
Philip II (May 21, 1527-Sept. 13, 1598)

Catharina van Hemessen (1528-After 1587)
Paolo Veronese (1528-Apr. 19, 1588)
Krishnadevaraya (d. 1529)
Juan de Herrera (c. 1530-Jan. 15, 1597)
Ivan the Terrible (Aug. 25, 1530-Mar. 18, 1584)
Grace O'Malley (1530-1603)

1531-1540

Amina Sarauniya Zazzua (c. 1532-c. 1610)
Sofonisba Anguissola (c. 1532-Nov., 1625)
Orlando di Lasso (1532-June 14, 1594)
Earl of Leicester (June 24, 1532 or 1533-Sept. 4, 1588)
Elizabeth I (Sept. 7, 1533-Mar. 24, 1603)
Michel Eyquem de Montaigne (Feb. 28, 1533-Sept. 13, 1592)
Stephen Báthory (Sept. 27, 1533-Dec. 12, 1586)
William the Silent (Apr. 24, 1533-July 10, 1584)
Isaac ben Solomon Luria (1534-Aug. 5, 1572)
Oda Nobunaga (June, 1534-June 21, 1582)
Sir Martin Frobisher (c. 1535-Nov. 22, 1594)

Edward VI (Oct. 12, 1537-July 6, 1553)
Hieronymus Fabricius ab Aquapendente (May 20, 1537-May 21, 1619)
Lady Jane Grey (Oct., 1537-Feb. 12, 1554)
Toyotomi Hideyoshi (Feb. 6, 1537-Sept. 18, 1598)
Hōjō Ujimasa (1538-Aug. 12, 1590)
Sir Humphrey Gilbert (c. 1539-Sept. 9, 1583)
José de Acosta (1540-Feb. 15, 1600)
Sir Francis Drake (c. 1540-Jan. 28, 1596)
Ana de Mendoza y de la Cerda (June 29, 1540-Feb. 2, 1592)
Joseph Justus Scaliger (Aug. 5, 1540-Jan. 21, 1609)

1541-1550

El Greco (1541-Apr. 7, 1614)
Bernardino de Mendoza (Feb. 21, 1541-Aug. 3, 1604)
Akbar (Oct. 15, 1542-Oct. 16, 1605)
Sir Richard Grenville (c. June 15, 1542-c. Sept. 3, 1591)
Saint John of the Cross (June 24, 1542-Dec. 14, 1591)
Mary, Queen of Scots (Dec. 8, 1542-Feb. 8, 1587)
William Byrd (1543-July 4, 1623)
William Gilbert (May 24, 1544-Dec. 10, 1603)
Torquato Tasso (Mar. 11, 1544-Apr. 25, 1595)
Sir Thomas Bodley (Mar. 2, 1545-Jan. 28, 1613)
Alessandro Farnese (Aug. 27, 1545-Dec. 2-3, 1592)
Barbarossa (d. 1546)
Tycho Brahe (Dec. 14, 1546-Oct. 24, 1601)

Mateo Alemán (Sept. 28, 1547-c. 1614)
Miguel de Cervantes (Sept. 29, 1547-Apr. 23, 1616)
Johan van Oldenbarnevelt (Sept. 14, 1547-May 13, 1619)
Giordano Bruno (1548-Feb. 17, 1600)
Oichi (1548-June 14, 1583)
Simon Stevin (1548-Feb., 1620)
Philippe de Mornay (Nov. 5, 1549-Nov. 11, 1623)
John Davis (c. 1550-Dec. 29 or 30, 1605)
Deganawida (c. 1550-c. 1600)
Kalicho (c. mid-1500's-late 1577)
John Napier (1550-Apr. 4, 1617)

1551-1560

Boris Godunov (c. 1551-Apr. 23, 1605)
Henry III (Sept. 19, 1551-Aug. 2, 1589)
Lavinia Fontana (1552-Aug. 11, 1614)

Alberico Gentili (Jan. 14, 1552-June 19, 1608)
Richard Hakluyt (c. 1552-Nov. 23, 1616)
Sir Walter Ralegh (c. 1552-Oct. 29, 1618)

Matteo Ricci (Oct. 6, 1552-May 11, 1610)
Rudolf II (July 18, 1552-Jan. 20, 1612)
Edmund Spenser (c. 1552-Jan. 13, 1599)
Henry IV (Dec. 13, 1553-May 14, 1610)
Luca Marenzio (1553-Aug. 22, 1599)
Richard Hooker (Mar., 1554-Nov. 2, 1600)
Sebastian (Jan. 20, 1554-Aug. 4, 1578)
Sir Philip Sidney (Nov. 30, 1554-Oct. 17, 1586)
Marietta Robusti Tintoretto (c. 1554-c. 1590)
Ludovico Carracci (baptized Apr. 21, 1555-Nov. 13, 1619; *see* The Carracci Family)
Sophie Brahe (Sept. 22, 1556, or Aug. 24, 1559-1643)

Giovanni Gabrieli (c. 1556-Aug. 12, 1612)
Agostino Carracci (Aug. 16, 1557-Feb. 23, 1602; *see* The Carracci Family)
Thomas Morley (1557 or 1558-Oct., 1602)
George Chapman (c. 1559-May 12, 1634)
Jacobus Arminius (Oct. 10, 1560-Oct. 19, 1609)
Elizabeth Báthory (Aug. 7, 1560-Aug. 21, 1614)
Annibale Carracci (Nov. 3, 1560-July 15, 1609; *see* The Carracci Family)
Thomas Cavendish (baptized Sept. 19, 1560-c. May, 1592)

1561-1570

Francis Bacon (Jan. 22, 1561-Apr. 9, 1626)
Isabella Andreini (1562-July 10, 1604)
John Dowland (1562 or 1563-Probably Feb. 20, 1626, London)
Hosokawa Gracia (1563-July 16, 1600)
First Earl of Salisbury (June 1, 1563-May 24, 1612)
Christopher Marlowe (Feb. 6, 1564-May 30, 1593)

William Shakespeare (Apr. 23, 1564-Apr. 23, 1616)
Barbe Acarie (Feb. 1, 1566-Apr. 18, 1618)
Mehmed III (May 26, 1566-Dec. 22, 1603)
Thomas Nashe (Nov., 1567-1601)
Aemilia Lanyer (Jan. 27, 1569-1645)
Guy Fawkes (Apr. 13, 1570-Jan. 31, 1606)

1571-1580

Caravaggio (Autumn, 1571-July 18, 1610)

John Fletcher (Dec., 1579-Aug., 1625; *see* Francis Beaumont and John Fletcher)

1581-1590

Francis Beaumont (c. 1584-Mar. 6, 1616)

Pemisapan (d. June 1, 1586)

CATEGORY INDEX

LIST OF CATEGORIES

ARCHITECTURE
Leon Battista Alberti, 18
Bess of Hardwick, 103
Donato Bramante, 132
Juan de Herrera, 445
Pierre Lescot, 565
Michelangelo, 682
Andrea Palladio, 753
Qāytbāy, 807
Raphael, 819
Jacopo Sansovino, 847
Diego de Siloé, 890
Sixtus IV, 893
Sixtus V, 895
Simon Stevin, 912
Giorgio Vasari, 953

ART
Leon Battista Alberti, 18
Andrea del Sarto, 39
Sofonisba Anguissola, 46
Giovanni Bellini, 97
Hieronymus Bosch, 120
Sandro Botticelli, 123
Pieter Bruegel, the Elder, 135
Caravaggio, 170
The Carracci Family, 175
Benvenuto Cellini, 202

Correggio, 249
Lucas Cranach, the Elder, 262
Albrecht Dürer, 297
Lavinia Fontana, 338
Giorgione, 383
El Greco, 390
Matthias Grünewald, 405
Charlotte Guillard, 413
Catharina van Hemessen, 421
Hans Holbein, the Younger, 453
Leonardo da Vinci, 561
Pierre Lescot, 565
Andrea Mantegna, 601
Aldus Manutius, 608
Michelangelo, 682
Piero della Francesca, 785
Raphael, 819
Sesshū, 865
Diego de Siloé, 890
Tintoretto, 931
Marietta Robusti Tintoretto, 935
Titian, 936
Giorgio Vasari, 953
Paolo Veronese, 959
Andrea del Verrocchio, 962

ASTRONOMY
Sophie Brahe, 126

Tycho Brahe, 128
Giordano Bruno, 138
Nicolaus Copernicus, 241
John Dee, 278
Girolamo Fracastoro, 343
Nostradamus, 728
Georg von Peuerbach, 773
Rheticus, 823
Matteo Ricci, 825
Simon Stevin, 912

CARTOGRAPHY
Álvar Núñez Cabeza de Vaca, 152
John Cabot, 155
Juan Rodríguez Cabrillo, 161
Jacques Cartier, 178
Gerardus Mercator, 678
Amerigo Vespucci, 969

CHEMISTRY
Paracelsus, 757

CHURCH REFORM
Barbe Acarie, 3
Anne Askew, 62
Anne Boleyn, 111
Martin Bucer, 142
George Buchanan, 146

HISTORIOGRAPHY

Geographical Index

Great Lives from History

Indexes

PERSONAGES INDEX

Subject Index

All personages appearing in **boldface type** in this index are the subjects of articles in *Great Lives from History: The Renaissance & Early Modern Era, 1454-1600*; Francis Beaumont and John Fletcher, The Carracci Family, Ferdinand II and Isabella I, The Pinzon Brothers, and The Tudor Family are the subjects of multi-person essays.